ENCYCLOPEDIA OF AMERICAN BUSINESS

GENERAL EDITOR

W. DAVIS FOLSOM

ASSOCIATE EDITOR

RICK BOULWARE

 Facts On File, Inc.

Encyclopedia of American Business

Copyright © 2004 by W. Davis Folsom

Facts On File, Inc.
132 West 31st Street
New York NY 10001

Library of Congress Cataloging-in-Publication Data

Encyclopedia of American Business / general editor, W. Davis Folsom ;
associate editor, Rick Boulware.
p. cm.
Includes bibliographical references and index.
ISBN 0-8160-4643-3
1. Business—Encyclopedias. 2. United States—Commerce—Encyclopedias. 3. Finance—
United States—Encyclopedias. 4. United States—Economic conditions—Encyclopedias.
I. Title: American business. II. Folsom, W. Davis. III. Boulware, Rick
HF1001.E463 2003
338.0973'03—dc21   2003048752

Text and cover design by Cathy Rincon
Illustrations by Sholto Ainslie

Printed in the United States of America

VB FOF 10 9 8 7 6 5 4 3 2 1

This book is printed on acid-free paper.

CONTENTS

LIST OF ENTRIES   iv

INTRODUCTION   x

CONTRIBUTING AUTHORS   xi

ENTRIES A–Z   1

BIBLIOGRAPHY   495

INDEX   498

LIST OF ENTRIES

Accounting Oversight Board
accounts payable, trade credit
accounts receivable
accrual basis, cash basis
achievement motivation
activity-based costing
adaptability screening
adjusting entry, trial balance, adjusted
    trial balance
administrative law
adoption process
advertising
affluent society
agency theory
agricultural support programs
Aid for Families with Dependent
    Children
American Bankers Association
American Bar Association
American Customer Satisfaction
    Index
American depository receipts
American dream
American Federation of Labor and
    Congress of Industrial
    Organizations (AFL-CIO)
American Industrial Revolution
American Institute of Certified Public
    Accountants
American Medical Association
American Society for Quality
American Stock Exchange
Americans with Disabilities Act
amortization
amortized loan
annual report
annuity
antitrust law
arbitrage
arbitration
assembly line

assembly plants
assessment center
assets
attention, interest, desire, action
    concept
attitudes, interests, opinions statements
auditing
automatic stabilizers
Auto Pact
bad debts, aging of accounts
balance of payments
balance sheet
Baldrige Award
banking system
Bank of International Settlements
barriers to entry
barter
benchmarking
beta coefficient, capital asset pricing
    model
Better Business Bureau
bill of lading
blind trust
blue-chip stocks
blue-collar
blue laws
board of directors
bonds
book value
Border Environmental Cooperation
    Commission
boycotts
Brady bonds
brands, brand names
break-even analysis
Bretton Woods
bribery
Buddhist economics
budgeting, capital budgeting
Bureau of Economic Analysis
Bureau of Labor Statistics

Bureau of Land Management
business and the U.S. Constitution
business cycles
business ethics
business failure
business forecasting
business language
business logistics
business plan
Business Roundtable
business taxes
business valuation
Buy American Act and campaigns
buy-grid model
buying-center concept
bylaws
cafeteria plans
callable bond
capital
capital expenditure, revenue
    expenditure
capital gain, capital loss
capitalism
capital markets, money markets
cartel
cash-flow analysis
cash management
Center for Science and the Public
    Interest
centrally planned economy
Certified Public Accountant
chain-of-command principle
Chamber of Commerce
Chicago Board of Trade
Chicago Mercantile Exchange
chief executive officer
chief financial officer
churning
circular flow model
Civil Aeronautics Board
Civilian Conservation Corps

civil procedure
Civil Rights Acts
class-action lawsuits
classical economics
Clayton Antitrust Act
Clean Air Acts
Clean Water Act
closely held corporation
Coalition for Environmentally
    Responsible Economies
collective bargaining
collusion
Commerce Business Daily
commerce clause
commercial law
commercial paper
Commodity Credit Corporation
Commodity Futures Trading
    Commission
commodity markets
common law
common stock, preferred stock,
    treasury stock
comparable worth
comparative advantage
compensation and benefits
competition
competitive advantage
compounding, future value
Comptroller of the Currency
computer-aided design, engineering,
    and manufacturing
Conference Board
conflict of interest
conglomerate
consent decree
consignment
consumer advocacy
consumer bankruptcy
consumer behavior
consumer buying process
consumer credit counseling service
Consumer Credit Protection Act
Consumer Price Index
Consumer Product Safety Commission
consumer protection
Consumers Union
consumption
consumption tax
contestable market theory
contract
cooperative
copy
copyright, fair use
corporate average fuel efficiency
corporate culture

corporate divestiture
corporate governance
corporate security
corporate social responsibility
corporate welfare
corporation
cost-benefit analysis
cost of goods sold
cost-of-living adjustment
cost-push inflation
costs
counterfeit goods
countertrade
countervailing power
country-risk analysis
Court of International Trade
credit cards
credit-reporting services
credit scoring
credit union
critical path method
cross-cultural communication
cross-price elasticity of demand
cultural industries
customer loyalty
customer-relationship management
customer relations/satisfaction
customs union
cyberspace
cycle time
damages
database management
Davis-Bacon Act
debit, credit
deceptive trade practices
decision tree
default
deflation
Delphi technique
demand
Deming's 14 points
demographics
Department of Commerce, U.S.
Department of Labor, U.S.
Department of the Interior, U.S.
Department of Transportation, U.S.
Department of the Treasury, U.S.
dependency ratios
depreciation, depletion,
    amortization
deregulation
derivative securities
direct investment
direct mail
direct marketing
disclosure duties

discounting, present value
discount rate
dispute settlement
distribution channels
diversification
dividends, retained earnings
document-retention policy
dot-coms
Dow Jones averages
downsizing
due diligence
due process
dumping
Dun & Bradstreet reports
duration
earnings management
e-business
e-commerce
economic conditions
economic development
economic efficiency
Economic Espionage Act
economic freedom
economic growth
economic policy
economic rent
economies of scale, economies
    of scope
efficient market theory
e-government
80/20 principle
elasticity of demand
electronic data interchange
Electronic Fund Transfer Act
electronic funds transfer
embargo
embezzlement
emerging markets
eminent domain
employee assistance program
employee benefits
employee motivation
employee recruiting
Employee Retirement Income
    Security Act
employee stock-ownership plan
employment
employment-at-will
empowerment
empowerment zones, enterprise zones
Endangered Species Act
entrepreneurship
environmental impact
    statement
Environmental Protection Agency
environmental scanning

equal employment opportunity and
    affirmative action
Equal Employment Opportunity
    Commission
Equal Pay Act
equation of exchange
equilibrium
equity
equity income theory
ergonomics
escalator clause
European Union
exchange-rate risk
exchange rates
exit strategies
expectancy theory
experience and learning curves
export controls
Export-Import Bank of the United
    States
exporting
externalities
extraterritorial jurisdiction
factoring
factory tours
Fair Debt Collections
    Practices Act
fair disclosure
Fair Labor Standards Act
Family and Medical Leave Act
family farm
family-friendly business
    practices
family life cycle
Farm Credit System
fast track
featherbedding
Federal Aviation Administration
federal budget
Federal Communications
    Commission
federal courts
Federal Deposit Insurance
    Corporation
Federal Financial Institutions
    Examinations Council
federal funds market
Federal Home Loan Bank System
Federal Home Loan Mortgage
    Corporation
Federal Mediation and Conciliation
    Service
Federal National Mortgage
    Association
Federal Reserve System
Federal Trade Commission

fiduciary duties
financial accounting
Financial Accounting Standards
    Board
financial instrument
financial intermediaries
Financial Planning Association
financial ratios
financial statements
first in, first out; last in, first out
first-mover advantage
fiscal policy
fiscal year
five Cs of credit
flowchart
flow of funds
focus groups
Food and Drug Administration
forced-ranking systems
Foreign Corrupt Practices Act
foreign exchange
foreign investment
Foreign Sovereign Immunities Act
foreign trade zones
401(k) plan
franchising
fraud
Freedom of Information Act
free on board
free trade
free-trade areas
futures, futures contracts
game theory
gap analysis
General Accounting Office
generally accepted accounting
    principles
General Services Administration
Gini ratio
glass ceiling
globalization
global shares
goal setting
goodwill, going concern
government debt
Government National Mortgage
    Association
government-sponsored enterprises
graphs
gray markets
Great Depression
green cards
green marketing
gross domestic product
growth stocks
guaranteed investment contract

harmonization
Harmonized Tariff System
Hawthorne experiments
health maintenance
    organization
hedge fund
hedging
Herfindahl Index
Hofstede's dimensions
holding company
human resources
import restraints
imports/exports
income
income elasticity of demand
income redistribution
income statement, gross margin
incorporation
independent contractors
Index of Consumer Expectations
indicators
individual retirement account
industrial-organizational psychology
Industrial Workers of the World
inflation
infomercials
infrastructure
initial public offering
injunctions
input-output
insider trading
Institute for Supply Management
Institute of Management Accountants
insurance
intellectual property
Inter-American Development Bank
interest rates
interlocking directorate
Internal Revenue Service
International Brotherhood of
    Teamsters
International Energy Agency
International Labor Organization
international management
international marketing
International Monetary Fund
International Trade Commission
Internet
Internet Fraud Complaint Center
Internet marketing
Internet surveys
internships
Interstate Commerce Commission
interviewing
inventory control
investment

investment banking
investment clubs
ISO standards
job satisfaction
joint venture
Jones Act
just cause
just-in-time production
Keogh plan
Keynesian economics
know-how
knowledge management
Kondratev waves
Kyoto Protocol
Labor/employee relations
labor force
labor markets
laissez-faire
Landrum-Griffin Act
layoff
leadership
leasing
letter of credit
leverage
leveraged buyout
liability
licensing
life cycle
limited liability company
limited liability partnership
loans
local option sales tax
Lorenz curve
macroeconomics
Madison Avenue
mail surveys
make-or-buy decisions
Malthusian trap
management
management gurus
managerial accounting
manufacturers' representatives
maquiladoras
marginal analysis
market concentration
market failure
marketing communications
marketing concept
marketing-information systems
marketing strategy
market intelligence
market research
market segmentation
market-share, market-growth matrix
market structure
market value

Marshall Plan
Maslow's hierarchy of needs
mass customization
mass merchandising
master of business
    administration
matrix management
mercantilism
mergers and acquisitions
metropolitan statistical area
microeconomics
middle managers
minimum wage
mission statement
mixed economy
Model Business Corporation Act
modern portfolio theory
monetary policy
money
money supply
monopolistic competition
monopoly
Montreal Protocol
Moody's ratings
moral suasion
mortgage
most-favored-nation clause
motivation theory
multilevel marketing
multinational corporation
mutual funds
mutual interdependence
National Association of Securities
    Dealers Automated Quotation
    System
National Bureau of Economic
    Research
national income accounting
National Industrial Recovery Act
National Labor Relations Board
National Mediation Board
negligence
negotiable instruments
nepotism
new-product development
New York Clearing House
    Association
New York Mercantile Exchange
New York Stock Exchange
nontariff barriers
Norris-LaGuardia Act
North American Agreement on Labor
    Cooperation
North American Development Bank
North American Free Trade
    Agreement

North American Industry
    Classification System
observation
Occupational Safety and Health
    Administration
Office of Federal Contract
    Compliance Programs
Office of Government Ethics
Office of Management and Budget
oligopoly
ombudsmen
open-market operations
opportunity cost
options, option contracts
organizational commitment
organizational theory
organization behavior
Organization for Economic
    Cooperation and Development
Organization of American States
Organization of Petroleum Exporting
    Countries
outplacement
outsourcing
Overseas Private Investment
    Corporation
owner's equity
packaging
parallel markets
parity
partnership
patent
payroll taxes
Pension Benefit Guaranty
    Corporation
perfect competition
performance appraisal
personal finance
personal-interview surveys
personal property
personal selling
peso crisis
Peter principle
poison-pill strategies
political action committee
pollution rights
Ponzi scheme
positioning
predatory lending
price ceilings, price controls
price discrimination
price fixing
price floors, price supports
price indexes
pricing strategies
primary markets, secondary markets

privacy
privatization
problem solving
process theories
Producer Price Index
product
production
production-possibilities curve
product liability
product life cycle
product-market growth matrix
product placement
product proliferation
profit
profit maximization
profit sharing, gain sharing
program evaluation and review
    technique
program trading
project management
promissory note
property taxes
proprietary information
proprietorship
prospectus
proxy
public administration
public relations
public service announcements
public utilities
purchasing
push and pull strategies
pyramid of corporate responsibility
quality control
questionnaires
queuing theory
Racketeer Influenced and Corrupt
    Organization Act
random-walk theory
real estate investment trusts
real income
recession
reciprocity
reductions in force
relationship marketing
repurchase agreements, reverse
    repurchase agreements
request for proposal, invitation to bid
research and development
reserve requirements
residual value
Resolution Trust Corporation
Resource Conservation and Recovery
    Act
resources
restraints of trade

restrictive covenants
retailing
retirement plan
right-to-know laws
right-to-work laws
risk management
risk, uncertainty
Robinson-Patman Act
rule of 72
rules of origin
safety and health
sales force compensation
sales forecasting
sales management
sales promotion
sanctions
saving
savings and loan associations
S corporation
Section 301, Special 301, Super 301
Securities and Exchange Commission
Securities Industry Association
securitization
seniority
services
sexual harassment
shareholders
Sherman Antitrust Act
short selling
shut-down point
simplified employee pension
sinking fund
Small Business Administration
Smoot-Hawley Tariff Act
social audit
social facilitation
socialism
social loafing
social responsible investing
Social Security
Society for Competitive Intelligence
    Professionals
stakeholders
Standard & Poor's
standard of living
Standard Rate and Data Service
stock market, bond market
stock options
stock-rating systems
strategic alliances
strategic planning
strengths, weaknesses, opportunities
    and threats (SWOT) analysis
Student Loan Marketing Association
Superfund
Supplemental Security Income

supply
supply rule
supply-side economics
sustainable growth and development
sweatshop
synergy
t-account
Taft-Hartley Act
takings clause
target markets
tariff
tax incremental funding
tax shelter
technical analysis
technology transfer
telemarketing
telephone surveys
tender offer
Tennessee Valley Authority
theory of constraints
Theory X and Theory Y
think tanks
360-degree feedback
time deposits
time management
tobacco settlement
total-quality management
trade-adjustment assistance
trade balance
trade barriers
trademark
trade secrets
trade shows
training and development
transaction costs
transfer payments
transfer taxes
trickle-down economics
trust
Truth in Lending Act
two-factor theory of motivation
tying contracts
underground economy
undertime
Underwriters Laboratory
underwriting
unemployment
Uniform Commercial Code
union
United Farm Workers
United States–Canada Free Trade
    Agreement
U.S. Agency for International
    Development
U.S. Census Bureau
U.S. Commercial Service

U.S. Customs Clearance
U.S. Customs Service
U.S. Trade Representative
U.S. Treasury securities
venture capital
vertical integration
viral marketing
visas
vision statement
wage and price controls
Wagner Act
Wall Street

warranty
wealth
welfare
Wheeler-Lea Act
wheel of retailing
whisper numbers
whistle-blower
white-collar
wholesaler
work council
Worker Adjustment and Retraining
    Notification Act

workers' compensation
Works Progress Administration
World Bank
World Intellectual Property
    Organization
World Trade Organization
Worldwide Web
wrongful discharge
yield curve
zero-sum game
zero-base budgeting
zoning

INTRODUCTION

The *Encyclopedia of American Business* is designed to assist students and other individuals in understanding the complex world of American business. The United States's economy, at more than $10 trillion in 2004, is the largest economy in the world. The many organizations, institutions, government agencies, laws, and business concepts that make up the U.S. economic system create a complex and confusing, yet exciting, business environment. The goal in creating this encyclopedia is to provide readers with a resource to help them understand the many facets of American business. With our focus on American business, this encyclopedia provides useful insight for businesspeople around the world learning about the U.S. system.

Two major resources were used in determining which topics to include in the encyclopedia. The first was the *Wall Street Journal,* the quintessential U.S. business newspaper. Issues, concepts, laws, and institutions discussed in the *Journal* were a major source of topics for this book. The second was "principles" texts used in beginning management, marketing, economics, finance, and accounting courses. Principles texts introduce students to concepts, laws, and institutions that make up the world of business. Our goal is to provide short summaries of these topics as a resource for students and individuals learning about American business.

We would like to thank many individuals who assisted with this project, including Dr. Robert Williams; Professor Megan Fox; Melissa Hudson; Judy Mims; Vera Basilone; Tom Odom; our Facts On File editor, Owen Lancer; and the many contributing authors who assisted this effort. Thanks also to the University of South Carolina Beaufort for the support and resources used in creating this work.

This book is dedicated to the many "teachers" who have influenced and enriched our lives. Davis Folsom would like to acknowledge and thank family members Myrtle and Morris Folsom; Ralph, Ellen, Roger, and Herb Folsom; Kathy and Brad Folsom; and special people including Dr. A. Robert Koch, Dr. Alpha Chang, Bertie Nelson "The Pro" Butts, Kathie Turick Robie, Jerry and Faye Rosenthal, Phil and Marilyn Ray, Bert and Lucille Keller, Helen Reece, Dr. Robert Botsch, Dr. Jim Snyder, and Dr. Mack Tennyson.

Rick Boulware would like to acknowledge and thank Gwen L. Boulware, Sheryl B. Blanks, and Kevin D. Boulware for their loving support over many years; and Dr. Gerald A. "Jerry" Merwin Jr., mentor, colleague, and friend.

CONTRIBUTING
AUTHORS

JOHN B. ABBOTT, PhD, SPHR, University of South Carolina Beaufort

RACHEL ARCHANGEL, University of South Carolina Beaufort

DONNA BEALES, Librarian CME, Coordinator Lowell General Hospital

PATTY BERGIN, MLS, Simmons College

DR. CAROL SEARS BOTSCH, Associate Professor, University of South Carolina Aiken

DR. ROBERT BOTSCH, Professor, University of South Carolina Aiken

BETH M. BRACCIA, MLS, Simmons College

JANET HADWIN BRACKETT, MLIS, University of Maine, Farmington

DR. LINDA BRADLEY, Professor, College of Charleston

JILL BRIGGS, University of South Carolina Beaufort

LAURA W. CARTER, Reference Librarian, Clark County Library

FRANK CHECK, University of South Carolina Beaufort

KAREN M. CIMINO, University of South Carolina Beaufort

TERRYE CONROY, MLIS, University of South Carolina

DR. ELIZABETH L. CRALLEY, Assistant Professor, University of South Carolina Beaufort

JOAN CUNNINGHAM, MLS, Simmons College

STEWART CURRY, MLIS, University of South Carolina

TODD DEVRIES, University of South Carolina Beaufort

MARGARET C. DUNLAP, MLIS, University of South Carolina

KAREN BRICKMAN EMMONS, MLIS, University of South Carolina

MEGAN D. FENNESSY, MLS, Simmons College

RALPH FOLSOM, JD, Professor, University of San Diego Law School

LEAH KNINDE FRAZIER-GASKINS, University of South Carolina Beaufort

LISA VINCENT GAGNON, Librarian, Simmons College

KRISTEN GAUDES, MLS, Simmons College

ABBEY GEHMAN, MLIS, University of South Carolina

PATRICIA GIDDENS, MLIS, University of South Carolina

STEPHANIE GODLEY, Reference Librarian, Nixon Peabody LLP

JONATHAN S. GOLDBERG, Management Decision Resource Center, VA Healthcare System

KAREN S. GROVES, MLIS, University of South Carolina

GAYATRI GUPTA, University of San Diego Law School

CINDY L. HALSEY, MLIS, University of South Carolina

R. JOSEPH HAROLD, University of South Carolina Beaufort

MELISSA HUDSON, University of South Carolina Beaufort

LINDSAY INGRAM, University of South Carolina Beaufort

KIMBERLY JEFFERS, University of South Carolina Beaufort

LINDA TRANT JOHNSON, MLIS, University of South Carolina

AARON S. JONES, Librarian, Simmons College

Alison Kaiser Jones, MLS, Simmons College

JOI PATRICE JONES, MLIS, University of South Carolina

ANDREW KEARNS, MLIS, University of South Carolina

JOSEPH F. KLEIN, Librarian, University of South Carolina

JAMES A. LAMEE, MLIS, University of South Carolina

JENNIFER R. LAND, MLIS, University of South Carolina

RICK LOCKETT, A. G. Edwards and Sons

JESSICA LUJICK, University of South Carolina Beaufort

MELISSA LUMA, University of South Carolina Beaufort

LAURIE MACWHINNIE, MLIS, University of South Carolina

THOMAS MADDEN, MLS, Simmons College

PAULA MALONEY, MLS, Simmons College

KATHERINE L. MAY, MSW, MLS, Newton, Massachusetts

TARA LYNN MCDONALD, MLS, Simmons College

JENNIFER MCGEORGE, MLS, Simmons College

DR. LEANNE MCGRATH, Associate Professor, University of South Carolina Aiken

CAROLYN MCKELVEY, MLS, Simmons College

DR. JERRY MERWIN, Assistant Professor, Valdosta State University

APRIL MILLER, MLIS, University of South Carolina

JUDY MIMS, Instructor, University of South Carolina Beaufort

MICHELLE MITCHELL, MLIS, University of South Carolina

MAUREN MURRAY, MLS, Simmons College

Beth MYERS, MLIS, University of South Carolina

JIM NIX, University of South Carolina Beaufort

LOURDES OWENS, University of South Carolina Beaufort

SUSAN POORBAUGH, MLIS, Medical College of Georgia

KATRINA V. REILING, MLS, Simmons College

JERRY ROSENTHAL, Zip's Business Services

JESSE ROSENTHAL, University of Chicago

DEBORAH J. ROTH, MLS, Simmons College

DR. HOWARD RUDD, Professor, College of Charleston

JEANNE SAWYER, Sawyer Partnership

LAURA M. SCOTT, Reference Librarian, Simmons College

SUSAN J. SLAGA, MLS, Simmons College

DAVID G. SPOOLSTRA, MLS, Simmons College

JONATHON R. SULLIVAN, University of South Carolina Beaufort

DR. MACK TENNYSON, Professor, College of Charleston

FRANK UBHAUS, JR., Valdosta State University

ASTA VAICHYS, MLS, Simmons College

GRETCHEN WADE, MLS, Simmons College

DANIEL P. WHICKER, University of South Carolina Beaufort

CARRIE WILSON, University of South Carolina Beaufort

DOMINQUE WINN, MLIS, Simmons College

STAN YOCCO, University of South Carolina Beaufort

KATE ANDERSON YOUNG, MLIS, Simmons College

DIANE ZYDLEWSKI, MLS, Simmons College

Accounting   See AUDITING; FINANCIAL ACCOUNTING; MANA-GERIAL ACCOUNTING.

Accounting Oversight Board

The Public Company Accounting Oversight Board (AOB) is a five-member board created when the Sarbanes-Oxley Act was signed into law on July 30, 2002. The AOB was established to protect the interests of the investors and the integrity of financial markets. It was set up in response to the recent scandals at Enron, WorldCom, and Andersen as a means for Congress to assure investors, employees, and pensioners that the hardships and losses they had suffered would not be repeated.

The AOB performs the following duties: registers public accounting firms; establishes AUDITING, QUALITY CONTROL, ethics, independence, and other standards relating to the preparation of audit reports for issuers; conducts inspections of accounting firms; conducts investigations and disciplinary proceedings, imposing appropriate sanctions; enforces compliance with the Sarbanes-Oxley Act and other professional standards; and sets the budget and manages the operations of the Board and its staff. The AOB is thus given the power to discipline accountants and issue subpoenas. It also has authority to amend, modify, repeal, and reject any standards suggested by the professional groups of accountants and any advisory groups. Some of these relevant groups are: the FASB (FINANCIAL ACCOUNTING STANDARDS BOARD), the IASB (International Accounting Standards Board), the FASAB (Federal Accounting Standards Advisory Board), the GASB (Governmental Accounting Standards Board), and the AICPA (AMERICAN INSTITUTE OF CERTIFIED PUBLIC ACCOUNTANTS). The AOB must report its standard-setting activity to the SECURITIES AND EXCHANGE COMMISSION annually. It requires registered public accounting firms to prepare and maintain files for a period of at least seven years, to audit work papers and other information related to an audit report in sufficient detail to support the conclusions reached in the report.

Members of the board are appointed by the Securities and Exchange Commission (SEC) in consultation with the Federal Reserve Chairman and the Secretary of the Treasury. The Sarbanes-Oxley Act states that board members must be "prominent individuals of integrity and reputation who have demonstrated commitment to the interests of investors and the public, and an understanding of the responsibilities and nature of financial disclosure . . . and the obligations of accountants with respect to the preparation and issuance of audit reports with respect to such disclosures." By law, two members of the board must be or must have been CERTIFIED PUBLIC ACCOUNTANTS and the three remaining members must not be and cannot have been certified public accountants. Members of the board are appointed for a five-year term during which time they will serve on a full-time basis.

Soon after the Accounting Oversight Board came into existence, controversy arose over the process of selecting board members. The SEC named William Webster, former director of both the FBI and the CIA, as chairman of the board in a divided vote (a 3-2 approval). Criticism mounted after the *New York Times* reported that Webster had warned SEC Chairman Harvey Pitt, but not to entire Commission, before the vote on his nomination that he had recently headed the auditing committee of a company facing FRAUD accusations from investors. Additionally, SEC Commissioner Harvey J. Goldschmid argued that Pitt had initially promised the chairmanship to John Biggs, head of the giant teachers pension fund TIAA-CREF, who had called for tight oversight of the accounting industry. Goldschmid further argued that Pitt had changed his mind under pressure from the industry and Republican lawmakers. There was general consensus among SEC members to open an investigation into the process used to select William Webster and other board members. Webster subsequently resigned his position as chairman.

The other current board members include Daniel Galzer, former general counsel at the SEC; Kayla Gillat, former attorney at Calpers, a large California pension fund; Willis Gradison, former member of Congress and former Undersecretary of the Treasury Department; and Charles Niemeier, a senior enforcement official at the SEC.

The Accounting Oversight Board is funded by assessed contributions from publicly traded CORPORATIONS. The Board collects a registration fee and an annual fee from every public accounting firm in amounts that are sufficient to recover the COSTS of processing and reviewing applications and ANNUAL REPORTS.

Further reading

American Institute of Certified Public Accountants. "Summary of Sarbanes-Oxley Act of 2002." American Institute of Certified Public Accountants website. Available on-line. URL: http://www.aicpa.org/info/sarbanes_oxley_summary.htm. Downloaded May 27, 2003. "Statement by SEC Commissioner: New Public Company Accounting Oversight Board by Commissioner Harvey J. Goldschmid," U.S. Securities and Exchange Commission, Open Committee Meeting, October 25, 2002. Downloaded May 27, 2003. URL: www.sec.gov/news/press.html.

—Beth Myers

accounts payable, trade credit

Accounts payable are a part of a firm's current liabilities, debts that must be paid within the short term. The accounts payable are the firm's trade credit. As the firm does business with its suppliers and other firms on a credit basis, accounts payable accrue. Trade credit is a source of CAPITAL for the firm. Using invoices instead of cash, trade credit facilities purchases from suppliers and others; cumbersome cash transactions aren't necessary when firms have good trade credit. When the accounts payable are kept current (i.e., paid on a timely basis), trade credit creates a good reputation for the firm among those with whom it does business.

To encourage the early payment of invoices, most suppliers' invoices contain sales discounts. There are percentages that can be deducted for the early payment of an invoice. A commonly used sales discount found on invoices is "2/10, net 30." This means that 2 percent may be deducted from the invoice if payment is made within 10 days of the invoice date; otherwise the full amount of the invoice is due within 30 days of the invoice date.

Sales discounts apply to short periods of time, usually 10 or 15 days, but when expressed as an annual percentage rate, these discounts are considerable and are powerful incentives for credit customers to pay early. The sales discount of "2/10, net 30" is greater than 36 percent when expressed as an annual percentage rate; "1/15, net 30" is approximately a 24-percent annual percentage rate. Consider a firm with a sizable amount of trade credit, which consistently pays its bills late, not taking advantage of the sales discounts. Such a firm is using its suppliers' money, borrowing it at INTEREST RATES more commonly associated with CREDIT CARDS and finance companies.

accounts receivable

Accounts receivable are part of a firm's ASSETS; they represent monies owed to the firm. (While receivables are assets, payables are liabilities to a firm. Payables are the firm's debt—that is, monies owed by the firm.) An account receivable is created when a firm sells a good or service to a customer on credit (see DEBIT, CREDIT). Rather than receiving an asset in the form of cash, the firm records an asset called an account receivable. The sum of all the monies owed to the firm by its customers collectively is called accounts receivable.

Because accounts receivable are assets, debit entries will increase accounts receivable, and credit entries will decrease accounts receivable. Because of the dual nature of a transaction (an exchange of equal-valued resources between two parties), for every account receivable in a firm's ledger, there is an equal-valued account payable in another firm's ledger.

Every firm that sells on credit will have an INVESTMENT in accounts receivable. The presence of accounts receivable, especially when sizable, creates a cash-flow problem for a firm. A sale was made; the merchandise was sold, but it was not liquidated (cash was not received). Thus, accounts receivable are in reality a pool of idle cash. To offset cash-flow problems, the accounts receivable need to be collected on a timely basis. Firms monitor their investment in accounts receivable by comparing their "days sales outstanding" (DSO) ratio with that of their industry.

A popular way firms attempt to offset cash-flow problems associated with receivables is to offer sales discounts on the invoices sent to their credit customers. Sales discounts are percentages that can be deducted for the early payment of an invoice. A commonly used sales discount found on invoices is "2/10, net 30." This means that 2 percent may be deducted from the invoice if payment is made within 10 days of the invoice date; otherwise, the full amount of the invoice is due within 30 days of the invoice date. These sales discounts apply to short periods of time, usually 10 or 15 days, but when expressed as an annual percentage rate, these discounts are considerable and are powerful incentives for credit customers to pay early.

Because it is impossible to predict with accuracy which customers are good credit risks, it is natural and expected that some of the accounts receivable will ultimately prove to be uncollectible, at which time they will be written off as BAD DEBTS. Bad-debt expense can be minimized by a tightening of a firm's credit policy. However, there is a trade-off: having a tight credit policy means that a firm will sacrifice sales to its marginal credit customers. Periodically a firm may review the status of its accounts receivable using an accounting method known as aging of accounts receivable (see BAD DEBTS, AGING OF ACCOUNTS), where the outstanding balance of each account and its DURATION are determined.

See also ACCOUNTS PAYABLE, TRADE CREDIT.

accrual basis, cash basis

GENERALLY ACCEPTED ACCOUNTING PRINCIPLES (GAAP) require accounting on the accrual basis, as opposed to the cash basis for accounting. In cash-basis accounting, revenues are recorded when the monies are received. Expenses are recognized and recorded only when they are paid. In other words, revenues and expenses are recorded only when there is a movement of cash either into or out of the firm, respectively. The use of cash-basis accounting is found in only a few types of businesses, namely restaurants, medical offices, and legal firms.

Accrual-basis accounting is based upon GAAP, primarily the revenue and matching principles. The revenue principle requires that revenues be recognized and recorded when they are earned; this may not be at the same time that the revenues are received. For example, suppose a firm sells a computer on credit in December 1999, and the customer pays for the purchase in January 2000. Using the accrual basis, the sale and revenue is recorded when the transaction occurs—that is, in 1999. When payment from the customer is received in the next year, this is an entirely separate transaction and is recorded with the other transactions of the firm for the year 2000. (If cash-basis accounting were used, the firm would not record the computer sale in 1999, although that is when the sale was made. It would record the computer sale in 2000, because that is when the firm received payment for the computer. Transactions in cash-basis accounting are not recorded unless there is either a receipt or payment of money.)

It is impossible for a firm to generate revenue without incurring some sort of expense. When a good is sold, the expense account—COST OF GOODS SOLD—is debited (increased). If a service is performed, labor and/or supplies expense is debited. The matching principle requires that the expenses incurred in the generation of a firm's revenue for a particular time period be recorded (included) in the same time period as the revenues to which they are related. For example, suppose a firm receives its telephone bill in January for its telephone expense that month, and the firm pays that bill two months later, in March. Even though the expense is paid in March, it is a January expense, not a March expense. The matching principle requires the expense to be recorded in January.

It is evident from the examples above that an accurate measurement of a firm's periodic revenues and expenses in only realized with accrual-basis accounting. In the accrual basis, revenues and expenses are recorded when the sale is made and the expense is incurred. Cash-basis accounting ignores the concept of periodicity by recording revenues and expenses only when money changes hands. For this reason, accrual-basis accounting is generally accepted.

achievement motivation

Achievement motivation has to do with how inspired people are to pursue and accomplish their goals. When an individual does accomplish a desired goal, it typically results in a sense of positive self-worth, which contributes to personal and professional growth and development. The motivation to achieve may be affected both by dispositional characteristics, such as individuals' perceptions of their abilities and potential to succeed; and by external forces, such as the promise of rewards for success or threat of punishment for failure.

Some individuals appear to have an intrinsically high level of achievement motivation. These people typically do not require the use of external incentives to prompt them to work towards their goals because they already have the desire to do so. People who are motivated mainly by a high need to achieve will seek out challenging tasks and work hard to succeed at them. People low in the need for achievement tend to pursue very easy tasks, where the chances of success are high; or they choose tasks that are extremely difficult, where no reasonable person could be expected to succeed. Thus when failure occurs, it is not attributed to the person's lack of skills or abilities but to the difficult nature of the task.

In contrast, some individuals are driven primarily by a fear of failure rather than a need to achieve. This fear of failure may lead them to avoid challenging tasks altogether. People who are motivated mainly by this fear will avoid the risks presented by difficult or complex tasks, precisely because they may result in failure. Instead, these individuals tend to prefer easy tasks where, even though the rewards may be small, the chances of success are great. A smaller subset of individuals may be motivated by a fear of success. People who fear success may worry that after succeeding at a challenging task, other people will raise their expectations of them. The pressure of these expectations, coupled with the individual's fear that he or she will be unable to continue success at that level, may lead these individuals to sabotage their own efforts to succeed in the first place. Thus they avoid the potential anxiety and pressure associated with success.

In addition, the nature of any given task may affect an individual's decision to pursue it and how hard that person tries to succeed. Specific tasks may elicit either intrinsic or extrinsic motivation, or both. Intrinsic motivation involves the desire to perform a behavior or task for its own sake, perhaps because the person finds it pleasurable or exciting. Extrinsic motivation involves performing a behavior or task in order to earn external rewards or to avoid punishments. Maximizing intrinsic motivation appears to be very effective for increasing and maintaining the performance of a desired behavior. Therefore employers or supervisors who try to make routine tasks more interesting or exciting may increase the chances that employees will want to work on those tasks.

On the other hand, providing external motivators for a task that is already intrinsically motivating may backfire, inadvertently decreasing the person's intrinsic motivation to perform it. For example, one study found that people who were given money as an external motivator for working on a puzzle found the puzzle to be less interesting than people who were not paid for working on it. Extrinsic rewards may change people's perceptions of how attractive or fun a particular task may be. In other words, once someone receives money for a task, it becomes more like work than like pleasure. In this respect the extrinsic reward may be interpreted as a control device used to entice a person into working on a task that has little intrinsic value.

However, the use of extrinsic rewards can be highly effective under certain conditions, such as when they are used to provide feedback or information concerning a person's performance. For example, when a salesperson receives an unexpected bonus for successful work, he may increase his future efforts, thus leading to improved performance rather than a decreased interest in continuing the task.

Finally, achievement motivation is linked to EMPLOYEE MOTIVATION in the sense that people motivated by a high need to achieve will likely seek out challenging tasks at work and strive to accomplish them. Employees with a high level of achievement motivation can contribute in significant ways to the success of any business.

See also MOTIVATION THEORY; PERFORMANCE APPRAISAL.

Further reading
Baron, Robert A., and Donn Byrne. *Social Psychology,* 10th ed. Boston: Allyn and Bacon, 2003; Myers, David G. *Exploring Psychology,* 5th ed. New York: Worth Publishers, 2002.

—Elizabeth L. Cralley

acquisitions   See MERGERS AND ACQUISITIONS.

activity-based costing
Activity-based costing (ABC) is a cost-accounting tool that attempts to determine the cost of each activity in the production or service process. Traditional cost accounting focuses on accumulating the total cost of the item produced by cost inputs (i.e., salaries, materials, overhead). ABC overcomes the deficiencies in this process by looking at the cost from an activity perspective instead of an inputs perspective. For example, a traditional cost-accounting system may say the painting department had the following COSTS for painting one appliance: direct labor, $20; direct materials, $10; assigned overhead, $20. An activity-based cost system would show the cost by activities: sanding, $5; cleaning, $5; spraying, $25; drying, $10; inspection, $5.

At the heart of this concept is the handling of overhead. Traditional cost accounting incorrectly assigns overhead based on some other cost such as direct labor. This often causes erroneous management data that assigns too much overhead to large jobs and too little to small jobs. It may allocate too much overhead to departments with less machinery and too little overhead to departments with more machinery.

Activity-based accounting tries to address this shortfall by allocating cost based on what it calls "cost drivers." Cost drivers are the items in the business that create overhead. Examples of cost drivers include number of production runs, number of engineering change orders, number of purchase orders, number of vendors, and number of parts. Activity-based costing requires the additional effort needed to determine what cost drivers are producing the overhead, and then it allocates the overhead to the activities based on the driver. This gives a much more accurate total cost calculation.

adaptability screening
Adaptability screening is identifying prospective employees who will be most likely to adjust to a company's work environment. Psychologist Dr. Saul Sells, who developed adaptability screening in the 1950s, emphasized the need to study behavior in its natural setting. In his first adaptability screening research, Dr. Sells tested pilots training for the U.S. Air Force and then assessed their performance in combat during the Korean War. His research became the basis for pilot selection and performance prediction.

Adaptability screening is now used in a wide variety of businesses. Predictive models help managers estimate the needed staffing level, adjusting for sick leave, relief, and physical conditions. Models can also predict which workers will adjust to shift work, changing schedules in factories operating 24 hours a day. By identifying those workers who can adjust to changes in sleep, fatigue, and health, adaptability screening can reduce absenteeism and improve safety and the work environment.

When combined with payroll systems and task load management, the results of adaptability screening can be used to optimize production operations. Screening also reduces training costs through more effective recruitment and retention rates.

See also INDUSTRIAL-ORGANIZATIONAL PSYCHOLOGY.

Further reading
Kaplan, D., and R. L. Venezky. *What Can Employers Assume About the Literacy Skills of GED Students?* Technical Publication of the National Center on Adult Literacy, September 1993; Simpson, D. Dwayne. "Founder and Former Director of IBR: Saul B. Sells," *American Psychologist* (December 1988): 1088.

adjusting entry, trial balance, adjusted trial balance
An adjusting entry is a journal entry made at the end of an accounting period to record accruals that have occurred during that time period. Adjusting entries are common to

ACCRUAL BASIS accounting, but they are not found in cash basis accounting. An accrual is an ASSET (other than cash), LIABILITY, equity account, revenue or expense that has accrued within a particular accounting period. In the case of a long-term note receivable, interest income will be earned each accounting period, although the interest income may not be received until the maturation of the note. Interest income will accrue over the life of the note, and it must be recorded as it is earned, not when it is received. In the case of a note payable, interest expense will accrue over time. As interest expense accrues, it must be recorded. The recognition and recording of such accruals is normally done at the end of the accounting period with adjusting entries.

As with most accounting entries, an adjusting entry is a double entry with one account being debited and another account credited. One of the entries will always be an INCOME STATEMENT account (either a revenue account or expense account), and the other entry will be a BALANCE SHEET account (either an asset, liability, or equity account). Because adjusting entries are necessary for the proper application of accrual-basis accounting, cash is never one of the accounts in an adjusting entry.

Frequently a trial balance is performed before the adjusting entries are made. The trial balance, consisting of a debit and a credit column, is a listing of all the ledger accounts with their net debit or net credit balances. The total of all the ledger accounts with debit balances should be equal to the total of all the accounts with credit balances. If the total debits are unequal to the total credits, an accounting error has been made. If there is equality, the trial balance signals the "green light" to proceed to the next step in the accounting cycle, the adjusting entries.

A trial balance constructed after the adjusting entries have been made is called an adjusted trial balance. As such, the adjusted trial balance includes all of the firm's revenue and expense transactions for that accounting period—that is, the cash transactions and the accruals. If the total debits are equal to the total credits, the adjusting trial balance again signals a "green light" to proceed to the next phase of the accounting cycle.

See also DEBIT, CREDIT.

administrative law
Administrative law is all law regarding administrative agencies, including rules, statutes, regulations, and agency and court interpretations of these activities. An administrative agency is any nonjudicial, nonlegislative government entity that creates and administers laws. Major administrative agencies affecting businesses in the United States include the FEDERAL TRADE COMMISSION (FTC), ENVIRONMENTAL PROTECTION AGENCY (EPA) and DEPARTMENT OF LABOR, to name a few.

Administrative agencies can be created by either statutes or executive orders. Most are created by statutes

known as organic acts, whereby a legislature recognizes a problem and creates an agency to address the problem. Administrative agencies are often created when

- legislatures and courts do not have the technical expertise to deal with specific issues
- ongoing oversight is needed for the protection of society from harm
- the weak and poor need assistance
- there is need for speed and efficiency in government decision making
- conflicts exist between groups and the judicial system

Some of the more important federal administrative law statutes include

- the Federal Register Act (1935), providing ways for citizens to access up-to-date information about agencies and regulations
- the Administrative Procedure Act (1946), setting requirements for conducting rulemaking and adjudication by agencies
- the FREEDOM OF INFORMATION ACT (FOIA, 1966), requiring agencies to disclose information in their possession to citizens
- the Federal Privacy Act of 1974, preventing agencies from disclosing about individuals without prior written consent
- the Sunshine Act (Government in Sunshine Act of 1976), or open meeting law, requiring agencies to conduct business in open forums
- the Civil Service Reform Act (1978), protecting many, but not all, civilian federal employees involved in WHISTLE-BLOWER complaints

Administrative law also includes sunset provisions, which terminate administrative agencies after a set period of time; and the creation of ombudspersons, agency representatives whose job is to ensure agencies operate for the purpose and benefit they were created.

Further reading
Fisher, Bruce D., and Michael J. Phillips. *The Legal, Ethical and Regulatory Environment of Business,* 8th ed. Cincinnati, Ohio: Thomson/South-Western, 2003.

adoption process
The adoption process is the series of stages through which consumers determine whether or not to become regular purchasers of a PRODUCT. When considering a new product, most consumers go through five stages in the adoption process: awareness, interest, evaluation, trial, and adoption/rejection. Marketers, recognizing which stage in the adoption process consumers are in, adjust their MARKETING STRATEGY to meet consumer needs.

During the awareness stage, potential consumers first learn that a new product exists, but lack complete information about the product. Marketers with new products attempt to create awareness through publicity, promotion, and word-of-mouth referral.

During the interest stage, consumers begin to seek information about new products. Often potential consumers will seek out consumer innovators—people they know who are knowledgeable about specific categories of products. Potential consumers will also request or look for information from the company or objective sources.

During the evaluation stage, consumers will consider the benefits of the product. For consumers in the evaluation stage, marketers attempt to demonstrate the benefits of their product, sometimes emphasizing the superiority of their new product compared to existing products. If the benefits meet the needs of the consumers, they will enter the trial stage. Samples, price discounts, and demonstrations are offered to encourage consumer trials. If the trial stage produces positive results, consumers will adopt the product and use it regularly; if not, it is rejected.

Consumers go through the adoption process for many categories of goods, including routinely purchased convenience goods, shopping goods, and specialty goods. Less time is involved for convenience goods and more time allotted for specialty goods. Consider the purchase of a new snack food (a convenience good). Usually consumers become aware of the existence of the new product through a store display or by being offered samples. Often they will only consider a new snack food when their favorite food is not available. Snack foods are not expensive, so people will try new products, which they will quickly adopt or reject. For specialty products, things people seek out and spend time evaluating before purchase, marketers recognize they will often need to use image ADVERTISING to generate awareness and interest and PERSONAL SELLING to move potential buyers through the evaluation and trial stages.

Further reading
Boone, Louis E., and David Kurtz. *Contemporary Marketing*, 10th ed. Fort Worth: Dryden Press, 2001.

advertising
Advertising—communication of a product or service through various media—is distinguished from publicity in that it is paid for and from PERSONAL SELLING in that it is nonpersonal and directed toward a group of consumers, the firm's target market. While many people think advertising and personal selling are essentially all there is to marketing, advertising is part of an organization's integrated MARKETING COMMUNICATIONS. Integrated marketing communications is the coordination of all promotional efforts, including advertising, DIRECT MAIL, personal selling, SALES PROMOTION, and PUBLIC RELATIONS. An organization's integrated marketing communications are, in turn, part of

the organization's marketing strategy, including pricing, distribution, and PRODUCT strategies as well as marketing communications.

Advertising in the United States began in the 18th century with craftsmen placing signs outside their dwellings to symbolize their trade. Cobblers used a shoe, gunsmiths used a rifle, and seamstresses used scissors to convey to consumers what product or service they offered. Especially in a market where many consumers were illiterate, symbols told consumers what was available. Even today these symbols can still be seen in company logos and small-town businesses. (Twentieth-century restaurateurs also used pictures of meal combinations to assist illiterate consumers.) Before billboard advertising, firms hired individuals to carry sandwich boards along city streets telling consumers about their products. Early print advertisements included newspaper ads and flyers distributed in markets.

Advertisements typically promote either products or institutions. Product advertisements promote particular products or SERVICES, while institutional advertisements promote ideas; concepts; philosophies; or the goodwill of an industry, firm, or organization. Advertising is used by both for-profit and nonprofit organizations. Major media are required to provide outlets for community-service advertising.

Generally there are three goals in advertising: to inform, persuade, or remind consumers and potential customers. Modern advertisements may consist of a billboard announcing a new business located nearby (inform), a television advertisement trying to convince diners to eat at a particular fast-food restaurant (persuade), or a postcard from the dentist to say a tooth cleaning is due (remind).

One variation of persuasive advertising is comparative advertising: efforts that directly or indirectly promote comparisons with competing products. Companies that are not the dominant firm in the industry often favor this form of advertising, comparing their products to the offerings of the leading firm in the industry. Avis car rentals was one of the early users of comparative advertising with their "We're #2, We Try Harder" campaign. FEDERAL TRADE COMMISSION regulations require advertisers to be able to substantiate claims made in comparative advertisements.

Few consumers realize how much effort and planning goes into advertising campaigns. Marketers start by defining objectives for an advertising effort. TARGET MARKETS are identified, advertising messages and media determined, and the new advertising campaign coordinated with other elements in the organization's marketing strategy.

Often considerable research is used in making advertising decisions. Consumer opinions and reactions are tested, and product features, market conditions, and competitors are all analyzed before executing an advertising campaign. Creative aspects of advertising—including wording, symbols, colors, and use of celebrities—are all carefully analyzed. FOCUS GROUPS are often asked to comment on advertising design before the campaign is implemented.

Print advertisements typically contain four elements: the headline, illustration, body COPY, and signature. The headline is a catchy word or phrase designed to gain attention. The illustration or images combine with the headline to gain interest as well as attention. The body copy serves to inform and then persuade consumers into taking action. The signature includes the company's name, address, and/or TRADEMARK to remind viewers who is sponsoring the advertisement.

Once advertising objectives are defined, tactical plans are developed, including budgets, media choices, and scheduling. Each step is critical to the success of an advertising campaign. A good message conveyed through the right media but at the wrong time will likely fail. For example, Campbell Soup Company once coordinated a radio campaign in the Northeast, scheduling messages with weather reports. The first message said, "Storms are coming, time to stock up on Campbell Soup." When storms arrived, the follow-up message said, "It's cold outside, time to stay warm with a cup of Campbell Soup." The same message delivered in the summertime would have failed.

There are seven media alternatives advertisers can use to convey their message to their target audience: television, radio, newspapers, magazines, direct mail, outdoor, and electronic/interactive. Each media alternative has advantages and disadvantages:

	advantages	disadvantages
television	mass coverage, prestige, repetition	expensive, temporary, lack of selectivity, zapping, public distrust
radio	low cost, targeted audience; quickly delivered	short life span; highly fragmented audiences
newspapers	community reputation, ability to refer to	image reproduction, life span
magazines	selectivity, long life, image reproduction	lack of flexibility
direct mail	selectivity, flexibility, personalized message	cost, consumer distrust, mailing list problems
outdoor	quick, visual, link to locations, repetition	brief exposure, environmental concerns, limited message
electronic/ interactive	two-way communication, cost flexibility, consumer-directed demographics	Internet problems, Web viewer acceptance

As portrayed on many television shows, most major advertisers hire advertising agencies to plan and prepare advertising campaigns (automobile manufacturers, the military, and beer companies are the largest spenders in the United States). Advertising agencies live and die with decisions by major clients to take their account to another agency. In today's global marketplace, ad agencies have emerged to become international service providers for their clients.

Further reading
Boone, Louis E., and David L. Kurtz. *Contemporary Marketing*, 10th ed. Fort Worth, Tex.: Dryden Press, 2001.

affluent society

The term *affluent society* comes from economist John Kenneth Galbraith's 1958 book *The Affluent Society*. Writing during a period when the United States maintained unilateral dominance of the global economy, Galbraith predicted a widening gap between rich and poor which, in turn, would destabilize economic systems. To overcome the disparities between the wealthiest and poorest Americans, Galbraith argued for significant public INVESTMENT in education, transportation, parks, and social needs.

The Affluent Society remains a classic analysis of the conflict between capitalism and society's needs. Using the language and logic of an economist, Galbraith articulated more expanded economic role for government than was generally accepted at that time. His book is credited with influencing such politicians as Bill Clinton and Tony Blair. The affluent society has come to symbolize widespread prosperity, sometimes referring to levels of conspicuous CONSUMPTION associated with 1980s in the United States.

Further reading
Galbraith, John Kenneth. *The Affluent Society*. Boston: Houghton Mifflin, 1958.

agency theory

Agency theory is a management and economic theory that attempts to explain relationships and self-interest in business organizations. In agency theory, principals contract with agents to perform tasks for the benefit of the principal. In making the CONTRACT with the agent, the principal delegates authority regarding how a task is to be accomplished, holding the agent responsible for attaining a certain outcome but not dictating the methods used to achieve the outcome.

Typical principal-agent relationships include shareholder-manager and manager-employee relationships. In a shareholder-manager relationship, the SHAREHOLDERS, through their BOARD OF DIRECTORS, set goals and managers allocate the company's RESOURCES to attain the goals. As evidenced in the Enron scandal, management's goals may be in conflict with those of shareholders. In the Enron case, managers manipulated financial arrangements among themselves, profiting significantly but ultimately bankrupting the company and leaving Enron shareholders (and many employees) with nothing.

Agency theory suggests that a system is needed to ensure managers operate in the best interests of the principals they represent. As in the Enron case, AUDITING is one agency cost principals incur in order to monitor the activities of managers. Limits placed by shareholders on the options managers can choose, such as private PARTNERSHIPS with executives, and bonus systems are also used to reduce the conflict of purposes between the self-interests of managers and the interests of shareholders.

Performance-based pay systems are designed to give agents—whether managers reporting to the board of directors of employees reporting to managers—incentives to work for the best interests of the principals. In many instances, these systems fail to attain the desired goal. MIT management professor Robert Gibbons describes three cases where incentive systems failed.

At the H. J. Heinz Company, for example, division managers received bonuses only if earnings increased from the prior year. The managers delivered consistent earnings growth by manipulating the timing of shipments to customers and by prepaying for services not yet received. At Dun & Bradstreet, salespeople earned no commission unless the customer bought a larger subscription to the firm's credit-report services than in the previous year. In 1989, the company faced millions of dollars in lawsuits following charges that its salespeople deceived customers into buying larger subscriptions by fraudulently overstating their historical usage. In 1992, Sears abolished the commission plan in its auto-repair shops, which paid mechanics based on the profits from repairs authorized by customers. Mechanics misled customers into authorizing unnecessary repairs, leading California officials to prepare to close Sears' auto-repair business statewide. In each of these cases, employees took actions to increase their compensation, but these actions were seemingly at the expense of long-run firm value.

Sales managers frequently face principal-agent conflicts. Straight salary systems would deter actions on the part of sales agents that are in conflict with the goals of the sales manager, but straight salary systems do not give salespeople positive work incentives.

Agency theory suggests that businesses operate under conditions of uncertainty and lack of complete information. Given these obstacles, two agency problems arise: the problem of employees not putting forth their maximum effort, referred to as moral hazard; and the problem of agents misrepresenting their ability to do the work for which they are being hired, called adverse selection. As in

the situations Gibbons described, tying compensation to performance or profits does not eliminate the problem of conflicting interests between principals and agents. While agency theory illustrates the economic conflicts between groups, few solutions beyond vigilance, on the part of principals, have been proposed.

See also PERFORMANCE APPRAISAL.

Further reading
Gibbons, Robert S., "Agency Theory, Part II: Getting What You Pay for." Available on-line. URL: http://web.mit.edu/rgibbons/www/903_1n2.pdf; Kaplan, B., "Transaction Costs vs. Agency Theory." Available on-line URL: http://wizrd.ucr.edu/~bkaplan/soc/lib/txcosta.pdf.

aging of accounts   See BAD DEBT, AGING OF ACCOUNTS.

agricultural support programs
Agricultural support programs are payments and incentives that subsidize agricultural businesses and growers. These subsidies include price supports, TARIFFS, and deficiency payments. Included in the system are incentives to conserve land and water resources, help stabilize the INCOME of farmers and ranchers, and enable new or disadvantaged farmers to get into the food production business. Agricultural subsidies, both in the United States and elsewhere, are political and highly controversial.

Agriculture is the world's most heavily subsidized trade sector. The WORLD TRADE ORGANIZATION (WTO) estimates that current government subsidies to farmers worldwide amount to $350 billion per year. The EUROPEAN UNION, United States, and Japan, in that order, are the major users of agricultural support programs. Government support and protection of industries has been increasing and all countries have felt the consequences. These programs impact ECONOMIC GROWTH, increase trade friction between nations, increase budget expenditures, and depress COMMODITY MARKETS. High price supports encourage surpluses, which distort global market prices. Restrictive import barriers keep some producers from being able to sell their products in certain markets.

The underlying reason for agricultural subsidies is to make sure, there is enough food and fiber on American tables and to ensure that American farmers can produce our food. When the U.S. population was still growing at a fast rate, the focus of the federal government's agricultural policy was on feeding its citizens. Many of the policy elements now in place were essential to accomplishing those goals.

Agricultural policy is political. U.S. government support for agriculture began in the late 1800s but became more structured and institutionalized after the GREAT DEPRESSION. Since the 1930s, agricultural support programs have been reexamined, and roughly every six years major new legislation has been passed. American farmers generally have resisted changes in subsidies and efforts to integrate the production and export market considerations.

The 1985 Farm Bill established the Conservation Reserve Program (CRP), providing incentives that encourage farmers to contract to set aside environmentally sensitive farmland for a period of time, usually 10 years. The Federal Agriculture Improvement and Reform (FAIR) Act (also known as the 1996 Farm Bill and "Freedom to Farm") was the first major attempt to get rid of much of the old structure in farm programs. Farmers had been chafing for years at the controls in place on what they could grow and how much they could produce. Many felt that efficient, productive farmers were penalized, and farmers who were poor managers or not as productive as others were rewarded. There had been major abuses in the system, with large agribusiness CONGLOMERATES getting much of the money intended for small-family farmers. The "Freedom to Farm" bill was intended to solve many of the problems that had been in the system up to that point. Farmers were optimistic about the bill, because it increased their flexibility in making choices about their farm operations by "decoupling" benefits. This meant they were not restricted to certain crops and they could make better use of their land. Because it rewarded land ownership, the 1996 Farm Bill had the unintended consequence of artificially inflating farmland prices.

One of the most unpopular elements of past farm legislation had been deficiency payments to producers, which, in essence, paid the farmer the difference between the commodity's market price and the allowance for it. A major thrust of the 1996 Farm Bill was to get rid of deficiency payments. However, large and well-funded lobbies and growers for some commodities managed to override this action by threatening to prevent passage of the entire bill unless their crops were exempted.

The Farm Security and Rural Investment Act of 2002, also known as the 2002 Farm Bill, reversed the 1996 Farm Bill and increased agricultural spending over the next 10 years by 80 percent, from just over $100 billion to more than $180 billion annually. Federal subsidies for the major program crops will rise by more than 70 percent. Throughout the world this was seen as a major reversal of President George W. Bush's FREE TRADE policy and of the U.S. commitment to reform world agriculture markets. Many predict that this will make negotiations at the next round of WTO talks much more difficult, since agriculture is to be the main focus of negotiations in the near future. The 2002 Farm Bill likely will result in the European Union keeping its higher levels of subsidies, and other countries will not lower theirs since the United States has increased theirs. Since American growers now depend on foreign exports as the major portion of their markets, domestic agricultural support policies will increasingly need to be addressed with consideration of international trade agreements.

Further reading

U.S. Department of Agriculture website. Available on-line. URL: http://www.usda.gov; "Food and Agricultural Policy: Taking Stock for the New Century," U.S. Department of Agriculture. Available on-line. URL: http://www.usda.gov/news/pubs/farmpolicy01/fpindex.htm; 2002 Farm Bill. Available on-line. URL: http://www. usda.gov/farmbill/; "U.S. Proposal for Global Agricultural Trade Reform." Available on-line. URL: http://www.fas. usda.gov/itp/wto/.

—Laura Carter

Aid to Families with Dependent Children

The Aid to Families with Dependent Children (AFDC) program was a federal WELFARE program that originated during the GREAT DEPRESSION as part of the 1935 Social Security Act. The SOCIAL SECURITY Act provided funds for the states to help the elderly, the blind, and underprivileged children. The provision to help states provide support for children was contained in Title IV of the act, and participation by any state was voluntary. With the original title "Aid to Dependent Children," the initial purpose of Title IV was to provide financial assistance for disadvantaged dependent children and did not provide assistance for parents or guardians involved in the child's raising. (There was, however, a requirement that the child live with an adult in order to be eligible for aid.) It was not until 1950 that the government began to provide funds to aid in the care of the adults responsible for the children. In 1960 states were allowed to claim federal reimbursement for funds used to aid the child of an unemployed parent *and* the unemployed parent, and in 1962 aid was allowed for a second parent in the family. Hence the name of the program was changed to "Aid to Families with Dependent Children."

Instead of setting apart a fixed amount of money each year to be divided among the states, Congress approved reimbursement of a certain percentage of state expenditures without any limit on the total amount. Originally each state with an approved plan was reimbursed by the Secretary of the Treasury for one-third of its benefit payments, up to maximum federal payment of $6 per month for the first child plus $4 for each additional child. This general plan went through several changes over the years, but the basic method of funding remained the same until the passage of the Temporary Assistance to Needy Families Act (TANF) in 1996.

In 1967 a set of formal rules for the program was published in the *Code of Federal Regulations*. This stated that each state was required to assign a single agency to be in charge of the administration of the program, that the state's program be available in all parts of the state, and that the rules be universally enforced. This prevented local governments from having the power to impose local rules and regulations. The states were also required to "provide an opportunity for anyone to apply for aid, to furnish aid with reasonable promptness to all eligible persons, and to provide the opportunity for a fair hearing to those denied assistance or not given a response within a reasonable period of time."

Eligibility for the program was regulated by the particular state of residence. Each state was required to establish a "standard of need" or maximum amount of INCOME and other resources a family could have and be eligible for assistance. These standards of need varied by the size of the family. Each state determined eligibility by comparing family income to the state's need standard. If the family had gross income that did not exceed 85 percent of the state's need standard, and gross income (less specified deductions) that did not exceed 100 percent of the need standard, then the family was eligible for assistance. All children through the age of 15 were eligible for assistance. Each state had the option of aiding children older than 15 if certain conditions were met. Children aged 16–17 had to be attending school regularly, students aged 18–20 had to be in high school or a course of vocational or technical training, and students aged 18–20 had to be in college or university. In 1981 changes were made which ended a child's eligibility on his or her 18th birthday or, if the state chose, on his 19th if still in high school. Also in 1981, Congress required states to calculate the income of a child's stepparent when figuring a family's needs, income, and resources, and allowed states to claim federal reimbursement for aid to an unborn child in the last trimester of pregnancy.

In 1962, for states that included unemployed parents in the program, Community Work and Training (CWT) programs were established for federally aided recipients age 18 and over. These programs were to pay wages comparable to those present in the community and were required to ensure that appropriate standards of health and safety were followed. In 1964, under Title V of the Economic Opportunity Act, Congress allowed the formation of CWT projects in states that had not yet included the unemployed parents category in their AFDC programs. In 1968, in conjunction with the Department of Health, Education, and Welfare (HEW) and the DEPARTMENT OF LABOR, Work Incentive (WIN) programs were created for certain AFDC recipients; all unemployed fathers had to be referred to the program. In 1971 the government required that all AFDC parents register for work or training with the WIN program (except for mothers of children under age six). Finally, in 1988 WIN was replaced by the Job Opportunities and Basic Skills Training (JOBS) program in a new part IV-F of the Social Security Act. This mandated that states engage most mothers with no children below age three in education, work, or job training.

Originally, in 1935, Congress set the federal share of AFDC payments at 33 percent, up to individual payments of $18 for the first child and $12 for additional children. As stated previously, this comes to a maximum federal share of $6 for the first child. Over the years matching maximums were increased and based on average spending per recipient. In 1956 variable rates were established, providing more generous federal reimbursement for states with lower per capita income. In 1965, with the creation of Medicaid, federal matching for each state dollar spent on the AFDC program was provided. Each state that implemented Medicaid was allowed to use the open-ended matching formula for claiming federal reimbursement of a portion of total AFDC benefits as well. Numbers provided for the years between 1971 and 1996 show that expenditures rose from $6 billion to $24 billion in actual dollars, however, when adjusted for INFLATION, total expenditures increased very slightly. In constant 1996 dollars, the amount spent on benefits actually declined from a high of $26 billion in 1976 to $20.4 billion in 1996 (Office of ASPE website, 2001).

Critics of the AFDC argue that the program created a set of incentives that were harmful to the nation's "social fabric." The welfare system was allegedly dehumanizing; encouraged dependency; supported female-headed families, divorce, and unmarried childbearing; and encouraged low levels of work effort among recipients. Supporters argue that the AFDC program helped to reduce poverty and provided work and skill training, in addition to its success in keeping intact poor female-headed families with young children.

On August 22, 1996, President Bill Clinton signed into law the Personal Responsibility and Work Opportunity Reconciliation Act (PRWORA) of 1996 (Public Law 104-193). PRWORA replaced the AFDC program that had been in existence for 60 years.

Further reading
Brandon, Peter D. "Did the AFDC Program Succeed in Keeping Mothers and Young Children Living Together?" *Social Service Review* 74, no. 2 (June 2000): 214; Office of the Assistant Secretary for Planning & Evaluation. "Aid to Families with Dependent Children: The Baseline," *Human Services Policy*, June 1998. Available on-line. URL: aspe.hhs.gov/hsp/AFDC/afdcbase98.htm. Downloaded on October 31, 2001; Social Security Administration. *Social Security Bulletin* (Annual 1994 57n SUPP): 114–37.

—April Miller

American Bankers Association

The American Bankers Association (ABA) is an organization representing banking interests at the national level. Created in 1875 to urge for the repeal of taxes on CAPITAL, deposits, and checks, the ABA is a powerful lobbying force in Washington on financial issues. ABA interests have changed with technological advances over the years. In the 19th century ABA efforts focused on banker education and advocacy. One of the early problems was bank robbers. In the 1890s an ABA program paying rewards for the conviction of bank robbers significantly reduced this problem and led to the death of notorious bank criminals, including Butch Cassidy and the Sundance Kid in Bolivia.

As telegraph technology became available, in the early 1900s the ABA created a cipher telegraphic code for use in banking communications. With today's INTERNET technology the ABA supported legislation creating the first Web-based bank in 1995. With the easing of GREAT DEPRESSION-era banking restrictions, the ABA is advocating new legislation expanding banking activities in the areas of INSURANCE and securities. In 1997 *Forbes* rated the ABA as the 12th most influential lobbying group in the country.

Further reading
American Bankers Association website. Available on-line. URL: www.aba.com.

American Bar Association

The American Bar Association (ABA) is the largest and most powerful law organization in the United States. Created in 1878 when 100 lawyers met in Saratoga Springs, New York, the ABA today has more than 370,000 members, including lawyers, judges, court administrators, law teachers, legal assistants, and law librarians. About half of the attorneys in the United States belong to the ABA. The percentage was higher in past decades but declined when ABA positions on major social and legal issues met with disagreement among its members.

The ABA publishes books, pamphlets, and brochures on almost every facet of the law, making it the largest legal publisher in the world. ABA publications are designed for the general public as well as members of the legal profession. The organization is also a major lobbying force in Washington and in state legislatures. ABA committees often create model legislation presented for adoption by legislatures. For example, The Model Business Corporation Act (1950) was drafted by the ABA Committee on Business Corporations.

While the ABA has over 150 committees, subcommittees and task forces, two of the most important functions of the organization are accrediting U.S. law schools and reviewing presidential nominations for judicial appointments. An ABA rating of "not qualified" is a major rebuke of a president's choice for a judgeship. In 2001 President George W. Bush announced he would no longer refer candidates for judicial appointments to the ABA review committee.

Further reading
American Bar Association website. Available on-line. URL: www.abanet.org.

American Customer Satisfaction Index

The American Customer Satisfaction Index (ACSI) is an indicator of changing customer satisfaction with the quality of goods and services available to households in the United States. The ACSI uses a national survey to measure customer satisfaction with 164 companies and 30 federal government agencies. ACSI conducts more than 50,000 interviews annually with customers of the companies and federal agencies included in the index. The scores for one or two sectors of the U.S. economy are updated quarterly.

For example, in August 2001 the updated scores for manufacturing and cable/satellite television were released. Using a 100-point scale, among automobile manufacturers Cadillac received the highest rating (88), while Jeep/Eagle received the lowest rating (76). Among personal computer manufacturers, Dell received the highest rating (78) and Compaq the lowest (69). When grouped, automobiles, consumer electronics, and household appliances had the highest average ratings (80, 81, and 82 respectively), while personal computers and cable/satellite television had the lowest average ratings (71 and 64). A *Wall Street Journal* writer concluded, "It shows that shoppers are happier with Old Economy products . . . than they are with New Economy [products and services]."

In the last quarter of 2000, the scores for federal agencies were updated (only those agencies that have significant interaction with consumers are included in the survey). Overall the government-wide index was 68.6, unchanged from the previous year, but significantly lower than the scores for the private sector. Among the federal agencies, Student Financial Assistance Education and NASA Education received higher ratings from the year before, while Head Start parents, the Census, and Veterans Administration all saw their ratings decline. The Internal Revenue Service and Occupational Safety and Health Administration perennially receive the lowest ratings among federal agencies.

The ASCI is produced through a partnership consisting of the University of Michigan Business School, the AMERICAN SOCIETY FOR QUALITY, and the CFI Group, a private consulting firm. The University of Michigan's School of Business is well known for its INDEX OF CONSUMER EXPECTATIONS. Like the Index of Consumer Expectations, the ASCI is used to predict CONSUMER BEHAVIOR. ASCI researchers developed an econometric model using the scores to predict customer complaints and CUSTOMER LOYALTY. Marketers know building and retaining relationships with customers is critical to long-term success. The developers of the ACSI have found their index is correlated with changes in the Dow Jones Industrial Index, and that companies rated in the upper half of the index have generated significantly greater shareholder WEALTH than those rated in the lower half of the index.

Further reading
American Customer Satisfaction Index website. Available on-line. URL: www.bus.umich.edu/research/nqrc/acsi.html; Hilsenrath, Jon E., and Joe Flint, "Consumers Find Fault with Products of New Economy," *Wall Street Journal*, 20 August 2001, p. A2.

American depository receipts

American depository receipts (ADRs) are certificates issued by a U.S. bank or brokerage firm, representing foreign shares held by the institution. One ADR may represent one share, a portion of a foreign share, or a bundle of shares of a foreign CORPORATION. ARBITRAGE, the simultaneous buying and selling of like securities in different markets to take advantage of slight price differences, keeps the prices of ADRs and underlying foreign shares essentially equal.

Most ADRs are "sponsored," meaning the corporation provides financial information and other assistance to the institution and may subsidize the administration of the ADRs. Institutions sponsoring ADRs act as custodian for the company issuing the stock and handle DIVIDEND payout, notifications, and processing. Depository receipts are registered with the SECURITIES AND EXCHANGE COMMISSION and trade like any other U.S. security in national exchanges or over-the-counter markets. Generally the foreign company approaches the institution requesting sponsorship. "Unsponsored" ADRs are issued by one or more depository institutions in response to market DEMAND but do not receive assistance from the corporation.

The U.S. financial market is the largest in the world. By selling shares of stock in their companies through ADRs, foreign corporations raise CAPITAL in U.S. markets for their business operations. In the year 2000, trading in ADRs exceeded $1 trillion for the first time. Ericson (Sweden), Nokia (Finland), Vodafone (United Kingdom), BP Amoco (United Kingdom), and Telephonos de Mexico were the highest-volume ADRs traded. During the year, 182 new ADR programs were established by companies from 38 countries, dominated by companies from the United Kingdom, Germany, and Hong Kong.

For investors, ADRs offer a low-cost opportunity to diversify their portfolios. Until the creation of ADRs, it was difficult for individual investors to purchase stocks of foreign companies. But ADRs are subject to a variety of risks: currency risk; the potential for decline in value as a country's currency declines in FOREIGN EXCHANGE markets; political risk, the potential for violence or DEFAULT of a government; and economic risk, the potential for decline in the foreign company's home economy.

See also GLOBAL SHARES.

Further reading

"ADR Trading Tops The $1 Trillion Mark For the First Time," *Wall Street Journal*, 2 January 2001, p. C10.

American dream

The American dream is the aspirations of working-class citizens, parents, and immigrant groups to attain their image of a middle-class STANDARD OF LIVING. Americans and people coming to the United States often desire home ownership, better jobs, education for their children, and perhaps their own business. Most working-class parents express the American dream by desiring that their children do better and have more than they did.

World War II, in which many poor and uneducated American soldiers traveled and interacted with people of different social classes and cultural backgrounds, strengthened their desire for a better standard of living for themselves and their children. Sometimes it was expressed as wanting a "bigger piece of the pie" as payment for their sacrifices during the war. Levittown, a major housing development created to meet the demands of veterans for their own homes, symbolized early images of the American dream. Subsequently, immigrant groups have pursued similar dreams, striving to educate their children and to succeed by standards known as the American dream.

American Federation of Labor and Congress of Industrial Organizations (AFL-CIO)

The American Federation of Labor and Congress of Industrial Organizations (AFL-CIO) is a voluntary league of national labor unions representing over 13 million workers. Its mission is to bring social and economic justice to America's workforce through political and legislative delegation. The AFL-CIO functions primarily to promote fair-trade legislation, affordable health care, quality public education, fair wages substantial enough to support a family, job safety, and retirement benefits including a pension program.

Sixty-four UNIONS make up the AFL-CIO, some of which include the Writers Guild of America, United Farm Workers of America, United American Nurses, Transport Union of America, Seafarers International Union of North America, and Association of Flight Attendants. Delegates elected by their local union govern the AFL-CIO along with an executive council. They meet every two years at a convention where policies are made and goals are set. Officers who run the AFL-CIO operations are elected at the convention every four years. John J. Sweeney, president of the AFL-CIO, was first elected in 1995.

The American labor movement began in the 1820s when skilled workers from various cities formed organizations in order to obtain better pay. National unions were formed in the 1850s when blacksmiths, machinists, printers, carpenters and other skilled laborers began a union organization named the Knights of St. Crispin. Philadelphia garment workers established the Knights of Labor, the first organized labor union to last more than a few years. Its main goals were to do away with the 10-hour workday, abolish child labor, and get equal pay for equal work.

In 1881 wage earners organized the union that became the American Federation of Labor (AFL). Samuel Gompers served as the AFL's president from 1886 to 1894 and from 1896 to 1924 for a total of 37 years. Gompers was not as politically active as other labor leaders had been. He stressed COLLECTIVE BARGAINING to obtain higher wages and better working conditions. The AFL campaigned to encourage the public to buy goods with the "union label," made by union employees.

Organized labor had many setbacks in the early 1900s, including violent strikes and unfavorable legislation, and union membership declined. The AFL was too conservative for those workers with a more socialist view. The union didn't begin to gain membership again until immigration was restricted with the Immigration Act of 1924. COMPETITION for jobs decreased and the bargaining power of the work force increased.

The GREAT DEPRESSION forced changes in the AFL. Business leaders were no longer in favor with workers because they could not bring about an end to the depression. Political leaders developed new laws to help the nation's economy. President Franklin Delano Roosevelt's New Deal program guaranteed a MINIMUM WAGE for all workers as well as the right to join unions, but the U.S. Supreme Court ruled it unconstitutional. In 1935 the National Labor Relations Act, also known as the WAGNER ACT, replaced the New Deal program. It established a board with the authority to punish unfair labor practices.

The AFL formed the Committee for Industrial Organization to organize mass-production industries. Union membership quickly grew in the steel, automobile, and rubber industries. Conflicts resulted with the AFL throwing out CIO union members. The Committee for Industrial Organization then changed its name to the Congress of Industrial Organizations and established its own league of unions under the leadership of John L. Lewis.

When the United States entered World War II, labor leaders agreed not to strike for the duration of the war. Wages did not increase during this period, but "fringe benefits" were established. After World War II, unions sought large wage increases through organized strikes, and the economy boomed. The TAFT-HARTLEY ACT in 1947 established government controls over unions. AFL leader George Meany and CIO leader Walter Reuther merged the two leagues in 1955, and they became known as the AFL-CIO.

The league of unions that make up the AFL-CIO has 13 departments, including the Safety and Health Department, the Organizing Department (which assists in the recruitment and training of union organizers), the Civil and Human Rights Department, the Field Mobilization Department (which coordinates a community services sector and mobilizes thousands of members across the nation to support political action), the Corporate Affairs Department (which assists national unions in collective bargaining), and the Legislative Department (which promotes equal pay for women, part-time workers, the minimum wage, public education, SOCIAL SECURITY, and economic policies).

The AFL-CIO goals remain much the same as they were when the AFL first was established:

- unionization of workers
- economic justice

- occupational safety and health
- education
- political lobbying

Civil rights and discrimination in all forms are also priorities of today's AFL-CIO. Through its Committee on Political Education, the AFL-CIO encourages members to vote on Election Day. An international department assists with organized labor in other countries. Under the leadership of John J. Sweeney, the AFL-CIO is committed to advancing the welfare of its membership, actively campaigns against RIGHT-TO-WORK LAWS, and continues to attempt to have the Taft-Hartley Labor Act repealed. The AFL-CIO's plan for the next century includes a restructured labor movement, INTERNET access for working families, and the preservation of workers' freedom to choose a union.

Further reading
Dark, Taylor E. *The Unions and the Democrats: An Enduring Alliance, Updated Edition.* Ithaca, N.Y.: Cornell University Press, 2001; Mangum, Garth L., *Union Resilience in Troubled Times: The Story of the Operating Engineers, AFL-CIO, 1960–1993.* Armonk, N.Y.: M. E. Sharp, 1994; Mort, Jo-Ann, ed. *Not Your Father's Union Movement: Inside the AFL-CIO.* New York: Verso, 1998; Tillman, Ray M. and Michael S. Cummings. *The Transformation of U.S. Unions: Voices, Visions, and Strategies from the Grassroots.* Boulder, Colo.: Lynne Rienner Publishers, Inc., 1999.

—Cindy L. Halsey

American Industrial Revolution
The American Industrial Revolution (1877–1919) was an era in which the nation was transformed from its agrarian, rural roots to an increasingly urban, mechanized, and innovative power. Marked by the escalating use of machines to perform work, expansion of transportation services and available markets, and the birth of labor UNIONS, the Industrial Revolution shaped the future face of American business.

During this period, deposit banking was born and delivered the funds necessary to bankroll technological improvements in transportation, agriculture, and manufacturing, which provided increased production at reduced COSTS. Profits were reinvested into each sector and paid for future innovations and technological changes. Meanwhile the labor movement was born in an effort to keep workers' needs in balance with big business's power. In all, five pillars evolved to bring about the foundations of U.S. business today.

BANKING
CAPITAL fueled the Industrial Revolution. The roots of change in the banking industry were planted by the federal government's search for Civil War financing, which led to the National Banking Act of 1863 and the revised

act of 1864. The 1863 act established a uniform national currency of federally chartered bank notes, backed by federal government BONDS to be sold to state banks. The revised act of 1864 created a tax on state bank-issued notes and led to the virtual elimination of state bank notes. However, the currency of national bank notes failed to adequately provide for the growing nation's need for flexible currency. Ten years later, loans in the form of bank notes gave way to deposit banking, in which banks delivered loan proceeds by crediting a depositor's account. Greenbacks, also known as paper money, were first issued as non-gold–backed legal tender in 1862 as part of the federal government's effort to raise money for the Civil War. Greenbacks became a permanent part of U.S. currency with the 1875 Resumption Act as well as 1878 congressional compromise that provided for paper money to be redeemable in gold and limited resumption of silver dollars, as proposed in the Bland-Allison Act. Multiple monetary panics closed the 19th century and led to the 1913 creation of the FEDERAL RESERVE SYSTEM: 12 regional, relatively independent banks to oversee regional monetary needs.

The increasing availability of loans allowed the nation's railroads to expand and add additional tracks between important cities and to invest in better equipment and technology. The expansion served to open new markets for agricultural products and industry, in addition to enhancing further development of the country's natural resources, including gold, silver, pig iron, and coal.

RAILROADS

America's first transcontinental railroad was completed by the Union and Central Pacific railroads in 1869. The nation boasted of 79,082 miles of railroad in 1877, and with the addition of five cross-country routes and extensive building of secondary and feeder tracks, railroad track mileage tripled to 240,293 miles by 1910. When completed, travel time from New York to Chicago was reduced from almost a month to two days. England's industrial accomplishments heavily influenced America's rail industry. Steel rails, available because of the steel manufacturing improvements by the Bessemer and open-hearth processes in England, were an improvement over the pre–Civil War rails. Steam locomotives (made practical by Englishman George Stephenson), air brakes, and automatic couplers to link cars together lengthened trains and, in turn, increased the tonnage each could carry. Additionally, the introduction of the refrigerated cargo car allowed for the transportation of perishable goods over longer distances. These improvements in technology increased individual freight train cargoes from 20 tons in the 1880s to 80 tons by 1914.

Farmers' dependence on railroads to get products to regional and urban markets led to increasing government regulation and consolidation of the railroad companies.

AGRICULTURE

While the Industrial Revolution signalled America's decreasing reliance on agriculture for its WEALTH, agriculture nevertheless remained prominent. Wheat, cotton, flour, and meat products held the greatest export value for farmers and were the bulk of U.S. exports, which rose in annual value from $590 million in 1877 to $1.37 billion in 1900. Technology again played an important role, as the "sodbuster," designed to break up virgin land, allowed farmers to plant crops on their new western farms, as encouraged by the Homestead Act of 1862. Refrigerated railcars carried perishables from local markets into regional markets and urban areas; fruit and vegetables from the Great Lakes, Florida, and California; dairy products from Michigan, Minnesota, New York, and Wisconsin; cattle to Chicago; and meat products from Chicago. Further mechanization occurred as farmers ploughed earnings into more land and newer equipment in an attempt to increase profitability.

MANUFACTURING

Improved railroad transportation allowed inexpensive coal delivery, which fueled steam-powered factories and freed factories from waterpower restrictions. As a result, factories spread throughout the Northeast. Manufacturing gained the largest benefit from technology, as business insisted on new processes, machines, products, and distribution methods. New PRODUCTS created new industries, as the period saw the successful installation of the gasoline internal-combustion engine (1893); automobile manufacturing (1900); aircraft production (1903); the electric light, patented by Thomas A. Edison (1890); and the telephone, radio, typewriter, phonograph, and cash register.

As productivity grew, the price of producing goods dropped, and improved mechanization increasingly accelerated the process of America's shift to manufacturing as a source of wealth. In 1860 leading manufacturing industries were, in order of rank, flour and meal, cotton goods, lumber, boots and shoes, and iron founding and machinery. By 1919 technology's influence had altered the top five industries to slaughtering and meatpacking, iron and steel, automobiles, foundry and machine shop products, and cotton goods. That same year the wealth derived from manufacturing was three times that of agriculture's wealth.

As industries grew so did COMPETITION, as many companies operated with varying levels of success and product quality. This situation resulted in overproduction, which led to lower prices and profits. To better control financial outcomes, industries began to operate collectively as TRUSTS. One of the earliest and most famous trusts was John D. Rockefeller's Standard Oil Company (1882), which was created when Rockefeller and associates bought nearly 90 percent of the country's kerosene industry. Similarly, James B. Duke invited competitors to join his American Tobacco Company or watch their markets be taken over by successful American Tobacco ADVERTISING campaigns.

As big business pooled the resources and interests of competing parties, by 1919 it was employing 86 percent of America's wage earners and created 87.7 percent of the value of goods manufactured. Additionally, the annual value of manufactured goods ballooned from $5.4 billion in 1870 to $13 billion in 1899.

Trusts faced opposition by state and federal governments. In 1911, the Supreme Court used the 1890 SHERMAN ANTITRUST ACT to decree Standard Oil and American Tobacco as monopolies, and further ruled the two companies be broken into smaller companies.

LABOR

In the face of the overwhelming power of trusts and big business, the labor movement took root as tensions between workers and employers increased. The Knights of Labor was the earliest influential group, founded in 1869 and designed to unify producers' interests. At its height (1884–85), the Knights claimed 700,000 members nationwide and backed successful strikes against the Southwest System, Union Pacific, and Wabash railroads, which prevented a reduction in wages and gained public sympathy. But the union's influence waned after 1886, when only half of 1,600 strikes involving 600,000 workers were successful. Additionally, strife within the union between skilled and unskilled workers weakened the Knights' membership and influence. As the Knights' power declined, the AMERICAN FEDERATION OF LABOR (AFL) gained the mantle of trade union leadership. Organized in 1881, the AFL had 548,000 members by 1900 and focused its efforts on economic gain for the membership, including better hours, wages, and working conditions. While the Knights attempted to meet goals through political influence and education, the AFL used economic means to meet its goals.

Further reading

Cleland, Hugh G., "Industrial Revolution." In *Encyclopedia Americana,* vol. 15, 122–27. Danbury, Conn.: Grolier Inc., 2002; Davis, W. N., Jr., "The Age of Industrial Growth, 1877–1919." In *Encyclopedia Americana,* vol. 27, 745–745r. Danbury, Conn.: Grolier Inc., 2002; Martin, Albro, "Economy from Reconstruction to 1914." In *Encyclopedia of American Economic History: Studies of the Principal Movements and Ideas,* vol. 1, 91–109. New York: Scribner, 1980; "United States of America: Industrialization of the U.S. Economy." In *The New Encyclopedia Britannica,* vol. 29, 242–43. Chicago: Encyclopaedia Britannica, 2002.

—Katrina Reiling

American Institute of Certified Public Accountants

The American Institute of Certified Public Accountants (AICPA), with over the 330,000 members, is the most prominent national professional association for CPAs (whose profession is the practice of FINANCIAL ACCOUNTING) in the United States.

AICPA qualifies individuals for the practice of public accounting by awarding its professional designation of "certified public accountant" (CPA). CPAs perform financial accounting services for the general public and charge professional fees for rendering them.

In addition to its professional designation activities, AICPA also supports its Accounting Standards Team and publishes *The Journal of Accountancy,* a monthly publication focusing on "the latest news and developments related to the field of accounting." Objectives of the Accounting Standards Team are "to determine Institute technical policies regarding financial accounting and reporting standards, and generally to be the Institute's official spokesperson on these matters; to provide guidance to members of the Institute on financial accounting and reporting issues not otherwise covered in authoritative literature; and to influence the form and content of pronouncements of the FINANCIAL ACCOUNTING STANDARDS BOARD . . . and other bodies that have authority over financial accounting or reporting standards."

Further reading

AICPA website. Available on-line. URL: www.aicpa.org.

American Medical Association

Founded in 1847, the American Medical Association (AMA), the leading organization representing medical doctors in the United States, is a powerful force influencing health-care policy and spending in the country. When first organized, the AMA focused on developing a code of ethics for medical practitioners. Later, in 1883, they established the *Journal of the American Medical Association* (JAMA), a premier medical journal highly quoted and influential among the medical establishment. In the early 20th century the AMA established its medical school accreditation program, controlling quality and growth of the number of physicians in the country.

U.S. health care accounts for over 13 percent of GROSS DOMESTIC PRODUCT annually, significantly more than the amount spent in other industrialized countries in the world. Critics of the AMA argue that the organization represents the interests of the medical industry at the expense of American consumers. Supporters counter that the AMA has a long history of ensuring high-quality medical care in the country. The AMA is a leading POLITICAL ACTION COMMITTEE in Washington.

Further reading

American Medical Association website. Available on-line. URL: www.ama-assn.org.

American Society for Quality

The American Society for Quality (ASQ) is the leading quality-improvement organization in the United States.

The ASQ has over 100,000 individual members and over 1,000 corporate sustaining members worldwide. Created in 1946, the organization is an outgrowth of efforts to improve production standards during World War II. Using the methods of Walter Shewhart, the War Production Board—later the American Society for Quality Control (changed to ASQ in 1997)—sponsored courses to train people in QUALITY CONTROL.

The ASQ now offers a variety of quality-control programs, including home study, conferences, certification, and administration of the BALDRIGE AWARD (Malcolm Baldrige National Quality Award). Through its Registrar Accreditation Board, the ASQ assists with the International Standards Organization's ISO 9000 and ISO 14000 accreditation and certification. ASQ training focuses on statistical process control, quality cost management, TOTAL QUALITY MANAGEMENT, failure management, and zero defects.

As stated on the ASQ website:

- Quality is not a program; it is an approach to business.
- Quality is a collection of powerful tools and concepts that is proven to work.
- Quality is defined by the customer through his/her satisfaction.
- Quality includes continuous improvement and breakthrough events.
- Quality tools and techniques are applicable in every aspect of the business.
- Quality is aimed at performance excellence; anything less is an improvement opportunity.
- Quality increases customer satisfaction, reduces CYCLE TIME and COSTS, and eliminates errors and rework.
- Quality is not just for businesses. It works in nonprofit organizations like schools, health care and social services, and government agencies.
- Results (performance and financial) are the natural consequence of effective quality management.

Further reading
American Society for Quality website. Available on-line. URL: www.asq.org.

American Stock Exchange

The American Stock Exchange (AMEX), a self-regulating organization registered with the SECURITIES AND EXCHANGE COMMISSION, is the second largest stock exchange in the United States. The AMEX originated in the late 1700s and was known as the New York Curb Market. In 1921 the curb market moved indoors in lower Manhattan. In the 1940s, after struggling through the depression years, the exchange was renamed the American Stock Exchange.

The NEW YORK STOCK EXCHANGE (NYSE) is the preeminent stock exchange in the country and in the world. The AMEX is much smaller and less prestigious; in the mid-1990s AMEX trading volume was only one-twentieth of NYSE volume. It has survived by being less expensive to list companies on the exchange and by introducing new products and services. In the 1950s the AMEX expanded into "satellite markets," began trading in commodities and monetary instruments, and introduced automated trading. In 1975 options trading was initiated, and in 1995 the AMEX, in conjunction with STANDARD & POOR'S, began offering Standard and Poor's Depository Receipts, or SPDRs, referred to as "spiders."

SPDRs were the first stock exchange–traded MUTUAL FUNDS. Mutual funds accept funds from savers by selling them shares and use the proceeds to invest in various financial securities ranging from short-term debt instruments to long-term BONDS and stocks. Purchasers of mutual funds own an interest in a pool of stocks or bonds. Owning an interest in a pool of ASSETS reduces investors' risk. Mutual funds are CORPORATIONS that manage and market their securities, charging investors a management fee, usually about 1 percent of the assets. "Load" funds charge investors an up-front fee, anywhere from 1 to 5 percent of the amount invested to purchase shares in the fund. By creating exchange-traded mutual funds, the AMEX allowed investors to buy and sell mutual fund products without having to go through a mutual fund.

In 1998 the American Stock Exchange, merged with the National Association of Securities Dealers (NASD), which operates the NATIONAL ASSOCIATION OF SECURITIES DEALERS AUTOMATED QUOTATIONS (NASDAQ) system, a growing, computer-based stock-exchange system. Since the AMEX was declining and in danger of going out of business, it now operates as part of the NASD.

See also COMMON STOCK, PREFERRED STOCK, TREASURY STOCK.

Further reading
American Stock Exchange website. Available on-line. URL: www.amex.com.

Americans with Disabilities Act

Enacted in 1992, the Americans with Disabilities Act (ADA) provides civil rights protections to individuals with disabilities. These rights are similar to those provided by the Equal Rights Act (1964). The ADA guarantees equal opportunity for people with disabilities in public accommodations, EMPLOYMENT, transportation, state and local government services, and telecommunications.

The ADA applies to government agencies and employers with 15 or more employees, protecting "qualified individuals with disabilities." Disabilities include physical or mental impairment that limits one or more life activities. Individuals with nonchronic conditions of short duration are not covered under ADA. Those who are covered must have a substantially limiting and permanent impairment, requiring employers to provide "reasonable accommodation."

"Qualified individuals" is defined by the act as people who meet legitimate skill, experience, education, or other requirements of an employment position and can perform "essential functions" of the position with or without reasonable accommodation. Reasonable accommodation is modification or adjustment to a job or work environment that will enable a qualified applicant or employee with a disability to participate in the application process or perform essential job functions.

The phrase "reasonable accommodation" has been the subject of considerable debate and interpretation. Critics claimed expensive adaptations to facilities for employees and customers would bankrupt small businesses. The act mandated modification of public-accommodation practices requiring provision for products and services such as assistive listening devices, note takers, written materials for people with hearing impairments, and materials in braille. The ADA requires removal of barriers to people with disabilities when removal is "readily achievable" and "easily accomplished without much difficulty or expense." The act has influenced the design of public facilities and fostered a positive change in social attitudes toward people with disabilities.

Further reading
U.S. Department of Justice ADA website. Available on-line. URL: www.usdoj.gov/crt/ada/qandaeng.htm.

amortization
Amortization is an accounting term used in three circumstances. Its most common use refers to the amortization of a loan or MORTGAGE. The series of loan payments associated with a loan or mortgage, along with the amount of each payment going to interest expense and to repayment of the principal, is known as an amortization schedule. Thus, to amortize a loan is to repay (pay off) that loan using a series of ANNUITY payments (payments of equal dollar amounts paid over regular intervals of time).

Another use of the term is associated with long-term, intangible ASSETS. While the systematic transfer of a firm's tangible assets from cost to expense over time is depreciation, the systematic transfer of a firm's intangible assets from cost to expense is amortization. One of the most fundamental of the GENERALLY ACCEPTED ACCOUNTING PRINCIPLES is the matching principle. It requires that a firm's expenses be matched with the revenues generated. Thus, as the intangible assets of a firm generate revenue (or some benefit), a portion of their costs must be amortized—that is, systematically transferred to expense, in this case amortization expense.

Amortization is also encountered in the accounting for non-interest-bearing notes payable. When funds are obtained with a non-interest-bearing note, the proceeds from that note are less than the face value of the note, requiring the creation of an account called Discount on Note Payable, a contra liability. The account Discount on Note Payable is amortized over the life of the note as interest expense accrues on the borrowed funds.

See also DEPRECIATION, DEPLETION, AMORTIZATION.

amortized loan
An amortized loan is one in which the principal and interest are repaid over time via a series of equal payments made over regular intervals of time. Because all the payments are equal in value and are due on the same day of each month over the DURATION of the loan, the stream of payments is considered an ANNUITY. The most common amortized loans are those for car and home purchases.

The payment schedule for an amortized loan typically includes a listing of each payment, indicating how much of each payment goes toward the repayment of principal, how much is interest expense, and the remaining principal. Especially for long-term loans such as 30-year home mortgages, most of each monthly payment for the first couple of years is interest expense, with very little of the payment remaining for the repayment of principal. However, with each successive payment, increasingly less of it is interest expense, leaving more for the repayment of principal. This pattern continues over the life of the loan, and as the end of the loan period approaches, most of each payment goes to the repayment of principal.

The majority of amortized loans are MORTGAGES (secured loans). Mortgages are backed by collateral, pledge ASSETS, titles, or deeds. With auto loans the lender retains title to the automobile until the last payment of the AMORTIZATION schedule is made. With the purchase of real property, the lender holds the deed to the real estate until the mortgage has been fully amortized (paid off).

annual report
The annual report is a collection of a firm's FINANCIAL STATEMENTS and other financial information, published yearly. All firms whose stocks are publicly traded are required by the SECURITIES AND EXCHANGE COMMISSION (SEC) to publish annual reports. Annual reports are attractive, well-designed booklets of financial data about a firm. Among the financial statements normally included are INCOME STATEMENTs for the current year and preceding year(s), BALANCE SHEET for the current year and preceding year(s), and cash-flow statements, all in accordance with GENERALLY ACCEPTED ACCOUNTING PRINCIPLES (GAAP). Written reports from the BOARD OF DIRECTORS and key management personnel are always an integral part of the annual report. When the report is distributed within a short time before the stockholders' annual meeting, it also includes election, voting, and PROXY information for the stockholders.

While annual reports are mailed to each stockholder within a firm, the annual report is also very useful to firms, individuals, creditors, and organizations outside of the firm being reported. Because of the SEC requirement that the financial statements be constructed and reported in accordance with GAAP, the comparison of financial statements among firms is possible when they all measure, record, and report accounting data in the same fashion and according to the same rules.

annuity

An annuity is a stream of equal payments (or receipts) of money over regular intervals of time. The most popular annuities are car payments and house payments. In these loans (which are actually MORTGAGES, i.e., secured loans), one makes the same payment on a particular day each month until the principal (the amount borrowed) and the interest expense have been satisfied according to the loan agreement.

Lottery and sweepstakes winners are often paid with an annuity. While the grand prize may be $1 million, it is common for the winner to receive the money over time—for instance, $25,000 a year for 40 years. The sum of the annuity payments over 40 years is $1 million, but the present value of such a payoff, the value of the annuity discounted for the time value of money, is less than $1 million.

Holders of long-term BONDS payable receive annuities in the form of coupon interest payments as stipulated on the face of the bonds for the life of the bonds or until they sell the bonds to another investor.

In a very real sense, retirees who receive SOCIAL SECURITY benefits are annuity recipients, getting a check for a fixed amount from the Social Security Administration each month. Unless a cost-of-living adjustment is made, the monthly payment remains fixed, creating a stream of income payments to retirees that constitute an annuity.

See also COMPOUNDING, FUTURE VALUE.

antitrust law

Antitrust law is the set of legal rules used to help promote COMPETITION in the economy. Antitrust law in the United States is a very distinct subject reflecting American economic history and perspectives. It has been borrowed, with variations, by many other countries around the world. Most U.S. antitrust litigation involves private actions taken for punitive remedies with treble DAMAGES. Thus, unlike other nations in the world, the United States does not rely principally upon public law enforcement in the area of antitrust.

One impact of U.S. antitrust law is its influence on business practices and the terms of business agreements. Most sales representatives' agreements and distributorships are drafted to minimize the risk of antitrust action and treble damages. This is often done by creating "areas of primary sales responsibility," a technique allowing con-

trol of an area but approved by the U.S. Supreme Court. Clauses in many distributorship agreements governing exclusive dealing, full-line coverage, purchase agreements, covenants not to compete, resale prices, and termination are written with careful consideration of avoiding antitrust actions. Similarly, joint ventures and licensing agreements are scrutinized for antitrust compliance, and many U.S. companies conduct "compliance reviews" of any business proposal.

The earliest antitrust statutes were created by states in the 1880s, and most adopted antitrust laws in the early 1900s. State antitrust laws typically prohibit TRUSTS (combinations in restraint of trade). The antitrust law of each state applies to activities affecting that state's commerce, including interstate or foreign activities.

Three major statutes govern federal antitrust law: the SHERMAN ANTITRUST ACT of 1890, the CLAYTON ANTITRUST ACT of 1914, and the FEDERAL TRADE COMMISSION Act of 1914. Federal and state antitrust laws are both applicable to most U.S. trade and commerce. Under recent antitrust law, there is very little subject matter covered exclusively by either state or federal law. This means businesses are subject to both state and federal interpretations in antitrust jurisdiction.

Interpretation of federal antitrust laws has varied over time. The Sherman Act initiated antitrust policy, but enforcement was minimal. Using the "rule of reason" standard, the anticompetitive effects of an action must be demonstrated to prove illegality. Just being a MONOPOLY or attempting to monopolize was not in itself illegal. The Clayton Act changed the basis of antitrust law to the "rule per se," where actions that could be considered anticompetitive were considered intrinsically illegal. Under the rule per se, activities attempting to monopolize markets were sufficient to be prosecuted. From 1914 until the Reagan Administration (1980–88), rule per se antitrust enforcement was used. The Clinton Administration (1992–2000) tightened antitrust enforcement.

Further reading

Boyes, William, and Michael Melvin. *Microeconomics*, 5th ed. Boston: Houghton Mifflin, 2002; Mallor, Jane P., A. James Barnes, Thomas Bowers, Michael J. Philips, and Arlen W. Langvardt. *Business Law and the Regulatory Environment*, 11th ed. Boston: McGraw-Hill, 2001.

arbitrage

Arbitrage—the practice of buying a product at a low price in one market and selling it at a higher price in another market—is as old as trade. A basic business maxim is: "Buy low and sell high." Knowledgeable middlemen, knowing the prices of products in different parts of the world, would buy from producers in one region and sell to consumers or merchants in another region. One motivation for the exploration of the New World was the control of land-based trade by merchants in the Middle East. European businesspeople and monarchs knew that new DISTRIBUTION CHANNELS would reduce the power of arbitrageurs.

Arbitrage is based on information. With today's global communications systems, the opportunities for arbitrage are both fewer and greater. In financial markets, arbitrageurs simultaneously buy and sell securities, commodity contracts, and currency contracts in two markets, with profits based on slight differences in prices in the markets. For example, currency exchanges operate in many countries around the world. The major currency markets are in New York (New York Mercantile Exchange—NYMEX) and London. If the U.S. dollar was being traded at a rate of $1.4225 dollars per British pound in New York and $1.4220 in London, an arbitrageur could buy British pounds in London and sell British pounds for U.S. dollars in New York, earning a small PROFIT ($0.0005) on the exchange. Five-hundredths of a penny is not much money, but when trading millions of dollars and British pounds, there is potential for profit. Increased access to global markets increases opportunities for arbitrage but also increases market knowledge, reducing disparities in market prices.

Arbitrage occurs in more than just financial securities and international trade. INTERNET auction sites are helping to bring together buyers and sellers, providing vast amounts of market information and opportunities for businesspeople using this resource. For many years classic cars have sold at a premium in California. Entrepreneurs often purchase cars in other parts of the country, hoping to sell them at a premium in the Golden State. Now automobiles, boats, and all kinds of products are being sold over the Internet.

arbitration

Arbitration is a method of business DISPUTE SETTLEMENT involving neutral "arbitrators." Arbitration is often required under business and consumer contracts and is seen as an alternative to litigation in courts. In most cases courts will honor arbitration clauses in CONTRACTS and refrain from entertaining lawsuits covered by arbitration.

The disputing parties typically choose the arbitrators, often with each side selecting one arbitrator and the two selected arbitrators choosing a third arbitrator. Alternatively, arbitrators may be chosen from an approved list through an "arbitration center," such as the American Arbitration Association or the International Chamber of Commerce in Paris. Together the arbitrators are a "panel." Arbitrators operate under rules of procedure regarding evidence, testimony, and the like that are more informal than court rules. Ultimately the arbitrators will render a decision that is binding upon the disputing parties. The binding nature of arbitration distinguishes it from mediation and conciliation, which is nonbinding. Mediators and conciliators act as "go-betweens," attempting to facilitate resolution of the dispute, not decide it.

The decisions of arbitrators are called "arbitral awards." Such awards are generally enforceable in courts under the U.S. Federal Arbitration Act and internationally, in the many countries like the United States that adhere to the "New York Convention" on judicial enforcement of arbitral awards. The enforceability of business-related arbitral awards around the globe is one of its key attributes.

Further reading
Folsom, Ralph H., Michael Gordon, and John Spanogle. *International Business Transactions in a Nutshell,* 6th ed. Eagan, Minn.: West Group, 2000.

assembly line

An assembly line is a manufacturing system where specialized workers focus on repetitive tasks, adding efficiency to the PRODUCTION of a PRODUCT. An assembly line is likely to be composed of numerous subassembly lines, taking raw materials and making parts and components, which are then used in producing the final product.

The idea behind assembly lines is division and specialization, which was first articulated by Scottish philosopher Adam Smith. Considered the father of modern economics and author of *The Wealth of Nations* (1776), Smith used a pin factory to describe assembly line production:

> One man draws out the wire, another straightens it, a third cuts it, a fourth points it, a fifth grinds it at the top for receiving the head; to make the head requires two or three distinct operation; to put it on is a peculiar business, to whiten the pin is another; it is even a trade by itself to put them into the paper.

As Smith noted, "it is even a trade by itself," suggesting the assembly-line system was an alternative to the existing trade and craft system of production. In the 18th century most goods were produced by craftsmen who worked alone or with apprentices, producing small quantities of specialized products. For example, Paul Revere, before his famous ride, was a silversmith; Benjamin Franklin was a printer. As Smith suggested, specialization and division of labor could be used to increase output.

Assembly-line systems used during the Industrial Revolution in Britain and then during the AMERICAN INDUSTRIAL REVOLUTION dramatically increased manufacturing output, decreasing the cost of production. The most famous American assembly-line system was initiated in 1913 by automobile manufacturer Henry Ford at his Highland Park, Michigan, plant. Within two years, by using conveyor systems to bring materials to workers and dividing tasks, Ford tripled production and reduced labor time per vehicle by 90 percent. This allowed him to reduce car prices, forcing thousands of small-scale automobile manufacturers to leave the industry.

Modern assembly-line production utilizes computerized coordination of materials and subassembly operations to maximize output. Managers at automobile factories know it costs thousands of dollars every minute the assembly line is not moving. Bells and whistles sound, and repairmen and managers run whenever the system stops. Assembly-line systems have added just-in-time (JIT) delivery systems, where suppliers ship parts and components to factories on an as-needed basis, reducing inventory costs for assembly-line manufacturers. Today, assembly-line efficiency is achieved in many organizations. Engineers and production managers constantly look for wasted time and motion, whether producing automobiles or hamburgers.

One of the problems associated with assembly-line production is repetitive stress syndrome. Workers doing the same task repeatedly often develop physical ailments.

Further reading
Miller, Roger LeRoy. *Economics Today*. Boston: Addison Wesley, 2001.

assembly plants
Assembly plants are factories located all over the world that bring together materials and machines to produce PRODUCTS. They are typically located where there is access to large numbers of low-cost workers. MAQUILADORAS, assembly plants located in the northern part of Mexico, take materials and parts produced around the world and produce components and final goods primarily destined for the North American marketplace. The primary manufacturer or a local production management company that agrees to manage PRODUCTION for another firm may own assembly plants.

Textile factories are another typical example of assembly plants. Textile equipment is relatively easily shipped and assembled anywhere in the world. Examination of labels in almost any U.S. clothing store will show that the clothes are made in Mauritius, Mongolia, Mexico, or the Northern Marianas. Entrepreneurs shift assembly-plant textile production based on cheap labor, transportation, and TARIFFs. Changes in international trade laws and regional ECONOMIC CONDITIONS frequently result in new, low-cost centers of assembly-plant production. Often developing countries initially expand their export production based on assembly plants. As market opportunities and workers' skills improve, they move into higher, value-added products for global markets.

assessment center
An assessment center is a tool or a service used in HUMAN RESOURCES management and designed to assist in career choice and development. In large organizations, assessment centers are part of a human resources department and are used to select new personnel, evaluate performance, and assist in internal promotion decisions.

With the advent of INTERNET technology, many on-line self-assessment centers assist workers and students with career path decisions. One on-line service, careers-by-design, offers four self-assessment tools. The most widely used tool, the Myers Briggs Type Indicator (MBTI), is used to assist in career change decisions and assess personality type. Personality type assessment can be used to determine the "fit" between an individual and the team or organization they are considering.

The Strong Interest Inventory (SII) is used to assist in career change decisions as well as college major and vocation choice decisions. As the title suggests, the SII measures peoples' interests, which then can be used to predict success and enjoyment in various career options.

The Fundamental Interpersonal Relations Orientation-Behavior (FIRO-B) is used for team building, leadership style, and management development purposes. FIRO-B helps assess individual behavior in work environments. The 16 PF Questionnaire assesses 16 personality factors, which influence management style. The 16 PF Questionnaire is used in corporate selection and career development decisions.

College placement offices and many job placement companies offer self-assessment tools along with résumé services, and interview preparation services.

See also PERFORMANCE APPRAISAL.

Further reading
Assessment Center website. Available on-line. URL: www.careers-by-design.com.

assets
Assets are revenue-generating resources owned by every firm. It is impossible for a firm to earn (generate) revenues without owning and using its assets.

Assets are divided into current assets and long-term assets. Current assets, which are the more liquid assets that a firm owns, have useful lives of one year or less. Examples of current assets are cash, ACCOUNTS RECEIVABLE, merchandise inventory, supplies, various prepaid expenses such as prepaid rent and prepaid insurance, and short-term investments.

Long-term assets are less liquid and have useful lives greater than one year. In other words, their useful lives will span several, if not many, accounting periods, and they are expected to generate revenues for the firm over many accounting periods. There are three classes of long-term assets: man-made assets (such as plant and equipment); natural resources (such as timber tracts, mineral deposits, mines, and oil wells); and intangible assets (legal rights and privileges such a PATENTs, COPYRIGHTs, TRADEMARKs, logos, franchises, and GOODWILL). Assets are increased by debits to those accounts and decreased by credit entries (see DEBIT, CREDIT).

In terms of the accounting equation *assets = liabilities + owners equity,* the assets are the uses of the firm's CAPITAL. The liabilities and owners' EQUITY are the sources of the firm's capital. Thus, the left and right sides of the accounting equation must always be in balance.

Because assets are used in the generation of a firm's revenues, most are transferred to expense over their useful life. While supplies reside in inventory, they are classified as assets (supplies inventory). When those supplies are used, their cost is classified as an expense (supplies expense). Likewise, when machinery is used, it is depreciated. When natural resources are used, they are depleted. When intangible assets help to generate revenue, they are amortized (see AMORTIZATION).

attention, interest, desire, action concept

The attention, interest, desire, action (AIDA) concept, first proposed by E. K. Strong in the 1930s, explains the process that individuals go through when making a purchase decision. The AIDA concept is a tool managers consider when designing their marketing strategies.

Attention, the first step, refers to marketer's efforts to make consumers aware that a firm's PRODUCTS and SERVICES exist. Consumers will not purchase goods or services they do not know about. Whether through SALES PROMOTION, PUBLIC RELATIONS, PERSONAL SELLING, or ADVERTISING, a first goal of marketers is to gain attention. Attention can be gained through simple efforts like a press release or major advertising expenditures like an ad aired during the Super Bowl. For many retail businesses, billboard advertising is used to make consumers aware that their business exists. Sometimes attention messages are designed to inform consumers of a problem; other times, of an opportunity.

The second step, interest, focuses on appealing to the needs and desires of consumers and addresses why they should care about the product or service. Humor and fear appeals are often used to capture consumer interest.

Desire, the third step, convinces consumers of the product's ability to satisfy their needs. Before and after advertising and dramatization of results are often used to increase consumer desire.

Finally, sales presentations, advertisements, and promotions attempt to produce action, hopefully resulting in a sale or at least providing additional opportunities for the marketer to continue a dialogue with the potential consumer. "Pick up your telephone now" and "Ask your doctor or pharmacist" promotional messages are calls to action.

Further reading
Boone, Louis E., and David L. Kurtz. *Contemporary Marketing,* 10th ed. Fort Worth: Dryden Press, 2001.

attitude, interests, opinions statements

Attitude, interests, opinions (AIO) statements are a type of market research survey designed to learn about consumers' attitudes, interests, and opinions. AIO statements are one method of developing psychographic profiles of market segments. The survey technique involves creating a series of statements with which respondents are asked to agree or disagree.

Market researchers often use AIO research to divide geographic or demographic groups into smaller segments. Different marketing strategies are then developed for each segment based on the groups' attitudes, interests, and opinions. For example, among today's college students aged 18–25 there are "traditionalists," people who have generally accepted the attitudes and opinions of mainstream America. There are also "experimenters," young people who are questioning traditional values and attitudes, exploring new interests, and open to new products and ideas. In addition there are "rejecters," people who are critical about mainstream opinions and values, often looking to subcultures within society. Each of these groups has different needs and wants. If a segment is large enough and has sufficient purchasing power, marketers will develop distinct marketing mixes to appeal to their attitudes, interests, and opinions.

Even within organizations there can be subsegments with different ideas. AIO surveys can be used to define groups with both common and different opinions and concerns. For example, a small church organization faced a typical set of problems: Should it expand services to every Sunday (they were only meeting twice a month), and should they first hire a full-time minister or build a church (they were meeting in a rented facility)? Using AIO statements like the ones below, the church group was able to identify the different "factions" within the organization.

1. The first priority of the church should be to get a full-time minister.
   strongly agree agree neutral
   strongly disagree disagree

2. Meeting twice a month is preferable to me.
   strongly agree agree neutral
   strongly disagree disagree

3. The first priority of the church should be to get our own building.
   strongly agree agree neutral
   strongly disagree disagree

4. Meeting every Sunday is preferable to me.
   strongly agree agree neutral
   strongly disagree disagree

5. The current facility meets the needs for our church.
   strongly agree agree neutral
   strongly disagree disagree

6. Having different ministers/speakers each Sunday is interesting.

strongly agree   agree   neutral

strongly disagree   disagree

See also DEMOGRAPHICS; MARKETING STRATEGY.

auditing

Along with bookkeeping, FINANCIAL ACCOUNTING, and MANAGERIAL ACCOUNTING, auditing is one of the branches of accountancy. Auditing—the process of examining the books and records of a business, agency, or organization to determine the accuracy of the accounts contained therein—verifies that the accounting system accurately represents and reports the transactions that have occurred over the past year.

External auditing is performed by accounting firms or by accountants who are not a part of the organization being audited. Fund-raising organizations, charities, and CORPORATIONS publishing their ANNUAL REPORTS regularly use external audits to provide impartial, objective reviews of their accounting systems.

Internal auditing is performed by accountants who are employees of the firm being audited. Internal audits check for conformance to a firm's own policies as well as to accounting standards. Because internal audits are performed by accountants within the firm or organization, such audits are not considered to be as impartial and objective as external audits.

automatic stabilizers (built-in stabilizers)

Automatic or built-in stabilizers are government programs and policies that cushion the impact of a change in spending in the economy. Technically automatic stabilizers reduce the multiplier effect of an autonomous change in spending.

FISCAL POLICY includes taxation and spending decisions by government designed to stimulate the economy during periods of RECESSION and to slow economic activity during periods of peak levels of output. In the United States, personal income taxes are slightly progressive, meaning the marginal tax rate increases as income increases. During periods of peak economic activity, the higher marginal tax rates reduce consumers' disposable INCOME, which in turn slightly reduces their consumption spending. This automatically slows the rate of growth in the economy, and economists suggest it helps reduce the potential for INFLATION.

Similarly, during recessions, when economic output is declining, workers are often laid off or put on temporary furlough. Most workers in the United States are then eligible for UNEMPLOYMENT benefits. These benefits allow workers to maintain some of the spending in the economy they were doing before they lost their job. During the GREAT DEPRESSION, unemployment and WELFARE benefits did not exist. When workers lost their jobs, their income dropped to zero, which in turn dramatically decreased their spending and reduced national income even further. Unemployment benefits and welfare benefits automatically offset some of the lost income and spending during a recession, cushioning its impact by supporting some level of consumer spending.

During periods of extreme economic decline, like the Great Depression, the federal government also engages in discretionary fiscal policy, tax cuts, and/or increases in government spending to stimulate economic activity when there is not sufficient consumer spending or private INVESTMENT. Automatic stabilizers, as the term suggests, occur without direct intervention of government policy makers.

Auto Pact

The United States–Canada Auto Pact (1965), formally entitled the Agreement Concerning Automotive Products between the Government of Canada and the Government of the United States, was a bilateral agreement liberalizing trade in automobiles and original equipment (OEM) parts. The Auto Pact was an important precursor to the Canadian-U.S. Free Trade Agreement (CFTA, 1989), which, in turn, was the "blueprint" for the NORTH AMERICAN FREE TRADE AGREEMENT (NAFTA).

Prior to the Auto Pact, Canada used British Commonwealth "content requirements" to impose significant TARIFFS against non-Commonwealth automobiles and parts. The "Big Three" U.S. automakers (DaimlerChrysler, Ford, and General Motors) manufactured cars and parts in Canada on this basis for the small Canadian market. This significantly reduced the ability of U.S. automobile manufacturers' ability to take advantage of economics of scale based on U.S. manufacturing, but it also protected Canada's small manufacturing industry.

During the 1960s, Canadian tariff refunds linked the degree of Canadian content of its automobiles and OEM parts to exports. U.S. manufacturers perceived this as an unfair trade subsidy and filed a complaint seeking the imposition of countervailing duties. With a trade war threatening this important industry, the Auto Pact was negotiated.

Under the Auto Pact, U.S. manufacturers could import on a duty-free basis regardless of origin only if 75 percent of their sales in Canada were manufactured there. In addition, each existing or subsequent automobile manufacturer had to meet "Canadian value-added content requirements," generally 60 percent. Manufacturers meeting these requirements attained Auto Pact status. The result of these requirements was expanded production of automobiles and OEM parts in Canada.

In the Auto Pact, the United States' criteria for duty-free entry were different. The United States required 50-percent

American-Canadian content, meaning Canadian vehicles and OEM parts could enter the United States without tariff if 50 percent of their appraised value was of Canadian or American origin (or both). The U.S. standard was based on fears of Japanese or other foreign automobile manufacturers using Canada as a production platform for entry into the U.S. market.

Generally, the Auto Pact was a successful industry-specific, bilateral trade agreement with the United States' largest trading partner. Under CFTA, the 50-percent appraised value was replaced with a 50-percent value based on value of materials plus direct processing costs, a more demanding standard.

Further reading
Folsom, Ralph H., and W. Davis Folsom. *Understanding NAFTA and Its International Business Implications.* New York: Matthew Bender/Irwin, 1996.

B

bad debts, aging of accounts

Bad debts, also known as uncollectible accounts, arise from ACCOUNTS RECEIVABLE that ultimately prove to be bad credit risks. When an account receivable is determined to be uncollectible, it should be written off—that is, removed from the collection of accounts receivable.

Periodically a firm estimates the amount of its bad-debt expense by an aging of its accounts receivable. This requires that the accounts and their outstanding balances be grouped according to their currency (how up-to-date they are): 0–30 days past due, 31–60 days past due, 61–90 days past due, etc. While it varies from firm to firm, there is some length of time overdue beyond which a firm will deem an account to be uncollectible.

An aging of accounts also helps the firm to control the amount of its INVESTMENT in accounts receivable. Accounts receivable, which actually represent an investment of a part of the firm's CAPITAL, are credit sales waiting to be liquidated; the sales have been made, but the cash has not yet been received.

If a firm believes its bad-debt expense is too large, it will tighten its credit policy, thereby decreasing the number of potential customers to whom it will sell on credit. Thus, a credit tightening will decrease revenues from credit sales. A lax credit policy will increase credit sales, but it will simultaneously increase bad-debt expense, illustrating the risk/return tradeoff that is prevalent in all business decisions.

balance of payments

Balance of payments is a summary of a country's economic exchanges with the rest of the world for a given period of time. Typically, countries trade goods, services, and financial ASSETS. The balance of payments shows whether a country is accruing debits or credits in its trade with other countries. For a country, exports of goods and services and investment INCOME from other countries represent credits against foreigners, while IMPORTS and investment income paid to foreigners are debits. Debits result in demand for FOREIGN EXCHANGE; credits generate supply of foreign exchange. Without offsetting activities, net trade balances influence foreign EXCHANGE RATES.

There are also unilateral transfers, gifts, and retirement pensions sent to and from countries for which there is no exchange of goods or services. Many foreign-born workers in the United States send money back to their families in other countries. For the United States there are more unilateral transfers out of the country than coming into the country.

Balance of payments, by definition, must balance or be equal, but different components of the balance of payments can have net positive or negative balances. The three most important components of a country's balance of payments are the merchandise account, current account, and capital account. The merchandise account records all international transactions involving goods. For decades the United States has run a negative net trade in merchandise. The merchandise account is also called the balance of trade. The current account is the sum of a country's trade in merchandise, services, investment income, and unilateral transfers. While the United States has a negative balance in merchandise trade, it has a positive balance of trade in services, and INVESTMENT income going out of the country is almost equal to investment income coming into the country. The United States has had a current account deficit for many years. In 2000, the U.S. current account was approximately $435 billion.

When a country like the United States has a current-account deficit, three things can occur. First, foreigners can exchange the excess dollars for their own currency. This increases the supply of dollars as well as the DEMAND for other currencies, causing the value of the dollar to fall in world currency markets. A decreasing dollar will make imports more expensive and exports cheaper to foreigners, reducing the current account deficit.

Second, foreigners can use the excess dollars to make DIRECT INVESTMENTs in the United States. For example, during the early 1990s foreign investors bought many visible symbols of Americana, including the Empire State building and the Pebble Beach Resort. In both cases they paid too much for these assets and subsequently sold them at a loss.

Third, foreigners can use the excess dollars to purchase financial assets, stocks, and BONDS in U.S. companies and U.S. TREASURY SECURITIES. These are known as portfolio investments. For decades foreigners have invested heavily in U.S. securities. Foreign investors hold almost 20 percent of U.S. Treasury securities. Alarmists fear this could lead to economic blackmail, where foreigners threaten to pull their funds out of the United States if the federal government does not follow policies they support. But foreigners, not foreign governments, are buying U.S. securities, and foreigners are buying these securities primarily because of the relative safety of financial investments in the United States. To try to undermine the authority of the U.S. government would be counter to their investment objective.

Because foreigners have primarily used excess dollars to purchase U.S. investments and securities, the value of the dollar has remained stable and even increased, and the capital account—net investment in the United States versus outside the country by U.S. investors—has been positive. This means the United States (businesses and the government) is selling more bonds and other financial assets to foreigners than it is purchasing from abroad. The media therefore portrays the United States as a "net debtor" nation. Since 1985 the U.S. net debtor status has grown annually. These financial assets represent claims against future income and output from the United States.

See also DEBIT, CREDIT.

Further reading
Boyes, William, and Michael Melvin. *Macroeconomics*, 5th ed. Boston: Houghton Mifflin, 2001.

balance of trade   See TRADE BALANCE.

balance sheet
The balance sheet is a statement of the financial position and net worth of a firm. Built on the accounting equation *assets = liabilities + owners' equity*, the balance sheet is a two-columned statement with ASSETS listed on the left side and liabilities and owners' EQUITY listed on the right side. Because the right side represents the sources of CAPITAL for the firm and the left side represents the uses of that capital, the two sides of the balance sheet must always be in balance.

On the asset side, current assets are listed at the top, followed by the long-term assets. The bottom of the left side of the balance sheet is called Total Assets.

On the right side of the balance sheet, liabilities—the firm's debt—are listed at the top, followed by the equity. The bottom of the right side of the balance sheet is called Total Liabilities and Equity. The left and right-side totals will be equal in dollar amount.

There is a physical significance to the arrangement of the right side of the balance sheet, with liabilities being listed above and before the firm's equity. This signifies and recognizes that the firm's creditors (represented by liabilities) have a priority to be paid in the event that the firm should have to liquidate (due to insolvency or bankruptcy, for example). The equity owners can receive payment from liquidation only after all the creditors have been paid in full. For this reason, the firm's equity is often referred to as the residual equity.

The idea of residual equity is also evident in the concept of net worth. With a simple transposition of the accounting equation *assets - liabilities = owners' equity*, it is evident that the equity is the firm's net worth. When debts are subtracted from assets, the residual, if any, is the firm's net worth.

Individuals and households can construct balance sheets, just as firms do. This is most useful if one wishes to determine his or her net worth. It should be noted that net worth can be negative when the liabilities (debts) exceed the assets. If a firm has a negative net worth, it is insolvent or bankrupt. If an individual or household has a negative net worth, the expression "living hand to mouth" describes the situation more aptly.

Baldrige Award
The Baldrige Award—formally known as Malcolm Baldrige National Quality Award—is an annual award designed to recognize quality management. It was created in 1987 and named after former Secretary of Commerce Malcolm Baldrige, who had died in a rodeo accident that year. During the 1980s the United States was perceived as not having products that could compete in world markets. U.S. products, symbolized by U.S. automobiles, were considered to be not "world class." As Secretary of Commerce, Malcolm Baldrige had led efforts to improve quality and productivity in U.S. industries.

The National Institute of Standards and Technology (NIST), part of the Department of Commerce, manages the Baldrige Award, criteria for which include

- leadership
- STRATEGIC PLANNING
- customer and market focus
- information and analysis
- human resource focus
- process management
- business results

Companies submit applications for the award and are evaluated by an independent Board of Examiners. Early recipients of the Baldrige Award have included Motorola Inc., Westinghouse Electric, Xerox, and Milliken & Co. Because of the public recognition associated with the Baldrige Award, some companies hire consultants and spend considerable sums attempting to win this symbol of quality. Winners often use the fact that their company won the award as part of their ADVERTISING efforts.

Winners are expected to share their organization's performance strategies and methods. Some state and local organizations have also created Baldrige Award competitions. The award is in some ways similar to Japan's Deming Award, named after American statistician W. Edwards Deming, who led in the development of TOTAL QUALITY MANAGEMENT (TQM) strategies in Japan during the 1950s and 1960s.

Further reading

Malcolm Baldrige Award website. Available on-line. URL: www.quality.nist.gov.

banking system

A banking system provides financial intermediation, taking deposits from individuals and households with excess cash balances and making LOANS to individuals and businesses wishing to borrow funds for CONSUMPTION or INVESTMENT. Banks also provide safekeeping for depositors' liquid ASSETS. Historically, banking systems evolved from early goldsmiths and silversmiths who provided depository and safekeeping services for merchants and traders. Metalsmiths often charged a fee for storing MONEY and issued a receipt to depositors. These receipts were often exchanged in commerce, becoming currency. Over time the receipts became standardized with respect to value, creating the first paper currency. Recipients could redeem them for gold or silver, but frequently held and used the receipts to make their purchases.

Metalsmiths, observing that not all receipts were redeemed during any time period, realized they could issue more receipts than the amount of gold or silver they had in their vaults. They could, in effect, create money. Money is anything people will accept as a means of payment. Since merchants and consumers had always been able to redeem these receipts for precious metals, they became accepted as money. Metalsmiths began making loans in the form of receipts to traders, accepting a note promising to repay the loan with interest, usually on completion of the trading venture. In the process, metalsmiths were engaging in fractional reserve banking, maintaining less gold or silver in their vaults than the exchange value of the receipts outstanding.

Today banking systems, as early metalsmiths did, create money through fractional reserve banking. Of course, there is the danger that depositors will all demand their money back at the same time. During the GREAT DEPRESSION there were many "runs" on banks, causing over 9,000

banks (more than 40 percent of the banks in the country) to fail during the period from 1930 to 1933.

Because of the risks involved, banking systems in any country are regulated. The first American bank was the Bank of North America, established in Philadelphia in 1782. The bank issued banknotes, convertible into gold or silver coins. Soon commercial banks were established in all major colonial cities, and the early American banks were controversial. Merchants and traders supported their creation as a means of access to credit (previously secured through British sources), but farmers perceived banking as a nonproductive activity and a source of INFLATION in the economy. Also, many colonists had come to North America to escape from their previous experiences with creditors and debtor prisons in Europe.

At the end of the American Revolution, part of the federalist/antifederalist debate concerned the development and control of banking. Federalists won the debate, resulting in the creation of the first central bank, the Bank of the United States, in 1791. Charged to regulate the MONEY SUPPLY in the public's best interests, the Bank of the United States operated both as a commercial bank and as a central bank. Like commercial banks, it took deposits, made loans, and issued banknotes, but it also controlled the amount of banknotes (money) state banks could issue and acted as the banking agent for the federal government. When its officials thought a state bank was extending too much credit, the bank would accumulate a large amount of the state bank's notes and present them for redemption. This decreased that bank's precious metal reserves, forcing the bank to reduce its lending activity or face bank failure. Antifederalists decried this policy, and in 1811 Congress failed to renew the charter of the Bank of the United States.

After a period of inflation, Congress established the Second Bank of the United States during the War of 1812. It operated as the central bank until President Andrew Jackson set out to destroy it, and after a protracted period known as the Bank War, the Second Bank's charter was not renewed in 1836. From this time until the establishment of the Federal Reserve in 1913, the U.S. banking system operated without a central bank. State chartered banks expanded during the period after 1836, but not without problems. Politics and corruption allowed state banks to operate without regulatory supervision, resulting in numerous bank failures and widespread distribution of banknotes of questionable worth; one publication, *The Bank Note Reporter and Counterfeit Detector,* reported the existence of over 1,000 counterfeit banknotes. In addition to counterfeiting problems, without a central bank the money supply varied widely, contributing to inflation and bank panics. States and regions attempted a variety of remedies, including bank reserves holding agreements, bank holdings of state BONDS, and state deposit insurance, but problems persisted.

The federal government's need to finance the Civil War resulted in the creation of a national banking system (the National Bank Act of 1862). (Readers who have seen the classic Civil War film *Gone With the Wind* may recall the South also created their own banking system. Ashley Wilkes patriotically exchanged his gold and silver assets for Confederate currency, but Rhett Butler shrewdly held his precious metals.) National banks were required to purchase bonds issued by the federal government, generating needed resources for the war effort. National banknotes printed by the U.S. Treasury were redeemable at any national bank. In addition to establishing nationally chartered banks and a common currency, the National Bank Act established CAPITAL requirements, placed restrictions on the type and amount of loans that could be made, set up minimum RESERVE REQUIREMENTS, and provided bank supervision by the COMPTROLLER OF THE CURRENCY.

State banks continued to exist, but their banknotes were driven out of existence by the imposition of a 10-percent tax in 1865. In response, state banks replaced banknotes with checks written on bank deposits. As a result, the United States developed a dual banking system, with both state chartered and nationally chartered banks but, until 1913, no central bank. After a series of financial panics that culminated in the panic of 1907, the FEDERAL RESERVE SYSTEM was created to act as the nation's monetary authority, lender of last resort to banks facing liquidity problems, manager of a bank payment system, and supervisor of bank operations.

Even with the creation of the Federal Reserve, the U.S. banking system continued to have problems, resulting in the creation of the FEDERAL DEPOSIT INSURANCE CORPORATION in 1934 and similar deposit insurance protection for other nonbank FINANCIAL INTERMEDIARIES. Historically (much less so today), commercial banks made loans to businesses but not to households. This left a need for other financial intermediaries, leading to the creation of mutual savings banks, SAVINGS AND LOAN ASSOCIATIONS, CREDIT UNIONS, and finance companies, all of which provide home MORTGAGES and consumer credit loans.

Further reading
Kidwell, David S., Richard L. Peterson, and David W. Blackwell. *Financial Institutions, Markets, and Money,* 7th ed. Fort Worth: Dryden Press, 2002.

Bank of International Settlements

The Bank of International Settlements (BIS) is an international organization supporting cooperation among central banks and other agencies. The Bank's mission is to ensure international monetary and financial stability. The BIS functions as:

- a forum for international central bankers,
- a provider of financial services for central banks,
- a center for monetary and economic research,
- an agent or trustee for implementation of international financial agreements.

Recently the BIS coordinated antiterrorism financial monitoring.

One of the major activities of the BIS is operating the Financial Stability Institute (FSI). The FSI, created in 1998, provides seminars and information programs training central bank personnel from around the world. As demonstrated in the CIRCULAR FLOW MODEL of an economic system, monetary flows are needed to facilitate the flow of resources and goods and services. Monetary authorities must provide the needed amount of funds to facilitate exchanges, savings, and INVESTMENT. Excessive or "tight" monetary policies impair economic performance. Financial stability is necessary for sustained ECONOMIC GROWTH. The FSI trains central bank personnel in areas concerning promotion of adequate CAPITAL standards, effective risk management, and transparency (openness) in financial markets. The best-known BIS agreement is the 1988 Basel Capital Accord. (The BIS is headquartered in Basel, Switzerland.) The accord strives for international convergence in the measurement of the adequacy of banks' capital and to establish minimum capital standards.

The BIS was created in 1930 as part of the Young Plan from the Treaty of Versailles ending World War I. The BIS took over responsibility for reparations payments imposed on Germany and was directed to promote cooperation among central banks. Responsibility for war reparations ended with the financial chaos in Germany during the 1930s, focusing BIS efforts toward central bank cooperation. The BIS supported the BRETTON WOODS system, with a gold standard and the dollar as the international reserve currency until the early 1970s, and it managed capital flows during the oil crises in the 1970s. The organization also assisted with the international debt crisis in the 1980s and with financial management associated with GLOBALIZATION in the 1990s.

In addition to providing training and a forum for central bank officials' discussion, the BIS provides banking services, such as reserve management and gold transactions for central banks and international organizations. At various times it has acted as the agent for EXCHANGE RATE agreements among European countries. It also hosts G10 (Group of 10, previously G7) central bank governors meetings. The G10 leaders attempt to coordinate monetary polices to stabilize world ECONOMIC CONDITIONS. The G10 includes Belgium, Canada, France, Germany, Italy, Japan, the Netherlands, Sweden, the United Kingdom, and the United States.

See also BANKING SYSTEM.

Further reading
Bank for International Settlements website. Available on-line. URL: www.bis.org.

bankruptcy   See BUSINESS FAILURE; CONSUMER BANKRUPTCY.

barriers to entry

Barriers to entry are restrictions preventing or discouraging new competitors from participating in a market. Barriers to entry most often occur in monopolistic and oligopolistic markets, reducing the number of competing firms and increasing prices and profits for those firms protected by barriers to entry. From a social perspective, barriers to entry generally harm consumers, reducing the number of choices available as well as price COMPETITION. From a business perspective, firms attempt to create and maintain barriers to entry. Economists use the term *rent-seeking* to describe the use of resources by firms on lobbying and influence-buying to acquire MONOPOLY rights from the government, creating a barrier to entry for future entrants. The government, particularly the Antitrust Division of the Justice Department and the FEDERAL TRADE COMMISSION, is responsible for monitoring anticompetitive practices in the United States. Potential competitors evaluate the cost of overcoming existing barriers to entry as part of their marketing strategy decisions.

Barriers to entry arise from a variety of sources.

- Product differentiation: This is any feature or perceived value to consumers that increases BRAND loyalty and reduces consumer consideration of alternatives in the marketplace. Marketers in the United States spend billions of dollars annually promoting the differences in their products, and offering price incentives for repeat and bulk purchases to existing customers.
- ECONOMIES OF SCALE: Products requiring a high initial capital cost, but with low variable costs production, allow existing producers to spread their fixed costs as output expands. Potential competitors are discouraged from entering the market because they cannot start small and later expand as DEMAND grows. Independent retailers such as hardware stores often join in buying franchises in order to obtain the economies of scale in PURCHASING and ADVERTISING of nationally owned competitors.
- Capital requirements: Products or services requiring significant initial INVESTMENT discourage potential competitors. Existing automobile manufacturers, steel producers, and communications companies have spent significant sums creating their enterprises. The investment CAPITAL required for new competitors is a barrier to entry.
- Access to DISTRIBUTION CHANNELS: Often existing firms control access to customers, either through ownership or contractual relationships. Small and new producers frequently have difficulty getting shelf space in retail stores and finding representatives to promote and sell their products through distribution channels.
- Other cost advantages: Through lower rents negotiated in long-term contracts, experience, access to materials,

and relationships in the industry, existing companies can often produce at a lower cost than potential competitors, discouraging entry into the marketplace.
- Government policy: LICENSING, PATENTs, safety and pollution standards, and access to distribution create barriers to entry. Patents give a firm a monopoly for a specified period of time. Licenses create costs and tests limiting entry. Many industries seek out government licensing as a way to restrict further entry into their market. Safety and pollution standards increase paperwork and initial costs for would-be competitors. Government restrictions on access to distribution act as a barrier to entry. For example, airline companies fight for government allocation of boarding space at airports around the country.

Information and gaining access to information has traditionally acted as a barrier to entry. Today's global INTERNET technology is changing this and also creating alternative distribution channels, reducing this barrier to entry.

See also OLIGOPOLY.

Further reading

Dwyer, F. Robert, and John F. Tanner Jr. *Business Marketing,* 2d ed. Boston: Irwin McGraw-Hill, 2002; Ruffin, Roy J., and Paul R. Gregory. *Principles of Economics,* 7th ed. Boston: Addison Wesley, 2000.

barriers to trade   See TRADE BARRIERS.

barter

Barter is the exchange of one service or commodity for another without exchanging MONEY. Barter was used by primitive peoples and is still practiced in some parts of the world. A barter economy requires a "coincidence of needs"—that is, a person having something to trade must find another who wants it and has something acceptable to offer in exchange. In a money economy, the owner of a commodity may sell it for money, which is acceptable in payment for goods, thus avoiding the time and effort that would be required to find someone who could make an acceptable trade. The money economy is considered the keystone of modern economic life.

Barter is still active, not only in countries with chronically weak currencies but also in western countries like the United States, where it made something of comeback with the onset of the INTERNET. Another reason for its revival is that barter can be attractive for smaller businesses to save money. For example, a painting contractor could paint the exterior of an auto body shop in exchange for car repairs.

Success in bartering requires finding an agreeable trading partner. Participants must agree on a fair value of the products or services that are being traded. It is best to put all bartering agreements in writing to avoid "he said, she said" kinds of problems. Bartering has become so accepted that even federal and state tax collectors recognize its value. Barter-system deals are included in taxes dollar for dollar, as if the two participants were simply exchanging checks for the amount of their trade.

The Internet has opened a vast array of bartering opportunities. Some sites for consumers to view are MrSwap.com, WebSwap.com, Switchouse.com, and SwapVillage.com.

See also COUNTERTRADE.

Further reading
Goff, Robert. "Swap 'Til You Drop . . . Or Drop Out." *Forbes* 11 September 2000, p. 62.

—Susan Poorbaugh

benchmarking

Benchmarking is the process of identifying and learning from the best business practices in a company, an industry, or the world. As stated by C. Jackson Grayson Jr., chairman of the American Productivity and Quality Center, the essence of benchmarking is, "Why reinvent the wheel if I can learn from someone else who has already done it?" The goals of benchmarking typically include cost reductions, quality improvement, and new product or process ideas.

Benchmarking involves a variety of considerations, including processing, legal issues, and limitations. Benchmarking is a structured analysis, starting with identification of the business or process to be benchmarked. In addition to comparing products with the "best in the business," companies also compare processes. For example, Wal-Mart is well known as a leader in inventory management. Many companies, including Amazon (which was sued for hiring away Wal-Mart inventory management executives), benchmark Wal-Mart as the leading firm in the area of cost control. Similarly, the United States is perceived by many nations as a leader in education. Education management personnel from other countries are often sent to the United States to study and bring back for adoption educational practices used in this country.

Once the product or process to be studied is identified, organizations develop a team to participate in the benchmarking process. Since benchmarking, by definition, is designed to create change, who is involved in the process is an important consideration. Team members must be knowledgeable, be open to new ideas, be able to analyze data, and have influence within the organization.

Once the team is formed, the benchmarking process typically involves data collection. For internal benchmarking, where similar operating units within an organization are compared, internal data is usually available. For example, many national sales organizations are broken down into dozens or hundreds of regional and local offices.

Sales, cost per sales, gross margins, and other performance measures can be compared. For competitive benchmarking, where companies compare their performance with direct competitors, data collection can be more difficult. Public data, observation, and surveys are often needed to collect needed information. Quality comparisons are often conducted using reverse engineering, purchasing and dismantling competitors' products in order to assess quality, and production processes.

Using the data collected, the benchmarking team looks for gaps between the company's processes and PRODUCTS and those of the leading unit, firm, or industry. Once gaps are identified, causes are searched for and hopefully identified. This leads to the final step in the process: taking action to change existing practices to match or exceed those of the benchmarked unit or competitor.

As Dean Elmuti et al. suggest, benchmarking can lead to legal issues. Especially in competitive benchmarking, copying the practices or processes of the leading firm in an industry can generate problems associated with PROPRIETARY INFORMATION and INTELLECTUAL PROPERTY. Groups of firms working together to improve industry standards and practices can violate antitrust and unfair trade practices laws.

Benchmarking peaked as a business management process in the 1990s. While many companies used the process to reduce costs and improve quality, benchmarking has its limitations. First, the focus of benchmarking is data. If the numbers are not accurate or do not allow valid comparisons, the process will fail. Also, focusing on data can distract managers from their need to address the desires of customers and needs of employees. With its emphasis on details, benchmarking can misinterpret the organization's "big picture," their reason for existing.

Typical areas of business practices where benchmarking is applied include billing and collection, customer satisfaction, distribution and logistics, employee EMPOWERMENT, equipment maintenance, manufacturing flexibility, marketing, product development, QUALITY CONTROL, supply chain management, and worker training.

Further reading
Elmuti, Dean, Yunus Kathawala, and Scott Lloyd. "The benchmarking process: assessing its value and limitations," *Industrial Management* 39, no. 2 (July–August 1997): 12–19.

benefits   See COMPENSATION AND BENEFITS; EMPLOYEE BENEFITS.

beta coefficient, capital asset pricing model

A beta coefficient is a measure of a stock's volatility relative to the market for all stocks. As an integral component of the theoretical capital ASSET pricing model that is used to determine the required return for a particular stock, beta coefficients are measures of a stock's risk.

The beta coefficient for all stocks collectively is 1, and a stock whose returns move with the market has a beta of 1. Thus, a beta coefficient of 1 indicates average volatility, and stocks with betas of 1 carry the same risk as the STOCK MARKET in general. If a stock's returns are more volatile than the average movements in the stock market, its beta is greater than 1. Stocks whose returns are less volatile than the average movements in the market have betas less than 1. (There are some stocks that are countercyclical, and their betas are negative.) Beta coefficients can be easily obtained for all stocks publicly traded.

The capital asset pricing model (CAPM) is based on risk aversion, the assumption that investors require compensation for assuming risk. CAPM is an equation used to calculate a stock's required return based upon the riskiness of that stock as measured by its beta coefficient:

$$k_s = k_{rf} + (k_m - k_{rf})b_s$$

where k_s is the required return for some individual stock s, k_{rf} is the theoretic return an investor would require in a risk-free world, k_m is the average return for all stocks in the market, and b_s is the beta coefficient of the stock s.

In the model, $(k_m - k_{rf})$—the difference between the average return for all stocks and the risk-free rate of return—is the stock market's average risk premium. The average risk premium is multiplied by a stock's beta coefficient to determine the risk premium associated with that particular stock. For example, when the beta is 1, the stock will have the same risk premium as the market's. When the beta is greater than 1, the stock's risk premium will be greater than the market's average risk premium, and when the beta is less than 1, the stock's risk premium will be less than the market's average risk premium. Thus the CAPM equation indicates that a stock's required return is the sum of the risk-free rate of return and the risk premium for that stock as determined by that stock's beta coefficient.

For example, assume a risk-free rate of return, k_{rf}, of 3 percent and an average return in the stock market, k_m, of 7 percent. Using the CAPM equation, if Stock A has a beta of 1, its required return, k_A, is $[3 + (7 - 3)1] = 7$ percent. Because Stock A is no more and no less volatile than the stock market in general (indicated by its beta coefficient of 1), the required return for Stock A is the same as the average return in the stock market. If Stock B has a beta of 2, its required return, k_B, is $[3 + (7 - 3)2] = 11$ percent. As indicated by its beta coefficient of 2, Stock B is twice as volatile and twice as risky as the average stock, and higher required return reflects the added riskiness of this stock's returns. If Stock C has a beta of .5, its required return is 5 percent. Stock C is less volatile and less risky, and as a result it has a lower required return.

Better Business Bureau

The Better Business Bureau (BBB) is a private, nonprofit organization with a mission to promote and foster ethical relationships between businesses and the public. The BBB is best known for its complaint service, where dissatisfied consumers contact local BBB offices to resolve disputes with businesses.

Established in 1912, the BBB today has 132 local bureaus and over 250,000 members nationwide. The national organization is the Council of Better Business Bureaus (CBBB). In 1997 the BBB received over 2 million complaints from American consumers. The bureau usually suggests consumers first contact companies directly. If they are not satisfied with the results, the BBB will intercede. The bureau has no power to force businesses to resolve disputes with consumers. Instead, it uses the fear of adverse publicity to pressure businesses to act promptly and ethically.

The major BBB activities include providing

- business reliability reports
- dispute resolution
- truth in advertising
- consumer and business education
- charity review

Business reliability reports provide consumers with information about past complaints involving local companies. Local BBBs collect and disseminate information about unanswered questions and unresolved complaints. For consumers the fact that a company has unresolved disputes registered with the local BBB is a signal that there may be problems. The CBBB plans to reliability report information on-line.

Dispute resolution services include buyer/seller mediation and ARBITRATION services. The BBB provides specialized on-line complaint services for auto-related and moving- and storage-related disputes. In addition it provides a customer assistance program. Along with auto and moving disputes, home-improvement and ordered products receive the greatest number of complaints.

One of the early functions of the BBB was to improve truth in ADVERTISING. False and misleading advertising by a few firms in a market hurts the public perception of all businesses. The BBB's Code of Advertising includes guidelines for ethical use of comparative pricing, savings claims, free offers, credit, distress sales, warranties, disclosures, bait and switch advertising, and even use of asterisks. The use of testimonials, superiority claims, contests, and extra charges, all issues that can lead to misrepresentation of products, are addressed by BBB codes.

A fourth function of the BBB is to provide consumer and business education. Knowledge improves business practices and consumer satisfaction. The CBBB writes and produces numerous alerts and press releases designed to inform businesses and consumers. Many newspapers include consumer-alert columns with information disseminated by the BBB. Recently, with the rapid growth of INTERNET commerce, the BBB established a Code of Online Business Practices for members. The code calls for on-line businesses to post privacy policies, protect user's security, and resolve consumer complaints promptly.

In conjunction with the Philanthropic Advisory Service, the BBB provides information about nonprofit organizations, educating private and corporate donors.

Further reading
Better Business Bureau website. Available on-line. URL: www.bbb.org.

bill of lading
A bill of lading is a document issued by a shipping company to acknowledge that the seller has delivered particular goods to it. Bills of lading are used in both interstate and international shipments. The Federal Bill of Lading Act (1916, formally called the Pomerene Act) governs the transfer and transferability of bills of lading, of which there are two types: a nonnegotiable or "straight" bill of lading; and negotiable bills of lading, known as "white" and "yellow" bills because of the colors of paper on which they are printed. Both types usually represent the seller's CONTRACT with the shipping company, setting the terms and TARIFFS of that contract.

In a nonnegotiable bill of lading, the carrier is obligated to deliver the goods to the designated destination point and is liable for misdelivery of the goods. Nonnegotiable bills of lading are sometimes called "air waybills," "sea waybills," and "freight receipts," depending on the intended method of transportation. Nonnegotiable bills are used when the seller is expecting payment upon delivery, not for payment based on bill-of-lading documentation.

The carrier issues a negotiable bill of lading to a person (consignee) or "order." This allows the person to endorse the bill of lading to "order" delivery of the goods to others. Negotiable bills can be endorsed to third parties, buyers or creditors, allowing the "holder" of the bill to receive the goods at the destination point. The shipping company is liable to the holder of a negotiable bill of lading for misdelivery if it delivers the goods to anyone but the holder. In this way the negotiable bill of lading is similar to a title document conferring ownership of the goods. Negotiable bills of lading are used when sellers are being paid at the time goods are shipped. In international business letters of credit are often used, obligating the buyer's bank to pay the amount of the contract once bills of lading are submitted, usually by the seller's bank to the buyer's bank. The banks use negotiable bills of lading to control title to the goods in their contracts with buyers and sellers. In the United States, negotiable bills of lading are most often used, but some countries only allow the use of nonnegotiable bills of lading.

Further reading
Folsom, Ralph H., and Michael Gordon. *International Business Transactions,* 6th ed. Eagan, Minn.: West Group, (2002).

blind trust
A blind trust exists when a beneficiary, the party for whom the benefit of a TRUST exists, turns over control of their ASSETS to a trustee, who is an independent third party, typically a professional money manager. The trustee is given broad discretion over the assets. The trust is "blind" because the beneficiary does not know the exact identity, nature, and extent of their financial interests within the trust's holdings. In other words, the beneficiary will become "blind" to the activity and makeup of the fund. The beneficiary will only receive a report on how the investments are performing, but no details on the actual investments. Blind trusts are typically set up when there is a CONFLICT OF INTEREST involving the beneficiary and the investments held in the trust.

The most common individuals to set up blind trusts are government officials, who arrange their assets this way so that no one can claim they are acting in their own self-interest when performing governmental service. All presidents and first ladies since Jimmy Carter have established blind trusts before taking office, with the exception of Bill and Hillary Clinton, who did not set up theirs until July 1993, and only then because of pressure due to conflict of interest. Without a blind trust, the Clintons were fair game for the media. It was revealed that when Hillary Clinton headed the health reform committee, her personal portfolio held more than $1 million in health stocks, and the portfolio was making money from sales of these health stocks. Soon after the news revelation of this $1 million conflict of interest, the Clintons created a blind trust naming Essex Investment Company, a Boston-based firm, as the trustee.

Ever since the Declaration of Independence, citizens have put their trust in government and have held that public officials should perform their duties in the public's interest and for the public's good. The ethics program within the executive branch of government helps to support this public trust and ensure that officials perform their duties impartially and free of conflicts of interest. The U.S. OFFICE OF GOVERNMENT ETHICS (OGE) was established by the Ethics in Government Act of 1978. This office oversees six major areas, including financial disclosure. Within the financial-disclosure area the OGE supervises the creation and operation of blind trusts and compliance with the Ethics in Government Act of 1978. The act permits two types of blind trusts: a qualified blind trust (QBT) and a qualified diversified trust (QDT). The difference between these two trusts is the level of restriction of the assets within the trust to the beneficiary's conflict of interest. In other words, with the QBT the initial assets may cause the beneficiary to be subject to conflict of interest, but these assets would be subsequently disposed of or valued at less than $1,000. In a QBT the beneficiary is then only blind to the subsequent assets purchased by the trustee. In a QDT the initial assets transferred into the blind trust are subject to more restrictions than the QBT. In other words, the initial assets cannot contain securities that may subject the beneficiary to conflict of interest. Both types of trusts are subject to rules of filing by the OGE and approval of both the actual blind trust and the appointed trustee.

Another example of when a blind trust is a remedy for a potential conflict of interest can be found within the financial industry. In 2000 the SECURITIES AND EXCHANGE COMMISSION (SEC) issued the Regulation FAIR DISCLOSURE (FD) and two new insider-trading rules. The latter rules (10b5-1 and 10b5-2) create insider-trading liability for anyone who may buy or sell stock in a company based on their knowledge of inside company information that has not been announced publicly. In order to comply with these new rules and protect themselves from insider-trading liability, many investment firms have instructed their traders to transfer their personal portfolios into blind trusts. Individuals such as CHIEF EXECUTIVE OFFICERS, company managers, members of a BOARD OF DIRECTORS, or holders of more than 10 percent of a particular company's shares would also establish blind trusts in order to avoid conflict-of-interest and insider-trading liability.

See also INSIDER TRADING.

—Maureen Murray

blue-chip stocks

Blue-chip stocks are COMMON STOCKs of nationally known companies that have a proven record of profitability, increases in stock value, and reputations for being leaders in their respective industries. Blue-chip stocks typically sell at a premium compared to other firms in their industry and usually pay moderate DIVIDEND yields. Blue-chip companies have quality management, products, and services. The term *blue chip* comes from poker, where the blue chip is the highest-valued chip.

International Business Machines (IBM), General Electric, General Motors, Dow Chemical, and DuPont are examples of traditional American blue-chip stocks. In recent years dominant firms in the technology industry, such as Microsoft and Intel, have also become known as blue-chip stocks. Ironically, Enron and MCI WorldCom were also considered blue chips. Sometimes business media refer to the Dow Jones Industrial Average (DJIA) as the blue-chip average. The DJIA, initially an index of manufacturing company stocks, has been reconfigured in recent years to reflect the growing importance of service and technology companies in the U.S. economy. Now the DJIA includes dominant firms from many nonmanufacturing U.S. industries, including McDonalds (fast food), Wal-Mart (discount retailing), and American Express (credit). AT&T, once the most widely held stock in the United States, has lost its blue-chip status to some investors.

Blue-chip stock is also an internationally used term. In Australia companies such as Australian Gas and Light, Amcor, National Australian Bank, Rio Tinto, and Qantas are known as blue-chip stocks.

blue-collar

The term *blue-collar* refers to workers who traditionally wear blue work uniforms, including ASSEMBLY LINE and other laborers. Laborers typically wear dark-colored clothing because it does not show dirt or sweat as easily as lighter colors. Blue-collar contrasts to WHITE-COLLAR professionals, administrators, and office workers. Blue-collar is often used to describe specific locations, groups, or products.

One news story described efforts to redevelop Warren, Michigan, a blue-collar city, "with its plethora of factories and industrial buildings and endless concrete ribbons that carry traffic." Blue-collar groups are stereotypically portrayed as hard-working people with relatively little education and minimal aesthetic tastes, and blue-collar products appeal to this market segment. Blue-collar workers are more likely to be unionized and working in manufacturing rather than in service industries. A blue-collar recession would be a decline in the manufacturing sector of the economy.

Further reading
Shine, Kim North. "General Motors Plans to Help Redevelop Downtown Warren, Mich.," *Detroit Free Press*, 16 May 2001.

blue laws

Blue laws are legislation regulating activities associated with the Sabbath (Sunday). In the Bible, the Sabbath, or holy day, is a day of rest. Blue laws got their name from 17th-century laws in Connecticut, which were written on blue paper. Some of the early laws included:

- No one shall cross a river on the Sabbath but authorized clergymen.
- No one shall travel, cook victuals, make beds, sweep houses, cut hair, or shave on the Sabbath Day.
- No one shall kiss his or her children on the Sabbath or feasting days.
- The Sabbath Day shall begin at sunset on Saturday.

Most blue laws have been eliminated based on questions of their constitutionality, economics, and practicality. Constitutional challenges are usually based on the First Amendment, which states, "Congress shall make no laws respecting the establishment of religion."

Economic realities and lost sales and tax revenues have also pressured governments into repealing blue laws. Some southern states, particularly South Carolina, retain blue-law restrictions. Title 53, Chapter 1, Section 53-1-40 of the

State of South Carolina Code of Laws reads in part: "On the first day of the week, commonly called Sunday, it shall be unlawful for any person to engage in worldly work, labor, business of his ordinary calling or the selling or ordering to sell publicly or privately or by telephone, at retail or at wholesale to the consumer any goods, wares or merchandise or to employ others to engage in work, labor or business or selling or offering to sell any goods, wares or merchandise, excepting work of necessity or charity." The act does allow the Sunday sale of tobacco, motor fuels, novelties, souvenirs, undergarments, and the operation of public eating places, funeral homes, and cemeteries.

Most Americans never encounter blue laws. Those who do are usually shocked or bemused to find they cannot purchase liquor in some southern states on Sundays. In South Carolina, counties can vote to overrule blue laws, and in most regions of the state where tourism is a significant source of INCOME, blue laws have been repealed or modified.

Further reading
"Blue Laws of South Carolina." Available on-line. URL: www.nobluelaws.org; "Connecticut Blue Laws." Available on-line. URL: www2.pitnet.net/primarysources/bluelaws.html.

board of directors
A company's board of directors makes its strategic decisions, including hiring and terminating executives, directing company policy, and considering proposals from outside investors or other companies to purchase or be purchased by the company. In the United States, a CORPORATION must have a board of directors elected by its SHAREHOLDERS, whose best interests the board of directors is charged to represent. (Many nonprofit organizations also have boards of directors providing similar functions to the organization but without responsibility to shareholders.)

A typical corporate board of directors creates at least three oversight committees: nominating, compensation, and audit. The nominating committee selects new candidates to be reviewed for positions on the board. The compensation committee determines the executive' pay. The audit committee reviews reports from independent audit firms and internal audits. In addition, some boards of directors create a finance committee to oversee CAPITAL investment decisions.

A board of directors can be large or small. Most corporate management specialists recommend that boards contain no more than 10 members. Larger boards allow for greater diversity but also slow decision making. Historically most U.S. corporate board of directors did not aggressively assert the interests of shareholders but instead generally accepted the recommendations of management. In the 1990s critics, especially giant pension-fund managers TIAA-CREF and CALPERS challenged the status-quo "rubber stamping" by corporate boards.

The Council of Institutional Investors (CII), created in 1985, developed a set of standards for board accountability and has acted as a "watch dog" group that oversees practices by boards. The CII developed a detailed set of recommendations, including core policies, general principles (shareholder rights, shareholder meeting rights, board accountability, and director and management compensation for board of directors), and positions.

CORE POLICIES

1. Confidential ballots counted by independent tabulators should elect all directors annually.
2. At least two-thirds of a corporation's directors should be independent. A director is deemed independent if his or her only non-trivial professional, familial or financial connection to the corporation, its chairman, CEO or any other executive officer is his or her directorship.
3. A corporation should disclose information necessary for shareholders to determine whether each director qualifies as independent.
4. Companies should have audit, nominating and compensation committees. All members of these committees should be independent. The board (rather than the CEO) should appoint committee chairs and members. Committees should have the opportunity to select their own service providers.
5. A majority vote of common shares outstanding should be required to approve major corporate decisions concerning the sale or pledge of corporate assets, which would have a material effect on shareholder value.

GENERAL PRINCIPALS

A. SHAREHOLDER VOTING RIGHTS

1. Each share of COMMON STOCK, regardless of class, should have one vote. Corporations should not have classes of common stock with disparate voting rights.
2. Shareholders should be allowed to vote on unrelated issues individually. Individual voting issues, particularly those amending a company's charter, BYLAWS, or anti-takeover provisions, should not be bundled.
3. A majority vote of common shares outstanding should be sufficient to amend company bylaws or take other action requiring or receiving a shareholder vote.
4. Broker non-votes and abstentions should be counted only for purposes of a quorum.
5. A majority vote of common shares outstanding should be required to approve major corporate decisions including:
   a. the corporation's acquiring, other than by TENDER OFFER to all shareholders, 5 percent or more of its common shares at above-market prices;
   b. provisions commonly known as shareholder rights plans, or poison pills;

c. abridging or limiting the rights of common shares;

d. permitting or granting any executive or employee of the corporation upon termination of EMPLOYMENT, any amount in excess of two times that person's average annual compensation for the previous three years; and

e. provisions resulting in the issuance of debt to a degree that would excessively LEVERAGE the company and imperil the long-term viability of the corporation.

6. Shareholders should have the opportunity to vote on all equity-based compensation plans that include any director or executive officer of the company.

B. SHAREHOLDER MEETING RIGHTS

1. Corporations should make shareholders' expense and convenience primary criteria when selecting the time and location of shareholder meetings.

2. Appropriate notice of shareholder meetings, including notice concerning any change in meeting date, time, place or shareholder action, should be given to shareholders in a manner and within time frames that will ensure that shareholders have a reasonable opportunity to exercise their franchise.

3. All directors should attend the annual shareholders' meeting and be available, when requested by the chair, to answer shareholder questions.

4. Polls should remain open at shareholder meetings until all agenda items have been discussed and shareholders have had an opportunity to ask and receive answers to questions concerning them.

5. Companies should not adjourn a meeting for the purpose of soliciting more votes to enable management to prevail on a voting item.

6. Companies should hold shareholder meetings by remote communication (so-called electronic or "cyber" meetings) only as a supplement to traditional in-person shareholder meetings, not as a substitute.

7. Shareholders' rights to call a special meeting or act by written consent should not be eliminated or abridged without the approval of the shareholders.

8. Corporations should not deny shareholders the right to call a special meeting if such a right is guaranteed or permitted by state law and the corporation's articles of INCORPORATION.

C. BOARD ACCOUNTABILITY TO SHAREHOLDERS

1. Corporations and/or states should not give former directors who have left office (so-called "continuing directors") the power to take action on behalf of the corporation.

2. Boards should review the performance and qualifications of any director from whom at least 10 percent of the votes cast are withheld.

3. Boards should take actions recommended in shareholder proposals that receive a majority of votes cast for and against.

4. Directors should respond to communications from shareholders and should seek shareholder views on important governance, management and performance matters.

5. Companies should disclose individual director attendance figures for board and committee meetings.

D. DIRECTOR AND MANAGEMENT COMPENSATION

1. Annual approval of at least a majority of a corporation's independent directors should be required for the CEO's compensation, including any bonus, severance, equity-based, and/or extraordinary payment.

2. Absent unusual and compelling circumstances, all directors should own company common stock, in addition to any OPTIONS and unvested shares granted by the company.

3. Directors should be compensated only in cash or stock, with the majority of the compensation in stock.

4. Boards should award CHIEF EXECUTIVE OFFICERS no more than one form of equity-based compensation.

5. Unless submitted to shareholders for approval, no "underwater" options should be re-priced or replaced, and no discount options should be awarded. (Underwater means option prices below the current market price of the company's stock.)

6. Change-in-control provisions in compensation plans and compensation agreements should be "double-triggered," stipulating that compensation is payable only (1) after a control change actually takes place and (2) if a covered executive's job is terminated as a result of the control change.

7. Companies should disclose in the annual PROXY statement whether they have rescinded and re-granted options exercised by executive officers during the prior year or if executive officers have hedged (by buying puts and selling calls or employing other risk-minimizing techniques) shares awarded as stock-based incentive or acquired through options granted by the company.

COUNCIL OF INSTITUTIONAL INVESTORS POSITIONS

A. BOARD SHAREHOLDER ACCOUNTABILITY

1. Shareholders' right to vote is inviolate and should not be abridged.

2. CORPORATE GOVERNANCE structures and practices should protect and enhance accountability to, and equal financial treatment of, shareholders.

3. Shareholders should have meaningful ability to participate in the major fundamental decisions that affect corporate viability.

4. Shareholders should have meaningful opportunities to suggest or nominate director candidates.
5. Shareholders should have meaningful opportunities to suggest processes and criteria for director selection and evaluation.
6. Directors should own a meaningful position in company common stock, appropriate to their personal circumstances.
7. Absent compelling and stated reasons, directors who attend fewer than 75 percent of board and board-committee meetings for two consecutive years should not be renominated.
8. Boards should evaluate themselves and their individual members on a regular basis.

B. BOARD SIZE AND SERVICE

1. A board should neither be too small to maintain the needed expertise and independence, nor too large to be efficiently functional. Absent compelling, unusual circumstances, a board should have no fewer than 5 and no more than 15 members.
2. Companies should set and publish guidelines specifying on how many other boards their directors may serve. Absent unusual or specified circumstances, directors with full-time jobs should not serve on more than two other boards.

C. BOARD MEETINGS AND OPERATIONS

1. Directors should be provided meaningful information in a timely manner prior to board meetings. Directors should be allowed reasonable access to management to discuss board issues.
2. Directors should be allowed to place items on board agendas.
3. Directors should receive training from independent sources on their fiduciary responsibilities and liabilities.
4. The board should hold regularly scheduled executive sessions without the CEO or staff present.
5. If the CEO is chairman, a contact director should be specified for directors wishing to discuss issues or add agenda items that are not appropriately or best forwarded to the chair/CEO.
6. The board should approve and maintain a CEO succession plan.

D. COMPENSATION

Pay for directors and managers should be indexed to peer or market groups, absent unusual and specified reasons for not doing so.

An important issue in governance of a board of directors is whether the board member is independent or not. The CII defines an independent director as someone whose only nontrivial professional, familial, or financial connection to the corporation, its chairman, CEO, or any other executive officer is his or her directorship. The CII's position on independent directors is based on the problems of conflicts of interest for board members who are also managers; and interlocking directorships, where board members represent the interests of shareholders for different corporations.

Further reading

Council of Institutional Investors website. Available on-line. URL: www.cii.org.

bond market   See STOCK MARKET, BOND MARKET.

bonds

Bonds are long-term debt instruments used by both the private and public sectors to raise funds. They are liabilities for the issuer and can be excellent INVESTMENT opportunities. In the private sector, corporate bonds are most common. In the public sector there are Treasury bonds and U.S. Savings Bonds issued by the federal government and municipal bonds issued by local governments and municipalities.

With the exception of bonds issued by the federal government, all bonds have some risk of DEFAULT. Moody's and Standard and Poor are the two major firms that rate bonds, both public and private sector, according to their default risk. Both organizations use two broad classifications of risk. Those bonds with ratings of "BBB" or "Baa" and higher are termed *investment grade* or *investment quality* bonds. These are the bonds with minimal default risk. Bonds with ratings less than BBB or Baa are termed speculations because of their considerable risk of default. The more common name for these speculative bonds is *junk bonds*.

All bonds have a maturity date and a face value, the amount that is paid to the bondholder on the maturity date. Most bonds, especially corporate bonds, also have a coupon-interest rate. The interest that a coupon bond pays is determined by multiplying the coupon-interest rate by the face value of the bond. Bonds may pay coupon interest annually, semiannually, or quarterly, depending on what is stipulated on the face of the bond.

The object of the bond issuer who is trying to raise CAPITAL is to get as much money for each bond as is possible while at the same time trying to minimize the interest expense associated with the bond. To accomplish this, the issuer sets the coupon-interest rate at the going rate of interest in the market at the time the bonds are issued. This helps to ensure that the bonds will sell "at par"—that is, for their face value. (If one looks in the newspaper at the reporting for the bond exchanges, one notices that there are many bonds outstanding, all with different coupon-interest rates. This is because there are bonds issued every day, and the various coupon-interest rates reflect the going rates of interest when the bonds were issued.)

A bond with a coupon-interest rate lower than the going rate of interest in the market, ceteris paribus (other things being equal), will not be viewed as an attractive INVESTMENT. Why should one purchase this bond when most any other investment in the market will yield a higher return? In order for the return on this bond to be more attractive, investors would only be willing to buy this bond at a discount (i.e., below its face value). This would add a CAPITAL GAIN to the bond's comparatively low interest yield. (At maturity, a bond will pay its face value, regardless of what was initially paid for it.) Thus, for organizations in need of funds, it makes no sense to issue bonds with coupon rates that are lower than current market rates.

A bond with a coupon-interest rate higher than the going rate of interest in the market, ceteris paribus, will be viewed as a very attractive investment. Investors will clamor to purchase such a bond, causing it to sell at a premium, or for more than its face value. Organizations in need of funds will not offer such high coupon-interest rates because this increases the interest expense they must pay on the borrowed funds.

Coupon-interest rates are also determined, in part, by default risk. Rational investors are risk-averse, and they demand to be compensated for assuming risk. Thus the higher the degree of default risk, the higher the bond's coupon interest rate, ceteris paribus.

Occasionally, a firm finds that it needs to raise funds during a period of high interest rates in the economy. In order for the bonds it issues to sell at par, the coupon-interest rate will be set at the current market interest rate. However, the bonds will most probably be callable. A CALLABLE BOND is one that will be called in by the issuer for redemption before the bond reaches it maturity date. The call period is normally stated on the face of the bond, and investors who own callable bonds expect not to be able to hold such an attractive bond until its maturity. The call provision allows firms to escape the costly interest expense of the high coupon-interest rates by allowing the bonds to remain outstanding only until their call dates. Often firms will use the funds obtained from newer, lower coupon-interest rate bonds to call in and redeem their callable bonds.

Some bonds are convertible bonds, which may be converted to shares of COMMON STOCK (as a fixed price) at the option of the bondholder. Because they offer the potential for a capital gain when the stocks are eventually sold, convertible bonds normally carry lower coupon-interest rates than bonds that are not convertible.

Some bonds have no coupon-interest rates. These are known as zero-coupon (or deep discount) bonds. When issued, they always sell at a discount. The return from investing in such bonds is a capital gain, because the face value received at maturity is more than the purchase price of the bond. Treasury bills and U.S. Savings Bonds are examples of zero-coupon bonds issued by the federal government.

Bonds may be secured or unsecured. Secured bonds have collateral or pledged ASSETS backing them, minimiz-ing their risk. Unsecured bonds have no such backing and are known as debentures. Ceteris paribus, secured bonds are less risky than debentures and, thus, offer lower interest yields than debentures.

Local governments and municipalities often sell bonds to finance INFRASTRUCTURE and to build schools. The interest earned on a municipal bond, called a muni, is exempt from federal taxation. Because the interest earnings on munis are not federally taxable, this allows local and municipal governments to issue their bonds at lower coupon-interest rates than other similar bonds, with the savings accruing to the local taxpayers.

The largest issuer of bonds is the federal government, selling Treasury securities and savings bonds. When there is a budget deficit, the federal government is forced to make up the shortfall by borrowing from the private sector. It does this by selling Treasury securities: Treasury bills with maturities up to one year; Treasury notes with one to five-year maturities; and Treasury bonds with five to thirty years. With the national debt at approximately $6 trillion, this is roughly the amount of money the federal government has borrowed (bonds outstanding) as a result of spending in excess of tax revenues in past years.

See also BRADY BONDS; STOCK MARKET, BOND MARKET.

book value (carrying value)

Book (or carrying) value is an accounting term that usually refers to a net amount, the remainder after a subtraction has occurred. Book values are commonly encountered in the accounting for ASSETS and liabilities.

For example, assume a firm has ACCOUNTS RECEIVABLE in the amount of $300,000. The related contra-asset account, Allowance for BAD DEBTS, has a balance of $25,000. The asset account has a debit balance, the contra-asset account has a credit balance, and the difference between the two is a net debit balance of $275,000. Because not all of the accounts receivable will prove collectible, the net realizable value of the firm's accounts receivable is $275,000, and this is the book, or carrying, value of the accounts receivable. Paying homage to the principle of conservatism (one of the GENERALLY ACCEPTED ACCOUNTING PRINCIPLES), the accounts receivable are being "carried" at $275,000, the amount that is more likely to be collected than the amount of $300,000 actually owed to the firm.

Assume Machine No. 3 has a cost of $900,000. The related contra-asset account, Accumulated Depreciation, has a credit balance of $350,000. The difference between the two amounts is a net debit balance of $550,000. This is the book (carrying) value of Machine No. 3.

For another example, assume a firm borrows money with a non-interest-bearing note payable. With such notes the interest rate is implicit, and the proceeds of the note are less than its face value. When the borrower records this LIABILITY as a note payable, a contra-liability account, Discount on Note Payable, is also established to record the difference between the face value of the note payable and the proceeds received from issuing the note. This will allow the book, or carrying, value of the note payable to be equal to the proceeds received from issuing the note.

See also DEBIT, CREDIT.

Border Environmental Cooperation Commission

The Border Environmental Cooperation Commission (BECC), a binational organization created in 1993 as a side agreement to the NORTH AMERICAN FREE TRADE AGREEMENT (NAFTA), helps states, localities, and the private sector develop and find financing for environment INFRASTRUCTURE projects along the U.S.-Mexico border. The BECC, which identifies, evaluates, and certifies affordable environment projects with the goal of improving the quality of life for citizens along the border, is an outgrowth of ideas put forth by UCLA urban planning professor Raul Hinjosa and others. The idea for the BECC was adopted by the Bush Administration in 1992 and superseded the 1983 Agreement on Cooperation for the Protection and Improvement of the Environment on the Border Area (the 1983 La Paz Agreement).

The Commission maintains offices in both El Paso, Texas, and Ciudad Juarez, Mexico, and is directed by a 10-member BOARD OF DIRECTORS, with five board members from each country. The Director of the U.S. Environmental Protection Agency is an ex officio member of the BECC board. Decisions of the board are based on a majority vote, thus requiring support from members representing both countries. A major role of the BECC is certifying projects for financing by the NORTH AMERICAN DEVELOPMENT BANK (NAD Bank). By 1998 the BECC had certified 16 projects, mostly water-treatment and municipal solid-waste projects. Many more projects were yet to be addressed, and financing problems, particularly for Mexican municipalities lacking authority to enter into public works financing and taxation agreements, limited the ability of the BECC and NAD Bank to address long-term problems.

Many U.S.-Mexico border problems stem from rapid growth of the MAQUILADORAS in Mexico. After the PESO CRISIS (1994–95), the reduced cost of Mexican labor for international firms and NAFTA increased access to the U.S. market and overwhelmed an already weak infrastructure. Although the BECC was created to address problems associated with border-area growth, it had limited impact in the 1990s.

Further reading

Folsom, Ralph H., and W. Davis Folsom. *NAFTA Law and Business.* The Hague: Kluwer Law International, 1998.

boycotts

Boycotts are organized attempts to influence a company, organization, or government through refusal to patronize a business or other group. Boycotts are frequently used to affect business practices. Sometimes boycotts are organized to challenge labor or environmental issues; other times they are used to sway social practices or policies.

In the United States, possibly the most famous boycott was organized by the United Farm Workers (UFW). During the 1960s, 1970s, and 1980s, led by charismatic UFW President Cesar Chavez, the UFW asked American consumers to not purchase table grapes, claiming unfair labor practices and poor working conditions by grape farmers. By 1975 an estimated 17 million Americans had stopped buying grapes. In another agricultural boycott, the UFW used a DIRECT MAIL campaign asking consumers to boycott Lucky Supermarkets because they were buying nonunion lettuce. The campaign targeted ethnic neighborhoods, areas with high agricultural EMPLOYMENT, and liberal, middle and high-income groups. After nine months Lucky agreed to stop buying nonunion lettuce but claimed the decision had nothing to do with the boycott.

Peace and environmental groups have often attempted to use boycotts to influence government policy. In 1990 Neighbor to Neighbor initiated a boycott of Folgers coffee, a Proctor and Gamble product, accusing P&G of prolonging the El Salvadoran civil war by buying Salvadoran coffee beans. The campaign brought attention to the plight of El Salvadorans but was actively opposed by the Bush Administration. (The war ended when the Clinton Administration withdrew financial support for the El Salvadoran military.) Similarly, American and other activists have long supported a boycott of Burma (now called Myanmar) because of its military rule and abuse of human rights. In 1995 U.S. environmental groups organized a short-lived protest of French products in reaction to France's nuclear tests in the South Pacific.

Boycotts are also used to influence social and political policies. The Boston Tea Party was one of America's first boycotts. Similarly, one of the hallmarks of the civil rights era was the 1950s boycott of buses in Montgomery, Alabama. The boycott of South Africa in the 1980s displayed the power of economic sanctions to influence social policies. As one author states, "Boycott. It's not blackmail. It's not censorship. What it is is capitalism. A boycott, after all, is merely a way to vote with our wallets."

In 1994 the National Organization of Women organized a boycott against orange juice when the Florida Citrus Commission decided to advertise on conservative Rush Limbaugh's talk show. Limbaugh supporters countered by increasing their purchases of orange juice. In 1996 Jesse Jackson threatened a boycott of Texaco stores in an effort to pressure Texaco to settle a racial discrimination suit. The next year Southern Baptists attempted to dissuade the Disney corporation from its gay-friendly employment policies by declaring a boycott against the company. In 1999 the NAACP organized a boycott of tourism in South Carolina because the state continued to fly the Confederate flag over its state capital. The National Collegiate Athletic

Association (NCAA) joined the boycott, refusing to bring collegiate athletic events to the state. Removal of the flag from the capital to a place on the capital grounds appeased some groups, but others continue to boycott the state.

Further reading
Kalisher, Jesse. "Art of Noise (Impact of Boycotts)," *Brandweek* 39, no. 18 (4 May 1998): 66.

Brady bonds

Brady bonds are debt instruments issued by governments and private lenders in developing countries as a means of restructuring their debt. Named after Nicholas Brady, secretary of the Treasury during the George H. W. Bush administration, these BONDS were first issued by the Mexican government as part of a plan to repackage loans made to Mexico during the 1980s. Many governments in developing countries had borrowed billions of dollars but were not able to pay back the loans. Poor INVESTMENT, management, and corruption led governments into situations where they owed significant amounts to foreign lenders and had few productive ASSETS to use or tax to pay off the loans. Just the interest due on the loans represented a significant portion of most government's budgets. Known as "debt overhang," these payments prevented governments from making new investments in education, INFRASTRUCTURE, and resource development needed to generate ECONOMIC DEVELOPMENT.

Under Nicholas Brady, a pool of funds from the United States, WORLD BANK, and INTERNATIONAL MONETARY FUND (IMF) was used to guarantee new bonds issued by the developing country government. The new bonds offered to lenders reduced the amount of debt owed and stretched payments over a longer period of time. This lowered the payments of the debtor country, allowing its government greater financial resources to be used in economic development plans. An alternative procedure provided no debt reduction but lower INTEREST RATES on the new debt than that paid for the old debt in return for guarantees of payment of the principal with the proceeds from long-term bonds provided by the United States and other developed countries. To lenders who faced DEFAULT by the borrowing country, the new debt plans, backed by the funds coordinated by Nicholas Brady, were better than default and more secure than direct loans to the borrowing government.

Brady plan restructurings were used in many developing countries in the late 1980s and early 1990s. As world ECONOMIC CONDITIONS improved, some countries, particularly Mexico, paid off their Brady bonds. On the other hand, in 1999 Ecuador became the first government to default on its bonds.

Once issued, Brady bonds became part of international financial debt instruments. A few MUTUAL FUNDS specialized in purchasing Brady bonds of various countries at deep discounts, hoping to profit from the eventual payoff of these high-risk bonds. These investors recognize the biggest concern associated with these bonds is political risk. The Brady plan was an outgrowth of an earlier strategy proposed by then-Secretary of Treasury James Baker, which emphasized economic reforms as a condition for new lending to developing countries.

Further reading
Appleyard, Dennis R., and Alfred J. Field, Jr. *International Economics*, 2d ed. Homewood, Ill.: Irwin Publishing, 1994.

brands, brand names

Brands are names, terms, designs, signs, symbols or some combination that identify a firm's PRODUCTs. Brands facilitate easy recognition of a company's products and increase consumer loyalty through repeat purchase. According to MARKET RESEARCH, consumers' brand loyalty goes through three stages: recognition, preference, and insistence.

A marketer's first objective is to gain brand recognition—that is, consumer knowledge of a company's brand. In ADVERTISING, marketers typically have three objectives: to inform, persuade, and remind consumers about the company's products. Brand recognition is consistent with informing customers about a brand. Gaining brand recognition in a national market like the United States is expensive. With a large geographic area, over 280 million people, and tremendous COMPETITION from other firms, marketers have to work hard to gain brand recognition. One option used by several small firms is advertising during the Super Bowl, the most widely watched television event in the United States. Super Bowl advertising is very expensive, but several small firms have successfully used it as a way to gain national brand recognition.

Brand preference is the stage where consumers select a particular brand over competing offerings. Typically brand preference is based on past experiences with a firm's products. In many categories of consumer products, customers tend to be very brand-loyal. Often brand loyalty is based on what peoples' parents purchased. For decades Sears's strongest MARKETING STRATEGY was brand preference and insistence based on consumers' past experiences with their tools and appliances.

Brand insistence is brand loyalty to the point where consumers refuse alternatives and seek out brands they most desire. Airlines and, more recently, hotel chains have successfully built brand loyalty through frequent-flyer/stay programs.

There are four types of brands: manufacturers, private, family, and individual. Manufacturers' brands, also called national brands, are those owned by the manufacturer. General Motors, Kodak, and Coca-Cola are all examples of national brands. Manufacturers protect and support their brands, often using price competition with private brands and cooperative advertising and promotion with retailers to maintain and expand brand loyalty.

Private brands are brand names created and marketed by WHOLESALERs and retailers. For example, Sears owns the Kenmore, Craftsman, and DieHard brand names. Sears contracts with manufacturers to make products to be sold under these private names. Traditionally manufacturers dominated brand marketing, but since World War II, retailers have greatly increased their control of DISTRIBU-TION CHANNELs and have used this market power to expand their use of private brands.

A family brand is a single brand name used to identify a group of related products. For example, Johnson & Johnson offers a variety of product lines all under one brand name. Many companies market a variety of individual brands. Proctor and Gamble's Tide is one of the longest-lasting individual brand names in cleaning products, and Crest Toothpaste is a leading brand in health products.

As previously noted, the goal of brands and brand names is to increase consumer loyalty. Marketers refer to this as gaining brand equity, which means DEMAND for a firm's product is less elastic. Loyal consumers are more likely to continue to purchase a product even when the price is raised. Brand equity makes it infinitely easier for a firm to introduce new products, since most consumers who have had a positive experience with a company's products are more likely to try new product offerings from that firm.

Marketers know developing effective brand equity is difficult and usually expensive. New brand names generally should be easy to pronounce, recognize, and remember. A brand name should also be consistent with the image a company wants to convey: status, safety, or confidence. TRADEMARKs are brands and brand names owned by a company.

Further reading
Boone, Louis E., and David L. Kurtz. *Contemporary Marketing*, 10th ed. Fort Worth: Dryden Press, 2001.

break-even analysis
Break-even analysis is a tool used by managers to estimate either the quantity they need to sell at a given price to cover all costs or the price they must charge to cover all costs for a given quantity of output. Break-even analysis is often used when managers are considering new INVEST-MENTs or new PRODUCTs.

Break-even quantity (BEQ) is estimated using the formula $BEQ = FC \div (P - AVC)$, where FC is total fixed costs, P is price per unit, and AVC is average variable cost per unit. Break-even analysis assumes a manager can estimate:

- the initial fixed costs (equipment, buildings, licenses; any cost that is required to get started but does not change with the level of output),
- the average variable cost (materials, labor, energy) in the range of output being considered.

If these costs can be estimated, a manager can then determine how many units must be sold at various prices to break even. For example, if FC is $1000 and AVC is $10, then at:

P = $20, BEQ = 100
P = $30, BEQ = 50
P = $40, BEQ = 33.3

Break-even analysis allows a manager to create a hypothetical DEMAND curve. Using the information from the BEQ analysis, managers then determine whether they think they can sell at least that quantity at a given price. Managers may then employ sales forecasting techniques to compare the results of BEQ analysis with potential market demand.

In the above formula, $P - AVC$ is often called the contribution margin. For each unit produced and sold, the difference between price and the average variable cost (if the difference is negative, the product should not be produced) contributes to "covering" fixed costs, and when all fixed costs are covered, ultimately contributes to profit. Break-even price (BEP) is estimated using the formula $BEP = (FC \div Q) + AVC$, which says that the BEP equals average total cost. Using this same example above, if FC are $1000 and AVC is $10 then at:

Q = 50, BEP = $30
Q = 100, BEP = $20
Q = 200, BEP = $15

Managers can use BEP analysis to answer the question, "If we produce and sell 100 units, what price do we have to get in order to at least break even?"

Retail store managers frequently use break-even analysis when considering new products. In RETAILING, firms often "keystone" products—that is, price their products at twice the cost to the store. If a manager orders 100 spring shirts at $10 each and prices them at $20 each, then they must sell at least 50 shirts to break even.

Another way to use break-even analysis is when considering ADVERTISING options. If a magazine ad costs $500, the product advertised sells for $10, and the average variable cost is $5, then the advertisement would need to generate 100 additional sales to break even.

Further reading
Dwyer, F. Robert, and John F. Tanner, Jr. *Business Marketing*. Boston: McGraw-Hill, 1999.

Bretton Woods
Bretton Woods, a small town in New Hampshire, was the host, in July 1944, for a major economic summit that has since transformed international economic relations. In economic discussions, the phrase "ever since Bretton

Woods" means ever since the creation of the INTERNATIONAL MONETARY FUND (IMF) and International Bank for Reconstruction and Development (IBRD, also called the WORLD BANK), which were created at the Bretton Woods conference at the Mount Washington Hotel.

Planning for the conference began in 1942 in the midst of World War II. Most world leaders agreed that weaknesses in the fixed EXCHANGE RATE system had contributed to the global depression and the rise of fascism. In response to the depression, governments expanded spending on public goods. But under the gold standard, where each country's currency was convertible to a specified amount of gold, government spending could over-stimulate an economy and result in a BALANCE OF PAYMENTS crisis. Over-stimulation led to increased IMPORTS and to price increases for export PRODUCTS. This resulted in a larger trade deficit and balance-of-payments problem. The gold standard, which was in effect during this time, required a country to send gold to trading partners, decreasing the country's MONEY SUPPLY. This constricted growth in the economy through higher INTEREST RATES. What was needed was an international monetary system that would allow domestic Keynesian economic stimulation without creating a monetary crisis.

British and American political and economic leaders proposed changes in the international monetary system. The British—led by John Maynard Keynes, by then the most widely acclaimed economist in the world—proposed a system with an international agency and a new currency, "bancors." Bancors would replace gold and U.S. dollars as the basic reserve currency for all national banks.

The British, and most of the 45 participating nations at Bretton Woods, recognized that the United States would be one of the few economically strong countries after World War II and would have a significant trade surplus with the rest of the world. Keynes proposed increasing the value of the dollar as a means of reducing the impending trade surplus and stimulating exports from war-torn countries. U.S. negotiators, led by Treasury Secretary Henry M. Morgenthau and Harry Dexter White, proposed that the trade deficit countries would have to devalue their currencies and/or cut government spending in order to balance international trade.

At Bretton Woods, the American proposal won out, resulting in the creation of the IMF. The IMF would assist countries with short-term problems in their international debt problems Funds for IMF operations were created by subscription. The United States, being the largest subscriber, became the dominating force in the organization.

Discussions over the creation of the World Bank were less controversial. While the IMF would minimize short-term trade problems, an organization was needed to provide long-term CAPITAL for INVESTMENT, particularly in developing countries. As envisioned, the World Bank would finance redevelopment of European economies and expand into assistance for other areas of the world. Like the IMF, the World Bank was established with funds by subscription, and the United States was the largest contributor. As planned, it would primarily guarantee loans made by private banks, thus stimulating investment in financially viable projects. The United States became the major source of funding for postwar European redevelopment.

Over time the World Bank became a leading source of funds for ECONOMIC DEVELOPMENT as well as a symbol of U.S. dominance in international economic affairs. The IMF, while initially created to support government deficit spending, later became the international "watchdog" against excessive government spending. The IMF continues to provide short-term international finance assistance but with stringent requirements. Countries in need of IMF assistance are often required to reduce spending and raise interest rates in order to put their financial affairs in order. This is usually accepted begrudgingly, adding to developing countries' disdain for the power of the United States and other industrialized countries over their economic affairs.

Further reading

Geisst, Charles. *The Encyclopedia of American Business History.* New York: Facts On File, 2004.

bribery

The crime of bribery is the offer or gift of money, goods, or anything of value in order to influence federal, state, or local public officials in the discharge of their duties. Bribery of foreign government officials may violate the federal FOREIGN CORRUPT PRACTICES ACT. Commercial bribery in the business world is an unfair trade practice.

Bribery is as old as civilization. One Egyptian pharaoh ruled that any priest or official taking a bribe was subject to the death penalty. One of the most widely reported bribery scandals involved International Olympic Committee officials accepting multimillion-dollar payments in exchange for their vote on locating the Winter 2002 Olympic Games.

Bribery is known by many names. It is called *dash* in West Africa, *la bustarella* (the little envelope) in Italy, *rishvat* in India, and *grease* in the United States.

The OFFICE OF GOVERNMENT ETHICS (OGE) proscribes government officials from taking anything of value from individuals or organizations affected by their government duties. Under the RACKETEER INFLUENCED CORRUPT ORGANIZATION ACT, predicate offenses that can be used to establish a pattern of FRAUD (and thus prosecution under the act) include bribery.

For businesses or government, detecting bribery is difficult, but a variety of "red flags" can be used to raise concern and investigation, including

- employee spending that surpasses INCOME
- unusually friendly relationships between an employee and an outside contractor

- employees who "stretch" or ignore standard operating procedures
- employees who repeatedly rationalize deficiencies on the part of suppliers
- employees who are under pressure due to external needs (family-member illness, drug or alcohol dependency, or gambling)

In 1999 the ORGANIZATION FOR ECONOMIC COOPERATION AND DEVELOPMENT (OECD) created a 17-article antibribery convention, which states:

Each Party shall take such measures as may be necessary to establish that it is a criminal offence under its law for any person intentionally to offer, promise or give any undue pecuniary or other advantage, whether directly or through intermediaries, to a foreign public official, for that official or for third party, in order that the official act or refrain from acting in relation to the performance of official duties, in order to obtain or retain business or other improper advantage in the conduct of international business.

Transparency International (TI), an organization that monitors international bribery, focuses on increasing awareness and providing information to individuals and institutions. TI has established an "Integrity Pact" for bidders and procures in government purchasing, creating a binding agreement among parties to conduct business in an ethical and legal manner. The organization also publishes a bribery index, rating countries on how likely bribes are paid to gain business. In 2002 Russia and China were rated most likely to pay bribes in developing countries, while Switzerland and Australia were least likely. According to *The Economist,* "Italy, America and Japan score poorly, despite their anti-bribery laws and conventions."

Further reading
The Authority. "The History of Corruption." Available on-line. URL: www.nznow.net.nz/Authority/1997/1997004.html; "Bribery Index," *The Economist,* 18 May 2002, p. 104; Organization for Economic Cooperation and Development website. Available on-line. URL: www.oecd.org; Podgor, Ellen S., and Jerold H. Israel. *White Collar Crime in a Nutshell.* 2d ed. Eagan Minn.: West Group, 1997; Transparency International website. Available on-line. URL: www.transparency.org.

Buddhist economics
Buddhist economics is the study of maximizing well-being while minimizing CONSUMPTION. This goal of Buddhist economics seems contradictory to modern Western economics, where increased consumption is perceived as analogous to improved well-being.

The German-born British economist E. F. Schumacher popularized Buddhist economics in the 1970s. In his classic book *Small Is Beautiful: Economics As If People Mattered*

(1973), Schumacher challenged standard assumptions of modern economic systems regarding labor, consumption, technology, peace, and the environment.

Labor, in the modern Western economic perspective, is a necessary evil. For an employer, labor is a cost to be minimized for workers, a sacrifice of one's energy and time. Employers would prefer output and INCOME without incurring the cost of labor, and workers would prefer the benefits of output and income without having to work. Labor, in the Buddhist economic perspective is necessary for the development of character and for overcoming ego. Work should be organized to benefit the needs of workers to develop their potential.

Consumption in the modern Western economic perspective, represents a better quality of life and therefore increased consumption is a major goal. According to Buddhists, consumption should support the goal of maximizing contentment. Attachment to WEALTH and desire for material goods are seen as causes of suffering, reducing contentment.

Technology, in the modern Western economic perspective, is seen as a source of increasing productivity. Improvements in technology are viewed as positive contributions to economic systems. Technology, in the Buddhist economic perspective, should enhance the natural capabilities and skills of workers. (Schumacher, a critic of blindly exporting industrial technology to developing countries, established the Intermediate Technology Development Group (1966).)

Peace, in the modern Western economic perspective, includes maintaining or increasing control over the resources needed to preserve a country's STANDARD OF LIVING. Resource conflicts arise as countries compete for control. Peace, in the Buddhist economic perspective, is enhanced through conservation and local control of resources.

The environment, in the modern Western economic perspective, is primarily a collection of resources to be used in maximizing production. Natural systems are perceived as constraints on ECONOMIC GROWTH. The environment, in the Buddhist economic perspective, is the natural system within which economic systems operate. Buddhist economics distinguishes between renewable and nonrenewable resources, emphasizing use of the first and using the latter sparingly. Exploitation of the environment is perceived as an act of violence.

Further reading
Schumacher, E. F. *Small Is Beautiful: Economics As If People Mattered.* New York: HarperCollins, 1973; Schumacher Society website. Available on-line. URL: www.schumachersociety.org.

budgeting, capital budgeting
Budgeting is the process of developing budgets, or financial plans that project a firm's inflows and outflows for a

future time period. Often budgeting results in the construction of pro forma statements, namely the budgeted INCOME STATEMENT and the budgeted BALANCE SHEET. Pro forma, as a matter of form, statements have generally accepted formats but are based on projections. A budgeted (pro forma) income statement is one that reflects projections rather than being based on prior transactions; thus it represents expectations rather than actual data. Likewise, a budgeted (pro forma) balance sheet is one that is constructed using projections rather than actual data. Pro-forma statements are important tools used in planning and decision-making. In banking, pro forma statements are commonly used as the basis for making loans of VENTURE CAPITAL and loans to new businesses.

Capital budgeting is the planning for a firm's fixed ASSETS in particular. How a firm decides to use its capital is the most important of all managerial decisions, and since fixed assets represent the majority of most firms' assets, capital budgeting is the most crucial of all budgeting activities.

While there are infinite uses for a firm's capital, its sources are limited, and capital budgeting determines its best uses. Payback period, net present value (NPV), and internal rate of return (IRR) are three capital-budgeting tools commonly used to determine a firm's most profitable INVESTMENT opportunities.

Payback period, the first capital budgeting tool to be developed, is the expected number of years required for a firm to recoup its original investment in a fixed asset or project. The decision rule when using payback is that shorter payback periods are preferable over longer ones. For example, suppose Project A requires an investment of $10,000 and will generate cash inflows of $3,000 per year for the next five years. Assuming that these inflows are evenly distributed over the next five years, the payback period for Project A is $10,000/$3,000 = 3.33 years. Suppose Project Z costs $10,000 and will generate cash inflows of $2,000 per year for the next 10 years. The payback period for Project Z is $10,000/$2,000 = 5 years. If payback is used to rank these two projects, Project A is the preferred investment opportunity because of its shorter payback period.

There are two major shortcomings of payback period as a capital-budgeting tool. Only the inflows required to recoup the original investment are considered; the inflows occurring after the payback period are ignored. For Project A above, returns continue for an additional 1.67 years beyond the payback period, but they aren't considered. For Project Z, returns continue for another five years beyond the payback period. Payback is particularly flawed when used to evaluate investment opportunities where the returns are slow for the first couple of years, but become significant in later years.

An even more serious flaw is that payback is not a discounted cash flow technique; it ignores the time value of money. In Project Z, for example, the $2,000 received in

Year 5 is viewed as just as valuable as the $2000 received in Year 1. Depending on the DISCOUNT RATE (cost of capital for the firm) used to determine the present value of the cash inflows, Project Z may, in reality, be a more profitable investment. This makes payback period a crude tool for evaluating and ranking profitable investment opportunities.

To incorporate the time value of money in capital budgeting, NPV and IRR were developed. These are discounted cash-flow techniques and are more valid tools for decision making than payback period.

NPV is the present value of a project's future cash inflows minus the initial cash outflow (original investment) required. The decision rule is to accept the project if its NPV is positive but reject if it is negative. If projects are not mutually exclusive, those with greater NPVs are ranked more preferable than those with lower NPVs. Suppose a project's NPV is +$50,000. The present value of the project's inflows are $50,000 greater than its initial cost, and this net return accrues to the firm's owners.

IRR, also a discounted cash-flow technique, is similar to NPV except that, while NPV is expressed in dollars, IRR is expressed in percentages. IRR is the discount rate that equates the present value of a project's expected inflows and its cost. The decision rule to follow when using IRR is to accept projects where the IRR is greater than the firm's cost of capital and reject those opportunities where the IRR is less than the firm's cost of capital. For example, if a project's IRR is 20 percent for a firm whose cost of capital is also 20 percent, undertaking and investing in the project will add nothing to the firm's PROFITS; the project's return exactly offsets the cost of the investment in the project. Thus the cost of capital is a "threshold" which must be exceeded when using IRR as a capital budgeting tool. If projects are not mutually exclusive, projects with higher IRRs are ranked more preferable than those with lower IRRs, and projects whose IRR is less than the firm's cost of capital are rejected.

See also FEDERAL BUDGETING; ZERO-BASE BUDGETING.

built-in stabilizers   See AUTOMATIC STABILIZERS.

Bureau of Economic Analysis

The Bureau of Economic Analysis (BEA) is an agency within the Department of Commerce that produces U.S. economic statistics. Each month the BEA estimates GROSS DOMESTIC PRODUCT (GDP); gross domestic income; and industry, regional, and international economic statistics. To make important policy, INVESTMENT, and spending decisions, government officials, business managers, and individuals use economic estimates produced by the BEA.

GDP and other important measures are usually first announced as press releases and widely quoted in the business media. GDP estimates are first released as a preliminary estimate followed by a first and second revision as more data become available. Financial markets watch GDP statistics closely, and analysts watch growth (or lack thereof) in the industries in which they are involved. Regional economic statistics provide estimates of personal INCOME, population, and EMPLOYMENT by state. International economic statistics include BALANCE OF PAYMENTS figures, U.S. DIRECT INVESTMENT abroad, and foreign direct investment in the United States.

The BEA's monthly journal, *Survey of Current Business*, presents detailed estimates, analyses, research, and methodology used by the agency to measure economic activity in the U.S. economy.

Further reading
Bureau of Economic Analysis website. Available on-line. URL: www.bea.gov.

Bureau of Labor Statistics
The Bureau of Labor Statistics (BLS), part of the DEPARTMENT OF LABOR, is the principal agency providing labor statistics in the United States. The most important BLS statistics generated each month are the CONSUMER PRICE INDEX (CPI), the UNEMPLOYMENT rate, and the PRODUCER PRICE INDEX (PPI). The CPI is the most widely used and quoted measure of INFLATION. Changes in the unemployment rate are a major indicator of strength or weakness in the economy. The PPI measures prices received by producers and is a leading indicator of future price changes for consumers. In addition, the BLS measures productivity; average hourly earnings; demographic characteristics of the LABOR FORCE; and wages, earnings, and benefits by area, occupation, and industry.

BLS statistics are available through the *Occupational Outlook Handbook* and other publications.

Further reading
Bureau of Labor Statistics website. Available on-line. URL: www.bls.gov.

Bureau of Land Management
The Bureau of Land Management (BLM), an agency in the Department of Interior, manages over 264 million acres of public land primarily in 12 western states and Alaska. In addition, the BLM manages 300 million acres of belowground mineral rights throughout the country. (Ownership of land is considered ownership of a "bundle of rights" to the land. Often, in areas of the United States where there are mineral deposits [oil, gas, gold, silver, etc.], developers and homeowners purchase surface rights, while other individuals or businesses own the right to extract subsurface minerals, which has led to conflicts.)

The BLM states its mission is "to sustain the health, diversity and productivity of the public lands for the use and enjoyment of present and future generations." On pub-

lic lands the agency manages a wide variety of resources and their uses, including energy and mineral extraction, timber, forage, wild horse and burro populations, wildlife habitats, and archaeological and historical sites.

The BLM's roots go back to the Land Ordinance of 1785 and the Northwest Ordinance of 1787, laws that provided for surveys and settlement of land beyond the original 13 colonies. In 1812 Congress established the General Land Office to oversee disposition of federal lands. Homesteading Laws and the Mining Law of 1872 expanded federal efforts to establish settlements in western territories.

By the end of the 19th century, with the creation of the first national parks, forests, and wildlife refuges, Congress withdrew these lands from settlement and also initiated a change in policy goals for public lands toward resource use. Acts in the early 20th century authorized mineral leasing, cattle grazing, and timberland management. In 1946 the Grazing Service was merged with the General Land Office to form the BLM, which operated under more than 2,000 laws, often in conflict with each other, until 1976. That year the Federal Land Policy and Management Act (FLPMA) was enacted, and Congress defined the BLM's role as "management of public lands and their various resource values so that they are utilized in the combination that will best meet the present and future needs of the American people."

While directed to achieve "multiple use management," the BLM remains a controversial federal agency. Traditional users of public lands, including grazing, timber, and mining interests, are often in conflict with increasing public calls for conservation, environmental management, and recreation. Supporters of the BLM point to the many conservation and environmental management actions taken by the bureau, while critics point to status quo practices subsidizing private development of public resources.

Further reading
Bureau of Land Management website. Available on-line. URL: www.blm.gov.

business and the U.S. Constitution
The parameters established by the U.S. Constitution affect business and commerce through federalism, judicial interpretation, and politics. Federalism is the relationship (division) of powers between the national government and state governments and, along with separation of powers and checks and balances, forms the foundation of the Constitution. Judicial interpretation resolves conflicting constitutional issues between national and state authority over business, namely through the COMMERCE CLAUSE (Article 1, Section 8), which gives Congress the power to regulate commerce among states. The policies of Franklin Delano Roosevelt's New Deal in the 1930s and of Lyndon B. Johnson's Great Society in the 1960s are examples of extending

national authority over business and commerce. Former Presidents Richard M. Nixon (1969–73) and George H. W. Bush (1989–93) supported transferring power from the national government back to state authority through the appointment of Supreme Court justices committed to limiting national power.

Although the theories of federalism provide a means of ensuring a federal system of government, politics ultimately determine the division of power between the national government and state governments. The two fundamental models of federalism are dual federalism and cooperative federalism. Dual federalism holds that the powers of the national government are fixed and limited and that all rights not explicitly conferred to the national government are reserved to the states. This model was appropriate for American society (business and commerce) from 1789 to 1933. The GREAT DEPRESSION, however, required a more cooperative relationship between the states and the national government in dealing with the social and economic deprivation of that era.

Cooperative federalism theory states that there is no discernment between state and national powers; their functions and responsibilities are intermingled. This model relies on the elastic clause of Article 1, Section 8 that gives Congress the power to "make laws which are necessary and proper for carrying into Execution the foregoing powers" and confines the Tenth Amendment to specific limitations not given to the national government. Cooperative efforts between the states and national government that influenced business and commerce in the 20th century have now shifted the power back to the states in the 21st century, limiting the national government's scope.

Since the 1960s the federal government's use of categorical and block grants has become prevalent as a means of shaping its relationships with state governments. Categorical grants are conditionally given for specific purposes; they increase national government power and reduce state government's power, because states must relinquish the freedom to set their own standards in order to receive financial assistance. Block grants are given for general purposes and allow greater flexibility in state spending, therefore increasing state powers and reducing national power. Greater discretionary state spending may also increase business enterprise with additional financial assistance available to businesses that work in cooperation with state agencies. Since the late 1960s, presidents have revised categorical and block grants in order to return business and commerce regulation to the states. Furthermore, the courts' interpretation of policies and society's social and economic welfare influence the continued shifting of business regulation and responsibilities.

Further reading

Baradate, L. P. "The Principles of the Constitution." In *Understanding American Democracy*, 20–44. New York: HarperCollins Publishers, 1992; Janda, K., J. Berry, and J. Goldman. "Federalism." In *The Challenge of Democracy*, 7th ed., 95–123. Boston: Houghton-Mifflin, 2002.

—Frank Ubraus and Jerry Merwin

business cycles

Business cycles are the patterns of increase and decreases in GROSS DOMESTIC PRODUCT (GDP) that occur in an economy. Most countries' economies have tended to grow over time, but within the trend of overall growth there have been periods of expansion, peaks, contractions, and troughs, followed again by expansion. The movement of an economy through periods of expansion and contraction is called a business cycle.

In the United States the longest period of economic expansion began with a trough in the first quarter of 1991 and continued until 2001. Since 1929 there have been 12 RECESSIONS, or periods of economic contraction. During the 1930 election, President Herbert Hoover claimed the country was not in a recession, just a mild depression. Since then a severe and prolonged recession has been called a depression. The longest period of recession in U.S. history, the GREAT DEPRESSION, lasted from 1929 to 1934. One saying suggested the distinction between a recession and a depression was that "in a recession your neighbor is unemployed; in a depression, you are too!"

During the Great Depression, GDP declined by one-third and UNEMPLOYMENT rose to 25 percent. Economists continue to analyze and debate the causes of the Great Depression and the causes of business cycles. Changes from economic expansion to contraction are caused by shifts in aggregate DEMAND, aggregate SUPPLY, or combinations of both. Changes in business INVESTMENT, CONSUMPTION spending, government purchases, fluctuations in EXPORTING, and IMPORTS, and changes in a country's MONEY SUPPLY all impact overall demand and supply in an economy. Discovery of new resources, wars, political upheavals, technological innovation, immigration, and population growth have all been suggested as factors contributing to business cycles. In the 19th century, sunspot cycles were suggested to have been similar to business cycles.

Economists try to predict business cycles. If businesses can anticipate changes in the economy, they can prepare for expansion and contractions in economic activity. If governments can anticipate changes in the economy, they can intervene with fiscal and MONETARY POLICY changes to reduce the severity of business cycle troughs and to sustain periods of economic expansion.

Economists use leading INDICATORS to predict changes in business cycles. Leading indicators, as the term suggests, shift in advance of changes in the economy. Changes in unemployment claims, stock prices, new plant and equipment expenditures, new building permits, and consumer expectations all tend to precede changes in economic output. Leading indicators are less than perfect predictors of business cycles, leaving business managers and policy makers uncertain about future changes in the economy.

Further reading
Boyes, William J., and Michael Melvin. *Macroeconomics,* 5th ed. Boston: Houghton Mifflin, 2001.

business ethics

PROFITS are the "bottom line" for businesses and CORPORATIONS, but should maximizing profits at any cost be the primary motivation of a business? Should responsibility to employees, customers, and the community be a concern as well? Can businesses act in ways that balance the duties they have to their SHAREHOLDERS with the duties they have to their STAKEHOLDERS?

Philosophers and other thinkers have contemplated ethics and ethical issues for thousands of years. However, it wasn't until the post-Watergate era that the development of ethical standards in business practices really began to evolve in response to highly publicized news about ethical issues in business. Some of these issues are: bribes and kickbacks, defective and harmful products, workplace discrimination and other unfair EMPLOYMENT practices, INSIDER TRADING, false ADVERTISING, deceptive accounting and AUDITING procedures, monopolies, whistle-blowing, hazardous work environments, and environmental pollution. These acts of misconduct have resulted in the creation and adoption of ethical standards into the structures of many businesses and corporations.

Just as individuals are guided by personal ethics when facing moral and other dilemmas, businesses (which are based on human activities, after all) also face challenges when they strive to earn profits and simultaneously try to maintain integrity in their practices in areas such as employee rights, workplace safety, and social responsibility. Therefore "business ethics" may be defined as the study and evaluation of both the moral implications of business behaviors and activities as well as the standards developed that promote moral policy-making at the individual, managerial, and organizational level.

Ethical business practices include acting within the law, providing a safe work environment for employees, treating employees fairly, giving back to the community through philanthropy, making safe products, and protecting the environment. To address these practices, businesses often codify ethical standards into the form of MISSION STATEMENTS, credos, or policies. Employees, managers, and executives may then refer to these policies for guidance when faced with situations that may have moral implications. Additionally, these policies may be applicable not only to existing and current problems but also to anticipated conflicts. These policies are then communicated to employees through handbooks and training, with notice that compliance with these policies is expected of employees, including the management and executives. Many companies also create ethics hotlines, committees, and training programs to further communicate their corporate values. Likewise, many professions and trade associations have their own codes of ethics developed in response to actual or anticipated ethical conflicts. These codes serve as guides for the professional behavior of members and set the standards of their profession.

An ideal world is one where businesses self-regulate according to ethical standards they have set and where corporations would always act ethically. However, external authority also exists to ensure adherence to legal standards addressing issues that are ethical in nature. Federal, state, and local laws, regulations, and codes are in effect to regulate business behavior and promote ethical practices. For example, OCCUPATIONAL SAFETY AND HEALTH ADMINISTRATION (OSHA) laws protect employees from hazardous work environments. The EQUAL EMPLOYMENT OPPORTUNITY COMMISSION (EEOC) oversees the legal protection of women, minorities, and the disabled against discrimination, harassment, and other injustices in the workplace. ENVIRONMENTAL PROTECTION AGENCY (EPA) legislation such as the CLEAN AIR ACTS and the CLEAN WATER ACT serves to protect the environment from industrial pollutants. The U.S. CONSUMER PRODUCT SAFETY COMMISSION is established to protect people from the risks of unsafe products. The SECURITIES AND EXCHANGE COMMISSION (SEC) has many rules and regulations that govern the financial disclosures of publicly traded companies.

With increasing GLOBALIZATION, business ethics must also extend internationally. Therefore the U.S. Department of Commerce has issued its "U.S. Model Business Principles" as a reference for businesses to use when framing their own ethical standards and policies—especially applicable in a global economy. Most recently, and in light of recent corporate scandals, the George W. Bush administration has initiated efforts to combat corporate FRAUD through its Corporate Fraud Task Force, to promote reforms to protect workers' pensions, and to protect stockholders through the "Ten-Point Plan to Improve Corporate Responsibility."

Today the media is reporting what seem like endless examples of unethical, illegal, and fraudulent corporate behavior by executives at Enron, WorldCom, Adelphia Communications, Tyco, Arthur Anderson, Qwest, and ImClone. These corporate scandals are probably the exceptions to the rule, since most businesses recognize that it benefits everyone to act ethically. An ethical business model will attract and keep high-quality employees, increase productivity, build a positive reputation for the business, inspire shareholder confidence, protect the environment, and make for good corporate citizenship in the form of philanthropy. All of these things have a tremendous impact on that bottom line: profits. It is therefore possible for businesses to adhere to high ethical standards and still please both their stockholders and stakeholders.

Further reading
Bender, David, pub. *Business Ethics*. Opposing Viewpoints Series. San Diego: Greenhaven Press, Inc., 2001; de George, Richard T. *Business Ethics*. Upper Saddle River, N.J.: Prentice Hall, 1999; Ethics Resource Center website. Available on-line. URL: http://www.ethics.org; Mauer, John G., et al., eds. *Encyclopedia of Business*. New York: Gale Research Group, 1995; Werhane, Patricia H., and R. Edward Freeman, eds. *The Blackwell Encyclopedic Dictionary of Business Ethics*. Cambridge, Mass.: Blackwell Business, 1997. For an excellent example of a corporate ethics credo, see the Johnson & Johnson website at http://www.jnj.com/our_company/our_credo/credo_heading.htm.

—Karen Brickman Emmons

business failure (bankruptcy)

Business failure or bankruptcy occurs when a firm cannot pay its debts on time or when liabilities exceed ASSETS. Bankruptcy is an ancient issue, critical to the development of an economic and social system. It is addressed both in the Old Testament of the Bible and the U.S. Constitution. The Bible states: "At the end of every seven years you shall grant a release and this is the manner of the release: every creditor shall release what he has lent to his neighbor . . ." The Constitution granted Congress the authority to establish "uniform laws on the subject of bankruptcies throughout the United States."

Business failure includes both legal and management issues. In the United States, The Bankruptcy Act, first passed in 1800 and amended numerous times since, serves several purposes:

- to ensure that the debtor's property is fairly distributed to creditors
- to ensure that some creditors do not obtain an unfair advantage
- to protect creditors from actions by the debtor to not relinquish assets to which the creditors are entitled
- to protect debtors from demands for payment by creditors

The Bankruptcy Code includes two levels or chapters of business failure status: straight liquidation (Chapter 7) and reorganization (Chapter 11). There are also statutes for FAMILY FARM bankruptcy (Chapter 12) and CONSUMER BANKRUPTCY (Chapter 13). Under Chapter 7, known as "straight bankruptcy," a firm must disclose all property owned and surrender the assets to a bankruptcy trustee. The trustee sets aside certain assets that the debtor is allowed to retain and then sells the remaining assets in order to pay off creditors. Either a voluntary or involuntary petition (filed by the debtor or the creditor, respectively) can initiate Chapter 7 proceedings. Individuals, PARTNERSHIPS or CORPORATIONS can file voluntary petitions. Involuntary petitions are sought by creditors seeking to have a debtor declared bankrupt and have their assets distributed to creditors. There are numerous legal details and exceptions in bankruptcy proceedings as well as attorneys that specialize in bankruptcy law.

Under Chapter 11 of the Bankruptcy Act, a debtor is allowed to work out a plan to solve its financial problems under the supervision of a court-appointed representative. The debtor agrees to a reorganization plan, usually including some debt relief from creditors. The goal of Chapter 11 is to allow debtors, primarily businesses, to continue to exist and return to solvency. During the 1980s and 1990s many U.S. companies seeking to avoid major liability claims used Chapter 11 proceedings. Johns-Manville Corporation filed for bankruptcy because of asbestos claims. A. H. Robins filed for protection because of birth control device LIABILITY. Some companies have filed Chapter 11 to get out of COLLECTIVE BARGAINING agreements.

As stated previously, business failure is also a management issue. As one official of the SMALL BUSINESS ADMINISTRATION (SBA) stated, "Poor management is the greatest single cause of business failure." Some common management mistakes include hiring the wrong people, inadequate employee training, trying to do too much, and misuse of management time. The SBA's Online Women's Business Center lists 11 common causes of business failure:

- choosing a business that is not very profitable
- inadequate cash reserves
- failure to clearly define and understand one's market, customers, and customers' buying habits
- failure to price one's PRODUCT or service correctly
- failure to adequately anticipate cash flow
- failure to anticipate or react to COMPETITION, technology, or other changes in the marketplace
- overgeneralization
- overdependence on a single customer
- uncontrolled growth
- believing one can do everything oneself
- putting up with inadequate MANAGEMENT

Further reading
Mallor, Jane P., A. James Barnes, Thomas Bowers, Michael J. Phillips, and Arlen W. Langvardt. *Business Law and the Regulatory Environment*. 11th ed. Boston: McGraw-Hill, 2001; U.S. Small Business Administration's Online Women's Business Center. Available on-line. URL: www.onlinewbc.gov/docs/starting/failure.html.

business forecasting

Business forecasting is analysis of past and current situations in order to anticipate the future. The most widely used type of business forecasting is sales forecasting, predicting future sales, but businesses engage in a variety of other forecasting efforts. Major forecasting concerns for businesses include predicting future workforce requirements, CAPITAL investment needs, and materials. Forecasts are typically incorporated in BUSINESS PLANS.

Business forecasting can be either qualitative or quantitative and subjective or objective. Qualitative forecasts are generalized predictions about the future, while quantitative forecasts result in a specified number, percentage change in sales, additional workers needed, etc. Subjective forecasting is based on peoples' opinions. Subjective forecasting techniques include jury of executive opinion, DELPHI TECHNIQUE, sales force composite, and surveys of buyers' intentions. Objective forecasting methods include trend analysis, market tests, and regression analysis. (These techniques are discussed in greater detail in the SALES FORECASTING entry.)

Whether quantitative or qualitative, subjective or objective, businesses use forecasting to make decisions in the current time period affecting production, sales, and profits in the future. Anticipating and then meeting the future needs of customers is critical to MARKETING STRATEGY.

business intelligence   See MARKET INTELLIGENCE.

business language
Business language is the combination of slang, jargon, and acronyms used in the business world. Americans use a variety of terms and phrases that are not standard English. Businesspeople are often in hurry. Slang and jargon are quick and easy ways to communicate. It saves time for people who know the terms, but for others it creates the potential for misunderstanding. A major problem in business communication is bypassing, where the speaker or writer knows what they want to communicate, knows what terms mean, and assumes the people they are communicating with also know the same terms. For example, a simple acronym AMA has at least three different meanings in American business: American Medical, Marketing, or Management Association. Similarly, "acid test" could mean the final decisive test or proof, or it could refer to a financial test for solvency. Users of business language need to consider their audience's level of understanding and the multiple meanings of terms and phrases.

Slang is a body of words intelligible to a large portion of the general public but not accepted as formal usage. *Jargon* is the technical vocabulary of a subgroup within the population. Slang and jargon are used more often in speech than in writing. "Baker's dozen," "bait and switch," and "bargain basement" are all examples of widely used slang phrases. "Keystone," "kicker," and "puff piece" are examples of jargon used in marketing but unfamiliar to most Americans.

Slang and jargon come from a variety of sources, usually industries or subgroups within society that are particularly important in a period of time. In the United States many colorful business language terms are historically rooted in the military (R&R, boot camp, deep six); sports (batting average, air ball, on the sideline, full-court press); immigrants (el jefe, fait accompli, schmuck, Chinese wall); and politics (kitchen cabinet, port barrel, brain trust). In recent years financial markets (zombie BONDS, dead cat bounce, elves, zeros) and technology (DOT-COMS, chip jewelry, platforms, URLs, desktops) have been the major sources of new business language in the United States. U.S. business domination of electronic commerce has often led to worldwide acceptance of American business-language terms. Business language is constantly changing, challenging consumers and industry members alike.

Further reading
American business language website. Available on-line. URL: www.islc.net/~folsom/language; Chapman, Robert. *New Dictionary of American Slang.* New York: Harper & Row, 1987.

business logistics (physical distribution)
Originally the term *logistics* described the strategic movement of military personnel and equipment. During World War II, General George Patton's army was stalled by a lack of fuel. Patton called his problem "the iron grip of logistics." Transporting a large number of troops and a lot of equipment quickly and efficiently is often the key to military success. The business world now uses logistics (also referred to as physical distribution) to describe the process of distributing final goods efficiently to the consumer to ensure a PROFIT.

Seven elements comprise the logistics (physical distribution) system:

- customer service—to ensure that customers get what they ask for
- INVENTORY CONTROL—to determine where and how much inventory should be kept on hand
- transportation—how and from where goods should be shipped
- processing orders—how long it should take for orders to be processed
- packaging—how goods should be packaged. Goods need to be packaged according to their method of delivery and in a manner that is visually attractive and environmentally conservative
- handling of materials—determining whether materials be kept in a warehouse, where orders will be filled later, or shipped and transferred to other trucks on the loading dock (cross-docking) and then delivered to stores
- warehousing—determining whether it will be more cost effective to keep materials in warehouses in different locations or ship from one location?

Optimally, these seven elements work together to ensure the logistics system runs effectively from both the customers' and the firm's perspectives. If one element is not working efficiently, the other elements will not run as smoothly.

U.S. companies spend approximately $700 billion on logistics yearly. In some cases businesses are able to reduce distribution costs by hiring third-party logistics firms, companies that specialize in handling logistics for other firms. Hiring a third-party logistics firm will allow a company to focus more on the manufacturing of the product rather than its distribution. By contracting other companies to distribute goods, the producer may use less manpower, leading to greater profits.

In order to make a profit, companies need to find the most cost-efficient way to produce and deliver their products to customers. Logistics can make or break a company. Amazon.com, for example, started as an INTERNET bookstore that was distributed from the house of its creator, Jeff Bezos, is now one of the largest domains for on-line shopping.

Consumers are more likely to do business with a producer who is able to get products to them in a timely manner. Consumers will often pay more in order to get a product in a shorter amount of time.

See also LOGISTICS.

Further reading
Boone, Louis E., and David L. Kurtz. *Contemporary Marketing,* 10th ed. Fort Worth: Dryden Press, 2001; Czinkota, Michael R., et al. *Marketing Best Practices.* 2d ed. Fort Worth: Dryden Press, 2002.

—Jessica Lujick

business plan
A business plan is a document that describes a company's overall plans. The phrase is sometimes used to describe a plan for a segment of the company or for a specific initiative. It can also describe the document prepared in an effort to raise VENTURE CAPITAL.

A business plan describes the current business environment, the company's goals, and the progressive milestones for how those goals will be reached. The plan specifically reports the marketing, operational, staffing, and financial steps to be taken to attain each of the goals.

Here is an outline commonly used in business plans:

1. Executive Summary. This section summarizes the rest of the document. It should be interesting enough to entice the reader to read the rest of the document.
2. Company Profile. This section, which provides a description of the business, includes the company's MISSION STATEMENT.
3. Competitive Analysis. This section describes the business's competitive environment, specifies what competitors are currently in the business, and looks at their likely response to the actions described in the business plans.
4. Marketing Strategy. This section describes the marketing strategy to accomplish the company's goals and includes discussion of pricing and distribution issues.
5. Operational Strategy. This section tells about the operational milestones needed to accomplish the company's goals. It describes the development of new processes or technology and the progress being made in these areas.
6. Staff Qualifications. This section—one of the plan's most important—describes the team that has been marshaled to carry out the plans. Potential investors are often more interested in the "who" of the plan than the "what."
7. Financial Information. The business plan needs to include any financial information that helps describe (a) the company's current financial situation, (b) cost data relative to carrying out the plan, and (c) the firm's financial condition if the plan is successful.
8. Appendices. This section contains any support documentation that makes the business plan more credible. For example, the financial information section may discuss the company's income growth over the past five years, and thus the appendix could contain the company's FINANCIAL STATEMENTS.

The sections described above serve only as an example of what often appears in a business plan. The more creative a person is in clearly presenting the plan, the more likely it is that the plan will get the attention of a potential investor.

Business Roundtable
The Business Roundtable is an association of CHIEF EXECUTIVE OFFICERS (CEOs) of major U.S.-based CORPORATIONS. The association's stated goal is "to promote policies that will lead to sustainable, non-inflationary, long-term growth in the U.S. economy." The Business Roundtable was formed in 1972 through the merger of three organizations: the March Group (a group of CEOs which had been meeting informally to discuss public issues), the Construction Users Anti-Inflation Round Table (a group focusing restraining construction costs), and the Labor Law Study Committee (a group of labor relations executives of major companies).

The Business Roundtable uses the power and visibility of major CEOs to influence government policies and regulations. At the annual meeting each June in Washington, D.C., Roundtable members discuss position papers developed by Task Forces on topics currently important to the group. In 2000, Roundtable Task Forces included Civil Justice Reform, CORPORATE GOVERNANCE, the Digital Economy, Education, Environment, Technology & the Economy, Fiscal Policy, Health & Retirement, Human Resources, and International Trade and Investment.

Roundtable position papers are often used by members in testimony before Congressional committees, lobbying efforts at Congress and the White House, and in media releases for the general public. The Business Roundtable is an important network for business executives, providing a forum for discussion of interests across industries and among competitors in the marketplace.

Further reading
Business Roundtable website. Available on-line. URL: www.brtable.org.

business taxes

Business taxation is a constantly changing and controversial subject covering a wide array of taxes. Some are imposed by the federal government, others by state and local governments. Some are paid directly by businesses, while others are added into the price of products and, depending on the market, paid by consumers, producers, or combinations of both consumers and producers.

Taxes have existed as long as organized societies have existed, and the most powerful people in a society usually control taxation. For example, the Earl of Mercia in 11th-century Coventry, England, only agreed to reduce taxes after his wife, Lady Godiva, agreed to ride through the village naked on a horse. In U.S. elementary schools, students learn about the early American colonists' protests against taxation without representation, dramatized by the Boston Tea Party.

At its conception in 1781, the federal government was given no power to tax citizens. When Congress, in 1791, allowed an excise tax on spirits, it resulted in a revolt by farmers in western Pennsylvania, known as the Whiskey Rebellion. In 1798 Congress levied a tax of $2 million, apportioned among the states based on population, to pay off part of the debt accumulated during the Revolutionary War. The tax was levied based on the value of ASSETS including dwellings, land, and slaves.

Throughout the 1800s, TARIFFs were the major source of federal tax revenue. Tariffs were generally easier to impose, since most ports were open and visible, and they were less controversial than PROPERTY TAXES or excise taxes. Tariffs were imposed for two purposes: to raise money for government and to protect domestic industries against foreign COMPETITION.

During the Civil War, the federal government imposed both property and INCOME taxes. After the war, the income tax was discontinued, but the Bureau of Internal Revenue continued to collect "sin and vice" taxes on tobacco and liquor. Tariffs remained the major source of federal tax revenue until World War I. Income taxation, reimposed in 1913 as a popular response to the concentration of power and WEALTH among elite industrialists, was expanded and used to pay for U.S. involvement in the war.

Today, while most of the federal government's tax revenue comes from personal income tax and SOCIAL SECURITY payments, business taxation remains a significant and complex part of our tax system. Some of the major taxes imposed by the federal government on businesses include corporate income tax, excise taxes, Social Security, and Medicare. Corporate income tax is, as the name suggests, a tax on the net income of companies. It is a progressive tax, or the percentage of corporate income paid as taxes, increasing as income increases. Numerous deductions and allowances reduce the income subject to taxation. The federal tax laws contain thousands of special provisions for CORPORATIONS reducing or eliminating their tax liability. Businesses can also avoid corporate taxation by either electing sub-S classification (for small businesses) and distributing profits to SHAREHOLDERS, who then declare the profits as personal income; or by creating PARTNERSHIPS, which also do not pay corporate taxes and, like sub-S corporations, distribute income to partners.

Excise taxes are taxes on the manufacture or sale of a PRODUCT. Businesses pay excise taxes to both the federal government and state governments. The major excise taxes in the United States are gasoline, tobacco, and alcohol taxes, taxed at a set amount per unit of output. For example, wine is taxed at $1.07 per gallon (for wine with less than 14-percent alcohol). Beer is taxed at $18 per barrel. As part of the TOBACCO SETTLEMENT, in 1998 the federal government significantly raised the excise tax on tobacco. There are also many obscure excise taxes, including taxes on coal, recreational vehicles, tires, and the production of machine guns and destructive devices.

To businesses, excise taxes are a cost of doing business, and as such they are included in the price of a product. How much of the tax is paid by consumers in the form of higher prices and how much is absorbed by businesses as a cost depends primarily on the ELASTICITY OF DEMAND for products. Elasticity of demand is consumers' sensitivity or responsiveness to price changes. For example, the government raised the excise tax on tobacco by 75 cents per pack in 1998 and settled the liability lawsuit costing the tobacco companies billions of dollars over the next 25 years. At the same time, the price of cigarettes went up an amount almost equal to the combined excise tax and settlement costs. Because demand for tobacco products is very inelastic (among addicted smokers), the tax was transferred to consumers. If, instead, consumers had significantly reduced their purchases of tobacco products in response to the higher price, much of the tax would have been incurred by the businesses.

The third major type of tax paid by businesses is Social Security. Employers and employees each contribute a set percentage of income, approximately 6 percent to Old Age, Survivors and Disability (OASDI), up to a limit of about $80,000 of wages and salaries annually. The limit increases with inflation. Both employers and employees contribute about 1.5 percent of wages, with no limit on income to pay for Medicare. Since these taxes are only paid on wage income, businesses, especially small businesses, can legally avoid paying some of these taxes by distributing income in the form of DIVIDENDS. On the other hand, self-employed people pay both the employer and employee's share of Social Security taxes.

Most states generate the majority of their tax revenue using sales, property, and personal income taxes. Business taxation varies considerably among states, with some states taxing business inventories and business income. Most cities impose property taxes on businesses but also offer tax breaks for companies bringing jobs to the community. Supporters of these practices call them incentives, while opponents call them CORPORATE WELFARE.

See also TAX SHELTERS.

Further reading
Legal Information Institute website. Available on-line. URL: http://taxes.about.com

—Jonathan S. Goldberg

business valuation

A business valuation is an estimate of the fair MARKET VALUE of a closely held business. There is no distinction between a valuation and an appraisal, but usually the term *valuation* is applied to estimating the value of a business and an *appraisal* is used to refer to estimating the value of a specific ASSET, such as real estate, jewelry, antiques, or art. *Fair market value,* an important term in business valuation, means what a willing buyer and seller would agree upon if neither had a particular compulsion to buy or sell and both had reasonable knowledge of all the facts.

Valuations are done for many reasons. The most obvious is the valuation done to assist in a genuine transaction, when, for example, a prospective buyer or seller hires a valuation expert to assist them in the process. But valuations are also done for other reasons. The estate tax levies a certain amount of tax on the value of property transferred to an heir, and so an estate must have a valuation of any family business that is inherited by the next generation. Sometimes the valuation of a family business is important in divorces. When the assets are being divided by the spouses, it is a relatively easy matter to establish a value for such things as cars and houses, but the value of the family plumbing business is a different matter. A valuation expert is important to guide the courts in the division of the assets.

In general there are three approaches used in estimating the value of a business: asset approach, INCOME approach, and the market approach. The asset approach is the easiest to understand: The company's individual are valued, then its debts are subtracted to find an overall fair market value.

The income approach estimates the company's future income and then uses DISCOUNTING techniques to estimate its current value. The difficulties with this approach include estimating the future income and determining an appropriate DISCOUNT RATE.

The market approach is theoretically very appealing. It compares certain characteristics of the company being val-

ued to companies that have been sold recently; the person doing the valuation tries to find a comparable company in the same industry, with about the same assets and income size. The difficulty with this method is both in finding a comparable company and understanding the elements of the comparable transaction, which may include other considerations besides the company being sold. For example, the CONTRACT to sell a comparable company may include a certain amount of work to be done by the previous owner or some special financing provision. Such things have to be stripped from the comparable transaction before it is used as a basis for valuing the business. Finding a comparable company and understanding the transaction makes the market approach most difficult to apply.

The American Society of Appraisers and the AMERICAN INSTITUTE OF CERTIFIED PUBLIC ACCOUNTANTS have specialty designations or valuation credentials that they confer on members who accomplish certain prescribed training and testing and have pertinent experience.

Buy American Act and campaigns

The Buy American Act (1933) and traditions favor the purchase of goods and services from domestic suppliers. Almost every time the U.S. economy begins to decline, local and national politicians, supported by business leaders, develop campaigns promoting the purchase of American-made products. The Buy American Act requires the federal government to purchase American products unless (a) the purchase is for use outside the United States (such as U.S. military bases abroad), (b) there are insufficient quantities of acceptable quality products available domestically, or (c) it results in unreasonable costs.

As currently applied, the act requires federal agencies to purchase domestic goods unless the domestic bids are more than 6 percent higher than bids from foreign producers. Bids from U.S. companies must contain 50-percent or more American materials to be considered domestic. These rules apply to civil purchases made by the U.S. government but are suspended for purchasing subject to WORLD TRADE ORGANIZATION rules.

The U.S. Department of Defense has its own Buy American rules giving preference to domestic suppliers. In addition, under the Small Business Act of 1953, federal agencies set aside 30 percent of their procurement for socially and economically disadvantaged businesses.

Many state and local purchasing requirements also support preferences for American producers. For example, California once had a regulation mandating purchase of American products, and cities in Massachusetts banned purchases from Myanmar (formerly Burma). These laws were declared unconstitutional on the grounds that they encroached on the federal power to conduct foreign affairs. State laws that copy the federal Buy American Act incorporating public interest and unreasonable cost exceptions have generally withstood legal challenges.

Many countries around the world have preferential buying laws similar to those of the United States. American laws can be used to deny procurement contracts to suppliers from countries that "maintain . . . a significant and persistent pattern of practice or discrimination against U.S. products or services which results in identifiable harm to U.S. businesses."

"Buy American" campaigns—business/political initiatives to encourage the purchase of American-made products—typically arise during downturns in the domestic economy. In the mid-1980s, Wal-Mart, the largest retail chain in the United States, initiated its "Keeping America Working and Strong" campaign. Led by founder Sam Walton, Wal-Mart directed buyers to seek out U.S.-made products and encouraged vendors to do business with U.S. manufacturers.

"Buy American" campaigns generate favorable publicity and are good PUBLIC RELATIONS strategies. The federal government estimates that each additional $1 million spent on U.S. products results in 23 additional jobs in the country. "Buy American" campaigns are frequently associated with trade deficits and efforts to increase protectionism in the country. Economists have conducted numerous studies showing the huge cost to consumers for each job saved through TARIFFS and other competition-reducing trade legislation.

Studies also show that, while Americans prefer U.S.-made products, they tend to purchase the best price/value products available regardless of where they are made. A frequent problem is determining what is American-made. For example, approximately half of the Japanese-brand cars sold in the United States are produced in this country. Similarly, many American-brand cars are produced elsewhere. Often consumers have to look on the inside passenger door to determine where their car was manufactured. In a controversial *Harvard Business Review* article entitled "Who Are US?," former Secretary of Commerce Robert Reich argued that if the goal is to create and maintain jobs in the United States, Americans should also support the many foreign companies producing products and employing workers in the country regardless of where the company is headquartered.

Further reading
"Buy American Campaign Gains Momentum," *Discount Store News* (9 December 1985): 24, 74; Folsom, Ralph H., and Michael Gordon. "International Business Transactions," 2d ed. Eagan, Minn.: West Group, 2002 (1999); Reich, Robert. "Who Are US?" *Harvard Business Review* (March–April 1991): 77.

buy-grid model
The buy-grid model is a business model depicting rational organizational decision making. Business marketers use the buy-grid model to portray the steps businesses go through in making purchase decisions. The model includes two components: buy phase and buy class.

Buy phase represents the logical eight steps businesses (or consumers involved in extensive problem solving) go through

- need recognition
- definition of PRODUCT type needed
- development of detailed specifications
- search for qualified suppliers
- acquisition and analysis of proposals
- evaluation of proposals and selection of a supplier
- selection of an order procedure
- evaluation of product performance

Business-to-business marketers recognize that at each step in the buying process, business buyers have different needs, and different groups within the organization may be involved. Business marketers anticipate which step organizational buyers are in and attempt to provide the needed information and support for that stage of decision making. Marketers who can become involved early in the decision-making process have a greater chance of being considered in the final selection process. Many organizations, including government agencies, have formal purchasing procedures incorporating the buy-grid model. Set-aside programs targeting small and minority-owned businesses and bid solicitation requirements for government offices follow a similar defined procedure for PURCHASING.

Most business-buying situations do not involve all of the steps in the buy-grip model. The number of steps varies with the buy-class, the type of buying decision. There are three buy-class categories: new buys, straight rebuys, and modified rebuys. While the complete buying process is typically used for new buys (purchases of products or services never used before), a majority of business purchasing decisions are either straight rebuys or modified rebuys. In straight rebuy situations, only the need recognition (the company almost out of the product) and reordering steps are used. For business marketers it is critical for their products or services to be listed as approved vendors for straight rebuys. Marketers will use reminder ADVERTISING, relationship-building entertainment and hospitality, and PERSONAL SELLING to maintain their status as the preferred provider. In modified rebuy decisions (where a buyer is willing to "shop around"), the buyer may go through some or all of the purchasing steps. For marketers desiring to be considered during modified rebuy situations, comparison advertising and demonstrations are used to influence business buyers. Incumbent firms will use relationships, special offers, and anticipation of or quick response to customer needs to maintain their status when business buyers are considering alternatives.

Further reading
Dwyer, F. Robert, and John F. Tanner, Jr. *Business Marketing,* 2d ed. Boston: Irwin McGraw-Hill, 2002.

buying-center concept

The buying-center concept is the idea that in businesses and organizations, many people with different roles and priorities participate in PURCHASING decisions. Unlike consumer buying, where the consumer, alone or with assistance or influence from acknowledged opinion leaders, makes his or her own purchase decisions, in business buying a group often determines which PRODUCTS or SERVICES are purchased.

The typical business buying center will include a variety of participants:

- initiators: people who start the purchase process by defining a need
- decision makers: people who make the final decision
- gatekeepers: people who control the flow of information and access to individuals in an organization
- influencers: people who have input into the purchase decision
- purchasing agent: the person who actually makes the purchase order
- controller: the person who oversees the budget for the purchase
- users: people who use the product or service

In many situations, people play more than one role in business purchasing decisions. Sometimes, buying centers are formal committees created to make a purchase decision, but more often they are defined by organizational relationships. Depending on an organization's structure and the importance of the decision being made, there could be many or few layers of management involved in a buying center. Some members of a buying center will participate throughout the decision-making process, while others will only be involved briefly.

Marketers attempt to define who is involved in buying-center decisions. For example, in the 1990s it was often difficult to determine which people made purchase decisions for business computer systems. In many organizations there was no formal computer-systems department. Often important influencers were individuals within an organization who had taken the time to learn about and analyze computers, even though it was not part of their job requirements. Influencers were often also initiators of computer-systems purchases and upgrades but sometimes were thwarted by gatekeepers resisting changes in technology. For a marketer of computer systems, it was important to identify who played which roles in business buying centers.

Marketers have also recognized the importance of "champions"—advocates for a company's products or services within an organization. During the latter 1990s and early 21st century, many organizations expanded the use of OUTSOURCING—contracting for specific products or services from outside the organization. The jargon term *pilot fish* refers to individuals and businesses created by former employees now providing outsourcing services to the companies they previously worked for. These pilot fish know the company's structure and the buying-center process in the organization and depend on their champions to continue to influence and send business to them.

Further reading

Dwyer, F. Robert, and John F. Tanner, Jr. *Business Marketing,* 2d ed. Boston: Irwin McGraw-Hill, 2002.

bylaws

Bylaws define the organizational and operational structure of a CORPORATION. In addition to the articles of INCORPORATION (sometimes called a charter), which state the rights and responsibilities of the corporation, bylaws provide greater definition regarding the powers of managers, SHAREHOLDERS, and the BOARD OF DIRECTORS. Jane P. Mallor et al. note that a typical set of corporate bylaws cover:

- the authority of directors and officers, specifying what they may or may not do
- the place and time at which the annual shareholders' meeting will be held
- the procedure for calling special shareholders' meetings
- the procedures for directors' and shareholders' meetings, including whether a majority is required for approval of specific actions
- provisions for the creation of special committees of the board of directors, defining their scope and membership
- the procedures for the maintenance of records regarding shareholders
- the mechanisms for transfer of shares of stock
- the standards and procedures for the declaration and payment of DIVIDENDS

Bylaws are the rules guiding the behavior of shareholders, management, and the board of directors. Without them many disputes are likely to arise among owners and managers, and they provide greater transparency in corporate business decision making. Even with well-defined bylaws, corporate disputes and lawsuits frequently arise. In the 1900s, shareholders in many companies proposed changes in bylaws, including "shareholder-rights bylaws," which would require the company's board of directors to "pull the pill" when confronted with a hostile acquisition—that is, implementing anti-takeover actions to prevent another company from taking control of the company. Known as POISON-PILL STRATEGIES, shareholder-rights bylaws would direct specific action by the board of directors, but many legal scholars question their legality.

Further reading

Goodchild, Seth, and Daniel J. Buzzetta. "Shareholder bylaws: a threat to the board?" *Corporate Board* 19 (May-June 1998): 10; Mallor, Jane P., A. James Barnes, Thomas Bowers, Michael J. Philips, and Arlen W. Langvardt. *Business Law and the Regulatory Environment,* 11th ed. Boston: McGraw-Hill, 2001.

C

cafeteria plans

Cafeteria plans allow employers to compensate employees by offering a combination of cash and tax-favored "fringe" benefits (health/disability INSURANCE, dependent care, or group term life insurance). Generally, when cash is an option, it is taxable. However, under a cafeteria plan the employee can choose a nontaxable benefit and receive it free of both federal INCOME and payroll (SOCIAL SECURITY and Medicare) taxes. Cafeteria plans provide flexibility for the employee to elect benefits that meet individual needs. This ability to choose allows the employee to select cash in the early career years, dependent-care assistance when children are young, and life insurance when dependent care is no longer needed. The employer is relieved of offering the maximum benefits to all the employees, but can instead offer to fund a minimum level of benefits and include a contribution to the cafeteria plan, which would allow the employee to choose which benefits to maximize. Long-term care insurance is one tax-favored fringe benefit that is not includable in a cafeteria plan.

—Linda Bradley

callable bond

A callable bond is a bond that the issuer can repurchase during certain time periods before its maturity date. To be callable, a bond must have a call feature, which enables the issuer to repurchase the bond before its maturity date. An issuer who chooses to call a bond generally pays the bond's holder a call premium upon repurchase, which is meant to compensate the holder for the disadvantage of having to find another way to invest his or her money.

Issuers like call features for several reasons. First, they can repurchase BONDS with call features and reissue them at a lower interest rate. If INTEREST RATES drop significantly, issuers sometimes need to repurchase and reissue their bonds to refinance their own debts. For example, if a 20-year callable corporate bond is issued at an 11.5-percent interest rate, and after five years interest rates drop to 8.5 percent, the CORPORATION could potentially waste a great deal of money if it did not recall the bond and reissue it at the lower rate. Issuers also sometimes like to recall bonds when they are rearranging their own capital structures or expanding. The flexibility afforded to issuers by the call feature enables them to do this.

A bond's call provision states whether the bond is noncallable, freely callable, or deferred callable. If a bond is noncallable, the issuer cannot repurchase it before the bond's date of maturity. Noncallable bonds are attractive to some investors because the issuer has to pay interest on them for the bond's full term, regardless of any prevailing level of interest rate. The drawback to these bonds for some investors, however, is that their interest rates are generally not as high as their callable counterparts. Noncallable bonds are sometimes referred to as bullets.

In comparison, an issuer can rescind a bond that is freely callable at any time. These types of bonds offer virtually no protection to investors and can be repurchased after as little as a few days.

A bond with a deferred call provision offers more protection to investors than a freely callable bond but less than a noncallable bond. Deferred callable bonds can be repurchased by the issuer, but only after the amount of time specified in the provision—for example, one, two, or 10 years after the date of purchase.

The only bonds that cannot be called are ones issued by the federal government. Other bonds, including state, municipal and corporate bonds, can be called when issuers are not able to meet interest rates, according to their own call provisions. Of the major types of bonds, corporate bonds are most likely to be called.

Further reading

Fabozzi, Frank J. *The Handbook of Fixed Income Securities,* 5th ed. New York: McGraw-Hill, 1997; Faerber, Esme. *All About Bonds and Bond Mutual Funds,* 2d ed. New York: McGraw-Hill, 2000;

"Investing Basics: Bonds." Available on-line. URL: http://www. motleyfool.com; "Other Types of Bonds: Callable Bonds." Available on-line. URL: http://www.cnet.com; "A Stock Buyer's Guide to Investing: Fourth Quarter 2001." Available on-line. URL: http://www.salomonsmithbarney. com; Woelfel, Charles J. *Encyclopedia of Banking and Finance,* 10th ed. Chicago: Probus Publishing Company, 1994; Wright, Sharon Saltzgiver. *Getting Started in Bonds.* New York: John Wiley & Sons, 2003.

—Carolyn McKelvey

capital

Along with labor, natural resources, and ENTREPRENEURSHIP (managerial ability), capital is one of the four factors of PRODUCTION. The sources of capital for a firm are represented by the items on the right-hand side of its BALANCE SHEET; debt, preferred stock, COMMON STOCK, and retained earnings. Capital is a major determinant of a firm's size. Since it is relatively more abundant for firms organized as CORPORATIONS than it is for PROPRIETORSHIPS and PARTNERSHIPS, the largest firms are corporations.

When various forms of debt, BONDS, and other liabilities are sources of capital, the cost of this borrowed capital is interest expense. When EQUITY (preferred and common stocks) and retained earnings are sources of capital, the cost of this capital is the return on equity to stockholders. On the other hand, the owners of capital earn interest income if they are creditors or bondholders; they earn DIVIDENDS and CAPITAL GAINs if they are stockholders.

Financial intermediation, the flow of capital from those who have to those who need, is necessary for ECONOMIC GROWTH. The more efficiently capital flows, the greater will be economic growth. A system of well-developed FINANCIAL INTERMEDIARIES is the cornerstone of all advanced economies, whose growth is attributable in large part to well-organized financial markets. Conversely, the lack of well-organized financial systems hinders economic growth. Lesser-developed countries are characterized by a paucity of financial intermediation. When financial intermediation is absent, capital is extremely scarce for those who need it.

See also VENTURE CAPITAL.

capital asset   See BETA COEFFICIENT, CAPITAL ASSET PRICING MODEL.

capital budgeting   See BUDGETING, CAPITAL BUDGETING.

capital expenditure, revenue expenditure

When a firm spends money, it is either for the purchase of an ASSET (a CAPITAL expenditure) or the payment of an expense (a revenue expenditure). Capital expenditures are recorded by debiting some asset account, and as a result, capital expenditures are reflected on the BALANCE SHEET.

Revenue expenditures are recorded by debiting some expense account, and as a result, revenue expenditures are reflected on the INCOME STATEMENT.

Ordinary repairs to equipment or other assets are normal expenses—that is, they are revenue expenditures. However, extraordinary repairs, such as overhauls and rebuilds, are capital expenditures. Rather than debiting an expense account for the extraordinary expenditures, the asset account for the item being overhauled or rebuilt is debited. Thus ordinary repairs are revenue expenditures and show up on the income statement as normal expenses, and extraordinary repairs are capital expenditures and show up on the balance sheet.

In accounting, "extraordinary" means both unusual and infrequent. Changing the oil and buying tires for the delivery truck are normal, usual expenses—that is, revenue expenditures. However, overhauling the delivery truck's engine is both unusual and infrequent. This is a capital expenditure, and when this is added to the asset account for the delivery truck, this will increase the BOOK VALUE of the delivery truck.

capital gain, capital loss

CAPITAL gain (or loss) is the result of the purchase and subsequent sale of a capital ASSET. If a stock, bond, or piece of real estate is sold for more than was paid for it, a capital gain on the sale of that asset is realized. If that asset has been held for less than a year, it is a short-term capital gain. If the asset has been owned for more than one year, it is a long-term capital gain. If less is received from the sale of a capital asset than was paid for it, this incurs a capital loss.

For tax purposes, short-term capital gains are treated as ordinary INCOME and taxed along with an individual's other income. However, preferential tax treatment is given to long-term capital gains, on which there is a tax cap (limit), which may be lower than an individual's marginal income tax rate. Currently, the maximum tax rate applicable to long-term capital gains is 20 percent. Tax caps on long-term capital gains are especially beneficial to taxpayers with high marginal income tax rates. For example, an individual paying a 36 percent marginal income tax rate will have his or her income from long-term capital gains taxed at only 20 percent. There is no benefit to taxpayers with lower marginal income tax rates. A taxpayer in the 15 percent marginal income tax bracket will have his or her long-term capital gains taxed at 15 percent. The long-term capital-gains tax cap is a maximum limit and becomes relevant only when an individual's marginal income tax rate rises above the 20 percent tax cap. Changes in capital-gains laws affect investor behavior.

capitalism

Capitalism is a social and economic system based on private property rights, private allocation of CAPITAL, and self-interest motivation. Capitalism is often referred to as a free enterprise or market system. Capitalism contrasts with SOCIALISM, in which most RESOURCES and industrial-PRODUCTION systems are state-owned or controlled; and with communism, in which most resources are state-owned and most decisions regarding output are made through central planning.

In the 18th century, capitalism replaced feudal control and MERCANTILISM as the primary basis for economic organization. Scottish philosopher Adam Smith described the benefits to society of rational self-interest, where producers would attempt to maximize their well-being by achieving the highest profit possible, and consumers would maximize their well-being by achieving the highest level of utility or satisfaction from the resources they controlled. Smith suggested that with private control and allocation of resources, ECONOMIC EFFICIENCY would result.

The distinguishing force of capitalism is self-interest motivation. Those individuals in control of capital will attempt to use it in a manner to maximize their profit, thereby increasing their WEALTH. Critics of capitalism, most notably 19th-century philosopher Karl Marx, suggested capitalism contained the seeds of its own destruction. Marx saw the English Industrial Revolution factory owners becoming increasingly rich, while workers, who were being replaced by machinery, were in excess SUPPLY and therefore were paid only minimal wages. Marx argued that capitalists, acquiring the "surplus value of labor," would add to the disparities between rich and poor, eventually leading to crises and social upheavals in which workers would overturn a minority's control of capital.

Ironically, the major characteristics of capitalism, private control and allocation of resources, depend heavily on the role of government. Many "free market" capitalists speak disparagingly about government, but without government laws and regulations defining who owns a resource, anarchy or dictatorial control would likely ensue. U.S. economic historians point to the excesses of the "robber baron" and AMERICAN INDUSTRIAL REVOLUTION eras as examples of the extremes of capitalism, and they credit the UNION movement and expansion of government control of resources as balancing forces in the evolution of U.S. capitalism.

Further reading
Ruffin, Roy J., and Paul R. Gregory. *Principles of Economics.* 7th ed. Boston: Addison Wesley, 2002.

capital markets, money markets
CAPITAL markets are those in which stocks and long-term debt instruments are traded. Examples of these securities having maturities of greater than one year are COMMON STOCKS and preferred stocks, corporate and government BONDS, U.S. Treasury notes and bonds, and MORTGAGES. Thus capital markets are comprised of both EQUITY and debt instruments.

Money markets are those in which short-term debt securities with maturities of one year or less are traded. Examples of these securities are consumer loans, U.S. Treasury bills, COMMERCIAL PAPER, negotiable certificates of deposit, and MUTUAL FUNDS investing in short-term debt securities. Thus money markets are comprised entirely of debt securities.

From the investor's perspective, money-market instruments are attractive during periods of rising INTEREST RATES. Investing for the short term allows the investor to continually replace lower interest-bearing securities with those of higher interest rates as rates continue to rise.

Conversely, capital-market investments are more attractive when interest rates are falling. Being able to "lock in" a high interest with a long-term security protects the investor better than a series of short-term money-market instruments.

carrying value   See BOOK VALUE.

cartel
A cartel is an organization comprised of members of an industry who once competed against each other. Cartel members usually agree to set production quotas, reducing total output available to the market, based on the percentage market share each participant had when the cartel was formed. By collectively reducing output, the market price for the cartel's output will rise and cartel members' profits will increase. Cartels, which can exist on local, regional, national, and international levels, are essentially formal agreements to restrict output, divide markets, or restrain price COMPETITION among firms in a market. As such they are illegal in the United States under the SHERMAN ANTITRUST ACT (1890).

Certain market conditions are necessary for creating and maintaining a cartel.

- few participants in the industry
- significant BARRIERS TO ENTRY
- similar PRODUCTS produced
- few opportunities to keep individual actions secret
- no legal barriers to production control agreements

Cartels are not easy to coordinate; if there are many members, it is difficult to gain consensus and cooperation. If new firms can enter the market once price has been driven up, the benefit of creating a cartel will quickly disappear. Likewise, if there are similar products that can be substituted for the cartel's product, the cartel will not be able to raise price because consumers will substitute other products. If members can cut special deals with customers, subverting the cartel agreement, the organization will quickly fall apart, and it will also disband or become an informal agreement if the agreement is deemed illegal in the markets where the cartel members participate.

Collusion, a secret agreement to restrict competition, has the same impact as a cartel and is also illegal in the United States. Most firms belong to industry associations and meet regularly to examine common issues. Frequently these meetings lead to discussion of prices. One industrial manufacturing lawyer cringed each time his company's executives went to annual industry gatherings, fearing they would return with secret agreements made with other executives in the industry.

The most famous cartel, ORGANIZATION OF PETROLEUM EXPORTING COUNTRIES (OPEC), is a group of countries (rather than firms) which coordinates oil production. When OPEC was formed in the 1960s, oil-producing countries were receiving $1–$2 per barrel of oil. In the 1970s OPEC members restricted SUPPLY while DEMAND was increasing, thereby raising oil prices to over $30 per barrel. (Oil prices vary slightly depending on the quality of the crude oil produced in different regions of the world.) Generally cartels contain the seeds of their own destruction, because members are reducing their output below their existing potential production. Once the market price increases, each member of the cartel has the capacity to raise output relatively easily. The tendency is for cartel members to "cheat" on their quota, increasing supply to the market and lowering the market price.

Most cartels are unstable agreements and quickly disband, returning the market to more competitive conditions. In the 1980s, OPEC began to fall apart, and the price of oil fell to $12 per barrel, when Saudi Arabia, the largest oil-producing country in OPEC, expanded output back to their agreed-upon OPEC quota. For most of the 1970s and 1980s, Saudi Arabia had cut its output below its quota to compensate for overproduction by other OPEC countries. This allowed OPEC to achieve the goal of higher prices but reduced Saudi Arabia's revenue. Frustrated with cheating by other members of the cartel, Saudi Arabia increased supply, and market prices plummeted. Reduced output due to the Iraq-Kuwait war in 1990, reduced cheating by OPEC members, and increased global demand brought oil prices back up over the $30-a-barrel level during most of the 1990s.

Over the years, many other cartels have been formed in tin, chrome, coffee, and diamonds. DeBeers controls the distribution of uncut diamonds, keeping prices high by restricting and coordinating supply to the market. Standard Oil—which in the 1890s gave John D. Rockefeller a near-monopoly in oil production and refining—created a cartel in petroleum distribution, shifting oil distribution among participants in the railroad cartel at agreed-upon levels. The railroads charged non-Standard Oil producers higher rates for oil distribution, facilitating Standard's acquisition of competitors and preventing new competitors from entering the oil-refining market. The Sherman Antitrust Act was a response to Standard Oil's monopolization activities.

While cartels are generally illegal in the United States, they are often legal in other countries and are sometimes sanctioned in the United States. The National Collegiate Athletic Association (NCAA) is a cartel of colleges and universities that sets athletic rules and behavior, determines distribution of television revenue from college sporting events, and penalizes institutions that violate NCAA rules. Many agricultural COOPERATIVES are legal cartels, raising prices for members' products or reducing costs through collective purchasing power. During bumper-crop years, one of the largest cooperatives in the United States, Sunkist, reduces market supply by mandating that members reduce production of citrus fruits. Cooperatives are legal in the United States.

Further reading
Boyes, William J., and Michael Melvin. *Microeconomics,* 5th ed. Boston: Houghton Mifflin, 2002.

case law See COMMON LAW.

cash-flow analysis
Cash-flow analysis is a planning device that looks at the cash flows into and out of a new project, new venture, equipment purchase, new product, etc. The manager analyzes the cash-flow predictions to determine the relative desirability of doing the new activity.

One method of analyzing the cash flow is called the "payback period." This simple technique evaluates the wisdom of carrying out a project by looking at the relative time it takes to pay back the initial INVESTMENT in the project. With this method, projects that pay back their original investment the quickest are considered superior to those that take longer. The major disadvantage of this method, which is often used by business and criticized by academics, is that it ignores cash flows after the payback period. Thus one project that brings in large cash flows after its payback period may be discarded in favor of a project that pays back the original investment rapidly. On the other hand, many business managers rightly want to minimize the time they are "at risk" with the investment, so they prefer projects that give them back their original investment rapidly.

More sophisticated techniques involve discounted cash-flow analysis. These techniques look at the time value of money and the effect of interest compounding, using relatively simple mathematical calculations to convert future cash flows to their "present value," which is the present worth of future cash flows given a specified interest rate. Financial calculators do these calculations.

The project that produces the highest present value is considered superior to those that produce a lower present value. Another way to use the same concept is to calculate each project's internal rate of return—that is, the interest rate that the original investment earns in producing the project's resultant cash flows. Often a company has a target internal rate of return that it demands from its projects and approves those projects that surpass the target or those with the highest internal rate of return.

These cash DISCOUNTING techniques add a disarming degree of mathematical rigor to the cash-flow analysis, leading the unwary manager to ignore the underlying uncertainty of the cash flows themselves. To try to deal with this, some cash-flow analyses include analyzing the probabilities of the resulting cash flows prior to their being discounted. This produces an expected value of the cash flows.

cash-flow statement See FLOW OF FUNDS.

cash management

Cash management is the cash collection, payment, and INVESTMENT activities involved in managing a business. This is done with the deliberate goal of minimizing the amount of cash the company has to borrow and maximizing its return from investments. Managers look for ways to hasten the collection of their ACCOUNTS RECEIVABLE, delay the payment of ACCOUNTS PAYABLE, and maximize the investment return of the resultant extra cash.

Hastening the collection of accounts receivable entails invoicing customers in a timely and accurate way, upon which the collected cash is hurried into investments. This happens in many different ways. The company must have an efficient way to process deposits. Banks offer a full array of services to speed cash into investments, such as bank lockboxes and sweep accounts. With a lockbox, a company lists the bank's address on its return envelopes used by its customers. The bank then directly receives all the payments on behalf of the company and immediately records these collections into the company's bank accounts, making copies of the collected checks and accompanying payment advices available to the company. This is now often done via an INTERNET site to which the company can, at its leisure, do its normal accounting for collections. Lockboxes are especially useful when the company's customers are widely dispersed. Strategically placed lockboxes minimize the amount of time the company's MONEY is tied up in the postal system instead of their bank account.

Another service offered by banks to maximize the amount of money in investments is a sweep account. The bank monitors needed cash levels in a cash account and then "sweeps" any excess into investments. Often this is done to sweep the account empty each night to get investment income on the otherwise idle cash.

To delay cash payments, the company maintains an accurate accounts payable system that carefully schedules payment dates and watches vendors' grace periods for taking cash discounts and avoiding late service charges. The payment is then made at the last possible moment.

At the heart of any cash management system is its cash accounting system and cash budget. Previously the cash account might be reconciled to the bank on a monthly basis, but today's accountants can download bank statements and reconcile them to the cash account almost daily. This close tracking of the cash account allows the company to keep a smaller cash safety cushion. As part of this focus on cash management, companies have dramatically reduced the number of bank accounts they maintain. This reduces the amount of cash that is tied up as safety balances for all of the accounts, and it allows the accounting staff to focus on the main accounts for the company.

Usually a cash budget is prepared as a part of a comprehensive BUDGETING process for the company. The cash budget predicts the inflow and outflow of cash and the resultant cash balances. This enables the company to minimize what it borrows and maximize the amount available for investments, but it involves more than just the simple scheduling of receivables and payables. Instead a good cash management system carefully studies each cash-flow item and determines the best strategy for its effective management.

International companies have developed an interesting cash management tool called *netting*. Instead of settling each transaction individually, where the receivable collected from the international client is collected, translated into the company's currency, and transmitted back to the company's main office, the company sets up a netting center where the company's collections for receivables in a certain currency are used to settle payables in the same currency. A version of this involves a joint-venture netting center where the receipts of one company are used to settle the payables of another. The resulting inter-company receivable/payable is settled between the two companies back in the home country. This solves some currency exchange and currency repatriation problems.

Center for Science in the Public Interest

The Center for Science in the Public Interest (CSPI) is an independent nonprofit organization focusing on food safety, nutrition, and alcohol abuse. Founded in 1971 by Michael Jacobson and headquartered in Washington, D.C., the CSPI has over 800,000 members and publishes *Nutrition Action Healthletter,* a widely read and respected source for information on health and nutrition.

In addition to disseminating information, the CSPI lobbies to pass health and nutrition legislation. The organization led efforts to pass the 1990 Nutrition Labeling and Education Act, which required all packaged and processed food sold in the United States to carry labels with nutritional information. Many food-industry leaders opposed the CSPI's efforts, arguing that the requirements would be expensive to comply with and were not necessary. The

Center also assisted with efforts to require warning labels on alcoholic beverages and to educate the public regarding the health dangers associated with fat, salt, and other substances in food.

In recent years the CSPI has gained widespread publicity for its efforts to educate consumers about high fat content in movie-theater popcorn and the questionable nutritional value of fast food and ethnic food restaurants. The CSPI is credited with gaining passage of the law requiring "Nutrition Facts" to be posted on packaged and processed foods sold in the United States. The center also has lobbied for increases in excise taxes on alcoholic beverages as a means to reduce alcohol consumption.

The CSPI has also influenced congressional legislation appropriating funds to reduce the risk of food-borne illnesses and to require safe-handling notices on meat and poultry products. The Center is currently assessing dangers associated with antibiotic resistance and biotechnology.

The CSPI informs consumers regarding improvements and advances in nutrition and safety. With their newsletter and publicity, the CSPI significantly influences Americans' eating habits and government regulation of the food industry. Products criticized for deceptive labeling or given negative reviews in the *Nutrition Action Healthletter* can expect to see their demand decrease.

Further reading

Center for Science in the Public Interest website. Available online. URL: www.cspinet.org.; Johanna T. Dwyer. "Center for Science in the Public Interest," World Book Online Americas Edition. Available on-line. URL: http://www.aolsvc.worldbook.aol.com/wbol/wbpage/na/ar/co/102850; *Nutrition Action Newsletter.* Available on-line. URL:http://www.cspinetorg.nah/index.htm.

—Leah Kninde Frazier-Gaskins

centrally planned economy

A centrally planned economy is an economic system where the factors of PRODUCTION (RESOURCES) are controlled by the state. Resource allocation plans and decisions are made by the central government and then promulgated through government agencies. Regional managers allocate resources to production managers and collective farms, which are given output goals. Centrally planned economies require significant government bureaucracies to control resource allocation, coordinate information flows, and measure performance.

Centrally planned economies are considered synonymous with communism but are also associated with fascism and SOCIALISM. Centrally planned economies contrast with capitalism, where most resources are controlled privately. Many U.S. politicians equate capitalism with democracy. CAPITALISM is an economic system, while democracy is a political system. Dr. David Korten of Stanford University, a critic of GLOBALIZATION, argues that, "Contrary to its claims, capitalism's relationship to democ-racy and to the market economy is much the same as the relationship of a cancer to the body whose life energies it expropriates." Korten suggests the American democratic political system has been overrun by rogue capitalism, focusing on "money and materialism over life itself."

Like capitalism, centrally planned economies are associated with a political system—in this case a single-party system—yet most European countries have a social democrat political party, advocating democracy but greater collective control and allocation of resources. There are probably no purely capitalist or centrally planned economies. The differences among countries are a matter of the degree of control and allocation of resources made privately versus centrally.

As of 2004, the major centrally planned economies in the world are Cuba and North Korea. In both countries, powerful leaders direct and control a central government making most decisions regarding resource allocation. Because of its international isolation, much less is known about North Korea than Cuba. In 2003 there were reports of severe food shortages in North Korea and fears of widespread starvation.

In 2002 Jimmy Carter became the first former American president to visit Cuba. In his farewell address, President Carter called for ending the American economic blockade of Cuba and increasing the freedom and rights of Cuban citizens. Cuba is a good example of the problems associated with centrally planned economies. When Cuban president Fidel Castro came to power in the early 1960s, he and his supporters overthrew the corrupt and dictatorial but pro-American Battista regime. Cuban resources, primarily land and tourism, were controlled by a wealthy elite, whereas communism advocates collective control of resources for the benefit of all of society. Castro had widespread support among Cuban citizens, because the vast majority of Cubans had few resources and a poor STANDARD OF LIVING.

After taking control of the government, Castro nationalized major industries in Cuba, mostly sugarcane plantations and rum factories. This infuriated the owners of these resources, in particular the Bacardi Rum family and the Boston-based United Fruit Company. Wealthy Cubans fled the country, and as the government seized control of the factors of production, many poor Cubans saw improved access to health care, education, and, initially, food supplies. But the major problem with centrally planned economies is efficiency. Private enterprise provides incentives for owners and managers to use resources efficiently and manage resources for long-term viability. If a business prospers, the owners profit, so efficient planning and allocating is desirable.

In a state-run enterprise, managers are given goals. If they achieve those goals, they may get some small bonus, a vacation at a government-run resort, or a larger apartment, but they do not get a share of any profit from achieving or exceeding the goal. Numerous stories report state farms being incredibly inefficient, but workers on the farms, given small plots of land for their own use, generate significant output which they then sell crops for their personal benefit. State-run enterprises also create rigidity. The *Wall Street Journal* once reported about the instructions given to a greenhouse manager near Moscow for his winter crop. He told the reporter he could grow a lot of cabbage but instead was told to grow tomatoes—so he did, using huge amounts of energy to heat the greenhouses.

Similarly, it was not long before the Cuban economy declined due to inefficiency, government bureaucracies, and U.S. sanctions. (Until 1961 Cuba was a larger trading partner with the United States than Mexico.) To support the Cuban economy, Castro entered into a BARTER agreement with the Soviet Union, trading sugar cane for oil. Before long the Soviet Union was subsidizing the Cuban economy for as much as $5 billion annually. In return, Cuba allied itself politically with the Soviets and provided troops in cold war-era regional conflicts.

With the collapse of the Soviet Union in 1989, Soviet subsidies ended and the Cuban economy plummeted. Declining world sugar prices also hurt Cuban efforts, and before long the Castro government began allowing various private enterprises, but this meant attracting investors, one of the problems with centrally planned economies. Since Cuba had nationalized private enterprises in the 1960s and not compensated the owners, foreign investors were reticent about dealing with the Castro government. Eventually Spanish investors led hotel and tourism investments, and individual Cubans were allowed to create some private businesses, including transportation and other services. At first Cuban college graduates were not allowed to participate, based on the argument that they had benefited from an education provided by the state and therefore should contribute their services to the state. Desperate for foreign exchange earnings, the Cuban government allowed all citizens to create private enterprises.

Centrally planned economies replace market systems with government systems. Market systems are chaotic, often ruthless, and impersonal, but they send signals to produce more of this and less of that. Private control, rather than collective control, provides incentives for business owners to manage their resources effectively and efficiently. While Cuba and North Korea remain the major examples of centrally planned economies, the Central European countries of the Warsaw Pact provide numerous examples of the problems involved in transitioning from a centrally planned economy to a market-based system.

The change from central planning to a market system requires addressing many issues including

- removal of price controls on necessities, usually food, housing, transportation, and utilities
- transfer of control of state-run enterprises to private enterprise

- changes in the legal system defining and enforcing property rights
- UNEMPLOYMENT and underemployment
- control of MONETARY POLICY
- privatization of finance and credit
- promises made by the state to retirees, military and others
- educating consumers and citizens about private enterprise

As the list suggests, the task is daunting. Some countries have adjusted better and more rapidly than others.

Further reading
Korten, David C. "Life after Capitalism." International Institute for Sustainable Development website. Available on-line. URL: http://iisd.ca/pcdf/1998/capitalism.htm.

certificates of deposit   See TIME DEPOSITS.

Certified Public Accountant

A Certified Public Accountant (CPA) is an individual who performs FINANCIAL ACCOUNTING services for the general public for a fee. While all CPAs are accountants, not all accountants are CPAs. Over 30,000 CPAs in the United States are members of the AMERICAN INSTITUTE OF CERTIFIED PUBLIC ACCOUNTANTS (AICPA). The AICPA was established in 1887 in New York City and originally had 31 members.

The AICPA Values and Vision Statement reads:

The AICPA is the premier national professional association in the United States. Our employees are a diverse, unified team who:

- Are committed to member service and the public interest, providing the highest quality products, services and support possible.
- Listen and respond to the needs and expectations of members, prospective members, the public and one another.
- Serve members with excellence.
- Act with the highest ethical behavior, performing with integrity and professionalism.
- Are committed to learning and using new or existing tools and technology to its maximum potential.
- Are responsive to others in a respectful and courteous manner.
- Embrace change and approach challenges with "can do" enthusiasm and creative thinking.
- Constantly seek opportunities to attract and retain members, offer additional products or services, reduce costs, and improve productivity.
- Are empowered to problem-solve and make decisions with the expectation of support by the AICPA.

The AICPA is committed to providing its employees with:

- Timely training to acquire the knowledge and skills needed for current and future jobs.
- Opportunity for professional and personal growth through job enlargement, rotation and education.
- A team environment that fosters participation, diversity, differences of opinion and a commitment to excellence.
- A system that recognizes and rewards outstanding performance, ongoing contributions and innovations of individuals and teams within the AICPA.
- EMPOWERMENT to problem-solve and make accountable and responsible decisions.
- A process that respects and utilizes contributions from staff throughout the Institute.
- Opportunities for promotion from within, when qualified and possible.
- Above all, a professional environment that values open and candid communications based on honesty, trust, respect, health COMPETITION and conflict resolution.

An accountant must earn the professional designation of CPA from the AICPA. As of 2002, the requirements to become a CPA included completing a program of study at a college or university with at least 150 hours of study; passing the Uniform CPA Examination; and completing required work experience in public accounting.

Further reading
American Institute of Certified Public Accountants website. Available on-line. URL: www.aicpa.org.

chain-of-command principle

The chain-of-command principle refers to the relationship of the reporting mechanism within an organization. A chain of command establishes the line of authority within the organization—i.e., who reports to whom and how all employees are linked within the company.

There are essentially two components that constitute a chain of command, namely unity of command and the scalar principle. "Unity of command" means that each individual reports to one (and only one) boss or supervisor. This is a vital issue in that all employees need to know from whom to accept commands and to whom they are directly accountable. Unity of command establishes the legitimate authority that a supervisor has over his/her workers. In reality, it legitimizes the right of the supervisor to make decisions, to allocate resources, and to direct an employee in his/her job. It gives authority to the supervisor to give an employee orders and then hold that person accountable in carrying out those orders. This legitimate authority is vested in the position and not the person.

Upholding unity of command in the organizational design provides structure and clarity for employees in the workplace. In MANAGEMENT, one organizational structure breaks the unity-of-command rule—specifically, the matrix design, which imposes a lateral reporting relationship on top of the traditional vertical reporting relationship that results from unity of command. Thus, a dual reporting relationship emerges, and the employee is accountable to two bosses or supervisors. A major disadvantage of the matrix is that it can result in inefficiency and discord if the two supervisors do not coordinate the employee's time. A major advantage is that the talents of one employee can be utilized more fully, resulting in greater efficiency in the use of a company's HUMAN RESOURCES. Ultimately, however, when an unresolved dispute arises between the two supervisors, the matrix design collapses to unity of command, with the one supervisor over the two disputing supervisors resolving the issue.

The second component in chain of command is called the scalar principle. This term means that an unbroken line can be traced from the lowest employee on the organizational chart to the CHIEF EXECUTIVE OFFICER (CEO). This unbroken line represents the line of authority and reporting relationship within the company.

Referring to the organizational chart, formal lines or channels of communication can be identified. Information within an organization is often passed through formal channels. This is especially the case with paperwork that needs approval to conform to company policies.

—Leanne McGrath

Chamber of Commerce

The U.S. Chamber of Commerce is federation of businesses and business organizations coordinated at local, state, regional, and national levels. A voluntary organization, its goal is to promote business interests. At each level, Chamber members typically include corporate, civic, and small-business owners.

The Chamber of Commerce grew out of a 1912 presidential commission review of the FEDERAL BUDGETING process. President William Howard Taft, in the first issue of *Nation's Business*, the official publication of the Chamber of Commerce, stated the need to "set forth periodically affirmative information and thought regarding our progress as a nation." Taft also cited the need for a single entity through which American businesses and government could deal with each other on a national level.

The most broadly represented business association in Washington, the Chamber of Commerce is an important voice in political, regulatory, and civil affairs affecting business. It has numerous committees that analyze and initiate policy positions in areas ranging from ANTITRUST LAW to taxation. The Chamber influences legislation through congressional testimony, lobbying, and the grassroots efforts of local and state chambers. One of its more effective mechanisms is its "action call," a memorandum outlining its position on an issue and urging members to contact their representatives.

During the 2000 election, the U.S. Chamber of Commerce spent $21 million supporting pro-business candidates. In the same year, it advocated normal trade relations with China and pressured Congress for regulatory relief for small businesses. In 1999 Chamber president Tom Donohue led a U.S. business mission to Cuba.

Local chambers of commerce provide members with information about business issues, resources, and opportunities to meet other businesspeople in their areas. The Chamber of Commerce is an important source of business information ranging from employee issues to taxes and money management. In many U.S. communities, the local chamber's "After Hours" receptions are an important chance for networking, exchanging ideas, and building relationships.

Further reading
"Affirmative information and thought regarding our progress as a nation," *Nation's Business* 80, no. 20 (September 1992): 83; Chamber of Commerce website. Available on-line. URL: www.chamberbiz.com.

Chicago Board of Trade
The Chicago Board of Trade (CBOT) is a market exchange where commodity and financial FUTURES and OPTIONS contracts are bought and sold. Created in 1848, the CBOT is used primarily by investors, managers, and broker/dealers to reduce risk in business transactions. Initially the CBOT focused on grain trade, allowing farmers and other agricultural-industry members to hedge or reduce their risk of price changes by using futures contracts.

Futures contracts—agreements to buy or sell a specific amount of a commodity at a particular price on or before a stipulated date—allow sellers to secure a price for their output and buyers to control the future cost of their inputs. If, in the time between their sale of the futures contract and when their products are ready for market, the commodity price goes down, farmers will be able to buy back their futures contract at a lower price. They profit by the difference and thus offset the lower market price for their product. If the price goes up, they will lose money on the futures contract but will profit from the higher price in the marketplace. Likewise, for a food-products company buying a futures contract, if prices rise in the interim, the value of their contract rises, offsetting the higher market price for their inputs. If prices decline, the food-products company's contract declines in value, but the cost of the inputs also declines in the marketplace.

Unlike stocks, which convey an ownership interest in a CORPORATION, futures contracts are standardized agreements defining the quantity, quality, delivery date, and location for a commodity or security. The CBOT estimates only 4 percent of all contracts result in delivery. The pri-

mary purpose of futures contracts is to provide protection against price changes for a specified period of time. As the maturity date of a futures contract approaches, traders who are "long" (having bought a futures contract) or "short" (having sold a futures contract) close their position by doing the opposite of their initial trade.

The CBOT is regulated by the COMMODITY FUTURES TRADING COMMISSION (CFTC), created to oversee the CBOT and other exchanges. In the last two decades, the CBOT, CHICAGO MERCANTILE EXCHANGE, Chicago Board of Exchange, NEW YORK MERCANTILE EXCHANGE, and other smaller regional markets have competed in providing new options and futures contracts to meet the needs of financial markets and managers. In addition to grains, the CBOT trades in U.S. Treasury bond futures, DOW JONES AVERAGES, silver, gold, and energy futures. In 1999 over 254 million contracts were traded on the CBOT.

Where futures contracts obligate the buyer and seller to a specified agreement, options contracts provide the buyer or seller the right to buy or sell at a specified price. If the option is not exercised by the maturity date, it expires with the buyer losing the amount of money they paid for the option. Prices of futures and options can be quite volatile. In addition to being used by managers to reduce risk, speculators add liquidity to commodity and futures markets and profit when they correctly anticipate price changes in the market.

There are over 85 commodity exchanges around the world. Most, like the CBOT, are colorful places where traders in a "pit" shout and use hand signals to communicate their buy and sell orders. Pit activity can be quite physical. Professional football players have been known to find second careers working in the pits of the CBOT and Chicago Mercantile Exchange.

Further reading
Chicago Board of Trade website. Available on-line. URL: www.cbot.com.

Chicago Mercantile Exchange
The Chicago Mercantile Exchange (CME) is a market exchange where commodity and financial FUTURES and OPTIONS contracts are bought and sold. Created in 1898 as the Chicago Butter and Egg Board, the CME is used primarily by investors, managers, and broker/dealers to reduce risk in business transactions. Traditionally farmers and other agricultural-industry members used futures contracts—agreements to buy or sell a specific amount of a commodity at a particular price on or before stipulated date—to hedge their risk. Initially the CME specialized in butter-and-egg markets, while the Chicago Board of Trade focused on grain markets. Today both exchanges compete in offering a wide array of futures contracts.

Farmers sell futures contracts for commodities they produce, thereby assuring themselves of a price for their products. If, in the time between their sale of the futures contract and when their products are ready for market, the commodity price goes down, farmers will be able to buy back their futures contract at a lower price. They profit by the difference, offsetting the lower market price for their product. If the price goes up, they will lose money on the futures contract but will profit from the higher price in the marketplace.

The CME is regulated by the COMMODITY FUTURES TRADING COMMISSION (CFTC), created to oversee the CME and other exchanges. In the last two decades, the CME, CHICAGO BOARD OF TRADE, Chicago Board of Exchange, NEW YORK MERCANTILE EXCHANGE, and other smaller regional markets have competed, providing new options and futures contracts to meet the needs of financial markets and managers.

Where futures contracts obligate the buyer and seller to a specified agreement, options contracts provide the buyer or seller the right to buy or sell at a specified price. If the option is not exercised by the maturity date, it expires with the buyer losing the amount of money they paid for the option. Prices of futures and options can be quite volatile. In addition to being used by managers to reduce RISK, speculators add liquidity to commodity and futures markets and profit when they correctly anticipate price changes in the market. In 2000, 231 million contracts valued at $155 trillion were traded on the CME.

Today the Chicago Mercantile Exchange facilitates trading in a wide array of agricultural, currency, interest rate, and indexes including butter, cheese, frozen pork bellies, Australian dollars, Japanese Yen, Euros, 90-day U.S. Treasury Bills, 10-year Japanese Government BONDS, STANDARD & POOR'S 500 Index, Russell 2000 Stock Price Index, and even heating and cooling degree indexes.

Further reading
Chicago Mercantile Exchange website. Available on-line. URL: www.cme.com.

chief executive officer

The chief executive officer (CEO) is the primary leader in an organization. Though he or she may be known by many other names, such as president, executive director, and chief administrator, the CEO's role is more or less the same. The CEO's scope of authority varies, depending on whether the organization is a CORPORATION, PARTNERSHIP, sole PROPRIETORSHIP, or nonprofit organization. In corporations or nonprofit organizations with a BOARD OF DIRECTORS, the board has controlling power of the corporation. The CEO reports to the members of the BOARD OF DIRECTORS and sometimes the CEO also serves as the president or chairman of the board.

There are no standardized lists of the major functions and responsibilities of a CEO, though there are some things almost every CEO is expected to do. A CEO is expected to be a visionary, information bearer, and decision maker. As a leader, the CEO advises the board of directors, identifies and promotes changes, and is chief motivator of the people within the organization. While the CEO rarely oversees day-to-day operations, he or she is responsible for overall design, promotion, and delivery of products and services to achieve the organization's objectives. The CEO is also expected to be a visionary, looking forward and anticipating changes needed for long-term survival and growth. CEOs are sometimes the major community spokesperson for an organization.

As a decision maker, the CEO is expected to oversee operations of the organization, implement plans, and manage HUMAN RESOURCES as well as financial and physical resources. The CEO recommends yearly budgets to the board of directors and manages resources with the guidelines determined by the board. Most CEOs are energetic, articulate, and creative thinkers and leaders, with the ability to quickly comprehend information and solve problems. Depending on the nature of the organization, CEOs may also require a technical background in addition to a sound understanding of business practices.

Further reading
"Free Management Library," The Management Assistance Program. Available on-line. URL: http://www.managementhelp.org. Downloaded on February 23, 2002; Carter McNamara. "Founder's Syndrome: How Corporations Suffer—and Can Recover." Available on-line. URL: http://www.mapnp.org/library/misc/founders.htm. Downloaded on February 23, 2002; "Organization Management Theory," Academy of Management. Available on-line. URL: http://www.aom.pace.edu/omt. Downloaded on February 27, 2002.

—Leah Kninde Frazier-Gaskins

chief financial officer

The chief financial officer (CFO), the highest-ranking financial executive of an organization, is responsible for all financial operations. The CFO oversees the preparation of budgets, treasury, internal AUDITING, forecasts, and qualitative information analysis for MANAGEMENT decisions; provides leadership to the financial services group; and contributes to the objectives of firm. The financial function includes internal and external reporting, treasury and tax matters, CAPITAL financing; contractual relations; the development of sound financial management systems and the management of investor/Wall Street relations.

Reporting to the CFO are the controller and treasurer, key leaders in the financial services group. The controller is the chief accounting executive who directs internal accounting programs, including cost accounting, systems and procedures, data processing, acquisitions analysis, and financial planning. The treasurer is concerned with the receipt, custody, INVESTMENT, disbursement, and protection of corporate funds and determines the ultimate cash position for the company. In smaller firms there may be an overlap of CFO and controller/treasurer responsibilities. While the CFO oversees the financial aspects of a business, the Chief Operating Officer (COO) oversees the company's production of goods and SERVICES. The CFO reports directly to the CHIEF EXECUTIVE OFFICER (CEO), the highest-ranking official of the company.

Typically the CFO position requires a bachelor's degree in accounting; an MBA, CPA, or equivalent postgraduate work; and a minimum 10 years of relevant, progressive experience. The experience may include numerous acquisitions, equity investments, divestitures, and JOINT VENTURES, both domestically and internationally.

Today's CFO requires a much broader knowledge base than just accountancy. The CFO job description is moving away from the super-accountant stereotype and towards someone more akin to a deputy chief executive officer. The changing global business environment has driven the trend towards diversification. In addition to being a financial manager, a CFO must be a strategic thinker, communicator, and team player, and must have an understanding of information technology (IT) systems.

The CFO must have the ability to clearly articulate the financial and operational results and strategic plans of the organization in a manner appropriate to a variety of audiences, including employee groups, the financial community, members of the BOARD OF DIRECTORS, and the corporate CEO. As a strategic planner, the CFO needs to understand the interrelationships between marketing, products, and production processes as well as understand the industry (market segment) in which the business operates.

The CFO's job has become more complex and demanding, and there are few general guidelines as to what one can expect when stepping into such a position. This will depend on the company—the nature of its business and its corporate structure, management style, strategic objectives, and executive resources.

—Asta Vaichys

churning

Churning is excessive trading in an investor's portfolio to generate commissions for the stockbroker. Sometimes brokers or INVESTMENT advisors are given discretionary authority over an investor's account. Many investors do not want to or do not have the knowledge necessary to actively manage their investments. These investors will often entrust their investment CAPITAL to a broker, giving him or her general instructions about their investment objectives. With discretionary authority a broker can move a client's funds into different investments in order to take advantage of market opportunities. During the DOT-COM era of the 1990s, many brokerage houses allocated shares of INITIAL PUBLIC OFFERINGS (IPOs) to only their best customers. Some investors gave discretionary authority in order to get their broker to include them in these hot-issue stocks.

Churning is illegal; SECURITIES AND EXCHANGE COMMISSION Rule 10b-5 can be the basis for claims for state and federal securities FRAUD, COMMON LAW fraud, NEGLIGENCE, breach of CONTRACT, and breach of fiduciary duty. Churning usually involves a large number of trades, but *large* is a debatable term. Courts often use turnover ratios, the number of times the value of the account is traded in a given time period, as a basis for determining that churning has occurred. Because churning is defined as trading that is done to benefit the broker rather than the investor, even one trade can be considered churning if it has no legitimate purpose. For example, if a broker moves a client's money from one family of MUTUAL FUNDS to another, he or she must have a good reason for doing so. This is why most brokers use written confirmation that the customer wants to switch funds in spite of the fees that will be incurred.

Brokers who churn accounts often use frequent in-and-out trades of the same stock and "wash" transactions (simultaneous or roughly simultaneous buy-and-sell transactions that nullify each other). When adjudicating a churning claim, the courts evaluate whether the broker or advisor had control over the account in the form of either discretionary authority or practical ("de facto") control. The broker or advisor has de facto control when, as a practical matter, the investor lacks the knowledge and sophistication to make his or her own independent investment decisions and instead always follows the broker's recommendations. Bruce D. Fisher and Michael J. Phillips describe a case where the broker engaged in 147 separate purchases and sales for a customer's account, resulting in over $24,000 in commissions, fees, taxes, and margin interest against an account that started with only $25,000.

In addition to churning, the other major investor complaint against stockbrokers is inappropriate recommendations. Unethical brokers often convince unsophisticated investors to purchase high-risk (and high-commission) investments ranging from real estate scams to shares in obscure foreign companies.

See also STOCK MARKET, BOND MARKET.

Further reading
Fisher, Bruce D., and Michael J. Phillips. *The Legal, Ethical and Regulatory Environment of Business,* 8th ed. Cincinnati: Thomson/South-western, 2003; Investor Recovery website. Available on-line. URL: www.investorecovery.com.

circular flow model

A circular flow model is a diagram illustrating how the major sectors in a mixed-CAPITALISM economy fit together. Circular flow models show how the value of output equals INCOME in an economic system. The model also demonstrates the MUTUAL INTERDEPENDENCE of the various participants in an economy.

The five sectors in the model are households, firms, FINANCIAL INTERMEDIARIES, the government, and foreign countries. Households own and determine how to allocate RESOURCES—human, CAPITAL, and natural. For example, household members decide where and how to use their labor resources; control the use of any equipment like a computer or a machine; and control the use of land, minerals, or other natural resources they own. In a noncapitalist economic system, households control only a small percentage of resources, while the government controls most resources.

In capitalist economies, households receive payments for the use of their resources from firms or the government, depending on who purchases the resource. Gross household income is the sum of resource payments received. Households with greater resources receive more income than those with fewer resources. The quality of resources also influences the amount of income received. Education, an improvement in human capital, typically results in greater income. Likewise, land with minerals, beautiful views, or a lakeside site is more valuable than barren or polluted natural resources.

Households take the resource payments they receive and primarily use this income for CONSUMPTION spending—payments to firms for products and services. Some household income is saved, usually by depositing a sum with financial intermediaries, and of course some household income is taken by government in the form of taxes.

A circular flow model shows that firms complement the actions of households. Firms purchase or rent resources, paying wages, interest, DIVIDENDs and PROFITs to households, and use the resources to produce goods and services, which are then sold to households, the government, and foreign buyers. Firms that produce goods and SERVICES most desired by consumers will receive a greater portion of the flow of payments, allowing these firms to purchase more resources, produce more goods, and, in essence, grow. Those firms that produce PRODUCTS consumers do not want or only will purchase at lower prices see their revenue decline and eventually will be forced out of business.

In a mixed-capitalism circular flow model, the government plays many roles. The government purchases resources from households and provides goods and services to both households and firms. Employing teachers is an example of a government resource purchase to provide services to households. The government taxes portions of income from both households and firms. Changes in taxation redistribute the burden of paying for government goods and services among households and between households and firms.

Financial intermediaries primarily aggregate savings from many households and provide INVESTMENT capital to firms. In the process financial intermediaries reduce investor risk through knowledge of investment alternatives and portfolio diversification. Intermediaries also adjust for the diverse needs of savers. Households have many different levels of savings and periods of time they are willing to lend their savings. The savers' time frame and dollar amount preferences are unlikely to mesh with the needs of firms borrowing funds for investment. Financial intermediaries smooth the process of lending and borrowing in financial markets.

Foreign countries, through relationships with U.S. businesses, sell products and services to American consumers and purchase products and services from U.S. firms. TRADE BALANCEs measure the net impact of EXPORTING and importing in the circular flow model.

Close inspection of a circular flow model shows that for each "real" flow of resources or goods and services, there is an opposite MONEY flow. One of the major roles of MONETARY POLICY is to provide the "right" MONEY SUPPLY to facilitate exchange of resources and goods in an economy. The "right" money supply is subject to debate and constant change as an economy grows or declines.

As stated earlier, one of the uses of circular flow models is to show how the value of output equals income in an economic system. Measuring either the flow of payments (income) or the value of goods and services (output) results in an estimate of the level of economic activity in an economy (GROSS DOMESTIC PRODUCT).

The circular flow model is analogous to the circulatory system in the human body. In the economy, the efficient flow of money between savers and borrowers is provided by financial intermediation, the process of bringing borrowers and savers together via financial intermediaries. Payments for goods and services (business revenues) flow in one direction, and payments for the factors of production (household incomes) flow in the opposite direction. One's spending becomes another's income. In the human body, blood flows from the heart via arteries and to the heart via veins. Just as leakages in the human circulatory system will cause declining performance, leakages in the circular flow model hamper the spending/income process, causing declining economic performance.

Civil Aeronautics Board

The Civil Aeronautics Board (CAB) regulated the U.S. airline industry until 1984. The CAB is most widely known as the first in a series of efforts toward government DEREGULATION, reducing government rules and regulations affecting American business.

The Civil Aeronautics Act (1938) mandated government regulation to promote "adequate, economical, and efficient service by air carriers at reasonable charges, without unjust discrimination, undue preferences or advantages, or unfair or destructive competitive practices." When passed, the U.S. airline business was similar to the pharmaceutical industry before creation of the FOOD AND DRUG ADMINISTRATION (1906); anyone with an airplane could and did establish an airline, flying wherever he/she wanted to, charging whatever the market would bear, and using equipment he/she deemed air-worthy. It was a classic "free market" industry.

Concerned over the airline industry's instability, safety record, and fierce price competition, Congress chose to regulate the industry. For almost 40 years the CAB regulated prices, routes, antitrust disputes, and CONSUMER PROTECTION. In the 1960s and 1970s, led by economic theorists, particularly Alfred Kahn, U.S. politicians began to question the role of government control of transportation industries. In response, in 1978 President Carter signed the Airline Deregulation Act, phasing out the CAB's role of controlling airline routes and prices by 1984. (Other roles of the CAB were transferred to the Justice and Transportation departments.)

Airline executives fought deregulation, arguing the United States had the strongest and safest airline industry in the world. Although they predicted chaos and disaster, the CAB was dismantled, and the U.S. airline market saw a surge in COMPETITION. Many new firms jumped into the market, and existing firms expanded into new service areas. There were both winners and losers as airlines learned how to compete and customers saw choices expand and prices decline.

Some areas with small populations saw airline service eliminated. Travel agencies, who were supported under CAB commission-fixing agreements, saw their fees cut by the airline companies. Throughout the industry, a new emphasis on marketing arose. American Airlines created the first frequent-flyer program, a practice emulated by other airlines and service industry providers. Southwest airlines is the low-cost leader and a model for many new airlines.

Further reading
Daube, Scott. "From Precept to Practice (History of Deregulation)." *Travel Weekly* 47 (30 September 1988): 47.

Civilian Conservation Corps

The Civilian Conservation Corps (CCC) was one of the most popular "New Deal" programs initiated by the Franklin Roosevelt administration during the GREAT DEPRESSION. Begun in 1933, the program eventually involved over 3 million unemployed Americans in planting trees, controlling forest fires, and building state and national parks. At the time, almost 25 percent of American workers were unemployed. The CCC and the Works Project Administration (WPA) were one of the government's stimuli to a failing economy. The idea of government stimulating economic activity during a RECESSION challenged the prevailing doctrine of CLASSICAL ECONOMICS but was strongly supported by KEYNESIAN ECONOMICS in 1936.

The CCC was operated by existing federal agencies. The DEPARTMENT OF LABOR selected participants, mostly

young men and women who were unemployed. (This broke traditional barriers of engaging women in the workforce.) The Departments of Interior and Agriculture planned the work projects. Participants were provided clothing, housing, and food and paid $30 per month but were required to send home $25 of their monthly earnings.

The CCC was the model for subsequent state conservation programs as well as the National and Community Service Trust Act enacted by President Clinton in 1993. The CCC was disbanded in 1942 due to U.S. involvement in World War II and the need for labor associated with the war effort. The results of its programs can be seen today in many state and federal parks.

Further reading
Pagan, Kathleen Waltson. "Viewpoint (Civilian Conservation Corps)." *Planning* 59 (November 1993): 46.

civil procedure

Civil procedure refers to the rules by which civil (as opposed to criminal) legal proceedings are conducted. The Federal Rules of Civil Procedure apply throughout the FEDERAL COURTS. The rules of civil procedure in state courts can vary considerably. In general, rules of civil procedure concern pretrial "discovery" of evidence, including documents, answers to interrogatories (questions), and depositions (pretrial taking of testimony under oath) of witnesses and experts. The allowance of extensive pretrial discovery in civil proceedings is almost unique to the American legal system.

Civil-procedure rules also concern the pleading (filing) of complaints, answers to complaints, motions to dismiss complaints, requests for summary judgments (pretrial judgments on the merits of the case), and rules for the conduct of civil trials by judges or juries. Since the vast majority of business disputes are settled in advance of trial, pretrial discovery is the primary point of contact for businesspeople involved in civil proceedings. Common business-law civil proceedings include products liability, CONTRACTS disputes, and EMPLOYMENT matters.

Further reading
Kane, Mary K. *Civil Procedure in a Nutshell,* 4th ed. Eagan, Minn.: West Group, 1996.

Civil Rights Acts

As defined in *Black's Law Dictionary* (7th ed.), Civil Rights Acts are "several federal statutes enacted after the Civil War (1861–1865) and, much later, during and after the Civil Rights movement of the 1950s and 1960s, and intended to implement and give further force to the basic rights guaranteed by the Constitution, and especially prohibiting discrimination in EMPLOYMENT and education on the basis of race, sex, religion, color, or age."

The Civil Rights Acts, which are often called the most important U.S. laws on civil rights since Reconstruction, were a highly controversial issue in the United States when President John F. Kennedy proposed them. Although Kennedy was unable to secure passage of the bill in Congress, a stronger version was eventually passed by his successor, President Lyndon B. Johnson, who signed the first bill into law in July 1964.

The Civil Rights movement of the 1960s resulted in some of the most significant civil-rights ruling and legislation in U.S. history. There had already been many civil-rights court cases tried in state and federal courts by mid-century, but the Supreme Court decision in *Brown v. Board of Education of Topeka Kansas* (1954) set the tone for new legislation by directly challenging the "separate but equal" principle established by the 1896 *Plessy v. Ferguson* ruling. In *Plessy* the Supreme Court had authorized separate facilities for blacks and whites as long as the facilities were equal. In the *Brown* decision, the Court challenged the earlier ruling by declaring that segregation in public schools was unconstitutional.

Beyond crucial court decisions like *Brown*, the Civil Rights movement also resulted in and benefited from new legislation in the 1960s that expanded the social and political rights of minorities and women. The Civil Rights Act of 1964 prohibited discrimination in public facilities and schools on the basis of race, religion, or national origin and mandated equal opportunities for all workers irrespective of race, religion, national origin, or gender. The Voting Rights Act of 1965 guaranteed the right to vote for all citizens who were qualified by age, thus striking down literacy requirements that had been used effectively to disenfranchise many blacks. Three years later the Civil Rights Act of 1968 outlawed racial discrimination in housing and jury selection.

The Civil Rights Act of 1964 contained specific titles with specific applications. Title I of the act guaranteed equal voting rights by removing registration requirements and procedures biased against minorities and the underprivileged. Title II prohibited segregation or discrimination in places of public accommodation involved in interstate commerce. Title III banned discrimination by trade UNIONS, schools, or employers involved in interstate commerce or doing business with the federal government. This section also applied to discrimination on the basis of sex and established a government agency, the EQUAL EMPLOYMENT OPPORTUNITY COMMISSION (EEOC), to enforce the provisions. Title IV called for the desegregation of public schools. Title V broadened the duties of the Civil Rights Commission. Title VI assured nondiscrimination in the distribution of funds under federally assisted programs. Title VII prohibited employment decisions based on stereotypes and assumptions about abilities, traits, or the performance of individuals of certain racial groups. Title VII also prohibited both intentional discrimination and neutral job policies that disproportionately exclude minorities or are not job-related.

Title 28 of the U.S. Code Sec. 1343, Civil rights and elective franchise, states that "the district courts shall have original jurisdiction over any civil action authorized by law to be commenced by any person (1) to recover DAMAGES for injury to his person or property, or because of the deprivation of any right or privilege of a citizen of the United States, by any act done in furtherance of any conspiracy mentioned in section 1985 of Title 42; (2) to recover damages from any person who fails to prevent or to aid in preventing any wrongs mentioned in section 1985 of Title 42 which he had knowledge were about to occur and power to prevent; (3) to redress the deprivation, under color of any state, law, statute, ordinance, regulation, custom or usage, of any right, privilege or immunity secured by the Constitution of the United States or by any Act of Congress providing for equal rights of citizens or of all persons within the jurisdiction of the United States; (4) to recover damages or to secure equitable or other relief under any Act of Congress providing for the protection of civil rights, including the right to vote."

—Joi Patrice Jones

Further reading
Civil Rights and Elective Franchise States, U.S. Code, vol. 28, sec. 1343; *Encyclopaedia Britannica,* 2002, "Civil Rights Act"; Garner, Bryan. ed. *Black's Law Dictionary,* 7th ed. Eagan, Minn.: West Group, 1999; "Race Discrimination," Equal Employment Opportunity Commission. Available on-line. URL: http://www.eeoc.gov. Downloaded on May 27, 2003.

class-action lawsuits
A class action is a device where large numbers of individuals whose interests are sufficiently related may bring suit. Thus it is more efficient to adjudicate their rights or liabilities as a group in a single action than to do so in a series of separate individual suits. Most class actions are called "plaintiff class actions," although in some cases the action may be brought against a defendant class as a defendant class action.

Most class-action lawsuits are filed for compensatory (money) DAMAGES. Class actions may also be filed to resolve disputes over a "limited fund," where the money available is inadequate to fully compensate all class members. A class action may seek injunctive relief, e.g., it may be filed to request that the court order the police or other authorities to discontinue an unconstitutional practice. Another type of class action is one that seeks a declaratory judgment, a court decision in a civil case telling the parties what their rights and responsibilities are without awarding damages or ordering any action be taken.

Generally, before a court certifies a class action (determines that the suit may proceed as a class-action suit), it must conclude that there are too many class members for them all to be named as parties in the lawsuit. The claims of the "class representatives" must arise from facts or law common to the class members. In most cases, class members do not technically join in the litigation but decide to participate by not "opting out." If the constitutional and procedural protections required for fairness are met in the underlying action, all absent class members are bound to the judgment or settlement of the case. However, if the action is primarily for compensatory damages, absent class members are entitled to notice and an opportunity to opt out (exclude themselves) from the proceedings. If a person opts out, he or she is not bound by any judgment or settlement of the class action.

The complex nature of many class actions and the danger of violating the DUE PROCESS rights of absent class members have led many rule-makers to provide the trial judge with authority to control and manage numerous aspects of the lawsuit. Further, in order to provide additional protection for absent class members, class-action provisions typically require court approval of any settlement or compromise of the class claims entered into between the class representatives and the defendant.

In recent years the subject of class actions has received more attention from the legal community and the media than any other area of CIVIL PROCEDURE, and it has even inspired film producers to make award-winning movies about them. Several high-profile cases involving tobacco litigation, asbestos claims, cases involving securities FRAUD, etc., have evoked public concern and stirred considerable debate. Some individuals claim that class actions should be used with greater frequency to spur major social change, to make CORPORATIONS pay up for their follies, and to provide recourse for those who otherwise would not find it economically feasible to litigate their grievances. Others argue that class actions are being brought not to defend the public interest but to enrich attorneys, force corporations into settlement with the threat of bigger jury awards, and waste the courts' valuable resources. They point to the fact that many of the suits have been extremely burdensome and expensive for litigants, and only a few have reached the stage of judgment.

Further reading
Friedenthal, Jack H., and Arthur R. Miller. *Civil Procedure: Sum & Substance.* 4th ed. Encino, Calif.: Herbert Legal Series, 1988; Klonoff, Robert H. *Class Actions and other Multi-Party Litigation in a Nutshell.* Eagan, Minn.: West Group, 1999.

classical economics
Classical economics is the macroeconomic school of thought that suggests that real GROSS DOMESTIC PRODUCT (GDP) is determined by aggregate SUPPLY, while the EQUILIBRIUM price level is determined by aggregate DEMAND. Classical economics was the predominant theory from 1776 to the introduction of KEYNESIAN ECONOMICS in 1936.

Classical economics is also defined as the study of an economy operating at full EMPLOYMENT, while Keynesian analysis portrays economies operating naturally at less than full employment.

According to classical theory, a major part of the self-correcting mechanism in an economy is flexible wages and prices. With this assumption, classical economists suggest real GDP is determined by the price of resources, technology, and expectations (the factors influencing aggregate supply). Prices would adjust depending on the overall level of demand. The assumption of flexible wages and prices distinguishes classical economics from Keynesian economics.

Classical economists believe economies tend to operate at or near full employment. Using Say's law (named after French economist Jean-Baptiste Say), supply creates its own demand; hence, desired expenditures will equal actual expenditures. According to classical economics, people produce goods and services because they desire to purchase other goods and services. The act of producing is based on their desire to trade their goods and services for other products, creating demand in the economy. From this reasoning, an economy would tend toward full employment of labor and other resources. Though temporary shocks may cause excessive UNEMPLOYMENT, this would be a temporary phenomenon.

Classical economists saw the GREAT DEPRESSION as a downturn in the BUSINESS CYCLE that would self-correct. Some politicians—U.S. president Herbert Hoover, for example—accepted classical theory. During the 1930 presidential election, Hoover said the current economic condition was just a mild recession, not a depression, suggesting this was a temporary situation that would self-correct. Political cartoonists compared Hoover to the Roman emperor Nero, famous for supposedly having fiddled while Rome burned. Hoover's opponent, Franklin Delano Roosevelt, advocated government intervention, a policy supported by Keynesian economics, leading to the New Deal.

See also MACROECONOMICS.

Further reading
Miller, Roger LeRoy. *Economics Today.* Boston: Addison Wesley, 2001.

Clayton Antitrust Act
The Clayton Antitrust Act (1914) specified and forbade activities that reduced COMPETITION. The act expanded on antitrust policy efforts initiated by the SHERMAN ANTITRUST ACT (1890), which was considered by many to be not specific enough and open to considerable judicial interpretation. Congress passed the Clayton Act to attack practices used by monopolists to acquire MONOPOLY power. Along with the FEDERAL TRADE COMMISSION Act passed in the same year, the Clayton Act prohibited four kinds of activities that would tend to lessen competition:

- PRICE DISCRIMINATION
- exclusive dealing and tying arrangements
- Certain types of MERGERS AND ACQUISITIONS
- Interlocking company BOARD OF DIRECTORS

Section 2 of the act prohibited local and territorial price discrimination by sellers. This was a practice often used by monopolists to bankrupt small competitors. A large company would sell its products at or below cost in markets where local competitors existed and at higher prices in markets where no local competitors existed. Small competitors were often driven out of business, allowing the monopolist to raise prices in markets where local competitors no longer existed. The ROBINSON-PATMAN ACT (1936) expanded and clarified anticompetitive PRICING STRATEGIES.

Tying agreements occur when a seller refuses to sell products to a buyer unless the buyer also agrees to purchase other products from the seller. If a firm has a monopoly on a critical product or component, it could use its monopoly power to pressure buyers into purchasing other products, for which the company does not have a monopoly, from them. Tying agreements reduce competition, and can be challenged under Section 3 of the Clayton Act, or under the Sherman Act. Exclusive dealing agreements require buyers of a particular service or product to purchase the product or service only from one seller. Like tying agreements, this reduces competition.

Section 7 of the Clayton Act bars mergers and acquisitions that may have an anticompetitive effect. To evaluate the impact of a merger or acquisition requires defining the market that would be affected. While this might seem simple, defining the relevant market or line of commerce is not always easy. Especially as technological advances allow markets to converge, defining who and how many competitors exist in a market is becoming increasingly difficult. For example, in the early 1990s the long-distance telecommunications market included three major firms—AT&T, Sprint, and MCI. A merger of any of these firms would have significantly increased MARKET CONCENTRATION. However, microwave, satellite, and fiber-optic cable company technologies are redefining telecommunications, thereby redefining competition in the industry.

Section 8 of the Clayton Act was designed to reduce the potential for price fixing or division of markets through coordination by INTERLOCKING DIRECTORATES. Section 8 prohibited any person from serving as a director of two or more corporations that were or had been competitors. The Antitrust Amendments Act of 1990 expanded the limitations on interlocking directorates by prohibiting individuals from serving as officers and/or directors of competing corporations.

See also ANTITRUST LAW.

Further reading
Mallor, Jane P., A. James Barnes, Thomas Bowers, Michael J. Philips, and Arlen W. Langvardt. *Business Law and the Regulatory Environment.* Boston: McGraw-Hill, 2001.

Clean Air Acts
The Clean Air Acts (1970, 1977, and 1990) initiated and then revised a variety of programs to reduce air pollution in the country. The acts require the ENVIRONMENTAL PROTECTION AGENCY (EPA) to set national health-based air-quality standards to protect against ozone depletion, sulfur emissions, carbon monoxide, lead, and other air-borne pollutants. The 1990 revisions created the first attempt at market-based systems, POLLUTION RIGHTS, to address air pollution.

According to former U.S. senator Edmund Muskie, "the Clean Air Act of 1970 defined the air pollution control program we have today. . . . In the 1960s, air pollution was widely perceived as a Los Angeles smog problem. . . . Earth Day occurred during the [1970] hearings. That summer, Washington suffered the worst and longest air pollution episode in its history. . . . Three fundamental principles shaped the 1970 law . . . protection of public health . . . industry should be required to apply the best technology . . . American people deserved to know when they could expect their health to be protected." The 1970 act established regulations of the auto industry and allowed citizens to file lawsuits against violators.

The 1970 act and subsequent revisions have been controversial. Industry groups—including oil companies, coal producers, service station operators and land developers—have often opposed the acts. Various groups have intervened to delay and change Clean Air Act statutes.

The acts require states to carry out most of the monitoring and permitting of air pollutants. States are required to develop implementation plans to meet the various criteria defined in the act. Through the EPA, the federal government provides research engineering designs and financial support for state implementation plans.

Some of the specific measures in the Clean Air Act include

- *Ozone.* The 96 cities failing for ozone are ranked from *marginal* to *extreme,* with the more severe cases required to institute more rigorous controls but given more time to attain them. States may have to initiate or upgrade inspection/maintenance (I/M) programs, install vapor recovery at gas stations and otherwise reduce hydrocarbon emissions from small stationary sources, and adopt transportation controls that will offset growth in vehicle miles traveled. Major stationary sources of nitrogen oxides will have to reduce emissions.
- *Carbon monoxide.* The 41 cities failing for carbon monoxide are ranked *moderate* or *serious.* States may have to initiate or upgrade I/M and adopt transportation controls.
- *Particulate matter.* The 72 areas failing to attain for particulate matter (PM-10) are ranked *moderate.* States will have to implement reasonably available control technology (RACT), and use of wood stoves and fireplaces may have to be curtailed.

The Clean Air Amendments of 1977 primarily established federal standards for various pollutants and regulation of emissions through state implementation plans. The 1977 act also defined Class I, II, and III areas restricting particulate emissions in the most polluted (Class I) areas.

The 1990 act required all air-pollution-control obligations of an individual source to be contained in a single five-year operating permit. States have three years to develop permit programs and submit them to the EPA, which has one year to issue regulations describing the minimum requirements for such programs. Sources must pay permit fees to the states to cover the costs of operating the programs. The 1990 act also addresses

- *Vehicle emissions.* Tailpipe emissions of hydrocarbons, carbon monoxide, and nitrogen oxides were to be cut beginning with the 1994 model year, and standards would have to be maintained over a longer vehicle life. On-board charcoal canisters to absorb evaporative emissions may be required.
- *Fuels.* In 1995 reformulated gasolines having less aromatics were to have been introduced in the nine cities with the worst ozone problems; other cities could "opt in." Beginning in 1992, oxyfuel gasolines blended with alcohol were to have been sold in winter in those cities having the worst carbon-monoxide problems.
- *Clean cars.* In 1996 a pilot program was introduce 150,000 cars to California that met tighter emission limits through a combination of vehicle technology and "clean" fuels (substitutes for gasoline or blends of substitutes with gasoline). Other states could "opt in."

According to the 1990 act, emissions of 189 toxic pollutants—typically carcinogens, mutagens, and reproductive toxins—had to be reduced within 10 years. The EPA was to publish a list of source categories within one year and issue Maximum Achievable Control Standards (MACT) for each category over a specified timetable. Companies that initiated partial controls before the deadlines set for MACT could receive extensions.

A two-phase, market-based system (pollution rights) was introduced to reduce sulfur-dioxide emissions from power plants. Electrical power plants account for approximately 70 percent of sulfur dioxide emissions. By the year 2000, total annual emissions were to be capped at 8.9 million tons, a reduction of 10 million tons from 1980 levels. Plants are issued allowances based on fixed emission rates set in the law and on their previous fossil-fuel use. Companies pay penalties if emissions exceed the allowances they hold. Allowances can be banked or traded. All sources are required install continuous emission monitors to assure compliance.

The 1990 act was rooted in the MONTREAL PROTOCOL, an international air-pollution agreement for restrictions on the use, emissions, and disposal of chemicals. It phased out production of chlorofluorocarbons (CFCs), carbon tetrachloride, and methyl chloride by 2000 and methyl chloroform by 2002; and it limited production of CFCs in 2015, phasing them out in 2030. Companies servicing air conditioning for cars were required to purchase certified recycling. The act mandated warning labels on all containers and products (e.g., refrigerators, foam insulation) that enclose CFCs and other ozone-depleting chemicals.

The Clean Air Acts have significantly impacted business in the United States and air quality in the country. According to the Clean Air Trust, a nonprofit organization established by former U.S. senators Edmund Muskie (Maine) and Robert Stafford (Vermont), the Clean Air Acts have been a "tremendous success." Lead emissions have been reduced by 98 percent primarily through removal of lead from gasoline in 1978. Emissions of sulfur dioxide (acid rain) and carbon monoxide emissions both decreased by 37 percent between 1987 and 1996.

Businesses have been required or motivated through pollution rights to change technology, production methods, disposal practices, and emissions levels. Changes in automobile technology, emissions from production processes, and smokestack emissions are examples of business responses to Clean Air act requirements. While not all goals have been achieved, as Senator Muskie stated, "[I]t was an 'experimental law.' It used innovative approaches to achieve the desired results on a more timely basis than provided under any previous law."

Further reading
"The Clean Air Act Amendments of 1990." Available on-line. URL: www.epa.gov/oar/cac/overview.text; Edmund S. Muskie. "NEPA to CERCLA The Clean Air Act: A Commitment to Public Health," Clean Air Trust website. Available on-line. URL: www.cleanairtrust. org./nepa2cercla.html.

Clean Water Act
Growing public awareness of water pollution and concern for controlling it led to enactment of the Federal Water Pollution Control Act Amendments of 1972. After being amended in 1977, this law became commonly known as the Clean Water Act, which established the basic structure for regulating discharges of pollutants into U.S. waters. It gave the ENVIRONMENTAL PROTECTION AGENCY (EPA) the authority to implement pollution-control programs such as setting wastewater standards for industry. The Clean Water Act continued requirements to set water-quality standards for all contaminants in surface waters, making it unlawful for any person to discharge any pollutant from a point source into navigable waters unless a permit was obtained under its provisions. It also provided billions of dollars for the construction of sewage treatment plants under a construction-grants program and recognized the need for planning to address the critical problems posed by non-point source pollution.

Subsequent laws modified some of the earlier Clean Water Act provisions. Revisions in 1981 streamlined the municipal construction-grants process, improving the capabilities of treatment plants built under the program. Changes in 1987 phased out the construction-grants program, replacing it with the State Water Pollution Control Revolving Fund, more commonly known as the Clean Water State Revolving Fund. This new funding strategy addressed water-quality needs by building on EPA-state partnerships. Other provisions in the 1987 revisions created programs to protect estuaries and focused attention on urban runoff issues.

For many communities, funding through the Clean Water Act facilitated needed construction of wastewater treatment centers both for community health and ECONOMIC DEVELOPMENT potential. When businesses look to create or relocate production facilities, wastewater treatment infrastructure is often a necessary component in those decisions.

Further reading
Environmental Protection Agency website. Available on-line. URL: www.epa.gov.

closely held corporation
A closely held or closed CORPORATION is a firm whose COMMON STOCK is owned by only a few individuals (often management) and is not publicly traded. PROPRIETORSHIPS and PARTNERSHIPS that eventually adopt the corporate form of organization often remain as closely held corporations with the original owners as the only stockholders. LEVERAGED BUYOUTS also result in firms being closely held.

In contrast are publicly owned corporations, large companies whose stocks are widely owned and are traded publicly. Usually closed corporations and publicly owned corporations are subject to the same state corporation laws. Many states, however, allow closed corporations greater autonomy in the operation of their business affairs than is granted to public corporations. For example, a closely held corporation may be allowed to operate without a BOARD OF DIRECTORS and be managed as if it were a partnership. The Close Corporation Supplement to the MODEL BUSINESS CORPORATION ACT (MBCA) allows SHAREHOLDERS in closely held corporations to have the same dissolution powers as partners in a partnership.

Closely held corporations may also institute supermajority voting requirements and restrictions on managerial discretion of the board of directors. Since most closely held corporations involve owner-managers, with some owners having more voting rights than others, sometimes closely held corporations establish rules such as requiring a three-fourths majority, unanimous approval to terminate owner-employees, or restricting management from reducing company DIVIDENDs.

See also STOCK MARKET.

Further reading
Mallor, Jane P., A. James Barnes, Thomas Bowers, Michael J. Philips, and Arlen W. Langvardt. *Business Law and the Regulatory Environment*, 11th ed. Boston: McGraw-Hill, 2001.

Coalition for Environmentally Responsible Economies
The Coalition for Environmentally Responsible Economies (CERES) is a group of environmental, investor, and advocacy groups coordinating efforts to promote sustainable development practices. (Ceres was the name of the Roman goddess of fertility and agriculture.) CERES is most known for its 10 principles, a 10-point code of environmental conduct. Companies that commit to these principles agree to "an ongoing process of continuous improvement, dialogue and comprehensive, systematic public reporting." Following are CERES' 10 principles.

Protection of the Biosphere   We will reduce and make continual progress toward eliminating the release of any substance that may cause environmental damage to the air, water, or the earth or its inhabitants. We will safeguard all habitats affected by our operations and will protect open spaces and wilderness, while preserving biodiversity.

Sustainable Use of Natural Resources   We will make sustainable use of renewable natural resources, such as water, soils and forests. We will conserve non-renewable natural resources through efficient use and careful planning.

Reduction and Disposal of Wastes   We will reduce and where possible eliminate waste through source reduction and recycling. All waste will be handled and disposed of through safe and responsible methods.

Energy Conservation   We will conserve energy and improve the energy efficiency of our internal operations and of the goods and services we sell. We will make every effort to use environmentally safe and sustainable energy sources.

Risk Reduction   We will strive to minimize the environmental, health and safety risks to our employees and the communities in which we operate through safe technologies, facilities and operating procedures, and by being prepared for emergencies.

Safe Products and Services   We will reduce and where possible eliminate the use, manufacture or sale of products and services that cause environmental damage or health or safety hazards. We will inform our customers of the environmental impacts of our products or services and try to correct unsafe use.

Environmental Restoration   We will promptly and responsibly correct conditions we have caused that endanger health, safety or the environment. To the extent feasible, we will redress injuries we have caused to persons or damage we have caused to the environment and will restore the environment.

Informing the Public   We will inform in a timely manner everyone who may be affected by conditions caused by our company that might endanger health, safety or the environment. We will regularly seek advice and counsel through dialogue with persons in communities near our facilities. We will not take any action against employees for reporting dangerous incidents or conditions to management or to appropriate authorities.

Management Commitment We will implement these Principles and sustain a process that ensures that the BOARD OF DIRECTORS and CHIEF EXECUTIVE OFFICER are fully informed about pertinent environmental issues and are fully responsible for environmental policy. In selecting our Board of Directors, we will consider demonstrated environmental commitment as a factor.

Audits and Reports We will conduct an annual self-evaluation of our progress in implementing these Principles. We will support the timely creation of generally accepted environmental audit procedures. We will annually complete the CERES Report, which will be made available to the public.

CERES was established in 1988 when the Board of the Social Investment Forum, an association of investment firms and pension funds supporting SOCIALLY RESPONSIBLE INVESTING, formed an alliance with environmental organizations. A year later the group created the 10 principles and began asking CORPORATIONS to endorse them.

Initially only environmentally friendly companies adopted the principles, but in 1993 Sonoco became the first Fortune 500 company to endorse them. By 2002 over 80 organizations and 70 companies have endorsed the principles, including 13 Fortune 500 companies, all of whom have benefited from endorsement of their companies. The coalition monitors the practices of participating companies to ensure compliance with the principles. As reported in a *Wall Street Journal* article, the relationship between CERES and major companies is not always harmonious.

The unlikely relationship between General Motors Corp. and the Coalition for Environmentally Responsible Economies . . . resulted in GM decreasing pollution at some of its factories—a step that the company says is saving money by cutting energy bills and precluding expensive government-mandated cleanups. The tie also sheltered the auto giant from some criticism of its environmental record. Along the way, the collaboration became a high-profile example of a growing trend within the environmental movement: using quiet negotiation rather than noisy protest to change boardroom behavior.

Further reading
Ball, Jeffrey. "Rocky Road: After Long Détente, GM, Green Group Are at Odds Again," *Wall Street Journal,* 30 July 2002; CERES website. Available on-line. URL: www.ceres.org.

collective bargaining

Collective bargaining is the process through which representatives of UNIONS and management negotiate a labor agreement. The WAGNER ACT (National Labor Relations Act, 1935) defines collective bargaining as follows.

For the purpose of (this act) to bargain collectively is the performance of the mutual obligation of the employer and the representative of the employees to meet at reasonable times and confer in good faith with respect to wages, hours, and terms and conditions of employment, or the negotiation of an agreement, or any question arising there under, and the execution of a written contract incorporating any agreement reached if requested by either party, but such obligation does not compel either party to agree to proposal or require the making of a concession.

This definition means that both labor and management are required by law to negotiate wages, hours, and conditions of EMPLOYMENT "in good faith"—that is, both sides are negotiating, putting forth proposals, and responding to proposals with counter proposals, though neither side is required to agree with what is proposed by the other side. Collective bargaining is seen by some economists as a countervailing force against the power of huge CORPORATIONS.

Through much of the early history of the United States, the few unions that existed had limited power to represent workers. Courts frequently treated unions as illegal criminal conspiracies and often sanctioned the use of police to counter union activity. In the early 20th century, with the expansion of industrialization in America, union membership grew and federal legislation began to recognize the rights of workers to organize and be represented by collective bargaining.

The Wagner Act was the third in a series of acts expanding the power of organized labor. In 1926 Congress passed the Railway Labor Act, regulating labor relations in the railroad industry. The NORRIS-LAGUARDIA ACT (1932) limited the circumstances in which FEDERAL COURTS could enjoin strikes and picketing in labor disputes and also prohibited federal-court enforcement of "yellow-dog" contracts (under which employees agreed not to join or remain a member of a union). The Wagner Act created the NATIONAL LABOR RELATIONS BOARD (NLRB), gave workers the right to organize and bargain collectively, and prohibited certain labor practices that were perceived to discourage collective bargaining, including

- interfering with employees' rights to form, join, and assist labor unions
- dominating or interfering with the formation or administration of a labor union
- discriminating against employees in hiring, tenure, or any term of employment due to their union membership

- discrimination against employees because they have filed charges or given testimony under the National Labor Relations Act (NLRA)
- refusing to bargain collectively with any duly designated employee representative

The NLRB and numerous court decisions have interpreted what is good-faith collective bargaining and what items are mandatory, permissible, and legal in collective-bargaining negotiations. ARBITRATION and mediation are often used to resolve collective bargaining disputes. The TAFT-HARTLEY ACT (Labor-Management Relations Act, 1947) rewrote NLRA powers, making secondary BOYCOTTS an illegal labor tactic, but also increased enforcement of collective-bargaining agreements.

In the 1980s, changes in the makeup of the NLRB reduced union power in collective-bargaining agreements. In the *NLRB v. Bildisco* (1984) case, the Supreme Court upheld a decision that employers may file a Chapter 11 bankruptcy petition and immediately break an existing collective-bargaining agreement without first communicating with the union. Congress then changed the bankruptcy code, requiring companies to consult with unions before using bankruptcy relief from collective-bargaining agreements. Bruce Fisher and Michael Phillips write "The Supreme Court has ruled that employers may shut down a plant permanently without committing an unfair labor practice, "provided the employer does not have the intent to discourage unionization elsewhere." Similarly, court decisions have addressed whether a successor company is liable for a collective bargaining agreement reached by the previous owners. Fisher and Phillips summarize the *NLRB v. Burns International Security Services* (1987) case, in which the NLRB ruled that "although the new employer is not bound by the substantive provisions of the predecessor's bargaining agreement, it has an obligation to bargain with the union so long as it is in fact a successor to the old employer and the majority of its employees were employed by the predecessor."

Employers can be charged with "Boulwareism," a violation of the duty to bargain in good faith. Named after a General Electric executive, Fisher and Phillips define Boulwareism as "an employer's careful study of all bargaining issues before meeting the union, and presenting its best offer to the union immediately on a take-it-or-leave-it basis." This process suggests a "closed-mind" attitude that violates good-faith collective bargaining.

Further reading
Dessler, Gary. *Human Resource Management.* 7th ed. Upper Saddle River, N.J.: Prentice-Hall, 1997; Fisher, Bruce D., and Michael J. Phillips. *The Legal, Ethical and Regulatory Environment of Business.* 4th ed. Eagan, Minn.: West Publishing, 1992; Mallor, Jane P., A. James Barnes, Thomas Bowers, Michael J. Philips, and Arlen W. Langvardt. *Business Law and the Regulatory Environment.* 11th ed. Boston: McGraw-Hill, 2001.

collusion
Collusion is an agreement between two or more parties in an effort to fraud or deceive. Collusion is often practiced to coordinate efforts among firms, effectively lessening the degree of competition among them. As a result, collusion can be found in many areas of commerce.

An interlocking directorate, where a director sits on the boards of competing corporations, is an example of collusion. Because interlocking directorates facilitate the flow of information between competing firms, this exchange of knowledge reduces the competition between the two firms. The result is that the relationship between the two firms becomes more cooperative and coordinated and less competitive. Because interlocking directorates lead to more concentrated (more monopolistic or less competitive) market conditions, they have been made illegal (Clayton Act, 1914).

Collusion occurs most often in oligopolistic market structures, where markets or industries are made up of only a few firms. The output of these markets is concentrated in only a few firms, making the actions of each firm much more significant than if these markets were competitive, that is, comprised of many firms. Oligopoly, the presence of only a few firms in an industry, provides an optimal climate for collusion; it is much easier to monitor the actions of a few competitors than it is to keep an eye on many firms.

Overt and covert agreements are common in oligopolies. They take the form of social gatherings among the industry leaders, trade association conventions, and lists of representative prices. The goal of each of these practices is to facilitate the exchange of information among the competing firms in the industry. Price leadership is also common, either in the form of the dominant firm being the price leader or the more subtle form of collusive price leadership. As stated by economist F. M. Scherer, "industry members must recognize that their common interest in cooperative pricing behavior overrides any centrifugal aspirations toward independent behavior."

The most overt form of collusion is the cartel. A cartel is formed when a group of previously competing firms or countries organizes to set prices and control aggregate output from its members. Rather than competing against each other, the members now cooperate and their actions are coordinated. The United States' motto is "E pluribus unum," translated "from many, one." It portrays one nation formed from many states. The same idea applies to a cartel. Where there once were many competitors, now there is the cartel of once-competing members. OPEC, the Organization of Petroleum Exporting Countries, and De Beers, the diamond cartel, are examples of successful cartels.

In general, because collusion leads to more market concentration rather than market competition, most forms of collusion have been made illegal in the U.S. The Sherman Antitrust Act (1890) and the Clayton Act

(1914), and a few other acts outlaw various forms of cooperation and collusion. These acts attempt to discourage anti-competitive practices improve and, thus, market performance.

Further reading
Scherer, F. M. *Industrial Market Structure and Economic Performance.* Chicago: Rand McNally, 1970.

Commerce Business Daily

Commerce Business Daily (CBD) is a federal government publication that lists notices of proposed government procurement actions, contract awards, sales of government property, and other procurement information. A daily publication, CBD usually contains 500–1,000 notices, each of which appears only once.

The U.S. government is the single largest purchaser of goods and SERVICES in the nation, buying approximately $1 trillion of products and services each year. Selling to the government can be an important part of a firm's business operations, and the CBD is its major source of information. Many businesses pay service companies to monitor the CBD and alert them when procurement notices are listed in their areas of interest. Selling to the government can be daunting, since government procurement often involves considerable paperwork and understanding a distinct coding system.

The idea behind the CBD is that, by using this form of public notice, the government increases companies' access to its procurement, improving openness and increasing competition to supply to the government. Only procurement actions and CONTRACT awards over $25,000 are listed in the CBD. Certain procurement activities are not reported, including classified services and supplies and those needed for an emergency. The CBD can be found in federal depository libraries and on-line.

Further reading
Commerce Business Daily website. Available on-line. URL: www.cbdnet.gov.

commerce clause

Section 8 of the U.S. Constitution grants Congress the power to "regulate commerce with foreign nations and among the several states, and with the Indian tribes." This section is referred to as the "commerce clause." Originally Congress was given this power in order to block protectionist state restrictions. The original 13 states were, in many ways, like small, independent countries and, without the commerce clause, could have chosen to restrict IMPORTS from other states. For example, for over 100 years New Jersey financed its state government by levying a transport tax on wagons moving goods from Philadelphia to New York.

The U.S. Supreme Court has indicated in recent decades that Congress has broad authority to regulate commerce under the commerce clause, and that even internal state commerce affecting interstate commerce can be regulated. Many federal statutes, including some civil-rights laws, are constitutionally based on the commerce clause. As a practical matter, the commerce clause, in conjunction with the supremacy clause, supports the common economic market of the United States by minimizing state regulatory TRADE BARRIERS.

Congressional regulation of U.S. foreign commerce, which has been much more controversial, is discussed under EXTRATERRITORIAL JURISDICTION.

Further reading
Engdahl, David E. *Constitutional Federalism in a Nutshell.* Eagan, Minn.: West Group, 1987.

commercial law

Commercial law concerns the sale and distribution of goods, the financing of credit transactions on the security of goods sold, and legal documents related to such transactions (NEGOTIABLE INSTRUMENTS). In the United States, most state commercial law is governed by the widely adopted UNIFORM COMMERCIAL CODE (UCC). The UCC was heavily influenced by civil law commercial code principles, particularly from Germany via Professor Karl Llewellyn.

Article 2 of the UCC details the law of commercial sales contract formation (offer, counteroffer, acceptance), contract excusal (unforeseen circumstances, force majeure), interpretation of CONTRACTS, and contract-breach remedies (DAMAGES, performance orders). Article 2A concerns lease contracts, their formation, effects, performance, DEFAULT, and remedies. Article 3 of the UCC governs "negotiable instruments" (transferable documents representing title to goods). Article 4 deals with bank deposits and collections, Article 4A with the transfer of funds. Article 5 covers the LETTER OF CREDIT, a bank-issued financing device common to international sales transactions. Article 6 governs bulk sales, Article 7 warehouse receipts and bills of lading. Article 8 deals with investment securities and their issuance and transfer. Article 9 concerns "secured transactions," such as when the buyer provides collateral to the seller to guarantee payment. Typically in sales transactions, the collateral is the goods being sold.

Further reading
Stone, Bradford. *Uniform Commercial Code in a Nutshell.* Eagan, Minn.: West Group, 2001.

commercial paper

Commercial paper is a debt instrument—that is, a PROMISSORY NOTE issued by large CORPORATIONS that are also financially strong. To minimize the risk associated with commercial paper, it is traded among only the largest, most financially stable corporations, MUTUAL FUNDS, INSURANCE companies, banks, and other large intermediaries. Commercial paper is unsecured and short-term, with maturities ranging from 30 to 270 days.

For firms with large amounts of excess cash, commercial paper is a convenient, relatively risk-free way of earning interest on otherwise idle balances for short periods of time. For example, a corporation may be saving up for the payment of a cash DIVIDEND or seeking to retire a bond issue. This pool of cash can be profitably and conveniently invested for a short term via commercial paper.

For the borrower, commercial paper is a relatively inexpensive source of short-term CAPITAL. The interest rate on commercial paper is always below the prime rate and, in recent years, has closely paralleled T-bill rates.

See also INTEREST RATES.

Commodity Credit Corporation

The Commodity Credit Corporation (CCC), a federally owned and operated entity, was created to stabilize, support, and protect American farmers' INCOME and prices. The CCC aids agricultural producers through LOANS, purchases, payments, and other operations to support PRODUCTION and marketing of agricultural commodities. Initially a modest and popular government-support program, it has recently become part of a controversial agricultural subsidy issue.

When established in 1933, the CCC helped farmers attempt to attain and maintain PARITY. During the GREAT DEPRESSION, prices for farm PRODUCTS dropped to near zero. While farmers' costs declined, farm incomes were severely depressed. As portrayed in John Steinbeck's classic novel *The Grapes of Wrath*, many farmers left agriculture in search of opportunities elsewhere. Initially incorporated as part of President Franklin Roosevelt's New Deal program to combat the depression, in 1939 the CCC was transferred to the U.S. Department of Agriculture (USDA). In 1948 it was reincorporated as a federal corporation within the USDA.

The CCC's programs and policies have changed many times as U.S. policy toward agriculture and other economic support programs has changed. When it was established in 1933, a majority of U.S. congressional districts had large agricultural constituencies. As the United States has become more urbanized, agricultural political interests have declined as consumer and taxation political clout has expanded, and farm lobby power has also diminished.

Major CCC programs include

- *Support activities.* These include loan, purchase, and payment programs for wheat, corn, oilseeds, cotton, rice, tobacco, milk and milk products, barley, oats, grain sorghum, mohair, honey, peanuts, and sugar. Farmers may receive nonrecourse commodity loans on most of these commodities at a designated rate per unit (price) by pledging and storing a quantity of a commodity as collateral. When the commodities are harvested, farmers can choose to either pay back the loan and sell on the open market or deliver the commodity to the government at the support price. In years when market prices are higher than the support price, farmers naturally sell on the open market. When support prices are higher than market prices, the government winds up owning large quantities of agricultural commodities.

Two of the more controversial support programs are sugar and tobacco. Support prices for sugar are frequently significantly higher than world market prices, creating subsidies for sugar producers and higher costs for consumers. Tobacco support programs are both expensive and ethically questionable. Paying U.S. farmers to produce a harmful product is a dubious role for government.

- *Inventory, disposal, and domestic food assistance programs.* When the CCC acquires commodities through either collateral acquisition or nonrecourse loans, it stores and processes commodities through contracts with commercial warehouses. Sometimes the CCC will make loan-deficiency payments to farmers, based on the difference between the support price and the market price, rather than having farmers deliver products to the agency. The CCC sells commodities through its Farm Service Agency office in Kansas City, Missouri. To reduce inventories, it donates food commodities acquired through its price support programs to the Bureau of Indian Affairs and federal, state, and private agencies. The commodities are used in school-lunch programs, summer camps, and assistance of needy persons. Some commodities are provided to the U.S. military and federal and state prisons.
- *Export programs.* Through a variety of sales, payments, export credits, and other activities, the CCC, along with the Foreign Agricultural Services, promotes and sells U.S. agricultural commodities abroad. Through the Export Enhancement Program, the CCC pays cash to U.S. exporters as a bonus, allowing them to sell in targeted countries at prices matching those of subsidizing competitors.

In 1996 the Freedom to Farm Bill, amending the CCC, intended to reduce government subsidies of commodity producers. Instead, when commodity prices declined to near-record lows, the CCC was authorized to increase support for farmers to prevent further foreclosures and bankruptcies among farmers. By 2001 farm subsidies, distributed primarily through the CCC, amounted to over $27 billion, but almost two-thirds of those funds went to wealthy farm individuals and farm CORPORATIONS.

Supporting agricultural producers is a common practice in both industrialized and developing countries. Many international trade disputes center on "unfair" subsidies of domestic producers. Support for agricultural producers traditionally has been a politically "sacred cow," but as the cost of subsidies and the balance of political power shifts, programs like the CCC have come under greater scrutiny.

Further reading
Farm Service Agency website. Available on-line. URL: www.fsa.usda.gov.; John Kelly, "Farm fund rules mean rich get richer," *Beaufort Gazette*, 10 September 2001, p. A1.

Commodity Futures Trading Commission

The Commodity Futures Trading Commission (CFTC) regulates FUTURES and OPTIONS markets in the United States, protecting market participants against market manipulation, abusive trading practices, and FRAUD. Created in 1974, the CFTC was a response to growing use and changes in futures and options markets. Traditionally, agricultural commodities dominated futures trading, but beginning in the 1970s, trading expanded to include FINANCIAL INSTRUMENTS, foreign currencies, U.S. government securities, and a variety of new commodity futures contracts. The CFTC's major activities include contract review, market surveillance, and regulation of futures market participants.

A futures contract is an agreement to buy or sell in the future a specific quantity of a commodity at a specified price. Most futures contracts consider that actual delivery of the commodity could take place; however, some futures contracts require cash settlement in lieu of delivery. For example, the NEW YORK MERCANTILE EXCHANGE offers an April contract in gold. Each contract is for 100 troy ounces, which at $300 per ounce represents $30,000 worth of gold. Most futures contracts are liquidated before the delivery date. An option on a commodity futures contract gives the buyer the right to convert the option into a futures contract. Futures and options must be executed through a commodity exchange and almost always through people and firms regulated by the CFTC.

The CFTC reviews all proposed futures and options contracts. Before an exchange is permitted to trade a future and option contract in a specific commodity, it must demonstrate that the contract reflects the normal market flow and commercial trading practices in the actual commodity. Normal trading practices are usually found in the "cash" market for a commodity, but if market norms are not well defined, the exchange must show why a contract should be structured as they propose.

The CFTC monitors trading in all commodity futures daily and can halt trading or take whatever action deemed necessary to restore order in any futures contract being traded. Trading in specific commodities is often conducted by relatively few individuals. Hedgers take a position in order to reduce the risk of financial loss due to a change in the price of their ASSETS, while speculators hope to profit by correctly anticipating changes in the price of an option or futures contract. In any market where there are relatively few participants, there exists the potential for market manipulation, raising or lowering prices by a few powerful individuals. For example, during the early 1980s, silver prices rose from $5 to over $50 per ounce, only to quickly fall back to the $5 range. Billions of dollars were made and lost in the silver market, and individuals were accused of market manipulation.

Companies and individuals who manage customer funds or give trading advice must apply to the National Futures Association, a self-regulating organization approved by the CFTC. The CFTC also requires registrants to disclose market risks and performance information to customers. One of the relatively new roles of the CFTC is to oversee trading in derivatives, contracts whose value is based on the value of the underlying financial asset or security. Derivatives LEVERAGE existing futures contracts, which in turn leverage the commodity they are based on. Leveraging allows buyers and sellers to benefit (or lose) from small changes in market prices while only having to pay a small percentage of the value of the contract being traded.

Further reading
Commodity Futures Trading Commission website. Available online. URL: www.cftc.gov.

commodity markets

Commodity markets are markets where basic goods and materials are exchanged. Commodity markets can be as small as a local farmers market or as large as the CHICAGO BOARD OF TRADE (CBOT), the first commodity exchange in the United States (established in 1848). Generally commodity markets are located near historic centers of PRODUCTION of major commodities or in major cities like Chicago and New York.

In the 19th century, the major commodity markets provided trading opportunities primarily in agricultural PRODUCTS. Initially the CBOT focused on grain trade, allowing farmers and other agricultural industry members to hedge or reduce their risk of price changes by using FUTURES contracts. Similarly, the CHICAGO MERCANTILE EXCHANGE (CME), created in 1898 as the Chicago Butter and Egg Board, allows investors, managers, and broker/dealers to reduce risk in business transactions. As ECONOMIC CONDITIONS changed, commodity markets like the CBOT and the CME expanded their trading to include currency futures, interest-rate futures, and stock-index futures.

Most commodity markets determine current market prices, called the cash price, by the interaction of buyers and sellers (DEMAND and SUPPLY). The CBOT and other commodity exchanges have colorful "pits" where traders, using hand signals, execute orders to buy and sell commodities and futures contracts. Within any major commodity market there is a variety of participants, including buyers, sellers, hedgers, floor traders, and speculators. Buyers are representatives of food companies purchasing commodities for use in production. Sellers are representatives of commodity producers.

Hedgers are firms and individuals who make purchases and sales in futures markets for the purpose of establishing a known price, weeks or months in advance, for commodities they intend to buy or sell in the cash market. HEDGING allows them to protect themselves against the risk of an unfavorable price change in the time before they are ready to buy or sell in the cash market. To a commodity producer, a decline in prices between the present and when the commodity will be available would be unfavorable. To a cereal company, where grains are input in production, a rise in commodity prices would be unfavorable. Both buyers and sellers of commodities can protect themselves against price changes.

For example, a farmer or farm corporation may plant 1,000 acres of winter wheat in the fall. Winter wheat is not harvested until the next year. The farmer knows that historically his/her land yields an average of 60 bushels per acre, so they expect to have 60,000 bushels at harvest time. The farmer can "lock in" the current price for wheat by selling 12 wheat futures contracts at the current price, say $2.90 per bushel. (The standard futures contract for wheat is 5,000 bushels.) If, in the interim, the price of wheat rises, the farmer will buy back the futures contracts at a higher price, losing money in the futures market, but then sell his or her wheat at the higher price in the cash market. If the price of wheat declines, the farmer will buy back the futures contracts at a lower price, profiting in the futures market, but then sell his or her wheat at a lower price in the cash market.

In addition to buyers, sellers, and hedgers, many commodity markets include floor traders and speculators. Floor traders are individuals who buy and sell for their own accounts. Like day traders in STOCK MARKETS, they buy and sell rapidly, hoping to earn PROFITS based on small changes in prices. Floor traders also provide liquidity to commodity markets. Speculators seek to profit based on anticipated changes in futures prices. Speculators will "go long," purchasing futures contracts, or "go short," selling futures contracts based on expectation that the price will decline, and profit by the difference. As one trading company states, "Commodity trading is risky and is not suitable for everyone."

Historically commodity-markets futures trading was designed to protect producers and manufacturers using commodities from price changes. Today commodity exchanges are used by a variety of nonagricultural buyers and sellers, such as power companies and airlines attempting to lock in their cost of fuel, multinational companies locking in their revenue or costs in other currencies, and investment companies locking in their cost or price of CAPITAL.

Further reading

"Understanding Opportunities and Risks in Futures Trading," National Futures Association. Available on-line. URL: www.nfa.org.

common law (case law)

Common law, also called case law or Anglo-American law, refers to the legal system developed in the common-law courts of England since the Middle Ages and transferred to much of the English-speaking world and Commonwealth nations, including the United States. It is distinguished from the civil-law system used in continental Europe and in the areas of other continents conquered and ruled by continental nations.

The common law evolved as a body of customary law based on judicial decisions and reports of decided cases of the common-law courts. Decisions by English grand juries, kings, magistrates and trial juries were written down and eventually catalogued according to the type of case. When the courts were called on to decide similar issues in subsequent cases, they reviewed the earlier decisions, and if they found one that was logically analogous to the contemporary case, they applied the principle of the earlier decision. This doctrine is called stare decisis—Latin for "to stand by decided matters." The common law thus consists of court opinions in specific disputes that state legal principles and must be followed in subsequent court cases about the same type of dispute.

The principle of stare decisis is the essence of common-law jurisprudence. Judges are usually reluctant to discard well-established rules. At the same time, the principles should reflect contemporary social values, and sometimes they have to be changed or modified to keep up with the times. For this reason, judges always attempt to write reasoned judgments, especially when their decisions mark a departure from the established precedent. However, different courts apply this general policy with varying degrees of strictness. The English courts, for instance, are inclined to be more rigorous than American courts in its application.

During America's colonial period, most of the English common-law tradition and many of the English statutes became firmly entrenched, though modified to some extent in accordance with the religious and cultural beliefs of the colonists. At the time of independence, the basic legal system did not change. The major difference was the creation of the U.S. Constitution, ratified in 1789. After that, the laws of Parliament and the edicts of King George III no longer had any power in the new United States. The Constitution became the foundation on which the American legal system was built. Both the law inherited from England and that enacted by Congress and state legislatures eventually had to stand the test of constitutionality in order to determine their validity.

In the centuries of American history following independence, the English common-law tradition has been modified to some extent. A number of common-law institutions have been rejected. For instance, in America, on death intestate (i.e., dying without leaving a will), all of the children inherited land and not just the eldest son, as was the case in England. Leaseholds owned by feudal landlords were replaced by freeholds in the American context, and there were no ecclesiastical (church) courts in America. Even in England, modern-day common law is considerably different from its feudal roots, and statutory law is widespread.

Especially during the past century, statutes and administrative regulations have become more important as instruments to make new law and to codify (put into a written, prescriptive form) broad principles developed by the case law. Even so, judge-made law remains an important component of American law. The courts in common-law jurisdictions have the right to interpret statutes, but they must do so in accordance with the rules of statutory interpretation. In the United States, the general policy of the courts has been to attempt to interpret the statute in the light of the legislature's intention. In England, on the other hand, the literal rule of interpretation is the predominant approach, i.e., the statute should be read literally, without reference to legislative intent.

Many laws affecting business evolve gradually through a series of court decisions. Major U.S. businesses closely watch product-liability, worker rights, environmental, and other court judgments. Companies and consumers (through their attorneys) often choose particular court venues where recent decisions have been advantageous to their interests.

One of the most widely reported issues involves tobacco companies' litigation. After decades of winning court decisions that smokers made the choice to smoke, in the mid-1990s, with new evidence that the companies knew their product was addictive, juries began finding in favor of smokers, creating an avalanche of lawsuits leading to the 1999 TOBACCO SETTLEMENT.

Further reading
Burnham, William. *Introduction to the Law and Legal System of the United States,* 3d ed. Eagan, Minn.: West Group, 2002; Meador, Daniel J., and Frederick G. Kempin, Jr. *Historical Introduction to Anglo-American Law in a Nutshell,* 3d ed. Eagan, Minn.: West Group, 1990.

common stock, preferred stock, treasury stock
Stock is an ownership interest in a corporation. If a CORPORATION issues only one type of equity security, it is called common stock, the kind normally issued by corporations. The common stockholders are the residual EQUITY in the corporation and are the only class of stockholders to have voting rights, one vote for each common share owned. Most common stock also carries a preemptive right, where existing stockholders have the privilege to purchase new issues before they are offered to the public for sale. This allows current stockholders to maintain the same percentage ownership in the corporation after a new issue is sold as they had prior to the new offering. The preemptive right is also crucial in preventing a dilution of value for existing stockholders when a new stock issue is sold at a lower market price than previous shares.

Par-value common stock and no-par-value common stock are issued by corporations. Originally conceived to establish a minimum legal CAPITAL to serve as protection for creditors, par value has little significance today. However, it still remains that if a common stock has a par value, that stock cannot be initially offered at less than its par value. When common stock is issued at a price above its par value, the excess of price over par value is recorded in the equity account: Contributed Capital in Excess of Par Value, Common Stock.

Preferred stock is also an equity security, but unlike common stock, it carries no voting rights. Preferred stocks have par values, a percentage of which is paid to the preferred stockholders when DIVIDENDS are declared. Preferred stock is named for the dividend preference that preferred stockholders enjoy over the common stockholders. The three types of dividend preference, listed here from the weakest to the strongest in terms of dividend-earning power, are current dividend preference, cumulative dividend preference, participating dividend preference.

Current dividend preference requires the preferred stockholders to receive dividends from a current dividend being paid and common stockholders to receive dividends only if there is any current dividend remaining after the preferred stockholders have been paid in full. In the case of a small dividend where there are insufficient funds to pay dividends to all stockholders, the preferred stockholders will receive dividends, and the residual, if any, will be shared by the common stockholders.

Cumulative dividend preference operates much in the same way as current dividend preference, but it is more powerful. In years when there is no dividend declared by the BOARD OF DIRECTORS or when the declared dividend has been so small as to be insufficient to pay in full the preferred dividends, the dividends which the preferred stockholders are entitled to but have not yet received are called "dividends in arrears." Cumulative dividend preference requires dividends in arrears to be paid before any other distributions of a current dividend. After the dividends in arrears are caught up and paid, then current dividend preference is applied to the remaining dividends to be distributed.

Participating dividend preference operates like cumulative dividend preference, except that when the cumulative dividend preference has been satisfied, the preferred stockholders then share the remaining dividends to be distributed with the common stockholders on a pro rata basis. By taking a larger share of the declared dividends, these dividend preferences benefit the preferred stockholders at the expense of the common stockholders.

Like common stock, when preferred stock is issued for more than its par value, the excess of price over par value is recorded in the equity account: Contributed Capital in Excess of Par Value, Preferred Stock. The issuance of common and preferred stocks is an important source of capital for corporations.

For a variety of reasons, occasionally a corporation will purchase (buy back) its own shares from the open market. Stock shares that have been previously issued but repurchased by the issuing corporation are called treasury stock. Treasury stock has the status of "issued, but not outstanding." The custom of "one vote per share" does not apply to treasury stock as long as it is held by the issuing corporation. Treasury stock is a contra equity account, has a normal debit balance, and reduces total stockholder equity as long as it remains not outstanding.

comparable worth (comparable pay, pay equity)

Comparable worth (also referred to as comparable pay or pay equity) is the idea that workers should receive equal pay for work of equal value. Comparable worth is most closely associated with differences in pay by gender. In the late 1960s, working women in the United States received only 59 percent of what working men were earning. During the 1980s, led by women in Oregon, pressure for pay based on comparable worth became a widely debated issue. Supporters argued women were shuttled into lower-paying professions, particularly education and nursing, and subjected to sex stereotyping, amounting to decades of undervaluing work done by women. In Oregon, women working for the state confronted the state legislature and described their job responsibilities. When asked to guess their pay, the legislators overestimated women's pay by at least 15 percent.

The efforts of women in Oregon led to pay-equity projects where jobs were evaluated and compared according to the level of skill, effort, and responsibility required for the job. This resulted in numeric rankings of jobs and equalization of pay based on rankings. While comparable-worth legislation grew in Canada, with most provinces passing legislation calling for achieving equal pay for work of equal value, in the United States comparable-worth laws have been limited to local and state public-sector workers. The EQUAL PAY ACT of 1963 has been interpreted in the courts as requiring equal pay only for workers in the same job and therefore has not affected efforts to equalize pay for jobs that are dissimilar but of equal skill and value.

By 1999 women workers in the United States were earning 75 percent of what men were earning, reflecting their increasing shift away from traditional, low-paying occupations. The change also reflects a robust economy that has raised most workers' wages, due largely to efforts achieving pay based on comparable worth.

Further reading

Hallock, Margaret. "Pay Equity: The Promise and the Practice in North America," *Labour & Industry* 10 (December 1999): 53.

comparative advantage

The law of comparative advantage is the principle that firms, people, or countries should engage in those activities for which their advantage over others is the largest or their disadvantage is the smallest. First articulated by English economist David Ricardo (1772–1823), the law of comparative advantage demonstrated that both weak and strong nations benefit from trade by doing those things they do relatively more efficiently than others. At the time, Ricardo's ideas were revolutionary. The predominant economic doctrine, MERCANTILISM, espoused accumulation of WEALTH in the form of precious metals and maintaining a favorable TRADE BALANCE. The idea of comparative advantage was used to convince the English parliament to replace protective TARIFFS with a FREE TRADE policy. England's success with these changes influenced other countries to change their policies.

Comparative advantage is based on relative COSTS and exchange. Considering the alternative, self-sufficiency, raises the question whether quality of life would improve or decline if one had to produce everything one consumed. There are few people who have the skills and other resources to come close to matching the quality of life they currently have in an economic system based on specialization and exchange.

Relative costs are also critical to the idea of comparative advantage. If one person (firm or country) can do something well, the OPPORTUNITY COST (the value of the output foregone) of not using those resources in that capacity is quite high. Meanwhile the opportunity cost of using personal skills and resources in production of what one does well is relatively low. For example, Tiger Woods plays golf exceptionally well and earns significant INCOME doing so. Knowing golf courses, Mr. Woods could also probably do an excellent job cutting the grass on the courses he plays. If he chose to cut grass, his opportunity cost would be the income foregone from playing and winning on a lot of golf courses. By playing golf, Mr. Woods sacrifices the income he could earn cutting grass, but that is quite small compared to his income from playing golf.

The same principal, relative costs, applies to specialization and trade among firms and countries. In the last decade, one of the trends in American business has been OUTSOURCING. Firms are finding it less expensive to pay others for skills or products that would be expensive to produce internally. Advances in communication technology are allowing firms to contract out a variety of service needs, including many human resource, accounting, and development functions. Increasingly U.S. countries are contracting for billing, engineering, and technology services with skilled English-speaking professionals around the world.

For the last two centuries, economists have studied the concept of comparative advantage, looking for the sources of relative-cost advantages. The Heckscher-Ohlim theorem suggests that relative factor endowments of countries are the principal determinant of comparative-cost differences. According to this theory, countries with highly skilled workers will have an advantage in the PRODUCTION of goods and SERVICES requiring skilled labor. Countries with significant mineral resources will have a comparative advantage in the production of those minerals. Empirical studies have both supported and challenged the Heckscher-Ohlim theorem. Other research suggests DEMAND considerations, ECONOMIES OF SCALE, and technology are important sources of comparative advantage. Governments sometimes attempt to create comparative advantage through subsidies to important domestic industries and tariffs placed on imported products.

Further reading
Folsom, Ralph H., and W. Davis Folsom. *Understanding NAFTA and Its International Business Implications.* New York: Matthew Bender/Irwin, 1996; Ruffin, Roy J., and Paul R. Gregory. *Principles of Economics,* 7th ed. Boston: Addison Wesley, 2001.

compensation and benefits

Compensation and benefits comprise the total rewards package that an employee receives for performing a job. Compensation is considered direct pay, since it is the amount of money the employee receives. Benefits are indirect pay, since they are monetary equivalents that can be converted later into cash or used to pay for selected expenses. For every dollar paid in compensation, the CHAMBER OF COMMERCE estimates that 39–40 percent is spent for indirect compensation, leaving 60–61 percent for direct compensation. These are composite averages; individual companies and specific situations may vary considerably.

Three factors influence the average pay for the organization and each employee's specific pay: (1) competitive pressures from forces outside the organization, (2) the company's desire to compensate all of its employees fairly and equitably, and (3) what the individual employee brings to the organization.

The primary external pressure affecting pay rates comes from other companies within the marketplace (the geographical region in which companies recruit applicants). Each employer is in competition with other companies for applicants of similar qualifications. The competition may group employees within common industries or by level of knowledge, skills, and abilities. Through area surveys, companies identify what the collective marketplace pays and set their pay scales accordingly. Companies can pay less than others, more than others, or at the market average. The most common philosophy is to pay competitively (e.g., "at" the market scale), but a primary factor is the

firm's ability to pay. Companies that can pay more than market scale are likely to be able to generate a larger pool of higher-qualified applicants, which translates to less required training time and higher operating efficiencies. Companies that pay less than market scale may be recent entrepreneurial start-up firms with limited CAPITAL. Sometimes these firms offer stock ownership incentives to attract highly qualified applicants. Compensation is directly linked the market's DEMAND for the products or services offered and the profits the company earns.

Every employee wants to be paid fairly in comparison with other employees. However, before pay rates are considered, each position needs to be studied and compared with other positions to assure an accurate hierarchy of jobs. This process assures internal equity, which is the second force that strongly shapes the company's compensation philosophy. Assuring internal equity requires that the company perform a thorough task analysis of each position. Task analyses look at the actual work performed by the job incumbent (job content) and the physical environment in which the work is performed (job context). In addition, the education, experience, knowledge, skills, and abilities of the desired job incumbent are identified. Common tasks are grouped and written into responsibility statements. Responsibility statements, budgetary responsibilities, reporting relationships, and a position summary statement are the bases for the job description. Care must be taken to ensure that essential job duties are accurately identified. (See EMPLOYMENT for additional information about this concern.) The job descriptions are then either compared to each other or to a predetermined measuring technique to determine their level of importance to the company. Job evaluations lead to the creation of a job hierarchy in which positions are listed in order of importance from most important to least important. Frequently positions are then grouped into labor (or salary) grades, and wage ranges are assigned using market survey data.

Individual considerations that are unique to each employee influence the actual salary or wage paid to the employee after the monetary range is defined. Individual salary determinants include the desire of the employer to hire the candidate, the level of performance as reflected by formal PERFORMANCE APPRAISALs, negotiating strength during the employment process and sometimes after employment, and SUPPLY and demand. Supply and demand recognizes the prevalence of applicants with unique knowledge and experiences in the recruiting area and the extent that the company needs someone with those unique capabilities.

A major portion of the employer's compensation expenses is allocated to pay for benefits that the company is either required to provide or offers voluntarily. Benefits that are voluntarily offered by employers are divided into three primary categories: (1) paid time off, (2) group INSURANCE, and (3) capital accumulation. Paid time off includes vacations and holidays but also may include work breaks, clean-up time at the end of the shift, sick pay, and personal time. Group insurance frequently includes medical, dental, life, and disability coverage. Capital accumulation includes the employers' portion of SOCIAL SECURITY payments and a wide variety of retirement benefit alternatives. Legally required benefits include Social Security, UNEMPLOYMENT insurance, WORKERS' COMPENSATION, and, in many cases, time off to attend to family medical needs. In a few states, employers are required to offer personal disability benefits, but this varies widely from state to state.

See also EMPLOYEE BENEFITS.

—John B. Abbott

competition

Competition has many meanings depending on the context in which the term is used. Almost all American businesspeople will say their market is highly competitive. Such business owners are concerned with both the actions of current competitors and the threats of potential competitors.

Companies often develop competitive strategies to differentiate themselves from other firms in their competitive environment. In this context, competition refers to the marketing strategies, product, pricing, distribution, or promotion strategies a firm uses to distinguish its offerings from competitors' offerings. A competitive environment is influenced by the actions of direct competitors, marketers of products that are substitutes for one another, and other marketers competing for the same consumers' purchasing power.

Sales managers use competition to motivate employees. In this context, competition is directed toward achieving a goal or measuring performance against other employees in the company. Sometimes sales managers will implement competitive PRICING STRATEGIES—that is, strategies designed to neutralize price as a competitive variable. A price-matching policy is one form of competitive pricing strategy.

The most common kind of competition is economic or market competition. This can range from a MONOPOLY, a market with only one seller, BARRIERS TO ENTRY, and no close substitutes; to PERFECT COMPETITION, a market with many sellers of similar products and ease of entry into the market. A market where there are many sellers of differentiated products is called MONOPOLISTIC COMPETITION. Perfectly competitive markets have the greatest degree of competition, while monopolistic markets have the least competition.

Business managers also use the term *nonprice competition*—that is, competing with other firms based on style, service, quality, availability, credit, or anything other than price. Nonprice competition is prevalent in markets where there are only a few firms (OLIGOPOLY).

See also MARKETING STRATEGY.

competitive advantage

Every day American businesses supply myriad products and services to consumers. The rational consumer is looking for the best value that can be found within his/her budget. Buyers evaluate products and services based on a variety of criteria. The primary purchasing criteria is the product's ability to satisfy the consumer's immediate need, but other decision criteria include price, appearance, quality, warranty, and service.

Producers understand consumers' buying habits and try to design into a product or service some unique characteristics that similar products from other producers do not have. Each producer hopes that the uniqueness of his or her product will induce the consumer to buy it instead of products made by other companies. This added uniqueness, intended to increase sales, is known as a *competitive advantage*.

Within the economic marketplace, producers also study products and services that compete with their own. If one company redesigns a product and includes new features, improves quality, or increases the product warranty, the changes are advertised with the goal of increasing the sales of their product and take potential sales away from the other producers. The uniqueness of competitive advantages like these, however, can be easily copied and duplicated by other producers. So most competitive advantages, such as quality, warranty, appearance, and product packaging, are short-lived.

Companies seek a competitive advantage that is not only unique but also is sustainable over extended periods of time. If the advantage cannot be easily duplicated, then it is sustainable over time. Probably the only sustainable competitive advantage that a company has is its employees—the human resources of the organization. It is only through a motivated, challenged, and rewarded workforce that the continuous stream of innovative new and improved products, with controlled manufacturing and distribution costs, can be developed and maintained.

—John B. Abbott

competitive intelligence   See MARKET INTELLIGENCE; SOCIETY FOR COMPETITIVE INTELLIGENCE PROFESSIONALS.

compounding, future value

Compounding is the process of finding an unknown future value from a known present value. Using a time line, compounding is moving forward in time from the present to some point in the future. Given the time value of money (assuming that INTEREST RATES are always positive), future values are always larger than present values.

For deposits and other INVESTMENTs where interest can, in turn, earn interest, compounding can be quite powerful, especially at higher rates of interest. Because INFLATION builds upon itself—that is, it compounds—uncontrolled inflation is quite damaging to the value of money and its PURCHASING power.

For a lump sum, the future value of some present amount is determined by the compounding formula $FV_n = PV[1+ir]^n$, where FV_n is the future value at some future point in time n, PV is the present value (the current amount of the lump sum), ir is the interest rate (expressed in decimal form) applicable to the situation in question, and the exponent n is the same future point in time for which the future value is to be determined. For instance, find the future value in three years of a current deposit of $100 at 10 percent compounded annually: $FV_3 = 100 [1.10]^3$. Simplifying the formula reduces this to $FV3 = 100[1.331] = 133.10$. Notice that 10 percent of $100 is $10, yet the future value adds more than $10 interest per year for three years to the lump sum. Compounding (interest earning interest) added $3.10 to this lump sum over three years.

It is sometimes necessary to determine the future value of an ANNUITY. While there is a formula for this, it is much easier to use a commonly published table of interest factors. For compounding, there are tables of future-value interest factors for lump sums (FVIFs) and for annuities (FVIFAs). To find the future value of a lump sum: $FV_n = PV[FVIF_{i,n}]$, where $FVIF$ is the lump-sum future-value interest factor for some interest rate i and for some time period n. To find the future value of an annuity: $FVA_n = PMT[FVIFA_{i,n}]$, where PMT is the regular annuity payment and $FVIFA$ is the annuity future-value interest factor for some interest rate i and for some time period n.

While using the published tables of future-value interest factors is easier than manually doing the number-crunching, it is much more convenient to find future values for lump sums and annuities using a financial calculator. Remembering that the interest factor tables carry the interest factors to only four digits to the right of the decimal, the results obtained from the use of a financial calculator are more accurate than using the tables. The published interest factor tables list interest factors only for whole-number interest rates. A financial calculator can compound using any interest rate.

See also RULE OF 72.

Comptroller of the Currency

The Comptroller of the Currency directs the Office of the Comptroller of the Currency (OCC), which charters, regulates, and supervises all national banks. The office also supervises the federal branches and agencies of foreign banks. Headquartered in Washington, D.C., the OCC has six district offices and an office in London to supervise the international activities of national banks.

The four objectives of the Comptroller of the Currency are

- to ensure the safety and soundness of the national BANKING SYSTEM

- to foster COMPETITION by allowing banks to offer new products and services
- to improve the efficiency and effectiveness of OCC supervision, including reducing regulatory burden
- to ensure fair and equal access to financial services for all Americans

In 1861 Secretary of the Treasury Salmon P. Chase recommended the establishment of a system of federally chartered national banks, each of which would have the power to issue standardized national bank notes based on U.S. BONDS held by the bank. In the National Currency Act of 1863, the administration of the new national banking system was vested in the newly created OCC and its chief administrator, the Comptroller of the Currency.

The law was completely rewritten and reenacted as the National Bank Act (1864), which authorized the Comptroller of the Currency to hire a staff of national bank examiners to supervise and periodically examine national banks. The act also gave the Comptroller authority to regulate lending and investment activities of national banks. Today the Comptroller is appointed by the president, with the advice and consent of the Senate, for a five-year term. The Comptroller also serves as a director of the FEDERAL DEPOSIT INSURANCE CORPORATION (FDIC) and of the Neighborhood Reinvestment Corporation.

OCC examiners conduct on-site reviews of national banks and supervise bank operations. The agency issues rules, legal interpretations, and corporate decisions concerning banking, bank investments, bank community development activities, and other aspects of bank operations. National bank examiners supervise domestic and international activities of national banks and perform corporate analyses. Examiners analyze a bank's loan and INVESTMENT portfolios, funds management, CAPITAL, earnings, liquidity, sensitivity to market RISK, and compliance with consumer-banking laws, including the Community Reinvestment Act. They review the bank's internal controls, internal and external AUDITING, and compliance with the law. They evaluate the bank management's ability to identify and control risk, particularly maturity matching (DURATION), and maintain collateral documentation.

In regulating national banks, the OCC has the power to

- examine the banks
- approve or deny applications for new charters, branches, capital, or other changes in corporate or banking structure
- take supervisory actions against banks that do not comply with laws and regulations or otherwise engage in unsound banking practices (i.e., remove officers and directors, negotiate agreements to change banking practices, and issue cease-and-desist orders as well as civil money penalties)
- issue rules and regulations governing bank investments, lending, and other practices

One of the reasons Congress passed the National Currency Act was to finance the Civil War. Although national banks no longer issue currency, they continue to play a prominent role in the nation's economic life. Today the OCC regulates and supervises more than 2,200 national banks and 56 federal branches and agencies of foreign banks in the United States, accounting for more than 55 percent of the total ASSETS of all U.S. commercial banks. Any bank with "national" in its name is chartered under the OCC. Banks can also choose to be chartered under state banking laws.

The OCC does not receive any appropriations from Congress. Instead, its operations are funded primarily by assessments on national banks. National banks pay for their examinations, and they pay for the OCC's processing of their corporate applications. The OCC also receives revenue from its investment INCOME, primarily from U.S. TREASURY SECURITIES.

Further reading
Office of the Comptroller of the Currency website. Available online. URL: www.occ.treas.gov.

computer-aided design, engineering, and manufacturing
Computer-aided design, engineering, and manufacturing (CAD, CAE, and CAM, respectively) are three stages in the industrial process that utilize computers to aid in the PRODUCTION of goods and SERVICES. CAD includes designing and drafting a product for manufacture. Many Americans have seen CAD systems in architects' offices, where architects take customers' ideas and requirements and create a computer model of the home or office. In a manufacturing environment, a client company or marketing division within the company will develop ideas for products which are then designed using a CAD system.

CAE is the use of computer systems to define and refine the tooling needed to produce a product. As Gary S. Vasilach reports, "If you can design for manufacturability, you are well on your way to minimizing variability and achieving zero defects. . . . Run the part through more electronic versions. Do more testing. Get it right. Pack more upfront engineering into the same time frame."

CAM, also called computer-integrated manufacturing (CIM), includes manufacturing engineering tasks such as programming numerically controlled machine tools and generating process plans outlining the steps needed to produce a part. CAM includes links to factory automation equipment and production management as well. CAM systems often include quality-control systems, materials and components testing, and monitoring of final products to ensure that they are within tolerance specifications.

CAD, CAE, and CAM flourished in the 1980s and early 1990s as computers became more powerful and able to handle more complex quantitative relationships. As Vasilach states, manufacturers adopted computer-controlled machine tools to improve efficiency and precision. Their problem "was being able to feed those machines with data in a timely manner. At the same time, people were looking at the ways and means to automate designs, to create drawings faster. Thus, there were two different systems." Since then CAD/CAM systems including hardware, software, networks, and factory floor equipment have been integrated into complete systems. Many computer companies developed specialized systems for each industry. One company, Policy Management Systems, Inc., developed software systems just for INSURANCE companies, allowing parent companies and agents throughout their system to write policies, assess risks, and manage operations. In some industries, like architecture, standardized, off-the-shelf CAD/CAM systems are available, while in many industries customized systems are designed. CAD/CAM systems are becoming increasing sophisticated and, with INTERNET communications, allow collaboration among design and manufacturing teams organized globally.

Further reading
Krouse, John, et al. "CAD/CAM basics," *Machine Design* 61, no. 15 (20 July 1989): C16–C22; ———. "CAE, CAD, and CAM at CMI." *Production*, 102, no. 5 (May 1990): 58–60; Vasilash, Gary S. "What Manufacturing Managers Should Know about CAD," *Production* 10, no. 1 (January 1989): 55–58.

Conference Board
The Conference Board is an international business organization headquartered in New York City. As stated on their website the Conference Board was created in 1916 during a period of intense criticism of "big business," and is a nonprofit group with a twofold purpose: "to improve the business enterprise system and enhance the contribution of business to society." Over 3,000 companies in 67 countries are members of the Conference Board.

While engaged in a variety of activities, the Conference Board is most widely known for its Consumer Confidence Index. Each month it sends a questionnaire to a sample of 5,000 households, with about 3,500 responses received. Households are asked to respond to five questions regarding

1. current business conditions in their area
2. expectations regarding business conditions in the next six months
3. current job availability in their area
4. expected job availability in the next six months
5. family income in the next six months

An index is constructed for each response covering the present situation and expectations, resulting in an overall Consumer Confidence Index, which is a leading indicator of future spending. Consumer confidence is closely correlated with UNEMPLOYMENT, INFLATION, and REAL INCOME changes.

Each month the index is compared to the previous month and a press release is issued and reported in the financial media. The base year is 1985, when the value was set at 100. In July 2000 the index was 141.7, a higher figure than the 139.2 rating for the previous month. Along with the University of Michigan's Consumer Sentiment Index, the Conference Board's Consumer Confidence Index is a closely watched statistic among STOCK MARKET analysts and investors. The dismalscientist.com website posts the current Conference Board index along with many other economic indicators.

Further reading
Conference Board website. Available on-line. URL: www.conferenceboard.org; Dismal Scientist website. Available on-line. URL: www.dismal.com/dismal/ ind_landing.asp.

conflict of interest
A conflict of interest can arise in almost any business situation where the well-being of individuals and businesses may differ. In business a conflict of interest exists when an employee's interests conflict with those of their employer, which may make the employee unable to represent the employer effectively. Employees are agents of the business they work for; implicitly or contractually, they are obligated to pursue the best interests of their employer. In a nonbusiness setting, the stereotypical example of a conflict of interest is the situation where a man or woman asks for advice about their loved one from a friend who is secretly in love with the same person.

Business law addresses numerous types of potential conflicts of interest. Agents are not allowed to deal with themselves as buyers. For example, a manager for a company that has a fleet of cars cannot sell a company car to himself. Similarly, employees in a grocery store will purchase something to eat from another cashier rather than themselves. In some situations conflict-of-interest rules extend to relatives of the agent, business associates, or other business organizations with which the agent is associated. If the employer consents to the sale, employees can sell company property to themselves. To avoid a potential conflict of interest, the employee must disclose all relevant information to the employer before dealing with the employer on his or her own behalf.

Another potential conflict of interest exists when an employee competes with the employer while acting as an agent for the employer. For example, employees generally cannot purchase property for themselves if their employer still desires to purchase the property, nor should they solicit customers for a planned competing business while still employed their current firm.

A third conflict-of-interest area exists when an employee acts on behalf of the other party to a transaction. Generally, an employee cannot act on behalf of the other party unless his or her employer knows about and consents to the action. As Mallor et al state, "Thus, one ordinarily cannot act as agent for both parties to a transaction without first disclosing the double role to, and obtaining the consent of, both principals."

The potential for conflict of interest exists in many business situations. The one most Americans encounter is in real-estate transactions. Only in the last decade have realtors been required to get signed acknowledgment from customers that they, the realtors, are agents of the seller. Also, in real-estate transactions it is common to have one closing attorney, acting on behalf of both the buyer and seller.

In recent years, conflicts of interest have become more important and visible in American business. In 2002, investment-banking firms were fined for pressuring company investment analysts to give favorable ratings to companies the investment-banking company was soliciting other business from. Investment-banking giant Merrill Lynch agreed to a $100 million fine and to change how it monitors and pays stock analysts, without admitting any wrongdoing. Similarly, accounting firms that audit companies and also provide business-consulting services to the same company are open to a potential conflict of interest. Since the Enron-Arthur Andersen case, many accounting firms have divested themselves of their business-consulting services, and many CORPORATIONS have discontinued the use of consulting services from their AUDITING company.

Part of the legal problems facing Enron Corporation involves company dealings with PARTNERSHIPS created and owned by company executives. These partnerships purchased ASSETS from the company and then sold them for significant profits for the partnership, not the company.

Conflict of interest may also arise for members of a company's BOARD OF DIRECTORS. Most boards include outside representatives, people who do not work for the company but are knowledgeable about the business and industry in which the company operates. Members of the board are not agents of the company and thus are not subject to the same conflict-of-interest rules. Under the MODEL BUSINESS CORPORATION ACT, board members can avoid conflict of interests when

- the transaction has been approved by a majority of the informed, disinterested directors
- the transaction has been approved by a majority of the shares held by informed, disinterested shareholders
- the transaction is fair to the corporation.

Further reading
Mallor, Jane P., A. James Barnes, Thomas Bowers, Michael J. Philips, and Arlen W. Langvardt. *Business Law and the Regulatory Environment,* 11th ed. Boston: McGraw-Hill, 2001; Schroeder, Michael, "Merrill Deal Spurs More Inquiries," *Wall Street Journal,* 23 May 2002, p. A3.

conglomerate

A conglomerate is a business that operates in more than one market. Usually conglomerates produce and sell many dissimilar PRODUCTs for different markets. Unlike VERTICAL INTEGRATION, in which a firm expands by acquiring or establishing company-owned operations at different stages of the production process; or horizontal integration, a combination of firms at the same level of COMPETITION, conglomerates represent corporate expansion into diverse areas, levels, and markets. Conglomerates are typically created by multiple mergers of previously independent companies.

In the United States, the creation of conglomerates was quite popular in the 1960s and again in the 1990s. In the 1960s, the economic logic for creating conglomerates was that a well-established MANAGEMENT team could efficiently operate many different types of businesses. Management efficiency would increase PROFITS and SHAREHOLDER value. During the 1990s, the sudden creation of CAPITAL by DOT-COM companies via INITIAL PUBLIC OFFERINGS allowed these companies to purchase many other similar and dissimilar firms. Company executives often cite SYNERGY and mutual benefits when creating conglomerates. Many Japanese corporations, including Mitsubishi and NEC, are considered conglomerates. U.S. companies such as Raytheon, United Technologies, and Disney are examples of conglomerates.

Legal challenges to conglomerates focus on the potential for reduced competition. Reciprocal trade agreements among member units in a conglomerate can limit the access of outside competitors. Conglomerate control of newspaper, radio, and television companies has raised fears of corporate censorship of journalists fearful of reporting negative news about their parent organization.

consent decree

Consent decree refers to a judicial order agreed to by all parties in a litigation. Thus it typically embodies a litigation settlement, most commonly the settlement of a public (government) prosecution. The defendant consents voluntarily to a court order mandating certain conduct on his or her part in order to avoid a court trial on the merits. For example, businesses charged with violations of U.S. securities and ANTITRUST LAWS often settle with government prosecutors in advance of trial. The terms of these settlements are embodied in consent decrees, sometimes referred to as consent orders.

Most consent decrees do not involve an admission of guilt by defendants. They merely agree to alter their activities to avoid the risk of being found guilty at trial, the costs of litigation, and the possibility that an adverse judgment might be used as precedent against them. Consent decrees are used to settle both criminal and civil prosecutions. The court issuing the decree retains the power to monitor compliance and sanction any noncompliance.

Further reading

Kane, Mary K. *Civil Procedure in a Nutshell,* 4th ed. Eagan, Minn.: West Group, 1996; Cammack, Mark E., and Norman, Garland. *Advanced Criminal Procedure in a Nutshell.* Eagan, Minn.: West Group, 2001.

consignment

Consignment is an arrangement in which the owner (consignor) delivers PRODUCTs to a seller (consignee), with the seller acting as agent for the owner in the sales process. The seller does not own the products; rather, the owner retains title to the products until they are sold. At that time the seller receives a commission for assisting with the sale of the item.

Consignment is typical in antique malls, art galleries, musical-instrument stores, and other businesses where an individual owner utilizes the skills and market contacts of an experienced businessperson to facilitate the sale of their possession. Consignment is one of three options within the category of sales transactions, called sales on trial. A sale on approval is an agreement in which goods are delivered to a buyer with the understanding that the buyer may use or test them to determine whether purchase is desirable. In a sale on approval, the title to the good and risk of ownership are not transferred until the buyer accepts the good. Because the title and risk of loss remain with the seller, goods held under a sale-on-approval agreement are not subject to claims from the buyer's creditors until the buyer accepts the good. Taking a car home from a dealership overnight would be an example of a sale on approval. If a buyer fails to notify the seller of his or her decision not to return the good, the buyer is considered to have purchased the good.

A second type of sales transaction is the sale or return in which goods are delivered to a buyer for resale to consumers with the understanding that the buyer has the right to return unsold items. Publishers and bookstores frequently use sale or return agreements allowing the bookstore to return for repayment unsold copies of a book. Since the buyer (the bookstore) has accepted the goods, the buyer is at risk for loss or damage, and the goods will be considered part of the buyer's ASSETS in any bankruptcy litigation.

Sales on consignment need to be clearly documented to avoid problems associated with the seller's creditors. Under the UNIFORM COMMERCIAL CODE (UCC), a consignor must (1) make sure that a sign indicating the consignor's interest is prominently displayed at the place of business, or (2) make sure that the merchant's creditors know that the merchant is generally in the business of selling goods owned by others, or (3) comply with the UCC's filing provisions. Most individuals are unlikely to be familiar with the requirements to protect their rights in consignment agreements. Many American consumers have found their assets attached as part of business bankruptcy proceedings from failure to comply with consignment regulations.

In international trade, many EXPORTING agreements are sales on consignment. The owner ships the product to the buyer, retaining title to the goods, and the importer pays for the goods when they are sold. The importer's bank will often act as trustee for the goods in this transaction.

Consignment has been scrutinized when used as a means to control the resale price of a manufacturer's product. This is known as vertical PRICE FIXING or resale price maintenance. Manufacturers are allowed to state a suggested retail price for products they sell to retailers, but it is illegal for the manufacturer to obligate a reseller to a specific price. If a consignment selling systems restrains price competition, it may be deemed unlawful.

Further reading

Mallor, Jane P., A. James Barnes, Thomas Bowers, Michael J. Phillips, and Arlen W. Langvardt. *Business Law and the Regulatory Environment,* 11th ed. Boston: McGraw-Hill, 2001.

consumer advocacy (consumerism)

Efforts to protect the rights of consumers are the basis of consumer advocacy, also called consumerism. Consumer advocacy has a long history in the United States. Upton Sinclair's book *The Jungle* (1906), describing deplorable worker-safety and unsanitary conditions in the meat-packing industry led "muckrakers" to challenge business practices. During the 1960s, Ralph Nader's book *Unsafe at Any Speed* (1965) challenged design practices in the U.S. automobile industry, particularly the design of General Motors' Corvair. Consumer advocacy is often not welcomed by industry. General Motors unsuccessfully used detectives to find information that would undermine Ralph Nader's claims.

Major U.S. consumer advocacy groups and agencies include the CONSUMER PRODUCT SAFETY COMMISSION (CPSC), the Office of Consumer Affairs, the Consumer Federation of America, and CONSUMERS UNION. As stated on its website, the CPSC is a federal agency created in 1972 to "protect the public against unreasonable risks of injuries and deaths associated with consumer PRODUCTS." The CPSC's most visible consumer-advocacy effort is its quarterly publication highlighting unsafe toys for children. The Office of Consumer Affairs addresses consumer complaints and provides consumer information services. Most states also have consumer-affairs offices.

The Consumer Federation of America, which includes over 260 organizations throughout the country, represents consumer interests in dialogues with policy makers and provides educational resources for consumers. Consumers Union, publisher of *Consumer Reports,* is a highly respected source of independent information for consumers. Unlike many industry magazines which derive their revenue from business advertisements, *Consumer Reports* is funded only by member contributions and grants. Consumers Union is well known for its independ-

ent testing of automobiles and other products. Positive and negative ratings by Consumers Union are closely watched by both consumers and businesses.

In addition to consumer education and publicity, consumer advocacy can include BOYCOTTS and CLASS-ACTION LAWSUITS. In the 1960s and 1970s, the UNITED FARM WORKERS, under the leadership of Cesar Chavez, gained support for farmworkers' unionizing efforts through boycotts. More recently, boycotts of tobacco-company products have been used by consumer advocates to influence business practices. Class-action lawsuits are increasingly used to challenge business safety and responsibility issues.

The BETTER BUSINESS BUREAU (BBB) is a business-sponsored organization providing services to consumers. The BBB attempts to resolve consumers' complaints against businesses and maintains files documenting such complaints.

Further reading

Consumer Federation of America website. Available on-line. URL: www.consumerfed.org; Consumer Product Safety Commission website. Available on-line. URL: www.cpsc.gov; Consumers Union website. Available on-line. URL: www.consumersunion.org.

consumer bankruptcy (insolvency)

Consumer bankruptcy or insolvency occurs when individuals with regular INCOMES can no longer afford to meet their payment obligations. Consumer bankruptcy is both a legal and business concern. Under Chapter 13 of the U.S. Bankruptcy Code, individuals can develop, under court supervision, plans to satisfy their creditors. Chapter 13 allows reductions in consumers' debts and/or extensions of time to pay debts. Consumers are also allowed to retain certain exempt ASSETS, usually their home, one motor vehicle, tools of their trade, and some other personal assets. Chapter 13 bankruptcy is available to individuals and sole proprietors of businesses, subject to limitations on unsecured debts and secured debts.

Chapter 7 of the U.S. Bankruptcy Code provides the option of liquidation or straight bankruptcy. Liquidation, selling all assets and dividing the proceeds among creditors, is available to individuals, partnerships or corporations operating in the United States.

Consumer bankruptcy is a major concern for U.S. businesses. CONSUMPTION spending represents two-thirds of U.S. GROSS DOMESTIC PRODUCT. Consumer spending is critical to the economy, but American consumers owe over $1 trillion to creditors. Business interests, particularly consumer-finance companies, complain U.S. personal-bankruptcy laws are too lenient. Early in 2001, the George W. Bush administration pushed for increased restrictions to consumer-bankruptcy laws.

CONSUMER ADVOCACY groups criticize lenders for inadequate disclosure of fees and rates to consumers and for irresponsible lending practices. Access to credit is critical to the sale of many consumer PRODUCTS. Businesses balance the need for sales against the credit-worthiness of customers. Lenders use the FIVE C'S OF CREDIT in evaluating lending requests and review credit-agency reports before extending credit. Nevertheless, consumer bankruptcy remains a major issue in the U.S. economy.

Further reading
Mallor, Jane P., A. James Barnes, Thomas Bowers, Michael J. Phillips, and Arlen W. Langvardt. *Business Law and the Regulatory Environment,* 11th ed. Boston: McGraw-Hill, 2001.

consumer behavior
Consumer behavior is comprised of the processes and factors consumers use to make purchase decisions. To most people, consumer behavior just "is." Many consumers only vaguely recognize the factors that influence their actions or the process they go through in making choices. But to marketers, understanding consumer behavior is critical to developing a successful MARKETING STRATEGY.

The first step in the CONSUMER BUYING PROCESS is problem or need recognition. Before consumers consider making purchases, a wide variety of social circumstances and psychological factors influence their problem or need recognition. This can be as simple as deciding one is thirsty or as complex as deciding to get married. In both situations, consumers are influenced by both personal and interpersonal forces in their decisions.

Personal or psychological factors—including needs, perceptions, attitudes, learning, and self-concept—can all influence people's actions. In MASLOW'S HIERARCHY OF NEEDS, there are basic physiological needs, such as thirst. People typically address their physiological needs before allocating time and money to meet higher-order needs. Perceptions are the process of receiving, organizing, and assigning meaning to stimuli detected by the five senses. Humans constantly receive stimuli from their environment. Some of the stimuli, like the sound of a bird, are natural, but others, like the roar of a jet, are man-made. Many man-made stimuli are marketing messages, and the typical American consumer is exposed to thousands of such messages daily—for example, commercials, signs, labels, and TRADEMARKS.

Marketers understand that one aspect of consumer behavior is reaction to stimuli. Consumers tend to pay selective attention to stimuli, screening out unpleasant or unfamiliar sensory information. As part of the perceptual process, people also distort meanings from stimuli, changing their interpretation to be consistent with their beliefs, in addition to selectively retaining sensory images. Relatively new studies indicate that significant events cause chemical changes in human brains, explaining why emotional situations can be recalled vividly many years later. Part of the task for marketers is to understand how people interpret stimuli. Understanding

consumers' perceptions can help in designing products, packaging, and promotions, especially when considering new TARGET MARKETS.

Learning takes place through changes in behavior resulting from experience and observation. A thirsty person will observe signs of water keenly. Attitudes are consumers' learned predispositions. Dentists, for example, know most of their customers come into their offices with fear and trepidation developed from past painful learning experiences.

A last psychological factor influencing consumer behavior is people's self-concept, or personal "picture." This can include their "real" self, self-image, and ideal self. Numerous popular psychology books have been written about the differences in men's versus women's self-image, usually suggesting that men see themselves as better and women as worse than their real selves. Consumer behavior is often influenced by self-image and by ideal self-image— that is, how we would like to be seen. Even a simple need like thirst can be influenced by self-concept. In recent years, marketers have made millions of dollars selling bottled water. Chemical studies usually show bottled water to be of no better quality than tap water, but blue bottles and French names appeal to consumers' self-image.

As stated earlier, consumer behavior is influenced by both psychological and social forces. The power of others to influence behavior is well known to marketers. Social influences are typically categorized into four groups: culture, social class, reference groups, and families.

Culture refers to values, norms, tastes, and preferences passed from one generation to the next. Many people, for instance, buy the same goods and services that their parents purchased. Marketers also recognize many distinct subcultures in the United States, which are often the source of new ideas and trends adopted into the mainstream culture. The fastest-growing subculture in the United States is the Hispanic population. Both the Republican and Democratic parties recognize the importance of Hispanic voters and develop specific messages to appeal to them. (American marketers are also beginning to distinguish subcultures within the Hispanic population.)

Social class is a powerful influence on consumer behavior. Social class includes peoples' education, occupations, and habitats. The phrase "keeping up with the Joneses" refers to the common practice of people striving to display a lifestyle equal to that of their neighbors. Realtors often quietly relate stories of people selling empty houses, which had originally been purchased in order to live in the "right" neighborhood, even if it cost more than the family could afford.

Similar to the factor of social class is that of reference groups—that is, groups with which consumers identify. The behavior of a reference group often influences individual consumer behavior, as in the purchase of conspicuous items such as automobiles. Few Americans recognize that U.S. products and trends are closely watched and influence consumer trends in other countries. American music, movies, and dress are copied by teenagers around the world, and the use of celebrity spokespeople in marketing campaigns is often aimed at people who aspire to be like those celebrities.

Lastly, families influence individual consumer behavior. In the United States changing family DEMOGRAPHICS—including more single-parent households, children returning to the "nest" households, and two-adult but unrelated households—influence purchasing decisions. Home builders have constructed more two-bedroom, two-bath dwellings for the two unrelated adults market. Numerous time-saving products have been created for the single-parent market, and parents are still adjusting to children returning home after college. One source stated that 35 percent of college graduates move home.

Further reading
Boone, Louis E., and David Kurtz. *Contemporary Marketing.* 10th ed. Fort Worth: Dryden Press, 2001; Etzel, Michael J., Bruce J. Walker, and William J. Staunton. *Marketing,* 12th ed. Boston: McGraw-Hill, 2001.

consumer buying process
The consumer buying process is the series of steps consumers typically go through in making a purchase decision. Often the whole process will only take seconds or a few minutes, while other times it may take years. Regardless of how long it takes, consumers generally go through six steps when making a purchase decision:

- problem or need recognition
- search
- alternative evaluation
- purchase decision and action
- post-purchase evaluation

Problem or need recognition initiates the buying process. Dissatisfaction with current PRODUCTS, running out of supply of an item, or a changed financial status can stimulate consumer needs. Most consumers are creatures of habit and will repurchase the product they always use. This helps firms who are the established leaders in their markets but creates a barrier for new competitors. New competitors look for dissatisfied customers; those who are new to an area; and those who, through inheritance, divorce, or other situations have significantly changed their purchasing power.

In the search stage, consumers identify different products that will solve their problem. For everyday purchases like milk or bread, consumers usually quickly determine alternative sources of products to meet their needs. For high-involvement purchases like homes or automobiles, the search process will take longer and probably include searching for objective sources of information. Many consumers will only consider a few possible choices when searching for products to solve their problem. Marketers refer to the choices considered as the "evoked set." Firms that have severely disappointed consumers in the past or who are new to the market often have difficulty even being considered by consumers. For many years a significant portion of American consumers would not even consider American-made automobiles, having been disappointed with the performance of their last American-made cars.

In the alternative-evaluation stage, consumers consider and weigh the choices available. Again, with everyday-type purchases this stage can take seconds, while for a specialty item it may take months. Marketers respond to the alternative-evaluation stage by providing and promoting features they hope will influence consumers' evaluation of their products.

There can be considerable variation in the evaluation stage. One marketer found that it took him half the time it took his wife to do the family grocery shopping. Going to the supermarket together, he found out why. His wife read the ingredient labels, while he just purchased what was on the shopping list.

The purchase decision and action is, as the term suggests, the determination of which product will best satisfy one's need and the action of making the actual deal. Salespeople refer to this stage as the "closing." For everyday purchases, the goal is to make the purchase as quickly and effortlessly as possible. For complex decisions like a real estate closing, the purchase process can take weeks.

Post-purchase evaluation addresses the questions "Did I make the right decision?" and "Did I get a good deal?" Marketers refer to this anxiety as cognitive dissonance. Good marketers, recognizing that word-of-mouth is almost always the best form of promotion and that new customers are almost always more difficult and expensive to find than maintaining existing customers, try to reduce consumers' cognitive dissonance. Realtors will offer buyer's insurance, protecting the purchaser against unforeseen problems. Service providers like dentists and doctors will often call clients to see how they are doing after a procedure. Thank-you notes convey appreciation and also remind consumers about their purchase process.

Further reading
Boone, Louis E., and David L. Kurtz. *Contemporary Marketing,* 10th ed. Fort Worth: Dryden Press, 2001.

consumer credit counseling service
A consumer credit counseling service (CCCS) is a nonprofit organization that assists individuals and families in the United States with BUDGETING and credit resolution. CCCSs are members of the National Foundation for Credit Counseling (NFCC), which was established in 1951 by

retail credit companies to provide financial counseling and education services. There are approximately 1,300 CCCSs in the country and over 1.5 million households who utilize their services annually.

CCCSs primarily provide debt-management services. In a debt-management plan, individuals document all of their financial liabilities as well as their INCOME and then voluntarily make payments to creditors through the CCCS. Payments are dispersed by the CCCS to creditors, who usually agree to eliminate interest and waive late or over-limit fees for consumers utilizing debt-management plans. Participants normally pay a $30 fee to set up a plan and are charged up to $24 per month to service the plan.

Debt-management plans are an alternative to filing for personal bankruptcy (Chapters 7 or 13), debt-consolidation loans, or home-equity loans. Personal bankruptcy filing is handled through the court system and stays on an individual's credit history for many years. Personal consolidation loans may reduce INTEREST RATES or monthly payments by extending the length of the loan, but they do not eliminate interest payments. Home-equity loans are tax-deductible and often at a lower interest rate than unsecured personal credit loans, but they use the borrower's home as security for the loan.

The major source of funding for CCCSs comes from the credit industry. Creditors who participate in CCCS programs contribute an amount equal to 15 percent of consumer payments to the local CCCS. The benefit to credit companies is they get their money back. The benefit to consumers is they restructure their loans into lower and usually interest-free payments that they usually can afford and thus get out of debt. The process also provides education to consumers about the use of credit. Excessive CREDIT CARD debt is a major problem in the United States, especially among young people with little knowledge of or experience in the use of credit.

See also PERSONAL FINANCE.

Further reading
National Foundation for Credit Counseling website. Available on-line. URL: www.nfcc.org.

Consumer Credit Protection Act

Passed in 1968, the Consumer Credit Protection Act (CCPA) protects employees from being discharged by their employers when their wages have been garnished and limits the amount of employees' earnings which may be garnished per week. Garnishment is the seizing of a person's property, wages, or money to satisfy a judgment. Generally creditors use garnishment as a last resort to gain payment from people they are owed money. Frequently there are few ASSETS available to garnish, aside from wages.

Employee earnings include salaries, commissions, bonuses, and INCOME from pension or retirement programs. The CCPA limits the amount a creditor can garnish

to 25 percent of the debtor's weekly disposable income or the amount by which the person's weekly take-home income exceeds 30 times the current federal MINIMUM WAGE. The smaller of the two choices is the limit on the amount that can be garnished. In court orders for child support or alimony, the CCPA allows up to 50 percent of an employee's disposable earnings to be garnished. Disposable income is defined under the act as income after deductions for taxes, SOCIAL SECURITY payments, and state retirement-system contributions.

The CCPA is administered and enforced by the Employment Standards Administration's Wage and Hourly Division, a division of the U.S. DEPARTMENT OF LABOR. Violations of the CCPA may result in reinstatement of a discharged employee with back pay and the restoration of garnished amounts. Employers who willfully violate the discharge provisions of the law may be prosecuted and subject to up to a $1,000 fine and imprisonment of up to one year, or both.

The Consumer Credit Protection Act applies to all states, but states are allowed to pass laws that eliminate garnishment, and many have. Often employers have fired workers whose earnings have been garnished, citing the added bookkeeping expense associated with complying with a judgment. The law allows states to prohibit firing of employees whose wages have been garnished.

The FAIR DEBT COLLECTION PRACTICES ACT (1977), an amendment to the Consumer Credit Protection Act, defines forbidden debt-collection practices, including harassment, false or misleading representation, and other unfair practices.

Further reading
Fisher, Bruce D., and Michael J. Phillips. *The Legal, Ethical and Regulatory Environment of Business,* 8th ed. Cincinnati: Thomson/South-Western, 2003; U.S. Department of Labor website. Available on-line. URL: www.dol.gov.siteindex.htm.

Consumer Price Index

The Consumer Price Index (CPI) is a statistical measure of the average prices paid by consumers for a typical "market basket" of goods and SERVICES. Measuring the rate of change in prices is important to policy makers. Price changes are a critical concern in MONETARY POLICY, essential in evaluating ECONOMIC CONDITIONS, and a major factor when indexing spending and taxes. The CPI is an important and controversial measure of price changes. The controversy centers on how the CPI is calculated and, thus, whether it is representative of INFLATION as experienced by American consumers. Most U.S. economists agree the CPI overstates the rate of inflation experienced by American consumers.

Calculated by the BUREAU OF LABOR STATISTICS (BLS) since 1917, the CPI is measured monthly by sampling prices around the country for a "typical market basket" of goods and services purchased. An average price for each good and service is derived from the sampling procedure, which is then multiplied by the assumed amount typical households purchase. This process "weights" the goods and services by the relative importance in consumers' budgets. The sum of the prices times quantities are then divided by the cost of the same goods and services in a base year to create a price index.

$$\text{Price index} = \frac{\text{cost of market basket today}}{\text{cost of market basket in base year}} \times 100$$

One of the problems with the CPI is what is "typical." Especially in the 1990s and early 21st century, rapid changes in technology have made many new products available to consumers. For example, cellular telephones, which have been available since the early 1990s, were not included in the CPI until 1998. Similarly, the CPI used the price of coal as a measure of the cost of heating long after it was replaced by heating oil and natural gas in most American homes.

Related to the problem of what constitutes typical purchases by consumers is the issue of quality changes. American consumers are paying more for health care but also have significantly improved products and services available to them. The CPI does not accurately distinguish between increased prices and higher prices for improvements in quality. The U.S. Congress created commissions to investigate the country's Consumer Price Index in 1961 (Stigler Commission) and again in 1997 (CPI Commission). The CPI Commission estimated changes in quality and introduction of new PRODUCTS resulted in approximately a half percentage point upward bias in the index.

Another problem is that the CPI does not always capture changes in CONSUMER BEHAVIOR. Because the amount of each product is fixed in the index, the CPI does reflect consumer substitution. For example, if citrus fruit prices rise rapidly due to a freeze in the southern part of the country, consumers will likely substitute other fruit products in their purchases, but the CPI reflects the amount of citrus fruits typically purchased. Consumers' cost of fruit will therefore be lower than the amount estimated in the index. In 1997 the CPI Commission estimated this substitution bias overestimated inflation by 0.4 percentage points.

The CPI Commission also reported two other smaller sources of bias measuring the index. Most sampling takes place during the week, but retailers often reduce prices on weekends, and thus the index does not accurately reflect the prices paid by consumers. Similarly, the Bureau of Labor Statistics rotates the retail stores included in the sampling procedure each year, but the Commission found that the process does not fully reflect consumers' substitution of discount and superstore outlets for traditional retailers.

As stated earlier, the CPI is used to measure the change in prices paid, reflecting the cost of living. The CPI is used to address the question: "How much more INCOME will consumers need to be just as well off at the current price level as compared to old prices?" Private contracts for products, borrowing, and approximately one-third of the FEDERAL BUDGET are automatically escalated each year by the change in the CPI. Many union wage agreements (COST OF LIVING ADJUSTMENTS) and SOCIAL SECURITY payments are examples of contracts tied to changes in inflation as measured by the CPI. Even small changes in the CPI, when compounded over time, result in large changes in wages and payments.

The Bureau of Labor Statistics produces two other inflation indices, the PRODUCER PRICE INDEX (PPI) and the GDP deflator.

See also PRICE INDEXES.

Further reading
Boskin, Michael J. "The CPI Commission," *Business Economics* 32, no. 2 (April 1997): 60–63.

Consumer Product Safety Commission

The Consumer Product Safety Commission (CPSC) is a federal agency created in 1972. The CPSC's mission is to "protect the public against unreasonable risks of injuries and deaths associated with consumer PRODUCTS." The commission has jurisdiction over 15,000 types of consumer products and issues safety standards for everything from bicycle helmets to matchbooks.

Certain consumer products (automobiles and food products, for example) are under the jurisdiction of other federal agencies (DEPARTMENT OF TRANSPORTATION and FOOD AND DRUG ADMINISTRATION, respectively.)

The CPSC uses a variety of methods to ensure product safety, including

- developing voluntary standards with industry
- issuing and enforcing mandatory standards; banning consumer products if no feasible standard adequately protect the public
- obtaining recall of unsafe products or arranging for their repair
- conducting research on potential product hazards
- informing and educating consumers

The CPSC administers five laws:

- Consumer Product Safety Act
- Flammable Fabrics Act
- Federal Hazardous Substances Act
- Poison Prevention Packaging Act of 1970
- Refrigerator Safety Act of 1956

The CPSC is composed of five members appointed by the president, by and with the consent of the Senate, for terms of seven years. The commission attempts to use voluntary standards and "product safety triangles"—government, industry, and consumers—to ensure product safety, and it will regulate industries when necessary.

Businesses do not want the negative publicity associated with the CPSC's determination that their product is unsafe. One of the most visible CPSC activities is the evaluation of toys that present choking hazards for children less than three years old. Some of the safety standards set by the CPSC include standards for lawn darts, swimming-pool slides, automated garage-door openers, insulation, and wood-burning appliances.

Further reading
Consumer Product Safety Commission website. Available on-line. URL: http://cpsc.gov.

consumer protection

Consumer protection refers to a wide variety of regulations, primarily issued and enforced at the federal level by the FEDERAL TRADE COMMISSION (FTC), affecting American consumers. Consumer protection includes regulation of consumer credit, product safety, warranties, and TELEMARKETING.

The major consumer-protection laws regulating consumer credit include the following:

- Fair Credit Reporting Act (1971): Requires credit-reporting SERVICES to maintain accurate, relevant, and recent information; provide access to credit information only to bona fide users; inform consumers who are turned down or have their interest costs raised and provide reasons for the change; allow consumers to review their files and correct any inaccurate information.
- Fair Credit Billing Act (1975): Requires creditors to mail bills at least 14 days prior to the payment-due date, customers to notify creditors in writing within 60 days regarding billing-error complaints; and allows merchants to give cash discounts.
- Equal Credit Opportunity Act (1975; expanded in 1977): Makes creditor discrimination based on sex, race, national origin, religion, age, receipt of public assistance, or marital status illegal.
- CONSUMER CREDIT PROTECTION ACT (1968): Requires prompt written acknowledgment of consumer billing complaints and investigation of billing errors by creditors.
- Consumer Product Safety Act (1972): Created the CONSUMER PRODUCT SAFETY COMMISSION as an independent regulatory agency issuing safety standards and rules banning hazardous products; the commission also brings lawsuits against producers of hazardous consumer products.
- Magnusson-Moss Warranty Act (1975): Requires simple, clear, and conspicuous presentation of certain information in written warranties to consumers. The act does not require sellers to provide warranties, only requires clear presentation of information in warranties.

- Telemarketing and Consumer Fraud and Abuse Prevention Act (1994): Requires the FTC to develop regulations defining and prohibiting deceptive and abusive telemarketing practices. One regulation allows telemarketing only during the hours of 8 A.M. to 9 P.M., local time. Another regulation prohibits threats, intimidation, or use of profanity in telemarketing activities.

See also WARRANTY.

Further reading
Mallor, Jane P., A. James Barnes, Thomas Bowers, Michael J. Philips, and Arlen W. Langvardt. *Business Law and the Regulatory Environment,* 11th ed. Boston: McGraw-Hill, 2001.

Consumers Union

Consumers Union (CU) publishes *Consumer Reports* magazine, a premier independent source of information for American consumers. Founded in 1936 by a group of concerned professors, labor leaders, journalists, and engineers, CU is known for its testing and rating of consumer PRODUCTS. To maintain its independence, CU purchases every product tested and does not accept grants. Instead it relies on member subscriptions, which were only 4,000 in 1936 but today exceed 5 million.

A positive Consumers Union review can create significant impact in the marketplace. In the mid-1960s CU's recommendation of the Toyota Corolla helped the Japanese manufacturer break into the U.S. market. Ralph Nader, author of *Unsafe at Any Speed* (1965), a highly critical assessment of General Motors' Corvair, was a member of CU's BOARD OF DIRECTORS for eight years. CU also supported the publication of *Silent Spring* (1963), Rachel Carson's environmental classic, with a special CU edition of the book.

CU's National Testing and Research Center in Yonkers, N.Y., is the largest nonprofit education and consumer product-testing center in the world. CU's safety and repair reports for automobiles are among their most widely used consumer-information service. CU also maintains three advocacy offices in Washington, D.C., San Francisco, and Austin, testifying before federal and state legislatures, petitioning government agencies, and filing consumer interest lawsuits.

Further reading
Consumers Union website. Available on-line. URL: www.consumersunion.org.

consumption

In everyday living, consumption is the act of using or consuming things, but in business consumption refers to the level of current spending for new goods and services; in economics and business statistics, it is the amount of spending by households for currently produced goods and SERVICES. The purchase of a used car or home is not included in current consumption statistics, because it was included during the period of time when it was purchased.

Consumption spending is the largest component of total spending in NATIONAL INCOME ACCOUNTING. Because consumption represents two-thirds of total spending, it is the most closely watched component. Economists analyze the level and changes in the level of consumption spending in the economy. They have developed numerous theories regarding what factors influence consumption, the major one being current INCOME, since without income most people do little consumption spending. A variety of other factors influence peoples' consumption decisions, including expectations, WEALTH, and access to credit.

Expectations play an important role in current spending decisions. College seniors often purchase a car on the expectation of graduating and getting a good-paying job. Nobel Prize–winning economist Milton Friedman proposed the permanent-income hypothesis, suggesting consumption is determined by what people consider to be their permanent income rather than their actual income. Permanent income is what people expect to earn annually, not including transitory income or sudden windfalls such as prizes or one-time tax cuts, which temporarily increase their income.

Since the late 1990s, wealth has become an increasingly important consideration in consumption spending by Americans, many of whom first invested in the STOCK MARKET in the early 1990s. By 1999 most investors had accumulated significant increases in the value of their portfolios, especially if they had invested in technology companies. Sales of luxury cars and high-priced California real estate soared based on newly acquired wealth. When technology stocks began to fall in early 2000, many Americans' wealth declined, and with it their consumption spending diminished. Alan Greenspan, chairman of the FEDERAL RESERVE SYSTEM, has frequently analyzed the "wealth effect" on consumer spending. Economists also recognize that expectations of wealth through inheritance influence current spending.

During the 1990s American consumers went on a credit binge, and one estimate at the end of the decade had consumer credit totaling $1.3 trillion. Credit and access to credit influences current consumer spending. Many college students have learned the hard way how easy it is to use credit for current consumption spending and become deep in debt as a result. Some consumer spending, of homes and automobiles particularly, is influenced by INTEREST RATES charged for financing, but much of this spending is limited by the maximum credit-level allowed.

Retail companies study changes in consumption spending to anticipate changes in DEMAND for their goods and services. Consumption of some products and services, such as health care, are relatively insensitive to changes in income or credit; while other products, leisure travel and appliances, are sensitive to changes in income. Manufacturers also study changes in consumption spending when making PRODUCTION-planning schedules and long-term CAPITAL investment decisions. Governments keep track of consumption spending in order to predict changes in sales tax revenue.

U.S. consumption statistics are available in the *Survey of Current Business Statistics,* published by the Department of Commerce.

Further reading
Department of Commerce website. Available on-line. URL: www.doc.gov.

consumption tax

Consumption taxes are the various taxes imposed on the purchase of goods and SERVICES. Sales, excise, and value-added tax (VAT) are the most common types of consumption taxes, with sales taxes being the most visible type. Many international visitors are shocked the first time a tax is added to the price of the PRODUCT they are purchasing. Americans, however, generally support the use of sales taxes over other forms of taxation, rationalizing that "everyone has to pay it" and "you only have to pay a little at a time." In the United States, sales taxes are commonly imposed by state and sometimes local governments, so sales-tax rates vary around the country. In addition, many states exempt certain categories of goods, usually food and clothing, from sales taxes.

A major controversy has arisen regarding whether to require E-COMMERCE businesses to collect and remit sales taxes. Presidents Bill Clinton and George W. Bush have both delayed implementation of INTERNET commerce sales taxation. Supporters argue taxation would discourage growth of this new industry, while opponents, including many state treasurers and retail "brick-and-mortar" companies, complain it reduces tax revenue and gives an unfair advantage to Internet-based companies.

Generally excise taxes which usually comprise a fixed amount per unit of a good, are imposed by the federal government. The federal excise tax on gasoline is charged in the form of cents per gallon. Excise taxes on liquor and cigarettes are similarly based on cents per gallon and cents per pack, respectively. Government agencies rarely collect consumption taxes directly. Instead, sales and excise taxes are typically collected by retailers and remitted to the respective government treasuries. Excise taxes are sometimes used to implement the benefits principle in government policy: the idea that those citizens who benefit from the government program or service should pay for it, while those citizens who do not utilize the program or service should not have to pay for it. The excise tax on gasoline, which is directed into the national highway TRUST fund for building and maintaining roadways, is an example of an excise tax based on the benefits principle. Excise taxes are also sometimes called "sin and vice" taxes and are imposed to discourage CONSUMPTION of certain products. Higher excise taxes increase the price of products, and, given the law of DEMAND and ELASTICITY OF DEMAND, a higher price will have a major or minor impact on quantity demanded.

The United States, unlike Canada and most of Europe, does not have a value-added tax (VAT). Many economists argue a VAT would be preferable to the myriad of income taxes currently used in the country. In a VAT system, goods are taxed at each stage of the production process with the tax incorporated as part of the cost to producers. For example, farmers produce wheat, which is sold to flour companies. The difference between the revenue from the sale and cost of seed, fertilizer, and other inputs the farmer used is the farmer's value added; this would then be taxed. Next, the flour company would take the wheat, convert it into flour, and sell it to a bread company. The difference between the cost of the wheat plus other inputs and the INCOME received from the bread company would be the flour company's value added, and the VAT would be applied. The bread company would pay a VAT based on their value added, and it would be incorporated in the price consumers would pay.

Economists argue a VAT would discourage consumption and therefore encourage savings. Savings provide funds for investment, which in turn increases a country's, CAPITAL resources, expanding its production capacity. Economists point to the current income-tax system as having almost infinite numbers of loopholes and discouraging productive activity through higher tax rates as peoples' incomes increase. Economists also recognize consumption taxes are regressive. Lower-income consumers typically spend a higher percentage of their income on sales-taxable items than upper-income consumers do, and therefore they pay a higher percentage of their income in the form of sales taxes.

Further reading
Ruffin, Roy J., and Paul R. Gregory. *Principles of Economics,* 7th ed. Boston: Addison Wesley, 2000.

contestable market theory

Contestable market theory suggests that in markets where the costs of entering and leaving are very low, existing firms are continually threatened by the entry of new competitors. Contestable market theory challenges one of the assumptions of PERFECT COMPETITION: that a large number of firms is needed to maintain COMPETITION and eliminate economic PROFITS.

A contestable market is one in which firms can enter and leave the market without incurring significant COSTS. Fixed costs—costs that are required to start a business and do not change as output expands—act as a barrier to entry to would-be competitors. If new competitors can enter and exit a market without large expenditures, they can take advantage of market conditions when prices and profits

are high and leave a market when prices are low. Many types of direct consumer sales, such as cosmetics, health-care PRODUCTS, and consumer information SERVICES, can be entered and exited at relatively little cost. When a new product or service suddenly becomes popular, the few existing firms make economic profits. Seeing opportunities, new competitors enter the market, driving down prices and eliminating profits. Once the market price has dropped, some firms will exit the market.

Recognizing the threat of potential entrants into contestable markets, existing firms will often cut prices and expand output to reduce the incentives for new competitors to enter their market. Contestable market theory is used to explain why firms with local monopolies or few competitors do not try to charge higher prices and maximize profits.

See also BARRIERS TO ENTRY; MONOPOLY.

Further reading
Miller, Roger Leroy. *Economics Today*. Boston: Addison Wesley, 2001.

contract

A contract is an agreement between two or more parties creating obligations (promises) that are recognized and enforceable by law. For example, the author of this book and its publisher have entered into a lengthy written contract detailing each others' obligations. Contracts may also be reached orally or electronically, but the Statute of Frauds incorporated as part of the Uniform Commercial Code and its successor statutes require certain contracts relating to realty, debts, marriage, sales, and those that take more than a year to perform to be in writing. Enforcement of contractual obligations is normally accomplished by means of court orders and remedies, although the parties to contracts may generally agree to submit their disputes to mediation or ARBITRATION or to pay a reasonable sum ("liquidated damages") in the event of a breach of contract.

There are many different types of contracts: sales, LICENSING, FRANCHISING, cost-plus, requirements, distribution, installment, procurement, etc. Some contracts, especially consumer contracts, are standardized on printed forms. Contracts and contract terms can be implied from the circumstances surrounding the parties' actions and have traditionally been governed by COMMON LAW doctrines regarding their formation, terms, and remedies. Most U.S. commercial contracts are governed by the UNIFORM COMMERCIAL CODE (UCC), a widely adopted statutory body of law. International commercial contracts may be governed by the Convention on the International Sale of Goods (CISG), to which the United States is a party.

Further reading
Rohwer, Claude, D., and Anthony M. Skrocki. *Contracts in a Nutshell,* 5th ed. Eagan, Minn.: West Group, 2000.

cooperative

A cooperative is a business owned and controlled by the people who use its SERVICES and whose benefits are derived and distributed equitably on the basis of use. Cooperative user-owners are generally called members. Cooperatives are similar to private businesses, but members benefit based on their use of cooperative services, and earnings are allocated to members based on the amount of business they do with the cooperative. Usually incorporated under state laws, cooperatives elect a BOARD OF DIRECTORS and hire a manager to run day-to-day operations, but unlike private enterprises, they do not seek to make a profit.

Cooperatives are organized to

- improve bargaining power
- reduce costs
- obtain products or services
- create new and expand existing marketing opportunities
- improve the qualities of products or services
- increase INCOME

Because cooperatives are state-chartered, cooperative members, like SHAREHOLDERS of CORPORATIONS, have limited LIABILITY. Unlike corporations, where voting is based on the number of shares of stock held, in most cooperatives each member has one vote. In the United States, cooperatives, like S CORPORATIONS, are subject to single-tax treatment. Most PROFITS from a cooperative are distributed to members as patronage refunds, which are taxable income for members. CAPITAL for a cooperative comes from the members rather than from outside investors. Cooperatives, like any private enterprise, also borrow funds as needed from traditional lending institutions; the largest single category of cooperatives in the United States is CREDIT UNIONS. In addition, there are thousands of health-care, news-service, consumer, and agricultural cooperatives.

In the United States, the Philadelphia Contributionship for the Insurance of Houses from Loss by Fire, created in 1752, is said to have been the first cooperative in the country. Organized by Benjamin Franklin this cooperative is still in existence. Many cooperatives follow the principles adopted by the Rochdale Equitable Pioneers Society, established in England in 1844 by 28 craftsmen and entrepreneurs to purchase supplies and consumer goods cooperatively.

- open membership
- one member, one vote
- cash trading
- membership education
- political and religious neutrality
- no unusual risk assumption
- limitation on the number of shares owned
- limited interest on stock

- goods sold at regular retail prices
- net margins distributed according to patronage

The Grange, founded in Washington, D.C. 1867, was a major agricultural cooperative, and by 1920 there were over 14,000 farmer cooperatives operating in the United States. By 1995 that number was reduced to 4,000, primarily farm-supply and grain and oilseed marketing coops. Farm Credit Service, established in 1916, is the country's oldest financial credit cooperative.

Further reading

U.S. Department of Agriculture. *Co-ops 101: An Introduction to Cooperatives.* Washington, D.C.: U.S. Department of Agriculture, Rural Development Cooperative Information Report 55, May 1999.

copy

Copy is a term for the words and illustrations used in an advertisement; *copy thrust* is what the words and illustrations should communicate to the target audience. A central part of any ADVERTISING campaign, copy is usually developed by advertising specialists for their clients.

Whether a part of billboard, brochure, television, radio, DIRECT MAIL, or other paid element of MARKETING COMMUNICATIONS, copy is generally designed to attract attention, hold interest, arouse desire, and result in action. This is known as the ATTENTION, INTEREST, DESIRE, ACTION CONCEPT (AIDA), and effective marketing attempts to accomplish one or more of these goals.

Author and copywriter Robert W. Bly states that his goal is to persuade buyers. He has collected numerous techniques he uses in writing copy, including the following:

- *The "so what" test.* If, after writing the copy for an advertisement, Bly thinks his target audience will respond, "So what," then he rewrites the copy until consumers will likely respond, "That is exactly what I am looking for."
- *Using key copy drivers.* The message should create one or more of the feelings that motivate people into action, including fear, greed, guilt, exclusivity, anger, salvation, or flattery.
- *The drop-in-the-bucket technique.* The copy should show that the price being asked is a "drop in the bucket" compared to the value it will provide.
- *Knowing the audience.* Use FOCUS GROUPS to probe into the feelings and motivations of target audiences.
- *Writing conversationally.* Use simple, easy-to-understand language that is appropriate for the target audience.
- *Leading with the strongest point.* Bly finds most writers end with their strongest point and suggests moving it to the beginning.
- *The tremendous whack theory.* If there is a strong point to make in the message, it is better not to be clever or subtle but to say it strongly, again and again.

Further reading

Bly, Robert W. "Persuasion Secrets of Marketing Pros." *DM News,* 21 October 2002; Perrault, William D., Jr., and E. Jerome McCarthy. *Basic Marketing.* Boston: Irwin McGraw-Hill, 1999.

copyright, fair use

The copyright law, Title 17 of the *United States Code,* includes all amendments enacted through the end of the second session of the 106th Congress in 2000. It includes the Copyright Act of 1976 and all subsequent amendments to copyright law; the Semiconductor Chip Protection Act of 1984, as amended; and the Vessel Hull Design Protection Act, as amended. The Copyright Office is responsible for registering claims under all three acts.

A copyright is a set of restricted, legal rights authors have over their works. Though copyright is most commonly applied to printed items like books and periodicals, it also includes music, videos, artwork, architectural works, software, databases, choreographic dances, pantomimes, images, graphics, and even sounds. Not only does copyright protect the use (copying) of these items, it also includes using parts of the work, distributing the work or performing the work as in a play. This protection is available to both published and unpublished works. The authors' rights begin when a work is created, and works published since March 1, 1989, do not have to bear a copyright notice to be protected under the federal law.

When an employee is creating a work as a job duty or on a commission, the employer, not the employee, is considered the author of the work. Examples of such situations could be a teacher creating a test, a graphic designer creating a company logo, a sound-effects recorder contributing to a motion picture, or a translator converting a text into English.

The copyright law does allow for a limited amount of an author's work to be copied or distributed without the author's permission; this is called fair use. The provisions outlined for fair use include the purpose of the use (mainly for educational purposes), i.e., students photocopying an article for a research paper or a teacher using a book, article, or artwork in the classroom; the nature of a work, i.e., a copy of a photo in a magazine or a clip of music from a CD selection; and using small "extracts" of a work that would not affect the value of a work. The idea of fair use is to copy or use a small portion of a work and not supplement or diminish its MARKET VALUE. Fair use does not allow for the user to distribute the work to the public, sale or lease the work, or profit from the work.

When using copyrighted material for personal or educational purposes, it is advised to make a reference to the authors of the materials, whether print, electronic, images, graphics, or sounds. If the material is used for a commercial venture, the author's permission should be obtained.

Some works that are not copyrighted include titles, names, slogans, familiar symbols, colloquialisms, colors, lettering, lists of ingredients, concepts, methods, and principles. Works that exclusively provide information, such as calendars, tape measures, rulers, height and weight charts and similar charts and tables, are not copyrighted.

Further reading

Copyright Office, Library of Congress. Available on-line. URL: http://lcweb.loc.gov/copyright/; Title 17 Copyright Law. Available on-line. URL: http://www.loc.gov/copyright/title 17/.

—Susan Poorbaugh

corporate average fuel efficiency

Corporate average fuel efficiency (CAFE) is a series of rules established by Congress in 1975 to increase fuel efficiency of automobiles produced and sold in the United States. Initiated as a response to the oil crises of that time, CAFE standards apply to all manufacturers who sell cars and light trucks in the United States. The standards are administered by the National Highway Traffic Safety Administration.

Initially, CAFE standards required manufacturers to gradually increase fuel efficiency, thereby decreasing U.S. dependence on imported oil. Over the years, the auto industry has blocked implementation of most changes in CAFE rules. As of 2002, the standards required manufacturers' cars to average 27.5 miles per gallon and light trucks to average 20.7 miles per gallon. The distinction between light trucks and cars, when established in the 1970s, emphasized differences in the style and use of the two groups of vehicles. Since then, with changes in market DEMAND, manufacturers have classified minivans and sport utility vehicles (SUVs) as light trucks, which then requires them to meet only the lower fuel-efficiency requirement. In 2002 the expanded light-truck category represented approximately half of new vehicle sales in the country. Together, light trucks and cars consume over 40 percent of all oil used in the United States.

In recent years the "Big Three" U.S. automobile manufacturers (General Motors, Ford, and DaimlerChrysler) have produced larger vehicles that have barely met fuel-efficiency standards. If standards are raised as part of new national-security goals, these manufacturers could face significant investment requirements or face penalties under CAFE. BMW and Mercedes-Benz (part of DaimlerChrysler) regularly do not meet CAFE standards and pay federal fines, but most Japanese manufacturers easily meet the current standards. Imposition of higher standards would result in a competitive advantage for Japanese manufacturers, who would not have to invest in new technology.

Further reading

Ball, Jeffrey. "Detroit Again Tries to Dodge Pressures for a 'Greener' Fleet," *Wall Street Journal,* 28 January 2002, p. A1;

National Highway Traffic Safety Administration website. Available on-line. URL: www.nhtsa.gov.

corporate culture

Culture can be described as the learned behavior patterns of any specific period, race, or people. Similarly, corporate culture refers to the beliefs, behaviors, values, and norms of an individual CORPORATION or of an organization. A corporation develops policies, procedures, and guidelines in order to establish and convey the concerns and priorities of the company. Corporate culture is what is "read between the lines" of those policies and procedures—that is, the "understood" or "unspoken" rules and regulations of a company. Informal, intangible, and ambiguous, corporate culture relates to the working environment or atmosphere of an organization and is very often based on the ideas and standards of the senior MANAGEMENT responsible for creating it.

For example, an organization's employee may understand that even though his or her boss is the nominal authoritarian figure, the boss's administrative assistant can often produce more results or has more "power" because he or she maintains more contacts throughout the company's INFRASTRUCTURE. Therefore she or he is the unofficial authority.

Corporate culture can be divided into four main categories: ritualized patterns, management styles and philosophies, management systems and procedures, and written and unwritten norms and procedures. Ritualized patterns refer to policies and procedures influenced by the political, economic, and social beliefs and behaviors of a society. An individual employee may affect a corporation's ritualized pattern when the employee brings his or her own ideas and beliefs to the organization. Collectively, the employee's work ethic, individuality, and relationships with fellow coworkers and customers create ideas and values that may shape a corporation.

LEADERSHIP, planning, motivation, and communication are all examples of areas influenced by management styles and philosophies. It is important that top managers constantly strive to improve and remain consistent in their management styles. Inconsistency can be seen by employees as unfair and frustrating. Motivating, training, and rewarding employees can provide a positive work experience, thereby causing them to be more productive and satisfied.

Management systems and procedures are those that are clearly stated as policy (in official documents) as well as assumptions made by staff for those instances that reach beyond the policy. Policies are developed in order to establish routines that employees should follow for certain situations. Training procedures followed during orientation and throughout the duration of EMPLOYMENT should be consistent with the established values of the organization. The organizational structure and company image are also important and can assist the firm when recruiting for new

workers. The physical structure of the building can also send a message to employees and visitors. For example, if it is physically open and has many windows, this can create a pleasant atmosphere in which to work. Similarly, dress codes should be established in order to ensure that the staff maintains a neat representation of the company image. However, if codes and policies are too strict, it can lead to a negative work environment. It is always important to remember that a balance of structure and freedom should be maintained.

Assumptions made by employees during situations not officially covered by company policy relate to the fourth category: unwritten and written norms and procedures. Generating a certain working environment or atmosphere for employees will equip them to make judgments and assumptions according to the already established guidelines for situations that have not previously been anticipated.

For example, a customer may have a complaint about a product. The employee has guidelines to follow when dealing with the situation, but the actual resolution to the problem may be an individual judgment based on the employee's knowledge of the customer as well as the company's values and policies.

A good corporate culture allows a company the opportunity to be more successful. Typically, if an organization establishes a positive corporate culture, it can boost staff morale and foster creativity among employees, which can be used as an excellent public-relations tool. If a corporation fails to create a good corporate culture, productivity may suffer and employees may become unsatisfied. This can lead to high employee turnover and lack of creativity. It is important to remember that a corporation's culture can be considered one of the most important aspects of business, and having a contented staff can lead to greater profitability.

Sometimes an organization has a corporate culture that is too strong, making it difficult to hire a diverse group of employees and to institute changes when necessary. It can also lead to hiring the same types of personalities, which might cause productivity to suffer for lack of ideas and make it harder for a new hire to fit in or feel comfortable.

Further reading

Goffee, Rob, and Gareth Jones. *The Character of a Corporation: How Your Company's Culture Can Make or Break Your Business.* New York: Harper Business, 1998; Sherriton, Jacalyn, and James L. Stern. *Corporate Culture/Team Culture: Removing the Hidden Barriers to Team Success.* Atlanta: American Management Association, 1997.

—Jennifer R. Land

corporate divestiture

Corporate divestiture is the disposing or relinquishing of a company's ASSETS or a portion of its business by way of sale, exchange, or liquidation. A CORPORATION may want to sell off a poorly performing division or spin off a subsidiary company through an exchange of stock with SHAREHOLD-ERS, or it may be forced to liquidate assets as a result of legal action.

A sell-off is one of the most common types of divestiture, where the divesting company sells a division or subsidiary to a third party for cash or some other asset such as stock. Companies usually sell off under-performing parts of the company and use the proceeds to strengthen other areas of the business. Likewise, if a company is experiencing financial trouble, it may decide to sell a segment of the business in order to generate INCOME.

Sometimes the business area is too small to sustain itself as an independent company and must be sold to another party. This leads to the second form of divestiture, a spin-off, which occurs when a parent company creates a new, independent company from a subsidiary company or division. Shareholders of the parent company are issued stock in the newly formed company to compensate for the asset loss of the parent company. This also serves the dual purposes of shifting some of the investment responsibility and risk away from the parent company and places it on the shareholders' shoulders. Additionally, debt from the parent company can be transferred to the spin-off company during its creation. A spin-off can improve the overall operations of both companies by reducing red tape and overhead costs, allow each company to focus on their PRIMARY MARKETS, and give greater freedom to the management of the spun-off company.

There is also a modified version of a spin-off known as a split-off. The two are very similar; however, unlike a spin-off, where all the shareholders receive shares in the new company, in a split-off shareholders can choose if they want to exchange the shares they own in the parent company for shares in the new company, although sometimes exchange is mandatory. This exchange of shares is often done on an unequal basis. For instance, a shareholder may receive two shares in the new company for each exchange share of the parent company.

Finally, there is the case of liquidation, also known as a split-or break-up. A split-up occurs when a parent company exchanges all of its shares for a stake in two or more subsidiary companies. This is then followed by the liquidation of the parent company. This arrangement is typical in antitrust cases, when a split-up is used to break up a company into individual and independent companies.

During the late 1980s there was a growing trend among companies to diversify operations and expand into new markets. However, some companies found they had spread themselves too thin and were no longer competitive in all areas of their business. Thus, in the 1990s there was a growing amount of corporate divestiture as companies tried to refocus their businesses on core competencies. For example, in 1997 PepsiCo decided to spin off three fast-food restaurants in an effort to focus more on its "core" soft-drink and snack-food business lines. This action was in part prompted by PepsiCo investors who believed Pepsi had expanded in too many directions and wanted to see the company reorganize its business.

While not as common as a spin-off or sale, a break-up is often more widely publicized in the general press, usually because of its association with litigation and antitrust cases. For example, in 2000 one of the proposed solutions in the Microsoft antitrust case was to split the company into two new companies. One company would focus on operating systems, while the other would focus on software. After the new companies had formed, the "original" Microsoft would be liquidated, ceasing to exist as a company. Shareholders of the original Microsoft were to be issued stock in both of the newly formed companies. However, this plan never came to fruition, and at the close of 2001 Microsoft continued to operate as normal.

Divestiture works as a foil against excessive growth and expansion and as a counterbalance to MERGERS AND ACQUISITIONS. Companies will always try to improve their businesses, often through trial and error. When companies find they have overextended their operations, become too large, or have come to the attention of government watchdogs, they will often rely on these different divestment strategies to make their businesses more efficient, easier to manage, or complaint with legal regulations.

—Aaron S. Jones

corporate governance

Corporate governance—the consideration and evaluation of business and social goals by corporate leaders—addresses the ways in which CORPORATIONS balance the interests of SHAREHOLDERS, workers, and the community. In recent years, although corporate governance has attracted considerable public interest, its concept is poorly defined because it covers a large number of distinct issues. As a result, different people have come up with different definitions that basically reflect their special interests. Some definitions of corporate governance include

- "Corporate governance . . . can be defined narrowly as the relationship of a company to its shareholders or, more broadly, as its relationship to society . . ." (*Financial Times,* 1997)
- "Corporate governance is about promoting corporate governance fairness, transparency and accountability." (J. Wolfensohn, President of the World Bank, *Financial Times,* 21 June 1999)
- "Corporate governance can also be described as the system that controls and directs business corporations. The structure specifies the distribution of rights and responsibilities among different participants in the corporation. Some examples of the participants are the board, managers, shareholders, and other STAKEHOLDERS. Corporate governance spells out the rules and

procedures for making decisions on corporate affairs. By doing this, it also provides the structure through which the company directives are set, and means of attaining those objectives and monitoring performance." (ORGANIZATION FOR ECONOMIC COOPERATION AND DEVELOPMENT, April 1999).

- As stated in the *OECD Principles of Corporate Governance*, "Some commentators take too narrow a view, and say it [corporate governance] is the fancy term for the way in which directors and auditors handle their responsibilities towards shareholders. Others use the expression as if it were synonymous with shareholder democracy. Corporate governance is a topic recently conceived, as yet ill-defined, and consequently blurred at the edges . . . corporate governance as a subject, as an objective, or as a regime to be followed for the good of shareholders, customers, bankers and indeed for the reputation and standing of our nation and its economy."

Further reading
OECD. *OECD Principles of Corporate Governance,* Paris, 1999; Organization for Economic Cooperation and Development website. Available on-line. URL: www.oecd.org.

corporate security
Corporate security aims to protect the safety and viability of a business organization. Since September 11, 2001, corporate security has become an increasingly important issue. A survey of corporate executives a few months after the World Trade Center attack reported increased concern about mail processing, travel, protection of employees and INFRASTRUCTURE, and other security issues.

With the anthrax mailings shortly after 9/11, mail processing has become a major concern. The U.S. Postal Service provides guidelines, cautioning recipients about mail from unknown sources with multiple stamps and no return address. Companies have instituted a variety of mail-security practices, from the use of latex gloves and masks to the use of a separate room with no connection to the central ventilation system.

Building security is another area of concern for businesses. Simple changes such as increased surveillance cameras, ID badges, and visible security guards are being used in many companies, especially in headquarter buildings and among companies more likely to be threatened by terrorism. Concrete barriers, shatterproof glass, controlled access, and protection of a building's ventilation system are additional building-security measures that companies are instituting. Some firms are constructing safe rooms, providing safety kits, and redesigning floor plans with security in mind. One architect says the new question being asked is, "How do you get the last person in the corner office of the top floor out of the building safely?"

Business travel is another worry for corporations. Since 9/11 many companies have reduced and even banned employee travel abroad. While executives continue to pursue international expansion plans, companies are offering travel-security advice, hiring bodyguards and bullet-proof limousines for executives and purchasing security and intelligence bulletins for areas of the world where they do business. The general travel-security rules are: be more discrete, do not dress lavishly, replace business luggage tags, move through open areas of airports to secure areas as quickly as possible, and do not have pick-up drivers displaying signs with the company's name at arrival areas.

Even before 9/11, computer security was a major corporate concern, especially given constantly changing technology. The many stories of hackers accessing sensitive company data or destroying important data files had already increased corporate computer security efforts. Major companies often hire "ethical hackers" who attempt to find weaknesses in the firm's computer security system. The American Society for Industrial Security reported on-site contractors as the major threat to a company's INTELLECTUAL PROPERTY. Current employees and former employees were ranked the second and third sources of corporate-security problems. Most corporate losses due to contractor or employee sabotage are never reported or prosecuted. One story described a disgruntled employee who, sensing he was about to be terminated, set up a program to crash the company computer and, when dismissed, called his assistant, who mistakenly activated the program at his request.

The value of continual back-up data storage became apparent to many companies after the events of 9/11. Data storage, back-up facilities, disaster plans, and the federal "shadow" government facilities are all part of increased efforts and concerns about corporate security.

Further reading
American Society for Industrial Security website. Available on-line. URL: www.asisonline.org; Hymowitz, Carol. "Business's New Agenda," *Wall Street Journal,* 11 March 2002, p. R6; Warren, Susan. "Tools to Protect . . . Buildings," *Wall Street Journal,* 11 March 2002, p. R6.

corporate social responsibility
Corporate social responsibility (CSR) is business decision-making linked to ethical values, compliance with laws and regulations, and respect for people, communities, and the environment. A relatively new concept in western capitalism, CSR recognizes that CORPORATIONS are a legal entity chartered by society. To operate (legally) in the United States, all businesses are required to have a business license, whether from a city, county or state government.

Some corporations perceive social responsibility to be part of PUBLIC RELATIONS, any action or contribution that makes the company "look good" in the minds of the public. Advocates of CSR consider it to be policies, practices, and programs integrated into business decision making. Some of the most widely quoted examples of CSR include

- Ben & Jerry's company policy of donating 7.5 percent of PROFITS to charity
- Levi Strauss exiting business in China as a protest of human rights violations
- Body Shop's decision to use natural ingredients harvested using environmentally responsible methods
- Calvert Group's decision to exclude investment in companies producing guns, cigarettes, and vodka

Supporters of corporate social responsibility suggest these practices benefit companies in a variety of ways. Several studies have correlated socially responsible business practices with improved financial performance. CSR efforts to reduce wastes frequently result in reduced COSTS. Similarly, reduced wastes improve productivity and product quality. Corporate social responsibility improves BRAND images and company reputations, resulting in increased CUSTOMER LOYALTY. Companies practicing CSR find it is easier to attract and retain employees.

In the 1990s CSR supporters developed standards and awards. Some of these groups include the following:

- The Global Reporting Initiative, established in 1997, designed guidelines for preparing enterprise-level sustainability reports.
- Social Accountability 8000, developed by the Council on Economic Priorities Accreditation Agency, has set standards that include monitoring child labor, forced labor, nondiscrimination, wages and benefits, working hours, health and safety, freedom of association, and MANAGEMENT systems.
- The Caux Round Table, a group of senior business leaders from around the world, produced "Principles of Business," a document expressing their standards for ethical and responsible business practices.
- The Interfaith Center on Corporate Responsibility published "Principles for Global Corporate Responsibility," a "collective distillation of the issues of concern" to religious-oriented institutional investors.
- The Sunshine Standards for Corporate Reporting to Stakeholders developed a list of information that the creators believe should be included in ANNUAL REPORTS to STAKEHOLDERS, including customer, employee, community, and society information needs to evaluate corporate performance.
- The Keidanren Charter for Good Corporate Behavior, produced by the Japanese Federation of Economic Organizations, created a 10-point charter directing behavior by corporations.

The Business and Society Review has developed a remarkable website detailing examples of corporate social-responsibility efforts, implementation steps, links to other CSR organizations, and model policies for companies considering CSR initiatives.

See also PYRAMID OF CORPORATE RESPONSIBILITY.

Further reading
Business and Society Review website. Available on-line. URL: www.bsr.org; Michael H. Green. "Corporate Social Responsibility: Balancing Bottom Lines with Social Responsibility." Available on-line. URL: www.ziplink.net/~mikegree/career/social/htm.

corporate welfare
Corporate welfare is a term used to describe special programs that benefit only specific CORPORATIONS or industries but not offered to others. In the United States, WELFARE—benefits to individuals or families for which no product or service is received in exchange—is a controversial area of social policy. Corporate welfare is less well-known and therefore less controversial, even though it represents billions of dollars annually. What critics call corporate welfare, supporters refer to as economic incentives, enterprise zones, or development assistance.

The federal government spends over $100 billion annually on corporate-welfare programs. In 2001 President George W. Bush's budget called for reductions in corporate welfare, including cuts in public-works projects, commercial-loan guarantees, shipbuilding programs, and export-import bank trade assistance programs. Supporters argue every country subsidizes exports and that export subsidies level and playing field in international trade.

In an ongoing NAFTA (NORTH AMERICAN FREE TRADE AGREEMENT) dispute, the United States and Canada have been challenging each country's support of timber production. Both countries provide low-cost access to public land and subsidize road development and other transportation. The dispute centers on which country is providing greater subsidies, unfairly reducing the cost of timber harvesting and creating an artificial COMPARATIVE ADVANTAGE in lumber markets. Similarly, in 2001 the WORLD TRADE ORGANIZATION (WTO) ruled U.S. foreign-sales corporations (FSCs), off-shore offices funneling paperwork for corporate exports to avoid federal income taxes on export PROFITS, unfairly subsidize U.S. corporations in world trade. The U.S. Congress responded by changing the language of laws allowing FSCs, hoping to continue to support the corporations without facing WTO sanctions.

In 1998 in a major exposé, *Time Magazine* devoted almost an entire issue to the subject of corporate welfare. In addition to federal subsidies, *Time* presented numerous examples of state and local governments competing with each other to attract corporations. Typical corporate-welfare packages include cash, low-interest LOANS, tax breaks, $1 real estate, and worker-training programs. States often compete to attract large corporations. In 2001 Boeing announced it was moving its corporate headquarters to Dallas, Denver, or Chicago. Chicago won the competition with a variety of "incentives." Among economic-development specialists, attracting Boeing or other large companies is known as an "elephant hunt." In the 1980s, to "bag" BMW, South Carolina leased land to the company for $1 a year, agreed to train workers, exempted the company from a variety of taxes, and even extended the runway on an area airport. Alabama subsequently offered hundreds of millions of dollars in incentives to bag Mercedes-Benz.

One of the problems with corporate welfare is the tendency for companies to "cut and run" once the incentive end. Throughout the southeastern United States, textile companies have long been known for this practice. *Time* describes the relocation of meat-packing operations around the Midwest. Rural communities lacking job opportunities build INFRASTRUCTURE (particularly waste-treatment facilities), spending millions to attract a company. When the company leaves for a better proposition, the community is left with huge indebtedness and little tax base to support the investment.

Critics say corporate welfare distorts allocation of RESOURCES and reduces ECONOMIC EFFICIENCY, but the question of how to stop it is difficult to answer. State officials from New Jersey and New York once agreed to stop "raiding" companies, but the truce was quickly ignored. Five possible measures have been suggested to reduce corporate welfare.

- Level a federal excise tax on incentives given to corporations from state and local governments. This would eliminate the value of the incentives and reduce the bidding war among communities.
- Challenge incentives as illegal under the COMMERCE CLAUSE of the U.S. Constitution.
- Create a special commission to propose ending corporate-welfare programs at the federal level.
- End funding for federal programs subsidizing loans to businesses.
- Challenge state and local incentive programs through lawsuits against companies receiving them.

See also EXPORT-IMPORT BANK OF THE UNITED STATES.

Further reading
Time Magazine, 30 November 1998, various pp.

corporation

A corporation is a legal entity owned by stockholders that is authorized by law to act as a single person. As such, the affairs of the corporation are separate from those of the owners, which gives them limited LIABILITY and thus a financial advantage. Under most circumstances, the owners' liability is limited to the CAPITAL they have invested in the company.

Corporations are created by acquiring a corporate charter from state offices, often the office of the secretary of state. In applying for a charter, a corporation submits its articles of INCORPORATION, listing the company name, address, number of shares of stock the company is authorized to issue, and usually the names and addresses of the individuals who will serve as the initial BOARD OF DIRECTORS. The board of directors represent the interests of stockholders and oversees the actions of managers. A corporation may have a few or many stockholders, based on who has purchased shares of COMMON STOCK in the company. For decades the most widely held stock in the United States was American Telephone & Telegraph (ATT), with over 80,000 shareholders. Only about 20 percent of businesses in the United States are incorporated, but they represent a majority of business activity in the country.

In addition to limited liability, the other major advantage of corporations is the ability to raise capital. Often a new business starts out as a sole PROPRIETORSHIP; expands by taking on partners; and, if promising or successful, funds further growth by incorporating. Selling shares of stock representing ownership interest in the company allows corporations to obtain funds needed to create or expand business operations without having to pay interest, but it reduces the ownership and control of initial owners of the business. Stockholders take an EQUITY interest in the company with the expectation of sharing in the company's future PROFITS, either through DIVIDEND payments or appreciation of the shares of stock in the marketplace as the company earns profits. Corporations also raise capital by selling BONDS and through bank LOANS issued in the corporation's name.

The selling of shares in a new corporation is called an INITIAL PUBLIC OFFERING (IPO). IPOs in technology stocks were highly sought after by investors during the rapid growth of the U.S. STOCK MARKET in the late 1990s. Since most new corporations often have only an idea, a BUSINESS PLAN, and little or no track record, shares of IPO companies are considered highly speculative investments.

Many times entrepreneurs create corporations to expand their PRODUCTS and SERVICES into larger markets. While they may have worked night and day for years developing their business and are reluctant to lose control of their enterprise, they need the capital and/or skill of managers to make their business grow. On the one hand, managers can provide new business expertise, but on the other they are unlikely to work as hard as the entrepreneur who created the business.

To overcome the problem of managers not being owners of companies, many U.S. companies offer employees STOCK OPTIONS—that is, the opportunity to purchase shares of stock at a specified price for a period of time. If the company does well and the stock price rises, employees can exercise their stock options, simultaneously buying stock from the company at the agreed-on price and selling the shares in the stock market at the current market price.

This allows employees to share in a company's profits. Software developers at Microsoft Corporation were known to have cots put in their office cubicles so they could sleep in their offices after working 15- and 20-hour days. Many of these employees have become Microsoft millionaires through stock options offered to dedicated employees. As demonstrated in the corporate corruption scandals in 2002, stock options also provide incentives for executives to artificially increase share prices in order to cash in stock options for personal gain.

A disadvantage of corporations is double taxation. Because they are recognized as a separate legal entity, corporations pay taxes on their INCOMES. When they distribute income in the form of dividends, SHAREHOLDERS must report these distributions and pay personal income tax on them. Thus, profits are taxed first as corporate income and second as personal income. Similarly, when shareholders sell their stock for a profit, they must report the gain on their personal tax return.

Further reading
Mallor, Jane P., A. James Barnes, Thomas Bowers, Michael J. Phillips, Arlen W. Langvardt. *Business Law and the Regulatory Environment,* 11th ed. Boston: McGraw-Hill, 2001.

cost accounting   See MANAGERIAL ACCOUNTING.

cost-benefit analysis
Cost-benefit analysis looks at proposed transactions from an economic viewpoint, comparing the cost of the improvement to the benefits derived from the improvement. At the very least, business wants the economic benefits of the improvement to be greater than the cost of the improvement. In American businesses, supervisors and managers ask their superiors for money to purchase more supplies, new equipment, additional employees, and a variety of other reasons. Money, however, is a scarce resource, and, usually, the total amount of money requested is greater than the money available to be spent. Higher level managers must evaluate the spending requests and decide which ones to approve.

Cost-benefit analysis is a frequently used technique to evaluate spending requests. For instance, if production levels can be increased by 60 percent with the purchase and installation of new automated manufacturing equipment and the cost of the equipment is $100,000, the return to the company must be $100,000 before there is a break-even point. If the company cannot earn a good financial return on the expenditure, then it may decide to leave the money in the bank to earn interest or spend it on other projects with a higher rate of return.

Companies often set standards for the desired rate of return for an expenditure. If that standard is 2.0, then the improvement must generate economic returns that are twice its cost in the first year of operation. This introduces the term *payback*. If an improvement generates returns of twice its cost in a year, then the improvement has paid for itself in six months. The returns earned during the second six months of operation are incremental profits to the company. Companies are more willing to spend money for improvements with shorter payback times than longer.

Cost-efficiencies are related to be both cost-benefit analyses and payback period. When a manager compares different potential improvements that have the same potential benefit, he/she should select the improvement that has the lowest overall cost. This results in requesting the improvement with the greatest cost-efficiency and, similarly, the shortest payback period. Determining the lowest overall cost is important because it goes beyond the immediate purchase price and includes additional considerations, such as projected life of the machine, equipment reliability, and potential cost of repairs. When costs are incurred initially with benefits expected to be realized over a longer period of time, present value analysis is used to adjust costs and benefits into the current time period.

Cost-benefit analysis is an important consideration, but not all purchase decisions are primarily driven by economic factors. Improvements may be authorized to assure a safe work place, free of recognized hazards or to protect the environment from pollution.

See also DISCOUNTING, PRESENT VALUE.

—John B. Abbott

cost of goods sold
Cost of goods sold is an expense account with a normal debit balance found in the ledger of merchandising firms that buy and resell finished goods. Using the perpetual inventory system, when an item is sold from inventory, the merchandise inventory account is credited for the cost of the item, and cost of goods sold is debited for the same amount.

Because cost of goods sold is often the most important of all the expense accounts in a retail or merchandising firm, it is separated from the other expense accounts and subtracted first from sales revenues, with the remainder called gross margin. All the firm's other expenses are then subtracted from gross margin.

A well-known model for determining the cost of goods sold is:

beginning inventory
<u>+ purchases of inventory</u>
inventory available for sale
<u>– ending inventory</u>
cost of goods sold

Cost of goods sold provides important data for manufacturing firms, and their INCOME STATEMENTS give the same treatment to the cost-of-goods-sold account—that is, subtracting it first from sales revenues to obtain gross margin.

cost-of-living adjustment

A cost-of-living adjustment (COLA) is an increase in INCOME to compensate for INFLATION. As the general level of prices rises (inflation), the purchasing power of a fixed amount of income decreases. COLAs protect against inflation by raising incomes, or benefits.

Almost all COLAs in the United States are tied to the CONSUMER PRICE INDEX (CPI). The most widely cited use of COLAs is by the Social Security Administration (SSA). SOCIAL SECURITY (Old Age Survivors and Disability Income, OASDI) and SUPPLEMENTAL SECURITY INCOME (SSI) are adjusted annually based on changes in the Urban Wage Earners and Clerical Workers Consumer Price Index (CPI-W). Since 1975 the SSA has used the third-quarter-to-third-quarter change in the CPI-W to adjust benefits at the beginning of each year. In 1980 Social Security benefits were increased by 14.3 percent, while in 1998 benefits were increased only 1.3 percent.

In addition to being used to adjust government benefits programs, COLAs are often incorporated into UNION contracts and child-support orders. COLAs are also used to adjust for regional differences in the cost of living. Companies often adjust salaries of workers when transferring them to high-cost areas. Manhattan (New York City), Honolulu, and Alaska are relatively expensive places to live in the United States, while most midwestern cities and smaller towns are less expensive. The U.S. military also uses COLAs when transferring personnel to high-cost areas around the world.

People whose major sources of income are not protected by COLAs face declining purchasing power over time and rapid decreases in purchasing power during periods of severe inflation. Many pensioners in former Soviet countries saw their incomes vanish during the break-up of the Soviet Union.

Further reading

Social Security Administration website. Available on-line. URL: www.ssa.gov.

cost-push inflation (supply-shock inflation, sellers' inflation)

Cost-push inflation, also referred to as supply-shock or sellers' INFLATION, is an increase in the general level of prices caused by a leftward shift of an economy's aggregate SUPPLY curve. Aggregate supply/aggregate DEMAND (macroeconomic) analysis describes the interrelationship of real GROSS DOMESTIC PRODUCT (GDP) and the general level of prices (inflation). Assuming nothing else changes, a decrease in aggregate supply will result in both higher prices and reduced level of output (GDP).

The most widely quoted example of cost-push inflation in the United States is the period from 1973 to 1980, during which the price of oil went from $2 to $30 per barrel. When the ORGANIZATION OF PETROLEUM EXPORTING COMPANIES (OPEC) effectively reduced the supply of oil, driving up oil prices, western countries experienced supply shocks. During the 1990s the United States imported approximately 50 percent of its oil needs. Because there are few substitutes available, the demand for oil and products derived from it are inelastic; higher oil prices do not significantly reduce the quantity demanded. The result is a double negative: higher prices and higher UNEMPLOYMENT associated with reduced GDP.

Cost-push inflation is also a result of other pressures increasing prices while decreasing output. Wage increases greater than increases in productivity increase the cost of PRODUCTION, causing inflation. Increased market power by firms, allowing them to raise prices while reducing supply, results in cost-push inflation. When either wages or market power increases in many sectors of an economy, the economic system will experience cost-push inflation.

See also MACROECONOMICS.

Further reading

Ruffin, Roy J., and Paul R. Gregory. *Principles of Economics,* 7th ed. Boston: Addison Wesley, 2000.

costs

When business managers change the level of output, they do so by changing the quantity of resources, called inputs, used to produce the output. As the number of inputs change, the firm's costs change. There are many types of costs: total costs (TC), total fixed costs (TFC), total variable costs (TVC), average total cost (ATC sometimes shown as AC), average variable cost (AVC), average fixed cost (AFC), and marginal cost (MC).

To understand the various costs, it is necessary to distinguish between fixed and variable costs. Fixed costs are those that do not change during the period of time and range of output under consideration. When the planning period is relatively short, some inputs, such as the size of the factory and number of machines, are constant; while other inputs—labor, materials, and energy—change with the level of output. Total costs can then be separated into fixed costs and variable costs. Using the table below, each of the cost concepts can be defined.

Units of Output(Q)	TC	TFC	TVC	ATC	AVC	AFC	MC
0	10	10	0	–	–	–	–
1	15	10	5	15	5	10	5
2	18	10	8	9	4	5	3
3	21	10	11	7	3.7	3.3	3

Total cost equals the sum of total fixed costs and total variable costs at each level of output: $TC = TFC + TVC$. Total fixed costs equal total costs minus total variable costs: $TFC = TC - TVC$. Note that in the table above, total fixed costs do not change as the units of output increase. By definition, fixed costs are fixed. Note also that when the firm has no output, total costs equals total fixed costs. When a firm has no output it has no variable costs, only fixed costs. For example, a new company, such as a bank, leases a building, gets a business license, obtains a charter with the banking authorities, hires office staff, rents computers and office equipment, and makes other expenditures before it ever opens its door for business. All of these costs are fixed costs.

Total variable costs equals total costs minus total fixed costs: $TVC = TC - TFC$. Variable costs are costs that change as the firm produces more output. For a bank, variable costs would include labor, communication costs, and costs of funds (interest paid).

Average total cost equals total cost divided by the number of units produced: $ATC = TC/Q$. Notice in the table above that there is no figure when the level of output is zero; division by zero is undefined. The same is true for average variable cost and average fixed cost.

Average variable cost equals total variable cost divided by the number of units produced: $AVC = TVC/Q$. Average fixed cost equals total fixed cost divided by the number of units produced: $AFC = TFC/Q$. Notice that AFC decreases as output increases. This is known as "spreading your fixed costs." One of the reasons a small business, like a new bank, will want to grow as fast as possible is to spread the initial start-up costs (fixed costs) over a larger volume of output (loans and other ASSETS).

Marginal cost equals the change in total cost divided by the change in output: $MC = change \ in \ TC/change \ in \ Q$. In the table above, there is no figure for marginal cost when output is zero; there is no information to compare the change in total cost and change in marginal cost. But when output increases to one unit, total cost increases from 10 to 15, a difference of 5, and output changes from 0 to 1, a change of 1. Therefore marginal cost is 5/1 = 5.

Marginal cost is a very useful concept to business managers. Often managers are faced with new choices or situations. Open a new location. Add a new line of products. Stay open additional hours. Have the employees work overtime. In each of these situations, a manager would like to know how much more will it cost to do this. Marginal cost answers this important question.

There are other ways to calculate costs. $TC = TFC + TVC$. Total cost also equals average total cost times the number of units of output: $TC = ATC \times Q$. Similarly, $TFC = AFC \times Q$, and $TVC = AVC \times Q$.

Average total cost can also be calculated by adding AFC + AVC at each level of output; therefore $AFC = ATC - AVC$ and $AVC = ATC - AFC$.

Often, in a business situation, a manager will only have limited information about what costs are or will be. If a manager can estimate cost per unit (average total cost) in a range of output and then compare to the price they expect to be able to sell the product for, they can make the decision whether or not to pursue that activity.

Summary of cost relationships:

$TC = TFC + TVC$, or $TC = ATC \times Q$
$TFC = TC - TVC$, or $TFC = AFC \times Q$
$TVC = TC - TFC$, or $TVC = AVC \times Q$
$ATC = TC/Q$, or $ATC = AFC + AVC$
$AVC = TVC/Q$, or $AVC = ATC - AFC$
$AFC = TFC/Q$, or $AFC = ATC - AVC$

See also MARGINAL ANALYSIS; PROFIT MAXIMIZATION; TRANSACTION COSTS.

counterfeit goods

Counterfeit goods are found in many markets, including the United States. Luxury brand-name articles are often counterfeited (Pierre Cardin, Louis Vuitton), but the phenomenon is by no means limited to them. Counterfeit auto and airplane parts, pharmaceuticals, and Levi jeans along with computer software, musical CDs and tapes, and even Apple and IBM computers exist. In China, a haven for counterfeiting, entirely counterfeit Jeeps have been produced.

Counterfeit goods are unlicensed and generally ride freely on the BRANDS identity and GOODWILL of TRADEMARK owners. Their quality, while often suspect, can be surprisingly good. Legal remedies against counterfeiting include customs seizures (the big problem being notice and identification of counterfeits), court orders, and DAMAGES. Members of the WORLD TRADE ORGANIZATION are required to provide such remedies, but their level of enforcement in developing countries varies substantially. Vested local interests (for example, the Chinese military) may block use of such remedies. The long-term solution is the emergence of local technology and brand-name supporters of INTELLECTUAL PROPERTY rights, as has occurred in Japan, Korea, and Singapore. When this occurs, counterfeiting as a cheap means of ECONOMIC DEVELOPMENT tends to move on to less-advanced nations.

Further reading
Folsom, Ralph H., Michael Gordon, and John Spanogle. *International Business Transactions in a Nutshell*, 6th ed. Eagan, Minn.: West Group, 2000.

countertrade

Countertrade is a reciprocal trading agreement between or among trading partners. In essence, countertrade is international BARTER. It is often used when there are problems with hard-currency generation and in TECHNOLOGY TRANSFER agreements. It is also often involved in the sale of aerospace and defense equipment.

Countertrade was the ancient basis for trade before MONEY was created and often became necessary during times of economic collapse. Between World War I and World War II, Germany was forced to barter for goods as its money became worthless. Countertrade became popular in the 1980s among companies wanting to trade with the Soviet Union and Eastern European countries. For example, PepsiCo traded billions of dollars worth of Pepsi PRODUCTS in exchange for Stolichnaya vodka and a few ships. Similarly, Coca Cola Company accepted Yugoslavian wine in exchange for their soft drinks.

In addition to straightforward barter agreements, there are many other types of countertrade transactions.

- *Counterpurchase.* This obligates the foreign supplier to purchase from the buyer goods and SERVICES unrelated to the goods and services sold, usually within a one- to five-year period.
- *Reverse countertrade.* This requires the importer to export goods equivalent in value to a specified percentage of the value of the imported goods—an obligation that can be sold to an exporter in a third country.
- *Buyback arrangements.* These obligate the foreign supplier of plant, machinery, or technology to buy from the importer a portion of the resultant production during a future time period.
- *Clearing agreements.* Two countries agree to purchase specific amounts of each other's products over a specified period of time, using a designated "clearing currency" in the transactions.
- *Switch arrangement.* Permission is granted to sell unpaid balances in a clearing account to a third party, usually at a discount; this may be used in producing goods in the country holding the balance.
- *Swap arrangements.* Products from different locations are traded to save transportation costs.

The American Countertrade Association includes over 100 U.S.-based companies. Countertrade specialists facilitate exchanges for companies wanting to sell products abroad but having no knowledge of products outside their industry.

Further reading

American Countertrade Association website. Available on-line. URL: www.countertrade.org; Boone, Louis E., and David L. Kurtz. *Contemporary Marketing*, 10th ed. Fort Worth: Dryden Press, 2001; "Nigeria: Market Will Not Be Easy to Do Business in This Year, As the Economy Continues To Face Difficulties," *Business America*, 14 April 1986.

countervailing power

Countervailing power is the economic concept that the power of a seller (buyer) in a market will eventually be off-set by an equal, opposite power among buyers (sellers). As developed by John Kenneth Galbraith, countervailing power suggests that initial market dominance will evolve into complimentary power, reducing the control and pricing power of the firm or group that originally prevailed in the market.

The most frequently discussed case of countervailing power is a bilateral MONOPOLY. In this market situation, a monopsonist, or single buyer of labor, is offset by a UNION, or single source of labor. U.S. union history contains many examples of workers organizing to counter the power and abuse of a "company town," where the factory owner controlled EMPLOYMENT, housing, stores, banking, and even education. Factory owners, logically not wanting to give up market power and often believing that they acted in the best interests of the people they controlled, resisted union attempts to offset their power.

Today professional sports leagues—with owners acting collectively (having been granted exemptions from U.S. ANTITRUST LAWS) and unions representing players—create a bilateral monopoly. For example, in major-league baseball, the players' union's power evolved in the 1970s and 1980s. Early leaders in the players' union were sometimes blacklisted by team owners, but eventually the union became an effective countervailing force. When players' demands were not met, a 1990s strike hurt both players and team owners but established the players' union as an effective balance to the initial dominance of team owners. The union's power led to increased players' salaries, and negotiating terms in players' clauses allowing them to sell their services in the free-agent draft.

country-risk analysis

Country-risk analysis is the assessment of the level of political and economic RISK associated with doing business in another country. Risk analysis is used when extending credit to foreign buyers making foreign DIRECT INVESTMENT decisions. Country-risk analysis includes analysis of

- the level of political stability
- regulation of businesses
- protection for private property
- government WAGE AND PRICE CONTROLS
- government budgets and deficits
- INFLATION
- UNEMPLOYMENT
- INTEREST RATES
- EXCHANGE RATES

Business managers do not like surprises. Each aspect of country-risk analysis is a potential source of uncertainty, which can lead to unpleasant surprises for anyone doing business abroad. One of the reasons foreigners have invested huge sums of CAPITAL in the United States for the last 20 years is the relatively low risk associated with

American business ventures. By comparison, investors in Indonesia, Malaysia, Thailand, Argentina and many other industrializing countries have, at times, lost money due to changes in political and ECONOMIC CONDITIONS. For example, many U.S.-based companies invested in Indonesia during the 32-year reign of President Suharto. His government imposed strict controls, creating, through force, a stable political and economic environment. The Indonesian economy grew rapidly, and its currency remained stable. In 1998 Suharto was forced out of office and replaced by President Wahid in national elections. With the Asian financial crisis that year, Indonesia's economy decreased by over 13 percent, its currency and STOCK MARKET plummeted, and political strife grew. In 2001, U.S. companies such as Newmont Mining and Exxon Mobil closed their Indonesian operations, citing risk of separatist revolt and conditions approaching anarchy.

Typically, MULTINATIONAL CORPORATIONS (MNCs) conduct country-risk analyses before making major financial investments in new areas of the world. MNCs also pay consulting services to monitor changes in political and economic conditions around the world. One service provides a weekly update summarizing events in each country and providing analysis of the significance to businesses operating there.

To reduce country risk, companies will hedge against EXCHANGE-RATE RISK, seek assistance from U.S. government agencies, and insure INVESTMENTs through government-sponsored corporations including the OVERSEAS PRIVATE INSURANCE CORPORATION and EXPORT-IMPORT BANK OF THE UNITED STATES.

Further reading
Schuman, Michael. "How Big Mining Lost a Fortune in Indonesia: The Locals Moved In," *Wall Street Journal*, 16 May 2001, p. A1.

Court of International Trade
The U.S. Court of International Trade (CIT) was created under Article III of the U.S. Constitution to provide judicial review of civil actions from import transactions and certain federal statutes affecting international trade. The CIT replaced the Board of General Appraisers, a unit of the Treasury Department, and the U.S. Customs Court, which together reviewed U.S. CUSTOMS SERVICE decisions concerning the amount of duties to be paid on IMPORTS. The president, with the approval of the U.S. Senate, appoints the nine CIT judges, with no more than five of the nine judges belonging to one political party.

The CIT has exclusive jurisdiction over civil actions taken against the United States, its agencies, or officers concerning any laws related to revenue from imports, duties, EMBARGOes, TARIFFs, or enforcement of customs regulations. Disputes regarding trade embargoes, quotas, customs classifications, and country of origin determinations are all heard by the Court of International Trade. Customs

classifications and country of origin decisions affect the tariff rate importing businesses must pay. Information regarding country of origin can be obtained from (for example) reading stickers on automobiles sold in the country. Customs classifications are also important. For example, a small Michigan company, Heartland By-Products, imported molasses from Canada after U.S. Customs agreed molasses was not sugar. The company then reprocessed the molasses into sugar, selling it to candy and soft-drink manufacturers. The U.S. sugar lobby protested and brought legal action before the CIT, but the court affirmed products should be classified according to the way they are imported, not their ultimate use.

The CIT has authority to review agency decisions concerning antidumping and countervailing duty matters as well as TRADE-ADJUSTMENT ASSISTANCE. For example, the United States, under the NORTH AMERICAN FREE TRADE AGREEMENT (NAFTA) Worker Safety Act, provides assistance for U.S. workers who have lost their jobs due to import COMPETITION. Workers can seek assistance if a significant number of company employees have been or are threatened with losing their jobs due to NAFTA imports or shifting of jobs to Mexico or Canada. The CIT reviews disputes regarding whether workers in a company are eligible for benefits. In 2000 Save Domestic Oil, a U.S. political-action group went before the CIT with charges against oil-rich countries for DUMPING. In the same year, the CIT affirmed a dumping determination against heavy hand tools being imported from China. CIT decisions can be appealed to the Court of Appeals for the Federal Circuit and ultimately to the U.S. Supreme Court.

Further reading
U.S. Court of International Trade website. Available on-line. URL: www.uscit.gov.

credit See DEBIT, CREDIT.

credit cards
Credit cards are a convenient method for consumers to secure short-term LOANS. In today's U.S. economy, credit cards and access to credit cards are ubiquitous; in many situations, such as hotels, it is difficult to purchase goods and services without use of a credit card. While most Americans probably cannot conceive of life without credit cards, they are a relatively recent phenomenon in U.S. business.

The AMERICAN BANKERS ASSOCIATION (ABA) credits Western Union with issuing the first consumer charge card in 1914. At the time there was no FEDERAL RESERVE SYSTEM, and the banking industry consisted of thousands of small-town banks and the large money-center institutions in New York. Credit was generally a locally based decision, and consumer credit was a new concept. Many hotels and department stores quickly followed Western Union's lead, issuing their own cards. Until the 1990s, locally based, high-interest-rate credit supported many main street businesses in small towns in the United States.

In 1950 Diners Club issued the first charge card accepted by a wide variety of merchants. Diners Club began the practice of charging merchants a small percentage "discount" for facilitating purchases by consumers. The next year Franklin National Bank (New York) issued its own card accepted by area merchants. Soon nearly 100 other banks issued similar cards for their market areas, but users were expected to pay their balances when presented with a statement.

In 1958 Bank of America issued its BankAmericard (later renamed Visa) for use throughout California. Bank of America was the first to offer credit rather than requiring consumers to pay their balances each month. By 1965 Bank of America had formed agreements with numerous banks, allowing them to issue BankAmericard outside of California. During the same period, a number of banks collectively created Master Charge (later renamed MasterCard).

The credit-card industry grew slowly until the advent of automated teller machines (ATMs). In the 1970s, American consumers did not readily accept ATMs; most preferred person-to-person bank transactions. Using both "carrots and sticks," incentives and disincentives, the industry gradually changed Americans' use of credit cards. Today Visa and MasterCard dominate the credit card industry in the United States, and in recent years they have been accused of anticompetitive behavior. The two associations have pushed the use of debit rather than credit cards, where consumers' accounts are directly debited and funds transferred to merchants as purchases are made. New technology now allows businesses to scan consumers' personal checks and directly debit their credit accounts.

Credit-card issuers are subject to a variety of legal requirements, most notably the TRUTH IN LENDING ACT (1968), which imposes a variety of disclosure requirements. They differ depending on how a credit-card application is solicited but basically require issuers to disclose the annual percentage rate (APR), annual fees, the grace period for paying without incurring a finance charge, and the method used for computing the balance on which a finance charge is based.

Credit-card usage is booming in the United States. Americans owe over $1 trillion, much of it borrowed using credit cards. Economists often predict that Americans saturated with credit will have to slow CONSUMPTION spending to pay off past credit-card debt. Studies show most American consumers are insensitive to or ignorant of the INTEREST RATES charged by credit-card lenders. In recent years card issuers have aggressively pursued "subprime" borrowers, people with poor credit histories or previous personal bankruptcy. Credit-"repair" and CONSUMER CREDIT COUNSELING SERVICES are expanding rapidly as Americans continue to increase their use of credit cards. In other countries, credit-card usage is much less prevalent, and consumer resistance to the use of credit cards has often surprised U.S. businesses expanding internationally.

See also DEBIT, CREDIT.

Further reading
"A History of Debit and Credit: How Plastic Cards Forever Changed our Lives," *Chain Store Age Executive with shopping Center Age* 68 no. 9 (September 1992): 22.

credit-reporting services (credit bureaus)
Credit-reporting services, also called credit bureaus, are firms that maintain credit-history information on consumers and businesses. Credit-reporting services collect data about Americans' bill-paying practices and public-record information such as tax liens, court judgments, and bankruptcies. In the United States there are three major credit-reporting companies: Trans Union, Equifax, and Experian (previously named TRW). These firms own, or work with on a contractual basis, over 1,000 local and regional credit bureaus around the country, maintaining databases with credit information on more than 170 million individuals and businesses and producing over 500 million credit reports annually.

Credit-reporting services are an important resource used by lending institutions in making loan decisions. A typical credit report identifies the individual or firm; provides bill-paying history with retail stores, banks, finance and mortgage companies; and includes any public record credit-related documents. Credit-reporting services do not make decisions on LOANS, but their reports are the primary basis for many lending decisions.

Credit-reporting services produce credit scores based on consumers' payment history and other credit information. Scores range from 300 to 850, with the higher score representing a lower credit risk to lenders. CREDIT SCORING has, at times, been a controversial issue, with consumer groups complaining about the use of inaccurate data. Many dubious businesses have promoted their "credit repair" services to consumers turned down for loans.

The number and type of inquiries made about an individual's credit history is an important factor. Lending firms often make promotional inquiries into credit-reporting databases, gathering mailing lists of consumers who meet their inquiry criteria. Creditors also make periodic account-management inquiries, reviewing changes in the credit status of their customers. While these two types of inquiries do not affect consumers' credit scores, credit inquiries generated by consumers' requests for credit affect peoples' credit ratings. Too many inquiries suggest consumers are seeking a large amount of credit or have too much available credit.

The Fair Credit Reporting Act (1971) regulates credit information, requiring credit-reporting services to

- maintain accurate, relevant, and recent information
- provide access to credit information only to bona fide users
- inform consumers who are turned down or have their interest costs raised the reasons for these decisions
- allow consumers to review their files and correct any inaccurate information

Further reading
Mallor, Jane P., A. James Barnes, Thomas Bowers, Michael J. Philips, and Arlen W. Langvardt. *Business Law and the Regulatory Environment,* 11th ed. Boston: McGraw-Hill, 2001; Trans Union website. Available on-line. URL: www.tuc.com.

credit scoring

Credit scoring is mathematical modeling used by CREDIT-REPORTING SERVICES to generate a number rating a customer's credit risk. Fair Isaac and Company (FICO) is the leading provider of credit scores in the United States. Their system generates credit scores, ranging from 300 to 850 for each individual, which are used by lenders to make millions of lending decisions annually. The benefit to most consumers is that credit scores allow lenders to make quick, on-the-spot decisions based on past credit behavior, reducing the potential for bias. But credit scoring is only as good as the data used to create the number and can be a conundrum: How does one get a good credit rating without having access to credit? Critics argue the use of credit scores penalizes poor people, immigrants, and seniors, all groups who tend to pay their bills in cash and therefore do not have credit histories.

Based on past experience, FICO developed a predictive model that is used by the major credit-reporting services. This model uses

- payment history
- amount owed
- length of credit history
- new credit
- number of CREDIT CARDS
- total available credit
- finance company loans
- bank-issued versus department-store cards

In addition to evaluating consumer LOANS and issuing credit cards, credit scoring is used in making MORTGAGE decisions and determinations for auto- and homeowners-INSURANCE policies. Based on a correlation between credit quality and insurance claims, many insurance companies adjust their rates for potential customers.

Compared to the traditional FIVE CS OF CREDIT, credit scoring introduces less potential for bias and less discretionary judgment.

Further reading
Quinn, Jane Bryant. "You Owe Yourself a Credit Check," *Washington Post,* 10 March 1996, p. H02; Simon, Ruth. "Looking to Improve Your Credit Score? Fair Isaac Can Help," *Wall Street Journal,* 10 March 2002, p. A1.

credit union

A credit union is a nonprofit cooperative financial institution that primarily provides consumer credit LOANS to its members, with funds deposited by its participants. Credit unions are mutually owned and run by their members, with a BOARD OF DIRECTORS, elected by the members, which sets policies and procedures. Most credit unions in the United States are members of the National Credit Union Association (NCUA), created to charter and supervise the industry; and participate in the National Credit Union Share Insurance Fund (NCUSIF), which insures credit union depositors.

The first credit unions were created in Germany during the 19th century. The first U.S. credit union was established by a group of Franco-American Catholics in Manchester, New Hampshire, in 1909. While banks provided business loans, and SAVINGS AND LOAN ASSOCIATIONS provided home MORTGAGE loans, credit unions grew to meet consumer-borrowing needs. In 1934 President Franklin D. Roosevelt signed the Federal Credit Union Act (FCUA), authorizing the establishment of federally chartered credit unions in all states.

After the FCUA was passed, Congress debated over which regulatory agency would preside over credit unions. Neither the COMPTROLLER OF THE CURRENCY (Treasury Department) nor the Federal Reserve Board wanted oversight of credit unions, so initially the Farm Credit Administration was responsible for managing them. Oversight then passed to bureaus within the FEDERAL DEPOSIT INSURANCE CORPORATION (FDIC); the Federal Security Agency; and the Department of Health, Education and Welfare. As the number of credit unions grew, responsibility for the system was shifted to the NCUA in 1970.

Because credit unions are nonprofit organizations, their INTEREST RATES on loans are typically lower than competing, for-profit, financial institutions. With DEREGULATION of the financial industry in the 1980s, credit unions expanded into mortgage and other lending activities. Like the savings and loan institutions, many credit unions failed during the 1980s, bankrupting the National Credit Union Share Insurance Fund (the credit union equivalent of Federal Deposit Insurance, FDIC). In 1985 the NCUSIF was recapitalized with deposits of member credit unions. The NCUSIF has three fail-safe features.

- Federal credit unions must maintain a one-percent deposit with the NCUSIF.
- Premiums are levied by the Board if necessary.

• When the equity ratio exceed 1.3 percent ($1.30 on deposit for every $100 insured), the Board sends a DIVIDEND to credit unions.

In 2001 there were over 12,000 credit unions with over $300 billion in ASSETS and 70 million members. Membership in credit unions is based on the principle of having a common bond. Workers in a particular factory, members of a local community or organization, or some other mutual relationship is usually required in order to join a credit union. During the 1990s credit unions greatly expanded membership, often redefining or relaxing the definition of the common-bond requirement. For-profit financial institutions challenged the actions of credit unions, and in 1998 the U.S. Supreme Court ruled against credit unions, stating government regulators too loosely defined the "field of membership" rule. In response, Congress passed the Credit Union Membership Access Act (1998), fostering local credit unions and expansion within "reasonable proximity" of existing credit-union service areas. Critics contend the NCUA continues to ignore and loosely interpret field of membership rules.

Further reading
American Banking Association Industry Issues website. Available on-line. URL: www.aba.com; National Credit Union Association website. Available on-line. URL: www.ncua.gov.

—Susan Poorbaugh

critical path method
Critical path method (CPM) was created in 1957 by J. E. Kelly of Remington Rand and M. R. Walker of DuPont to assist in the building and repairs of DuPont's chemical plants. In the following year, the Special Projects Office of the U.S. Navy created PROGRAM EVALUATION AND REVIEW TECHNIQUE (PERT) to help coordinate the duties of the thousands of contractors working on the Polaris missile program. Today CPM and PERT are essential planning tools used to help managers overcome the limitations of Gantt charts (horizontal bar charts used to track the progress of projects) and to determine which critical activities must be completed in order for a project to be finished in a timely and cost-effective manner. Although CPM and PERT do have some differences, which will be pointed out, they are often discussed synonymously because both are necessary quantitative techniques used for effective PROJECT MANAGEMENT.

In project management, determining CPM and PERT requires the creation of a network diagram, which gives the order of critical activities and the estimated time for completion of each activity. Loosely defined, a critical activity is any job in a project's schedule whose completion is necessary in order to have the entire project completed on time. Critical activities are found along a critical path, which therefore is "the longest path route through the network" because it is the path that will take the most time to complete. To reduce the time needed to complete a project, the number of activities found on the critical path would first have to be reduced.

Critical path method uses two time estimates for determining the time it will take to finish a project. The first is the "normal completion time" and the other is the "crash time." As the name implies, the normal completion time is the estimated time it will take to complete a project under "normal" conditions, or rather, a situation in which nothing unexpected happens to interrupt the course of the project. The crash time is the shortest time it would take to finish an activity if more money and other resources where added to complete the project.

Finding CPM and PERT requires project managers to perform a few simple calculations. CPM requires managers to find four quantities.

1. *Earliest Start Time (ES):* the earliest time an activity can start without violating any of the initial requirements for beginning the activity.
2. *Earliest Finish Time (EF):* the earliest time an activity is expected to end.
3. *Latest Start Time (LS):* the latest time the activity could begin without having the entire project lag.
4. *Latest Finish Time (LF):* the latest an activity could end without having the entire project lag (Render and Stair Jr., p. 635).

To calculate the earliest start and finish times for each activity in a project, project managers should begin by drawing a graph that looks something like this:

(Earliest Start Time) $\underline{0}$ 2 (Earliest Finish Time)
$$0 \underline{\hspace{2cm}} 2$$
$$t = 2$$

The Earliest Start Time is set at zero. Project managers should keep in mind that the earliest start time for each activity in the project will always be set at zero. Say, for instance, that activity "A" takes two weeks to complete; therefore, its earliest finish time is represented as 2. The following calculation can be used to find the Earliest Finish Time: *Earliest Finish Time = Earliest Start Time + Expected Activity Time, or EF = ES + t.*

When computing the ES and EF for the activities in a project, there is one rule that must be followed. Before project managers begin one activity, all critical activities preceding that one must be completed first. For CPM, project managers are looking for the "longest path to an activity in determining ES" (Render and Stair Jr., p. 636). To calculate the ES and EF times for each activity in the entire project, project managers will make a "forward pass" through the network, where at each step EF = ES + t. Thus, say a project consists of projects A, B, C, D, E, and F; activity "F" cannot begin until the 11th week after starting the project, and it is expected to take two weeks to complete. The whole project will take exactly 13 weeks to be finished, since EF = ES + t; in this case, 13 = 11 + 2.

However, once the earliest finish time has been calculated, project managers still need to calculate the latest start and finish times for each activity in order to find the critical path. Now they will begin at the last activity, in this case activity "F," and work backward to activity "A." The formula used to find the latest start time is *Latest Start Time = Latest Finish Time – Expected Activity Time,* or LS = LF – t. For example, because LF equals 13 for activity "F," the latest start time for the activity is 11 weeks since LS = 13 – 2. The general rule here is that "the latest finish time for an activity equals the *smallest* latest starting time for all activities leaving that same event" (Render and Stair Jr., p. 637).

Another calculation that should be determined when finding the critical path of a project is the slack time, or the amount of time an activity can be put on hold without holding up the project as a whole. The calculation for slack is: *Slack = LS – ES* or *Slack = LF – EF.* However, it cannot be stressed enough that no critical activities can have any slack time because they are critical, and any delay in completing them will delay the completion of the entire project. Slack time can only be applied to those activities that are not considered critical to the outcome of the project.

Once the times for all activities on the critical path are computed, managers will apply PERT techniques to each activity to determine the variance of the entire project. Project variance is found by adding all the variances for each critical activity. Project variance equals sigma variances of each activity found on the critical path. The standard deviation for the project is the square root of the project variance. Once these calculations are made, project managers can determine whether the project will be completed on time.

While using CPM and PERT techniques is a necessary part of project management, it may not be necessary for a company to apply these tools to every job undertaken. Clearly there is a lot of analysis involved finding both CPM and PERT, and it takes a lot of experience on the part of the project managers to make the correct calculations. Managers who have little skills and knowledge working with the projects will surely make plenty of mistakes applying CPM or PERT because these techniques assume that managers already have plenty of understanding about the projects at hand and that each critical activity will be done in a known sequence, independent of one another. If the sequence is disrupted for any reason, the project could easily fail. Only when a job is expensive or important should this kind of detailed analysis be applied. Once these skills are crafted, however, project managers will have an extremely valuable tool that will enable them to remain in control of their projects from start to finish (Anderson, p. 338).

Further reading

Anderson, Carl R. *Management: Skills, Functions, and Organization Performance.* Boston: Allyn and Bacon, 1988; Cammarano, James. *Project Management: How to Make It Happen. IIE Solutions* 29, no. 12.

Available from Dialog, Expanded Academic ASAP, article A20331320, 1997; Render, Barry, and Ralph M. Stair Jr. *Quantitative Analysis for Management.* Boston: Allyn and Bacon, 1988.

—Allison Kaiser Jones

cross-cultural communication

Cross-cultural communication is the ability to successfully form and maintain relationships with members of a culture different from one's own. Many factors contribute to success in communicating with a person of another culture; these include manners, social structure, and values.

Understanding cross-cultural communication is vital if one is pursuing a career in international business, and the best way to achieve this is by practice. Reading about other cultures is helpful, but understanding them cannot be done by reading alone. Practice, instruction, and experience are the three keys to success. Many U.S. CORPORATIONS send personnel who are being transferred abroad to cultural training seminars before they leave the country; often spouses also attend the seminars. Around the world, thousands of language-training centers offer immersion courses in local languages and culture.

Communication is the act of sharing information, often using both oral and written symbols as well as nonverbal symbols such as body language. For example, handshaking is a common form of nonverbal communication. In the United States, a solid, firm handshake is customary, whereas Orientals and Middle Easterners generally use a gentle grip. To many non-Westerners, using a firm grip may suggest that one is unnecessarily aggressive.

Another form of nonverbal communication is eye contact. Eye contact is used throughout the world, but the way it is interpreted varies. Americans are taught to look directly at people when speaking; not doing so suggests one is either not sure oneself or is trying to conceal something. In other cultures, making direct eye contact can convey disrespect or even convey sexual messages.

Culture also affects verbal communication. For example, the general tone in which one speaks varies among groups around the world. Many Americans consider raised voices to be rude and inappropriate, but other groups consider an increase in volume to be a sign of enthusiasm.

Even with accurate translation in business communications, many misunderstandings are caused by bypassing, where the sender and receiver "bypass," or miss, each other's meaning. Management professor Naoki Kameda writes that bypassing in cross-cultural communication is caused by the absence of general agreement, egocentric interpretation of received communications, and self-conceited conception of communications. People give their own meanings to words, and cultural differences result in misinterpretations. Even among English speakers there exists a strong potential for miscommunication. Language specialists often refer to

"Englishes," recognizing that each country injects its own culture into the language.

Americans are often accused of being presumptuous in international business settings, assuming that others understand English and, in particular, American English. One area of frequent cultural miscommunication is in the use of acronyms. People situated within the "beltway" surrounding Washington, D.C. (Interstate 495), are masters of acronym-speak, a language that few people outside the beltway, never mind outside the United States, comprehend.

Marcelle DuPraw and Marya Axner describe six fundamental patterns of cultural differences that influence cross-cultural communication.

- *Communication styles.* Meanings of words, nonverbal communication, and BUSINESS LANGUAGE vary among cultures.
- *Attitudes toward conflict.* In the United States, conflict is generally avoided, but when necessary, it is dealt with directly. In many other cultures, conflict is considered embarrassing and addressed discreetly.
- *Approaches to completing tasks.* Americans are known for being task-oriented and developing relationships while working together. People from Asian and Hispanic cultures generally prefer developing relationships first and then approaching tasks together.
- *Decision-making styles.* In the United States, decision-making authority is often delegated, while in many other cultures it is highly centralized. Majority-rule decisions are common in the United States, while in Asian cultures consensus is preferred.
- *Attitudes toward disclosure.* In the United States, most businesspeople are up-front, willing to discuss issues and problems. In many other cultures, candid expression or questioning can be considered shocking and inappropriate. Probing questions, often used to better understand a problem, may seem intrusive to non-Americans.
- *Epistemologies (approaches to knowing).* Americans emphasize cognitive knowledge gained through counting or measuring while other cultures incorporate transcendent knowledge gained through meditation, or spiritual understanding.

Further reading

DuPraw, Marcelle E., and Marya Axner. "Working on Common Cross-cultural Communication Challenges." Webster's World of Cultural Democracy website. Available online. URL: www.wwcd. org/action/ampu/crosscult.html; Folsom, Ralph H., and W. Davis Folsom. *Understanding NAFTA and its International Implications.* New York: Matthew Irwin/Bender, 1996; East-West Business Strategies website. "What Is Cross-cultural Communication?" Available on-line. URL: www.ewbs. com/descr.html. Sabath, Ann Marie. *Business Etiquette, in Brief.* Avon, Mass.: Adams Media, 1996.

—Stan Yocco

cross-price elasticity of demand

Cross-price elasticity of demand is the responsiveness of DEMAND for one PRODUCT or service to changes in the price of another good or service. Cross-price elasticity is calculated by dividing the percentage change in demand for one product by the percentage change in the price of a related product.

$$E_{xy} = (\text{\% change in demand good X}) / (\text{\% change in price of good Y})$$

In most markets, managers can change price whenever they want. Managers of businesses selling related products will usually see a change in demand for their product in response to another firm's price change. One easy example is hot dogs and hot-dog rolls. If the price of hot dogs increases because hot dog manufacturers begin using higher-quality meat in their products, by the law of demand, fewer hot dogs will be sold, and sellers of hot-dog rolls (commercial bakeries) will see a decrease in demand for their products. Using the cross-price elasticity formula, a 20-percent increase in the price of hot dogs might cause a 15-percent decrease in demand for hot dog rolls. The cross-price elasticity is $-.15/.20 = -.75$. As would be expected, the two products are complimentary goods, and the cross-price elasticity is negative. If the two products were substitutes, an increase in the price of one good would result in an increase in demand for the other good, and the cross-price elasticity would be positive. If the cross-price elasticity is zero, the two products are not related.

Managers know changes in prices affect their business. Few small-business managers take the time to calculate the impact of price changes by other companies, but cross-price elasticity can be used to measure the degree of response to changes in prices of complements or substitutes for their products. This can be used in planning inventories, projecting sales, and developing PRICING STRATEGIES.

Examples of cross-price elasticity estimates include:

butter and margarine	0.67
natural gas and fuel oil	0.44
beef and pork	0.28
cheese and butter	–0.61

Further reading

Ruffin, Roy J., and Paul R. Gregory. *Principles of Economics,* 7th ed. Boston: Addison Wesley, 2000.

cultural industries

Cultural industries are those industries considered critical to maintaining the cultural heritage of a region or country. Most often the term refer to the exclusion of certain industries from FREE TRADE agreements. (Citizens and politicians in many countries fear U.S. cultural dominance.) In addition to challenging existing cultural norms, cultural industries are a significant source of revenue. Many governments, including the United States, subsidize cultural industries in order to maintain them.

The U.S.-CANADA FREE TRADE AGREEMENT (1989) and NORTH AMERICAN FREE TRADE AGREEMENT (NAFTA) (1994) both contain provisions protecting primarily Canadian cultural industries. The acts restrict trade and control of publishing, distributing, or selling books, periodicals, newspapers, films, videos, audio or video music recordings, and printed or machine-readable music. The acts also define public-radio communications and all radio, television, and cable TV broadcasting as cultural industries; and allow unilateral retaliation against actions affecting cultural industries.

NAFTA also protects certain cultural products such as Mexican tequila and Kentucky bourbon. Under the agreement, only producers in each country can use these terms to describe their products.

Further reading
Folsom, Ralph H., and W. Davis Folsom. *Understanding NAFTA and its International Business Implications.* New York: Matthew Bender/Irwin, 1996.

customer loyalty (customer retention)

Customer loyalty (or customer retention) is the degree to which a company keeps its existing customers. Customer loyalty can be measured through repeat business and customer referrals. In most marketing environments, it is significantly more expensive to find and acquire a new customer than it is to retain an existing customer. Yet according to Paul R. Timm, author of *Seven Power Strategies for Building Customer Loyalty,* few companies measure customer retention rates or evaluate why customers do not return. Dr. Timm's research suggests three categories of "turnoffs" reducing customer loyalty: value, systems, and people.

Value turnoffs are situations in which customers think they are not getting what they paid for. Value turnoffs include inadequate guarantees, high prices relative to the perceived value, and a failure to meet quality expectations. A few years ago, a fast-food chain introduced a new "deluxe" hamburger, but in reality it only added lettuce and a tomato to its existing burger. The price was significantly higher, and consumers could easily see what they were paying extra for. Consequently, the product was a flop. Marketers of SERVICES often need to explain what they are providing in order to assure customers that they are getting good value for their purchase.

Systems turnoffs are situations where the purchase or distribution of PRODUCTs disappoints customers. Anyone who has gone through a telephone menu and, after spending five minutes on the phone, not found the desired choice has experienced systems failure. INTERNET marketers know

they have about five seconds to catch viewer's attention. Simple features on websites, like "back" and "return to main menu" buttons are basic to facilitating consumers' needs. Slow service, lack of delivery choices, and unnecessary paperwork all reduce customer satisfaction and loyalty.

People turnoffs include lack of courtesy, failure to attend to the needs of customers, and unprofessional behavior. One retailer directed his employees to tell customers that any item the store did not have in stock was "on back order." People returned, expecting to find the product available and were usually disappointed; they soon went elsewhere. A television story described a telephone customer-service contractor in India using a scene with Jack Nicholson in the film *A Few Good Men* to train employees how to respond professionally and courteously to an angry customer. Occasionally a business will choose to lose a rude customer, but it is more expensive to replace a customer than retain one. Customers who have a poor experience with a firm are highly likely to tell others about their experience.

People turnoffs can also be subtle rather than blatant. Jeff Mowatt suggests customer loyalty is often affected by first impressions, including whether the business or business representative looks different from a customer expected. Bankers know that clients like them to look professional and dress conservatively; flashy dress suggests that the banker might take excessive risks with their funds. Similarly, an electrician who shows up in a suit and driving a luxury car brings fear of fleecing to consumers. Mowatt also suggests consumer retention is affected by employees' communication skills and promises made to customers. If people do not understand what is being said, either through excessive use of technical jargon or inability to understand accents, they are likely to walk away and not return.

Many marketers also recommend understating promises to customers as a way of not building high expectations and setting an expectation that can be exceeded. When asked what advice he had for young people, new in marketing, one marketer said simply, "Be on time for your appointments and return your phone calls. You would be surprised how few people do this."

See also RELATIONSHIP MARKETING; GAP ANALYSIS.

Further reading
Keenan, William, Jr. "Customer Turnoffs," *Industry Week* 250 (11 June 2001): 25; Mowatt, Jeff. "The Shocking Truth About Your Image," *Canadian Manager* 26 (Fall 2001): 15.

customer-relationship management

Customer-relationship management (CRM) is an organization's efforts to build and maintain relationships with the people who buy their products and services. CRM became a popular buzzword among marketers in the last decade as new technology improved the ability of firms to gather information about and communicate with their customers using a variety of methods. But as Stephen Horne suggests, "In essence, CRM is your corner grocer knowing you by name, remembering what grade your child is in and suggesting that you pick up extra batteries for the big storm."

Customer-relationship management is based on the reality that, in most markets, it is much cheaper to maintain existing customers than to find new ones. Retailers know they spend hundreds or thousands of dollars for each new customer, but a thank-you note, sample, or discount coupon can stimulate additional purchases from existing customers.

A good customer-relationship management program involves applying the MARKETING CONCEPT, thinking of the customer in every aspect of the business, and involving everyone in the organization. Horne defines CRM as "process discipline," remembering and treating people well.

Customer-relationship management involves collecting and using information about existing customers to extend and strengthen relationships. In the 1990s, many marketers jumped on new CRM technology: DATABASE MANAGEMENT, INTERNET customization, and e-mails. But CRM is a process, not a technology. New technologies facilitate building relationships.

One of the major issues in American business today is PRIVACY. CRM is based on knowing one's customers, but some consumers are concerned about the use of technology to invade privacy and distrust institutions involved in collecting information. Direct marketers Michael Staten and Sheila Colclasure report one researcher has found that familiarity fosters trust. Those institutions with which consumers maintain positive relationships are trusted to act responsibly with information about them. "Thus, paradoxically, acquiring more information and showing greater interest in your customers can reduce privacy concerns."

See also CUSTOMER RELATIONS/SATISFACTION.

Further reading
Horne, Stephen C. "Cutting Through the CRM Hype." *DMNews*, 30 July 2001, p. 32; Staten, Michael, and Sheila Colclasure. "Using CRM to Enhance Privacy." *DMNews*, 30 July 2001, p. 38.

customer relations/satisfaction

Customer relations/satisfaction involves meeting or exceeding customer needs and expectations. CUSTOMER-RELATIONSHIP MANAGEMENT (CRM) is a philosophy and process of building and maintaining relationships with customers.

Customer relations and satisfaction begins with knowing what customers want, need, or expect. Most marketers develop a sense of understanding of their customers through experience. With good communications, marketers can often anticipate customers' needs and wants

and, by fulfilling these needs, develop enduring business relationships. Understanding customers can be difficult, especially in new TARGET MARKETS. A common mistake is to assume new customers think and feel the same as past customers. Economic, demographic, and cultural differences, as well as lack of knowledge of a PRODUCT or service, can lead to different customer expectations.

Effective marketers constantly measure customer satisfaction through SURVEYS, complaints, and employee input. In almost every retail business, customers are offered customer-comment cards. These cards, if they have postage-paid mailing, are usually processed by marketing-research firms, which provide monthly summaries to the client. Some retailers have drop-in boxes at the checkout counter, while others ask customers to just leave their comment cards at their table. Like all MARKET RESEARCH, obtaining and interpreting information about customer satisfaction (or lack thereof) can be difficult. One restaurant had customers leave their comments at their table. Waiters and waitresses would read the comments and, if they were not complimentary, discard the cards. Some managers may overreact, using one complaint to change policy or procedures. Anyone who has worked in retailing knows it is impossible to please everybody. Market researchers recommend using complaints on customer-comment cards as a signal that there might be a problem.

In addition to customer-comment cards, some companies conduct surveys of their customers, assessing changes in perceptions and expectations. Whether conducted by mail, telephone, or personal interview, customer-satisfaction SURVEYS can provide valuable information to marketers. Armed with information about their customers, companies can develop better FAQ (Frequently Asked Questions) websites and information brochures, train call-center personnel, and adjust their MARKETING STRATEGY to better meet customer expectations.

The University of Michigan, along with the American Society of Quality Control, developed the AMERICAN CUSTOMER SATISFACTION INDEX, which tracks customer satisfaction across a broad range of companies, industries, and government agencies. Major companies watch the index and track their ranking relative to other competitors in their industry.

Improving customer satisfaction leads to better relationships. In almost every marketplace it is significantly more expensive to find new customers than retain existing customers. Effective customer-relationship management reduces marketing COSTS and improves word-of-mouth referrals. One study found that 95 percent of dissatisfied customers do not complain directly to the company but instead, on average, tell 11 friends or acquaintances about their negative experience. Marketers know word-of-mouth is almost always the most important source of promotion. Customer relations and relationship management can directly impact the success of marketing efforts.

With advanced DATABASE MANAGEMENT techniques in recent years, companies have adopted customer-relationship management strategies. CRM involves using information about customers to better meet and exceed their expectations. In the past, many times different divisions or individuals within a company had information about customers that was not centrally organized or accessible. CRM can tell managers simple things like which of the company's products and services the customer is already purchasing, leading to opportunities to cross-sell. It can tell marketers when customers have made most of their purchases, allowing predictions of when they will be ready to reorder. It can report which MARKETING COMMUNICATIONS and promotional methods customers respond to.

Some companies install CRM technology but do not institute a customer-relationship philosophy. A customer-relationship philosophy involves centering company efforts on the needs of their customers. Together, CRM and a customer focus can lead to enhanced customer satisfaction and retention and profitable business relationships.

Further reading

Boone, Louis E., and David L. Kurtz. *Contemporary Marketing,* 10th ed. Fort Worth: Dryden Press, 2001.

customs union

A customs union is an agreement between or among countries to reduce or eliminate TRADE BARRIERS among its members and have a common set of external TARIFFS for trade outside the union. A customs union is one step beyond a FREE TRADE agreement but below a common market. A free-trade agreement only reduces or eliminates barriers to trade, while a common market also allows the free flow of CAPITAL and resources (including labor) among participating nations.

The most widely known customs union is Mercosur, an agreement among Argentina, Brazil, Paraguay and Uruguay, established in 1995. By this agreement, reductions in trade barriers among the four countries increased regional trade, and a common set of external trade barriers stimulated regional investment. Because a customs union is not an economic union (such as the EUROPEAN UNION), it does not include the creation of a common currency. In 2000 and 2001, currency crises in Brazil and Argentina altered EXCHANGE RATES, undermining the basis of trade within the customs union.

The only other major customs union is the Southern African Customs Union (SACU), which includes South Africa, Botswana, Lesotho, Swaziland, and Namibia.

cyberspace

Cyberspace is the electronic network of communications that includes the INTERNET and the WORLD WIDE WEB. Cyberspace is growing rapidly and creating a variety of new issues and concerns for global businesses.

In general, economists applaud the rapidly diminishing barriers to COMPETITION resulting from increased communication and access to market and other information through cyberspace. As with any revolution, rapidly changing market conditions are resulting in problems that did not exist just a few years before. Cyber-attacks (viruses diffused through cyberspace, crippling computer networks or gaining unauthorized access to proprietary computer systems) are a growing problem. Responding to fears of cyber-attacks on U.S. financial and electronic business systems, in 2001 President George W. Bush created the position of cyberspace security advisor, thus recognizing that cyberspace is both a concrete foundation of 21st century business and a vulnerable network of electronic communication.

Another major issue concerns domain names in cyberspace. Domain names are unique Internet addresses. In the United States, initially one company, Net Solutions, was the sole registry for domain names. Other companies now provide domain-name registration, but a variety of problems, including cybersquatting, cyberhustling, and typosquatting, have emerged. Cybersquatting is the registration of a domain name that has no meaningful relationship to the person or company registering it. Cybersquatters hope to either sell the domain name to someone who wants it or use it to draw traffic to their websites. One cybersquatter received $7.5 million for business.com, while Bank of America paid $3 million for loans.com.

Related to cybersquatting is the more recent practice of cyberhustling. Cyberhustlers purchase the rights to domain names that are not renewed by the original owner. In an embarrassing situation, a technical college that switched its URL (universal resource locator) later found its old URL was purchased by a cyberhustler and then used to sell space to a variety of website promoters. People visiting the technical school's old URL found a variety of noneducational promotions, including pornography links.

Typosquatting is the registration of common misspellings. Cyberspace visitors typing in the wrong URL wind up at a typosquatter's site. Amazon.com challenged a typosquatter who had registered amazo.com. Businesses and individuals faced with typo- and cybersquatters can file complaints with the WORLD INTELLECTUAL PROPERTY ORGANIZATION (WIPO) and other arbitrators of names in cyberspace. The WIPO, an agency of the United Nations, uses three criteria in determining whether a complainant has been harmed.

- The domain name is identical or confusingly similar to a TRADEMARK or service mark in which the complainant has rights.
- The person who registered the domain name has no rights or legitimate interests in it.
- The domain name was registered or is being used in bad faith.

Cyberspace, like space itself, provides infinite possibilities for global businesses. Business use of cyberspace will continue to be a dynamic and important force requiring careful and continual scrutiny by managers.

Further reading
Harper, Timothy. "Cybersquatters." *Sky Magazine* (October 2001): 113; World Intellectual Property Organization website. Available on-line. URL: www.wipo.org.

cycle time
Cycle time—the minimum amount of time necessary for a task or series of tasks to be completed—is usually associated with manufacturing systems and depends on whether tasks are accomplished in a series or as parallel units. For example, in a textile factory production of a shirt requires cutting, sewing, and packaging. Assuming cutting requires 3 minutes per shirt, sewing 12 minutes per shirt and packaging 5 minutes per shirt, if the work is being done by one person (in a series of steps) then the minimum cycle time is 20 minutes. If three people are working in parallel, each performing one task, the minimum cycle time is 12 minutes, the time it takes to do the longest task.

PRODUCTION managers use the concept of cycle time to estimate the minimum amount of time needed to produce PRODUCTS, the maximum output in a fixed time period, and the coordination and allocation of resources to maximize efficiency. In the example above, the minimum time depends on whether the operations are conducted simultaneously or not. If it takes 12 minutes for a team of workers to make a shirt working in parallel, then in 8 hours the maximum number of shirts that could be produced is 8 hours ÷ 12 minutes = 480 minutes ÷ 12 = 40 shirts. But to maximize output, a manager would have to shift workers from one task to another. At 3 minutes per shirt, it will take only 120 minutes to cut the material for 40 shirts and only 200 minutes to package the 40 shirts.

In order to maximize output with a given level of workers and machines, production managers allocate machines and workers to fully utilize resources in production. In materials management, cycle time is defined as the time it takes from when materials enter the production process to when they leave the system. Similarly, one retail company sets as its goal to never have products in their distribution center for more than 24 hours. Recognizing that customers do not buy products from distribution centers, minimizing the time products are in storage increases the availability of products on the company's retail shelves. Reducing cycle time increases productivity. In complex production systems, statistical models are used to minimize variation in production and reduce cycle times.

Further reading
Stevenson, William J. *Production Operations Management,* 6th ed. Boston: McGraw-Hill, 1999.

D

damages

Damages, for legal purposes, are compensatory or punitive monetary awards. Persons suffering loss or injury (for example, in a car accident) sue in court to recover damages to which they are entitled by law. Damages can be awarded by court order for personal or property losses, for breach of CONTRACTs, and the loss of legal rights (such as COPYRIGHT infringement). Damages will only be awarded if the defendant acted unlawfully, negligently or in breach of contract and caused the damages alleged.

"Actual damages" refers to real damages suffered. In some cases, courts and juries may award "punitive" or "exemplary" damages when the defendant's conduct was outrageous and future deterrence is desired. Punitive damages are often a multiple of actual damages. At the other extreme, "nominal damages" may be awarded when little actual loss occurs. Some statutes, such as the federal ANTITRUST LAWs, mandate automatic trebling of actual damages, a kind of controlled version of punitive damages.

Further reading

O'Connell, John F. *Remedies in a Nutshell,* 2d ed. Eagan, Minn.: West Group, 1985.

database management

Database management is the process of organizing and manipulating a database. A database is a collection of organized data that is alterable (create, update, and delete), accessible, has a purpose, minimizes/eliminates redundancy, imports and exports data, has data independence, and has data integrity. It usually collects large amounts of data, which it organizes and stores in a computer system. The data are organized so the information can be searched or accessed quickly and efficiently.

The terms *database* and *database management* first appeared in the early 1960s with the introduction of computers into the business world. Computers allow businesses to store and retrieve large amounts of information in a database. Companies require a database-management system that is reliable and easy to maintain. This is a software package that assists in the organization and management of a database. Database-management systems were developed when existing systems no longer met the demands of businesses. The existing flat-file system was (and still is) ineffective, slow, inefficient, and unreliable, and the data were easily compromised. As databases increased in size, the flat-file system became even more redundant, unable to maintain the information in the database.

A flat-file system is unable to organize and manage data or to link them to other data. For example, a customer comes into a bank and asks for her checking account balance. She provides the bank teller with the checking-account number, and receives the account balance. Then the customer asks the bank teller for her savings-account balance, but she does not have the savings-account number. The bank teller is unable to give the customer the savings account balance without the account number. A flat-file system is unable to link the customer's checking account and savings account, whereas a database-management system allows the customer access to both the checking- and savings-account balances with only one of the account numbers. A database-management system allows for linking and flexibility in accessing information.

A database-management system also allows for multiple people to access, query, and update data simultaneously. A query or search retrieves specific information from the database. For example, several bank tellers can access the database simultaneously to assist numerous patrons. They can also query or search, all at one time, on specific account numbers to determine if patrons have accounts with that bank. If the information queried takes too long to retrieve, or if the information about a certain account is corrupted, patrons may determine the bank is unreliable and take their business elsewhere. The information in the database has to be accessed effectively and efficiently in order to better serve the customer.

A database-management system has to be organized properly or it may be just as inefficient and ineffective as a flat-file system. A downside to organizing a database-management system correctly is that it takes time, money, and resources. The database-management system has to be continually monitored and updated at regular intervals to maintain data integrity and efficiency.

Businesses now buy database-management software systems instead of creating a system from scratch, because it is more cost effective. There are two primary types of database-management systems: relational database-management systems (RDBM) and object-oriented database-management systems (ODBM).

The difference between ODBMs and RDBMs is how much the programmer can affect the data. Object-oriented databases can be fast and simple if the programmer is experienced in retrieving the information and understands the structure of the data storage, although a downside is that the programmer can also easily corrupt the data in the database. Relational-database programmers are restricted from interacting directly with the data, and the chance of corrupting the database is lower. Overall, relational databases tend to be faster and more efficient.

Not all database-management systems are created equal. Cost is an important factor in choosing the system that is right for an individual or business. For example, Oracle is an expensive database-management system to own and would rarely be purchased by an individual. Existing hardware and software are also factors in choosing a database-management system. Microsoft databases are not able to run on an Apple computer; Microsoft database systems are only able to run using a Microsoft operating system. Some database-management systems cater to individuals or small companies such as Microsoft Access, MySQL, and Progressql. Other systems cater to large CORPORATIONS such as Oracle, IBM's DB2, SYBASE, and Microsoft SQL server.

Further reading
Paul McJones SystemR website. URL: http://www.mcjones. org/System_R/; Date, C. J. *Introduction to Database Systems,* 7th ed. Addison-Wesley, 2000; Hoffer, Jeffrey A., Mary Prescott, and Fred R. McFadden. *Modern Database Management,* 6th ed. Englewood Cliffs, N.J.: Prentice Hall, 2002.

—Deborah Roth

Davis-Bacon Act
The Davis-Bacon Act, signed by President Herbert Hoover in 1931, requires contractors working for the federal government to pay the "prevailing" local wage. Expanded to include projects receiving federal funding or loan guarantees, the act effectively requires contractors to pay UNION scale wages. Rather than hire workers independently and pay union rates, most contractors rely on local unions to provide labor for federally supported construction projects. The act was later expanded to provide EMPLOYEE BENEFITS and require contractors or subcontractors to make necessary payments for these benefits. In right-to-work states, the act often accounts for the vast majority of union membership.

Originally the Davis-Bacon Act was intended to prevent itinerant labor from undercutting wages during the GREAT DEPRESSION. Supporters of the act argue it helps ensure stability in construction-market wages and provides skilled labor for federal projects. Opponents argue the act increases the cost of federal construction projects, costing taxpayers billions annually.

Further reading
"Should the Davis-Bacon Act Be Repealed," *Nation's Business* 71 (March 1983): 75.

debit, credit
The accounting terms *debit* and *credit* mean "left" and "right," respectively. Abbreviated *dr.* (from the Latin *debere*) and *cr.* (from the Latin *credere*), debits and credits are integral parts of financial or double-entry accounting.

When a transaction is recorded in the journal, the book of original entry, debit entries precede credit entries, and the dollar amount of the debit entry is placed in the debit (left) column of the journal. Credit entries follow the debit entries, and they are indented. Their dollar amount is placed in the credit (right) column of the journal.

In the ledger, the book of final entry, debit entries are recorded on the debit (left) side of the T-ACCOUNT; credit entries are recorded on the credit (right) side of the t-account.

Debit and credit by themselves do not signify an increase or a decrease in an account. It is only when debits and credits are associated with particular accounts that they take on the added meanings of increase or decrease. For example, to increase an ASSET account requires a debit to that account, because all asset accounts have normal debit balances. To decrease an asset account requires a credit to that account, because credit entries will offset the normal debit balances found in all asset accounts.

The converse holds true for the LIABILITY and owners' EQUITY accounts. Since they have normal credit balances, credit entries into these accounts will increase them. Debit entries will offset their normal credit balances, thereby reducing the balances in these accounts.

All of this is part of the double-entry accounting system developed in 1494 by Fra Luca Pacioli, a Venetian considered to be one of the most learned men of the Renaissance. Double-entry accounting has become the standard for FINANCIAL ACCOUNTING.

debt collection   See FAIR DEBT COLLECTIONS PRACTICES ACT.

deceptive trade practices

Also known as deceptive acts, deceptive practices, and deceptive sales practices, deceptive trade practices are methods of doing business that are likely to mislead individual consumers or other businesses, usually through the use of deceitful, false, incomplete, or otherwise misleading statements. In other words, deceptive trade practices occur when someone in business acts in a misleading manner toward another party, often a buyer, in a commercial transaction. For example, sellers of a weight-loss product were recently found to have violated a federal law prohibiting deceptive acts and practices by falsely representing that their product could cause substantial weight loss in a short period of time without the need for diet or exercise. Another example would be an outlet store selling reconditioned blenders or stereos, without any indication that they were actually used and reconditioned rather than new.

Consumers and other businesses are protected from deceptive trade practices through laws prohibiting and punishing such practices. For example, today, many companies include explanatory statements in their ADVERTISING and product PACKAGING that are designed to prevent the misleading of consumers. Statements such as "some assembly required" in television advertisements for children's toys, "quantities limited" in sale circulars, and "serving suggestion" on boxes of breakfast cereal are the result, in part, of laws against deceptive trade practices.

Deceptive trade practices are prohibited by both federal and state laws. Enacted by Congress in 1914, the Federal Trade Commission Act (FTCA), which can be found at 15 United States Code § 45, prohibits "[u]nfair methods of COMPETITION in or affecting commerce and unfair or deceptive acts or practices in or affecting commerce." As the quoted text suggests, commercial acts or practices may be found to be unfair, deceptive, or both, but an act or practice need not be both deceptive and unfair to violate the FTCA. The FEDERAL TRADE COMMISSION is the federal agency primarily responsible for enforcing the FTCA.

While the FTCA governs unfair or deceptive trade practices occurring across state lines, all 50 states have also enacted laws prohibiting deceptive trade practices. Such laws may be known as consumer protection acts, unfair trade practices acts, or consumer fraud acts, among others.

While the specific provisions of each state's laws differ, they often have the following common features. First, both the state governmental authorities and private consumers or businesses can enforce the laws. The government can bring enforcement actions and individual consumers or businesses can bring lawsuits against those who engage in deceptive trade practices. For example, in Massachusetts both the Attorney General's Office of Consumer Protection and injured consumers or businesses can enforce the state's consumer protection act. Second, the government, consumers, or businesses may be able to get an INJUNCTION against deceptive trade practice through a court order requiring that the offending party stop engaging in the deceptive trade practice. Third, victims of deceptive trade practices may be entitled to sue for double or triple DAMAGES and attorney's fees for knowing violations of their state's deceptive trade practices laws.

Under some states' laws, the standards for what constitutes a deceptive trade practice may be different in the business-to-consumer context and the business-to-business context. Such standards are more protective of consumers than of other businesses. For example, courts in Massachusetts have decided that business conduct considered unfair or deceptive toward a consumer would not necessarily be unfair or deceptive toward another business. As one court put it, in the business-to-business context, "[t]he objectionable conduct must attain a level of rascality that would raise an eyebrow of someone inured to the rough and tumble world of commerce." (*Levings v. Forbes & Wallace*, 396 N.E.2d 149, 153, 1979)

Many states have adopted the Revised Uniform Deceptive Trade Practices Act (UDTPA), which was originally drafted and approved by the National Conference of Commissioners on Uniform State Laws, approved by the American Bar Association in 1964, and approved in its revised form in 1966. The original purpose of the UDTPA was to reconcile and update the states' conflicting laws in the area of deceptive trade practices. The UDTPA's drafters subdivided the types of business conduct that constitute deceptive trade practices under the act into conduct involving either misleading trade identification or false or deceptive advertising. More specifically, the UDTPA enumerates 12 types of business conduct that constitute deceptive trade practices.

Under the UDTPA, a "person" (which includes individuals, CORPORATIONS, and many other entities) "engages in a deceptive trade practice when, in the course of his business, vocation, or occupation, he

1. passes off goods or SERVICES as those of another;
2. causes likelihood of confusion or misunderstanding as to the source, sponsorship, approval, or certification of goods or services;
3. causes likelihood of confusion or misunderstanding as to affiliation, connection, or association with, or certification by, another;
4. uses deceptive representations or designations of geographic origin in connection with goods or services;
5. represents that goods or services have sponsorship, approval, characteristics, ingredients, uses, benefits, or quantities that they do not have or that a person has a sponsorship, approval, status, affiliation, or connection that he does not have;
6. represents that goods are original or new if they are deteriorated, altered, reconditioned, reclaimed, used, or second-hand;

7. represents that goods or services are of a particular standard, quality, or grade, or that goods are of a particular style or model, if they are of another;
8. disparages the goods, services, or business of another by false or misleading representation of fact;
9. advertises goods or services with intent not to sell them as advertised;
10. advertises goods or services with intent not to supply reasonably expectable public DEMAND, unless the advertisement discloses a limitation of quantity;
11. makes false or misleading statements of fact concerning the reasons for, existence of, or amounts of price reductions; or
12. engages in any other conduct which similarly creates a likelihood of confusion or of misunderstanding."

Further reading
Sheldon, Jonathan, and Carolyn L. Carter. *Unfair and Deceptive Acts and Practices,* 5th ed. Boston: National Consumer Law Center, 2001.

—Laura M. Scott

decision tree
A decision tree is a map of the reasoning process business-people use to make choices. Decision trees are excellent tools for making financial or number-based decisions where a lot of detailed data needs to be considered. They provide guidelines in which alternative decisions and the implications of choosing those decisions can be organized and reviewed. Decision trees help people form an accurate and more realistic picture of the risks and rewards associated with a particular choice.

Creating a decision tree requires time. The first step is determining what decision needs to be made; a small square representing the decision is drawn on the left side of the paper. From this square lines are drawn toward the right for each possible solution, which are written on separate lines. The results of each solution are then considered. If the result is unknown, a circle is drawn; a different decision needs to be made, a square is drawn. When creating decision trees, squares represent decisions and circles represent unknown factors. The decision tree will thus expand until all possible outcomes and unknowns are included.

When the tree is completed, it is necessary to review the diagram and challenge each square and circle to see if there are solutions or outcomes that have not been considered. At this point, a decision tree will provide a range of possible outcomes. The next step is to evaluate the tree and calculate the decision that has the greatest worth. Once the values of expected outcomes have been established and the probability of the unknown outcomes have been assessed, it is possible to calculate the values needed to make the best decision. The benefit of each solution is its probability multiplied by its worth. When the benefit of each solution is calculated, the decision with the greatest benefit is selected.

Creating and using decision trees have many advantages when trying to make an important decision. Though it takes time to calculate the outcomes and probabilities, it is often time well spent. Decision trees allow managers to view all possible choices. They should be used in conjunction with common sense, identifying all considerations associated with a decision and recognizing that probabilities are usually professional judgments and subject to variation.

Further reading
"Decision Theory and Decision Trees," Mind Tools Ltd. Available on-line. URL: www.mindtools.com/dectree.html; "Decision Tree," Mighetto & Associates. Available on-line. URL: www.eskimo.com/~mighetto/1sttree.htm.

—Melissa Luma

default
Default is the failure of a debtor to meet the provisions agreed upon in a loan agreement. Typical consumer default involves the failure to make payments on a personal, automobile or home loan. Business default involves failure to make timely interest and principal payments on BONDS or corporate LOANS. When default occurs (which is usually defined in the lending agreement), the lender may make claims against the borrower's ASSETS in order to recapture the funds loaned to the individual or business.

In consumer credit markets, lenders often apply the FIVE CS OF CREDIT: character, capacity, CAPITAL, conditions, and collateral. When a consumer defaults on a loan, lenders usually foreclose on the collateral provided by the borrower, entailing repossession of the asset. The repossession process varies from state to state depending on consumer-lending laws.

Lenders recognize that a certain percentage of loans will end in default. Most consumer defaults are caused by "trigger events" such as death, divorce, disease, or business downsizing. When making loans, the likelihood of failure to receive payments is referred to as default risk. Higher-risk loans are assessed higher INTEREST RATES. Consumer advocates are especially critical of lending practices in the subprime market, where borrowers are sometimes are sold products with payments they cannot feasibly make, resulting in excessively high default rates. Lenders in subprime or nonprime mortgage markets frequently repossess homes, sometimes literally towing manufactured housing off a borrower's property.

In securities markets, bonds are evaluated for the likelihood of default by MOODY'S RATINGS, STANDARD AND POOR'S, and other rating services. Junk bonds, considered riskier than investment-grade bonds, have a higher risk of default. In 2001 corporate bond defaults were predicted to rise primarily in the telecommunications industry due to over-investment in telecommunications delivery systems.

Default is not limited to businesses and consumers. In the largest public-sector default action, Washington Public

Power Supply System (WPPSS, known as Whoops) borrowed billions of dollars to construct nuclear power plants. In 1983 cost overruns, changing market conditions, and poor management led to the failure to complete construction and thus default on the WPPSS bonds. Many bondholders first learned about the difference between general obligation (backed by the taxation power of the government agency that issues them) and revenue bonds (backed by the anticipated revenue from the project they are used to fund) from experience with the default of the power-plant bonds.

Default rules are regulated by the UNIFORM COMMERCIAL CODE. Article 9 of the code is a set of rules that govern the taking of most types of collateral for loans, how to protect lenders' rights to collateral against claims by others, how to describe collateral in security agreements and FINANCIAL STATEMENTS, where to file financing statements, and what rights a lender has after default. Default rules are a complex but critical part of sound lending decisions.

Further reading

McElroy, John M. "Enforcing the Security Interest: The Lender's Rights & Duties After Default," *The RMA Journal* 83 (February 2001): 84.

deflation

Deflation is a sustained decrease in the general level of prices in an economy. It is the opposite of INFLATION, an increase in the general level of prices. Falling prices are a result from either increasing productivity, which allows producers to increase output and INCOME; or declining DEMAND. Increasing productivity benefits both the economy and producers, but decreasing demand results in lower prices and lower incomes. As illustrated in the CIRCULAR FLOW MODEL, when demand declines, output declines, and household income declines even further, causing further decreases in demand. The result can be a downward spiral in the economy.

Deflation has what economists call *distributive effects*. People with fixed incomes, including bondholders, benefit from deflation because it raises the value of the money income they are receiving, and thus their REAL INCOME or purchasing power increases. People with savings also see their purchasing power increase. Deflation hurts debtors because they are paying back money that has increased in purchasing power while their incomes have not increased commensurately.

Deflation can hurt creditors if declining prices put borrowers in a situation where the amount they owe exceeds the now-reduced value of the ASSETS they borrowed against. In the United States during the 1980s, when oil prices fluctuated dramatically, in some communities housing prices declined so much that owners "walked away" from their MORTGAGES. Banks and SAVINGS AND LOAN ASSOCIATIONS were forced to liquidate these mortgages and take

losses, contributing to the savings and loan crisis and the creation of the RESOLUTION TRUST CORPORATION to bail out the industry. Similarly, declining prices in Japan have bankrupted many financial institutions, crippling the Japanese economy for over a decade. The most severe period of deflation in the U.S. economy occurred during the GREAT DEPRESSION, between 1929 and 1934, when prices decreased by 24 percent. Business bankruptcies skyrocketed, 9,000 banks failed, homeowners defaulted on mortgages, and UNEMPLOYMENT rose to 25 percent.

During a period of high debt levels, deflation is of particular concern to economic policy makers. With high debt levels, the potential for business and household DEFAULTS increases. In 2002 total debt in the United States equaled 158 percent of GROSS DOMESTIC PRODUCT (GDP). According to the *Wall Street Journal*, "the last time debt rose to that level was in the late 1920s."

Policy makers fear deflation from decreased demand because it can make it hard for them to stimulate the economy. INTEREST RATES tend to change with inflation rates. When there is negative inflation (deflation), interest rates cannot go below zero. The Federal Reserve, the monetary authority in the United States, lowers interest rates to stimulate borrowing and spending, but the Fed cannot lower rates below zero. Without monetary policy options, the only ways to stimulate the economy are fiscal policy options, increasing government spending, and/or decreasing tax rates. These choices, though, increase budget deficits, increasing the national debt.

Generally businesspeople prefer stable prices. Increasing or decreasing prices create uncertainty, increasing the risk of business ventures.

Further reading

Ip, Greg. "Inside the Fed, Deflation Draws a Closer Look," *Wall Street Journal*, 6 November 2002, p. A1.

Delphi technique

The Delphi technique—named after the Oracle of Delphi, to whom ancient Greeks would travel to seek advice about the future—is a marketing-management tool used by businesses for forecasting. Developed by the Rand Corporation, a major U.S. "think tank," the Delphi technique utilizes an anonymous group of knowledgeable individuals to estimate future trends or sales. Like the jury of executive opinion, in the Delphi technique managers solicit the opinions of people both inside and outside the organization. A series of QUESTIONNAIRES is used, and the results of each round of surveys are aggregated and returned to the participants until a consensus forecast is reached.

The Delphi technique is more time-consuming and expensive to administer than a simple jury of executive opinion. Because the individual responses in early rounds are anonymous, it prevents one individual, often a senior executive, from influencing the others in the group. As individuals compare their initial forecast, either for sales or predictions about some future trend, they can modify or justify their estimates in future rounds. As a consensus is being reached, often the final rounds are conducted by bringing the group together for discussion.

Further reading

Etzel, Michael J., Bruce J. Walker, and William J. Staunton. *Marketing*, 12th ed. Boston: McGraw-Hill, 2001.

demand

Demand, or the law of demand, is the relationship between price and quantity demanded for a good or service in a market. The law of demand states there is an inverse relationship between price and quantity demanded; that is, the higher the price the lower the quantity demanded, and the lower the price, the higher the quantity demanded.

A number of conditions are implicit in the analysis of demand. First, the market under consideration needs to be defined. For example does the term *automobile market* refer to the local, regional, national, or global market? Further, does it refer to the retail, wholesale, or manufacturing level? Demand relationships are usually studied with the assumption ceteris paribus (all other things being equal, or assuming nothing else has changed).

A demand schedule or graph shows the relationship between price and quantity demanded in a market in a period of time, ceteris paribus. In most markets, businesspeople have the power to change prices. Consumers respond to the changing prices by changing the quantity they are willing and able to purchase. Price is the independent variable, and quantity demanded is the dependent variable. A change in price causes a change in quantity demanded.

While a change in price causes a change in quantity demanded, other factors can cause a change in demand, which is a shift of the whole price/quantity relationship in a market. An increase in demand means that at every price, consumers are willing and able to purchase more of the good or service. Likewise, a decrease in demand means consumers are willing to purchase less of the good at each price.

Economists have identified six factors that can cause a change in demand:

- tastes and preferences
- INCOME
- price of compliments and substitutes
- expectations
- number of consumers
- EXCHANGE RATES

It is easy to envision how changing tastes and preferences affect demand in a market. Consider what were the most popular gift products in past holiday seasons. Some

years it was a stuffed animal, other years a new electronic game. When PRODUCTS are "hot," they experience an increase in demand. Products that are no longer fashionable and those that receive unfavorable publicity experience a decrease in demand.

Income can affect market demand in two ways. Most often an increase in consumers' income increases demand for goods and services; if we have more money, we spend more. American business managers know that the demand for expensive products, automobiles, appliances, and electronic equipment is sensitive to changes in income. Automobile manufacturers consider changes in income when planning production levels. For some products, called economically inferior goods, as income increases, demand decreases. As an example, if someone wins the lottery, what would that person buy less of? College students often respond fast food, instant noodles, and used cars. A shrewd manager of an automobile repair business once observed that his business prospered during downturns in the economy. He recognized that when peoples' incomes decreased, they held on to their cars longer, creating an increase in demand for repair services.

The prices of complementary goods and substitute goods affect the demand for a product. For example, if the price of hot dogs increases, it would cause a decrease in the quantity of hot dogs demanded. This would cause a decrease in demand for hot-dog rolls. Business managers keep track of the prices of complementary products affecting the demand for their products. Similarly, managers monitor the prices of substitute products. Chicken producers know an increase in the price of beef products will increase demand for their products.

Economists have observed that consumer expectations affect demand for some goods and services. While most consumers will purchase basic goods and necessities without considering changing ECONOMIC CONDITIONS, the demand for home purchases, automobiles, and other significant purchases are affected by consumers' comfort and security about the future. The University of Michigan Survey of Consumer Expectations is a widely studied and quoted index of American consumers' attitudes.

Logically, the more consumers in a market, the greater the demand for most goods and services. Back in the 1950s, Aiken, South Carolina, then a town of 5,000 people, suddenly had an influx of 30,000 workers constructing the Savannah River Site Nuclear Weapons facility. The huge increase in number of consumers overwhelmed local markets. Landlords rented the same bed to two people, one working the day shift, the other working the night shift. Local grocery stores put canned goods out in boxes, never stacking the shelves. There were so many new customers, they opened and emptied the boxes themselves. Midwestern oil towns experienced the same boom, but it declined in the 1980s when low oil prices sent workers elsewhere.

Changes in exchange rates can increase or decrease demand for a product. DEPRECIATION of the Japanese yen makes products from Japan cheaper for American consumers, increasing this demand and decreasing demand for substitute products made by American businesses. Similarly, appreciation of the U.S. dollar increases demand for foreign products and decreases foreign demand for U.S. products.

While only a price change causes a change in quantity demanded, the above examples were changes in demand for a product.

Deming's 14 points

Deming's 14 points comprise a philosophy about business and efforts to achieve quality devised by Dr. W. Edward Deming (1900–93), a mathematical physicist. In 1950 Deming was invited to Japan to teach. His statistical quality-control methods were quickly adopted by Japanese manufacturers, and in 1951 a Deming Prize was established in his honor. Deming has had a significant impact on business managers, first in Japan and more recently in the United States.

Deming's 14 points, referred to as "A System of Profound Knowledge," are a basis for transformation for industry. Quality advocates suggest they apply anywhere, to small and large organizations, to the service industry, and to the manufacturing. As one of the first MANAGEMENT GURUS, Deming brought together ideas from many sources and emphasized the importance of human factors in achieving excellence. The 14 points are:

- Create constancy of purpose toward improvement of product and service.
- Adopt the new philosophy. We are in a new economic age.
- Cease dependence on mass inspection to achieve quality.
- Constantly and forever improve the system.
- Remove barriers.
- Drive out fear. Create trust and a climate for innovation.
- Break down barriers between departments.
- Eliminate numerical goals.
- Eliminate work standards (quotas).
- Institute modern methods of supervision.
- Institute modern methods of training.
- Institute a program of education and retraining.
- End the practice of awarding business based on lowest price alone.
- Put everybody in the company to work to accomplish the transformation.

Further reading

American Society for Quality website. Available on-line. URL: www.asq.org.

demographics

Demographics are population measures such as age, race, gender, occupation, and INCOME. Demographics are often used by businesspeople to define market segments on which to focus their efforts. No business has the resources to be "all things to all people"; marketers therefore use segmentation to identify which groups of consumers are or are likely to be most interested in their PRODUCTS and SERVICES.

Segmentation of markets based on demographics allows marketers to make more efficient use of RESOURCES. Consider the alternative, broadcast marketing—that is, promoting and distributing a company's products wherever and whenever possible. Also known as "spaghetti marketing" (throw it up on the wall and see if it sticks), broadcast marketing wastes resources and reduces the likelihood of success.

Often obtainable from U.S. CENSUS BUREAU data, demographics—in exacting detail for anywhere in the country—are a basic tool for marketing. Segmentation by gender is commonplace and logical. Some products, such as computerized action games, appeal more to males; while other products, such as cosmetics, appeal more to women. In the 1980s, racetracks, traditionally thought of as a male-dominated spectator sport, studied their demographics and found almost 50 percent of their patrons were female. This led to a huge increase in sponsorships by firms targeting women.

Age is also a basic demographic characteristic affecting CONSUMER BEHAVIOR. In the 1980s, Chrysler recognized that "baby boomers," Americans born after World War II (1945–64), were finally starting to have children. Chrysler's vans appealed to this demographic group who needed room for a baby seat but did not want to drive station wagons like their parents. Demographers have come up with a variety of age-based labels, including "Generation X," people born between 1965 and 1976 perceived to be more egalitarian and environmentally oriented; and "Generation Y," young people in the 1990s, considered more conservative and materialistic than their predecessors.

Similar to age and gender segmentation, race, income, and occupational demographics are useful ways to look at consumer groups. Almost any television show or commercial radio station will have ADVERTISING that targets different demographic groups. Most advertising media maintain a listener, reader, and viewer demographic profile, allowing marketers to match their customer demographics with similar advertising media demographics.

Business markets are also divided based on demographic characteristics: size, geographic location, end-use applications, and customer type. Business marketers often use the NORTH AMERICAN INDUSTRIAL CLASSIFICATION SYSTEM to identify business customer groups. Business marketing organizational structures are typically based on business demographics. Sales organizations are usually divided based on customer types, geographic location, and business size, with representatives assigned to each group.

See also MARKET SEGMENTATION; TARGET MARKETS.

Further reading

Boone, Louis E., and David L. Kurtz. *Contemporary Marketing.* 10th ed. Fort Worth, Tex.: Dryden Press, 2001.

Department of Commerce, U.S.

The U.S. Department of Commerce (DOC) is the major department managing the federal government's domestic and international trade policies. Created in 1903 as the Department of Commerce and Labor, it has gone through numerous changes in activities as the U.S. economy has changed over the last 100 years. In 1913, a separate Department of Labor was created. In 1925 the Patent Office was transferred from the DEPARTMENT OF THE INTERIOR to the DOC. The Bureau of Mines has been moved in and out of the Commerce Department. The Radio Division was created in 1927 and then abolished in 1932. At various times the DOC has included bureaus of lighthouses, air commerce, weather, and marine inspection.

In 2003 the major organizations within the Commerce Department include the following:

- Bureau of Industry and Security
- Economics and Statistics Administration
- Bureau of Economic Analysis
- Bureau of the Census
- Economic Development Administration
- International Trade Administration
- Minority Business Development Agency
- National Oceanic & Atmospheric Administration
- National Telecommunications & Information Administration
- Patent and Trademark Office
- Technology Administration
- National Institute of Standards and Technology
- National Technical Information Service.

The most widely known parts of the Commerce Department are probably the Bureau of the Census, the Patent and Trademark Office, and the National Oceanic and Atmospheric Administration (NOAA). The Census Bureau is charged with managing the U.S. population census, which is used to determine political representation and allocation of funds for many federal programs. The Patent and Trademark Office oversees patent and trademark applications in the United States. NOAA is widely known for its hurricane advisory service but also manages a variety of science, fisheries, and ocean management programs.

Most of the other bureaus and agencies within the Commerce Department manage federal functions explained by their titles. The International Trade Administration promotes exports of U.S. products, the Economic Development Administration stimulates economic growth in distressed communities, and the Minority Business Development Agency promotes growth and competitiveness of minority-owned businesses.

Further reading

U.S. Department of Commerce website. Available on-line. URL: www.commerce.gov.

Department of Labor, U.S.

The U.S. Department of Labor (DOL) is a cabinet-level agency in the federal government created in 1913 with a mission "to foster, promote, and develop the welfare of the wage earners of the United States, to improve their working conditions, and to advance their opportunities for profitable employment." The DOL was created by transferring four bureaus—Labor Statistics, Immigration, Naturalization, and Children's—from the old Department of Commerce and Labor.

Over the years, changing political and ECONOMIC CONDITIONS have expanded the DOL's role in addressing the needs of workers in the United States. During World War I, the department was placed in charge of the War Labor Administration, and during the Depression it operated EMPLOYMENT services and many New Deal-era programs. Some DOL responsibilities, including veterans' employment rights and immigration, have been shifted to other federal agencies. Today the DOL administers and enforces over 180 federal laws. Following are some of its major responsibilities.

- The FAIR LABOR STANDARDS ACT prescribes standards for wages and overtime pay. The act requires employers to pay covered employees at least the federal MINIMUM WAGE and overtime at a rate of at least 1½ times the regular wage. The act also restricts employment of children under age 16.
- The OCCUPATIONAL SAFETY AND HEALTH ACT (1970), administered by the OCCUPATIONAL SAFETY AND HEALTH ADMINISTRATION (OSHA), defines and regulates safety and health conditions for workplace environments in most industries in the United States. Additional acts protecting miners, longshore and harbor workers, and child labor are also administered by OSHA.
- The EMPLOYEE RETIREMENT INCOME SECURITY ACT (ERISA) regulates employers who offer pension or WELFARE benefit plans for their employees. Before passage of ERISA, unscrupulous employers would "raid" employee pension funds for corporate and personal use, often bankrupting workers' funds. ERISA mandated fiduciary and disclosure requirements and created the PENSION BENEFIT GUARANTY CORPORATION requiring employers to insure retirement benefits with payments in to guaranty fund.
- The LABOR-MANAGEMENT REPORTING AND DISCLOSURE ACT (also known as the LANDRUM-GRIFFIN ACT) created safeguards for the use and management of union funds. Protection of WHISTLE-BLOWERS—workers who report or

complain about unsafe or illegal actions by their companies—is administered under OSHA.

- The WORKER ADJUSTMENT AND RETRAINING NOTIFICATION ACT (WARN) requires employers to provide employees with early warning of impending LAYOFFS or plant closings.
- The EMPLOYEE POLYGRAPH PROTECTION ACT (1988) prohibits most employers from using lie detectors on employees.
- The CONSUMER CREDIT PROTECTION ACT (1968) regulates the garnishment of wages by creditors.
- The FAMILY AND MEDICAL LEAVE ACT (1993) requires certain employers to provide up to 12 weeks of unpaid leave for eligible employees for the birth or adoption of a child or serious illness of the employee or a family member.
- The DAVIS-BACON ACT (1931) mandates payment of prevailing wages and benefits to employees of contractors engaged in U.S. government construction projects.
- The MCNAMARA-O'HARA SERVICE CONTRACT ACT (1965) sets wage rates and other labor standards for employees of contractors furnishing services to the U.S. government.
- The WALSH-HEALEY PUBLIC CONTRACTS ACT (1936) requires the DOL to settle disputes of awards to manufacturers supplying products to the U.S. government.
- The MIGRANT AND SEASONAL AGRICULTURAL WORKER PROTECTION ACT (1983) regulates hiring and employment of agricultural workers.
- The IMMIGRATION AND NATIONALITY ACT (1952) requires employers who want to hire foreign temporary workers to obtain certification that there are insufficient available and qualified Americans to do the work.
- The FEDERAL MINE SAFETY AND HEALTH ACT (1977) covers all people who work on mine property.
- The COPELAND ACT (1934) precludes "kickback" requirements, payments demanded from employees as a condition for employment with a federal contractor.
- The LONGSHORING AND HARBOR WORKERS' COMPENSATION ACT (1927) requires employers to assure that WORKERS' COMPENSATION is funded and available to eligible employees.

The DOL has many other regulatory and advisory responsibilities related to workers and working conditions in the United States. Critics of government involvement in the workplace often cite DOL regulations as bureaucratic interference that creates inefficiency.

See also BUREAU OF LABOR STATISTICS; LABOR FORCE.

Further reading
U.S. Department of Labor website. Available on-line. URL: www.dol.gov.

Department of the Interior, U.S.
The U.S. Department of the Interior (DOI) is the principle federal agency managing public land RESOURCES in the United States. Created in 1849, the DOI manages almost half a billion acres of federal property. The Department states as its mission:

1. to encourage and provide for the appropriate management, preservation, and operation of the Nation's public lands and natural resources for use and enjoyment both now and in the future;
2. to carry out related scientific research and investigations in support of these objectives;
3. to develop and use resources in an environmentally sound manner, and provide an equitable return on these resources to the American taxpayer;
4. to carry out trust responsibilities of the U.S. Government with respect to American Indians and Alaska Natives.

Since its inception, the DOI has managed a wide array of public projects including the water system and jail in the District of Columbia, the 1850s boundary with Mexico, U.S. trust territories, schools, hospitals, patents, and public parks. Today it is divided into 8 bureaus, each managing different aspects of federal natural resources. The roles of most DOI bureaus are obvious by their name: the National Park Service, Fish and Wildlife Service, Indian Affairs, Geological Survey, Land Management, Minerals Management, and Surface Mining. The Bureau of Reclamation manages federal dams, power plants, and canals, mostly in the western United States. The Bureau of Reclamation is the largest WHOLESALER of water and second-largest producer of hydroelectric power in the country.

Over the years, many DOI bureaus have been the center of controversy. The Bureau of Indian Affairs has been criticized for heavy-handed treatment of Native Americans and misuse of funds. The Bureau of Land Management has been criticized for mismanagement and subsidizing animal grazing on federal lands. Surface Mining has been challenged for not protecting natural resources during mining operations; and Reclamation has been denounced for water subsidies to western farmers, impairing salmon fisheries, and damming natural waterways. James Watt, DOI Secretary during the Reagan administration, became the focus of environmental critics. Drilling in the Arctic National Refuge, proposed in 2000 by the George W. Bush administration, is under the DOI's direction.

Further reading
Department of Interior website. Available on-line. URL: www.doi.gov.

Department of Transportation, U.S.
The U.S. Department of Transportation (DOT) is a federal agency responsible for national transportation policy. The DOT, established in 1966, oversees numerous federal regulatory programs ranging from intermodal transportation

to the St. Lawrence Seaway. The DOT negotiates and implements international transportation agreements, ensures the safety of U.S. airlines, and regulates interstate surface-transportation systems. Changes in DOT regulations affect location and distribution decisions of U.S. and international business managers and safety standards for vehicles in the United States.

Following are some major DOT programs.

- The Bureau of Transportation Statistics compiles, analyzes, and publishes national transportation statistics. Commodity flow and American travel statistics are used to analyze changing patterns of U.S. business and consumer transportation.
- The U.S. Coast Guard, most widely known for rescuing stranded sailors, also manages waterway systems, intercepts illegal drug traffic, and promotes boater safety.
- The FEDERAL AVIATION ADMINISTRATION (FAA) oversees the safety of civil aviation. FAA regulations direct aircraft and airport management and maintenance procedures. FAA allocation of airport terminal space significantly affects airline market competition. The FAA has been criticized for lagging in upgrading airport traffic control systems.
- The Federal Highway Administration (FHWA) coordinates interstate highway programs. The Federal-Aid Highway Program, financed with gasoline taxes, is a major source of funding for highway development around the country. Critics of U.S. transportation policy often point to FHWA funding of highways, rather than mass transportation systems, as an example of misguided federal priorities.
- The Federal Motor Carrier Safety Administration, created in 2000, focuses on commercial motor vehicle safety.
- The Federal Railroad Administration promotes and inspects railroads, with a focus on safety and environmental concerns.
- The Federal Transit Administration assists in developing mass-transportation systems in urban areas.
- The Maritime Administration promotes the maintenance of U.S. merchant-marine (domestically owned marine transportation) resources through preferences for U.S.-flag vessels in transportation of goods involving federal funding or support; and provides subsidies for maintaining U.S.-flag vessels, repair, and shipbuilding facilities.
- The National Highway Traffic Safety Administration (NHTSA) directs highway safety programs, including defining and enforcing safety performance standards for motor vehicles, investigating safety defects, and setting and enforcing fuel economy standards. The NHTSA has frequently been criticized for capitulating to automobile manufacturers' demands, resulting in reduced fuel-economy standards.
- The Research and Special Programs Administration oversees rules governing safe transportation and packaging of hazardous materials.

- The St. Lawrence Seaway Development Corporation operates and maintains the Saint Lawrence Seaway.
- The Surface Transportation Board is responsible for economic regulation of interstate shipping, primarily rail transportation. The board adjudicates complaints regarding the pricing practices of railroads.
- The Transportation Administrative Service Center provides technical support for DOT administration of other government agencies.

Further reading

U.S. Department of Transportation website. Available on-line. URL: www.dot.gov.

Department of the Treasury, U.S.

The U.S. Department of the Treasury is the major financial management department for the federal government. As stated on its website, the major functions of the Treasury Department are:

- managing federal finances
- collecting taxes, duties and monies paid to and due to the U.S. and paying all bills of the U.S.
- producing all postage stamps, currency and coinage
- managing government accounts and the public debt
- supervising national banks and thrift institutions
- advising on domestic and international financial, monetary, economic, trade and tax policy
- enforcing federal finance and tax laws
- investigating and prosecuting tax evaders, counterfeiters, forgers, smugglers, illicit spirits distillers, and gun law violations
- protecting the president, vice president, their families, candidates for those offices, foreign missions resident in Washington and visiting foreign dignitaries

The most widely known bureaus of the U.S. Treasury are the Internal Revenue Service (IRS), the U.S. Mint, and the Bureau of Engraving and Printing, and the Alcohol and Tobacco Tax and Trade Bureau. The Internal Revenue Service (IRS) is probably the most controversial bureau, charged with administering income tax laws and collections. The U.S. Mint produces coins, while the Bureau of Engraving and Printing creates currency. The Alcohol and Tobacco Tax and Trade Bureau (ATF) was divided by The Homeland Security Act of 2002 Bureau of Alcohol, Tobacco and Firearms into two new agencies, the Bureau of Alcohol, Tobacco, Firearms, and Explosives, which moved to the Department of Justice, and the Alcohol and Tobacco Tax and Trade Bureau (TTB), which remains in the Department of the Treasury. The TTB, as ATF did before it, administers and enforces the existing Federal laws and tax code provisions related to the production and taxation of alcohol and tobacco products. These taxes amount to approximately $15 billion in excise taxes, including $100 million in occupational tax on the manufacture of firearms and ammunition.

Historically, the TTB was one of the most important parts of the U.S. Treasury. The department was created by an act of Congress in 1789. During the early post–American Revolutionary era, Congress levied excise taxes on distilled spirits, tobacco, snuff, and other products to pay for the debts incurred during the Revolution. The TTB became the federal bureau responsible for collecting these taxes and enforcing tobacco and alcohol laws. During Prohibition, the TTB became known as the federal revenue agents, closing down and destroying thousands of illegal alcohol production operations. As tax laws changed, increasing the importance of income and employment taxes, the IRS became the major tax revenue bureau with the Treasury Department.

Today, as the major department managing federal finances, the U.S. Treasury oversees the government's budget, borrowing to finance the national debt (more than $6 trillion in 2003), and international financial and trade policy. In 2003, statements by the new treasury secretary, John Snow, signaled to the global financial market that the U.S. would no longer support a strong dollar (a high exchange rate of the dollar with other currencies). Within two months the dollar dropped more than 20 percent against the euro.

Further reading
United States Department of the Treasury website. Available online. URL: www.ustreas.gov.

dependency ratios
Dependency ratios are statistics estimating the number of people in various dependent groups per 1,000 working-age adults. Dependency ratios are used by demographers to predict changing relationships and social patterns. The two most common are the youth-dependency and elderly-dependency ratios.

The youth-dependency ratio in the United States, or the number of children under age 18 per 1,000 adults between the ages of 18 and 64, is expected to decline by 11 percent between 1996 and 2020. This will lead to reductions in demand for public-school education as well as reduced SUPPLY of teenage labor, critical to many retail-business employers. In Indonesia a reduction in the youth-dependency ratio was found to alleviate household budget constraints and boost savings rates in the country. China's one-child-per-family policy significantly reduced the youth-dependency ratio but is contributing to a crisis in the pension system, with fewer workers per pensioner.

The elderly-dependency ratio, the number of people over age 65 per 1,000 working-age adults, is expected to increase by 43 percent in the United States between 1996 and 2020. Political debates over SOCIAL SECURITY and Medicare begin with the reality of a declining ratio of contributors to recipients in the system. In the 1990s demographers found an increase in the mortality rate among working-age Russians resulted in an increase in the elderly-dependency ratio, further exacerbating problems with their social WELFARE system.

Further reading
"Fountains of Youth," *American Demographics* 18, no. 7 (July 1996): 60.

depreciation, depletion, amortization
Depreciation, depletion, and AMORTIZATION are accounting techniques associated with the long-term ASSETS of a firm. When a long-term asset that is used in the course of business helps to generate revenue, a portion of its purchase cost is systematically apportioned to expense to satisfy accounting's matching principle. The systematic apportionment from cost to expense for the firm's man-made, tangible assets is called depreciation. The systematic apportionment from cost to expense for the firm's natural resources in depletion, and for the firm's intangibles it is amortization.

When a long-term asset is purchased, this is a CAPITAL EXPENDITURE, and an asset account is debited for the purchase. When that asset is then used in the generation of revenue, a part of that purchase cost must be transferred to expense, a revenue expenditure. Thus the accounting for long-term assets requires an understanding of both capital and revenue expenditures.

Contra asset accounts are created when depreciation, depletion, or amortization expense is recorded as accumulated depreciation, accumulated depletion, and accumulated amortization. These contra asset accounts serve to systematically reduce the book (carrying) value of the long-term assets over their useful lives. When the BOOK VALUE of a long-term asset declines to the level of its residual (salvage) value, then the asset is considered to be fully depreciated, depleted, or amortized.

See also RESIDUAL VALUE.

deregulation
Deregulation is the reduction of government rules regulating business activities; it is a response to previous government decisions to regulate certain industries in the economy. Deregulation and PRIVATIZATION were popular political-economic policies in the United States during the latter half of the 20th century. In the United States, a variety of industries have undergone deregulation, including airline, railroad, banking, and trucking industries. Advocates of deregulation call for further action in such industries as helium, power PRODUCTION, and the U.S. Postal Service.

The debate over regulation and deregulation centers on the COSTS and benefits associated with government intervention into markets. Free-market economists argue that government intervention creates inefficiencies and that competitive markets will adjust and eliminate market problems. Most economists agree that one role of government is to correct for MARKET FAILURE—situations where there is a lack of COMPETITION, a misallocation of resources, and economic PROFITS. In the late 19th century, the social costs of living in an unregulated market environment were visible to all citizens. Large CORPORATIONS used their market power to extract higher prices from consumers, drive out competitors from markets, gain concessions from workers and suppliers, and procure support from the political establishment. Defective and dangerous products were sold to the public, and MONOPOLY profits concentrated in the hands of a few who became known as the "robber barons."

With a loss of trust in market solutions, public calls for business regulation became louder. The INTERSTATE COMMERCE COMMISSION (ICC), established in 1887, became the first in a series of government regulatory agencies. Earlier government subsidies had resulted in over-expansion of some rail routes and monopoly control in communities serviced by only one railroad. Some railroad owners colluded to fix prices in markets in which they were, in theory, competing, while in other markets competition drove prices to below operating costs. In response to the proposal to create a regulatory commission, railroad owners supported price stabilization at profitable levels, while grain shippers and small communities supported control over monopoly service. The ICC was seen as the solution to market failure at both extremes.

In Europe, rather than regulate private companies, many countries created government monopolies. Like regulation, the goal was to provide services on a least-cost basis. It clearly did not make sense to have two railroads connecting the same destinations or to have multiple sets of telephone lines in a community. In many industries where ECONOMIES OF SCALE exist, providing an ability to produce at a lower cost per unit as output expands, political leaders chose to either regulate existing firms or create government-run monopolies. With greater numbers of government monopolies, in recent decades European governments have expanded privatization efforts rather than deregulation.

When railroads were first regulated in the United States, there were few alternative means of transportation. Automobiles and trucks did not exist, and waterways were limited by seasonal changes. With the advent of trucking, the monopoly power of railroads declined. Initially interstate trucking was included in ICC regulation. Similarly, AT&T was a regulated monopoly in the long-distance telephone market until the development of microwave technology created new sources of competition in long-distance communication.

In the 1960s and 1970s, critics of regulation cited the cost of huge regulatory bureaucracies, the slowness of regulators in approving changes, and the need to compete on a global basis, many times with firms that faced less regulation than U.S. firms, as reasons for government to deregulate. The ICC was disbanded, deregulating trucking and railroad transportation. The CIVIL AERONAUTICS BOARD (CAB) was dissolved, deregulating airline markets, and interstate banking restrictions were reduced and/or eliminated. Supporters of deregulation often point to the airline example citing lower fares that resulted from deregulation. Critics of deregulation point to increased airline overbooking practices, elimination of service to some communities, and increased safety problems.

In 2000 California experimented with deregulation of electrical power production. Prices power producers could charge were deregulated, while distribution fees and, more importantly, retail prices remained regulated. When, in 2000-2001, wholesale prices rose and retail prices were not allowed to also rise, a crisis occurred, severely challenging the financial survival of the power companies in California.

Further reading
Mallor, Jane P., A. James Barnes, Thomas Bowers, Michael J. Philips, and Arlen W. Langvardt. *Business Law and the Regulatory Environment*, 11th ed. Boston: McGraw-Hill, 2001; Moore, Thomas G. "Deregulation, privatization, and the market," *National Forum: Phi Kappa Phi Journal* 70 (Spring 1990): 5.

derivative securities

In their basic form, derivative securities are agreements between two or more parties. The parties agree to pay each other based on some agreed benchmark. For example, two businesses agree to pay each other based on the behavior of INTEREST RATES. If interest rates rise above a previously agreed level, one company pays the other. On the other hand, if the interest rates fall below the agreed level, the other company pays the first. The amount that each company must pay is derived by the terms of the agreement, hence the name *derivatives*. Usually the higher the rate goes above the benchmark rate, the more one company must pay the other, and vice versa. This is similar to betting on a football game where the bet varies based on the difference in scores. To complicate things even more, the agreement can specify the way that payment is made—in currency; securities; or a physical commodity such as gold, silver, corn, or pork bellies (used to make bacon).

Although derivative securities are nothing more than complicated gambling, they can serve a useful business purpose. To illustrate, suppose a resort hotel negotiates a CONTRACT with a Japanese tour operator, who wants to have the contract stipulate payment in yen. This protects the tour operator if the value of yen falls. The operator is charging his customers so many yen to come on the tour. If the value of yen falls and the hotel rooms were priced in dollars, the tour operator would lose. To avoid this risk, the tour operator forces the RISK onto the hotel. To get the tour operator's business, the hotel must accept payment in yen, but it does not want the risk of the yen falling in value, because when it exchanges the yen into dollars, it gets fewer dollars than it bargained for. On the other hand, the hotel could make an unexpected profit if the yen increased in value. To shift this risk, in essence it sells to someone else by using a derivative. The derivative contract specifies that the hotel will pay if the value of the yen increase, but if it falls the other party pays the hotel. They are essentially betting on the change in the yen EXCHANGE RATE. The hotel puts the agreement together in such a way that the derivative contract will produce profits that make up for the amount it loses on the yen deal with the tour operator. If the hotel should make money on the agreement with the tour operator because the yen went up in value, it would lose a corresponding amount on the derivative arrangement. This effectively shifts the risk of the fluctuating yen to the other party to the agreement.

See also FUTURES; HEDGING.

developing countries   See EMERGING MARKETS.

direct investment

Direct INVESTMENT has two meanings in business: the creation of a business enterprise in another country or direct transfer savings from households to businesses without the use of FINANCIAL INTERMEDIARIES. In its first meaning, direct investment is one alternative for a business considering expansion abroad. Direct investment is an alternative to either EXPORTING or LICENSING. It usually involves a larger and longer-term commitment of CAPITAL and resources than either of those two alternatives.

Direct investment in foreign economies is typically done for any of three reasons. First, investment may be needed to extract or make use of raw materials. In the 1960s and 1970s, many U.S.-based oil and mining companies established facilities around the world to extract resources.

Second, many MULTINATIONAL CORPORATIONS (MNCs) establish manufacturing facilities in countries to take advantage of less-expensive, trained labor resources. For example, MAQUILADORAS, the production-sharing factories in northern Mexico employ over a million workers at significantly lower cost than in the United States or Canada. In recent years, many U.S. computer companies invested in software development facilities in India to take advantage of a highly skilled, English-speaking workforce.

Third, direct investment is often used as a means of overcoming TRADE BARRIERS protecting domestic industries. Production in a country, even by a foreign-owned com-

pany, is usually exempt from restrictions. In the 1980s, Japanese automobile manufacturers, fearing trade barriers, invested heavily in factories in the United States.

Globally direct investment is dominated by the United States, Europe, and Japan. For a developing country, direct investment brings new technology and production capacity. It also provides access to management and marketing methods used in international trade. But FOREIGN INVESTMENT is made based on earning profits, which are withdrawn from the country, and foreign companies are often criticized for lack of respect for cultural values and for creating and leaving behind environmental damage.

The second meaning of direct investment refers to direct interaction between lenders and borrowers. In the United States most savings are deposited with financial intermediaries, banks, CREDIT UNIONS, and SAVINGS AND LOAN ASSOCIATIONS, which then lend these funds to consumers and businesses. Financial intermediaries provide the benefits of aggregating funds, reducing risks through lending to multiple borrowers, and knowledge of sound lending practices. Like any business, financial intermediaries attempt to earn a profit for the services they provide. Since the 1980s, many U.S. financial intermediaries have experienced disintermediation: the withdrawal of funds by savers, who then directly purchase securities.

direct mail

Direct mail is the use of letters, brochures, samples, postcards, catalogs, and other printed material sent by mail to potential and current customers. Direct mail is a multibillion-dollar industry in the United States. If one person set aside all the direct mail received in a month, in one month he would probably have a huge pile of solicitations, depending on how many lists he is on.*

Marketers use direct mail because they can be highly selective in deciding which TARGET MARKETS to send MARKETING COMMUNICATIONS. The other advantages of direct mail as compared to other traditional media (television, radio, and magazine ADVERTISING) are as follows.

- The circulation can be controlled by the advertiser.
- Each mailing can be personalized.
- Consumers see only the company's message, not a competitor's as well.
- It is relatively easy to measure response rates.
- It can be used to stimulate a direct response.

Disadvantages of direct mail:

- It is considered "junk" by many recipients.
- It is expensive.

---

* To reduce the amount of direct mail received, write to Mail Preference Service, DMA, PO Box 9008, Farmingdale, NY 11735-9008. Consumers should specify whether they want their names to be removed from commercial lists, nonprofit lists, or both.

- It can be considered an invasion of privacy.
- It is only as effective as the list being used.

Mailing lists are the "lifeblood" of direct-mail marketing. Lists come from many sources: internal company lists of customers and requests, associations, and list-service agencies. Each issue of *DMNews*, a weekly newspaper for direct marketers, includes advertisements for thousands of direct-mail lists. List brokers represent businesses and organizations willing to rent out their mailing lists. Rental rates vary, but lists usually cost $100–$200 per thousand names. List renters usually agree to pay only for new names and addresses: the names remaining after they "merge and purge" the list received against their existing database. The selling of information about people is an important issue in business PRIVACY.

In the United States, direct mail traditionally has been used effectively by companies offering CREDIT CARDS, through magazine subscriptions, and via music clubs. With today's increasingly sophisticated database systems, many small businesses and nonprofit organizations are using direct mail to identify new customers and supporters and to sell their products. Contests are often a great way to generate names for future mailings.

Direct mail is expensive. In 2001 the U.S. Postal Service offered discount rates for bulk mailings of 200 or more pieces of mail. But bulk-rate mail is easily identified by recipients and often is not even opened. Direct-mail marketers know the typical piece of direct mail is evaluated for only four seconds before people decide whether to throw it away or consider it further. The design of direct mail—including whether a label or hand-written address is used, a message on the outside of the envelope conveying the benefits of the product or service being offered, and the material included in the mailing—are critical to the effort's success. Direct-mail campaigns are often considered successful if the response rate is 2 percent.

Direct e-mail is becoming an increasingly effective form of direct mail. Companies are starting to ask consumers for their e-mail addresses and permission to send messages, then are collecting and renting lists of consumers who have agreed to receive direct e-mail solicitations. On-line newsletters and message-alert services allow companies to collect addresses and expand marketing communication using e-mails.

Further reading
DMNews website. Available on-line URL: www.dmnews.com; Etzel, Michael J., Bruce J. Walker, and William J. Staunton. *Marketing*, 12th ed. Boston: McGraw-Hill, 2001.

direct marketing

Direct marketing is MARKETING COMMUNICATIONS other than direct selling between consumers and companies. Although there is no consensus regarding what constitutes

direct marketing and what is ADVERTISING, direct marketing includes catalog marketing, DIRECT MAIL, TELEMARKETING, direct-response television, and on-line retailing.

Catalog marketing, begun in the United States by Montgomery Ward in 1872, allows consumers to evaluate choices in a catalog and make purchases either by mail or telephone. There are over 7,000 catalog-marketing companies in the United States. American consumers spend over $100 billion annually on catalog sales. Many consumers in rural areas with few shopping alternatives, those in urban areas where travel is often congested, and people working long hours and only able to shop for personal needs late in the evening prefer catalogs. Catalog marketers maintain extensive databases about their customers, customizing the catalogs consumers receive based on past purchases, mailing catalogs based on the timing of past purchases, and analyzing the effectiveness of each photograph used and number of items per page. Catalogs are expensive, so marketers attempt to maximize the effectiveness of their efforts.

Direct mail is the use of letters, brochures, samples postcards and other printed material sent by mail to potential and existing customers. Mailing lists are critical to the success of direct-mail marketing. Most companies maintain extensive databases about their customers, consumer requests for information, and other prospective customers. List brokers rent the names and addresses of magazine subscribers, association members, contributors to campaigns, credit-card applicants, and a variety of other groups. Direct marketers rent lists most likely to include people similar to their current customer groups. While expensive, direct mail allows marketers to personalize messages and focus on those consumers most likely to be interested in their goods and services.

Dedicated TV channels and INFOMERCIALS are forms of direct marketing. QVC and Home Shopping Network are the leading direct-response television marketers. Jewelry, housewares, clothing, and electronics products have been successfully marketed using direct-response television. Infomercials and dedicated television shopping networks are expensive but continue to be popular.

On-line retailing, often predicted to surpass all other forms of direct marketing, is the sale of products through computer connections. In the late 1990s, many companies created websites, promoted them through banner advertisements and other traditional advertising, and waited for consumers to come. To a large extent it did not happen. U.S. consumers frequently use the World Wide Web to research companies and products but are reluctant to purchase products through computer connections. Even with on-line security systems, only a few product categories—primarily books, music, and travel—are gaining consumer acceptance of on-line retailing. The electronic retailing world is replete with DOT-COMS, which were unable to gain consumer acceptance. Some on-line retailers are adding hyperlinked toll-free numbers at each stage of the on-line buying process, attempting to reduce the "bailout rate" (the high percentage of customers who begin to purchase online but do not complete the transaction). Many on-line retailers are using their websites to increase and improve communications with customers.

Further reading
Etzel, Michael J., Bruce J. Walker, and William J. Staunton. *Marketing*, 12th ed. Boston: McGraw-Hill, 2001.

disclosure duties

Disclosure duties in the context of the U.S. business environment ordinarily refer to information that companies and corporate officers must disclose on a timely basis to the public. Many disclosure duties originate in U.S. securities law and cover, for example, the PROSPECTUS that any stock, bond, or security buyer must receive. These disclosure duties relate to publicly traded companies, not privately held businesses. Other disclosure duties concern corporate accounts, ANNUAL REPORTS, materially significant events, and the securities transactions of company "insiders."

Some disclosure duties are specific to certain industries. For example, franchisers are obligated under federal and some state laws to disclose to prospective franchisees the nature of their franchise system and CONTRACT obligations. Other disclosure duties are consumer-oriented, such as the energy efficiency of household appliances and the fuel efficiency of automobiles. The economic premise behind disclosure duties is that information helps perfect markets by leveling the knowledge of buyers and sellers.

Further reading
Ratner, David L. *Securities Regulation in a Nutshell*, 7th ed. Eagan, Minn.: West Group, 2001.

discounting, present value

Discounting is the often-encountered process of finding an unknown present value from a known future value. Using a time line, discounting is moving backward in time from a given point of time in the future to the present time. Given the time value of money (that INTEREST RATES are always positive), present values are always smaller than future values.

Lottery and sweepstakes winners may be offered their winnings not as a lump sum paid presently but as a future stream of ANNUITY payments. For example, a sweepstakes participant may have won the grand prize of $1 million to be paid in yearly installments of $25,000 for the next 40 years. While the sum of the 40 payments is $1 million the present value of such a payoff is considerably less than $1 million. Finding the present value of this future stream of annuity payments will determine the true value for the

grand-prize winner. Using a discount rate of 10 percent, the present value of receiving $25,000 each year for the next 40 years is only $244,476.27.

For a lump sum, the present value of some future amount is determined by the discounting formula $PV = FV_n \div [1+ir]^n$, where PV is the present value, FV_n is the future value at some future point in time n, ir is the interest rate (expressed in decimal form) applicable to the situation in question, and the exponent n is the same point in time for which the future value is known. For instance, find the present value $133.10 to be received three years from now, given a 10 percent interest rate, compounded annually: $PV = 133.10 \div [1.10]^3$. Simplification reduces the formula to $PV = 133.10 \div 1.331 = 100.00$.

It is sometimes necessary to determine the present value of an annuity. While there is a formula for this, it is much easier to use a commonly published table of interest factors. For discounting, there are tables of present value interest factors for lump sums (PVIFs) and for annuities (PVIFAs). To find the present value of a future lump sum: $PV = FV_n[PVIF_{i,n}]$, where $PVIF$ is the lump sum present interest factor for some interest rate i and for some time period n. To find the present value of an annuity: $PVA = PMT[PVIFA_{i,n}]$, where PMT is the regular annuity payment and $PVIFA$ is the annuity present value interest factor for some interest rate i and for some time period n.

While using the published tables of present value interest factors is easier than manually doing the number-crunching, it is much more convenient to find present values for lump sums and annuities using a financial calculator. Remembering that the interest-factor tables carry the interest factors to only four digits to the right of the decimal, the results obtained from the use of a financial calculator are more accurate than using the tables. The published interest-factor tables list interest factors only for whole-number interest rates. A financial calculator can compound using any interest rate.

discount rate

The discount rate is the interest rate charged by the FEDERAL RESERVE SYSTEM to member banks for short-term loans. Changing the discount rate is one of three "tools" used by the Federal Reserve (known as the Fed) to manage the MONEY SUPPLY. The discount rate is not a major tool; rather it is more of a "pencil tool." Like a builder changing the construction plans, changing the discount rate is a signal that the Fed is encouraging or discouraging banks to make more loans.

Banks are expected to exhaust alternative sources before the Fed provides discount-rate credit. Discount-rate borrowing is closely scrutinized. Excessive borrowing suggests a bank is not carefully managing its funds, and frequent borrowing might lead to closer evaluation of a bank's business activities by the Federal Reserve.

In the Fed's early days, banks would borrow funds for their short-term liquidity needs at the discount window of the New York Federal Reserve. In recent years, as banks have become better at managing their cash needs, fewer have utilized the Fed's borrowing at the discount window. A falling discount rate encourages banks to make more loans and signals that the Fed is practicing expansionary MONETARY POLICY. A rising discount rate signals contractionary monetary policy.

After September 11, 2001, the Federal Reserve publicly announced the discount window was available to provide liquidity to the BANKING SYSTEM. With the stock exchanges closed and major banks scrambling to reestablish operations, there was a liquidity problem in U.S. financial markets. The Fed stepped in to provide liquidity by providing loans through the discount window. As reported in the *Wall Street Journal,* that week the Fed loaned $45 billion, compared to a typical weekly amount in the range of $25–$300 million.

By opening up access to the discount window, the Fed was attempting to reduce volatility in the FEDERAL FUNDS MARKET, the short-term (usually overnight) lending among U.S. banks to meet the Fed's RESERVE REQUIREMENTS. Despite its name, the Federal Reserve does not operate or control the federal funds market. The Fed requires banks to keep a set percentage of their deposits as cash or other specified U.S. TREASURY SECURITIES. These required reserves, which are available when customers want their deposits returned, act as a source of liquidity for banks.

As banks receive more deposits, their reserve requirements increase. At the end of each business day, bank managers calculate their required reserves, determine whether they have excess or insufficient reserves, and lend or borrow reserves electronically in the federal funds market. Loans made in the federal funds market are returned the next business day.

Banks borrowing to meet their reserve requirement will compare rates in the market, attempting to minimize their costs. Federal funds rates tend to be uniform among participating banks and increase or decrease, depending on the demand for and supply of funds available.

In 2002 the Fed announced it would change its discount-rate policies. Federal Reserve governor Edward Gramlich was quoted as saying, "There is an alleged stigma to the discount window, and we intend to get rid of that." The Fed proposed setting the discount rate 1 percent above the targeted federal funds rate. Financially sound banks would be allowed to borrow at the new rate with "few questions asked and without requiring a bank to first exhaust alternatives." With the discount rate above the federal funds rate, banks will not likely borrow, but if a financial crisis arose, raising the federal funds rate temporarily, banks could borrow at the discount window, reducing pressure in the federal funds market. The new Fed proposal would also allow less financially sound banks to borrow at a rate one-half percentage point above the pri-

mary discount rate. The Fed goal is to reduce interest-rate volatility.

See also OPEN MARKET OPERATIONS.

Further reading
Ip, Gregg. "Fed Is Overhauling Procedure for Discount-window Loans," *Wall Street Journal,* 20 May 2002; Mishkin, Frederic S. *The Economics of Money, Banking, and Financial Markets,* 6th ed. Boston: Addison Wesley, 2001.

dispute settlement
There are many ways to settle business disputes. Litigation in courts is common in the United States, much less common elsewhere. Mediation and friendly consultations, which are not binding, are increasingly used and predominant in Asian countries like China. ARBITRATION is growing rapidly as a business dispute-settlement method in the United States and globally. Arbitration is typically binding and precludes going to court in most instances, although enforcement of arbitral awards in court may be required. One reason for the growth in the use of commercial arbitration to settle international business disputes is the so-called New York Convention. This international agreement, to which the United States and over 100 nations are parties, greatly facilitates the enforcement of arbitration awards across borders.

The U.S. Supreme Court has repeatedly demonstrated deference to arbitration as a method of settling business disputes, notably in the securities industry. Antitrust disputes can also be arbitrated. As a practical matter, many arbitrations result in compromises as opposed to the "winner-take-all" approach of litigation before courts.

Arbitrators are often chosen ad hoc by the disputing parties, say one for each side with a third arbitrator chosen by those two selected arbitrators. There are many arbitration centers, where the arbitrators and their procedural rules come prepackaged. The American Arbitration Association hosts a wide range of business dispute-settlement options.

Further reading
Nolan-Haley, Jacqueline M. *Alternative Dispute Resolution in a Nutshell,* 2d ed. Eagan, Minn.: West Group, 2001.

distribution channels (marketing channels)
Distribution channels, also called marketing channels, are the systems used to move PRODUCTS and SERVICES from producers to consumers. At first glance, distribution seems like a simple and obvious process for a business: Find out where the customer is and get the product to him or her. But distribution channels can involve numerous structures depending on the needs of customers and producers.

Generally distribution channels involve two to five levels. In the simplest two-level system, manufacturers provide their good or service directly to consumers. With expanded use of the INTERNET, direct sales from producers to consumers are becoming more prevalent. Because of the direct contact needed, many service businesses have short, two-level distribution systems. Doctors, dentists, and lawyers rarely have market intermediaries between them and the customer.

Many manufacturers do not have the resources or skills needed to effectively market directly to consumers. These firms will sell to WHOLESALERS who then market the products to retailers, who in turn sell the product to customers. In recent years some U.S. retailers have used their market power to eliminate wholesalers, instead buying directly from manufacturers.

In addition to wholesale and retail levels in distribution channels, some markets have manufacturer's representatives who act as intermediaries between producers and wholesalers; in some markets jobbers or rack jobbers act as intermediaries between wholesalers and retailers. Manufacturers' representatives are often used for complex products where considerable explanation is needed. Rack jobbers provide physical distribution of products to small retail outlets that are not being serviced by wholesalers.

The number of levels in a distribution channel depends on who is performing which marketing channel functions. To be successful, all marketing functions must be accomplished. A manufacturer selling directly to consumers will need to advertise and promote the product, manage inventory and assortment, provide physical distribution, monitor customer satisfaction and feedback, and handle all financial aspects of the selling process. Many small E-COMMERCE entrepreneurs have learned there are reasons why intermediaries exist in distribution channels. The intermediaries provide benefits by managing distribution functions. Retailers assist with ADVERTISING and promotion, maintain an assortment of products available directly to consumers, manage returns, often offer credit, and complete the sales transaction. Wholesalers typically manage inventory and storage functions, have distribution systems, sometimes provide credit, and assist with advertising and promotion.

Sometimes a firm will want to control various aspects of its distribution channels. A manufacturer that creates or purchases retail outlets or creates its own wholesaling system is involved in VERTICAL INTEGRATION. For example, many U.S. cosmetic manufacturers lease space within retail department stores and hire their own sales staff to sell their products to customers in these stores, and oil companies now refine, distribute, and own the retail stores selling gasoline. Retailers sometimes contract to have products made by manufacturers to the retailer's specifications and with the retailer's brand name. Vertical marketing systems can also be created through contractual relationships. Many independent hardware stores are part of a voluntary wholesaling system, buying most of their merchandise from the group wholesaler and pooling funds for advertising.

Within distribution systems there exists channel power. One or more of the members of the distribution channel will determine which products are placed on retailers' shelves, which products are promoted, and which stores will be selected to sell exclusive products. Historically in the United States, manufacturers dominated distribution channels, determining how products were distributed and often dictating product and pricing decisions. In recent years, with an abundance of new products and limits to retail space, retailers have increased their power to influence manufacturers' and wholesalers' actions. Price concessions, shelving fees, and advertising allowances are a few examples of the increased channel power of retailers. Distribution channels are a dynamic part of a marketing system. Members of distribution channels are at the same time resistant to change, trying to maintain their part and power in the system but constantly changing in response to new threats and opportunities.

See also BRANDS, BRAND NAMES; ENTREPRENEURSHIP; RETAILING.

diversification

Diversification has two very different meanings depending on the business context. In personal finance, diversification is investing in a variety of assets. Diversification reduces risk. If one or a few companies go bankrupt, the investor does not lose all his or her assets. Investing in mutual funds that hold financial assets in many companies is one form of diversification. In 2002, Enron, WorldCom, and employees of other companies learned a painful lesson in the value of diversification. Many of these employees had, in addition to their livelihoods, all or most of their retirement funds in company stock. When the companies went bankrupt, they lost both their jobs and their pensions.

In a product/market growth matrix, diversification is expansion of a company into new markets with new products. This strategy for growth is more risky than expanding into new markets with existing products or expansion with new products into existing markets. While business diversification is more risky, if successful, it reduces a firm's business risk because, like personal financial investing, the company is less vulnerable if one product or one market fails. In the 1960s many U.S. conglomerates were formed, owning a diverse array of businesses. Conglomerate strategy was based on the idea that better management and financial backing would yield stronger growth than small, independent firms. In the 1980s and 1990s, many conglomerates, in an effort to become more efficient, sold off divisions, returning to their core business activities.

divestiture   See CORPORATE DIVESTITURE.

dividends, retained earnings

Dividends are a distribution of a corporation's earnings to its stockholders. A CORPORATION can do two things with its earnings: Pay them out in the form of dividends or retain them. Most corporations choose some combination—that is, they pay out a portion of earnings as dividends and retain the rest. A financial ratio called the *dividend payout ratio* measures dividends as a percentage of earnings.

The payment of dividends involves three dates. The first is the declaration date, the day on which the BOARD OF DIRECTORS announces the dividend and the time line for its processing and payment. A LIABILITY, dividends payable, is created by the announcement, and retained earnings are reduced on this date by the amount of the dividend.

Second is the holder-of-record date. The roster of stockholders as of this date determines who will receive the forthcoming dividend. Assume the holder-of-record date is June 24. Several days before June 24, the corporation's stock goes *ex dividend*. Sales of shares after this date will not include the upcoming dividend payment. If an investor buys shares of this stock on June 22, for example, the transaction is too close to the holder-of-record date for the new owner to be listed on the roster of stockholders to receive the dividend. As a result, the new owner will not receive the forthcoming dividend. The new owner is said to have purchased the stock *ex dividend,* that is, without the dividend. When a stock is purchased *ex dividend,* the price paid per share is normally the market price less the dividend not received.

The last date in the time line is the payment date. Checks are cut and mailed, effectively distributing a portion of the firm's earnings. The liability created on the declaration date is satisfied by the payment of cash dividends.

Retained earnings are the corporation's PROFITS not distributed as dividends. The cumulative amount of retained earnings accrues in an EQUITY account of the same name. Retained earnings belong to the stockholders and have the effect of increasing the value of the firm and the WEALTH of the common stockholders. Retained earnings do not usually exist in the form of cash. Rather, most firms use the retained earnings for CAPITAL EXPENDITURES— that is, to purchase ASSETS to foster growth and enhance the firm's profitability.

document-retention policy

A document-retention policy is a firm's written policies regarding which documents to retain and where and how to retain them. Document-retention policies serve a number of purposes, including maintaining whatever is needed to conduct business, what is needed for legal and regulatory purposes, and what is needed in case of litigation.

The first rule in creating a document-retention policy is to be constantly saving everything that is needed to conduct business. Following the September 11 tragedy, most companies operating in the World Trade Center were able to reestablish their operations due to continuous data backup systems located elsewhere. Many CORPORATIONS have since reviewed and revised their document-retention systems.

The second rule in document-retention policies is retaining what is required by law. For example, the SECURITIES AND EXCHANGE COMMISSION (SEC) and INTERNAL REVENUE SERVICE (IRS) regulate how long companies and individuals must retain financial documents. The IRS can audit tax-related records for up to seven years back.

The third rule in document-retention policies is to retain anything that may be subject to existing or pending litigation. In the United States, courts usually notify defendant parties when a lawsuit is initiated. Destroying documents once litigation has begun is called "spoilation." Attorney Brett Dorny defines spoilation as "the intentional destruction of evidence that is material to an ongoing or imminent litigation matter." Once litigation has commenced, both sides to a lawsuit engage in discovery, where each party is allowed to interrogate witnesses, take depositions, and request documents from the opposing party.

Discovery often is expensive. In most cases each party to a lawsuit bears its own expenses of discovery, including the costs of producing the documents requested. A well-organized document-retention system can mitigate these costs and allow a firm access to documents needed for its defense. One of the problems associated with document-retention policies is constantly changing technology. Often firms find they cannot easily access old documents saved under different software platforms.

Document-retention policies became widespread in the 1990s and drew public attention in 2002 during the Arthur Andersen LLP-Enron Corporation collapse. In the aftermath, former Arthur Andersen executive David Duncan pleaded guilty to obstruction-of-justice charges. He admitted participating in a meeting where Andersen partners decided to advise staff members assigned to Enron that they should begin implementing the firm's documentation-retention policy. The Andersen policy required personnel to destroy all files that were not supposed to be included in the firm's permanent records, including draft memos that often provide insight into the firm's decision-making process. Duncan testified that another Andersen executive suggested staff members be told to take care to not do "any more or any less" than the document-retention policy required.

The government's case against Andersen was based on the theory that when Andersen partners and employees directed staff members to implement the policy, they knew that an investigation of Andersen's audit of Enron was imminent. Ironically, Arthur Andersen, one of the country's "big five" accounting firms, created a nearly 500-page source book entitled "Document Retention . . . in the Face of Pending or Threatened Litigation," which has been licensed to many Fortune 500 corporations.

Further reading

Dorny, Brett. "Pitfalls for Pack Rats and Purgers." *CIO Magazine* 13, no. 19 (15 July 2000): 64–65; Jonathan Weil and Richard Schmitt, "Andersen Auditor Avoids Testifying," *Wall Street Journal*, 21 May 2002.

dot-coms

Dot-coms are businesses that operate primarily or solely on the INTERNET. The term *dot-com* comes from the suffix for business domain names (.com). Dot-coms compete with traditional store-based businesses (called "bricks and mortar"), providing alternatives to consumer and business markets. Dot-coms have been more successful in fulfilling the needs of business customers who make repeat purchases of similar items and need relatively little customer assistance in making purchase decisions.

Because there are relatively low start-up costs associated with many dot-com businesses, the industry has attracted a wide array of entrepreneurs. In the late 1990s, the United States experienced a dot-com frenzy. Any business with even a whimsical Internet MARKETING STRATEGY was able to register a domain name and begin promoting itself as a global enterprise. Initially dot-coms used registration with Internet search engines and traditional media promotion to attract visitors and potential customers to their sites. Some dot-coms then used their click-rates (number of visitors to the site) to sell banner ADVERTISING to other dot-coms. Other early dot-coms also offered wireless modems, specialty hand-held gadgets, and Internet currencies for consumer purchases.

One dot-com offered up to 100-percent rebates for highly overpriced merchandise, betting few customers would collect the paperwork necessary for reimbursement. Another company's hand-held device offered entertainment and dining listings. When the company went bankrupt, the devices, which were not compatible with other hand-held technology, became worthless. The possibilities seemed endless, and almost any dot-com entrepreneur could find financial backing. INITIAL PUBLIC OFFERINGS (IPOs) of dot-coms created huge sums of money for businesses with meager sales and no PROFITS. Many companies with an Internet strategy changed their names, adding dot-com, hoping to attract investor interest and stock-price escalation.

The industry coined the term *burn rate* to quantify the rate the dot-com was using up investor CAPITAL in their quest for profitability. In March 2000 the dot-com "bubble" burst as investors finally recognized the lack of earnings and lack of prospects for future earnings among the vast majority of dot-coms. Media reports described the demise of dot-com millionaires whose paper WEALTH vanished as stock prices dwindled.

Many successful dot-coms use drop-shipping (taking orders from customers and then forwarding them to producers that ship directly to customers) along with traditional wholesaling channels to offer a wide array of products while maintaining minimal inventory. Amazon.com became the most successful dot-com using this business model.

See also ENTREPRENEURSHIP.

Further reading

Kaplan, Karen. "On Junk Heap of the Net," *Los Angeles Times,* 1 October 2001, p. 1.

double-entry accounting   See FINANCIAL ACCOUNTING.

Dow Jones averages

Dow Jones averages are the most widely quoted INDICATORS of the U.S. STOCK MARKET. There are three Dow Jones averages: industrials, transportation, and utilities. The Dow Jones Industrial Average (DJIA) is the oldest and best-known indicator.

In 1882 Charles Dow, Edward Jones, and Charles Bergstresser began producing a market newsletter delivered by messenger to subscribers in the WALL STREET area of New York. At the time the stock market was not highly regarded, being perceived as the province of speculators and market manipulators. Dow, Jones, and Bergstresser provided information to investors, and in 1884 they created their first index with 11 stocks, mostly railroad companies. Their business grew, and the newsletter quickly became a newspaper that would be called *The Wall Street Journal.*

In 1896 Dow Jones created their industrial average. At the time it included 12 stocks. The DJIA was calculated by adding up the closing price of these companies and dividing by 12. On May 26, 1896, the DJIA was 40.94. The average was increased to include 20 stocks in 1916 and 30 stocks in 1928. While the number of stocks in the DJIA has remained constant since then, the companies included in the index change infrequently. The editors of *The Wall Street Journal* select which stocks are included in the industrial average. The definition of "industrial" has changed as the U.S. economy has shifted away from primarily manufacturing to, increasingly, a service economy. Any stock (other than utility and transportation companies, which are included in the other Dow Jones averages) can be considered for inclusion in the index. In 1999 four companies—Union Carbide, Goodyear Tire & Rubber, Sears Roebuck, and Chevron—were removed from the DJIA, and Home Depot, Intel, Microsoft, and SBC Communications were added. A few companies have been added and deleted more than once, including General Electric, DuPont, U.S. Rubber, and IBM.

Changes to the index usually occur when a company is acquired by another company eliminating that stock from the market. While almost all other stock-market indexes are weighted by the market capitalization (price times the number of shares outstanding) of the stocks included in the index, the DJIA is an unweighted index. The DJIA is a relatively narrow indicator of the U.S. stock market, but because it is the oldest index, it is the most widely quoted. While it is well known, changes in the DJIA are neither a reliable indicator of future stock market changes nor a reliable predictor of changes in the economy. Generally changes in the stock market precede changes in the economy, but not always and not exactly by the same amount of lead time.

The Dow Jones Transportation Average (DJTA) and utilities average (DJUA) are, as their names indicate, industry-sector averages. Stock-market analysts use changes in the transportation and utilities averages as indicators of change in the larger market.

Dow Jones is a leading U.S. financial information service company. In addition to publishing *The Wall Street Journal*, they publish *Barrons, Far Eastern Economic Review,* Dow Jones newswires, and WSJ.com.

Further reading

Dow Jones website. Available on-line. URL: www. dowjones.com.

downsizing

Downsizing is the reduction of staffing levels necessitated by business reasons such as low sales or low profits. The number of employees required to build products is a variable expense directly related to the number of units being built. So if fewer people are on the company's payroll, labor expense is reduced, resulting in stabilized or increased profits.

People are a primary resource in virtually all businesses. People perform work necessary to the firm's success. Having either too few or too many employees may result in lower operating efficiencies and lower profits for the business. Determining the number of employees needed to operate the business is a primary management responsibility.

The following employee planning process is for a manufacturing firm; however, the process for a service company is virtually the same. With the best business forecast available, management estimates by product line the number of units that are projected to be sold over a time period of six months or more. Projected sales are totaled and existing finished goods inventory is subtracted to determine the number of units that need to be manufactured. Using existing manufacturing standards, by type of job and work station, management then estimates the number of positions needed and the requisite knowledge, skills, abilities (KSAs), and experience. After the positions, KSAs, and experience levels are identified, the employees are evaluated to determine which ones have the required background to perform the work. In the aggregate, if there are fewer employees than needed, new employees are hired; if there are more employees than needed, downsizing occurs.

The downsizing process can occur in several ways. If the sales forecasts, initially used by management to plan production levels, project a protracted slump in sales (that may last for a year or more), then those employees not needed are usually terminated. If the sales slump is expected to be relatively short and then sales are expected to rebound, then excess employees are usually laid-off. When an individual is laid-off, the assumption is that the person will be needed back within a reasonable period of time. The return to work process is known as a recall. A termination assumes that the employee will not return to work at that company.

Attrition is an attractive alternative to downsizing. Attrition occurs when an individual leaves a company's employment through either a voluntary resignation or being terminated for reasons other than low sales or low profits. The position is vacant, but the company does not fill the position with a newly hired employee. Total number of employees will decrease; however, this process is very slow and will not reduce the total number as quickly as downsizing.

—John B. Abbott

due diligence

Due diligence refers to any in-depth investigation, review, or effort to comply with requirements, expectations, or requests. The phrase originated in U.S. securities law. The laws require companies and the accountants, lawyers, and bankers who assist in the process issuing securities to provide accurate information about the securities. The company and its accountants, lawyers, and bankers must show that they were careful in complying with the disclosure requirements of these laws. The courts said that these groups must show due diligence in their efforts to comply with the law.

The phrase is now applied to any situation where in-depth information about a company is needed. For example, U.S. banking laws designed to reduce money laundering require banks to really know their customers fully, not just on a superficial level. To do this, banks employ due diligence to learn all they can about their clients, including such things as credit checks and background checks on a company's officers.

Due diligence also describes the procedure before one company buys another. It is common for the buyer and seller to agree on the selling price and other aspects of the deal based solely on the information the seller provides about the company. After both parties agree on a price, they have a due diligence period that allows the buyer and seller to check out the details of the transaction, ensuring that all the information is complete and accurate.

Due diligence can thus be interpreted as "to check something out to make sure it is true." Today it is often used just this way within a company. For example, a company adopts a tentative business plan to take a new initiative, such as starting a new product line. Before implementing the plan, a due diligence period will ensure its validity and check all its details.

due process

Under the Fifth and Fourteenth Amendments of the U.S. Constitution, everyone is guaranteed legal due process (fair treatment) under certain circumstances. There are two major subcomponents: procedural due process and substantive due process. Procedural due process refers to the constitutional provisions that prohibit federal and state governments from depriving persons of life, liberty, or property without a fair legal process. Substantive due process refers to the constitutional provisions that require all laws, federal and state, to be reasonable.

The Fifth Amendment to the U.S. Constitution, the part of the Bill of Rights that includes the due-process principle, applies only to the federal government—that is, it prohibits the federal government from violating the requirements of due process. In 1833, in the landmark case of *Barron v. Baltimore,* the U.S. Supreme Court determined that the Bill of Rights applied only to the federal government. However, due process, as provided in the Fifth Amendment, applies to state governments via the Fourteenth Amendment to the constitution, which is also known as the due-process clause.

The Fourteenth Amendment's due-process clause allows several provisions of the Bill of Rights to be applicable to state governmental conduct, including the Fifth Amendment's due-process provision. The Fourteenth Amendment's due-process clause "incorporates" several of the provisions of the Bill of Rights and makes them applicable to state governments. Thus, this function of the Fourteenth Amendment is known as incorporation.

The principles of due process under the Fifth and Fourteenth Amendments are very similar. However, a due-process case involving federal governmental conduct must be brought before the court by using the Fifth Amendment as the basis for the case, whereas a due-process case involving state governmental conduct must be brought before the court by using the Fourteenth Amendment. Failure to refer to the appropriate amendments in a due-process action may lead to the case being delayed or dismissed.

Procedural due process deals with the fairness of criminal and civil proceedings. Fair legal process generally includes providing notice of the proceeding to the relevant parties, bringing the case before an impartial tribunal or arbiter, and providing the parties with an opportunity to present evidence before the tribunal or arbiter hearing the case.

First, when a private, nongovernmental party deprives another of life, liberty or property, there is no due-process claim. However, there may be some other criminal or civil claim against that party, such as false imprisonment, theft, or WRONGFUL DISCHARGE. Corporate human resource managers often are involved with employee terminations in order to document that due process procedures were followed.

Second, if the deprivation involves something other than life, liberty, or property, there is no due-process claim. The U.S. Supreme Court is in charge of interpreting the meaning of "life, liberty, and property" for due-process purposes. The definitions of "liberty" and "property" have undergone periods of being both broadly and narrowly defined by the court, depending on the political climate or the sociopolitical beliefs of the majority of the court's justices.

When a federal or state government attempts to deprive a person of life, liberty, or property, some sort of fair legal process is required. However, whether the process is required before or after the deprivation occurs depends on the severity of the deprivation. The more severe the deprivation, the more likely predeprivation notice and a hearing will be required to satisfy procedural due process.

"Liberty" is defined as a significant freedom provided by the U.S. Constitution or state laws, including the right to CONTRACT, the right to engage in gainful EMPLOYMENT, the right to be free from unjustified intrusions of personal security, and the right to refuse medical treatment. One recent due process issue is employers' and employees' rights regarding use of a company's computer.

"Property" is defined as an entitlement right—that is, an interest that a person may reasonably expect to receive on a continuing basis. State laws may also create property interests, and where this is the case, those interests may not be terminated without procedural due process. The definition of property includes common-sense possessions such as PERSONAL PROPERTY, real property (land), and money, but it also encompasses less obvious interests such as

- the continued receipt of WELFARE benefits. If the government wishes to terminate a person's welfare benefits, there must be a pre-termination hearing that approves the termination.
- uninterrupted public education. When a public school attempts to suspend a student, that student must be given notice of the charges and an opportunity to explain his side.
- continued public employment. A public employee who has tenure, or who reasonably believes that his employment may be terminated only on sufficient grounds for termination, may not be terminated from employment without notice and a hearing.

Another component of due process, substantive due process, concerns the substance of laws. Substantive due process prohibits federal and state governments from creating laws that unreasonably infringe upon a person's fundamental rights and freedoms (generally involving matters related to sexual relations, marriage, bearing children, and child rearing). When a law restricts or regulates a person's fundamental rights, the court applies a standard called *strict scrutiny* in evaluating the validity of the law under substantive due process. Under strict-scrutiny evaluation, the government must prove to the court that the law is necessary to achieve a compelling state interest. As its name implies, strict scrutiny is very strict in its application and usually serves to invalidate state laws. Security changes since September 11, 2001, have redefined many areas of due process law.

Due process is still an evolving concept, and its boundaries will no doubt be continually tested in the U.S. Supreme Court in the future.

Further reading

Tribe, Laurence H. *American Constitutional Law,* 2d ed. Mineola, N.Y.: The Foundation Press, 2001.

—Gayatri Gupta

dumping

Dumping, in its most frequently used meaning, involves the sale of goods or SERVICES in a foreign market at prices that are below those in the seller's home country. Popular reports often refer to a specific country as the offending party, but in fact dumping is generally practiced by private businesses.

Dumping can also be viewed as PRICE DISCRIMINATION or predatory pricing. Price discrimination is the practice of charging different groups of consumers different prices for the same product or service. Price discrimination is based on market considerations, consumers' willingness and ability to pay for a product, and differences in price ELASTICITY OF DEMAND among consumer groups. Generally price discrimination is not against the law in the United States, but when done internationally, price discrimination and dumping appear to be very similar practices.

Predatory pricing is a pricing strategy where low prices are used to drive weaker competitors out of a market. Once the competitors have been eliminated (they are often sold to larger companies), the predatory-pricing firm can raise its prices and earn higher PROFITs. When practiced in international trade, predatory pricing can result in antidumping claims being filed by businesses and industries hurt by the actions of the exporting company. In the United States, the domestic steel industry has often filed charges of dumping against international competitors.

Dumping can also be the result of government subsidies to exporters, which artificially reduce the cost of production. Governments often subsidize export industries in order to create domestic jobs and INCOME. Consumers in importing countries benefit from lower-priced products, subsidized by foreign governments, but domestic producers are forced to compete on an unfair basis. Domestic businesses then ask their government to invoke antidumping statutes.

Antidumping laws have evolved since World War II through each "Round" of General Agreement on Tariffs and Trade (GATT) negotiations and through regional trade agreements such as the NORTH AMERICAN FREE TRADE AGREEMENT (NAFTA). Since the Uruguay Round in 1993, antidumping action can be brought against an importer if sales are at "less than fair value" and "material injury to a domestic industry" occurs. These phrases are open to interpretation, which has resulted in many dumping claims and counterclaims.

In the United States, dumping charges are forwarded to the U.S. INTERNATIONAL TRADE COMMISSION (ITC) for consideration. The ITC investigates PROFIT margins of the exporter in their home country versus in the United States and whether the exporter has injured or potentially could injure an existing U.S. industry. If the ITC concludes that dumping has occurred, representatives from the country are contacted to remedy the situation. If no agreement is reached, the U.S. president can order higher TARIFFs be placed on products from the offending country. While individual firms and industries are accused of dumping, government-to-government negotiations and dispute-resolution mechanisms are used to resolve dumping claims.

Another use of the term *dumping* refers to the selling of securities in financial markets. If a seller orders the sale of a large number of securities at whatever price he or she can get, the seller is said to have "dumped" the securities in the market.

Further reading

Folsom, Ralph H. and W. Davis Folsom. *Understanding NAFTA and its International Business Implications.* New York: Matthew Bender/Irwin, 1996; Hill, Charles W. L. *Global Business Today.* New York: Irwin/ McGraw-Hill, 1999.

—Gayatri Gupta

Dun & Bradstreet reports

Dun & Bradstreet (D&B) reports provide information about the creditworthiness of businesses around the world. D&B reports are the most widely used financial reports used by businesses in the United States in determining credit, marketing, purchasing, and receivables management decisions. D&B dominates the commercial credit-data market. Many corporate financial officers rely solely on D&B reports to make credit decisions.

Created in 1841, Dun & Bradstreet is a long-established U.S. business that maintains files of information on more than 10 million firms worldwide. D&B analysts gather data by reviewing customer-supplied information, INTERVIEWING company executives, examining public documents about businesses, and reviewing credit references.

Over 100,000 companies use D&B reports to

- target market prospective companies
- assess risk of doing business with other companies

- set credit terms
- define collections methods for credit
- analyze COMPETITION
- evaluate potential vendors

Having a D&B report is often a prerequisite for doing business with major U.S. CORPORATIONS. Business managers tend to be RISK averse, not wanting to be surprised by either competitors or suppliers. Bankruptcy of an important supplier can create chaos and be costly to a company. Financial reports like those D&B supplies are used to reduce uncertainty.

D&B reports typically include a summary BALANCE SHEET, an INCOME STATEMENT, and a payments record indicating how timely the firm has been paying its bills. Background information about the company, its history, facilities, owners, litigation, bankruptcies, and settlements are also included.

D&B also published MOODY'S RATINGS, reports focusing on the status and details of corporate securities, but in 2000, Moody's was separated into its own publicly traded company.

Further reading
Dun & Bradstreet website. Available on-line. URL: www.dnb.com.

duration

Duration is a measure of interest-rate RISK (bond price volatility) that includes both the coupon rate and the time to maturity of the bond. Most BONDS, both government and corporate debt instruments, are issued with a fixed interest rate (the coupon rate) for a set period of time (maturity). Duration incorporates both these features. A weighted average of each of the coupon payments plus final payment (return of principal) at the maturity date, duration is calculated by the formula

$$D = \frac{PB\,(t)}{PB}$$

where:

D = duration of the bond
PB = price of the bond = $\sum CF_t/(1 + i)^t$
CF = coupon or principal payment at time t
i = interest rate
t = time period in which the principal or coupon payment is made

In the formula, duration is the present value of all cash flows discounted according to the length of time until they are received and divided by the price of the bond, which is the present value of all cash flows.

Duration is directly related to maturity and inversely related to the coupon rate. The longer the time until maturity, the higher the duration, and the higher the coupon rate, the lower the duration. Since duration measures interest rate risk, financial managers can match the duration of their ASSETS and liabilities. Thus if INTEREST RATES rise (causing a decline in bond prices), decline values of financial assets will be offset by declining costs of liabilities. During the 1980s, many SAVINGS AND LOAN ASSOCIATION managers, faced with increased competition for deposits from nonbank financial institutions (particularly stock brokerage firms), used short-term deposits to finance long-term LOANS. When interest rates continued to rise, the value of their assets (loans) declined while their liabilities did not decrease, contributing to the S&L crisis.

Further reading
Kidwell, David S., Richard L. Peterson, and David W. Blackwell. *Financial Institutions, Markets and Money,* 7th ed. Fort Worth: Dryden Press, 2000.

E

earnings management

Earnings management is the controversial practice among publicly held corporations of adjusting the timing of reporting certain revenues and expenses by the company. In recent years, under pressure to meet WALL STREET analysts' earnings estimates, many U.S. corporations have deferred expense recognition or counted as revenue funds from sales that have not been fully completed. In 2000 the SECURITIES AND EXCHANGE COMMISSION (SEC), sensing an increase in abusive earnings-management practices, proposed new Supplemental Financial Information rules to address these abuses. The SEC recognized such problems were largely caused by a lack of transparency (openness and easily understood) in financial reporting, including problems associated with

- failure to comply with the disclosure requirements for changes in accrued liabilities for certain costs to exit an activity during periods subsequent to the initial charge
- grouping dissimilar items into an aggregated classification
- recurring "nonrecurring" charges
- inadequate disclosure of changes in estimates and in underlying assumptions during the period of change
- inconsistent application of SEC-required disclosures of valuation and loss accruals
- insufficient information about expected useful lives, changes in useful lives, and salvage values of long-lived ASSETS

A company's failure to comply with disclosure rules for changes in accrued liabilities can increase or decrease reported net INCOME. Information explaining changes provides investors with better estimates of present and future obligations. Grouping dissimilar items into an aggregated category has sometimes been used by companies to conceal something that is unfavorable and potentially a risk for investors. Reporting "recurring" charges as nonrecurring charges can be a misrepresentation of costs. Typical nonrecurring charges include restructured charges, merger expenses, and write-down of impaired assets. Investors assume nonrecurring charges are one-time costs, not costs that will have to be included in the future. Inadequate disclosure of changes in estimates is often associated with bad debt estimates or product returns. Increases in bad debt or product-return allowances reduce corporate income, but without adequate information, investors cannot easily assess the significance of the change being made. Inconsistent application of SEC-required disclosures of valuation and loss accruals is often associated with the value of future income-tax benefits. Lack of consistency in valuation can lead to over- and understatements of net income. During the late 1990s, many of these problems were particularly evident among DOT-COMS attempting reach profitability or minimize losses and operating in markets where rapidly changing technology made standard depreciation allowances subject to considerable variation.

A related issue is the use of "pro forma" earnings. Companies issue pro forma (projected) earnings by adjusting net earnings reported using GENERALLY ACCEPTED ACCOUNTING PRINCIPLES (GAAP). Pro forma earnings exclude items such as restructuring charges, employee severance expenses, and write-offs of fixed assets that have declined in value (impairment charges). This increases a company's earnings and makes it look better to investors. The problem is there are no definitions of what pro forma earnings include or exclude. Thus investors looking at companies' pro forma earnings cannot easily compare them. In December 2001 the SEC warned companies they could face civil-FRAUD lawsuits for issuing misleading earnings numbers, and directed companies to fully explain how their pro forma results are calculated.

See also LEVERAGE; PROFITS.

Further reading

Cassell Bryan-Low, "Pro Forma Forecasts Are Hard to Decipher for Investors," *Wall Street Journal,* 28 May 2002, c1, Securities and

Exchange Commission website. Available on-line. URL: www.sec.gov; Stanko, Brian B. "Improving Financial Reporting and Disclosure," *Business & Economic Review* 47, no. 4 (July-August, 2001).

e-business

The term *e-business* is often used synonymously with the term *e-commerce*. Technically e-business is a broader term that encompasses not only e-commerce but, importantly, all the internal processes of an organization—such as production, inventory, and HUMAN RESOURCES—that become digitally based functions. This often necessitates a rethinking of every aspect of the business. When the organization establishes its strategy and goals to include e-business concepts, the result is often a radical redesign of how the entire organization conducts business.

The entire business/economic environment has changed with the evolution of e-business and the introduction of digital-based design (DBD) models; many have described the new environment as dynamic, rapid, and reinventive. The speed at which information is exchanged globally has also increased the intensity and fierceness of business COMPETITION. Many companies have begun to think about competitors as partners in order to ensure their own survival. At the very least, many such businesses are building alliances and/or collaborating with competitors for survival.

E-business strategy involves system-wide integration from suppliers through customers. This entails many aspects within the organization and its interface with other organizations with whom it has a business relationship. Specifically, on-line sharing of information with customers, suppliers, manufacturers, and partners is an integral part of e-business. Terms such as enterprise-resource planning (ERP), CUSTOMER-RELATIONSHIP MANAGEMENT (CRM), supply-chain management, and KNOWLEDGE MANAGEMENT (KM) are common in e-business.

ERP integrates the entire organization's resource planning, payroll and accounting, inventory, PURCHASING, manufacturing, marketing, distribution, and so forth into one digitally based management system. ERP changes the way that almost everyone in every department in the organization does his/her job.

CRM involves all possible encounters with the customer. Designing a fully integrated system throughout the entire organization, regardless of the source of the interface, is often done with a call center. Interface originating on-line (e-mail and order form) or through telephone contacts resulting from catalogs or store visits can be handled from one location. This is sometimes achieved regionally or nationally to achieve economies.

Marketing is another area that has substantially changed with e-business. Use of the computer allows information tracking that has not been easily done with past processes. One-to-one marketing with individualized promotions targeted to the specific customer's needs has emerged because detailed information about the customer and his/her buying habits, interests, and so forth are readily available with data gathered on-line. Banners, affiliate programs, links, to promote the organization are new channels of marketing possible with e-business. Viral marketing, e-mail messages designed to encourage recipients to forward the message to their friends and colleagues, is emerging as an important marketing strategy. Multichannel marketing, such as Web, catalog, and storefront, is linked and piggybacked.

Knowledge management changes the way information is gathered, shared, and disseminated throughout the entire organization and with customers, suppliers, manufacturers, and partners. The term *collaborative commerce* is being used to identify this information exchange on-line with business partners.

Supply-chain management involves the information exchange about product flow and services, from suppliers, through the organization, and ultimately to customers and end users, i.e., the consumers. System compatibility becomes a major issue for this aspect of conducting e-business.

Overall, e-business requires structural changes in the way organizations conduct business. The sharing of information and resources across the organization changes the way people do their jobs. This also changes the relationship of the organization with other businesses for full integration to occur. Because it breaks down barriers and often necessitates a radical cultural shift for the organization, e-business changes the entire way that an organization conducts business. This new approach needs to be integrated into the strategy of the organization for successful implementation to occur.

See also INTERNET MARKETING.

—Leanne McGrath

e-commerce

Although the terms *e-business* and *e-commerce* are frequently used interchangeably, e-commerce is actually one component of e-business. Generally e-commerce covers the aspects of conducting business transactions via the INTERNET. This would include on-line marketing, sales, processing orders, customer issues, and supplier issues. From using the Internet, both business-to-business (B2B) and business-to-customer (B2C) relationships have evolved from traditional forms into a digital interface. To the extent that this interface involves sales and sales support and the exchange of goods and services for money or BARTER, it is defined as e-commerce.

An integral part of e-commerce is the website on the World Wide Web. There are various levels for which a company may use its website. The simplest level entails ADVERTISING an informational presence and display of products worldwide. Intermediate levels would be adding such features as e-mail and/or data-driven capabilities. The most complex level constitutes e-commerce, comprising a fully functional storefront that allows ordering and payment capability on-line. The latter requires addressing issues for payment security for the customer. Options for ordering on-line include CREDIT CARDS, electronic wallets, electronic cash, and smart cards.

A secure server protects information that is stored on it, and for some businesses like banks or investment brokers, this issue is a mandatory requirement for the customer. Use of encryption, for example a two-key public key system, protects the customer's information while it is being transmitted across the Internet.

The success of an e-commerce website includes development of effective INTERNET MARKETING for the website. Attracting traffic and building customers involve adding some new approaches to the traditional marketing approach. These include use of banners, links to other websites, affiliate programs, viral marketing, and search-engine registration. The use of one-to-one marketing has become common because of the ease with which data can be accumulated, sorted, weighted, and evaluated through use of the computer. This one-to-one approach allows specific tailoring of SALES PROMOTIONs to the individual's need or area of interest. Of course, customer consent to gather and use personal information should be acquired before using this promotional technique. Including a policy statement on an e-commerce site concerning use of information gathered helps create a vital comfort level for the customer.

When a bricks-and-mortar company also establishes a presence on the Web, the term "bricks and clicks" is often applied to define the new multichannel e-commerce venture. Some businesses, however, exist only on the Web. For example, Amazon.com does not have any physical retail outlets. It conducts only e-commerce and exists as an e-business, utilizing its computer software for all aspects of its existence. In contrast, Talbots.com is a "bricks and clicks" example, with physical stores, a catalog, and an Internet presence.

See also DOT-COMS.

—Leanne McGrath

economic conditions
Economic conditions are the current state of the economy and are usually characterized by macroeconomic measures, including aggregate output, INFLATION, UNEMPLOYMENT, and INTEREST RATES.

Aggregate output is measured by GROSS DOMESTIC PRODUCT (GDP). Changes in aggregate output and changes in aggregate INCOME are closely related. Changes in GDP are the most widely watched measure of current economic conditions. The U.S. Department of Commerce issues monthly estimates of percentage change in GDP. Changes in GDP result in changes in DEMAND for

natural resources, workers, and credit, causing prices to rise or fall.

Declining GDP reduces DEMAND for oil and in LABOR MARKETS, and it tends to reduce interest rates. Because the United States is the largest economy in the world, changes in U.S. economic conditions impact industries and economies globally. OPEC (Organization of Petroleum Exporting Countries) oil ministers know expanding or declining output in the United States directly affects demand for oil. Major trading partners of the United States are also affected by changing conditions in the United States. One exaggeration frequently used is: "If the United States sneezes, the world economy gets a cold."

As changes in aggregate output/income cause changes in demand, the overall level of prices, inflation, also changes, and as inflation changes, interest rates change. Inflation causes lenders to demand higher interest rates to compensate them for the reduced purchasing power associated with inflation.

Changes in output also cause changes in demand for workers. Cyclical unemployment is unemployment caused by changes in BUSINESS CYCLES, the ups and downs of economic activity. A 1-percent decrease in GDP results in over a million jobs lost in the U.S. economy.

Economic conditions are usually evaluated using leading and coincident INDICATORS. Coincident indicators change at the same time as changes in real output in the economy. Coincident indicators include

- payroll employment
- industrial production
- personal income
- manufacturing and trade sales

Leading indicators project future economic conditions. Leading indicators of the U.S. economy include

- average workweek
- UNEMPLOYMENT claims
- manufacturers' new orders
- stock prices
- new plant and equipment orders
- new building permits
- delivery times of goods
- interest-rate spread
- money supply
- consumer expectations

STOCK MARKET reporters frequently say, "The stock market anticipates changes in the economy." Historically, the U.S. stock market has gone up or down six to eight months in advance of changes in economic conditions. Similarly, consumer expectations are measured by the University of Michigan's Consumer Expectations Index and the CONFERENCE BOARD's Consumer Confidence Index.

See also MACROECONOMICS.

Further reading
Boyes, William, and Michael Melvin. *Macroeconomics,* 5th ed. Boston: Houghton Mifflin, 2001; Conference Board website. Available on-line. URL: www.conference-board.org.

economic development

Economic development is the process by which a country's economic system changes. This includes ECONOMIC GROWTH, an increase in a country's output, and changes in resource allocation and control, improvement in a country's INFRASTRUCTURE, and expansion of CAPITAL formation. Economic development occurs in all countries but is most closely associated with the process of change in poorer countries. Development economists study the process by which countries' economic systems grow or fail to grow, labeling them lesser-developed, underdeveloped, or developing economies.

To understand economic development, consider first the circle of poverty: low INCOME leads to low levels of savings, which leads to low levels of investment, which leads to low levels of income. In many developing countries, few households have sufficient income to save. If savings were available, households could choose to send their children to schools, expanding human capital and the productivity of future generations. With savings, farmers could purchase new equipment, seeds, simple tools, or storage bins to improve their productivity, but with only subsistence levels of income, most households in poorer countries cannot afford to save.

Development economists ask the question, "Why are some countries so much poorer than others?" Obviously some areas of the world are endowed with greater quantities of natural resources and more hospitable climates, but geographic differences only explain some of the differences in economic development among countries. Differences in political and social systems also contribute to explaining differences in economic development. One of the roles of a government in a capitalist economic system is to define and enforce property rights. Without control over their resources, households cannot effectively and efficiently allocate RESOURCES. Many resource-allocation decisions involve a long-term commitment of resources, which, if undermined by political instability, encourages people with portable resources, knowledge, and financial capital to seek alternatives elsewhere. With political instability, owners of land and other nonportable resources will attempt to extract as much income as possible in the short term, often at the expense of SUSTAINABLE GROWTH AND DEVELOPMENT of their resources.

Social customs and practices also influence economic development. Social systems that encourage maintaining existing social structures and customs such as limitations on work roles based on gender, restrictions to access to education, or nonacceptance of entrepreneurial efforts influence economic development. Corruption adds to the cost of doing business, limiting resource and business development.

Countries pursuing economic development typically adopt one or more of three strategies: primary production, import-substitution-industrialization, or export promotion. Many Mideast countries have developed their primary natural resources, oil and natural gas, as a means to economic growth and development. The kingdom of Saudi Arabia, until the 1930s a series of small tribal groups, grew rapidly with a joint agreement to extract oil from its land with ARAMCO (Arab American Oil Company), a consortium of U.S. oil companies. ARAMCO provided the capital and technology to develop Saudi Arabia's natural resources. MULTINATIONAL CORPORATIONS (MNCs) frequently participate in primary production development around the world. Supporters argue that without foreign capital and technology, developing countries would not be able to expand development of their primary products. Supporters contend MNCs are an agent of change and modernization. Critics argue that MNCs align themselves with the political elite in developing countries, maintaining the status quo, and once the primary products are depleted, they leave the developing country, sometimes in worse economic and environmental condition than when it arrived.

A second development strategy is import-substitution-industrialization (ISI). This strategy focuses on replacing previously imported products with domestically produced substitutes. Many developing countries have assisted domestic industry development through combinations of low-cost capital and TARIFFS on competing imported products. ISI development can stimulate domestic production and income but has two inherent problems: market limits and lack of COMPETITION. The assisted producers can produce for the domestic market, but if the market is small, they may not be able to achieve ECONOMIES OF SCALE. Domestic producers protected from global competition often will produce goods of sufficient quality to sell domestically but not up to global standards, when or if the company tries to expand internationally. Mexican leaders, fearful of U.S. economic dominance, pursued ISI development in the 1960s and 1970s. Only in the 1980s, after a series of economic collapses, did Mexico move away from ISI and gradually toward export promotion.

Since the 1950s, many developing countries, particularly the so-called Asian Tigers (Japan, Korea, Hong Kong, Taiwan, and Singapore), have stimulated economic growth and development through export promotion. With government support and subsidies, domestic producers are encouraged to produce output for sale in global markets. Although export promotion requires producers to meet world-class standards, is vulnerable to changing prices and FOREIGN EXCHANGE problems, and requires access to major markets, it has been a successful development strategy for many countries. At some point government subsidies have to be withdrawn, which has created problems for many countries and companies.

Critical to economic development is access to capital. There are five general ways businesses and governments pursuing economic development acquire capital. Foreign direct investment (FDI), the development of factories or purchase of interests in existing businesses, is sometimes encouraged and sometimes discouraged. One of the major features of the NORTH AMERICAN FREE TRADE AGREEMENT (NAFTA) was the reduction in restrictions on FDI in Mexico. In the 1990s, portfolio INVESTMENT became an increasingly popular way to raise capital, particularly in countries like Mexico, where there was some existing level of industrialization. U.S. investors, often pursuing diversification, bought shares of stock or AMERICAN DEPOSITORY RECEIPTS in business around the world. Before the expansion of portfolio investment, commercial bank LOANS were a major source of capital for development. In the 1980s, U.S. banks were close to bankruptcy when loans to foreign businesses and governments failed. Trade credit, the extension of short-term loans by exporters to importers, is often an important source of capital to businesses in developing countries. Foreign aid acts as a source of capital, mostly for governments in developing countries. The WORLD BANK and U.S. AGENCY FOR INTERNATIONAL DEVELOPMENT are major sources of foreign aid for economic development.

Further reading
Boyes, William, and Michael Melvin. *Microeconomics*. 5th ed. Boston: Houghton Mifflin, 2002; Folsom, Ralph H., and W. Davis Folsom. *Understanding NAFTA and its International Implications*. New York: Matthew Irwin/Bender, 1996.

economic efficiency

Economic efficiency is defined in a variety of ways. Most simply stated, efficiency is the lack of waste. Economic efficiency in production is using the method that requires the least amount of resources to produce a given level of output. Efficiency is also associated with producing at the lowest point on a firm's average total-cost curve, producing at the least cost per unit possible.

Economic efficiency is also defined as a situation in which any reallocation of resources cannot make one person better off without harming someone else. This is known as Pareto Optimality, named after the Italian economist Vilfredo Pareto. Optimality is a bit misleading in that it usually infers the "best" outcome possible, whereas in reality many economic situations present multiple outcomes that are nearly equally efficient.

Economists also use a PRODUCTION POSSIBILITIES CURVE (PPC) to portray efficiency for an economic system. A country or business is said to have achieved economic efficiency when it has produced any combination of output that maximizes their production capability with existing RESOURCES and technology. Economic growth is portrayed by a rightward shift of the PPC through expansion of the quantity of resources, improvements in technology, or improvement in the quality of resources.

The 18th-century Scottish philosopher Adam Smith is credited with first describing economic efficiency of markets. In his famous "invisible hand" analogy, Smith suggested that self-interested individuals, both sellers and buyers, act as if driven by an invisible hand to produce economic efficiency. Buyers will attempt to maximize their benefits from the scarce resources they own. Sellers will attempt to maximize their return from the products they produce and sell. In the process, sellers and buyers will reduce and eliminate waste, producing what is most desired in the marketplace and purchasing those goods that maximize utility.

Advocates of LAISSEZ-FAIRE economic theory argue that economic efficiency is maximized when markets are allowed to act freely without government control or intervention. Critics counter that economic efficiency depends on having competition, and the assumed goal of businesses, maximizing PROFITS, is best achieved by reducing competition. Therefore government is needed to ensure markets operate as competitively as possible in order to achieve economic efficiency.

Further reading
Boyes, William, and Michael Melvin. *Macroeconomics*, 5th ed. Boston: Houghton Mifflin, 2001.

Economic Espionage Act

The Economic Espionage Act of 1996 was enacted to protect economic PROPRIETARY INFORMATION. With the end of the cold war in 1990, many governments and former espionage agents redirected efforts from political to business espionage. The act established penalties of up to $500,000 and 15 years in prison for agents of foreign powers and up to $10,000,000 in fines for organizations in cases where any "foreign government, foreign instrumentality, or foreign agent knowingly:

1. steals, or without authorization appropriates, takes, carries away, or communicates, or by FRAUD, artifice, or deception obtains TRADE SECRETS;
2. without authorization copies, duplicates, sketches, draws, photographs, downloads, uploads, alters, destroys, photocopies, replicates, transmits, delivers, sends, mails, communicates, or conveys a trade secret;
3. receives, buys, or possesses a trade secret, knowing the same to have been stolen or appropriated, obtained or converted without authorization;
4. attempts to commit any offense described in any of the paragraphs 1 through 3."

In cases of commercial espionage the same actions are illegal, but the penalties are: for persons, $500,000 and 10 years; for organizations, $5 million.

Like U.S. drug-smuggling laws, the act adds the potential of criminal forfeiture, meaning the seizure and disposition of property associated with the economic espionage activity. The act also directs prosecutors to "take such other action as may be necessary and appropriate to preserve the confidentiality of trade secrets," consistent with the requirements of federal laws. Civil court actions are also possible under the act. The act exempts law enforcement activity that might be in violation of the act.

See also MARKET INTELLIGENCE; SOCIETY FOR COMPETITIVE INTELLIGENCE PROFESSIONALS.

Further reading
Society for Competitive Intelligence Professionals website. Available on-line. URL: www.scip.org.

economic freedom

Economic freedom is the ability of individuals to exercise control over their property. Though there is no single, accepted definition Steve Hanke and Stephen Walters found that economic freedom includes

- secure rights to property
- freedom to engage in voluntary transactions both domestically and internationally
- freedom from governmental control of the terms on which individuals transact
- freedom from governmental expropriation of property

Economic liberty is perceived as distinct from political liberty, when people are free to participate in the political process on an equitable basis; and civil liberty, which involves protection against unreasonable searches and the right to fair trials, free assembly, free speech, and the practice of religion.

In the 1980s economists and political-interest groups became increasingly interested in measuring economic freedom and the relationship of economic freedom to ECONOMIC GROWTH. Part of the interest is ideologically based. Free-market advocates and critics of government scrutiny of business practices wanted to demonstrate a relationship between economic freedom and economic growth. Three organizations—Freedom House, Fraser Institute, and the Heritage Foundation—all developed measures of economic freedom by country. Each organization identified crucial elements of economic freedom, quantified measures of these elements, and weighted the elements in order to create an index or score of economic freedom.

The first attempt to measure economic freedom was developed by Raymond Gastil and Lindsay Wright for Freedom House in 1983. Their efforts grew out of Freedom House's annual assessment of political and civil liberties. Since 1972 Freedom House has published an ANNUAL REPORT categorizing countries as "free," "partly free," or "not free" based on an average of the political- and civil-liberties ratings. Gastil and Wright supplemented this data with estimates of property rights, labor rights, business-operation rights, investment freedom, international trade openness, and antidiscrimination, and absence of corruption. Since 1995 Freedom House has published a separate *World Survey of Economic Freedom*. In the 1995–96 survey, only 27 nations were rated as free, representing only 17 percent of the world's population but over 80 percent of total world output.

Fraser Institute publishes its Economic Freedom Index using five indices of economic liberty based on weighted averages of 21 components. In 2002 the Institute published *Economic Freedom of the World: 2002 Annual Report*. Their index uses measures of

- sound money
- size of government
- legal structure and security of property
- regulation of credit, labor, business
- freedom to exchange with foreigners.

Money supply growth, INFLATION rate, foreign currency accounts, and bank accounts abroad measure sound money. Size of government is measured by government spending as a share of total CONSUMPTION, transfers, subsidies as a share of GROSS DOMESTIC PRODUCT (GDP), private versus state-run enterprises, and marginal tax rates. Judicial independence, impartial courts, protection of INTELLECTUAL PROPERTY, and military interference with the rule of law measure legal structure. Regulation of credit, labor, and business is measured by credit, labor, and business market regulations. Level of TARIFFS, regulatory TRADE BARRIERS, absence or presence of black-market EXCHANGE RATES, size of the trade sector, and absence of CAPITAL controls measure freedom to exchange with foreigners.

Beginning in 1994, the Heritage Foundation started publishing its annual *Index of Economic Freedom*. The Heritage Foundation's goal is to provide evidence on the impact of externally funded development assistance on facilitating economic growth. The foundation wants to discredit foreign-aid programs. The Heritage ranking of countries from mostly free to mostly unfree was then correlated with receipt of foreign aid and showing that many countries receiving foreign aid also lacked economic freedom and had not developed economically.

While some variation exists depending on the emphasis given to size of government and monetary stability, economic freedom index rankings are fairly consistent. Ironically, in 1996 Hong Kong (then independent of China) was ranked as one of the most economically free countries. New Zealand, Switzerland, the Netherlands, and the United Kingdom were also ranked high on each scale, followed closely by the United States. Not surprisingly, North Korea, Cuba, and Myanmar (Burma) ranked among the least free countries.

Part of the interest in economic freedom comes from the question "How does economic liberty contribute to economic growth?" After each economic-freedom index was developed, economists correlated economic freedom ratings with measures of prosperity, usually GDP per capita. As expected, economic freedom (as defined by each organization) and economic growth are positively related. As Hanke and Walters observed, "They [economic researchers] have focused on the nature of institutions and on the structure of rules and norms that constrain economic behavior as a way of understanding the development process. And they have rediscovered [Adam] Smith's ancient insight that economic liberty is a crucial precondition for sustained, vigorous economic growth."

Further reading

Fraser Institute website. Available on-line. URL: www.fraserinstitute.ca; Freedom House website. Available on-line. URL: www.freedomhouse.org; Hanke, Steve H. and Stephen J. K. Walters, "Economic Freedom, Prosperity, and Equality: A Survey," *Cato Journal* 17, no. 2 (1998).

economic growth

Economic growth, in its most limited definition, is an increase in real GROSS DOMESTIC PRODUCT (GDP), the primary measure of output in an economy. GDP comprises the total MARKET VALUE of final goods and services produced in an economy in a period of time, and increases in GDP are economic growth. Economies tend to go through periods of expansion and contraction of GDP.

Economic growth can be either extensive (resulting from greater quantity of labor, materials, and CAPITAL input) or intensive (resulting from technological advances and more efficient use of existing RESOURCES). Whether as a result of increasing quantities of resources or more efficient use of resources, output increases. Studies have documented growth in industrial economies as being largely attributable to intensive factors, while growth in developing economies tends to be derived from extensive sources. In an often-cited study, economist Edward Denison analyzed U.S. economic growth during the 20th century. He found that in the period from 1929 to 1948, over 50 percent of the growth in GDP was attributable to increases in the quantity of labor, with capital contributing to less than 5 percent of overall economic growth. From 1948 to 1973, the overall U.S. economic growth rate was 40-percent higher than the earlier period, but the contribution of labor to growth was almost unchanged. The quantity of capital accounted for over five times as much growth, and technological change accounted for three times as much growth in the later period. Denison attributed the added economic growth to the combination of increased capital, incorporating knowledge gains and technological advances in the period. Similarly, most economists attribute U.S. produc-

tivity gains in the 1990s to capital and human investment in computer technology.

Developing economies often face numerous obstacles in pursuit of economic growth. In many developing countries, resources for investment are concentrated among a small wealthy class and government. If these resources are spent on current CONSUMPTION, future economic growth will be limited. In what economists call the circle of poverty, low investment leads to low levels of output, which results in low levels of saving, which leads to low levels of investment.

In *The Stages of Economic Growth,* economist Walt Rostow posited that economies go through a series of five stages of economic growth: traditional society, preconditions for takeoff, takeoff, drive to maturity, and mass consumption. In the traditional-society stage, well-established economic and social systems and customs limit economic change and growth. In the preconditions stage, traditional constraints are removed and new methods and technology introduced. In the takeoff stage, an economic growth begins and investment expands rapidly. The takeoff stage is a period of intensive development. Rostow dated the takeoff stage in the U.S. economy as the period from 1843 to 1860, when major railroad investment opened new markets and expanded access to resources throughout the country. In the drive to maturity stage, an economy shifts from its original industrial base to expanding into new products and services. In the fifth stage, mass consumption, an affluent population leads to a well-developed consumer goods and SERVICES economy.

Austrian economist Joseph Schumpeter argued that economic growth depends on creative destruction. Schumpeter suggested that, in competitive markets, businesses attempt to find new ways to produce goods and better PRODUCTs in order to survive and prosper. In the process, existing methods and products are constantly being replaced. During periods of rapid economic growth, new technologies and new products are constantly being introduced. During periods of economic stagnation, innovation and INVESTMENT are low.

See also BUSINESS CYCLES; SUPPLY-SIDE ECONOMICS; TRICKLE-DOWN ECONOMICS.

Further reading

Folsom, Ralph H., and W. Davis Folsom. *Understanding NAFTA and its International Business Implications.* New York: Matthew Bender/Irwin, 1996; Rostow, Walt W. *The Stages of Economic Growth,* 3d ed., Cambridge, Eng.: Cambridge University Press, 1991; Ruffin, Roy J., and Paul R. Gregory. *Principles of Economics,* 7th ed. Boston: Addison Wesley, 2001.

economic policy

Economic policy is a nation's use of its RESOURCES and power to achieve economic goals and objectives. Generally the central government has three types of economic policies—fiscal, monetary, and INCOME—that it can utilize.

FISCAL POLICY is the use of government taxation and/or spending to achieve economic objectives. For example, in early 2002 Congress and the White House could not reach an agreement on "economic stimuli" to help get the U.S. economy out of the RECESSION. The two groups differed on the composition of fiscal policies each considered best for economic recovery. One group proposed greater tax cuts for businesses, the other lower tax rates for households.

MONETARY POLICY is controlling the MONEY SUPPLY to achieve economic growth with stable prices. In the United States, the primary goal of monetary policy is to attain and maintain price stability. Monetary policy is based on monetarism, a school of macroeconomic thought emphasizing the impact of changes in the supply of MONEY on the aggregate economy. Economic policies regarding the control of the money supply are often referred to as "tight money" or "easy money" plans. Generally the goal of monetary policy makers is to increase the money supply, but the question is at what rate to increase the supply. In the United States, the FEDERAL RESERVE SYSTEM determines monetary policy.

Income policies, also called WAGE AND PRICE CONTROLS, are government-imposed limits on increases in wages and prices. Income policies are typically imposed during wartime to limit INFLATION. during wars, government spending usually expands rapidly to provide the materials and weapons needed for defense. This increases DEMAND for labor and products and, in absence of wage and price controls, would likely result in inflation.

Economic policies can be directed to achieve a variety of objectives. As already stated, common economic objectives include price stability and ECONOMIC GROWTH. Other objectives include full EMPLOYMENT, economic choice and freedom, economic security for the elderly and ill, improvement in economic well-being, and equitable distribution of income among members of society. Some of these objectives are complimentary. Economic growth leads to increased employment and income, but some objectives present potential for conflict. Many economists, using Philips curve analysis, suggest there is a tradeoff between price stability and economic growth in the short run. A more significant conflict exists between ECONOMIC FREEDOM and social objectives. Economic freedom implies individual control and allocation of resources and receiving the rewards and returns from those resources. Economic security for the elderly and ill and equitable distribution of income in a society require economic policies that take resources or income from one group and provide resources and income to another group. Economic policies significantly affect what is produced, how it is produced, and who gets the output of an economic system.

economic rent

Economic rent is any payment to an owner of a productive resource in excess of the minimum amount necessary to keep the resource in its current use. In capitalist economic systems, individuals and households control most RESOURCES and choose how to allocate those resources. To keep a resource (land, labor, or CAPITAL) in its current use, the resource owner will demand, as minimum payment, a price equal to what they could receive for the best alternative use of that resource (OPPORTUNITY COST).

Economists distinguish between economic rent and quasi rents. Economic rent is the price paid to a productive resource that is perfectly inelastic in supply. Perfectly inelastic SUPPLY means there is a fixed quantity of the resource, and a higher price will not increase the quantity supplied in the market. The standard example of pure economic rent is agricultural land. There is a fixed quantity of useable land, and competing sources of DEMAND for the land determine the market price. A high percentage of agricultural land in the United States is rented out. Depending on the expected profitability of crops that can be grown, demand will increase of decrease and price will rise or fall, depending on demand. In many areas of the country, nonagricultural uses, generating higher use values for agricultural land, result in the conversion of agricultural property into commercial or residential areas. This activity, once approved by zoning officials, increases the economic rent to the resource holder.

Quasi rent is a payment in excess of the resource owner's short-run opportunity cost. The difference between economic rent and quasi rent is the response of suppliers to changing prices. Economic rent assumes quantity supplied does not change with price, while quasi rent assumes higher prices induce greater quantities supplied. Quasi rent is the difference between the current price and the price suppliers would have accepted. For example, if an employer offers a job-seeker $10 per hour more than he or she would have accepted, that is a quasi rent. In most markets, word will get out that higher-than-expected wages are being paid by an employer or industry, resulting in an increase in supply and a lowering of market wages. Thus the quasi rent is a short-run phenomenon, disappearing in the long run.

Further reading
Ruffin, Roy J., and Paul R. Gregory. *Principles of Economics*, 7th ed. Boston: Addison Wesley, 2001.

economies of scale, economies of scope
Economies of scale are production efficiencies realized when per-unit costs are reduced as the quantity produced increases. In business, scale is size, and in many business situations, as a company produces more output, the average cost of that output declines. Economies of scale are the result of efforts that improve efficiency.

Generally specialization and use of larger machines allow firms to become more efficient. Greater levels of output allow firms to spread the fixed COSTS associated with specialized equipment or personnel. For example, a manager is a fixed cost to a business; it does not change over a range of output (until the business is large enough to need a second manager). Every business needs a manager, and a manager's salary has to be included in the cost of doing business. If a company produces more output (in a manufacturing firm) or generates greater sales (in a retail firm), the cost of the manager per unit of output or sales decreases.

Economies of scale result in lower average costs of PRODUCTION up to the point where a firm reaches its minimum efficient scale (MES). MES is the level of output where the firm's average cost is lowest. Many times there is a range of output over which a firm achieves its MES. Production levels beyond MES result in diseconomies of scale, or rising costs per unit. Diseconomies of scale occur when the cost of additional RESOURCES rises, managers face so many demands that work slows, or new equipment is necessary to expand output.

Economies of scale are an important factor in market COMPETITION. Often cost advantages from large-scale production act as a BARRIER TO ENTRY in oligopolies and monopolies. Potential competitors are forced to start out with large levels of production in order to compete with existing firms.

Government often allows the creation of a regulated MONOPOLY in order to achieve economies of scale. Economists call these situations natural monopolies. Electric utilities, local cable and telephone service, and water companies are all examples of situations where one large firm can produce at a lower cost per unit than many competing firms. In many countries these services are directly provided by government, but in the United States private companies whose prices are regulated (public utilities) are more prevalent.

While economies of scale are the result of specialization, economies of scope are the result of production of similar products. A firm producing shirts can use the same equipment to also produce blouses or pants. A farmer growing one crop has the land and much of the equipment needed to grow other crops. These firms have an advantage, economies of scope, over other potential competitors based on their existing knowledge and resources.

See also OLIGOPOLY.

Further reading

Ruffin, Roy J., and Paul R. Gregory. *Principles of Economics,* 7th ed. Boston: Addison Wesley, 2001.

efficient market theory (efficient market hypothesis)

Otherwise known as the efficient market hypothesis, this theory concludes that investors cannot expect to outperform the STOCK MARKET over an extended period of time. This is not to say that some investors cannot outperform the stock-market indexes. The theory does suggest, however, that investors will not outperform the market on a RISK-adjusted basis over a longer time frame.

The efficient market theory is based on the assumptions that securities markets are highly competitive, information for research purposes is readily available at low cost, and transactions may be executed at low cost. Since securities prices adjust rapidly to new information and other market-driven effects, day-to-day price changes are unpredictable. The RANDOM-WALK THEORY suggests that the pricing pattern of securities is accidental, and techniques such as charting, moving averages, or purchases relative to sales will not lead to superior selection. The term *random walk* is occasionally misunderstood to mean that securities prices are randomly determined. To the contrary, securities prices are efficiently determined by the markets. It is the changes in securities prices that are random, as is new and unpredictable information. If new information were predictable, then securities price changes would also be predictable and investors could consistently outperform the market, assuming the same risks, and securities markets would not be efficient.

Further reading

Mayo, Herbert B. "The Valuation of Common Stock." In *Investments—An Introduction.* Greenwood Village, Colo.: College for Financial Planning, 2000.

e-government

E-government refers to government initiatives to provide information and SERVICES electronically and over the INTERNET; the means used include websites and e-mail. E-government has been linked to efforts to change or reform government in order to provide services to citizens, other governments, and the business community more efficiently and effectively.

The federal government, all of the state governments, and many cities and counties established a presence on the Internet by developing websites that provide information about their mission and how to obtain services. Many people have no idea how to reach various government agencies or even what services are available. Government websites provide much of this information to the public through on-line links to other government agencies and services. In many cases, government entities are able to streamline service provision for the general public and the business community as well.

In 2000 the federal government established a gateway, or portal website, to provide the public with one central location for accessing information about federal government agencies and services. For example, consumers can print up a passport application, find a zip code, or obtain information about many government benefits. Businesses can file taxes electronically, learn about subcontracting opportunities, and report employee wages electronically. The federal government's website can be accessed at http://www.firstgov.gov. In response to a presidential directive on improving e-government, the U.S. DEPARTMENT OF

LABOR established a new website entitled GovBenefits.gov in 2002 that initially provided links to 55 programs. The site was intended to meet individual needs and to be user-friendly. After answering a set of questions, an individual will have a better idea as to his or her eligibility for various government benefits and programs.

Most states and many local governments provide a variety of information on their websites. The virtual visitor can learn a great deal about a state's history, culture, and laws, places to visit, the organizational structure of its government, and the services it provides. Typical services include information about business opportunities, taxes, EMPLOYMENT opportunities, and public health. Some state and local governments provide on-line forms and information to reduce waiting and travel time as well as time spent on telephone queries. For example, a government entity may provide information about how to obtain a copy of a birth or death certificate or a marriage license. The library system in one major city has experimented with an on-line pay research service to fill requests for information from other governments and from businesses. A West Coast county allows contractors to apply for permits on-line and then schedule an appointment with a building inspector. In one East Coast city, traffic violators can track their case on-line through all the stages of the legal process. E-mail links contribute to government responsiveness by allowing consumers to contact government officials with specific questions and concerns that may save multiple trips to a bricks-and-mortar facility. City and county websites vary from those with an extensive presence to those with minimal websites or no presence on the World Wide Web at all, but the trend is toward at least a minimal presence.

Technology is changing the ways that citizens and the business community interact with government in other respects. Some communities provide on-line coverage of government meetings, either live or through archives, so citizens can "watch" a meeting from the comfort of their own homes or at their convenience. A few high schools and many colleges offer "virtual" classes where students never meet their teachers face to face. A traffic court goes paperless, and offenders can track each step of their cases on-line. Some communities are integrating a mapping and data-analysis technique known as geographic information system (GIS) with the Internet. In one community, citizens can use GIS to report the exact location of a pothole. In other communities, economic development offices are using GIS to provide information to businesses searching for new locations. In the spirit of open government, one southern city that has placed cameras at busy intersections makes specific information about camera placement available on its website. A number of states are at various stages of changing from a paper to an on-line procurement process (e-procurement).

E-government also provides new opportunities for businesses to establish partnerships with government entities by contracting for technology-related services. For example, the U.S. Postal Service contracted with several private companies to upgrade its hardware and software as it moved toward Web-based services.

New problems have developed along with the new technology. One key concern is how to balance the needs for national security and the free flow of information in a democratic society. In an effort to make government more "customer-friendly," federal and state government agencies provided public access to an enormous amount of information on topics as varied as nuclear power plants, chemical site security, pipeline mapping, and crop dusters. Following the terrorist attacks of September 11, 2001, government agencies began to reexamine what information was made available to the public through the Internet and other means, including via federal FREEDOM OF INFORMATION ACT requests. Subsequently, federal and state officials removed some information from the Internet that was deemed too sensitive and subject to abuse by terrorists. To what extent limits should be placed on public access to information about government is a subject for debate in the political arena.

A second concern is how to ensure the security of a website. Staying a step ahead of hackers who maliciously attack and damage websites for fun or for profit is a challenge for experts in computer security in both the public and the private sectors. Computer-savvy criminals may hack into websites to gather data that will allow them access to personal finances and to engage in identity theft. Hackers have breached thousands of computer systems around the world, including many government websites. A terrorist attack on the nation's computer network would have serious ramifications for government operations and for the economy. Security experts use a variety of mechanisms to keep hackers from gaining access to data stored on computers, including firewalls, secure configuration of software, keeping security patches up to date, and designing "trust relationships" that prevent hackers who break into a system from accessing all the computers in a network (i.e., someone using a computer in the network must provide proof of identity in order to access other computers). Hackers also gain access to computer systems through social engineering—i.e., by tricking people into giving them their usernames and passwords. Experts agree that one of the best ways to prevent social engineering is by educating computer users to exercise care in giving out such information. Another security issue is related to transmission of data over the Internet, where it is readily accessible. Security experts recommend encryption of sensitive data so that it will be meaningless gibberish to those who are not authorized to use it, although hackers may develop new computer programs to gain access.

A related concern is maintaining the PRIVACY of personal data that may be available through the Internet and electronic records. A wide variety of information about clients, citizens, and government employees exists in both paper and electronic form. A widespread belief in the right to privacy exists in the society at large, buttressed by laws and court decisions. Many citizens object when government agencies gather personal data and fear that it will be misused by both government entities and by the private sector if they obtain this information. However, government agencies seeking to prevent terrorism may need to share data in order to better coordinate their activities. Maintaining confidentiality and ensuring appropriate safeguards of such data while at the same time allowing public officials access to the information needed for homeland security and national defense is difficult. Governments may also have a legitimate need for client data in order to determine what services a particular client is receiving from other agencies. For example, a county in an east-coast state purchased a program that allows it to track homeless people and lets social workers determine which benefits clients are receiving without contacting each separate service provider. They encrypted the data to maintain confidentiality.

A different kind of concern centers on the growing divide between those people who have Internet access and those who do not. Lower-income persons are less likely to have home computers. Some state and local governments have addressed this problem by providing more computers in places like libraries and shopping malls. Sometimes joining with partners in the private sector, government initiatives have made more computers available to schools in poorer communities. However, the cost of providing and maintaining technology is a problem when the economy slows and there are more demands on limited dollars.

E-government has its limitations. In and of itself it will not solve all the problems inherent in service delivery. But ultimately it may change the way governments operate. New issues arise along with the new technology. For example, as governments become paperless, public officials must determine what records have to be retained under federal and state laws. Questions will be raised about what should be saved for the historical record as well. Another issue that may arise is that of increased citizen participation in government. Governments are already subject to many demands from a wide range of interest groups and from the general public. As government becomes more "user-friendly," the public may find it easier to understand how it operates and to access more specific information about how government spends the public's money. Government officials may find themselves responding to a new set of constituents who will closely question the day-to-day operations of government organizations. A challenge for governments at all levels will be how to best use new and changing technology to coordinate and maximize service provision.

Further reading
Daukantas, Patricia. "What on Web merits saving?" *GCN Government Computer News*. Available on-line. URL: http://www. gcn.com/cgibin/udt/im.display.printable?client.id=gcn2&story.id =18754. Downloaded on May 28, 2002; Davies, Thomas R. "Throw E-Gov a Lifeline," *Governing* (June 2002): 72; Gurwitt, Rob. "Behind the Portal," *Governing online*. Available on-line. URL: http://www.governing.com/8egweb.htm. Downloaded on May 28, 2002; Harris, Shane. "Bridging the Divide," *Governing* (September 2000): 36; ———. "E-Commerce at the Library," *Governing* (April 2000): 56, 58; Kittower, Diane. "Welcome to Cyber High," *Governing* (April 2000): 52, 56; Jason Miller. "USPS looks to travel light via Web," *GCN Government Computer News*. Available on-line. URL: http://www.gcn.com/cgi-bin/udt/im. display.printable?client.id=gcn2&story.id=18709.; Newcombe, Tod. "Conservative Growth," *Government Technology* (March 2002): 26, 28; Palumbo, John. "Social Engineering: What is it, why is so little said about it and what can be done?" SANS Institute, Information Security Reading Room. Available on-line. URL: http:// rr.sans.org/social/social.php. Downloaded on June 3, 2002; Perlman, Ellen. "Gavel to Gavel Online," *Governing* (April 2000); 52; Perlman, Ellen. "Maps that Sell," *Governing* (December 2000): 68, 70, 7; Stanton, Sam, and Ted Bell. "Hacking bares key data on all state employees," *The Sacramento Bee* (25 May 2002). Available on-line. URL: http://www.sacbee.com/content/politics/story/ 2882520p-3704154c.html. Downloaded on May 25, 2002; Swope, Christopher. "Total Disclosure," *Governing* (April 2000): 58; Walsh, Trudy. "Software helps Lancaster, Pa., aid its homeless," *GCN Government Computer News*. Available on-line. URL: http://gcn.com/21_11/statelocal/18634-1.html. Downloaded on May 28, 2002; Zanko, Pete L. "Labor Department Launches New Web Site," *Washington Post On-line. Available on-line. URL: http://www.washingtonpost.com/ac2/wp-dyn/A2566-2002Apr29? language=printer. Downloaded on May 28, 2002.*

See also the entire February 2002 issue of *Government Technology*, which focuses on network security.

—Carol Sears Botsch

80-20 principle

The 80-20 principle is the general observation that, in many markets, the vast majority (80 percent) of sales and/or PROFITS come from a small percentage (20 percent) of a firm's customers. Likewise, 20 percent of a firm's sales and/or profits come from 80 percent of its customers.

Italian economist Vilfredo Pareto first articulated the 80-20 principle in the 1890s. Pareto observed that 80 percent of the WEALTH in Italy was owned by 20 percent of the population. More recently marketers have utilized the 80-20 principle to evaluate and design marketing strategies. One example is the growth of affinity programs. First developed nationally by American Airlines, frequent-flyer programs reward the small percentage of customers who generate a large percentage of sales. Recognizing the benefits of catering to their most important customers, other airlines, hotels, and auto rental companies quickly adopted similar programs.

With today's CUSTOMER-RELATIONSHIP MANAGEMENT systems, marketers can better evaluate which customers are generating the lion's share of their profits. Personal sales efforts, customized products, specialized services, and alternative delivery systems are just a few of the many marketing strategies that can be used to retain and cultivate relationships with a firm's most important customers. Ultimately, the goal is to win and maintain the trust of valued customers.

Another example of the 80-20 principle can be used in MARKET RESEARCH surveys. Sometimes a marketer may not want a random sample of all of their customers. Instead, the opinions of their important customers (the 20 percent generating 80 percent of the company's profits) may be needed. Marketer Tony Cram makes an important insight about the 80-20 principle. Some customers may not generate significant sales or profits but may benefit a firm by sharing its planning process, collaborating on NEW PRODUCT DEVELOPMENT, or being a source of referrals and recommendations; they thus also prove valuable to a marketer. Like many aspects of business, the 80-20 principle should not be taken as an absolute guide for MARKETING STRATEGY decisions.

Of course, the 80 percent of customers who generate 20 percent of sales or profits should not be ignored. Manufacturers often use independent representatives to call on small customers. Catalog companies change the size, composition, and frequency of mailing depending on past customer purchases. College textbook publishers provide 800-number services for small campuses while sending sales reps to major institutions. The INTERNET allows companies to customize offerings for different customer groups.

Further reading
Cram, Tony. "How to care for customers who count the most." *Marketing* (12 July 2001), 21; Etzel, Michael J., Bruce J. Walker, and William J. Staunton. *Marketing,* 12th ed. Boston: McGraw-Hill, 2001.

elasticity of demand
In most market situations, business managers raise or lower price as they judge in their best interest. Elasticity of demand is a quantitative way to measure consumers' sensitivity or responsiveness to price changes.

Starting from the current price a firm charges, elasticity of demand is measured by the percentage change in quantity demanded in response to a percentage change in price. If, for example, price is raised by 10 percent and quantity demanded decreases by 10 percent (the law of DEMAND states the higher the price the lower the quantity demanded and vice versa), the increase in revenue from the higher price is exactly offset by the decrease in quantity demanded. Total revenue for the firm will remain the same, though PROFITS may increase because the firm is now selling less quantity of their product and receiving the same amount of revenue. When a price change results in

no change in total revenue, the elasticity-of-demand coefficient is one or unitary.

The elasticity-of-demand coefficient is the absolute value of the percentage change in quantity demanded divided by the percentage change in price.

$$E_D = \text{(\% change in quantity demand) / (\% change in price)}$$

The elasticity-of-demand formula initially appears quite daunting, but looking closely it is just a percentage divided by a percentage. If the percentage change in quantity demanded is greater than the percentage change in price, demand is said to be elastic, or people responded significantly to the price change. However, demand is inelastic if consumers do not respond much when a business changes price.

For example, if a firm raises its price by 10 percent and quantity demanded goes down by 5 percent, the elasticity of demand is the absolute value of 5/10 or 0.50. This is less than 1.0 and considered inelastic. If, instead, when the firm raises price by 10 percent, the quantity demanded decreases by 50 percent, the elasticity coefficient is the absolute value of 50/10 or 5.0. This is considered very price-elastic; when the firm raises prices by 10 percent, people significantly reduce their quantity demanded.

The assumed primary goal of a business is to maximize profits, which are the excess of total revenues over total costs. Since elasticity of demand measures relative changes in quantity demanded in response to a change from an initial price, it can be used to estimate what happens to total revenue when price is changed. In the example of inelastic demand above, a 10-percent increase in price resulted in a 5-percent decrease in quantity demanded. The firm is now selling 5 percent less of their product but receiving a price that is 10-percent higher than what they were charging previously. The increase in price has more than offset the decrease in quantity sold. Their total revenue, therefore, is increased. In the example of elastic demand, the firm is charging 10-percent more for their product, but the number of products sold decreased by 50 percent. They are getting a higher price but losing a lot of sales. Their total revenue has decreased.

An easier way to remember the relationship of price elasticity is this axiom: For inelastic demand, price and total revenue move in the same direction, and for elastic demand, price and total revenue move in opposite directions.

Large companies often hire economists and MARKET RESEARCH professionals to estimate the price elasticity of demand for their products, but small-business owners can also use this concept. There are four rules of thumb used to make an educated judgment whether the demand for a product will be sensitive or insensitive to price changes.

- necessities versus luxuries
- short time frame versus long time frame

- few competitors versus many competitors
- inexpensive items versus expensive items

Generally people are more likely to purchase necessity goods even if the price of those goods rise, but they are less likely to buy luxury goods when those prices go up. For example, airlines keep some seats open on flights for last-minute business travelers who need to get to some destination to conduct business. Business travel is price-inelastic, while vacation travel is generally price-elastic; when the price of vacations increase, more people will decide not to travel for their vacation.

People are less likely to respond to a price change initially but more likely to change given time to adjust. When oil prices rose in the early 1970s, American consumers did not respond significantly to the price increase. But when they were ready to trade in their cars, they bought smaller, more fuel-efficient cars, reducing their demand for gasoline. Thus, over time consumers were more responsive to oil-price increases than they were in the short run.

If monopolists raises prices, especially for necessity goods like electricity or water, people will reduce their quantity demanded very little, as they have few or no other choices. But if one fast-food company raised their price, consumers would fairly quickly substitute competitors' products. When there are few substitutes, demand tends to be price-inelastic, and when there are many substitutes demand tends to be price-elastic.

If the price of an ice cream cone goes up by 50 percent, most people will buy it anyway. But if the price of a new car goes up by 50 percent, many will keep driving their old clunkers. What one person considers expensive could be considered inexpensive to someone with significant INCOME, but generally consumers are more sensitive to price changes for expensive items than inexpensive items.

Using these four rules of thumb, business managers can estimate the degree of response to a price change. Small-business managers learn over time which customers are sensitive to price changes and also how much of a price decrease they need to make in order to sell end-of-the-year items. Though a theoretical concept associated with economics, price elasticity of demand has many practical uses for business managers.

Further reading

Boyes, William, and Michael Melvin. *Microeconomics,* 5th ed. Boston: Houghton Mifflin, 2002.

electronic data interchange

Electronic data interchange (EDI) is the electronic transfer of business documents such as purchase orders, invoices, and bills of lading between companies using a structured, machine-readable data format. A manufacturer using EDI can transmit purchase orders directly from its company computer to a supplier's company computer over a

telecommunications network or the INTERNET, eliminating the time-consuming and expensive manual processing of paper documents. By streamlining data flow within an organization, companies can reduce inventory, lower labor costs, shorten CYCLE TIME, and enhance customer service.

The U.S. shipping industry first implemented electronic data interchange in the 1970s. EDI grew rapidly in the 1980s, especially in large manufacturing industries such as the automotive sector. For example, as a key step in streamlining their manufacturing processes to remain competitive, General Motors Corporation, Chrysler Corporation, and Ford Motor Company implemented EDI. They also expected their suppliers to use EDI to automate the procurement cycle, reducing inventory in support of a just-in-time (JIT) production philosophy.

However, EDI was often complex and expensive to implement, since large companies typically used many suppliers. It was common for each company to use different types of computer systems and software packages and to require different features from an EDI application, all of which complicated EDI implementation. Generally only large companies could afford to implement EDI, sometimes with only limited success. In the mid-1990s the growth of the Internet fueled the first attempts at E-COMMERCE, introducing a simpler, less-expensive way for smaller companies to conduct business transactions electronically. Today implementing Web-based EDI is a viable alternative for small and medium-sized companies pressured by their larger customers who prefer to complete their business transactions electronically using EDI. In the future it is likely that businesses not using EDI will be at a competitive disadvantage, as CORPORATIONS continue to embrace flatter, decentralized organizational structures in an effort to remain competitive in the global marketplace.

The EDI process itself is quite simple: companies, or trading partners, first agree on the specific format of each EDI transaction, including the format, content, and structure of the business document. Standardized formatting ensures that each trading partner's computer can correctly interpret the data it sends or receives. Document content standards such as ANSI X.12 or EDIFACT typically provide the standard format for EDI transmissions. Most American companies adhere to the American National Standards Institute (ANSI) X.12 standard, while global business partners use the international EDI for Administration, Commerce, and Trade (EDIFACT) standard supported by the United Nations. Computer software applications translate each trading partner's documents into the proper standardized format.

After translating the business document into machine-readable form, one business partner can electronically transmit it to the other. A direct telecommunication line between trading partners, telecommunication lines via an intermediary value-added network (VAN), and the Internet are all methods used to transmit electronic data. Using a third-party value-added network, companies can transmit all of their EDI transactions for all of their trading partners at the same time. The VAN separates the EDI transactions by company and places them in each trading partner's electronic mailbox. At regular intervals, each trading partner's company computer dials the VAN's computer and extracts any pending EDI transactions. Translation software then transforms the EDI transaction into the specific format used internally by the trading partner.

Increasingly, smaller companies are turning to the Internet for EDI transmissions. Web-based EDI uses the Hypertext Markup Language (HTML) as a document format standard and maintains security during transaction transmission over the Web through the Secure Hypertext Transfer Protocol (SHTTP) or Secure Sockets Layer (SSL) protocol. As more vendors embrace the concept of e-commerce and offer inexpensive Web-based EDI software and VAN services, Web-based EDI has become a less costly and more attractive alternative to traditional EDI for even the smallest companies.

Further reading
Busby, Michael. *Demystifying EDI.* Plano, Tex.: Wordware Publishing Inc., 2000; Jilovec, Nahid. *The A to Z of EDI & Its Role in E-Commerce,* 2d ed. Loveland, Colo.: Twenty Ninth Street Press, 1998.

—Karen S. Groves

Electronic Fund Transfer Act
The Electronic Fund Transfer Act (EFTA, 1978) defined the LIABILITY rules governing electronic fund transfers. As defined in the act, electronic fund transfers are "any transfer of funds, other than a transaction originated by check, draft, or similar paper instrument, which is initiated through an electronic terminal, telephone instrument, or computer or magnetic tape so as to order, instruct, or authorize a financial institution to DEBIT or credit an account. Such term includes, but is not limited to, point-of-sale transfers, automated teller machine transactions, direct deposits or withdrawals of funds, and transfers initiated by telephone."

At the time it was passed, the EFTA was far-reaching legislation, affecting the E-COMMERCE that is commonplace today. The act provides CONSUMER PROTECTIONS requiring financial institutions providing EFT services to inform the customer regarding

- the customer's liability for unauthorized transfers caused by loss, or the loss of the card, code, or other access device
- whom to call and the phone number if there is a theft or loss
- the charges for using the EFT system
- what systems are available, including limits on frequency and dollar amounts

- the consumer's right to see transactions in writing
- ways to correct errors
- the consumer's right to stop payments
- rules concerning disclosure of account information to third parties

Probably the EFTA's most important aspect to consumers is the $50 limit on their liability when their access device is lost, stolen, or misplaced. This limit applies if the consumer notifies the financial institution within two business days of learning of the loss or theft. A consumer's liability rises to $500 if notification is made after two business days, and unlimited liability occurs if notification does not take place within 60 days after receiving a periodic statement reflecting the unauthorized transfer.

The act also provides sanctions and DAMAGES against financial institutions that violate the EFTA. Actual, punitive, and criminal sanctions can result from failure to comply with the act.

Further reading
Fisher, Bruce D., and Michael J. Phillips. *The Legal, Ethical and Regulatory Environment of Business,* 8th ed. Cincinnati: Thomson/South-Western, 2003.

electronic funds transfer
Electronic funds transfer (EFT) is the movement of funds using an encrypted electronic format. Moving money electronically is generally more efficient, more secure, and less costly than handling cash or paper checks. Although payments by cash and checks still dominate in the United States, nonpaper, or "e-payments," are growing rapidly through integration of existing and new electronic technology.

The predominant means of electronic funds transfer are CREDIT CARDS, debit cards, and automatic clearing house (ACH) transactions. Credit cards are used in almost 20 percent of all customer-business transactions and are growing annually. In a credit-card transaction, cardholders, merchants, card-issuing banks, merchants' banks, and credit-card companies are all linked electronically. Scanning credit cards simply activates accounts of participants in their banking and credit-card companies, recording the transaction that is taking place.

Debit cards are similar to credit cards, but the electronic funds-transfer system is more direct. Debit cards create point-of-sale (POS) transactions, eliminating the issuance of credit between the buyer and seller and instead directly debiting the buyer's account and crediting the seller's account. Like automated teller machine (ATM) transactions, debit cards are linked to a customer's bank account.

In the 1990s the federal government began using electronic funds transfer systems to provide electronic benefits transfer (EBT) programs, in part to reduce costs and also to reduce FRAUD. Most states have joined the federal program and provide cash entitlement assistance (AID FOR FAMILIES WITH DEPENDENT CHILDREN) and food assistance (Food Stamps), using cards that allow recipients to make cash withdrawals from designated ATM machines or to pay for food purchases at grocery stores using the equivalent of a debit card.

Another category of electronic funds transfer involves wire and ACH systems. Wire transfers are payments made among banks and other financial institutions through either of two electronic payments systems, CHIPS and Fedwire. CHIPS (Clearing House Interbank Payment System) is operated by the NEW YORK CLEARING HOUSE ASSOCIATION and is primarily used to settle FOREIGN EXCHANGE transactions among major banks. Fedwire is operated by the FEDERAL RESERVE SYSTEM and is used to settle interbank transactions.

ACH is a nationwide electronic funds-transfer system facilitating payments among individuals, businesses, and governments. Created in the 1970s, ACH is a network used for payroll direct deposit, automatic bill payments, and corporate tax payments. It is also used as the settlement mechanism for ATM, credit card, and debit card transactions. Settlement means balancing of debits and credits. During the course of any business day, there are likely to be thousands of electronic payments on the behalf of customers and businesses between any two large banks. Settlement determines which bank transfers funds electronically to compensate for the balance in exchanges between the two institutions. Each bank settles with all other banks with which it had funds transfers, also done electronically through the clearinghouse.

There are four ACH operators in the United States. The largest is the Federal Reserve, which clears almost 80 percent of all ACH transfers. The major ACH transfer is direct deposit of employee salaries. Approximately 50 percent of employees in the U.S. utilize payroll-deposit programs, and 75 percent of Social Security recipients utilize electronic transfer. The second major use of ACH transfer is cash concentration. Companies with many branches or sales outlets lose ACH to aggregate funds into a central cash account. The third major use of ACH operators is bill payment by the federal government, businesses, households. The Debt Collection Improvement Act (DCIA, 1996) directed the federal government to expand its use of electronic funds-transfer systems. As per the DCIA:

1. The government should be able to maximize on collection of delinquent accounts.
2. Debt-collection costs can be minimized by consolidating functions and activities.
3. The reduction of losses from debt-management activities is achieved by conducting proper screening for potential borrowers, monitoring accounts, and sharing information between federal agencies.

4. The federal government will ensure the public is fully aware of their debt-collection policies so debtors are cognizant of the obligation to repay amounts owed.
5. Debtors are afforded all DUE PROCESS rights, including the ability to challenge, verify, and compromise claims and have access to administrative appeals procedures.
6. When appropriate, agencies are encouraged to sell any delinquent debt, especially debts with underlying collateral.
7. The experience and expertise of private-sector professionals should be employed to help provide debt-collection services for federal agencies.

Relatively new uses of electronic funds transfer include electronic bill presentment and payment and e-money. In the increasingly popular method of electronic bill presentation and payment, bills are received over the computer, and payment is initiated or authorized electronically. Bills received in the mail may also be paid via the computer or telephone.

E-money has been attempted by a number of electronic service providers, with minimal success to date. One type of e-money system is prepaid stored-value cards, by which consumers pay in advance for set dollar amounts, which are then scanned to execute purchases. Most stored-value cards are designated for specific purchases, such as telephone, photocopying, and mass-transit cards. Multipurpose stored-value cards are gaining acceptance in Europe but more slowly in the United States. E-cash systems, including DigiCash and PayPal, have attempted to create an on-line currency exchanged among customers and merchants, thus avoiding the use of credit cards and the potential for credit-card FRAUD. These forms of electronic funds transfer have not yet been widely accepted.

See also DEBIT, CREDIT; E-COMMERCE.

Further reading

Electronic Funds Corporation website. Available on-line. URL: www.achnetwork.com; Financial Management Service website. Available on-line. URL: www.fms.treas.gov/eft; Weiner, Stuart E. "Electronic Payments in the U.S. Economy: An Overview," *Economic Review* 16, no. 2 (1999): 44.

embargo

An embargo is a government-sponsored INJUNCTION against the sale of goods to a foreign country and/or the importation of goods from another country. Though embargoes are designed to adversely affect the economy of another country, they are usually motivated by political reasons—i.e., to punish an offending country. Embargoes are less costly than military intervention, both in money and lives, and they are less likely to be opposed by other countries in the region or world.

The United States' use of embargoes against specific goods is justified on the grounds of national security.

Under Section 232 of the Trade Expansion Act of 1962, the president is authorized to take actions to "adjust the IMPORTS" of any good that may impair the national security. In addition to national defense, economic welfare is considered part of national security under the act. In the United States, complete embargoes of goods from some nations are undertaken through the International Emergency Economic Powers Act, or the Trading with the Enemy Act. U.S. embargoes against goods from North Korea, Libya, Vietnam (until 1994), and Cuba all originated under the Trading with the Enemy Act.

In the 20th century, the longest-lasting and most famous U.S. embargo has been the ban against trade with Cuba. Enacted in the early 1960s, the Cuban embargo was a reaction to the expropriation of private businesses, many of them owned by Americans, and the communist rhetoric of Fidel Castro's government. For over 40 years, the United States has prohibited trade with Cuba.

An embargo is not a blockade; it is an economic sanction. For any embargo to be effective, other countries must agree to cooperate with the sanction. Before the rise of Fidel Castro, Cuba was a major trading partner with the United States. In 1959 Cuban exports to the United States exceeded those from Mexico. After the embargo, Cuba expanded trade relations with the then Soviet Union and Eastern Bloc countries under Soviet control, trading sugar for oil and other goods previously imported from the United States. With the collapse of the Soviet Union, trade and Soviet subsidies of the Cuban economy ended. The Cuban government then turned to other trade partners, primarily Spain and Mexico, developing new business arrangements and investments.

In 1992 the U.S. government attempted to expand its embargo against Cuba, passing the Cuban Democracy Act. Designed to force developing countries to adhere to the U.S. embargo, the act prohibits trade by subsidiaries of U.S. firms with Cuba and bars ships using Cuban ports from entering U.S. ports for six months after leaving Cuba. A provision of the act also terminates eligibility for U.S. economic aid, debt reduction, and debt forgiveness for any country providing assistance to Cuba. Most U.S. trading partners objected strongly to the Cuban Democracy Act, passing legislation prohibiting U.S. subsidiaries operating in their countries from complying with the act.

Sometimes the United States has banned specific products from entering the country, including oil imports from Iran (1979) and Libya (1982) and wheat from the Soviet Union (1978). The wheat embargo, in response to the Soviet invasion of Afghanistan, had little impact as Soviet buyers found ready suppliers of grains from South American producers.

Further reading
Folsom, Ralph H., and Michael Gordon. *International Business Transactions,* 5th ed. Eagan, Minn.: West Group, 2002.

embezzlement

Embezzlement occurs when employees steal from a company. Whereas theft and larceny involve an outsider's taking funds or property, embezzlement is the misappropriation of funds or ASSETS by someone within an organization. Most business owners actively work to reduce shoplifting (called *shrink,* short for inventory shrinkage, by retailers), but fewer businesses develop policies and strategies to reduce embezzlement.

Almost any business is vulnerable to embezzlement. Experts report that it most often occurs in financial institutions and small businesses. A typical case of embezzlement involves a bookkeeper who, using multiple accounts, electronic transfers of funds, and phony paperwork, removes funds from the company into his or her own accounts. Once established, an embezzler can repeatedly extract funds, covering his acts with receipts and accounting transfers. This type of WHITE-COLLAR crime is rarely prosecuted and often repeated at subsequent places of EMPLOYMENT. Logically, a thorough review of references would prevent embezzlers from repeating their crimes, but given the potential LIABILITY associated with a negative reference and without a criminal conviction, former employers usually will volunteer little information beyond dates of employment.

To reduce embezzlement, experts recommend establishing

- policies and procedures regarding cash-handling and internal accounting controls, and rotating responsibilities in sensitive areas where embezzlement is most likely to occur, segregating office shipping, sales, and bookkeeping functions
- a code of conduct for personnel, including notice the company will conduct periodic credit checks on employees and all applicants
- a documentation system that restricts access to FINANCIAL INSTRUMENTS allowing transfer of funds and an AUDITING system to ensure accuracy of information
- control of access to facilities, including having a least two people open and close the facility, and documentation of who has keys, security, and alarm-system information
- review of a fidelity bonding company's reputation and performance

One of the largest cases of embezzlement in the United States involved a group of executives in Phar-mor, a chain of retail drug stores. In 1992 the company lost $350 million in a FRAUD and embezzlement scheme. The company was forced into Chapter 11 bankruptcy protection, fired 16,000 employees, and closed 200 stores to recover from the crime.

Further reading
Turner, Dana, and Richard G. Stephenson. "Embezzlement: Practicing Prevention," Bankinfo.com. Available on-line. URL: www.bankinfo.com/security/embez2.html.

emerging markets

Emerging markets are economies that present high RISK but also potentially high rates of growth; they have low per capita GROSS DOMESTIC PRODUCT (GDP). Economists and investors use a variety of terms to differentiate among economies. In the 1960s, economies were divided among first-, second-, and third-world countries. Considered elitist by many, these terms were replaced with industrialized, newly industrialized (NICs), and developing countries. With increased GLOBALIZATION and the end of cold-war economic barriers, many developing countries are now referred to as emerging markets.

In recent years many U.S. mutual fund companies have created emerging-market funds. Emerging markets are predominantly capitalist political/economic systems, with the potential for growth. In addition to relatively low per capita GDP, emerging markets tend to have lower literacy rates, lower life expectancies, and higher infant mortality rates. Most emerging markets also lack INFRASTRUCTURE, roads, ports, and utilities needed for ECONOMIC GROWTH.

Emerging markets differ from agrarian economies in that there is the potential for growth. In very low-INCOME countries, the circle of poverty limits the potential for economic growth. Low incomes prevent households from saving. Lack of savings limits INVESTMENT. Lack of investment limits the potential for economic growth.

One problem for many emerging markets is the dependence on commodities. Except for hydrocarbon resources, most World Commodity prices have been declining for decades; with declining prices for their exports, emerging markets have lower income. In many emerging markets, people have become the major export, called guest workers in the Middle East and temporary workers in Europe. Throughout the later part of the 20th century, remittances sent home to developing countries from these young men and women working abroad have been a major source of hard-currency income.

In his *The Stages of Economic Growth,* William Rostow describes how economies go through a series of five stages of economic growth: traditional society, preconditions for takeoff, takeoff, drive to maturity, and mass CONSUMPTION. In the traditional society stage, well-established economic and social systems and customs limit economic change and growth. In the preconditions stage, traditional constraints are removed and new methods and technology introduced. In the takeoff stage, an economic growth begins, and investment expands rapidly; this is a period of intensive development. Rostow dated the takeoff stage in the U.S. economy as the period from 1843 to 1860, when major railroad investment opened new markets and expanded access to resources throughout the country.

Today many emerging markets are in what Rostow would label the preconditions for take-off. Removal of centrally planned economic systems, creation of STOCK MARKETS, and economic aid to stimulate infrastructure development are all occurring in emerging markets around the world.

One source of CAPITAL for emerging markets is MULTINATIONAL CORPORATIONS (MNCs). These are firms that operate in more than one country. The common image of an MNC is a giant CORPORATION engaging in business around the world. The *Forbes* 2000 list of "The World's Largest Corporations" is led by General Motors, followed by Wal-Mart, ExxonMobil, Ford, and DaimlerChrysler. Of the top 25 MNCs on the list, eight are U.S.-based companies, 10 are based in Japan, four are Germany-based, and there are one to two each from Britain, the Netherlands, and France.

The contribution of multinational corporations and their subsidiaries to the emerging markets they operate in is debatable. Two contrasting theories center on issues of dependency versus modernization. The dependency theory suggests that market CAPITALISM in the form of large MNCs entering small, less-developed countries leads to exploitation and dependency on the MNCs and inhibits indigenous ENTREPRENEURSHIP. Dependency theorists argue that MNCs monopolize local industrial, capital, and LABOR MARKETS. Economic growth occurs, but it is largely to the benefit of the "triple alliance": MNCs, government-owned enterprises, and the local capital elite.

Modernization theorists, on the other hand, suggest multinational corporations are agents of change, promoting economic growth and development. When a multinational corporation enters an emerging market, it brings with it new technology, managerial training, infrastructure development, and access to modern business practices. Management scholar Peter Drucker contends MNCs are "the only real hope" for less-developed countries (LDCs). They alter traditional value systems, social attitudes, and behavior patterns and encourage responsibility among political leaders of LDCs. Some economists, however, question whether replacing traditional systems with "modern" values is always beneficial to the local population.

In today's economy, global sourcing is a common practice. MNCs purchase materials and components around the world, assembling and producing wherever costs are lowest. With INTERNET communications, corporations now hold vendor auctions, inviting selected suppliers to bid on production of parts and products. Managers argue this results in increased COMPETITION and lower prices. Critics counter that it leads emerging economies to cut their prices by ignoring social costs, including pollution, in the race to keep any EMPLOYMENT and income in their economy.

In addition to lack of capital and potential exploitation by multinational corporations, emerging markets face a variety of other hurdles to economic growth and development. Political instability, corruption, protection of property rights, and other risks impair investment and growth in emerging markets.

Further reading
Folsom, Ralph H., and W. Davis Folsom. *Understanding NAFTA and Its International Implications.* New York: Matthew Bender/Irwin, 1996; Lamb, Charles, Joseph Hair, and Carl McDaniel. *Marketing.* 5th ed. Cincinnati, Ohio: Thomson, 2000.

eminent domain

A legal term for one of the "sovereign" powers inherent in all governments, eminent domain allows for the taking (with "just compensation") of private property for public use without the consent of the owner. The government exercises this right, by either judicial or administrative proceedings, through condemnation.

The need for eminent domain is predominately based on growth. As population increases, the demand for land use also grows, along with increasing needs for all kinds of public goods and SERVICES such as sewage-treatment systems, hospitals, bridges, highways, cemeteries, and other forms of INFRASTRUCTURE.

The idea of eminent-domain compensation comes from 17th-century judges and legal scholars, such as Hugo Grotius and Samuel Pufendorf. In the early 1600s, the English Parliament would authorize the taking of property and the amount to be paid as compensation, or it would provide a judicial review to determine the amount. In the American colonies, legal proceedings evolved allowing for landowners to make statements concerning the question of compensation.

Unlike Anglo-American law, the French and German systems require that compensation be paid in advance of the takings. There are fewer general statutes allowing for blanket authorization of condemnation for specific public projects (such as highways) than there are in the United States, and often each case of condemnation has to be authorized by that country's government.

The U.S. Constitution deals specifically with eminent domain in the last clause of the Fifth Amendment, stating: " . . . nor shall private property be taken for public use, without just compensation." The issue of property takings is not limited to those at the federal level. Section 1 of the Fourteenth Amendment extends the limits to state and local levels by declaring: " . . . nor shall any State deprive any person of life, liberty, or property, without the DUE PROCESS of law."

Additionally, several state constitutions limit eminent-domain powers. As the Industrial Revolution developed in the United States, quasi-public CORPORATIONS such as railroads were able to acquire private property for their own use. Some STATE COURTS reacted to this by interpreting the "public use" clause in its strictest sense, that public access must be allowed to the property taken, while other states required only that the public benefit in some manner from the taking. This situation created a legal debate that lasted for decades, although current U.S. courts' interpretation of the amendment tends towards the "public benefit" theory. Until the 1930s, "public use" was defined to include schools, roads, dams, government buildings, and other public entities. Lately the concept has been expanded to include the resale of private property to private owners for urban renewal, housing developments, and similar programs that generally benefit the public. Critics claim that governments often tread a fine line between what benefits the public and what is essentially ECONOMIC DEVELOPMENT in the guise of public interest.

In a basic condemnation situation, a single person owns the property; however, a great deal of property in the United States is not held in such a simple manner. Often ownership involves holders of easements, MORTGAGES, OPTIONS, and leases. Leaseholders are particularly significant in number, since land is often leased for residential, agricultural, industrial and commercial reasons. This situation creates a two-step legal situation: the government is only required to settle with the landowner, but often another hearing determines how those LEASING the property are compensated. Many states and the federal government have "quick taking" statutes that allow the government to take title and possession before the price is decided by the courts, provided an adequate security deposit is offered.

Generally the amount of compensation due is the fair MARKET VALUE of the property taken. Fair market value is interpreted as the price for which the property would have sold in the absence of condemnation, including not only the existing use value but also the best use for which the property may be utilized. Problems often arise from the definition of a fair market: when there is no market or DEMAND for the condemned property; when adjacent properties rise or fall in value because of the government projects (some of which end up being condemned at a later date); or when the taking involves less than full ownership of the property. Some states, such as California, allow for the compensation for business GOODWILL losses (based on the reputation and location of the business), but these are not recoverable in federal-takings cases.

Probably the biggest eminent-domain issue in recent years has been the case of regulatory takings. In this situation, a new law, regulation, or government action under an existing statute (such as the ENDANGERED SPECIES ACT) results in a decrease in the value of the property, generally because of restrictions placed on its utility and development. This instance, where land has not actually been formally seized under eminent domain, is known as inverse condemnation, and critics maintain that the owner is still entitled to compensation for the loss of property value. As of this writing, almost every state in the union has introduced legislation regarding regulatory-takings compensation.

Further reading
Fellows, James A. "The legal doctrine of regulatory takings: an evolving issue," *Appraisal Journal* 64 October 1996 p 363

(12); Guidry K., and A. Quang Do. "Eminent domain and just compensation for single-family homes." *Appraisal Journal* 66 July 1998 p. 231(5) Melton, B. "Eminent domain, 'public use' and the conundrum of original intent." *Natural Resources Journal* 36 (1996): 59–85.

—Patricia Giddens

employee assistance program

An employee-assistance program (EAP) is a series of company-sponsored services designed to address employees' work and personal problems affecting their performance. In the 1980s many U.S. companies, recognizing the benefits of healthy, focused employees, implemented EAPs as part of EMPLOYEE BENEFITS packages. Most often employee assistance programs are associated with counseling services, which help to address stress, family difficulties, drug abuse, and other problems. The North Dakota Public Employees Retirement System works to give employees assistance "in guidance and counseling and to determine appropriate diagnosis and/or course of treatment to employees and their eligible dependents in cases of alcoholism, drug abuse and personal problems." The North Dakota program, like most EAPs, allows employees a set number of visits per year. EAPs can also include wellness programs, financial counseling, and legal advice.

The economic logic behind providing employee assistance programs is productivity. Focused workers not distracted by personal crises will be more productive, and burnout and work frustration is lessened, improving worker loyalty and reducing turnover costs. EAPs provide a confidential resource for employees, rather than employees having to discuss personal issues with their managers. After the events of September 11, 2001, employees at many U.S. companies, most of them far removed from the direct impact of terrorism, utilized employee assistance programs to deal with emotional stress.

Most companies contract with independent providers of employee assistance programs. Typically employers pay a set dollar amount per month per employee to the EAP provider, regardless of how often employees use the service. Kevin Host, director of Family Services Employee Assistance Program, suggests employers use five criteria in choosing an EAP provider.

• *Location.* Is the EAP provider local or national? Which is best suited for the particular business?
• *Contract terms.* Is it subcontracted? Will employees interact directly with the EAP or a variety of subcontractors?
• *Pricing and value.* Different levels of service result in varying prices and benefits.
• *Accessibility.* How easily accessible is the EAP? How long will employees have to wait to gain assistance?

• *Relationships.* How does the EAP provider's philosophy and practice fit with the mission and philosophy of the company?

One of the difficult parts of employee assistance programs is evaluating their effectiveness. Simple measures like reduced absenteeism and turnover are a starting point; reductions in conflicts and accidents can also be measured. In *Human Resource Management,* Cynthia Fisher, Lyle Schoenfeldt, and James Shaw describe the approach taken by Phoenix, Arizona. A company determined its average annual wage costs and then multiplied this by 0.17, which is the national average percentage of troubled employees. They then multiplied this figure by 0.25 on the assumption that personal problems reduce performance by 25 percent. Assuming EAP intervention could reduce losses due to troubled employees by 50 percent, the savings from their EAP would be 50 percent of the calculated improvement in performance. Net benefits would then be the savings minus the cost of the program, which the city estimated to be $2.5 million annually.

Further reading

Fisher, Cynthia D., Lyle F. Schoenfeldt, and James B. Shaw, *Human Resource Management,* 5th ed. Boston: Houghton Mifflin, 2003; Host, Kevin. "How to choose an employee assistance plan." *Puget Sound Business Journal,* 17 August 1998.

employee benefits

Benefits are one part of the COMPENSATION AND BENEFITS package that an employee receives as a member of the workforce of a particular company. Total compensation costs to an employee include salary or wages, incentives, and benefits. During the time around World War II, the description was "fringe benefits," because the benefits constituted a minor part of an employee's compensation, but this has changed overtime. As the new millennium dawns, employee benefits can add an average 40 percent or more of salary (payroll) costs to the employer's costs. In current economic times, shrinking of benefit packages through cost cutting, cost sharing, deductibles, and fewer benefits offered is occurring. Some major categories of benefits are discussed below, although the list of possibilities is broad, and employers have the flexibility to customize for their specific company needs.

Benefit packages called CAFETERIA PLANS or flexible-benefit packages are common today. With these the company pays a certain dollar amount per pay period for the purchase of various benefits. Any coverage chosen above the company limit can be purchased by the employee at the company's group rates. Thus the employee has a benefits package that is tailored to his or her needs.

INSURANCE is a broad category that includes such items as hospital, medical, dental, vision, life, disability, and long-term care coverage. Each of these can include several choices as to level of coverage. For the medically related insurances, usually several options are offered involving a range of costs for employees. In general a higher deductible and co-pay are associated with a lower premium for the employee. Preferred Provider Organizations (PPOs) and HEALTH MAINTENANCE ORGANIZATIONS (HMOs) are common options offered by most employers today.

RETIREMENT PLANS, if offered, are guaranteed when an employee becomes vested with a company. Vesting traditionally comes after a designated number of years of service, although it can be part of a phased-in system. For example, an employee can earn 20 percent per year with full vesting at five years or another time schedule designed by the company. Pension plans can be fully funded by the employer or be proportionately funded by both employer and employee. Some companies are using the option of a 401K program as their total pension benefit for employees. In this arrangement the employer contributes some dollar amount such as 30 or 50 cents per dollar contributed by the employee up to a certain limit—for instance, 6 percent of earnings. This is further capped by law as to the maximum amount that can be contributed to a 401K plan per year. It is possible and preferable for a company to offer both the traditional pension plan and a 401K plan.

In many companies, "leave banks" have replaced the traditional separate programs for vacation, sick leave, and holidays. Commonly these forms of paid absence from work have been combined into a maximum number of days per year for the employee in his/her leave bank. Whether an employee uses these days for vacation, sickness, or other purposes is immaterial to the employer. The FAMILY AND MEDICAL LEAVE ACT is a separate issue. This is unpaid leave that, by law, an employee may take under certain circumstances and within certain specified guidelines.

Finally, additional leave areas that are traditionally paid by the employer include jury duty, leave due to death of an immediate family member, and military service.

A partial listing of other areas for benefits would include memberships in various clubs like Sam's Club or country clubs; paid educational expenses; paid travel expenses; programs or assistance for child care and elder care; employee discounts; food services; use of a company car; membership in CREDIT UNIONS; and EMPLOYEE-ASSISTANCE PROGRAMS for such items as counseling, financial planning, or legal advice.

Legally required benefits include SOCIAL SECURITY insurance, UNEMPLOYMENT compensation (most employees are eligible), and WORKERS' COMPENSATION (compulsory in most states).

—Leanne McGrath

employee motivation

Employee motivation involves the willingness of people to work towards and obtain their goals at work. Multiple factors affect employee motivation, including the nature of the organization's formal reward structure, perceived pay equity, employee benefits, interesting work, leadership style and quality, and individual needs.

The formal structure of the company's reward system, or the means through which employees earn promotions, salary increases, or other rewards, can either increase or decrease employee motivation. As discussed in MOTIVATION THEORY, incentives or external rewards often motivate people, provided that the incentives are used in an informative manner rather than a controlling manner. Reward structures that promote professional development and provide recognition for employees' contributions to company success are associated with higher levels of JOB SATISFACTION and likely increase employee motivation. On the other hand, inadequate or unfair reward structures may decrease motivation and tempt employees to reduce their efforts at work.

Perceived equity in rewards, such as pay, is a key factor in determining employee motivation. Good wages, which are distributed fairly, serve as an important external motivator. People tend to make social comparisons with other individuals or groups, comparing the level of their own contributions and subsequent rewards with those of their peers. When employees feel either over- or underpaid for their work, it affects motivation. People who feel overpaid may increase their outputs in order to match the high level of pay, benefiting the organization. On the other hand, employees who feel underpaid may respond in a variety of ways. They may decrease their efforts to match the low pay, ask for a raise, try to change the contributions or rewards garnered by other individuals, or search for another job.

Part of the perception of pay equity depends on whether employees believe that their supervisors are qualified to assess their work and that they make fair use of objective standards in evaluating employee performance. Although many employees agree that merit-based pay, or pay related to actual performance, is appropriate and desirable, few believe that such systems are successful when applied to them. In addition, perceptions of pay equity sometimes depend on the appropriateness of the comparison group. Because many companies keep salary information confidential, it may be difficult for employees to select an appropriate comparison group when assessing pay equity. For example, women tend to compare their salaries with those of other women performing the same job, especially if this information is more readily available to them, rather than compare their pay with men performing the same job. In cases where pay inequity does exist between men and women for the same job and level of experience, women may be relatively unaware of the difference.

Although many organizations may have a difficult time raising employees' salaries due to budget constraints, there are other actions they can take to motivate their workers. Supervisors can strive to maximize the intrinsic value of a job by making it more intellectually stimulating, challenging, or interesting for employees. In addition, providing clearly defined goals for the employees and stating how their performance will relate to potential rewards helps reduce ambiguity about job responsibilities. Providing interesting and stimulating work is as essential to employee motivation as providing fair and equitable pay.

Leadership style and quality also affect employee motivation. Directive leaders, or those who are task-oriented, tend to do the best when the organizational needs include defining a problem or goal and keeping employees focused while working on it. Of course the success of this type of leader depends in part on the leader's ability to provide clear direction to employees. However, leaders who adopt a more democratic style, for instance including employees in the decision-making process, may be more effective at promoting motivation and morale. These leaders are concerned both with the employees' needs and relations and with the organizational goals. Research indicates that leaders who are flexible enough to use either style when the situation dictates, or who at least can recognize when a situation is not well matched for their style, tend to be the most effective.

Finally, employees vary in their individual needs for different kinds of motivating rewards. For example, some employees are high in ACHIEVEMENT MOTIVATION and thrive on accomplishment. Providing these employees with challenging or complex tasks may increase their motivation. Other employees derive motivation primarily from recognition for a job well done. Although organizations should strive to provide full recognition for the work of each employee, extra praise and attention may work especially well in motivating these employees. For others, the need for belonging and affiliation is important. These employees may be highly motivated when working in democratic groups where they can play a role in making decisions and in shaping the group outcome. Still other employees are competition-oriented and may be motivated most when they are provided with opportunities to compete and succeed. Tailoring rewards to employees' personal needs can be an effective means of motivation. However, employing this one-on-one strategy requires a perceptive, creative, and highly effective supervisor.

The importance of facilitating employee motivation should be underscored. Organizations that treat their employees well by providing fair and equitable wages, a stimulating atmosphere, high-quality LEADERSHIP, and full and suitable appreciation for a job well done will be the most successful at retaining talented and motivated employees.

Further reading

Myers, David G. *Exploring Psychology.* 5th ed. New York: Worth Publishers, 2002; Schemerhorn, John R. Jr., James G. Hunt, and Richard N. Osborn. *Basic Organizational Behavior.* 2d ed. New York: John Wiley and Sons, 1998; Schultz, Duane, and Sydney Ellen Schultz. *Psychology and Work Today: An Introduction to*

Industrial and Organizational Psychology, 8th ed. New York: Macmillan Publishing, 2001.

—Elizabeth L. Cralley

employee recruiting

People are the one resource that every organization needs to accomplish its mission successfully. How, when, and where to find these people; determination of appropriate COMPENSATION AND BENEFITS; and then securing their EMPLOYMENT constitute the essence of employee recruitment. Effective recruiting begins with HUMAN RESOURCES planning. This includes (but is not limited to) determining job tasks and duties; the education, skills, and experience required of the hired individuals; the level of responsibility for process, people, and product; and the market prices for specific talent. In implementing the organizational strategy, the need for certain employee talent becomes evident for success.

In order for hiring to be effective, it must be tied to organizational goals and result in the desired performance (accomplishing the mission). The human resources that a company hires can provide the sustainable competitive advantage needed to win in the marketplace. No two individuals will bring to the organization identical abilities, experience, or skills, and what they bring will be unique for each and every company. For this reason alone, the recruiting process should be a top priority for all companies. Any and all parts of the process must adhere to all employment laws, including but not limited to the 1964 CIVIL RIGHTS ACT as amended, Age Discrimination Act, Pregnancy Act, and EQUAL PAY ACT.

Many times the initial screening for employees involves reading or scanning résumés, which is done to get a preliminary idea of the person's suitability for a position. Résumés, however, contain only the information that a candidate wants to reveal, and this is always presented in a most positive light. In contrast, a carefully designed application form tells an employer what he/she wants to know about the candidate. This consistency of information gathering allows better comparison of candidates and helps in the event of legal challenge to the final hire.

Tests are used frequently by employers to measure candidates' intangible dynamics as well as job-performance skills. These tests need to be both reliable and valid to be useful and to pass possible legal challenge. The available battery of tests is quite extensive, including paper-and-pencil integrity or honesty tests, personality tests, physical-ability tests, mental-ability tests, and job-knowledge tests.

INTERVIEWING is a common screening step used in the hiring process. Because of cost considerations, a two-step process is often used. The first pass can be a phone call to screen candidates; this often includes asking behavioral-type questions to gain insight into the candidate's work performance. The second step often consists of a series of face-to-face interviews that occur at the company with managers and those with whom the new hire would be working. A consistent set of questions should be employed and used for all candidates for the position, and the scores of raters should be checked for interrater reliability.

Reference and background checks are another integral part of the recruiting process. Failure to do such checks can result in charges against an employer for negligent hiring if the new hire proves unfit or harms a third party. Both personal and work references are sources for candidate information. Again, specific and consistent questions need to be asked about all candidates to allow accurate comparison. A check of employment facts for verification of information given should also be done. Other types of background checks include credit, educational credentials, and criminal background.

Drug tests are common today as a preliminary screen done early in the recruiting process. A complete medical examination, if required of all new hires, is completed after the offer of hire is extended. The offer then is made contingent upon passing the medical exam successfully.

The list of possible sources for qualified candidates for a job opening is very extensive and includes the following: private employment agencies; public employment agencies; ADVERTISING venues such as newspaper, radio, and television; bulletin boards; professional publications; INTERNET employment sites; employee referral; recruitment from competitors; unsolicited applicants; current (in-house) employees; and universities, colleges, and other educational institutions. Using as many of these sources as possible helps the organization find qualified candidates.

Overall the employee recruitment process needs to be designed well and to be understood by all managers. Then its implementation can result in effective hiring.

—Leanne McGrath

Employee Retirement Income Security Act

The Employee Retirement Income Security Act (ERISA, 1974) imposed requirements, on covered employers, to manage employee pension funds for the benefit of their workers. For years many U.S. employers engaged in a variety of practices such as arbitrary termination in pension-plan participation, arbitrary benefit reductions, and mismanagement of pension-fund ASSETS. ERISA was passed to address many of these abuses. The act does not require an employer to establish or fund a pension plan but does impose FIDUCIARY DUTIES for fund managers.

Three important rules within ERISA include the "prudent man" rule, which stipulates that employee pension funds cannot be invested in FINANCIAL INSTRUMENTS that prudent trustees of other pension funds would not purchase. This was intended to reduce the risks taken by pension-fund managers with employees' retirement funds. Under the prudent man rule, most fund managers diversify investments as way to reduce risk.

The second rule requires ERISA fund managers to be registered brokers with the SECURITIES AND EXCHANGE COMMISSION (SEC). This often prevents fund managers from investing in FUTURES markets, because futures-market managers are regulated by the COMMODITY FUTURES TRADING COMMISSION, not by the SEC.

Third, ERISA only applies to pension funds for private-sector employees, not public pension funds. While many states have adopted ERISA guidelines, state employees' pension funds have often been "tapped" to purchase risky investment decisions. In one of the more famous cases, New York City employee pension funds were loaned to the city to prevent the city from filing for bankruptcy. If the prudent man rule had applied to the New York City pension fund managers, it is unlikely that they would have made that investment decision.

The DEPARTMENT OF LABOR (DOL) is charged with enforcing ERISA. Most companies hire professional fund managers to oversee investment of pension funds, but the DOL has ruled that corporate directors and officers are still liable for prudent management of their employees' retirement funds. ERISA requires record-keeping, reporting, and disclosure requirements on companies, as well as requirements guaranteeing employee participation and vesting in pension plans.

Further reading
Gold, Jackey. "The rape of public pensioners: or why public pension funds aren't under ERISA, and what happens as a result." *Financial World* 160 (23 July 1991): 22; Mallor, Jane P., A. James Barnes, Thomas Bowers, Michael J. Philips, and Arlen W. Langvardt. *Business Law and the Regulatory Environment*. 11th ed. Boston: McGraw-Hill, 2001.

employee stock-ownership plan

Employee stock-ownership plans (ESOPs) are programs where a CORPORATION contributes shares of the company's stock into a TRUST, which then allocates the stock to employee accounts within the trust.

Shares are typically allocated in proportion to compensation and employees usually begin receiving allocations after one year of service, the shares must vest, meaning the employees become entitled to the shares, before the employee can choose to diversify his or her account. By law, vesting must occur within seven years of service, but many companies vest empolyees within shorter waiting periods. Employees waiting receive the vested portion of their accounts at termination, disability, death, or retirement. In publicly traded companies employees may sell their distributed shares on the market. In privately held firms, the company must give employees an option to sell the stock to the company. In the United States, ESOPs, created by the EMPLOYEE RETIREMENT INCOME SECURITY ACT of 1974, allow both publicly owned and closely held corporations to transfer ownership interest in the company to its employees.

ESOPs are typically used to buy the stock of a retiring owner in a privately held company and as an employee benefit or incentive plan.

Employees can also benefit from the creation of ESOPs, which are often used to establish a pension plan and add incentives for workers. ESOP distributions and DIVIDENDS are tax-deferred, and laws require financial disclosure to employees. Researchers have found that employee ownership heightens worker involvement and productivity. Drawbacks to ESOPs include the cost of starting a plan, administrative expenses, and compliance with government regulations.

Further reading

Dessler, Gary. *Human Resource Management.* 9th ed. Saddle River, N.J.: Prentice Hall, 2003. Employee Stock Ownership Association. Available on-line. URL: www.esopassociation.org.

employment

Every organization needs to be staffed with knowledgeable personnel. When evaluating applicants, there are two major concerns: hiring the right person for the available position and being sure that the applicant is right for the company. The person-job fit evaluates whether the applicant has the appropriate knowledge, skills, abilities, and other requirements to perform the job. Factors such as education, experience, and the applicant's desire to perform the job duties are also included in the evaluation. The person-company fit looks beyond the applicant's immediate capacity to perform the current open position and evaluates such factors as the long-term potential of the applicant with the company. Important questions to be answered include: Is the applicant capable of assuming greater responsibilities that are inherent with promotions? Will the applicant fit in with the CORPORATE CULTURE and appreciate the organization's guiding beliefs and values?

The employment process typically consists of three phases: EMPLOYEE RECRUITING, selection, and socializing. Recruiting assures a supply of qualified applicants from which the appropriate selection(s) of new hire(s) can be made. While recruiting and selection are the two steps in employment that receive the most attention, the process of socializing—acclimating the new employee into the organization—should also be an integral part of the employment process. Socialization reduces the potential of psychological shock that the new employee may experience during the first few weeks or months of employment.

Applicants can be recruited from either within or outside the organization. Many companies emphasize developing and promoting their own employees, so these firms conduct an internal search before looking elsewhere. There are several techniques for notifying employees that a position is open and will be filled. Job-posting and job-bidding systems allow the individual employee to tell the company that he/she is interested in the position. Other internal recruiting techniques include data and skills banks that the company may maintain. This information may have been encapsulated from career discussions the employee had with his/her supervisor. The company typically has many applicants for only one opening, so another valuable technique is to maintain information from earlier applicants for previous jobs.

Regardless of whether the position is to be filled with an internal or external candidate, knowledge of the position's availability is crucial. Many applicants are drawn to apply because other individuals already employed by the company have told their friends and family members about the position. Current employees are an effective source of applicants because the referring employee often believes if his/her recommendation results in an unsatisfactory hire, it could negatively reflect on him- or herself. More common external-recruiting methods include ADVERTISING available positions in newspapers and technical journals, on radio stations, and on the INTERNET. Public and private employment agencies are frequent sources of candidates. State employment security commissions are the primary public employment agencies; their services are provided without fees since they are publicly funded. Private employment agencies are paid for their services either by the applicant or the potential employer. Finally, many candidates simply walk into the office and ask if the company is hiring individuals with their qualifications.

Evaluating the applicant's qualifications and determining to whom the employment offer will be made is the purpose of the selection phase. Selection usually involves multiple steps including (1) a series of interviews with the HUMAN RESOURCES representative, the supervisor and/or manager with the opening, and other knowledgeable individuals; (2) verbal and written comprehension and ability tests; and (3) a physical examination that may include a screen for illegal drug use. A unique type of interview is the realistic job preview (RJP). This interview technique involves the employee in performing actual job duties on the job site. The applicant sees where the work is done and is encouraged to ask questions of current employees whom he/she will be working alongside. RJPs give the applicant more information about the job than would be otherwise obtained. Companies vary widely, however, in their use of these specific techniques.

"Job relatedness" is a critical concern in determining which selection techniques will be used. The ultimate purpose of interviews, tests, and other screening techniques is to predict the potential on-the-job success of the applicant. If a specific question or technique does not predict success, then it should not be used. Employment techniques must be both reliable and valid. Reliability is concerned with the consistency of results if the test or technique is used multiple times. Validity asks the question, "Did the test measure what it was supposed to measure?"

Employment specialists must be careful that the employment process conforms to the requirements of the

AMERICANS WITH DISABILITIES ACT. This federal law was passed to help applicants with physical or emotional limitations find meaningful employment. The applicant, after reviewing an up-to-date job description based on a thorough job analysis, is asked whether he/she can perform the essential job duties. At this time the candidate can ask the company to make reasonable accommodations in the job to enable him/her to perform the duties. The company must then evaluate the applicant's request(s) and decide whether it can implement the requested accommodation. Duties that are not essential to the position may be reassigned to other positions.

—John Abbott

employment-at-will

Employment-at-will is the concept that EMPLOYMENT is a CONTRACT between an employer and an employee and therefore subject only to the terms of the agreement between the two. As such, workers are hired for an indefinite duration, and either the employee or the employer may end the relationship for any reason and at any time. Implicit in employment-at-will is the idea that government does not determine employment relationships.

The concept of employment-at-will evolved out of the AMERICAN INDUSTRIAL REVOLUTION as workers and employers shifted from small-scale, local craft guilds to an industrial system employing hundreds and thousands of workers. Employment-at-will became part of American COMMON LAW based on rulings in the 1870s and 1880s.

Most discussion of employment-at-will focuses on an employer's right to terminate a worker without having to justify the action. Contracts, union agreements, and federal discrimination laws limit the right of employers to terminate employees. Until the WAGNER ACT of 1935, UNIONS had relatively little power. Union strikers were often prosecuted under criminal conspiracy laws. The Wagner Act gave union members the right to COLLECTIVE BARGAINING and through these contracts; workers often gained protection from being fired, except for JUST CAUSE.

Law Professor Jane Mallor and her coauthors note that public employees are also often protected from termination without just cause. In what is called the public-policy exception, recognized by about 80 percent of the states, terminated public employees can claim WRONGFUL DISCHARGE based on "(1) refusal to commit an unlawful act, (2) performance of an important public obligation (jury duty or whistle-blowing), (3) exercise of a legal right or privilege (e.g., making a WORKERS' COMPENSATION claim or refusing top take an illegal polygraph test)."

Other limitations on employment-at-will relationships are based on federal antidiscrimination laws. Generally workers are protected against termination based on personal traits, age, and disabilities. In some states, promises by employers and implied good faith and fair-dealing covenants also limit employment-at-will. But as Cynthia Fisher, Lyle Schoefeldt, and James Shaw summarize, " . . . between 70 and 75 percent of employees in the United States have no such explicit protection."

Further reading
Fisher, Cynthia D., Lyle F. Schoenfeldt, and James B. Shaw. *Human Resource Management*, 5th ed. Boston: Houghton Mifflin, 1990; Mallor, Jane, A. James Barnes, Thomas Bowers, Michael Philips, and Arlen Langvardt. *Business Law and the Regulatory Environment*, 11th ed. Boston: McGraw-Hill, 2001.

employment taxes   See PAYROLL TAXES.

empowerment

Empowerment in business is participatory decision making and teamwork within organizations. Empowerment includes greater worker control, accountability, and, often, flexibility in scheduling, work hours, and prioritizing of tasks.

Empowerment became a popular management concept in the United States during the 1990s. One story reported that in an empowered work environment, managers were called vision supporters. Empowerment is an alternative to hierarchical work environments, which many portray as places where bosses think they know more than they do and subordinates say what they think boss wants to hear, rather than saying what they believe is true. Hierarchical work environments discourage creativity and risk taking, essential to long-term growth and viability of the organization. MANAGEMENT consultants often advocate greater empowerment of workers. Managers frequently may say they encourage worker participation but instead fear and react against workers who suggest changes with which they are uncomfortable.

Empowerment can also refer to improving the choices available to minority groups struggling for equal opportunity, both in the work environment and in society. In this context, empowerment refers to taking greater control of personal decision making.

empowerment zones, enterprise zones

Empowerment and enterprise zones are areas identified by the Secretary of Housing and Urban Development or the Secretary of Agriculture that have a condition of persuasive poverty, UNEMPLOYMENT, and general distress. To help rebuild these distressed urban or rural areas, tax incentives encourage businesses to locate in these areas and to hire the people who live there. In the United States there are 95 enterprise communities and 29 empowerment zones where these tax benefits are in place. These regions meet certain criteria concerning population, size (urban, less than 20 square miles; rural, less than 1,000 square miles), and poverty rate (minimum 20 percent).

Businesses operating within the designated areas are entitled to an empowerment-zone employment credit (EZEC) of 20 percent for the first $15,000 of wages paid to employees who are residents of the empowerment zone, with a maximum credit per employee of $3,000 per year. The employer's deduction for wages must be reduced by the amount of credits allowed. To further encourage development, businesses within an enterprise zone are entitled to increase from $24,000 to $44,000 the amount they can expense under the Internal Revenue code for the purchase of tangible business property that is not real estate.

—Linda Bradley

Endangered Species Act

The Endangered Species Act, passed by Congress in 1973, provides for the protection and conservation of endangered species and their habitats. The act refers to all species of plants and animals with the exception of pest insects.

The Fish and Wildlife Service (FWS) in the DEPARTMENT OF THE INTERIOR and the National Marine Fisheries Service (NMFS) in the Department of Commerce administer the act and are responsible for identifying and listing "endangered" and "threatened" species. The act defines "endangered species" as "any species which is in significant danger of extinction throughout all or a significant portion of its range." A "threatened species" is "any species which is likely to become an endangered species within the foreseeable future throughout all or a significant portion of its range."

Before a species is listed, its status is evaluated by biologists, scientists, and government agency officials using set criteria. Factors considered when determining species status are: habitat instability, disease or predation, overutilization, inadequacy of existing regulatory mechanisms, and "other natural or manmade factors affecting its continued existence." The Endangered Species Act requires all proposed and officially listed species to be published in the *Federal Register.* Once listed officially, conservation programs are designed for the species' ultimate recovery.

The Endangered Species Act of 1973 builds upon two previous species-protection acts: the Endangered Species Preservation Act of 1966 and the Endangered Species Conservation Act of 1969. Although these acts were important because they established endangered-species listings, they did little to protect the listed species. The Endangered Species Act of 1973 provides enforceable rules for endangered-species protection. All federal agencies are required to participate in the conservation of listed species and are prohibited from taking any action that could harm listed species or their habitats. Additionally, under the 1973 act, the importing or EXPORTING of endangered species is illegal.

One widely publicized controversy involving the Act erupted in 1990 between conservationists and the timber industry when the northern spotted owl of the Pacific Northwest forests was listed as a "threatened" subspecies. (The northern spotted owl is a subspecies of the spotted owl.) Because the owl's "critical habitat," the old-growth federal forestland in the Pacific Northwest, is protected under the provisions of the act, the U.S. government proposed limits on the harvesting of timber in the area. The timber industry protested the limits, fearing the loss of jobs. Conservationists proposed that not enough of the forestland was being protected from logging. As of 2002, the northern spotted owl has not been removed from the "threatened" species list and the controversy between forest workers and conservationists continues.

Further reading

U.S. Fish & Wildlife Service Website. http://endangered.fws.gov/esa.html.

—Paula Maloney

enterprise zones   See EMPOWERMENT ZONES, ENTERPRISE ZONES.

entrepreneurship

Entrepreneurship is the ability and urge to find new, creative solutions to problems. Entrepreneurs forsake the security of regular EMPLOYMENT in pursuit of their dreams. Their compensation is measured by their initiative, skill, and performance. An academic definition states that entrepreneurs are individuals willing to risk investing time and money in a business activity that has the potential to make a PROFIT or incur a loss. Entrepreneurs are innovators who make things happen. The potential for success often blinds an entrepreneur to obstacles, creating a single-mindedness hard to ignore and nearly impossible to stop.

CAPITALISM provides endless opportunity to achieve business success and accumulate WEALTH. People who are excited about profitable opportunities and vigorously pursue them are a business force of unquenchable desire and inexhaustible energy. Economic textbooks typically categorize resources as human, natural, and capital. Some texts use the land, labor, CAPITAL, and entrepreneurship categories. Entrepreneurship is a resource. In the 1990s, as they discarded socialist economic systems, many Central European countries recognized the need to develop entrepreneurial resources. Often the first entrepreneurs were the people who previously had been operating in the black market.

In the United States, people like Bill Gates, Mary Kay, Jeff Bezos, and Steve Case fit the definition of *entrepreneur.* Their dreams involved risking time and money on an idea with no guarantees. Destiny, freedom, and money motivated them. Today Microsoft, Mary Kay Cosmetics, Amazon.com, and AOL are household names.

Entrepreneurs are not held to the restrictions of corporate rules and regulations; they decide how to manage their personal lives and businesses. Many people crave the freedom from direct supervision, and this is very important to entrepreneurs. Entrepreneurs answer to consumers and the requirements of their individual business; their supervisor is the person who stares back at them from the mirror. Even though money is important, it is hardly ever at the top of the list of entrepreneurial motivation. Entrepreneurs simply want to be rewarded in direct proportion to their own efforts. Most realize that profitability is usually not immediate but can be the end result of hard work, a good idea, and perseverance.

What exactly is an entrepreneur? Marketing professor Dr. Jerry Moorman has a unique definition: "An entrepreneur is simply a capitalist in heat!" Ignoring the crudeness of this analogy, it is probably an accurate description.

Further reading
Moorman, Jerry, and James W. Halloran. *Contemporary Entrepreneurship*. Cincinnati, Ohio: Southwestern, 1995.

environmental impact statement

An environmental impact statement (EIS) is a public report of a government-funded project, usually industrial, and its potential impact on the environment. An EIS summarizes the project's long-term and short-term effect on noise, water, and air pollution as well as the impact on EMPLOYMENT and living, social, and local service standards. An EIS explains the proposed project and describes any alternatives to it.

An EIS is written by any federal agency either on its own behalf or on the behalf of a state agency and, given the complexity of the report, is usually authored by numerous professionals including scientists, social scientists, and engineers. The drafting of an EIS is required by the National Environmental Policy Act of 1969 (NEPA). The NEPA created a Council on Environmental Quality (CEQ), a three-member board that advises the President with respect to environmental matters. The CEQ directed the creation of guidelines used in writing environmental impact statements. An EIS is required if a project involves federal licensing or federal funding or is undertaken by the federal government.

An EIS is required to address all the possible questions a "reasonable person" might ask. Most environmental impact statements are lengthy documents containing a wealth of information from experts, community groups, and individuals affected by the proposed action. As a brief example, there is the St. Augustine (Florida) Bridge of Lions (details available at www.fdotbridgeoflions.com). The EIS begins by outlining the bridge's importance, the history of the city, and the importance of the bridge for tourism, together with a description of the action that must be taken to rehabilitate, replace, or continue to maintain the existing bridge. The EIS explains three alternatives and their effect on the environment, the public, and businesses and individuals who would have to be relocated. The report states the cost of land acquisition, the method of appraising land values, and additional costs to be paid

to individuals affected by the project. The potential economic impact of the bridge project is also evaluated.

Initially the requirement for federal projects and agencies to conduct environmental impact studies was seen as a way to minimize community and activist opposition to federal activities. Businesses benefitting from federal contracts are often closely involved in EIS development. A whole industry has now developed to provide consulting services to federal agencies required to produce environmental impact statements. Opponents of particular federal projects have learned to use the EIS requirement to stall projects they oppose and bring public attention to questionable practices.

Further reading
St. Augustine Bridge of Lions Draft Environmental Impact Statement. Available on-line. URL: www.fdotbridgeoflions.com.

—Karen M. Cimino

Environmental Protection Agency

The Environmental Protection Agency (EPA) is the major federal agency responsible for protection of the natural environment. The EPA's mission is "to protect human health and to safeguard the natural environment—air, water, and land—upon which life depends. For 30 years, EPA has been working for a cleaner, healthier environment for the American people."

The EPA employs over 18,000 people in 10 regional offices and 17 laboratories around the country. As stated on their website, "The EPA is responsible for researching and setting national standards for a variety of environmental programs and delegates to states and tribes responsibility of issuing permits, and monitoring and enforcing compliance. Where national standards are not met, EPA can issue sanction and take other steps to assist the states and tribes in reaching the desired levels of environmental quality. The agency also works with industries and all levels of government in a wide variety of voluntary pollution prevention programs and energy conservation efforts."

The EPA was established in 1970 in response to public outcries for better management of air, water, and land. A major contributing factor to this pressure was the publication of *Silent Spring*, Rachel Carson's 1962 classic about the indiscriminate use of pesticides and their impact on bird reproduction. Though skeptics accused Carson of "shallow science," her passionate concern and "literary genius" lead to calls for environmental protection. At the time, environmental management was spread among a wide array of federal agencies. In response to the public pressure, in 1969 Congress passed the National Environmental Protection Act (NEPA), calling for the creation of a Council on Environmental Quality (CEQ) and

- "To declare a national policy which will encourage productive and enjoyable harmony between man and his environment."

- "To promote efforts which will prevent or eliminate damage to the environment and biosphere and stimulate the health and welfare of man."
- "To enrich our understanding of the ecological systems and natural resources important to the Nation."

President Richard Nixon, not known for environmental leadership, signed the NEPA on January 1, 1970, beginning what became known as the "environmental decade." The first Earth Day, April 22, 1970, brought out 20 million citizens demonstrating for environmental reforms, and by the end of the year the Environmental Protection Agency was formed.

The EPA was initially cobbled together from personnel and programs at other federal departments. Responsibility for air and water pollution came from Department of Health, Education, and Welfare (HEW) and the DEPARTMENT OF THE INTERIOR. Pesticide management came from the FOOD AND DRUG ADMINISTRATION (FDA) and the Department of Agriculture. EPA website history notes the National Air Pollution Control Administration (NAPCA) and the Federal Water Quality Administration (FWCA) "represented the core of the federal government's pollution-control apparatus prior to the birth of EPA." Both the NAPCA and the FWCA "gained enforcement and standard-setting powers in the 1960s, but the actual exercise of these powers fell far short of expectations."

On December 1, 1970, William Ruckelshaus was confirmed as the first EPA Administrator, and by the end of that month the first major piece of environmental legislation, the CLEAN AIR ACT of 1970 was signed. This act required the EPA to establish national air-quality standards as well as standards for significant new sources and for all facilities emitting hazardous substances. The act focused on automobile emissions.

The 1970s are sometimes considered the heyday of environmentalism, yet Ruckelshaus blames the idealism of the time for subsequent problems. In an interview he said,

> "We thought we had technologies that could control pollutants, keeping them below threshold levels at a reasonable cost, and that the only things missing in the equation were national standards and a strong enforcement effort. All of the nation's early environmental laws reflected these assumptions, and every one of these assumptions is wrong . . . the errors in our assumptions were not readily apparent in EPA's early days because the agency was tackling pollution in its most blatant form."

Since then the Clean Air Act has been amended twice, in 1977 and 1990. In addition, other major environmental acts enforced by the EPA include the

- Federal Insecticide, Fungicide and Rodenticide Act (1996)
- Food Quality Protection Act (1996)

- Toxic Substances Control Act (1976)
- National Environmental Policy Act (1969)
- Pollution Prevention Act (1990)
- Environmental Research, Development and Demonstration Authorization Act (1976)
- RESOURCE CONSERVATION AND RECOVERY ACT (1970)
- CLEAN WATER ACT
- Marine Protection, Research and Sanctuaries Act
- Rivers and Harbors Act (1899)
- Safe Drinking Water Act

The EPA is involved in all major international environmental negotiations, including global warming and ozone-depletion efforts. It has also been involved in cleanup after major environmental disasters, including Love Canal, *Exxon Valdez,* Times Beach, and Three Mile Island. Love Canal was a small ditch dug in the early 1900s to create electrical power using water from Niagara Falls. When the project failed, it became a municipal and industrial chemical dump. In 1953 Hooker Chemical Company filled in the canal and sold it to the city for $1, and in the late 1950s houses were built on the land. In the late 1970s Lois Gibbs and other area home owners began documenting and questioning the exceptionally high rate of birth defects among Love Canal residents. Eventually, using SUPERFUND monies, the EPA relocated 1,000 residents. The Superfund was created by its federal government in 1980 to clean up abandoned and accidentally spilled hazardous waste.

The *Exxon Valdez* was the infamous oil tanker that had a disastrous spill in Prince William Sound, Alaska, in 1989. The EPA oversaw bioremediation efforts, while Exxon paid over $1 billion in fines. Less well known than the *Exxon Valdez* was Times Beach, a small community south of St. Louis, Missouri. Dioxin-contaminated oil had been sprayed on area roads in the 1970s in efforts to control dust. The EPA managed permanent relocation of Times Beach residents and brought a portable thermal incinerator to the area to burn dioxin-laced soil.

The EPA was actively involved in the aftermath of the 1979 Three Mile Island nuclear accident. Mechanical failure at the nuclear power plant near Harrisburg, Pennsylvania, created the potential for nuclear meltdown, which fortunately did not occur. No nuclear power plant has been built since then. The EPA is responsible for long-term monitoring of the impact of radioactive releases from Three Mile Island.

Environmental critics of the EPA often complain the agency does not conduct "good science" research, leading to lax environmental regulations. Social critics complain about the lack of enforcement of environmental laws. Business and industry groups complain about the cost of reporting and compliance with EPA regulations.

See also GREEN MARKETING.

Further reading
Environmental Protection Agency website. Available on-line. URL: www.epa.gov.

environmental scanning

Environmental scanning is the process of monitoring and collecting information about business conditions affecting a market. As marketers develop and then implement their marketing strategies—combinations of pricing, PRODUCT, distribution, and SALES PROMOTION decisions for each target market—businesses must keep track of changes in the marketplace. Yet most business managers have more than enough to do directing day-to-day operations; one analogy of a typical businessperson's day is that it is spent swatting mosquitoes. In addition a manager must also hire new workers, meet government requirements, decide which products to produce or terminate, and cultivate relationships with customers and distributors, resulting in workweeks that are often 70–80 hours long. Often managers can become so consumed with these necessary activities that they fail to notice the "lion"—some change in the marketplace that can create a major new opportunity or a dire threat to their enterprise. Thus, environmental scanning is needed to look beyond all the mosquitoes and see if there are any lions coming.

The main purpose of environmental scanning is to track changes in ECONOMIC CONDITIONS, GROSS DOMESTIC PRODUCT, INFLATION, UNEMPLOYMENT, technology, COMPETITION, international trade agreements, and other cultural, political, and legal factors that affect business decisions. Businesses consider changes in economic conditions, which usually do not change very quickly, when making long-term planning decisions. On the other hand, changes in technology can rapidly redefine markets and sources of competition or of COMPARATIVE ADVANTAGE. For example, while the U.S. Postal Service has a MONOPOLY in mail service, the fax machine and cellular and INTERNET technologies are changing the ways people communicate, often bypassing standard mail service.

When conducting competitive environmental scanning, marketers consider three types of competition: direct competitors producing similar products, competitors producing substitute products, and firms competing for the same consumers' spending. Most marketers can name their direct competitors instantly, and they are usually aware of producers of substitute products. Many companies maintain MARKET INTELLIGENCE efforts to monitor the activities of these sources of competition.

Changing social and cultural conditions require marketers to be aware of and sensitive to changing values and to changes in market DEMOGRAPHICS. For example, in 2001 California no longer had a majority population as Hispanic and Asian Californians together represented a majority of the state's residents. Cultural groups have different values, consumer preferences, and buying activities. Some groups, such as Japanese consumers, are reluctant to use CREDIT CARDS, and many cultural groups in the United States tend to be very brand-loyal consumers. During environmental scanning, marketers attempt to identify changing social and cultural trends and adjust their marketing strategies to meet changing market opportunities.

Political and legal changes can harm or help a business. Often firms or business organizations will attempt to influence regulatory processes affecting their markets. Industry associations use environmental scanning to monitor proposed changes in laws, testify at public forums for and against legislation, and lobby on behalf of their interests.

See also MARKETING STRATEGY.

Further reading

Boone, Louis E., and David L. Kurtz. *Contemporary Marketing*, 10th ed. Fort Worth: Dryden Press, 2001.

equal employment opportunity and affirmative action

Two terms commonly used in American business but often misunderstood are *equal employment opportunity* and *affirmative action*. In general, "equal employment opportunity" means that individuals will be considered for jobs or employment actions without any regard to their race, color, religion, sex, or national origin. These five demographic criteria are specifically named in Section 703 of the Civil Rights Act (CRA) of 1964, (see CIVIL RIGHTS ACTS) as amended. Considering one or more of the criteria in personnel activity is to engage in discrimination, which is prohibited by the act. The definition of covered employers, governments, labor unions, employment agencies, and training and apprenticeship sponsoring groups is so extensive that equal employment opportunity is considered a fundamental principal in employment law.

Since equal employment opportunity prohibits the use of artificial criteria (race, color, religion, sex, or national origin) in personnel activities, the concept is considered to be facially neutral. Affirmative action, however, is not facially neutral. Affirmative action encourages giving special consideration because of an individual's membership in a protected category, such as racial or sexual. Affirmative action is a voluntary program. It is above and beyond equal employment opportunity and intended to help correct injustices that occurred in the past. Through this concept when qualified applicants have similar qualifications for the same job opportunity, additional consideration is given to the minority and/or female applicant.

The practice of affirmative action was promulgated with the issuance of Executive Order 11246 in 1965. Issued by President Lyndon Johnson, this Executive Order established regulations for companies doing business with the federal government. Covered federal contractors and primary subcontractors are prohibited from discriminating based on race, color, religion, sex, or national origin. Covered companies which employ 50 or more people and have more than $50,000 in government contracts must have a written affirmative action program for minorities and females, with identified goals and timetables. The plans include a comparison of the internal utilization of minorities and females, by job group, compared with their external availability. When the external availability is greater than the internal utilization, underutilization exists and a goal to eliminate the utilization must be developed. Companies with government contracts of $10,000 or less are exempted from this executive order.

The elimination of discrimination in America was the goal of the 1964 Civil Rights Act. It is a very broad and far-reaching act. Section 7 specifically addresses employment. Other laws such as the 1968 Federal Fair Housing Act, as amended, assures equal housing opportunities regardless of race, color, religion, national origin, gender, as well as handicap and familial status. This act prohibits the red-lining of geographic areas (an area where loans are not made) or failure to finance housing to people living in inner cities or low-income census tracts.

—John B. Abbott

Equal Employment Opportunity Commission

The Equal Employment Opportunity Commission (EEOC) is a federal agency created by the passage of the CIVIL RIGHTS ACT of 1964. The EEOC's mission is "to promote equal opportunity in EMPLOYMENT through administrative and judicial enforcement of the federal civil rights laws and through education and technical assistance." In addition to enforcing Title VII of the Civil Rights Act of 1964, which prohibits discrimination in employment based on race, color, religion, sex, or national origin, the EEOC enforces the following statutes.

- The Age Discrimination in Employment Act of 1967 makes it illegal for employers to discriminate against individuals 40 years of age and older.
- The EQUAL PAY ACT of 1963 prohibits discrimination based on gender in compensation for similar work performed under similar conditions.
- Title I of the AMERICANS WITH DISABILITIES ACT of 1990 makes it illegal for employers in the public and private sector, excluding the federal government, to discriminate on the basis of disability.
- The Civil Rights Act of 1991 provides for monetary DAMAGES in cases where intentional discrimination can be proved and clarifies legislation regarding disparate impact actions. (Disparate impact actions are those which, although not intentionally discriminatory, can be shown to have a disproportionately negative effect on a group defined by race, color, religion, sex, or national origin.)
- Section 501 of the Rehabilitation Act of 1973 prohibits discrimination in employment against federal employees with disabilities.

In order to fulfill its mission, the EEOC

- investigates charges brought by individuals who believe they have experienced discrimination in employment, as well as charges initiated by Commissioners themselves

- attempts to "conciliate" substantiated charges by negotiating voluntary resolution between the party bringing the charge and the employer
- brings suit in federal court in cases where conciliation is not successful
- interprets the laws it enforces by means of regulations and other forms of guidance
- provides funding and support to state and local agencies, as well as training and assistance programs to employers

Individuals may file charges of employment discrimination at the EEOC headquarters in Washington, D.C., or at any one of the commission's 50 field offices. Once charges have been filed, the commission assigns them to one of three categories. Category A charges receive highest priority, in terms of investigation, resource allocation, and settlement effort. Category B charges are identified as those needing more investigation before action is taken. Category C charges are those over which the commission does not have jurisdiction or where the charges are unsupported. Category C charges are not pursued by the EEOC, although complainants are free to file civil suits in such cases.

The EEOC encourages all parties to negotiate settlements without resorting to litigation, and it has instituted a program to help individuals and employers reach mutually acceptable solutions with the help of trained mediators. When mediation fails, the commission represents victims of employment discrimination in federal court, obtaining monetary judgments against employers of all types and sizes who violate the statutes under the EEOC's jurisdiction.

In addition to investigating and resolving employment discrimination cases at the federal level, the EEOC contracts with state and local fair-employment practices agencies (FEPA's) to handle charges and claims that arise under state and local statutes. The commission's Federal Sector Program provides for the enforcement of antidiscrimination laws on behalf of employees of the federal government and serves as the point of appeal for complainants against federal agencies. Additionally, the commission coordinates individual federal departments' and agencies' equal-opportunity programs, policies, and regulations.

The EEOC offers education and training to employers, employees, groups representing companies and workers, community organizations, and the general public. Its outreach and education programs include speakers, seminars, booths and displays, a website, and interactive workshops, which are provided free of charge to small businesses, employee groups, job fairs, cultural festivals, and other interested parties. Technical assistance and training programs are fee-based (with fees limited to the cost of providing training and producing training materials) and cover a wide variety of seminars and training courses on general and customer-specific topics aimed at the private sector as well as local, state, and federal government agencies. The goal of the commission's outreach and education programs is to provide information that will clarify the requirements of the laws and encourage voluntary compliance.

The EEOC is also responsible for gathering, tabulating, and publishing data on the employment status of women and minorities in a wide variety of private- and public-sector occupations. An important component of this effort is the annual Employer Information Survey, which requires certain employers and government contractors to complete and file an EEO-1 report with the EEOC every year. In addition to processing the information generated by these reports, the commission provides guidance and training for employers in completing the EEO-1.

The EEOC is made up of five commissioners who are appointed by the U.S. president, subject to the consent of the U.S. Senate. Commissioners serve for five years; terms are staggered, and a chairman and vice chairman are chosen by the president. Other key positions include an executive officer, general counsel, inspector general, and legal counsel, as well as directors of communications and legislative affairs; equal opportunity; federal operations; field programs; financial and resource management; HUMAN RESOURCES; information resources management; and research, information, and planning. The EEOC budget for FISCAL YEAR 2002 was $310.406 million; the budget requested by the president for fiscal year 2003 is $323.516 million. Approximately 90 percent of the commission's budget is spent on personnel costs (salaries, benefits) and rent. At the end of fiscal year 2001, the commission had the equivalent of 2,704 full-time employees, down from a high of 3,390 in 1980.

EEOC statistics for fiscal year 2001 indicate that

- 35.8 percent of the 80,840 individual charge filings in that year alleged race-based discrimination
- 31.1 percent of cases were for gender-based discrimination
- 9.9 percent alleged discrimination on the basis of national origin
- gender-based discrimination charges included pregnancy-related discrimination as well as allegations of SEXUAL HARASSMENT; of the sexual harassment charges filed in FY2001, 13.7 percent were filed by males
- the commission resolved 90,106 cases, reducing the existing backlog by 5 percent
- 57.2 percent of the resolutions were dismissals based on the commission's determination that no reasonable cause existed
- 20.7 percent of the resolutions were administrative closures involving cases where the charging party could not be located, withdrew the charges, or refused full relief, or cases where the EEOC did not have jurisdiction
- successful resolutions resulted in monetary benefits of $247.8 million for victims of employment discrimination in fiscal year 2001, excluding monetary benefits from litigation
- 3,233 EEOC-sponsored educational and training events reached more than 257,000 people, including employers and employees in the public and private sector as well as employee representatives and community organizations.

Further reading

EEOC website. Available on-line. URL: http://www.eeoc.gov/; Office of the Federal Register, National Archives and Records Administration. *The United States Government Manual, 2000/2001.* Washington, D.C.: United States Government Printing Office, 2000; Quain, Anthony J. *The Political Reference Almanac, 2001/02.* Arlington, Va.: PoliSci Books, 1999; Rothstein, Mark, et al. *Employment Law,* 2d ed. St. Paul, Minn.: West Group Publishing, 1999.

—Janet Hadwin Brackett

Equal Pay Act
The Equal Pay Act (1963), which makes pay discrimination based on gender illegal, was designed to correct the wage gap for women. At the time female workers were being paid 60 percent of what male workers were making. By 1999 women were earning 75 percent of men's wages. Until 1999 the Equal Pay Act had rarely been a major concern for businesses. In that year the Clinton administration pushed for expanded use of equal-pay auditors, raising the importance of addressing pay discrimination.

In 1999, after the DEPARTMENT OF LABOR conducted a "glass ceiling" audit, Texaco paid female employees over $3 million. Other companies and government agencies scrambled to assess and address pay discrimination. The general provisions of the Equal Pay Act (referred to as the EPA in HUMAN RESOURCES literature) requires equal pay for equal work and prohibits paying an employee of the opposite gender less if the work both employees in an establishment do is the same or substantially the same.

Close examination of the act requires legal assistance, but according to the law, "same or substantially the same work" refers to job content, not job titles or descriptions. "Opposite gender" means the EPA protects both men and women from pay discrimination. Under the EPA, pay refers to all payments and benefits including PROFIT SHARING, bonuses, and expense accounts. An establishment is defined as a distinct physical place of business. Thus employers can pay different wages to people doing the same work at different locations. the act exempts certain categories of employees, but in 1999, when faced with the potential of a pay audit, many companies were forced to look closely at their pay practices.

While the EPA challenges gender-based pay discrimination, generally pay differences are legal when based on

- differences in level of skill
- unequal effort

- differences in responsibility
- differences in working conditions
- differences based on a SENIORITY system
- differences based on a merit system

Many pay-discrimination lawsuits have defined and redefined the legal parameters associated with the Equal Pay Act. The EPA is enforced by the EQUAL EMPLOYMENT OPPORTUNITY COMMISSION.

Further reading
Bland, Timothy S. "Equal pay enforcement heats up," *HRMagazine* 44, no. 7 (July 1999): 138; Mallor, Jane P., A. James Barnes, Thomas Bowers, Michael Philips, and Arlen Langvardt. *Business Law and the Regulatory Environment,* 11th ed. Boston: McGraw-Hill, 2001.

equation of exchange
The equation of exchange is a mathematical statement showing that the MARKET VALUE of all goods and services sold equals the amount of money paid for the goods and services. The equation is $MV = PQ$, where M is the MONEY SUPPLY, V is the velocity of circulation of money (the number of times that money changes hands during a year), P is the level of prices (in most circumstances, retail prices), and Q is quantity of goods and services sold to final consumers. In the equation of exchange, P times Q is the monetary value of final goods and services—that is, national INCOME. The equation of exchange is used to relate monetary aspects of an economy and ECONOMIC POLICY to output and INFLATION in the economy.

The quantity theory of money, developed by Yale economist Irving Fisher (1867–1947), stated that under most circumstances V and Q are constant, and therefore an increase in the money supply will cause an increase in the price level (inflation). Historical data do not support Fisher's theory. Velocity, while often assumed to be constant, varies over time with changes in technology and CONSUMER BEHAVIOR. The quantity of goods and services sold (Q) also cannot be assumed to be constant.

Monetarists, led by Milton Friedman, use the equation of exchange to demonstrate the importance of the money supply in affecting inflation. They assume velocity is constant, at least over short periods of time, suggesting that changes in the money supply result in changes in the price level and/or changes in real output of an economy. Most monetarists believe economies tend toward EQUILIBRIUM at the level of potential real GROSS DOMESTIC PRODUCT; thus, changes in MONETARY POLICY primarily affect inflation. Because of the time lag between a change in the money supply and its impact in the economy, monetarists argue government intervention heightens peaks and troughs of BUSINESS CYCLES, rather than smoothing out variations in the level of economic output. Milton Friedman and many other monetarists suggest establishing a fixed rate of growth in the money supply, thereby eliminating money-supply changes as an uncertainty in the business environment.

Further reading
Boyes, William, and Michael Melvin. *Macroeconomics,* 5th ed. Boston: Houghton Mifflin, 2001.

equilibrium
In economics, equilibrium refers to situations in which individuals, firms, markets, and systems are operating at optimal level and there is no current need or motive to change. One analogy to equilibrium is dropping a marble into a bowl. The marble will roll back and forth but will eventually come to rest. Unless something disturbs the bowl, the tendency will be for the marble to stay in the same place. Similarly, when circumstances change for individuals, firms, or societies, economic systems adjust to attempt to attain a new equilibrium.

At the individual level, equilibrium is attained when consumers allocated their INCOME among available choices to obtain the maximum level of satisfaction. Also at the individual level, a firm achieves equilibrium when it chooses levels of inputs and outputs that maximize PROFITS, given current market conditions.

Market equilibrium is portrayed by the Marshallian cross, named after British economist Alfred Marshall. Market equilibrium is achieved where there is a market-clearing price, meaning a price at which those consumers who want to purchase the PRODUCT can do so, and those producers who want to sell their product at that price can find buyers. It is the price at which quantity demanded equals quantity supplied, ceteris paribus (other things being equal).

Macroeconomic equilibrium occurs when all the markets within the economic system are in balance. Like market equilibrium, macroeconomic equilibrium is a price level at which aggregate demand equals aggregate supply. Changes in monetary and FISCAL POLICY, consumer and business decisions, and global social, political, and climatic conditions are major causes of changes in equilibrium of economic systems.

Realistically, economic forces are in constant change. In the time it takes to read this entry, markets, economic policies, and individual and household priorities are changing. Nevertheless, equilibrium is an important concept portraying the direction of efforts within economic systems. A story in the *Wall Street Journal* once described pricing activity by airline companies, noting that managers changed 1 million airline-ticket prices each day. These firms were adjusting their price, attempting to maximize profits depending on market forces: the number of people who bought tickets that day, the time until the flight departed, the actions of competing firms, the capacity of the plane, and past experience with last-minute DEMAND.

While most markets do not change as rapidly as that for airline tickets, markets are nonetheless constantly changing, and therefore equilibrium, the state of balance, is also changing.

Further reading

Ruffin, Roy J., and Paul R. Gregory. *Principles of Economics,* 7th ed. Boston: Addison Wesley, 2002.

equity

Equity has different meanings, depending on the business context. In general, equity is the ownership interest of SHAREHOLDERS; in accounting it is the portion of a company's ASSETS owned by shareholders, as opposed to the amount the company has borrowed. In this context, equity equals assets minus liabilities, or net worth. This is also referred to as stockholders' equity. Similarly, in banking equity is the MARKET VALUE of a property minus the loans against the property. Equity LOANS are based on this type of equity.

Equity, equity interest, and equity markets are all a critical part of any capitalistic economic system. By definition, CAPITALISM is a social and economic system based on private property rights, private allocation of CAPITAL, and self-interest motivation. Capitalism is often referred to as a free-enterprise or market system. Capitalism contrasts with SOCIALISM, in which most RESOURCES and industrial PRODUCTION systems are state-owned or controlled; and with communism, in which most resources are state-owned and most decisions regarding output are made through central planning. Equity and the ability to transfer equity interests are essential to the flow of capital. In the CIRCULAR FLOW MODEL of an economic system, households provide savings, either directly or indirectly, through FINANCIAL INTERMEDIARIES to businesses. Businesses use savings to purchase capital to produce goods and services, which in turn are purchased by consumers. In exchange for their savings, households receive either interest INCOME for loans or an ownership interest in the business—equity.

Equity interests are often exchanged among investors in stock exchanges. While these venues create new equity interests through INITIAL PUBLIC OFFERINGS (IPOs), most stock trading is a transfer of ownership interests. In the United States the oldest and most prominent stock exchange is the NEW YORK STOCK EXCHANGE (NYSE). Established in 1792, along a wall that had been used to keep wild pigs out of settlers' gardens in lower Manhattan, the NYSE is the largest stock exchange in the world based on dollar value of shares traded. In 2000 the exchange traded 262.5 billion shares, valued at $11.1 trillion dollars.

While NYSE dominates the stock exchanges in dollar volume traded, the over-the-counter (OTC) market is the largest stock exchange in terms of the number of different CORPORATIONS whose stocks are traded there. The backbone of the OTC market is NASDAQ, the NATIONAL ASSOCIATION OF SECURITY DEALERS AUTOMATED QUOTATIONS. Geographically dispersed securities dealers connected by computers are the intermediaries for the OTC stock traders. The enormous size of the OTC market is illustrated by the fact that NASDAQ surpasses NYSE in annual share volume.

As important as equity markets are to the U.S. economy, they are sometimes even more important to countries that are transitioning from socialism to capitalism. In the 1990s Mongolia, with the advice of former Secretary of State James Baker, privatized its few industries, issuing each adult shares of stock in what had been government-controlled industries, including the electrical company, railroad, and a few factories. The old opera house in Ulan Batur, Mongolia's capital, was converted into the national stock exchange. Government representatives held numerous education forums, explaining what shares of stock were and what value they might have.

Romania was one of the last post-communist countries to move toward capitalism. After the assassination of dictator Nicolae Ceaușescu, Romania was pressured by the INTERNATIONAL MONETARY FUND (IMF) and WORLD BANK to "establish the INFRASTRUCTURE for a market economy." In response, Romania created two small stock exchanges modeled after the U.S. system. One, the Bucharest Stock Exchange (BSE), trades "listed securities." Starting with six listings and 24 brokerage companies, by 2002 the BSE had 60 companies listed and 100 brokerage firms. The other, the Rasdaq, like the NASDAQ, acts as an over-the-counter electronic exchange. Romanian managers were initially shocked that the exchanges required financial transparency; disclosure of the BALANCE SHEETS, and other financial information. They quickly learned that attracting equity investment in EMERGING MARKETS like Romania required transparency. The Romanian stock exchange remains tiny, with a market capitalization of only the equivalent of $1.3 million, but it represents a starting point for creating equity ownership.

The Securities and Exchange Act of 1934 defines an equity security as "any stock or similar security, certificate of interest or participation in any profit sharing agreement, pre-organization certificate or subscription, transferable share, voting trust certificate or certificate of deposit for an equity security, limited partnership interest, interest in a JOINT VENTURE, or certificate of interest in a business TRUST or any security convertible, with or without consideration into such a security, any such warrant or right; or any put, call, straddle, or other option or privilege of buying such a security from or selling such a security to another without being bound to do so."

See also OWNER'S EQUITY.

Further reading

"The Securities Lawyer's Deskbook." Available on-line. URL: www.law.uc.edu/CCL/34actRls/rule3a11.1.html; "Romania Builds Infrastructure for Economic Reform," *Securities Industry News,* 11 March 2002.

equity income theory

Equity income theory suggests that employees determine whether they are being fairly treated by management by comparing their own input/outcome ratio to the input/outcome ratio of others. Inputs are the experience, education, effort, time worked, and special skills workers bring to a job. Outcomes are pay, benefits, recognition, and other rewards given to workers.

Equity income theory attempts to address almost every worker's question, "Am I being treated fairly?" People develop a sense of inequity when a comparison of inputs and outcomes leads to a perceived imbalance relative to others. For example, teachers frequently complain that relative to their education and responsibilities, they are not paid equitably. In situations where employees perceive they are not being paid equitably, they often resort to any of three alternatives:

1. Reduce effort.
2. Work with colleagues to lobby for higher pay for each member of the affected group.
3. Seek EMPLOYMENT where pay is better.

Successful employee COMPENSATION AND BENEFITS systems incorporate the concept of equity income theory. Equitable compensation plans address internal, external, and individual equity concerns. Internal equity is the pay relationship among jobs within the organization. Employees expect senior executives to earn more than production workers, but when the differences become huge, the system is not perceived as internally equitable. Ben & Jerry's Ice Cream company was legendary in the 1980s for mandating that the president receive no more than seven times the INCOME of the lowest paid worker. Enron executives apparently did not adhere to that sense of social, internal equity.

External equity refers to workers' comparisons of similar jobs in different organizations. In many rural areas of the United States, federal government jobs pay more than similar local, private-sector jobs. Local businesses often hire, train, and then lose employees to government and government-funded jobs in the area. In the 1990s, U.S. postal workers threatened to strike. When the postal workers' pay scale became known, public ire over perceived pay inequity relative to the skills and effort required created resentment against postal workers, leading to such comments as "I will do their job for that pay."

Individual equity refers to comparisons among individuals doing the same or very similar job within an organization. Those in HUMAN RESOURCES management suggest this is the most important comparison. In the United States, most workers accept the concept of paying senior employees more than newer employees and paying more-productive employees more than less-productive employees. Problems arise in defining and differentiating productivity. In service environments, measuring differences in productivity are difficult. Subjective evaluations often become popularity contests and create resentment among the workforce. Equity income theory suggests managers need to address all three types of equity concerns. Unionized work environments address pay differences in COLLECTIVE BARGAINING. New workers understand the pay system before they choose to join the workforce. In nonunion environments, pay inequities are a frequent source of conflict and sometimes litigation.

The EQUAL PAY ACT (EPA, 1963) made illegal any pay discrimination based on gender. The act was designed to correct the wage gap for women at a time when women workers were being paid 60 percent of what men workers were making. By 1999 women were earning 75 percent of men's wages, and many companies were closely evaluating their pay practices.

See also FORCED RANKING SYSTEMS; UNION.

Further reading
Fisher, Cynthia D., Lyle F. Schoenfeldt, and James B. Shaw. *Human Resource Management.* 5th ed. Boston: Houghton Mifflin, 2003; Mallor, Jane P., A. James Barnes, Thomas Bowers, Michael Philips, and Arlen W. Langvardt. *Business Law and the Regulatory Environment,* 11th ed. Boston: McGraw-Hill, 2001.

ergonomics

Ergonomics is an engineering science concerned with the psychological and physical relationship between workers and their work environment. Ergonomics evolved after World War II as production managers recognized the physiological impact of workers' repetitive actions. The term *ergonomics* comes from the Greek words *ergon,* meaning work, and *nomos,* meaning laws. Initially ergonomics focused on improving productivity through developing a more worker-friendly environment, but in recent years with increased concern about repetitive stress syndrome, it has grown increasingly important in workplace health and safety.

Ergonomics is most closely associated with repetitive-stress syndrome, encompassing such injuries as carpal-tunnel syndrome; lower back pain; and problems with tendons, nerves, ligaments, and joints from performing the same manual task over and over. In 2000 the OCCUPATIONAL SAFETY AND HEALTH ADMINISTRATION (OSHA) issued over 300 pages of new ergonomics regulations. The new rules detail which job categories, what activities are covered, and the minimum number of hours per day a worker can do a repetitive task before they are covered by the OSHA rules. For example, workers using a keyboard are covered if they work at that task for four or more hours per day. Workers who lift 55-pound objects over 10 times per day are also covered by the new regulations.

OSHA justified the new ergonomics rules using benefit-cost analysis, claiming it would cost U.S. businesses $4.5 billion to comply but result in over $9 billion saved annually from reductions in lost employee time due to injuries and lost productivity from long-term disabilities. Business managers differed with the OSHA analysis, claiming the cost of compliance would be significantly greater. Business managers complained they would have to frequently shift workers to different job activities, losing work time and the benefits of specialization.

Further reading
Calderwood, James A. "Ergonomic Rules Become Final," *Ceramic Industry* 151, no. 3 (March 2001): 24.

escalator clause
An escalator clause is a stipulation in CONTRACTS that adjusts the agreed-on price when costs change. Generally business transactions include an agreed price, but often market conditions are volatile, and the seller can potentially lose money if his or her costs increase between the time the price is agreed on and when the transaction is completed. Escalator clauses protect sellers against this risk.

Escalator clauses are common in business-supply contracts, labor agreements, utility pricing, and lease arrangements. Usually an escalator clause is tied to changes in a cost index such as the CONSUMER PRICE INDEX (CPI), the price reported in a market exchange such as the CHICAGO MERCANTILE EXCHANGE or some other industrial cost index to which both parties agree.

Escalator clauses are more common during periods of uncertainty and INFLATION. In recent years, with dramatically changing oil and natural gas prices, utility companies, airlines, and chemical manufacturers have all resorted to escalator clauses. In the 1980s, most union contracts added escalator clauses to protect workers' wages against inflation. Many long-term rental agreements contain clauses raising the rent a set percentage annually.

Critics contend escalator clauses reduce producers' incentives to operate efficiently, instead just passing along cost increases to customers. When escalator clauses are used, it is important to clearly define what index or price is to be used and how often prices are to be adjusted. In multimillion-dollar transactions, small details such as using the national CPI or regional index, end-of-the-day or average for the day price on a commodity exchange can significantly affect costs and PROFITS.

ethics   See BUSINESS ETHICS; OFFICE OF GOVERNMENT ETHICS.

European Recovery Program   See MARSHALL PLAN.

European Union
The European Union (EU) comprises 15 European countries joined in economic and political cooperation. The member countries are Austria, Belgium, Denmark, Finland, France, Germany, Greece, Ireland, Italy, Luxembourg, the Netherlands, Portugal, Spain, Sweden, and the United Kingdom. While each country retains its independence and own political system, member states of the EU join together to establish policies they abide by for mutual benefit. Today, while the driving force of the European Union continues to be economic, its goals include issues of law, citizenship, and social justice.

The European Union has five main objectives: (1) to promote economic and social progress; (2) to assert the identity of the European Union on the international scene; (3) to introduce European citizenship; (4) to develop geographic area of freedom, security and justice; and (5) to maintain and build an established EU law (http://europa.eu.int/abc-en.htm).

Annual meetings take place between members of the EU's governing bodies and U.S. government representatives. The United States and the European Union are interdependent on one another regarding trade and because of this have established a number of areas of cooperation and conflict.

Combined, the gross domestic product (GDP) of EU countries is equal to that of the North American countries (United States, Canada, and Mexico). The evolution and expansion of the EU created a fear of "fortress Europe," with increased power and economic integration within the union and barriers to businesses outside of the union. The North American Free Trade Agreement (NAFTA) was, in part, a response to fears about the growing economic power of the EU. Though all countries in the EU and NAFTA are members of the World Trade Organization (WTO) there are continuing trade conflicts. Two of the more publicized disputes were the banana wars, preferential access to European markets for bananas from former European colonies, and the bovine growth hormone (bgh) restriction on U.S. meat exports to the EU. While trade disputes gain headlines in the news, historically the EU countries and the United States have been closely linked.

After World War II, there was a desire to integrate the economies of European countries in order to avoid another war in Europe. Leaders believed that by fostering cohesion among European nations through unified trade and economic policies, countries would be less likely to fight against one another. In the early 1950s, proposals for how to establish a united Europe were developed. In 1951 Belgium, France, Germany, Italy, Luxembourg, and the Netherlands signed the European Coal and Steel Community Treaty (ECSC), which came into effect on January 1, 1952. This treaty created an official body known as the High Authority that regulated coal and steel production, creating a single economic market for these products for all of the member countries. This group was extremely successful, and coal and steel trade increased dramatically, benefiting all six countries. Based on this success, the countries started working towards creating a common market for additional goods for mutual economic benefit.

The EU's common currency, the euro, was introduced on January 1, 1999, and has been adopted by eleven countries: Austria, Belgium, Finland, France, Germany, Italy, Ireland, Luxembourg, the Netherlands, Portugal, and Spain. Denmark, Sweden, and the United Kingdom have not yet agreed to adopt the euro. On January 1, 2002, the euro became the official legal tender of participating states, and each country's individual currency was permanently replaced by the common currency.

Further reading
European Union website: Europa. Available on-line. URL: http://europa.edu.int.

—Stephanie Godley

exchange-rate risk

Exchange-rate risk is the effect on profitability and ASSETS that can occur as a result of changes in EXCHANGE RATES. Exchange rates are the value of one country's currency in terms of another country's currency. As the value of one currency increases, the value of the other currency decreases. For most of the 1990s, the U.S. dollar appreciated against most of the other world currencies. As the dollar increased in value, U.S. companies doing business in other parts of the world saw their PROFITS, earned in other currencies, decrease when converted to dollars. For example, in 2000 Coca-Cola Company warned investors of declining profits from foreign operations due to appreciation of the dollar. By contrast, foreign companies earning profits in dollars saw their earnings increase when converted to their home country's currency.

Many factors influence exchange rates, including changing DEMAND for U.S. products and foreign products, changes in investment opportunities both in the United States and elsewhere, and changes in expectations of speculators in FOREIGN EXCHANGE markets. Most business manager try to make profits not by successfully predicting the direction of exchange rates but by selling their products and services. To reduce exchange-rate risk, managers

- hedge in foreign exchange markets
- diversify operations
- borrow in the currency used for investing

HEDGING involves buying or selling FUTURES currency contracts. Many exchanges (in the U.S., particularly the CHICAGO MERCANTILE EXCHANGE) offer currency futures contracts. A company, expecting payment in another currency six months from now, when the job is completed, could sell a futures contract for that amount of the currency. If, in the interim six months, the value of that currency declined, they will be able to buy back the futures contract at a lower price, offsetting the decline in value of the payment they receive.

By diversifying operations, MULTINATIONAL CORPORATIONS (MNCs) can also reduce their exchange-rate risk. Many global automobile manufacturers have set up factories in the markets they sell in. By producing in markets where they sell, companies incur their costs and generate their revenue primarily in the host country's currency. This reduces the impact of changing exchange-rate values.

Similarly, MNCs reduce exchange-rate exposure by borrowing in the currency they are investing in. By borrowing in U.S. dollars, Japanese automobile manufacturers building plants in the United States incur their financial costs in the same currency as their received revenue.

While most of this discussion has focused on MNCs involved in or exposed to exchange-rate risk, almost every business is vulnerable to changing exchange rates. In the early 1990s, when the U.S. dollar was declining, a *Wall Street Journal* article described the impact of the dollar decline against the Japanese yen in Troy, Ohio.

- Japanese automobiles were $2,000 more than comparable domestic models.
- The price of pearls and cameras also rose.
- Japanese robots used in the production of U.S. cars became more expensive.
- Farmers hoped the declining dollar would increase demand for local corn and soybeans.
- A local economic development officer speculated Japanese companies would be more interested in building factories in the area.

Further reading
Hill, Charles W. L. *Global Business Today.* Boston: McGraw-Hill, 1999; Reitman, Valerie. "Global Money Trends Rattle Shop Windows in Heartland America," *Wall Street Journal,* 26 November 1993, p. A1.

exchange rates

Exchange rates are the domestic price of a unit of foreign currency. Exchange rates impact international trade, part of a country's CIRCULAR FLOW MODEL of economic output and INCOME. When the value of a country's currency rises relative to another country's currency, the currency is said to have appreciated. Likewise, when a currency decreases in value relative to another currency, it has depreciated. For most of the 1990s and early 21st century, the U.S. dollar appreciated against most of the other world currencies. For example, on January 9, 1998, the Canadian dollar was worth 0.6992 U.S. dollars; on April 30, 2001, it was worth 0.6483 U.S. dollars, 7.3 percent less than a little over three years earlier. The same relationship can be expressed in terms of how many Canadian dollars are required to be exchanged for one U.S. dollar. In 1998, 1.4303 Canadian dollars equaled one U.S. dollar, while in 2001 it took 1.5425 Canadian dollars to equal one U.S. dollar.

In 1957 two treaties were signed by the six members of the ECSC, establishing the European Economic Community (EEC) and the European Atomic Energy Community (EAEC or EURATOM). The EEC established common markets for goods in addition to those already established for coal and steel. EURATOM established agreements regarding atomic and nuclear energy with regards to research. These treaties came into effect on January 1, 1958. In 1967 the members of these three treaties (the ECSC, the EEC, and the EAEC) established one governing authority known as the European Communities (EC) that had four divisions: the European Commission, the Council of the European Union, the European Parliament, and the European Court of Justice. The EC existed until 1993, when it was incorporated into what is now the European Union.

In 1973 Denmark, Ireland, and the United Kingdom officially joined the EC. In 1981 Greece joined, followed by Spain and Portugal in 1986.

Due to the success of the trade policies created by the EC and growing interest in establishing even more integration, the countries continued to work together to create a more unified governing structure. The Treaty on the European Union, more commonly known as the Maastricht Treaty, came into effect on November 1, 1993. The Maastricht Treaty essentially revised the original treaties that were effective under the EC and created the European Union, as it is known today. The treaty established what are termed the three pillars of the European Union. The first pillar incorporates the original three treaties, the second pillar created the Common Foreign and Security Policy, and the third pillar created the Justice and Home Affairs Policy. One of the most important outcomes of the Maastricht Treaty was the establishment of the European Monetary Institute (EMI), which, created a FREE TRADE zone known as the European Economic Area (EEA), effective January 1, 1994. In addition, the treaty included the plan to create a single currency and citizenship for all member countries. The United Kingdom and Denmark only agreed to the treaty once they had been exempted from some of its provisions.

Austria, Finland, and Sweden joined the EU in 1995. Any European country can join the EU provided it has a stable democratic government, a decent human-rights record, a functioning economy, and the ability to follow the membership requirements. Many Eastern European countries, such as Poland and the Czech Republic, are expected to join the EU in the coming years.

The EU's structure is based on a democratic system to ensure that member states and citizens are represented fairly while at the same time the institutions work for the good of the whole union. There are five main governing bodies.

- The European Commission consists of 20 commissioners including the president of the union, Romano Prodi.

The commission proposes legislation; implement directives, regulations, and the budget; and acts as th EU's official representative.

- The European Council, also referred to as the Counc of Ministers, is made up of representatives of each of th 15 member countries and is considered the EU's mai decision-making body. Council meetings cover variou topics such as the environment, finance, and foreig affairs. The council enacts legislation for the union as whole in conjunction with the European Parliament. I addition, the council makes decisions on foreign polic and deals with cooperation among member countries i criminal matters.

- The European Parliament is a political body whos members are elected by the citizens of the EU countri every five years. Representation in the Parliament based on the population size of each member countr The Parliament deals with the legislative process, pla a role in the budget process, approves the nominatio to the European Commission, and supervises the oth governing bodies.

- The Court of Justice operates as the EU's supreme cou The court makes decisions regarding treaty interpret tions and is made up of one justice from each memb country.

- The Court of Auditors oversees the management of tł EU budget and controls expenditures.

There are additional governing bodies to support the fiv main branches of the EU.

- The Committee of Regions addresses issues of loc identities and plays a role in decisions involvin regional policies, the environment, and education.

- The Economic and Social Committee has 222 membe and represents the views of organizations and grou that deal with topics such as labor and consumer right

- The European Central Bank handles the EU's monetar policies.

- The European Investment Bank is the EU's financia institution.

- The European Ombudsman handles complaints fron EU citizens regarding the EU's administration.

Common policies adopted by member countries have allowed for freer movement of both goods and peopl throughout member countries. For example, citizens o member countries now have EU passports rather than passports from their individual countries, allowing for freer travel. Common policies deal with topics such as agriculture, the environment, education, and transportation. The EU has established uniform foreign policies and plays an active role in distributing humanitarian aid. It collects revenue from the value-added tax (VAT), import duties, and contributions from each of the member countries.

Two important questions when studying exchange rates are: What is the impact of appreciating and depreciating currencies, and what exchange-rate policies can and do governments pursue?

When a country's currency appreciates, its exports become more expensive to foreign buyers and IMPORTS become less expensive. This increases DEMAND for imports and decreases demand for exports. In recent years the U.S. TRADE BALANCE, both the merchandise trade balance and the current account, have been negative, reflecting the relative value of the U.S. dollar against world currencies. In 2003 the United States' current account deficit was approximately $400 billion, meaning foreigners held more ($400 billion worth) claims against the U.S. output than U.S. sellers had against foreign output. Ceteris paribus (other things being equal), the U.S. dollar should fall in value as foreigners increase the supply of U.S. dollars in exchange markets and increase demand for their currencies. Instead foreigners have been buying U.S. securities, both government BONDS and corporate stocks and bonds, and purchasing U.S. ASSETS, mostly U.S. companies. Because foreigners are not exchanging the U.S. dollars, the value of the dollar has not declined.

Economists are quite concerned about the potential impact of a change in international investment in the United States. A sudden shift in international sentiment would decrease the supply of investment CAPITAL and thus the value of the dollar in world markets, increasing the price of imports and adding to INFLATION. This can happen in a system of floating exchange rates. Since 1973, when the gold standard created at BRETTON WOODS at the end of World War II was abandoned, a variety of exchange-rate policies have evolved in world trade, including floating, fixed, pegged, and managed floating exchange-rate systems.

Floating exchange-rate systems, as stated earlier, allow SUPPLY and DEMAND for a country's currency to determine the exchange rate. Floating exchange rates create uncertainty for businesses engaged in foreign trade, allow countries to pursue independent economic policies, and tend to ease balance-of-payments adjustments. Fixed exchange-rate systems reduce business uncertainty but require government intervention to maintain the fixed exchange rate (buying or selling currencies to adjust for the imbalance of supply and demand for the currency). If two countries have similar rates of inflation, they will be able to maintain a fixed exchange-rate policy. If one country's inflation rate is consistently greater than the other country's inflation rate, the first country's currency will be overvalued in a fixed exchange-rate system. The PESO CRISIS was largely a result of higher inflation in Mexico than in the United States, without sufficient devaluation of the Mexican peso.

At the time of the peso crisis (1994), Mexico had a crawling-peg exchange-rate system: a predetermined monthly rate of DEPRECIATION of the peso against the U.S. dollar. Some countries that have experienced rapid infla-tion have "pegged" their currency to another country's currency, creating a fixed exchange rate. Argentina and Ecuador pegged their currencies to the U.S. dollar. Many former French colonies peg their currencies to the French franc.

The EUROPEAN UNION, through the European Monetary System, negotiated a fixed exchange rate among the participating members and a floating exchange rate with respect to the rest of the world. Not all members of the EU agreed to the terms of the historic Maastricht Treaty, but those that did agreed to coordinate domestic macroeconomic policies including budget deficits and inflation rates as part of agreement to create a unified currency.

See also EXCHANGE-RATE RISK; FOREIGN EXCHANGE; MACRO-ECONOMICS.

excise tax   See BUSINESS TAXES; CONSUMPTION TAX.

exit strategies

Exit strategies are methods used by companies to discontinue PRODUCTS, businesses, or relationships with customers or suppliers. They are generally not considered as part of a company's BUSINESS PLAN; rather, they are decisions made when a business plan does not work as anticipated.

One of the trends in the United States is RELATIONSHIP MARKETING—development and maintenance of long-term, cost-effective exchange relationships with customers, suppliers, employees, and partners. Most businesspeople are optimists, rarely accepting the end of a project, product, or enterprise. An often-neglected part of relationship marketing is establishing when, how, or on what terms the relationship will end. Exit strategies devised in advance are like prenuptial agreements, easing the pain of breaking up.

Exit strategies are important because they influence consumers' and business partners' image of a company. In the 1970s, when Texas Instruments announced it was abandoning its line of early computer equipment, many consumers expressed distrust for the company. It took decades for the company to recover its reputation.

Marketers recognize most products and product categories go through what is known as the PRODUCT LIFE CYCLE (PLC)—market stages that include introduction, growth, maturity, and decline. Exit strategies are part of the decline stage. Generally as sales and PROFITS decline, firms can sell the product line to another company, create a separate company (called spinning-off), or abandon the product line. Which exit strategy is chosen depends on market conditions, the current status of the product line, and company resources. Sometimes products in the decline stage gain new life as "retro" products sought out by a small number of loyal consumers. These consumers are often willing to pay more for the product, creating a profitable niche market. For example, the Coca-Cola Company still sells Tab, their early diet drink, even though sales represent less than 1 percent of Diet Coke sales. A small, vocal group of consumers continues to prefer Tab, and rather than chance losing those customers to their rival Pepsi, Coca-Cola continues to produce the soda.

expectancy theory

Expectancy theory states that motivation depends on an individual's expectations of his or her ability to perform a job and the relationship between performance and attaining rewards valued by that individual. First proposed by management specialist Victor Vroom, expectancy theory can be used in sales management to stimulate sales-force productivity. Sales managers apply a five-step process.

1. Provide each salesperson with detailed information regarding what management expects in terms of selling goals, service standards, and other areas of performance. For example, one study found that sales performance was enhanced by setting goals more frequently. In many companies, sales representatives are given annual goals. Quarterly or monthly goals can increase sales-force motivation.
2. Assign salespeople to appropriate tasks by assessing the needs, values, and abilities of each salesperson. For example, some salespeople like to travel while others do not. Some people are great at getting to know clients but poor at closing a deal.
3. Make goals achievable. Sales managers should provide the LEADERSHIP, training, and support salespeople need to be successful.
4. Provide specific and frequent feedback to salespeople.
5. Offer appropriate rewards that reinforce the values of each salesperson. Most salespeople are motivated by making money, but recognition, prizes, vacation time, and other incentives motivate some people.

Further reading
Boone, Louis E., and David L. Kurtz. *Contemporary Marketing,* 10th ed. Fort Worth: Dryden Press, 2001.

experience and learning curves

Experience and learning curves are behavioral models demonstrating that individuals and organizations learn and become more efficient through work. Experience and learning curves are a source of COMPARATIVE ADVANTAGE in competitive markets.

The concept of improved efficiency and productivity through learning is relatively easy and can be understand by considering some new activity that has been initiated (learning a new software, language, sport, etc.). The more often one practices or studies, the more proficient one becomes at the activity. Generally everybody learns by doing, and while the results can be dramatic initially, eventually doing more of an activity results in smaller marginal improvement.

The early 20th-century management consultant Frederick W. Taylor studied productivity under different working conditions, focusing on the size of shovel used at a coal company. He believed the company would be much more efficient if each worker learned to do a smaller portion of the entire job, which would increase overall workers' productivity. Using observation and experimentation, he answered a few key questions:

1. Will a first-class worker do more work per day with a shovelful of 5, 10, 15, 20, 30, or 40 pounds?
2. What kinds of shovels work best with which materials?
3. How quickly can a shovel be pushed into a pile of coal and pulled out properly loaded?
4. How long does it take to swing a shovel backward and throw the load a specified horizontal distance at a specified height?

Experience and learning curves can be used to measure the productivity improvement of individual workers and organizations. Critical to the success of any organization is being able to respond quickly to opportunities and challenges. The collective knowledge within a business provides information about what has been done before, who knows where resources exist to meet an opportunity or challenge, or why something failed in the past. This collective experience allows a firm to act faster than competitors with no experience and to be more efficient by avoiding mistakes from the past.

Experience and learning curves as a source of comparative advantage depend on retaining that knowledge and experience within an organization. With greater use of OUTSOURCING, contract workers, and turnover, particularly in knowledge-based businesses, it is often difficult to control the transfer of knowledge and experience among industry competitors.

Further reading
Hellriegel, Don, Susan E. Jackson, and John W. Slocum Jr. *Management,* 8th ed. Cincinnati: South-Western College Publishing, 1999.

export controls

The United States has a detailed system of export controls intended to protect scarce RESOURCES, further U.S. foreign policy, and enhance national security. The controls are contained in the Export Administration Act (2001) as implemented by a host of regulations. Broadly speaking, all exports from the United States are controlled under two categories, those permitted with or without a license. These categories reflect country of destination and product-type analyses.

The first step in ascertaining whether a license is needed is to examine the "Country Control List." This list specifies which destination countries are license-free and which are not. For example, Libya, Iraq, Iran, Cuba, and North Korea are countries for which an export license is often required. Canada, Mexico, France, South Africa, and Japan are not ordinarily on the Country Control List.

The second step is to examine the "Commerce Control List" to ascertain which products require a license for EXPORTING. Supercomputers and military goods will almost always require licenses. Personal computers and most consumer goods will not. If a U.S. export is not on the Commerce Control List and the country of destination is not subject to licensing, the goods may be freely shipped subject to completion of a Shipper's Export Declaration form.

If the country or the PRODUCT (or both) is on a control list, then a license from the U.S. Bureau of Export Administration is required. Obtaining such a license takes considerable time and expense. Violations of the Export Administration Act can incur very large company fines and penalties. Individual violators can be sentenced criminally. In extreme cases, the right of U.S. businesses to export can even be revoked. These sanctions are severe.

Further reading
Folsom, Ralph H., Michael Gordon, and John Spanogle. *International Business Transactions in a Nutshell,* 6th ed. Eagan, Minn.: West Group, 2002.

Export-Import Bank of the United States
The Export-Import Bank of the United States (Ex-Im Bank) is a government-held CORPORATION created in 1934 to finance and facilitate U.S. exports. To stimulate exports to the former Soviet Union at the end of World War II, the Ex-Im Bank supported reconstruction of Europe and Asia. More recently, the Ex-Im Bank shifted its focus to supporting exports to developing countries. The Ex-Im Bank is managed by a BOARD OF DIRECTORS chosen by the U.S. president and confirmed by the Senate.

The primary goal of the Ex-Im Bank is to support exports and in the process stimulate ECONOMIC GROWTH in the United States. The bank has three primary programs: working-CAPITAL loans, LOANS to foreign purchasers, and credit guarantees. Working-capital loans provide funds for companies to bid on projects, facilities, build production, or complete foreign CONTRACT awards. Loans to foreign purchasers provide financing subject to U.S. content rules, generally 50 percent, and other restrictions. Credit guarantees protect U.S. exporters against debtor DEFAULT for political or commercial reasons.

Critics contend the Ex-Im Bank is a form of CORPORATE WELFARE, subsidizing U.S. MULTINATIONAL CORPORATIONS. Private-sector banking and business INSURANCE companies contend the Bank unfairly competes with their lending

business. In 2001 President George W. Bush surprised many critics and supporters by recommending significant cuts in federal support for the Ex-Im Bank.

Further reading
Export-Import Bank of the United States website. Available online. URL: www.exim.gov.

exporting
Exporting—the production and sale of goods from one country to another—is both a business decision and part of a country's economic and political policies. Businesses export PRODUCTS and SERVICES to markets where they expect to earn PROFITS. From a business perspective, exporting is part of a firm's MARKETING STRATEGY. Countries exchange goods and services based on COMPARATIVE ADVANTAGE.

Because the U.S. market is the largest in the world, for many years American companies did not feel the need to participate in global markets; domestic DEMAND created sufficient opportunities. For some U.S. companies, export expansion resulted from needs generated by World War II; for others creation of the General Agreement on Tariffs and Trade (1947), now part of the WORLD TRADE ORGANIZATION, led to export expansion.

Most trade is conducted among industrialized countries and among large MULTINATIONAL CORPORATIONS (MNCs). MNCs often produce raw materials, components, and partially assembled products in many different countries, shipping these products to other factories and markets around the world. Intrafirm trade is a major part of total exports. One of the issues associated with this type of trade is transfer pricing, the price assessed for goods "sold" from one division of a company to another in a different country.

Exporting contributes to a country's GROSS DOMESTIC PRODUCT, adding output and INCOME to an economy. Many countries create TRADE BARRIERS, blocking IMPORTS while supporting domestic exporting activity. In the 1980s Japanese automobile manufacturers, fearing the creation of new BARRIERS TO ENTRY into the U.S. market, agreed to voluntary export constraints, limiting the number of cars shipped annually. With decreased SUPPLY and increasing demand, retailers of Japanese cars raised prices in the United States. One study found this voluntary export constraint program cost American consumers $250,000 for every domestic job saved.

Exporting depends heavily on price competitiveness in world markets, and this, in turn, depends on EXCHANGE RATES. The relatively high-valued dollar in the 1990s reduced U.S. exports while stimulating demand for imports, contributing to a continuing U.S. trade deficit. The United States (as well as the governments of most other industrialized countries) provides support for business exporting. The OVERSEAS PRIVATE INVESTMENT CORPORATION and the EXPORT-IMPORT BANK OF THE UNITED STATES provide

INSURANCE and investment CAPITAL for U.S. companies. The Department of Commerce and many state commerce departments provide a variety of trade seminars, trade-show services, and other assistance to businesses attempting to expand their export-marketing efforts. The U.S. State Department provides assistance through commercial attaches to U.S. businesses seeking opportunities abroad.

See also EXPORT CONTROLS.

externalities (spillover effects)

Externalities, also called spillover effects, are COSTS (negative externalities) or benefits (positive externalities) associated with a market but not included in the price of a good or service. An external cost occurs when the PRODUCTION or CONSUMPTION of a good inflicts a cost on someone other than the producer or consumer. A standard example of an external cost is pollution. Many producers are allowed to dump wastes into streams or send emissions up their smokestacks. By releasing their wastes into the environment, these firms are avoiding costs of pollution control or mitigation. Because they do not have to bear them, market prices do not reflect these costs, and this encourages greater consumption of their products. Instead, the cost of pollution is transferred to others, either people trying to use the water downstream from the polluter or people breathing the polluted air.

Business groups sometimes argue that forcing them to reduce their emissions will make them unable to compete in global markets. Referring to demands for reduction in emissions associated with the use of oil products, President George H. W. Bush once said, "I am an environmentalist too, but we cannot afford these new regulations." From a business perspective, unless everyone, including international competitors, has to incur the same costs, they will become higher cost producers and less competitive. Developing countries, eager to have new jobs and sources of INCOME, are often willing to ignore negative externalities (spillovers of costs and negative effects onto society) in the name of ECONOMIC GROWTH.

The air and water pollution examples illustrate MARKET FAILURE, with an overallocation of resources into production of the polluting firm's products. These two examples can also be used to illustrate how society can correct the problem. In a market environment, a downstream user of water could simply pay the upstream user not to pollute the water. Naturally the downstream user does not want to pay, but faced with no other choice and needing clean water, paying is one option. More likely the downstream user will complain to a government agency, which in turn will force the polluter to stop.

Regulation is one option to correct the problem, but that requires the government agency to develop an appropriate set of regulations and enforce them. Often it is difficult to come up with a standard set of rules that can be applied among many firms and across various industries.

In the United States, business managers frequently complain about the time, cost, and lack of logic in many government environmental regulations. Another option is for government to tax the polluting firm based on the amount of pollution it creates. This will encourage the firm to reduce its pollution, alleviating the problem for the downstream user of the water.

In the case of water pollution, the third party, the downstream user of the water, can easily be identified and will pressure the upstream polluter to pay to clean up its pollution or internalize the externality. In the case of air pollution from the same factory, it probably will be more difficult to identify the people hurt by the air pollution. If these people do not recognize the impact of the pollution on them, or if only a few citizens complain, the company may not be forced to stop polluting the air. This is the problem of lack of clearly defined property rights. The downstream water user demanded the right to clean water, but no one person or group owns the air.

Beginning in the 1970s, the U.S. ENVIRONMENTAL PROTECTION AGENCY (EPA) experimented with an alternative to regulation or taxation of pollution. Recognizing that the environment can accept some level of pollution without being significantly harmed (called environmental carrying capacity) and that some firms can reduce their pollution more cheaply than others, the EPA helped create a market for pollution credits. After defining an acceptable level of overall pollution, firms were given an allocation of pollution credits. Firms that could reduce their emissions most cheaply did so and sold their pollution credits, while firms that would have to incur significant costs to reduce their pollution bought credits. A market for pollution credits was established, allowing firms to choose which was a more efficient method of achieving the government-imposed standard. Some environmental groups also bought pollution credits, reducing the overall supply of credits, thereby increasing the price of polluting, making it more efficient for firms to clean up the air than to continue to pollute.

Like an external cost, external benefits are not reflected in the price of a product. An external benefit is derived when some of the benefits of consumption of a good or service are enjoyed by a third party. If, for example, just as Mr. Smith is ready to put his home up for sale, his neighbor cleans up her house and yard, Mr. Smith receives a benefit from her action—that is, his house will probably sell for a higher price due to his neighbor's efforts. Similarly, everybody benefits from other people being more educated. Education enhances peoples' productivity, increasing their incomes, reducing overall taxes, and providing the public with better products and services. Recognizing that society benefits from having educated people, U.S. education DEMAND and SUPPLY are both subsidized. This results in a greater quantity of education being produced than would be if consumers had to pay the full cost of education. This is called internalizing a positive externality.

Further reading

O'Sullivan, Arthur, and Steven M. Sheffrin. *Economics: Principles and Tools*. Upper Saddle River, N.J.: Prentice Hall, 2001.

extraterritorial jurisdiction

Extraterritorial jurisdiction most often refers to laws that are applied to activities, businesses, and persons located outside the United States. These activities, businesses, and persons may or may not involved Americans, but they are subject to U.S. laws reaching beyond U.S. territorial boundaries. Laws regarding antitrust, securities, export control, EMPLOYMENT, and TRADEMARKS provide good examples of U.S. extraterritorial jurisdiction. The SHERMAN ANTITRUST ACT does so by being specifically applicable to U.S. "foreign commerce."

Extraterritorial jurisdiction has been extremely controversial among U.S. trading partners. Many, including Britain, France, Canada, and Australia, have enacted "blocking statutes" intended to make it difficult to apply U.S. laws extraterritorially. These statutes typically deny access to documents, people, and information; deny enforcement of U.S. extraterritorial judgments; and sometimes retaliate by authorizing in local courts actions for DAMAGES against successful U.S. extraterritorial plaintiffs.

In an increasingly integrated global economy, the effects of business are often felt beyond territorial boundaries. The EUROPEAN UNION applies its competition (antitrust) laws extraterritorially, doing so specifically to block the U.S.-based General Electric/Honeywell merger in 2001, although U.S. antitrust authorities had already approved that same merger. Resolving extraterritorial conflicts like this one is a major problem. The United States has "antitrust cooperation" agreements with Canada, Australia, Germany, and the European Union, which attempt to reduce the potential for conflicts over extraterritorial jurisdiction in that field.

See also ANTITRUST LAW.

Further reading

Folsom, Ralph H., Michael Gordon, John Spanogle. *International Business Transaction in a Nutshell*, 6th ed. Eagan, Minn.: West Group, 2000.

F

factoring

Factoring is selling ACCOUNTS RECEIVABLE to another business in order to obtain cash payment before the due date on the account receivable. In many businesses, cash flow—the stream of revenues and expenses—is a major problem. Creditors want payment on delivery or shortly afterwards, and customers tend to delay payment, often for 30–90 days after receiving the good or service. Factoring allows businesses to get their money (at a discount) by selling the right to receive the future payment from a customer.

Once factored, the account receivable becomes the property of the company (factor) purchasing the CONTRACT. The factor, assuming the risk that a customer may delay or DEFAULT on payment, pays the seller a discounted amount below the amount owed. To effectively assess RISK, factors have to be familiar with the firms and practices in the markets they operate in. Factoring is most associated with the garment industry and is conducted primarily by large factoring finance companies.

Further reading

Kidwell, David S., Richard L. Peterson, and David W. Blackwell. *Financial Institutions, Markets, and Money,* 7th ed. Fort Worth: Dryden Press, 2000.

factory tours

Factory or industrial tours show consumers how a company's PRODUCTs are manufactured. Sometimes used as part of a firm's MARKETING STRATEGY, factory tours are a relatively new promotional tool as many companies are just beginning to realize the benefits of demonstrating to consumers how their products are made. One company, Celestial Seasonings Tea, opened their manufacturing facilities to customers in the mid-1990s. Within five years more than 500,000 people were visiting the factory annually. The company sells teas, mugs, t-shirts, and other company-logo products in the factory tour store and also includes visitors in taste tests of new products it is considering.

Three business concerns when considering creating a factory tour include INSURANCE, plant organization, and MARKET INTELLIGENCE. Having nonworkers walking around a factory creates a potential insurance liability. Plant design can incorporate factory tours by including showcase windows and walkways to facilitate visitors. One company discontinued factory tours when competitors used the tours to gain access to the facility and view proprietary production technology.

The book *Watch It Made in the USA* (1998) lists hundreds of factories around the country open to the public. York County, Pennsylvania, promotes itself as the United States' factory-tour capital, with 14 free factory tours. HowStuffWorks.com has developed virtual tours of U.S. factories. Many factory managers offer tours when asked but consider factory tours a distraction from their primary activity; production.

See also SALES PROMOTION.

Further reading

Axelrod, Karen, and Bruce Brumberg. *Watch It Made in the USA,* 2d ed. Santa Fe, N. Mex.: John Muir Publishing, 1998.

Fair Debt Collections Practices Act

The Fair Debt Collections Practices Act (FDCPA, 1977, and amended since then) is a federal law designed to prohibit abusive practices by debt collectors. Congress stated, "It is the purpose of this title to eliminate abusive debt collection practices by debt collectors, to ensure that those debt collectors who refrain from using abusive debt collection practices are not competitively disadvantageous, and to promote consistent State action to protect consumers against debt collection abuses." The act applies to debts incurred by consumers involving money, property, INSURANCE, or services. At the time, Congress found that

(A) There is abundant evidence of the use of abusive, deceptive, and unfair debt collection practices by many debt collectors. Abusive debt collection practices contribute to the number of personal bankruptcies, to marital instability, to the loss of jobs, and to invasions of individual PRIVACY. (B) Existing laws and procedures for redressing these injuries are inadequate to protect consumers. (C) Means other than misrepresentation or other abusive debt collection practices are available for the effective collection of debts. (D) Abusive debt collection practices are carried on to a substantial extent in interstate commerce. Even where abusive debt collection practices are purely intrastate in character, they nevertheless directly affect interstate commerce.

The act generally prevents debt collectors from contacting anyone other than the person who incurred the debt. Previously debt collectors often contacted relatives, employers, and friends, attempting to intimidate or embarrass people into paying the debt. The act states that any debtor communicating with any person other than the consumer for the purpose of acquiring location information about the consumer shall "only ask location information; not state that the consumer owes any debt; not use postcards or any symbols or language in mailings referring to debt collection; and not communicate with any person other than the attorney, after the debt collector knows the consumer is represented by an attorney."

Without the prior consent of the consumer given directly to the debt collector, a debt collector may not communicate with a consumer at the consumer's place of EMPLOYMENT or at any unusual time. (Generally debt collectors can only contact consumers between 8 A.M. and 9 P.M. local time.) The act also requires the collector to provide details regarding the debt within five days of initial contact. If a consumer notifies a debt collector in writing that they refuse to pay a debt or that they wish the debt collector to cease further communication with the consumer, the debt collector must not communicate further with the consumer regarding the debt.

The act states that the debt collector may not engage in any conduct to harass, oppress, or abuse any person in connection with the collection of a debt. The following list provides an idea of the types of practices utilized before the FDCPA.

- The use or threat of use of violence or other criminal means to harm the physical person, reputation, or property of any person.
- The use of obscene or profane language or language the natural consequence of which is to abuse the hearer or reader.
- The publication of a list of consumers who allegedly refuse to pay debts, except to a consumer reporting agency.
- The advertisement for sale of any debt to coerce payment of the debt.

- Causing a telephone to ring or engaging any person in telephone conversation repeatedly or continuously with intent to annoy, abuse, or harass any person at the called number.

The act states further: a debt collector may not use any false, deceptive, or misleading representation or means in connection with the collection of any debt, including

- the character, amount, or legal status of any debt
- any services rendered or compensation which may be lawfully received by any debt collector for the collection of a debt
- the false representation or implication that any individual is an attorney or that any communication is from an attorney
- the representation or implication that nonpayment of any debt will result in the arrest or imprisonment of any person or the seizure, garnishment, attachment, or sale of any property or wages of any person unless such action is lawful and the debt collector or creditor intends to take such action
- the threat to take any action that cannot legally be taken
- the false representation or implication that a sale, referral, or other transfer of any interest in a debt shall cause the consumer to lose any claim or defense to payment of the debt, or become subject to any practice prohibited by this title
- the false representation or implication that the consumer committed any crime or other conduct in order to disgrace the consumer
- communicating or threatening to communicate to any person credit information which is known or which should be known to be false, including the failure to communicate that a disputed debt is disputed
- the use of distribution of any written communication which simulates or is falsely represented to be a document authorized, issued, or approved by any court, official, or agency of the United States, or which creates a false impression as to its source, authorization, or approval
- the use of any false representation of deceptive means to collect or attempt to collect any debt or to obtain information concerning a consumer
- the false representation or implication that accounts have been turned over to innocent purchasers for value
- the false representation or implication that documents are legal process
- the use of any business, company, or organization name other than the true name of the debt collector's business, company, or organization
- the false representation or implication that documents are not legal process forms or do not require action by the consumer
- the false representation or implication that a debt collector operates or is employed by a consumer reporting agency

The FEDERAL TRADE COMMISSION is the primary federal agency responsible for enforcement of the FDCPA, which also allows individual civil actions and class actions by consumers or consumer groups.

See also CONSUMER CREDIT PROTECTION ACT.

Further reading
Mallor, Jane P., A. James Barnes, Thomas Bowers, Michael J. Philips, and Arlen W. Langvardt. *Business Law and the Regulatory Environment,* 11th ed. Boston: McGraw-Hill, 2001.

fair disclosure (SEC Regulation FD)
Fair disclosure is providing information to all parties at one time. The SECURITY AND EXCHANGE COMMISSION's (SEC) Regulation FD, effective October 2000, is designed to eliminate "selective disclosure" of financial information by officials of publicly traded CORPORATIONS in the United States. Historically, STOCK MARKET analysts "cover" stocks in particular industries, analyzing trends, making predictions about future profitability, and offering recommendations to investors. These WALL STREET insiders get to know managers and officials of the companies they cover and are often provided reports from and interviews with company executives, thus obtaining information in advance of individual traders in the marketplace. For decades this was standard practice on Wall Street, but with the advantage of on-line trading and the huge increase in individual traders, non-Wall Street investors complained about the unfair advantage given to industry analysts and the firms they represented.

In addition to eliminating selective disclosure, the fair disclosure regulation, as SEC Regulation FD is known, also addresses "analyst independence," recognizing that the firms analysts work for often have other business relationships with the companies they evaluate. The SEC and the SECURITIES INDUSTRY ASSOCIATION direct stock market firms to separate analysts' pay from other relationships with the companies they cover.

The fair disclosure guidelines provide flexibility for companies to comply with disclosure requirements. The guidelines allow companies to issue press releases through conventional media and encourage firms to announce in advance website disclosures and teleconferencing announcements. Companies continue to have investor conferences, but with the new fair disclosure rules, all information provided at these conferences must also be made available to the general investing public.

Further reading
Securities and Exchange Commission website. Available on-line. URL: www.sec.gov.

Fair Labor Standards Act
The Fair Labor Standards Act (FLSA), passed in 1938 and amended many times since then, is a major labor-management law regulating wages and hours, child labor, equal pay, and overtime pay. The act entitles covered employees to a specified MINIMUM WAGE and a time-and-a-half rate for work exceeding 40 hours per week.

One of the critical and complicated aspects of FLSA is the question of who is covered by the act. Generally, hourly employees for business engaged in interstate commerce or producing goods and services for interstate commerce are covered by the act. Federal employees were added to coverage in 1974. Most executive, administrative, and professional personnel are exempted from coverage. Whether or not an employee is covered is important in determining which workers can be expected to work beyond 40 hours per week without compensation and which employees must be compensated.

FLSA also contains provisions regarding child labor. "Oppressive" child labor is considered to include most EMPLOYMENT of children below the age of 14. Employment in certain occupations is allowed for children aged 14–15, and the act contains restrictions for employment of children aged 16–17 in certain hazardous occupations. Changes in minimum-wage laws are amendments to the original FLSA.

Interpreting the FLSA is a complex process with numerous legal precedents. Whole books have been written and are continually updated regarding labor-law requirements under the act. International businesses opening operations in the United States need to become familiar with labor practices acceptable and unacceptable under FLSA.

Further reading
Mallor, Jane P., A. James Barnes, Thomas Bowers, Michael J. Philips, and Arlen W. Langvardt. *Business Law and the Regulatory Environment,* 11th ed. Boston: McGraw-Hill, 2001.

fair use   See COPYRIGHT, FAIR USE.

Family and Medical Leave Act
One of the first legislative acts signed by President Bill Clinton in 1993, the Family and Medical Leave Act (FMLA), entitles eligible employees to take up to 12 weeks of unpaid leave in a 12-month period for specific family and medical needs such as the birth of a child, adopting or fostering a child, serious health care for immediate family (spouse, parent, or child), and medical leave when an employee has a serious health condition. The employer has a choice of using either a calendar year or the company's FISCAL YEAR. The law protects the employee who takes the leave by guaranteeing job continuation after the leave, health benefits during the leave, and the right to take the leave.

This law applies to all employees who work for public agencies; local, state, and federal government employers; and educational institutions such as local public schools, colleges, and universities. For employees in the private sector, their company must have 50 or more employees and have 20 or more workweeks in the current or preceding calendar year and be engaged in commerce or any industry or activity that affects commerce.

For employees to take leave under the FMLA, they must have worked in the job for 12 months, have worked at least 1,250 hours for those 12 months, and worked in the United States or any territory or possession of the United States. For spouses employed by the same employer, they are jointly entitled to a combined total of 12 workweeks.

Under some conditions, the family leave may be taken in blocks of time (intermittently) or by reducing their normal workday. Intermittent leave must be approved the employer. Employees may also combine earned leave (vacation or sick time) with the FMLA upon approval of the employer.

It is unlawful for any eligible employer to interfere or deny their employees' rights to the FMLA. It is also illegal to fire or discriminate against the employee for participating in the FMLA. The DEPARTMENT OF LABOR will bring action against any eligible employer for denying an employee participation in the FMLA.

The FMLA does not take the place of state or local laws, which offer better leave provisions, nor does it prevent an employer from offering better benefits to their employees.

Further reading
Flynn, Gillian. "The Latest Focus on the Fuzzy FMLA," *Workforce* (February 2001): 94–95; U.S. Department of Labor website. Available on-line. URL: http://www.dol.gov.

—Susan Poorbaugh

family farm

A family farm is officially defined by the 1998 Agricultural Resource Management Study as any farm organized as a sole PROPRIETORSHIP, PARTNERSHIP, or family CORPORATION. Family farms exclude those organized as nonfamily corporations or COOPERATIVES or firms with a hired manager. Family farms are those legally controlled by one operator, or the person who makes daily decisions, and are run by their family or household. The U.S. Department of Agriculture (USDA) defines small family farms as those with sales of less than $250,000, large family farms as those with sales of $250,000–$499,999, and very large family farms as those with sales of $500,000 or more. Farms were first defined for census purposes in 1850, and their definition has changed nine times. The current definition of a farm is any place from which $1,000 or more of agricultural PRODUCTs are sold or would normally have been sold in a given year.

The 2001 Family Farm Report by Economic Research Services of the USDA illustrates that there is a wide variety of small family farms. These include are limited-resource farms with sales less than $100,000 and an operator

household of less than $20,000; retirement farms, whose owners are retired; and residential/ lifestyle farms, which are small farms where the majority of household INCOME comes from an occupation other than farming.

Family farms declined dramatically in number during the 20th century. The census of agriculture has shown that the number of farms decreased by two-thirds between 1935 and 1974, from 6.8 million to 2.3 million. The average farm was 155 acres in 1934; it was 487 acres in 1998. Agricultural PRODUCTION is heavily concentrated on large and very large family farms. While these two groups accounted for only 8 percent of all farms in 1998, they made up 53 percent of the total production of agricultural products. Although the limited-resource, retirement, and residential/lifestyle types make up 62 percent of farms in the United States, they produce only 9 percent of farm output. Family farms in the United States also tend to specialize in production, and half of all farms produce just one commodity.

In addition, family farmers are an aging and mostly rural population. The average age of a family farmer is typically around 50 years old. Many younger people have moved off family farms as more nonfarm EMPLOYMENT became available. Almost two-thirds of U.S. farms are in nonmetropolitan counties. One of the biggest problems that these farms face is a heavy debt burden. A USDA-recommend strategy for these farmers by the USDA is to lease land and farm equipment rather than purchase it in order to eliminate the need for CAPITAL financing. A large number of family farms are simply too small for their owners to do anything other than supplement other types of employment.

Farm policy has always been a difficult issue for the United States, especially in the 19th century when the populist movement was a major force in U.S. politics. This movement lasted until the early 20th century and was widely supported by farmers who hoped to have some control over crop prices and determining credit policies toward farmers. During the New Deal of the 1930s, legislation was passed that was designed to protect farmers from wide price changes during the GREAT DEPRESSION, and a farm policy called the Parity Program was developed. This resulted in the COMMODITY CREDIT CORPORATION (CCC), which made LOANS to farmers whenever prices fell below the cost of production. Farmers could consequently hold crops back from the market to force prices back up and repay their loans with interest. This program also regulated farm production in order to balance crop supply with DEMAND and created a national grain reserve.

Controversial legislation passed in 1996 sought to alleviate the problems of family farmers. The Federal Agriculture Improvement and Reform Act (FAIR), also known as the Freedom to Farm Act, is a seven-year farm program that put an end to New Deal production controls and eliminated federal price supports. FAIR gave farmers a guarantee of fixed but declining payments that were to end in 2002 as well as the flexibility to plant whatever crops they want. By eliminating PRICE FLOORS and production controls, FAIR was supposed to give farmers some control over the price of their crops so that they could increase EXPORTING by offering more competitive prices on the world market. Critics of this legislation have argued that in the last four years, exports of key crops such as corn, wheat, and soybeans have dropped 10 percent. They also suggest that this law has not allowed farmers a means of controlling the SUPPLY of crops on the market, even if there is already a surplus that has greatly depressed prices. Finally, critics argue that legislators have failed to consider the reality of increased production by other exporting countries, and that lower commodity prices do not increase overall demand.

The decline in the profitability and number of family farms has also led to great debate over their future role in the American economy. Some economists have argued that in a global economy, small family farms have simply become too inefficient and that those who support them cling to a romantic notion rather than economic reality. In the last 20 years the agriculture industry has seen a great deal of concentration. In 2000 the top packing companies in the beef business accounted for 81 percent of cattle slaughtering, up from 30 percent in 1980. In hog processing, four farms control 56 percent of the market. Several recent mergers have also created huge new CONGLOMERATES, often referred to as agribusiness companies. In 1999 Cargill Inc., the country's largest grain processor, acquired Continental Grain Company, the third largest. In order to prevent this new conglomerate from becoming a complete MONOPOLY, the Justice Department required that they make some significant CORPORATE DIVESTITURES of ASSETS.

As corporate farms have become steadily larger, some critics have warned about potential environmental and health dangers associated with them. Factory farms such as hog farms often create pools of waste that can leak into ground water and rivers. While agribusiness companies insist that that mergers will lead to a growing efficiency in production and lower consumer prices, many small farmers argue that such mergers are driving them out of business.

Supporters of agribusiness suggest that family farms are simply unproductive and outdated in face of the large-scale efficiency offered by large corporations. They suggest that family-farm supporters exaggerate the environmental threat, that America is no longer a rural culture, and that agriculture policies should be developed to favor international trade, rather than small rural farmers. FAIR was passed in great measure to support the U.S. commitment to the WORLD TRADE ORGANIZATION and the General Agreement on Tariffs and Trade (GATT). Nonetheless, some staunch family-farm supporters, such as Senator Bryan Dorgan of North Dakota, argue that family farms do not

struggle because they are inefficient but because of inappropriate federal legislation and trade agreements that favor agribusiness. He suggests that the most important element family farms provide to the country is a sense of community and family values. The place of family farms in American life was important throughout the 18th and 19th century, but their decline in the 20th century has been significant, and their future economic viability remains in question.

Further reading
Dorgan, Byron. "Don't Be Down on the Farm." *The Washington Monthly,* January/February 2000; Ghent, Bill. "Agriculture: Mergers Squeeze Family Farms," *National Journal* (15 July 2000): 32; "Structural and Financial Characteristics of U.S. Farms: 2001 Family Farm Report," U.S. Department of Agriculture Economic Research Service. Available on-line. URL: http://www.ers. usda.gov/publications/aib768/. Downloaded on May 31, 2001.
—Alison Jones

family-friendly business practices
Family-friendly business practices are policies and benefits provided to employees to assist them with their family needs and obligations. The idea of family-friendly business practices was part of the 1992 presidential debates regarding "family values" and the FAMILY AND MEDICAL LEAVE ACT (FMLA), vetoed by President George H. W. Bush and later passed under the Clinton administration. Under FMLA, a covered employer must grant an eligible employee up to 12 workweeks of unpaid leave during any 12-month period for one or more of the following reasons.

- for the birth and care of the employee's newborn child
- for placement of a son or daughter with the employee for adoption or foster care
- to care for an immediate family member (spouse, child, or parent) with a serious health condition
- to take medical leave when the employee is unable to work because of a serious health condition

Beyond the Family and Medical Leave Act, there is no one definition of what constitutes a family-friendly business, but two surveys provide guidelines. A group in Horry County, South Carolina, created the *Employee Certified Family-Friendly Business Initiative.* To be certified at their minimum (bronze) level, a firm needs to offer

- health INSURANCE with the organization paying at least 50 percent of the premium and offering some dependent coverage
- paid time off for critical family needs
- dependent care assistance
- some type of savings program
- school/educational support
- community/neighborhood support

- paid vacation or leave
- opportunity for skill development and progression
- some type of dissemination of family, work/life information
- sponsored seminars or workshops on family/work/life topics
- employee recognition for work service, community work, and personal events
- life insurance for employees
- selected benefits for part-time/seasonal employees
- a written MISSION STATEMENT emphasizing employees and family

By 2001, 21 area organizations had been certified as family-friendly.

In a second study, 28 benefits or policies were identified as family-friendly business practices, including

- timing of employee training
- equal pay for equal work
- vacation time
- time for family emergencies
- MINIMUM WAGE
- health insurance
- COMPARABLE WORTH
- flexible working hours
- college tuition reimbursement
- overtime guidelines for salaried employees
- family counseling services
- moving expenses reimbursement
- preretirement planning services
- freedom to refuse transfers
- family leave
- pretax account for dependent care
- consideration of spouse in transfers
- voluntary reduced time
- CAFETERIA PLAN for benefits
- benefits for part-time workers
- job-sharing opportunities
- satellite offices/branches
- work-at-home capability
- release time or flexible hours for sick-dependent care
- release time or flexible hours for elderly care
- paid time off for volunteer work
- dependent care provision or referral
- career break plan

Relatively few firms offer all or most of these benefits or policies. Traditionally in the United States, employees were expected to "leave their personal problems at the door." During the labor shortage that occurred in many industries in the 1990s, many U.S. companies became more flexible in accommodating and supporting their employees' personal needs. Surveys show that companies offering family-friendly work environments have greater worker loyalty, initiative, and teamwork.

Further reading
Department of Labor Family and Medical Leave Act Fact Sheet. Available on-line. URL: www.dol.gov/esa/regs/compliance/whd/whdfs28.htm; Folsom, Davis, and Robert Botsch. "Is Your Company Family Friendly?" *B&E Review*, April–June 1993; Rogers, Jim R. "Is Your Business Family-Friendly?" *B&E Review*, July–September 2001.

family life cycle
The family life cycle is a series of typical stages that families go through, from family formation to dissolution. At each stage individual and family needs and wants differ, creating opportunities for marketers to change and provide what will best suit their customers.

The family life cycle can comprise up to eight stages, including bachelor, young married, full nest, single parent, divorced and alone, middle-aged and married, full nest again, and empty nest. The usefulness of family life-cycle analysis is looking at customer groups based on their life stage rather than age or other demographic measure. For example, in the United States the average age at which people get married for the first time has been increasing, which means consumers remain in the bachelor stage for a longer period of time. Bachelors are more likely to need apartment furnishings, purchase economy or sports cars, and pursue adventure travel. Another phenomenon within the bachelor stage is that young people are staying longer in their parents' home. Especially in areas where housing costs are high, many young singles live at home and will have different needs than those moving into their own dwellings.

Young married couples are an attractive group to many marketers. Anyone who has recently become engaged has probably been overwhelmed with a vast array of promotions from wedding services, jewelers, travel agents, and INSURANCE companies. Many new choices and decisions are made in a short period of time among young married couples, creating needs and opportunities for marketers.

Even before the arrival of first children, full-nest families (and filling-the-nest families) change their CONSUMER BEHAVIOR. Sports cars often cannot hold safety seats and are traded in for vans and SUVs. Larger apartments and first-home purchases create changing needs for products. Insurance, health care, and other service needs also change.

Single parent and divorced and alone are two similar and typical family life-cycle stages. The splitting up of households creates changing needs for products and services and undoes many existing CONTRACTs, including home ownership and insurance coverage.

Those families that make it through the full-nest stage or remarry after the single-parent stage become the middle-aged and married segment. These households tend to have higher INCOMEs, established relationships with firms, and greater interest in quality and timesaving products. Often, within a few years, these families are surprised to find themselves in the full-nest-again stage, as college-graduate children return home. This can create needs for remodeling, changing insurance needs, and a variety of products to accommodate different needs under one roof.

Eventually the family life cycle leads to the empty-nest stage. At this point families often shift from homes to condominiums or purchase a second home in a warmer climate, leaving offspring behind to take care of the homestead. Travel demand increases, and at some point health-care needs grow.

Of course, many adult groups do not go through the family life cycle. Marketers refer to DINKS (Double Income, No Kids) as one segment of affluent consumers who choose to not have children.

Further reading

Boone, Louis, and David Kurtz. *Contemporary Marketing,* 10th ed. Fort Worth: Dryden Press, 2001; Etzel, Michael J., Bruce J. Walker, and William J. Staunton, *Marketing,* 12th ed. Boston: McGraw-Hill, 2001.

Fannie Mae   See FEDERAL NATIONAL MORTGAGE ASSOCIATION.

Farm Credit System

The Farm Credit System (FCS) is a national financial cooperative providing LOANS to farmers, COOPERATIVES, rural homeowners, agribusinesses, and rural utility systems. In 2002 the FCS made over $62 billion in loans to 500,000 borrowers and provided approximately one-fourth of the credit extended to U.S. agricultural producers.

The Farm Credit System, the earliest government-sponsored enterprise (GSE), sells FCS BONDS and notes and then lends funds through a network of 200 Farm Credit lending institutions. The Farm Credit Administration (FCA) based in McLean, Virginia, is an independent federal regulator responsible for examining and ensuring the FCS's financial soundness. The FCA's three-member BOARD OF DIRECTORS are nominated by the U.S. president and confirmed by the Senate.

To people not involved in agriculture, the FCS is a maze of acronyms. To anyone involved in agriculture, the FCS is a major source of government support and funding. The FCS includes a variety of financial institutions including Farm Credit Banks, CoBank, Federal Land Bank Associations (FLBAs), Federal Land Credit Associations (FLCAs), Production Credit Associations (PCAs), Agricultural Credit Associations (ACAs), and Farm Credit Council (FCC).

There are six Farm Credit Banks (FCBs), including AgAmerica and Western FCBs (western and northwestern U.S.), Agribank, FCB (midwestern states), AgFirst, FCB (primarily southeastern U.S.), FCB of Wichita (south-central states), and FCB of Texas (Louisiana to parts of New Mexico). The FCBs provide financial services and finds to local associations, which in turn lend those funds to agricultural and rural borrowers.

The CoBank, created in 1989 through the merger of 10 of the 12 district cooperative banks, is one of three Banks for Cooperatives. A Bank for Cooperatives in turn provides lending and other financial services to farmer-owned cooperatives and rural utility systems.

The Federal Land Bank Associations (FLBAs) are affiliates of the Farm Credit Bank and provide long-term MORTGAGE loans to farmers, ranchers, and rural homebuyers. The Federal Land Credits Associations (FLCAs) provide lending for long-term loans. The Production Credit Associations (PCAs) provide short- and intermediate-term loans to farmers and ranchers. The Agricultural Credit Associations (ACAs), formed through mergers, are the successors to the FLBAs and PCAs, providing long- and short-term agricultural and rural loans. The Farm Credit Council (FCC) is the national trade association of the FCS, representing the interests of the FCS with respect to federal agricultural policies and providing INSURANCE and business services to the FCS.

The history of the Farm Credit System began with the Country Life Commission created by President Theodore Roosevelt in 1908. At that time, lending for agricultural real estate was extremely limited. In 1913 federal law prohibited national banks from making loans with maturities greater than five years. (The government was attempting to reduce interest-rate RISK in banking and reduce bank failures after the crash of 1907.) The Commission's report eventually led to the passage of the Federal Farm Loan Act of 1916, which created the 12 Federal Land Banks, using $125 million in government funds and private CAPITAL to create credit institutions for agricultural producers. The land banks prospered with World War 1 and increased DEMAND for food products but collapsed in the postwar economic decline. In response Congress created 12 Federal Intermediate Credit Banks, but they faltered with the GREAT DEPRESSION. The Agricultural Marketing Act of 1929 provided support prices for agricultural products and financial support for agricultural cooperatives. By 1933 the government consolidated federal farm programs into the Farm Credit Administration, creating the basis for today's Farm Credit System.

Historically, support for U.S. agriculture has been strong, based on widespread political representation. In recent decades, as agricultural interests have been supplanted by manufacturing, technology, service industries, and greater consumer interests, support for farm programs have been sometimes challenged in the political arena. In response the Farm Credit System has come under greater scrutiny to become financially sound and self-sustaining.

See also GOVERNMENT-SPONSORED ENTERPRISES.

Further reading

Farm Credit Council website. Available on-line URL: www.fccouncil.com.

fast track (trade promotion authority)

Fast track is the media term for the authority, granted by Congress to the U.S. president, to negotiate trade agreements. Fast track allows the president to negotiate a trade agreement with the understanding that Congress will ratify or reject the treaty but will not amend the agreement. By granting the president fast-track authority, Congress limits its right and duty under the U.S. Constitution to ratify any agreement the president enters into.

Every U.S. president since 1974 has been granted fast-track authority. Ronald Reagan used fast-track authority to negotiate the U.S.-CANADA FREE TRADE AGREEMENT (1989), and Bill Clinton used his fast-track authority to complete the NORTH AMERICAN FREE TRADE AGREEMENT (NAFTA), initiated by George H. W. Bush in the early 1990s. At the 1994 Conference of the Americas in Miami, President Clinton assured Chile that they would be the next country allowed to join NAFTA. Congress then refused to renew Clinton's fast-track authority, ending the expansion of NAFTA for the rest of his presidency.

In 2001 President George W. Bush met with the leaders of 33 Western Hemisphere countries in Quebec, Canada, to initiate plans for the Free Trade Area of the Americas (FTAA). At the conference, the president renamed fast-track authority "trade promotion authority." Even though the leaders agreed to create a FREE TRADE AREA by 2005, unless Congress grants the president fast track/trade promotion authority, it is unlikely the effort will succeed.

featherbedding

The term *featherbedding* describes UNION efforts to require employers to hire more workers than needed for the task. Featherbedding agreements require companies to pay union members wages whether their work is needed or not. As LABOR MARKETS change, often certain skills and tasks are no longer needed. However, if the union/MANAGEMENT agreement calls for workers to be employed, then the company is required by the CONTRACT to pay the workers. A classic example was firemen on trains. In the days of wood and coal engines, having a fireman on board a train was a reasonable requirement. But as diesel and electric engines came into use, railroad companies were often required by the union contract to continue to employ firemen.

The TAFT-HARTLEY ACT (1947) attempted to outlaw featherbedding by making it an unfair labor practice to demand payment of wages for services that are not performed or will not be performed. Nevertheless, featherbedding exists. In one case the Supreme Court ruled that only payments for workers not to work are prohibited. A union may require that the employer pay workers for useless or totally unnecessary work, as long as the work is actually performed. For example, a newspaper accepted ads from customers that had been prepared by the customer. However, the union agreement required the employer to recopy the prepared work using union workers. In another case, companies have been forced to pay union workers who do nothing as long as they remain willing to work. For example, a theater that brought in out-of-town orchestras still had to pay union musicians, even though no work was performed.

Featherbedding is a basis for major criticism of labor unions in the United States. In recent years many unions have become more flexible in union/management negotiations about minimum crew sizes and "make-work" agreements.

Further reading

Regulation of Economic Pressure. Available on-line. URL: http://web./missouri/edu/~labored/1997-30.html.

Federal Aviation Administration

The Federal Aviation Administration (FAA) is an agency in the U.S. DEPARTMENT OF TRANSPORTATION responsible for the safety of civil air transportation. Its other roles include RESEARCH AND DEVELOPMENT, implementing programs to control noise pollution resulting from air traffic, and regulating launches of commercial space payloads.

Originally called the Federal Aviation Agency, the FAA was created when Congress passed the Federal Aviation Act of 1958. Its responsibilities included overseeing licensing and certification of pilots and aircraft, development of air navigation and air traffic-control systems, and adopting the safety rules and policy-making functions of the CIVIL AERONAUTICS BOARD. In 1967 it became part of the Department of Transportation and took its present name.

The FAA is comprised mainly of seven organizations whose leaders report to the administrator and deputy administrator. Other significant programs are managed by assistant administrators. The FAA's primary role is to enforce safety and security policy within the industry. The National Transportation Safety Board frequently makes recommendations for safety inspections and aircraft repair as a result of accident investigations. It is at the FAA's discretion to enforce such recommendations.

The FAA oversees all activities with regard to aviation operations, and its activities are a pivotal part of the business aspects of the aviation industry. Airlines and the aviation industry in general are strongly affected by FAA mandates. Inspection orders, requirements for hiring policies for employees and contractors, upgrades to equipment, and updated procedures are some of the common directives issued by the FAA. These directives can be determining factors in how safe or successful the industry will be. Ordered inspections, for example, are time-consuming and costly for airlines. Grounding aircraft for inspection and repair often requires cancellation of flights and incurred costs ultimately reach the consumer.

Past air disasters, particularly the TWA Flight 800 explosion over Long Island, New York, in July 1996, have raised questions about the FAA's performance in maintaining air safety and security. Many critics claim that mandates for inspection, upgrades, and policies regarding aging aircraft have come only in response to tragedy. However, in 1998 the FAA responded immediately by ordering the inspection of older Boeing 737s when frayed wiring was found during routine maintenance.

Following the TWA disaster, when initial evidence suggested terrorism, President Bill Clinton directed the FAA to put into operation specific recommendations dealing with airport and airline security. Few have been fully implemented, others not at all. Scrutiny regarding security increased after the terrorist attacks on September 11, 2001.

Other FAA functions include promoting aviation safety abroad, constructing and maintaining navigational facilities, developing new aviation technology, providing air-travel advisories, awarding grants and scholarships, and participating in outreach programs.

Further reading
Federal Aviation Administration website. Available on-line. URL: http://www.faa.gov.

—Jennifer McGeorge

federal budget
The federal budget is the spending activity of the U.S. government. At almost $2.2 trillion in 2002, the federal budget is larger than the GROSS DOMESTIC PRODUCT (GDP) of every country in the world except Japan, China, and Germany. Yet federal government spending represents only about 21 percent of U.S. GDP, a smaller percentage than almost every other industrialized country in the world.

The federal budget is a source of constant debate. While politicians often complain the federal government is too big, few political leaders are willing to cut spending programs for fear of offending important constituents. Until 1998 there were often cries to cut the federal budget as a means of achieving a balanced budget. Beginning that year, budget surpluses (a result of modest growth in the federal budget), tax increases, use of the presidential line-item veto, and increased government revenue and reduced spending from a growing economy allowed political leaders the option of reducing the GOVERNMENT DEBT.

The major components of the U.S. federal budget include defense spending, SOCIAL SECURITY, Medicare and Medicaid, other INCOME security, and interest on the government debt. The federal government groups budget spending into mandatory and discretionary spending. The year 2000 budget is summarized below.

Outlays:	Billions of Dollars
Discretionary:	
Department of Defense (DoD)	278
Non-DoD discretionary	339
Mandatory:	
Social Security	403
Medicare and Medicaid	316
Means-tested entitlements	110
Other	123
Net interest	220
Total	1,790
Receipts (taxation)	1,956
Unified budget surplus	167

The budget process begins in the government's executive branch. Every January the president sends to Congress a budget containing spending proposals for all departments and agencies for the coming FISCAL YEAR, which begins October 1. The OFFICE OF MANAGEMENT AND BUDGET represents the president in budgetary matters, and proposed allocations in the federal budget are examined by committees in Congress. Hearings are held with representatives of the government departments and other interested parties testifying for or against the budget proposal. Congress must approve funding for each budget allocation. Some years, when political control is divided between Democrats and Republicans, the approval process has been contentious and often delayed past the beginning of the fiscal year. Congress then passes continuing resolutions, allowing government agencies to operate under the last budget allocation.

Because of the federal budget's size, nearly every industry or business group in the United States watches it closely and attempts to influence spending. The U.S. CHAMBER OF COMMERCE represents the interests of U.S. business groups in general, while industry associations focus on specific parts of federal legislation and spending. Industry association newsletters, websites, and magazines generally summarize pending federal legislation affecting their industry.

Further reading
U.S. Office of Management and Budget website. Available on-line. URL: www.whitehouse.gov/omb.

Federal Communications Commission
The Federal Communications Commission (FCC) is a government agency regulating interstate and international communications by radio, television, wire, satellite, and cable. The FCC was established by the Communications Act of 1934 as part of government regulation of evolving technologies. Like the FEDERAL AVIATION ADMINISTRATION and the Nuclear Regulatory Commission, the FCC was created to regulate the growth and use of communications systems, such as television and radio, that require the use of an electrical frequency spectrum transmitted through the air.

Like other federal agencies, the FCC is directed by a five-member commission, with no more than three members from one political party and one member rotating off annually. Commissioners are nominated by the U.S. president and confirmed by the Senate. The FCC has seven bureaus organized by function, including Cable Services, Common Carrier (telephone), Consumer Information, Enforcement, International, Mass Media (AM-FM radio and television broadcast stations), and Wireless Telecommunications (cellular and PCS phones, pagers, and two-way radios). Each bureau develops and implements regulatory programs, analyzes complaints, conducts investigations, and processes licenses.

One of the most important functions of the FCC is LICENSING. Mass-media companies are required to file license renewal requests every eight years, demonstrating that they are serving local communities. Licenses are limited in most mass-media markets. In recent years the FCC also expanded the sale of broadcast frequency licenses. These licenses sold for billions of dollars to telecommunications companies anticipating expanded wireless communications systems. The Telecommunications Act of 1996 attempted to increase COMPETITION in the communications industry. The act directed incumbent local exchange carriers (telephone companies) to lease part of their network "at cost" to competitors. Numerous legal challenges have blocked many of the act's goals.

Further reading

Federal Communications Commission website. Available online. URL: www.fcc.gov.

federal courts

The U.S. judicial system, which is based on England's system of COMMON LAW, was established by the authority found in Article I and Article III of the U.S. Constitution. In England between A.D. 476–1450, judges developed common law through their procedures and rulings. Eventually laws passed by legislatures replaced common law. Article I of the Constitution, provides the legislature (Congress) authority to establish courts inferior to the supreme Court [sic]—legislative courts. Constitutional courts are established by Article III, which states that the "judicial power of the United States, shall be vested in one supreme Court," but allows Congress the authority to "ordain and establish" inferior courts when necessary.

Common-law principals are still important to the American federal court system in that they emphasize protecting the individual from state abuse in two ways. First, the individual is presumed innocent until proven guilty; the burden of proof rests upon the state, and therefore the individual need not prove innocence. Second, common law provides individual protection from state abuse through a jury system (grand and petit juries).

Grand and petit juries consist of panels of ordinary citizens. Federal courts cannot prosecute defendants unless they are first indicted (charged with a crime) by the grand jury. The grand jury determines whether enough evidence exists to prosecute the individual for the charged crime in a trial court (petit jury). Petit juries consist of jurors who hear evidence from the prosecution and defense attorneys and then render a verdict of guilty or not guilty. Once a defendant is convicted, the judge imposes the sentence, or punishment. As previously noted defendants are protected from state abuse during these two stages of the judicial process.

Federal courts are distinguished by two major criteria: (a) the authority that establishes the court—constitutional and legislative courts, and (b) the jurisdiction the court has when hearing cases—original and appellate jurisdiction. Article III established constitutional courts, specifically the Supreme Court, but also gave Congress the power to establish lesser federal courts deemed necessary to exercise the "judicial power of the United States" (Article III Section 1). Constitutional courts include the Supreme Court, the U.S. Court of Appeals, and the U.S. District Courts. Legislative courts are lesser federal courts established by Congress with their vested authority in Article I. These special courts have limited jurisdictions to areas as defined by Congress. Examples of legislative courts include Military Courts, U.S. Tax Courts, U.S. Courts of Appeals, and the U.S. Claims Court. When cases are heard in court for the first time, they are heard under original jurisdiction. If an individual appeals the decision from the lower federal court, the case is then heard under appellate jurisdiction. Attorneys for major corporations monitor court decisions, particularly Tax and Claims court rulings, for their potential impact on business actions and strategies. Tax court rulings often influence accounting and business location decisions.

The United States has 89 Federal District Courts, each state having at least 1 and larger states having as many as 5. These courts are the country's major federal trial courts in which a single judge presides and a jury decides a verdict.

There are 12 circuit Courts of Appeal throughout the country. Precedence is determined by three judges (no jurors, witnesses, or attorneys present) and interpretation of the law, rather than case facts, is used to establish (hand down) an opinion. In most cases, decisions of the federal appellate courts are final—only a small number of cases are accepted (heard) by the Supreme Court proceeding appellate court rulings.

Further reading

Baradat, Leon P. "The Judiciary." In *Understanding American Democracy.* New York: HarperCollins, 1992; Janda, Kenneth, Jeffrey M. Berry, and Jerry Goldman. "The Constitution." In *The Challenge of Democracy,* 7th ed. Boston: Houghton Mifflin Company, 2002.

—Frank Ubhaus Jr. and Jerry Merwin

Federal Deposit Insurance Corporation

The Federal Deposit Insurance Corporation (FDIC) is a government agency administering federal deposit INSURANCE funds and regulating state-chartered "nonmember" banks. The FDIC is directed by a five-member BOARD OF DIRECTORS, appointed by the U.S. president and approved by the Senate. The FDIC was created in 1934 in response to the collapse of more than 9,000 U.S. banks between 1929 and 1933. Less than two days after Franklin Roosevelt was elected president, he declared a "banking holiday," closing all banks in the country while Congress enacted legislation to strengthen the BANKING SYSTEM. The FDIC, part of the 1933 Glass-Steagall Act, created insurance for bank depositors.

Banks play important roles in any economic system, including acting as FINANCIAL INTERMEDIARIES, aggregating funds from depositors, and making LOANS to businesses for INVESTMENT. In the CIRCULAR FLOW MODEL of an economy, most households save a small portion of their INCOME for varying periods of time, but they do not have the time or expertise needed to evaluate business investment proposals. Without a sound banking system, it is difficult for businesses to find the needed CAPITAL to make investments. Fearful of bank failure, individuals store their savings under the mattress, bury it in jars, or hold precious metals, none of which provides the capital most needed for investment and thus ECONOMIC GROWTH.

The bank failures of the GREAT DEPRESSION were not the first experience with problems in the U.S. financial system. Bank panics had occurred almost every 20 years beginning in 1819. Between 1929 and 1933, almost 40 percent of U.S. banks closed their doors, with depositors losing their savings. In 1934 the FDIC began by insuring deposits up to $2,500 per depositor, the goal being to restore bank customers' confidence. Over time FDIC insurance was raised to the current limit of $100,000 per depositor. Insurance premiums are paid by member banking institutions into an FDIC-managed fund that contains only a small portion of the outstanding guarantees but is backed by the federal government.

The $100,000 insurance amount is available per depositor per institution. This means if one customer has savings, checking, and certificate of deposit accounts in an FDIC-insured institution, the sum of that depositor's accounts is insured for $100,000. (INDIVIDUAL RETIREMENT ACCOUNTS and KEOGH PLANS are insured separately.) During the 1980s, when almost 3,000 banks and SAVINGS AND LOAN ASSOCIATIONS failed, invariably individuals and groups lost parts of their deposits. In one case, a church group saving for a new building had over $200,000 in one account but received only the $100,000 maximum coverage. Since FDIC insurance is applied on a per-depositor per-institution basis, consumers with deposits exceeding $100,000 frequently spread their savings among financial institutions in order to be covered by FDIC insurance.

In addition to insuring bank customer deposits, the FDIC monitors about 6,000 state-chartered "nonmember" banks. These are commercial and savings banks that are not members of the FEDERAL RESERVE SYSTEM. The FDIC audits these financial institutions for sound banking practices and, when necessary, manages the liquidation of failed institutions. Typically the FDIC comes in and reorganizes a failed institution by merging it with a financially sound institution. The FDIC will often provide subsidized loans and buy questionable ASSETS of the failed institution from the merger partner. In the purchase-and-assumption method, customers of the failed bank become customers of the new bank, with their deposits continuing to be insured by the FDIC. When the FDIC cannot find another institution to assume the role of the failed institution, it will take over the failed bank, pay depositors, and liquidate the institution's assets.

Further reading

Federal Deposit Insurance Corporation website. Available online. URL: www.fdic.gov; Mishkin, Frederic S. *The Economics of Money, Banking, and Financial Markets,* 6th ed. Boston: Addison Wesley, 2001.

Federal Financial Institutions Examinations Council

As stated on their website, the Federal Financial Institutions Examinations Council (FFIEC) is a "formal interagency body empowered to prescribe uniform principles, standards, and report forms for the federal examination of financial institutions by" the major regulatory agencies responsible for supervision of the financial industry in the United States. The five member agencies of the Council are the Board of Governors of the FEDERAL RESERVE SYSTEM (FRS), the FEDERAL DEPOSIT INSURANCE CORPORATION (FDIC), the National Credit Union Administration (NCUA), the Office of the COMPTROLLER OF THE CURRENCY (OCC), and the Office of Thrift Supervision (OTS).

While the FFIEC has existed since 1979, it has rarely attracted public attention or industry concern. In July 2002, however, the council released draft guidelines on account management and loss-allowance guidance for credit-card lending. The council "found disparities in the quality of account management practices and inconsistencies in the application of existing guidance. The practices can increase institutions' credit RISK profile to imprudent levels. Further, the inconsistent application of accounting and regulatory guidance can affect the transparency and comparability of financial reporting for all institutions engaged in credit card lending."

As the *Wall Street Journal* reported, the FFIEC "issued new guidelines in an attempt to clean up inconsistent accounting methods, slow down the providing of credit to consumers who can't pay it back and to insure credit-card companies are adequately reserved for bad loans and fees tied to the loans." The council's actions followed the numerous financial accounting scandals that arose during 2002.

The FFIEC also has the responsibility to facilitate public access to depository institution data required under the Home Mortgage Disclosure Act of 1975. As required in the statute creating the group, the council has established an advisory State Liaison Committee composed of five representatives of state financial supervisory agencies.

See also CREDIT CARDS; CREDIT UNION.

Further reading
Federal Financial Institutions Examinations Council website. Available on-line. URL: www.ffiec.gov; Mollenkamp, Carrick. "New Scrutiny on Credit Cards Already Squeezes Some Lenders," *Wall Street Journal,* 19 August 2002.

federal funds market

The federal funds market is the short-term (usually overnight) lending and borrowing among banks in the United States to meet the FEDERAL RESERVE SYSTEM's reserve-requirement ratio. Though it is called the federal funds market, the Federal Reserve does not operate or control the market. Banks are required by the Federal Reserve to keep a set percentage of their deposits as cash or other specified U.S. TREASURY SECURITIES. These required reserves are available when customers want their deposits returned and act as a source of liquidity for banks.

As banks receive more deposits, their RESERVE REQUIREMENTS increase. At the end of each business day, bank managers calculate their required reserves, determine whether they have excess or insufficient reserves, and lend or borrow reserves electronically in the federal funds market. LOANS made in the federal funds market are returned the next business day.

Banks borrowing to meet their reserve requirement will compare rates in the market, attempting to minimize their COSTS. Federal-funds rates tend to be uniform among participating banks, but they increase or decrease depending on the DEMAND for and SUPPLY of funds available. Depending on the Federal Reserve's MONETARY POLICY, the Federal Reserve will increase or decrease the supply of funds in the federal funds market through OPEN-MARKET OPERATIONS. By purchasing securities from banks, the Federal Reserve increases the supply of funds in the market, which tends to decrease the federal-funds rate. Sale of securities by the Federal Reserve would have the opposite effect. Increasing federal-funds rates increases the costs to banks, which in turn increases rates charged to borrowers, decreasing borrowing from banks.

Further reading
Mishkin, Frederic S. *The Economics of Money, Banking, and Financial Markets,* 6th ed. Boston: Addison Wesley, 2001.

Federal Home Loan Bank System

The Federal Home Loan Bank System (FHLBS) was created by Congress in 1932 to stimulate housing financing in the United States. Through its 12 regional Federal Home Loan Banks, the FHLBS provides support to member financial institutions for residential MORTGAGE lending by providing access to CAPITAL MARKETS. In 2001, over 7,700 commercial banks, thrift institutions, CREDIT UNIONS, and INSURANCE companies were members of the FHLBS.

The Federal Housing Finance Board regulates the 12 Federal Home Loan Banks and has regulatory oversight for the Office of Finance, which supervises its members' financial practices. The 12 Federal Home Loan Banks are privately capitalized, government-sponsored enterprises. Each member of the regional banks is a shareholder in the institution, which receives no direct funding from the federal government. The FHLBS sells debt securities in capital markets, generating funds that are used by the regional FHL banks to provide mortgage credit to home buyers.

The FHLBS, like the FEDERAL RESERVE SYSTEM, serves as lender of last resort for its members, but it also provides long-term mortgage funds and provides advances to member institutions at competitive INTEREST RATES. In 1989 the mission of the FHLBS was expanded to include lending for affordable housing and community development.

Most SAVINGS AND LOAN ASSOCIATIONS (S&Ls) are members of the FHLBS. Unlike the Federal Reserve System, where loans are made for short periods of time at the discount rate, the FHLBS provides long-term loans at rates lower than the S&L would have paid in the open market. In this way the FHLBS subsidize mortgage lending.

This system of government-sponsored, privately owned financial institutions supported growth in residential housing for almost 50 years. In the early 1980s, new financial PRODUCTs, negotiable order of withdrawal (NOW) accounts, money-market funds, junk BONDS, and SECURITIZATION threatened traditional business lending practices by commercial banks and S&Ls. The Depository Institutions Deregulation and Monetary Control Act (1980) and the Depository Institutions (Garn-St. Germain) Act of 1982 allowed banks and S&Ls to move into risky lending areas while still protecting depositors through the FEDERAL DEPOSIT INSURANCE CORPORATION (FDIC) and the Federal Savings and Loan Insurance Corporation (FSLIC) insurance.

S&L managers increased investment in new areas of real estate lending beyond their traditional market, residential housing. RISKS were either ignored or not understood by S&L managers and regulators. A RECESSION in 1981–82 combined with a collapse in oil prices resulted in huge DEFAULTs on S&L LOANS, bankrupting many S&Ls. The Federal Home Loan Bank Board and its deposit insurance subsidiary, FSLIC, failed to close insolvent institutions. Finally, in 1989 the George H. W. Bush administration proposed new legislation (the Financial Institutions Reform, Recovery, and Enforcement Act [FIRREA]) eliminating the FHLB Board and the FSLIC. The act created a new fund, the Savings Association Insurance Fund; and a new agency, the RESOLUTION TRUST CORPORATION, to manage and liquidate insolvent thrifts.

Bailout of S&Ls cost an estimated $150 billion, with funding coming partly from FHLBS member institutions but mostly from the sale of government debt securities. FIRREA imposed new restrictions on S&L lending practices and new supervision of the thrift industry.

Further reading
Federal Home Loan Bank website. Available on-line. URL: www.fhlb.gov; Mishkin, Frederic. *The Economics of Money, Banking, and Financial Markets,* 6th ed. Boston: Addison Wesley, 2001.

Federal Home Loan Mortgage Corporation (Freddie Mac)
The Federal Home Loan Mortgage Corporation (FHLMC), better known as Freddie Mac, is a government-sponsored enterprise that purchases MORTGAGES from lending institutions and packages them into securities sold to investors (SECURITIZATION). Freddie Mac and Fannie Mae (FEDERAL NATIONAL MORTGAGE ASSOCIATION), the two major competitors in the mortgage securitization market, grew out of government desire to support mortgage lending and help stimulate economic activity. Freddie Mac was established in 1970 to buy conventional (not federally insured) mortgage LOANS. In 1989 it became a private stockholder-owned CORPORATION, but with a mixture of oversight. Freddie Mac's BOARD OF DIRECTORS includes 13 members elected by stockholders and five members appointed by the president of the United States. Freddie Mac is the 27th largest corporation in the country, with over $500 billion in ASSETS.

In addition to purchasing mortgages for its own portfolio, Freddie Mac creates pass-through securities (called participation certificates) and guaranteed mortgage certificates. The participation certificates are similar to GOVERNMENT NATIONAL MORTGAGE ASSOCIATION (Ginnie Mae) pass-through certificates, except that they contain conventional mortgages. The mortgage pools are assembled directly by Fannie Mae (not mortgage lenders). The mortgages are usually much larger than government-insured mortgages, and participation certificates are sold in minimum amounts of $100,000.

Freddie Mac's government mortgage certificates (GMCs) are also pass-through securities, guaranteed by the FHLMC. As such, GMCs are similar to conventional BONDS where the borrower guarantees payment of principal and interest over the life of the security.

Like Fannie Mae, Freddie Mac is subject to market and government scrutiny. In 1992 Congress passed the Federal Housing Enterprises Financial Safety Act to provide regulatory oversight over Freddie Mac and Fannie Mae. The act did not go into effect until 1995, and the

initial report was published in 2002. Critics of Freddie and Fannie, most notably the lobbying group FM Watch, argue that GOVERNMENT-SPONSORED ENTERPRISES compete unfairly in the secondary mortgage market due to their implied government sponsorship. This allows Freddie Mac and Fannie Mae to borrow at lower rates in the market. Critics also contend the FHLMC has undermined the private lending industry through creation of Loan Prospector, an automated underwriting system created by Freddie Mac. In recent years Freddie Mac has expanded into subprime (higher RISK) mortgage lending and the financial derivatives market. Critics contend lack of oversight of these activities creates potential government risk through implied guarantes as a government-sponsored enterprise.

Further reading
Freddie Mac website. Available on-line. URL: www.freddiemac.com; Kidwell, David S., Richard L. Peterson, and David W. Blackwell, *Financial Institutions, Markets, and Money,* 7th ed. Fort Worth: Dryden Press, 2000.

Federal Mediation and Conciliation Service
The Federal Mediation and Conciliation Service (FMCS) is a federal agency created by the TAFT-HARTLEY ACT (1947) to assist labor and MANAGEMENT relationships. The FMCS offers six categories of services, as follows.

- mediation of disputes and CONTRACT negotiations for private, public, and federal sectors
- preventive mediation, providing services and training in cooperative labor and management relationships
- alternative dispute resolution, providing services and training in a variety of problem-solving approaches that can be used in lieu of litigation, agency adjudication, or traditional rule-making by federal, state, and local governments
- ARBITRATION services, maintaining a computerized roster of qualified arbitrators
- labor-management grants, administering a grants program to fund cooperative, innovative joint labor-management committees
- international services, providing international dispute resolution and international labor education

The goal of the FMCS is to minimize labor-management conflict and, in the process, support ECONOMIC GROWTH. The FMCS is a very small agency, with less than 300 workers and a budget of less than $40 million annually. Its director is appointed by the U.S. president with the advice and consent of the Senate.

Further reading
Federal Mediation and Conciliation Service website. Available on-line. URL: www.fmcs.gov.

Federal National Mortgage Association (Fannie Mae)

The Federal National Mortgage Association, better known as Fannie Mae, is the nation's largest secondary MORTGAGE financial institution. Fannie Mae was initially chartered during the GREAT DEPRESSION as a government-owned enterprise to buy federally insured mortgage LOANS. In 1968 Fannie Mae became a private, shareholder-owned company trading under the symbol FNM. It is the United States' third-largest company in terms of ASSETS ($859 billion in 2002).

Fannie Mae's principal activity is SECURITIZATION of mortgage loans. Securitization is the purchase of loans from lenders in the United States and then issuing securities, backed by the loan agreements, to investors. Fannie Mae buys mortgage loans from SAVINGS AND LOAN ASSOCIATIONS, commercial banks, mortgage bankers, CREDIT UNIONS, and state and local housing-finance agencies. Fannie Mae then sells mortgage-backed securities to investors and mortgage lenders. Mortgage-backed securities, which provide low-risk, diversified portfolio returns to investors, are liquid investments that can be bought and sold through securities dealers. Mortgage lenders sell loans to Fannie Mae but receive a fee for handling mortgage payments and use the proceeds from the sale of the loan (the principal) to make new loans.

The 1934 National Housing Act established the Federal Housing Administration (FHA), to be headed by a federal housing administrator. As one of the principal functions of the FHA, Title II of the act provided for the INSURANCE of home mortgage loans made by private lenders. Title III of the act provided for the chartering of national mortgage associations by the administrator. These associations were to be private corporations regulated by the administrator, and their chief purpose was to buy and sell the mortgages to be insured by FHA under Title II. Only one association was ever formed under this authority: the National Mortgage Association of Washington, formed on February 10, 1938, as a subsidiary of the Reconstruction Finance Corporation, a government CORPORATION. Later that same year its name was changed to the Federal National Mortgage Association.

By amendments made in 1948, the charter authority of Fannie Mae's administrator was repealed, and Title III became a statutory charter for the Federal National Mortgage Association. By revision of Title III in 1954, Fannie Mae was converted into a mixed-ownership corporation, its preferred stock to be held by the government and its COMMON STOCK to be privately held. It was at this time that Section 312 was first enacted, giving Title III the short title of Federal National Mortgage Association Charter Act.

By amendments made in 1968, the Federal National Mortgage Association was partitioned into two separate entities: GOVERNMENT NATIONAL MORTGAGE ASSOCIATION (Ginnie Mae) and Federal National Mortgage Association. Ginnie Mae remained in the government, and Fannie Mae became privately owned by retiring the government-held stock.

Fannie Mae and its competitor, Freddie Mac (FEDERAL HOME LOAN MORTGAGE CORPORATION) are often at the center of financial-industry controversy. Because they were created as GOVERNMENT-SPONSORED ENTERPRISES and continue to have the implied backing of the federal government, Fannie Mae and Freddie Mac are able to raise funds in CAPITAL MARKETS at lower costs than competitors. They also maintain significant lobbying and campaign finance operations in Washington, D.C., designed to protect other benefits. (Fannie Mae and Freddie Mac donate millions of dollars annually to the major political parties.) Though Fannie Mae is not connected to the federal government, it is exempt from PROPERTY TAXES and from SECURITIES AND EXCHANGE COMMISSION (SEC) securities registration fees. (Fannie Mae and Freddie Mac are the second- and third-largest issuers of securities behind the U.S. Treasury.) Fannie Mae is also exempt from SEC quarterly and annual disclosure requirements.

When it was created in the 1930s, Fannie Mae was needed to restore confidence to failing financial markets. Since it became a private corporation in 1968, other FINANCIAL INTERMEDIARIES have questioned the fairness of retaining special benefits for one private enterprise. Competitors have pressured Congress to restrict Fannie Mae's advantages, including efforts to eliminate its emergency line of credit with the U.S. Treasury, ending its property-tax exemption, and requiring SEC disclosure.

General Electric Capital, Wells Fargo, Household Finance, JP Morgan, Chase, and other financial institutions have funded FM Watch, an industry-lobbying group to challenge Fannie Mae and Freddie Mac. Fannie Mae refers to FM Watch as a "group of mortgage insurers, high-cost lenders and their allies who want to roll back Fannie Mae policies that cut costs to consumers." Though it is a for-PROFIT business, Fannie Mae claims it "is in business to lower consumer costs and expand home ownership."

Another controversy surrounding Fannie Mae is its use of derivatives and purchase of lower-quality debt. Derivatives are CONTRACTS based on the changes in value of some underlying financial asset. Stock-options values are derived from the value of the stock they are tied to. Financial derivatives are complex, highly leveraged investments. In 1999 the Federal Reserve led the bailout of Long Term Capital Management, which became insolvent when its derivatives on the spread between short- and long-term INTEREST RATES proved wrong. Because Fannie Mae is exempt from some SEC disclosure requirements but also has a line of credit with the U.S. Treasury, congressional critics have asked whether Fannie Mae is creating RISK exposure for the federal government. In 1992 Congress created the Office of Federal Housing Enterprise Oversight (OFHEO) to ensure the CAPITAL adequacy and financial safety of Fannie Mae and Freddie Mac.

Further reading
Federal National Mortgage Association website. Available on-line. URL: www.fanniemae.com; O'Leary, Christopher. "Bush Budget Raps Fannie Mae: Political grousing causes stir in mortgage, agency bond markets," *Investment Dealers Digest,* 18 February 2002.

Federal Reserve System

The Federal Reserve is the central bank of the United States, issuing currency, directing MONETARY POLICY, and supervising commercial banks in the country. The Fed, as it is often called, is a uniquely American institution that was created in 1913 after a series of financial panics and bank failures. Given the long history of distrust in centralized control of political and ECONOMIC POLICY in the United States, Congress created the Federal Reserve System, an independent agency, to oversee commercial banks and coordinate monetary matters in the country.

The key word in the Federal Reserve System is *system.* Unlike most industrialized countries where control of banking and monetary policy is a cabinet-level function within the central government, the United States has a decentralized, semiautonomous system to direct these critical economic functions. The three important parts of the Fed are the Board of Governors, Federal Reserve Banks, and Federal Open Market Committee.

The Board of Governors includes seven members, nominated by the president of the United States and confirmed by the U.S. Senate. The Board members serve 14-year terms, staggered so that a new appointment is made every two years. A two-term president nominates four member of the Board of Governors, and the chairperson of Board of Governors is appointed by the president for a four-year term. In recent times the president has frequently renewed that appointment. The chairman of the Federal Reserve has considerable influence and is often referred to as "the second most important person in Washington."

There are 12 Federal Reserve District Banks in the system. Located in Boston, New York, Philadelphia, Cleveland, Richmond, Atlanta, Chicago, St. Louis, Minneapolis, Kansas City, Dallas, and San Francisco, these banks are technically separate CORPORATIONS owned by their members, commercial banks in each district. All national banks—banks given a charter to operate by the COMPTROLLER OF CURRENCY in the U.S. Treasury—and some state-chartered banks in each district purchase shares in their District Federal Reserve Bank. The members of each district bank elect a BOARD OF DIRECTORS who then appoint a district bank president.

Together, the Fed's Board of Governors and five of the 12 Federal Reserve District Bank presidents form the Federal Open Market Committee (FOMC). The FOMC, whose goals are to maintain price stability and support ECONOMIC GROWTH, meets on a regular basis in Washington and directs monetary policy. Its primary activity, OPEN-MARKET OPERATIONS, involves buying and selling government securities in order to increase or decrease the MONEY SUPPLY in the economy.

The Fed's monetary-policy decisions, which affect all Americans and many other people around the world, are made in secrecy by seven people, appointed by the President for long terms, and five Federal Reserve District Bank presidents. Some people argue that monetary policy is too important to be left in the hands of this group of bankers and economists largely removed from the democratic process. Others have argued that monetary policy is too important to be left in the hands of politicians. However, critics and supporters of the Federal Reserve System have generally complimented the Fed's decisions and leadership in recent years.

See also DISCOUNT RATE; MONEY.

Further reading
Boyes, William, and Michael Melvin. *Fundamentals of Economics,* 2d ed. Boston: Houghton Mifflin, 2002.

Federal Trade Commission

The Federal Trade Commission (FTC), created in 1914, provides administrative enforcement of ANTITRUST LAWS. Section 5 of the Federal Trade Commission Act prohibits "unfair methods of COMPETITION." While the CLAYTON ANTITRUST ACT, enacted in the same year, created judicial remedies for some anticompetitive activities, the FTC Act created a commission to review and regulate unfair competition.

The FTC is composed of five people nominated by the U.S. president and confirmed by the Senate; no more than three members can be from the same political party. While structured as an independent agency, the FTC is subject to political influence, most often through budgetary constraints imposed by Congress. The commission's primary antitrust remedy is issuance of "cease and desist orders" against parties found to violate Section 5 of the FTC Act. The commission can also impose civil penalties and restitution requirements. In recent years its primary activity has been evaluating mergers under the premerger-notification rules of the Clayton Act. When major companies announce a merger, the announcement almost always includes the statement "subject to government approval." This approval includes review by the Antitrust Division of the U.S. Justice Department and review by the FTC.

While review of mergers is the FTC's primary activity, the commission is charged to enforce 46 laws in three categories: statutes relating to both competition and CONSUMER PROTECTION, statutes principally related to competition, and statutes principally related to consumer protection. Statutes relating to both competition and consumer protection include

- the Federal Trade Commission Act
- the Energy Policy and Conservation Act, which directs the commission along with the Justice Department to develop, implement, and monitor plans established by oil companies to deal with emergency international oil shortages. The act also addresses "energy efficiency ratings" on appliances, and, with the DEPARTMENT OF TRANSPORTATION, assesses penalties against automobile manufacturers for violating fuel-economy standards
- portions of the Lanham Trade-Mark Act (1946), authorizing the FTC under specified conditions to apply to the PATENT and TRADEMARK Office for the cancellation of registered trademarks
- the Packers and Stockyards Act, extending FTC jurisdiction to some activities of meat packers

The FTC enforces 10 acts related to competition.

- the Clayton Antitrust Act, preventing and eliminating unlawful TYING CONTRACTS, corporate mergers and acquisitions, and INTERLOCKING DIRECTORATES
- the Hart-Scott-Rodino Antitrust Improvements Act of 1976, establishing waiting periods for certain acquisitions and requiring premerger notification to the FTC and the Antitrust Division of the Justice Department
- the Webb-Pomerene Act, providing for supervision of export-trade associations allowed under the act and allowing collaborative trade activities among companies that compete in the U.S. market
- the Deepwater Port Act of 1974 along with the Attorney General, mandates the FTC to assess the expected competitive effects of proposed licenses for deepwater ports
- the Defense Production Act of 1950, by which the FTC participates in establishing and monitoring voluntary agreements by oil companies to deal with domestic oil shortages, along with the Department of Justice
- the Conservation Service Reform Act of 1986, allowing the FTC to adjudicate complaints concerning the supply and installation of energy conservation measures by public utilities
- the Deep Seabed Hard Minerals Act (1980), providing the FTC with the opportunity to review and make recommendations regarding the antitrust implications of proposed licenses for extraction of minerals from deep seabed sites
- the National Cooperative Research and Production Act of 1993, providing regulatory protection for joint research and development ventures
- the International Antitrust Enforcement Assistance Act of 1994, authorizing the FTC and the Justice Department to enter mutual assistance agreements with foreign antitrust authorities
- the Interstate Commerce Commission Termination Act of 1995 along with other agencies the FTC files reports regarding possible anticompetitive features of rate agreements among common carriers.

The Federal Trade Commission administers 31 statutes related to consumer protection.

- The Wool Products Labeling Act (1939) concerns the manufacture, introduction, sale, transportation, distribution, or importation of misbranded wool. The statute requires that wool-product labels indicate the country in which the product was processed or manufactured and that mail-order promotional materials clearly and conspicuously state whether a wool product was processed or manufactured in the United States or was imported.
- The Fur Products Labeling Act (1998) requires that articles of apparel made of fur be labeled and that invoices and ADVERTISING for furs and fur products specify, among other things, the true English name of the animal from which the fur was taken and whether the fur is dyed or used.
- The Textile Fiber Products Identification Act (1960) requires disclosure in the labeling, invoicing, and advertising of textile fiber products.
- The Federal Cigarette Labeling and Advertising Act of 1966 requires the FTC to submit ANNUAL REPORTS to Congress concerning (a) the effectiveness of cigarette labeling, (b) current practices and methods of cigarette advertising and promotion, and (c) recommendations for legislation. The act also establishes the text of four health-related warning labels and requires that cigarette packages and advertisements carry these warnings on a rotating basis.
- The Fair Packaging and Labeling Act (1966) directs the FTC to issue regulations requiring that all consumer commodities other than food, drugs, therapeutic devices, and cosmetics be labeled to disclose net contents, the commodity's identity, and the name and place of business of the product's manufacturer, packer, or distributor. The act authorizes additional regulations where necessary to prevent consumer deception (or to facilitate value comparisons) with respect to descriptions of ingredients, slack fill of packages, use of "cents-off" or lower-price labeling, or characterization of package sizes.
- The TRUTH IN LENDING ACT (1968) gives the FTC responsibility for assuring compliance by nondepository entities with a variety of statutory provisions, including certain written disclosures concerning all finance charges and related aspects of credit transactions (i.e., disclosing finance charges expressed as an annual percentage rate). The act also establishes a three-day right of rescission in certain transactions involving the establishment of a security interest in the consumer's residence and establishes certain requirements for advertisers of credit terms.
- The Fair Credit Billing Act (1975), amending the Truth in Lending Act (1968), requires prompt written acknowledgment of consumer billing complaints and investigation of billing errors by creditors. The amendment prohibits creditors from taking actions that

adversely affect the consumer's credit standing until an investigation is completed, and it affords other protection during disputes. The amendment also requires that creditors promptly post payments to the consumer's account and either refund overpayments or credit them to the consumer's account.

- The Fair Credit Reporting Act (1971) protects information collected by consumer reporting agencies such as credit bureaus, medical information companies, and tenant-screening services.
- The Fair Credit and Charge Card Disclosure Act (1988), amending the Truth in Lending Act (1968), requires credit- and charge-card issuers to provide certain disclosures in DIRECT MAIL, telephone, and other solicitations to open-end credit and charge accounts and under other lending circumstances.
- The Equal Credit Opportunity Act (1976) prohibits discrimination on the basis of race, color, religion, national origin, sex, marital status, age, receipt of public assistance, or good-faith exercise of any rights under the CONSUMER CREDIT PROTECTION ACT.
- The FAIR DEBT COLLECTION PRACTICES ACT (1977) prohibits third-party debt collectors from employing deceptive or abusive conduct in the collection of consumer debts incurred for personal, family, or household purposes.
- The ELECTRONIC FUNDS TRANSFER ACT (1978) establishes the rights, liabilities, and responsibilities of participants in electronic fund-transfer systems.
- The Consumer Leasing Act (1976) regulates personal property leases that exceed four months in duration and that are made to consumers for personal, family, or household purposes.
- Magnuson Moss Warranty-FTC Act (1975) authorizes the Federal Trade Commission to develop regulations for written and implied warranties.
- The Hobby Protection Act (1973) outlaws manufacturing or importing imitation numismatic and collectible political items unless they are marked in accordance with regulations prescribed by the Federal Trade Commission.
- The Petroleum Marketing Practices Act authorizes the FTC to prescribe requirements for the calculation and posting of gasoline octane ratings by gasoline distributors and retailers.
- The Postal Reorganization Act of 1970 authorizes the FTC to prosecute any use of the mails to send unordered merchandise as an unfair or deceptive practice in violation of the FTC Act.
- The Comprehensive Smokeless Tobacco Health Education Act of 1986 requires manufacturers, packagers, and importers of smokeless-tobacco products to place one of three statutorily prescribed health-warning labels on product packages and in advertisements. It also prohibits advertising of smokeless tobacco products on radio and television.
- The FEDERAL DEPOSIT INSURANCE CORPORATION Improvement Act of 1991 amends the Federal Deposit Insurance Act to impose certain disclosure requirements on non-federally insured depository institutions and to require that the FTC prescribe the manner and content of those disclosures.
- The Dolphin Protection Consumer Information Act (1990) makes it unlawful under section 5 of the Federal Trade Commission Act for any producer, importer, exporter, distributor, or seller of any tuna product that is exported from or offered for sale in the United States to deceptively claim that its tuna is "dolphin safe."
- The Energy Policy Act of 1992 requires the FTC to issue disclosure rules regarding the energy efficiency of lightbulbs, plumbing fixtures, and other energy-related products.
- The Telephone Disclosure and Dispute Resolution Act of 1992 regulates advertising, operation, and billing for "900 number" services.
- The Telemarketing and Consumer Fraud and Abuse Prevention Act (2001) regulates deceptive TELEMARKETING practices.
- The Violent Crime Control and Enforcement Act of 1994 establishes domestic content requirements for products labeled "Made in America" or "Made in USA."
- The Telecommunications Act of 1996 expands the definition of "pay-per-call service."
- The Home Equity Loan Consumer Protection Act requires creditors to provide certain disclosures for credit plans secured by consumers' dwellings and imposes limitations on such plans.
- The Home Ownership and Equity Protection Act (1994) establishes disclosure requirements and protection from abusive practices in connection with high-cost MORTGAGES.
- The Credit Repair Organizations Act (1996) prohibits untrue or misleading representations regarding "credit repair" services.
- The Children's Online Privacy Protection Act (1998) provides protection of information from children collected online.
- The Identity Theft Assumption and Deterrence Act of 1998 directs the FTC to create a central clearinghouse for identity-theft complaints.
- The Gramm-Leach-Billey Act requires the FTC and other agencies to issue regulations ensuring that financial institutions protect the PRIVACY of consumers' personal financial information.

Further reading

Federal Trade Commission website. Available on-line. URL: www.ftc.gov; Folsom, Ralph H., and Michael Gordon. *International Business Transactions*, 5th ed. Eagan, Minn.: West Law, 2002.

fiduciary duties

Fiduciaries are people and businesses that by law owe others a high duty of care when acting on their behalf.

Corporate officers are fiduciaries for SHAREHOLDERS; trustees are fiduciaries for TRUST beneficiaries; executors are fiduciaries for estates and heirs; conservators and guardians are fiduciaries for wards. Fiduciaries can be individuals or CORPORATIONS, and sometimes cofiduciaries are both. They owe duties of loyalty, prudent INVESTMENT, disclosure, accounting, and integrity to those whom they benefit. Unless specifically authorized, for example, fiduciaries should not undertake speculative investments with other people's money.

The powers of fiduciaries are controlled by the legal documents creating the fiduciary relationship and by statutory law. Other commonly existing fiduciary relationships include attorneys and their clients, stockbrokers and their customers, and persons acting for others under powers of attorney.

Further reading
Mennell, Robert L. *Wills and Trusts in a Nutshell*. Eagan, Minn.: West Group, 1994.

financial accounting (double-entry accounting)
Financial accounting, also called double-entry accounting, is the system of collecting, processing, and periodically reporting a firm's transactions. First described in 1494 by a Franciscan monk, Fra Luca Pacioli, double-entry accounting was largely an oral tradition which, for centuries, was passed down through the generations. In the 20th century, two organizations, the FINANCIAL ACCOUNTING STANDARDS BOARD (FASB) and the AMERICAN INSTITUTE OF CERTIFIED PUBLIC ACCOUNTANTS (AICPA), were instrumental in codifying the accounting principles that had become widely accepted and generally agreed upon over time. No longer an oral tradition, this comprehensive set of published rules and methods is now referred to as GENERALLY ACCEPTED ACCOUNTING PRINCIPLES (GAAP). The establishment of GAAP has served to standardize the practice of accounting among all firms and organizations, and the federal government, most notably the INTERNAL REVENUE SERVICE (IRS) and the SECURITIES AND EXCHANGE COMMISSION (SEC), requires that all published accounting information be collected, processed, and reported in accordance with GAAP.

Accounting is often called double-entry accounting because of the nature of the data (a firm's transactions) that are collected and processed in an accounting system. Since a transaction is an exchange of equal-valued RESOURCES between two parties, a double entry is required to record a transaction: one entry recording what is received in the transaction and one entry recording what is given up. The first entry is the debit (abbreviated *dr.* from the Latin *debere,* meaning "left") and the second entry, which is indented to the right, is the credit (abbreviated *cr.* from the Latin *credere* meaning "right"). Because equal-valued resources are exchanged in a transaction, the dollar amount of the debit entries must equal the dollar amount of the credit entries.

While account names have evolved over time and new accounting principles have been added to comply with governmental and tax regulations, the practice of accounting today is in many ways much the same as what was developed over 500 years ago.

See also DEBIT, CREDIT; INCOME STATEMENT, GROSS MARGIN.

Financial Accounting Standards Board
The Financial Accounting Standards Board's mission is "to establish and improve standards of FINANCIAL ACCOUNTING and reporting for the guidance and education of the public, including issuers, auditors, and users of financial information." It serves the "investing public through transparent information resulting from high-quality financial reporting standards, developed in an independent, private sector, open due process."

Since 1973 the Financial Accounting Standards Board (FASB) has been the designated organization in the private sector for establishing standards of financial accounting and reporting that govern the preparation of financial reports. The FASB is officially recognized as authoritative by the SECURITIES AND EXCHANGE COMMISSION and the AMERICAN INSTITUTE OF CERTIFIED PUBLIC ACCOUNTANTS.

In further explaining its mission, the FASB states that "accounting standards are essential to the efficient functioning of the economy because decisions about the allocation of resources rely heavily on credible, concise, and understandable financial information. Financial information about the operations and financial position of individual entities also is used by the public in making various other kinds of decisions."

Further reading
Rutgers Accounting Web; http://accounting.rutgers.edu/raw/fasb/main.html; http://accounting.rutgers.edu/raw/fasb/facts/fasfact1.html.

financial instrument
Financial instrument is a broadly used term to refer to almost any obligation of one party to give financial ASSETS to another. There are three types of financial instruments, the first of which is cash. The second type is any agreement that is settled only with the payment of a financial instrument (usually cash); this would make LOANS, BONDS, notes, derivatives, and receivables all financial instruments. The third type of financial instrument is EQUITY securities, which represent ownership in a company; this makes COMMON STOCK and preferred stock in a company financial instruments. Equity securities give owners residual rights (remaining assets after all liabilities have been satisfied) in the company and the right to share the company's PROFITS.

CONTRACTS between two parties that are not settled with financial instruments (including cash) are not themselves financial instruments. For example, contracts to buy a piece of real estate, equipment, or inventory or to deliver services are not financial instruments.

Many financial instruments are negotiable. There are dozens of types of negotiable financial instruments, and more are created every day as others pass off the scene. Some of the more common type of NEGOTIABLE INSTRUMENTS would be COMMERCIAL PAPER, bonds, corporate debt securities, banker acceptances, treasury bills, repurchase agreements, and some PROMISSORY NOTES.

These financial instruments are created in a primary market and traded in a secondary market. The primary market consists of INVESTMENT banks that enter into the agreements with the issuing companies and then sell a portion of the negotiable instruments to other investors who are free to trade the instruments with others; this is the secondary market. Thus an investment bank may buy all the new stock issued by a company and then sell it to investors. When these investors then sell, these are secondary-market transactions.

See also U.S. TREASURY SECURITIES.

financial intermediaries

Financial intermediaries are institutions that take funds saved by households and in turn make LOANS to others. The process of taking savings and providing funds to borrowers is called intermediation, or indirect finance. While most people think of banks as financial intermediaries, in the United States, SAVINGS AND LOAN ASSOCIATIONS, mutual INSURANCE companies, CREDIT UNIONS, pension funds, finance companies, MUTUAL FUNDS, and money market funds all function as financial intermediaries.

Generally financial intermediaries specialize in particular types of lending practices and provide services for certain segments of the overall market. For example, savings and loan associations came into existence to provide lending to consumers for the purpose of building or purchasing homes. Early savings and loan organizations (many were mutual organizations rather than for-PROFIT businesses) were established by groups of immigrant workers who brought together their savings, which were then loaned to other members of their group. Until the 1980s savings and loan crisis (see RESOLUTION TRUST CORPORATION), one group of German Americans in Cincinnati, Ohio, ran their savings and loan out of a bar where they and their ancestors had socialized for almost 100 years.

Financial intermediaries perform the following basic services.

- denomination divisibility: providing lending and savings options for different dollar amounts
- maturity flexibility: providing lending and savings options for different time periods

- credit RISK diversification: reducing risk through lending to multiple borrowers
- liquidity: providing access to funds when needed by depositors

Financial intermediaries pool the funds of many small savers and make loans in varying amounts to borrowers. This is preferable to the alternative, where a borrower would have to find and negotiate with tens or hundreds of savers in order to get sufficient funds. Financial intermediaries create securities with a wide range of maturities, from overnight to 50 years and also reduce RISK through diversification. Lending money to one person results in concentrated risk—that is, it depends on the repayment of one borrower. Financial intermediaries make loans to many borrowers, spreading the risk of DEFAULT among many loans and thereby reducing risk through diversification. Intermediaries also provide liquidity, facilitating the conversion of financial ASSETS into money.

In the 1990s many Americans and American businesses decreased their use of financial intermediaries. With greater information obtained through INTERNET technology, more lenders and borrowers interacted directly with each other, with individuals buying shares of stock, businesses purchasing COMMERCIAL PAPER issued by CORPORATIONS, or direct placement of tax-exempt BONDS by state agencies. Nevertheless, financial intermediaries provide three basic benefits over direct borrowing and INVESTMENT: ECONOMIES OF SCALE, reduced transaction costs, and information.

Because they handle a large volume of transactions, financial intermediaries can spread the fixed costs and start-up COSTS associated with lending. With their experience in lending, financial intermediaries lower the cost of searching and evaluating information associated with saving and lending actions. Most importantly, financial intermediaries generally have better knowledge of credit criteria and risk associated with particular financial instruments and borrowers.

See also FIVE CS OF CREDIT.

Further reading
Kidwell, David S., Richard L. Peterson, and David W. Blackwell. *Financial Institutions, Markets, and Money,* 7th ed. Fort Worth: Dryden Press, 2000.

Financial Planning Association

The Financial Planning Association (FPA) is an organization that trains and certifies financial planners. Financial planning is the process of establishing personal financial goals and allocating resources to obtain those goals. The FPA was created in 2000 through a merger of the Institute of Certified Financial Planners and the International Association for Financial Planning.

The FPA and its earlier organizations grew rapidly in the 1980s and 1990s due to changes in business pensions and changes in STOCK MARKET trading. Until the 1980s, most corporations in the United States provided defined-benefit pensions for their employees (see RETIREMENT PLAN). The employer put aside funds in a TRUST account to meet future obligations to retirees based on a percentage of what salary employees were receiving when they retired. Depending on how much the trust fund earned, a company could have either an over-funded pension plan or unfunded pension liabilities.

With the advent of 401(K) PLANS, employers shifted the RISK associated with pension LIABILITY to employees. The 401(k)s, along with similar 403b and 457 plans, allow employees to contribute a portion of their salary into a tax-deferred retirement fund. The money can be invested by the employee in MUTUAL FUNDS, individual stocks, and other INVESTMENT options. The employee's pension benefits are determined by how well their investments do and are not the responsibility of the employer.

The new retirement plans led to tremendous growth in the DEMAND for and SUPPLY of financial planners. Virtually every personal finance-related salesperson, from INSURANCE representative to stockbroker, began to call himself a financial planner. Since a planner's INCOME depended on how many policies or stock trades he or she made, it often led to a CONFLICT OF INTEREST when the best objective advice did not generate sales commissions.

The Financial Planning Association's major role is to certify financial planners. Members must pass the FPA examination and acquire three to five years of financial planning–related experience to become a Certified Financial Planner (CFP). In addition, members ascribe to the FPA code of ethics and obtain a minimum of 30 hours of continuing education every two years.

The second factor contributing to the rapid expansion in the financial-planning industry was the advent of discount stock-brokerage firms. Pioneered by Charles Schwab Company, discount-brokerage firms allow individuals to trade stocks without paying huge commissions to full-service brokerages. Today individuals can buy or sell stock for $10 per trade or less, but in the 1980s trades often cost $100 to $200 each and had to be conducted through a full-service broker. Brokers acted as financial planners for people with investment funds, recommending strategies and appraising risks for investors. Discount brokers offer fewer financial planning services creating a need for, and opportunity for professional financial planners.

The Financial Planning Association states the following as their "core values."

- competence
- integrity
- relationships
- stewardship

The objectives of the FPA are

- Unify the voice, focus and resources of the financial planning community.
- Grow the organization by bringing together those who champion the financial planning process.
- Cultivate the body of knowledge of financial planning.
- Advance brand awareness for professional financial planners, building the CFP credential as the hallmark brand.
- Define and effectively communicate a common understanding of the discipline of personal financial planning and the benefits of its use.
- Facilitate the success of our members.

Further reading
Financial Planning Association website. Available on-line. URL: www.fpanet.org.

financial ratios
FINANCIAL STATEMENTS are analyzed by MANAGEMENT and investors to predict and plan for the future. Financial ratios, fractions that show relationships between accounts found on the financial statements, are the tools used in financial-statement analysis. Some ratios are useful in the analysis of a single firm, while other ratios have meaning only when compared to those of other firms or to industry averages. A few of the more common financial ratios follow.

A firm's credit worthiness—that is, its ability to service its debt on a timely basis—can be determined by the current ratio and the acid-test ratio. A rough measure of a firm's ability to pay its debt on time is the current ratio: current ASSETS divided by current liabilities (CA/CL). The numerator is the firm's current assets and the denominator is the firm's current liabilities (current debt). The current assets are the firm's resources it will use to pay its current debts. If the current assets exceed the current liabilities, the current ratio will have a value greater than 1, an indicator that there are sufficient current assets to pay the current liabilities. Thus current ratios greater than 1 indicate that a firm can take on more debt. If the current assets are equal to the current liabilities, the current ratio will have a value of 1. All of the firm's current assets are used to cover (pay) the current liabilities, and the firm has no excess assets with which to assume additional debt. If the current assets are less than the current liabilities, the current ratio will have a value less than 1, and the firm is having problems paying its current debt. In fact, a current ratio less than 1 is indicative of a firm that is slow in paying its bills.

Working CAPITAL is the current assets of a firm: cash, short-term investments, ACCOUNTS RECEIVABLE, and inventories. Net working capital (CA–CL) is a measure of a firm's liquidity, the amount of current assets remaining after the current debt of the firm is paid. The current ratio (CA/CL) can be used to compare net working capital among firms.

Included in a firm's current assets are merchandise inventories, but in reality inventories aren't very liquid. If a buyer is found, the sale may be a sale on credit, in which case no monies are currently received. Many creditors understand the lack of liquidity associated with inventories, and as a result they prefer using the acid-test (quick) ratio, in which inventories are not included with the current assets of the firm: (CA–inventories)/CL. Because inventories are subtracted from the current assets, the acid-test numerator is smaller than the one used in the current ratio. This causes the acid-test ratio to be a stricter measure of the debt worthiness of a firm; the acid-test ratio is more commonly than the current ratio for this purpose.

The debt ratio (total liabilities/total assets) is an indicator of a firm's capital structure. For example, a debt ratio of 60 percent indicates that debt (liabilities) comprises 60 percent of a firm's capital and EQUITY (stocks) comprises 40 percent.

The days' sales outstanding (DSO) ratio (accounts receivable/average sales per day) analyzes a firm's accounts receivable by determining its average collection period, the average number of days a firm waits after making a credit sale before receiving cash. The number of days' sales tied up in accounts receivable is compared with that of other firms or with industry averages to determine how well a firm manages its investment in accounts receivable.

The asset-turnover ratio (sales/total assets) measures a firm's sales volume relative to its INVESTMENT in total assets. For example, a firm with an asset-turnover ratio of 1.4 times operating in an industry with an industry average of 1.7 times is not generating sufficient sales volume, given its investment in total assets.

The price/earnings (P/E) ratio (price per share/earnings per share) indicates how much investors are willing to pay per dollar of current earnings. When compared to industry averages, a low P/E ratio generally indicates that investors view the firm as being riskier than other firms in its industry. A high P/E ratio relative to the industry average generally indicates that investors view this firm as having a greater potential for growth and, therefore, less riskier.

PROFIT margin is the relationship between a firm's net INCOME and its sales volume, indicated by the profit-margin ratio (net income/sales). This ratio measures a firm's income per dollar of sales. A firm's relative profitability can be determined by comparing its profit margin ratio with that for the industry.

Return on equity (ROE), the ratio of net income to common equity, measures the rate of return earned by the common stockholders' investment in a firm. The ROE ratio is net income/total common equity. In order for a firm to attract the interest of investors and thus retain their investment in the firm, its ROE must be greater than or equal to its industry average. A firm with a low ROE as compared to its industry average will be viewed by investors as an unattractive investment, and investors will be attracted to those firms with greater earnings potential.

Financial Stability Institute See BANK OF INTERNATIONAL SETTLEMENTS.

financial statements

FINANCIAL ACCOUNTING is the system of collecting, processing, and periodically reporting a firm's financial information; thus, its ultimate purpose is the dissemination of a firm's financial data. This is accomplished by the publication of financial statements, all of which must be constructed in accordance with GENERALLY ACCEPTED ACCOUNTING PRINCIPLES (GAAP). The more common financial statements are the INCOME STATEMENT, the statement of OWNER'S EQUITY, the BALANCE SHEET, and the statement of cash flows.

The income statement measures the performance and success (or lack thereof) of a firm for a specific period of time, usually a year. When the accounting period coincides with the calendar year (January 1–December 31), the firm is said to be reporting on a calendar-year basis. If the accounting period is any other 12-month period (say, July 1–June 30), the firm is reporting on a FISCAL YEAR basis. The equation upon which the income statement is based is *revenues – expenses = net income*. Revenues are resources flowing into the firm from the sale of goods and/or services. Expenses, necessarily incurred in the process of earning revenue, are resources flowing out of the firm. The difference between revenues and expenses is "the bottom line"—i.e, net INCOME. Whether the firm has made a PROFIT or a loss for the period being reported, the bottom line is always labeled "net income."

The statement of owner's (or owners') equity illustrates the changes that occurred in owner's equity during the accounting period being reported. Positive net income and additional investment by the owner are the primary factors that increase owner's equity. Negative net income and withdrawals will decrease owner's equity.

The balance sheet measures the assets, liabilities, and owner's equity of the firm at a point in time that is the last day of the accounting period. The equation on which the balance sheet is based is *assets = liabilities + owner's equity*. Assets are resources owned by the firm; they are necessary for the generation of revenue. Liabilities are the firm's debts; they are one major source of CAPITAL for the firm. Equity is the firm's ownership and forms the other major source of capital for the firm. The right side of the balance-sheet equation represents the sources of capital; the left side, the uses of that capital. Thus, the equation must always be in balance. The format for the balance sheet is identical to the balance sheet equation: assets on the left side of the balance sheet, liabilities and equity on the right side. Just as the equation is always in balance, the two sides of the balance sheet are also always in balance.

Important for effective liquidity management, the statement of cash flows details the cash flowing into and out of the firm for the accounting period being reported. This is not the same as an income statement. The income statement, constructed on the ACCRUAL BASIS as required by GAAP, includes more than just cash flows; it also contains accruals (such as revenues earned but not yet received and expenses incurred but not yet paid). The income statement also contains many non-cash expenses such as DEPRECIATION, DEPLETION, AMORTIZATION. The statement of cash flows makes adjustments for accruals and noncash expenses to give a true picture of a firm's actual flows of cash.

The SECURITIES AND EXCHANGE COMMISSION requires CORPORATIONS whose stocks are publicly traded to publish their financial statements at least annually. To meet this requirement, a corporation will group these financial statements and others with reports from management and the BOARD OF DIRECTORS to form the ANNUAL REPORT.

first in, first out; last in, first out

First in, first out (FIFO) and last in, first out (LIFO) are inventory-costing methods. Inventory costing methods are used to assign values to a firm's ending inventory and to COST OF GOODS SOLD. For tax purposes, a firm will use the inventory-costing method that maximizes its cost of goods sold and minimizes the value of its ending inventory. When unit costs are rising, as is normally experienced with INFLATION, LIFO is the inventory costing method of choice.

To illustrate the effects of FIFO and LIFO, assume the following inventory data where unit costs are rising:

Jan. 1	Beginning inventory	
	100 units @ $10 each	$1000
Jan. 12	Inventory purchase	
	100 units @ $12 each	$1200
Jan. 23	Sale 150 units	

For the month of January, what is the firm's cost of goods sold? What is the value of the ending inventory at the end of the month? To answer these questions, the firm must first select an inventory-costing method.

Using FIFO, cost of goods sold and the value of ending inventory are determined as follows:

Beginning inventory	
100 units @ $10 each	$1000
+ Purchases	
100 units @ $12 each	1200
Goods available for sale	
200 units	$2200

Units sold	
100 units @ $10	$1000
50 units @ $12	600

Cost of Goods Sold	
150 units	**$1600**

Ending inventory	
50 units @ $12 each	$600

Using LIFO, cost of goods sold and the value of ending inventory are determined as follows:

Beginning inventory	
100 units @ $10 each	$1000
+ Purchases	
100 units @ $12 each	1200
Goods available for sale	
200 units	$2200
Units sold	
100 units @ 12	$1200
50 units @ $10	500

Cost of Goods Sold	
150 units	**$1700**
Ending inventory	
50 units @ $10 each	$500

Using FIFO, cost of goods sold is $1,600; using LIFO, $1,700. In order to maximize cost of goods sold and, in turn, reduce gross margin and taxable INCOME, a PROFIT-maximizing firm uses LIFO when unit costs are rising.

When unit costs are falling over time, FIFO is the inventory-costing method that maximizes the cost of goods sold.

first-mover advantage (first-to-market)

First-mover advantage, also called first-to-market, is the benefit a company gains by being first to market with a new PRODUCT or service. First-mover advantage is part of MARKETING STRATEGY—the coordination of product, pricing, promotion, and distribution decisions for each target market.

In the late 1990s many of the frenetic marketing efforts of DOT-COMS were based on the idea of first-mover advantage. The first company offering a new INTERNET product or service gained significant publicity, attracted additional financial support, and created a BARRIER TO ENTRY for other potential competitors. As Latin American Internet expert Lucas Graves states, "It's absolutely true that nothing can make up for first-mover-advantage, and the proof is that Yahoo! remains where it is today and eBay remains where it is, despite the entry of many other companies into those vertical categories."

First-mover advantage is based on attracting consumer innovators—customers who purchase a product as soon as it reaches the market. Often people are consumer innovators in specific categories of products. Serious photographers try out the latest equipment, committed golfers are always looking for something new, and fashion-conscious consumers keep abreast of the latest styles. With today's Internet communications technology, consumer innovators quickly evaluate and recommend or reject products. Marketers recognize that word-of-mouth referrals from consumer innovators can ensure the success of their new product.

First-mover advantage is offset by the potential for mistakes from rushing a product or concept to the marketplace. An old saying in marketing is, "You only have one chance to make a first impression." Many dot-coms and other companies died quickly when the promised benefits of their new products did not meet consumer expectations.

Further reading

Hemlock, Dorren. "Mass Production Hits the Web," *Sun-Sentinel*, December 3, 1999.

fiscal policy

Fiscal policy is the use of the federal tax and spending process to influence the level of economic activity. In its simplest form, fiscal policy involves changing taxes and/or government spending in order to expand or contract aggregate DEMAND towards a targeted level of equilibrium national INCOME. Contractionary fiscal policy dictates a decrease in spending and/or an increase in taxes in order to reduce economic activity. Expansionary fiscal policy is the opposite, an increase in spending and/or a decrease in taxes in order to stimulate economic activity.

In the United States, fiscal policy became an accepted, important part of macroeconomic policy during the GREAT DEPRESSION. In the absence of private CONSUMPTION spending and business INVESTMENT, government spending was used as an alternative source of demand. As advocated by the British economist John Maynard Keynes, President Franklin Roosevelt's "New Deal" administration greatly expanded government spending through programs such as the CIVILIAN CONSERVATION CORPS and the WORKS PROGRESS ADMINISTRATION. Many of today's state parks and older government buildings were created during the Depression.

When estimating the impact of fiscal policy, economists consider how the policy is financed and the indirect impacts of the fiscal-policy measure. For example, if an increase in government spending is financed by an increase in taxes, the increase in government spending will be largely offset by a decrease in consumption spending. An increase in government spending financed through borrowing will have a larger immediate impact on the economy but will also likely increase INTEREST RATES due to the government's increased demand for funds. This, in turn, will likely increase interest rates, reducing consumption spending and private investment. Economists call this the crowding-out effect.

Many economists support the use of discretionary fiscal policy along with a consistent MONETARY POLICY to stabilize the overall economy. Other economists argue the time lag between the implementation of fiscal-policy measures and their impact causes these efforts to exacerbate rather than mitigate peaks and troughs in BUSINESS CYCLES.

In addition to discretionary fiscal policy, the U.S. political economic system also includes AUTOMATIC STABILIZERS. During periods of economic expansion, progressive tax rates—tax rates that increase as income increases—automatically reduce consumers' incomes, reducing their spending and slowing the rate of growth in aggregate demand. During periods of economic contraction, UNEMPLOYMENT and WELFARE benefits offset some of the loss of income and spending when workers lose their jobs. These are referred to by economists as automatic stabilizers.

In the U.S. political system, the use of fiscal policy during periods of economic decline to stimulate the economy is widely accepted. The logical corollary is to advocate a decrease in government spending and/or an increase in taxes during periods of an inflationary, full-employment economy. Few politicians want to run for reelection after having increased taxes or to cut voters' favorite government programs, which is why monetary policy is often needed to counterbalance excessively expansionary fiscal policy.

fiscal year

In the United States most CORPORATIONS are legally required to report the results of their business activities at least once a year. In their initial INCORPORATION documents, companies define when their business year starts and ends; this is their fiscal year. Some retail businesses end their business year at the end of January, corresponding to the end of the holiday sales season. Companies usually also conduct inventories at the end of each fiscal year.

The U.S. government begins their fiscal year on October 1. Many U.S. agencies engage in a flurry of PURCHASING just before the end of the government's fiscal year, and frequently Congress and the executive branch will fail to pass spending legislation in time for the beginning of the next fiscal year. In those years government agencies will be allocated funds based on the previous fiscal year's budget. State governments also have varying fiscal years, with many states starting new budget years in July.

In recent years STOCK MARKET watchers have closely scrutinized the quarterly earnings reports of leading companies. The release of quarterly earnings statements are tied to corporations' fiscal years, which is why the statements do not all appear at the same time. When a leading company in any industry reports unexpectedly high or low earnings, the stocks of other companies in the same industry are usually affected by the one company's report.

five Cs of credit

The five Cs of credit are character, capacity, CAPITAL, collateral, and conditions. To analyze the risk of DEFAULT by a borrower, lenders typically evaluate a customer's five Cs. *Character* refers to a borrower's integrity, credit history, and past relationships with the lender. Credit history is an important determinant in predicting whether a borrower will default or not. In the United States, three major CREDIT-REPORTING SERVICES provide lenders with information about customers' past credit experiences. *Capacity* is the borrower's ability to pay off the loan requested. Lenders often use ratios of loan payment to monthly INCOME and total monthly payments to income in evaluating a borrower's ability to pay.

Capital is a borrower's net worth or WEALTH, some of which may be offered as collateral against a loan. *Collateral* is comprised of ASSETS that the lender could seize and sell if the borrower defaulted on the loan. *Conditions* refer to ECONOMIC CONDITIONS. Lenders know from experience that borrowers' ability and likelihood of paying off LOANS are influenced by changes in the economy. U.S. banking institutions are regulated by state banking commissions or the FEDERAL RESERVE SYSTEM. During declining economic conditions, regulatory authorities often examine more closely how lenders apply the five Cs of credit in making loan decisions.

By the nature of their business, banks and other lending institutions consider borrowers their most important customers. Generally lenders can attract deposits or capital by offering competitive INTEREST RATES. Finding good borrowers is more difficult. Lenders make a PROFIT by the spread, the difference between the cost of funds and the rate being received for LOANS or INVESTMENTS. Because lenders are RISK-averse, borrowers whose five Cs indicate a higher potential for default are charged higher interest rates, compensating lenders for the higher percentage of defaults. During the 1990s many U.S. lending institutions made money through credit-card lending to low-quality customers at very high interest rates.

Further reading

Kidwell, David S., Richard L. Peterson, and David W. Blackwell. *Financial Institutions, Markets and Money,* 7th ed. Fort Worth: Dryden Press, 1997.

flowchart

A flowchart is a graphic illustration of the steps to follow in the process of production. Flowcharts are important in understanding a project and the different sequences to follow. They are also important for decision making, helping people better understand a project, the possible outcomes, and possible solutions to consider.

A flowchart consists of various standard-shaped boxes, circles, or other shapes that are interconnected by flow lines. The flow lines have arrows indicating the direction of flow between the boxes, and if flow continues elsewhere, connector lines show this. Flowcharts are drawn on white, unlined paper on one side only.

Some of the standard flowchart symbols include

- circles representing the on-page connector (used to connect remote parts of the flowchart to one another)
- rectangles representing processing or activities (each activity is represented by a separate rectangle)
- diamond shapes used to represent decisions or questions
- rounded-edge rectangles representing the beginning and terminal activities (start or end)

Constructing a flowchart involves a series of steps, the first of which is determining the process and the purpose of the diagram. The next step is determining who will work in constructing the flowchart and how accurate and reliable the information available is, an important consideration. Defining the relationship between each of the diagrams and how they are connected is a third step.

Flowcharts are convenient because they are easy to read and understand. Flowcharting in business is useful because it helps a business consider all its possibilities and all the outcomes of the decision they might or might not make. Flowcharts are often created by teams within an organization to coordinate new projects.

Further reading

Chaneski, Wayne S. "Process Flow Chart: A Tool for Streamlining Operation," *Modern Machine Shop* 72 (March 2000): 52.

flow of funds

The term *flow of funds* has both business and economic meanings. In business, flow of funds refers to a statement of the sources and application of funds in the organization. In this context it is often referred to as a funds-flow statement or cash-flow statement. More often flow of funds refers to data showing the movement of savings and the sources and uses of funds through the economy.

Since 1955 the FEDERAL RESERVE SYSTEM has published quarterly and annual data on flow-of-funds accounts. These data measure the financial flows across sectors of the economy, tracking funds as they move from those sectors that serve as sources of CAPITAL through FINANCIAL INTERMEDIARIES (such as banks, MUTUAL FUNDS, and pension funds) to sectors that use the capital to acquire productive and financial ASSETS.

The flow-of-funds accounts are useful in identifying economic trends. They show, for example, how the growth of debt for each sector changes in the sources of household credit as well as the development of new FINANCIAL INSTRUMENTS for providing credit. In recent years flow-of-funds data have been used to document the widely discussed "WEALTH effect"—the effect of change in households' net worth on savings and CONSUMPTION decisions. The data are also used to estimate the impact of changing credit conditions on output and spending in the economy.

The Federal Reserve's flow-of-funds accounting system tracks over 40 types of financial instruments, including savings accounts, MORTGAGES, corporate BONDS, STOCK MARKET shares, mutual fund shares, and bank LOANS. Financial transactions are recorded for 30 economic sectors, including nonfinancial sectors (households, nonprofit organizations, businesses, and government) and financial sectors (banks, INSURANCE companies, pension funds, and other financial intermediaries). In flow-of-funds accounting, total sources of funds must equal total uses of funds. Analysis of the data allows macroeconomic forecasters to estimate the impact of policy measures and project the impact of changing market conditions on output and INCOME in the economy.

Further reading
Teplin, Albert M. "The U.S. Flow of Funds Accounts and Their Uses." *Federal Reserve Bulletin,* July 2001, p. 431.

FOB   See FREE ON BOARD.

focus groups
Focus groups are small groups of individuals brought together by market researchers to discuss a particular topic. Most focus groups include 8–12 people and a moderator. Individuals are chosen based on interest or involvement with the subject to be discussed and are often paid $50–$100 to participate in the session. A typical focus group will last 1–2 hours, be taped for later detailed review, and observed by market researchers and the client through a one-way mirror.

Focus groups are often used during the exploratory stage of the MARKET RESEARCH process to provide quick, in-depth information about people's attitudes and motivations. They are often used to screen ADVERTISING designs, learn about the interests and values of hard-to-research market segments, provide feedback during NEW PRODUCT DEVELOPMENT, and help structure market-research SURVEYS. Marketers recognize they are often "too close" to a particular project or PRODUCT to be objective about it. Focus groups can be used to get consumers' opinions before a product is launched, helping to avoid costly marketing failures.

Focus groups are vulnerable to a variety of problems. First, they only include a small number of participants and therefore may not be representative of the ideas and opinions of the larger target market. Second, the moderator must be chosen carefully, since his or her role is critical in successfully probing participants' feelings and controlling group dynamics. Third, critics contend focus groups tend to result in people saying what they think the sponsor wants to hear rather than honest opinions. Finally, there are "professional" focus groupers, people who participate in numerous studies and tend to dominate group discussion.

Further reading
Boone, Louis E., and David Kurtz. *Contemporary Marketing,* 10th ed. Fort Worth, Tex.: Dryden Press, 2001.

Food and Drug Administration
The U.S. Food and Drug Administration (FDA) is a federal agency charged to protect public health. The agency, created by the 1906 Food and Drugs Act, defines its mission as

1. To promote the public health by promptly and efficiently reviewing clinical research and taking appropriate action on the marketing of regulated products in a timely manner;
2. With respect to such products, protect the public health by ensuring that foods are safe, wholesome, sanitary, and properly labeled;
3. Participate through appropriate processes with the representatives of other countries to reduce the burden of regulation, harmonize requirements, and achieve appropriate reciprocal arrangements.

The original act prohibited interstate commerce in misbranded and adulterated foods, drinks, and drugs; the Meat Inspection Act was passed the same day as the Food and Drugs Act. The historian James Harvey Young describes the evolution of pure-food regulations as a combination of seven Cs: change, complexity, COMPETITION, crusading, coalescence, compromise, and catastrophe.

Change refers to the rapid industrialization in the United States during the late 1800s, including discoveries in chemistry leading to synthetic medicines and changes in markets as consumers moved away from the village merchants they knew and trusted for pure food. *Complexity* refers to the problem of how the federal government should address the problems of deceptions and hazards in food and drugs. Some products were regulated under individual laws, but how could the government address the many products that existed and the continuing flow of new products coming into the market?

Competition refers to the reality at the time that adulterated food could be produced and sold more cheaply than healthier and safer foods. With lower prices, questionable and unsafe foods were competing with reputable food makers, and an uninformed public had little basis for judging the difference in quality. Throughout the 1890s, business groups pressured Congress for protection. Many state laws were enacted, but they were often contradictory, creating inefficiency for national producers.

The fourth C, *crusading,* evolved when animal-rights groups, the National Consumer League, and the General Federation of Women's Clubs began pushing for tougher food-and-drug safety laws and the U.S. Department of Agriculture (USDA) began to oversee food-adulteration practices. Initially food adulteration was perceived as a harmless FRAUD, but with USDA research, the threat to consumers' health was explored and articulated. Harvey Wiley, a chemist and physician who became the chief chemist for the USDA, joined forces with other agricultural groups, medical professionals, and sympathetic journalists, creating the fifth C, a *coalescence* of forces for reform. *Compromise* recognized the many different groups and interests among government, business, and consumer interests. Wiley organized three National Pure Food and Drug Congresses between 1898 and 1900 to work out agreements.

As James Harvey Young states, "In the end it took the seventh 'C,' *catastrophe*, to fuel the final compromise and get the law enacted." Investigations showing that "embalmed beef" had been shipped to troops in the Spanish-American war and the publication of Upton Sinclair's *The Jungle,* describing filthy conditions in meat-packing plants, pressured politicians into passing the Food and Drug Act.

Since the act's passage, numerous responsibilities have been assigned to the Food and Drug Administration, including medical labeling, narcotic-substance control, cosmetic and therapeutic device supervision, ADVERTISING of FDA-regulated products, hazardous-substance labeling, sanitation programs, and many others. In 1997 Congress pressured the FDA to speed up its drug-review process. Consumers and pharmaceutical industry representatives pointed to European drug-review processes, which often took one or two years less than the FDA's system, allowing new therapies to be available sooner.

Recent "hot topics" confronting the FDA include buying medicines over the INTERNET, mad-cow disease, LASIK surgery, and radiation of foods.

Further reading

Food and Drug Administration website. Available on-line. URL: www.fda.gov; Young, James Harvey. *"The Long Struggle for the 1906 Law."* Available on-line. URL: www.cfsan.fda.gov/~lrd.history2.html.

forced-ranking systems (forced distributions, "rank and yank")

Forced-ranking systems are employee performance review systems where workers within groups or departments are rated best to worst with the lowest ranked workers either terminated or considered for termination. Also called forced distributions or "rank and yank," forced-ranking systems were popular in the 1990s among many major companies including General Electric, Cisco Systems, Ford, Microsoft and Intel. Even the infamous Enron Corporation had a forced-ranking system. At Enron workers rated "needs improvement" meant "you have one leg

hanging out the window," while "there are issues associated with an employee" meant "you're gone."

Ford's system probably received the most negative publicity and was dropped after numerous employee complaints and lawsuits. The most common criticism has been that forced-ranking systems are biased, often using subjective criteria and favoring younger and majority employees over minorities. These systems can also be demoralizing, especially when their criteria are not well understood. Another criticism is that forced ranking might make a mediocre employee in a poorly performing unit look good and penalize a strong performing employee in an exceptional unit.

Many senior managers like forced-ranking systems. Legendary General Electric CEO Jack Welch Jr. touted the system as the best way to eliminate the least productive employees. Welch is quoted as saying, "A company that bets its future on its people must remove that lower 10 percent, and keep removing it every year—always raising the bar of performance and increasing the quality of its LEADERSHIP."

An Intel spokesperson says of forced ranking systems, "It rewards good performance, not seniority, not cronyism, not teacher's pets. We think it is a pretty accurate reflection of people's performance."

However, as Bonnie Kabin, a workforce-training consultant, notes, "What happens with forced distribution is that there is no place to hide. If your performance is poor, a manager is forced to make a decision." Often managers, especially first-line supervisors, are reticent to make critical evaluations and decisions. Called the "halo effect," or "Lake Wobegon" evaluations, everyone is rated above average.

See also 360-DEGREE FEEDBACK.

Further reading

Bruman, John. "Performance Reviews: Perilous Curves Ahead." Available on-line. URL: http://deming/eng.clemson.edu/pub/den/archive/2001.05/msg00114.html; Johnston, Mark, Neil M. Ford, Greg W. Marshall, Orville C. Walker, and Gilbert A. Churchill. *Sales Force Management,* 6th ed. Boston: McGraw-Hill/Irwin, 2002.

Foreign Corrupt Practices Act

The Foreign Corrupt Practices Act (FCPA, 1977) makes it illegal for any U.S. firm to offer, promise, or make payments or gifts of anything of value to foreign officials. The FCPA was a response to a 1970s investigation documenting that over 400 American companies had given bribes or made otherwise questionable payments in excess of $300 million to foreign officials for the purpose of obtaining or keeping business. The act is one of the toughest anti-BRIBERY laws among trading countries in the world.

The FCPA, technically an amendment to the Securities and Exchange Act of 1934, applies to issuers of registered securities in the United States and "domestic concerns" (any individual who is a citizen, national, or resident of the United States). Payments are prohibited if the person making the payment knows or should know that some or all of the funds will be used to influence government decisions. The FCPA prohibits payments to foreign political parties and candidates as well as officials. Payments to foreign companies and executives are not prohibited unless it is known or should be known that the payments will be distributed to government officials.

As amended in 1988, the FCPA allows "facilitating payments" for "routine governmental action." This may include payments for obtaining permits, licenses, or other official documents; processing of governmental papers; providing public services; and scheduling inspections.

As documented in the investigation, many U.S. companies hid bribes for foreign government officials, accounting for these payments as commissions or payments rendered for professional services. As part of the FCPA, U.S. firms engaged in international trade are subject to periodic disclosure requirements. The act requires the making and keeping of records and accounts "which, in reasonable detail, accurately and fairly reflect the transactions, and disposition of the ASSETS."

Criminal penalties for violation of the FCPA are significant. Firms are subject to fines up to $2 million; officers, directors, employees, and agents are subject to fines up to $100,000 and imprisonment up to five years. Civil penalties are also possible as well, and other federal criminal laws apply for bribery of international officials. While bribery remains a global business issue, the FCPA has significantly influenced American international business practices.

Further reading
Business Information Service for the New Independent States (BISNIS) website. Available on-line. URL: www.bisnis.doc.gov; Mallor, Jane P., A. James Barnes, Thomas Bowers, Michael J. Philips, and Arlen W. Langvardt. *Business Law and the Regulatory Environment,* 11th ed. Boston: McGraw-Hill, 2001.

foreign exchange
Foreign exchange is the trading of one country's currency for another's. There are many reasons why this must be done in the normal course of business. For example, a company may need a foreign currency to purchase items priced and sold in another currency. Also some people (often poorer people) see holding the currency of another country as a hedge against the INFLATION in their own currency. Most U.S. currency is held outside the United States, probably for this reason.

Many countries try to manage the rate at which their currency exchanges with other countries. A too-weak currency makes the purchase of foreign goods more expensive and indicates a weak economy. A too-strong currency makes the purchase of foreign goods cheaper, leading the country's citizens to buy IMPORTS instead of domestically made goods. (The 1994 PESO CRISIS in Mexico is an example of what happens when a currency becomes overvalued.)

Some countries try to control currency value fluctuations by establishing fixed or legal EXCHANGE RATES that currency exchanges must use. This usually produces devastating results in the local economy. In most cases there emerges an illegal black market where the common people and small businesses exchange the country's currency. The degree of seriousness of this situation depends on how vigorous the government enforces the official exchange rate. In some cases an "official" exchange rate is set, but everyone, including the government, uses the unofficial market rate. This has little impact on the economy, allowing the country's officials to delude themselves that the economy is behaving well. On the other hand, if the government strictly enforces the dictated exchange rate, large business may not be able to function in the country, and no foreign investor would dare invest money there.

A less disruptive way to manage the exchange rate is for the government's central bank to manage it by open-market activities. The central bank will purchase its own currency in an attempt to raise its value in the market and then sell its currency in an attempt to lower its value. This behavior is less troublesome but is usually only effective to manage minor currency fluctuations on an ongoing basis. It is largely ineffective in managing large shocks to an economy. For this reason, small countries are becoming more wary of draining their foreign-currency reserves by buying large amounts of their own currency to support its value.

The reasons for the foreign-currency exchanges discussed above are the results of normal economic activity within a country. However, for years foreign-exchange markets (some very informal) have existed for solely speculative reasons. People in France are buying Indian rupees from people in Australia solely in anticipation of gains in the value of Indian rupees. These speculative exchanges combined with the routine ones discussed earlier have produced a financial market of gigantic proportions. The worldwide foreign-exchange market has a typical volume of $1.5 trillion per day, more than three times the amount of stocks and BONDS traded in the United States per day. Unlike STOCK MARKETs, which have central exchanges, the foreign-exchange market has no physical location. It operates 24 hours a day, solely through an electronic network of banks, CORPORATIONs, and individuals. Even though there are some regulations on the participating banks and corporations, the foreign-exchange market is virtually unregulated.

foreign investment
Foreign investment includes both portfolio INVESTMENT and DIRECT INVESTMENT; these two investment types vary in the degree of RISK and control.

Foreign-portfolio investment is investment in foreign stocks, BONDS, and other FINANCIAL INSTRUMENTS. Usually there is no intention on the part of the investor to be involved in the MANAGEMENT of the company in which he or she is investing. Investing in the stock of, say, an Indian company can be lucrative, but it involves risks that do not exist in investing in a domestic company. Here is a short list of such risks.

Currency risk. Changes in the currency EXCHANGE RATES will affect the profitability of the investment. The Indian company may pay its normal 10,000-rupee DIVIDEND. If the rupee strengthens in value relative to the dollar, the value of the dividend increases to the U.S. investor, and vice versa.

Political risk. Favorable political actions, government changes, and events or increased stability will increase the value of the stock, and vice versa.

Diplomatic risk. Diplomatic relations between the two countries will affect the value of the investment. Improved relations and an openness of currency exchange between the United States and India will improve the value of the stock, and vice versa.

Information risk. Changes in the regulatory environment in either the United States or the foreign country can affect the value of the foreign investment. The foreign investment carries what could be characterized as an information premium. This could be stated in terms of the increased returns the foreign company must pay because of the low quality or quantity of information it provides compared to a U.S. company. So if information is improving just in the United States, this premium widens and the price will fall in order to provide the needed return to compensate the investors for the poorer quality information from the foreign investment, and vice versa.

Foreign-direct investment occurs when an investor company in, say, the United States invests in a subsidiary company or project with intentions of being involved in the management of that company. Typically the investing company invests in the ASSETS directly by providing EQUITY funding to a subsidiary in the foreign country. Foreign-direct investment also includes the parent company leaving INCOME in the subsidiary company or loaning money to the subsidiary.

Most developing countries consider foreign-direct investment an important part of their development strategy. Consequently they spend a great deal of energy in providing incentives and reforming their legal systems, all in an effort to attract foreign-direct investment.

See also EMERGING MARKET.

Foreign Sovereign Immunities Act

Immunity can be defined as being exempt from or not responsible for things such as illness, problems, or gover-

nance. Specifically, the Foreign Sovereign Immunities Act states that foreign countries are immune to the U.S. judicial system, with the exception of certain limitations.

The Foreign Sovereign Immunities Act (FSIA) refers to Title 28, Section 1330, and Sections 1602-1611 of the U.S. Code. This law, passed by Congress in 1976, is complex and states the exceptions with which the United States and its citizens have the right to file suit against a foreign country. Some of these general exceptions include a waiver of immunity by a foreign state, commercial activity of a foreign country which involves the United States, and the personal injury or death of a U.S. citizen caused by any foreign entity.

The need for a law such as the Foreign Sovereign Immunities Act has grown throughout the last century. With increased international commercial activity and GLOBALIZATION, obtaining the ability to hold a foreign country responsible in case of illegal actions is necessary.

Earlier in the history of the United States, foreign countries were given almost absolute immunity. In 1812 Chief Justice John Marshall, ruling in *The Schooner Exchange v. McFaddon*, developed the theory of foreign-sovereign immunity. Eventually the United States adopted the "restrictive theory" or "absolute theory," which gave foreign countries immunity for public acts of government offices but not for commercial or private activity. The U.S. courts found this difficult to apply because of a lack of standards and the frequent deference of cases to the State Department. Political considerations often influenced decisions, and during the 1950s many countries were competing unfairly by treating commercial activities as government actions to remain immune. In 1976 Congress passed the Foreign Sovereign Immunities Act to provide clear standards, making it more difficult to hide commercial activities and avoiding the use of political branches, such as the State Department, when making decisions.

The purpose of the FSIA is not only to establish standards but also to define "foreign state." According to the U.S. Code, a "foreign state" is considered any political subdivision, agency, or instrumentality of a foreign country. This act also sets forth standards for the extent of LIABILITY and counterclaims.

Through the years the FSIA has been amended several times with the most recent being in 1999, when it was amended to include terrorist actions by foreign countries. It is under this amendment that victims' families from September 11, 2001, are provided the ability to file suit against the country or countries sponsoring such terrorist actions.

Further reading

Fisher, Bruce D., and Michael J. Phillips. *The Legal, Ethical and Regulatory Environment of Business.* 8th ed. Cincinnati: Thomson/South-Western, 2003; *Foreign Services Immunities Act U.S. Code.* Vol. 28, sec. 1330 (1976): 1602–11; Lowenstein, Andrew. "The Foreign Sovereign Immunities Act and corporate subsidies of agencies or instrumentalities of foreign states," *Berkeley*

Journal of International Law 19 (Spring 2001): 350; Tessitore, Michael A. "Immunity and the Foreign Sovereign: An Introduction to the Foreign Sovereign Immunities Act," *Florida Bar Journal* 73, i10 (November 1999): 48.

—Jennifer R. Land

foreign-trade zones

Foreign-trade zones (FTZs), also known as free-trade zones, are facilities, usually established in enclosed areas near U.S. ports of entry that receive special treatment with regard to taxation of imported of goods. Technically FTZs are treated as being outside the customs territory of the United States and are subject to local and state labor, public health, and other laws. However, state regulations regarding food, drugs, or cosmetics do not apply to imported goods transshipped through foreign-trade zones.

Although FTZs have existed in Europe since the 1800s, they were first established in the United States after passage of the Foreign Trade Zone Act in 1934 as an attempt to mitigate the impact of protective TARIFFS imposed during the GREAT DEPRESSION. FTZs were not widely used until the 1980s and 1990s. In 1970 there were only eight FTZ projects; by 2001 there were over 230 FTZs.

Goods imported into FTZs are treated for tariffs primarily as either "privileged foreign merchandise" or "nonprivileged foreign merchandise." Privileged foreign merchandise is assessed tariffs based on condition upon the entry into the zone, but the actual duties are deferred until the merchandise is removed from the FTZ and enters the United States. In addition to having the tariffs deferred, privileged foreign merchandise status continues even if the goods are manufactured or processed before leaving the zone. This avoids additional tariffs if the good is changed from one classification to another and would otherwise be subject to a higher tariff.

Nonprivileged foreign merchandise is not categorized for tariff purposes until it leaves the FTZ. Thus its value, classification, condition, and applicable tariff rate are determined by the PRODUCT leaving the zone. Because of the ability to take advantage of differences in the U.S. tariff structure, there has been substantial growth in the use of foreign-trade zones in the United States. In one case, Japanese steel plates were brought into an FTZ on a nonprivileged basis and left the zone as barges. The steel plates would have been subject to a U.S. tariff, but barges are not subject to tariffs.

Another advantage of foreign-trade zones is that U.S. quotas do not apply. If an import quota has been filled, FTZs can be used to store products until the next quota period. Goods from countries not subject to most-favored-nation status can be brought into foreign-trade zones and, if they are transformed into products subject to lower most favored nation (MFN) tariffs, receive the lower tariff rate. Even though foreign-trade zones are intended to benefit U.S. exporters, allowing them to bring products into the U.S. for processing and then reexport without having to pay tariffs, many foreign companies use FTZs to bring products into the United States subject to lower tariffs.

The National Association of Foreign Trade Zones list of FTZ benefits include

1. duty deferral
2. exports
3. reduced or eliminated duties related to defects, damage, obsolescence, waste, and scrap
4. nondutiability of labor, overhead, and PROFIT
5. inverted customs duty savings
6. international returns
7. spare parts
8. U.S. quotas
9. simplification of import/export procedures
10. QUALITY CONTROL
11. cargo insurance
12. security
13. INVENTORY CONTROL
14. consumed merchandise (generally not subject to duties)
15. inventory taxes
16. exhibition of market goods before payment of duty
17. reduced INSURANCE costs
18. country of origin marking and labeling
19. zone-to-zone transfer
20. transfer of title.

See also RULES OF ORIGIN.

Further reading

National Association of Foreign Trade Zones website. Available on-line. URL: www.naftz.org; U.S. Customs website. Available on-line. URL: www.customs.ustreas.gov.

401(k) plan

The term *401(k)* comes from a section of the Internal Revenue Code allowing special tax consideration to help people save for retirement. Americans, particularly "baby boomers," have relatively low savings rates. The 401(k) plan was created to induce Americans to increase their savings. This plan, along with similar 403b and 457 plans, allows employees to contribute a portion of their salary into a tax-deferred retirement fund. The funds can be invested by the employee in MUTUAL FUNDS, individual stocks, and other INVESTMENT options.

A 401(k) plan has a maximum pretax amount that an employee can contribute each year. For 2002 the limit was $11,000, with increases of $1,000 per year allowed through 2006. 401(k) rules also allow a "catch-up" provision of an extra $1,000 for people 50 or older in 2002. This catch-up also increases by $1,000 per year through 2006.

Another change made in 2002 eliminated the 25-percent limit to 401(k) contributions. This means anyone can contribute up to $11,000 per year to their 401(k), even if their total INCOME was only $11,000 for the year. (Previously, someone earning $11,000 per year would only be able to contribute 25 percent of the $11,000 to their 401(k).)

401(k) plans offer a variety of benefits. Tax deferment means contributors do not have to pay taxes on their contributions until the funds are withdrawn, usually during retirement. Tax deferment also reduces workers' current taxable income. In addition, 401(k)s facilitate savings, since the funds are taken out of a worker's pay. Many companies also match workers' contributions to 401(k)s, increasing the amount set aside for retirement.

In the 1990s, 401(k)s and other defined-contribution RETIREMENT PLANS replaced traditional defined-benefit plans. In a traditional retirement plan, a worker's retirement pension was a set percentage of their salary, often 50–60 percent of their highest three-year average salary. In defined-contribution plans, employers match employees' contribution. If an employee elects to contribute 3 percent of their salary, the employer would match that amount. The employee's retirement pension would be the future value of those funds and would depend on the growth in value of the investments chosen.

Employers often put contingencies on their contributions to employees' 401(k)s—for instance, not allowing employees access to the employers' contributions until they had been with the company a set amount of time, often 3–5 years (vesting) and making employer contributions in the form of company stock. (Beginning in 2002, the longest a company can require is three years.) These contingencies contributed to the hardship of Enron employees who, in 2001, seeing their 401(k)s "vaporizing," were unable to sell their Enron stock.

Most 401(k) plans allow employees access to funds in an emergency through LOANS or withdrawals. Loans, which are paid back, are not subject to taxes or penalties, but they have their own danger; if an employee leaves or is laid off, he or she will probably have to repay the loan immediately. Withdrawals are restricted by INTERNAL REVENUE SERVICE (IRS) rules and are subject to taxes. The IRS allows withdrawals for

- certain nonreimbursable medical expenses
- purchase of primary residence
- payments for post-secondary education
- to prevent eviction or foreclosure on a home

401(k)s are also portable, meaning they can be carried with an employee when they change employers. When changing jobs employees can

- directly roll an old 401(k) plan into the new employer's plan
- keep the old 401(k) account and start a new one

- directly roll the old 401(k) into an INDIVIDUAL RETIREMENT ACCOUNT (IRA), and start a new plan with the new employer.

Further reading
PAI-Pension Services website. Available on-line. URL: www. paipension.com; Fidelity Investments' 401K website. Available on-line. URL: www.401k. com; CNN money Mutual Funds website. Available on-line. URL: www.mutual-funds.com.

—Rachel Archangel

franchising
Franchising is a contractual agreement between a manufacturer or business-idea owner—the franchiser—and a WHOLESALER or retailer—the franchisee. The franchiser sells to the franchisee the right to market its products or ideas and to use its TRADEMARKS and brand names. The franchisee agrees to meet the franchiser's operating requirements, usually pays an initial fee for the franchise, and agrees to pay a percentage of sales to the franchiser.

Franchising is big business in the United States. While it has existed for centuries, it boomed in the country after World War II. Growth of the interstate highway system in the 1950s and 1960s stimulated travel in the United States, and franchises offered travelers the expectation of standardized PRODUCTS or levels of service. Ray Kroc's McDonald's fast-food restaurants and the many hotel chains symbolized the growth of this type of business. Today over one-third of all retail sales in the United States are transacted through franchises. Critics argue the growth of franchising is creating "sameness" in America, reducing local and regional differences and creating cultural homogenization.

Franchising is a business strategy that allows rapid and flexible penetration of markets, growth, and CAPITAL development. In the United States, franchises are typically distinguished as either product franchises or business-format franchises. Product franchises involve manufacturers who produce goods that are distributed through franchise agreements. Many ice-cream stores, soft-drink bottling outlets, and gasoline retailers are product franchises. Business-format franchises involve the LICENSING of INTELLECTUAL PROPERTY rights in conjunction with a unique "formula for success" of a business. Many service businesses, including hotels, fast food restaurants, and employment services, are examples of business-format franchising.

Franchising provides both advantages and disadvantages to the franchiser and franchisee. Based on the growth of franchising in the United States, generally both sides benefit from this type of business relationship. For the franchisee the benefits include use of trademarks and brands that are recognized and preferred by customers, support and training from the franchiser organization, national ADVERTISING, a protected territory, reduced costs through bulk buying, and reduced risk from a proven business concept. The disadvantages for the franchisee include payments for use of the franchise trademark or brands, restrictions on business practices, and the potential to be hurt by actions taken by the franchiser or other franchisees.

From the franchiser's perspective, franchising allows faster growth into new markets before competitors copy its ideas, expansion without additional CAPITAL EXPENDITURES, royalty payments from franchisees, and ECONOMIES OF SCALE through larger operations. Franchising also allows firms to expand internationally in conjunction with franchisees who understand and adapt to cultural differences.

Franchises are subject to significant government regulation both from state and federal agencies. Many states and the FEDERAL TRADE COMMISSION enacted disclosure statutes for franchise agreements. The typical franchise-disclosure statute created criminal penalties for material misrepresentation or omission in franchise promotions. It usually permits withdrawal from any franchise agreement if the franchisee did not receive a copy of the PROSPECTUS. In the 1950s and 1960s, franchising was known for having many unscrupulous operators promising instant success and making unsubstantiated claims to potential franchisees. Franchising was and is often promoted as a way for people who do not have business experience to start their own enterprise, and it does reduce the RISK for new businesspeople through the knowledge gained by the franchiser.

Most state franchise-disclosure laws require the franchiser to register with an agency by filing a franchise-offering circular. The state agency reviews the circular to ensure it meets the necessary disclosure requirements. Once registered, the franchiser is licensed to sell franchises in that state. Many states also review franchisers' capitalization before permitting the sale of franchises. This is done to protect potential investors from franchisers who have made little initial investment in the proposed franchise system. States have also enacted laws dealing with the termination of franchise agreements. These laws typically prohibit franchisers from initiating termination of the franchise CONTRACT without "good cause," which is usually defined as a material breach of the franchise agreement.

Franchising is designed to provide standardized products and services even though the parent company (franchiser) does not own all the business outlets. Franchise agreements protect the image and reputation of the franchiser and the other franchisees from inappropriate actions by individual franchisees.

See also BRANDS, BRAND NAMES.

Further reading

Boone, Louis E., and David L. Kurtz. *Contemporary Marketing.* 10th ed. Fort Worth: Dryden Press, 2001; Folsom, Ralph H., and Michael Gordon. *International Business Transactions,* 5th ed. Eagan, Minn.: West Group, 2002.

fraud

Fraud is intentional misrepresentation and has long been a major problem both for businesses and consumers. In 17th-century England, a law on oral contracts prohibited parties to a lawsuit from testifying on their own behalf. This frequently led to third parties offering false testimony about the existence of an oral CONTRACT. To reduce this problem, in 1677 Parliament enacted the Statute of Frauds, requiring written evidence before certain types of contracts would be enforced.

American legislatures adopted similar rules, and today statutes of frauds vary from state to state. Most contracts covered by statutes of fraud require written evidence. Contracts for sale of real estate are the most common written agreement Americans encounter. Fraud statutes also cover executor or administrator contracts, contracts associated with marriage, and collateral contracts (in which a person promises to perform another person's obligation).

Today fraud against businesses includes a variety of misrepresentations with the intent to deceive. Employee EMBEZZLEMENT is a constant problem for businesses. Sham transactions, by which a company executive sells a PRODUCT, division, or other ASSET in order to record a PROFIT while agreeing to purchase the asset back in some future time period, is another type of fraud. Early evidence in the Enron fiasco of 2001 indicated significant use of sham transactions to boost reported earnings in order to bolster the firm's stock price while executives were selling their shares.

Bogus invoices are another serious type of fraud against businesses. Large companies are often fooled into paying what appear to be legitimate business expenses. Bogus checks, counterfeit currency, and devious contract agreements all challenge business managers. Misrepresentation in EMPLOYMENT is another problem. One sales representative courted a young woman, offering her a fantastic job with his company. Fortunately the woman was shrewd enough to contact the company's HUMAN RESOURCES department in the company and find out that the sales rep had no authority to hire anyone.

While businesses contend with a variety of frauds, criminals posing as businesses confront American consumers with numerous fraudulent representations. The FEDERAL TRADE COMMISSION has identified what they call their "Dirty Dozen" of fraudulent solicitations likely to be received by consumers by bulk mail or e-mail, including

- business-opportunity scams offering financial success with little or no effort. Often these are pyramid schemes, requiring the individual to find and sell the business opportunity to others in order to create a "downline" and profit from sales to others.
- making money by sending bulk e-mail—that is, offers to sell the consumer bulk e-mail distribution lists and products, services, or software to promote through e-mail.

- chain letters, a classic fraud received through the mail or e-mail, asking people to send money to the person on the top of the list. The recipient adds his or her name to the bottom of the list, and supposedly, when that name rises to the top, he or she will receive huge sums of money. Sometimes these solicitations include some type of information package designed to suggest that something of value is being exchanged and therefore it is not fraud.
- work-at-home schemes, which usually involve stuffing envelopes with promises of earning hundreds and even thousands of dollars per month. These are often advertised in classified ads and on signs tacked onto telephone poles. Like the old saying, "If it sounds too good to be true, it probably is too good to be true," these solicitations prey upon the least sophisticated and usually poorest people in society.
- health and diet scams—miracle cures for every ailment that have been around for centuries. In the 19th century, tonics often included codeine and a high percentage of alcohol to numb anyone who might doubt their efficacy.
- effortless income—offers that promise ways to earn huge profits, usually from currency exchange. Charles Ponzi, after whom the PONZI SCHEME was named, promised investors a 40-percent profit on their investment in 90 days. At the time, prevailing INTEREST RATES were around 5 percent, making the Ponzi proposition very attractive to investors. Ponzi's proposition was based on International Postal Reply Coupons, which were redeemable at fixed rates of exchange negotiated by the participating governments. However, EXCHANGE RATES for currency fluctuate. Ponzi convinced investors he would take their funds, invest in International Postal Reply Coupons in countries where the currency had depreciated significantly, and then redeem the coupons in strong-currency countries, making a significant profit. After being caught and sent to jail, Ponzi moved to Florida to sell real estate.
- free-goods offers that promise expensive products such as computers for free if one pays to join the club and get so many other people to join.
- offers for investment opportunities, which, like Ponzi schemes, promise huge returns using "scientifically proven" trading methods or inside information of some upcoming breakthrough. Like health and diet claims, these are "snake oil" schemes for an INVESTMENT portfolio.
- cable descrambler, INTERNET services, pay-per-call scams, and other communications service offers that either do not work or contain hidden clauses costing unsuspecting consumers much more than they thought.
- guaranteed LOANS or credit scams offering, for instance, home-equity loans and CREDIT CARDS to anyone regardless of credit history. One of the worst types is the PREDATORY LENDING scheme in which homeowners are conned into refinancing their MORTGAGES with low interest rates but huge fees, leaving the homeowner (often an elderly person) with payments that cannot be sustained.

- credit repair schemes involving companies that claim they will repair someone's credit rating with the credit-rating services. Under U.S. law, consumers are allowed to request a copy of their credit-rating reports once a year for free and submit documentation refuting claims made to the reporting agency by any creditor.
- vacation prize promotions, a classic fraud that involves claims of deluxe accommodations on luxury cruise ships and other sorts of misrepresentations.

To reduce the chances of being defrauded, experts recommend the following.

- Use common sense. If it sounds too good to be true, it is probably a scam.
- Watch out for "processing fees," whether to borrow money, register for prizes, or to receive "free" things.
- Do business with companies one knows and trusts.
- Protect financial information. One of the latest frauds is a bogus form saying it is from the INTERNAL REVENUE SERVICE, looking to update personal information.
- Scrutinize charitable solicitations. Two common frauds are sound-alike charitable organizations—i.e., the soliciting group sounds like a well-known national charity—and the use of a paid, professional solicitor, with the charity receiving only a small percentage of the donations received. After September 11, 2001, many fraudulent solicitations duped millions from well-meaning Americans.
- Avoid the classic Nigerian money order fraud, in which callers or e-mailers requests help getting money that is "theirs" but need help transferring the funds to a U.S. bank account—the consumer's. With that account information, they liquidate the account.

A relatively new area of fraud is Internet fraud. See the INTERNET FRAUD COMPLAINT CENTER entry for discussion of this topic.

Further reading

Mallor, Jane P., A. James Barnes, Thomas Bowers, Michael J. Philips, and Arlen W. Langvardt. *Business Law and the Regulatory Environment*. 11th ed. Boston: McGraw-Hill, 2001; National Consumers League website. Available on-line. URL: www.nclnet.org; Scam Watch Organization. Available on-line. URL: www.scamwatch.org.

Freddie Mae   See FEDERAL HOME LOAN MORTGAGE CORPORATION.

Freedom of Information Act

The Freedom of Information Act (FOIA), which can be found in Title 5 of the U.S. Code, Section 552, was enacted in 1966 and provides that any person has the right to request access to federal agency records or information.

FOIA requires government agencies to respond to public requests for documents within 20 days after the request is received. All states have their own statutes governing public access to state and local records. Federal agencies unwilling or unable to respond within the 20-day period must justify their denial of a FOIA request. The FOIA exempts from public disclosure documents that:

1. are of national security interest
2. concern internal agency personnel practices
3. are specifically exempted from disclosure by federal statute
4. contain TRADE SECRETS or other confidential information
5. reflect internal agency deliberations on matters of proceedings or policies
6. are part of personnel or medical files
7. jeopardize law enforcement investigation's or individual's rights to a fair trial
8. relate to regulation or supervision of financial institutions
9. contain geological or geophysical data

All agencies are required by statute to make certain types of records created by the agency on or after November 1, 1996, available electronically. FOIA requests are not needed to obtain access to (1) final opinions and orders made in adjudicating cases, (2) final statements of policy and interpretations which have not been published in the *Federal Register,* (3) administrative staff manuals and instructions to staff that affect a member of the public, (4) copies of records that have been the subject of a FOIA request and that are of sufficient public interest or curiosity that the agency believes other persons are likely to request them, and (5) the agency's annual FOIA report.

There is no initial fee to file a FOIA request, and in the majority of requests made to the Justice Department, no fees are ever charged. By law, however, an agency is entitled to charge certain fees, which depend on the requestor's category.

FOIA is important to businesses in that media, public-interest groups, companies, and industry trade associations use FOIA requests to learn about their competitors. Competitive intelligence professionals "mine" government documents, whether EPA documentation or SECURITIES AND EXCHANGE COMMISSION reports, to gather public information about competitor's products and activities.

Further reading
Mallor, Jane P., A. James Barnes, Thomas Bowers, Michael J. Philips, and Arlen W. Langvardt. *Business Law and the Regulatory Environment,* 11th ed. Boston: McGraw-Hill, 2001; U.S. Department of Justice website. Available on-line. URL: www.doj.gov.

free on board (FOB)

Free on board, most commonly called FOB, is a shipping term that has much significance in the accounting for a firm's ASSETS. There are two FOB situations: FOB shipping point and FOB destination. When a seller needs to ship goods to a buyer, the two parties will negotiate the manner in which the goods are transported, either FOB shipping point or FOB destination. The shipping point is usually the seller's shipping docks, and the destination is usually the buyer's receiving docks.

When goods are transported FOB shipping point, the title (ownership) to the goods being shipped is passed to the buyer at the shipping point—that is, when the goods leave the seller. Though the buyer may not receive the goods for several days or weeks, it is the buyer who now owns the goods and must include them in his inventory, despite the fact that he doesn't have physical possession of them. It is also the buyer who is liable for the goods while in transit, as it is he who owns them. Because the goods were shipped "free on board," the shipping agent (transportation company) will send the freight bill to the buyer, the owner of the goods while in transit.

When goods are transported FOB destination, the title (ownership) to the goods being shipped is not passed to the buyer until the goods reach their destination. Thus the seller owns the goods while they are in transit, and it is she who is liable for the goods while they are being transported. The seller will continue to include the shipped items in her inventory until such time as they reach their destination. The freight bill will be sent to the seller, the owner of the goods while in transit.

free trade

Free trade is international trade without restraints imposed by governments. For a variety of reasons, governments often impose limitations on trade, and thus totally free trade does not exist in the world. Limitations on trade include TARIFFS, quotas, and other NONTARIFF BARRIERS. Tariffs can be used to generate revenue or increase the price of imported PRODUCTS, making domestically produced products cheaper and more competitive in the marketplace. Quotas are quantitative limits on the amount of a specific import that can be brought into a country during a period of time. To protect domestic textile jobs for decades the United States imposed quotas on textiles coming into the country.

Today nontariff barriers are often the biggest restraint on free trade. Nontariff barriers include labeling requirements, "voluntary export quotas," technical standards, and health and safety constraints. For example, the United States, ignoring rulings by the NORTH AMERICAN FREE TRADE AGREEMENT (NAFTA) and the WORLD TRADE ORGANIZATION (WTO), used safety concerns to prohibit Mexican trucks from having full access to U.S. highways. In the 1980s Japan, fearing the imposition of quotas, voluntarily restricted automobile shipments to the United States for several years.

The argument for free trade is based on the ideas of Adam Smith, author of the *An Inquiry into the Nature and*

Cause of the Wealth of Nations (1776), and 19th-century economist David Ricardo. Smith argued against MERCAN-TILISM, the idea that a country's WEALTH and power could be increased through the accumulation of precious metals and by maintaining a favorable balance of trade. Mercantilism was the dominant economic doctrine of his time, but Smith proposed free trade, or unrestricted access to markets, instead. (Ironically, he ended his career as port tax collector in his native Scotland.)

David Ricardo, building on Smith's ideas, was the originator of the concept of COMPARATIVE ADVANTAGE. The law of comparative advantage is the principle that firms, people, or countries should engage in those activities for which their advantage over others is the largest or their disadvantage is the smallest. Trade is then based on doing those things that can be done relatively more efficiently than others can do. Logically, free trade encourages individuals, firms, and countries to specialize in doing those things they can do well and trading for those that they cannot do as efficiently. Also, logically, comparative advantage depends on access to markets to make exchanges—free trade.

The other arguments for free trade are that exports pay for IMPORTS and the cost of protection of domestic industries. Countries that attempt to limit imports usually find that their exports face similar restrictions, offsetting any economic gain from reducing imports. Restricting free trade also creates a strange dichotomy. Using the example of Japan's voluntary export limits in the 1980s, economists found for each American automobile industry job retained because Japanese producers were limiting exports, American consumers paid approximately $250,000 more for cars. The benefits of trade restrictions usually are concentrated, in this case in the U.S. automobile industry, while the costs are dispersed among consumers in general. Because of this dichotomy, there is often a strong, vocal group of supporters for restricting free trade and no strong group opposing it on an economic basis.

Trade among countries has existed for thousands of years, well before the ideas of Smith and Ricardo, but there are many economic and social-justice reasons countries and individuals do not always support free trade (as evidenced in the WTO meetings in Seattle in 1999). One argument against free trade is to prevent unfair foreign COMPETITION. Free trade and fair trade do not mean the same thing. Free trade, as stated earlier, is trade without restraints, whereas in fair trade everyone "plays by the same rules." Sometimes referred to as a market with a "level playing field," fair trade precludes DUMPING, export subsidies, and, more recently, abuse of workers and the environment. As the largest economy in the world, the U.S. market is important to any multinational firm. U.S. businesses often ask government to restrict access to the U.S. market, claiming unfair trade practices on the part of firms from other countries. Under section 301 of U.S. trade rules, the U.S. trade representative must investigate and report findings regarding claims of unfair trade practices.

NAFTA, the NORTH AMERICAN FREE TRADE AGREEMENT, is often cited as an example of the benefits of free trade. Since 1995 NAFTA has significantly increased trade among the United States, Canada, and Mexico, but close inspection of the agreement (more than 1,100 pages long) shows a myriad of exceptions and limitations. Free trade would be trade without limitations; NAFTA significantly reduces the barriers to trade but does not eliminate restrictions. The World Trade Organization's goal is to increase world free trade. More than 100 countries are members of the WTO, but free trade is still a vision for the future among those who support that vision.

Further reading

Ruffin, Roy J., and Paul R. Gregory. *Principles of Economics*, 7th ed. Boston: Addison Wesley, 2000.

free-trade areas

Free-trade areas are regional agreements to reduce TARIFFS, quotas, and other barriers to trade among the participating nations while retaining national TRADE BARRIERS with respect to other countries. The goal in creating areas for FREE TRADE is to stimulate ECONOMIC DEVELOPMENT and increase economic bargaining power.

Since World War II, numerous free-trade areas have been established. The most widely known are the 130+-member WORLD TRADE ORGANIZATION (WTO), the 14-member EURO-PEAN UNION (with plans to expand membership in the near future), and the 3-member NORTH AMERICAN FREE TRADE AGREEMENT (NAFTA).

Each region of the world has attempted to create regional agreements. In 1966, five Central African countries created the Customs Union of Central Africa (Union Douaniere et Economique de l'Afrique Centrale, UDEAC). The following year Kenya, Tanzania, and Uganda created the East African Community (EAC). In 1974, six French-speaking West African countries formed the West African Economic Community (known by its French initials CEAO). The following year the CEAO became part of the Economic Community of West African States. In 1991, 51 African nations established the Organization of African Unity (OAU).

In Latin America and the Caribbean, the first free-trade area was the Central American Common Market (CACM), established in 1958. Many Latin American countries participated in the Latin American Free Trade Association (LAFTA, 1961). Eight island nations plus Belize created the Caribbean Community (CARICOM, 1973). In 1994, 37 nations became members of the Association of Caribbean States, agreeing to long-term economic integration.

The Persian Gulf states formed the Gulf Cooperation Council (GCC) in 1984 implementing trade and investment rules among participating states. In South America, two free trade areas have been established: MERCOSUR (Southern Cone including Brazil, Paraguay, Argentina, and Uruguay in 1991 and later joined by Chile and Bolivia); and ANCOM, the Andean Common Market established in 1969 by Bolivia, Chile, Columbia, Ecuador, and Peru. In South Asia the most prominent free trade area is ASEAN, the Association of Southeast Asian Nations, formed in 1967.

Most regional free-trade areas have had limited success in stimulating economic development. Often they are created as a counter-balance to the political and economic power of the United States, Japan, and European nations. Many countries retain special trade agreements based on historic and colonial relationships and political-military alignment. For example, the United States has a special trade agreement with Israel, established in 1985. The United States and the European Union (EU) got into what was known as the "banana wars" over preferential access to the EU for banana producers in former European colonies and Commonwealth countries.

Further reading
Folsom, Ralph H., Michael Gordon, and John Sproagle. *International Business Transactions in a Nutshell*, 6th ed. Eagan, Minn.: West Law, 2000.

futures, futures contracts

Futures or futures contracts are sales of commodities for delivery at some later time. In the United States, futures generally refer to CONTRACTS specifying a fixed quantity and quality of a commodity to be delivered to a location at a certain date. Futures contracts are traded under the rules of the COMMODITY FUTURES TRADING COMMISSION (CFTC).

Futures contracts eliminate or reduce the RISK associated with future price changes. Initially they were used by farmers and food-industry processors to hedge against the risk of price changes. Farmers would sell a futures contract at a specified price, "locking in" that price for the PRODUCT between planting and harvesting time; this is referred to as HEDGING. Food processors would buy futures contracts locked in the cost of raw materials. Over time a wide variety of futures contracts have been developed, including those concerned with FINANCIAL INSTRUMENTS, STOCK MARKET indices, INTEREST RATES, energy products, foreign currency, and precious metals.

In a futures market like the CHICAGO BOARD OF TRADE, someone who buys a futures contract is said to have "gone long." If, after going long, the price of the underlying commodity or ASSET rises, the price of the futures contract will rise, and the buyer profits. In the example

of the food-processing company, the PROFIT from buying a futures contract would offset the increase in price of the commodity in the cash market. If, instead, the price of the commodity declined, the value of the futures contract would decline, causing a loss for the food processor, but the cash-market price would also have decreased, offsetting the loss associated with purchasing the futures contract.

Someone who sells a futures contract is said to have "gone short." If the price of the underlying commodity or security rises, the short seller loses, but if the price declines, the short seller can buy back the futures contract at a lower price and profit by the difference.

In most situations, buyers and sellers of futures contracts "close out" their trades before the expiration date of the contract. They could also take or make delivery of the commodity or security, as per the stipulations in the contract.

In addition to hedging, futures contracts are widely used as speculative investments. Holders of futures are required to pay an initial margin, usually equal to 10 percent of the value of contract. Thus, futures contracts provide significant LEVERAGE. For example, if a contract is worth $100,000, a buyer is only required to put up $10,000. Should the value of the underlying ASSET increase by 5 percent, the investor earns $5,000 (5 percent of $100,000), a 50-percent return on their INVESTMENT. The buyer could also lose money in the same leveraged manner if the value of the contract decreased by 5 percent. If the value decreased, the investor would receive a margin call, requiring him to put up additional funds or have the contract closed. The most famous recent example of the potential for profit from futures market speculation was the report that Hilary Clinton earned approximately $100,000 from an initial investment of only a few thousand dollars.

Futures markets are known for their widely varying prices. Changes in weather, political turmoil, and rumors cause rapid changes in futures markets, resulting in huge profits and losses. Futures markets are also known for their "pits," intense bidding rooms where brokers shout and use hand signals to exercise trades for their customers. Prior experience as a football player is considered a valuable training for work in futures market pits.

Further reading
Futures Contracts, Strategic Opportunities Fund. Available online. URL: www.neoware.com.

—Todd Devries

future value   See COMPOUNDING, FUTURE VALUE.

G

gain sharing   See PROFIT SHARING, GAIN SHARING.

game theory

Game theory is a mathematical representation of situations in which two or more players strategize and make choices that affect the choices and outcomes for other players. There are many forms of game theory, and in a business environment it is defined by boundaries, players, and a set of rules within which outcomes are determined.

Game theory is often used in marketing to describe the results of strategies depending on strategies other participants in the market employ. Understanding the rules and theory of game theory, which occur in every business, are essential for success. Consumers, entrepreneurs and managers, regulators, courts, and other participants contribute to a market's design, directly or indirectly. Any change, either within the company or outside the company, will be reflected throughout the business system.

In game theory, nothing is fixed. The marketplace is constantly evolving, and players are constantly creating new markets. Buyers and sellers do not take products or prices as given. Game theory differs from conventional economic assumptions by which consumers are thought to behave in simple stimulus-response, i.e., sellers determine prices and consumers respond accordingly.

Mathematicians John Von Neumann and Oskar Morgenstern first developed game theory. Their theories were restricted to games in which no players could gain except at the expense of others. In the process of the game, each player strategized in order to gain what he or she wanted out of the interaction. For example, when purchasing a car, buyers go to the car dealership looking for the lowest price they can possibly obtain, while the salesperson will ask for a higher price than the minimum they will accept up to the point when he fears they will walk away. Buyers will continue to negotiate as long as they believe the seller still might come down on their price.

Nobel Prize–winning economist John F. Nash (portrayed in the Academy Award-winning film *A Beautiful Mind*) clarified the distinction between cooperative and uncooperative games. In an uncooperative game (unlike cooperative games), there are strategies that are used by players in such a way that neither player can benefit by changing the strategy if the strategies of the other players remain unchanged. Nash introduced the concept of "bargaining negotiation," or agreement between two players to produce an outcome, with both participants believing they will benefit from the ultimate outcome.

See also ZERO-SUM GAME.

Further reading
Roth, Alvin E. "Game Theory as a Tool for Market Design." Available on-line. URL: http://www.economics.harvard.edu/~aroth/design.pdf.

—Karen M. Cimino

gap analysis

Gap analysis is a managerial tool used to compare a company's performance or customer expectations with current outcomes. It is used both in product MANAGEMENT and SERVICES marketing to evaluate and improve business performance.

In product management, gap analysis can be used to measure current PRODUCT quality against desired standards. Any difference between product quality and desired standards reveals a gap. Managers sometimes create product specifications based on PRODUCTION technology or regulatory standards, but they do not create product specifications consistent with their understanding of consumer's expectations. Changing product quality can take time and be costly, but it can also make the difference between success and failure.

Marketers use service gap analysis to measure the difference between expectations and perceived outcomes. One potential gap is the difference between management perceptions of consumer expectations and actual consumer expectations. Many marketers are surprised when consumers occasionally express their expectations (usually an expression of their disappointment with the service received).

A second potential gap can be the difference between managers' perceptions of consumer expectations and the service quality specifications that managers create. Service quality includes timeliness, accuracy, friendliness, and attentiveness. Managers who emphasize fast service may miss consumers' need for friendliness or attentiveness. United Parcel Service (UPS), known for its hustling employees, learned customers would like to talk longer with UPS delivery people. The company adjusted expected deliveries per hour to allow delivery people to take time to communicate with customers.

A third potential gap can exist between service quality standards set by management and the actual service quality delivered. Just because managers set a standard does not mean it will be attained or maintained. Another service quality gap can exist between what is provided and what is promised. Many marketing people have learned from customers about assurances made by senior managers. Communications gaps are a common problem between all levels of organizations.

An additional service quality gap can exist between received service and expected service. Consumers develop expectations regarding service quality through experience and observation. Miscommunication and misinterpretation can lead to a gap between expectations and perceived service received.

Gap analysis can help define problems. It often involves creating rating scales used to survey both internal staff members and external constituents. Differences in the average ratings between customers and companies signal a potential gap for further evaluation. Reducing and eliminating gaps improves CUSTOMER RELATIONS/SATISFACTION, leading to repeat purchases and stronger marketing relationships.

See also RELATIONSHIP MARKETING.

Further reading
Boone, Louis E., and David L. Kurtz. *Contemporary Marketing,* 10th ed. Fort Worth: Dryden Press, 2001.

General Accounting Office

The General Accounting Office (GAO) investigates problems and issues for members of Congress. The GAO examines the use of public funds, evaluates federal programs and activities, and provides analyses, options, recommendations, and other assistance to Congress. Where the Office of Management Budget (OMB) provides analytical support to the executive branch of government, the GAO works for the legislative branch of government. The GAO is sometimes called the "congressional watchdog," investigating how the federal government spends taxpayer dollars. GAO reports are often used by members of Congress as a basis for drafting legislation, supporting or opposing legislation, and evaluating the economic impact of proposed policies.

Companies doing business with the federal government monitor and attempt to influence GAO reports. Critical GAO reports can hinder business-favorable legislation or result in termination of current government contracts with a business.

Since the U.S. Senate and House of Representatives contain members from both major political parties, the GAO faces challenges providing unbiased analyses. The GAO

- evaluates how well government policies and programs are working
- audits agency operations to determine whether federal funds are being spent efficiently, effectively and appropriately
- investigates allegations of illegal and improper activities
- issues legal decisions and opinions

The GAO releases over 1,000 documents annually, often in the form of "blue book" reports, in response to requests for analysis of current issues being debated by Congress.

The GAO was created in 1921 in response to financial management problems after World War I. The Budget and Accounting Act transferred AUDITING responsibilities, accounting, and claims from the Treasury Department to the new agency. The agency grew rapidly during the New Deal era of President Franklin Roosevelt and the expanded government spending associated with World War II.

The GAO is directed by the Comptroller General, appointed for a 15-year term to insure the independence of the GAO from political pressures.

Further reading
General Accounting Office website. Available on-line. URL: www.gao.gov.

General Agreement on Tariffs and Trade   See WORLD TRADE ORGANIZATION.

generally accepted accounting principles

A double-entry system of accounting (now called FINANCIAL ACCOUNTING) was first described in 1494 by a Franciscan monk, Fra Luca Pacioli, living in the Tuscany region of Italy. As a result of his extensive treatment of the double-entry system, then known also as the Venetian system, Pacioli is regarded as the father of accounting. Born in 1445, he was one of the greatest minds of the Renaissance, distinguishing himself as a mathematician, college professor, and author. The accounting process Pacioli described is called a double-entry system because it takes two entries to record a transaction.

Drawing upon the nature of a transaction, an exchange where equal-valued RESOURCES are simultaneously received and given up, the accounting system uses one entry to record the resource received in a transaction and another entry to record the resource given in exchange. The first entry of the double entry is known as the debit, and the dollar figure of the first entry is placed in the left column of the journal. (Debit comes from the Latin word *debere* meaning "left" and is abbreviated *dr.*) The following entry is the credit, and the dollar figure of this entry is placed in the right column of the journal. (Credit comes from the Latin word *credere* meaning "right" and is abbreviated *cr.*) Because the double entry represents a transaction, an exchange of equal-valued resources, the amount of the debit entry is equal to the amount of the credit entry, and at any given time in the accounting cycle, the sum of all the debit entries must equal the sum of all the credit entries.

For centuries, accounting existed as an oral tradition passed from one generation to the next. The rules, methods, and formats for accounting became widely known and generally accepted over time by accounting practitioners. It was not until the 20th century that accounting rules were made more formal, rather than accepted as an oral tradition. Largely due to the efforts of the FINANCIAL ACCOUNTING STANDARDS BOARD (FASB) and the AMERICAN INSTITUTE OF CERTIFIED PUBLIC ACCOUNTANTS (AICPA), perhaps the two most important organizations governing the practice of financial accounting today, the rules for the practice of accounting are now codified and are regarded as "generally accepted accounting principles" (GAAP).

The SECURITIES AND EXCHANGE COMMISSION (SEC) requires that all published FINANCIAL STATEMENTS be constructed in accordance with GAAP. The INTERNAL REVENUE SERVICE (IRS) requires that the accounting for businesses follow GAAP. Because of the long oral tradition, the codification of GAAP, the various organizations concerned with the practice of financial accounting, and its backing from the SEC and IRS, financial (double-entry) accounting has become the standard among today's businesses and organizations.

See also DEBIT, CREDIT.

General Services Administration
The General Services Administration (GSA) is a major purchasing agent for the federal government. The GSA was created in 1949 through the consolidation of four small agencies involved in PURCHASING services, space, and PRODUCTS to support the activities of federal employees. After World War II the GSA directed disposal of war-surplus materials and managed emergency preparedness and stockpiling of strategic materials. Emergency-preparedness functions were later transferred to the Federal Emergency Management Agency (FEMA), and stockpiling functions were transferred to the Department of Defense.

Rather than have each of thousands of federal offices procure rental space, office equipment and supplies, and business services, the GSA oversees and coordinates these actions with the goal of obtaining the best value for federal expenditures. The GSA also provides travel and transportation services, manages the federal motor vehicle fleet, oversees telecommunication centers and federal child-care centers, preserves historic buildings, manages a fine-arts program, and develops, advocates, and evaluates government-wide SERVICES. The GSA employs 14,000 people, has an annual budget of $16 billion, and directs $66 billion in federal spending. Businesses wishing to sell to the U.S. government must learn GSA's methods of purchasing, including paperwork and bidding procedures.

Further reading
General Services Administration website. Available on-line. URL: www.gsa.gov.

Gini ratio
A Gini ratio is a measure of the distribution of INCOME in an economy. A Gini ratio (also called Gini coefficient) can range between 0 and 1. Zero means all families have the same income; 1 means one family has all of the income. Gini ratios are used in conjunction with LORENZ CURVES. Lorenz curves plot the cumulative income by quintiles (one-fifths) of the population in an economy. If each fifth of the population had 20 percent of the income, the Lorenz curve would be a 45-degree line and the Gini ratio would be 0.

Since no economy has an equal distribution of income, the Lorenz curve, with quintiles on the horizontal axis and cumulative percent of income on the vertical axis, is a bow-shaped line beneath the 45-degree line. The Gini ratio measures the gap between the Lorenz curve and the 45-degree line. The higher the Gini ratio, the greater the disparity of income in an economy. Since the area between the 45-degree line and the Lorenz curve is an irregular-shaped half ellipse, calculating the area requires a complex mathematical formula. See "Gini says: measuring income inequality" in the *Left Business Observer* (October 18, 1993) for details.

The Census Bureau calculates the Gini ratio for the U.S. economy. As the table below shows, income inequality decreased for approximately two decades after World War II, but beginning in the 1960s it has steadily increased. Economists suggest stagnant and declining minimum wages (in real terms) and increased executive compensation explain much of the changing distribution of income. Government Gini ratios are calculated using cash income and therefore do not take into account changes in tax laws and noncash benefits such as food stamps, AID FOR FAMILIES WITH DEPENDENT CHILDREN, and employer-provided noncash benefits. Opponents of government WELFARE programs suggest that when noncash benefits are included in income-distribution statistics, lower income groups are receiving an increased share of national income.

U.S. Gini Ratios for 1967 to 2000

2000	0.460	1988	0.427	1977	0.402
1999	0.457	1987	0.426	1976	0.398
1998	0.456	1986	0.425	1975	0.397
1997	0.459	1985	0.419	1974	0.395
1996	0.455	1984	0.415	1973	0.397
1995	0.450	1983	0.414	1972	0.401
1994	0.456	1982	0.412	1971	0.396
1993	0.454	1981	0.406	1970	0.394
1992	0.434	1980	0.403	1969	0.391
1991	0.428	1979	0.404	1968	0.388
1990	0.428	1978	0.402	1967	0.399
1989	0.431				

Further reading

U.S. Census Bureau website. Available on-line. URL: www.census.gov; "Gini says: measuring income inequality." *Left Business Observer,* 18 October 1993.

Ginnie Mae   See GOVERNMENT NATIONAL MORTGAGE ASSOCIATION.

glass ceiling

While there are many definitions of the term *glass ceiling,* the DEPARTMENT OF LABOR has concluded that it is most clearly defined as those artificial barriers based on attitudinal or organizational bias that prevent qualified individuals from advancing upward in their organization into MANAGEMENT-level positions. The phrase was first used in a 1986 *Wall Street Journal* article describing the invisible barriers women confront as they attempt to be promoted up to the top corporate hierarchy.

As part of the 1991 CIVIL RIGHTS ACT, the Department of Labor was directed to establish the Federal Glass Ceiling Commission, which issued its report in 1995. The commission found that the glass ceiling was real, and in many instances it existed lower in business organizations than expected. Evan Kemp, the chairman of the EQUAL EMPLOYMENT OPPORTUNITY COMMISSION (EEO) stated, "I believe the glass ceiling is real, that it destroys morale, and that though we have made some progress, we are a long way from shattering it." In the report John W. Snow, President and CEO of CSX Corporation is quoted as saying, "It's clear that progress is possible when top management addresses the importance of women and minorities in a straightforward manner with real commitment to finding answers . . ."

The basic finding of the commission was: "Qualified minorities and women are all too often on the outside looking into the executive suite." Lynn Martin, secretary of labor in the George H. W. Bush administration, summarized the glass ceiling's impact: "The glass ceiling, where it exists, hinders not only individuals but society as a whole. It effectively cuts our pool of potential corporate leaders by eliminating over one-half of our population. It deprives our economy of new leaders, new sources of creativity the 'would be' pioneers of the business world."

The Glass Ceiling Commission pilot project randomly selected nine Fortune 500 establishments for review reviews that were conducted by senior officials from the national and regional offices of the Department of labor. They found that their conclusions generally applied to all nine companies, despite the vast differences that existed among them in terms of organizational structure, CORPORATE CULTURE, and business sector and personnel policies.

- If there was not a glass ceiling, there certainly was point beyond which minorities and women had not advanced in some companies.
- Minorities had plateaued at lower-levels of the workforce than women had.
- Monitoring for equal access and opportunity, especially as managers move up the corporate ladder to senior management levels where important decisions were made, was almost never considered a corporate responsibility or part of the planning for developmental programs and policies.
- Appraisal and total compensation systems that determined salary, bonuses, incentives, and perquisites for employees were not monitored.
- Placement patterns were consistent with research data.
- There was a general lack of adequate records.

Among the attitudinal and organizational barriers identified were

- recruitment practices involving reliance on word-of-mouth and employee-referral networking as well as the use of executive search-and-referral firms in which affirmative action/EEO requirements were not made known
- a failure to make available to minorities and women such traditional precursors to advancement as developmental practices and credential-building experiences, including advanced education, as well as career-enhancing assignments such as to corporate committees and task forces and special projects
- the failure of senior-level executives and corporate decision-makers to be accountable for Equal Employment Opportunity responsibilities

To help support the removal of glass ceilings, the Department of Labor annually honors outstanding federal contractors and contractor associations that have demonstrated innovative efforts to increase EMPLOYMENT opportunities for minorities, women, individuals with disabilities, and veterans. The OFCCP Exemplary Voluntary Efforts (EVE) Awards are presented for highly successful good-faith efforts and action programs.

The United States is not the only country facing the problem of glass ceilings. The Australian Human Rights & Equal

Opportunity Commission studied "Glass Ceilings and Sticky Floors" in the finance sector. They found that "women were concentrated in part-time, lower-grade work with limited opportunities for training and advancement." The commission recommended the introduction of career and gender-awareness programs, development plans for managerial and nonmanagerial women employees, appropriate training, and examination of lateral and vertical career paths.

Further reading
Australian Human Rights & Equal Opportunity Commission website. Available on-line. URL: www.humanrights.gov.au; Lynn Martin. "A Report on the Glass Ceiling Initiative." Available on-line. URL: http://www.mith2.umd.edu/WomensStudies/Gender Issues/GlassCeiling/LaborDeptInfo/glass-ceiling-initiative.

globalization
Globalization is an economic and cultural process in which countries are increasingly integrated through economic and political connections. Globalization began to grow after World War II, when falling TARIFFS and more efficient means of air travel promoted both an expansion and a reliance on world trade. In the immediate postwar era, TRADE BARRIERS were eased through international agreements, such as the General Agreement on Tariffs and Trade (GATT, 1947), as part of an effort by industrialized nations to reinvigorate the world economy. More recently, technological advances have linked financial markets, and today financial transactions can occur in an instant from across the world. As global markets have been established and become profitable, new open markets continue to emerge in countries that have formerly been closed and highly regulated.

With globalization there has been an increase in the number of regional trade agreements, such as the EUROPEAN UNION (EU), the NORTH AMERICAN FREE TRADE AGREEMENT (NAFTA), and the Asia-Pacific Economic Cooperation (APEC). These agreements serve to enhance international economic opportunities for their member nations by easing economic barriers to international trade and business operations. In 1994 the WORLD TRADE ORGANIZATION (WTO) was created out of GATT negotiations. With over 130 participating countries, the WTO is currently the most prominent international organization responsible for setting and enforcing global-trade rules intended to lower trade barriers, institute international product standards, and provide a forum to settle international trade disputes.

With globalization there has been an increase in foreign direct investment by MULTINATIONAL CORPORATIONS, large companies with operations in more than one country. These CORPORATIONS take advantage of economic opportunities by utilizing variations in local conditions, such as lower wages, to promote a competitive advantage in the PRODUCTION, distribution, and marketing of their PRODUCTS. Some labor organizations have feared that globaliza-

tion will allow corporations to exploit unequal standards of workers' rights in less developed countries and EMERGING MARKETS. For example, if workers were to strike in the United Kingdom or France, employers could move their operations to countries where workers have lower expectations. This has caused some labor organizations to be resistant to globalization forces.

Concerns over the negative impact of globalization have increased in recent years. A 1999 WTO Conference in Seattle, Washington, was met with thousands of protesters who claimed that the WTO should leverage trade sanctions against nations with poor labor or environmental practices. In 2001 similar protests were made at the meeting of the Group of Eight industrialized nations in Genoa, Italy, where over 100,000 antiglobalization demonstrators congregated and one was killed in clashes with police. On the other hand, many developing countries have resisted the demonstrators' efforts, claiming that eased trade restrictions bring much-needed FOREIGN INVESTMENT to poorer countries, and that strict environmental and labor regulations would be prohibitively expensive for less-developed countries.

CONSUMER BEHAVIOR has also been influenced by globalization. The growth of the mass media and an increase in international travel has heightened cultural exchanges, which in many cases has made it easier for companies to operate and train personnel abroad. Many multinational corporations have developed brand awareness with consumers worldwide; for example, McDonald's, Coca-Cola, Fosters Lager, and Marks and Spencer have products that are sold in numerous countries. The INTERNET has also permitted some consumers to purchase products from other countries on-line.

As the world becomes smaller through international coalitions, electronic exchanges from across the globe in a matter of seconds, the development of E-COMMERCE and E-BUSINESS, the proliferation of mass media, and the development of worldwide consumer tastes, globalization will continue to shape the world economy and culture in the years to come.

—Margaret C. Dunlap

global shares
Global shares are COMMON STOCK shares that trade in multiple currencies around the world. Introduced in 1998 with the merger of DaimlerChrysler, global shares are an alternative to AMERICAN DEPOSITORY RECEIPTS (ADRs), which are indirect holdings of stock in a foreign company. With ADRs, a U.S. custodial bank holds the shares of stock of the foreign company and issues receipts to stock purchasers. Because ADRs are indirect holdings, they must be converted back to local shares if sold outside the United States. Also, holders of ADRs do not always have the same rights, including shareholder resolutions and sometimes voting privileges.

The market for creating ADRs is dominated by J. P. Morgan, Citibank, and Bank of New York. In 1998 Bank of

New York, along with Deutsche Bank, created global shares as an alternative to ADRs. Global shares were seen as part of the process linking STOCK MARKETS around the world and a way for the two banks to gain a greater share of the lucrative foreign stock-trading market.

Between 1998 and 2001, only three companies—DaimlerChrysler, Celanese, and UBS Financial Services—issued global shares, while over 500 companies issued ADRs. Both ADRs and global shares offer the benefits of allowing companies to issue dollar-denominated stock to its U.S. employees, opportunities to broaden their investor base, and the use of proceeds to acquire companies in the United States. Most companies considering both alternatives have found global shares more expensive to initiate and requiring more coordination with back-office systems and regulatory agencies.

Further reading
Karmin, Craig. "What in the World? Global Shares May Leave Obscurity," *Wall Street Journal,* 20 August 2001, p. C1.

goal setting

In business, goal setting—the establishment of personal or professional objectives—can be an individual or organizational activity. Managers often use goal setting as a means of motivating employees. Many MANAGEMENT writers provide guidelines for people or groups attempting to set goals.

Selling magazine recommends not setting goals that are easily attained, suggesting that these types of goals do not inspire people. Instead they suggest:

- "Create a big-picture goal"—some long-term important objective.
- "Break it down into basics"—divide the overall goal into smaller more manageable tasks.
- "Be unreasonable"—goals should be appropriate but should also take effort to achieve.

Tom Ritchey, author of *I'm Stuck, You're Stuck: Break Through to Better Work Relationships and Results by Discovering Your DiSC Behavioral Style,* suggests that managers need to understand first what drives their own behavior and then what motivates their employees. Ritchey states there are four behavioral styles: dominance, influence, supportiveness, and conscientiousness.

For dominance-style employees, people who see problems and attempt to solve them, Ritchey suggests goal setting should include such questions as "What do you think needs to be done?" and "What can you do to help the company?" Dominance-style employees prefer autonomy and need only clearly stated rules and expectations to work effectively.

Influence-style employees take more time, as they want to discuss everything that is going on in the com-

pany and are more emotional than dominance-style workers. Influence-style employees are likely to be better at goals associated with working with others and generating enthusiasm for the objectives.

Supportiveness-style workers prefer to make lists and check off accomplishments; these workers need more guidance in goal-setting. Finally, conscientiousness-style employees tend to be careful and more reserved, needing specific information related to goals and time in order to achieve them.

Most people think of goal setting as having a New Year's resolution. Whether setting personal or business goals, *Investor's Business Daily* writer Linda Stockman-Vines suggests reviewing past goal-setting using statements like "I learned (fill in the blank) this past year." She then suggests asking oneself, "What risks am I running by going along just as I have been?" Experts in HUMAN RESOURCES state that working Americans will have, on average, seven major career changes in their professional life. Without setting goals and striving for them, businesspeople can leave themselves unprepared for change. Stockman-Vines also suggests going through lists of goals and eliminating any "shoulds," which are obligations, not goals.

Like almost every other aspect of business, there are a variety of websites that attempt to provide assistance with goal setting. *Business Week* writer Francesca Di Meglio reviewed several sites and came away unimpressed, noting, "All these sites have spiritual jive in common, instructing visitors to do things like overcome their fears and move metaphorical mountains. Of course, no Web site can move the mountains for you. This may not be a shock. But it's still worth saying."

See also PROBLEM SOLVING.

Further reading
Di Meglio, Francesca. "This Self-Help Site Needs Help." *Business Week Online.* Available on-line. URL: www.businessweek.com. Downloaded on January 2, 2002; "Set 'unreasonable' goals." *Selling* (January 2002) p. 2; Stockman-Vines, Linda. "Decide on your Dreams: Help Workers Set Goals." *Investor's Business Daily,* 22 January 2002: p. 6. Ritchey, Tom. *I'm Stuck, You're Stuck: Break Through to Better Work Relationships and Results by Discovering Your DiSC Behavioral Style.* San Francisco: Berrett-Koehler, 2002.

goodwill, going concern

A going concern is an established business with a developed clientele and/or reputation. Because the business is "up and running" and has a following, such a business, if sold, will command a price higher than the BOOK VALUE of its ASSETS as listed on its BALANCE SHEET. The excess of price over the book value of the firm's assets is called goodwill, which can be recorded only when it is purchased; that is, a buyer may claim goodwill only when he or she pays for it. Goodwill is a long-term, intangible asset and is listed with the other long-term assets of the newly purchased firm.

Until 2002, goodwill was amortized over a period of time not to exceed 40 years. Under new rules, companies can leave goodwill on their balance sheets indefinitely, as long as it does not become impaired. After the Enron fiasco, many companies are taking a closer look at their accounting practices and incurring "impairment" charges under the new rules. Companies are now required to test the value of goodwill they carry on their FINANCIAL STATEMENTS every year and write it down if it is excessive. Discounted cash flow is often used to test the value of assets acquired.

It is not the seller of a going concern who determines the amount of goodwill associated with the firm; rather, goodwill is market-determined. If the market (selling) price is above the book value of the assets of the firm being sold, then the market views the established nature of the firm and its clientele as desirable and more profitable than a new, start-up firm. If the firm's selling price is in line with the book value of its assets, then the market does not view that any goodwill has developed over the life of that firm.

Further reading
Sender, Henry. "Flood of Firms to Take Goodwill Write-downs," *Wall Street Journal,* 24 April 2002. p. A1.

government debt
The government debt, also referred to as the federal, public, or national debt, is the cumulated sum of outstanding IOUs that a government owes its creditors. In the United States, the government debt refers to indebtedness of the federal government. (State governments have balanced-budget laws limiting or prohibiting the state government from running persistent budget deficits and creating a state-owed debt.) The federal debt, approximately 6.3 trillion in the year 2003 is the result of past budget deficits. Historically the U.S. government ran budget deficits during periods of war and RECESSIONs. Government spending and deficits rose during the GREAT DEPRESSION and World War II but declined after each period. However, beginning in the mid-1970s, the federal government began running persistent and expanding deficits, averaging $50 billion during the Jimmy Carter administration, almost $200 billion per year during the second Ronald Reagan administration, $290 billion during the last year of the George H. W. Bush administration (1992), and approaching $450 billion per year in the George W. Bush administrations (2003). Each year the U.S. Treasury Department borrows additional funds to pay for the difference between government revenue and government spending (the deficit). These additional amounts are added to the federal debt. Unlike households and individuals, the federal government rarely pays off its debt but does have to pay interest on it; otherwise creditors, primarily U.S. citizens, would no longer lend money to the government. Interest payments on the debt are included in the FEDERAL BUDGET and are generally the third- or fourth-largest category of federal government spending.

In 1998, for the first time in almost 30 years, the federal government began accumulating a budget surplus. Economic logic suggests it is normal for governments to run budget surpluses during periods of economic expansion, when government spending on programs for the poor tends to decline and revenues from progressive taxation tend to increase. If budget surpluses are used to pay off portions of the government debt, it can create what economists call a "virtuous circle." Decreased government borrowing reduces market INTEREST RATES, which in turn reduces government spending on interest payments. This increases budget surpluses, which then can be used to pay off more of the debt.

In recent years budget surpluses have been replaced by deficits. When the government increases its borrowing to fund deficit spending it can lead to higher interest rates, reducing business borrowing and investment. This is called the crowding-out effect and is a hotly debated topic among business economists.

There are several ways to consider and measure government debt. While the gross public debt was approximately $6.3 trillion in 2003, much of it was interagency borrowing—for example, the FEDERAL RESERVE SYSTEM lending surplus funds to the U.S. Treasury and accumulating Treasury securities in return for the funds loaned to the government. Another way to look at the government debt is as a percentage of GROSS DOMESTIC PRODUCT (GDP). Like a growing business, it is normal and logical for government borrowing to increase as the economy grows. When compared to the size of the economy, the national debt peaked at the end of World War II at approximately 115 percent of GDP, declined to about 30 percent of GDP during the 1970s, and rose to about 60 percent in 1994 before beginning to decline.

A third way to look at the debt is consider to whom is it owed. One common myth is that foreign governments control much of the U.S. debt, which could lead to political "blackmail" and international lenders dictating policies to the U.S. government. The overwhelming majority of the national debt (80 percent) is owed to Americans. Of the remaining 20 percent, most of it is held by foreign individuals, investors who decided the U.S. government was a good credit risk.

Another common question is: Why would people lend money to a government that already owed over $6 trillion? The U.S. economy is the largest and, by many measures, the most productive in the world. When private individuals borrow money, they are often required to provide collateral, ASSETS the lender could take title to and sell if the borrower defaulted on the loan. The federal government has the authority to tax its citizens, so in effect the collateral of the U.S. government is the assets and productive capacity of its citizens.

This leads to the question of whether the government debt is a transfer of indebtedness from present citizens to future generations. The Congressional Budget Office has developed "generational accounts" estimating the net-payment burden on future generations if the government debt is eventually paid off. This analysis showed that current retirees are, in fact, receiving benefits in excess of tax payments they have made, while younger workers' lifetime tax payments will likely exceed the present value of the benefits will receive.

Further reading
Ruffin, Roy J., and Paul R. Gregory. *Principles of Economics*, 7th ed. Boston: Addison Wesley, 2001.

Government National Mortgage Association (Ginnie Mae)

The Government National Mortgage Association, better known as Ginnie Mae, is a government-owned CORPORATION that primarily provides INSURANCE for MORTGAGES originating through Federal Housing Administration (FHA) and Veterans Administration (VA) government-loan programs.

Ginnie Mae does not make mortgage LOANS; its mission is "to support expanded affordable housing in America by providing an efficient government-guaranteed secondary market vehicle linking the CAPITAL MARKETS with Federal housing markets." Ginnie Mae helps make mortgage-backed securities more attractive to investors, thereby increasing the availability of mortgage credit.

Ginnie Mae was created in 1968 as a wholly owned corporation within the Department of Housing and Urban Development (HUD). Its purpose is to serve low-to-moderate-income homebuyers. The National Housing Act was enacted on June 27, 1934, as one of several economic recovery measures during the GREAT DEPRESSION. It provided for the establishment of a Federal Housing Administration (FHA) to be headed by a federal housing administrator. Title II of the act provided for the insurance of home-mortgage loans made by private lenders as one of the FHA's principal functions.

Title III of the act provided for the chartering of national mortgage associations by the federal housing administrator. These associations were to be private corporations regulated by the administrator, and their chief purpose was to buy and sell the mortgages to be insured by FHA under Title II. Only one association was ever formed under this authority, the National Mortgage Association of Washington, which was created on February 10, 1938, as a subsidiary of the Reconstruction Finance Corporation, a government corporation. That same year the association's name was changed to the FEDERAL NATIONAL MORTGAGE ASSOCIATION (known as Fannie Mae). By revision of Title III in 1954, Fannie Mae was converted into a mixed-owner-ship corporation, its preferred stock to be held by the government and its COMMON STOCK to be privately held. By amendments made in 1968, the Federal National Mortgage Association was partitioned into two separate entities, one known as the Government National Mortgage Association

(Ginnie Mae), the other, Federal National Mortgage Association. Ginnie Mae remained in the government, and Fannie Mae became privately owned by retiring the government-held stock. Ginnie Mae has operated as a wholly owned government association since the 1968 amendments.

Ginnie Mae issues securities that pass through payments of principal and interest received on a pool of federally insured mortgage loans. These pools of loans are originated by commercial banks, mortgage bankers, and other mortgage-lending institutions. Ginnie Mae dictates the specifications regarding which loans can be placed into the pool; does not purchase the loans from originators; and guarantees that payments will be made on a timely basis, reducing the risk to investors. Because most mortgages are repaid before their maturity (on average, Americans change homes every seven years), holders of Ginnie Mae securities recover most of their principle investment well before the scheduled maturities of the pool of loans.

In 2002 proposed legislation would allow Ginnie Mae to securitize conventional mortgage loans. SECURITIZATION is the process of aggregating a pool of debt instruments and issuing securities backed by the pool of loans. The legislation would authorize Ginnie Mae Choice and allow the government-owned corporation to compete directly with Fannie Mae and Freddie Mac (the FEDERAL HOME LOAN MORTGAGE CORPORATION) in the secondary mortgage-loan market.

Further reading
Government National Mortgage Association website. Available on-line. URL: www.ginniemae.gov. Fernandez, Tommy. "Just Where Does the MBA Stand on GNMA Choice?" *The American Banker* (22 March 2002).

government-sponsored enterprises

Government-sponsored enterprises (GSEs) are government-created institutions designed to close perceived gaps in the country's capital markets for agriculture and housing. The major GSEs are the FEDERAL NATIONAL MORTGAGE ASSOCIATION (Fannie Mae), the FEDERAL HOME LOAN MORTGAGE CORPORATION (Freddie Mac), the FARM CREDIT SYSTEM, STUDENT LOAN MARKETING ASSOCIATION (Sallie Mae), and the FEDERAL HOME LOAN BANK SYSTEM. Most GSEs are WHOLESALERS in financial markets, buying securities from retail lenders and packaging them for resale to investors and INVESTMENT groups. The Farm Credit System (FCS) is an exception, in that it is a retail lender to agricultural and rural customers.

The need for GSEs grew out of the GREAT DEPRESSION. Over 10,000 banks failed during a two-year period, creating a credit crisis in the country. The 1934 National Housing Act established the Federal Housing Administration (FHA). Title III of the act provided for the chartering of national mortgage associations by the federal housing administrator. These associations were to be private CORPORATIONS regulated by the administrator, and their chief purpose was to buy and sell MORTGAGES to be insured by FHA under Title II. Only one association, Fannie Mae, was ever formed under this authority.

By revision of Title III in 1954, Fannie Mae was converted into a mixed-ownership corporation, its preferred stock to be held by the government and its common stock to be privately held. By amendments made in 1968, the Federal National Mortgage Association was partitioned into two separate entities, the GOVERNMENT NATIONAL MORTGAGE ASSOCIATION (Ginnie Mae) and the Federal National Mortgage Association (Fannie Mae). Ginnie Mae remained in the government, and Fannie Mae became privately owned by retiring the government-held stock.

Freddie Mac, known as the smaller cousin of Fannie Mae, was established in 1970 to buy conventional (not federally insured) mortgage LOANS. In 1989 Freddie Mac became a private stockholder-owned corporation, but with a mixture of oversight. Freddie Mac's BOARD OF DIRECTORS includes 13 members elected by stockholders and five appointed by the president of the United States. Freddie Mac is the 27th-largest corporation in the country, with over $500 billion in ASSETS.

The Farm Credit System (FCS) was the first GSE, established under the Federal Farm Loan Act of 1916. The FCS was funded with government CAPITAL and tax-exempt BONDS to extend long-term loans to agriculture. Over the years, FCS has expanded and contracted with changes in the agricultural industry, but it continues to provide direct lending in rural areas of the country.

The Federal Home Loan Bank (FHLB) System includes 12 regional banks that provide loans ("advances") to retail financial lenders. While commercial banks make up the majority of FHLB System members, proposed changes in federal laws would expand credit to small community banks, allowing them to utilize new categories of collateral for loans and meet lesser standards for entry into the FHLB System. Private lenders are challenging these proposed changes as well as a new program that would allow direct lending through the System.

The fifth major GSE, Sallie Mae, was established in 1972 as a federally chartered, stockholder-owned corporation. Sallie Mae controls a variety of education-lending programs, the most widely known being the Student Loan Marketing Association (SLMA), from which Sallie Mae's name was derived. In 1997 it was reorganized with SLM Holding Company, and in 2000 it was renamed USA Education, Inc. Through a variety of subsidiaries, Sallie Mae is the leading student lending, servicing, and loan-guaranteeing organization in the country. The GSE part of Sallie Mae must be dissolved by 2008.

The major issue facing all GSEs is the implied federal guarantee of their securities. This decreases the perceived market RISK, reducing the cost of capital for GSEs. With lower-cost borrowing, GSEs can earn greater gross-PROFIT margins than competing lending institutions. A second issue to "mission creep," the expansion of GSEs beyond their original intent. Direct lending, on-line loan applications, home-mortgage INSURANCE, and other lending-related activities that are traditionally the domain of commercial, retail financial institutions are an increasing source of conflict between GSEs and the financial market.

Further reading
"Government-sponsored Enterprises." Available on-line. URL: www.aba.com; "About Us." Student Loan Marketing Corporation. Available on-line. URL: www.salliemae.com.

graphs
In business and economics, graphs are used to convey information and ideas quickly. The most frequently used types are line graphs, bar graphs, and pie charts. Typical line graphs include time-series and cause-and-effect relationship graphs. As a matter of convention, time-series graphs put time on the horizontal axis and whatever is being compared over time on the vertical axis.

Generally cause-and-effect relationship graphs show the dependent variable on the horizontal axis and the independent variable on the vertical axis, but not always so. The independent variable is the variable whose value is not determined by the value of other variables. The dependent variable is the variable whose value is determined by the value of the independent variable. For example, a demand curve shows the relationship between price and quantity demanded in a market in a period of time, ceteris paribus (other things being equal, unchanged). The amount of a product purchased depends on its price, which is the independent variable, determined by the business offering the good. Quantity demanded is the dependent variable, changing in response to changes in price.

In the example of a DEMAND curve, there is an inverse relationship between price and quantity demanded. As price rises, the quantity demanded decreases. As price decreases, the quantity demanded increases. (The degree to which quantity demanded responds to a price change is measured using the ELASTICITY OF DEMAND concept.) A direct, cause-and-effect relationship is one where a positive change in the independent variable causes a positive change in the dependent variable, and a decrease in the independent variable causes a decrease in the dependent variable. Two typical examples of direct relationships are supply curves and CONSUMPTION functions. In response to a higher price, producers will provide greater quantity. In response to an increase in INCOME, consumers will purchase more goods and services.

Graphs are used frequently by businesspeople and economists. Some students call economics courses "graphs and laughs." Others refer to economics as the "dismal science." Marketers use graphs to quickly display relationships like the growth in sales or market share over time. Unethical businesspeople use graphs to impress or "snow" consumers. Graphs are created using data, and the quality of the data used to create a graph determines the validity of the information or concept being portrayed. In statistics there is an old saying, "Garbage in, garbage out." The same is true in the use of graphs.

gray markets

Gray (or parallel) markets are markets where legitimate (as opposed to counterfeit) trademarked goods are distributed and sold through unauthorized channels. Many U.S. manufacturers license their technology and BRANDS to companies in other countries. If there are significant differences in the price of domestically made goods and the same PRODUCT made under license by a foreign manufacturer, it can encourage the transshipment of the foreign-made product back into the U.S. market. For example, in the 1990s when the Mexican peso fell against the dollar (see PESO CRISIS), the price of consumer products like Colgate toothpaste made in Mexico was approximately one-third the price of the same product made in the United States. Similarly, Parker Pen authorized the PRODUCTION and sale of their pens to a Japanese manufacturer. If those pens are then shipped back into the U.S. market, they compete with the American-manufactured items. Most companies, in their CONTRACTS with international manufacturers, prohibit the shipment of products made under license back into the licensing company's home market, but it is debatable whether such actions violate U.S. importation, TRADEMARK, PATENT, or COPYRIGHT laws.

Sometimes consumer DEMAND creates gray markets. When Canon shifted supply of its copiers for the Russian market from factories in Japan to a company factory in China, sales plummeted. Canon dealers in Russia found gray marketers willing to ship them copiers made in Japan. Sometimes gray markets are created by company attempts at MARKET SEGMENTATION, in which marketers try to divide the total market into relatively homogeneous groups and charge a higher price to those groups who are willing and able to pay more for the product. Markets where the higher price is charged encourage ARBITRAGE, buying the product in the lower-priced market and reselling it in the higher-priced market.

With the speed and access of INTERNET communications, price differentials are quickly recognized, creating opportunities for gray marketers. Gray markets have even developed for computer chips, providing computer manufacturers alternatives to the authorized dealer when looking for components. Gray markets differ from markets for counterfeit products in the fact that they are made under license from the original company. Gray markets are not "black markets" because they are not trading illegal products. While price differences are the major factor in creat-

ing gray markets, customers concerned with service and warranties are not likely to purchase gray market products. Because these products are purchased through unauthorized marketing channels, service and warranties are difficult to obtain. One study found that gray markets benefit manufacturers because sales in those markets are mostly to price-sensitive customers who would not have purchased their product through the authorized and higher-priced channel.

Further reading

Champion, David. "The bright side of gray markets," *Harvard Business Review* 76, no. 5 (September-October 1998): 19.

Great Depression

The Great Depression (1929–41) was the most severe period of economic decline in the history of the United States. During the Great Depression, U.S. output declined by one-third, the unemployment rate reached 25 percent, the STOCK MARKET declined by 40 percent, and over 9,000 banks failed. The depression brought an end to the Roaring Twenties, a period of euphoria in the country marked by increasing output and INCOME, Federal Reserve management of the MONEY SUPPLY, and significant technological advances.

The causes of the depression are still being debated, and economists' lists of the contributing factors include

- TARIFFS
- overproduction
- the FEDERAL RESERVE SYSTEM
- the gold standard
- malinvestment
- rigid wages and prices
- distribution of WEALTH and power

During the economic boom of the 1920s, U.S. manufacturers significantly increased their export activity. Previously there was sufficient domestic DEMAND for new industrial output, and U.S. firms largely ignored EXPORTING. With the decline in 1929, Congress passed the infamous SMOOT-HAWLEY TARIFF ACT increasing tariffs an average of 60 percent. European countries and Canada quickly reciprocated causing a collapse in international trade.

Overproduction during the 1920s, both in industry and agriculture, resulted in declining prices. Declining prices are generally considered beneficial, reducing costs and controlling INFLATION. However, when price declines are widespread, DEFLATION occurs, and when deflation reaches a critical stage, it impacts financial markets, primarily banks. (At one point during the depression, prices fell 10 percent a year). Today many financial institutions make LOANS to businesses and deposit INSURANCE protects accounts, but in the 1920s, commercial banks almost exclusively provided business loans and FDIC insurance did not exist. When deflation occurs, the value of ASSETS decline. Eventually (as in Japan in the 1990s), banks have loans for which the collateral is worth less than the amount loaned; the result is bank failure.

In the early 1930s, over 9,000 U.S. banks failed, with depositors losing everything they had in the failed banks. Seeing their life savings disappear, many reacted by withdrawing any funds left in existing banks, contributing to a run on the BANKING SYSTEM. Future savings were also hoarded, buried in Mason jars, stuffed in mattresses—put anywhere but in banks. Savings are needed for INVESTMENT, but without funds being deposited in banks, banks cannot lend anything to businesses for investment and thus increase the supply of MONEY, leading to problems for the Federal Reserve, the nation's manager of MONETARY POLICY. In 1928 the Fed increased INTEREST RATES in order to discourage stock-market speculation. When the stock market finally crashed in October 1929, panic struck. Banks raised their interest rates on business loans, further discouraging private investment. The Fed "tightening" of the money supply again in 1931 exacerbated the situation, which one economist described as a period of "collective insanity." There was no work, therefore there was no demand. Without market demand, there was no output and therefore no income.

The flow of output and income in an economic system requires money, which is not an asset but primarily a medium of exchange between producers and consumers and among traders in international transactions. During the Great Depression, the world was on the gold standard, and each country limited its money supply based on its gold reserves. In the United States, 1 ounce of gold equaled $20. Under the gold standard, a country with a trade surplus received gold and therefore could expand its money supply. A country with a trade deficit transferred gold to its trading partners, reducing its money supply and, in theory, correcting its trade imbalance through lower prices. Since gold was in relatively fixed supply, the world's money supply was more or less fixed. Thus monetary authorities had limited ability to increase the money supply when, during an economic downturn, an increase in the money supply could lower interest rates and stimulate economic activity.

With the booming economy of 1920s, the Fed allowed a 60 percent increase in the money supply, a decision that critics suggest abetted stock market speculation and contributed to the collapse in 1929. According to the Austrian school of economic theory, it also led to malinvestment— investments that were not justifiable at prevailing interest rates but were considered rational when interest rates declined. Monetary policy designed to stimulate investment is a temporary action, and when interest rates later rose, these investments were no longer profitable and therefore liquidated.

According to economists, rigid wages and prices contributed to the depression by not allowing markets to adjust. With the collapse of the stock market in 1929, con-sumers reduced their spending, causing a decrease in aggregate demand. Decreased spending along with flexible wages and prices would lower both, but businesses maintained prices in order to cover costs and workers resisted wage cuts, leading to both reduced sales and increased UNEMPLOYMENT.

Probably the most controversial theory regarding the causes of the Great Depression is the issue of wealth and power distribution. The 1920s saw the heyday of the industrial capitalists. Even with constraints imposed by the SHERMAN ANTITRUST ACT (1890) and the CLAYTON ANTITRUST ACT (1914), a relatively small number of individuals and companies controlled significant amounts of the country's wealth. Some economists suggest this contributed to the depression by concentrating demand in the hands of a small percentage of the population who, when the stock market crashed, pulled back their spending, furthering the decline. In addition, with a small number of large CORPORATIONS producing significant portions of the national output, the economy was adversely affected when a few of these companies declined.

As British economist John Maynard Keynes observed in 1930, the world was ". . . as capable as before of affording for every one a high standard of living. . . . But today we have involved ourselves in a colossal muddle, having blundered in the control of a delicate machine, the working of which we do not understand."

Further reading

Delong, J. Bradford. "The Great Crash and The Great Slump," UC-Berkeley. Available on-line. URL: http://econ161.berkeley.edu/TCEH/Slouch_Crash14.html; Nordeen, Ross. "America's Great Depression." Available on-line. URL: www.ametecon.com/greatdepression.html. Smiley, Gene. *Rethinking the Great Depression.* Chicago: I. R. Dee, 2002.

green cards

Green cards are immigrant VISAS giving foreigners permanent-resident status in the United States. Unlike visas, which are granted for a specific length of time to engage in specific business activities, green cards allow non-U.S. citizens to reside in the country indefinitely. Green-card status also allows individuals to become U.S. citizens after five years (three years if the immigrant acquired the green card through marriage to a citizen).

Most green cards, named such because of their color, are allocated based on the relationship of the applicant to U.S. citizens, but some are available based on business criteria. Employment-based green cards called First Preference Petition are issued to foreigners with extraordinary ability, including outstanding professors and researchers and certain executives and managers of MULTINATIONAL CORPORATIONS. Second Preference Petition cards are issued to members of professions holding advanced degrees and people of exceptional ability in the sciences, arts, and business. Third Preference Petition cards are available to skilled workers, professionals, and other workers, while Fourth Preference Petition cards are for special immigrants, including religious workers. Finally, Fifth Preference Petitions, known as million-dollar green cards, are available for people actively investing in a new business that will create at least 10 new full-time jobs for U.S. workers. The million-dollar requirement is reduced to half that amount for investment in low-population or high-unemployment areas of the country.

Green cards are difficult to obtain and often require hiring specialized legal assistance. Foreigners in the United States on visas are sometimes subject to different rules when applying for permanent-resident status. In the 1990s the United States created a lottery system for 50,000 green cards annually.

Further reading
U.S. Immigration and Naturalization Service website. Available on-line. URL: www.ins.usdoj.gov.

green marketing
Green marketing is the PRODUCTION, promotion, and reclamation of environmentally sensitive PRODUCTS. Green marketing includes a variety of activities and strategies, including recycling, pollution control and reduction, product development, POSITIONING, and reclamation systems.

The emergence and importance of green marketing in the United States is associated with a series of events over the last three decades of the 20th century. When Americans protested the use of pesticides on the first Earth Day in 1970, they sent a message to marketers that they wanted chemical-free food products. Earth Day influenced the 1970 formation of the ENVIRONMENTAL PROTECTION AGENCY. The Love Canal tragedy came to light on the late 1970s when Lois Gibbs documented diseases among residents in a housing development built on top of a toxic-waste dump. Three Mile Island, the 1979 nuclear-reactor crisis in Pennsylvania, galvanized environmentalist fears, and Exxon became a symbol of environmental irresponsibility with the Alaskan oil spill created by its ship, the *Exxon Valdez,* in 1989. The Brundtland Report (World Commission on Environment and Development, 1987), the Earth Summit in Rio (1992), and former vice president Al Gore's book *Earth in the Balance* (1993) added information and pressure to change business strategies.

Initially most American businesses responded to pressure from consumers and citizenry by instituting bottom-up pollution-prevention programs to reduce wastes and environmental pollutants. In the process many firms found environmental management could generate cost savings. Green-market concerns were framed in terms of risk reduction, reengineering, or cost cutting. In addition to companies, communities across the country initiated recycling programs to expand the supply of recyclable

materials, sometimes beyond the industry capacity to use them in the production of new products.

Later some companies found green marketing could be used as a strategy to differentiate companies from their competitors. In the 1990s, whether through efforts to reduce pollution, increased use of renewable resources, donations to protect the rainforest, or new environmentally friendly products, American businesses began to develop green-marketing strategies. Most had to first overcome the problems of educating consumers about company products and green strategies, demonstrating tangible efforts and impacts and providing opportunities for choosing environmentally friendly products. The FEDERAL TRADE COMMISSION developed Guides for Use of Environmental Marketing Claims, providing green marketers with assistance in complying with truth-in-ADVERTISING regulations.

Early green-marketing efforts included organically grown produce, which some remember for being overpriced and of lower quality than nonorganic products. The utility industry is an often-cited example in green marketing. In the 1990s, many utilities, often under mandates from regulatory commissions, reluctantly developed sources of renewable energy, including solar, wind, and geothermal systems. Because these sources cost more to produce, companies charged a higher price. Consumers, who could not see the product, had to be shown the benefit of renewable energy sources and convinced the utility company was truly investing in environmentally friendly sources of energy. Consequently, green-marketing efforts by electric utilities have been only modestly successful.

In the late 1990s, the Green Gauge Report, conducted by Roper Starch Worldwide, reported that Americans' attitudes toward green marketing were changing. The report, which tracked Americans' environmental knowledge and concerns since 1990, showed the percentage in most environmentally dedicated groups, labeled the "True-Blue Greens," remained constant at 10 percent of the adult population. But the percentage of "Greenback Greens"—people willing to pay more for green products—had declined from 11 percent in 1990 to 5 percent in 1996. Some former Greenback Greens were now found in what Roper called the "Sprouts Group," people who still cared but were unwilling to pay more; this group represented 33 percent of adults. The third group, "Passive Grousers"—those who viewed the environment as someone else's problem—shrank from 24 percent to 15 percent in the 1990–96 period, but many of these consumers became "Basic Browns," or environmental deadbeats—people who did not care much, if at all, about the environment. This group grew from 28 percent to 37 percent.

Green marketing must appeal to consumers, but with increasing consumer apathy or indifference to environmental concerns, it has become less important among business concerns. Nevertheless, in a highly praised 1997 *Harvard Business Review* article, management professor

Stuart Hart argues, "Rarely is greening linked to strategy or technology development, and as a result, most companies fail to recognize opportunities of potentially staggering proportions." Hart outlines a current strategy based on pollution prevention and product stewardship, leading to clean technology and a sustainability vision for future strategies. Interest in and growth of green marketing will likely move in cycles as world economic, political, and environmental conditions change.

Further reading

Hart, Stuart L. "Beyond greening: Strategies for a Sustainable World." *Harvard Business Review*, V75N6 January–February 1997; 66. Speer, Tibbett L. "Growing the Green Market." *American Demographics*, V19N8 August 1997, 45–50.

gross domestic product

Gross domestic product (GDP) is the estimated MARKET VALUE (the price paid for goods and services) of all final goods and SERVICES produced in a country in a year. Generally, only those goods and services exchanged in markets for which there is taxable INCOME are included in GDP; most bartered services, illegal activities, household efforts, and in-kind transactions are not included. Some goods, particularly goods and services produced and sold to government, have no marketplace price. In this situation the cost to government is assumed to be the market value. For example, complex weapons systems only sold to the military are included in GDP at their cost.

Final goods and services are those that available to consumers. Since GDP is used to estimate the output of goods and services available to final consumers, primary goods such as raw materials and intermediary goods (which are used in the production of final goods) are not included in GDP. For example, few Americans buy wheat or flour; they purchase bread. Wheat is a primary PRODUCT, and flour is an intermediate product.

GDP can be calculated by either the sum of all expenditures for final goods and services or the sum of income received for the goods and services. These are known as the expenditures and income approaches, respectively. Recognizing in the CIRCULAR FLOW MODEL that businesses, households, and government are connected by flows of money, resources, and goods and services, the sum of expenditures for final goods and services will equal the income received for those products (with some statistical adjustment). Using the income approach, GDP equals the sum of wages, interest, rent, corporate PROFITS, capital CONSUMPTION allowance (the estimated value of DEPRECIATION of capital goods used in production), and indirect BUSINESS TAXES (taxes collected by businesses for government agencies), and net-factor income from abroad.

Using the expenditures approach, GDP equals the sum of consumption, INVESTMENT, and government spending, plus spending for exports minus spending for IMPORTS.

Economics textbooks use the equation $GDP = C+I+G+(X–M)$ to show the expenditures approach. In the United States, consumption expenditures (C) represent approximately two-thirds of all spending. Changes in consumer spending can dramatically change GDP. Reports describing changes in consumer income, confidence, and credit levels are INDICATORS of likely changes in consumption spending. Investment spending (I), spending on capital goods, represents approximately 15 percent of U.S. GDP, but it is often the most volatile component of GDP. Business investment is made in anticipation of growing and changing DEMAND for consumer goods. Investment spending is also influenced by INTEREST RATES, the percentage of factory capacity currently being utilized, and changes in technology. Government spending (G) is that portion of government budgets used to purchase goods and services. The U.S. FEDERAL BUDGET is approximately $2 trillion, but transfer payments, redistribution of purchasing power from one group to another, is not a government expenditure. SOCIAL SECURITY and other government-sponsored WELFARE programs are subtracted from the budget to estimate government expenditures. Net trade (X–M) adds expenditures for exports and subtracts expenditures for imports from GDP. Since GDP measures the value of output in an economy, foreign purchases of U.S. output are part of GDP, but U.S. consumers' purchases of imports is not part of GDP. Net trade is influenced by EXCHANGE RATES, levels of income in other countries, barriers or reductions in TRADE BARRIERS, and consumer preferences.

In the United States, GDP is calculated quarterly by the Department of Commerce. Each quarter the department issues a preliminary estimate, followed by a first and then second revision for GDP. GDP and percentage changes in GDP are the most widely watched measures of economic performance, influencing American business and MONETARY POLICY.

GDP is also often used as a measure of the economic well-being of a country and its citizens. But since GDP is a measure of output in an economy, it does not include

- nonmarket activities
- black-market exchanges
- changes in the quality of goods and services over time
- distribution of income and goods and services
- depletion of natural resources
- environmental degradation
- distinction between the use of renewable and nonrenewable resources
- Composition of spending, i.e., spending on negative deterrence (defense and personal safety) versus positive benefits (such as recreation, culture, or education)

Advocates of sustainable development challenge the widespread acceptance of the idea that if GDP is growing, people are better off, and have offered a variety of alternatives to GDP to measure well-being in a society. The most widely quoted alternative is the Index of Sustainable Economic Welfare (ISEW). Created by former World Bank economists Herman Daly and John Cobb Jr., the ISEW adjusts GDP to account for environmental and social factors, including income distribution, value of household Labor, and environmental damage.

Further reading

Boyes, William J., and Michael Melvin. *Macroeconomics,* 5th ed. Boston: Houghton Mifflin, 2001; Folsom, W. Davis, and Rick Boulware. "Sustainable Development: Toward a Sustainable Environmental Index." Paper presented at the Mountain Plains Management Conference, Cedar City, Utah, October, 2000.

gross margin   See INCOME STATEMENT, GROSS MARGIN.

growth stocks

Growth stocks are COMMON STOCK equities in companies perceived by investors as having above-average current- and projected-earnings growth. These stocks typically have very high price-earnings ratios and very low DIVIDEND yields; they have higher BETA COEFFICIENT ratios and are riskier INVESTMENTS, with greater upside and downside potential. The counter-investment strategy is value stocks. These stocks generally have low price-earnings ratios, higher dividend yields, and have a market capitalization (price times the number of shares outstanding) equal to or less than the value of the company's assets.

There are several ways a company can be a proven growth company, and several more in which it can be perceived by investors as having growth potential. If a company has an existing record of quarter-to-quarter (or year-to-year) above-average increases in sales, earnings, or gross PROFIT margins, investors will project these increases over many quarters or years and bid up the price of the stock well above current values in comparison to other investments. Companies without a verifiable record may project that their growth in sales or earnings will dramatically increase. They may also have investment analysts, bankers, or other promote their stock. Sometimes, because they are in the same industry or specific manufacturing or service category as other companies that have experienced superior growth in recent years, they feel they "deserve" a high price/earnings ratio or even a high price without any current earnings or substantial sales. Many U.S. DOT-COMS rationalized their high prices based on this reasoning.

The reward for investors in a company that is proven (or widely perceived) as a growth company is that the stock commands higher price/book, price/earnings, and price/sales ratios than its peers. The risk for investors in buying a growth stock is that the projection may be wrong, the premium paid for projected growth is withdrawn, and the stock falls substantially. More RISK is

entailed buying smaller companies that have no current earnings or high debt.

Growth companies have arisen in many fields, from retailing to technology, tobacco to perfume. In some cases the company developed a concept or idea that set it apart from existing COMPETITION; or it became the most efficient and drove out or bought up the competition; or it invented an entire new field and was the first (or best of the first group of companies) to succeed in it, dominating the new industry. Examples of large, successful companies considered to be proven growth companies (i.e., those that have demonstrated above-average growth in sales and earnings over many years) are Intel, Microsoft, Philip Morris, and Wal-Mart.

—Jerry and Jesse Rosenthal

guaranteed investment contract (guaranteed income contract)

A guaranteed investment contract (GIC), also referred to as a guaranteed income contract, is a CONTRACT between an INSURANCE company and a pension plan (i.e., 401(K) PLAN) or corporate PROFIT-sharing plan that guarantees a specific rate of return on the invested CAPITAL over the life of the agreement. The insurance company guarantees the rate of return and earns a profit by investing the funds in securities of similar DURATION (time to maturity) as the length of the agreement. For example, with a 10-year, 5-percent GIC, the pension plan will receive, on the employee's behalf, a 5-percent yield for 10 years. The insurance company will invest in BONDS, MORTGAGES or other debt securities that mature in 10 years. If the INVESTMENTS yield 7 percent, the insurance company profits by the spread, 2 percent between the guaranteed return and the yield.

The insurance company assumes all credit, market, and interest-rate RISKS. Credit or DEFAULT risk is the potential for a borrower to not repay their loan. Market or systematic risk is the risk associated with changing values in all securities in a class. STOCK MARKET risk is measured by the BETA COEFFICIENT, a statistical measure of the variability in a stock's price relative to the overall variability of stock-market prices. Interest-rate risk is the potential for fixed-interest-rate securities to decline in value if INTEREST RATES rise.

The term *guaranteed* refers to the rate of interest to be paid over the life of the contract, but it does not guarantee repayment of principal (the amount invested). Americans are used to FEDERAL DEPOSIT INSURANCE CORPORATION (FDIC) guarantees on bank deposits. The FDIC, a government-sponsored CORPORATION, guarantees depositors' savings should the bank fail. Insurance companies are not federally guaranteed. As a group, there have been relatively few defaults among GICs, and even when a GIC has failed, investors got most if not all of their principal returned.

As an investment in a RETIREMENT PLAN, GICs are referred to as stable-value ASSETS. GIC yields are almost always higher than money-market funds and similar to bond funds. Because investors are accepting a guaranteed rate, they are taking less risk than if they put their money in stock MUTUAL FUNDS. Stock mutual funds have historically generated higher yields than bonds or other fixed-income securities, but with greater variation in the short run. During the "go-go" years of the stock market during the mid-to-late 1990s, many employees removed their retirement investments from GICs and put them into stock mutual funds. With the decline of the stock market in early 2000, GICs again became popular.

Further reading

Younkin, Timothy Owen. "Understanding GIC's." Available on-line. URL: www.timyounkin.com/articles/GIC.html; "Stable Comeback." *Pensions and Investments* 30 (7 January 2002): 10.

H

harmonization

In general, harmonization means "to bring into common accord or agreement." In business, particularly international business, harmonization of laws, agreements, definitions, and specifications is an important consideration. Having common rules and specifications reduces uncertainty and reduces the problems businesspeople face when entering markets. Harmonization of rules and specifications increases both efficiency for business and market fairness, with each participant operating under the same standards.

Business literature includes many harmonization issues. For example, European and U.S. accounting systems still differ, adding to the difficulty in interpreting figures from one company to another. With the NORTH AMERICAN FREE TRADE AGREEMENT (NAFTA), the United States, Canada, and Mexico agreed to the NORTH AMERICAN INDUSTRIAL CLASSIFICATION SYSTEM (NAICS), defining products by the same classification system. NAICS is used in the HARMONIZED TARIFF SYSTEM (HTS), by which goods that are transformed from one product category to another are then subject to a different TARIFF classification.

As part of the WORLD TRADE ORGANIZATION, the United States agreed to harmonize its PATENT system with that of the EUROPEAN UNION (EU). Similarly, the EU harmonized taxation on interest INCOME in order to reduce the impetus for tax evasion. (A company or individual with interest income from several EU countries would rationally try to declare that income in the country with the lowest tax rate.)

The United Nations has helped to harmonize labeling and classification of products as a way to reduce miscommunication and misunderstanding of materials and chemicals. For example, in recent years the United States and the European Union have debated what criteria to use in defining organic foods. The International Standards Organization attempts to harmonize technical standards among global manufacturers, in the process increasing the substitutability of one firm's products for another, increasing market competition and reducing the need to produce different components and parts for each manufacturer.

Harmonization is a controversial issue in international business. Each company or country favors harmonization based on their own rules and specifications, which gives their firms a competitive advantage over other firms that would have to adjust to the new rules or standards.

Further reading

Leebron, David W. "Claims for Harmonization: A Theoretical Framework," *Canadian Business Law Journal* 27 (July 1996): 63; Lohr, Luanne. "Implications of organic certification for market structure and trade," *American Journal of Agricultural Economics* 80 (December 1998): 1125.

Harmonized Tariff System

The Harmonized Tariff System (HTS) is an international system of numeric classification of PRODUCTS. With HTS, products are classified using a 6- to 10-digit number. The first six digits are standardized worldwide, while some governments use additional numbers to further distinguish products. Each nation applies its own TARIFF rates on products. HTS classification is important, because most countries apply different tariff rates for different categories of goods. For example, having a product classified as a component rather than a finished product may significantly reduce the tariff on imported goods.

Most tariffs are percentage rates applied ad valorem (according to value) of the imported product. Some prices are quoted CIF, meaning the price includes the cost of the goods, INSURANCE, and freight; while other goods are priced FOB (FREE ON BOARD), meaning cost of the goods and all transportation costs to the port of departure plus loading. Some tariffs are applied to the CIF value, while others are added to the FOB value for each HTS classification.

The U.S. INTERNATIONAL TRADE COMMISSION publishes the *Harmonized Tariff Schedule of the United States Annotated,* which provides categories and applicable rates for imported products.

Further reading
U.S. International Trade Commission website. Available on-line. URL: www.usitc.gov.

Hawthorne experiments
The Hawthorne experiments, conducted from 1924 to 1932, were designed to assess whether improvements in physical working conditions would increase employee productivity. Scientist Elton Mayo and his colleagues manipulated multiple aspects of the work environment for a selected group of workers at the Hawthorne Plant of the Western Electric Company and subsequently measured their productivity.

Six women who regularly assembled telecommunications relays from a number of small electronic parts were selected from the general population of workers at the plant. They began working in a special testing room where factors such as the level of lighting, workday length, and the number and duration of rest periods were each changed. Productivity then was measured in terms of the number of relays each woman assembled.

Results indicated that brighter light, shorter hours, and the addition of two rest periods during the day all increased productivity, theoretically by helping workers see and by preventing fatigue. But much to the researchers' surprise, productivity did not revert to lower levels when these changes were reversed. Rather, it climbed to an even higher level.

These unexpected results initially led Mayo and his colleagues to conclude that the workers became more productive simply because they were under observation. However, subsequent analyses of the testing situation revealed that several important social factors also differed markedly from the workers' previous environment, contributing to higher productivity. For example, the testing-room supervisor behaved in a friendlier fashion than did other company supervisors, and the testing personnel solicited participants' opinions about the upcoming changes as opposed to simply forcing new changes upon them.

Presumably these positive social conditions increased participants' self-esteem and made them feel like an important part of a team, unlike ASSEMBLY LINE workers. In essence, participating in the experiments led to more positive attitudes towards work in general and a higher level of commitment to working hard for the company. These factors, along with being under constant observation, help explain the high levels of productivity observed even after the changes were reversed.

Today, individuals who modify their behavior when they are being observed or when participating in research are said to be using the Hawthorne effect. This falls under the broader category of SOCIAL FACILITATION, which describes any behavioral changes that are due to the presence of other people or an audience.

The Hawthorne experiments were highly influential in expanding the scope of the field of INDUSTRIAL-ORGANIZATIONAL PSYCHOLOGY. The experiments led industrial-organizational psychologists to consider for the first time how social factors such as quality of supervision, informal groups, and employee satisfaction affect people's behavior in the business environment.

Further reading
Forsyth, Donelson R. *Group Dynamics,* 3d ed. Belmont, Calif.: Wadsworth Publishing, 1998; Mayo, Elton. *The Human Problems of an Industrial Civilization.* Cambridge, Mass.: Harvard University Press, 1933; ———. *The Social Problems of an Industrial Civilization.* Cambridge, Mass.: Harvard University Press, 1945.

—Elizabeth L. Cralley

health maintenance organization
A health maintenance organization (HMO) provides comprehensive health care to its members on the basis of a prepaid CONTRACT. HMOs function both as INSURANCE companies, collecting periodic premium payments; and as health-care providers, contracting with doctors and hospitals to provide services at predetermined rates. As such the HMO is an example of managed care, the goal of which is high-quality medical care at a reasonable cost.

HMOs are financed through a "capitated" system in which care is provided for each member at a fixed rate. In employer-supplied plans, this rate is paid by the employer through a contract with the HMO. Each member of an HMO selects a primary-care physician who is contracted to the plan, provides basic health care, and acts as a "gatekeeper" to specialists who may be consulted only on his or her referral. Sometimes, a small copay, or fee, is charged for each office visit. HMOs traditionally have stressed preventive health care, offering physicals and checkups at little or no extra cost as well as extra health and fitness programs or classes that address a variety of health concerns, such as helping members to lose weight or stop smoking.

There are currently several variants of the HMO scheme. In the classic HMO, the company owns most of its own facilities and hires all medical personnel. In a second type, the group-model HMO, the company contracts with a group of doctors who form their own professional CORPORATION. A more flexible variant of the second type, the individual-practice association, allows doctors in individual practices to form corporations with other doctors in their area to provide services to the HMO at predetermined fees. Point-of-service (POS) plans and preferred provider organizations (PPOs) are similar schemes that allow members to see doctors and use medical facilities outside of the network at an additional cost; they sometimes do not require a referral from the primary-care physician to see a specialist.

The industrialist Henry J. Kaiser created the prototype of the HMO when he teamed up with Dr. Sidney Garfield to provide a prepaid health plan to Kaiser's workers at the Grand Coulee Dam construction site in 1938. During World War II they offered a similar plan to 30,000 West Coast shipyard workers and their families. The popularity of the plan encouraged Kaiser and Garfield to offer it to the public after the war.

The postwar boom encouraged employers to offer health insurance as part of their EMPLOYEE BENEFITS package. Because of tax incentives (the premiums paid were tax deductible), most employers found traditional insurance supporting fee-per-service health care to be cost-effective. By the 1970s, though, rising health costs were becoming a burden for employers and the government. The Health Maintenance Organization Act of 1973 encouraged the creation of HMOs as a means of controlling medical costs. In the early 1970s, less than 3 percent of Americans were enrolled in an HMO, a number that rose to 30 percent by 1992. In the face of the economic stagnation and INFLATION of the late 1970s, many employers had to reduce benefits in traditional health plans and shift more of the burden of health-care costs to their employees, a situation that continued throughout the 1980s. But neither the increased reliance on HMOs and other types of managed-care plans nor the shifting of more costs to employees did much to rein in the spiraling health-care costs. Not only was there an increasing financial burden on employers, employees, and insurance companies, but an estimated 37 million Americans were uninsured or had lost their health insurance by the early 1990s. Health care became a major issue in the presidential campaign of 1992, but the Clinton administration's attempts at comprehensive health-care reform ended in a debacle that left managed care as the only viable alternative to the pay-per-service model. During the 1990s, employers moved rapidly away from traditional insurance to various kinds of managed care.

The proponents of HMOs, PPOs, and other kinds of managed care stress the plans' ability to contain costs while providing SERVICES like preventive medicine not usually associated with pay-per-service health care. They make the point that managed care is better able to prevent unnecessary medical procedures and to encourage more cost-effective alternatives to expensive procedures where appropriate. Opponents, on the other hand, have focused on what they see as compromises in the quality of care provided by such plans through practices such as subjecting physicians' requests for certain medical procedures to review by gatekeepers within the company (who were sometimes alleged not to be qualified to make major medical decisions) or giving doctors financial incentives and bonuses to choose less-expensive options.

Many of the more controversial aspects of managed-care plans have been addressed by legislation on the state and federal level and by numerous lawsuits. Some see a trend towards dismantling managed care, although a majority of insured Americans are still in managed-care plans. According to a Kaiser Family Foundation study released in 2002, health costs continue to soar ($1.3 trillion in 2000). The study also showed a shift away from the traditional HMO (28 percent) to PPO networks (48 percent) and found that most people were enrolled in plans offered by for-profit companies. In addition, 91 percent of doctors had a contract with a managed-care provider.

Further reading

Gail Carlson. "What is a Health Maintenance Organization?" HES Extension website, University of Missouri. Available on-line. URL: http://outreach. Missouri.edu/hes/fmhlth/whatishmo.htm; Glaser, William A. "Health Maintenance Organizations and Managed Care," Grolier Online Encyclopedia. Available on-line. URL: http://gme. grolier.com/cgi; Gustavson, Sandra G. "Health Insurance," Encyclopedia Americana. Available on-line. URL: http://ea-ada. Grolier. com/cgi; "Health insurance options." In *Encyclopedia of Business,* edited by John G. Maurer, Joel M. Schulman, Marcia L. Ruwe, and Richard C. Becherer. New York: Gale Research, 1995; Kaiser Permanente History. Available on-line. URL: http://www. kaiserpermanente.org/locations/northwest/newsroom/history. html. Downloaded on November 8, 2002; "Kaiser Study: Managed Care Enrollment Shifting as Costs Rise," *BestWire,* 6 June 2002. Available on-line. URL: http://web.lexis-nexis.com/ universe; Makoverb, Michael E. *Mismanaged Care.* New York: Prometheus Books, 1998; Smith, Richard Dean. *The Rise and Fall of Managed Care.* Lima, Ohio: Wyndham Hall Press, 2001.

—Andrew Kearns

hedge fund

A hedge fund in the United States is a private PARTNERSHIP that engages in a variety of high-risk INVESTMENT strategies for PROFIT. Investors should not think that a hedge fund provides them with protection against risk; in fact the opposite is true. Hedge funds operate under different rules from most MUTUAL FUNDS and engage in such activities as ARBITRAGE, investments in EMERGING MARKETS, SHORT SELLING, PROGRAM TRADING, swaps, and other financial investments.

Because they are private-investment partnerships, hedge funds in the United States are typically limited to 99 investors and a general partner. The general partner is paid a small management fee, usually 1 percent of ASSETS under MANAGEMENT, and given a significant share of the profits earned by the hedge fund, often 20 percent or more. Hedge funds are exempt from the Investment Company Act of 1940, meaning they not subject to the standard reporting requirements of CORPORATIONS or mutual funds. Taxation of hedge funds' profits is constantly changing.

At least 65 percent of the investors must be "accredited," meaning that each investor should have a net worth of at least $1 million and an INCOME of at least $200,000 in the previous year. Most hedge funds require a minimum investment of $25,000 or more and have lock-up periods (times during which investors cannot get their money back) of one year or more. The most famous hedge fund in the United States, Long Term Capital Management (LTCM), had a minimum investment of $5 million and a lock-up of two years.

As previously noted, hedge funds engage in high-RISK investment strategies, hoping to earn significant profits. One strategy, arbitrage, is the practice of buying a product at a low price in one market and selling it at a higher price in another market. Arbitrage is as old as trade. A basic business maxim is "buy low and sell high." Knowledgeable middlemen, knowing the prices of products in different parts of the world, would buy from producers in one region and sell to consumers or merchants in another region. One motivation for the exploration of the New World was the control of land-based trade by merchants in the Middle East. European businesspeople and monarchs knew that new DISTRIBUTION CHANNELS would reduce arbitrageurs' power. Hedge-fund managers are, typically, knowledgeable international traders who take advantage of price differentials, earning small profit margins on large sums of money. One of the most famous hedge-fund operators is George Soros, a Hungarian-born manager who made billions of dollars in currency and interest-rate markets in the United States.

A second hedge-fund strategy is investment in emerging markets. Often markets like Central European countries and Russia after the collapse of the Soviet Union offer tremendous profit opportunities for high-risk investors. Most small, individual investors do not have the time or knowledge to make investments in emerging markets.

Hedge funds also engage in short selling, the sale of borrowed securities, betting that the price of those shares will decline. If the share price does decline, the hedge fund repurchases the shares at the lower price, earning a profit on the difference.

Because they control significant sums of MONEY and additional borrowed funds based on their CAPITAL, hedge-fund managers can influence market prices through their buying and selling. Hedge funds often engage in program trading, the purchase and sale of large volumes of shares or other securities at preset prices. Computers are used to purchase and sell shares automatically, moving the hedge fund into and out of markets rapidly. Program trading was implicated in the massive 1987 sell-off of stock, when the Dow Jones Industrial Average declined over 500 points in one day.

Swaps are the exchange of securities with the agreement to repurchase them at some future time. Hedge funds engage in interest-rate and currency swaps, hoping to profit on changing market conditions. LTCM's demise came when the hedge fund bet that the spread between short-term and long-term INTEREST RATES would narrow. Instead the spread increased, and because the fund was highly leveraged, it lost billions of dollars.

Hedge funds control billions of dollars worth of assets and have significant influence on financial markets. They tend to profit during downturns in the economy and financial crises. Because they are exempt from SECURITIES EXCHANGE COMMISSION reporting requirements, there is relatively little information available about them.

Further reading
Baker Library Guide to Hedge Funds. Available on-line. URL: http://library.hbs.edu/hedgefunds.htm.

hedging

Hedging is any business and INVESTMENT activity entered into to reduce RISK rather than to produce earnings. For example, a farmer makes a decision on how much wheat to plant. At the current price of wheat, he will make a good PROFIT, and if the price of wheat rises, it will be especially profitable, but if the price falls, it will be unprofitable. To hedge for this uncertainty, he can enter into a FUTURES contract for wheat, which will be profitable to him if the price of wheat falls and unprofitable if the price rises. The risk of this futures CONTRACT offsets the risk of growing the wheat. In essence, the farmer has shifted the risk of the falling prices to the other person in the futures contract.

An investor must not think that a HEDGE FUND provides the investor any sort of protection against risk; in fact, the opposite is true. A hedge fund takes on risk by entering into contracts that hedge the risk for other businesses, so it would possibly be the other party in the contract with the farmer in the above example. If that is so, the investors in the hedge fund now have the risk of changes in wheat prices.

Hedging does not apply only to investment instruments; it should also be part of any sound BUSINESS PLAN. To hedge against bad economic times, a cruise-ship line can invest in a chain of movie theaters. During slow economic times, the cruise ships will lose money, but the movie theaters will make a profit, and vice versa. Each division serves as a hedge for the other.

Herfindahl Index (Herfindahl-Hirschman Index)

The Herfindahl Index, also referred to as the Herfindahl-Hirschman Index, is a measure of MARKET CONCENTRATION, the degree to which a few firms control the pricing and output in a market. In perfectly competitive markets there are many firms, and no one firm is large enough to influence the market outcome. In a MONOPOLY, however, there is only one firm, and its actions determine the market outcome.

Herfindahl Indices are most often associated with oligopolies, markets where there are only a few competitors. A market's Herfindahl Index is the sum of the squares of the market shares of each firm in the industry. For example, if there are only four firms in a market and two firms each have 30 percent of market sales, and the other two firms each have 20 percent of market sales, then the Herfindahl Index is:

$$30^2 + 30^2 + 20^2 + 20^2 = 2600$$

This market would be considered highly concentrated by the antitrust division of the U.S. Justice Department, which considers any market with a Herfindahl Index of less than 1800 to be competitive. When deciding whether to allow the merger or acquisition of companies, the Justice Department calculates the Herfindahl Index that would result if the merger or acquisition. One of the problems is defining the market in question. For example, the main competitors in the U.S. retail telecommunications market are the three large telephone companies AT&T, MCI, and Sprint, but consumers also use cellular phones and the INTERNET to communicate. If only these three large telephone companies are used to calculate the Herfindahl Index, it will be much higher than if the market is defined more broadly.

Before the development of the Herfindahl Index, the traditional measure of market concentration was the four-firm concentration ratio. This index was created by adding the market shares (percentage of market sales) of the four largest firms in the industry, a measurement that did not account for the size distribution of firms in the market.

See also OLIGOPOLY.

hierarchy of needs   See MASLOW'S HIERARCHY OF NEEDS.

Hofstede's dimensions

Hofstede's dimensions refer to a well-known study of five dimensions of international cultural differences in work-related values. The five dimensions, first published in 1980, include uncertainty avoidance, power distance, masculinity-femininity, individualism-collectivism, and Confucian dynamism. Using existing survey data (sample size of 116,000) collected from a MULTINATIONAL CORPORATION, Hofstede, an IBM psychologist, developed a score for each dimension for employees from 40 different countries.

Uncertainty avoidance refers to the levels of people's comfort with ambiguity. Cultures with high uncertainty avoidance prefer formal rules and relationships, reducing uncertainty and anxiety, while cultures with low uncertainty avoidance are more comfortable with lack of structure in an organization. In countries with a high level of uncertainty avoidance (such as Greece and Japan), business environments tend to have formal rules and procedures, and managers more often choose low-risk alternatives. In countries with lower levels of uncertainty avoidance (such as Denmark and Great Britain), business activities are less structured and managers tend to take greater risks. The United States ranks moderately low on Hofstede's uncertainty avoidance scale.

Power distance refers to the extent to which less powerful members of institutions accept and expect that power will be distributed unequally. In a workplace, inequality of power is normal, as evidenced in hierarchical boss-subordinate relationships. In Hofstede's study, Mexican and Malaysian work environments had high power distance, employees acknowledging the manager's authority and seldom bypassing the chain of command. Austrian, Israeli, and Danish workplaces exhibited lower power distance, while the United States ranked in the middle.

Masculinity-femininity refers to the extent to which society values assertiveness (masculinity) versus caring (called femininity by Hofstede). In this dimension, Hofstede evaluated expected gender roles in a culture. "Masculine" cultures tend to have distinct expectations for males and females, while "feminine" cultures have less-defined gender roles. Japan and Austria rated high in masculinity, while Denmark and Chile rated low. The United States ranked in the middle on the masculinity-femininity scale.

Individualism-collectivism refers to the degree to which ties among individuals are normally loose rather than close. In more individualistic cultures, all members of society are expected to look after themselves and their immediate families. Collectivist cultures have stronger bonds beyond immediate families. The United States and Australia are considered individualistic, while Indonesia and Pakistan are considered collectivist cultures.

Confucian dynamism refers to the degree a culture promotes ethics found in Confucian teachings, including thrift, perseverance, a sense of shame, in addition to how it follows a hierarchy. According to Hofstede, rapid ECONOMIC DEVELOPMENT in Asian countries is in part attributable to this workplace cultural dimension.

Further reading

Deresky, Helen. *International Management*, 2d ed. Reading, Mass.: Addison-Wesley, 1997; Hofstede, Geert. *Culture's Consequences: International Differences in Work-related Values*. Newbury Park, Calif.: Sage Publishing, 1980.

holding company

A holding company is a CORPORATION that owns other companies or corporations. Holding companies typically own stock in or otherwise exercise managerial control over the companies they own; their controlling interest is usually at least 50 percent. For tax reasons, individuals sometimes create personal holding companies for their investments.

Holding companies are often created to separate a corporation's regulated and unregulated industries. For example, most PUBLIC UTILITIES in the United States are owned by holding companies. The utility part (an electrical or water supply company) operates as a regulated MONOPOLY, while the land development or other INVESTMENT part of the business operates as a regular corporation. Beginning in the 1960s, many U.S. banks created holding companies, which allowed them to expand over state lines and bypass laws limiting the number of bank branches allowed. Like utility companies, banks could also diversify into nonbanking activities, and holding-company status reduced some types of tax liability.

Further reading
Hamilton, Robert W. *The Law of Corporations in a Nutshell,* 5th ed. Eagan, Minn.: West Group, 2000; Kidwell, David S., Richard L. Peterson, and David W. Blackwell. *Financial Institutions, Markets and Money,* 7th ed. Fort Worth: Dryden Press, 2000.

human resources

The term *human resources* has two different meanings. It may refer to the people within an organization who are performing the work or it may refer to the human resources (HR) function—a collection of related activities that pertain to the management of personnel within the organization. It is the second reference that is being discussed here.

The HR function has developed significantly in recent years. In many organizations today, human resources is considered an essential, strategic business function as well as an integral part of a company's administrative staff. This arm of the business is involved in ensuring that the employees accept responsibility; perform at high levels of efficiency; and make decisions within their area of responsibility, knowledge, and expertise. Senior MANAGEMENT expects HR to add unique, sustained value to the organization, thus helping the business improve its position over its competitors. Providing this competitive advantage helps the firm increase PROFITS, enhance CUSTOMER RELATIONS/SATISFACTION, and improve market share. Many HR functions work closely with management to help structure jobs so that the work is challenging and satisfying. HR also helps create the culture and shape the organization's management style.

Although HR professionals may place different emphases on core activities in accordance with the organization's current needs, there are five traditional HR activities: EMPLOYMENT, TRAINING AND DEVELOPMENT, COMPENSATION AND BENEFITS, employee and labor relations, and health and safety. These five activities comprise the HR function, although motivation, communication, and job and organization design are often delegated to HR. Following are brief definitions of the core areas.

1. Employment consists of recruiting and selection. Recruiting ensures a supply of qualified applicants from which the appropriate selection(s) of new hire(s) can be made. Often the process of socializing the new employee into the organization is a part of the employment process. Socializing reduces the potential of psychological shock the new employee may experience during the first few weeks or months of employment.
2. Training and development ensure that the organization has employees with the appropriate knowledge, skills, and abilities to perform the necessary job duties. Training often has the connotation of learning specific job skills necessary to perform the current job. Development, however, has a longer-term focus to educate employees to perform future jobs that require higher knowledge, skills, and abilities.
3. Compensation and benefits comprise the total rewards package that an employee receives for performing the job. Compensation is considered direct pay, since it is the amount of money the employee receives. Benefits are indirect pay, since they are monetary equivalents that can be converted later into cash or cash equivalents. Benefits that are voluntarily offered by employers often include vacations, holidays, group INSURANCE (e.g., health and life insurance) and pension programs. Legally required benefits include SOCIAL SECURITY, UNEMPLOYMENT insurance, WORKERS' COMPENSATION, and in many cases time off to attend to family medical needs (see FAMILY AND MEDICAL LEAVE ACT). For every dollar paid in compensation, the CHAMBER OF COMMERCE estimates that 39–40 percent is spent for indirect compensation, leaving 60–61 percent for direct compensation. This is a composite average; individual companies and specific situations may vary considerably.
4. Employee relations is concerned with assuring that each employee is treated fairly, and if there is a concern or problem, those issues are addressed quickly. Employees are encouraged to discuss their concerns with either their supervisor or HR representative. The term *employee relations* is usually used when the organization's employees are not represented by a UNION. The term *labor relations* is used when specific employee groups are represented by a union. Individual union members are represented by a union representative called a union steward or committee person, although employees can still discuss issues with their supervisor or HR representative. When a union does represent groups of employees, the wages, hours, terms, and conditions of work are negotiated jointly by union and company representatives in a process called COLLECTIVE BARGAINING.
5. Health and safety standards ensure that employees work in an environment that is free from recognized hazards. Although safety and health activities are usually management-led, safety is everyone's responsibility. Safety committees are often established within each department to implement safety programs and assist in accident investigations. The Occupational Safety and Health Act (1970), a federal law, has many industry-specific safety regulations, but even when there are no specific guidelines, the act contains the General Duty Clause, which requires employers to conform to the law's intent of the law—safe and healthful working conditions.

See also OCCUPATIONAL HEALTH AND SAFETY ADMINISTRATION.

—John Abbott

I

import restraints

The United States, like many countries, uses a variety of methods to restrain IMPORTS into the country, including TARIFFS, quotas, tariff-rate quotas, and NONTARIFF BARRIERS. Tariffs are taxes or duties applied to imported products, paid by the importing company, increasing the cost of imported PRODUCTS. Quotas are limits on the number of units of a good that can be imported into the United States. Tariff-rate quotas allow a lower tariff rate on in-quota quantities of imports and a higher rate on over-quota levels of imports. Some imports are restrained through nontariff barriers, the rules and regulations with which imported products must comply. Nonconforming products are often banned from importation.

Many U.S. quotas were created to protect American agriculture. These quotas, mostly on animal feeds, dairy products, chocolate, cotton, peanuts, and selected syrups and sugars, are utilized to coordinate U.S. farming price-support programs. For example, the United States supports domestic sugar production by paying sugar producers prices significantly higher than world prices. In absence of import quotas, domestic sugar users, such as candy and soft-drink manufacturers, would purchase sugar on the world market instead of higher-priced domestic supplies. Some U.S. agricultural quotas are being "tariffed," converted into tariff-rate quotas, under the WORLD TRADE ORGANIZATION's Agreement on Agriculture.

Under the Trade Expansion Act of 1962, the United States authorized the president to "adjust imports" whenever necessary to the country's national security. Trade EMBARGOes, such as those against Iraq and Cuba, are conducted under this legislation. Narcotic drugs, "immoral" goods, and goods produced by forced, child-bonded, or convict labor are excluded from importation into the United States. Certain goods from the People's Republic of China have been banned based on these restrictions.

There are numerous nontariff barriers to imports into the United States. These barriers often arise out of state or federal health and safety concerns. Others are based on environmental, CONSUMER PROTECTION, product standards, and government procurement. Many nontariff barriers were created for legitimate consumer-protection reasons, but others are attempts by domestic producers to restrict COMPETITION. In addition to health and safety concerns, restrictions on imports are often justified based on saving domestic jobs, creating "fair trade," national defense interests, infant-industry arguments (protecting new domestic industries from established international competitors), and strategic trade-policy goals.

During the debates on the NORTH AMERICAN FREE TRADE AGREEMENT (NAFTA), then presidential candidate Ross Perot claimed NAFTA would create a "giant sucking sound," as U.S. jobs were drawn away to Mexico. Perot argued that Mexico's cheaper labor costs would cause the loss of millions of American jobs. Steel import restrictions are rationalized as being necessary so the United States will have a domestic source of steel in times of war. Countries sometimes justify protecting new industries, arguing the industries need time to become competitive with the rest of the world. In the mid-1980s, the United States negotiated voluntary import restrictions with Japanese automobile producers so that U.S. producers would have time to catch up to Japanese quality and technology.

Strategic trade policy is the use of trade restrictions or subsidies to allow domestic firms with decreasing costs per unit of output (ECONOMIES OF SCALE) to gain a larger share of the world market. Producers in many countries around the world argue they need access to the huge U.S. market in order to become large enough to effectively compete with giant U.S. CORPORATIONS.

Further reading

Boyes, William J., and Michael Melvin. *Microeconomics*, 5th ed. Boston: Houghton Mifflin, 2002; Folsom, Ralph H., and W. Davis Folsom, *Understanding NAFTA and its International Business Implications*. New York: Mathew Irwin/Bender, 1996.

imports/exports

Imports are the goods produced in another country (foreign goods) that are brought into a home country (e.g., the United States) for sale. Exports are the goods produced by the home country (domestic goods) that are shipped to another country for sale. Thus one country's exports are another country's imports. Balance of trade occurs when a country's imports equal its exports.

A simplified explanation of why trade takes place is because the foreign country can produce a certain good cheaper than the importing country. The law of comparative advantage, however, states that the item will be made in a more expensive location as long as its relative cost of production is cheaper than in the importing country. For example, suppose a country could manufacture computers very efficiently and profitably but could less efficiently and profitably produce automobiles. If it did produce automobiles, though, they would be cheaper than those produced by its neighbor country. Yet in spite of the higher cost, it imports automobiles from its neighbors instead of moving workers and capital from its more profitable computer industry to produce domestic automobiles.

As demonstrated by the decline in the value of the U.S. dollar in 2003, imports and exports are sensitive to changes in currency exchange rates. With the decline in the dollar, foreign car imports declined and sales U.S. products abroad expanded. U.S. tourism abroad dropped significantly while foreign visitors to the United States grew. In many countries the value of exports and imports can equal or exceed a country's GROSS DOMESTIC PRODUCT (GDP). While trade represents approximately 6 percent of GDP in the United States, export income and competition from imported products contribute to the growth in the economy. Countries often attempt to maintain a positive trade balance in order to create and expand domestic jobs and income. The United States has run a significant (in 2003, more than $400 billion) current account deficit (the sum of merchandise, services, investment income, and unilateral transfers) since 1980.

The U.S. imports significantly more merchandise than it exports but exports more services than it imports. The United States perennially has a trade surplus in certain categories, including agricultural and technology products, and a trade deficit in energy and textile products. The major trading partners of the United States are Canada, Mexico, and Japan, with China becoming an increasingly important source of imports. Canada has long been the United States's leading trading partner, but trade with Mexico grew with the passage of the NORTH AMERICAN FREE TRADE AGREEMENT (NAFTA) in 1994.

income

The *Income* has many definitions, depending on the context in which it is used. Definitions of income can be separated into four categories: income related to personal taxes, business INCOME STATEMENTS; aggregate income in an economy; and money versus REAL INCOME.

In the U.S. personal-income tax system, the INTERNAL REVENUE SERVICE uses three definitions of income: total or gross income, adjusted gross income (AGI), and taxable income. Total income is, as the term suggests, money received by the taxpayer from all sources. For most U.S. taxpayers, total income is the sum of wage, salary, interest, and DIVIDEND income along with CAPITAL GAINS in a given year. Some taxpayers also have rents, royalties, distributions from INDIVIDUAL RETIREMENT ACCOUNTS (IRAs), refunds, alimony, business income, pensions, annuities, PARTNERSHIP income, and SOCIAL SECURITY benefits included in their total income.

Adjusted gross income is total income minus a variety of deductions, including IRA contributions, student-loan interest, medical savings-account deductions, moving expenses, self-employment tax, health Simplified Employee Pension (SEP) payments, and alimony payments. Taxable income is adjusted gross income minus tax credits, including standard or itemized deductions and personal exemption allowances. Taxable income is the net amount of total income subject to U.S. personal income taxes.

Business income statements, which can be quite complex, measure a firm's income for its accounting period. Businesses compare revenue with expenses and allowances for DEPRECIATION to develop a statement of the company's income.

While accountants calculate a company's income, the U.S. Department of Commerce estimates the country's aggregate income, the total value of all claims against output. Aggregate income (GROSS DOMESTIC PRODUCT [GDP]) equals the sum of wages, rents, dividends, and PROFITS less net-factor income from abroad, plus capital consumption allowance and indirect BUSINESS TAXES. National income is GDP minus factor income, CAPITAL consumption allowance and indirect business taxes. Personal income is national income adjusted for income that is received but not earned and earned but not yet received. Finally, disposable personal income is personal income minus personal-income taxes, or what people have available to spend or save.

Money income is income measured in dollars received in the current period of time, while real income is measured by the purchasing power of income received. Real income is money income adjusted for INFLATION. Economists use PRICE INDEXES such as the CONSUMER PRICE INDEX to compare the purchasing power of money income over time.

Further reading

Boyes, William, and Michael Melvin. *Macroeconomics*, 5th ed. Boston: Houghton Mifflin, 2001.

income elasticity of demand

Income elasticity of demand is the responsiveness of DEMAND for a good or service to changes in INCOME. As consumer income rises, the demand for most goods and SERV-ICES will increase. For example, the demand for new cars and homes is quite sensitive to changes in income. Manufacturers of these PRODUCTS incorporate estimates of changing income when forecasting demand and making long-term planning decisions. Income elasticity of demand is calculated as follows:

$$E_y = (\% \text{ change in demand for good X}) / (\% \text{ change in income})$$

In the 1990s Americans' income rose steadily, and demand for most products also increased. If income rose 4 percent and demand for a product increased 6 percent, the income elasticity of demand would be .06/.04 = 1.5. If, as one source states, the income elasticity of demand for automobiles were 1.7, then with a 4 percent increase in income, demand would be expected to increase by 6.8 percent (.04 × 1.7).

Economists call goods for which an increase in income results in an increase in demand "normal" goods. There are also goods for which an increase in income will result in a decrease in demand; economists call these "inferior" goods. The label has nothing to do with the quality of the product or service, just the fact that they have negative income elasticity. The classic "inferior" good is potatoes. However, as consumers' incomes rise, people substitute stuffing, gourmet rice, and other starches for potatoes. When consumers' incomes decline, they purchase more potatoes.

Another example comes from a very shrewd independent automobile mechanic. He observed that as the economy boomed, demand for his repair services declined, since people were buying new cars, trading in their "clunkers" and not creating work for him. But when the economy slowed, demand for his services increased as people held on to their cars longer.

Since income tends to change slowly, most managers do not consider income elasticity of demand in daily or operational plans but do incorporate the impact of changing incomes in their STRATEGIC PLANNING. Some examples of estimated income elasticity include

movie tickets	3.4
foreign travel	3.1
wine	1.6
beef	0.5
beer	0.4
lard	−0.1

Further reading

Ruffin, Roy J., and Paul R. Gregory. *Principles of Economics.* 7th ed. Boston: Addison Wesley, 2001.

incomes policies   See WAGE AND PRICE CONTROLS.

income redistribution

Income redistribution is government action to transfer money and/or goods and SERVICES from some groups in a society to others. Income redistribution involves the transfer of money payments or goods and services with no requirement or expectation of exchange of RESOURCES or services by the recipients. In the United States, major income-redistribution programs include transfer-payment systems such as WELFARE, SOCIAL SECURITY, and UNEMPLOYMENT benefits; and transfer-in-kind programs such as food stamps, public housing, and medical care. Compared with most industrialized countries in the world, U.S. income-redistribution programs are quite modest, but they are a controversial part of U.S. public policy.

At the beginning of the 21st century, the fastest-growing income-redistribution programs in the United States were Medicare and Medicaid. Medicare subsidizes medical care for the elderly, while Medicaid provides health-care services for poorer Americans. However, the largest income-redistribution program in the United States is Social Security. When it was created, Social Security was intended to be a modest income INSURANCE program, by which workers paid into the program and later received benefits based on their contributions. Because of growth in the U.S. economy after World War II, there soon were many more workers relative to beneficiaries, creating surpluses in the program. Congress then expanded the benefits and programs under Social Security well beyond its initial objective, and as a result, most retired Americans now get all they paid into Social Security plus interest within 3–4 years. Though most American retirees don't like the word, they are actually receiving welfare.

Today Social Security is an intergenerational income-transfer program, with current retirees being given money payments from current workers. Some analysts compare this system to a PONZI SCHEME, in which initial investors are paid with the funds collected from subsequent investors. The system works as long as there are new contributors to the system. With the ratio of retirees to workers increasing in the United States, officials anticipate problems with the Social Security program.

Further reading

Miller, Roger LeRoy. *Economics Today.* Boston: Addison Wesley, 2001.

income statement, gross margin

An income statement measures a firm's profitability (or lack thereof) for a period of time known as the accounting period, which can be monthly, quarterly, yearly, or any other length of time. If the accounting period coincides with the calendar year, the firm's INCOME is reported on a calendar-year basis. If the accounting period is a 12-month period of time other than the calendar year (say July 1–June 30), the income is reported on a FISCAL YEAR basis.

Because the income statement is one of the FINANCIAL STATEMENTS used to convey information about the firm to entities outside the firm, it must be constructed using the ACCRUAL BASIS and in accordance with GENERALLY ACCEPTED ACCOUNTING PRINCIPLES (GAAP).

An income statement consists of three major sections: revenues, expenses, and net income. Revenues are RESOURCES accruing to the firm as a result of the sale of goods and/or SERVICES, both for cash and on credit. Expenses are resources flowing out of the firm as a result of the revenue-earning process. Included in expenses are those that have been paid in cash and those that have not yet been paid but nonetheless were incurred during the accounting period being reported.

At the bottom of an income statement is the section stating net income. The difference between revenues and expenses is always called net income, both when there is a PROFIT and when there is a loss for the period. In corporate income statements, it is customary for the net income to be reported in total and per share. Earnings per share (EPS) is determined by dividing net income by the number of common shares outstanding.

Income statements are generally organized as multiple-step statements, as follows:

Revenues
Less: Cost of Goods Sold
Gross Margin
Less: Operating Expenses
Earnings before Interest and Taxes (EBIT)
Less: Interest Expense
Earnings before Taxes (EBT)
Less: Income Tax Expense
Net Income
EPS

The difference between revenues and COST OF GOODS SOLD is the gross margin—the excess (or mark-up) of a firm's prices for goods and services over their cost to the firm. A firm's gross margin is closely monitored and given a prominent place on the income statement. The gross margin must be sufficient to cover the firm's remaining expenses and to ultimately contribute to net income. If the gross margin is insufficient, the firm must raise prices (if possible), reduce expenses (including cost of goods sold), or implement some combination of these two. Gross margin is routinely expressed not only in dollars but as a percentage of sales. Firms in extremely competitive markets find it most useful to compare gross-margin ratios to monitor their profitability.

Cost of goods sold is a crucial element in the determination of a firm's gross margin. It is the most important and closely watched of all the expenses within a firm. While a firm has little, if any, control over its revenues (a customer cannot be forced to buy), it does have control over its expenses. For this reason, cost of goods sold is sep-arated from the other expenses and subtracted from revenues before the other expenses to determine the firm's gross margin.

Income statements, like all financial statements, are excellent tools of comparison among firms. Because revenues and expenses are reported on the accrual basis and statements must adhere to GAAP, the practice of accounting is standardized and interfirm and interindustry comparisons are possible.

See also FINANCIAL ACCOUNTING.

incorporation

Incorporation is the process of creating a CORPORATION. The rules on incorporating vary somewhat from state to state, with Delaware often perceived to be the most desirable state in which to incorporate because its fees tend to be low. The "articles of incorporation" typically create the company name, designate its corporate officers, identify its headquarters, indicate the amount of CAPITAL involved, and establish BYLAWS (rules of CORPORATE GOVERNANCE). A main reason for incorporating is to obtain "limited financial liability," which restricts, under most circumstances, owners' LIABILITY to their capital INVESTMENT. The two major reasons some businesses do not incorporate is its cost and being subject to corporate taxation.

To incorporate, generally a business organizer

- prepares articles of incorporation
- signs and authenticates the articles
- files the articles with the state's secretary of state and pays filing fees
- receives a "filed" copy of the articles from the secretary of state
- holds an organization meeting for the purpose of electing officers, adopting bylaws, and transacting other business

Although a corporation may do business in many states, usually the relationship among the corporation, its SHARE-HOLDERS, and its managers is regulated by the state in which it was incorporated. The American Bar Association prepared a model statute that has been used by most states as the basis for their incorporation statutes.

Further reading
Hamilton, Robert W. *The Law of Corporations in a Nutshell,* 5th ed. Eagan, Minn.: West Group, 2000; Mallor, Jane P., A. James Barnes, Thomas Bowers, Michael J. Philips, and Arlen W. Langvardt. *Business Law and the Regulatory Environment,* 11th ed. Boston: McGraw-Hill, 2001.

independent contractors

Independent contractors are individuals or companies that provide SERVICES for consumers, businesses, or government. Most professionals are independent contractors, who are best defined by what they are not: employees. Independent contractors typically are paid by the task, while employees are paid by the hour. Independent contractors contract with the consumer or business to produce some result, while employees are told how to conduct their work. The distinction between independent contractors and employees has many legal, tax, and INSURANCE implications.

As cited in *Mallor et al.*, U.S. courts use five factors in determining whether workers are independent contractors or employees. First is the degree of control exercised by the alleged employer. Does the employer determine when, where, what, and how a worker does their job? Independent contractors generally determine when and how work is done.

Second, what are the relative investments of the worker and alleged employer? If the worker provides equipment, transportation, and other ASSETS necessary to the task, they are more likely to be considered an independent contractor. In a factory where the company provides almost all of the materials and machinery needed to produce the products, workers are more likely to be considered employees. In the case described by *Mallor et al.*, topless dancers for the Circle C organization provided their own costumes and locks for their lockers, but Circle C provided the nightclub. The dancers' investments were relatively small compared to those of the business.

Third, to what degree does the alleged employer determine the workers' opportunities for PROFIT and loss? Independent contractors generally profit by their ability to gain CONTRACTS and complete their work. In the Circle C case, the dancers' initiative, hustle, and costumes significantly contributed to their income, but the club's ADVERTISING, location, aesthetics, and food and beverage service gave the club control over customer volume and therefore provided the dancers with opportunities for profit.

Fourth, what skills and initiative are required in performing the job? Most independent contractors provide a distinct skill that the consumer or business needs and wishes to hire for a specific purpose. Employees are generally trained to do tasks required by their employer.

Fifth, what is the permanency of the relationship between the worker and the alleged employer? Independent contractors generally have a short-term, task-specific relationship, while employees have a longer, hours-per-week commitment with the employer.

Independent contractors are typically liable for their work, while the consumer or business hiring them is generally not liable for the contractor's actions. There are exceptions to this distinction, such as when a firm hires an incompetent independent contractor or when the contractor is negligent in taking "special precautions needed to conduct certain highly dangerous or inherently dangerous activities."

Another important distinction between independent contractors and employees is eligibility for WORKERS' COMPENSATION and other benefits. Workers' compensation protects employees but not independent contractors against the risk of injury on the job. Many companies hire independent contractors in order to avoid the workers' compensation costs and liabilities. Independent contractors are also not eligible for a company's health-care program, RETIREMENT PLAN, vacation time, or other benefits. In the 1990s many companies reduced their number of employees, often rehiring laid-off workers, at a lower cost, as independent contractors. In the business world, these new independent contractors were called "corporate pilot fish."

Independent contractors are also treated differently under the federal tax code. Employees pay Federal Insurance Contributions Act (FICA) taxes based on wages, and their contributions are matched by their employers. Independent contractors are considered self-employers. If a contractor has employees, then he, she, or it could be a PROPRIETORSHIP, PARTNERSHIP, or CORPORATION. Many businesses prefer to classify workers as independent contractors in order to avoid the benefits and taxes paid on employees. The FAIR LABOR STANDARDS ACT (FLSA), passed in 1938 and amended many times since then, is a major labor-management law regulating wages and hours, child labor, equal pay and overtime pay, and employee-versus-independent contractor status.

Further reading
Mallor, Jane P., A. James Barnes, Thomas Bowers, Michael J. Philips, and Arlen W. Langvardt. *Business Law and the Regulatory Environment,* 11th ed. Boston: McGraw-Hill, 2001.

Index of Consumer Expectations
The Index of Consumer Expectations is a measure of how consumers view prospects for their financial situation and the general economy over the near term and long term. The index is part of the University of Michigan's monthly Surveys of Consumers. Created in 1946 by George Katona, the surveys document the importance of consumer spending and saving decisions as a major part of the national economy. Consumer spending represents two-thirds of GROSS DOMESTIC PRODUCT. Changes in consumer expectations influence spending decisions and have significant impact on the overall economy.

Each month a minimum of 500 telephone interviews are conducted by staff members at the University of Michigan survey center; the survey includes approximately 50 questions. One question consumers are asked is, "No one can say for sure, but what do you think will happened to INTEREST RATES for borrowing money during the next 12 months—will they go up, stay the same, or go down?" When consumers' responses are compared to the change in the prime rate (the interest rate charged by banks for short-term unsecured loans to top-quality commercial customers), consumer expectations change on average two quarters (six months) in advance of the change in the prime rate. Consumers generally anticipated interest rate changes six months in advance of the actual change.

Another question asked is, "How about people out of work during the coming 12 months—do you think that there will be more UNEMPLOYMENT than now, about the same, or less?" Survey results show consumers anticipate changes in the unemployment rate nine months in advance of the actual change. In a similar question about INFLATION, consumers predict changes in prices (as measured by the CONSUMER PRICE INDEX) by three months. Survey results also show consumers generally anticipate changes in home buying and vehicle sales by six months.

Business managers watch the Index of Consumer Expectations closely. Manufacturers of durable goods and housing-related products recognize the Index is an effective planning tool when making production decisions. Following the STOCK MARKET crash in October 1987, respondents to the survey displayed less panic than prognosticators on WALL STREET. Managers trusting the survey correctly concluded that stock-market fears would not greatly influence consumer-spending decisions.

The Index of Consumer Expectations is included in the Leading Indicator Composite Index published by the Department of Commerce. INDICATORS included in the Commerce Department index are based on their economic significance, statistical accuracy, consistency in timing the peaks and troughs of BUSINESS CYCLES, conformity to business expansions and contractions, consistency, and prompt availability. The Index of Consumer Expectations is the only consumer survey included in the composite index. Many other countries have developed consumer expectations indices based on the Index of Consumer Expectations model.

Further reading
Surveys of Consumers website. Available on-line. URL: www.umich.edu.

indicators
In the business world, economic indicators are measures associated with BUSINESS CYCLES. Business indicators are statistical measures used by individual firms or industry groups to measure and predict changes in business activity. There are three categories of indicators: leading, coincident, and lagging. Leading indicators change in advance of changes in real output—i.e., GROSS DOMESTIC PRODUCT (GDP). Coincident indicators change as real output changes following which lagging indicators will change.

The Department of Commerce index of leading indicators includes

- average workweek
- UNEMPLOYMENT claims
- manufacturers' new orders
- stock prices
- new plant and equipment orders

These statistical measures tend to move in advance of changes in the economy. Declining workweek hours, manufacturers' new orders, stock prices, and new plant and equipment orders tend to precede a decline in GDP. Unemployment claims tend to rise in advance of declining real output.

Coincident indicators include

- payroll EMPLOYMENT
- industrial production
- personal INCOME
- manufacturing and trade sales
- new building permits
- delivery times of goods
- interest-rate spread
- MONEY SUPPLY
- consumer expectations

Logically these indicators change at the same time as changes in real output. Some coincident indicators, such as payroll, personal income, and consumer expectations, affect primarily consumer spending; while other indicators, such as industrial PRODUCTION, trade sales, and delivery time of goods affect primarily business spending.

Lagging economic indicators include

- labor cost per unit of output
- inventories-to-sales ratio
- unemployment duration
- ratio of consumer credit to personal income
- outstanding commercial LOANS
- prime interest rate
- inflation rate for SERVICES

These indicators typically do not change until after real GDP has changed. Economists use lagging and leading indicators to distinguish the peaks and troughs in business cycles.

Major U.S. CORPORATIONS usually have a team of economists to analyze economic indicators and use these indicators to develop forecasts for future DEMAND for a company's products based on changes in real GDP. Many firms and industries develop customized sets of indicators for forecasting. For example, convenience-store operators know gasoline prices affect the demand for other PRODUCTS in their stores. Because the ELASTICITY OF DEMAND for gasoline is inelastic, or relatively unresponsive, consumers continue to purchase almost as much gasoline at a higher price as compared to when the price was lower. Higher prices reduce consumers' discretionary spending on candy, drinks, and other impulse purchases. Similarly, universities know changes in high-school graduation rates and federal loan and grant programs, as well as changes in the economy, affect demand for their services. One owner of a traditional men's clothing store noticed that demand for his products shifted depending on which business groups were doing well. At times he had many real-estate developers, other times business executives, lawyers, and doctors. He adjusted his MARKETING STRATEGY based on indicators predicting which segment of the market would continue to prosper.

Further reading
Boyes, William, and Michael Melvin. *Macroeconomics,* 5th ed. Boston: Houghton Mifflin, 2001.

individual retirement account

In 1974 the Employee Retirement Security Act created the Individual Retirement Account (IRA), allowing eligible persons to establish their own tax-deferred retirement savings plans from which withdrawals can be made after age 70½. These so-called "traditional IRAs" offer an immediate tax benefit by deducting the allowed amount saved from the annual taxable INCOME, though there are some exceptions. When funds—principal and interest—are withdrawn, they are taxed. Early withdrawals, unless exempt, are subject to an additional 10-percent excise tax. The Roth IRA, established in 1998 and named for Delaware senator William Roth, does not offer investors an immediate tax write-off but allows them to make tax-free withdrawals after the mandatory age of 59½.

In June 2001 President George W. Bush signed the Economic Growth and Tax Relief Reconciliation Act (EGTRRA), which changed tax and labor laws, including an increase in the maximum dollar amount of contributions to traditional and Roth IRAs. Contributions can be made only from earned income, wages, salaries, and tips. Married couples who file joint income-tax returns are excepted; even if one does not work, each may make a contribution for their "combined" income, with some limitations (see below). Until the passage of EGTRRA, the maximum annual contribution had been $2,000 per individual; the amount increased to $3,000 for 2002–04, to $4,000 for 2005–07, and to $5,000 for 2008 and beyond. For 2002–03, individuals 50 and older may take an additional $500, for a total of $3,500.

A married couple's contributions to the traditional IRA may not be tax-deductible, depending on their enrollment in a qualified RETIREMENT PLAN and their adjusted gross income (AGI) level. A nonworking spouse's tax deduction is phased out if the working spouse is in a retirement plan and their joint AGI falls between $150,000 and $160,000 (filing jointly); the phase-out begins limiting the deduction starting at $150,000 and increases so that there is no deduction at $160,000 or more. Similarly, if the working spouse is in a retirement plan, his or her deduction is decreased once the AGI reaches $54,000, with total phase-

out at $64,000. If neither is in a retirement plan, deductions are allowed, regardless of AGI. If both work and are in retirement plans, deductions again are phased out from $54,000 to $64,000. The range is $95,000–$110,000 for single filers.

Future traditional IRA phase-out ranges for married couples filing jointly with a working spouse in a retirement plan are

2003: $60,000–$70,000 ($40,000–$50,000 single filer);
2004: $65,000–$75,000 ($45,000–$55,000 single filer);
2005: $70,000–$80,000 ($50,000–$60,000 single filer);
2006: $75,000–$85,000 ($50,000–$60,000 single filer);
2007: $80,000–$100,000 ($50,000–$60,000 single filer).

Though tax deductions are not an option with Roth IRAs, a taxpayer's AGI can limit eligibility. Eligibility to contribute to a Roth is phased out between $150,000 and $160,000 for married couples filing jointly, between $95,000 and $110,000 for single filers, and between $0 and $10,000 for married couples filing individually. Roth IRA investors can be penalized both for making early withdrawals and for failing to make withdrawals after age 70½. "Unauthorized" withdrawals made before age 59½ incur a 10-percent tax, and failure to make minimum withdrawals after 70½ are penalized 50 percent on the amount not taken. There are exceptions to the 10-percent early-withdrawal tax, although these are still subject to regular income tax. The exempted withdrawals are those made

- because of the disability or death of the IRA holder
- that represent a series of "substantially equal periodic payments" made over the life expectancy of the owner
- that are used to pay medical expenses not reimbursed and exceeding 7½ percent of the AGI
- that are used to pay medical INSURANCE premiums after the owner has received UNEMPLOYMENT compensation for more than 12 weeks
- that are used to pay the costs of a first-time home purchase (lifetime limit of $10,000)
- that are used to pay for the qualified expenses of higher education for the IRA owner and/or eligible family members
- that are used to pay back taxes from an IRS levy against an IRA

Types of IRAs include the following.

1. A traditional or Roth Individual Retirement Account is set up through a bank, broker, or mutual fund. INVESTMENTS may be made in stocks, BONDS, money markets, and certificates of deposit (CDs).
2. An Individual Retirement Annuity is the same as a traditional or Roth IRA, except that a life insurance company sets up the account through an ANNUITY contract.

3. A group IRA, or Employer and Employee Association Trust Account, works like a traditional IRA but is run through an employer, UNION, or other employee association.

4. A Simplified Employee Pension (SEP-IRA) is a traditional IRA set up by a business for its employees. The employer may contribute up to $30,000, or 15 percent, of an employee's compensation annually to his/her IRA.

5. A Savings Incentive Match Plan for Employees IRA (SIMPLE-IRA) is a traditional IRA set up by a small employer for its employees. The contribution limit will increase each year through 2005, when it will stop at $10,000. The limit will increase by $500 a year from 2006 on. Employers may also match a percentage of their workers' contributions, with the combined amount not to exceed a set limit each year.

6. A Spousal IRA is either a traditional or Roth IRA funded by a married taxpayer in the name of his or her nonworking spouse. The couple must file a joint tax return in the year of the contribution. The limits established under EGTRRA hold true for the nonworking spouse.

7. A Rollover (Conduit) IRA is a traditional IRA that receives a distribution from a qualified retirement plan. Distributions are not subject to any contribution limits and may be eligible for transfer into a new employer's qualified retirement plan.

8. An Inherited IRA is either a traditional or a Roth IRA acquired by the nonspousal beneficiary of a deceased IRA owner. A tax deduction is not allowed for contributions to this IRA.

9. An Education IRA (EIRA) is established to allow a beneficiary to attend an institute of higher education. Contributions aren't tax-deductible, but withdrawals to pay the costs of higher education are not taxed or penalized. Beginning in 2002, EIRA funds also can be used to pay for education for kindergarten through 12th grade, with a maximum contribution of $2,000 (in addition to any other IRA contributions).

See also SIMPLIFIED EMPLOYEE PENSION.

Further reading

BISYS Retirement Services website. Available on-line. URL: http://www.bisysretirement.com/news/AlertIRA05302001.asp; H&R Block website. Available on-line. URL: http://www.hrblock.com/part7856124con974632SI3647816/tax_law/ira_contributions.html; IRA Investor website. Available on-line. URL: http://www.irainvestor.com/individualinvestors/rothira/index.asp; Internal Revenue Service website Forms and Publications. Available on-line. URL: http://www.irs.gov/formspubs/page/0,,id%3D12563,00.html; Internal Revenue website. Available on-line. URL: http://www.irs.gov/businesses/small/industries/article/0,,id=98765,00.html; Motley Fool website Motley Fool website IRA glossary information. Available on-line. URL: http://www.fool.com/money/allaboutiras/allaboutirasglossary.htm; http://www.fool.com/money/allaboutiras/allaboutiras01.htm; Smart Money website IRA information. Available on-line. URL: http://www.smartmoney.com/retirement/ira/index.cfm?story=spousal.

—Andrew Kearns

industrial-organizational psychology

The field of industrial-organizational (I/O) psychology includes the study of all aspects of human behavior in the business environment. Because people spend a considerable amount of time at work and often with other people, understanding work-related experiences and attitudes is critical for improving the overall quality of work life and employee performance within an organization. I/O psychologists study important organizational issues such as personnel selection, job-related training, employee PERFORMANCE APPRAISAL, group work, MANAGEMENT and LEADERSHIP quality, and general working conditions.

Personnel selection involves INTERVIEWING, selecting, and hiring job candidates who are suitably matched for particular jobs. Many organizations employ testing procedures to screen applicants beforehand, helping to ensure that an applicant has the necessary skills and abilities to perform a job before making any hiring decisions. I/O psychologists work to develop reliable and valid tests for job placements so that both the employer and the employee benefit from their use. In addition, I/O psychologists study the interview process itself, identifying variables that affect its success, such as the applicant's appearance and the interviewer's expectations.

I/O psychologists also study job-related training so employers know how and when to provide the necessary training for their employees. In addition, they work to ensure that additional training opportunities are provided, allowing employees to update and improve their job-related skills and knowledge.

Evaluation of employee performance is another critical concern. I/O psychologists review the procedures for performance evaluation and feedback, seeking to ensure that employees are evaluated fairly and accurately on job performance and not on extraneous or irrelevant factors. Ultimately performance evaluations feed into decisions about salary increases and promotions, both of which affect employees' satisfaction with their jobs and their commitment to the company.

I/O psychologists also study how groups function in the workplace, trying to increase productivity and decrease the occurrence of SOCIAL LOAFING. They seek to identify the variables that affect the quantity and quality of group work, such as feelings of cohesion, and assist in deciding whether particular projects are better suited for group work or for individual efforts.

Management and leadership quality have important effects on the business environment. I/O psychologists study how good managers motivate employees and make suggestions regarding what style of leadership is best suited for a given situation. Training can then be provided to enhance managers' leadership skills.

I/O psychologists are also interested in how the general working conditions in an organization affect employees and productivity. Safety on the job, exposure to workplace violence, general health concerns, absenteeism, and stress are all important concerns in the work environment. The HAWTHORNE EXPERIMENTS were highly influential in alerting I/O psychologists to social and physical factors that could affect worker productivity and satisfaction in general.

I/O psychology is a rapidly growing field. Ultimately research that helps organizations understand and improve their work environment can be of tremendous value in determining a company's success or failure.

See also SOCIAL FACILITATION.

Further reading
Oskamp, Stuart, and P. Wesley Schultz. *Applied Social Psychology.* 2d ed. Upper Saddle River, N.J.: Prentice-Hall, 1998; Schultz, Duane, and Sydney Ellen Schultz. *Psychology and Work Today: An Introduction to Industrial and Organizational Psychology,* 8th ed. New York: Macmillan Publishing, 2001.

—Elizabeth L. Cralley

Industrial Workers of the World

The Industrial Workers of the World (IWW) was a major U.S. UNION during the early 20th century; today it is a small international union. Established in Chicago in 1905, the IWW (or "wobblies" as they came to be called) was one of the first industrial unions. These differed from CRAFT UNIONS in that industrial unions attempted to organize all workers in a factory or industry, while craft unions limited membership to workers with a particular skill. One IWW pamphlet stated, "The directory of unions of Chicago shows in 1903 a total of 56 different unions in the packing houses, divided up still more in 14 different trades unions of the AMERICAN FEDERATION OF LABOR. . . . What a horrible example of an army divided against itself in the face of a strong combination of employers."

The IWW defined itself as "One Big Union" undivided by sex, race, or skills. At the time this was a radical goal, earning IWW members labels as anarchists and socialists. Big Bill Haywood, leader of the Western Federation of Miners, stated at the 1905 meeting, "The aims and objects of this organization shall be to put the working-class in possession of the economic power, the means of life, in control of the machinery of production and distribution, without regard to the capitalist masters."

IWW membership probably never exceeded 10,000 people at any one time. Its leaders moved from one industrial conflict to another, and many were arrested frequently, often under anti-speech ordinances imposed to stifle union efforts. Joe Hill, an IWW organizer among western railroad workers, was accused of killing a grocer in Salt Lake City. Convicted and executed in 1915, he became famous to recent generations through a Joan Baez ballad.

Joe Hill was an African American. One of the IWW principles was the inclusion of workers from any race or nationality, a revolutionary practice at the time. When Big Bill Haywood was invited to speak to the Brotherhood of Timber Workers in Louisiana in 1912, he asked why there were no blacks present and was told it was illegal to have interracial meetings. Haywood argued, "If it is against the law, this is one time when the law should be broken," and blacks were invited to the convention.

With the outbreak of World War I, union activity declined, and the IWW diminished as an agent of change in the American labor movement. Today the IWW describes itself as "a union dedicated to organizing on the job, in our industries and in our communities both to win better conditions today and build a world without bosses, a world in which production and distribution are organized by workers ourselves to meet the needs of the entire population, not merely a handful of exploiters."

Further reading
Industrial Workers of the World website. Available on-line. URL: www.iww.org.

inflation

Inflation is a sustained rise in the average level of prices that causes a decrease in the PURCHASING power of a country's currency. By decreasing the purchasing power of money, inflation has what economists call redistributive effects. During periods of inflation, people who are on fixed INCOMES, such as pensioners, as well as holders of BONDS and other fixed-interest credit instruments are paid with MONEY that has lost part of its purchasing power. During the economic upheaval in 1990s Russia, retirees with fixed incomes saw their pensions become almost worthless as inflation eroded the purchasing power of their money.

People who borrow in advance of inflation pay back their LOANS with less valuable money. People who are able to increase their income equal to the increase in inflation do not lose their purchasing power. UNIONS frequently negotiate wage increases to protect their members' incomes. Often the owners of resources can increase the price of their resources to keep up with inflation.

Inflation is caused by an excess of DEMAND relative to SUPPLY, or a reduction in supply relative to demand. COST-PUSH INFLATION, sometimes called supply-shock or sellers' inflation, occurs when a decrease in supply of many or important resources causes an increase in the price of these resources resulting in price increases. The OPEC (ORGANIZATION OF PETROLEUM EXPORTING COUNTRIES) oil EMBARGO that caused huge increases in oil prices in the 1970s is an example of supply-shock inflation. Demand-pull inflation occurs when overall demand exceeds supply. One way to describe demand-pull inflation is "too many dollars chasing too few goods." "Too many dollars" in an economy is caused by an expansionary MONETARY POLICY or FISCAL POLICY, or some combination of both.

The most extreme example of demand-pull inflation occurred in Germany in the 1920s. At the end of World War I, the German economy was in a shambles. During the war the German government had issued bonds borrowing significant amounts from its citizens, and afterwards it was required to make reparation payments to the Allies. Having little economic activity to tax, the German government literally cranked up the presses, printing deutsche marks. They paid off their debt, but in the process the currency became worthless as inflation increased 100 trillion times between 1914 and 1924. During the worst periods, German workers insisted on being paid twice a day so they could spend their money before it lost more of its purchasing power. One apocryphal story described a German consumer leaving a wheelbarrow full of money outside a bakery while making purchases in the store. Someone stole the wheelbarrow, dumping the money on the sidewalk. The deutsche mark became worthless during this period of hyperinflation.

Inflation in the United States is measured using three indexes: the GROSS DOMESTIC PRODUCT (GDP) DEFLATOR, THE producer price index (PPI) and the CONSUMER PRICE INDEX (CPI). The GDP deflator measures price changes of all goods and SERVICES produced. The PPI measures changes in prices received by producers; inflation at the producer level usually precedes inflation at the consumer level. The CPI uses a "market basket" of typical goods and services purchased by households in the United States to measure inflation at the consumer level. The CPI is the most widely watched and quoted measure of inflation and is used in making COST-OF-LIVING ADJUSTMENTS.

Further reading

Boyes, William, and Michael Melvin. *Macroeconomics*, 5th ed. Boston: Houghton Mifflin Company, 2001.

infomercials

Infomercials are program-length TV commercials, usually devoted solely to one product, that resemble regular programming; the name is derived from "information" and "commercials." Infomercials are used to increase public awareness, develop brand-name recognition, and create a direct consumer response. They traditionally have been viewed with cynicism by the ADVERTISING industry. Early infomercials offering miracle products and get-rich plans were sometimes accused of marketing PONZI SCHEMES. However, Microsoft's use of an infomercial to promote Windows 95 is credited with "legitimizing" this form of MARKETING COMMUNICATIONS.

Typical infomercials employ the television format to demonstrate PRODUCTS and provide testimonials. Often celebrities are used to bolster the credibility of marketers' claims.

Infomercials are expensive, costing on average at least $300,000 to develop and more to air, depending on how often and in what time slots they will appear. On a per-minute basis, infomercials cost a fraction of the price of a 30-second television commercial.

Combined, infomercials and home-shopping networks (now called direct-response television) are big business in the United States, generating over $1.25 billion in revenue in 2000. *Infomercial Marketing Report,* an industry newsletter, tracks the leaders each year. In the past, leading infomercials included

- Fitness Breakthroughs with Jane Fonda
- Hidden Keys to Loving Relationships with Kathie Lee and Frank Gifford
- Psychic Friends Network
- Deal-a-Meal with Richard Simmons

Further reading

Boone, Louis E., and David L. Kurtz. *Contemporary Marketing,* 10th ed. Fort Worth: Dryden Press, 2001.

infrastructure

Infrastructure is man-made products services that facilitate production and distribution of other goods and services. The term was originally used to refer to the basic systems that support a community. Roads, bridges, railroad tracks, power lines, sewer systems, and water systems are considered part of a community's infrastructure. Over time the phrase has expanded to include such things as postal and prison systems and the national defense system, but recently it has become widely used in the information technology industry, referring to the basic system of computing in general and to the INTERNET in particular.

In the United States, development of the railroads in the 1800s, the interstate highway system in the 1950s, and expansion of communication systems in the 1990s all were major infrastructure investments leading to economic growth. The decaying national infrastructure is a popular discussion topic in public-administration circles. This refers to the decay of the bridges, roads, and sewer systems on which communities depend. Often governments will defer improving infrastructure as a way to address a financial crisis, which could leave them in a situation of what is termed *hidden debt.* One government may have the exact same financial situation as one of its neighboring governments; however, it could be in serious hidden financial trouble because of decaying infrastructure that needs to be dealt with to keep the community viable. During economic declines, organizations such as school systems and businesses also defer infrastructure maintenance and replacement, hoping better ECONOMIC CONDITIONS or a crisis event will result in the needed resources to make infrastructure improvement. During economic expansions, managers are faced with the difficult choice of whether to increase output using existing technology, expanding work hours, or adding additional work shifts; or to replace existing CAPITAL with new technology. Often infrastructure constraints influence these business decisions.

—Mack Tennyson

initial public offering

"Going public" is when the stock of a closely held CORPORATION, PROPRIETORSHIP, or PARTNERSHIP is offered for sale to the public for the first time. This sale of formerly closely held shares is known as an initial public offering (IPO). IPOs are used to raise additional CAPITAL and result in publicly held corporations. In the late 1990s, initial public offerings of INTERNET companies dubbed DOT-COMS were compared to "feeding frenzies," with investors wildly bidding up the prices of new companies that had no earnings record and untested MANAGEMENT. Early investors in dot-com IPOs often "flipped" their shares, quickly selling them for a huge PROFIT. Insiders were prevented by SECURITIES AND EXCHANGE COMMISSION (SEC) rules forcing them to hold onto their shares for a period of time, usually six months. When the dot-com bubble burst in 2000, many SHAREHOLDERS watched as the value of their paper holdings disappeared. The SEC is investigating whether executives from clients of securities firms received preferential treatment in the allocation of shares in initial public offerings.

injunctions

Injunctions are judicial orders to cease and desist from certain activities—for example, destroying documents relevant to litigation. Injunctions can also order persons and businesses to do certain acts, such as releasing documents. Injunctions can be "temporary" or "permanent," "preliminary" or "final," depending on the circumstances. Injunctions are considered a type of "equitable remedy" at law, meaning they can be fashioned to meet many judicial needs. They are available only when irreparable injury is likely to occur in absence of an injunction.

Failure to obey an injunction can lead to severe penalties, such as fines and penalties for being in contempt of court. For example, the TAFT-HARTLEY ACT allows the U.S. president to seek an injunction imposing a 60-day "cooling-off" period, delaying a UNION's strike in a labor dispute if the president determines the activity would harm national security or welfare.

Further reading

Dobbyn, John F. *Injunctions in a Nutshell.* Eagan, Minn.: West Group, 1974.

input-output (I/O)

In all businesses that produce a product or service there is an input-output process. This process includes all the resources needed to create the product or services that are then transformed into finished items that are sold in the marketplace. The process of taking the raw materials and other items necessary for production (inputs) and converting (transformation) them into finished goods and services (outputs) is an open, systematic approach to production. This process is often abbreviated as the I/O system.

Inputs in the I/O system include raw materials, technical information, financial resources, and people. Within the transformation process there are numerous subsystems. In a manufacturing environment raw materials are converted into a product by a production subsystem that includes all the equipment necessary to make the product. The building and the manufacturing equipment are maintained by a maintenance subsystem. Management, responsible for coordinating and controlling work, is another subsystem.

I/O systems are considered to be open systems if they are open to and respond to their outside environment. The environment is dynamic and, therefore, constantly changing. Open systems are constantly looking for changes in their environment (boundary spanning) and adapt to those impending changes. Forward-looking companies anticipated the growth of the Internet and electronic means of conducting business. They looked for changes in the legal and regulatory environment and were able to manage those changes through their adaptation subsystem. Closed systems rely on themselves and ignore their environment. These organizations are in an entropic state and will eventually collapse.

insider trading

Insider trading is the buying and selling of shares of stock in a CORPORATION by the company's managers, BOARD OF DIRECTORS, or other individuals with a financial interest in or knowledge of the company. Some insider trading is legal and closely watched in the marketplace, while other insider trading is illegal and closely scrutinized by securities-industry authorities. Managers, directors, and individuals who own 10 percent or more of a company's shares must disclose the purchase or sale of shares to the SECURITIES AND EXCHANGE COMMISSION (SEC) by the 10th of the month after their action. However, it is illegal for insiders to buy or sell stock based on their knowledge of material corporate developments that have not been made public. Material corporate developments may include MERGERS AND ACQUISITIONS, NEW PRODUCT DEVELOPMENT, divestitures, key personnel departures or appointments, and any other news that could affect the price of a company's stock.

In 1984 the Insiders Trading Sanctions Act imposed penalties of up to three times a trader's PROFITS on any trader who intentionally "tips" private market-sensitive information to a third party who then profits by trading based on that information. In 1988, incensed over continued insider-trading abuse on WALL STREET, Congress unanimously passed the Insider Trading and Securities Fraud Enforcement Act, extending penalties to employers or "controlling persons" who do not take steps to prevent illegal employee trading. Controlling persons are subject to civil penalties up to the greater of $1 million or three times the amount of illegal-trading profit. In addition to civil penalties, insider trading is subject to criminal prosecution, and professionals (accountants and lawyers) may be suspended or barred from practice.

Over the years, the SEC has been given increased power to oversee and curtail insider trading. One of the most notorious cases of insider trading involved Ivan Boesky, an arbitrageur who bought shares of stock in companies that were about to be taken over by another firm at an above-market price. Boesky learned in advance of these transactions through Dennis Levine, an investment banker, who worked in a company providing the financing for the takeovers. When confronted by the SEC in 1986, Boesky agreed to an out-of-court settlement banning him from securities trading, payment of a $100 million fine, and three years in jail.

Determining what is insider trading is generally based on the answers to three questions:

- Is the information public?
- Is the information material?
- Is there a fiduciary relationship?

Information is considered public when it has been distributed through the media, allowing the public to learn about it. Press releases, wire-service reports, and reports through business newspapers allow buyers and sellers in the STOCK MARKET to learn about and interpret information. If the public does not know about the information, it would be illegal to trade based on that information if it is significant enough to influence the stock's price.

What is and is not material information is a difficult question to answer. The SEC analyzes trading in stocks before and after important announcements. Using statistical variation from the norm, the commission looks for larger-than-normal trading activity just before a material event. After September 11, 2001, U.S. and global securities regulators analyzed stock and options trading in airline, INSURANCE, and financial stocks just prior to the attack. While trading volume was higher than normal, to date no known links have been made between terrorists and the individuals engaging in the stock-market transactions.

The third question of fiduciary relationship addresses whether or not an individual with information is an "insider." Any officer, director, or employee of a company is considered a "traditional insider," who must either make the information available to the public or refrain from trading or tipping other people who might trade.

"Temporary insiders" include auditors, lawyers, brokers, and investment bankers who do not work for the company but often have access to sensitive, nonpublic information.

As previously stated, insider trading can also be a legal activity watched closely by stock-market investors. For years investors have monitored the ratio of insider (officers and directors) sales to purchases of company stock, but like all investors, insiders have many reasons for buying and selling stock that don't rely solely on their perceptions of the company's future profitability. For example, in the late 1990s, Bill Gates, Microsoft's CHIEF EXECUTIVE OFFICER, announced that he would sell shares of his company over time, both to diversify his ASSETS and to finance the endowment he and his wife, Melinda, were establishing. Nevertheless, investors and financial news services often track insider-trading activity.

When insiders sell shares, stockholders worry that there is impending trouble ahead. But as managers of companies are increasingly offered STOCK OPTIONS, the reported statistics distort the reality of insider trading. Options are not included in purchases of shares, but sales based on the exercising of options are included in insider trading.

Further reading
Rosen, Robert C. "An Accountant's Guide to the SEC's New Insider Trading Regulations," *CPA Journal* 63 (February 1993): 67.

Institute for Supply Management
Formerly the National Association of Purchasing Managers, the Institute for Supply Management (ISM) is the leading professional organization of PURCHASING and supply-chain MANAGEMENT professionals; the organization changed its name in 2002. The ISM's mission is "to educate, develop, and advance the purchasing and supply management profession." Established in 1915, the association has over 48,000 members, provides a variety of publications, and offers seminars, conferences, and two certification programs: Certified Purchasing Manager (CPM) and Accredited Purchasing Practitioner (APP).

The ISM is most noted for its Purchasing Managers' Indexes (PMI), which are based on surveys of purchasing managers around the country and recognized as important INDICATORS of economic activity. The PMIs include production, new orders and backlog of new orders, supplier, prices, inventories, new exports, and import of materials. Because purchasing managers are directly involved in production management and must order materials and supplies in advance of actual production activity, their assessments are good predictors of near-term manufacturing activity.

The ISM's standards of supply-management conduct provide a number of valuable insights into ethical conflicts in business. Some of their standards include

- perceived impropriety—avoid the intent and appearance of unethical or compromising conduct in relationships, actions, and communications
- CONFLICT OF INTEREST—avoid any personal business or professional activity that would create a conflict between personal interests and the interests of the employer
- personal INVESTMENT—ownership of stock by a supplier of goods or services, competitor, or customer should be reported to the employer for review and guidance to avoid the potential for impropriety
- issues of influence—avoid soliciting or accepting money, LOANS, credits, or preferential discounts, and the acceptance of gifts, entertainment, favors, or services from present or potential suppliers that might influence, or appear to influence, supply-management decisions
- confidential and proprietary information—handle confidential or proprietary information with due care and proper consideration of ethical and legal ramifications and governmental regulations.

Further reading
Institute for Supply Management website. Available on-line. URL: www.ism.ws.

Institute of Management Accountants
The Institute of Management Accountants (IMA) is "the leading professional organization devoted exclusively to MANAGERIAL ACCOUNTING and financial management." As set forth on its website its mission and vision statements, its goals are "to help members develop both personally and professionally, by means of education, certification, and association with other business professionals." Instrumental in shaping managerial accounting concepts and standards, the IMA also influences ethical practices and the development of ethical standards for practitioners.

The IMA offers two certifications: the CMA (Certified in Management Accounting) and the CFM (Certified in Financial Management). Earning and maintaining IMA certifications document test individuals' competence and expertise in management accounting and financial management.

Further reading
Institute of Management Accountants website. Available on-line. URL: www.imanet.org.

insurance
Insurance is an asset purchased by individuals and organizations to protect them from loss and provide them with a way to reduce the risk of exposure to possible injury or loss. There are three classifications of RISK—personal risk, property risk, and LIABILITY risk—and it is possible to be insured against all three types. Personal risk entails the loss of INCOME and/or ASSETS because the individual or organization can no longer work or operate. Property risk entails the loss of property (i.e., anything that an individual or organization owns). Liability risk entails the loss of assets or income due to an individual's or organization's NEGLIGENCE, as determined by law. Insurance transfers an individual's or an organization's risk to the insurer.

Insurance has been practiced in one form or another for thousands of years. In ancient Babylonian society, it was common for merchants to purchase bottomry CONTRACTS, or LOANS that did not have to be repaid if the purchased merchandise did not make it to its final destination. This evolved into a more sophisticated marine (shipping) insurance system. Modern marine insurance was introduced in Italy during the 13th century, when banks and merchants formed syndicates to protect themselves from shipping losses. In the 18th century a former coffeehouse named Lloyds developed into a major marine insurance group, and London developed into a center for marine insurance. The 18th century also introduced other types of insurance, including life, fire, and casualty insurance. The astronomer Edmond Halley made life insurance possible with the development of the first mortality table in 1683. The first insurance company in the United States was the Philadelphia Contribution, formed by Benjamin Franklin in 1752. The 1820s saw enormous growth in the insurance industry in the United States.

Today insurance is an international business dominated by huge companies. In the United States there are several thousand insurance companies employing millions of people. The insurance business uses statistical probabilities, usually in the form of actuarial tables, to determine if something or someone is insurable and to set premiums. The larger the number of individuals or organizations insured, the easier it is to set a reasonable premium. Higher premiums are assigned when an insurance company deems someone or something to be a larger risk. Some insurance companies then reinvest this premium money in revenue-producing projects, and for this reason some of the United States' largest institutional investors are insurance companies.

The McCarron-Ferguson Act (1945) left the regulation of U.S. insurance companies to the individual state, and for this reason insurance regulation is not as uniform as that in other industries. The McCarron-Ferguson Act affects Title 15, Chapter 20 (Regulation of Insurance) of the U.S. Code. It states that "the business of insurance, and every person engaged therein, shall be subject to the laws of the several States which relate to the regulation or taxation of such business" (U.S. Code Title 15, sec. 1012a). Some uniformity in state regulation does exist, however, due primarily to the National Association of Insurance Commissioners (NAIC), which works toward creating a uniform standard.

There are various types of insurance to protect against the three types of risk. To protect against personal risk, there is life insurance and health insurance, both of which most closely resemble the insurance model described above. Large groups of people contribute to a fund, and if an individual in that group is injured, gets sick, or dies, monetary relief is provided to him, her, or his/her beneficiaries.

Homeowners and commercial insurance are two types of protection against property risk, providing monetary relief if an individual or organization suffers accidental property loss; these types include fire and flood insurance. In many cases creditors require an individual or organization is required to obtain property insurance.

Liability insurance entails several types of insurance, including automobile, theft, and aviation, all of which may be legally required and will compensate others if personal negligence leads to their injury or loss. WORKERS' COMPEN-SATION is an additional type of liability insurance that protects employers from monetary loss in case of employee injury; it is mandatory for all employers to have workers' compensation insurance for all employees. Credit insurance and title insurance are two additional types of liability insurance that protect individuals and organizations from financial loss due to the negligence of others.

There is an additional type of insurance called "surety ship" that protects companies from losses due to their employees' dishonesty. Athletes' bodies, musicians' hands, and even weather for outdoor events are some examples of things that are currently being insured. As computers allow for the more accurate computation of risk, it will become possible for insurers to develop policies for almost anything.

Further reading
Vaughn, Emmett J., and Therese M. Vaughn. *Fundamentals of Risk and Insurance*, 9th ed. New York: Wiley, 2002.

—Joseph F. Klein

intellectual property

Intellectual property is a broad category of intangible property rights created by law. COPYRIGHTS, PATENTS and TRADEMARKS are examples of intellectual property.

Patents for inventions are adjudicated exclusively under federal and statutory law. A patent application results in a search of the "prior art" (state of knowledge) in the field. U.S. patent awards grant exclusive rights to make, use, and sell the invention for 21 years from the date of filing for the patent. In recent years patents for computer programs and "business methods" have grown in number.

Copyrights are likewise exclusively federal and statutory under U.S. law. Copyrights, such as the one on this book, last from the creation of a work to 70 years after the death of the author/creator. Copyrights protect the author/publisher from copying by others.

Trademarks and service marks are recognized under COMMON LAW by state registration and by federal registration. Trademarks and service marks are words and symbols that distinguish particular goods and SERVICES from oth-

ers—Coca-Cola, for instance. Once registered and actively used, trademarks and service marks can be maintained indefinitely.

Other intellectual-property rights recognized in U.S. law and sometimes by international agreement include TRADE SECRETS, integrated circuits, industrial designs, and geographic indicators of origin like Kentucky bourbon and Mexican tequila.

See also WORLD INTELLECTUAL PROPERTY ORGANIZATION.

Further reading
Miller, Arthur R., and Michael H. Davis. *Intellectual Property—Patents, Copyrights and Trademarks in a Nutshell*, 6th ed. Eagan, Minn.: West Group, 2000.

Inter-American Development Bank

The Inter-American Development Bank (IDB) is a regional, multilateral development organization. Established in 1959 with 20 members, including the United States and 19 Caribbean and Latin American countries, the IDB's mission is to "promote and support development of the private sector and CAPITAL MARKETS in its Latin American and Caribbean member countries by investing, lending, innovating and leveraging RESOURCES."

IDB lending grew from $294 million in 1961 to $5.3 billion in 2000. Membership has also grown to 46 countries, 26 borrowing countries, and 20 nonborrowing countries. Initially the bank's lending focused on agriculture and INFRASTRUCTURE projects. Its current lending priorities include "poverty reduction, social equity, modernization, and the environment."

Within the IDB, two groups focus on private-sector lending. The Inter-American Investment Corporation (IIC) finances small- and medium-scale private enterprises, while the Multilateral Investment Fund (MIF) promotes INVESTMENT reforms and supports private-sector investment.

Headquartered in Washington, D.C., the IDB is largely funded by the United States and supports U.S. political agendas. When the IDB was created, most Latin American countries were controlled by dictators, some of whom were friendly to the United States and others hostile to U.S. interference and economic and domination. The IDB acts as a nongovernmental means of supporting political and economic change in the Caribbean and Latin America.

See also ECONOMIC DEVELOPMENT.

Further reading
Inter-American Development Bank website. Available on-line. URL: www.iadb.org.

interest rates

In economic theory, interest is what is paid to induce a person with MONEY to save it and invest it in long-term ASSETS rather than spend it or a payment by borrowers for the use of funds. The rate of interest is a product of the interaction between the DEMAND for CAPITAL and the SUPPLY of savings. A higher demand for capital relative to the supply for savings produces higher interest rates, and vice versa.

Economic theory also makes a distinction between real and nominal interest rates. A nominal rate is the rate stated in the loan agreement. Real rates are nominal rates minus the rate at which money is losing its value. Thus, a loan agreement may have a rate of 10 percent, but if money is losing its purchasing power at the rate of 1 percent per year, the real rate is only 9 percent. In a loan of $10,000, the borrower will pay the lender $1,000 at a nominal rate of 10 percent, but since the loan is being paid back using dollars that are 1-percent less valuable, the real cost of the loan to the borrower is only 9 percent. Therefore the interest rate of 10 percent can be considered to be made of two parts: the basic rate and a 1-percent adjustment for inflationary pressure.

Another important factor in the level of interest rates is RISK. If a particular loan has a higher risk, creditors will require a higher interest rate to induce them to make the loan. To continue the example started in the last paragraph, suppose that the risk-free interest rate is 6 percent. The closest thing to a risk-free rate is the loan of money to the federal government via the purchase of Treasury bills. The 10 percent nominal rate would then be a product of three things: (1) the risk-free rate of 6 percent, (2) a risk premium of 3 percent, and (3) an adjustment for inflationary pressure of 1 percent.

Interest rates are also viewed in terms of the loan's DURATION. Borrowing for up to a week is often referred to as the "overnight" rate. Short-term rates apply to LOANS intended to last up to a year, and long-term rates are for loans lasting over a year. In general, with longer-term loans, there is upward pressure on each of the three elements comprising the interest rate. The risk-free rate is higher, while the longer-term loan has more potential time for something to go wrong. Thus the risk premium is higher and inflationary pressure is more observable over a long period of time. Usually long-term debts have a higher interest rate, but there have been notable exceptions.

Rates are usually stated in terms of a percentage payable and as an annual percentage rate. This is true even if the borrowing is for shorter than a year. A 10-percent interest rate infers 10 percent a year. For example, if a loan was for $10,000 for six months, the interest cost would be $500 ($10,000 x 6/12).

The federal-funds rate is the rate that banks charge each other when they are making short-term loans to each other. The prime rate is the rate that banks charge their best customers for short-term loans.

In the 1970s, lenders were using hidden fees and weird calculations to calculate interest as a way of stating a low interest rate in order to induce someone to borrow from them; however, they then charged a higher interest rate. In response to this, the U.S. government passed a series of CONSUMER PROTECTION laws, including the Fair Credit Billing Act (1975) and the CONSUMER CREDIT PROTECTION ACT (1969). These laws allow lenders to continue their practices, but they must disclose what is termed the annual percentage rate (APR). In addition to standardizing the way that interest is calculated, the APR also considers all the hidden fees in the loan. Consequently, a lender may calculate interest and impose fees as it likes, but it must disclose the APR to its borrowers before they agree to the loan. The law specifies how the disclosure should be made; the simplest way is to ask the lender the APR on the loan and to compare this rate with the APRs quoted by other lenders.

Another issue relative to consumer interest rates is their duration. Some low rates are merely introductory and will adjust after a few months to more typical rates. As a result, a loan that was initially appealing may adjust to an unacceptable rate after the introductory period. The intent of most of these types of interest rates is to deceive unwary customers.

Introductory rates should not be confused with indexed or adjustable rates—that is, loans with flexible interest rates. In this case the interest rate is indexed to some rate not under the control of either the lender or the borrower, i.e., the prime rate. If an interest rate is stated as "two percentage points above prime," and the prime rate is 6 percent, then the loan rate is 8 percent. This allows the lender to reduce some of its risk in lending the money. For new loans, the interest rate for an adjustable-rate loan will be lower than the rate for a fixed-rate loan. This is because the lender in an adjustable-rate loan has shifted some of the risk of changing rates to the borrower. Usually the rate is subject to an annual "cap," or maximum that can be adjusted in one year, and a lifetime cap, over the life of the loan.

See also YIELD CURVE.

—Mack Tennyson

interlocking directorate

An interlocking directorate is a network of business leaders who are members of boards of directors of CORPORATIONS. Any situation in which a director sits on the board of two or more companies simultaneously creates an interlocking directorate. While interlocking directorates are most associated with Japanese business, they are a powerful force in U.S. business practices.

Individuals serving on more than one BOARD OF DIRECTORS provide an informal means of communication and facilitate the building of business relationships. The old saying "It's not what you know but who you know that counts" summarizes the benefits of interlocking directorates. Depending on how information and influence is used, interlocking directorates can aid small companies attempting to build strategic relationships or assist large companies in finding new sources of ideas, talents, or products.

Members of a corporate board of directors have a fiduciary responsibility to direct corporate policy in the best interest of the SHAREHOLDERS. Corporate ANNUAL REPORTS usually state directors' financial interests in the company but rarely state their other financial and managerial relationships. An individual who sits on the board of two companies has access to advance knowledge of what each company intends to do. In advising on policy, the board member is likely to use his or her inside information to guide business-strategy decisions, even without directly revealing the other company's plans. This could benefit either both companies the board member represents or one company at the expense of the other.

Research into the impact of interlocking directorates is limited by lack of information regarding the use of information to influence corporate policy. Studies suggest interlocking directorates

- have been responsible for rapid diffusion of POISON-PILL STRATEGIES
- influence corporate-structure decisions
- influence corporate acquisitions
- influence the decision to pursue ISO STANDARDS
- influence decisions on corporate charitable contributions

Further reading
"New Corporate Governance: The Role of Director Interlocks." Mind Theme. Available on-line. URL: www.mindtheme.com/knowledge/interlock.asp.

Internal Revenue Service
The Department of the Treasury is responsible for administering and enforcing the internal revenue laws of the United States. The Secretary of the Treasury has delegated most revenue functions and authority to the Commissioner of Internal Revenue, the CHIEF EXECUTIVE OFFICER of the Internal Revenue Service (IRS). The president of the United States appoints the commissioner to a renewable five-year term. The commissioner is responsible for overall planning, directing, and coordinating of IRS programs, as well as policy control. The IRS is one of about a dozen bureaus within the Department of the Treasury, and with more than 100,000 employees, it is the second-largest federal government agency (after the Department of Defense).

The history of the IRS dates from President Abraham Lincoln and the Civil War. Congress created the office of Commissioner of Internal Revenue in 1862 and passed an income tax to pay expenses associated with the war: a 3-percent tax on INCOMES between $600 and $10,000 and 5 percent on incomes exceeding $10,000. This income tax was repealed 10 years later. The Wilson Tariff Act of 1894 revived the income tax, but the Supreme Court ruled it unconstitutional the next year. Early in the 20th century, Congress sought ratification of an amendment to allow the collection of a tax on income. Wyoming became the last state needed to ratify the amendment in 1913, and that year saw the introduction of a 1 percent tax on personal income greater than $3,000 and an additional surtax of 6 percent on incomes of more than $500,000. Later, the Revenue Act of 1918, in efforts to finance World War I, produced a top income-tax rate of 77 percent.

A reorganization of the IRS in 1952 replaced the patronage system—in which politicians had control of who was hired to do the agency's work—with independently hired professional career employees. A year later President Dwight D. Eisenhower changed the agency's name from the Bureau of Internal Revenue to the Internal Revenue Service.

The next major change for the system came in 1992, when taxpayers were allowed to file income tax returns electronically. Responding to a public outcry concerning a growing insensitivity on the part of the IRS and its possible abuse of power, Congress passed the Internal Revenue Service Restructuring and Reform Act in 1998, intended to protect taxpayer's rights. The act reorganized the IRS from a geographically based structure into four major operating divisions aligned according to types of taxpayers: the Wage and Investment Income Division, serving taxpayers who file individual and joint tax returns; the Small Business and Self-Employed Division, serving the approximately 45 million small businesses and self-employed taxpayers; the Large and Mid-Size Business Division, serving CORPORATIONS with ASSETS of more than $10 million; and the Tax Exempt and Government Entities Division, serving nonprofit charities and governmental entities. The 1998 act also set up a Taxpayer Advocate Service as an independent agency within the Internal Revenue Service to help resolve taxpayer problems.

In 1998 Congress also instituted a nine-member IRS Oversight Board, consisting of the secretary of the Treasury, the IRS commissioner, a representative of IRS employees, and six private-sector representatives; the president of the United States appoints all board members to five-year terms. The Oversight Board's duties are to review the IRS mission, strategic plans, operational functions, and processes; to review and approve the IRS budget; to recommend candidates for commissioner; and to ensure the proper treatment of taxpayers.

The IRS is an important component in the development of tax law. The IRS annually produces thousands of releases that explain and clarify tax law, including regulations, revenue rulings, letter rulings, revenue procedures, and technical advice memoranda. IRS publications, many of which are updated annually, are interpretations written in general terms using understandable language to provide guidance to the public. Although they do not bind the IRS and are not considered substantial authority, these publications can be very helpful for a taxpayer endeavoring to determine the best way to report a given transaction.

The IRS has the power to impose interest and penalties on taxpayers for noncompliance with tax law. Provisions such as the penalty for failure to pay a tax or file a return that is due, the NEGLIGENCE penalty for intentional disregard of rules and regulations ("substantial authority"), and various penalties for civil and criminal FRAUD serve as deterrents to taxpayer noncompliance.

Another deterrent to taxpayer noncompliance is the IRS audit process, which can take the form of correspondence audits, office audits, or field audits. While field examinations are common for business returns and complex individual returns, most returns are audited in an office audit. An audit notice indicating which items the IRS will examine and what information the taxpayer should bring are sent in advance. The IRS employee and the taxpayer and/or taxpayer's representative then meet at a nearby IRS office.

The IRS also has a computerized matching program through which the tax information filed on taxpayers' individual returns is compared with the information filed by payers or employers. Wages, interest, alimony, pensions, UNEMPLOYMENT compensation, SOCIAL SECURITY benefits, and other items of income are reported to the IRS by the payers. In addition, payees report deducted items, including state income taxes, local real-estate taxes, home MORTGAGE interest, etc. However, taxpayers who report only these items generally face a 100 percent audit rate.

Further reading
Internal Revenue Service website. Available on-line. URL: http://www.irs.ustreas.gov/; Pope, Thomas R., Kenneth E. Anderson, and John L. Kramer. *Prentice Hall's Federal Taxation 2003.* Upper Saddle River, N.J.: Pearson Education, Inc., 2003; Nellen, Annette. *Tax Aspects of Business Transactions, A First Course.* Upper Saddle River, N.J.: Prentice Hall, 1999; Raabe, William A., Gerald E. Whittenburg, John C. Bost, and Debra L. Sanders. *West's Federal Tax Research.* Cincinnati, Ohio: South Western College Publishing, 2000; Tax History Project website. Available on-line. URL: http://www.taxhistory.org.

—Linda Bradley and Stewart Curry

International Bank for Reconstruction and Development   See WORLD BANK.

International Brotherhood of Teamsters (Teamsters Union)
The International Brotherhood of Teamsters (IBT), also known as the Teamsters Union, is a major industrial UNION in the United States with a long and contentious history. Created in 1903, with Cornelius Shea elected as president, the Teamsters Union grew to represent over 1 million workers. Teamsters were men who drove horse-drawn wagons. The initial teamsters were quickly replaced with truck drivers, and the union expanded to represent different groups of transportation-related workers.

The Teamsters describe their goal as follows: "To make life better for Teamster members and their families—and for all working families—the Teamsters organize the unorganized, make workers' voices heard in all corridors of power, negotiate CONTRACTS that make the AMERICAN DREAM a reality for millions, protect workers' health and safety, and fight to keep jobs in North America."

After their initial meeting in 1903, the Teamsters met with considerable opposition, the bloodiest of which was a 100-day strike against Montgomery Ward in 1905, during which 21 lives were lost. The union has a long history of dissent and conflict both internally and externally. Local unions, opposed to national corruption and manipulation, have often seceded from the national union. The most famous Teamsters president was Jimmy Hoffa, who was elected in 1957 and disappeared in 1975.

With DEREGULATION of the trucking industry in the 1980s, Teamsters Union membership declined along with union membership in general in the United States. The 1997 United Parcel Service (UPS) strike brought a surprising resurgence in the Teamsters Union's influence as UPS management underestimated public and business support for UPS drivers. Businesses and consumers knew their UPS drivers by name, respected their fast and professional service, and supported union demands for increased EMPLOYMENT of full-time workers.

Further reading
International Brotherhood of Teamsters website. Available on-line. URL: www.teamster.org; Witwer, David. "Local Rank and File Militancy: The Battle for Teamster Union Reform in Philadelphia in the Early 1960s," *Labor History* 41, no. 3 (August, 2000): 263.

International Energy Agency
The International Energy Agency (IEA) is an alliance of 26 nations created in the 1970s to ensure energy security for its members. The United States, Japan, Korea, and most European countries are members of the IEA, which works in conjunction with the ORGANIZATION FOR ECONOMIC COOPERATION AND DEVELOPMENT (OECD). The IEA's objectives are

- to maintain and improve systems for coping with oil-supply disruptions
- to promote rational energy policies in a global context through cooperative relations with nonmember countries, industries, and international organizations
- to operate a permanent information system on the international oil market
- to improve the world's energy supply and demand structure by developing alternative energy sources and increasing the efficiency of energy use
- to assist in the integration of environmental and energy policies.

The IEA publishes the monthly *Oil Market Report* and the biannual *World Energy Outlook* and reports regularly on the energy policies of its member states and those of selected nonmembers.

Most of the IEA members are major oil-importing countries. As such, they oppose restrictions made on oil production, particularly the actions by the ORGANIZATION OF PETROLEUM EXPORTING COUNTRIES (OPEC) to reduce supplies and raise market prices. However, the IEA has no power to direct policies by member countries. Norway, an IEA member, changed from a net-importing country to the world's third-largest oil-exporting country. In 1998 and 2002, Norway reduced oil output along with OPEC countries in an effort to increase the world price of oil. The IEA reviewed Norway's actions but took no action.

Most industrial nations were caught by surprise during the energy crises in the 1970s. Working together through the IEA, member countries attempt to offset the market power of oil-exporting countries. One of the agreements among IEA members is to maintain a stockpile of oil to be released during emergencies. The United States maintains a stock of petroleum reserves in caverns in the western part of the country.

Further reading
International Energy Agency website. Available on-line. URL: www.iea.org.

International Labor Organization

The International Labor Organization (ILO) is a global international labor association with a primary goal of improving working conditions, living standards, and equitable treatment of workers in all nations. Most of the major industrialized countries in the world, including the United States, are members of the ILO, which was created in 1919 at the Versailles peace conference, ending World War I. The ILO's constitution is included in the Treaty of Versailles.

When it was created, the ILO's goals included humanitarian, political, and economic objectives; or, as its constitution states, "conditions of labor exist involving . . . injustice, hardship and privation to large numbers of people." The constitution also refers to "unrest so great that the peace and harmony of the world are imperiled." The ILO hoped to reduce worker-industrialization tension and in the process reduce social unrest. It further hoped to gain worldwide acceptance of basic rights and reforms, recognizing that countries where workers were exploited could produce goods more cheaply. Therefore, global acceptance of basic rights and working conditions would "level the playing field" in economic COMPETITION. At the Versailles peace conference, a fourth justification for creating the ILO emerged: "[U]niversal and lasting peace can be established only if it is based upon social justice."

Headquartered in Geneva, Switzerland, the ILO became a specialized agency of the United Nations in 1946. It issues conventions to recommend international labor standards when there is substantial agreement among members. It also issues recommendations in situations where the issue is complex or when there is not a consensus regarding proper labor practices. Member states are obliged to provide ANNUAL REPORTS to verify their compliance with ILO conventions they have ratified. The ILO's Committee of Experts on the Application of Conventions and Recommendations reviews submissions and compiles a "special list" of governments that have defaulted on their obligations to the ILO agreements. The list is then presented to the General Conference for review and approval. In 1974 the Soviet Union was included on the list for breach of the 1930 Convention Concerning Forced or Compulsory Labor. After considerable debate, the General Conference failed to adopt the committee's recommendations, leading to U.S. withdrawal from the ILO in 1977. The United States rejoined the organization in 1980.

In recent years the ILO has focused on human rights, stating as its strategic objectives to

- promote and realize standards and fundamental principles and rights at work
- create greater opportunities for women and men to secure decent EMPLOYMENT and INCOME
- enhance the coverage and effectiveness of social protection for all
- strengthen tripartism (government, labor, and industry cooperation) and social dialogue

In 1969 the ILO received the Nobel Peace Prize for its work.

Further reading
August, Ray. *International Business Law.* 2d ed. New York: Prentice Hall, 1997; International Labor Organization website. Available on-line. URL: www.ilo.org.

international management

International management is the process of applying MANAGEMENT concepts and techniques in a multinational, multicultural environment. Large, medium, and small firms are seeing increasingly more of their overall revenue coming from overseas markets. International management is changing rapidly, due in part to the fact that managers are increasing their contact with other countries as foreign INVESTMENT and trade are increasing and TRADE BARRIERS among countries continue to fall. Businesses are also depending more on international markets for larger percentages of their total revenues. Managers face challenges and problems in the economic, political, legal, technological, and cultural areas of doing business in a global environment.

A lack of ECONOMIC GROWTH in some countries makes it difficult for MULTINATIONAL CORPORATIONS to continue to do business there. Elements that contribute to the economic RISK of doing business globally include trade barriers, weak savings, inadequate INFRASTRUCTURE, and unavailable or unskilled labor force. Governments can mismanage their country's economy, or it can be hurt by global factors such as an increase in INTEREST RATES worldwide.

A country's political environment is very complex and can change rapidly; international managers must therefore be aware of the impact of both the existing situation and political changes on their business. Foreign firms doing business in a country can be harmed when its leaders interfere in their operations, taking over ASSETS, practicing policies and regulations that adversely affect foreign investors, and allowing political upheaval to disrupt foreign business. With such risks, government leaders at home may not encourage international trade and investment.

Legal issues affecting international management include determining which country's laws will govern expatriates, how INTELLECTUAL PROPERTY is protected, and how disputes are resolved. Managers must be aware of INTERNATIONAL LAW and extensions of home-country law, in addition to learning the host-country laws and regulations with which they must comply, including those relating to foreign investment, labor, and EMPLOYMENT. Other legal challenges include corrupt foreign governments, restrictive foreign bureaucracies, inefficient government controls, and PRIVATIZATION of state-run companies.

International managers face challenges in a rapidly changing technological environment. Increasing numbers of people now have access to the INTERNET and can obtain information more quickly than ever before. Security issues and E-COMMERCE pose additional challenges. Technology affects the number and nature of employees in international firms and also makes work more portable. Advances in telecommunications offer EMERGING MARKETS new opportunities to engage in international transactions.

The world's many cultural differences also affect managing in the international arena, and therefore it is vital for international managers to have an understanding of the impact of culture on behavior. Culture can affect managers' attitudes, business-government relations, how people think and behave, employees' work values and attitudes, and the local practices. Managers must be aware that different approaches may be necessary, depending on the country where business is being transacted. The success of the company and its employees depends on a thorough understanding of both the cultural differences and the similarities between the home and host countries.

Managing HUMAN RESOURCES across cultures is another challenge in international management. Processes for selecting, training, motivating, monitoring, and compensating foreign employees will differ by country. Specific approaches to labor relations in the international arena will also vary from country to country.

Further reading
Hodgetts, Richard M., and Fred Luthans. *International Management: Culture, Strategy, and Behavior,* 4th ed. New York: Irwin McGraw-Hill, 2000; Sullivan, Jeremiah J. *Exploring International Business Environments,* New York: Pearson Custom Publishing, 1999.

—Judy Mims

international marketing

International marketing is marketing products and SERVICES to customers outside a company's home country. It is important to both businesses and countries and involves a variety of strategy issues, laws, and other considerations.

International marketing is as old as civilization. Almost any issue of *National Geographic Magazine* will include a story about trade, whether it concerns an ancient sailing ship being raised from the ocean bottom or travel along centuries-old trails where merchants carried goods from one civilization to another. International trade exists and has existed for a variety of reasons, including access to products not available domestically, COMPARATIVE ADVANTAGE among producers in one country, foreign DEMAND, saturation of domestic demand, and technological advantage.

Historically the United States has not been a leader in international trade. As a colony it was subject to British laws requiring marketers to use British ships and requiring some products to be sold only to British merchants. With independence, U.S. producers focused mostly on meeting local demand. As the country grew and INFRASTRUCTURE expanded marketing opportunities, most U.S. manufacturers were content to work in domestic markets, while international trade was predominantly with Britain and later Canada. U.S. expansion into international markets grew rapidly after World War II, with the increasing dominance of American manufacturers and the growth of MULTINATIONAL CORPORATIONS. Today international trade represents a little more than 15 percent of U.S. GROSS DOMESTIC PRODUCT; most industrialized countries have a much higher percentage. While the U.S. percentage is small, on a dollar basis the United States is the largest trading country in the world, and U.S.-based companies dominate many international markets.

Companies expand into international markets either by careful analysis of the options and opportunities or almost by accident. Often international marketing begins with a request from a foreign company or a proposal from a foreign supplier. Many U.S. companies expanded internationally based on the MARSHALL PLAN programs for redeveloping Europe and Japan.

Many companies use MARKET RESEARCH to first assess opportunities when considering whether to expand into international markets. Market research is used to answer questions such as

- How is the social and cultural environment different?
- Are there infrastructure constraints?

- Who are the competitors and how competitive are they?
- Are there sufficient numbers of potential customers with sufficient purchasing power?
- What political and legal issues are likely to be a concern?
- What operating laws, standards, and taxes need to be considered?

Each of these questions needs to be analyzed carefully. Numerous articles describe INTERNATIONAL MANAGEMENT blunders—mistakes made by companies "going international." A classic example notes how Chevrolet marketed its Nova car in Spanish-speaking countries where *no va* means "no go." An Asian manufacturer shipped sandals to the Middle East with a tread pattern that closely resembled the Arabic word for Allah (god). Kodak attempted to sell their film in Japan by charging a lower price than Fuji, but later research revealed that Japanese film buyers perceived the lower price as meaning the PRODUCT was of lower quality.

Once international marketing opportunities have been identified, companies then address the question of how to expand internationally. The choices include EXPORTING, LICENSING, FRANCHISING, foreign direct INVESTMENT (FDI), JOINT VENTURES (JVs), and wholly owned subsidiaries. The choice will usually depend on a company's resources and willingness to take on RISK. Exporting—selling directly to a foreign buyer or to a middleman—requires little CAPITAL and, if managed properly, involves relatively little risk. Licensing—granting the right to a foreign producer to manufacturer a product for sale through foreign companies—also involves few resources and little risk. However, one risk is the potential creation of GRAY MARKETS, where licensed products made in other countries are returned into the company's domestic market, competing with domestically made products.

Franchising is a contractual agreement between a manufacturer or business-idea owner, the franchiser, and a WHOLESALER or retailer, the franchisee. It requires little capital on the part of the franchiser and relatively little risk. The franchiser sells to the franchisee the right to market its products or ideas, and to use its TRADEMARKS and BRANDS. The franchisee agrees to meet the franchiser's operating requirements, usually pays an initial fee for the franchise, and agrees to pay a percentage of sales to the franchiser. There is a potential risk if the franchisee harms the franchiser's reputation through shoddy products or dubious business practices.

Foreign direct investment (FDI) is the purchase of production, distribution, or retail facilities in another country. FDI requires capital, and because it generates physical ASSETS in another country, it creates greater risk. FDI also provides greater control and PROFIT potential than other less-risky international marketing options.

Joint ventures (JVs) are a popular method of expansion among U.S. companies; many U.S. companies first expanded into China and Mexico using JVs. Often the U.S.

firm provided the capital and technology, while the Chinese or Mexican firm provided the contacts and distribution or retailing capability. Influence, connections, and relationships—called *guanxi* in China—are often as important as money in making business happen in international markets. Joint-venture agreements require capital and involve risk. There is an old saying that CONTRACTS are only as good as the people signing them. In many international markets, contracts are seen as establishing a relationship, not defining the terms and agreements of each party to a joint venture. Because of this, many U.S. businesses have been surprised or disappointed in their international joint ventures.

The last option for expanding internationally is the creation of a wholly owned subsidiary. Investment in foreign manufacturing or in an ASSEMBLY PLANT provides company control but requires investment capital and involve risk. Many companies create foreign operations as a means to overcome BARRIERS TO ENTRY. In the early 1900s, U.S. companies often created what were called "branch plants" in Canada as a way to sell goods there.

Basically, international markets are divided into three known spheres of influence in Europe, North America, and Asia, plus one unknown. The EUROPEAN UNION (EU) is called "fortress Europe." Companies wanting to market there often find it to their advantage to create manufacturing or assembly operations in one or more of the EU countries. North American international marketing is heavily influenced by the NORTH AMERICAN FREE TRADE AGREEMENT (NAFTA). Trade diversion, the shifting of production facilities in response to changes in international trade laws, grew with NAFTA's passage; other foreign companies frequently establish production facilities in North America in order to have access to the U.S. market. South Asia has historically been called "Japan Inc." dominated by Japanese multinational corporations. With the decline in the Japanese economy and the ascension of China to the WORLD TRADE ORGANIZATION (WTO) in 2001, Japanese dominance is being challenged by the relatively unknown, China.

While identifying opportunities for international marketing and deciding what type of international organization or option to use, marketers develop an international MARKETING STRATEGY, a firm's overall plan for selecting and meeting the needs of a target market. Marketing planning begins with comparing opportunities against the firm's resources, then developing objectives and mapping strategies, including tactical plans for implementation and control, to meet those objectives.

Marketing strategy includes decisions regarding product, promotion, pricing, and distribution (called the four Ps of marketing). When expanding into international markets, basic assumptions should be questioned and confirmed and minute details addressed. When considering product decisions, the easiest option would be to sell the same product in new markets. Depending on the country, marketers may need to change the size of the product, language, symbols, colors, and usually labeling. International marketers often hire labeling specialists to address the requirements of the country they are targeting. Since most of the rest of the world uses the metric system, weights and measures as well as container sizes probably will need to be changed. Packaging laws and environmental requirements can also necessitate product changes.

Pricing is a second strategy consideration. Logically marketers would like to charge a price similar to domestic prices but will consider adjusting prices based on consumer INCOMES in the new market. Other pricing factors need to be considered as well. For example, in many markets higher prices convey an image of better quality, so having the lowest or competitive price may not be the best strategy. Markups also vary from country to country, and the number of participants in the marketing chain may influence pricing decisions. For example, because lower incomes are normal in many South Asian countries, U.S. snack-food marketers reduced the size of their packages and then reduced prices.

As mentioned above, the number of participants in DISTRIBUTION CHANNELS may vary in international markets. Major retailers like Wal-Mart will alter their distribution strategy depending on the country they are entering. In Canada, Wal-Mart bought the Woolworth chain of stores but, rather than bring in its own distribution system, contracted with a Canadian-based company to distribute products to the stores. In many countries, distributors and their connections to government agencies require international marketers to hire local service providers. A fine line exists between hiring for distribution and customs services and paying bribes to get products into the market.

Promotion can be the most difficult challenge for international marketers. Symbols, colors, and expressions are all possible sources of confusion or misinterpretation, in addition to the obvious problem of language translation. Even in English-speaking countries, promotional messages need to be "translated." For example, in the United States to say people are "on the job" means they are there and actively working; in England the phrase refers to prostitution. There are many such "Englishes," and symbols also have many meanings. In Bali there is a lovely hotel called Hotel Swastika, bearing what Americans call the Nazi symbol—yet in Bali this symbol refers to the four forces on Earth. Color is another issue. While white is associated with purity and cleanliness in the United States, in many countries it is associated with death and funerals.

Even after addressing promotional message issues, international marketers have to consider media options. Newspaper, television, and radio options are likely to be different, and billboards and the use of premiums may not be allowed. Promotional specials may be regulated, and PERSONAL SELLING may be more important in some interna-

tional markets. International marketing strategy is a classic example of Murphy's Law, "if it can go wrong, it will go wrong."

See also FOREIGN INVESTMENT.

Further reading
Folsom, Ralph H., and W. Davis Folsom. *Understanding NAFTA and its International Business Implications*. New York: Matthew Bender/Irwin, 1996.

International Monetary Fund
In 1945, 45 countries established The International Monetary Fund (IMF) to

1. promote international monetary cooperation
2. expand and balance international trade
3. promote currency-exchange stability
4. establish a system of international exchange payments
5. make resources available to assist countries having BALANCE OF PAYMENTS difficulties

There are now 183 member countries in the IMF. In contrast with the WORLD BANK, the IMF does not focus directly on development issues but is responsible for stabilizing the international monetary and financial system.

In its program called "Surveillance," the IMF each year evaluates each member country's exchange-rate policy within the overall framework of the member's economic policies. The IMF operates from the conviction that strong and consistent economic policies within a country will lead to stable EXCHANGE RATES and a growing and prosperous world economy.

In addition to the surveillance program, the IMF will extend credits and LOANS to a member country if it has balance-of-payment problems. It only extends such credits and loans to help a country bring about needed monetary and economic reform. In addition to this standard loan program, the IMF has a loan program designed to alleviate poverty and another designed to assist heavily indebted poor countries.

The IMF also has a training program to assist countries in stabilizing their economy and effecting ECONOMIC GROWTH. This includes giving technical assistance in such matters as FISCAL POLICY, MONETARY POLICY, and other macroeconomic efforts.

Recently the IMF has been criticized on three fronts. Critics complain that because of the IMF, some poorer countries are indebted in such a way that they cannot possibly serve their citizens. In addition, the IMF stated purpose of advancing the global economy is opposed by many who think that a global economy damages such things as the ecology, worker rights, and national identity.

The IMF also receives a great deal of criticism from debtor nations who think the organization meddles in decisions to which the nations themselves have a national prerogative. For example, often the IMF will make a loan contingent on a country carrying out some economic reform. Such reforms, which critics call austerity programs, can cause economic suffering for the country's citizens and thus creates resentment against the IMF for dictating internal country economic policies.

Further reading
International Monetary Fund website. Available on-line. URL: www.imf.org.

—Mack Tennyson

International Organization for Standardization   See ISO STANDARDS.

International Trade Commission
The United States International Trade Commission, created by an act of Congress as the U.S. Tariff Commission in 1916, is an independent bipartisan commission that investigates matters of trade. The ITC conducts research and specialized studies of U.S. commercial and international trade policies and is charged with preparing reports analyzing international economics and foreign trade for the executive and congressional branches of government, other government agencies, and the public. ITC activities include

- determining whether U.S. industries are materially harmed by IMPORTS priced at less than fair value or by subsidization
- directing actions against unfair trade practices such as TRADEMARK, PATENT, or COPYRIGHT infringement
- analyzing trade and TARIFF issues and monitoring import levels
- participating in the development of an international harmonized commodity code (Harmonized Tariff Schedule of the United States, or HARMONIZED TARIFF SYSTEM)
- making recommendations to the U.S. president regarding domestic industry injury determinations
- advising the president whether agricultural imports conflict with the U.S. Department of Agriculture's price-support programs

The ITC also advises the president regarding the probable economic impacts of proposed trade agreements with foreign countries.

The commissioners of the ITC are appointed by the president and confirmed by the U.S. Senate for nine-year terms. To increase its independence from the executive branch, no more than three commissioners may be from the same political party, and the ITC submits its budget directly to Congress, exempting it from review by the OFFICE OF MANAGEMENT AND BUDGET.

Further reading
U.S. International Trade Commission website. Available on-line. URL: www.usitc.gov.

Internet
The complex matrix of globally connected computer networks known today as the Internet is the product of past national-defense projects whose goals were to keep the United States ahead in the cold war's arms race. Following the 1957 launch of the Soviet Union's first satellite, Sputnik I, the U.S. Department of Defense (DoD) created the Advanced Research Projects Agency (ARPA), which would develop a nationwide communications network to help protect the United States against nuclear attacks from space.

The 1960s saw the development of more advanced methods of data transfer, so that by 1969 the first wide-area computer communications network, called Advanced Research Projects Agency Net (ARPANET) was born. Through the 1970s, standards and protocols for communications were set in place, and the addition of England and Norway to the network made it truly global. Electronic mail (e-mail) became a reality, allowing computer users to send "instant" messages around the world.

By the 1980s, ARPANET was being used by universities and research institutions to share information, changing the network's functions from primarily military to educational uses. Also during this decade, the first news groups and on-line interactive games were created as the network continued to develop many useful applications. In 1990 a faster network called NFSNet, allowing more users to get connected to the growing network, replaced ARPANET.

This growth in the number of users throughout the 1980s, thanks mainly to the availability of desktop computers during this period, led inevitably to the network's commercialization by 1994. With more than 3 million Web locations or hosts connected, on-line retailers, banks, and entrepreneurial businesses were established daily, and by 1995 the U.S. government had handed control of the network over to private organizations. The WORLD WIDE WEB (WWW) was born out of this growth, as privatization and the development and standardization of a hypertext computer language allowed users to "browse" the network quickly and efficiently.

Business interest in the Internet first began when companies created network "browsers," computer programs that allowed users to move among the Internet's "website pages" easily. Then, coupled with the greater availability of desktop computers, businesses offering dial-up connections began to sell their SERVICES, facilitating the Internet's expansion. By 2001 there were over 31 million Internet host sites.

During the 1990s, as more hosts and users became connected, businesses began researching how they could use the Internet for both the transfer of information in and between markets, as well as for direct commerce. Scores of companies, called DOT-COMS (referring to their Internet address endings of .com), sprung up seemingly overnight, selling everything imaginable to "on-line customers." The excitement over the potential of a new global market that was opening up to businesses of every size and geographic location created an electronic commerce (E-COMMERCE) frenzy. It was not long before the new market was flooded with competitors. However, by 2000, when on-line shopping had become less novel, many of the dot-coms suffered decreasing PROFITS or ceased to exist altogether, creating what was called the "dot-com burnout" and a market crash.

In spite of the failures of many eager E-BUSINESSes, the Internet has continued to be a source of high profits for the firms who established themselves on the Internet early and were able to set themselves apart from their competitors. The Internet has also created new markets, specifically in ADVERTISING and communication. Advertisers understand that with more and more people becoming "connected" to the vast network, there will be greater potential to reach them with their messages.

In areas of communication, the early 2000s have seen the creation of handheld computers that allow users to receive e-mail messages almost anywhere on the planet. Further development is expected to allow for a "wireless" Internet, thus removing more geographical and physical barriers to the network.

By 2001 analysts had agreed that there still remained a great deal of research to be done into how businesses could use Internet technology and INTERNET MARKETING to increase profits. However, continued growth in the number of Internet hosts and users supports the visions of many people who continue to view it as a greatly untapped resource and marketplace frontier.

—Daniel P. Whicker

Internet Fraud Complaint Center

The Internet Fraud Complaint Center (IFCC) is an organization that takes Internet FRAUD complaints from consumers and reports cases to authorities for investigation. The IFCC is a joint project between the National White Collar Crime Center and the Federal Bureau of Investigation (FBI). The center maintains a database tracking Internet fraud complaints and biannually publishes and publicizes INTERNET fraud activities.

In 2001 the highest percentage of complaints was auction fraud (42.8 percent) followed by nondelivery of merchandise or payment (20.3 percent). Internet auction fraud, the misrepresentation of products for sale through on-line auctions, has been the number-one type of Internet fraud since the creation of such auctions. Often, the fraud involves the sale of name-brand merchandise, which when received is a "knockoff" (an illegally produced copy of inferior quality), like the $15 Rolex watches and $25

Gucci bags Americans have purchased abroad on the street or in flea markets. In 2001 the average on-line auction fraud cost consumers $478. The major on-line auction companies have attempted to reduce this problem through buyer-rating surveys and increased policing of their auction services, but it remains a major problem.

In 2001 the IFCC ranked an Internet version of the "Nigerian money-order scam" as its third most frequent complaint. In the Nigerian money-order scheme (named after the 1980s letter scams frequently starting from Nigeria), the solicitor claims to be a Nigerian government official or widow of an official with access to an unclaimed bank account with a huge amount of money. The solicitation offers a percentage of the funds if the recipient will help transfer them to a U.S. bank account—the recipient's account. After getting the account information, the defrauder takes the money. In 2001 the average Nigerian money-order fraud cost consumers $6,542. A variation on the Nigerian money-order fraud involves a Russian claiming a loved one died in the World Trade Center after depositing millions that must now be claimed.

Internet fraud tends to be similar to other consumer fraud. In addition to the top three categories, other types of reported Internet fraud involve Internet access services, information adult services, computer equipment/software, work-at-home offers, advance-fee loans, credit-card issuing, and business opportunities/franchises.

Other groups also track Internet fraud, including the Department of Justice and the National Fraud Information Center. In addition to the kinds of Internet fraud already mentioned, the Department of Justice scrutinizes market-manipulation schemes. In this type of fraud, criminals use investment chat rooms to "pump" up interest and speculation in a stock and then sell their shares before the company whose shares are being touted refutes the false rumors. A variation in this scheme involves selling a company's stock short and then disseminating negative false information, driving the stock price down.

Further reading

"Internet Fraud." Available on-line. URL: www.internetfraud.usdoj.gov; Internet Fraud Complaint Center. Available on-line. URL: www1.ifccbi.gov/index.asp; Internet Fraud Watch. Available on-line. URL: www.fraud.org/internet/intset.htm.

Internet marketing

Internet marketing is the use of the INTERNET to promote, distribute, and price goods and SERVICES for target audiences. While uses of the Internet are constantly changing, several successful Internet marketing models are evolving to facilitate E-COMMERCE and E-BUSINESS.

First, the Internet as a means of promotion is clearly established. Early Internet marketers had dreams of putting up a site on the WORLD WIDE WEB and drawing customers from around the world. In many ways, it was like the production mentality of the AMERICAN INDUSTRIAL REVOLUTION: build it and they will come. The implosion of the DOT-COMS industry in 2000 brought marketers and investors back to reality, but the use of the Internet to promote goods and services is still expanding daily. Early Internet marketers often created what were known as "billboards" a Web page listing the phone number and address of the company and its logo. These were quickly replaced by informational sites that allowed consumers to access a wide array of information about the company, thus saving time and personnel for marketers. Since the goals of promotion are typically to inform, persuade, and/or remind consumers about a company, Internet marketers quickly learned to use the new medium in such a way that consumers could gather helpful information for their purchase decisions.

Some Internet marketers found they could do more than just promote their PRODUCTS; they could also take and confirm orders, and even deliver products electronically. The airline, hotel, and auto-rental industries quickly developed the capability to make reservations over the Internet. In the process, distribution systems changed. Travel agents and other service-industry intermediaries are disappearing as Internet direct sales are expanding. Automobile manufacturers have also been tempted to use the Internet for DIRECT MARKETING, but to date, having established distribution relationships with car dealerships, most have opted to direct Internet customers to retail outlets.

One of the Internet's most amazing uses is on-line auctions. eBay and other Web auction systems are dramatically changing a wide variety of markets. The market prices for antiques and collectibles have plummeted with expanded market access through the Internet. In addition, Internet auction sites are important sources of market price information, reducing the ARBITRAGE possibilities used by many retail antique dealers. While some auction systems like Priceline.com have not been fully accepted by consumers, businesses are expanding their use of Internet auctions both to sell excess inventory and to purchase standardized products.

Another use of the Internet is the expansion of specialty merchants on-line. Several years ago, one merchant created a Web business solely for marketing hot sauces. Amazon.com started as a new-book retailer, holding minimal inventory but using relationships with major publishers to quickly fulfill Internet orders. Comparison-shopping websites expanded, allowing consumers to search multiple Web merchants for the best price for the product or service they desired.

Pricing strategy using the Internet is just beginning to evolve. Airlines are now ADVERTISING discount rates for Internet users both on their own sites and through group sites. Orbitz.com, created by airline companies, competes with other discount-pricing sites. Hotel and auto-rental companies have been slow to recognize the Internet as a distinct market segment and a way to discount services.

Some products and services like software and information can be delivered over the Internet. Relatively few firms are making a PROFIT using the Internet for delivery, but products such as Norton antivirus software, information distributors such as the *Wall Street Journal,* and agencies such as the INTERNAL REVENUE SERVICE are using the Internet to reach consumers. Access to secondary data, whether from government or private sources, is one of the major products available through the Internet. This information access is allowing entrepreneurs throughout the world to compete in major markets like the United States. For example, data processing and accounting services for U.S. firms are now being subcontracted to Indian businesses.

One of the visions of Internet marketing was a global marketplace in which a small entrepreneur with the right strategy could compete with the multinational giants. To some degree this is possible, but like BRANDS in a store, name recognition, preference, and loyalty is an evolving trend on the Internet. Major Internet marketers are buying up failing competitors' domain names (their identifying Web address), increasing their market dominance. International trade restrictions are to some degree limiting global COMPETITION. Because Internet markets are changing so rapidly, global trade agreements regarding Internet marketing lag behind market advances.

Establishing and maintaining loyal Internet customers is a challenge for many marketers. With a click consumers can move from one competitor to the next. Contests, newsletters, and frequent-user programs are all being tested to increase Internet customer loyalty. Many different models are being used in Internet marketing, as evidenced in the wide variety of hotel Web sites. Some are "designer" sites—i.e., "come look and see how fabulous your stay will be with us" sites. Another group of sites will be more direct—"Let us take your order." A third group of sites will display everything there is to do and see in or know about the cities or areas where the hotels are located.

One successful Internet marketing strategy is target e-mail. By using opt-in e-mail distribution lists, lists of e-mail recipients who have agreed to receive marketing messages, marketers are quickly and efficiently communicating with target audiences. For example, one car dealership purchased an e-mail list for consumers in its geographic area and sent a message to 20,000 addresses, offering a price reduction to anyone who responded and offering a contest for a free car. Recipients enthusiastically entered the contest, forwarded the e-mail solicitation to friends, and generated more than enough new customers to justify the cost.

Like most marketing methods, Internet marketing is not without controversy and concern. The two major issues are PRIVACY and spam (junk e-mails and ads). Most ethical marketers reframe from spam, and most Internet marketers have established and posted clearly stated privacy policies. Other Internet marketing issues include "cyber hustlers," "cyber squatters," and "typo squatters." Cyber hustlers are marketers who legally purchase rights to domain names that are not renewed. Like TRADEMARKS, domain names have value and are obtained on a first come, first served basis. In the United States domain names are registered through domain registry companies, licensed by the government to allocate specific Web addresses. If a company does not renew its domain name, it gives up its rights to the name, which then goes back into the available domain-name pool. Cyber squatters purchase potentially popular domain names and sell them to late-entry marketers. For example, an entrepreneur who learned about the new South Carolina lottery registered a number of logical domain names for the new program. Typo squatters register domain names that misspell or approximate a popular domain name, hoping to sell them to businesses at a profit. For example, one typo squatter registered amaza.com.

According to Net Solutions, the first domain registry company in the United States, in November 1999 the U.S. Court of Appeals (Ninth Circuit) ruled that the company had "no responsibility or duty to police the rights of trademark owners concerning domain names." Questions about domain-name disputes are referred to www.domainmagistrate.com., which lists the new Uniform Domain Name Resolution Policy (UDRP). The site also suggests that viewers go the U.S. Patent and Trademark Office site (www.uspto.gov) to see if the domain name in which they are interested is similar to a trademark registered with the office.

The WORLD INTELLECTUAL PROPERTY ORGANIZATION (WIPO), one of a number of organizations handling domain-name disputes, reports increasing disagreement between cyber hustlers and previous owners of domain names. WIPO has no specific measure to address the problem, and instead the disputes have been referred to the UDRP.

Three of the many newer Internet marketing strategies are customization of websites, use of pop-up promotions, and viral marketing. Web sites can be customized based on viewers' past visits or current movement within a site. For example, Amazon.com welcomes returning visitors. Pop-up promotions appear on computer screens after viewers visit particular sites. Pop-ups are considered annoying and force viewers to have to close the ad on their screen. Viral marketing is e-mail messages sent to groups asking recipients to forward the message to others. With relatively low entry costs, the Internet will continue to evolve and become an important part of almost any organization's MARKETING STRATEGY.

Further reading
Wilson Internet. Available on-line. URL: www.wilsonweb.com.

Internet surveys
Internet surveys provide an efficient and inexpensive means of collecting marketing information from a large number of people. Internet surveys are often used to collect demographic information and viewer opinions regarding products, services, or core issues. Researchers may either post SURVEYS on websites or e-mail them to potential respondents. However, there are both advantages and disadvantages to the use of INTERNET and e-mail surveys.

Perhaps the most important benefit of using Internet or e-mail surveys is that both types of surveys are inexpensive. Without printing, paper, and mailing expenses, these surveys typically are more cost-efficient than their traditional paper counterparts, MAIL SURVEYS. In addition, Internet and e-mail surveys can reach a very large and potentially diverse group of people who otherwise might not be accessible for survey research. For example, Internet or e-mail surveys may be the best way to reach people with specific characteristics or backgrounds, such as highly intelligent members of the population, people with unusual illnesses, or people from different countries. The use of these types of surveys also allows researchers to collect information around the clock, as the respondents choose when they wish to complete the survey.

However, Internet and e-mail surveys do have disadvantages. Although they allow researchers to reach unique groups of people, the typical Internet sample is not representative of the general public. For instance, current Internet samples tend to include more men than women and are restricted to people who have Internet access. To the extent that some people either cannot afford computer access or tend not to use the Internet, such as people from lower socioeconomic levels and the elderly population, certain groups may be excluded from an Internet sample.

In addition, Internet and e-mail surveys offer researchers less control over who completes the survey. Several potential participants may use the same e-mail address, and any one participant may use multiple computers. Technical variation in computers, monitors, browsers, and Internet connections also may affect responses to any given survey. Recent research suggests that there is a high attrition rate for Internet surveys, which means that although many participants may start the survey, many do not complete it. Finally, there is typically no opportunity for participants to ask the researcher any questions, as they might in a TELEPHONE SURVEYS or PERSONAL-INTERVIEW SURVEYS.

There also are important considerations for researchers when choosing between Internet and e-mail surveys. Although e-mail surveys tend to be simple to construct and easy to distribute, most are limited to plain text. Many standard QUESTIONNAIRE-layout techniques, such as tables and GRAPHS, either cannot be created in an attractive format or viewed properly as an attachment file. E-mail surveys are also restricted to people with e-mail accounts, the currency of which must be updated frequently. On the other hand, while Internet surveys usually require more time during the construction phase, they may save time at a later point if the data can be directed automatically into an electronic database.

In general, Internet and e-mail surveys are applicable in many areas of research. Businesses that make use of these means of collecting information can use the data to better target marketing promotions, improve product quality, and test new product ideas.

Further reading
Birnbaum, Michael H., ed. *Psychological Experiments on the Internet.* San Diego: Academic Press, 2000.

—Elizabeth L. Cralley

internships

Business internships are opportunities for students to experience working in a company or industry; they can be paid or unpaid, part-time or full-time, and can last a semester, a summer, or a year. Because schools and businesses define internship programs differently, it is important for students considering internships to carefully consider the expectations and benefits of internships at their institutions.

For students, internships provide

- a great way to learn about a career direction before leaving school
- a way to differentiate oneself from students who do not have relevant work experience
- job opportunities
- opportunities to explore specialized business professions

Business internship programs have become popular in the United States; over 40,000 internship opportunities are available annually. Especially in times of low unemployment, businesses are eager to have the added help of interns and also benefit by bringing in people with fresh ideas and new skills, in addition to considering and recruiting future employees. Many companies compete to recruit summer interns from prestigious schools and professional programs.

A good internship program should include

- meaningful work
- projects that can be completed in the time of the internship
- broad exposure for the intern within the organization
- time set aside to learn about the company in general
- the expectation that the intern will present the results of his or her project

Some industries have been accused of exploiting interns, using them for low- or no-cost labor. The U.S. DEPARTMENT OF LABOR's Wage and Hour Division provides guidelines distinguishing interns from employees.

Further reading
Ryan, Cathy, and Roberta H. Krapels. "Organizations and Internships," *Business Communication Quarterly* 60, no. 4 (December 1997): 126–132.

Interstate Commerce Commission

The Interstate Commerce Commission (ICC) was established in 1887 to regulate surface transportation in the United States as a response to market manipulation and control of railroads during the AMERICAN INDUSTRIAL REVOLUTION. The ICC was the first regulatory commission in U.S. history, but from 1887 until 1906 it had little control over the transportation industry. Vague wording in the initial legislation and lack of enforcement power limited the commission's effectiveness.

With the passage of the Hepburn Act in 1906, the ICC's functions and power grew, giving the commission control over interstate railroads, trucking, bus lines, freight forwarders, water carriers, oil pipelines, transportation brokers, and express agencies. The ICC was allowed to set prices for interstate transportation and, like public utility commissions, to determine fair rates of return for industry firms. In the 1950s and 1960s, the ICC oversaw the consolidation of railroad systems and enforcement of desegregation in public-transportation systems.

Beginning in the 1970s, government regulation of interstate transportation declined. With the Motor Carrier Act of 1980, the ICC's control over the trucking industry was diminished, and subsequent legislation reduced its control over railroads, bus lines, and other transportation markets. The ICC's decline was one of the first steps in the movement away from government regulation of business. The commission was eliminated in 1995, and some ICC functions were conveyed to the DEPARTMENT OF TRANSPORTATION, while others were transferred to the newly created National Surface Transportation Board.

Further reading
Records of the Interstate Commerce Commission. Available online. URL: www.archives.gov/research_room/federal_records_guide/interstate_commerce_commission_rg134.html.

interviewing

Interviewing job candidates is an important part of any business organization's efforts to succeed and prosper. From an employer's perspective, numerous issues and legal concerns are involved in business interviewing. From a job candidate's perspective, interviewing is a skill that can be developed for successful hiring.

Well before interviews take place, managers must address a variety of questions. Who will participate in the hiring process? Who has the authority to make the final decision? Companies then conduct a job analysis, addressing the questions of what activities, tasks, and responsibilities are involved in the job to be filled. For unique, new positions in a company, job analysis can be a detailed process. For companies hiring additional people to do a common task, job analysis is standardized.

From the job analysis, job descriptions and a statement of job qualifications are written. Most companies first advertise the new position within the organization but will also look at outside applicants. Before interviewing candidates, companies screen applications and creates a list of top candidates to interview. Major companies are often flooded with applications and use computerized software designed to pick out key words in applicants' résumés as an initial basis of screening.

When interviewing is scheduled, managers need to decide whether to use structured or unstructured interviews; most prefer unstructured interviews, asking candidates about a variety of subjects. Sometimes candidates are asked to demonstrate their ability in an area related to the job description. Candidates for sales positions should anticipate being asked to make an on-the-spot sales presentation. MANAGEMENT candidates should anticipate being given hypothetical situations. Unstructured interviews will often put candidates in different situations, including group interviews, one-on-one conversations, and discussions over meals.

In structured interviews, each candidate is asked the same predetermined questions. Well-developed questions help managers gain insight into a candidate's capability. Many public organizations, using teams of staff members not used to interviewing, will employ structured interviews, which provide an advantage in comparing candidates. Often when a group is involved in interviewing, rating forms are used to evaluate each candidate's response to specific questions. Structured interviews have the potential disadvantage of not probing or drawing out unique qualities during the interview process, but they help the interviewing team to avoid asking inappropriate questions.

Numerous federal laws impact business interviewing. The CIVIL RIGHTS ACT of 1964 prohibits discrimination based on race, color, religion, national origin, or gender. The Age Discrimination in Employment Act (1967) prohibits discrimination against people ages 40–70. The AMERICANS WITH DISABILITIES ACT (1990) prohibits discrimination based on handicaps or disabilities, either mental or physical.

These laws and others lead to a list of "do not ask" questions during the interviewing process, including

- *religion.* Candidates should not be asked about their religious beliefs or whether the work schedule would interfere with their religious activities.
- *sex and marital status.* Sex is obvious, but a common mistake is asking candidates about their marital status, including questions about whether their spouses work, their children, or whether a woman would prefer to be addressed as Ms., Mrs., or Miss.

- *age.* Candidates may be asked whether they are a minor or over 70, because special laws affect those people. Otherwise candidates should not be asked their age or date of birth.
- *nationality and race.* Questions or comments about race, color, or national origin should not be asked of the applicant or his/her spouse. Candidates can be asked if they are U.S. citizens, but not whether they, their parents, or their spouses are naturalized or native-born citizens. Applicants who are not citizens may be asked if they have the proper VISAS to work in the United States.
- *physical characteristics.* Questions related to disabilities, handicaps, or health problems should be avoided. Candidates can be asked if they are capable of performing tasks stated in the job description.
- *bankruptcy or garnishments* (directed payments from wages to a creditor). Generally, these questions should be avoided because the U.S. bankruptcy code prohibits discrimination against people who have filed for bankruptcy.
- *arrests and convictions.* Questions about past arrests are not legal. Candidates can be asked about past convictions.

From a job candidate's perspective, interviewing can be an intimidating experience. Numerous interviewing "tips" articles provide ideas and guidelines when preparing for a job interview. The first step is to learn about the company; like the Boy Scout motto, "be prepared." Applicants should use the INTERNET, local newspapers, CHAMBER OF COMMERCE, or stockbrokers to learn basic information such as the number of employees, history of the company, major products, and competitors.

The second step is dressing appropriately; there is only one chance to make a first impression. What is appropriate dress for an interview will vary depending on the organization, the region of the country, and the type of position for which one is interviewing. One salesman tells the story of wearing a conservative suit for the interview, which went well. He was invited to the second round of interviews, but as he only owned one quality suit, he went to the local men's clothing store and bought a second suit on credit. After the second interview went well, he was invited for a third set of interviews at the regional office. After buying another suit on credit, he got the job. Afterwards his new manager confided that they almost did not hire him because he dressed too well, and they thought he was too affluent to work hard in sales.

Common advice for job candidates in an interview is to answer one question at a time and take time answering questions. One should also be prepared to talk about past employment and to stress the positive aspects of those jobs. Other advice is to ask questions, make good eye contact, and avoid telling jokes. A common technique interviewers use is to tell a slightly off-colored or inappropriate joke and watch the candidate's response. Job candidates should think of an interview as an opportunity to sell themselves.

Common questions asked in business interviews include

- What is your greatest strength?
- What is your greatest weakness?
- What makes you different from other candidates with similar background and education?
- If you were hiring someone for this position, what qualities would you look for?
- Are you more comfortable working alone or as part of a team?
- Describe one of your experiences working in a team.
- Why are you leaving your current position?
- Describe a situation where something went wrong and how you handled the situation.

Further reading

Churchill, Gilbert A., Neil M. Ford, and Orville C. Walker. *Sales Force Management.* Boston: Irwin McGraw-Hill, 1999; "Interviewing." Cuyahoga Valley School to Career Consortium. Available on-line. URL: www.schooltocareer.com; "Interviewing with Confidence!" Allan-Jones Associates. Available on-line. URL: www.jobsinplastic.com.

inventory control

Inventory control is the management of raw materials, work in process, and final goods. Inventory control attempts to minimize costs while avoiding production stoppages, the cost of idle workers, and the potential for lost sales due to not having sufficient PRODUCT available to meet market DEMAND. In many business environments, inventory control is a complex, dynamic process that requires continual oversight and decision making.

Logistics management specialist Jeroen P. Van den Berg divides inventory control into two parts: planning and control. In his article Van den Berg states "Planning refers to MANAGEMENT decisions that affect the intermediate term (one or multiple months), such as inventory management and storage location assignment. Control refers to the operational decisions that affect the short term (hours, day) such as routing, sequencing, scheduling and order-batching." Adjusting final goods inventory to meet anticipated changes in demand would be part of inventory planning, while changes in raw materials and work-in-progress levels would be part of inventory control.

One method of assessing inventory control is called materials-requirements planning (MRP) and materials-resource planning (MRPII). MRP is an operational planning system in which, by looking at the end product and working backward, all the labor, materials, and other RESOURCES needed to produce the product are determined. Computer models are used to assess the complex relationships among the production processes, including timing, energy requirements, machine and worker-production capacities, and shipping and handling. MRPII takes the resource requirements estimated from MRP, analyzes the production costs at various levels of output, and coordinates resource controls with estimated market demand.

In the 1970s many companies shifted emphasis from PRODUCTION improvement to inventory reduction. MRP and MRPII led to the concept of just-in-time (JIT) inventory minimization. In Japan the Toyota Production System, "kanban," or time-based management, called for eliminating inventories, with suppliers delivering materials and components, sometimes within 30 minutes of when the inputs were needed for production. The system saved money for Toyota, but as correspondent Roger Schreffler states, "The savings realized through kanban, however, aren't necessarily passed on to Japanese suppliers. In fact, much of the cost for ensuring on-time delivery of precise quantities of components and materials falls directly on the suppliers' shoulders." JIT inventory-control systems work better when suppliers and customers are in close proximity, but as Toyota learned in the 1990s, such systems create risks. When Toyota's only brake-part supplier's factory burned, its ASSEMBLY PLANT had only a few hours' worth of parts to use, and production stopped. Other suppliers quickly created alternative sources of parts, but Toyota lost millions of dollars' worth of production.

In the United States, Dell Computer Corporation and Wal-Mart are recognized leaders in inventory control. In the 1980s Wal-Mart developed an often-copied electronic sales, ordering, and warehousing system. Scanning systems constantly transmit sales from each store to Wal-Mart headquarters in Bentonville, Arkansas. Reorders based on sales are automatically transmitted to vendors, who then ship to Wal-Mart's distribution centers. Distribution centers are expected to maintain no inventory but instead constantly coordinate shipments from vendors to individual stores. As an old saying goes, "Nothing gets sold in the warehouse." A story in the *Wall Street Journal* about sales on September 11, 2001, provides insights into both American CONSUMER BEHAVIOR and Wal-Mart's inventory-control system. The article reported that during the morning of September 11, sales of all goods plummeted as Americans were transfixed to their television screens. In the afternoon sales of water, batteries, canned goods, and ammunition skyrocketed. By evening, sales of American flags had exhausted stores' inventories.

Dell Computer Corporation is another example of the importance of inventory control. Relatively few Dell customers realize the company does not produce computers or computer parts. Instead, when customers go on-line and order a Dell computer, their orders automatically send other orders to Dell suppliers to produce and send the needed components. By maintaining no inventory, Dell reduces their costs, allowing them to adjust for market conditions and also to avoid inventory obsolescence.

With such methods, many companies wind up with products or components that are out-of-date. Managing inventory has been critical to minimizing costs of production, especially in the personal computer market during the late 1990s, when the "state of the art" technology was being replaced every 12–18 months.

See also MASS CUSTOMIZATION.

Further reading
Schreffler, Roger. "Kanban isn't perfect—really!" *Chilton's Distribution,* August 1987; Stoner, James, and R. Edward Freeman. *Management,* 5th ed. Upper Saddle River, N.J.: Prentice Hall, 1992; Van den Berg, Jeroen P. "A literature on planning and control of warehousing systems." *IIE Transactions,* August 1999.

investment

Investment can refer to either economic investment or financial investment. Economic investment is the purchase of new productive ASSETS—buildings, equipment, computers, etc.—that are used to produce goods and SERVICES. Financial investment is the use of CAPITAL (MONEY) to generate hoped-for PROFITS. Financial investment includes the purchase of shares of stock in a company, other securities, or assets with the goal of selling them at a higher price.

Economic investment is part of aggregate expenditures in an economy. In NATIONAL INCOME ACCOUNTING, aggregate expenditures are the sum of CONSUMPTION, investment, government, and net trade spending for final goods and services in an economy in a year. In the U.S. economy, investment spending represents approximately 17 percent of total spending annually, but it is the most volatile component of aggregate expenditures. Business managers determine economic investment. The decision whether or not to invest in new productive assets is primarily influenced by expected profits. Managers make their best projections of future sales of output from the new investments and compare expected sales with estimated COSTS. Like the oracles in ancient societies, managers seek out "divine wisdom" when making investment decisions.

In addition to being influenced by expected profits, economic investment decisions are also affected by changes in technology, capacity utilization, and the cost of borrowing. Often managers will replace existing equipment, even though the existing equipment is fully operational. If new technology can result in a better-quality product, managers are forced to purchase the new equipment in order to remain competitive. Capacity utilization is the percentage of existing productive capacity that is currently being used. The Department of Commerce maintains an overall capacity utilization rate for U.S. manufacturers; generally 85-percent capacity utilization is considered close to full capacity. If, when operating at full capacity, managers think DEMAND for their PRODUCTS will continue to grow, they will decide to invest in new productive capacity. New

investment is also influenced by INTEREST RATES, or the cost of borrowing. As interest rates decline, the cost of new productive assets decreases, stimulating additional investment spending.

As stated earlier, financial investment is the use of money to generate hoped-for profits. Financial investment can lead to economic investment, but not necessarily. Often people will say, "I invested in a new car." Almost always this is an incorrect use of the term *investment.* If someone bought a car for use in his or her business, say for delivery of goods to customers, then yes, it would be an economic investment. But most often when people purchase a car, it is what economists call durable consumer expenditure, the purchase of a product for personal benefits with an expected use life of more than one year. An example of a financial investment would be a person who bought an antique car with the expectation of selling it for a profit.

Financial investment decisions involve a comparison of RISKS versus returns. Returns are expected profits, often expressed by a percentage return on investment (ROI). Risks can include DEFAULT, exchange, INFLATION, interest-rate, liquidity, and political risks. Default risk is the likelihood that the borrower will not repay the loan. Exchange risk is the potential for losses due to an unfavorable change in EXCHANGE RATES. Inflation risk is the potential loss if the value of the asset or money loses value due to increased inflation. Interest-rate risk is the potential decreased value of a fixed-rate debt like a bond, due to rising interest rates. Liquidity risk is the potential problem of not being able to find a buyer for the investment. Owners of small businesses and obscure investments often face liquidity risks. Political risk is the potential for nationalization (takeover) of investments by a government or the potential for political instability causing a decrease in value of an investment. For example, the major unresolved issue in the long-standing U.S. EMBARGO of Cuba has been the 1960s nationalization of businesses by the Castro government.

Financial investment can also take place through either direct or portfolio investments. DIRECT INVESTMENT is the purchase of a business or assets by an investor; portfolio investment is the purchase of securities representing an ownership (EQUITY) interest in an enterprise. Direct investment generally involves a long-term commitment of resources, while portfolio investment can be sold quickly in STOCK MARKETS. Stock markets are exchanges, which facilitate the transfer of financial investments.

Investment can also refer to INVESTMENT CLUBS, INVESTMENT BANKING, and investment grade. Investment clubs are groups that pool their funds and analyze investment choices before allocating the club's money. Investment bankers are FINANCIAL INTERMEDIARIES assist in merger acquisitions, offer securities brokerage services, and who help CORPORATIONS and governments raise capital through UNDERWRITING and distributing new securities. Investment grade refers to BONDS issued by corporations that are rated above a specified level by bond-rating agencies.

investment banking (I-banking)

Investment banking, also called I-banking, refers to the financial services provided by investment bankers. Until 1933, commercial banks participated in activities that are now purely investment-banking activities, such as UNDERWRITING. The 1929 STOCK MARKET crash and the resulting GREAT DEPRESSION led U.S. lawmakers to pass several laws between 1933 and 1940 that aimed to regulate the securities industry, since bankers and financial institutions were perceived as having created the crash and depression. Laws aimed at regulating the securities industry included the Glass-Stegall Act of 1933, the Securities Act of 1933, and the Securities Exchange Act of 1934.

The term INVESTMENT BANKER was created in 1933 when the Glass-Stegall Act prohibited commercial bankers (i.e., those whose functions included making LOANS and accepting deposits) from participating in risk-taking activities such as underwriting and dealing in corporate securities and certain governmental securities. The act also aimed to encourage the stability of commercial banks in that entities that pursued underwriting and dealing in securities were considered investment bankers and could not offer services such as providing loans or accepting deposits. Conversely, entities that provided loans and accepted deposits were commercial bankers and could not underwrite or deal in securities. Thus, after 1933 the financial-services industry was divided into investment banking and commercial banking.

Investment bankers are not investors or bankers. Rather, they are firms that provide a wide range of financial services, including underwriting and distributing new securities issues to help CORPORATIONS and governments raise CAPITAL or obtain financing, MERGERS AND ACQUISITIONS services, and wholesale and retail broker services.

Corporations and government entities sometimes issue securities such as stocks, BONDS, and OPTIONS in order to raise capital or funds for their operations. Investment bankers act as FINANCIAL INTERMEDIARIES between the investing public and corporate and government securities issuers. Generally investment bankers buy new securities issued by a corporation or a government entity and resell those securities to the public. Firm-commitment underwriting refers to the practice of investment bankers purchasing new issues of securities (purchase price) and reselling those securities at a higher price than the purchase price. The investment bankers' PROFIT is the spread (or the difference) between the purchase price and the selling price of the securities. Investment bankers may also sell new securities issues on a "best effort" basis, which refers to the practice of their marketing and selling new securities issues on a commission basis rather than underwriting.

Investment bankers may assist businesses with mergers, acquisitions, and divestitures—for instance, identifying possible merger opportunities, negotiating the purchase of another business, and structuring the purchase. Investment bankers may also offer wholesale and retail broker services to assist institutional investors, such as entities that manage large groups of funds like pension funds or MUTUAL FUNDS, in buying or selling securities for their portfolios; retail brokerage services for individuals who are interested in creating and managing their individual investment portfolios; and private, brokerage and money-management services for very wealthy individuals.

There are three major categories of investment bankers based on the types of service they offer and where they offer those services: full service, regional, and boutiques. Full-service investment bankers are large organizations that operate on a global basis and offer a full range of investment banking services. Some full-service investment bankers are known as "super-bulge" bracket firms because they have major market share in the industry and relationships with most of the leading corporations. Goldman Sachs and Merrill Lynch are examples of super-bulge bracket firms.

Regional investment bankers are those investment bankers that operate in a particular region or city. Boutiques are investment bankers that specialize in a particular function of investment banking, such as advising on mergers and acquisitions.

The Securities Act of 1933 regulates public offerings of securities and requires full disclosure of information with regard to new security issues. Under this act, issuers of new securities are required to file a "registration statement" with the SECURITIES AND EXCHANGE COMMISSION (SEC) and receive approval from the SEC before the securities can be sold. Issuers are also required to furnish prospective investors with a PROSPECTUS, which is typically incorporated into the registration statement. Criminal and civil penalties will be imposed for false or misleading statements in the registration statement or prospectus, or for noncompliance with the registration and prospectus requirements. Thus, before an investment banker can sell new issues of securities, it must ensure that the new securities issues have been properly registered with and approved by the SEC.

The Securities Exchange Act of 1934 regulates secondary trading of securities listed on national securities exchanges and securities that are traded over-the counter and therefore not listed. This act requires disclosure of information on securities traded on national securities exchanges and over the counter. Further, representations of securities must be accurate.

See also BANKING SYSTEM.

Further reading

"Beginner's *Guide to Investment Banking: Overview.*" Available online. URL: http://www.personal.umich.edu/~bquah/IBanking/

Overview.htm; Downes, John, and Jordan Elliot Goodman. *Finance and Investment Handbook.* 3d ed. New York: Barron's, 1990; Gitman, Lawrence J. *Principles of Managerial Finance.* 6th ed. New York: HarperCollins, 1991; Hayes, Samuel L., and Philip M. Hubbard. *Investment Banking: A Tale of Three Cities.* Boston: Harvard Business School Press, 1990; Kessler, Robert A. "The Effect of the Securities Laws upon the Small Business," *The Practical Lawyer,* 1 September 1982: 11. *Reprinted in* Larry D. Sonderquist, et al. *Corporations and Other Business Organizations: Cases, Materials, Problems,* 5th ed. New York: LEXIS Publishing, 2001.

—Gayatri Gupta

investment clubs

Investment clubs are a popular way for Americans to learn about and become involved in STOCK MARKET investing. In an investment club, members agree to contribute a set amount of MONEY each month, often $50; review and evaluate stock choices; and make INVESTMENT decisions based on member voting.

Many Americans, especially before 1990, had little involvement in the stock market. Until then, stock-market investing could only be done through brokerage houses, which provided investment management and advice but also charged significant fees for purchases and sales of stock. In addition, until the 1990s, most American workers were part of defined-benefit rather than defined-contribution RETIREMENT PLANS. In a defined-benefit plan, a worker's retirement pay is a percentage of his or her pay. In a defined-contribution plan, workers contribute a set percentage of their pay into a retirement plan, which is usually matched by their employer, but each worker determines how the funds are invested. The movement away from expensive, full-service brokers and the increase in worker-controlled retirement investment contributed significantly to the growth of investment clubs.

The National Association of Investment Clubs (NAIC) was established in 1951. Interest in investment clubs grew rapidly in the 1990s, and, by 1998 there were over 36,000 NAIC clubs with 600,000 members. Membership has declined since 1998, but NAIC clubs have over $190 billion invested in the stock market. Typical NAIC investment-club membership is majority female, with an average age of 54.

The NAIC's mission is to provide a program of sound investment information, education, and support that helps create successful, lifetime investors. Its four basic investment principles are as follows.

> Invest regularly, regardless of the present outlook for the economy or the stock market.
> Reinvest all earnings, letting the power of COMPOUNDING work for you.
> Discover growing companies so that your WEALTH can grow as their sales and earnings grow over the years.

> Diversify your holdings, and don't put all your eggs in one basket, regardless of how carefully you watch that basket.

There is also a World Federation of Investors.

Further reading
National Association of Investment Clubs website. Available online. URL: http://better-investing.org.

invitation to bid   See REQUEST FOR PROPOSAL, INVITATION TO BID.

ISO standards

The International Organization for Standardization (ISO) is a nongovernmental worldwide federation whose mission is to promote the development of standardization (have weights, measures, etc., conform to a standard). The ISO believes standardization facilitates the international exchange of goods and SERVICES; its efforts result in international agreements reducing or eliminating technical barriers to global trade. For example, through the ISO a uniform thickness of 0.76 millimeters was agreed on for credit, debit, and phone cards. This has created greater efficiency for both consumers and businesses as CREDIT CARDS can be used in almost any country in the world, in part because the size of cards were standardized.

The ISO includes national standards bodies from 130 countries, each of which has one organization representing it in the ISO. The U.S. representative is the American National Standards Institute (ANSI), a private, nonprofit organization, which administers and coordinates U.S. private-sector voluntary standardization. ANSI was founded by five engineering societies and three governmental agencies in 1918. Its goal is to "enhance global competitiveness of U.S. businesses and American quality of life by promoting voluntary consensus standards and conformity assessment systems."

International standardization began in electromagnetics with the creation of the International Electrotechnical Commission (IEC) in 1906. The International Federation of the National Standardizing Associations (ISA), emphasizing mechanical engineering standards, was set up in 1926. The ISA effort ceased with the beginning of World War II and was replaced by the ISO in 1947.

The acronym ISO is, in itself, a standardization. In English the organization's initials would be IOS, but in French, the other standard language of the ISO, its initials would be OIN (from Organization International de Normalization). Instead, ISO, which comes from the Greek *isos,* meaning "equal," is the group's global acronym.

A few years ago not many people had ever heard of the ISO. Today, trade liberalization, GLOBALIZATION, interconnections among market sectors, worldwide communications systems, global standards for emerging technologies, and the needs of developing countries for INFRASTRUCTURE standardization all contribute to the expanding need for technology standards. As a result, the ISO's role is growing rapidly.

Within industries, suppliers, users, and sometimes governments participate in the process of defining standards. The ISO's goals are to "facilitate trade and TECHNOLOGY TRANSFER through:

- Enhanced product quality and reliability
- Reduced waste
- Greater compatibility and interoperability of goods and services
- Simplification for improved usability
- Reduction of the number of models
- Increased distribution efficiency and ease of maintenance."

The process of creating ISO standards involves thousands of people, including ISO committees, representatives of industries, research institutes, government authorities, consumer groups, and international organizations. The need for a standard is usually proposed by an industry sector, which communicates their need to their national member body (ANSI in the United States), which then proposes study of the issue to the ISO. Once accepted for evaluation, the first phase involves definition of the technical scope of the future standard.

Over 30,000 experts participate in ISO-sponsored meetings annually. The organization's members group themselves into standards committees, and the views of all interest groups are solicited. Groups within the ISO negotiate the detailed specifications within a standard. During the final phase, a draft international standard must be approved by three-fourths of all voting members. By the year 2000, there were over 12,000 international standards.

As their goals suggest, the ISO is primarily a business organization. Standardization reduces the cost of doing business. For example, anyone who has worked on both an American-made and a foreign-made car knows two sets of wrenches are required. Similarly, anyone who has traveled abroad knows U.S.-made appliances cannot be used in most foreign electrical systems. Standardization eliminates such problems. The ISO facilitated the creation of standards for:

- film-speed code
- freight container sizes
- paper sizes
- symbols for automatic controls
- codes for country names, currencies, and languages

In the last decade, two of the ISO's major efforts were ISO 9000, which provides a framework for quality management and quality assurance; and ISO 14000, which provides a framework for environmental management. First adopted by European manufacturers in the 1990s, ISO 9000 standards of quality assurance have become widely accepted and are often a condition for doing business with companies. To become ISO 9000-certified, a company must conduct an on-site audit, including inspection, to ensure that documented quality procedures are in place and that all employees understand and follow those procedures. Once certified, a company is periodically audited to verify it is in compliance with ISO standards.

The ISO 9000 series standards include nine principles of quality management.

- customer focus
- LEADERSHIP
- involvement of people
- process approach
- system approach to MANAGEMENT
- continual improvement
- factual approach to decision making
- mutually beneficial supplier relationships

The ISO 14000 series, first published in 1996, is a result of the ISO's focus on sustainable development. The 14000 series has 21 published standards, including an audit of a firm's environmental management system; monitoring and measuring environmental performance of its activities, PRODUCTS, and services; and LIFE CYCLE assessment. Both the 9000 and 14000 series are in the process of being reviewed and revised, reflecting changing technology and lessons learned in QUALITY CONTROL and environmental management.

The ISO is headquartered in Geneva, Switzerland, which is also the headquarters of the WORLD TRADE ORGANIZATION (WTO). It is "building a strategic partnership" with the WTO, providing technical agreements to support WTO trade agreements. The ISO also maintains ISONET, the ISO Information Network, a global network of national standards information centers.

Further reading
Boone, Louis E., and David L. Kurtz. *Contemporary Marketing,* 10th ed. Fort Worth: Dryden Press, 2001; International Organization for Standardization website. Available on-line. URL: http://www.iso.ch.

J

job satisfaction

Job satisfaction has to do with employees' attitudes towards and liking for their work. Measures of job satisfaction are often used to predict how long employees will continue working for a particular company, as well as their level of ORGANIZATIONAL COMMITMENT. Variables affecting job satisfaction typically include both organizational and personal factors.

There are numerous organizational factors that affect job satisfaction. First, the structure of the company's reward system—the means through which employees earn promotions, salary increases, or other rewards—is important in determining satisfaction. Reward structures that hinder professional development or provide little recognition for employees' contributions to company success lead to lower levels of satisfaction. On the other hand, reward structures that provide reasonable and adequate opportunities for employees' contributions to be recognized and rewarded are associated with more positive attitudes about the job.

Both the actual and perceived quality of the supervision at work also affect job satisfaction. Competent supervisors who treat employees with respect and consider the needs and interests of the employees when they make decisions tend to foster high levels of job satisfaction on the part of the company's employees. Company executives who are flexible and recognize when a particular situation calls for them to change their tactics tend to provide the most effective LEADERSHIP. Sometimes a leader may need to be autocratic when directing employees in order to accomplish a task or resolve a problem. However, at other times the key to success may involve a democratic approach, with employees participating in decision making and helping to shape outcomes. Unfortunately, some leaders are rigid about their preferred approach and may miss opportunities for more successful interactions with employees. Poor leadership or supervision is associated with low levels of job satisfaction and higher levels of job turnover, which may ultimately cost the company in terms of money and reputation.

The specific characteristics of the job also affect satisfaction. Monotonous and hectic tasks and those assignments that do not stimulate employees are all related to lower levels of job satisfaction. Employees in these types of positions, such as people who work on ASSEMBLY LINES in factories, report higher levels of psychological distress and tend to have a high number of absences from work. High-quality supervision is especially important in these types of jobs, as it can help increase productivity and satisfaction when workers perceive that their contributions are valued. The HAWTHORNE EXPERIMENTS demonstrated positive effects on productivity when management simply showed an interest in their factory workers.

Many personal factors also affect job satisfaction—for example, higher levels of status and SENIORITY. Employees who have been with a company for longer periods of time typically tend to also have and seniority and are more satisfied than are newer employees. In addition, when the responsibilities of a particular job are well matched to the employee's personal interests, job satisfaction tends to increase. Finally, job satisfaction is linked to employees' personal satisfaction with life outside work. People who are happy in their personal lives tend to have more positive attitudes toward work than those who are unhappy.

There are many ways a company may try to increase job satisfaction for its employees. For example, rewarding an employee with a deserved raise in a timely fashion or amending a job description so that it more closely matches the employee's interests will likely increase satisfaction both at work and at home. Given that job satisfaction is such an important aspect of working life, leaders who carefully consider how their decisions affect both the company and its employees should promote the success of both.

See also EMPLOYEE MOTIVATION.

Further reading

Baron, Robert A., and Donn Byrne. *Social Psychology*, 10th ed. Boston: Allyn and Bacon, 2003; Oskamp, Stuart, and P. Wesley

Schultz. *Applied Social Psychology,* 2d ed. Upper Saddle River, N.J.: Prentice-Hall, 1997.

—Elizabeth L. Cralley

joint venture

A joint venture is the combined effort of two or more business entities for a limited purpose. Joint ventures are frequently established for coordinated research, international expansion, and specialized PRODUCTION. Creating a joint venture involves both legal and strategic MANAGEMENT implications.

In the United States, joint venture agreements are similar to PARTNERSHIPS. Generally partnership law applies to joint ventures, including personal LIABILITY for its debts and treatment for federal income-tax purposes. The most significant difference between a joint venture and a partnership is that participants in a joint venture usually have less implied and apparent authority than partners, because of the limited nature of the joint-venture activity. For example, a joint venture among pharmaceutical companies to conduct research would limit the actions and decision-making authority of managers to research-related activities, and not include marketing or production decisions.

Joint ventures are also scrutinized under ANTITRUST LAW. Joint ventures, by definition, involve integration of resources between or among firms. Joint ventures hope to yield improved efficiencies through collective effort, more than could be achieved by any one firm. While a joint sales agency created to fix prices would be illegal, a joint research and development venture is more likely be legal. In 1984 Congress passed the National Cooperative Research Act (NCRA), requiring firms contemplating a joint RESEARCH AND DEVELOPMENT venture to notify the Department of Justice and the FEDERAL TRADE COMMISSION in advance. The act limited the antitrust liability of firms engaged in joint research and development ventures. The act was later amended to include joint production ventures as well.

Joint ventures often enter into strategic management decisions when they are used or considered in international expansion. Frequently U.S. businesses expanding abroad will choose to form joint-venture agreements with host-country firms. After the passage of the NORTH AMERICAN FREE TRADE AGREEMENT (NAFTA) in 1994, many U.S. firms entered Mexican markets through joint ventures. Wal-Mart partnered with Cifra, a chain of discount stores in Mexico, which provided knowledge of local markets, customs, rules, and regulations, as well as an existing distribution system. Wal-Mart provided financial RESOURCES, buying power, and systems management experience and efficiency. Some U.S. firms entered Mexico through joint-venture agreements and then bought out their partner or expanded on their own.

Management specialist caution companies entering into joint ventures to carefully define the rights and responsibilities of each participant and to develop a working relation-

ship before entering into a joint venture. In the 1990s, many U.S. firms rushed into joint ventures as a means to enter the Chinese market, only to be disappointed with the results.

Further reading
Mallor, Jane P., A. James Barnes, Thomas Bowers, Michael J. Philips, and Arlen W. Langvardt. *Business Law and the Regulatory Environment.* 11th ed. Boston: McGraw-Hill, 2001.

Jones Act (Merchant Marine Act)

The Jones Act (officially named the Merchant Marine Act of 1920) and related statutes require that vessels used to transport passengers and cargo between U.S. ports be owned by U.S. citizens, built in U.S. shipyards, and manned by crews of U.S. citizens. According to the wording of the act, its purpose "is to maintain reliable domestic shipping services and to ensure the existence of a domestic maritime industry available and subject to national control in time of need." The Jones Act is also known as the "cabotage" law. Cabotage, from the old French word for "cape," means navigation along a coastline and now refers to all navigation within a country's waters. Most major maritime countries have cabotage laws similar to the Jones Act.

Enacted after World War I, the Jones Act, like other industry-protection laws, reduces market competition in the name of national security. When World War II began, the existing shipping industry and ship-building INFRASTRUCTURE became the basis for naval military resources. More recently, during the 1990 Gulf War, the U.S. military chartered domestic cargo ships and tankers from the "Jones Act fleet" and used American merchant seaman to supply U.S. forces in the Middle East.

One question associated with the Jones Act is: What is a vessel? According to the Louisiana Workers' Compensation corporation Jones Act case history defines a vessel as "a structure designed for and being used for the transportation of passengers, cargo, or equipment across navigable waters." Determining what constitutes a Jones Act vessel has significant implications. The act's critics contend the United States' fleet of vessels is miniscule, and it is unrealistic to think the Jones Act is helping to protect national security in an emergency. The Jones Act Reform Coalition claims, ". . . the United States today has no more than 128 privately owned vessels over 1,000 tons in domestic service . . . all but 33 of these vessels are tankers or tub-barge combinations carrying liquid bulk cargoes." The act's supporters contend the United States has "more than 44,000 vessels in the U.S. Jones Act fleet." Both sides agree that foreign-flagged vessels transport 97 percent of all cargoes moving into and out of American ports.

Critics argue the act has not worked and has increased the cost of goods to consumers. They use examples like the reduction in U.S.-flagged tankers bringing oil from the Caribbean as a major factor in raising the cost of transportation of fuel oil to the Northeast. Other critics point out the act does not allow foreign-flagged shippers to stop in Hawaii on their way to the West Coast, forcing goods to go to the West Coast and then back to Hawaii. One University of Hawaii economist estimated abolishing the Jones Act shipping rules would save $500 to $600 per Hawaiian household. The act also prevents foreign-flagged cruise ships from operating in the Hawaiian Islands unless they add one foreign stop to the cruise itinerary—a difficult requirement, given how far Hawaii is from any other foreign port of call. Yet cruise companies are adding foreign destinations because it is cheaper than complying with U.S. merchant laws that would force them to hire U.S. crews and conform to U.S. environmental and labor laws.

Supporters of the Jones Act, such as Representative Neil Abercrombie, contend that "the dependability of Hawaii's maritime links to the mainland would vanish . . . Our now-dependable shipping would be under the control of whatever foreign government was most willing to subsidize its shipping. We could find Hawaii-mainland shipping routes under the control of a hostile nation."

As Representative Abercrombie suggests, many foreign governments are actively involved in subsidizing shipbuilding and shipping. Shipping is part of international trade infrastructure and almost always the cheapest form of bulk transportation. Countries that have access to international shipping have a COMPARATIVE ADVANTAGE over those that do no shipping. Shipbuilding is labor-intensive, creating thousands of jobs, and many countries subsidize shipbuilding as a means to ECONOMIC DEVELOPMENT. In the United States, one controversial "boondoggle," according to Arizona senator John McCain, was the proposal supported by Mississippi senator Trent Lott for the U.S. Navy to take over the CONTRACT for cruise ships being built in Mississippi boatyards.

Further reading
Dicus, Howard. "Rough sailing for shipping. Cloudy future for Jones Act," *Pacific Business News,* 26 October 2001; "Jones Act heightens supply risk," *LatAm Energy,* December 1, 2000; "The Jones Act: Fact and Fiction," Maritime Cabotage Task Force. Available on-line. URL: www.mctf.com.; Louisiana Workers' Compensation Corporation website. Available on-line. URL: www.LWCC.com/articles_legal.cfm?A=76&C=3. Downloaded June 2, 2003.

just cause (sufficient cause)
Just cause is the dismissal or termination of an employee with good reason. Just-cause dismissal (also referred to as sufficient cause) can be based on any of four reasons: unsatisfactory performance, lack of qualifications, changed requirements for the job, or misconduct.

Unsatisfactory performance is failure to do the job as expected. It can include excessive absenteeism, tardiness, or failure to meet the job requirements. Human Resource professor Gary Dessler adds unsatisfactory performance can also be claimed when an employee displays an "adverse attitude toward the company, supervisor, or fellow employees."

Lack of qualification for a position exists when an employee diligently attempts to perform the job but is unable to do so. Changed job requirements as a basis for dismissal occurs when the needed tasks change or are eliminated. Workers who become unemployed due to changing job requirements are referred to as structurally unemployed.

Misconduct, which is usually defined as deliberate violation of the employer's rules, can include theft and insubordination. Insubordination is often used as a basis for just-cause dismissal of employees. Author Gary Dessler lists a variety of employee actions that can be labeled as insubordination:

- direct disregard for the employer's authority
- refusal to follow a supervisor's orders
- deliberate defiance of clearly stated company rules and policies
- public criticism of the employer
- blatant disregard for the supervisor's reasonable instructions
- disregard for the organizational chain of command
- participation in efforts to undermine and remove the supervisor

Just-cause dismissal contrasts with WRONGFUL DISCHARGE, dismissal that does not comply with laws or contractual arrangements between the employer and employee. Union CONTRACTS state the procedures and bases for employee dismissal in great detail. In nonunion workplaces, employee manuals, employment contracts, and promises between the employer and employee define just-cause dismissal. WHISTLE-BLOWER laws protect employees from wrongful discharge, but workers who engage in whistle-blowing often are dismissed, suffer ruined reputations, and spend years attempting to gain redress in the legal system.

Just-cause dismissal also contrasts with EMPLOYMENT (or termination) at will, a common legal doctrine in the United States, allowing either employers or employees to terminate a work agreement for any reason. State and federal laws vary, limiting termination-at-will doctrine in many situations.

Further reading
Dessler, Gary. *Human Resource Management,* 9th ed. Upper Saddle River, N.J.: Prentice Hall, 2003.

just-in-time production
Just-in-time production (JIT) is a MANAGEMENT philosophy that embraces eliminating all waste and continually upgrading and improving PRODUCTION processes. The basic concept of JIT is that materials and supplies are replen-

ished exactly when they are needed rather than too early or too late, thus ensuring an efficient flow of production. JIT reduces the cost of having expensive materials sitting idle while waiting for production and eliminates the cost of having expensive equipment sitting idle while waiting for materials. It also reduces or eliminates related production costs such as scrap materials, defective PRODUCTs, unnecessary inventory, and wasted space, so that a company expends the least amount of RESOURCES—including materials, personnel, and facilities—to produce its final products. While traditional companies focus more on planning than control, expending tremendous time and energy planning inventory level, materials and parts shipments, production schedules, etc., a just-in-time company emphasizes control more than planning by developing flexible, fast operations and processes that enable quick response to changing market conditions.

The Toyota Motor Company developed the just-in-time production strategy in Japan in the mid-1970s. The Japanese approach to JIT is to make products "flow like water" through a company. JIT readily exposes problems common in traditional companies, such as defective parts, lost orders, late shipments, and an over-reliance on overtime, by eliminating the excessive inventory levels and management practices used to compensate for these problems. The Japanese compare inventory to a lake, and these types of problems to boulders beneath its surface. As the "water" (inventory) recedes, the "boulders" (problems) are exposed and "removed," or resolved. By reducing inventory to minimal levels, a JIT company achieves a constant work pace with products "flowing" through the production facility. Using the JIT philosophy, Toyota reduced the time required to produce an automobile from 15 days to 1 day.

While JIT emphasizes the importance of reducing material inventories to support the concept of "the right parts, at the right place, at the right time," it is more than just an approach to dealing with materials. Just-in-time production affects all aspects of a company's operations, from product design and manufacturing operations to parts-suppliers and CUSTOMER RELATIONS. A JIT production environment requires a company to develop close relationships with selected vendors who participate in the design process and will ensure consistently high quality and on-time delivery of materials. JIT product engineering and design emphasizes standardization and continuous process improvements. The just-in-time production philosophy also changes the role of the labor force and of management. JIT strives to develop flexible, broadly skilled workers who are capable of solving production problems and initiating process improvements. In a non-JIT environment, management typically makes all production-related decisions. In a JIT production environment, teams comprised of workers and management make decisions jointly through consensus. Eliminating many of

the status symbols traditionally reserved for management such as the executive dining room, reserved parking places, and executive bonuses creates a less adversarial relationship between workers and management, enhancing cooperation.

The just-in-time production concept, or management philosophy, is very much a part of the competitive strategy of most large companies today. Often referred to by other names such as "continuous flow manufacturing," "stockless production," "cellular manufacturing," or "lean production," JIT simplifies production and lowers costs, giving JIT companies a competitive edge. Current management literature suggests that implementing JIT offers many advantages to companies, including

- maintaining minimum inventory levels
- establishing customer order-driven production planning and scheduling
- purchasing materials in small-lot sizes only when required
- performing simple, quick, and inexpensive machine setups
- developing a flexible, multiskilled, and empowered workforce
- creating a flexible manufacturing system that quickly adapts to changing market conditions
- improving and maintaining product quality
- developing time- and cost-effective preventive maintenance
- promoting continuous process improvements
- improving worker morale
- reducing labor, material, and overhead costs

In spite of the obvious advantages of just-in-time production, many U.S. manufacturers have still not adopted a JIT philosophy. The dominant reason is that JIT requires an overall change in CORPORATE CULTURE at every level of an organization. JIT demands new types of relationships with suppliers, customers, and employees that render traditional methods and processes obsolete. Additionally, implementing JIT requires an ongoing commitment to continuous improvement, not only in a company's products but also in its processes.

Further reading
American Production & Inventory Control Society, Incorporated. *Just-In-Time Reprints, Articles Selected by the Just-In-Time Committee of the APICS Curricula & Certification Council.* Alexandria: APICS, 1998; Monden, Yasuhiro. *Toyota Production System, An Integrated Approach to Just-in-Time,* 3d ed. Norcross, GA: Engineering & Management Press, 1998; Wheatley, Malcolm. *Understanding Just in Time.* Business Success Series. Hauppauge, New York: Barron's Educational Series, 1997.

—Karen S. Groves

K

Keogh plan

A Keogh plan is a tax-deferred savings vehicle serving as a RETIREMENT PLAN for unincorporated businesses, usually small businesses or people who are self-employed. Keogh plans (which are also sometimes called "qualified plans" or "H.R. 10" plans) were named after New York Representative Eugene James Keogh and were first introduced in the 1960s. Keogh plans offer significant benefits over traditional INDIVIDUAL RETIREMENT ACCOUNTS (IRAs) and 401(K) PLANS for self-employed individuals and their employees. Like traditional IRAs and 401(k)s, Keogh plans allow for contributions to a retirement account, and the employee's contribution is pretax, which reduces his or her taxable INCOME. This MONEY can be invested, and the interest from INVESTMENTS is tax-free until the money is withdrawn from the plan. There is an additional tax advantage to employers who receive a "dollar for dollar" tax write-off for any money contributed to an employee's plan.

The chief advantage of a Keogh plan over traditional retirement accounts is the fact that it is possible to contribute more money annually. The amount of contribution possible depends on the Keogh plan chosen, but in 2002 it was generally a maximum of $40,000 per year. However, this changes often due to legislation and INFLATION.

There are two different Keogh plan options: the defined-benefit plan, and the defined-contribution plan. The defined-benefit plan is set up to give individuals a desired income upon retirement. There is a complex actuarial formula that is created individually for each employee to reach this income level, which cannot be more than the lesser of 100 percent of the employee's average compensation for the three highest consecutive calendar years, or $135,000 of income per year.

The more common defined-contribution plan allows for a maximum contribution of 100 percent of the employee's actual compensation, or $40,000. With defined-contribution plans, there are several ways that the money can be contributed. The most popular is the PROFIT SHARING plan, which allows employers to contribute up to 25 percent of all compensation per year to all participants in the plan. The employer also has the discretion to contribute nothing. Another option is a money-purchase plan in which the employer is required to contribute a set percentage of the employee's compensation regardless of whether the company makes a profit or not. It is also possible to combine the profit-sharing and money-purchase options so that a portion is at the discretion of the employer and a portion is set. One important note is that if a self-employed individual has a net loss for any year, that individual cannot contribute to his or her plan but may still contribute to his or her employee's plan.

Because Keogh plans are so complicated, it is usually necessary to have a retirement specialist set them up. Such specialists are a good source for more detailed information regarding Keogh plans. Details about the most current versions of Keogh plans can be found on the Internal Revenue Services website in Publication 560, available in PDF format on the INTERNET at http://www.irs.gov/pub/irs-pdf/p560.pdf; the information is in the section entitled "Qualified Plans."

—Joseph F. Klein

Keynesian economics

Keynesian (pronounced Canes-e-an) economics refers to the macroeconomic theories of John Maynard Keynes (1883–1946), considered by many to be the greatest economist of the 20th century. Lord Keynes, knighted for his work on behalf of Great Britain, developed much of the framework of modern macroeconomic theory.

Keynesian economics focuses on aggregate expenditures rather than aggregate SUPPLY in an economy. Aggregate expenditures are divided into four categories: CONSUMPTION, INVESTMENT, government, and net trade. In the Keynesian economics income-expenditures model, the price level is assumed to be fixed, and changes in aggregate expenditures determine the EQUILIBRIUM level of output. Later economists relaxed the assumption of fixed prices, arguing that as an economy approaches a full-EMPLOYMENT level of output, increases in aggregate expenditures will increase both INCOME and prices.

The Keynesian model challenged the prevailing classical theory, which suggested that an economy was always at or near a full-employment level of output and that adjustments in prices and wages would alleviate any temporary surpluses or shortages in the market.

Focusing on aggregate expenditures, the Keynesian economic model suggests that any source of expenditure stimulates output, income, and employment. Developed in the 1930s during the height of the GREAT DEPRESSION, Keynesian economics supported government intervention into the marketplace during periods of insufficient private-sector DEMAND. Keynesian economic thinking was consistent with the efforts of Franklin Roosevelt's "New Deal" programs, creating huge increases in government spending. (In Keynesian economics, when an economy is at or above a full-employment level of output, it is logical for government to reduce spending and/or increase taxes as a means of reducing inflationary pressure.)

Keynesian economics focuses on short-run adjustments in aggregate expenditures and income. In possibly his most famous quip, Keynes justified his approach by saying, "In the long run we are all dead."

Monetarists challenge Keynesian economic theory regarding the role and importance of INTEREST RATES. In Keynesian theory, changes in interest rates affect overall aggregate expenditures by changing levels of investment. Monetarists suggest changes in interest rates have a greater impact in an economy.

Further reading
Boyes, William, and Michael Melvin. *Macroeconomics,* 5th ed. Boston: Houghton Mifflin, 2001.

know-how
Know-how is valuable business knowledge; it may or may not be a trade secret, and may or may not be patentable. Know-how often refers to technical, scientific, or engineering fields. An engineer who specialized in industrial coatings once said, "I am more than willing to show my ideas and inventions to potential partners and investors. They could try to steal my ideas, but they do not have the know-how that comes from experience to make these things work without me." Know-how can also be more general in character, encompassing marketing and MANAGEMENT skills as well as simple business advice.

Legal protection for know-how is limited. Unlike PATENTS, TRADEMARKS, and COPYRIGHTS, individuals cannot obtain exclusive rights to know-how by registration. Knowledge is a public good; once it is made available to others, it can generally be used by anyone and is nearly impossible to retrieve. Because know-how is so difficult to protect, preserving its confidentiality is often an important business strategy. If competitors gain access to critical knowledge about a firm's production or operations, the firm loses some of its competitive advantage. For example, one of Wal-Mart's secrets of success is its inventory management system. When Amazon.com hired away some of Wal-Mart's inventory-management executives, Wal-Mart sued, claiming loss of company know-how. Similarly, one of the best-kept business secrets is the Coca-Cola formula. Only a few people in the company know the formula, a necessary precaution to prevent loss of this critical knowledge.

Protecting business know-how is usually done through confidentiality CONTRACTs, civil law, and use of trade-secret law. It is often difficult to sue for the loss of know-how, so employers' best efforts focus on protecting knowledge. In the United States, the ECONOMIC ESPIONAGE ACT (1996) created criminal penalties for misappropriation of financial, business, scientific, technical, economic, or engineering information whose owner has taken reasonable measures to keep it secret and whose "independent economic value derives from being closely held." MARKET INTELLIGENCE experts advise that people are the sources of information, and the best protection of know-how is clear instructions to company personnel.

knowledge management
Knowledge management (KM) is a business activity through which organizations generate value utilizing their explicit and tacit intellectual assets. This is accomplished through the dissemination and utilization of knowledge. The practice of KM involves combining explicit assets (information technologies) with tacit assets (competencies and experiences possessed by employees).

In one form or another, knowledge management has been around for as long as people have been conducting business. Elements of KM exist in all work environments. SENIORITY systems explicitly place a value on the knowledge gained over time by employees who have worked longer in the organization. Companies often have someone who is known and deferred to for his or her knowledge of company history. In many societies, philosophers, priests, teachers, and politicians act as the source of knowledge for their organization. In the 1990s, KM became popular among "new economy" companies, where the rapid pace of technology led to almost continual improvement of software, computer, and electronic technology. Firms that did not retain their RESEARCH AND DEVELOPMENT personnel quickly lost their knowledge base and competitive advantage.

Knowledge management helps organizations gain knowledge from its own experiences and the experiences of its employees. This knowledge is then merged into the organizational structure and existing technology, which in turn produces new knowledge, continuing the organization's evolution.

Many companies have attempted to formulate explicit knowledge-management programs. In any organization it is difficult to determine what is known and who knows it. MARKET INTELLIGENCE professionals recommend determining what information is most valuable and deciding who should have access to that information. KM professionals attempt to determine where information is gathered and coordinate access to that knowledge in order to achieve company goals. With today's electronic information systems, many professionals are experiencing information overload. Effective DATABASE MANAGEMENT systems allow managers to access explicit information as needed and combine tacit knowledge to explore new opportunities, address problems, and achieve objectives.

Further reading

Hallriegel, D., S. E. Jackson, and J. W. Slocum, Jr. *Management: A Competency-Based Approach,* 9th ed. Cincinnati: South-Western Publishing, 2002; McFarland, Dalton E. *Management and Society.* Saddle River, N.J.: Prentice-Hall, 1982.

—R. Joseph Harold

Kondratev waves

Kondratev waves are 50-year periods of expansion and contraction in Western countries during the period from 1790 to 1940. These long-term BUSINESS CYCLES were first observed and analyzed by the Russian economist and statistician Nikolay Kondratev.

Kondratev's analysis showed three cycles.

1. 1792–1815
2. 1850–1896
3. 1896–1940

The third cycle included expansion from 1896 to 1920 and then contraction from 1920 to 1940, the period of Joseph Stalin's rule over the Soviet Union. This did not endear Kondratev to Russian leaders, and in 1928 he was dismissed from his post as director of the Institute for the Study of Business. He was later arrested, imprisoned, and received a death sentence.

Business-cycle scholars have studied Kondratev's work and developed a variety of hypotheses regarding these long-term waves, but no general consensus explanation has developed.

Kyoto Protocol (Kyoto Accord, Climate Change Treaty)

The Kyoto Protocol is a treaty intended to reduce the impact of human activity on the earth's environment. The focus of the treaty is global warming, but it also contains goals to reduce poverty and shepherd water RESOURCES. It is also called the Kyoto Accord or the Climate Change Treaty. This agreement was signed on December 11, 1997, in Kyoto, Japan, and was ratified by 160 countries by September 2002, the time of the United Nations World Summit on Sustainable Development in Johannesburg, South Africa. The Kyoto Protocol is significant for its emphasis on economic development in a manner that can be sustained by the planet's resources.

The Kyoto Protocol sets targets to reduce greenhouse gas emissions 8 percent below 1990 levels in the EUROPEAN UNION and 6 percent in Japan. Less-developed countries are not obligated to limit their emissions under the agreement. Under the Clinton administration, the United States agreed to a 7 percent reduction below 1990 levels, but the second Bush administration argued that this target would curtail its economy too much and withdrew from negotiations in March 2001.

HISTORY

The United Nations Framework Convention on Climate Change (UNFCCC) resulted in the creation of the Kyoto Protocol. In 1974 an English atmospheric scientist, Brian Gardiner, hypothesized that the earth's stratosphere was developing a hole in it due to chlorofluorocarbons (CFCs), chemicals found in emissions resulting from burning fossil fuels (coal or petroleum). The decade from 1970 to 1980 saw an increased awareness in the damage to the earth's stratosphere, as the "hole" in the ozone layer over Antarctica grew.

The Kyoto Protocol evolved out of many earlier steps.

- Vienna Protocol (1981). This summit was convened to acknowledge and discuss the problem with the ozone layer, and it organized a working group.
- MONTREAL PROTOCOL (1987). This measure identified offending chemicals by name and stipulated that industrial activities continue on the condition that industry produce fewer CFCs. The Montreal Protocol added halon (an ingredient in fire extinguishers) to the list of offending chemicals.
- London Amendment to the Montreal Protocol (1990). The London Amendment mandated complete phaseout of the production of chemicals degrading the atmosphere (CFCs, halon, carbon tetrachloride by 2000, and methyl chloroform by the year 2005). This was a more aggressive approach, in place of reductions in production levels.
- The Copenhagen Agreement (1992). This was significant for its establishment of a WORLD BANK fund to assist EMERGING MARKETS in seeking alternatives to CFCs. The fund's contributors were developed countries such as United States.

In 1997 the Kyoto Protocol set the following environmental goals: to slow the rate at which emissions are accumulating in the earth's atmosphere, to decrease the world's reliance on fossil fuel, to stop deforestation, and to explore renewable energy more actively. Industrialized nations argue that too drastic a reduction in the rate of increase in emissions will stagnate the world economy. Environmentalists counter that all nations enjoy the benefit of the clean air, therefore all must join in the effort to end global warming.

PARTICIPANTS IN THE DEBATE
OVER THE KYOTO PROTOCOL

Scientists, on whose work legislators rely but whose word is sometimes disputed, play an important role in defining environmental problems. Participants in the Kyoto Protocol who are held accountable for environmental degradation challenge the credibility of scientific data or deny the environmental problem altogether. Lawmakers who do not understand or trust data they are being given, however good that data may be, postpone decisive action. With each environmental summit called by the United Nations, countries review new developments from scientific research (either privately funded or government-funded) and revisit questions on pollution costs.

Members of industry, whose PRODUCTION processes create harmful emissions, argue that the cost of providing their communities with goods and services will go up if the standards of the Kyoto Protocol are enforced. The threat of putting employees out of work leads to some vociferous arguments against environmental standards that are seen as too harsh. The biggest consumers of fossil fuels are power plants, energy-intensive industries, and motorized vehicles. History shows that an industry or a utility, left on its own, is very slow to change its manufacturing practices if it must incur a cost.

Southern countries (Australia and New Zealand) whose land mass is closest to the Antarctic, where the ozone hole is located, suffer higher rates of skin cancer due to exposure to too much ultraviolet light. (Australia did not ratify the Kyoto Protocol, although it was to be permitted to increase its levels of emissions to +8 percent of the 1990 levels.)

Developing countries (e.g., India, Thailand) need to develop INFRASTRUCTUREs, generate electricity, and grow economically to catch up to a STANDARD OF LIVING more like that of industrialized nations. The social agenda of the Kyoto Protocol is complex because there must be increased productivity to raise developing nations out of poverty. That is why the developing countries have no emissions caps set in their portion of the agreement, something the developed nations perceive as unfair COMPETITION. A long-standing struggle between industrialized nations and developing nations concerns the proposition that the most-polluting nations should own the biggest share of the cost.

The emissions of developed countries (European Union, United States, and Japan) constitute the bulk of the problem plaguing the environment. These nations wish to continue to grow and also retain a competitive presence in the world economy. In 2002 California's emissions equaled Germany's, at 12 percent of the world's output. The United

States' emissions contribution was 36 percent of the world's output.

The withdrawal of the United States from the Kyoto Protocol has drawn criticism from most quarters, especially U.S. environmentalists. Their skepticism comes from doubt regarding the United States' ability to control its level of greenhouse emissions by government programs inside the country. The Kyoto Protocol contains numerous compliance-related elements, such as reporting requirements and an expert-review process to assess implementation and identify potential cases of noncompliance.

To satisfy critics, the United States opted in 2001 to allocate money to research on advanced energy technology and research on climate change. Under the second Bush administration, the Office of Energy Efficiency and Renewable Energy had its budget increased by $1.2 billion. Its mission has been to investigate the use of wind power, solar power, and renewable energy.

The Kyoto Protocol strives for reduction in the rate of growth of emissions so that all countries can continue to have clean, healthy air without making the problem of global warming worse. The protocol also addresses the need for people to rise from poverty in developing nations. It presses for respect for the environment while achieving sustainable development so that the earth's resources are not exhausted prematurely. The levels of emissions prescribed in the treaty, tolerable to the environment if not world governments, are set to allow the world's rate of ECONOMIC GROWTH to continue, even if more slowly. As long as there are industries, utilities, and cars serving people, greenhouse gasses will persist.

Further reading

Buchanan, Rob. "1984: The Sky Is Falling," *Outside Magazine* 27, no. 10 (October 2002): p. 114; Department of Energy Office of Energy Efficiency and Renewable Energy website. Available online. URL: http://www.eren.doe.gov. Downloaded on November 15, 2002; "Kyoto Protocol" Washington, D.C.: Congressional Quarterly Press, 2001; *Federal Regulatory Directory, 9/E.* Washington, D.C.: Congressional Quarterly Press, 1999; Harvard University International Environmental Policy Reference Guide. Available on-line. URL: http://environment.harvard.edu/guides/intenvpol/indexes/treaties/FCCC.html. Downloaded on November 15, 2002; "Kyoto Conference/Protocol." In *International Encyclopedia of Environmental Politics.* Edited by John Barry and E. Gene Frankland. London, New York: Routledge, 2002; United National Framework Convention on Climate Change: Kyoto Protocol Text from the UNFCCC. Available on-line. URL: http://unfccc.int/resource/convkp.html. Downloaded on November 18, 2002; "Global Warming," Environmental Protection Agency. Available on-line. URL: http://yosemite.epa.gov/oar/globalwarming.nsf/content/index.html. Downloaded on November 17, 2002; United Nations Environment Programme. Available on-line. URL: http://www.unep.ch/ozone/vienna.shtml. Downloaded on November 15, 2002.

—Dominique Winn

L

labor/employee relations

Employee relations is concerned with assuring that each employee is treated fairly and that concerns and problems are addressed quickly. Employees are encouraged to discuss their concerns with either their supervisor or a HUMAN RESOURCES representative. The term *employee relations* is usually used when the organization is union-free, meaning the employees are not represented by a UNION. The term *labor relations* is used when specific employee groups are represented by a union. Individual union members are represented by a member called a union steward or a committee person, although employees can still discuss issues with their supervisors or human resources representatives. When a union does represent groups of employees, the wages, hours, and terms and conditions of work are negotiated jointly by union and company representatives in a process called COLLECTIVE BARGAINING.

The product of collective bargaining is the CONTRACT between the company and the union. Both the employee handbook in a union-free organization and the union contract in a unionized organization contain essentially the same topics and information. In both documents the employee will find information about the rules of the organization, how to get questions answered and problems solved, the role of employee representatives, SENIORITY, wages, increases in pay, and hours of work, to list only a few considerations.

The process that a union typically follows to gain legal authority to represent employees of a given location is under the regulation of the NATIONAL LABOR RELATIONS BOARD (NLRB). In most instances, employees who are disgruntled over one or more issues with their current employer will contact a union representative and ask, if in the union's opinion, there is valid cause for concern. If the union agrees with the disgruntled employees, the union estimates the number of other similarly dissatisfied employees. Frequently these dissatisfied employees will assist in the union's organizing campaign and encourage other employees that union representation is needed to assure fair treatment. The purpose of this action is to project the likelihood of winning a secret-ballot election that would give the union authority to represent the employees. Like any business, before the union undertakes an organizing campaign, it wants to feel it has a good likelihood of success and that the effort will be financially worthwhile (i.e., there will be enough dues-paying members).

There are three important steps that the union must achieve. First, union is to have at least 30 percent of the prospective bargaining unit (potential union members) sign authorization cards giving the union exclusive rights to represent individual employees in all matters concerning wages, hours, and terms and conditions of work. With this valid display of union support by the employees, the NLRB will conduct a secret-ballot election.

Winning the election is the union's second major hurdle; in order to win, the union must receive a simple majority of the votes cast, or 50 percent plus one of the votes cast. If the union does not receive a majority of the cast votes, then it has lost the election. Just as the union is campaigning for the employees to vote "yes" and bring the union in, the company is also vigorously campaigning for the employees to vote "no" and keep the union out.

If the union wins the representation election, the third important step is for representative of the union and the company to jointly negotiate a contract. Simply winning the representation election does not mean the union represents the employees; a contract must be negotiated and ratified by the union members. After negotiating and ratifying the contract, the focus then shifts to its administration, which is often more difficult than the negotiations.

—John B. Abbott

labor force (workforce)

In the United States, the labor force (or workforce) is defined as individuals age 16 or older who either have jobs or can work and are looking for jobs. People under 16 are not considered part of the workforce, even though many young people in the United States work. Another way of defining the labor force is the sum of people employed plus the number of unemployed. This does not, however, distinguish between part-time and full-time EMPLOYMENT. During RECESSIONS people can often only find part-time work, causing labor-force statistics to underestimate the true level of UNEMPLOYMENT. To be part of the labor force, one has to be employed or looking and available for a job. Some people choose to leave the labor force, usually after their unemployment benefits have ended but sometimes for health or personal reasons. Others, discouraged because they cannot find the employment they want, simply drop out of the workforce.

The definition of labor force may vary among countries. In the United States, the DEPARTMENT OF LABOR's BUREAU OF LABOR STATISTICS (BLS) surveys and estimates labor-force and related statistics. The labor-force statistic is used to calculate the country's unemployment rate; the number of people unemployed divided by the labor-force number, is the nation's unemployment rate expressed as a percentage.

The BLS also calculates labor-force participation rates, the percentage of working-age individuals who are working or seeking work, by category. One of the trends in the American labor market has been the increase in the participation of women in the workforce, rising from less than 40 percent in 1950 to over 60 percent in 2000. During the same period, the labor-force participation rate among males actually declined slightly, from over 80 percent to approximately 75 percent. As would be expected, the participation rate is low among people under 20 years old and over 55 years old, and slightly lower among minority groups in the United States.

Further reading
Bureau of Labor Statistics website. Available on-line. URL: http://stats.bls.gov.

Labor-Management Relations Act   See TAFT-HARTLEY ACT.

labor markets
Labor markets are markets where workers are the source of SUPPLY and employers are the source of DEMAND. Labor is one category of RESOURCES. Along with CAPITAL and natural resources, labor is necessary to produce goods and SERVICES. Employers hire workers based on the expected output and revenue they will generate. If only one worker staffed a fast-food restaurant, that person would have to take orders, prepare the food, take payment, inventory supplies, and clean the eating area, spending a considerable amount of their time moving from one task to the next. Adding more workers would increase output through task specialization and reduction in wasted motion. The addi-

tional output from adding one more unit of labor is the marginal product of labor. The value of that marginal product, the extra output multiplied by the market price of that output, is the marginal revenue product of labor.

The demand for labor is based on the marginal revenue product of labor. Using the fast-food restaurant example again, adding more workers will increase output up to a point, but as workers start jostling with each other in the confined space and competing for limited machinery, the marginal product of labor would begin to decline and even become negative. Employers are unlikely to hire more workers when they do not increase output.

Labor markets are different from other resource markets in that a higher price will not always result in a greater quantity supplied. The law of supply states that, ceteris paribus (other things remaining constant), a higher price will result in a greater quantity supplied and a lower price will result in less quantity supplied. But workers look at work as a source of INCOME with which to purchase goods and services. If people are constantly working, they will not have time to use and enjoy their purchases. During peak economic times, when wages are rising rapidly, some workers will work less (primarily choosing not to work overtime) as wages increase. Economists refer to this as a backward-bending supply curve.

Labor markets, like markets for goods and services, vary greatly. Local supply-and-demand conditions result in considerable wage variation. College students often find local markets (around big universities) are overcrowded with qualified people. This excess supply allows employers to hire highly skilled people at relatively low salaries. Similarly, in many remote areas, subsidies are often needed to attract skilled workers.

In addition to labor supply and demand conditions, working conditions and risks, certification requirements, and occupational segregation contribute to wage differences. Many professions attempt to restrict entry into their specialized labor markets as a means of reducing supply and generating higher incomes. In one state, realtors tried to pass a requirement that real-state agents have a four-year degree (although they grandfathered themselves, allowing existing realtors to avoid the requirement). A few years ago, accounting students were shocked when they learned they now needed 150 college credits (rather than the previous 120 credit hours) in order to sit for CERTIFIED PUBLIC ACCOUNTANT (CPA) exams. Cosmetologists fought legislation designed to do away with licensing of workers in their industry. U.S. antidiscrimination laws prohibit discrimination in labor markets based on race, gender, age, and national origin. The EQUAL EMPLOYMENT OPPORTUNITY COMMISSION (EEOC) oversees labor market discrimination complaints.

labor relations   See LABOR/EMPLOYEE RELATIONS; WAGNER ACT.

laissez-faire

Laissez-faire is an economic philosophy advocating limited government involvement in an economy. Advocates of "free enterprise economics" and "free market systems" often invoke the term *laissez-faire* in their criticism of government. Translated as "let them do" or "leave it alone," laissez-faire originated in the protests of 18th-century French businessmen against government regulation of trade and industry.

Laissez-faire economic ideas were first advocated by 18th-century French economists known as physiocrats. Led by François Quesnay, physiocrats challenged the dominant economic doctrine of the time, MERCANTILISM, by which increasing exports and collecting precious metals in return maximized the WEALTH and power of a nation. Physiocrats argued that nature was the true source of an economy's wealth and saw government laws, TARIFFS, and privileges granted to individuals as interfering with the natural flow of commerce, hindering economic and social prosperity.

The Scottish philosopher Adam Smith (1723–90), author of *The Wealth of Nations* and considered the father of modern economic thought, incorporated the ideas of laissez-faire CAPITALISM in his work. Smith emphasized the role of self-interest in the functioning of markets—that is, self-interest would guide individuals to use their resources wisely. Consumers would attempt to maximize their well-being with their limited INCOMES, purchasing products at the lowest possible price and offering their resources to the highest bidder. Producers would attempt to purchase RESOURCES at the lowest possible price and sell their products to the highest bidders. Smith theorized that in markets, buyers and sellers would benefit society by efficiently allocating resources and goods as if guided by an "invisible hand." COMPETITION would lead to efficiency without government oversight or control.

In the 19th century, classical economic theory argued that laissez-faire markets would keep economies at close to the natural level of real output. Flexible prices and wages would adjust market prices, eliminating shortages and surpluses. Since markets would be self-correcting, there would be no need for government intervention during ups and downs in economic activity. Classical economic theory dominated macroeconomic thought into the 20th century but could not explain the GREAT DEPRESSION. Keynesian economic theory, challenging the assumption of flexible wages and prices and advocating government spending during periods of reduced private-sector spending, replaced classical theory for most of the second half of the 20th century.

During the 1970s and 1980s, there was a resurgence of the laissez-faire philosophy in the United States. Articulated by the Nobel Prize-winning economist Milton Friedman in his classic film series *Free to Choose* and adopted by the Reagan administration, laissez-faire supporters called for reduction in the size of government and government rules and regulations. Libertarian Party members had long advocated similar measures. Recent pressure for the PRIVATIZATION of public goods and SERVICES, including SOCIAL SECURITY, are based on laissez-faire ideas.

See also CLASSICAL ECONOMICS; KEYNESIAN ECONOMICS; MACROECONOMICS.

Further reading

Boyes, William, and Michael Melvin. *Macroeconomics,* 5th ed. Boston: Houghton Mifflin, 2001; Ruffin, Roy J., and Paul R. Gregory. *Principles of Economics,* 7th ed. Boston: Addison-Wesley, 2000.

Landrum-Griffin Act (Labor Management Reporting and Disclosure Act)

The Landrum-Griffin Act, officially titled the Labor Management Reporting and Disclosure Act (1959), created a "bill of rights" for UNION members, including freedom of speech, secret elections, and fiduciary reporting requirements for union officials. Landrum-Griffin was an outgrowth of the McClellan Corruption Committee investigations of organized-crime involvement in a few U.S. labor organizations. The committee found evidence of collusion between employers and union officials, diversion and misuse of union funds, and use of violence by labor leaders against others within the union movement.

The Landrum-Griffin Act was the first significant legislation directed toward internal union activities, limiting union officials' use of funds and requiring disclosure of union spending. At the time, some union leaders overpowered and intimidated anyone within the organization who questioned their decisions. The act also restricted unions' use of secondary boycotting (union BOYCOTTS of companies that did not use union labor) and picketing at companies where another union was already representing workers.

Landrum-Griffin was opposed by most union groups for what was perceived as strengthening antilabor provisions in the TAFT-HARTLEY ACT. In particular, Landrum-Griffin authorized states to handle all cases that were outside the province of the NATIONAL LABOR RELATIONS BOARD.

layoff

A layoff is the reduction in the number of workers due to changes in DEMAND for the firm's PRODUCTs or changes in MANAGEMENT strategy but not due to cause. Layoffs can be temporary or permanent. Historically they were most often associated with changes in BUSINESS CYCLES. As the economy grew, so did EMPLOYMENT; but as the economy declined, workers would be laid off.

In the 1990s, a decade of continually growing GROSS DOMESTIC PRODUCT, many companies reduced their number of employees. A new language evolved, with many colorful and cynical words and phrases to describe being laid off, including "attrit," "ax," "given the boot," "canned," "get bounced," "get the pink slip," "house-cleaning," and "riffed." During this period, many companies experienced new challenges, often in the form of global competitors. In response, executives jettisoned divisions or products that did not compete effectively and flattened management hierarchies. One manager of a fiberglass factory described how there had previously been seven layers of management between him and the CHIEF EXECUTIVE OFFICER, and now there were only three layers. Executives chanted the mantra "lean and mean" to support their decisions to lay off middle-management people and outsource functions that had previously been handled by employees.

In UNION work environments, layoffs are addressed in the labor-management CONTRACT and are almost always based on SENIORITY; workers with the most seniority are the last to be laid off and the first to be rehired. Occasionally union and nonunion groups will agree to adjust hours rather than lay off people. After September 11, 2001, many employees, particularly in airline- and tourism-related markets, faced the choice of cutting back hours or facing mass layoffs. Cutting back hours provides employment for people and also retains skilled workers for when the economic situation turns around. It usually means workers get to retain their benefits, but it also means these workers are not unemployed and therefore not eligible for UNEMPLOYMENT benefits.

In addition to unemployment-benefit rules, two sets of federal laws affect layoffs. The WORKER ADJUSTMENT AND RETRAINING NOTIFICATION ACT (WARN) requires employers covered by the act to provide 60-day advance notice of large-scale employment loss, generally resulting from plant closings and mass layoffs. WARN became law in 1989, and in general it applies to companies and nonprofit groups with 100 or more employees. Hourly, salaried, and managerial workers are all entitled to notification under WARN. In addition, if the sale of a business results in mass layoffs or plant closings, the parties to the sale must give WARN notice to the state dislocated worker unit and the local government where the employment site is located.

WARN provides a variety of exceptions, including when a company is faltering or suffering unforeseeable business circumstances or in the event of a natural disaster. Failure to give notice can lead to penalties, including back pay and benefits for the period of violation of the act. Many states have WARN-like disclosure laws alerting workers to the possibility of layoffs.

TRADE-ADJUSTMENT ASSISTANCE (TAA) refers to government-sponsored training programs and supplemental cash unemployment compensation provided to workers who lose their jobs due to increased foreign COMPETITION. TAA grew out of programs intended to aid Americans who were dislocated when the European Community (now the EUROPEAN UNION) was established. The first assistance program was authorized in the Trade Expansion Act of 1962; however, no assistance was actually provided until 1969. It was not until the Omnibus Trade and Competitiveness Act of 1988 that significant funding was committed to TAA.

Under TAA, workers may petition the U.S. secretary of labor for assistance. The secretary must certify that workers have been or are threatened with job losses, that the sales or production or both of the firm in question have decreased absolutely, and that increased IMPORTS of articles like or directly competitive with those made by the workers or the firm for which the workers provide essential goods or services "contributed importantly" to job separation or decline.

The most visible trade-adjustment assistance program is NAFTA-TAA. Between 1994 and 1997, almost 100,000 American workers were certified for trade-adjustment assistance. This number was often used to show the adverse impact of the NORTH AMERICAN FREE TRADE AGREEMENT (NAFTA), but TAA certification does not necessarily mean workers have been displaced, only that there is the potential for workers to lose their jobs due to imports. In the first three years of NAFTA, slightly more than 12,000 workers received NAFTA-TAA. Many workers who have lost their jobs are encouraged by state officials to apply for TAA, thereby reducing the state costs for unemployment compensation.

See also OUTSOURCING; REDUCTIONS IN FORCE.

Further reading
Folsom, Ralph H., and W. Davis Folsom. *NAFTA Law and Business.* The Hague: Kluwer International, 1999; Folsom, W. Davis, and Bradley P. Folsom. *American Business Language.* Beaufort, SC: Kalmia Publishing, 2000; U.S. Department of Labor. Employment & training websites. Available on-line. URL: www.doleta.gov/programs/factsht/warn.htm and www.doleta.gov/layoff/.

leadership
Although it is difficult to agree on a precise definition of leadership, it can be described as the process of influencing people to direct their efforts toward the achievement of some particular goal or goals. Good leaders encourage people to perform at higher levels and to achieve their goals, whereas ineffective leadership can contribute to lackluster performance. Researchers generally agree that to be a great leader, one has to be able to exert influence over other members of a group or organization as well as help a group or organization to achieve its goals.

Early studies of leadership identified personal characteristics that distinguish effective from ineffective leaders. These traits include intelligence, self-confidence, the ability to exert influence and control over others, knowledge of what has to be done and how, high energy levels, the ability to tolerate stress, honesty, integrity, and being emotionally mature enough to handle criticism. Individuals who possess these traits are more likely to become effective leaders although it does not guarantee that an individual will become an effective leader.

The behavior approach to effective leadership focuses on specific behaviors that good leaders have that contribute to their effectiveness. Most leader behaviors involve two main categories: consideration and initiating structure. *Consideration* is behavior that demonstrates leaders respect, trust, and value good relationships with their followers. *Initiating structure* is what leaders do to make sure subordinates perform their jobs and the work gets done. While hard to define or measure, effective leadership is easily recognized when present in an organization.

—Judy Mims

leasing

Leasing involves temporary grants of the right to possess, use, and occupy real estate or PERSONAL PROPERTY in exchange for rent or other payments. Leasing is a widespread business and consumer practice. Apartments, automobiles, trucks, equipment, facilities, mining claims, and many other forms of property are leased. To businesses and consumers, leasing offers the benefit of reduced initial expenditure. Many manufacturers provide leasing as an option for their customers. As the cost of durable goods, particularly automobiles, has risen, many U.S. consumers now lease cars. Changes in U.S. tax laws, no longer allowing deduction of interest expenses from personal income taxes for consumer purchases other than home-MORTGAGE interest deduction, has helped stimulate consumer leasing activity.

Leases can be long- or short-term, but never more than the owner's rights extend. The owner is called the "lessor"; the temporary user, the "lessee." Financed leases, a type of secured transaction, are governed by Article 2A of the UNIFORM COMMERCIAL CODE.

The sale of property with the understanding that the seller will lease it back, known as a "leaseback" transaction, is often driven by tax considerations. A tenant's temporary interest in realty is called a "leasehold," and in the practice of "subleasing," the holder of lease rights transfers them to a third party, the "sublessee." This can only be done with permission of the lessor.

Further reading
Stockton, John M., and Frederick H. Miller. *Sales and Leases of Goods in a Nutshell,* 3d ed. Eagan, Minn.: West Group, 1992.

letter of credit

A letter of credit is commercial tool through which a bank or other financial institution instructs a suitable institution to advance a specified sum of money to the bearer. It is primarily used by importers to offer secure financing to exporters. The letter of credit refers to the document representing the goods, not the goods themselves. It is called a circular letter of credit when it is not addressed to any particular corresponding institution.

In effect, a letter of credit is a draft indicating a dollar (or other currency) amount as a maximum that is not to be exceeded. Letters of credit greatly simplify nonlocal business transactions. Institutions that issue such letters are generally well-known FINANCIAL INTERMEDIARIES, and any bank will honor the letter upon verification of proper identification.

There are several types of letters of credit. A commercial letter of credit is typically written with payment designated to a third party, possibly a creditor financing the transaction between the importer and exporter. A performance letter of credit is issued to guarantee performance under an agreement. A confirmed letter of credit is one that guarantees payment by the issuing bank. A revolving letter of credit is one that is renewed automatically within the time frame and amount limits specified. A traveler's letter of credit lists banks at which drafts against the letter of credit will be accepted.

All letters of credit contain specific elements, including the name of the issuing bank, the buyer's name, the seller's name, a specified amount, specific time limits, terms and conditions of documentation, and a specific place to present documents. When all conditions are met, the issuing bank guarantees to pay the seller the specified amount. In effect the bank is substituting its credit for the buyer's credit, reducing the seller's risk.

Although letters of credit are a common mode of payment, there are many problems associated with them, including the possibility that the seller's documents will be rejected by the bank at presentation. This can be extremely aggravating to both the importer and exporter and can result in loss of potential customers.

Banks act to protect their customers but are usually not concerned whether the CONTRACT between the buyer and seller is performed exactly as per the terms. A bank's concern is that the documents presented by the seller conform to the documents required under the letter of credit and whether they are presented within the time period required.

Further reading
Moses, Margaret L. "Controlling the Letter of Credit Transaction." Available on-line. URL: http://global-trade-ltd.com/loccontol.html; "Practical solutions for payment and collections." Tradecorp Finance. Available on-line. URL: www.tradecorp.com/letter_of_credit.

—R. Joseph Harold

leverage

In business a person with leverage is someone who can influence a company's operations and get things done, usually with only minimal effort. Within a firm there are two kinds of leverage: operating leverage and financial leverage.

Operating leverage arises from the use of fixed costs within the firm's total cost structure. The higher the percentage of fixed COSTS relative to variable costs, the higher the degree of operating leverage for the firm. With high operating leverage, small changes in sales cause larger changes in a firm's operating INCOME (called earnings before interest and taxes, or EBIT). For example, if a firm has a degree of operating leverage equal to 3, a 1-percent increase (or decrease) in sales results in a 3-percent increase (decrease) in its EBIT. Operating leverage thus magnifies the effects of increases and decreases in sales. Typically firms with high degrees of operating leverage are CAPITAL-intensive with automated production. Such firms have a heavy INVESTMENT in plant and equipment, creating large fixed costs relative to variable costs.

Financial leverage arises from the proportion of debt within the firm's capital structure. The higher the percentage of debt relative to ASSETS (that is, the higher the firm's debt ratio), the higher the degree of financial leverage. With financial leverage, small changes in EBIT cause larger changes in earnings per share (EPS). For example, if a firm has a degree of financial leverage equal to 2, a 1-percent increase (decrease) in EBIT results in a 2-percent increase (decrease) in EPS. Like operating leverage, financial leverage magnifies the effects of increases and decreases in sales. Typically firms with high degrees of financial leverage are those acquired in LEVERAGED BUYOUTS and those with stable sales, such as PUBLIC UTILITIES.

For firms with high degrees of both operating and financial leverage, small changes in sales will lead to volatile fluctuations in its EPS.

leveraged buyout

A leveraged buyout (LBO) is the takeover of a company using borrowed funds. In an LBO, the ASSETS of the company being acquired are used as collateral to secure LOANS needed to finance the company's purchase. The takeover company or group then repays the loans using the PROFITS from the company being acquired or by selling off part or all of the assets of the targeted company.

In the United States, leveraged buyouts were quite popular during the 1980s. Kohlberg, Kravis, Roberts (KKR), the leading LBO group, analyzed companies, looking for situations where a company's assets were greater than the current capitalization (price of the company's stock times the number of shares outstanding). By 1990 KKR had acquired 36 firms using $58 billion of borrowed funds. Their pinnacle acquisition was RJR-Nabisco for a record $25 billion. Critics contended KKR contributed nothing to the economy and were undermining American CAPITALISM. Supporters suggested KKR and other LBO specialists increased efficiency and improved MANAGEMENT by replacing overpaid executives closely tied to their BOARD OF DIRECTORS with new LEADERSHIP. In some instances, the companies' management initiated leveraged buyouts themselves, taking their companies "private," using borrowed funds to pay stockholders a premium over the current price to repurchase shares in order to gain control and avoid layouts by firms such as KKR.

BONDS rated below investment grade by MOODY'S RATINGS and STANDARD & POOR'S were often used in leveraged buyouts. The two firms rate bonds, both public and private sector, according to their DEFAULT risk, and both use two broad classifications of RISK. Those bonds with ratings of BBB or Baa and higher are termed investment-grade or investment-quality bonds and have minimal default risk. Bonds with ratings less than BBB or Baa are termed speculations because of their considerable risk of default. The more common name for these speculative bonds is junk bonds. Because the acquiring company used loans to take over the targeted company, the company's debt rating usually fell below investment grade.

Often leveraged buyouts are "hostile takeovers" in which the company being targeted does not want to be acquired. With the proliferation of LBOs in the 1980s, the board of directors of many U.S. companies instituted POISON PILL STRATEGIES—also called shareholder rights plans—to make their company unattractive to a hostile acquisition. "Poison pills" create rights (or options) for shareholders to purchase stock at a discount when certain events are triggered by the bidder (the individual or company initiating the takeover), such as purchasing a certain percentage of stock. They thus make the target company prohibitively expensive for the bidder to buy.

By the 1990s the use of LBOs declined as the number of attractive companies for takeover disappeared and companies developed strategies to avoid being acquired.

liability

Liability is the status of being responsible or obligated under the law. Persons and businesses can be subject to both civil (private) and criminal liability. Liability can be "joint and several" with each liable party individually responsible for the entire legal obligation; and "derivative" or "vicarious" acts involving other persons and businesses, such as when an agent acts on behalf of another or an employee acts on behalf of an employer.

Products liability refers to the liability of manufacturers and distributors when users of their PRODUCTS are harmed. Products liability may be based on NEGLIGENCE, or it may be "strict" (not based on negligence) as a matter of law. Liability for very hazardous activities is often based on strict liability principles, as are "no fault" WORKERS' COMPENSATION and auto-accident laws.

Limited liability concerns the restriction of liability by CONTRACT terms or by statutory or regulatory law. The most notable form of limited liability is that of stockholders whose liability cannot exceed the CAPITAL they have invested in an incorporated business.

Liabilities are represented by the various payables accounts found in the liabilities section on the top right-hand side of a BALANCE SHEET. ACCOUNTS PAYABLE, notes payable, wages payable, interest payable, and BONDS payable are examples of various forms of debt.

It is customary to group debts into current liabilities and long-term liabilities. Current liabilities are accruals that arise and must be satisfied within the current accounting period. Long-term liabilities are usually more formal debt instruments such as PROMISSORY NOTES and bonds, and they will not come due during the current account period. In fact, there may be several years before some longer-term liabilities reach their maturities.

The debt is owed to the firm's creditors, and these lenders have a priority over the firm's EQUITY members (stockholders) in the event of liquidation or bankruptcy. For this reason the liabilities are always placed before the equity accounts on the balance sheet.

Further reading
O'Connell, John F. *Remedies in a Nutshell.* 2d ed. Eagan, Minn.: West Group, 1984.

licensing

Licensing is an agreement offering the right to use a manufacturer's process, trademark, patent, or trade secret by a Licensee in a foreign market. Licensing arrangements are often considered in a company's international expansion efforts, since it offers the opportunity to generate royalties without INVESTMENT in resources or the assumption of RISK associated with market development. For a licensee, a licensing agreement provides name-brand recognition, association with foreign products, and access to proprietary technology.

Licensing agreements involve many business considerations, including

- royalty structure
- licensed territory
- length of agreement
- provisions for termination
- assignment rights to third parties
- extent and timeliness of support by the licensor
- currency of payment
- protection of INTELLECTUAL PROPERTY

Licensing agreements usually state either a fixed payment per unit sold or a percentage of revenues or operating PROFIT from the sale of licensed products. Fixed- payment agreements are easier to administer but do not increase royalties as prices or profits increase. Royalties based on a share of operating profit require careful definition of what costs are included and excluded in calculating profits from licensed products. Defining the territory in which the licensee is allowed to sell the product is another important consideration. Often licensing agreements result in the creation of GRAY MARKETS, where licensed products find their way back into the market of the licensor. One new licensing issue is the sale of licensed products over the INTERNET, crossing all geographic boundaries. The WORLD TRADE ORGANIZATION (WTO) passed the Agreement on Trade-Related Aspects of Intellectual Property in 1995 to increase protection of PATENTS, COPYRIGHTS, TRADE SECRETS, and TRADEMARKS by member nations.

In the United States, brand-licensing agreements tend to fall into three categories: first-tier licenses for exclusive, limited distribution products such as Calvin Klein and Ralph Lauren; second-tier licenses for more widely distributed and lower (in category) priced products, such as Guess and Nautica; and third-tier licenses for mass market products such as Adolfo and Gloria Vanderbilt. In one of the widely quoted licensing disputes, Calvin Klein sued Warnaco, complaining that its high-end image was harmed by the appearance of Calvin Klein apparel in mass-market stores.

Further reading
Johnson, Howard E. "Establishing Royalty Rates in Licensing Agreements," *CMA Management* 75, no. 1 (March 2001): 16.

life cycle

According to Webster's *New World Dictionary,* life cycle is "the series of changes in form undergone by an organism in development from its earliest stage to the recurrence of the same stage in the next generation." In business, life cycle is the series of stages individuals, products, and organizations go through from the beginning to the end of its existence.

Individuals go through stages of career development involving formal education and training, on-the-job education, or training and continuous career development. Recent studies suggest American workers will change careers on average seven times during their lifetime. Many professions have developed licensure or appropriate certification to practice in addition to instituting continuing professional education requirements that help professionals remain current and sustain the knowledge and skill sets expected by the profession.

PRODUCT LIFE CYCLES include introduction, growth, maturity, and decline. During the introduction stage, businesses face little COMPETITION but also have to educate customers about product features and benefits. During the growth stage, firms expand sales and PROFITs but begin to see competition. During the maturity stage, sales begin to decline and profits drop as increased competition creates added price competition. During the decline stage, managers decide whether to discontinue existing PRODUCTS or revive market interest through revisions and improvements.

Organizational life cycles are analogous to products. Many dynamic, leading companies of 50 years ago no longer exist today. Statistics from the Dow Jones Industrial Average (DJIA), a composite of the leading companies in the United States, demonstrate this. In the 1980s, service companies like McDonald's were added, while U.S. Steel and Gulf Oil were eliminated as they were taken over by other companies. In the 1990s, technology companies were added to the DJIA as they became major contributors to the economy.

To avoid decline, organizations often engage in redesign (restructuring/reengineering), repackaging (PUBLIC RELATIONS), or creative destruction/obsolescence/termination (relocation or merger). According to James A. Champy, changes in the marketplace in the 1990s created needs for restructuring, reengineering, management specialist or other organizational alternatives in order to manage customer-driven needs and in response to increased competition due to GLOBALIZATION. These factors have reduced the length of the organizational life cycle, forcing organizations to rethink how they deliver their products or SERVICES. The solution, according to Champy, is to utilize X-engineering principles, including concepts like HARMONIZATION, "know what your customers are going through," and "fish upstream." Some enlightened enterprises, described as learning organizations, even build into their organizational processes opportunities for employee learning in order to prevent employee obsolescence (referred to by economists as structural UNEMPLOYMENT).

Further reading

Champy, James A. "From Reengineering to X-Engineering." In *Organization 21C: Someday All Organizations Will Lead This Way.* Edited by Subir Chowdhury. Upper Saddle River, N.J.: Prentice Hall, 2003; Dunphy, Dexter. "The Sustainability of Organizations." In *Organization 21C: Someday All Organizations Will Lead This Way.* Edited by Subir Chowdhury. Upper Saddle River, N.J.: Prentice Hall, 2003; Robbins, Stephen P. *Organizational Behavior.* Upper Saddle River, N.J.: Prentice Hall, 2003.

—Howard Rudd

limited liability company

A limited liability company (LLC) is a business form that combines some of the advantages of the corporate business form with the favorable tax treatment of business PARTNERSHIPS. Like a CORPORATION, a limited liability company is a legal entity existing separately from its owners, creating limits to their LIABILITY. Owners of LLCs, called members, have no personal liability for LLC obligations. Like a partnership, an LLC may elect to distribute all PROFITS and losses to its members, who in turn report these losses and INCOME on their personal tax returns. LLCs thus allow the benefits of limited liability and the ability to avoid corporate income taxes.

Typically LLCs are used by wealthy investors as TAX SHELTERS to reduce their taxable income. Members can deduct losses to the extent they are at RISK—that is, their CAPITAL contributions to the LLC. Passive losses—losses in excess to their at-risk capital—can be used to offset income from other passive investments.

In 1977 Wyoming passed the first laws allowing limited liability companies. Since then every state has adopted LLC statutes. To establish an LLC, one or more people must file articles of organization with the secretary of state. The term *limited company* or *LLC* must appear in the name of the company. When being established, LLCs usually include an operating agreement stating how the company will be managed. Like a BOARD OF DIRECTORS for a corporation, members of an LLC select managers to operate the company. Voting in an LLC is based on the capital contributions of each member. Unlike a corporation, in which ownership interests can be sold to other investors, in an LLC there is limited ownership transferability. Unless agreed by other members or provided for in a provision in the LLC's creation, ownership interest cannot be transferred to other individuals.

LLCs differ from limited liability partnerships (LLPs) in that LLCs have limited liability, while in LLPs partners retain personal liability.

Further reading

Mallor, Jane P., A. James Barnes, Thomas Bowers, Michael J. Philips, and Arlen W. Langvardt. *Business Law and the Regulatory Environment,* 11th ed. Boston: McGraw-Hill, 2001.

limited liability partnership

A limited liability partnership (LLP) is a form of business where partners retain individual liability but have no LIABILITY for most LLP obligations. An LLP is similar to a PARTNERSHIP except for the LLP's lack of liability. LLPs are used by many professional groups as a means of maintaining a partnership while not being liable for each partner's actions.

Limited liability partnerships are a relatively new form of business. Texas passed the first laws permitting LLPs in 1991. Almost all states and the District of Columbia now have LLP statutes. In most states partners in an LLP are required to file with the secretary of state, pay an annual fee, and add the letters LLP or RLLP (R meaning *registered*) to their partnership name. Some states also require the LLP to maintain professional liability INSURANCE.

LLPs can choose to have the LLP taxed as a partnership or a CORPORATION. If taxed as a corporation, the LLP pays corporate income taxes and partners pay personal income taxes only on compensation and partnership PROFITS distributions. Like a corporation, LLPs are unaffected by death or the withdrawal of partners. They continue to exist as a legal entity. Partner interests are not transferable in LLPs.

Further reading
Mallor, Jane P., A. James Barnes, Thomas Bowers, Michael J. Philips, and Arlen W. Langvardt. *Business Law and the Regulatory Environment,* 11th ed. Boston: McGraw-Hill, 2001.

loans

Loans are generally represented by PROMISSORY NOTES (unconditional promises to pay). Loans may be for the long term (maturities greater than one year) or short term (less than one year) and may be secured (backed by collateral, ASSETS pledged to lessen the loan's RISK) or unsecured (such as a signature loan).

The cost of a loan is interest expense, determined in several ways: simple interest, discount interest, and compensating balance. With a simple-interest loan, the borrower receives proceeds equal to the face value of the loan; the loan's principal and interest are paid at maturity. This is called a simple-interest loan because its effective interest rate is equal to the stated, nominal interest rate. Many consumer loans, such as automobile loans, are simple-interest loans.

With a discount-interest loan, the lender deducts the interest expense from the loan's proceeds, and thus the borrower receives less than face value. Because the interest expense is calculated on the face value of the loan, but the borrower receives less than the face value, the effective interest rate is higher than the nominal interest rate.

A compensating balance is a minimum amount of funds that must be kept in a deposit account with the bank over the life of the loan. The presence of this compensating balance lessens the loan's riskiness of the loan and increases its effective interest rate. For example, with a $100,000 loan that has a 10 percent compensating balance, the borrower has use of only $90,000, because $10,000 must remain on deposit at the lending institution. However, the interest expense is calculated on the face value of the loan—that is, on $100,000—which causes the effective interest rate to be higher than the loan's nominal interest rate.

local option sales tax

A local option sales tax (LOST) is an addition to an existing sales tax made by a local government or municipality for a specific purpose. Local option sales taxes, usually ranging from 0.5 to 1.5 percent, are enacted to pay for special projects, typically things like roads, bridges, and schools.

Generally sales taxes are imposed by state governments and used for financing state-level activities. In the 1990s, states began allowing cities and counties to add on local taxes. Sales taxes are collected by retail businesses and then forwarded to state treasuries. Added amounts from local option sales taxes are then remitted by the state treasurer to the local governments. In states that do not have sales taxes, local governments would not be likely to impose a local sales tax because of the cost of creating and managing a collection system.

Most local option sales taxes are created through referenda. City or county political leaders propose a referendum stating the amount, the use, and how long the tax will be imposed. Around the country, most LOST referenda have been successful. While American taxpayers are generally resistant to increased taxes, LOST referenda succeed when they demonstrate a specific local benefit.

A Georgia county promoted a LOST referendum to pay for school construction. Supporters argued local option sales taxes would allow taxpayers to "pay as you go," only paying a small amount each time they purchased goods locally. Another slogan used by LOST advocates is "a penny for education," suggesting that a 1-percent increase in the sales tax is a small price to pay. Opponents of local option sales taxes point out that sales taxes are regressive, meaning lower-INCOME people pay a higher percentage of their income in sales taxes than higher-income consumers.

Many local governments impose very high accommodations and hospitality and tourism taxes. In fact, these are two of the few types of tax citizens usually like to see increased. Similar to a LOST, accommodations, hospitality, and tourism taxes are imposed as a percentage of the price of the hotel or restaurant meal and are used for local initiatives, often things like tourism promotion or development.

Further reading
"LOST: Still a bad idea." North Carolina Justice website. Available on-line. URL: www.ncjustice.org.

logistics   See BUSINESS LOGISTICS.

Lorenz curve

The Lorenz curve, named after statistician Max Otto Lorenz, shows the portion of total money INCOME accounted for by different proportions of the nation's households. The Lorenz curve displays the cumulative percentage of households on the horizontal axis and cumulative percentage of household income on the vertical axis. If income were distributed equally among all households, the Lorenz curve would be a straight line at a 45-degree angle, but since income is not equally distributed in any country, the Lorenz curve is bowed or curved, falling below the 45-degree line and creating what is called the *inequality gap.* The Lorenz curves for countries with greater income disparities have greater curves representing larger inequality gaps in those countries.

In the United States, the disparity between rich and poor households has increased. In 1947 the lowest quintile (20 percent group) of Americans received 5.1 percent of

MONEY income, while in 1998 the same group received only 3.6 percent of income. During the same period, the richest one-fifth of American households received 44.3 percent of money income in 1947 and 49.4 percent in 1999. These figures can also be used to create a ratio of income of the richest 20 percent to the poorest 20 percent. In 1998 the U.S. ratio was 13.7, higher than any other develop country in the world.

Critics note that the Lorenz curves

- do not include income in kind, such as government food stamps, public housing, or education
- do not take into account differences in the size of households or number of wage earners
- do not take into account age differences
- measure income before taxes, not disposable income

- do not include the value of household labor and unreported income

Lorenz-curve statistics are often used to justify greater government intervention to reduce income inequality in the United States. Americans' attitudes toward income-inequality programs have changed over time, but they continue to be less supportive of such programs when compared to other industrialized countries. Current figures for U.S. income distribution can be found on the U.S. Census Bureau website.

Further reading
Miller, Roger Leroy. *Economics Today*. Boston: Addison Wesley, 2001; U.S. Census Bureau website. Available on-line. URL: www.census.gov.

M

macroeconomics

Macroeconomics is the study of aggregate economic systems, most often the study of a nation's economy. Macroeconomics includes analysis of an economy's INCOME, output, EMPLOYMENT (and UNEMPLOYMENT), and INFLATION. Often economists use the CIRCULAR FLOW MODEL to portray the relationships among households, businesses, and government interacting in consumer, financial, and resource markets.

Macroeconomists develop or study complex mathematical models constructed using past economic data to predict the impact of changing conditions in the economy. Macroeconomic analysis typically begins with estimation of an economy's GROSS DOMESTIC PRODUCT (GDP), the value of final goods and SERVICES produced in the economy in a year. GDP can be estimated using either the income or expenditures approach. In the 1930s, President Franklin Roosevelt directed the future Nobel Prize economist Simon Kuznets to develop a system to measure changes in the economy. Kuznets' NATIONAL INCOME ACCOUNTING system is the basis for macroeconomic analysis. Using the income approach, a nation's output is equal (with adjustments) to the sum of wages, rents, PROFITS, and interest payments paid for the production of goods and services. Using the aggregate expenditures approach, a nation's output is the sum of the CONSUMPTION, INVESTMENT, government, and net trade expenditures for the output in an economy. This results in the standard formula $AE = C + I + G + (X–M)$, which all students learn in their first macroeconomics course.

Macroeconomic models are used to assist in business- and government-policy decisions. Large CORPORATIONS often employ macroeconomists to develop models to predict the impact of changing market conditions on DEMAND for their products. For example, producers of durable goods (things like automobiles and washing machines) know that demand for their products is highly influenced by consumers' income. Changes in national income result in changes in demand for their product, which in turn leads to a host of MANAGEMENT decisions including investment in new equipment, expansion into new markets, purchase of materials and hiring of workers.

Government also uses macroeconomic analysis to support changes in fiscal and MONETARY POLICY. Alan Greenspan, chairman of the FEDERAL RESERVE SYSTEM, is famous for his in-depth analysis of the Fed's "beige book," a compilation of the latest statistics measuring the status of the country's economy. In 2001, sensing a slowdown in the growth of GDP, Greenspan and the Federal Reserve lowered short-term INTEREST RATES, a common monetary policy prescription to stimulate investment and interest-rate-sensitive consumer spending. During the same period, President George W. Bush justified tax cuts, a common FISCAL POLICY option, in part by stating reduced taxation would increase consumers' income and stimulate expenditures.

Macroeconomic analysis is largely based on KEYNESIAN ECONOMICS, the ideas formulated by British economist John Maynard Keynes (1883–1946). Keynes challenged the existing macroeconomic doctrine, CLASSICAL ECONOMICS, emphasizing the importance of aggregate demand rather than aggregate SUPPLY in determining the level of aggregate output in an economy. Classical economists thought economies were self-adjusting, full-employment systems. In classical theory, unemployment and inflation were temporary phenomena, and changing prices would eliminate surpluses and shortages in an economy. Keynes, observing the GREAT DEPRESSION, argued that wages and prices were not as flexible as classical economists suggested. He argued in a time of prolonged economic decline there is a role for government to help an economy return to EQUILIBRIUM through management of aggregate demand.

Many other economists have debated and expanded upon Lord Keynes's work. Keynesians and monetarists continue to debate the role of government and the effectiveness of fiscal versus monetary policy in having the desired effect on the economy.

Further reading

Miller, Roger LeRoy. *Economics Today*. Boston: Addison Wesley, 2001; Boyes, William, and Michael Melvin. *Macroeconomics*, 5th ed. Boston: Houghton Mifflin, 2001.

Madison Avenue

In most business contexts, Madison Avenue refers to the major ADVERTISING agencies with offices on Madison Avenue in New York City. It is also a major retail shopping district in the city. During the 20th century, New York City dominated world financial markets, was headquarters for most U.S. businesses, and competed with Paris as the center of Western fashion design. Advertising agencies evolved in New York City to support the MARKETING COMMUNICATIONS needs of major companies located there.

During the latter part of the 20th century, many U.S. companies moved their headquarters out of New York and at the same time became MULTINATIONAL CORPORATIONS (MNCs). Most Madison Avenue agencies retained offices in the city but merged with other ad agencies in order to service multinational clients. Madison Avenue agencies are mostly named after the individuals and groups who founded them: Ogilvy & Mather; Young & Rubicam; J. Walter Thompson; Leo Burnett; and Saatchi & Saatchi. In recent years these and other agencies have merged, creating global marketing services firms such as WPP and Omnicom.

mail surveys

Mail SURVEYS are a method market researchers use to collect customer and potential customer information. Like other data-collection methods (TELEPHONE SURVEYS, PERSONAL-INTERVIEW SURVEYS, OBSERVATION, INTERNET SURVEYS, and tests), mail surveys have both advantages and disadvantages.

The major advantages of mail surveys include the amount of information that can be collected, the low cost of the mailings, the lack of interviewer bias, and anonymity for respondents. While response rates decline as the number of questions in a survey are increased, compared to other methods mail surveys are relatively inexpensive.

The major disadvantages of mail surveys are the low response rate, lack of control over the data-gathering effort, the inability to clarify questions, and the inability to probe for in-depth information. Response rates for mail surveys are often quite low, sometimes as little as 10 percent, which leads to the potential for nonresponse bias. If only those people who are very interested in the topic respond to the mail survey, the results are not representative of the total population. Market researchers use a variety of techniques to increase response rates, including multiple mailings of QUESTIONNAIRES, sponsorship of the survey by a group or firm known and respected by those being surveyed, and incentives to respond. Almost every American receives mail surveys. If the subject is one that interests the recipient, it came from an organization to which the recipient belongs, a postage-paid envelope is included, a donation to a charity is made for responding, or the recipient is included in a contest for participating, he or she is more likely to respond.

Market researchers also know that the person they want to respond to the questionnaire may not actually be the person responding. Careful attention is given to the mailing list to reduce this problem. Questionnaires are also pretested to avoid including questions that are misleading or could be misinterpreted. The order of questions asked is important to response rates and gathering in depth information. Generally researchers try to use closed-end rather than open-ended questions. Closed-end questions allow easier data tabulation and analysis, but occasionally valuable information can be derived from comments added by respondents. Even simple design factors such as organizing rating scales from poor to excellent versus excellent to poor can influence responses.

On-line surveys are similar to mail surveys, but there is less control over who is responding and "ballot stuffing" is achieved through multiple submissions. For example, *Time* magazine conducted an on-line survey asking people to name the most important people of the 20th century. They received thousands of responses naming Mustafa Attaturk, the leader of Turkey during the 1930s and 1940s. It is also difficult to determine who is responding to Internet surveys, which often are not representative of the population the researcher is trying to study.

One criticism of surveys, both mail and other types, is their use as a disguised selling technique. Unethical marketers will conduct surveys whose purpose is really to stimulate DEMAND for their products.

Further reading

Etzel, Michael J., Bruce J. Walker, and William J. Staunton. *Marketing*, 12th ed. Boston: McGraw-Hill, 2001.

make-or-buy decisions

Make-or-buy decisions are concerned with whether PRODUCTS or components should be made in-house or purchased from external sources. These decisions are a simple economic decision based on COSTS. However, in many instances make-or-buy decisions are more strategic and can affect a company's competitive position. To determine whether a product should be purchased or produced, managers consider

- the role of the process technology in providing a competitive advantage for the firm
- the maturity of the process technology
- competitors' technology position

OUTSOURCING of process technology can often lead to the creation of suppliers who have the ability to become competitors in the marketplace. Thus, a supplier may internalize enough of the process technology to start doing RESEARCH AND DEVELOPMENT on the process. With the improved technology, the supplier may then use the technology to supply current competitors; and, finally, if the technology is a core part of the business, these suppliers can emerge as competitors. A classic example of this strategy can be seen in computer vendors from Taiwan. Initially these vendors were utilized as low-cost suppliers of components and circuit boards. They then expanded to producing computers, which were sold under different labels. Eventually these companies began marketing computers under their own brand names.

The maturity of the process technology also plays a key role in the make-or-buy decision. Even if the technology is new in the industry, there might be other industries where the technology is routinely used. For example, when fire-reinforced composites were being developed, the weaving process required was new to this industry but fairly well advanced in the textile industry. If the technology is mature, there is not much to be gained from research and development, since competitors can simply acquire the technology from other sources.

Finally, it is important to gauge the ability of competitors to develop/acquire and assimilate the new technology. Such assessments are typically done using BENCHMARKING studies, by reverse-engineering a competitor's product, and by searching through literature to identify use of the technology by other companies. If proprietary technology is involved or if the technology represents a core competency of the firm, special thought should be given to the outsourcing decision.

Once assessment is made of the key decision variables, the make-or-buy decision falls into one of the following categories: make, marginal make, develop internal capability, buy, marginal buy, and develop suppliers.

Further reading
Cooper, Robin, and Robert Kaplan. *Cost and Effect: Using Integrated Cost Systems to Drive Profitability and Performance.* New York: Harvard Business School Publishing, 1997; Zant, Peter. *Microchip Fabrication.* New York: McGraw-Hill, 2000.

Malthusian trap

The Malthusian trap, named after the 19th-century political economist Thomas Malthus, is the idea that population can or will outgrow the means to feed itself. The result would be widespread famine. (Malthus is one of the reasons economics is called "the dismal science.")

Malthus observed that plants and animals produced significantly more offspring than could survive. He argued that the potential existed for population to increase exponentially, while resources were finite, limiting the ability of society to increase food production. He concluded that humans, unless restricted, could also overproduce and, with limited food production, outstrip their ability to feed themselves.

Living in 19th-century England, Malthus saw declining living conditions and high birth rates among the poor. Malthus advocated regulation of birth rates so that poor families did not produce more offspring than they could support.

Most criticism of the Malthusian trap centers on Malthus' apparent inability to foresee the tremendous advances in technology and the ability to increase food production with a finite amount of land. Many economists and sociologists dismiss Malthus as being exceedingly pessimistic about humankind's ability to adapt and overcome resource constraints.

Recently sociologist William Catton Jr. and others have suggested that Malthus could not have foreseen the advances in technology that allow economic systems to temporarily "overshoot" their long-term PRODUCTION capacity. Catton contends, "Human economic growth and technology have only created the appearance that Malthus was wrong. . . . What our technological advances have actually done was to allow human loads to grow precariously beyond the earth's long-term carrying capacity by drawing down the planet's stocks of key RESOURCES accumulated over 4 billion years of evolution." He adds, "By drawing down 'savings accounts' (i.e., using resources faster than their rates of renewal), populations can (and do) temporarily exceed carrying capacity. When the stockpile runs out, the once-thriving population finds itself in dire straits."

The British economist John Maynard Keynes also suggested that economies could temporarily expand output beyond their long-term capacity by extending the use of CAPITAL and HUMAN RESOURCES for short periods of time. Increasing resource prices due to increased DEMAND would then reduce aggregate SUPPLY back to the potential level of output, but at higher prices. Catton suggests the adjustment time frame is longer as economies continue to produce using large amounts of finite resources, particularly hydrocarbons, and CONSUMPTION of renewable resources beyond sustainable limits, thus overshooting the ecosystem's carrying capacity.

Malthus is credited with stimulating the idea of natural selection, developed by Charles Darwin and others. In his autobiography, Darwin states, "In October 1838, that is, fifteen months after I had begun my systematic inquiry, I happened to read for amusement Malthus on *Population*, and being well prepared to appreciate the struggle for existence which everywhere goes on from long-continued observation of the habits of animals and plants, it at once struck me that under these circumstances favorable variations would tend to be preserved, and unfavorable ones to be destroyed. The results of this would be the formation of a new species. Here, then I had at last got a theory by which to work."

See also SUSTAINABLE GROWTH AND DEVELOPMENT; KEYNESIAN ECONOMICS.

Further reading
Catton, William R. Jr. "Malthus: More Relevant Than Ever." Available on-line. URL: www.greatchange.org/ ov-catton,malthus.html.

management

Management is the essence of an organization, responsible for the accomplishment of its mission. In particular, management, like medicine, is both a science and an art. It is a science because research has documented certain management principles and theories that have a scientific basis. At the same time, because each management situation is encountered in a different situational context, it is an art to diagnose the presenting situation and decide what managerial principles to apply for resolution to the issue. Furthermore, on a larger conceptual basis, the overall process of management includes causing and directing a transformation or conversion process. Basically the resources— i.e., human (both physical and intellectual RESOURCES), plant and equipment, CAPITAL, and information—are transformed or converted into outputs (SERVICES or products). All levels within the organization—first-line, middle, and top managers—practice management. During the transformation, the application of the major principles of management occurs in the functions of planning, organizing, leading, and controlling. The goal is to accomplish the entire management process efficiently and effectively.

Planning is the intellectual process that determines the anticipated use of resources, methodology, projected outcome, and time line of occurrence. Planning begins with setting goals derived from the organization's mission. The collective management of a company then is charged with the overarching process of measurably achieving those goals within a determined time frame.

Organizing, an essential function for management, involves decisions concerning the best allocation and utilization of RESOURCES for implementing the strategic plan. Coordinating the assignment of people and the use of capital, information, and physical resources are part of this process.

Leading is a more complex function because it strictly involves the HUMAN RESOURCES (people) of an organization. Leaders possess the ability to influence and motivate followers in accomplishing the organization's goals. Managers with LEADERSHIP ability are able to get employees to follow willingly in the achievement of those goals. The managers/leaders of an organization are responsible for everything that "goes on," both collectively and individually, in relation to the organization.

Controlling, a function that takes place throughout the management process, involves the monitoring, checks and balances, and course corrections necessary to the achievement of established goals. Preliminary control is practiced during the input phase as management screens for quality materials, workers, and information. During the transformation process, controlling involves comparing accomplishments at certain intervals of time against goals set. If any deviation or gap is discovered, then management takes corrective action. At the output level, post-action control occurs when the finished service or product is again inspected for quality. An effective control system will involve a control dimension in each of the three stages, specifically input, transformation, and output.

All of the four functions of planning, organizing, leading, and controlling are performed simultaneously and by all managers at every level within the organization.

—Leanne McGrath

management gurus

Management gurus are influential teachers, educators, and even mentors on such topics as global business, HUMAN RESOURCES, and productivity. They study a company's operations and recommend improvements in such things as CUSTOMER RELATIONS/SATISFACTION, MANAGEMENT practices, organizational structure, EMPLOYEE/LABOR RELATIONS, etc. Management gurus share their knowledge and expertise through writing books, consulting, speaking at conferences, and teaching workshops. Following are some of the top management gurus in the United States.

KENNETH BLANCHARD

Dr. Kenneth Blanchard is a business writer, consultant, and cofounder of the Ken Blanchard Companies of Escondido, California. He has made many contributions in the field of human resources development and formulated the situation LEADERSHIP model and several management styles. Blanchard is most famous for coauthoring the book *The One Minute Manager* (1981). This book shows how managers can set goals and give feedback to employees with advice such as "Everyone is a winner" and "Catch someone doing something right." The book states that one should look at the goals set and then look at performance to see if performance matches goals. Managers should praise employees for what they are doing right and, if they are doing something wrong, tell them how to fix it and reaffirm them.

Kenneth Blanchard also coauthored *Management of Organization Behavior: Utilizing Human Resources* (1969).

STEPHEN COVEY

Stephen Covey is a lecturer, author, and founder of the Covey Leadership Center in Provo, Utah. He focuses on subjects including leadership and personal and organizational effectiveness. He has a unique style of personal-development teaching that involves promoting individual development, discipline, and self-control, and he challenges organizations to treat their employees more holistically as a way to achieve greater productivity.

In *The Seven Habits of Highly Effective People* (1989) Covey states:

1. Be proactive. Be responsible and take the initiative.
2. Begin with the end in mind. When you start anything such as a day at the office or a meeting, make a mental image of an outcome that conforms to your values.
3. Put first things first. Discipline yourself to subordinate your feelings, moods, etc.

4. Think win/win.
5. Seek first to understand, then to be understood. Listen with the intent to empathize, not with intent to reply.
6. Synergize. Create a whole that is greater than the sum of its parts.
7. Sharpen the saw. Engage one's mental, emotional, physical and spiritual capabilities.

Stephen Covey is also the author of *How to Succeed with People* (1971); *Principle-Centered Leadership* (1991); and *Daily Reflections for Highly Effective People* (1994).

W. EDWARD DEMING

Deming (1900–93) was a mathematical physicist, a teacher, and a management consultant. He had a significant impact on business managers, first in Japan and then in the United States. He was an advocate of QUALITY CONTROL methods and industrial PRODUCTION.

DEMING'S 14 POINTS, referred to as "A System of Profound Knowledge," are a basis for transformation for industry. They can apply to small and large organizations, to the service industry as well as to the manufacturing. Deming brought together ideas from many sources and emphasized the importance of human factors in achieving excellence and the importance of continuous improvement.

Deming also wrote *Out of the Crisis (1986).*

PETER DRUCKER

Peter Drucker is a management consultant, economist, author, and teacher specializing in strategy and policy for businesses and nonprofit organizations and in the work and organization of senior management. One of the most influential writers and speakers on organization and management, Drucker thinks management is an important component to all organizations in society.

The Essential Drucker (2001) summarizes key points from Drucker's works from 1954 to 1999. It covers such topics as management in the organization, society and management, and management and the individual. Highlights of Drucker's thoughts on management include:

- Management is about human beings. It makes people capable of making their weaknesses irrelevant and their strengths effectual—this is what an organization is about and what makes management important.
- Management is a part of culture. It deals with uniting people in a common venture.
- An enterprise or business does not exist unless there is a commitment to common goals and shared values.
- TRAINING AND DEVELOPMENT must be ongoing for businesses and enterprises so that their members can grow as needs and opportunities change.
- Every business or enterprise should be built on individual responsibility and communication amongst its members.

- In addition to the amount of output and the bottom line, productivity, market standing, development of people, and good financial results are important to an organization's performance and survival.
- One of the most important results of a business is a satisfied customer.

Other books by Peter F. Drucker include

- *The Concepts of the Corporation* (1946, rev. 1972)
- *The New Society: The Anatomy of the Industrial Order* (1950)
- *The Practice of Management* (1954)
- *The Effective Executive* (1967)
- *Management Challenges for the 21st Century* (1990)
- *The Executive in Action* (1996)

DR. ELIYAHU M. GOLDRATT

Dr. Eliyahu Goldratt is an Israeli physicist, business consultant and chairman of the Goldratt Institute in New Haven, Connecticut. He is a recognized leader in developing new management concepts and systems.

One of Goldratt's most famous philosophies is the THEORY OF CONSTRAINTS (TOC). It argues that every organization has something (a constraint) that is preventing it from making bigger PROFITS. Examples of constraints could be a machine that is working inadequately or employees that aren't directed well. If the constraint is removed, production rates are increased, which can help increase profits.

TOC also focuses on the importance of time, or throughput, which is the rate at which a system generates money. If time is reduced and a company's product can be manufactured quicker, that means faster throughput and increased revenues.

Other books by Eliyahu Goldratt include

- *The Goal: A Process of Ongoing Improvement* (1986)
- *The Race* (1986)
- *The Haystack Syndrome: Sifting Information Out of the Data Ocean* (1990)
- *An Introduction to the Theory of Constraints: The Production Approach; Workshop Description* (1992)

DR. MICHAEL HAMMER

Dr. Hammer is a management consultant, author, lecturer, former MIT computer science professor, and president of Hammer and Company in Cambridge, Massachusetts. He is the originator of the business concept called "reengineering," which in the 1990s encouraged many companies to restructure themselves.

Reengineering is the redesign of a company's important business processes after thorough analysis. It achieves substantial performance improvements in quality, service, speed, and cost and enables the company to better meet the demands of the economy.

In his 2001 book, *The Agenda: What Every Business Must Do to Dominate the Decade*, Hammer presents these core principles:

1. Make your company easy to do business with.
2. Provide more added value for your customers.
3. Obsess about your company's process in order to achieve high performance for your customers.
4. Turn innovative work into process work.
5. Use measurement for improving, not accounting.
6. Loosen up the structure of your organization.
7. Sell through your DISTRIBUTION CHANNELS.
8. Push past boundaries in the pursuit of efficiency.
9. Lose your identity in an extended enterprise.

Other books by Dr. Michael Hammer include

- *Reengineering the Corporation: A Manifesto for Business Revolution* (1993)
- *The Reengineering Revolution: A Handbook* (1995)
- *Beyond Reengineering: How the Processed-Center Organization is Changing Our Work and Lives* (1996)
- *The Agenda: What Every Business Must Do to Dominate the Decade* (2001)

TOM PETERS

Tom Peters is a management consultant, author, and lecturer. He founded the Tom Peters Company in California in the early 1980s. His books focus on successful corporate practices.

In his book *In Search of Excellence* (1982), Peters discusses eight principles for companies to stay on top:

1. a bias for action—a preference for doing something
2. staying close to the customers—knowing what they prefer and catering to them
3. ENTREPRENEURSHIP and autonomy—separating the CORPORATION into smaller companies encourages them to be competitive and independent
4. productivity through people—telling employees how essential their best efforts are and how they'll share the rewards of the company's success
5. hands-on value-driven—demanding that management keeps in touch with the firm's essential business
6. stick to the knitting—the company should stick with the business it knows best
7. simple form, lean stuff—there should be few administrative layers and only a small number of people at upper levels
8. simultaneous loose-tight properties—fostering a climate where there is dedication to the central values of the company combined with the tolerance for all employees who accept these values

Tom Peters also wrote *A Passion for Excellence: The Leadership Difference* (1985).

Further reading

American Society for Quality website. Available on-line. URL: www.asq.org; Walton, Mary. *The Deming Management Method*. Berkeley, Calif.: Berkeley, 1999.

—Susan Slaga

managerial accounting (cost accounting)

Managerial accounting is sometimes called cost accounting. Unlike FINANCIAL ACCOUNTING, whose ultimate purpose is to report financial information about the firm to parties external to it, managerial accounting focuses on internal control and planning. While financial accounting is governed by GENERALLY ACCEPTED ACCOUNTING PRINCIPLES (GAAP) to ensure accounting consistency among firms, managerial accounting need not conform to GAAP because it is used strictly internally.

Because of its emphasis on COSTS, managerial accounting is an excellent tool for internal decision making, BUDGETING, and planning. Drawing on MICROECONOMICS, managerial accounting makes use of budgets and cost-volume-PROFIT analysis to fully explore not only break-even relationships but those volumes or activity levels necessary to generate target levels of profit.

In financial accounting, GAAP requires that the INCOME STATEMENT use the report format, in which the firm's expenses are organized by function, e.g., administrative expenses and selling expenses. In managerial accounting, the expenses are grouped according to cost behavior (fixed or variable), a type of income statement known as the contribution format. Income statements using this format are not generally accepted can be used only internally.

Following are examples of financial accounting's report format and managerial accounting's contribution format for the income statement.

Report format	*Contribution format*
Expenses organized by function	*Expenses organized by cost behavior*
Sales	Sales
Less Cost of Goods Sold	Less Variable Expenses
Gross Margin	Contribution Margin (CM)
Less Operating Expenses:	Less Fixed Expenses
Administrative	Net Income
Selling	
General	
Net Income	

In the contribution format, contribution margin is the revenue remaining after the variable expenses have been covered. The contribution margin must serve two purposes: to cover the fixed expenses and ultimately to contribute to net INCOME. Once the fixed expenses are covered (that is, when the contribution margin is equal to the fixed expenses), all of any additional contribution margin goes directly to net income. In financial accounting, break-even occurs when the bottom line, net income, is zero. In managerial accounting, break-even occurs when the contribution margin is equal to the fixed expenses.

The following four formulas arise from the contribution format for the income statement and constitute the core of managerial accounting's cost-volume-profit analysis.

Break-even point in units = FC/CM per unit

Break-even point in sales dollars (revenue) = FC/CM ratio

Units to be sold to earn a desired amount of net income (DNI) = [FC + DNI]/CM per unit

Sales dollars (revenue) required to earn a desired amount of net income = [FC + DNI]/CM ratio, where FC is the firm's total fixed costs, CM is the firm's contribution margin expressed in dollars, CM ratio is the firm's contribution margin expressed as a percentage of sales, and DNI is the targeted or desired amount of net income.

These formulas give immediate answers to complex questions regarding break-even and other levels of volume or activity. This is why managerial accounting lends itself well to internal planning, control, and decision making.

See also BREAK-EVEN ANALYSIS.

manufacturers' representatives (manufacturers' agents)

Manufacturers' representatives (also called manufacturers' reps or manufacturers' agents) are independent sales people who work for a number of manufacturers of related by not competing PRODUCTS. Manufacturers' reps are paid on a commission basis for the sales they generate. They are typically given a specific territory or represent manufacturers to relatively small firms in an industry, while the manufacturers' sales representatives (company employees) sell to large customers.

Because they operate independently, manufacturers' reps do not report directly to marketing managers and usually do not oversee delivery, credit, or other financial aspects of a sales transaction. Manufacturers' reps offer the advantage of no overhead, since they are INDEPENDENT CONTRACTORS; their disadvantage lies in less control and less loyalty to a specific manufacturer. Unlike selling agents, who have authority over pricing and promotional expenditures and may contract for worldwide selling rights, manufacturers' representatives have little control over these marketing decisions. In addition to their function of calling on small businesses, manufacturers' reps also create a low-risk method for firms to expand internationally. While the use of selling agents is declining because manufacturers want greater control over marketing efforts, the use of manufacturers' reps is expanding in the United States.

Further reading
Boone, Louis E., and David Kurtz. *Contemporary Marketing*, 10th ed. Fort Worth: Dryden Press, 2001.

maquiladoras (twin plants, in-bond production operations)

In 1965 Mexico created the Maquiladora (or Border Industrialization) Program. The program was initially a modest attempt to shift PRODUCTION activities away from the Mexico City area in response to changes in U.S. TARIFFS that limited customs duties on U.S.-fabricated components shipped abroad for assembly and then returned to the United States.

Also called twin plants or in-bond production operations, maquiladoras (from the spanish verb *maquilar*, meaning to collect a fee or toll for grinding grain at a mill) are factories that assemble parts and components produced around the world and then ship the finished and semifinished PRODUCTS, primarily to North American countries.

Under the maquiladora program, foreign CORPORATIONS initially could import equipment and raw materials into Mexico without paying taxes, but they were required to export all of the output. Asian and North American companies established maquiladoras, but the program did not take off until a Mexican financial crisis in the early 1980s. Declining oil prices combined with excessive international borrowing forced the Mexican government to look for new sources in hard currency to meet debt obligations. With devaluation of the Mexican peso, maquiladora labor became cheaper than in developing Asian countries.

Maquiladoras boomed in the mid-1980s and again after the PESO CRISIS in 1994. In the late 1980s Mexico relaxed the requirement that all maquiladora production be shipped out of the country, providing access to Mexican markets through those operations. In the 1990s, with new trade agreements with Chile, Mercursor countries (Argentina, Brazil, Uruguay, Paraguay) and most recently the EUROPEAN UNION, Mexico became an export platform for U.S.-based MULTINATIONAL CORPORATIONS. Exports from Mexican plants can enter countries like Chile without tariffs, while exports to Chile from U.S. factories do face tariffs.

In the year 2000 there were over 1.2 million workers in 3,562 maquiladora operations. Employment in maquiladoras doubled in the period from 1995 to 2000. Tijuana, Mexico, is the global center of television production. Maquiladoras are now found way beyond border areas as manufacturers seek new locations with sufficient labor supplies. In November 2000, as part of the NORTH AMERICAN FREE TRADE AGREEMENT (NAFTA), only parts and materials originating in the three North American countries could enter Mexico tariff-free. In anticipation of this change, multinational corporations, particularly Asian companies, have expanded production activities in Mexico, diverting production from other areas of the world.

The success of the maquiladora program significantly influenced Mexican domestic and trade policy. Until the 1970s, Mexico was one of the most closed markets in the world and particularly fearful of U.S. domination. The maquiladora program now exceeds oil as the most import source of export revenue in Mexico. While INFRASTRUCTURE still lags, working conditions have sometimes been highly criticized, and environmental conditions are less than healthy, maquiladoras have provided a new source of opportunity for Mexican workers.

Further reading

Folsom, Ralph H., and W. Davis Folsom. *Understanding NAFTA and Its International Implications.* New York: Matthew Irwin/Bender, 1996.

marginal analysis

Marginal analysis is an analytical method developed in which the impact of small economic changes is evaluated. Marginal analysis includes discussion of marginal utility, contribution margin, marginal cost and revenue, marginal benefit and cost, marginal propensity to consume and save, and marginal product and marginal revenue product.

The first widely recognized application of marginal analysis was developed by the English economist Stanley Jevons who, in 1862, used marginal utility analysis to explain why the price of diamonds was so much higher than a necessity good such as water. Jevons demonstrated that the price of a good was determined by its marginal utility, the extra benefit obtained from an additional unit of the good, not its total utility. While the total benefit or utility of water was clearly greater than that of diamonds, because water is in much greater abundance than diamonds, the marginal utility of purchasing and consuming an additional unit of water was less than that of diamonds, which are much more scarce.

During the late 1800s and early 1900s, economists led by Alfred Marshall used the concept of diminishing marginal utility to explain the law of DEMAND, the inverse relationship between price and quantity demanded that exists in markets. The law of diminishing marginal utility states that the more of a good one obtains in a period of time, the less the additional utility derived from each additional unit of that good. Therefore to induce people to purchase more of a good, the price would have to be lowered. In what is called the equi-marginal principle, to maximize utility or well-being, consumers allocate their scarce INCOMES among goods so as to equate the marginal utilities per dollar of expenditure on the last unit of each good purchased. If the price of a good decreases, the marginal utility per dollar spent on that good increases, and consumers will adjust their allocation by purchasing more of that good.

Contribution margin, part of BREAK-EVEN ANALYSIS, is the difference between average revenue and average variable cost at various levels of output. Average revenue (price for competitive firms) is total revenue divided by quantity sold. Average variable cost is the firm's total variable costs divided by output. Variable costs are costs that change with the level of output (as opposed to fixed costs, which do not change over a range of output). Contribution margin provides firms with income over the cost of the product, to be used to pay fixed costs and contribute to the firm's overall PROFITS.

Marginal analysis also includes comparison of marginal cost and marginal revenue. Marginal cost is the added cost of producing one more unit of a good. Marginal revenue is the added revenue from the sale of one more unit of a good. Most business decision making includes marginal analysis. Questions—such as should the firm add another worker, stay open an additional hour, or add a new line of PRODUCTS—are marginal decisions. In each of these situations, managers consider how much more will it cost and how much more revenue will it generate. Many times it is difficult to accurately measure marginal costs and revenues, but conceptually many business decisions are made based on marginal analysis.

Marginal benefit and cost are part of benefit-cost analysis. Benefit-cost analysis is widely used in public-sector decision making. Marginal benefit and cost differ from private decision making in that some benefits or costs to society may not be included in a firm's analysis, while public-sector resource allocation tries to include direct and indirect benefits and costs, called EXTERNALITIES.

In his *General Theory of Employment, Interest, and Money* (1936), John Maynard Keynes introduced the concepts of marginal propensity to consume (MPC) and marginal propensity to save (MPS). Marginal propensity to consume is the percentage of additional INCOME individuals will use for CONSUMPTION expenditures, while marginal propensity to save is the percentage of additional income individuals will use for savings. Together an individual's MPC plus MPS equals 1. Keynes stated that the impact of a government policy such as a tax cut would depend on consumers' MPC. A tax cut increases peoples' incomes, and the higher consumers' MPC the greater the stimulus effect of a tax cut. Studies have shown that younger people and people with lower income tend to have higher MPCs, which would suggest that tax cuts for college students would have greater impact on an economy than tax cuts for their parents.

Marginal product is the additional output obtained from using one more unit of a variable input in a fixed-PRODUCTION process. For example, marginal product is the extra food produced from adding one worker in a fast-food restaurant. The cooking system is the fixed-production process, and as more workers are added to the system, more food is produced up to the point where workers start bumping into each other and reducing each other's productivity. At that point marginal product is zero or even negative. Marginal revenue product is the value of the output from using one more unit of a variable input in the fixed-production process. In the above example, marginal revenue product is the value of the extra food produced as more workers are added to the process.

See also COMPETITION.

Further reading
Boyes, William, and Michael Melvin. *Microeconomics,* 5th ed. Boston: Houghton Mifflin, 2001.

market concentration

Market concentration is the control of a large proportion of total sales by a small number of firms in an industry, leading to reduced COMPETITION. Economists and government regulators monitor market concentration closely. The FEDERAL TRADE COMMISSION and the Antitrust Division of the U.S. Justice Department sometimes block mergers of firms in an industry based on reduced competition through market concentration. While there was a significant increase in mergers among major CORPORATIONS in the United States during the 1990s, most economists think market concentration has declined since the 1930s.

Market concentration is measured using two concentration ratios. The U.S. Department of Commerce developed a four-firm ratio adding together the percentage of output by the four largest U.S. firms. The closer the sum of their output is to 100 percent, the more concentrated the industry. For example, in 1992 the top four U.S. firms produced 93 percent of cigarettes, 85 percent of the cereal PRODUCTS, and 90 percent of beer produced in the country. Each of the markets is highly concentrated, and participating firms engage in many OLIGOPOLY market practices, including nonprice competition, price matching, and price leadership. These PRICING strategies reduce price competition, creating higher prices for consumers.

The most commonly used market concentration ratio is the HERFINDAHL INDEX, which measures concentration using the sum of the squares of the market shares of firms in an industry. Using the sum of the square of a firm's market share increases the weight in the index in markets where one or two firms have a major share of the market. The U.S. Justice Department has stated that markets with a Herfindahl Index of less than 1,000 are highly competitive; those with indexes between 1,000 and 1,800 are moderately competitive; and those with indexes greater than 1,800 are highly concentrated. Herfindahl Index values are often cited by the Justice Department when deciding whether or not to intervene in a corporate merger or takeover proposal.

The problem with market-concentration ratios is defining the market. In 2001, three firms—AT&T, Sprint, and MCI WorldCom—dominated the long-distance telephone-communications market. But increasingly Americans are communicating by use of the INTERNET, fax, and wireless systems. How the U.S. telecommunications market is defined significantly affects any measure of market concentration.

Further reading
Boyes, William, and Michael Melvin. *Microeconomics,* 5th ed. Boston: Houghton Mifflin, 2001.

market failure

Market failure is a situation where the forces of SUPPLY and DEMAND in a market result in an outcome that is not efficient, not equitable, or not acceptable. The most common type of market failure occurs when a market does not include all the COSTS or benefits associated with the PRODUCTION or CONSUMPTION of a good. EXTERNALITIES exist in this situation, meaning there is a difference between the private costs and benefits and society's costs and benefits. In theory, competitive markets allocate production and consumption so that marginal social benefits equal marginal social costs, resulting in an efficient allocation of RESOURCES, but market power and lack of clearly defined property rights often results in inefficient resource allocation, creating market failures.

In the United States, governments use ANTITRUST LAWS, public utility regulation, subsidies, taxes, and environmental regulations to correct for market failure due to inefficient allocation of resources. Antitrust laws and utility regulation reduce or control the market power of monopolists, lowering prices and increasing market output. Taxes and environmental regulations motivate or force businesses to include environmental costs in their market decisions, increasing prices and reducing the allocation of resources in those market; pollution credits are also being used to correct for market failure due to inefficient resource allocation. Those businesses that can reduce their pollution most do so efficiently and then sell pollution credits to firms that cannot reduce their pollution as easily.

The second type of market failure occurs when the market outcome is not socially acceptable, although this depends on people's political/economic philosophy and has shifted over time in the United States. Market failure associated with socially unacceptable distribution of INCOME and consumption is corrected through progressive taxation and income-transfer programs.

Markets can also fail to create and maintain stability. Rapidly increasing prices (INFLATION) or increasing levels of UNEMPLOYMENT are generally unacceptable market outcomes. Government fiscal and/or monetary policies are utilized to even out fluctuations in BUSINESS CYCLES correcting for this form of market failure.

See also FISCAL POLICY; MONETARY POLICY; PUBLIC UTILITIES.

Further reading
O'Sullivan, Arthur, and Steven Sheffrin. *Economics: Principles and Tools.* Upper Saddle River, N.J.: Prentice Hall, 2001.

marketing channels   See DISTRIBUTION CHANNELS.

marketing communications (integrated marketing communications)

Marketing communications is the combination of personal and nonpersonal efforts companies use to inform and influence customers. Marketing communications, also referred to as integrated marketing communications, is a relatively new industry term created to emphasize the fact that promotion is more than just ADVERTISING and PERSONAL SELLING. Often consumers and some businesspeople perceive marketing to be simply these two activities, but marketing communications is a coordinated effort that includes SALES PROMOTION, DIRECT MARKETING, and PUBLIC RELATIONS.

Generally the goal of any marketing communications effort is to inform, persuade, or remind consumers about a company's offerings. Advertising is one element within an overall marketing communications strategy. Advertising is paid, nonpersonal communication using any mass-communication channel to try to gain awareness and adoption of a company's PRODUCTS. Sometimes, especially in business-to-business marketing, advertising is not an important or effective way to promote a product, and there may be limited advertising options in some markets.

In markets where advertising is not effective or available, often personal selling is a critical element in marketing communications. Whether conducted face-to-face or electronically, personal selling allows marketers to measure the effectiveness of their message, tailor the presentation to the specific audience, and generate immediate results. While personal selling is often quite effective, it is relatively expensive and depends on the ability of the salesperson.

Sales promotion, an important part of a firm's marketing communications strategy, uses coupons, samples, premiums, point-of-purchase displays, contests, rebates, and TRADE SHOWS for marketing communications purposes. Coupons, samples, and rebates often are needed to get consumers to try a different product from the one they usually purchase. Point-of-purchase displays appeal to consumer impulse purchases; and premiums, items given or provided at a discount price, are likewise used to encourage purchases. Like each of the other aspects of marketing communications, sales promotions should be coordinated to achieve the overall marketing goal.

Direct marketing communications are, as the term suggests, efforts targeted directly to final customers. DIRECT MAIL, TELEMARKETING, e-mail, and direct-response television are popular methods of direct marketing.

Public relations are also part of marketing communications. In the last decade, U.S. businesses have increased their public-relations communications to customers, employees, DISTRIBUTION CHANNEL members, stockholders and community members. With today's electronic communications, firms can respond quickly to public concerns, rumors, and market changes. Businesses often cultivate relationships with media representatives in the hope of generating positive publicity, which is almost always more credible than paid advertising. When coordinated, effective public relations reinforce the marketing message companies want to present to consumers. The concept of marketing communications emphasizes coordination of each aspect of a firm's promotion strategy.

Further reading

Boone, Louis E., and David L. Kurtz. *Contemporary Marketing*, 10th ed. Fort Worth: Dryden Press, 2001.

marketing concept

The marketing concept is a company-wide consumer-orientation policy with the objective of achieving long-run commercial success. While this may seem like common sense, in fact the idea that a business exists to anticipate, meet, and exceed the needs of its customers is a relatively new concept in American business.

From the beginnings of the AMERICAN INDUSTRIAL REVOLUTION (1870s) to about 1925, most businesses operating in the United States (and other industrialized countries as well) focused on producing goods. Marketers refer to this as the PRODUCTION era, in which a good PRODUCT would sell itself. Prior to the 1870s, production was mostly done by small-scale craft businesses, but the Industrial Revolution brought factory systems and constant reductions in the cost of production through job specialization and ASSEMBLY LINE techniques. Manufacturers focused on reducing the cost of production, recognizing that consumers would buy more because the price was now lower. The production era is epitomized by the Henry Ford saying that customers "can have a car any color they want so long as it is black."

Eventually initial consumer DEMAND was satisfied and manufacturers recognized their products would not just sell themselves. In the 1920s, many companies adopted a sales orientation, putting salespeople on the road to convince consumers to buy what the company was producing. But selling is only one part of marketing, and eventually even a good sales force could not convince consumers to buy what they did not need or want.

Beginning in the 1950s (some companies did not catch on until much later), American businesses started focusing on customer needs, General Electric's 1952 *Annual Report* stated a new management philosophy.

[The concept] introduces the [marketer] at the beginning rather than at the end of the production cycle and integrates marketing into each phase of the business. Thus, marketing, through its studies and research, will establish for the engineer, the design and manufacturing [person], what the customer wants in a given product, what price he [or she] is willing to pay, and where and when it will be wanted. Marketing will have authority in product planning, production scheduling, and INVENTORY CONTROL, as well as in sales, distribution, and servicing of the product.

A "company-wide consumer orientation" emphasizes the fact that every job in the organization exists to meet the needs of customers. "Achieving long-run commercial success" reinforces the idea that to succeed a company has to build and maintain relationships with its customers and anticipate rather than respond to customer desires, thus recognizing the lifetime value of customers.

Further reading
Boone, Louis E., and David Kurtz. *Contemporary Marketing,* 10th ed. Fort Worth: Dryden Press, 2001.

marketing-information systems
Marketing-information systems provide a continuous flow of information designed to assist decision making. Marketing-information systems differ from MARKET RESEARCH in the fact that they are continuously updated and utilized as opposed to being designed to address a specific problem. Marketing-information systems are or should be integrated into MANAGEMENT-information systems.

Marketing-information systems typically focus on sales and customer information. Sales managers often want a monthly or quarterly report on sales by each product group, region, or salesperson. This type of information is used to determine performance, SALES PROMOTIONS, and pricing changes. In addition, information regarding sales per customer or TARGET MARKETS is used to evaluate past marketing strategies and potential growth areas.

One important use of marketing-information systems is to provide company history. With changing personnel, downsizing, and OUTSOURCING, organizations often lose the collective knowledge of past marketing efforts. A good information system can provide insights from past experiences. For example, one company sells collectible plates and figurines through advertisements in magazines; over the years, it is advertised hundreds of items in dozens of magazines. When considering new PRODUCTs, the company's marketing people search their information system for similar products and then the response rate in various magazines. When combined with the current ADVERTISING cost in those magazines and the gross margin for the item being considered, the company has reliable information to determine the likely profitability of ad placements for the new product.

Another use of marketing-information systems is CUSTOMER-RELATIONSHIP MANAGEMENT (CRM). CRM is a philosophy and process of building and maintaining relationships with customers. The more a firm knows about its customers, the better it can anticipate and meet their needs. One simple marketing-information method is a date-"tickler" system, which many salespeople use to remind them when it is time to communicate again with their customers. Dentists send reminder cards, and business send time-to-change/renew/upgrade notices. Using an information system organizes basic informa-

tion to effectively maintain customer communications and relationships.

Marketing-information systems can also be used as part of decision-support systems, which integrate, analyze, and interpret information. While a marketing-information system typically allows access to the company's database, a decision-support system allows managers to conduct statistical analyses and manipulate the database to meet their specifications. One use of the information is called data mining, or statistical analysis designed to identify patterns and relationships. With today's electronic-scanning systems, companies often have billions of pieces of information about their customers. Data mining can cluster groups of customers with similar buying patterns, identify regional changes in CONSUMER BEHAVIOR, and also track short-term changes. One story connected with the events of September 11, 2001, concerns sales at Wal-Marts around the country that day. From the first attack until about noon, sales plummeted, but in the afternoon, sales of necessities like batteries and bottled water expanded, as did sales of guns and ammunition. By the evening and next day, sales of U.S. flags had skyrocketed.

See also CUSTOMER RELATIONS/SATISFACTION; DATABASE MANAGEMENT; MARKETING STRATEGY.

Further reading
Etzel, Michael J., Bruce J. Walker, and William J. Staunton. *Marketing,* 12th ed. Boston: McGraw-Hill, 2001.

marketing strategy
Marketing strategy, part of an organization's marketing-planning process, is a firm's overall plan for selecting and meeting the needs of TARGET MARKETS. Marketing planning begins with comparing opportunities against the firm's resources, then developing objectives and strategies to meet those objectives. Tactical plans for implementation and control are used to outline how the objectives will be achieved.

When developing marketing strategies, firms spend considerable effort evaluating potential target markets—groups of buyers toward whom the firm directs its efforts. Target markets are usually defined by MARKET SEGMENTATION—division of the total market into smaller, more homogeneous groups. Different marketing strategies are developed for each market segment, which involves adjusting the firm's marketing mix: its pricing, SALES PROMOTION, PRODUCT, and distribution strategies for different groups of consumers.

For example, the primary target markets for this encyclopedia are high school and college libraries. The product is a reference book, not likely to be purchased by individuals. The publisher, Facts On File, is a major provider of reference materials for these target markets. Being a known, credible publisher will facilitate acceptance of this encyclopedia in this target market. Additionally, the publisher knows from experience what pricing strategy is appropriate and has existing promotion and distribution strategies for these markets. A second target market for this book is libraries in other countries. Because of the emphasis on institutions and organizations of American business, this book would be an excellent resource for students and businesspeople wanting to learn about U.S. business practices. For the publisher, this target market will involve evaluating a variety of marketing questions. For example, are international libraries more or less price-sensitive? How is the book promoted to international libraries, DIRECT MAIL, PERSONAL SELLING, or industry TRADE SHOWS? Would having distributors in the major countries facilitate distribution? Should the product or title be changed for different international markets?

Firms moving into international markets face the problem of GLOBALIZATION versus customization. Should the firm use strategies that treat the world as a single market or adjust for local and regional differences? Global strategies are cheaper, requiring few changes in product and promotion. Because the United States is the largest market in the world, and because U.S. BRANDS and cultural norms heavily influence consumers around the world, global marketing strategies often work for U.S. companies. But colors, symbols, and language can have different meanings in different cultures. A now-defunct U.S. airline once used a band of purple around the cockpit of their planes as part of their color scheme. In South American countries, consumers interpreted the purple band as a funeral shroud and refused to board the plane. The swastika, a reviled symbol of Nazism in Europe and the Americas, is the symbol of the four elements of the earth in Indonesia.

Recognizing cultural differences, marketers often adjust their marketing strategies for local conditions. In many countries, homes have smaller kitchens and less storage space, and U.S. companies have found that large containers at reduced per-unit costs are not accepted in many markets. Similarly, U.S. measurements and container sizes must be adjusted for ISO STANDARDS.

Nonprofit organizations also create and adapt marketing strategies. Because such groups target both clients and supporters, their marketing strategies will likely be quite different for each group. Often a difficult part of nonprofit marketing is effectively communicating with the people towards whom the organization intends to direct its efforts.

Further reading
Pride, William M., and O. C. Ferrell. *Marketing Concepts and Strategies.* Boston: Houghton Mifflin, 2000.

market intelligence (competitive intelligence, business intelligence)
Market intelligence, also referred to as competitive intelligence or business intelligence, is the information one company is able to accumulate about another based on data gathered from public sources and effective interviewing. Market-intelligence systems are used to help managers assess their COMPETITION but do not constitute corporate espionage since the ethics and legality of methods used to collect information are different. The SOCIETY FOR COMPETITIVE INTELLIGENCE PROFESSIONALS has a code of ethics that includes compliance with all laws, respect for confidentiality requests, avoiding CONFLICT OF INTEREST, and abiding by company policies.

Most major American companies have market-intelligence units monitoring and assessing information from a variety of sources about their competitors. The data gained through market intelligence and ENVIRONMENTAL SCANNING (collecting information about the external marketing environment) are used in making decisions; the goal is to become a more efficient and effective competitor. U.S. automobile manufacturers sometimes note that the first purchasers of their new cars are competitors who will then take the car apart looking for ideas, methods, and features that can be used in their PRODUCTS.

Market intelligence can be derived from a variety of sources, including

- articles written about a company
- advertisements
- published interviews with company executives
- government agencies, including PATENT, environmental, and local ZONING offices
- reporters and analysts who cover a company
- company employees
- consultants
- suppliers
- TRADE SHOWS
- direct observation of competitors' businesses
- customers
- use of "secret shoppers"
- job INTERVIEWING

Business managers use many of the above market-intelligence practices. In one survey of small businesses, discreetly observing a competitor's firm and asking suppliers and delivery people about competitors were the most widely used market-intelligence methods. The amount of information vendors can obtain about other businesses can be amazing. For example, the same trucking company often supplies appliance retailers, and printers frequently provide marketing materials for competing firms. Sales representatives always know what competitors are doing and often what their plans include.

Generally if a firm uses a method of gaining intelligence, they assume their competitors also utilize the same method; and if they use a certain method, they think it is ethical. Asking customers to solicit bids from competitors, using job interviews to learn about competitors, and hiring people away from competitors are considered the least-ethical market intelligence practices.

To reduce market-intelligence leakage, most business managers instruct their employees on not divulging company plans or procedures. Some firms disguise their marketing strategies in order to reduce competitors' knowledge of their actions. One sales representative knew his competitors were finding his prices through his customers' office staff. He sometimes would quote a price to a customer and then fax a written confirmation with a higher price. He would then follow up the fax with a call correcting the information and a second bid quotation sent by mail. Competing sales representatives sitting in customers' offices would quote a price under his faxed quotation and not understand why they were not the low bidder.

New businesses generally utilize public sources of information, including tax records, government documents, and ADVERTISING. As they become established and develop industry contacts, firms replace public-information sources with industry contacts such as sales representatives and delivery people. Frequently businesses have market-intelligence information available within their organization but fail to ask employees for it. Market-intelligence professionals know that ultimately people are the best source of information.

Further reading
Folsom, Davis. "Market Intelligence in Small Businesses," *Marketing Intelligence & Planning* 9, no. 2 (1991): 16–19; Society for Competitive Intelligence Professionals website. Available on-line. URL: www.scip.org.

market research

Market research is the development, interpretation, and communication of decision-oriented information for business managers. It is used to solve problems, identify opportunities, support promotional efforts, and improve CUSTOMER RELATIONS SATISFACTION. Market research is distinguished from MARKETING INFORMATION SYSTEMS in that it is undertaken to accomplish a specific objective, while marketing information systems provide an ongoing source of information used to make marketing decisions. Market research can be valuable to nonprofit groups as well as businesses.

Market research is often conducted to understand why sales have decreased and how consumers perceive a company's products as well as to identify new market segments, test consumers' responses to new PRODUCTS and new promotional messages, and evaluate customer satisfaction with existing products and SERVICES. Companies often use syndicated market research (research data collected by a specialist detailing industry trends) to address many issues and concerns syndicated services. Marketers of retail products subscribe to services providing monthly sales data for their own and their competitors' products by region and type of retail outlet. Other syndicated services like Nielsen and Arbitron provide television-viewer and radio-listener data,

respectively. Some market-research firms also maintain a database of U.S. consumers, allowing marketers to send samples or surveys to particular groups of consumers whose opinions and responses they are interested in.

When existing information, either within the organization or from syndicated sources, will not sufficiently answer the problem, and the problem or objective is of significant importance, market research is undertaken.

The market research process involves a seven-step procedure.

- Define the objective.
- Conduct a situation analysis.
- Conduct an informal investigation.
- Plan and conduct a formal analysis.
- Plan the sample.
- Collect the data.
- Analyze and report the data.

Market research usually is conducted for one of three objectives: learning about a market or situation, describing market segments or customer behavior, or estimating the effectiveness of a MARKETING STRATEGY or the impact of a change in the marketing environment. Situation analysis addresses the question of what is known. Often the research objective can be accomplished by conducting an informal investigation. Review of existing published studies, discussions with personnel and customers, and analysis of existing data can (and should be) utilized before launching a formal market-research analysis.

Formal market research studies can be expensive. If the problem or opportunity can be sufficiently evaluated using informal investigation, it is usually less costly and less time-consuming than conducting a full market study. After determining what information is needed, market researchers usually choose among six methods of gathering data: OBSERVATION, experimental design, PERSONAL INTERVIEW SURVEYS, TELEPHONE SURVEYS, MAIL SURVEYS, or INTERNET SURVEYS. Each method has its advantages and disadvantages.

Observation does not interfere with CONSUMER BEHAVIOR, but it sometimes requires training of observers and can be expensive and time-consuming. Consumer-behavior studies using one-way mirrors, parking lot license plate-number collection, and people-flow patterns in buildings are all common observation methods.

In experimental designs, researchers change one or more variables and measure consumers' response. Price, ADVERTISING message, lighting, and product location within a store are examples of experimental designs used by market researchers.

Personal interview surveys offer the advantage of in-depth discussion, use of open-ended questions, and observation of respondents' nonverbal responses. However, they are expensive and time-consuming, and they have the potential of interviewer bias. Telephone surveys are faster and less costly than personal interviews but limited in length, and with call screening and message machines, they may not generate a representative sample. Mail surveys are even less costly than telephone surveys, but they are slow and often result in a low response rate. This introduces the problem (called nonresponse bias) of whether those people who did not respond have different opinions from those who did. INTERNET surveys are an increasingly popular form of research but can result in a nonrepresentative sample. If a few respondents log-in and fill out the survey form repeatedly, the results will be of little use to the researcher. An old saying in market research (and in any data-collection effort) is "garbage in, garbage out."

The choice of data-collection method and the decision of what samples to take often influence each other. Ideally market researchers would like to have information from the target audience they are studying, but many times limitations restrict the sampling process. A random sample gives each member of the population an equal chance of being chosen for the survey. Random samples allow researchers to use their data to make judgments about the total population. Convenience samples (samples of readily available people such as colleagues, employees, and friends) or mall-intercept studies (random interviews with people at malls) are nonprobability samples and are not necessarily representative of the group being studied. The classic study using a convenience sample was the 1980s research by Coca-Cola regarding whether to replace the formula for Coke. Using a mall-intercept survey, researchers asked consumers which sample they liked best. Respondents chose the new formula by a small margin, but the researchers did not ask respondents whether they were Coke drinkers, and they did not say the purpose was to evaluate an alternative formula. By not sampling Coke drinkers and by not asking the right questions, Coca-Cola's research was flawed and when Coca-Cola introduced the new formula consumers were outraged.

While retailers chant the mantra "location, location, location," market researchers repeat "pretest, pretest, pretest." Researchers should pretest the survey instrument, sampling procedure, data-collection process, and data analysis. In the process, market researchers hope to avoid Murphy's Law—"if it can go wrong, it will go wrong." How the data is going to be evaluated should be established in advance, facilitating analysis and reporting of research results.

See also SURVEYS.

Further reading
Boone, Louis E., and David Kurtz. *Contemporary Marketing,* 10th ed. Fort Worth: Dryden Press, 2001.

market segmentation
Market segmentation—dividing the total market into smaller, relatively similar groups—is essential to target

marketing, in which a company's efforts are focused on meeting and anticipating the needs of those segments of the total market most likely to purchase their goods and SERVICES. No business or organization has sufficient RESOURCES to market their PRODUCTS or services to everyone. Market segmentation directs MARKETING STRATEGY to those groups who provide the best possibilities for success. It is applicable for consumer and business markets as well as for nonprofit organizations.

Four criteria are necessary for successful market segmentation.

- The market segment must have a measurable size and PURCHASING power.
- The segment must be accessible to the marketer with effective SALES PROMOTION and distribution.
- The segment must be sufficiently large enough to be profitable.
- The segment must match the firm's marketing capability.

Consumer markets are generally segmented based on DEMOGRAPHICS, geographic, psychographic, or product-related characteristics. Demographic segmentation divides consumer groups based on age, gender, occupation, education, household size, and stage in the FAMILY LIFE CYCLE. Most DIRECT MAIL promotions are targeted based on demographics; the products being promoted are geared to the gender, age, income level, or education of the recipient. For example, someone's age and stage in the family life cycle will create changing needs. In the 1980s Chrysler astutely anticipated demographic changes by developing minivans for aging baby boomers who found child car seats did not fit well in their sports cars. While Toyota had the first minivans in the U.S. market, Chrysler developed a better product to meet the needs of this changing demographic group. Anyone who announces a wedding or a birth will be inundated with marketing promotions as a result of entering a new market segment.

Geographic segmentation is simply dividing the total market based on population locations. Marketers adjust their strategies based on regions of the country and urban/suburban/rural locations. Wal-Mart, the largest U.S. retailer, grew by locating stores on the perimeters of larger towns and small cities, rather than attempting to locate within major urban areas. A favorite question in RETAILING is, "What are the three most important considerations in retailing?" The answer is "location, location, location." One firm expanding into Mexico used three different distribution strategies depending on location. In large cities it opened company stores and service centers. In smaller cities it contracted with local, independent stores to sell and service its products, while in rural areas only mail-order sales were available.

Psychographic segmentation divides consumers into groups based on psychological characteristics, lifestyles, and personal values. One common method used is ATTI-TUDES, INTERESTS, OPINIONS STATEMENTS (AIO), which segment consumer groups in a way that provides marketers with more information to better target consumers. AIO statements also help marketers to develop lifestyle profiles of customer groups, overcome consumer reservations about products, and appeal to specific segments of the market.

Product-related segmentation involves dividing the consumers into groups based on usage rates, benefits received, and loyalty to BRANDS/BRAND NAMES. Marketers of INTERNET services modify their strategies depending on whether the targeted group wants speed, reliability, or least-cost service. A common usage-rate concept in marketing is known as the 80/20 PRINCIPLE, whereby 80 percent of a company's sales come from 20 percent of its customers. Marketers who can identify the 20 percent of the customers generating the majority of their revenue will offer special SERVICES, discounts, and added attention to these groups. For example, airline companies have lounges for valued customers, allow frequent flyers to board the plane ahead of the others, and offer upgrades to heavy-user groups. Airline, hotel, and other frequent-visitor programs are also used to build and maintain brand loyalty.

Businesses that sell to other businesses (b-to-b) also use market segmentation. B-to-b marketers typically segment based on geographic area, business demographics, customer type, or end use of their products. If a firm has a limited product line or its products are not complex, it may use geographic segmentation, having one sales representative calling on all businesses in an area. Many b-to-b marketers segment based on the size of companies with executive sales representatives for large companies, and TELEMARKETING efforts for smaller companies. If the needs of one industry are unique, a company might segment by customer type. If each user of a firm's products has unique specifications, a company might group customers based on the end use of their products.

See also TARGET MARKETS.

Further reading
Boone, Louis E., and David L. Kurtz. *Contemporary Marketing*, 10th ed. Fort Worth: Dryden Press, 2001.

market-share, market-growth matrix
The market-share, market-growth matrix, created by the Boston Consulting Group, is a model used by companies to evaluate components (business units or PRODUCT groups) of their organization. This model allows firms to classify business units within the firm based on the company's market share (high or low) and industry-growth rate (high or low). Market share is the percentage of market sales a company controls. Market growth is the annual percentage growth in sales for that market category.

As shown below, the matrix classifies company components into four categories: colorfully labeled stars, cash cows, question marks, and dogs.

Stars represent high industry-growth rate and high market-share parts of a company's business. Almost every

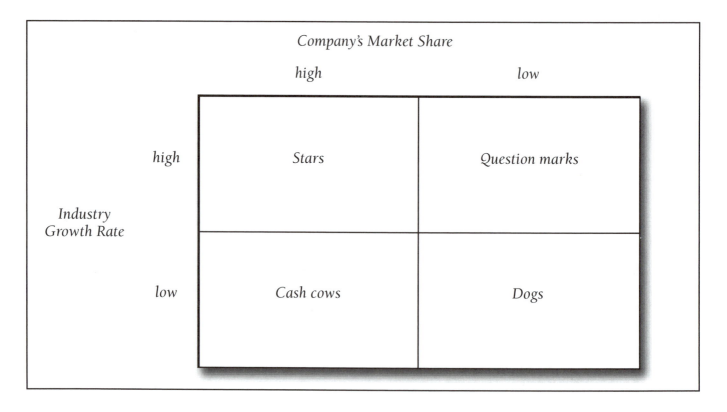

business involves more than one product. Stars are the firm's leading products with the greatest potential for growth. Like movie stars, a company's stars are pampered; additional RESOURCES are usually allocated to parts of the company that have the greatest potential to provide growth. In large CORPORATIONS, future CHIEF EXECUTIVE OFFICERS often rise through the star units of the organization.

Cash cows are parts of a company that have high market shares but are in low-growth markets; they are typically the mature parts of a company's business—i.e., well-established customers in slow-growth markets. Because cash cows provide little growth opportunities, managers "milk" the PROFITS from them to invest in other parts of the company. Most alcohol and tobacco products are mature products with slowly growing markets. The well-established companies in these markets are using the revenue from their cash cows to expand into other food and beverage markets.

Question marks, sometimes referred to as problem children, are business units with low market shares in high-growth markets. These parts of a company provide potential based on high market growth but are not currently living up to their potential. Managers closely evaluate question marks, deciding whether to invest additional resources to improve sales and profits or liquidate or divest that part of the company.

Dogs are parts of a company with low market shares and low growth. MANAGEMENT questions regarding dogs include whether this part of the company can become profitable and if not, how to get rid of it. Dogs rarely get infusions of new CAPITAL. Instead, COSTS are often cut in attempts to make this part of the business profitable.

Further reading
Etzel, Michael J., Bruce J. Walker, and William J. Staunton. *Marketing*, 12th ed. Boston: McGraw-Hill, 2001.

market structure
Virtually all businesspeople claim the markets they operate in are highly competitive. Colorful terms like *dog-eat-dog, cutthroat* COMPETITION, and *economic Darwinism* are used to describe behavior in markets. Market structure refers to models representing the degree of competition that exists in a market. Economists use the following five criteria to define four market-structure models.

- number of firms in the market
- whether the firms are acting independently or not
- presence or lack of knowledge of market conditions (prices and variations in quality)
- ease with which new competitors can enter a market
- degree to which producer's PRODUCTS are similar or different (product differentiation)

The four models of market structures are PERFECT COMPETITION, MONOPOLISTIC COMPETITION, OLIGOPOLY, and MONOPOLY.

A perfectly competitive market has many independently operating firms, consumer and producer knowledge of market conditions, ease of entry, and standardized products. Markets for agricultural products are often used as examples of perfectly competitive markets. Because of knowledge of market conditions and ease of entry, perfectly competitive markets result in lower prices, greater output, and only normal levels of PROFIT. Logically business managers prefer not to be in this type of market, which is why many firms attempt to differentiate their products from competitors' products.

Monopolistic competition is a market structure very similar to perfect competition, differing only in product differentiation rather than standardization. With product differentiation, firms gain a small degree of pricing power. If consumers perceive a product as being different from competitors' products in some positive manner, they will likely be willing to pay more for the product and less willing to switch to other products with a price increase. This allows the firm to earn above-normal profits, at least for a short period of time. Ease of entry and knowledge of market conditions prevent businesses in monopolistically competitive markets from earning long-term economic profits. Retail clothing and fast-food markets are often good examples of monopolistic competition. New variations on products and services and significant amounts of SALES PROMOTION are used in these markets in efforts to continually create product differentiation.

Oligopoly is a market structure characterized by few firms, BARRIERS TO ENTRY, and either standardized or differentiated products. Economists have developed concentration ratios to measure the market share held by firms in oligopolistic markets. Markets with only a few firms quickly recognize that each firm's actions affect the other firms in the market. This is called market interdependence, whereby each firm has to consider competitors' actions and reactions to their decisions. In oligopolies firms are reluctant to raise prices for fear that their competitors will not also do so. However, they will match price decreases because they do not want to lose customers and market share. Therefore oligopolists find price competition is not to their advantage and instead engage in nonprice competition—competing based on service, reputation, and product variations. Automobile and steel manufacturing markets in the United States are examples of oligopolies.

Monopolies are markets with only one firm because of considerable, if not overwhelming, barriers to entry. Control of a critical resource or technology can give a firm monopoly power. Because of considerable pricing power and the presence of strong barriers to entry by other firms, monopolists earn economic profits even in the long run. ANTITRUST LAWS and regulations are often used to control or reduce the power of monopolists. Local utility companies are often regulated monopolies, while firms with a PATENT for a unique product have temporary monopolies.

Markets characterized by perfect competition and monopolistic competition generally result in lower prices and greater output than those characterized by oligopoly or monopoly.

market value

The term *market value* is easy to throw into a business conversation but correspondingly difficult to define precisely. Since market value is often cited in CONTRACTS, law courts have developed a very precise definition that has been adopted in many valuation settings. The courts have ruled that market value is the probable price that a buyer and seller would agree to if

1. both the buyer and seller are acting prudently (considering their own best interest)
2. both are motivated to buy and sell
3. both are well informed and well advised about all aspects and potential uses of the property
4. neither are affected by undue stimulus or any special compulsion to buy or sell
5. the market is competitive
6. the ASSETS have had reasonable time and exposure in the market
7. the price is in terms of MONEY consideration and does not reflect the value of any extraneous factors such as seller financing or covenants not to compete

—Mack Tennyson

Marshall Plan (European Recovery Program)

To advance economic recovery in Europe following World War II, the Marshall Plan, or the European Recovery Program, was established. A draft of this plan took form in a commencement speech given at Harvard University on June 5, 1947, by U.S. Secretary of State George C. Marshall, who spoke of the importance of restoring "economic health" in order to assure "political stability" in the region. He also urged European countries to determine their economic "requirements" before the United States could proceed in supporting recovery to the area.

> The truth of the matter is that Europe's requirements . . . are so much greater than her present ability to pay that she must have substantial additional help or face economic, social, and political deterioration. . . . It would be neither fitting nor efficacious for this Government to undertake to draw up unilaterally a program designed to place Europe on its feet economically. The initiative must come from

Europe. The role of this country should consist of friendly aid in the drafting of a European program and of the later support of such a program.

World War II and its aftermath left the countries of Europe in ruins. Throughout the continent, homes, factories, INFRASTRUCTURE, and farmlands were destroyed, reduced to rubble after years of bombardment. With national economies having been diverted to the war effort, the European nations' financial systems were also devastated, and famine endangered stability.

In Eastern Europe, the Soviet Union posed another postwar threat. After the war, Germany was governed by the victorious powers of the United States, the Soviet Union, Great Britain, and France, each with its own zone of occupation. As these various sectors became increasingly expensive to maintain, the United States, Great Britain, and France merged their zones. This divided Germany in two, the Allied zone in the West and a Soviet zone in the East, a division that would last until reunification in 1990. Old, unresolved conflicts between the United States and the Soviet Union resurfaced. This discord and the growing influence of communism as well as the cold war posed further challenges for restoration efforts. It was crucial that economical, societal, and political stability be restored.

Following Secretary Marshall's commencement speech, and because the plan called for Europe to show the first initiative, Great Britain's foreign secretary, Ernest Bevin, visited the French foreign minister, Georges Bidault, in Paris. The Soviet foreign minister, Vyacheslav Molotov, also attended the meeting but returned home after five days without reaching an agreement. The Kremlin blocked Poland, Yugoslavia, Romania, and Czechoslovakia from attendance, further deepening their division with the Allies.

Bevin and Bidault invited representatives from 16 nations to meet in Paris to form a committee for European Economic Cooperation. By September 1947, with the assistance of the United States, the committee had developed a budget and drafted a planning strategy. Participating countries would work to raise agricultural and industrial production to prewar levels, reduce TRADE BARRIERS, and stabilize their domestic finances.

President Harry S. Truman convened a committee of businessmen, statesmen, and military leaders to study the Marshall Plan's merits. Upon receipt of their report, he submitted a plan to the 80th Congress, which met in January 1948. Various political events shortly thereafter threatened positive development of the plan, including a communist coup in Czechoslovakia that further hastened the debate. On April 3, 1948, President Truman signed the Foreign Assistance Act, authorizing the European Recovery Program; it became known as the Marshall Plan in honor of Secretary of State George C. Marshall, who had first suggested it.

Paul G. Hoffman was named the economic cooperation administrator to supervise the allocations. The plan called for approximately $13 billion in the form of grants and LOANS that were to be paid out over a four-year period. In addition to the financial aid, assistance was to be offered in the form of foodstuffs, building materials, machinery, and advice and expertise. Participating countries included Austria, Belgium, Denmark, France, West Germany, Great Britain, Greece, Iceland, Italy, Luxembourg, the Netherlands, Norway, Sweden, Switzerland, Turkey, Portugal, Trieste, and Iceland.

The first shipment of foreign aid was wheat, vitally needed to feed Europe's desperate refugees. Future shipments included such items as tractors for farms, coal for generators, turbines for dams, iron for locomotives, and electrical equipment for PUBLIC UTILITIES—all necessary RESOURCES to increase the productivity that would make Western Europe once again self-supporting and help bring political stability to the region.

The Marshall Plan continued through 1951 and dispensed over $12 billion in assistance. Transferred to the Mutual Security Agency in 1951, and later to other agencies, the plan's aid was extended to less-developed countries. Historians regard the program as a great success and credit the plan as a turning point toward the restoration of the democratic nations of Europe.

The plan greatly contributed to the expansion of U.S. multinational corporations (MNCs). During the Great Depression protectionist trade policies increased U.S. economic isolation. The Marshall Plan was a major reversal from those policies. The plan resulted in significant purchases of U.S. capital goods by European companies. In addition, U.S. service businesses, accounting, finance, insurance, and architecture expanded internationally with their manufacturing customers.

George C. Marshall was awarded the Nobel Peace Prize in 1953 for his part in instituting the Marshall Plan. When he accepted the award, he modestly proclaimed it was not an individual triumph and that he was merely a representative of the American people whose support and money had made the program a success.

Further reading
Donovan, Robert J. *The Second Victory: The Marshall Plan and the Postwar Revival of Europe.* New York, Madison Books, 1987; Price, Harry Bayard. *The Marshall Plan and Its Meaning.* Ithaca, N.Y.: Cornell University, 1955.

—Linda Trant Johnson

Maslow's hierarchy of needs
Psychologist Abraham Maslow formulated a theory of motivation based on humans working to meet their needs. The individual will start with efforts to meet the lowest-level basic needs and as those are met will work up to meeting the highest level of needs. This is the hierarchy of needs often referred to in relation to Maslow's theory.

According to Maslow, a human being will first work to meet basic, biological, or physiological needs, such as food and water. When these needs are met, the individual will next address safety needs, such as shelter and security. After safety needs are met, the person will work toward social needs, such as love and affection.

Robert P. Vecchio and other authors have grouped the physiological, safety, and social needs into "deficiency needs," meaning that they are based on something the person lacks. The upper two sets of needs are called "growth needs" and include esteem and self-actualization. Humans can get by without the growth needs being met, and according to Vecchio, not all people work toward the higher two levels.

If social needs have been achieved, the individual will move on to esteem needs, which are based on the view others have of him or her. High or low self-esteem generally comes from feedback received from others.

If the esteem needs are met, the person may work toward self-actualization. The concept of self-actualization (self-development and realization) is based on an individual's reaching his or her potential based on personal expectations. Few humans can reasonably be described as self-actualized, although some individuals may feel this level of satisfaction for a short time based on some major accomplishment.

The concept of the hierarchy of needs is often taught to students in MANAGEMENT so they can use it in motivating their employees. If they understand at what level of needs the person is currently operating, the manager will better understand the employee. For instance, an employee may miss work because his or her home has been destroyed in a fire and the family is in need of food and shelter. This prioritization on the employee's part would be something the manager can understand within the framework of Maslow's theory. Once the manager learns that the employee has met his or her basic needs, the manager might then be able to come up with appropriate ways to motivate the person as the employee returns to work.

Comparisons are often made between Maslow's hierarchy of needs and the motivational theories of Henry A. Murray, David McClelland, and Frederick Herzberg. According to Vecchio, all are examples of "achievement motivation theory" in that all are based on people motivated by efforts to meet needs. Herzberg's TWO-FACTOR THEORY OF MOTIVATION is the closest, with hygiene factors and motivator factors roughly corresponding to Maslow's hierarchy as described by Vecchio. The deficiency needs are the basic needs, or hygiene factors, and the growth needs are the higher-level needs, or motivator factors.

Further reading
Vecchio, Robert P. *Organizational Behavior.* Fort Worth: Dryden Press, 1991.

—Jerry Merwin and Frank Ubhaus Jr.

mass customization

Mass customization is providing customers with high-quality, competitively priced goods and SERVICES tailor-made to their specifications or needs. Mass customization attempts to deliver the ECONOMIES OF SCALE of mass PRODUCTION along with the special attention associated with custom-made PRODUCTS and services.

While marketers emphasize the fact that the customer is king or queen, businesses have often relied on a significant degree of guesswork about their customers. Clearance sales, rebates, and discounts are testimony to the lack of accurate knowledge of customer wants and needs. With the help of the INTERNET and software systems known as "choiceboards," companies are now allowing customers to design their own products.

First popularized by Dell Computer Corporation, choiceboards provide a menu of components, attributes, prices, and delivery options. Choiceboards anticipate consumer questions, offering advice and signaling when customers make questionable selections. Consumer decisions are sent directly to the firm's manufacturing center for production, reducing ordering time and allowing manufacturers to minimize inventory. Dell Computers maintains less than a week's worth of inventory at any time, reducing costs and avoiding becoming stuck with out-of-date components. Michael Dell envisions a time when companies will maintain no inventory and only produce on demand what customers order.

While mass customization generally requires use of sophisticated technology systems, the concept can be used for many nontechnology-based products. Amazon.com epitomizes customization of book selection, and service industries from banking to communications use mass customization to personalize service offerings. Proctor & Gamble created Reflect.com, allowing consumers to create customized beauty-care products, each labeled with the customer's name. Customfan allows consumers to design their own licensed apparel with choices of sizes, color, style, and graphics.

One of the important considerations in mass customization is organization-wide coordination. Mass-customization systems often require redesign of manufacturing systems. Modular production processes allow companies to quickly assemble products on demand. While Dell Computers has successfully adopted mass customization, automobile manufacturers continue to struggle.

In addition to reducing inventory levels, mass customization also provides valuable information about customers and helps build CUSTOMER LOYALTY. Marketers recognize it is almost always easier and less expensive to keep an existing customer than to try to find new customers. Mass customization provides firms with valuable information to use in anticipating their customers' future needs.

See also INVENTORY CONTROL.

Further reading
"All yours (mass customization as manufacturing trend)." *The Economist* 355, no. 8164 (1 April 2000): 57.

mass merchandising

Mass merchandising is a method of RETAILING is characterized by high-volume, fast-turnover selling of staple goods for less than conventional prices. Establishments that satisfy these selling criteria are called mass merchandisers, discount department stores, discount variety stores, general merchandise discount stores, full-line discounters, or discount "houses."

Ordinarily mass merchandisers are organized in a departmentalized format, present their merchandise in massive displays, provide minimal customer assistance within each department, and provide a centralized checkout service. Their structure is typically single-level and between 10,000 and 100,000 square feet. The "Big Three" mass merchandising chains are Wal-Mart, Kmart, and Target.

Mass merchandising emphasizes PRODUCTs whose markets are not highly segmented. Typical merchandise that is sold through mass merchandisers includes apparel, hardware, housewares, auto supplies, small appliances, toiletries, sporting goods, toys, pharmaceuticals, and electronics, as well as any product line that is in popular demand.

The discount-store industry began in the early 1900s and started to pick-up after World War II due to an increasing DEMAND for new consumer goods such as record players and television sets. In the 1960s, industry leaders as well as a standard store format were established and sales were around $2 billion. By the 1980s, Wal-Mart, Kmart, and Target dominated the industry and by the 1990s the industry surpassed $200 billion in sales.

The emergence of the mass-merchandising industry, which has relied heavily on technological advances to improve productivity and cost cutting, has had a huge impact on the financial health of full-price retailers. This trend has established a competitive environment between traditional department stores and discount retailers, resulting in a battle for market share. The August 1999 *Chain Store Age State of the Industry Supplement* sums up this scenario, noting that "discount stores continue to be in the catbird seat in the retail industry. As long as they continue to provide customers with value and quality merchandise, they will be hard to beat."

—Kirsten Gaudes

master of business administration

The master of business administration (MBA) is a graduate degree offered by American and other universities around the world. Dartmouth's Tuck School of Business created the first MBA program in 1900. In 2001 there were 344 accredited business schools in the United States, of which 188 graduated 50 or more MBA students in the previous year.

In major CORPORATIONS, the MBA is often a requirement for advancement into the upper ranks of MANAGEMENT. Many junior executives have liberal arts or technical backgrounds. As these people progress in their careers beyond their initial area of expertise and into positions supervising other workers, an MBA provides the needed skills to survive and prosper.

In the United States, MBA programs come in several varieties: full-time, part-time, executive, and on-line programs. Traditionally MBA programs were either full-time or part-time night programs. Some business schools would not accept students who did not have at least three years of business experience. Since MBA programs generally do not assume students have an undergraduate degree in business, they typically start with condensed (and intense) background courses in the basic areas of business: management, marketing, finance, economics, and accounting. Students then choose areas to study further: HUMAN RESOURCES, production management, INTERNATIONAL MARKETING, LOGISTICS, or other specialized business areas. Executive MBA programs meet less frequently than traditional programs, often for long weekends with Web-based assignments and communication in between meetings. Most MBA programs emphasize teamwork and use case study methods to train students.

There is intense competition among MBA programs for national recognition. A 2000 poll of MBA recruiters rated Dartmouth's Tuck school as the top program in the country, followed by Carnegie Mellon University, Yale University, the University of Michigan, and Northwestern University. Rounding out the top ten were Purdue University, the University of Chicago, Harvard University, Southern Methodist University, and the University of Texas at Austin. Graduates of these and other major MBA programs command starting salaries often in excess of $100,000 per year. Management consulting firms are the major recruiters of new MBA graduates, though just a few years ago start-up DOT-COMS were hiring many new MBAs.

Further reading
"The Top Business Schools," *Wall Street Journal,* 30 April 2001.

matrix management
Matrix management is the use of a different MANAGEMENT structure for each type of work environment. It combines both functional and PRODUCT-organizational structures. In matrix management, an employee may report to several managers for different projects assigned to him or her. Because employees report to more than one manager, communications skills and interpersonal skills are extremely important. By pooling employees from different areas of the organization, the matrices combine diverse expertise, skills, and abilities.

In a simple form, a matrix structure can look like the table below.

In this matrix, it is the job of customer management to ensure that the individual customer's needs are taken care of and that the customer receives the product; it is the product-management team's responsibility to design,

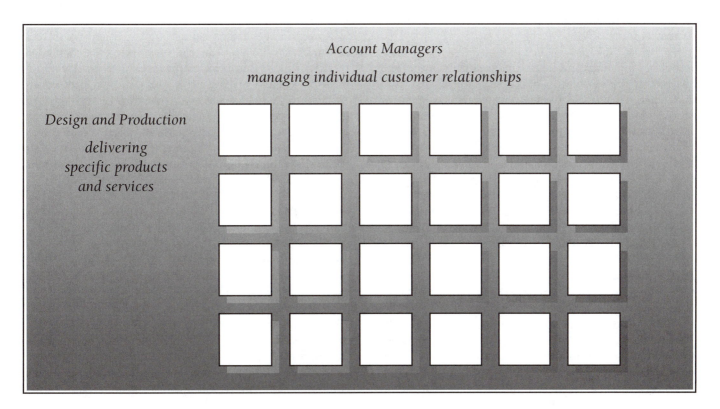

Account Managers

managing individual customer relationships

Design and Production

delivering specific products and services

research and develop the product. This type of structure aligns a product manager with a business manager in the expectation that they will work together to ensure cost-effectiveness, coordination, and productivity. In the 1960s, the U.S. Defense Department developed a project-management system requiring the coordination of components in the production of missile systems, in effect creating a matrix-management system.

There is the potential for significant conflict in a matrix-management structure, because there are overlapping lines of responsibility and reporting among groups that have different goals. Senior managers will likely need to resolve conflicts among groups involved in the matrix.

Because workers are organized in groups, it is difficult to distinguish and reward the efforts and accomplishments of individual employees. From an employee's perspective, this can impede efforts to advance in the organization. When a matrix-management structure is first implemented, management and staff have to understand that, in there will be new role relationships and difficulty adjusting to the system.

Ronald Gunn, in "Five Not-So-Easy Pieces of Matrix Management," recommends five efforts needed when implementing matrix management.

1. Clarify roles and matrix principles and methods, both within and outside of the internal service unit.
2. Clarify cross-divisional priorities and implement a streamlined forum for priority setting and resource allocation.
3. Clarify internal, cross-divisional partnership agreements.
4. Improve the response capability of internal service personnel assigned to the matrix.
5. Smooth cultural transitions involved in moving to a matrix form.

Before implementing matrix management, a thorough analysis of the advantages and disadvantages should be conducted. On the positive side, matrix management can provide integrated activities, lowered costs by eliminating the duplication of key functional activities for each product line, diversity, and quicker completion of tasks. It can also help companies adapt rapidly to changing COMPETITION and address complex problems with a multiskilled team. On the negative side, matrix management can include communication problems and conflicts among team members.

See also ORGANIZATIONAL BEHAVIOR.

Further reading
Gunn, Ronald A. "Five Not-So-Easy Pieces of Matrix Management." Available on-line URL: www.strategicfutures.com/articles/matrix/5pc-1.htm; Hellriegel, D., S. Jackson, and J. Slocum. *Management*. 8th ed. Cincinnati: South-Western Publishing, 1999; Management Learning. Available on-line URL: www.managementlearning.com/topi/mngtmtrx.html.

—Lindsay Ingram and Karin M. Cimino

mercantilism

Mercantilism was an economic theory based on the idea that national WEALTH and power could be increased through the accumulation of precious metals (primarily gold) and by maintaining a favorable TRADE BALANCE (an excess of exports over imports). Mercantilism, the dominant political and economic philosophy in Europe from the 16th and 19th centuries, evolved along with the development of Europe from feudal communities to crown-controlled nations.

In mercantilist countries, state control of commerce expanded through granting corporate charters and trading companies. The royal "one-fifth" of PROFITS from any enterprise became part of the cost of doing business. Early North American Land grants to lords proprietors by English royalty were based on enriching the monarchy. In return the crown protected business interests through its armies and navies. Since a country's wealth was associated with the amount of precious metals it acquired, mercantilist doctrine supported expansion by colonization. Colonies that produced and shipped gold and silver back to the mother country were of first importance. Other colonies were valuable only if they produced raw materials, which could then be used to create PRODUCTs for trade among European economies. In England the Navigation Acts required colonies to ship products only on British or colonial vessels, forced certain products to be sold to Britain, and required exports from European countries to pass through England. As a result, industrial production and shipping industries grew in mercantilist countries, but colonial economies had few choices and many restrictions. The famous Boston Tea Party was a response to new tax measures imposed by England on its colonies.

As economists later pointed out, rapid expansion of a country's MONEY SUPPLY can lead to INFLATION. Prices tended to rise in most European countries with each new shipment of gold and silver returning to port. Also, protectionist measures emphasizing EXPORTING over IMPORTS ignored the mutual benefits of trade based on COMPARATIVE ADVANTAGE. Later LAISSEZ-FAIRE economists, led by Adam Smith (*Wealth of Nations*, 1776), pointed out that trade, whether domestic or international, benefits both buyers and sellers.

Merchant Marine Act   See JONES ACT.

mergers and acquisitions

Mergers and acquisitions (M&As) are the joining together of two or more firms. Mergers generally bring together two similar-sized firms, while acquisitions usually involve larger firms taking control of smaller firms. In either case, the purpose of mergers and acquisitions is to increase shareholder value. When M&As are announced, company leaders typically argue the new combined companies will increase shareholders' value through synergies, the combined correlated force of the new enterprise, resulting in a more efficient and profitable operation.

Typical examples of synergies expected from mergers and acquisitions include

- ECONOMIES OF SCALE—one larger firm being able to produce at a lower cost per unit
- VERTICAL INTEGRATION—control of the means of PRODUCTION and distribution of PRODUCTS
- increased market share and power
- the acquisition of new technology
- gaining access to new customers
- increased geographic presence
- consolidation of markets

Mergers and acquisitions activity evolved out of the AMERICAN INDUSTRIAL REVOLUTION. Before the advent of the large industrial CORPORATIONS, small-business enterprises rarely merged or were acquired. Management professor David M. Schweiger states, "Since the beginning of the twentieth century, M&As have become a common part of the business landscape. During this relatively short period of time, trillions of dollars in deals have been struck and tens of millions of people have been affected." Most early mergers were "horizontal consolidations," the combination of two or more competing companies that produce the same goods and SERVICES in the same geographic area. These early mergers led to ANTITRUST LAWS and the creation of the FEDERAL TRADE COMMISSION (1914). Today, whenever a major firm in an industry announces a merger or acquisition, the announcement will include the statement "subject to antitrust approval."

Mergers and acquisitions activity gained increased public notice during the 1980s. Michael Milken, of the INVESTMENT BANKING firm Drexel Burnham Lambert, was a leader in the use of "junk BONDS" to purchase companies. These were speculative-grade high-RISK bonds backed by the ASSETS of the company being acquired. Often a company's MANAGEMENT puts up small amounts of their own CAPITAL and issues junk bonds to finance their gaining control of the company. The biggest M&A was the takeover of RJR Nabisco by the firm Kohlberg Kravis Roberts & Co. (KKR). Labeled "corporate raiders" by opponents, KKR argued managers were not doing their job and new LEADERSHIP was needed to improve the efficiency and profitability of businesses.

Mergers and acquisitions activity peaked in the United States during the late 1990s. As Schweiger reports, "From 1992 through 2000 there were eight straight record years of worldwide M&A activity." Some of the biggest M&A activity during that period included

- AOL–Time Warner
- Chevron–Texaco
- BP–Amoco–Arco

- AT&T–TCI
- SBC–Ameritech
- Sandoz–Ciba Geigy
- Bell Atlantic–GTE
- Daimler–Chrysler

The joining of Daimler-Benz AG and Chrysler Corporation to form DaimlerChrysler was a typical merger effort. At the time, the CEOs of both companies pronounced the deal as a joining of equals and that power would be shared as equals. Daimler-Benz, manufacturer of Mercedes-Benz automobiles, is known for quality products. Chrysler is known as the least-cost U.S. auto manufacturer. Combined, the two companies expected to benefit from each other's strength but have struggled in their implementation efforts.

Numerous studies have found that, M&As tend to benefit the target's SHAREHOLDERS, but not the acquirer's shareholders. . . . Studies also have shown that M&As often result in job losses, as acquirers reduce costs through elimination of redundant jobs. . . . M&As can affect employees' well-being. Increased stress, can reduce, productivity, and loyalty lead to greater absenteeism.

If M&As have been shown to be of no benefit to most acquiring companies, the obvious question is: Why do businesses pursue this activity? Many factors influenced the large amount of M&A activity during the late 1990s. M&A efforts were driven by GLOBALIZATION and the expansion of the WORLD TRADE ORGANIZATION. It was also driven by advances in technology, expanding global communications, and the ability to outsource work to least-cost areas around the globe. M&A efforts were also driven by DEREGULATION in many industries and countries and by skyrocketing STOCK MARKET prices, allowing many companies, particularly technology companies, to use shares of stock to acquire other companies.

The goal in the M&A frenzy was to create value. Value can be created by

- purchasing a target firm for less than its intrinsic, or stand-alone, value
- from synergies that can be created by integrating the firms

To evaluate a merger or acquisition, Schweiger suggests adding a variety of costs associated with the M&A. These costs include the

- acquisition premium, the portion of the purchase price that exceeds the intrinsic value of the firm
- restructuring COSTS, typically including severance benefits for workers terminated
- transactions costs and attorney, investment banker, and consultant fees
- value leakage, the loss of cash flow during M&A due to lost sales, decreased productivity, and employee turnover

Mergers and acquisitions involve what Schweiger calls "the integration process." The five stages of integration include

- strategic and financial objectives
- the transaction stage
- the transition stage
- the integration stage
- evaluation

During the strategic and financial objectives stage, companies evaluate potential candidates through discreetly collecting information through primary sources (e.g., knowledgeable personal contacts) or secondary sources (e.g., public databases and periodicals). Once contact is made with the potential firm, negotiations, DUE DILIGENCE evaluation, and analysis of integration planning and potential begin.

In the transactions stage, the two companies evaluate each other and typically sign a merger or acquisition agreement. Many colorful financial terms are associated with the transactions stage. A "friendly takeover" occurs when the company being acquired does not oppose the takeover. A "hostile takeover" occurs when the company being acquired opposes the effort. Companies opposing a takeover can use a variety of defense mechanisms. Shareholder amendments can block potential takeovers and companies can swallow a "poison pill" to make the acquisition unattractive. POISON-PILL STRATEGIES can come in many varieties, but all alter the financial position of the company being acquired. Another strategy is known as the "white knight" suitor, whereby the company being acquired sells itself to another firm, sometimes perceived as saving the company from an unacceptable suitor.

Once a merger or acquisition has been completed, the transition stage begins. During this stage, decisions are made regarding the new structure of the combined business, what parts to integrate and what to allow to remain unchanged, and implementation strategies and time lines are determined. As Schweiger states, "No matter how well transition planning was conducted, many elements cannot be forecasted accurately. Executives and managers must therefore be prepared to make adjustments to plans as events change." In other words, like a marriage, mergers and acquisitions contain many surprises. In fact, Schweiger reports, "Various consulting firms have also estimated that from one-half to two-thirds of M&As do not live up to the financial expectations of those transacting them. . . . One study even estimated that the merger and acquisition failure rate is equivalent to the divorce rate in the United States!"

During the evaluation stage, the merged firms address the question, "Did it work?" Often it has not lived up to expectations, leading to portions of the company being sold off. With the deflation of the dot-com bubble in spring 2000, followed by the RECESSION in 2001, M&A activity dropped precipitously. As the *Wall Street Journal*

reported, "there was no market. You couldn't sell a company. . . . Better to not do a deal rather than do a deal that winds up looking stupid." While M&A activity has remained slow, it will probably pick up again as market conditions change.

See also SYNERGY.

Further reading
Reed, Stanley Foster. *The M&A Deskbook*. New York: McGraw Hill, 2001; Schweiger, David M. "Merger Right." *Business and Economic Review*, April–June 2002; Whitman, Janet. "No Deal: M&A activity among small firms plunged last year. Is it poised for a turnaround?" *Wall Street Journal*, 27 March 2002.

metropolitan statistical area
A metropolitan statistical area (MSA) is freestanding area with an urban center containing at least 50,000 people and a total MSA population of 100,000 or more. The U.S. CENSUS BUREAU defines and identifies MSAs, which are frequently used by marketers in developing geographic segmentation strategies. Because MSAs are freestanding areas (surrounded by rural areas), they generally contain residents with similar social and economic characteristics. This allows marketers to develop specific marketing strategies for a large, homogeneous, geographically isolated group of consumers. Peoria, Illinois, and Moorhead, Minnesota, are examples of MSAs.

In addition to MSAs, the Census Bureau also defines CMSAs, Consolidated Metropolitan Statistical Areas; and PMSAs, Primary Metropolitan Statistical Areas. A CMSA is a major population concentration. The United States has 25 CMSAs, including New York, Los Angeles, and Chicago. A CMSA contains at least two PMSAs, which are urbanized counties or clusters of counties with strong internal social and economic links, and close ties to other urban areas. For example, Nassau and Suffolk Counties are part of New York's CMSA.

Many retail companies use geographic data including MSAs, PMSAs, and CMSAs as a starting point for locating new outlets. For example, a retail discount store like Wal-Mart or Kmart, from past marketing experience, may know that to support a new store, they need at least 50,000 residents within a 10-mile radius with an average annual INCOME of at least $20,000.

See also MARKETING STRATEGY.

Further reading
Boone, Louis E., and David L. Kurtz. *Contemporary Marketing*, 10th ed. Fort Worth, Tex.: Dryden Press, 2001; U.S. Census Bureau website. Available on-line. URL: www.census.gov.

microeconomics
Microeconomics is the study of decision making by individuals and businesses. Microeconomics includes the

study of resource allocation, output decisions, and pricing by businesses; how businesses respond to COMPETITION; and the different types of competitive environments within which businesses operate. It also includes the behavior of individuals and households; their CONSUMPTION decisions; response to price changes; and the impact of changes in WEALTH and expectations on consumer decisions.

In studying microeconomics, economists use a variety of concepts, including DEMAND and SUPPLY schedules, ELASTICITY OF DEMAND, marginal COSTS, fixed and variable costs, EQUILIBRIUM, marginal revenue, and PROFIT MAXIMIZATION. Demand schedules represent the law of demand, an inverse relationship between price and quantity demanded by consumers in a market in a period of time. Supply schedules represent the law of supply, a positive relationship between price and quantity supplied by producers in a market in a period of time. Elasticity of demand measures the sensitivity or responsiveness of quantity demanded to a price change. Marginal cost is the additional cost, or change in total cost, due to producing one more unit of output. Fixed COSTS are costs that do not change when output changes, while variable costs change as output increases or decreases. Marginal costs are variable costs. Equilibrium is the price at which quantity demanded equals quantity supplied in a market. It is often called the "market clearing" price. Marginal revenue is the change in total revenue from the production and sale of an additional unit of output. Profit maximization is the level of output at which a business realizes the greatest positive difference between total revenue and total cost. Profit maximization also occurs when marginal revenue equals marginal cost.

Most microeconomic activity takes place in markets. MARKET STRUCTURES vary from PERFECT COMPETITION to monopolies. Perfectly competitive markets are characterized by many knowledgeable buyers and sellers, operating independently, producing the same product with ease of entry. At the other extreme, a MONOPOLY is a market with one producer, BARRIERS TO ENTRY, and no close substitutes. Businesses in perfectly competitive markets have no market power and are referred to as "price takers," while monopolists have full market power and are called "price makers." Microeconomics includes the study of how businesses behave under varying market conditions. Most markets are characterized by either MONOPOLISTIC COMPETITION (many producers but differentiated products) or oligopolies (a few interdependent firms whose actions influence those of their competitors).

Microeconomics also includes resource market behavior, in which individuals and households are the source of supply (labor, land, and CAPITAL) and businesses are the source of demand. Microeconomic analysis can be used to predict prices, output, profitability, and resource allocation. The impact of taxes, subsidies, barriers to entry, and social policies can also be predicted using microeconomics.

See also OLIGOPOLY.

Further reading
Boyes, William, and Michael Melvin. *Microeconomics*, 5th ed. Boston: Houghton Mifflin, 2001.

middle managers
Middle managers are the people in an organization whose authority and LEADERSHIP lie below top MANAGEMENT and above first-level supervisors. In traditional settings, the middle manager is responsible for developing operational plans and procedures to implement the broader goals, objectives, and strategies of top management.

After World War II, middle managers were considered to be one of the driving forces behind the economic success of the major industries in the United States. Companies like US Steel and Ford Motor Company had hierarchical management structures. Middle managers were often promoted from the ranks of the workers, had operational experience, and could translate the directives of top management into activities to be carried out by front-line workers. A good analogy used to describe the middle manager was "the neck" that connects "the body" (the line worker) to "the head" (the policy-making top manager).

With industrial GLOBALIZATION in the 1970s, experts brought the "team approach" from Japan to the management circles of the United States. Instead of middle managers, there were "team leaders," usually technically skilled but inexperienced managers who were promoted from the ranks. The middle manager thus became the first person to be downsized in the flatter, leaner organizations of the 1980s. Considered obsolete, middle managers were labeled as saboteurs of change in many organizations. In the 1980s and 1990s, heavy industry was replaced by high-tech industry as the foundation of the U.S. economy. These high-tech companies favored "flat" organizational structures, which have in fact proven to be less efficient. In the late 1990s, top-level managers were often heard saying, "There's nobody around here who knows how to get things done!"

There is now a new respect for the middle manager. Many organizations are structured around teams, and the middle manager's leadership skills have become increasingly important. Many middle managers have new titles like "business leader," and their value in the leaner, flatter organizations of today comes from a unique knowledge base and ability to integrate strategic and operating-level information. With high turnover in the upper levels of management, middle managers tend to be keepers of "institutional memory." Leading from the middle, these managers are closest to the front lines as well as the customers. With their understanding of the problems and challenges of change, they can communicate objectively with the upper levels of management and offer insight into how to solve problems. This ability to communicate across the organization is a major strength of the middle manager's role, especially in times of change and economic stress.

Further reading
Floyd, Steven W., and Bill Woolridge. *The Strategic Middle Manager: How to Create and Sustain Competitive Advantage.* San Francisco: Jossey-Bass Publishers, 1996; Huy, Quy Nguyen. "In Praise of Middle Managers," *Harvard Business Review* 79, no. 8 (September 2001): 72–80.

—Katherine May

minimum wage

The minimum wage is based on a federal law that sets the lowest wage an employer can pay an employee. In the United States, the FAIR LABOR STANDARDS ACT (FLSA), passed in 1938 and amended many times since then, is a major labor-management law regulating wages. The act, which also contains directives regarding hours, child labor, equal pay, and overtime pay, entitles covered employees to a specified minimum wage and a time-and-a-half rate for work exceeding 40 hours per week.

One of the critical and complicated aspects of the FLSA is the question of who is covered by the act. Generally employees paid by the hour for businesses engaged in interstate commerce or that produce goods and SERVICES for interstate commerce are covered by the act. Federal employees were added to coverage under the act in 1974, but most executive, administrative, and professional personnel are exempt from coverage. Whether or not an employee is covered is important in determining which workers can be expected to work beyond 40 hours per week without compensation and which employees must be compensated.

When first legislated, the federal minimum wage was $.25 per hour; in 1998 it was raised to $5.15. The intent of the minimum-wage law was to help poor working people. Economists are in constant disagreement about whether minimum-wage laws achieve this objective. Generally, PRICE FLOORS (a minimum wage is a price floor in LABOR MARKETS) above the prevailing wage cause a surplus in labor markets. If a minimum-wage law raises the market price for labor, there will be less quantity demanded (employers hiring workers) and greater quantity supplied (people willing to work for the new, higher wage), resulting in a surplus.

The idea that minimum wages result in more unemployed people assumes the prevailing market wage was lower than the new minimum wage. Even during the 1990s' economic expansion in rural and higher-UNEMPLOYMENT areas, the prevailing wage was close to the minimum wage. In these labor markets, increasing the minimum wage reduced the number of workers hired, but those still working received a greater INCOME. Opponents of minimum-wage laws suggest that in this situation the government forced a transfer of income from those who lost their jobs to those who remained employed at the higher wage.

If, instead, the prevailing wage is higher than the minimum wage, it will have no impact on the market for workers. Throughout most of the 1990s' market expansion, most urban and suburban area employers had to pay more than $5.25 per hour to find workers. At upscale, labor-short Hilton Head Island, South Carolina, many fast-food chains closed early because they could not find workers, even at $8.00–$9.00 per hour. In any market where the price of labor is expensive, employers are encouraged to substitute alternative RESOURCES when possible. Fast-food companies purchase technology to reduce and replace workers. Some companies outsource low-skilled operations to other areas of the country and even other parts of the world where the cost of labor is less than in the United States.

One of the issues associated with the minimum-wage debate is: "Who benefits from increasing the minimum wage?" Most full-time workers are paid more than the federal minimum wage. In the United States, it is primarily part-time working adults who are paid the minimum wage. This group includes second-income earners, retirees, and teenagers. Opponents of increasing the minimum wage argue that increases do not go to working poor people. University of Chicago economist George Stigler reportedly told the story of the farmer who thought sick pigs tended to have straight tails. The farmer tried to cure them by chopping off their tails. By analogy, Stigler suggested, raising the minimum wage addresses the symptom of low pay but not the cause. Generally employee pay is based on the value of the output produced by the worker, the worker's marginal revenue product. Efforts to increase worker productivity would then be likely result in increased income.

Nevertheless, social advocates argue that workers should be paid a living wage, pay that is high enough to provide a basic STANDARD OF LIVING and would vary depending on the cost of living in each community.

Further reading
Coons, James W. "Minimum Wage: a Tail of Two Cities," *ABA Banking Journal* (June 1996): 17; Mallor, Jane P., A. James Barnes, Thomas Bowers, Michael J. Philips, and Arlen W. Langvardt. *Business Law and the Regulatory Environment,* 11th ed. Boston: McGraw-Hill, 2001.

mission statement

A mission statement is a business or organization's declaration of purpose—i.e., why they exist. It generally defines the key values and guiding principles for the organization. Written for a variety of audiences, including customers, employees, and investors, statements are usually short (30–60 words) and describe the organization's TARGET MARKET, philosophy, and public image. They should avoid the use of company or industry jargon, be simple to understand, and identify the organization in a unique way. Many MANAGEMENT specialists recommend beginning a firm's STRATEGIC PLANNING process with development of a mission statement and then conducting ENVIRONMENTAL SCANNING, followed by prioritizing goals and objectives.

A mission statement differs from a vision statement in that a vision statement portrays what the organization is striving to become, pushing it toward a future goal. A mission statement directs current organizational planning and efforts. A good statement is used as a guiding force to determine an organization's goals and directions and can be used to direct and redirect a firm's resources. During the ECONOMIC GROWTH of the 1990s, many U.S. businesses expanded into new markets and new products, often moving away from their core competency (the things that they did well and their initial reasons for creating a business). Mission statements help to reinstate direction.

Mission statements are applicable for individuals, organizations, and CORPORATIONS. Nonprofit organizations can benefit from the development of a mission statement to use in defining and directing the group's charitable activities. Developing a mission statement before creating a corporate website, can be useful determining its purpose—i.e., ADVERTISING, information, sales, or building customer relationships. Critics, however, contend mission statements are expensive exercises that result in a framed wall-hanging read by visitors in a company's waiting area but are rarely utilized in management decision making.

Further reading
Drohan, William M. "Writing a Mission Statement," *Association Management* 51 (January 1999); 117.

mixed economy

A mixed economy is an economic system containing both state and private control of RESOURCES and output. Political-economic systems can be characterized along a continuum ranging from pure SOCIALISM to laissez-faire CAPITALISM. In a purely socialistic economy, all resources are controlled collectively, usually by a government. In a LAISSEZ-FAIRE system, almost all resources are privately owned.

Every country in the world operates under the conditions of a mixed economy, with differences being the degree of government control of resource decisions. In the United States, the federal government controls a little over 20 percent of the country's economic activity through taxes (which are then used to purchase goods and SERVICES). In most Scandinavian countries, government spending represents about 40 percent of total national economic activity; the difference is that in Scandinavian countries, health care is a public good and education is almost a public expenditure. In many countries, natural resources, PUBLIC UTILITIES, and transportation systems are developed and controlled by government.

Until it was returned to Chinese control, Hong Kong often exemplified the laissez-faire economic system. Cuba and North Korea are examples of highly centralized economies, but in recent years Cuba has encouraged foreign private INVESTMENT, particularly in resort developments.

Model Business Corporation Act

The Model Business Corporation Act (MBCA), 1950 is a model statute created by the AMERICAN BAR ASSOCIATION for adoption by state legislatures. The MBCA, as revised, is the basis for corporate law in most states. California, New York, and Delaware (a state attractive to many businesses because of its INCORPORATION laws) do not follow the MBCA.

The MBCA includes numerous important legal issues associated with creating and managing CORPORATIONS in the United States. According to the authors Bruce D. Fisher and Michael J. Phillips, the act is considered supportive of MANAGEMENT power "at the expense of corporate SHAREHOLDERS and creditors." Among many provisions in the MBCA is the requirement that corporations designate registered agents, who act as their legal representatives. Many times companies incorporate in states where tax laws and incorporation statutes are least costly but then operate in other states. The registered-agent requirement allows creditors to find and file litigation against companies through these agents. The act also defines when a company begins to exist—that is, when the public official issues the certificate of incorporation. It also addresses LIABILITY for preincorporation CONTRACTS made by the corporation's promoter.

Several important aspects of the MBCA concern the definition of the BOARD OF DIRECTORS' activities as well as their responsibilities to shareholders, and corporate officers. The MBCA declares that the board of directors are the corporate managers, fixes the number of members on the board, and grants the first board authority to manage the company until the shareholders meet to elect a board. The act also lists the steps involved in incorporating a business and outlines the contents of corporate articles of incorporation and BYLAWS and addresses problems of CONFLICT OF INTEREST when board members engage in transactions with the company, indemnification of directors, and shareholders' rights.

Further reading
Fisher, Bruce D., and Michael J. Phillips. *The Legal, Ethical and Regulatory Environment of Business,* 8th ed. Cincinnati: Thomson/South-Western, 2003; Mallor, Jane P., A. James Barnes, Thomas Bowers, Michael J. Philips, and Arlen W. Langvardt. *Business Law and the Regulatory Environment,* 11th ed. Boston: McGraw-Hill, 2001.

modern portfolio theory

In 1952 Yale professor Harry Markowitz published a study now regarded as the origin of the modern portfolio theory (MPT). His work revolutionized the INVESTMENT world and won him a Nobel Prize.

According to Dr. Markowitz, RISK was as important as return. Investors, considering the risk/return tradeoff, had a higher probability of making more money over the long term. Before this concept was revealed, investors generally measured the desirability of an investment solely by its expected return in the short term. They subsequently used the new discovery to construct better portfolios. If risk versus return could be calculated, then ASSETS could be distributed in a way that could maximize returns and minimize RISK for various investors' unique goals.

In modern portfolio theory, return is measured by a percentage gain over a period of time; risk is measured by the percentage of fluctuation (or deviation) from the particular investment's average rate of return. A good investment might demonstrate a return of 20 percent and a standard deviation of 15 percent. A less-desirable investment might have a 10-percent return and a 20-percent standard deviation. If the risk/return characteristics of various investments are known, then the MPT practitioner should be able to find the optimum mixture of assets for the client's objectives, providing the highest possible return for the amount of risk the client could accept.

The MPT framework has created the following terminology.

- *capital asset pricing model,* the investment equation that establishes the expected return link to the risk of the investment (beta)
- *capital market line,* a graph showing the risk/reward relationship for a portfolio of risky assets when combined with a risk-free asset
- *efficient frontier,* a graph that represents various combinations of assets plotted so that a maximum expected return is shown for each incremental risk level
- *optimal portfolio,* the portfolio that maximizes an investor's expected return within the investor's given level of acceptable risk
- *security market line,* a graph showing the relationship between "systematic risk" and return for investment

—Rick Lockett

monetary policy

Monetary policy is controlling the MONEY SUPPLY to achieve policy makers' goals. Most often these goals include ECONOMIC GROWTH with stable prices. In the United States, the primary goal of monetary policy is to attain and maintain price stability. Monetary policy is based on monetarism, a school of macroeconomic thought emphasizing the impact of changes in the SUPPLY of MONEY on the aggregate economy. Monetarism is closely associated with economic thought from the University of Chicago, most notably with the Nobel Prize winner Milton Friedman.

Monetary theory and policy is based on the quantity theory of money, expressed by the equation $MV = PQ$, where M = money supply, V = velocity of money, the average number of times each dollar is spent on final goods and services in a year, P = price level, and Q = the quantity of output (real GROSS DOMESTIC PRODUCT [GDP]).

According to the quantity theory, if the velocity of money (V) is constant (an economic assumption), then changes in the money supply (M) will cause changes in the price level (INFLATION or DEFLATION) and/or changes in real output in the economy (Q). If the money supply is increased, it will result in an increase in nominal GDP. If an economy is already operating at maximum output (potential GDP), an increase in M will result in an increase in P, inflation. If, instead, the economy is operating at less than potential GDP, an increase in the money supply will cause an increase in Q and/or an increase in P.

During the 1950s, KEYNESIAN ECONOMICS, based on the ideas of John Maynard Keynes, dominated macroeconomic theory. Keynesian theory emphasized aggregate DEMAND, the spending on goods and services in an economy by households, businesses, and government. Keynesians argued that during a RECESSION, government should step in as a source of aggregate demand to stimulate the economy (FISCAL POLICY). During the GREAT DEPRESSION, Franklin Roosevelt's "New Deal" administration followed Keynes's recommendations by becoming an employer of last resort, implementing a variety of programs known as the alphabet agencies, including the WPA (WORKS PROGRESS ADMINISTRATION) and CCC (CIVILIAN CONSERVATION CORPS).

Modern Keynesian economists (also known as neo-Keynesians) recommend using the monetary policy, in addition to fiscal policy, to influence the level of aggregate demand. Keynesians believe increases in the money supply will primarily affect aggregate demand by decreasing INTEREST RATES and stimulating INVESTMENT. This is known as the "Keynesian transmission mechanism."

Monetarists believe monetary policy has a powerful impact on an economy, much more than just affecting investment, and also suggest when and how much monetary policy will impact an economy are difficult to predict. Due to these uncertainties, most monetarists advocate a monetary rule—an agreed-upon constant rate of increase in the money supply—suggesting that, since the primary function of money is to facilitate exchanges, and more money is needed as an economy grows, a constantly rising money supply equal to the growth rate in the economy will fuel economic growth without fueling inflation.

Policies regarding the control of the money supply are often referred to as "tight money" or "easy money" plans. Generally the goal of American monetary policy makers is to increase the money supply, but the question is the rate at which to do this. To increase the money supply, monetary authorities (in the United States, the Federal Open Market Committee of the FEDERAL RESERVE SYSTEM, known as the Fed) have three tools: RESERVE REQUIREMENTS, DISCOUNT RATE, and OPEN-MARKET OPERATIONS.

Like a builder changing construction plans, changing the discount rate—the rate charged by the Federal Reserve to member banks for short-term LOANS—is a Fed signal that encourages or discourages banks to make more loans. Changing the reserve requirement, the percentage of bank deposits (liabilities) a bank is required to keep on reserve, is a powerful but rarely used tool of monetary policy. In construction it would be analogous to bringing in the heavy equipment to weed a flowerbed. Increasing the reserve requirement would reduce a bank's reserve funds, drastically reducing their ability to make loans and slowing the rate of growth in the money supply.

The Fed's most frequently used tool to implement monetary policy is open-market operations, the buying and selling of government BONDS in order to increase and decrease the nation's money supply. People often think money consists of only coins and currency, but money is anything people will accept as a means of payment. For example, most Americans pay for a majority of their purchases using checks. Checking-account balances, called demand deposits, are money.

People also think that the government is printing more money, but in fact money is created in the BANKING SYSTEM. The process of banks creating money is called the deposit-expansion multiplier. The deposit-expansion process begins with an open-market operation in which the Fed buys bonds from a bank, paying it by an electronic transfer of funds called an injection. The bank now has more funds, a portion of which it has to keep in reserve (the reserve requirement). The bank would not have agreed to sell the bond to the Fed unless it had something better to do with the funds, i.e., loan them to a customer, which is done by either giving the customer a check or adding the loan amount to the customer's checking account. This new checking-account balance is money.

Customers usually borrow money in order to buy things, which they pay for by writing checks. Their checks are deposited in the accounts of the businesses they paid. This adds to those businesses' checking-account balances, and they will write checks to workers and other businesses to pay for the materials that went into producing the products they sold. These checks will become additions to workers' and vendors' checking-account balances. This process will repeat itself quite rapidly through the economic system. Each time new money is deposited, the bank receiving it will hold a portion, the reserve requirement, and then lend most of the rest of the funds.

The amount of money created by the Fed's initial injection of funds is expressed by the equation $1/(reserve\ requirement\ ratio) \times amount\ of\ initial\ injection$.

Until the late 1980s, monetary policy was primarily followed by WALL STREET investors. Once, in the mid-1980s, a rumor spread among Wall Street traders that then-Federal Reserve Chairman Paul Volcker had suffered a heart attack. The STOCK MARKET fell precipitously, and Mr. Volcker, who was well and in a meeting, came out before news cameras to announce, like Mark Twain, "The reports of my death are premature!"

In the last decade, monetary policy has become widely recognized and even closely followed by individuals, investors, and policy makers. Alan Greenspan, chairman of the Fed since 1987, has become a well-known near-celebrity to Americans. Often referred to as the second most powerful person in Washington, Mr. Greenspan is widely credited with managing a 10-year-plus period of sustained economic growth. Many people refer to the Fed chairman as the most important individual affecting the U.S. economy, a statement implying the significance of monetary policy.

Further reading
Miller, Roger Leroy. *Economics Today*. Boston: Addison Wesley, 2001.

money

Money is anything people will accept as a means of payment for goods or services. Money's primary function is to facilitate exchanges and is infinitely easier to use than BARTER, which requires one person to want what another person has to offer in exchange. To find a person who is willing and able to make a barter exchange often takes considerable time and effort. Money allows producers to sell to any customer wanting their PRODUCT and then buy from other producers. It also allows people to retain their purchasing power during the time between they sell goods and make other purchases.

In addition to serving as a medium of exchange, money serves as a unit of account, store of value, and unit of deferred payment. Relative values are measured by the price of various goods; money serves as the unit of account. It is simpler to say something costs $10 than it is to say it cost 10 chickens or five goats. The store-of-value function allows producers and consumers to defer their purchases. Of course, during periods of high inflation, money's purchasing power can decrease rapidly, and as a result, it does not serve well as a store of value during periods of high INFLATION. Money also serves as the standard of deferred payment. Debt obligations are assessed in terms of money owed and interest payments due to the creditor.

In the United States, many different commodities and tokens have served as money. In the prerevolutionary period, Native American groups used wampum, made from the shells of a type of clam, to make exchanges. Some nations specialized in drilling holes in clamshells so they could be strung together as beads. In 1637 the Massachusetts Colony declared white wampum as legal tender, which meant colonists could pay their taxes and make other exchanges using clamshells. European immigrants brought with them steel drills, which allowed colonists to create and expand the supply of wampum, causing a dramatic decrease in its value.

Early Virginia residents paid taxes in the form of hogsheads of tobacco; while in South Carolina, indigo and rice served as a means of payment. In many areas furs, wheat, and maize were exchanged. In New England, fish served as money to some degree, but because it was perishable, fish was not an effective store of value.

During the British colonial period, there was a chronic shortage of coins. In addition to British coins, Spanish, French, and Portuguese gold and silver coins all freely circulated in the colonies. The shortage was so drastic that in 1775 North Carolina declared 17 different forms of money as legal tender. While many different commodities were used as a medium of exchange, the common unit of account was British pounds, shillings, and pence.

In 1690 Massachusetts became the first American colony to issue paper currency. The colony issued notes ("bills of credit") to pay soldiers involved in an expedition to Quebec; the notes promised payment in gold or silver and could be used to pay taxes. Unfortunately for the colonial government, the expedition returned before the government had secured sufficient reserves to convert the notes, causing significant disgruntlement among the soldiers and a market discount on the face value of the notes.

Other colonies also experimented with paper currency. Tobacco notes, certificates indicating the quality and quantity of tobacco deposited in a warehouse, circulated as currency throughout Virginia in the 18th century, and Benjamin Franklin became printer for notes issued by the Pennsylvania Land Bank. Eventually the British government restricted the rights of colonies to issue paper currency.

The American Revolution ended British control over money in the former colonies, and the new American government issued Continentals, a paper currency, to pay for the war. By the end of the revolution a Continental was worth one-tenth of one percent of its nominal value, sparking the phrase "not worth a Continental."

The new Congress chartered the Bank of North America in 1781, which was followed by the creation of several state banks. Financial chaos and conflict after the end of the revolution led to the creation of a national currency, replacing state-issued currency. Banking was a hotly debated topic in the new, independent America. Alexander Hamilton led the argument for a strong central bank and establishing the new government's financial credibility, while Thomas Jefferson led the advocates of state control over banking and the issuing of paper money. The first national bank, the Bank of the United States, was forced to close in 1805 when its 20-year charter was not renewed.

The U.S. Civil War led to the creation of two currencies. The Union government issued "greenbacks," which were not convertible into gold or silver but were authorized as legal tender for most purposes. Greenbacks lost some of their value but were obviously worth more than the currency issued by the defeated Confederate government. A scene in the classic American film *Gone With the Wind* shows Scarlet O'Hara visiting Rhett Butler in a Union prison after the war. She has come to beg for money to save her family plantation, Tara, because her patriotic husband bought Confederate—and now worthless—war BONDS. Rhett, on the other hand, is well off because he kept his ASSETS in gold and silver.

After the Civil War, the United States used both gold and silver as money, but by 1873 gold had replaced silver as the standard money measure. The lawyer William Jennings Bryan eloquently but ineffectively argued for a bimetal standard, trying to support silver and silver-mining interests. In the late 19th century, checks replaced coins and paper currency as the primary form of money in the United States. Banks, of course, issued checks, and, after a series of bank failures, the U.S. Congress created the FEDERAL RESERVE SYSTEM (known as the Fed) in 1913.

The Federal Reserve System, the nation's central bank, supervises banking practices, manages the amount of credit available in the BANKING SYSTEM, and issues Federal Reserve Notes, today's paper currency. Early Fed leadership was widely criticized for contracting the supply of money during the STOCK MARKET collapse in 1929, contributing to the subsequent severe decline in the U.S. economy called the GREAT DEPRESSION. More recent Fed leaders are credited with effective control of the MONEY SUPPLY and contributing to the economic expansion throughout the 1990s.

Further reading

Davies, Roy. "Money in North American History." Available online. URL: http://www.ex.ac.uk/~Rdavies/arian/northamerica.html.

money markets   See CAPITAL MARKETS, MONEY MARKETS.

money supply

The money supply in an economy is all the MONEY held by the nonbank public at any point in time and is important in the determination of MONETARY POLICY. Money is anything people will accept as a means of payment. Most consider the money supply to be the sum of all the coins and currency circulating in the economy, but in fact money is anything accepted as a medium of exchange. In today's "cashless" society, most people make a majority of their purchases using checks and CREDIT CARDS rather than hard currency. Credit cards are not considered money because they are in effect LOANS, allowing purchases based on credit that will probably be paid in the near future with a check.

The FEDERAL RESERVE SYSTEM (known as the Fed) defines, measures, and controls the money supply in the U.S. economy. As technology and new forms of money have changed, they have adjusted their definitions of the money supply. Currently the Fed uses three measures of the money supply, referred to as monetary aggregates M1, M2, and M3. The narrowest definition of money, M1, includes currency, checking-account balances (often referred to as demand deposits), other checkable balances, and traveler's checks. All of these ASSETS are readily used as mediums of exchange. Currency is simply coins and Federal Reserve notes. Demand deposits are usually business checking-account balances drawing no interest. Other checkable deposits are checking-account balances that pay interest, including negotiable order of withdrawal (NOW) accounts and various other consumer checking accounts with banking institutions. Traveler's checks are a minor part of the M1 measure of the money supply. As of December 1999 the total M1 measure was $1,092.3 billion, as follows.

M1 Component	$ billions
Currency	460.1
Traveler's checks	8.3
Demand deposits	376.7
Other checkable deposits	247.2
Total	1,092.3

The M2 measure equals the M1 plus other assets that are considered "near money." These assets generally cannot be used for payment but can be quickly converted into liquid assets accepted as a means of payment. Small-denomination TIME DEPOSITS (certificates of deposit for $100,000 or less), savings deposits, money-market deposit accounts, and money market MUTUAL FUNDS are part of the M2 monetary aggregate. As of December 1999, the M2 measure was

M2 Component	$ billions
M1	1,092.3
Small-denomination time deposits	953.2
Savings deposits and money-market deposit accounts	1,604.5
Money-market mutual funds (non-institution)	702.4
Total	4,412.3

The M3 measure includes the M2 and adds other less-liquid financial assets, as listed below for December 1999.

M3 Component	$ billions
M2	4,412.3
Large-denomination time deposits	624.4
Money-market mutual-fund shares (institution)	511.6
Term repurchase agreements	283.4
Term Eurodollars	150.7
Total	5,982.5

Large-denomination time deposits are certificates of deposit (CDs) of $100,000 or more. Money-market mutual-fund shares are of mutual funds invested in money market (short-term) instruments. Money-market mutual funds shares held by individuals are reported in the M2 measure, while those held by institutions are reported in the M3 measure. Term repurchase agreements (repos) are arrangements by which the Federal Reserve or another financial institution purchases securities with the understanding that the seller will repurchase them in a short period of time, usually a week. Repurchase agreements provide liquidity in the financial system. Term Eurodollar agreements are similar repurchase agreements involving U.S. dollars deposited in foreign banks outside the United States or in foreign branches operating in the country.

The Federal Reserve studies changes in the money supply and other measures when making monetary policy. The Federal Open Market Committee tends to focus on the M2 and M3 measures. Usually the Fed sets a quarterly targeted range for growth in the money supply, and then, through OPEN-MARKET OPERATIONS, increases or decreases the supply of reserves in the BANKING SYSTEM. Increasing the reserves available in the banking system allows banks to expand their lending activity and in the process create new checking-account balances, expanding the money supply.

Further reading

Mishkin, Frederic S. *The Economics of Money, Banking and Financial Markets*, 6th ed. Boston: Addison Wesley, 2001.

monopolistic competition

Monopolistic competition is a MARKET STRUCTURE in which there are many producers of differentiated products and ease of entry into the market. Monopolistic competition is similar to PERFECT COMPETITION, but with each firm selling slightly different PRODUCTS or SERVICES. In the United States, many retail clothing, food, sporting goods, and lodging markets are characterized by monopolistic competition.

The essential feature of monopolistic competition is product differentiation. Producers attempt to create real or perceived positive differences in their products compared to competitors' offerings. Businesses use brand images, PACKAGING, product variations, and considerable ADVERTISING and SALES PROMOTION to convince consumers that their product is superior and therefore worth a higher price.

The goal in monopolistic competition is to sufficiently differentiate the firm's products so that consumers will not substitute competitors' products when the firm's products are priced higher. Businesses try to develop CUS-TOMER LOYALTY in a market that offers many choices for consumers. Economists describe this effort as attempting to reduce the ELASTICITY OF DEMAND for the firm's products. Often in monopolistically competitive markets, individual firms can earn substantial economic PROFITS for a short period of time, but with ease of entry, competitors seeing a firm making profits will enter the market, taking away part of the market DEMAND and reducing the first firm's profits.

The clothing industry is a good example of monopolistic competition. One firm will introduce a new product, style, or color; just having a celebrity endorse something creates demand for the product. When it becomes a hit, competitors will quickly enter the market with very similar products.

Toys are another monopolistically competitive market. When a new stuffed animal or electronic game becomes popular, competitors will rapidly create almost exact copies of the hit item. Because there are many competing firms and it is easy for firms to enter the market, monopolistically competitive firms will earn economic profits only in the short run.

monopoly

A monopoly is a MARKET STRUCTURE where there is one producer, no close substitutes, and considerable BARRIERS TO ENTRY. In the United States, PUBLIC UTILITIES (electricity, telephone, cable, and water) are monopolies. These and many other monopoly markets are created by a variety of conditions.

Public utilities are what economists call "natural monopolies." In these markets it is natural or makes sense to have one large firm because it can produce at a lower average cost than many small firms (ECONOMIES OF SCALE). Telephone service in the early 1900s was initially a competitive market, with many producers using a variety of telephone equipment, often incompatible with each other. In some cities there were as many as five telephone companies. A business wishing to be able to communicate by phone with its customers and suppliers would have five different phones in their office and pay for service to five different companies.

Because telephone systems involve significant CAPITAL investments in equipment and lines, telephone companies have huge fixed COSTS but relatively low variable costs. If the company could spread its fixed costs over a large customer base, it could reduce its average cost of telephone service and achieves economies of scale. It was inefficient and redundant to have many small telephone companies, so with government approval, monopolies were created in regional markets, and AT&T was given monopoly control in long-distance markets. With price regulation, consumers received lower costs and better service.

Government also creates monopolies through PATENTS and licenses. Patents give an inventor monopoly rights on new devices or processes for a specified period of time. Until recently in the United States, patents gave monopoly rights for 17 years from the time the patent was granted. Recently, in order to comply with the General Agreement on Tariffs and Trade (GATT), U.S. patent rights are now issued for 20 years from the time the application is filed. Patents are an incentive for producers to create new and improved products, because monopoly control over a useful device usually results in significant PROFITS for the patent holder.

Like patents, licenses received from government result in monopolies. For example, hospitals wanting to expand their service offerings are required to get a certificate of need from state authorities. Neighboring hospitals that already provide a service will often oppose allowing a new hospital to offer the same service, as they do not want to lose their monopoly.

Another source of monopoly power is control over a critical resource. For years DeBeers has dominated the diamond market, controlling almost all of the world's supply of raw diamonds. In 1999 Microsoft was accused by the U.S. Justice Department of abusing its monopoly power in personal-computer operating systems.

Since by definition a monopoly is a market with only one firm and no close substitutes, monopolists have considerable market power, which often allows them to charge higher prices and earn significant profits. However, just because a firm is a monopolist does not necessarily mean that it will earn economic profits. If there is no sufficient DEMAND for the firm's products, the monopolist may not be able to earn a profit at all. These are other common myths about monopolists as well, including:

- Monopolists always charge the highest price.
- Monopolists can ignore consumers.
- Monopolies go on forever.

Even though they are a monopoly, monopolists do not control consumers and therefore cannot force consumers to pay whatever price they want to charge. Like all firms, monopolists face a market demand curve, in which higher prices lead to lower quantities demanded. Monopolists therefore cannot ignore consumers. The earlier example of telephone service illustrates the fact that monopolies do not go on forever. In the 1980s, when new technology allowed alternative (microwave and later satellite) delivery of communication, AT&T's monopoly ended.

The telephone-service example also illustrates the question of whether monopolies are good or bad for society. Without regulation, monopolies generally result in higher prices and lower output as compared to competitive markets. But with regulation monopolies can result in lower prices and greater output. Monopolies are also an incentive to provide new goods and SERVICES for consumers and increases in productivity. Much of the ECONOMIC GROWTH during the 1990s in the United States is attributable to the development and utilization of new technology. Monopolists who use their market power to prevent new competitors to enter the market harm society. The SHERMAN ANTITRUST ACT of 1890 and subsequent acts make attempts to monopolize trade a criminal offense.

Further reading
Slavin, Stephen L. *Economics*, 6th ed. Boston: Irwin-McGraw Hill, 2001.

Montreal Protocol

The Montreal Protocol (1987) is an international agreement that controls the production and CONSUMPTION of substances that cause ozone depletion. The full title of the agreement is the Montreal Protocol on Substances that Deplete the Ozone Layer. Ozone (three oxygen atoms, chemical formula O_3) is a rare but important compound found in the earth's atmosphere. In the 1980s, scientists identified chlorofluorocarbons (CFCs) as a major source of ozone depletion. (CFCs were mainly used in refrigeration and air conditioning systems.) The ozone layer in the earth's atmosphere filters solar radiation, absorbing ultraviolet sunlight, and its depletion contributes to global warming. The Montreal Protocol and subsequent agreements were the first major international agreements forcing businesses to change PRODUCTION processes in response to fears of global warming. Since 1987, when the protocol was signed by 29 countries and the EUROPEAN UNION (then the European Economic Community), the production and consumption of ozone-depleting substances has been reduced more rapidly than that required hydrochlorofluorocarbons (HCFCs) and hydrofluorocarbons (HFCs) have been introduced to provide alternatives to CFCs.

Global cooperation for the protection of the ozone layer began with the negotiation of the Vienna Convention for the Protection of the Ozone Layer in 1985. The details of the international agreement were defined in the Montreal Protocol, which was signed in 1987 and became effective in 1989. It contains provisions for regular review of the adequacy of control measures, based on assessments of existing and new scientific, environmental, technical, and economic information.

At a meeting in London in 1990, the parties to the Montreal Protocol agreed to a phase-out of additional controlled substances, including halons, carbon tetrachloride, methyl chloroform, HCFCs, hydrobromofluorocarbons (HBFCs), and methyl bromide. At a 1992 meeting held in Copenhagen, the participating countries agreed to accelerate the phase-out schedules of these controlled substances. The 1997 Montreal amendments banned export and import of controlled substances, and the 1999 Beijing amendments added reporting requirements and further restrictions on ozone-depleting substances. By 1999, 172 countries had signed the Montreal Protocol, and a multilateral fund was established to provide RESOURCES for developing countries to meet their commitments under the accord.

Under the protocol, developed countries were given a specified period to phase out the use of CFCs. Developing countries agreed to eliminate CFCs, but were given an additional 10 years to reach compliance. Developing countries are allowed to continue to produce and purchase CFCs and carbon tetrachloride for use until 2010 and methyl chloroform until 2015. Developed nations can continue to produce CFCs up to 15 percent of their 1986 baseline for sale to developing countries to meet their domestic needs and for essential uses. In addition to the Montreal Protocol, the U.S. ENVIRONMENTAL PROTECTION AGENCY and the European Union have imposed stricter regulations and phase-out schedules.

Parties to the protocol identified a number of essential uses that are deemed necessary for the health and safety of society and for which there are no technically and economically feasible alternatives available or substitutes that are environmentally acceptable. Production for such uses is still permitted under the protocol; this provision is reviewed annually.

Further reading
United Nations Environment Programme (UNEP). Available online. URL: www.unep.org/ozone/montreal.shtml

Moody's ratings

Moody's Investors Service (along with STANDARD & POORS'S Corporation) ranks BONDS according to their DEFAULT risk. Investors want information in order to assess the RISK versus return of financial securities. Moody's Investor Service's widely used rating system provides investors with default risk information.

In Moody's system, corporate bonds are rated from Aaa to C, with Aaa signifying highest quality (lowest default risk) and C being the lowest grade. The full Moody's rating scale is Aaa, Aa, A, Baa, Ba, B, Caa, Ca, and C. Bond ratings are based on the firm's expected cash flow, the firm's other contractual cash obligations, how profitable the firm has been, and the variability of the firm's earnings. Any corporate bond rated Baa or above is considered "investment grade" with relatively low risk of default. Any bond rated below Baa is considered a speculation and is referred to as a "junk bond" in financial markets.

The distinction between investment-grade and speculative-grade bonds is important because many INVESTMENT groups (MUTUAL FUNDS, commercial banks, INSURANCE companies, and pension funds) direct their investment managers to invest only in investment-grade bonds.

Companies issuing debt (that is, selling bonds) pay a rating service to get their securities rated. The charge to a company can easily be $50,000–$100,000, but the benefit can be significant. Bonds with higher ratings will be purchased by investors at lower INTEREST RATES, while bonds with lower ratings (greater potential of default) will have to pay investors a higher interest rate. While the difference in a few basis points (each basis point equals one-hundredth of one percent) may not seem significant to individual investors, to corporate financial officers charged with borrowing hundreds of millions of dollars, it is a considerable amount of money.

Once Moody's has issued a bond rating, the rating is reviewed periodically. Moody's will sometimes issue a rating alert, signaling to investors that a company's bonds are being reviewed for either an upgrade or downgrade. If a bond is downgraded, the bond price typically will decrease as investors demand a higher rate of return to hold riskier securities. In the 1990s many companies' bonds were downgraded when they took on additional debt in order to acquire other companies.

Some companies in poor financial condition will choose to not have their debt securities rated. In addition, companies issuing small amount of bonds will sometimes find it cheaper to issue unrated securities rather than pay the cost for having them rated.

Moody's also rates COMMERCIAL PAPER—short-term, unsecured obligations issued by banks and CORPORATIONS to meet temporary financial situations. Moody's commercial-paper rating system ranks securities from P-1 to P-3.

Further reading

Kidwell, David S., Richard L. Peterson, and David W. Blackwell. *Financial Institutions, Markets and Money,* 7th ed. Fort Worth: Dryden Press, 2000.

moral suasion

Moral suasion is the use of influence to affect behavior. Business moral suasion is most often associated with public statements by individuals with authority, ADVERTISING campaigns, and educational programs. President John F. Kennedy attempted moral suasion in his classic statement, "Ask not what your country can do for you. Ask what you can do for your country." The powerful antismoking campaigns by the American Legacy Foundation and others since the 1999 TOBACCO SETTLEMENT also provide examples of moral suasion. In addition to ad campaigns, educational programs and testimonials from respected community, sports, and entertainment leaders are among the most effective moral-suasion efforts.

One of the major users of moral suasion is the FEDERAL RESERVE SYSTEM (often called the Fed). Many times the Fed, usually through statements by its chairman, will suggest what they would like banks to do or not do, without instituting a regulation or policy. In 1999 the Fed's chairman, Alan Greenspan, used the famous phrase "irrational exuberance" when describing the skyrocketing STOCK MARKET prices of technology companies. In 2002 Mr. Greenspan suggested that STOCK OPTIONS given to executives be included as a cost in company accounting practices. In both instances he was stating his opinion on subjects that were related to banking and finance but out of his sphere of control, MONETARY POLICY. In effect, he was attempting to use moral suasion to influence others.

In 1998 the Federal Reserve initiated a major moral-suasion effort when it intervened in the rescue of the international HEDGE FUND Long Term Capital Management (LTCM). In "Costs and Benefits of Moral Suasion: Evidence from the Rescue of Long Term Capital Management," Craig Furfine suggests that the Fed's use of moral suasion to prevent the liquidation of LTCM may not have been necessary. The Fed organized and hosted a series of meetings between LTCM and 14 institutions, including nine large commercial banks that ultimately provided the financial resources to bail out the hedge fund. The Fed itself did not provide funding; instead it persuaded lenders to provide funds, and the Federal Reserve Bank of New York, through provision of its "good offices," facilitated the rescue. In fact, financial leaders worked through the critical weekend to put together a plan. The Fed's use of moral suasion was based on the idea of "too big to fail," the perception that failure of the hedge fund would destabilize financial markets and create a domino effect, threatening the solvency of commercial banks and other financial institutions.

mortgage

A mortgage is a loan secured by real property in which the lender obtains the legal right to liquidate (sell) the property to recover its funds in the event the borrower fails to make payment on the loan. The purchase of a home is often a consumer's single largest purchase in his or her life. Generally mortgage lenders will lend an amount two to three times the annual household INCOME, depending on a borrower's savings and other debts. Mortgage payments usually should not exceed 30 percent of a household's monthly disposable income.

Mortgage payments include three components: payment on the principal of the loan (the amount borrowed); payment on the interest owed; and payments to special accounts (called an escrow account) for payment of INSURANCE, PROPERTY TAXES, and other recurring charges. Combined, this is called PITI (Principal, Interest, Taxes, Insurance).

One major question in securing a mortgage is how much the borrower will "put down." The down payment reduces the amount of the mortgage and acts as security for the lender against the possibility that the value of the house might decline. Most mortgage lenders require at least 5 percent of the value of the property as down payment, though there are special programs for veterans, active members of the military, and first-time home buyers that allow 0 percent down. Borrowers who put at least 20 percent down can often avoid certain mortgage-related costs, such as principal mortgage insurance (PMI).

There are two general types of mortgages: fixed rate and adjustable rate. Fixed-rate mortgages retain the same interest rate over the life of the mortgage. They are typically 30 years or 15 years in length, though some are as short as 10 years. Many homebuyers choose a mortgage length to coincide with when they expect to retire. Shorter length mortgages significantly reduce the total amount of interest paid but result in higher monthly payments. One way to shorten a mortgage is to agree to biweekly payments of half the monthly amount, rather than monthly payments. Biweekly payments result in 13 equivalent payments per year (26 ½ payments equals 13 "months" worth of payments).

Adjustable-rate mortgages (ARMs) allow the interest rate to change over the life of the mortgage. In the late 1990s, with falling mortgage rates, many households saw their INTEREST RATES and monthly payments decline. In the early 1990s, when interest rates rose, adjustable-rate mortgage payments also rose. There are many different kinds of ARMs. The most common type combines a fixed rate for a specified period of time with an annual cap (limit) on how much the rate can change after the initial time period and a life of the mortgage cap on how high the rate could go. For example, a 1/2/6 ARM would hold the interest rate fixed for the one year, then have a 2 percent annual limit to how much the interest rate could change and a 6 percent limit on how high the rate could go from the initial rate charged.

The advantage of an ARM to a borrower is that the initial rate is usually 2–3 percent lower than the fixed-rate mortgage, which lowers the initial payments for the borrower. The advantage to the lender is that it has transferred interest rate risk to the borrower. Therefore if interest rates go up in the future, the lender will get a higher return. Pre-1980, almost all mortgages in the United States were fixed-rate mortgages. In the late 1970s and early 1980s, INFLATION increased, and interest rates increased with it. Lenders, particularly, SAVINGS AND LOAN ASSOCIATIONS, found that, like BONDS, when interest rates rise, the value of a fixed-payment security (a fixed-rate mortgage) declines. For example, an 8 percent $100,000 mortgage generates $8,000 interest income the first year. If mortgage interest rates rise to 16 percent (which they did in 1980), then an investor would only be willing to pay $50,000 for a mortgage paying $8,000 per year ($8,000 ÷ $50,000 = 16 percent return). They would not pay $100,000 for the mortgage, because they could also purchase a new mortgage yeilding 16 percent.

Another confusing issue for consumers seeking mortgages is "points"—fees charged by lenders, expressed as a percentage of the amount being borrowed. Many lenders charge a 1 percent initiation fee (in addition to a loan application fee). Borrowers can also reduce their interest rate by paying more points; this is known as a "buy-down discount." By paying a higher fee, the borrower reduces his

or her interest rate and therefore the monthly payment. Whether to pay the higher points depends on how much lower the interest rate will be and how long the homebuyer thinks he/she will own the property.

Whether to choose a fixed-rate or variable-rate mortgage depends on a variety of factors, including

- the borrowers' current financial situation
- how the borrower expects his or her finances to change in the future
- how long the borrower expects to own the home
- the borrower's willingness to risk higher payments in the future

Households where one family member is temporarily not working may choose a variable-rate mortgage for the lower current payment, knowing they will probably have more income in the future. Similarly, borrowers who are in the process of paying off student loans or other short-term payments will know when those payments end and be able to make higher payments in the future, should interest rates rise. Borrowers who expect to move in a few years will probably benefit from an adjustable-rate mortgage. Borrowers who think they will stay in a home a longer period of time or who are uncomfortable with the risk of rising mortgage payments would likely choose a fixed-rate mortgage.

The mortgage process can be quite daunting to first-time homebuyers. There are now many websites where monthly payment schedules can be calculated and where borrowers can shop for a mortgage lender. Before starting the mortgage process, usually homebuyers find a home they wish to purchase and sign a real-estate sales CONTRACT. This is the most critical stage in the buying process and should not be entered into without independent expert advice. One part of a real-estate sales contract stipulates the mortgage financing the buyer will secure. When signing a contract, buyers often attempt to "lock in" a specified interest rate with a mortgage lender, contingent on the sale going through.

Further reading
Gitman, Lawrence J., and Michael D. Joehnk. *Personal Financial Planning*, 9th ed. Cincinnati, Ohio: South-Western, 2001; Mortgage Bankers Association website. Available on-line. URL: www.mbaa.org.

most-favored-nation clause
A most-favored-nation (MFN) clause in an international trade agreement requires participants in the agreement to offer all other participants treatment as favorable as that extended to any other country. Therefore most-favored-nation clauses, with some exceptions, eliminate discrimination among countries on the basis of TARIFFS and duties and provide freedom for INVESTMENT.

In the 19th and early 20th centuries, most-favored-nation clauses were generally reciprocal agreements between two countries. Sometimes powerful Western countries unilaterally imposed MFN clauses on Asian nations. With the creation of the General Agreement on Tariffs and Trade (GATT, 1947) and the WORLD TRADE ORGANIZATION (WTO, 1995) with over 100 member nations, most-favored-nation status has become a widespread basis for trade arrangements. Occasionally WTO members will ignore most-favored-nation clauses, allowing other members to impose higher tariffs or other restrictions. Logically most-favored-nation clauses expand trade, and equal trading opportunities favor the economically strongest countries. The United Nations and GATT deliberations have led to special concessions to EMERGING MARKETS.

In recent years in the United States, the most controversial aspect of MFN clauses has been the annual renewal of MFN status for China. Critics often cite labor and human-rights abuses as well as unfair trading practices on China's part, whereas supporters of MFN for China note it is one of the largest economies in the world and therefore needs to be part of a global trading agreement. As of 2001 the United States stopped opposing China's application to join the World Trade Organization. When China became a WTO member, in 2002 gained access to most-favored-nation trade access without annual renewal through the U.S. Congress.

Further reading

Mallor, Jane P., A. James Barnes, Thomas Bowers, Michael J. Philips, and Arlen W. Langvardt. *Business Law and the Regulatory Environment*, 11th ed. Boston: McGraw-Hill, 2001.

motivation theory

Motivation describes a state of being in which an individual experiences the energy and desire to pursue a specific goal. Motivation theory includes different explanations for how motivation helps propel and direct people's behavior and addresses possible reasons for why people try to achieve goals. The explanations of motivation range from physiological states in the human body, such as hunger or thirst, to cultural and social interactions with other individuals, such as the needs for approval, recognition, or respect from others.

Drive-reduction theory suggests that motivation results from a state of tension that occurs in the body when a particular need is not met. For example, hunger would suggest a need to eat, which would create a state of tension in the body, motivating the person to seek out food. Once the behavior is performed, it should reduce the drive, or the need to eat. Although such a theory is useful for explaining many behaviors, such as why people may take a break from work in order to eat, it cannot explain why people sometimes eat when they are not hungry.

Arousal theory suggests that there is a certain level of arousal—a state of tension, energy, or excitement—that people seek to maintain. Thus people may be motivated to engage in certain behaviors in order to change their level of arousal. The theory suggests that people perform their best when they experience a moderate level of arousal. Indeed, there seems to be an optimal level of arousal, below which people do not perform well because they may be disengaged from the task and above which people are too aroused to perform well. If an individual is bored or otherwise not intellectually stimulated, he or she may try to seek arousal by engaging in exciting or fun activities. However, too much arousal can be aversive and may hinder performance or motivate the individual to leave a situation in order to decrease the high level of tension. Ideally employees experience a moderate level of arousal in their jobs, such that they are neither bored nor experiencing very high levels of stress.

Some motivation theories focus less on such bodily states as drive-reduction and arousal and instead incorporate dynamic social factors. For example, incentive theory suggests that external motivators, or incentives, help increase an individual's interest in performing a particular behavior. Incentives can include a variety of desirable rewards, such as money, recognition, status, or acceptance, and are often used in the workplace to motivate employees to perform tasks relevant to their jobs and the company's goals. Many incentives are related to social factors or relationships with other individuals, as opposed to biological drives or arousal.

In order to understand the relationships among both biological and social needs, psychologist Abraham Maslow proposed a hierarchy of human needs that incorporated multiple levels. At the bottom of the hierarchy, representing the most basic human needs, are physiological needs, such as those for food and water. Maslow suggested that when an individual has met the lowest-level needs, then he or she may focus on safety needs, such as the needs for shelter and security. Above safety needs, Maslow proposed needs for belonging and love, suggesting that once the lower levels are met, an individual can focus on social relationships. Esteem needs, or the needs for self-respect and being valued by others, represent the next-higher level, and the top of the hierarchy represents the need for self-actualization, or the ultimate state of self-knowledge and development. Maslow suggested that when lower-levels needs were satisfied, people would be motivated to seek the higher needs, although he acknowledged that not all people would reach self-actualization.

As useful as MASLOW'S HIERARCHY OF NEEDS may be in helping people understand and identify what human needs are important, there are some shortcomings. For example, individuals may place different priorities on certain needs, resulting in a different hierarchy. Individuals who put esteem needs before love and belonging needs may sacrifice the quality of their family relationships in exchange for their work. Additionally, homeless people, who may struggle each day with their basic needs for food and shelter, still may desire to be loved and have friends.

There are many different theories of motivation, no one of which can adequately explain all of human behavior. However, taken together, each theory contributes an important part to our overall understanding of the reasons why people are motivated to pursue certain goals.

See also ACHIEVEMENT MOTIVATION; EMPLOYEE MOTIVATION; PROCESS THEORIES; THEORY X AND THEORY Y TWO-FACTOR THEORY OF MOTIVATION.

Further reading

Myers, David G. *Exploring Psychology*, 5th ed. New York: Worth Publishers, 2002.

—Elizabeth L. Cralley

multilevel marketing (network marketing)

Multilevel marketing (MLM), also known as network marketing, is a home-based marketing system based on selling to friends and recruiting others to sell and distribute the company's products. In the United States, multilevel marketing is a multibillion-dollar industry. MLM was started by Carl Rehnborg who, in 1941, created Nutrilite Products, Inc., to sell food supplements through networks of friends and distributors. Perhaps the most famous MLM company, Amway Corporation, founded by former Nutrilite distributors, became the most widely known multilevel marketer.

Multilevel marketing is based primarily on recruiting others to also sell the PRODUCT. Its advantages include low COSTS for getting started (often $500 or less), a chance to make significant INCOME (many MLMs offer testimonials describing people who became millionaires), and a relatively simple BUSINESS PLAN.

Few multilevel marketers actually become wealthy selling products. The key to success in MLM is having a large "downstream"—salespeople who are selling products and the MLM system to others. In multilevel marketing, a person is paid a percentage of the sales of downstream participants, which can rapidly increase one's income. For example, if someone recruits five people who in turn also recruit five people, who then recruit five people, in most MLM systems the first person will receive a percentage of the sales of the 125 people downstream from him or her.

There are many problems associated with MLM. Like the old maxim, "if it sounds too good to be true, it probably isn't true," some multilevel marketing systems involve products that can easily be purchased at lower prices in retail stores or SERVICES of questionable value. Often MLM programs are "get-rich-quick schemes" foisted on unsophisticated consumers looking for opportunities. Dubious MLM schemes tend to expand during RECESSIONs as people who lose their jobs look for alternative ways to make a living. Like most business organizations, people at the top of MLM systems make the most money, and people on the bottom often find it much more difficult than they imagined recruiting others to the system.

Multilevel marketing grew rapidly following a 1979 ruling by the FEDERAL TRADE COMMISSION that it was a legitimate marketing technique. Some of the most successful MLM programs include Amway, Mary Kay, Avon, Tupperware, and NuSkin. The INTERNET has resulted in a new generation of multilevel marketing programs using electronic rather than direct sales to recruit participants.

Further reading

Bononma, Thomas. "This snake rises in bad times (multi-level marketing schemes," *Marketing News* 25, no. 4 (18 February 1991): 16.

multinational corporation

A multinational corporation (MNC) is a firm that operates in more than one country. The common image of an MNC is a giant CORPORATION engaging in business around the world. The *Forbes* 2000 list of "The World's Largest Corporations" is led by General Motors, followed by Wal-Mart, ExxonMobil, Ford, and DaimlerChrysler. Of the top 25 MNCs on the list, eight are U.S.-based companies, 10 are based in Japan, four are in Germany, and one or two each are from Britain, Netherlands, and France. While each of these companies has its headquarters in the country where it started, they all produce and sell goods and SERVICES in almost every country in the world.

Multinational enterprises have existed for hundreds of years but began to flourish in the 19th and early 20th centuries. Until World War II, British, German, and Dutch trading companies were the major multinationals. At the beginning of the 20th century, overproduction by U.S. manufacturers led to development of export markets, and some U.S. businesses, including the powerful United Fruit Company, expanded their control of minerals and agricultural products from Central and South America.

The MARSHALL PLAN, designed to assist in the rebuilding of European economies after World War II, greatly contributed to the evolution of U.S. MNCs. In the 1930s, the United States, in response to the GREAT DEPRESSION, imposed increased protective TARIFFs (see SMOOT-HAWLEY TARIFFS ACT) and isolated itself both politically and economically from the world marketplace. The Marshall Plan represented a major reversal from those policies. One result was that a substantial portion of aid was spent in the United States for the purchase of capital goods from U.S. manufacturers. This international activity combined with new U.S. military alliances, and European allies were "encouraged" to buy U.S. military hardware. Foreign accommodation of U.S. multinational corporations thus changed the business strategies of many companies.

In addition to the sale of U.S. capital and military goods, American service, finance, accounting, INSURANCE, and architecture businesses, among others, "followed the flag," expanding internationally to meet the needs of their corporate customers. By the 1960s, these corporations were "as global as American diplomacy." Generally, the goals of U.S. MNCs were to penetrate foreign markets, avoid tariff and nontariff barriers, access cheap labor, and/or gain direct control of vital RESOURCES (often oil). The U.S. press rarely reports the fact that much of OPEC (ORGANIZATION OF PETROLEUM EXPORTING COUNTRIES) oil was initially developed by U.S. multinationals. During the 1970s and 1980s, U.S. manufacturing multinationals began to lose out to new sources of COMPETITION, but American service-based MNCs continue to dominate global trade, contributing to a U.S. trade surplus in services.

The contribution of multinational corporations and their subsidiaries to global ECONOMIC DEVELOPMENT is debatable. One controversy centers on the dependency-versus-modernization theory. Dependency theory suggests that market CAPITALISM in the form of large MNCs entering small, less-developed countries result in exploitation and dependency on the MNCs and inhibits indigenous ENTREPRENEURSHIP. Dependency theorists argue MNCs monopolize local industrial, capital, and LABOR MARKETS. ECONOMIC GROWTH occurs, but largely to the benefit of the "triple alliance": MNCs, government-owned enterprises, and local capital elite.

Modernization theorists, on the other hand, suggest multinational corporations are agents of change, promoting economic growth and development. Multinational corporations bring new technology, managerial training, INFRASTRUCTURE development, and access to modern business practices when they enter a developing country. Management scholar Peter Drucker contends MNCs are "the only real hope" for lesser-developed countries (LDCs). They alter traditional value systems, social attitudes, and behavior patterns and encourage responsibility among political leaders of LDCs. Some economists, however, question whether replacing traditional systems with "modern" values is always beneficial to the local population.

Developing countries' governments may attempt to access the benefits of multinational corporations without creating dependency through the use of JOINT VENTURES (JVs). At times both China and Mexico have mandated joint ventures for any company wishing to expand into their country. Often the MNC provides the CAPITAL and technology, while the domestic country partner provides labor, local knowledge, and access to domestic distribution systems. With the signing of the NORTH AMERICAN FREE TRADE AGREEMENT (NAFTA, 1994), Mexico reduced and agreed to eventual elimination of join-venture requirements. With China's ascension to the WORLD TRADE ORGANIZATION (WTO) in 2001, joint ventures and other restrictions on international access to Chinese markets are expected to be diminished.

Changes in international trade agreements are critical to the expansion of multinational corporations. In 1995, after eight years of negotiation, the General Agreement on Tariffs and Trade (GATT) was replaced by the WTO. Today over 90 percent of international trade is governed by WTO rules. In addition to efforts to reduce tariffs, the WTO is committed to eliminating nontariff barriers. Critics contend the WTO is an agent of multinational corporations, facilitating their dominance of the global economy.

In today's economy, global sourcing is a common practice. MNCs purchase materials and components around the world and assemble and produce wherever costs are lowest. With INTERNET communications, corporations now hold vendor auctions, inviting selected suppliers to bid on PRODUCTION of parts and products. Managers argue this results in increased competition and lower prices. Critics counter that it leads developing countries to cut their prices by ignoring social costs, including pollution, in the race to retain EMPLOYMENT and INCOME in their economies.

Generally large MNCs have an advantage over smaller, domestic producers based ECONOMIES OF SCALE, production efficiencies realized when per-unit costs are reduced as the quantity produced increases. In business, scale is size. In many business situations, as a company produces more output, the average cost of that output declines. Economies of scale are the result of efforts that improve efficiency. Generally specialization and the use of larger machines allow firms to become more efficient. Greater levels of output allow firms to spread the fixed costs associated with specialized equipment or personnel.

MNCs already producing for large domestic markets (like U.S. multinationals) tend to have an advantage when entering smaller markets. For decades many smaller countries restricted access to their markets in order to protect domestic producers. For example, in the 1890s, Canada imposed the Fielding Tariffs on imported products. In response, U.S. manufacturers established "branch factories" in Canada, and by 1970 they dominated FOREIGN INVESTMENT in Canada. With the passage of the U.S.-CANADA FREE TRADE AGREEMENT in 1985, Canadian leaders feared U.S. multinationals would "rationalize" that is, consolidate their North American operations, removing factories and jobs from Canada. By that time the branch factories had been integrated into most MNC business strategies and continued to flourish.

In Mexico, MNCs expanded greatly even before NAFTA. The MAQUILADORAS program, like Canada's branch-factory tariffs, attempted to create jobs and income in Mexico while limiting access to Mexican markets. Established in 1965, the maquiladoras (or Border Industrialization Program) allowed foreign firms to import materials and parts into Mexico with no tariff if the resulting products were then exported. Asian and North American companies established maquiladoras, but the program did not take off until a Mexican financial crisis in the early 1980s. With devaluation of the Mexican peso, maquiladora labor became cheaper than in developing Asian countries. Maquiladoras boomed in the mid-1980s and again after the PESO CRISIS in 1994.

In the late 1980s, Mexico relaxed the requirement that all maquiladora production be shipped out of the country, providing access to Mexican markets through maquiladora operations. In the 1990s, with new trade agreements with Chile, Mercursor countries, and the EUROPEAN UNION, Mexico became an export platform for U.S.-based multinational corporations. Exports from Mexican plants could enter countries like Chile without tariffs while, exports to Chile from U.S. factories face tariffs. As of November 2000, as part of NAFTA, only parts and materials originating in the three North American countries could enter Mexico tariff-free. In anticipation of this change, multinational corporations, particularly Asian companies, expanded production activities in Mexico, diverting production from other areas of the world.

Further reading

Folsom, Ralph H., and W. Davis Folsom. *Understanding NAFTA and its International Implications*. New York: Matthew Irwin/Bender, 1996; Lamb, Charles, Joseph Hair, and Carl McDaniel. *Marketing*, 5th ed. Cincinnati, Ohio: Thomson, 2000.

mutual funds

Mutual funds, organized as CORPORATIONs and regulated by the SECURITIES AND EXCHANGE COMMISSION, are major FINANCIAL INTERMEDIARIES in today's world. They accept funds from savers by selling them shares and then use the proceeds to invest in various financial securities ranging from short-term debt instruments to long-term BONDS and stocks. In order to meet the needs and desires of the various savers, each mutual fund specializes in investing in a particular type or a unique mix of securities. Generally there are income funds, growth funds, and mutual funds made up of a mix of income and growth funds. Money-market mutual funds invest only in short-term securities and operate like interest-bearing checking accounts for the savers.

Income funds are mutual funds investing in lower-risk securities, usually bonds. They attract savers who are looking for stability and regular INCOME from their INVESTMENTs, rather than growth or higher rates of return. Growth funds invest in higher-risk securities, such as stocks. These mutual funds attract savers who are less RISK-averse, willing to assume greater risk for the potential of higher returns from their investments.

By pooling the funds of many savers, a mutual fund realizes ECONOMIES OF SCALE in the purchasing, selling, and management of its securities portfolio. Such portfolios also offer the benefits of diversification for the savers. Perhaps the greatest benefit offered by mutual funds is that they allow small investors to enjoy the same rates of return normally available only to larger investors. The saver who invests $5,000 in a mutual fund receives the same percentage return as a saver with $5 million in the fund. A small investment in a mutual fund can offer a yield much higher than if that same amount were invested in a certificate of deposit, for example.

A mutual fund may be organized as an open-ended fund or a closed-end fund. In the more common open-ended fund, shares may be redeemed at any time at a price determined by the ASSET value of the total fund. A closed-end fund is comprised of a fixed number of nonredeemable shares which, after their initial offering, are traded like COMMON STOCK. Closed-end shares are less liquid than one-ended shares and are therefore less popular with investors.

Originally mutual funds were load funds, in which a sales commission is charged and paid when the shares are purchased. Today, however, most mutual funds are no-load funds, in which shares are sold directly and no commission is charged.

The administrators of mutual funds are called managers. They earn income by charging management fees ranging from .5 percent to 2 percent of the asset value of the total fund. Most SHAREHOLDERS consider management fees of 1.5 percent or greater to be relatively excessive, and as a result, the more common management fees are less than 1 percent.

mutual interdependence

In a market with only a few large firms, mutual interdependence is the reality that the actions of one firm affect the choices and actions of the other firms. Mutual interdependence is associated with oligopolistic markets—markets with BARRIERS TO ENTRY, few competitors, and either similar or differentiated PRODUCTs.

In perfectly competitive and monopolistically competitive markets, where there are many competing firms, the actions of one firm have very little impact on the overall market. If one firm lowers its price, increases or decreases its output, or expands its ADVERTISING or distribution network, it will have little impact on its market because it represents only a small part of the overall output. If, on the other hand, one firm is a significant part of the overall market, its actions can affect its competitors. If one firm lowers its prices and the other firms do not match the price decrease, the one firm will increase sales, taken from the few other competitors in the market.

Mutual interdependence leads to a variety of market behaviors, including price leadership, kinked-demand curves, nonprice competition, collusion, and CARTELs. Using price leadership, one firm announces a price change; usually an increase in price, and the other firms match the price increase. In the United States, steel, banking, and airline prices are often changed through price leadership.

Kinked-demand curve behavior is the matching of price decreases but not price increases. This leads to two different responses to changes from the existing price. If one firm raises its price and the few other firms do not match the price increase, the firm will experience a significant decrease in sales as consumers switch to competitors' products. If the firm lowers a price, competitors, recognizing they will lose sales if they do not lower their own price, will match the decrease. This leads to two different elasticities of demand at the current price, resulting in a kink in the DEMAND curve.

Recognizing that competitors will match a decrease but not an increase in price frequently results in "sticky" prices. The few firms will instead compete on a basis other than price. Nonprice competition can include efforts to attract customers based on image, BRANDS, service, warrantees, hours of operation, quality—anything but price. One of the classic studies in nonprice competition analyzed the U.S. cereal industry. Dominated by four firms (Quaker, Kellogg, Post, and General Mills), for years the industry competed based on PRODUCT PROLIFERATION, constantly creating new or slightly different products, attempting to differentiate their products from competitors' products but not competing on a basic of price.

Mutual interdependence can also lead to collusion—secret agreements to reduce COMPETITION and thereby increase PROFITS. Collusion typically involves arrangements to divide up markets or rig prices. With only a few competitors, it is possible to agree to measures that will benefit each participant. As one sales representative once said, "We all call on the same customers and stay in the same hotels. At night we are down in the bar talking with each other, and eventually the discussion comes around to price." Collusion is tempting but also illegal in the United States.

Cartels are open arrangements among firms to reduce output in order to raise prices. Like collusion, cartels work when there are a few mutually interdependent producers. The most famous cartels are the ORGANIZATION OF PETROLEUM EXPORTING COUNTRIES (OPEC) and the illegal drug cartels. Both groups operate by controlling supply.

Recognizing mutual interdependence, economists and mathematicians (including John Nash, portrayed in the film *A Beautiful Mind*) have developed theories about the actions and reactions of participants in a market. GAME THEORY attempts to describe the various possible outcomes in a situation involving two or more interacting individuals when those individuals are aware of the interactive nature of their situation and plan accordingly. Games can be either cooperative or noncooperative and can be zero-sum, negative-sum, or positive-sum. Cooperative games involve participants who agree to work together; noncooperative games exist when competitors neither cooperate nor negotiate. A ZERO-SUM GAME exists when the gains of one player come at the expense of other participants, while a negative-sum game is one where players as a group lose in the end, and a positive-sum game results in players as a group gaining in the end. Game theory can be used to construct a payoff matrix, measuring the outcomes, or consequences of the strategies available to participants.

See also ELASTICITY OF DEMAND; OLIGOPOLY.

Further reading
Miller, Roger LeRoy. *Economics Today*. Boston: Addison Wesley, 2001.

N

National Association of Purchasing Managers See
INSTITUTE FOR SUPPLY MANAGEMENT.

National Association of Securities Dealers Automated Quotation System

The National Association of Securities Dealers Automated Quotation System (NASDAQ) is the world's largest electronic stock market. Created by the National Association of Securities Dealers (NASD) in 1971, NASDAQ is a computerized market system allowing 11,000 traders at 790 firms to buy and sell shares of stock. The NASDAQ processes 5,000 transactions per second. NASDAQ is called an over-the-counter market because there is no central location where shares are traded. On a typical day, 6.5 million quotes and 2.5 million trades are executed. In 2001 471 million shares were traded over the system.

In 1971 NASDAQ began trading shares of 2,500 companies. Generally, companies listed on NASDAQ are smaller, less well-known corporation, which, when they grow in assets, leave the NASDAQ for the "big board," the New York Stock Exchange (NYSE). Unlike the NYSE, where Wall Street specialists make a market in particular stocks, raising and lowering prices depending on the number of buy and sell orders, on the NASDAQ dealers list buy and sell orders on linked computer terminals. Sales are executed when there is a match between bids (buy) and offers (sell). There are 400,000 terminals in 83 countries, providing a huge, global market with liquidity and transparency. Liquidity, in a stock market, is the ease and speed of buying and selling shares. Transparency is openness, the ability to view buy and sell orders in the market.

In 1994 NASDAQ surpassed the NYSE is yearly volume of shares traded. In 1999 it became the world's biggest stock market in dollar volume. In the 1990s NASDAQ became the major market for new technology companies. The NASDAQ 100, an index of the 100 largest nonfinancial companies trading on the NASDAQ exchange, is considered the major technology index. Microsoft, one of the world's largest companies, chose to remain on the NASDAQ rather than move to the NYSE. On many days Microsoft is the highest dollar-volume stock traded on the NASDAQ.

Further reading
National Association of Securities Dealers Automated Quotation System website. Available on-line. URL: www.nasdaq.com.

National Bureau of Economic Research

The National Bureau of Economic Research (NBER) is a private, nonpartisan, nonprofit economic research organization whose mission is to provide unbiased economic research among public policymakers, business professionals, and the academic community. Created in 1920, the NBER initially focused on the NATIONAL INCOME ACCOUNTING work of Simon Kuznet. Early NBER studies included Wesley Mitchell's analysis of BUSINESS CYCLES and Milton Friedman's monetary theory research. NBER analysis states there have been 31 business cycles in the period from 1854 to 1999, 26 during peacetime and five during periods of war.

The NBER is a prestigious organization with a membership of more than 500 economists, including 12 American recipients of the Nobel Prize in economics and numerous chairs of the President's Council of Economic Advisers. NBER associates focus on four areas of empirical research: developing new statistical measurements, estimating quantitative models of economic behavior, assessing the impacts of public policies on the U.S. economy, and projecting the effects of alternative policy proposals. The current major NBER research programs focus on aging, ASSET pricing, children, corporate finance, U.S. ECONOMIC DEVELOPMENT, economic fluctuations and growth, health care and economics, international finance, international trade and INVESTMENT, labor, monetary economics, productivity, and public policy. The NBER is a major analytical THINK

TANK whose research is closely watched and highly respected.

Further reading

National Bureau of Economic Research website. Available online. URL: www.nber.org.

national income accounting

National income accounting refers to a series of statistical measures of aggregate national INCOME or output. These statistical measures are estimated and published by the Department of Commerce on a monthly basis and are used by economists, business analysts, and government officials to forecast future changes in the economy. These predictions are then used in making policy decisions regarding ECONOMIC GROWTH and stimulation, and to make projections for the DEMAND for companies' and industry output.

National income accounting was developed in the 1920s by the NATIONAL BUREAU OF ECONOMIC RESEARCH. When Franklin Roosevelt became president, he directed the bureau to devise estimates of the country's national income. Without a measure of national income and output, it was impossible to evaluate the impact of the New Deal programs Roosevelt initiated to stimulate the economy out of the GREAT DEPRESSION. Simon Kuznets, a Russian-born American economist, led the development of national income accounting and in 1971 was awarded the Nobel Prize in economics for his work.

In the CIRCULAR FLOW MODEL of an economic system, income flows from businesses and government to households in exchange for the use of resources. Households then use their income to make purchases (CONSUMPTION), save, and pay taxes, leading to government spending. Logically the level of economic activity in an economy could be measured by the amount of income generated or the amount of spending. In national income accounting, the level of output is estimated by the sum of expenditures for that output. The aggregate expenditures (AE) approach to national income accounting is expressed by the equation

$$AE = \text{consumption (C)} + \text{Investment (I)} + \\ \text{Government (G)} + \text{exports} - \text{imports (X-M)}$$

In the United States, consumption spending is the largest portion of aggregate expenditures, accounting for two-thirds of all spending in the economy. Often economic news will include comments about the importance of consumers to the future of the economy. After the September 11, 2001, terrorist attacks, most economists feared consumers would significantly reduce their spending. A significant decrease in the most important source of spending would lower national income. President George W. Bush even went so far as to suggest to Americans that what they could do for the country was to continue to spend.

Consumption spending is primarily determined by income. As household income rises, spending rises. Consumption spending is also influenced by changes in WEALTH, expectations, INTEREST RATES, and DEMOGRAPHICS. During the 1990s, economists and the FEDERAL RESERVE SYSTEM debated the "wealth effect," the degree to which current spending was influenced by increases in wealth from rising STOCK MARKET prices. When the DOT-COMS "bubble" burst in spring 2000, many consumers' wealth declined, contributing to the RECESSION that followed.

Expectations about the future affect consumption spending in the present. Economists and business forecasters closely watch the two major indexes of American consumer expectations, the University of Michigan's Consumer Sentiment Index and the CONFERENCE BOARD's Consumer Confidence Index. After September 11, understandably Americans' confidence fell, but by December it had begun to rise again. Each spring, positive expectations are often also evident in college student parking lots as many college seniors, expecting to graduate and anticipating higher incomes, purchase cars.

Interest rates also influence consumer spending, particularly for durable goods such as homes and automobiles. MONETARY POLICY can be used to stimulate aggregate expenditures through lower interest rates. For example, many Americans barely notice the price of a car, asking only what the monthly payments will be. After September 11, auto sales grew in response to zero-percent interest-rate financing.

Lastly, consumption spending is influenced by demographics. For example, most young people and lower-income people (of any age) spend a greater portion of their disposable income than do older more affluent citizens. Tax cuts that increase the disposable income of younger, lower-income consumers will result in more consumption spending than tax breaks for upper-income groups.

Economic INVESTMENT is the second component of aggregate expenditures in an economy. In the U.S. economy, investment spending represents approximately 17 percent of total spending annually but is the most volatile component of aggregate expenditures. The decision whether or not to invest in new productive ASSETS is primarily influenced by expected PROFITS. Managers make their best projections of future sales of output from the new investments and compare expected sales with estimated costs.

In addition to being influenced by expected profits, economic investment decisions are also affected by changes in technology, capacity utilization, and the cost of borrowing. Often managers will replace existing equipment, even though the existing equipment is fully operational. If new technology can result in a better-quality product, managers are forced to purchase the new equipment in order to remain competitive. Capacity utilization is the percentage of existing productive capacity that is currently being used. The Department of Commerce maintains an index of overall capacity-utilization rate for U.S. manufacturers.

Generally, 85-percent capacity utilization is considered close to full capacity. If, when operating at full capacity, managers think demand for their products will continue to grow, they will decide to invest in new productive capacity. New investment is also influenced by the cost of borrowing (interest rates). As interest rates decline, the cost of new productive assets decreases, stimulating additional investment spending.

Government spending is the third component of aggregate expenditures. Unlike estimating consumption spending and business investment, which are done through SURVEYS and trend analyses, government spending is the record of expenditures for goods and SERVICES by various levels of government and is determined by the budgetary negotiation process. At the national level, every January the executive branch of the federal government promulgates a proposed budget. If the opposition party controls Congress, they will declare the president's budget proposal DOA (dead on arrival). The two branches of government will then debate the level and composition of government spending and reach a compromise, usually by June for the beginning of the FISCAL YEAR or October 1.

Some government programs act as AUTOMATIC STABILIZERS in overall aggregate spending. UNEMPLOYMENT benefits soften reductions in income and spending among households when people lose their jobs. Progressive tax rates (rates that increase as income increases) reduce consumers' ability to spend as their income increases, slowing the growth of aggregate spending. Government redistribution of income (transfer payments) is not part of government spending. It simply transfers purchasing power from one group of consumers to another.

Finally, exports are added and IMPORTS are subtracted to estimate national income. Since national income accounting measure the value of output in an economy, exports are part of the country's output; imports are not, since they were produced somewhere else. Exports are influenced by the level of income in other countries, the relative rate of INFLATION, EXCHANGE RATES, and government policies. Imports are determined primarily by domestic income but also influenced by exchange rates and government policies.

GROSS DOMESTIC PRODUCT (GDP), the MARKET VALUE of final goods and services produced in an economy in a year, is the primary measure estimated using national income accounting. In addition to GDP, national income accounts provide estimates of

- gross national product (GNP): GDP plus factor-income receipts from foreigners and minus factor-income payment to foreigners
- net national product (NNP): GNP minus DEPRECIATION (capital consumption allowances)
- national income: NNP minus indirect BUSINESS TAXES
- personal income: national income plus transfer payments and government interest payments, minus cor-

porate taxes, SOCIAL SECURITY contributions, and undistributed corporate profits
- personal disposable income: personal income minus personal taxes

See also EXPORTING.

Further reading

Bureau of Economic Analysis website. Available on-line. URL: www.bea.doc.gov; Ruffin, Roy J., and Paul R. Gregory. *Principles of Economics*, 7th ed. Boston: Addison Wesley, 2001.

National Industrial Recovery Act

The National Industrial Recovery Act (NIRA, 1933) allowed price and output agreements among firms in an industry and permitted greater labor organizing and COLLECTIVE BARGAINING. In effect, NIRA suspended ANTITRUST LAWS regarding restraint of trade. Price and output agreements were designed to increase producers' INCOME during a time of falling prices. Almost 900 industry agreements were written.

UNION organizing and collective bargaining would increase workers' incomes, allowing them to increase their purchases. NIRA was the first major federal legislation recognizing workers' right to organize. It was a radical step, contrary to the then-prevalent doctrine of CLASSICAL ECONOMICS. Classical economic theory suggested economies would tend to operate at a full-EMPLOYMENT level of output and income, and prices and wages would adjust to maintain a full-employment level of output.

NIRA was a centerpiece of President Franklin Roosevelt's policies to address the GREAT DEPRESSION. Along with government-spending programs like the WORKS PROGRESS ADMINISTRATION (WPA) and youth-employment programs like the CIVILIAN CONSERVATION CORPS (CCC), NIRA was designed to reverse the 33 percent decline in output (GROSS DOMESTIC PRODUCT) and 25 percent UNEMPLOYMENT rate. In 1935 the Supreme Court ruled NIRA unconstitutional on the grounds that the act affected primarily local markets and industries, not interstate commerce. Thus, the actions allowed under NIRA were outside the power of Congress to control. The court also ruled that, with NIRA, Congress had delegated excessive powers to the president.

See also SHERMAN ANTITRUST ACT.

National Labor Relations Act   See WAGNER ACT.

National Labor Relations Board

The National Labor Relations Board (NLRB) is a federal agency created in 1935 to enforce the WAGNER ACT (National Labor Relations Act, NLRA), the primary law governing relations between UNIONS and employers in the private sector of the U.S. economy. The NLRB engages in a wide range of activities, including conducting secret-ballot elections to determine whether employees of a company want union representation and investigation and adjudication of unfair labor practices by employers and unions. NLRB jurisdiction generally applies to all employers engaged in interstate commerce other than airlines, railroads, agriculture, and government.

Since its inception, the NLRB's role has been amended by Congress, by its board's actions, and by court decisions. The board has five members and primarily acts as a quasi-judicial body deciding cases on the basis of records from administrative proceedings. Board members are appointed by the U.S. president to five-year terms with Senate approval. The term of one board member expires each year.

When an unfair labor-practice charge is filed with the NLRB, the appropriate field office conducts an investigation to determine if there is reasonable cause to believe the NLRA has been violated. If the regional director finds reasonable cause, the region seeks a voluntary settlement to remedy the alleged violations. If the settlement effort fails, a formal complaint is issued and the case goes to hearing before an NLRB administrative law judge, who issues a written decision that may be appealed to the full NLRB. Of approximately 35,000 charges filed annually, approximately one-third are found to have merit, of which over 90 percent are settled.

Changes in the TAFT-HARTLEY ACT (1947) gave the NLRB power to seek court INJUNCTIONS to temporarily prevent unfair labor practices by either unions or employers and restore the status quo, pending a full review of the case by the NLRB. The act requires the NLRB to seek a temporary federal-court injunction against certain forms of union misconduct, principally involving secondary BOYCOTTS (boycotts of companies with which unions are not directly negotiating) and recognitional picketing (picketing of a company in order to establish union representation).

Further reading
Mallor, Jane P., A. James Barnes, Thomas Bowers, Michael J. Philips, and Arlen W. Langvardt. *Business Law and the Regulatory Environment*, 11th ed. Boston: McGraw-Hill, 2001; National Labor Relations Board website. Available on-line. URL: www.nlrb.gov.

National Mediation Board
The National Mediation Board (NMB), established by the 1934 amendments to the Railway Labor Act of 1926, is a federal agency that facilitates labor-MANAGEMENT relations within two of the nation's transportation modes: railroads and airlines. Pursuant to the Railway Labor Act, NMB programs provide a dispute-resolution process to meet the objective of minimizing work stoppages in the airline and railroad industries. The NMB's processes are designed to promote three statutory goals:

- prompt and orderly resolution of disputes arising from the negotiation of new or revised COLLECTIVE BARGAINING agreements
- achievement of employee rights to self-organization where a representation dispute exists
- prompt and orderly resolution of disputes over the interpretation or application of existing agreements

The purpose of mediation is to foster the prompt and orderly resolution of collective-bargaining disputes in railroad and airline industries. These disputes, referred to as "major disputes," involve the establishment or revision of rates of pay, rules, or working conditions. Management and UNIONS should first attempt to resolve collective-bargaining disputes through direct negotiation. Failing that, either party may request the NMB's services or the board may involve itself on its own initiative. The objective of mediation is to assist the parties in achieving agreement. NMB expertise in mediation and its discretion to determine when mediation has been exhausted ensures that bargaining disputes escalate only rarely into disruptions of passenger service and the transportation of commerce. Historically some 97 percent of all NMB mediation cases have been successfully resolved without interruptions to public service. Since 1980 only slightly more than 1 percent of cases have involved a disruption of service.

In rare situations, when a distribution of essential transportation services looms, the NMB may recommend that the U.S. president create a Presidential Emergency Board. This board temporarily prevents a work stoppage or a lockout for up to 60 days and provides recommendations for resolving the dispute.

The NMB is responsible for achieving employee rights to self-organization where a representation dispute exists. Its primary representation-dispute responsibilities are to

- conduct initial investigation of representation applications
- determine and certify employees' collective-bargaining representatives
- ensure that the process occurs without interference, influence, or coercion

The NMB is also involved in alternative dispute-resolution and dispute-prevention activities, such as training and education that includes interest-based bargaining and facilitation, predispute mediation, and grievance mediation, among other services.

Further reading
National Mediation Board website. Available on-line. URL: www.nmb.gov.

negligence

Webster's defines *negligence* as habitual failure to do the required things or carelessness in manner or appearance. Business law authors Jane Mallor et al. define *negligence* as "conduct that falls below the level necessary to protect others against unreasonable risks of harm." In the United States, negligence law grew out of the American industrial revolution, when railroads, machinery, and new technology increased injuries to workers. Initially, courts generally ruled against plaintiffs, under the belief that there should be no tort liability to employers. Over time, negligence liability shifted, becoming more pro-plaintiff and leading to calls for tort reform. Lawsuits and insurance against liability are a major cost of doing business in the United States. Many would-be entrepreneurs find that the cost of protecting against liability is prohibitive and discourages business initiative.

Critical to the definition of negligence is what constitutes failure. The most common definition of failure is not using reasonable care—doing something that a reasonably prudent person would not do or failing to do something that a reasonably prudent person would do under like circumstances or a departure from what an ordinary reasonable member of a community would do in the same community. Mallor et al. write that to prove negligence, a plaintiff must demonstrate a breach of duty, actual injury suffered by the plaintiff, and actual and proximate causation between the breach and the injury.

In cases involving allegedly defective, unreasonably dangerous products, the manufacturer may be liable even though it exercised all reasonable care in the design, manufacture, and sale of the product in question. Manufacturers are not required to produce a product that is "accident-proof." They are required to make a product that is free from defective and unreasonably dangerous conditions.

The two traditional defenses manufacturers take in negligence cases are contributory negligence and assumption of risk. Contributory negligence is failure by the user to take reasonable care for his or her safety. Assumption of risk is the legal argument that the user voluntarily exposed him- or herself to a known danger. More recently, negligence defense has included comparative fault and comparative negligence. Comparative fault involves plaintiffs' and defendants' overall fault rather than either's negligence alone. Comparative negligence argues that damages should be apportioned based on each party's relative fault. Often, settlements of negligence cases are based on comparative negligence.

Further reading

Mallor, Jane, A. James Barnes, Thomas Bowers, Michael Philips, and Arlen Langvardt. *Business Law and the Regulatory Environment.* Boston: McGraw-Hill, 2001.

negotiable instruments

Negotiable instruments are financial securities that may be transferred by endorsement or by the holder's simple delivery. The primary example of a negotiable instrument is a check. The UNIFORM COMMERCIAL CODE, which has been adopted by all states, specifies the laws that govern negotiable instruments.

A FINANCIAL INSTRUMENT must contain the following characteristics in order to be negotiable.

1. The instrument must be in writing.
2. It must contain an unconditional promise to pay a specific sum of money.
3. It must either be payable "upon demand" of the holder or at a specific point in time.
4. It must be made payable to bearer or to the order of someone.
5. It must be signed.

There are two types of negotiable instruments. The first is called a draft, which orders a payment to be made. A check is a good example of the "draft" type of negotiable instrument involving three players: a drawer, a payee, and drawee. The drawer is the party that creates the draft (i.e., writes the check), telling the drawee to pay the payee on behalf of the drawer. The payee receives the check from the drawer and presents it to the drawer's bank, which is the drawee. The drawee then pays the payee on behalf of the drawer.

The other type of negotiable instrument is a CONTRACT that promises a payment will be made. There are two parties to this type of negotiable instrument. The first is the maker of the note—that is, the one who signs the note promising to pay. The payee is the person whom the maker promises to pay.

With both types of negotiable instruments, the payee can be listed as "bearer." This basically says that whoever is holding the note on the due date is entitled to be paid by the drawee or maker. If a draft or note is made to a specific payee instead of to bearer, the payee can "negotiate" the note by signing it. This endorsement transfers the note or draft to a subsequent holder. Whoever holds it on the due date can collect on the note or draft from the maker or drawee.

—Mack Tennyson

nepotism

Nepotism refers to the practice of people, usually executives and managers, giving relatives preferential treatment in EMPLOYMENT. Such people are in a position to heavily influence various employment-related decisions, such as hiring, firing, promotions, COMPENSATION AND BENEFITS, and discipline. A relative may be a blood relative, such a grandparent, parent, sibling, niece, nephew, uncle, or aunt; or a relative through marriage, such as a husband, wife, brother-in-law, or sister-in-law. Nepotism is usually regarded as legitimate in family-owned businesses.

Nepotism can occur in the public and private sectors. In the public sector, officials may give preferential treatment to their relatives in employment-related decisions. For example, a public official who approves a bid for a government contract submitted by her husband's firm is engaging in nepotism if other firms had submitted lower bids for the contract.

In the private sector, members of MANAGEMENT may give preferential treatment to their relatives in hiring or promotion decisions. For example, a senior manager of a CORPORATION who hires her brother for a position in the corporation is probably engaging in nepotism if her brother is less qualified for the position than other candidates who applied for the job.

A manager who engages in nepotism may be subjecting his organization to inefficiencies or ineffectiveness in business operations, because he is not basing business decisions on criteria that would ensure that the organization's RESOURCES are maximized. For example, a manager of a corporation who hires his brother instead of a more qualified candidate has failed to maximize the organization's HUMAN RESOURCES because he has failed to hire the best possible candidate for the position.

In order to reduce problems associated with nepotism, such as the appearance of favoritism, some organizations have implemented antinepotism policies. Generally such policies prohibit department leaders from hiring their immediate family members for positions that are supervised by those department leaders and limit the ability of family members in the same organization to work together.

Organizations must exercise care in crafting and implementing antinepotism policies so as to avoid lawsuits alleging violation of privacy rights, unlawful restraints on marriage, or employment discrimination. States differ in their treatment of antinepotism policies, and thus organizations with operations in more than one state should draft antinepotism policies with regard to the legality of such policies in each of the states in which they operate.

Further reading

Black, Henry Campbell, et al. *Black's Law Dictionary.* 6th ed., abridged. St. Paul, Minn.: West Publishing Co., 1991; Russ, Lee R. "What Constitutes Employment Discrimination on Basis of 'Martial Status' for Purposes of State Civil Rights Laws." In *American Law Reports,* 4th ed. Eagan, Minn.: West Group, 2001; *TI Source Book 2000: Chapter 21: Conflict of Interest, Nepotism and Cronyism.* Transparency.org. Available on-line. URL: http://www.transparency.org./sourcebook/21.htm; Downloaded on March 9, 2002.

—Gayatri Gupta

network marketing   See MULTILEVEL MARKETING.

new-product development

New-product development is the process companies go through in creating, changing, and repositioning PRODUCTs for their TARGET MARKETS. Given the dynamics of changing markets and changing technology, almost every business needs to be constantly evaluating new products. Studies show leaders in any industry are the firms that are creating new products. As one saying goes, "If you are not creating, you are decaying." STOCK MARKET analysts, particularly in industries like pharmaceuticals, closely watch what each company is spending on RESEARCH AND DEVELOPMENT and how many new products companies have "in the pipeline." Pharmaceutical companies' new-product development is relatively easy to observe because new drugs must go through various stages in FOOD AND DRUG ADMINISTRATION approval.

For most businesses, new-product development is a closely held secret. The process of development can be either formal or informal, but in major companies it tends to be structured. Recognizing new-product failure rates and the cost of bringing new products to market, companies generally go through a six-step process.

1. *Idea generation.* Ideas can come from anywhere. Typically they come from either consumers or organization employees. Many businesses actively seek the ideas and opinions of consumers and front-line staff who interact directly with consumers. Some ways new products can be created include adding something to existing products, taking something out, answering consumer complaints, changing the shape or size, making a task easier, using products in a new way, substituting one product for another, or looking in other markets for ideas.
2. *Idea screening.* Marketers report that one idea in 100 becomes a new product. As marketing teams go through the development process, COSTs go up. Therefore marketers screen ideas, using questions such as, "Is the idea in a field or market the company is engaged in? Can the product be made with materials or machinery the company already owns or has access to? Can the new product be marketed through the organization's existing sales and distribution system? Is there sufficient market potential? Is there sufficient PROFIT potential?"
3. *Business analysis.* At this stage the new-product development team conducts an in-depth analysis of the market potential and profitability. Sometimes consulting firms are used to conduct market-feasibility studies.
4. *Product development.* At this stage a company commits to creating prototypes of the new product. Sometimes this can be quite expensive, other times it can be done with minor adaptations to existing products.
5. *Test marketing.* For large CORPORATIONS, it can be quite expensive to introduce new products. Many companies conduct tests in a few outlets or markets before doing a

full rollout. One problem with test marketing is that competitors will learn quickly about the new product. Sometimes test marketing is skipped in order to get new products to market ahead of the COMPETITION. Almost any new-product development is going to need adjustment, and test marketing provides opportunities to address problems early in the marketing process.

6. *Commercialization.* At this stage the new product is fully introduced to the target market. Depending on the type of new product involved, at the commercialization stage SALES PROMOTION efforts will focus on generating interest or awareness of the new product.

Generally there are five categories of new products, ranging from new-to-the-world goods people have never seen before to repositioning and targeting existing products to new markets or new uses. Most new-product development falls in between, including products new to the firm (i.e., adding a product line to a retail store), additions to a product line (i.e., adding fruit juices to a convenience store's beverage offerings), and product improvements (i.e., new and improved XYZ). Each of these new-product development strategies builds upon existing knowledge and strengths within the organization and therefore are less risky than introducing totally new products.

See also POSITIONING; TARGET MARKETS.

Further reading
Etzel, Michael J., Bruce J. Walker, and William J. Staunton. *Marketing,* 12th ed. Boston: McGraw-Hill, 2001.

New York Clearing House Association
The New York Clearing House Association is the oldest and largest bank clearinghouse in the United States. Established in 1853, the Clearing House was created to provide "clearing" operations for the burgeoning network of New York banks. New York City has been the center of commerce in the United States since the American Revolution. Each day, porters from the banks would carry bags of gold and silver coins from bank to bank to settle accounts based on the checks drawn and deposited by the banks' customers. With the gold rush in California and development of the railroad system, the number of banks in New York grew from 24 to 57 in the period from 1849 to 1853. This expanded the number of exchanges exponentially.

Using the London Clearing House system as a model, a bank bookkeeper named George D. Lyman proposed the creation of a central office to clear accounts. Bankers quickly created the New York Clearing House, with 52 members participating in the exchange. The first day the Clearing House exchanged $22.6 million in checks. Clearing House members agreed to weekly audits, minimum reserve levels, and daily settlement of balances.

For most of the 19th century, there was no central bank, and the United States experienced economic panics, fre-

quently due to lack of liquidity in the financial system. During the panic of 1857, the Clearing House created loan certificates that could be used to settle accounts. In effect these certificates were currency, adding the needed liquidity. Certificates continued to be used into the early 1900s, until Congress passed legislation creating the FEDERAL RESERVE SYSTEM. The Fed replaced many of the Clearing House's functions, including supervision of banks and providing liquidity to the financial system.

Today the New York Clearing House processes an average of $20 billion worth of checks daily and is expanding with the growth of the U.S. economy. In 1970 the organization created the Clearing House Interbank Payments System (CHIPS), facilitating real-time FOREIGN EXCHANGE transactions. CHIPS transfers an average value of $1.2 trillion daily, handling 95 percent of all U.S. dollar payments among countries around the world. In addition, the Clearing House operates the Electronic Payments Network and Electronic Check Clearing System, which is a major wire-transfer and clearinghouse provider in the country, in addition to the Federal Reserve's Fedwire.

Further reading
New York Clearing House Association website. Available on-line. URL: www.nych.org.

New York Mercantile Exchange
The New York Mercantile Exchange (NYMEX) is a market exchange where precious metals and energy FUTURES and OPTIONS contracts are bought and sold. Created in 1872 as the New York Butter and Cheese Exchange, it was renamed the New York Mercantile Exchange in 1882, and in 1994 it merged with COMEX (Commodity Exchange Inc.) to become the largest physical commodity futures exchange. Today NYMEX is used primarily by managers and broker/dealers to reduce RISK in business transactions.

Traditionally merchants and other industry members used futures CONTRACTS—agreements to buy or sell a specific amount of a commodity at a particular price on or before stipulated date—to hedge their risks. Producers sell futures contracts for commodities they produce, thereby assuring themselves of a price for their products. If, in the time between when they sell the futures contract and when their products are ready for market, the commodity price goes down, producers will be able to buy back their futures contract at a lower price. They PROFIT by the difference, offsetting the lower market price for their product. If the price goes up, they will lose money on the futures contract but profit from the higher price in the marketplace.

As distribution systems for agricultural products changed in the 1930s and 1940s, NYMEX and many other commodity exchanges declined in importance. The exchange moved away from trading in agricultural commodities and added futures markets for gold, silver, and platinum as well as energy-related products including crude oil, heating oil, gasoline, and natural gas. With the rapid changes in energy prices during 2000–01, companies often used futures contracts or options on futures contracts to reduce their risk of higher energy COSTS.

Where futures contracts obligate the buyer and seller to a specified agreement, options contracts give the buyer or seller the right to buy or sell at a specified price. If the option is not exercised by the maturity date, it expires with the buyer losing the amount of money paid for the option. Prices of futures and options can be quite volatile. In addition to the reduction of risk, speculators add liquidity to commodity and futures markets and profit when they correctly anticipate price changes in the market.

The NYMEX is regulated by the COMMODITY FUTURES TRADING COMMISSION (CFTC), created to oversee commodity exchanges. In the last two decades, NYMEX, the CHICAGO BOARD OF TRADE, CHICAGO MERCANTILE EXCHANGE, and other smaller regional exchanges have competed to provide new options and futures contracts to meet the needs of financial markets and managers.

Further reading
New York Mercantile Exchange website. Available on-line. URL: www.nymex.com.

New York Stock Exchange

The New York Stock Exchange (NYSE) is the oldest stock exchange in the United States. Established in 1792 along a wall that had been used to keep wild pigs out of settlers' gardens in lower Manhattan (WALL STREET), the NYSE is the largest stock exchange in the world based on dollar value of shares traded. In 2000 the exchange traded 262.5 billion shares, valued at $11.1 trillion dollars.

In 1971 the NYSE became a nonprofit CORPORATION directed by a 25-member BOARD OF DIRECTORS. The board of directors includes the CHIEF EXECUTIVE OFFICER, 12 public members, and 12 members from the securities industry. The mission of the NYSE (also known as the "Big Board," "Wall Street," and "the Exchange") is "to add value to the CAPITAL-raising and ASSET-management process by providing the highest-quality and most cost-effective and self-regulating marketplace for the trading of FINANCIAL INSTRUMENTS . . ."

As the country's premier stock exchange, the NYSE's listing requirements are more stringent than most exchanges, precluding many small and unproven corporations. To be a listed company on the NYSE (there were 2,862 companies in 2000), a domestic company must, among other requirements

- have a minimum of 2,000 round-lot (100 shares) SHARE-HOLDERS
- have an average trading volume of at least 100,000 shares in the previous six months
- have at least 1.1 million public shares

- have a MARKET VALUE for public companies of at least $100 million
- have minimum pretax earnings of $6.5 million in the last three years

There are other requirements and slightly different rules for non-U.S. companies. Many corporations consider it a status symbol to become large enough to be traded on the Big Board. Most of the DOT-COMS created in the 1990s never met the NYSE standards. Some major technology companies, like Microsoft, have chosen to remain on the NATIONAL ASSOCIATION OF SECURITIES DEALERS AUTOMATED QUOTATIONS (NASDAQ) system rather than be listed with the NYSE.

While the NYSE is the largest stock exchange in dollar volume, the NASDAQ is the largest exchange based on number of shares traded. At the end of 2000, the stocks on the NYSE had a global market capitalization (number of shares multiplied by price per share) of $17.1 trillion. By comparison, the NASDAQ had a market capitalization of $3.6 trillion, the Tokyo exchange had $3.2 trillion, and the London exchange had $2.6 trillion in market capitalization.

In addition to trading shares of U.S. corporations, foreign companies, and AMERICAN DEPOSITORY RECEIPTS (ADRs, receipts representing shares of foreign corporations) are also traded on the exchange.

There are over 1,300 members (called "seats") of the New York Stock Exchange, which are owned by securities-industry executives. NYSE members execute trades for their clients, though a few members trade only for their own accounts. Trading posts on the floor of the exchange are manned by specialists. When stockholders order or sell shares of NYSE-listed stocks, the brokerage firm forwards the order to the floor specialist, who sets the market price based on the number of buy and sell orders for that stock that day. Specialists are charged to provide an orderly market, facilitating the exchange of shares. They maintain a portfolio of their own in order to execute trades when there is no liquidity in the market. Floor specialists have significant market power, earning comfortable livings providing market transactions.

In 2000, the NYSE changed market pricing from measurement in eighths to a decimal system. Members also debated converting into a for-profit publicly held corporation but did not follow through on that initiative. Becoming a for-profit corporation would have changed the exchange's relationship with the SECURITIES AND EXCHANGE COMMISSION, which oversees the securities industry. In response to competition from NASDAQ, the NYSE instituted off-hours off-hour trading.

See also EQUITY; STOCK MARKET, BOND MARKET.

Further reading
New York Stock Exchange website. Available on-line. URL: www.nyse.com.

nontariff barriers

Nontariff barriers (NTBs) are limits on trade other TARIFFS, including quotas, regulations, and technical requirements. While many countries claim to embrace FREE TRADE, most continue to use a variety of nontariff barriers to restrict the entry of imported goods and SERVICES.

Quotas are limits on the quantity of a good that may be imported into a country. Immigration restrictions are a form of quotas, as are voluntary export restraints. Each year the United States limits the number of immigrants from different regions of the world. In the 1980s, fearing the imposition of quotas or tariffs, Japan coordinated a "voluntary" export limit of automobiles into the United States. U.S. political leaders had pressured the Japanese government into the quota, hoping to protect American auto-industry jobs. Facing increased DEMAND in the United States along with restricted supply, car dealers simply raised prices.

Regulations are another form of NTB. For decades U.S. exporters to Japan have complained about Japanese regulatory requirements and tedious inspection demands as a form of trade barrier. Limits on the size of retail stores and distribution systems that are difficult to access are also forms of nontariff barriers.

Developing countries claim labor and environmental standards imposed by industrialized countries impose nontariff barriers. Eco-labeling requirements in the EUROPEAN UNION have been challenged as a barrier to trade. The International Organization for Standardization's ISO 9000 quality standards and ISO 14000 environmental-management standards limit entry to those companies that can afford to meet ISO STANDARDS. Critics suggest this effectively limits COMPETITION and is a nontariff barrier. In addition, health and safety concerns are often used to justify barring imports; in the 1990s, the EUROPEAN UNION challenged U.S. dairy products containing bovine growth hormones. U.S. health and safety laws also restrict entry into the country. In 2001, Mexican trucks were still restricted from transporting goods into the U.S. beyond a limited border area even though access was permitted in the NORTH AMERICAN FREE TRADE AGREEMENT (NAFTA). Safety concerns were stated as the U.S. justification to ignore that provision of the agreement.

In addition to reducing tariffs, the WORLD TRADE ORGANIZATION attempts to reduce nontariff barriers through greater HARMONIZATION of global trade rules.

See also TRADE BARRIERS.

Norris-LaGuardia Act

The Norris-LaGuardia Anti-Injunction Act (1932), better known simply as the Norris-LaGuardia Act, restricted the power of FEDERAL COURTS to intervene in labor disputes. Until its passage, actions by groups of employees (UNIONS) such as picketing, strikes, or BOYCOTTS were considered criminal conspiracies and subject to prosecution. The Norris-LaGuardia Act was a major change, reducing industrial managers' use of federal courts to seek INJUNCTIONS against union activity. At that time federal injunctions frequently lead to deputation of employer agents or the use of federal troops to disperse union groups, often resulting in violence and deaths.

The Norris-LaGuardia Act reduced employers' power over workers, specifically prohibiting federal court injunctions involving

- striking
- becoming a member of a labor organization
- paying or withholding strike or UNEMPLOYMENT benefits
- providing lawful assistance to people engaged in legal action in federal courts related to a labor dispute
- publicizing a labor dispute
- peaceful assembly associated with a labor dispute
- notifying or agreeing with another person to engage in labor-dispute actions

In cases where an injunction was sought against union activity, the act included specific procedural steps that must be taken by a federal court considering an injunction request. Injunctions could still be sought against acts of violence or FRAUD. The act also prohibited "yellow dog" contracts in federal courts, whereby workers agreed to not join a union as a precondition for their EMPLOYMENT.

In 1932 the Norris-LaGuardia Act removed federal court jurisdiction over injunctions in labor disputes, but the TAFT-HARTLEY ACT (1947) gave the NATIONAL LABOR RELATIONS BOARD, a federally created agency, power to seek injunctions against unfair labor practices.

Further reading

Mallor, Jane P., A. James Barnes, Thomas Bowers, Michael J. Philips, and Arlen W. Langvardt. *Business Law and the Regulatory Environment,* 11th ed. Boston: McGraw-Hill, 2001.

North American Agreement on Labor Cooperation

The North American Agreement on Labor Cooperation (NAALC) is one of the two side agreements to the NORTH AMERICAN FREE TRADE AGREEMENT of the United States, Canada, and Mexico. The labor agreement affirmed the right of each country to establish its own "high" labor standards and "guiding labor principles" but did not establish common minimum standards. The agreement created a Commission on Labor Cooperation and Secretariat charged to "effectively enforce" labor law.

The NAALC Secretariat, headquartered in Dallas, Texas, monitors and reports labor law issues among the NAFTA countries. Under the NAALC, each country is obligated to provide

- access, transparency and DUE PROCESS of law
- public information and awareness

- cooperative activities
- national administrative office (NAO) reviews, consultations, and evaluations

Complaints about labor practices are submitted to national administrative offices (NAOs) established by each country as part of the agreement. The first complaint filed by UNIONS with the U.S. NAO alleged that U.S. subsidiaries (Honeywell and General Electric) had fired Mexican workers for union-organizing activities. The NAO found no evidence of failure to enforce Mexican labor law. Later the Telephone Workers Union of Mexico filed a complaint with the Mexican NAO regarding worker dismissals and a plant closing at a Sprint subsidiary in San Francisco. The complaint, upheld by the Mexican NAO, alleged Sprint had thwarted unionization. The complaint led to consultation between the two countries.

Under the NAALC, if a complaint is not resolved by ministerial consultations, the next option is to establish a three-person Evaluation Committee of Experts (ECE). The ECE reports to the Labor Council of Ministers, part of the Commission on Labor Cooperation. Depending on the nature of the labor issue being evaluated by the ECE, different dispute resolution mechanisms are utilized. The ECE examines labor legal matters including laws on

- occupational safety and health
- equal pay for men and women
- forced labor
- EMPLOYMENT standards
- child labor minimum wages
- employment discrimination
- migrant workers

If, after consideration of a final ECE report, a country believes that there is still a persistent pattern of failure by another country to effectively enforce labor laws, it may request further consultation and, eventually, the establishment of an independent arbitral panel. After considering the matter, the arbitral panel may issue a ruling, as a result of which the parties agree on an "action plan." If the action plan is not implemented, the panel may impose a monetary enforcement assessment, the fine to be used to improve labor law enforcement by the offending party. Generally the labor side agreement of NAFTA is much more limited in scope and remedial authority than the environmental side agreement (BORDER ENVIRONMENTAL COOPERATION COMMISSION).

Further reading

Folsom, Ralph H., and W. Davis Folsom. *Understanding NAFTA and Its International Business Implications.* New York: Matthew Bender/Irwin, 1996; North American Agreement on Labor Cooperation website. Available on-line. URL: www.naalc.org.

North American Development Bank

The North American Development Bank (NADBank) is a binational financial institution that provides financial assistance to projects certified by the BORDER ENVIRONMENTAL COOPERATION COMMISSION (BECC). NADBank's primary functions are to

- promote public and private CAPITAL investment in BECC projects
- supplement such INVESTMENTS with NADBank loans and guarantees
- provide technical assistance for financing BECC projects

NADBank's BOARD OF DIRECTORS include three members from the United States and three from Mexico, with decisions requiring two supporting votes from members representing each country. U.S. directors are the secretary of state, secretary of the Treasury, and administrator of the ENVIRONMENTAL PROTECTION AGENCY (EPA). NADBank's headquarters are in San Antonio, Texas.

Initial plans for NADBank anticipated $8 billion in border environmental INFRASTRUCTURE needs in the decade from 1995 to 2005 with financing from federal, state, local, and private sources. The U.S. government appropriated $450 million to be directed by the EPA in the first five years. At the beginning of 2001, NADBank was involved in 43 infrastructure projects administering $339 million in EPA construction funds, 26 on the U.S. side and 17 on the Mexican side of the border. Only six projects had been completed at that time, representing a small fraction of the infrastructure needs of the region.

Further reading

U.S. Environmental Protection Agency BECC and NADBank website. Available on-line. URL: www.epa.gov/oia/mex2.htm.

North American Free Trade Agreement (NAFTA)

The North American Free Trade Agreement (NAFTA) is an agreement governing trade among the United States, Canada, and Mexico in effect since January 1, 1994. NAFTA negotiations began in July 1991 and were completed in August 1992 under the George H. W. Bush administration. The agreement was negotiated under FAST TRACK authorization, meaning Congress agreed to vote yes or no on the trade agreement as negotiated, without making changes to it. NAFTA is both a radical change in U.S. policy and a minor "tinkering" of an existing U.S. trade policy. To understand it, it is necessary to review the context within which the agreement was negotiated.

NAFTA is an expansion of the UNITED STATES–CANADA FREE TRADE AGREEMENT (CFTA) of 1989. The United States and Canada have a long history of trade, with the U.S. accounting for more than 70 percent of Canadian exports.

In the mid-1980s, trade negotiations under the General Agreement on Tariffs and Trade (GATT; see WORLD TRADE ORGANIZATION) were stalled. Traditionally Canada had found it to its advantage to negotiate trade agreements with the United States as part of a larger world organization rather than as a smaller nation negotiating with a larger nation (Canada's economy is about one-tenth the size of the United States). Before NAFTA, Canada and Mexico engaged in very little trade. (Some PRODUCTS made or assembled in Mexico were used in producing products in the United States, which were then shipped to Canada.) But when President Bush indicated interest in including Mexico in a trade agreement, Canadian leaders joined the initiative rather than being left out of the process.

For Mexico, NAFTA represented a radical change in trade policy. Trade relations between Mexico and the United States have often been strained or at best minimal. (The Mexican economy is approximately one-twentieth the size of the U.S. economy.) While Mexico is a huge country with over 100 million citizens, has vast quantities of oil and gas resources, and is contiguous to the United States, until the 1980s its trade was largely limited to energy and agricultural commodities. Though the U.S.-Canada border is open and largely unmonitored, the U.S.-Mexican border is highly monitored. An old story illustrates the traditional relationship between the United States and Mexico (as well as other Latin American countries). If a Latin American manager is asked what he watches, he will say he keeps one eye on his cash register and the other eye looking north to see what is happening in the United States. Although Mexicans know they cannot control what the United States does, they also know changes there will affect them.

Part of the strained relationship between the United States and Mexico dates back to the Treaty of Guadalupe Hidalgo (1848) and the Gadsden Purchase (1853), which together Mexicans refer to as the "War of North American Invasion." Following the defeat of General Santa Anna in the Texas Revolution (1836) and the addition of Texas to the United States (1845), war broke out, and U.S. forces were sent to Vera Cruz, Monterey, and Mexico City. After gaining control of most of Mexico, the United States negotiated the Treaty of Guadalupe Hidalgo and subsequently the Gadsden Purchase, acquiring much of what are now parts of Arizona, New Mexico, and California.

Another reason for the historically limited trade relations between Mexico and the United States was due to past Mexican trade policies. During World War II, the United States sought support from Mexico, primarily for oil RESOURCES, but trade relations were neglected after the war. Mexico then instituted a policy of import-substitution-industrialization (ISI), protective TARIFFS, and other TRADE BARRIERS, targeted to reduce their dependence on foreign IMPORTS and growth through domestic production of what was previously imported. The three major problems with ISI are that it limits

COMPETITION to just domestic producers, does not require domestic manufacturers to be competitive on a global basis, and limits growth to the size of the domestic market.

Mexican interest in a FREE TRADE agreement with the United States was initiated by President Carlos Salinas. After being rebuffed in attempts to attract greater INVESTMENT from Europeans and with a stagnating domestic economy, President Salinas contacted President George H. W. Bush in 1990, and NAFTA discussions began.

A free-trade agreement is much less than what it first appears. Countries agree to reduce and/or eliminate trade barriers among members of the agreement. Each country retains its own trade agreements (and barriers) with respect to trade with other countries, and restrictions on the movement of labor among the trade partners typically are retained.

With more than 1,000 pages, NAFTA contains 22 "chapters" and two major side agreements. Although it was negotiated in a little over a year, each sentence of the agreement was closely scrutinized both by the government representatives negotiating the agreement and business interests affected by the agreement's terms. The objectives of NAFTA listed in Article 102 are to

a. eliminate barriers to trade in, and facilitate the cross-border movement of, goods and services between the territories of the Parties;

b. promote conditions of fair competition in the free trade area;

c. increase substantially investment opportunities in the territories of the Parties;

d. provide adequate and effective protection and enforcement of INTELLECTUAL PROPERTY rights in each Party's territory;

e. create effective procedures for the implementation and application of the Agreement, for its joint administration and for the resolution of disputes; and

f. establish a framework for further trilateral, regional and multilateral cooperation to expand and enhance the benefits of the Agreement.

One significant aspect of NAFTA is that it emphasizes trade in SERVICES as well as goods. At the time, GATT negotiations were stalled, and U.S. negotiators saw NAFTA as a model for future GATT treaties. (The United States is a dominant force in international trade in services, and while it has a large trade deficit, it also has long had a trade surplus in services.) NAFTA also emphasizes increasing investment opportunities. At the time the agreement was signed, Mexico had significant barriers to international investment and bans on FOREIGN INVESTMENT in certain industries, particularly oil. In addition, NAFTA is envisioned as a blueprint for expansion of trade throughout the Americas. In the 1995 Summit of the Americas, President Bill Clinton promised Chile it would be the next nation allowed to join NAFTA. (The U.S. Congress then failed to renew the president's fast-track authorization, effectively ending NAFTA's expansion for the rest of the Clinton administration.)

Just a month before NAFTA's implementation, Mexico succumbed to what is known as the PESO CRISIS: an overvalued peso leading to an international financial crisis and a huge $50 billion bailout. Because the peso crisis occurred at the same time as NAFTA, many people blamed the agreement for the crisis. However, many economists think that because Mexican leaders chose to adhere to NAFTA during the crisis, it was not as prolonged as previous financial crashes in the country had been. As the Mexican peso lost its value relative to the U.S. dollar, MAQUILADORAS (Mexican factories of goods intended primarily for the U.S. market) rapidly expanded, creating jobs and INCOME.

In addition to the 22 chapters in the agreement, NAFTA included two unique side agreements creating the BORDER ENVIRONMENTAL COOPERATION COMMISSION and the NORTH AMERICAN AGREEMENT ON LABOR COOPERATION. Although President Bush negotiated NAFTA, after the 1992 presidential election, it was left to President Clinton to gain ratification of the agreement from Congress. The two side agreements on labor and the environment mollified traditional Democratic opposition to free trade and allowed for the treaty's passage.

Most economists consider NAFTA a success. It has led to increased trade among the participating countries; trade diversion, particularly the movement of production facilities out of Asian countries and into Mexico to gain access to the U.S. market; and expanded investment opportunities. NAFTA has also contributed to declines in some U.S. industries, particularly textiles and other labor-intensive manufacturing.

See also FREE-TRADE AREAS.

Further reading
Folsom, Ralph H., and W. Davis Folsom. *Understanding NAFTA and its International Business Implications.* New York: Matthew Bender/Irwin, 1996.

North American Industry Classification System
The North American Industry Classification System (NAICS) is a system for classifying businesses based on their economic activity. Introduced in April 1997, NAICS replaced the Standard Industrial Classification System (SIC) used since the 1930s.

NAICS is based on the concept of grouping businesses that use similar processes to produce goods and SERVICES. The system allows statistical agencies in the United States to produce data that can be used for measuring productivity, unit labor cost, and capital intensity of production. Classification of industrial activity is an important component of the economic census produced by the U.S. CENSUS BUREAU.

NAICS was developed in a combined effort involving the U.S. OFFICE OF MANAGEMENT AND BUDGET, Statistics Canada, and Mexico's Instituto Nacional de Estadistica. The effort began in the early 1990s as a result of criticism claiming the SIC was outmoded and not reflective of economic changes in the United States. Increased economic integration since the passage of the NORTH AMERICAN FREE TRADE AGREEMENT (NAFTA) in 1994 added to the interest in improving measurement and reporting industrial production in North America.

NAICS includes a greater number of service-based industries and greater compatibility with the United Nations—sponsored International Standard Industrial Classification System (ISIC) than the old SIC system. NAICS is a six-digit system classifying economic activity according to sector, subsector, industry group, and NAICS industry. The sixth digit is reserved for classification within respective countries.

For example, in NAICS

31 = manufacturing
312 = beverage and tobacco products manufacturing
3121 = beverage manufacturing
31211 = soft-drink and ice manufacturing
312111 = soft-drink manufacturing
312112 = bottled-water manufacturing

In addition to being used by government agencies to measure input and output relationships, NAICS is an important tool for marketers looking for prospective customers. Business-to-business marketers recognize that businesses using similar production processes are likely to need similar materials, machines, and SERVICES. Lists of businesses using NAICS codes provide a basis for identifying TARGET MARKETS for a firm's products.

Further reading
Development of NAICS. Available on-line. URL: http://www/census.gov/epcd/www/naicsdev.htm.

O

observation

Observation is a method market researchers use to record people's overt behavior. Researchers use a variety of observation methods, from simply looking at car license plates in parking lots to rigging special cameras to detect the order in which consumers read and time spent reading parts of an advertisement. Observation provides information about how people behave, but not what motivates them. Results can be biased by the researcher conducting the observation study and also by subjects if they know they are being observed.

In states with license plates issued by county, parking-lot observation can tell marketers where people live and the amount of business competitors are doing. One company measured the rust on rail ties to estimate how often a competitor was shipping PRODUCTS. The Louvre museum in Paris studied the wear patterns on their wood floors to determine which exhibits were the most popular.

Mechanical devices can be used to determine the number of people entering a store or department. Most state highway departments use mechanical counters to measure the volume of traffic moving along roads; traffic-flow data is useful for businesses choosing new locations. In-store scanners record sales electronically and, combined with store bonus cards, allow marketers to determine who is purchasing what products. Double-click Corporation developed software to track website viewer patterns; its data have been the subject of numerous privacy debates.

Video cameras are also used in observation research. Companies study CONSUMER BEHAVIOR in bars, clothing stores, and other environments to better understand who is buying their products and what choices and comparisons people make. Observation methods are limited by the capabilities of the methods available and may not provide insights into why people behave the way they do.

See also MARKET RESEARCH.

Further reading

Pride, William O., and O. C. Ferrell. *Marketing Concepts and Strategies,* 12th ed. Boston: Houghton Mifflin, 2003.

Occupational Safety and Health Administration

The Occupational Safety and Health Administration (OSHA) is the primary federal agency responsible for workplace SAFETY AND HEALTH. Created under the Occupational Safety and Health Act (1970) to be part of the DEPARTMENT OF LABOR, OSHA's mission is to prevent injuries, protect workers, and save lives. OSHA operates in 24 states, while 26 states have state-run OSHA offices. OSHA and its state partners employ over 2,400 inspectors nationwide, in addition to discrimination investigators, engineers, educators, physicians, standards writers, and other technical and support personnel working in 200 offices around the country. In 2001 combined state and federal OSHA personnel conducted more than 90,000 inspections. Almost every worker is covered by OSHA regulations. Exceptions include miners, transportation workers, and self-employed people.

OSHA attempts to gain employee cooperation and MANAGEMENT commitment to comprehensive workplace safety and health programs. Among business managers and owners, OSHA rules and regulations are perceived as a burden, requiring significant time demands and massive amounts of paperwork. When industry leaders speak about reducing the "red tape" associated with doing business, they are often referring to OSHA regulations.

As with any set of federal regulations, what seems appropriate in one setting may be cumbersome or even illogical in another setting. OSHA regulations are often criticized for their conflict with efficiency and even safety. Like many government regulatory agencies, OSHA was created because businesses were not addressing workplace problems and issues.

OSHA regulations include penalties for noncompliance. Businesses can be fined for violations leading to worker injuries. Repeat violations increase both OSHA penalties and scrutiny of the offending firms. Employers with 11 or more employees must keep some type of record of on-the-job injuries and illnesses. Exceptions are given to employers in low-hazard industries such as service, retail, finance, INSURANCE, and real estate.

OSHA violations are placed in one of five categories: willful, serious, repeat, failure to abate, and others. Willful violations, where a company intentionally and knowingly violates OSHA regulations, are subject to fines ranging from $5,000 to $70,000; violators can also be subject to criminal charges. Serious violations (68 percent of all 2001 violations were in this category) are conditions involving a substantial probability of death or serious injury. Repeat violations are violations of any standard or regulation for which a substantially similar violation is found upon reinspection. Failure to abate is simply failure to correct a situation.

Further reading
Occupational Safety and Health Administration website. Available on-line. URL: www.osha.gov.

Office of Federal Contract Compliance Programs
The Office of Federal Contract Compliance Programs (OFCCP) is part of the U.S. DEPARTMENT OF LABOR's Employment Standards Administration. It has a national network of six regional offices, each with district and area offices in major metropolitan centers. The OFCCP enforces three equal employment opportunity (EEO) programs: Executive Order 11246 (as amended), Section 503 of the Rehabilitation Act of 1973 (as amended), and the affirmative-action provisions of the Vietnam Era Veterans Readjustment Assistance Act of 1974. The OFCCP also shares enforcement authority for regulations requiring EEO and affirmative action in apprenticeship programs, immigration programs, and the FAMILY AND MEDICAL LEAVE ACT.

Signed by President Lyndon B. Johnson in 1965, Executive Order 11246 prohibits discrimination in hiring or EMPLOYMENT decisions on the basis of race, color, gender, religion, and national origin. It applies to all nonexempt government contractors and subcontractors as well as federally assisted construction CONTRACTs and subcontracts in excess of $10,000. Contractors and subcontractors with a federal contract of $50,000 or more and 50 or more employees are required to develop a written affirmative-action program that is designed to ensure equal employment opportunity and sets forth specific and action-oriented programs to which a contractor commits himself with good faith.

Section 503 of the 1973 Rehabilitation Act prohibits discrimination and requires affirmative action in all personnel practices for qualified individuals with disabilities. It applies to all firms that have a nonexempt government contract or subcontract in excess of $10,000. An affirmative-action program is required.

The Vietnam Era Veterans Readjustment Assistance Act prohibits discrimination and requires affirmative action in all personnel practices for all veterans who served on active duty in the U.S. military—ground, naval, or air service—or who are special disabled veterans, Vietnam-era veterans, recently separated veterans, or veterans who served on active duty during a war or in a campaign or expedition for which a campaign badge has been authorized. It applies to all firms that have a nonexempt government contract or subcontract of $25,000 or more. An affirmative-action program is required.

The Immigration Reform and Control Act (IRCA, 1986) requires employers to maintain certain records pertaining to the citizenship status of new employees. These records are examined during the course of compliance reviews and complaint investigations. Results are reported to the Immigration and Naturalization Service.

When Title I of the AMERICANS WITH DISABILITIES ACT became effective in July 1992, most qualified individuals with disabilities attained protection against employment discrimination through that act and the Rehabilitation Act of 1973.

In carrying out its responsibilities, the OFCCP uses a variety of enforcement procedures, including

- technical assistance to federal contractors and subcontractors to help them understand the regulatory requirements and review process
- compliance evaluations and complaint investigations of federal contractors' and subcontractors' personnel policies and procedures
- obtaining conciliation agreements from contractors and subcontractors who are in violation of regulatory requirements
- monitoring of contractors' and subcontractors' progress in fulfilling the terms of their agreements through periodic compliance reports
- linkage agreements between contractors and Labor Department job-training programs to help employers identify and recruit qualified workers
- recommendation of enforcement actions to the Solicitor of Labor

The ultimate sanction for violations is debarment—the loss of a company's federal contracts. Other forms of relief to victims of discrimination may also be available, including back pay for lost wages.

The OFCCP works with many other federal agencies, including the Department of Justice, the EQUAL EMPLOYMENT OPPORTUNITY COMMISSION, and the Department of Labor. It coordinates with the Office of the Solicitor, which advises on ethical, legal, and enforcement issues; the Women's Bureau, which emphasizes the needs of working women; and the Bureau of Apprenticeship and Training, which establishes policies to promote equal opportunities in the recruitment and selection of apprentices. The

OFCCP also works with the Employment and Training Administration, which administers Labor Department job-training programs for current workforce needs.

Further reading
Fisher, Cynthia D., Lyle F. Schoenfeldt, and James B. Shaw. *Human Resource Management.* 5th ed. Boston: Houghton Mifflin, 2003; Office of Federal Contract Compliance Programs website. Available on-line. URL: http://www.dol.gov/eas/public/aboutesa/hisotyr/ofccp/ofcphist.htm.

Office of Government Ethics
The Office of Government Ethics (OGE), established by the Ethics in Government Act (1978), is a small, executive branch agency created to prevent conflicts of interest on the part of government employees and to resolve conflicts of interest when they occur. Executive-branch employees hold their positions as a public trust and are expected to place loyalty to the Constitution, U.S. laws, and ethical principles above their private gain. By executive order (President George H. W. Bush, 1989), public employees cannot use public office for private gain and must impartially (i.e., not give preferential treatment to any private organization or individual).

When new government officials are appointed, the news media will frequently provide information about financial disclosures, BLIND TRUSTS, and potential conflicts of interests. The OGE processes government employee financial-disclosure statements, reviews blind trusts established to avoid a CONFLICT OF INTEREST, and advises government officials when it would be appropriate to recuse or remove themselves from a particular government policy decision because of such a conflict.

The OGE is responsible for a variety of ethical guidelines for government employees, including

- gifts from outside sources, generally allowing anything under $20 in value or from family or personal relationships
- gifts between employees, generally allowing gifts valued at no more than $10 or food and refreshments shared in an office among employees
- conflicting financial interests, including the employee, his or her family or general partner, or the organization in which the employee serves as an officer, director, trustee, or general partner
- outside activities, prohibiting an employee from being paid for teaching, speaking, or writing related to their official duties, except at accredited teaching institutions
- honoraria, generally allowing payments for an appearance, speech, or article, provided that the activity does not relate to the employee's official duties
- Post-EMPLOYMENT regulations barring employees from representing others that in any way relates to their official capacity for two years after leaving government.

Certain high-level officials are barred from making any appearance on behalf of any person before their former agency for one year. (This is known as the "revolving-door syndrome," in which former officials become high-paid consultants for clients seeking benefits from government agencies.)

- financial disclosure, requiring certain senior officials to file a report detailing their interests in property, INCOME, gifts and reimbursements, liabilities, agreements, and outside positions

Further reading
Office of Government Ethics website. Available on-line. URL: www.oge.gov.

Office of Management and Budget
The primary function of the Office of Management and Budget (OMB) is to prepare the annual U.S. federal budget. The federal budget, over $2.2 trillion in 2003, is approximately 22 percent of all spending in the U.S. economy. Spending and tax recommendations by the OMB are closely watched and influenced by business leaders. The OMB serves the president of the United States, developing fiscal and MANAGEMENT policies and coordinating government-wide program analysis and implementation. The OMB's major responsibilities include

- preparation of the president's budget
- oversight of financial management, federal procurement, and information technology
- review and clearance of proposed legislation, regulations, and executive orders
- oversight of program management
- implementation of other statutory responsibilities
- providing continuity during transitions to new presidential administrations

While the OMB serves the president of the United States, the GENERAL ACCOUNTING OFFICE (GAO) serves the U.S. Congress. Depending on which parties are in control of Congress and the White House, the GAO and OMB can play important roles in FISCAL POLICY decisions. Often analysts at the two agencies will disagree about the projected level of government tax revenue and the potential cost of proposed legislation. During the 1990s, in debates regarding balanced budgets and, later, the use of budget surpluses, OMB and GAO projections were frequently used to argue for and against policy measures.

In addition to politically sensitive budget and tax issues, the OMB develops policies to improve government statistics and information management.

Further reading
Office of Management Budget website. Available on-line. URL: www.whitehouse.gov/omb.

oligopoly

An oligopoly is a MARKET STRUCTURE in which there are BARRIERS TO ENTRY, allowing for only a few firms. Oligopolies occur in those industries in which it is difficult for new competitors to get established. CAPITAL, technology, or LICENSING frequently restricts entry into oligopolistic markets, which can have either standardized or differentiated PRODUCTS.

The critical characteristic of oligopolies is that there are only a few competitors in the market. Because of this, the actions of each individual firm usually affect the other firms in the market. This creates what economists call MUTUAL INTERDEPENDENCE.

In competitive markets there are many small firms, so if one firm lowers its price or increases its output, it has virtually no impact on the overall market conditions. But in an oligopoly, because each firm is a significant part of the industry output, if one firm lowers its price, its actions affect the DEMAND for the other oligopolists' products. If one oligopolist lowers its price below the existing market price and the other firms do not match that price decrease, the one firm will see an increase in sales and the other oligopolists will lose sales. But business managers do not like to lose their share of the market, so logically the other firms in the industry will match the one oligopolist's price decrease. Conversely, if one oligopolist raises its price, the other firms will be happy to take away new customers from that firm. This interdependence creates what is known as a kinked-demand curve, whereby oligopolists will match a price decrease but will not usually follow a price increase. The result of market independence is price rigidity. It usually does not benefit an oligopolist to compete on a price basis.

Mutual interdependence among the few firms in an oligopoly is overcome by a variety of methods, some legal and some illegal in the United States. Recognizing that competing on a price basis will not benefit them, oligopolists frequently compete on a nonprice basis. A classic example of this is found in the cereal industry. Examination of the cereal aisle in grocery stores and supermarkets will show that four companies—Kellogg, Post, General Mills, and Quaker Oats—produce almost all of the choices, and their prices are amazingly similar. These four competitors attempt to increase their sales and PROFITS through PRODUCT PROLIFERATION.

Another legal way for oligopolists to compete is through price leadership. One firm announces a price change, and the other firms quickly match the leading firm's actions. Occasionally the other oligopolists will not match the leading firm's price change, and usually a few days later the firm will rescind that price. The U.S. airline industry and banking industry frequently use this method of changing prices. In the 1990s, one airline began a practice of signaling price changes in advance to the few competing firms on specific routes. The competitors would then signal whether they would also increase their price.

This procedure, called collusion, is illegal in the United States.

The U.S. automobile-manufacturing industry is often cited as an example of an oligopoly. Each year (usually in August) manufacturers announce their price changes for the new model year; invariably the prices are very similar. Automobile manufacturers compete primarily on a basis of product differentiation such as image, safety features, environmental-control devices, and having the largest or most fuel-efficient models. Near the end of the model year, manufacturers begin to compete on a price basis, offering rebates and below-cost financing to sell existing inventory before the new model year begins. When the prices for the new models are announced, they are once again amazingly similar.

Further reading

Boyes, William L., and Michael Melvin. *Microeconomics*, 5th ed. Boston: Houghton Mifflin, 2002.

ombudsmen

Ombudsmen are people designated in organizations to provide alternative means of resolving problems. Translated as "people's representative," the term comes from Old Norse and was first used in 1809, when Sweden established a government ombudsman to serve the needs of the public. While other countries followed Sweden's example, only in recent years has the use of ombudsmen expanded in American business.

Today many government agencies and several hundred CORPORATIONS have established ombudsmen offices. Frustrated with the ENVIRONMENTAL PROTECTION AGENCY, Congress created an independent ombudsman to help communities file grievances against the agency. In New Jersey the secretary of state created a business ombudsman's office to assist businesses with the layers of state government. The INTERNAL REVENUE SERVICE renamed their ombudsman Taxpayer Advocate, while the FEDERAL DEPOSIT INSURANCE CORPORATION (FDIC) has an office of more than 60 people addressing questions and concerns from consumers, bankers, and employees.

At the FDIC and elsewhere, the ombudsman's role is to work toward problem resolution, acting as an impartial listener. To appease employee concerns, some corporations hire independent suppliers for ombudsmen services. From a business perspective, ombudsmen

- increase employee participation
- alert companies to ethical problems
- provide an outlet for SEXUAL HARASSMENT complaints
- provide an alternative for dispute resolution

Further reading

Martin, Justin. "New tricks, for an old trade," *Across the Board* 29, no. 6 (June 1992): 40.

open-market operations

Open-market operations are the buying and selling of U.S. TREASURY SECURITIES by the FEDERAL RESERVE SYSTEM (known as the Fed) to implement MONETARY POLICY. The Fed, through the Federal Reserve Bank of New York, buys and sells securities, primarily U.S. Treasury bills, notes, and BONDS, in order to increase or decrease the financial reserves in the BANKING SYSTEM. The New York Fed trades with 40 primary dealers, who then resell or purchase securities with other financial institutions.

Economies need MONEY to facilitate transactions and support ECONOMIC GROWTH. The goals of monetary policy are economic growth and price stability, and open-market operations are the primary tool of monetary policy. The Fed uses open-market operations on a daily basis to adjust the amount of money in the economic system.

When the Fed buys securities, it pays for the securities with a check, drawn on the Federal Reserve Bank. This adds money to the financial system, which banks then lend to borrowers, who spend the funds, which are in turn deposited in banks by the recipients of the checks received from the borrowers. The Fed's initial injection of funds multiplies through the economy in a process called the demand-deposit multiplier. The simple demand-deposit multiplier is one divided by the reserve-requirement ratio—the percentage of deposits a bank is required to keep either in cash or on deposit with the Fed.

When the Fed sells securities, primary dealers pay for the securities with funds, reducing the amount of money available to lend. This is called a withdrawal of liquidity in the banking system, reducing growth in the MONEY SUPPLY. Reductions in the money supply increase INTEREST RATES, in turn decreasing the DEMAND for INVESTMENT and consumer borrowing. This slows economic activity and reduces inflationary pressure. Similarly, increases in the money supply reduce interest rates, stimulating investment and consumer borrowing. Most often, the Fed is increasing the money supply through open-market operations to facilitate exchanges in an expanding economy. The Fed wants the "right" money supply, but "right" is a judgment determination, and controlling the money supply is not an exact science. The Federal Open Market Committee meets on a regular basis to review changes in ECONOMIC CONDITIONS. Open Market Committee members receive an updated "beige book" containing statistics and reports on current economic conditions to use in making decisions. After their deliberations, the committee directs the New York Federal Reserve Bank regarding open-market operations until the committee meets again.

Further reading

Federal Reserve System website. Available on-line. URL: www.federalreserve.gov.

opportunity cost

Opportunity cost is the value of the best thing you must give up when you make a decision. As Rutgers University economist Dr. A. Robert Koch once stated, whether for decisions made by individuals or collectively by society, "there is always an opportunity cost." The concept of opportunity cost is critical to economic analysis. Economists assume RESOURCES are scarce. The labor used to produce an airplane cannot be used to make windmills; likewise, the materials used to produce the airplane are also not available to build windmills. Thus the cost of choosing one alternative use of a set of resources is the highest-valued alternative use of those resources.

Both individuals and countries incur opportunity costs. For years, critics of the U.S. military-industrial complex argued that the salaries paid at greater than the market rate to U.S. scientists working in military laboratories drained needed talent from the production of nondefense goods, sacrificing development of new consumer goods for new weapons systems. Supporters of defense spending responded by pointing out the spillover benefits of new technology developed for military purposes. For example, the INTERNET was initially a military project to improve communication among specialists located throughout the country.

Individuals also face opportunity costs. When time is spent on one activity, it is not available for other efforts. Economists use opportunity costs to estimate the value of leisure time, assuming the value of leisure is equal to or greater than the INCOME foregone when not working. Even wealthy individuals incur opportunity costs. One of the criticisms of the U.S. economic system is the time demand made on workers. Stories abound of hard-working people who have little time left for their families. The opportunity cost of a day spent with family is the value of work not done. In the DOT-COMS industry, employers seek out "zero drag" workers—people without families who will work 15–20 hour days for low pay with hopes to benefit if the firm succeeds. Dot-com employers recognize these workers have relatively low opportunity costs.

When evaluating the true cost associated with a business endeavor, economists include the value of owner resources. Often in small, family-owned businesses, owner CAPITAL, land, and family labor are not explicitly paid. Each of these resources has a value that could be measured by what they would be paid in the marketplace. The opportunity cost of owner capital is the return on INVESTMENT that could have been earned in a similar business venture. The opportunity cost of owner land is the rent another business would have paid to use that land, and the opportunity cost of family labor is what they could have earned working elsewhere.

Sometimes large companies also incur opportunity costs. In 2000, Delta & Pine Land Company brought a lawsuit against Monsanto, seeking up to $1 billion in DAMAGES, claiming that its stock plunged and it passed up an acquisition bid from another company while their proposed merger with Monsanto was under regulatory review. The lawsuit, filed after Monsanto withdrew its request for clearance from the Antitrust Division of the U.S. Justice Department, demanded compensation in part for diversion of its MANAGEMENT's time to the unsuccessful merger. Delta & Pine's opportunity cost was the time, resources, and talent spent on one activity, precluding their use for other benefits.

Further reading
Sikora, Martin. "Trying to Recoup the Cost of Lost Opportunities," *Mergers & Acquisitions* 35, no 3 (March 2000): 12.

options, option contracts
An option is the right to select a particular action among choices. In business the term most often refers to "option contracts" to buy or sell stock, called STOCK OPTIONS. Options are also referred to as derivative or contingent claims, because the option instrument is derived from or contingent on the value of the asset with which they are associated.

Typical options are "put" or "call" CONTRACTs. A put is the right to sell a fixed amount of the underlying asset at a fixed price for a set period of time. A call is the right to buy a certain of "fixed" amount of an underlying asset at a fixed price for a set period of time. An option contract's seller has the obligation to buy (in the case of a put) or sell (in the case of a call) if the purchaser decides to exercise the option. The buyer gains the right to exercise the option, while the seller gets the payment for the option rights. The payment for the option is referred to as the option "premium." The fixed price at which the purchase or sale may be executed is called the "strike price."

Whether an option has any value as its expiration date approaches depends on whether it is "in the money" or "out of the money." "At the money" is when the strike price of the option equals the market price of the stock. An option is in the money if the current market price is above the strike price. Logically the owner of a call option would want to exercise his option to buy the stock from the call-option seller, if he could then turn around and sell the shares on the open market for more than he paid for them. For example, if ABC stock is selling for $26 per share and an option investor has a call option to purchase 100 shares (each option is typically for 100 shares) for $25 per share, she will buy the shares at $25 and sell at $26, earning $100 fewer commissions. If, however, the market price on the last day of the option contract is $24 per share, the holder of the call option will not exercise her call option because she could purchase the stock at a lower price on the open market.

One conservative INVESTMENT strategy used by investors is called "writing covered calls." In this strategy an investor sells call options against shares of stock owned.

The investor receives the option premium, and if the price of the stock remains stable or declines, he will probably not have his shares called by the option buyer. When the option expires, the investor can write or sell new options against his shares. However, should the price of the stock rise, he will have to deliver the stock to the buyer of the option or purchase the option back at a higher price reflecting the rise in the value of the stock (the underlying asset). Very few options are actually delivered. Instead, near the expiration date, an opposite transaction (purchase of a call for someone who sold a call, or sale of a put for someone who bought puts) takes place, with the investor earning a PROFIT or loss by the difference in the value of the option.

A risky but potentially profitable strategy is to sell call options without owning the stock against which the option is being sold. This is called "going naked," and like the term suggests, it exposes the seller to significant RISK but also the potential for profit without investment CAPITAL. Professional options investors also engage in ARBITRAGE, the simultaneous buying and selling of options in different markets when there are small price differences. Individual investors rarely engage in arbitrage because the TRANSACTION COSTS are too high, but with market LEVERAGE, market professionals sometimes find opportunities for arbitrage.

In recent years the term *financial engineering* has been used to describe complex, innovative FINANCIAL INSTRUMENTS and strategies utilizing options and other financial leverage investments. In the late 1990s, Long Term Capital Management (LTCM) was a global leader in financial engineering, using mathematical models developed by Nobel Prize-winning economists Myron Scholes and Robert Merton to buy and sell options and other financial derivatives. At their peak, LTCM had capital of $4.8 billion, a portfolio of $200 billion, and derivatives with a nominal value of $1,250 billion. In less than a year, though, the company was bankrupted when it bet that short-term and long-term rates would converge, but instead the spread between rates expanded. Fearing a collapse in the global securities market, the president of the New York Federal Reserve Bank orchestrated a $3.5 billion bailout of the company.

Most stock brokerage firms offer options trading, which is guaranteed and cleared through the Option Clearing Corporation (OCC). The Chicago Board of Options Exchange (CBOE) is one of the major exchanges providing options trading.

Options for other ASSETS can also be bought or sold. Commercial real-estate developers often purchase an option to buy a piece of property contingent on receiving development approval or finding financing to make the purchase. Companies frequently offer employees and primarily executives options to purchase company stock. Options are also available on U.S. TREASURY SECURITIES, STOCK MARKET indexes, precious metals, and a variety of other assets. As option trading has expanded into commodities and other assets beyond stocks, regional stock exchanges and the major commodity FUTURES exchanges compete to provide markets for these new securities.

Further reading
Chicago Board of Options Exchange website. Available on-line. URL: www.cboe.com; Ibrahim Warde, "LTCM, a hedge fund above suspicion," *Le Monde diplomatique,* November 1998.

organizational charts See CHAIN-OF-COMMAND PRINCIPLE.

organizational commitment
Organizational commitment has to do with how much employees identify with and are involved with the company they work for, as well as how hard they are willing to work for the organization. Many factors affect such commitment, including whether an employee accepts and endorses the company values and goals, how willing he or she is to exert extra effort on the company's behalf, and whether he/she has a strong desire to remain affiliated with the organization.

Employees tend to have higher levels of commitment when there is a strong match between their personal values and goals and those of the organization. An employee who believes in, accepts, and internalizes the company goals is more likely to be committed to the organization than someone with conflicting values or goals. For example, an employee who takes tremendous pride in developing a superior product may feel a low level of commitment to an organization that sacrifices quality for the sake of quantity, but he or she may be much more committed to a company whose primary focus is product quality. Although the values and goals of both the employees and the organization may change over time, having a close match is beneficial for both parties in the long term.

In addition, some employees are more willing to engage in extra work for their employers than others when they experience levels of JOB SATISFACTION and perceive that the organization treats them in a fair and just manner. Also important are organizational citizenship behaviors, which include voluntary helping behaviors that aid the organization, such as speaking well about the organization to others, attending optional functions, and staying current in company changes and policies. Citizenship behaviors may also include voluntarily helping other employees by, for example, easing a coworker's workload during a busy time, volunteering for assignments, and being efficient in order to avoid wasting others' time. Although citizenship behaviors may not be recognized in the organization's formal reward system, research suggests that when employees believe that their supervisors notice such behaviors and reward "good team players" they may be more inclined to perform citizenship behaviors.

Other factors can affect how strongly an employee wants to stay affiliated with a company. Older employees with a high ACHIEVEMENT MOTIVATION, tend to have high levels of organizational commitment and presumably have a stronger desire to maintain their affiliation, in large part due to having higher levels of SENIORITY and status and more financial INVESTMENT in the company than younger or newer employees have. Younger employees tend to be more mobile in the workforce and may be less likely to forfeit significant contributions to pension plans or high levels of seniority by leaving an organization. Because it costs the organization money to recruit, select, and train new employees, retention of high-performing individuals at all levels is desirable.

There are several ways that an organization may try to increase their employees' level of commitment. Providing opportunities for job enrichment or the chance to learn and use new skills, providing sufficient opportunities for advancement, and increasing workers' autonomy in their positions are ways organizations can show their employees that the company is committed to them. When employees believe that the organization cares about their needs, it may lead to a reciprocal increase in employees' loyalty. Indeed, increasing commitment tends to reduce employee turnover and is associated with fewer employee absences from work.

However, having a high level of organizational commitment is not always beneficial to the organization or the employee. Commitment that is too intense can inhibit an employee's personal and professional growth and development. Employees with extremely high levels of commitment may be resistant to changes in the organization, ultimately diminishing their contributions to achieving organizational goals. Job turnover in these situations may be helpful to both the organization and the employee.

In general, companies that treat their employees well tend to promote employee loyalty and commitment, benefiting the organization in terms of higher levels of citizenship behaviors and lower levels of job turnover.

See also EMPLOYEE MOTIVATION; MOTIVATION THEORY.

Further reading
Baron, Robert A., and Donn Byrne. *Social Psychology,* 10th ed. Boston: Allyn and Bacon, 2003; Schultz, Duane, and Sydney Ellen Schultz. *Psychology and Work Today: An Introduction to Industrial and Organizational Psychology,* 8th ed. New York: Macmillan Publishing, 2001.

—Elizabeth L. Cralley

organizational theory
There are many ways to view organizations, so researchers, professors, and students need some structure and guidance to aid discussions on the topic. Organization theory offers a structured way to talk about the organization as a unit and the subunits, groups, and individuals who work

within an organization. Organizations and the people who work in them are the focus of study in organization theory. There are many different "models" used to represent organizations, and one that is currently used is called the contingency model, meaning different organizations types are likely to be most effective in different situations.

Researchers in business administration, psychology, and sociology conduct studies of individuals and groups in organizations, the purpose of which is to attempt to identify typical behavior patterns. The focus may be on the total organization, groups of employees such as departments or divisions, or on individual employees. Other topics of research related to organization theory include ORGANIZATION BEHAVIOR, HUMAN RESOURCES management and organization development. The primary differences relate to the level of analysis and the focus on either theory or practice.

In organization behavior, the level of analysis mainly concerns the group and the individual rather than the total organization, and the focus is on theory. Both human resources management and organization development focus on application to real situations (practice). Human resources management emphasizes the individual level of analysis, while organization development works at the level of the full organization or large groups within the organization.

One key aspect of modern organizational theory is the emphasis on the environment in which the organization operates, which is often referred to in terms of a systems approach. This general frame of reference comes from biology and can be applied to organizations in a purely theoretical way. In the early days of study and research on organizations, managers and even researchers took what may be termed a closed-system approach, meaning they tried to consider only those aspects of the organization itself in relation to its functioning and success or failure. They seldom tried to evaluate the environmental influences on the organization or vice versa.

The newer approach, called the open-systems view, makes it clear that organizations can only be studied in terms of how they interact with their environment. There are many aspects of the environment to consider; for instance, there is the immediate community in which the organization operates for such important factors as the labor market; and there are also the variables in the organizations' own industries, such as competitors, suppliers and technical specialty organizations. All of these entities will be influenced by and will likewise influence the organization. In order to make sense of the organization and its operation, factors from the environment must be included, and thus an open-systems view is essential to current understanding of organization theory.

Effectiveness in organization functioning may be measured in many different ways. The traditional methods focus on productivity, quality, and earnings for private organizations. Some newer and more widely focused methods of measuring success include the satisfaction of both customers and employees, the organization's STAKE-HOLDERS, and the actual stockholders and BOARD OF DIRECTORS. Others who might be considered when viewing the organization's environment would include bankers who lend money to the organization and might view it in terms of its success in maintaining credit. Suppliers might add the view that payment of invoices is a measure of success. This type of extension of the way organizations are viewed is a factor that has developed in the way organization theory has grown as a study specialty.

Organization theory is often used to study the ways that organizations sets goals and then plan how to meet those goals. This focus is generally called STRATEGIC PLANNING or strategic MANAGEMENT. These are primarily internal factors but are clearly influenced by external variables such as COMPETITION; general economic factors (for example, INTEREST RATES); and, for international organizations, TRADE BALANCES with other countries.

Further reading
Daft, Richard L. *Organization Theory and Design.* Eagan, Minn.: 6th West Group Company, 1997.

—Jerry Merwin

organization behavior
Organization behavior (OB) is the study of the actions of individuals and groups within organizations. Important considerations are the individual employee and how he or she relates to others, both as individuals and groups within the organization. From this standpoint, most analyses are performed on the individual or group level. Each employee's personality, values, and attitudes influences their behavior in group processes involving the performance of work, making decisions, and designing jobs. OB, however, should also be considered from the viewpoint of the entire organization, especially given the need for diversity and BUSINESS ETHICS as well as the impact of the global environment on the business.

Motivation, leadership, the implementation of teams to perform work, communications, GOAL SETTING, and PERFORMANCE APPRAISALS are important components of OB. Motivation is the process of getting employees to focus on achieving the organization's goals. There are two broad types of motivation: content and process. Content motivation looks at what specific things motivate employees. One theory advanced by Abraham Maslow postulated that an individual's needs and wants ranged from a low of basic physiological needs (i.e., the things necessary for survival) to a high of self-actualization (i.e., becoming everything one is capable of becoming). Instead of addressing specific things that motivate people, PROCESS THEORIES look at how people are motivated. Psychologist Victor Vroom proposed a motivation process in which the employee made a decision regarding whether or not to work hard. If the employee wanted to get ahead, he/she would work harder. The increased effort would result in greater output, which in turn would result in the company offering the employee a variety of rewards. The employee accepted the reward that had the greatest value to him/her.

LEADERSHIP is the process of guiding people to perform the organization's work. Leaders use motivation as one of the techniques to inspire followers. Leadership roles are not confined to managers or executives; anyone in the organization can be a leader. While there are many different approaches to leadership, recent research finds that leaders can effectively challenge the way work is done because they have a long-term vision of where the organization needs to be for the business to be successful and grow, and thus they inspire and develop others to achieve the transformation. Throughout the process of accomplishing a goal, the leader sets the example to follow and the standard to achieve.

Today many organizations are changing the decision-making process. Traditionally if there was a problem, the employee asked his/her superior or manager and then was given the appropriate directions. This process forced decision making up into higher organizational levels so that many day-to-day decisions were being made by individuals who were somewhat removed from the operations. The new approach in decision making is to reverse the process so that decisions are made at the lowest appropriate level, empowering employees who are closest to the problem to do what is best to solve it and assure good customer service. Frequently these decisions are not made by a single person but by a team of people. Self-directed teams are groups of individuals who come together to achieve common goals. They are knowledgeable in the unit's work, share information, and help each other succeed. Members of a self-directed team work together to achieve organizational goals. In addition to helping each other, self-directed teams may also set their own goals and assess the performance of the group and the individual team members.

See also MASLOW'S HIERARCHY OF NEEDS; MOTIVATION THEORY.

—Melissa Hudson

Organization for Economic Cooperation and Development

The Organization for Economic Cooperation and Development (OECD) provides a forum for discussion and development of public-sector and corporate policy making. The OECD consists of 30 member countries and maintains relationships with other countries and nongovernment organizations (NGOs) involved in social and economic policies. Best known for its economics publications and statistics including its country surveys, the OECD is involved in a wide array of international development issues from price transparency to pesticides.

The OECD produces internationally agreed decisions and recommendations, which are then utilized by policy makers in individual countries. OECD recommendations reduce variations in economic and government policies among member countries and provide a basis for sound government decision making in EMERGING MARKETS without resources to individually analyze and evaluate issues. OECD guidelines are available for issues such as SUSTAINABLE GROWTH AND DEVELOPMENT, food safety, energy, biotechnology, electronic commerce, health, and even money laundering. While the WORLD TRADE ORGANIZATION focuses on reductions in TRADE BARRIERS, the OECD focuses on issues that facilitate or constrain social and ECONOMIC DEVELOPMENT.

The OECD superseded the Organization for European Economic Co-operation, which was formed after World War II to administer U.S. and Canadian aid for Europe under the MARSHALL PLAN. For most of its existence, the OECD focused on ECONOMIC EFFICIENCY and market systems among member countries. More recently OECD efforts have expanded to include support for countries transitioning from centrally planned to market economies and developing countries in Asia and Latin America. Critics of OECD view the organization as an extension of western capitalist interests. Supporters argue the organization is a forum for dialogue and debate regarding the impact of GLOBALIZATION.

Further reading
Organization for Economic Cooperation and Development website. Available on-line. URL: www.oecd.org.

Organization of American States

The Organization of American States (OAS) is a regional political organization for discussion and cooperation on social and economic issues. Comprised of 35 member states representing North, Central, and South America and the Caribbean, the OAS was created in 1948, originally with 21 member countries. The group meets annually to discuss such issues as peace, democracy, human rights, the drug trade, sustainable development, and FREE TRADE.

Free trade is the most important business issue involving the OAS, and the 1994 Summit of the Americas in Miami was the most visible OAS effect in recent years. At the summit, President Bill Clinton focused on free trade, promising Chile that it would be the next country considered for acceptance into the NORTH AMERICAN FREE TRADE AGREEMENT (NAFTA). When Congress repealed the president's FAST TRACK authority to negotiate trade agreements, the expansion of NAFTA in the Americas died. Subsequently, individual countries and regional groups in South and Central America developed free trade agreements among themselves without including the United States.

The OAS General Assembly meets annually, and its permanent council is headquartered in Washington, D.C. Critics portray the OAS as a mechanism for the North (United States) to further manipulate and exploit the

South (Central and South American countries) in the interest of corporate PROFITS, with little concern for the environment or human rights.

Further reading

Organization of American States website. Available on-line. URL: www.oas.org.

Organization of Petroleum Exporting Countries

The Organization of Petroleum Exporting Countries (OPEC) is a CARTEL of 12 nations that seek to influence oil prices through control of the supply of oil to world markets. OPEC was created in 1960 with initial members including Iran, Iraq, Kuwait, Saudi Arabia, and Venezuela. At the time, oil prices were less than $5 per barrel. (Prices vary slightly, depending on oil's sulfur content.) Algeria, Gabon, Indonesia, Libya, Nigeria, Qatar, and the United Arab Emirates subsequently joined OPEC. (Ecuador also joined but later left the organization.)

Unlike the United States, in most countries oil and other subsurface RESOURCES are considered public ASSETS. Early in the 20th century, U.S. British, and Dutch companies entered into agreements to explore and drill for oil resources in developing countries; at the time, many of these countries were European colonies. Along with the independence movement of the 1950s came the demand by newly formed countries to control their natural resources.

Humorist Art Buchwald once argued that the creation of OPEC was Harvard's fault because the sons of royalty from oil-producing nations attended Harvard, where they learned about the benefits of forming cartels. OPEC was created as a cartel to control oil supplies and thereby raise the price received by oil-producing countries. While OPEC countries control less than 40 percent of the world supply of oil, they control nearly 100 percent of the world's short-term marginal production. Slight increases or decreases in the supply of oil, ceteris paribus (other things being held constant), result in significant changes in the price of oil. OPEC, like other cartels, allocates production quotas among its members, attempting to achieve a desired SUPPLY and thereby controlling the price of oil.

Raising the price of oil significantly increases revenue for OPEC members as well as other oil-exporting countries, particularly Norway and Mexico. One estimate suggested that OPEC would earn nearly $250 billion in 2000, more than double its oil income from 1998, when oil prices declined below $10 per barrel. In March 1999 OPEC agreed to cut oil production by 2.1 million barrels per day, about 8 percent of member output. For most of its history, OPEC has been a fractious organization with constant conflict among members. Economic theory suggests cartels tend to be unstable and fail because once prices rise, members have incentives and capacity to increase output. Cheating on agreed production quotas increases market supplies, driving down prices.

OPEC's longevity is directly attributable to Saudi Arabia, its leading oil-producing country. Saudi Arabia has acted as the "swing producer" in the cartel, often reducing its output to offset over-quota production by other OPEC members. It also controls most of the spare capacity in OPEC, an estimated 3 million barrels per day in 2000. When Saudi Arabia has increased its production, as it did in 1986, world oil prices have fallen. When it has reduced output, oil prices have tended to rise. During the Gulf War (1990), Saudi Arabia stepped in and increased output, offsetting reduced output from Iraq and Kuwait during the conflict. Because of the role Saudi Arabia plays, some economists argue OPEC is not a cartel but instead represents a price-leadership OLIGOPOLY. In July 2000 Saudi Arabia unilaterally announced it would increase output by 500,000 barrels per day in an attempt to lower oil prices. Saudi leaders feared continued high oil prices might push the fragile global economy into a RECESSION.

While OPEC reduces market supplies in order to achieve higher prices, market prices are established by the interaction of supply and DEMAND. New supplies of oil from the North Sea, Arctic wilderness area, and other parts of the world also influence world oil prices. Global demand for oil depends primarily on the level of global output. In adopting their production quotas, OPEC attempts to forecast world market conditions. Often changes in OPEC output decisions create huge swings in market prices, which in turn threatens ECONOMIC GROWTH, the source of demand for their product.

In recent years European countries have paid even higher prices for OPEC oil. OPEC prices are payable in U.S. dollars, and as European currencies have depreciated against the dollar, the cost of oil has increased. Continued high oil prices can adversely affect OPEC by stimulating additional oil exploration and increasing the benefits of energy conservation. Sheik Zaki Yamani, the former Saudi Oil Minister, recognized the potential danger of high oil prices with the statement, "The stone age didn't end because the cavemen ran out of stone."

Further reading

Kaletsky, Anatole. "Fall in oil prices is now in interests of OPEC and West," *The Times* (London), 12 September 2000.

outplacement

Outplacement is employer-provided assistance for employees who are about to lose their jobs. With corporate downsizing, rightsizing, and "return to core competencies," many U.S. companies will lay off large numbers of employees. Many companies feel an obligation to try to support former employees. Specialists in HUMAN RESOURCES suggest former workers who talk to employment counselors are less likely to be talk to attorneys about WRONGFUL DIS-CHARGE.

Outplacement can be provided either internally or externally; many companies prefer to pay outside providers. In the 1980s many employment services added outplacement services to their corporate offerings. Outplacement efforts to help workers find new jobs focus on two major activities, counseling and training in job-search skills, which include personal counseling, résumé-preparation and job-application workshops, recruiting services, job fairs, and office and support facilities. Employees at the managerial and executive levels will often negotiate having an office, answering service, and other support services during the transition from one job to another.

The federal government, through the Office of Personnel Management Employment Service, offers downsizing planning and outplacement programming assistance. Even former presidential appointees may receive outplacement support. The comptroller general (CG) has ruled that an agency may not provide outplacement assistance to political appointees unless it generally offers these services to all its employees. The CG decision says that "an agency may not expend public money for the specific purpose of helping political appointees return to private life. . . . although an agency may offer its existing outplacement assistance program to political appointees, it may not provide outplacement services exclusively to appointees of the outgoing Administration."

Further reading

Fisher, Cynthia D., Lyle F. Schoenfeldt, and James B. Shaw. *Human Resource Management,* 5th ed. Boston: Houghton Mifflin, 2003.

outsourcing

Outsourcing takes place when an organization contracts out functions, tasks, or services. Typically the goals of outsourcing include circumventing distractions from the company's core activities, acquiring specialized expertise, and reducing COSTS.

Outsourcing involves the substitution of part-time, CONTRACT, and other contingency workers for a company's full-time employees. Some types of outsourcing are common practices that have existed for decades in American business, while other types became growth industries during the 1990s. Traditionally companies hire temporary personnel, often through employment agencies, to meet seasonal labor needs. Specialized functions such as HUMAN RESOURCES, payroll processing, and even sales representation are also types of outsourcing. Outsourcing provides the benefits of flexibility, lower human resource costs, the ability to try out workers before hiring them permanently, and the reduction of overhead

costs through not having to pay INSURANCE and retirement benefits to temporary personnel.

In the late 1990s Outsourcing reached into new areas with the concept of a virtual CORPORATION, in which a small group of entrepreneurs employ very few workers, instead contracting for services wherever and whenever needed. Outsourcing allows the virtual corporation to change personnel and locations its their MARKETING STRATEGY evolves. During the late 1990s, many technology companies used outsourcing because skilled workers were not available in local markets. With INTERNET connections available around the world, technology companies subcontracted a wide array of services to highly skilled, lower-cost sources.

Sometimes outsourcing has been used as a means to circumvent existing salary structures, particularly UNION wage agreements. During the peak frenzy of technology advances during the 1990s, many companies paid dearly for information technology (IT) expertise. When salary structures restricted a firm's ability to pay market wages, IT services were outsourced.

While outsourcing continues to grow, it is not without costs. First, many companies fail to recognize the administrative cost associated with finding, comparing, contracting, supervising, and evaluating outsourcing activities. A second hidden cost is the impact on employee morale and productivity, when workers are laid off and replaced by outsourcing services. Third, employees tend to be more loyal than contract workers. Fourth, outsourcing increases the likelihood of losing company knowledge and leakage of sources of competitive advantage. Finally, outsourcing can challenge a company's ethical standards. In the United States, executives perceive many outsourcing decisions to be a betrayal of workers, as threats of outsourcing have been used to extract wage and work-rule concessions.

Further reading

Garaventa, Eugene, and Thomas Tellefsen. "Outsourcing: The Hidden Costs," *Review of Business* 22 (Spring 2001): 28.

Overseas Private Investment Corporation

The Overseas Private Investment Corporation (OPIC) is a U.S. government agency created to support private INVESTMENT by U.S. firms abroad. OPIC's primary activities include

- insuring investments overseas against political risks
- financing overseas business investments
- financing private investment funds that provide equity to businesses overseas
- advocating American business interests overseas

OPIC insurance reduces business RISK. Insuring against political risks stimulates U.S. businesses to invest in EMERGING MARKETS where the potential for changing business rules, government expropriation, or political turmoil would otherwise preclude investment. User fees, charged to participating CORPORATIONS, finance political-risk insurance.

OPIC offers direct LOANS—up to $200 million per project—and loan guarantees for U.S. businesses investing abroad. Since it was created in 1971, the agency has supported $138 billion worth of investments. OPIC programs are justified on the basis of generating U.S. exports, creating domestic jobs through exports, and generating host-country ECONOMIC GROWTH.

OPIC also provides private investment funds for developing countries. In 1999 the agency initiated the New Africa Infrastructure Fund, with $227.5 million from OPIC and $122.5 million of institutional-investor funds. The fund, managed by a consortium of financial advisors, invests in telecommunication and other INFRASTRUCTURE needs on the African continent.

OPIC's advocacy mission is conducted through seminars and conferences to increase awareness among U.S. companies and interaction with other agencies and organizations involved with investment in emerging markets. The agency's critics, point to its support of socially and environmentally harmful projects, including timber, mining, and fishing ventures around the world. OPIC provided political risk insurance for Freeport McMoRan's controversial copper and gold mine in Irian Java, Indonesia. Critics also object to a U.S. government agency providing financial support for private investment ventures outside the country.

See also U.S. TRADE REPRESENTATIVE.

Further reading
Overseas Private Investment Corporation website. Available online. URL: www.opic.gov.

owner's equity (owners' equity)
Owner's equity is the term appropriate for PROPRIETORSHIPS, while *owners' equity* applies to PARTNERSHIPS and CORPORATIONS. Both terms represent the owners of a firm. Equities represent internal claims against a firm's ASSETS (the investors/owners), while liabilities represent external claims (the firm's creditors). Often a firm's EQUITY is referred to as the residual equity. If the firm were to become insolvent, go bankrupt, or for some reason have to liquidate its assets, the liabilities must be repaid in full before the equity owners receive any proceeds from selling off the assets. A transposition of the accounting equation *Assets = Liabilities + Owners' Equity* to *Assets – Liabilities = Owners' Equity* illustrates the concept of residual equity; any assets remaining after satisfying the firm's debts belong to the firm's owners.

In proprietorships and partnerships, revenues and the investment of CAPITAL by the owner(s) increase equity. Expenses and withdrawals by the owner(s) decrease equity. Along with liabilities, equity is an important source of capital for these firms.

In corporations, owners' equity is increased by revenues and by the sale of stock. Expenses and the repurchase of a firm's stock (called treasury stock when repurchased) decrease owners' equity. On corporate BALANCE SHEETS, owners' equity is divided into two sections to clearly indicate the sources of the equity capital: contributed capital and retained earnings. Contributed capital comes from the sale of the firm's stock. Retained earnings arise when the firm does not distribute all of its earnings to stockholders in the form of dividends. Rather than paying dividends, the firm is retaining its earnings. Along with liabilities, owners' equity is an important source of corporate capital.

See also DIVIDENDS, RETAINED EARNINGS; LIABILITY.

P

packaging

Packaging is one of many issues a firm must address when developing a MARKETING STRATEGY. At first glance, packaging seems like a relatively simple concern; it is needed to protect the PRODUCT and communicate what is inside. However, marketers have learned that, in addition to protecting and promoting a product, packaging needs to be cost-effective and environmentally sensitive.

The first packaging consideration is protecting the product. Consumers do not like to purchase damaged goods; returning such products is a hassle for them and is also an expense for businesses, creating the potential to lose customers. Businesses often test product packaging to avoid selling damaged goods. In addition to protecting against damage, packaging can prevent spoilage, reduce pilferage, protect against being opened by children, and guard against product tampering. The Tylenol scares in the 1980s, when Johnson & Johnson removed their product from shelves after a few bottles had been laced with poison, was one of the most dramatic examples of protective-packaging concerns in recent American business.

A second consideration in packaging is its role in marketing. In some consumer goods categories, colorful, descriptive packaging is a major factor in a product's success. As part of their mission, Celestial Seasonings Company states that their packaging is "aesthetically pleasing." Packaging should bring attention to the product, allow a good fit on store shelves, and provide information about the product and its benefits. The Fair Packaging and Labeling Act (1966) requires firms to provide adequate information about the contents of a package and facilitate consumer comparisons with competing products. The Nutrition Labeling Act of 1990 requires a uniform format for labeling of food products.

Cost-effectiveness is an important consideration in packaging decisions. Packaging should be lightweight and should facilitate unitizing (gathering of cartons into one unit), palletizing (placing cartons on a pallet), and stack-ing. Today most large manufacturers have automated unitizing and palletizing systems, greatly reducing the cost of packaging. Whether the work is done manually or with an automated system, businesses compare the COSTS and benefits of customized packaging versus standardized box sizes and the many alternative kinds of dunnage, the protective material that goes into a carton (i.e., wood, paper, plastic, foam, air, or starch). Increasingly firms are using air, because it is inexpensive and lightweight.

A few firms are using denatured cornstarch, a biodegradable type of dunnage. This and other environmental considerations are becoming more important in packaging considerations. The EUROPEAN UNION Directive for Packaging and Packaging Waste (1996) set packaging targets of recovery, recycling, and reuse. While the United States has not set environmental packaging mandates, some states and municipalities are requiring recycling. Some European firms operating in the United States, such as BMW, require their suppliers to be responsible for any packaging used to ship products to the BMW factory in South Carolina.

parallel markets

Parallel markets are two or more markets where the same PRODUCT, produced by the same company, are sold at different prices. Parallel markets are more common in Europe than in the United States and are the result of government price setting.

Pharmaceutical products are often sold in parallel markets due to differences in government-dictated prices. Many countries regulate the price of medicines and other necessity goods. In Europe, where there is close proximity and few TRADE BARRIERS, consumers will often travel to the lowest-priced country in the EUROPEAN UNION and purchase large quantities of drugs. For pharmaceutical companies, the result is increased sales in countries with low regulated prices and reduced sales in countries with high regulated prices. To combat the problem, drug companies are considering limiting supplies to an amount equal to the estimated DEMAND in each country.

Parallel markets are based on the principle of ARBITRAGE, the practice of buying a product at a low price in one market and selling it at a higher price in another market. Arbitrage is as old as trade; a basic business maxim is "buy low and sell high." Knowledgeable middlemen, knowing the prices of products in different parts of the world, would buy from producers in one region and sell to consumers or merchants in another region. One motivation for the exploration of the New World was the control of land-based trade by merchants in the Middle East. European businesspeople and monarchs knew that new DISTRIBUTION CHANNELS would reduce the power of arbitrageurs. The distinction between arbitrage and parallel markets is how the price difference is created. In parallel markets, price differences are the result of government price controls, while arbitrage is based on the differences in SUPPLY and demand and market knowledge.

Parallel markets differ from parallel or underground economies in that parallel markets are open, legal, and regulated market exchanges; parallel economies are unregulated and untaxed exchanges in both legal and illegal products. In parallel markets, the products are produced by the same firm, unlike GRAY MARKETS in which similar or identical products are produced by another firm under LICENSING agreements. Many U.S. consumers flock to Mexico to purchase pharmaceutical drugs produced under license from U.S. companies but sold at much lower prices.

Parallel markets create the same CONSUMER BEHAVIOR as that occurring when different taxes are applied to products. In Europe, tax differences on wine and gasoline create a constant flow of consumers back and forth across the English Channel. In the United States, variations in cigarette taxes create interstate smuggling. In the 1990s, Canada significantly raised its tax on cigarettes, only to see tax revenue decrease as consumers stocked up during visits to the United States.

See also UNDERGROUND ECONOMY.

parity

The most common definition of parity is equality in price or value. Workers often ask for pay parity when they are transferred to another part of the country. Software companies offer parity with competing products. Parity can also refer to parity price of BONDS, or stocks, PURCHASING power parity, and parity payments.

The parity price of a bond equals the number of shares of stock (in exchange) times the current price of the stock share. Convertible bonds are those that can be exchanged for a specific number of shares of stock in the company, usually any time until the bond reaches maturity. For example, if XYZ Corporation issues a convertible bond exchangeable for 20 shares of the company's stock, and the current price of the stock is $45, the parity price of the bond is $45 × 20 = $900. Companies offer convertible bonds as a way to attract investors and pay a lower interest rate to borrow funds.

The parity price of a stock is the bond's MARKET VALUE divided by the conversion ratio. In the example above, if XYZ's bond is selling for $1,000, the parity price for the stock is $1,000 ÷ 20 = $50.

Purchasing power parity is the exchange rate between the currencies of two countries that equalizes the purchasing power of both currencies. The idea behind purchasing power parity is called the "law of one price." When there are no transactions COSTS, the prices of products in competitive markets tend to be equal. When purchasing power in one country is greater than purchasing power in another country, that country's currency is considered overvalued, while the other country's currency is considered undervalued. Consumers with overvalued currencies increase their purchases of IMPORTS, which in turn tend to decrease the value of the currency, if it is allowed to fluctuate. The PESO CRISIS in Mexico during the mid-1990s was largely due to a disparity in the peso's purchasing power, leading to increasing trade deficits.

The term *parity payments* refers to a system of support for agricultural producers. Under parity-payment programs, the U.S. Department of Agriculture uses price supports and production quotas to increase farmers' INCOME, allowing farmers to maintain parity with nonfarmworkers. Parity payments were instituted in the Agricultural Adjustment Act of 1938, authorizing the secretary of agriculture to make payments to producers of corn, wheat, cotton, rice, and tobacco. Over time, parity-payment programs have been modified or eliminated.

See also EXCHANGE RATES; INTEREST RATES.

Further reading

"Purchasing Power Parity," Pacific Exchange Rate Service. Available on-line. URL: http://pacific.commerce.ubc.ca/xr/PPP.html.

partnership

A partnership is an association of two or more persons for the purpose of conducting business, with each contributing money, property, labor, or skill, and with all expecting to share in PROFITs and losses. Partners can be individuals, CORPORATIONS, estates partnerships, or TRUSTS. The federal-taxation advantage in the partnership form of business is that partnership losses generally pass through to the partners for deduction on their tax returns (subject to basis, at-risk, and passive limitations described below), whereas partnership gains are not subject to double taxation (as they are in the corporate form of business).

The term *partnership* includes a syndicate, group, pool, joint venture, or other entity that exists for the purpose of making a profit in a business or financial operation. The rights and responsibilities of the individual partners include (1) the right of each partner to act as an agent of the partnership (mutual agency); (2) the personal responsibility of each partner for the debts of the partnership (unlimited LIABILITY); (3) the termination of the partnership by the withdrawal, death, insanity, or bankruptcy of any partner (limited life); and (4) the right to share profits in some mutually agreeable manner (profit motive).

The partnership form of business allows a great degree of flexibility in the conduct of an enterprise. Partnerships generally operate as general partnerships, limited partnerships, LIMITED LIABILITY PARTNERSHIPS, or limited liability companies. All four enjoy pass-through taxation and thus avoid the double taxation inherent in a corporation's division of profits (as DIVIDENDS).

A general partnership has two or more partners who share ownership, profits, losses, and liability. Although one or more of the partners manage the day-to-day affairs of the partnership, they still share equally the profits, losses, and liability for DAMAGES caused by employees or partners. General partners are often required to sign personal guarantees for business and equipment leases and bank lines of credit. Each partner has full authority to bind the partnership. In essence, one partner can make each of the other partners liable on business and equipment leases and bank lines of credit (joint and several liability). No one may join a partnership without the approval of a majority of the existing partners.

A limited partnership has one or more limited partners in addition to at least one general partner. Typically only the general partners are liable to creditors; each limited partner's risk of loss is restricted to that partner's EQUITY investment in the entity. Limited partners by definition are not involved in the MANAGEMENT of the partnership enterprise. A limited partnership is often used for acquiring CAPITAL in activities such as real-estate development.

Partners in a limited liability partnership (LLP) are treated much like general partners, with the exception that an LLP partner is not liable for torts or malpractice committed by the other partners. The LLP partners are liable for the other partners' CONTRACT violations.

A LIMITED LIABILITY COMPANY (LLC) combines the best features of a partnership and a corporation, even though it is neither. It is taxed like a partnership while providing the limited liability of a corporation; this limited liability extends to all the LLC owners, called members. Similar to an unlimited partnership with no general partners, the LLC can elect to be taxed as either a corporation or a partnership under check-the-box regulations, but most LLCs elect to be taxed as a partnership. The LLC entity form protects the members from both tort liabilities arising from the actions of other members as well as any liabilities arising from CONTRACTs entered into by other members. Members are always liable for their own tort and contract acts as well as for the acts of others under their direction.

Partnership taxation blends the entity concept with the aggregate concept, with the central tax advantage being that the partnership items of net INCOME or loss flow through (pass through) to the partners' tax returns. The partnership files a Form 1065 as an information report to the INTERNAL REVENUE SERVICE (IRS), but partnerships do not pay any tax. The tax is paid by the partners, with the information reported on the Form 1065 K-1 filed for each partner disclosing the partner's name and federal identifying number (e.g., SOCIAL SECURITY number or employer's ID number).

Approximately 2 million partnership returns are filed with the IRS annually. The tax law addressing the transaction of partners and partnerships is found in Subchapter K of the Internal Revenue Code. However, most partnership tax-law details have evolved through extensive IRS regulations and a large number of court cases.

In many cases, a partnership may be formed and liquidated tax-free. Immediately after its formation, a partner's basis in the partnership interest is the carryover basis of the amounts contributed to the partnership, less the share of debt assumed by the other partners, plus the share of partnership debt assumed by the contributing partner. During the life of a partnership (or an LLC electing to be taxed as a partnership), the partners are taxed on the distributive share of partnership income, whether or not the amount is actually received by the partner. The income and loss items are added and subtracted to the partner's basis in the partnership interest. Withdrawals by a partner are not taxed as long as the partner has sufficient basis in the partnership interest (capital recovery concept). The partner's basis in the partnership interest is reduced by the distributions received from the partnership.

The partner's share of partnership losses are passed through for potential deduction on the individual partner's return. The partner's ability to reduce his/her taxable income with this allocated loss will depend on (1) the partner's basis in the partnership interest, (2) the partner's at-risk basis, and (3) the partner's passive-loss limitations. In many cases a loss will not be allowable for a given year because of these restrictions, and the partner will then carry the loss forward into a future year for potential deductibility.

The LLC and LLP are existing new forms of business that are able to combine partnership taxation, limited liability, and flexible management. As a result of this development, many businesses organized after the late 1990s will be taxed as partnerships. Many businesses organized before that time are C and S corporations, and will continue to operate in the C or S corporation form due in part of the tax cost of liquidating these corporate entities.

See also JOINT VENTURES; S CORPORATION.

—Linda Bradley

patent

A patent is a protective right given to inventors by the federal government. Under patent law, inventors receive exclusive rights to their invention for a limited period of time. To obtain a patent, inventors provide information about their PRODUCT to the government. Because individual governments give patents, an inventor seeking a patent will need to decide whether to seek a patent only in their home country or in other countries around the world.

Patent laws vary among nations. For example, some developing countries traditionally refuse to grant patents on pharmaceuticals. U.S. nationals receive tens of thousands of patents in other countries, and over half of the patents issued in the United States are given to residents of foreign countries. In many countries, patent practice is a specialized branch of law.

In the United States, the U.S. Patent Office issues patents. U.S. patents grant the inventor exclusive rights to the product for 20 years from the date of application. (U.S. law used to give a 17-year patent from the date the patent was granted, but in the 1990s the United States changed its patent laws in order to comply with the General Agreement on Tariffs and Trade [GATT].) The patent allows the patent holder (patentee) to exclude everyone from making, using, or selling the patented invention without the permission of the patentee. Unlike many countries, the United States grants patents to the "first to invent" not the "first to file." Some countries issue patents upon registration, without review of the application. Other countries, including the United States, issue patents after careful examination of the inventor's patent request. A patent can be sought for a process, machine, manufacturing method, composition of matter, improvement of any of these, ornamental design, and plant produced by asexual reproduction. Naturally occurring things such as wild plants, abstract ideas, scientific laws, and other mental laws are not patentable.

To receive a patent in the United States, the inventor must demonstrate that the inventions are novel, useful, and nonobvious. In 1998, more than 150,000 patents were issued, a 33 percent increase over the year before. Much of the growth is attributable to U.S. technology industries, including computer-software and business-methods patents.

A patent provides a short-term legal MONOPOLY for the inventor, but often competitors find noninfringing ways to create similar products. When seeking a patent, inventors must disclose valuable information about their product. This information is available to the public and is often used by competitors in creating new and improved versions of the original product. Some inventors, particularly those of technically sophisticated products, choose not to seek patents, hoping others will not easily copy their KNOW-HOW.

Challenges to a patentee's rights are called patent infringement litigation. Patentees often seek INJUNCTIONS and DAMAGES against competitors infringing on their rights. U.S. patent holders against foreign-made patent-infringing goods often seek exclusion orders, which are often issued by the INTERNATIONAL TRADE COMMISSION and enforced by the U.S. CUSTOMS SERVICE.

Further reading
Mallor, Jane P., A. James Barnes, Thomas Bowers, Michael J. Philips, and Arlen W. Langvardt. *Business Law and the Regulatory Environment,* 11th ed. Boston: McGraw-Hill, 2001.

pay equity   See COMPARABLE WORTH; EQUAL PAY ACT; EQUITY INCOME THEORY.

payroll taxes (employment taxes)
Payroll taxes, also known as EMPLOYMENT taxes, are levied on wages and salaries and are assessed on both employers and employees. Payroll taxes are collected by state governments and the federal government. Employers are required to withhold state and federal income taxes as well as SOCIAL SECURITY and Medicare taxes from employees' salaries, paying these taxes on the employees' behalf as well as paying a matching amount of Social Security and Medicare taxes. Employers also pay 100 percent of state and federal UNEMPLOYMENT taxes and WORKERS' COMPENSATION taxes. These social INSURANCE programs provide cash payments to help replace INCOME lost as a result of retirement, unemployment, disability, or death, and are financed by required contributions from both employers and employees.

Employment taxes imposed by the federal government are FICA (Federal Insurance Contributions Act) and FUTA (Federal Unemployment Tax Act) taxes. FICA governs taxes for Old Age Insurance and Survivor's and Disability Insurance (OASDI, aka Social Security) and hospital insurance (Medicare). These taxes are paid by both the employer (7.65 percent of wages in 2002) and the employee (7.65 percent of wages). A self-employed person pays a tax of 15.3 percent of earnings (7.65 percent + 7.65 percent) under the Self-Employment Contributions Act (SECA).

FUTA taxes pay for unemployment insurance coverage. An employee, if laid off without cause, may apply for unemployment compensation. FUTA taxes are 6.2 percent of an employee's first $7,000 of wages and are paid solely by the employer. State Unemployment Taxes (SUTA) are levied by the state where the EMPLOYMENT occurred and are calculated as a varying percentage of wages, depending on the number of unemployment claims that have been filed by employees terminated by the employer. A credit is provided in the calculation of FUTA for the SUTA taxes paid, up to 5.4 percent. This results in a minimum net-FUTA tax rate of 0.8 percent. Self-employed individuals are not covered under the FUTA system and thus do not pay FUTA taxes on their earnings.

The OASDI contributions finance the Social Security system. During their working lives, members of the system and their employers make contributions via payroll taxes.

Employees' share of the tax is withheld from their paychecks. Upon retirement, members are eligible for payments based in part on their contributions. Social Security also provides benefits for disabled workers and for dependents and survivors of disabled and retired individuals. Medicare provides health-care coverage for individuals aged 65 and older.

In addition to FICA tax withholding on employee's wages, an employer is required to withhold federal and state income taxes from employees' paychecks. Each new employee must complete an IRS form W-4, which provides information concerning his or her marital status and the number of dependents he/she is allowed to claim. A new W-4 can be used whenever there are changes to an employee's filing status and/or number of dependents. The federal and state withholding will be based on withholding tables provided by the INTERNAL REVENUE SERVICE (IRS) and each state.

Information on federal payroll-tax requirements can be found in IRS Publication 15, Circular E. Information on state payroll taxes can be found in each state's taxation and revenue department. FICA taxes are reported on an IRS form 941, submitted quarterly. However, FICA and federal income-tax withholding payments must be remitted during the pay period as payroll checks are issued. The deposit schedule is dependent on the dollar amount of the deposit and/or the day of the week the payday occurs. Most employers use the Electronic Federal Tax Payment System to make deposits to an authorized financial institution. FUTA taxes are reported on IRS form 940.

Social Security (OASDI) is the largest domestic-spending program. It provides retirement incomes and minimum incomes for the aged (SUPPLEMENTAL SECURITY INCOME [SSI]). Social Security benefits are calculated in two steps. Average indexed monthly earnings (AIME) are derived from the worker's earnings history and determine the primary insurance amount (PIA). To compute actual benefits, the PIA is adjusted according to retirement age, family status, and other earnings. Benefits are paid not out of a fund of previous contributions but out of current payroll taxes. This pay-as-you-go financing transfers income from younger to older citizens. SSI adds to the transfer aspect by including an income guarantee.

There have been calls to reform the Social Security system, both to reduce its impact on SAVING and work incentives and to insure its solvency. Fundamental reforms under consideration would separate the forced savings-and-transfer aspects of the program.

—Linda Bradley

Pension Benefit Guaranty Corporation

The Pension Benefit Guaranty Corporation (PBGC) is a little-known but important federal agency that provides INSURANCE guarantees for private, defined-benefit RETIREMENT PLANS. The PBGC was created by the EMPLOYEE RETIREMENT INCOME SECURITY ACT of 1974 and is financed primarily from insurance premiums paid by companies whose retirement plans they insure.

Until the 1990s, many U.S. CORPORATIONS (and government agencies) provided defined-benefit retirement plans. Defined-benefit plans offered employees fixed, monthly retirement INCOME, usually based on an employee's salary and number of years of service. Employers set aside funds and collected contributions from employees to provide for future payments to retirees and their beneficiaries. Many of these employer-sponsored funds flourished during the 1990s' growth in the U.S. economy. Some employers used excess funding in retirement funds to finance other business activities. During the 1970s, some employers' underfunded retirement plans or pension plans were poorly managed, and if the company went bankrupt, employees and retirees faced the loss of their retirement income.

The PBGC was created to protect the retirement income of private-sector workers in defined-benefit programs. Retirement plans for many small companies (fewer than 26 employees), professional-service firms (doctors and lawyers), and nonprofit organizations are usually not insured by the PBGC. As more and more companies move away from defined-benefit to defined-contribution plans (employers and employees set aside fixed percentages of their income into a 401(K) PLAN or other retirement fund), the PBGC's role has decreased.

Further reading

Pension Benefit Guaranty Corporation website. Available on-line. URL: www.pbgc.gov.

perfect competition

Perfect competition (PC) is a term used to describe a market with many sellers of similar products and ease of entry into the market. Consumers and producers in perfectly competitive markets act independently and have knowledge of market choices and conditions. To most economists, perfect competition is the ideal level of COMPETITION against which markets are compared. Perfectly competitive markets have the greatest degree of competition, while MONOPOLY markets have the least competition.

The benefit of perfect competition is efficiency. With many independent producers of the same PRODUCT and knowledge of market conditions, no one firm can charge a higher price, because consumers will choose to purchase from competing firms. If individual firms cannot produce the product at the market price, they leave the market. Only those firms that can produce efficiently will remain in the market.

Like *always* and *never,* the word *perfect* is an absolute term. Economists sometimes say there are about as many truly perfectly competitive markets as there are people in Antarctica. Usually agricultural COMMODITY MARKETS, particularly ones where there are no government price-support programs, are given as examples of perfect competition. There are thousands of producers of most agricultural commodities. If they are not part of a COOPERATIVE, they act independently and have knowledge of market prices through market-reporting services; and unless technical expertise or huge amounts of CAPITAL act as a barrier to entry, it is relatively easy to enter the market.

Few managers want to be part of perfectly competitive markets. Because there are many competitors producing the same product, no one firm has any pricing power. PC firms are known as price takers because managers in PC markets are constantly trying to cut COSTS and become more efficient. With no power to raise prices, managers can only increase PROFITS by cutting costs or differentiating their product. A market where there are many sellers of differentiated products is called MONOPOLISTIC COMPETITION. If a firm has a product that is different from competitors' products (either really different or perceived as different by consumers), increasing its price will not result in losing all customers. Firms in PC markets constantly attempt to differentiate their products by emphasizing they are home-grown or chemical-free, or just by providing better service than competitors.

performance appraisal (performance evaluation)

A performance appraisal or evaluation is a structured, formal interaction between a supervisor and a subordinate in which the subordinate's work performance is evaluated and discussed. Performance appraisals are primarily used to determine pay raises, as tools to identify weaknesses and develop corrective actions, and as a means of motivating employees to improve their work performance.

The performance appraisal evolved out of management specialist Frederick Taylor's early 20th-century time and motion studies, the goal of which was to improve workers' productivity. Taylor's classic study analyzed the output of workers shoveling coal using different-sized shovels. He calculated how much output workers should be able to achieve with the equipment and materials available and then encouraged employers to pay more productive workers at a higher rate than other workers.

In the 1940s, performance appraisal began to be recognized as a distinct MANAGEMENT function. It is now used primarily to justify paying some workers more than others and attempts to define and utilize objective standards for evaluation. The alternative is informal evaluation, which can lead to a variety of problems, including arbitrariness, and bias. This discourages motivation among workers who perceive the process to be unfair, and it can lead to legal disputes.

With the performance appraisal's early focus on justifying pay differentials, developers ignored the potential for it to be used as a basis for EMPLOYEE MOTIVATION and development. Research showed that although pay for performance often worked, it did not always totally explain employee performance. Self-esteem and morale also contributes to workers' productivity, but early performance-appraisal systems did not include these considerations.

Beginning in the 1950s, managers attempted to move beyond pay-for-performance appraisal systems. Some management scholars suggest performance appraisal must be linked to pay, or workers will not take it seriously. Others argue performance appraisal should be used for development of workers' potential but not linked to pay. Some organizations use it to identify TRAINING AND DEVELOPMENT opportunities and define supervisor-employee agreements on work expectations, but it is still most often used to determine monetary rewards. The appraisal is also used for promotions, transfers, and LAYOFFS. In the 1990s, Ford Motor Company established a controversial appraisal system, mandating that employees who were consistently ranked the lowest in their part of the organization be terminated. Only after considerable disgruntlement among managerial workers was the system scrapped.

Performance appraisal involves two parts: evaluation and feedback. From a supervisor's perspective, evaluation attempts to identify any performance gaps—that is, divergences between what a worker is responsible for and what they accomplish. From an employee's perspective, performance appraisal addresses four questions.

- What am I expected to do?
- How well am I doing?
- What are my weaknesses and strengths?
- How can I do better and get rewarded for doing so?

Employers use a wide variety of performance-appraisal methods, including rating scales, essays, management by objective pre- and post-evaluations, and ranking systems. Each method has its advantages and disadvantages and may or may not be appropriate, depending on situation and the appraiser's skill and integrity.

Usually workers' direct supervisors conduct performance appraisals, which can lead to a variety of issues and situations. One problem is known as the game of feedback-seeking. Some employees frequently seek out informal confirmation from their supervisors that what they are doing meets or exceeds expectations. The supervisor is caught off guard, being asked for an appraisal without the time or often the full information needed to evaluate the individual objectively. When the supervisor does conduct a formal performance appraisal, if the worker receives a less-positive evaluation, he may claim he was "ambushed" by the supervisor after receiving consistently positive signals.

Another issue in performance appraisal is a tendency for supervisors not to make critical evaluations or to "fudge" the evaluations, because they fear such appraisals will make them look bad then fear legal action from the employee, or employees will respond poorly. Especially in the United States, where work environments tend to be less formal and where teamwork is valued and promoted, supervisors are frequently hesitant to make harsh judgments about coworkers' performance standards, since this can be seen as interference with their staff-coaching function. In addition, some supervisors see performance appraisal as wasted paperwork if the upper administration does nothing with the information provided.

See also ACHIEVEMENT MOTIVATION; INDUSTRIAL-ORGANIZATIONAL PSYCHOLOGY; 360-DEGREE FEEDBACK.

Further reading
"Performance Appraisal." Archer North's Performance Appraisal website. Available on-line. URL: www.performance-appraisal.com; Stoner, James F., and R. Edward Freeman. *Management,* 5th ed. Saddle River, N.J.: Prentice Hall, 1992.

personal finance
Personal finance is the management of individual or family resources to achieve financial security and other goals. Personal finance includes five basic activities: BUDGETING, SAVING, INVESTMENT, retirement planning, and estate planning. Most Americans engage in only a few personal financial-planning activities, leaving themselves and their dependents vulnerable to risks and surprises.

Personal finance begins with budgeting, which involves analyzing how one's INCOME is being spent and making decisions on how to control and allocate it. A typical budget will include allocations for housing, utilities, food, transportation, health care, clothing, INSURANCE, taxes, entertainment, and savings. When first analyzing current expenditures, many people are surprised to find how much of their income is already committed to recurring expenses. Families in financial difficulty may learn they are committed to spending in excess of current income. The CONSUMER CREDIT COUNSELING SERVICE is a banking industry–run service assisting individuals and families who are heavily in debt.

Frequently households become overextended through the use of CREDIT CARDS. Until about 1980, credit cards were not aggressively marketed and not issued to individuals who did not have good credit history or a strong personal finance situation. The proliferation of credit cards in subsequent years has facilitated credit PURCHASING but also tested the personal financial management of many families.

The second part of personal financial planning is making provision for saving, which is needed for unexpected expenses (the proverbial "rainy day" fund), to provide for replacement of durable goods (items that are used for over a year before being replaced), for uncertainties such as loss of job, and for retirement. Collectively, Americans are terrible savers who often lack the discipline necessary to saving. Most personal financial advisors recommend families have an amount equal to 3–6 months' average expenditures set aside for emergencies and uncertainty. They also recommend setting aside a percentage of monthly income as part of a personal financial plan.

The third part of personal financial management is investing. Investment by individuals and households can have multiple objectives and involve a variety of ASSETS. Typically households invest to earn CAPITAL GAINS from the increase in value of stocks or real estate, or to provide income to support a certain lifestyle and spending pattern. An ever-popular investment question is, "How long will it take for my money to double?" or "How long will it take for the account to double?" The RULE OF 72 estimates with a surprising degree of precision how long it will take for a sum to double at some given rate of interest, compounded annually. The number 72 is the numerator and the denominator is the rate of interest applicable to the situation in question. For example, at 10 percent interest compounded annually, it will take approximately 72/10 = 7.2 years for a sum to double. At 7 percent interest compounded annually, the sum will double in approximately 72/7 = 10 years.

The major investment for most Americans is their homes. The U.S. personal income-tax system encourages the purchase of homes by allowing taxpayers to deduct home MORTGAGE interest as an expense if they itemize their tax deductions. Depending on the marginal tax rate a taxpayer is subject to, the deductibility of mortgage interest can reduce the effective long-term interest cost of home ownership.

A second area of investment for most Americans is through their RETIREMENT PLANS. Many companies provide matching programs, whereby employees set aside a percentage of their income, which is matched by their employer. Although these programs have restrictions, they effectively double the employees' investments.

When considering investment as part of a personal financial plan, individuals should also consider liquidity and effective rate of return. Liquidity is how easily an asset can be turned into MONEY. Company retirement programs are generally nonliquid investments. As the employees of Enron learned, when the company's stock went down, their retirement accounts went into a blackout period during which the company was changing retirement-plan administrators. They also found their STOCK OPTIONS and company stock payments into their retirement investments had become worthless.

While the U.S. STOCK MARKET, over longer periods of time, has yielded approximately an 8 percent rate of return, the effective yield will be lower, depending on taxes and expenses. During the stock market boom of the late 1990s, many individuals borrowed heavily to invest in the market, often earning significant returns. In recent years, average stock market yields have been considerably lower than those in the 1990s, making paying off credit-card debt secured at high INTEREST RATES an attractive alternative to stock market investment.

Another personal investment option is MUTUAL FUNDS. Organized as CORPORATIONS and regulated by the SECURITIES

AND EXCHANGE COMMISSION, mutual funds are major FINANCIAL INTERMEDIARIES in today's world. They accept funds from savers by selling them shares and then use the proceeds to invest in various financial securities ranging from short-term debt instruments to long-term BONDS and stocks. In order to meet the needs and desires of the various savers, each mutual fund specializes in investing in a particular type or a unique mix of securities. Generally there are income funds, growth funds, and mutual funds made up of a mix of income and growth funds. Money-market mutual funds invest only in short term securities and operate like interest-bearing checking accounts for the savers.

Insurance should be considered as part of personal financial budgets, retirement options, and estate planning. Insurance is primarily designed to protect individuals and families against the risk of losses or significant expense. Most households use insurance to protect the value of their investment in their home and other PERSONAL PROPERTY, to protect against medical expenses, and to compensate for the death of family members who contributed to the household's welfare and expenses. Insurance products such as GUARANTEED INVESTMENT CONTRACTS (GICs) are sometimes used as part of a retirement income plan. Life insurance is also used as part of estate planning. Wealthy individuals purchase life insurance to pay estate taxes, allowing inheritors to retain other valuable family assets.

In addition to using insurance as part of estate planning, personal finance management includes wills, TRUSTS, and power of attorney documents to facilitate the transfer of assets from one generation to the next. Many family conflicts have arisen over the failure to execute clear estate plans.

The FINANCIAL PLANNING ASSOCIATION (FPA) is an organization that trains and certifies people to assist with personal finance. Financial planning is the process of establishing personal financial goals and allocating resources to obtain those goals. The FPA was created in 2000 through a merger of the Institute of Certified Financial Planners and the International Association for Financial Planning.

Further reading

"Building A Balanced Financial Plan." Available on-line. URL: www.aboutmoney.com; Gitman, Lawrence J. and Michael D. Joehnk. *Personal Financial Planning,* 9th ed. Cincinnati, Ohio: South-Western, 2001.

personal-interview surveys

Personal-interview SURVEYS are one method market researchers use to collect information. Personal interview surveys are often conducted to collect information about customer needs and wants, opinions, demographics, and financial status. Personal-interview research can be conducted in peoples' homes, businesses, prearranged focus-group locations, or public places. One of the most popular forms of personal-interview research is the mall-intercept method, where researchers set up in the walkway or in a booth at shopping center and ask shoppers to take part in the survey.

Personal-interview surveys allow for in-depth questioning of respondents and the use of visual materials. They also allow for flexibility in collecting data and can be conducted quickly, yielding fairly high response rates. Respondents can be shown videotapes, pictures, and prototypes of new PRODUCTS. In addition to their responses to survey questions, respondents' nonverbal responses—e.g., expressions of surprise, concern, or excitement—can also be assessed. Personal-interview questions are usually structured to gather additional information from respondents. In addition to asking typical questions about what products people use or do not use, like or dislike, interviewers can ask about motivations—e.g., why people do or think the way they do.

The disadvantages of personal-interview surveys are the expense and the potential for interviewer bias. Except for the focus-group method, only one respondent can be interviewed at a time, and interviewers often spend considerable time traveling to meet respondents. Since personal-interview methods are expensive, companies often use them when they cannot obtain the information using other methods and when the information is critical to business decisions. An additional cost is interviewer training. To obtain consistently objective data, interviewers must be trained to avoid interjecting bias through the tone of language used or nonverbal cues.

Personal-interview methods, particularly mall-intercept surveys, are used to test product and promotional concepts. In the famous 1980s Coke/new Coke disaster, researchers used a mall-intercept method to ask people to taste samples of the cola and state which they preferred. A slight majority preferred the new Coke formula, and based on this research, Coca-Cola Company replaced the traditional formula. When consumers protested, the company realized they had not asked consumers how they felt about traditional Coca-Cola. Using the personal-interview method, this information could have been gathered and the problem avoided.

See also FOCUS GROUPS; QUESTIONNAIRES.

Further reading

Pride, William M., and O. C. Ferrell. *Marketing Concepts and Strategies.* 12th ed. Boston: Houghton Mifflin Company, 2003.

personal property

All property that is not real estate is personal property. Personal property can be tangible or intangible and includes stocks, BONDS, RETIREMENT PLANS, cash, furnishings, vehicles, boats, jewelry, clothing, electronics and goods of all sorts, animals, COPYRIGHTS, PATENTS, TRADEMARKS, and CONTRACT rights, among many other things. Ownership of personal property conveys the exclusive right to possess, enjoy, and use it and to sell or transfer it. In most situations, personal property is not subject to seizure in corporate lawsuits, although it is vulnerable in business disputes involving PARTNERSHIPS and PROPRIETORSHIPS.

Further reading
Burke, Bartow, D. *Personal Property in a Nutshell,* 2d ed. Eagan, Minn.: West Group, 1993.

personal selling
Personal selling—direct interaction between a seller and a buyer—is a critical component in MARKETING COMMUNICATIONS. Salespeople help to generate a company's revenue by providing information to consumers and feedback to manufacturers. Personal selling includes field sales; making calls on existing and potential customers at their businesses; over-the-counter sales in retail or wholesale locations; and electronic sales, telephone, or INTERNET communications with customers. Personal selling, especially field sales, can be expensive, which is why companies are using electronic sales communications whenever appropriate.

The stereotypical salesperson is someone who uses high-pressure, fast-talking tactics. But selling has many facets, most of which are ethical and beneficial to society. Increasingly businesses attempt to build relationships with customers though their sales representatives. Selling involves listening to customers and helping them solve problems even if it does not immediately result in a sale. Selling is often a team process, with many specialists contributing to the organization's overall goal. Personal selling is also part of nonprofit marketing. People who believe in their organization's goal can often be very effective representatives when soliciting donations.

Personal selling is a seven-step process. Individual salespersons may or may not be involved in all seven steps, but someone in an organization needs to be responsible for accomplishing each step in the process, as follows.

- prospecting and qualifying
- approach
- presentation
- demonstration
- handling objections
- closing
- follow-up

Prospecting—identifying potential customers—is sometimes managed by company headquarters, which provides leads for its salespeople. Prospecting and then qualifying customers can be time-consuming, but it is a critical first step, since it reduces wasted effort by determining which prospects are potential customers. Real-estate agents will often offer to prequalify buyers before showing them properties. Buyers give the agent INCOME and expense information, allowing the agent to estimate the maximum loan the buyer will likely be able to get from a lending institution. This eliminates wasted time showing customers properties they cannot afford and also provides the agent, a representative of the seller, valuable information about what buyers can afford to pay.

Once a salesperson identifies a qualified prospect, she or he makes initial contact with the prospective customer. The approach stage is carefully planned utilizing whatever information the salesperson can obtain. Business salespeople will often spend considerable time learning about a company before approaching the firm. Retail salespeople frequently have limited information about prospects but will quickly engage potential customers to better define their approach.

Presentations, describing a PRODUCT's features and benefits to customers, are designed to stimulate interest. In some sales organizations, representatives memorize and use canned presentations. Others use a features-benefits framework, in which the seller presents the product in terms of how the features of their product will meet the customer's needs.

In face-to-face personal selling, the seller can demonstrate the good or service to a potential buyer, which reinforces the benefits that the salesperson has already discussed. Auto sales almost always involve test-driving vehicles. Television INFOMERCIALS and shopping networks show consumers how to use and benefit from the product being sold. Sometimes, however, demonstrations can fail. In 2000, Microsoft's CHIEF EXECUTIVE OFFICER, Bill Gates, attempted to demonstrate one of his company's new products at the important Comdex Trade show, only to have the product fail in front of thousands of technology industry customers and competitors.

Handling objections is the next stage in the selling process. Well-trained salespeople know in advance most of the objections potential customers will have and are prepared to address those objections. Once objections are answered, the "moment of truth" in the sales process, the closing, takes place: The salesperson asks the customer to buy the product. Salespeople have learned a number of techniques to close a sale, including

- the "if I can show you . . ." suggestion
- the "which do you like better" alternative decision
- the "buy now or it might not be available later" teaser (called the Standing Room Only technique)
- the sweetener—adding something to the offer
- silence

Salespeople generally use one or more of the above techniques. However, one study found salespeople often fail to close when the buyer is ready.

The last stage in the sales process is follow-up. Post-sales efforts often determine whether the customer will become a repeat customer. In most marketing situations, it is much more expensive and time-consuming to find new customers than it is to sell to existing customers. Follow-up also cultivates word-of-mouth referral, which is almost always the best form of promotion a company can get. Good follow-up practices make personal selling easier.

Further reading

Boone, Louis, and David Kurtz. *Contemporary Marketing*, 10th ed. Fort Worth: Dryden Press, 2001.

peso crisis

The peso crisis was the Mexican government's near DEFAULT on its international debt obligations in 1994–95. The frightening but largely unreported aspect of the Mexican peso crisis was how dangerously close Mexico came to defaulting on all its debt. The unprecedented U.S.-IMF (INTERNATIONAL MONETARY FUND) financial support package was the largest international aid response since the MARSHALL PLAN in 1948.

While the peso crisis was a Mexican economic problem, it is included in an encyclopedia of American business for three reasons. First, Mexico is the United States' second-largest trading partner (after Canada). Second, the U.S. government was heavily involved in Mexico's bailout during the crisis. Third, the peso crisis is instructive of the risks associated with international business in EMERGING MARKETS.

In 1994 Mexico was widely heralded as one of the success stories of ECONOMIC GROWTH through export expansion. For decades the nation had pursued import-substitution-industrialization (ISI), by which economic growth is attained through substituting domestic production for foreign IMPORTS. The logical limit of ISI economic development is the size of the domestic economy. At the time, the Mexican economy was about one-twentieth the size of the U.S. economy. When the Mexican economy stagnated in the 1970s and again in the 1980s, Mexican economists and later political leaders began to reduce TRADE BARRIERS and support export expansion. However, Mexico had a long history of financial crises coinciding with changes in political leadership every six years.

In 1994 the outgoing Mexican president, Carlos Salinas, who was lobbying hard to become the first president of the WORLD TRADE ORGANIZATION, chose to ignore a growing liquidity crisis. (A liquidity crisis occurs when currency reserves are insufficient to offset trade deficits.) Early that same year, international investors led by U.S.-based banks began reducing their holdings of Mexican peso debt securities. In an effort to maintain CAPITAL inflow, the Mexican government expanded the use of tesebonos, short-term peso-denominated securities convertible to U.S. dollars. In effect, the Mexican government assumed the RISK of currency devaluation by guaranteeing payment in dollars. In early 1994, the expanded use of tesebonos combined with an overvalued Mexican peso, which stimulated greater

imports and reduced exports, increased the current-account deficit. This further reduced Bank of Mexico currency reserves. At the time, Mexican exchange-rate policy was a "crawling peg"—that is, the peso was being devalued on steady rate within a prescribed range or band. But Mexican INFLATION was greater than the rate of devaluation of the currency. Thus, the peso became overvalued.

In December 1994, when the new government took office, it quickly became evident that peso devaluation was needed. Finance Minister Dr. Guillermo Ortiz, hoping to gradually reduce the imbalance, announced an expansion of the band of peso/dollar devaluation. While the new Mexican leadership hoped this would be seen as a minor adjustment and not panic in the financial markets, it was seen as a radical step and became front-page news. Investors rapidly pulled funds out of Mexico, and the peso immediately fell by 35 percent.

Because of the tesebonos guarantees, the Mexican government now owed billions more in dollars while the peso was worth significantly less. The U.S. government stepped in with a $6 billion currency swap credit, but that was only the beginning. By the end of January 1995, President Bill Clinton had orchestrated a $52 billion bailout plan, including funds support through the Exchange Stabilization Fund (U.S.), the International Monetary Fund (IMF), the BANK OF INTERNATIONAL SETTLEMENTS (Switzerland), and lesser amounts from commercial banks and other countries. One Mexican commentator called the plan "at least the greatest event in Mexico since the arrival of Cortes."

Two unique features of the plan were the requirement for Mexican finance managers to report weekly to the U.S. Treasury and a provision tying the revenue from Mexican oil sales as collateral for the loan. In Mexico, oil is a public resource that is controlled by the government through Petroleos Mexicanos (PEMEX). The 1917 Mexican Constitution prohibits foreign exploration for oil in the country, but the constitution does not say what the government can do with the proceeds from the sale of oil. The bailout required deposit of payments by foreign customers for Mexican oil to be made into an account with a U.S. bank that would be under "irrevocable instructions" to transfer funds to the Banco of Mexico account at the Federal Reserve Bank of New York. The U.S. Treasury was entitled to file claims against these funds if Mexico failed to repay the loan.

In addition to the financial guarantees, the Mexican government was forced to implement a series of IMF-dictated economic reforms to increase government revenues and reduce government spending. Unlike past Mexican financial crises, when recovery often took a decade or longer, this time the Mexican economy recovered quickly with the growth of the MAQUILADORAS program, the signing of the NORTH AMERICAN FREE TRADE AGREEMENT (NAFTA), and other new export-directed trade policies. By the late 1990s, the government had paid off its peso-crisis bailout.

See also EXCHANGE RATES.

Further reading

Folsom, Ralph H., and W. Davis Folsom. *NAFTA Law and Business*. The Hague: Kluwer Law International, 1998.

Peter principle

The Peter principle, named after Dr. Laurence Peter, is the MANAGEMENT theory that people tend to be promoted to one level beyond their competency. As stated in Peter's book *The Peter Principle—Why Things Always Go Wrong* (coauthored with Raymund Hull), "In a hierarchy every employee tends to rise to his own level of incompetence."

The Peter principle is a widely quoted concept. Even though it was written in 1969, today many Dilbert cartoons portray management incompetence, with executives often not knowing what they are doing. As frequently observed in business, great salespeople do not always make great sales managers, hard-working laborers may be poor foremen, and some great teachers have been lousy administrators.

Peter and Hull developed most of their ideas from observations of academic bureaucracies. They also contributed 19 other theories about business behavior, including the idea that people in businesses dislike super-competent people who seem to know everything and do everything well as much as they dislike incompetent workers.

Critics counter the Peter principle by questioning how anything gets done in organizations where people are incompetent. Peter and Hull respond that people rise to their level of incompetence, so at any given time, there are numerous employees who are still working within their level of ability. People at the top of an organization who have not reached their level of incompetence frequently leave the organization seeking new challenges, while "Petered" managers are often promoted out of the way.

Further reading

Peter, Dr. Laurence J., and Raymond Hull. *The Peter Principle—Why Things Always Go Wrong*. New York: William Morrow, 1969.

physical distribution   See LOGISTICS.

poison-pill strategies (shareholder rights plans)

Poison-pill strategies, also called shareholder rights plans, are a common defense used by companies to stop hostile takeovers. A poison pill makes the target company prohibitively expensive for the bidder (the individual or company initiating the takeover) to buy. Poison pills create rights (or OPTIONS) to purchase stock at a discount, when the bidder triggers certain events, such as purchasing a certain percentage of stock. For example, a company could have a poison pill that goes into effect when a hostile bidder acquires 20 percent of the company. Poison pills are usu-

ally set up to last for 10 years, after which they can be renewed or allowed to expire.

Martin Lipton, a lawyer who defended companies against hostile takeover attempts, invented poison pills in 1982. He realized that a company could make a takeover more expensive by offering SHAREHOLDERS rights to buy preferred stock at a discount if the takeover attempt succeeded. By 1985 Lipton had perfected the technique by issuing COMMON STOCK instead of preferred stock, and poison pills have been a popular defense against takeovers ever since.

There are two types of poison pills: flip-over and flip-in. The flip-over strategy allows shareholders to buy stock at a discount after the takeover occurs. The right to buy shares is created when the bidder buys a certain percentage of stock. The rights don't become exercisable until the bidder buys 100 percent of the outstanding shares.

The problem with flip-overs is that they can be overcome by buying less than 100 percent of the shares. An example of this is Sir James Goldsmith's takeover of timber company Crown Zellerbach. Shareholder rights would be activated when a bidder bought 20 percent of the outstanding stock, and once the rights became active, they would not expire for 10 years. Rights would not become exercisable (shareholders could not actually buy the stock) until the bidder bought 100 percent of Crown Zellerbach's stock. To get around the pill, Goldsmith purchased only 50 percent of outstanding stock. This activated the pill but wasn't enough to make the rights exercisable. Goldsmith gained a controlling interest in Crown Zellerbach but did not have to pay the price of the poison pill.

To close this loophole, the flip-in poison-pill strategy was invented. In this strategy, once the bidder buys the triggering percentage of shares, the target company issues more stock. Current shareholders, except for the bidder, are allowed to buy these new shares at a discounted price before the merger. The increase in the number of outstanding shares reduces the bidder's percentage.

In the United States, a BOARD OF DIRECTORS without shareholder approval can still adopt poison-pill plans. Many companies put strategies in place as a preventative measure, so they will be ready if a takeover attempt occurs. Most prison pills are adopted with the view that they will never be triggered, but since they can be roadblocks to welcome takeovers, boards can also rescind poison pills without shareholder approval.

There is much debate over whether poison pills are good or bad for a company and its shareholders. For example, they can make it harder to get rid of incompetent MANAGEMENT who may fear losing their jobs if a takeover occurs. In addition, shareholders may see the takeover as being good for the company and would not want it to be blocked. The management could use a poison pill to protect themselves at the shareholders' expense.

Some poison pills have a deadhand provision that blocks new directors from rescinding pills adopted by previous directors. Only the directors who adopted the pill, or their chosen successors, can rescind it. Any new directors (who have probably been chosen by the bidder) are unable to get rid of the pill on which the previous directors voted.

Poison pills can also be inconvenient to large institutional investors, such as pension-fund managers, who must be careful not to trigger the pill by accidentally purchasing the triggering percentage of shares. To prevent this, some companies include a provision that excludes institutional investors from triggering the pill.

As demonstrated, poison pills can be an effective defense in repelling hostile takeovers. They can give the targeted company greater bargaining power and will usually increase the bid price, preventing the company from being bought at a bargain price. This is good for shareholders, who will see the value of their shares rise.

There have been many legal challenges to poison pills, and their legality and provisions are determined on a state-by-state basis. In 1985 the Delaware Supreme Court decided that poison pills were legal. Given that so many companies are incorporated in Delaware, this was a crucial decision. Since then courts have focused on the legality of the particulars in some pills, like the deadhand provision, but overall poison pills continue to be a very popular defense mechanism against hostile takeovers.

Further reading
"Corporate Governance: Bid Blockers," *The Economist* 349, no. 8099 (19 December 1998): 90; "Pills Gain More Corporate Adherents," *Mergers & Acquisitions Journal* 35, no. 7 (July 2000): 17.
—Joan Cunningham

political action committee

A political action committee (PAC) is a legal entity created for the purpose of raising MONEY for political purposes. PACs have become a central feature of the American political landscape at both the national and state levels. Tip O'Neil, the legendary Speaker of the House of Representatives, once quipped that "money is the mother's milk of politics." If so, then PACs are a major mammary gland, as much of the money for political activities comes through PACs.

At the national level, PACs play a relatively larger role in congressional campaigns than in presidential campaigns. This is because the presidential election campaign is partially funded through public funding, a system created by the Federal Election Campaign (FEC) Act of 1974. In congressional campaigns during the 1997–98 campaign cycle, candidates raised a little over $710 million. Of this total, about 30 percent came through PACs (calculations based on FEC figures). The major single source of money is individual contributions, but it should be remembered that almost all individuals also have ties to interest groups, so PAC giving grossly underestimates the monetary influence of interest groups.

Interest groups (some of which represent the interests of American corporations) and the PACs that are associated with them have found ways to exert influence in presidential campaigns as well as in congressional campaigns. They can contribute money to candidates during the primary stages of campaigns; they can contribute to political parties and to other PACs that may be supporting or opposing a candidate; and until the passage of a major campaign finance bill in 2002, they could contribute unlimited amounts of money through a soft-money loophole. Soft-money contributions are unlimited donations to the political parties from corporations, labor unions and wealthy individuals. The soft-money loophole was opened by a 1978 Federal Election Commission (FEC) ruling designed to strengthen political parties by allowing them to use unrestricted funds for such activities as voter registration drives and get-out-the-vote efforts. Soft money was used primarily for this purpose throughout most of the 1980s, but by the 1992 election cycle, clever attorneys for the parties determined they could use soft money to pay for massive amounts of television attack ads while remaining within the letter, if not the spirit, of the law.

The overwhelming majority of PAC money goes to incumbents. In the 2000 elections, incumbents in the House of Representatives enjoyed more than an 8 to 1 advantage in PAC contributions. In the House, 392 of 399 incumbents won reelection. On the Senate side, incumbents had a 6 to 1 advantage in PAC contributions, and 23 of 28 won reelection. Although victory cannot be attributed solely to money advantages, it certainly helps.

In close contests, PACs frequently contribute to both candidates, because no matter who wins, they want access to the officeholder. Thus the contributions serve two separate but related functions. First, they help those who hold views favorable to the group get elected and stay in office. Second, they assure access to the officeholder so that the PAC or associated group can provide information on issues of concern.

A number of watchdog groups keep track of all contributions, including those from PACs. These include Common Cause (www.commoncause.org), Political MoneyLine (www.tray.com), Open Secrets (www.opensecrets.org), and the Campaign Finance Institute (www.cfinst.org/index.html). All of these groups base their reports on data provided by the Federal Election Campaign Commission (www.fec.gov).

PACs have been on the political scene since the 1900s, when federal laws banned contributions directly from CORPORATIONS (contributions banned in 1907) and labor UNIONS (contributions banned in 1943). Union PACs were formed first as a way of offsetting large contributions made by corporate leaders. Union leaders solicited contributions from members and then presented the money to candidates as contributions. Some of the largest contributors are the Teamsters Union and the American Federation of Labor.

Business PACs outspend labor PACs by almost 2 to 1. The National Association of Business Political Action Committees (NABPAC), an association of more than 100 special-interest political action committees (PACs) that represent American corporations. Among NABPAC's leading special-interest givers to congressional campaigns are:

- The National Association of Realtors, one of the largest PAC givers in politics today, which has contributed more than $14 million to congressional candidates since 1985.
- The American Medical Association, another long-time major player in money politics, having given $13.8 million to congressional candidates since 1985.
- Some of the country's largest defense contractors, who have made their mark in Washington with big-money PAC contributions to congressional candidates since 1985. Among them are Lockheed Martin, which has given $4.5 million since 1985; Northrop Grumman, at $3.4 million; General Electric, at more than $2.4 million; Textron, at $2 million; Boeing, at $1.6 million; United Technologies, at $1.5 million; and AlliedSignal, at $1.2 million.
- Insurance companies and their lobbying groups, which are among the biggest PAC players in Washington. Among them are the National Association of Life Underwriters, which has given $6.9 million in PAC contributions to congressional candidates since 1985; Blue-Cross/BlueShield Associations, which has given $1.6 million; and the National Association of Independent Insurers, the Professional Insurance Agents and CIGNA Corp, which have given more than $1 million each.
- Oil companies, which have pumped millions of dollars into the Washington influence money system. NABPAC's biggest oil industry PAC contributors to congressional candidates since 1985 include: Chevron, at more than $1.6 million; AMOCO, at $1.5 million; ARCO, at more than $1.3 million; and Mobil Oil and Occidental Petroleum (OXY USA), both at more than $1 million.
- The nation's top two tobacco manufacturers—RJR Nabisco and Philip Morris—which each contributed more than $3.5 million in PAC contributions to congressional candidates since 1985.
- Telephone companies—both long distance and local Baby Bells—including a number of million-dollar PAC givers. Heading the list is AT&T, which contributed $7 million to congressional candidates since 1985. Also on the million-dollar list are: GTE, at $2.8 million; Bell-South, at $2.7 million; Pacific Telesis and Sprint, at more than $1.3 million; and US West and SBC Communications, both at more than $1.1 million.

The campaign finance reforms that came in the 1970s following the Watergate scandals encouraged the growth of PACs of all kinds because the reforms banned direct contributions from any group other than PACs. Technically the law says that groups must create a "separate segregated fund," which cannot have any "membership dues or other money as a condition of EMPLOYMENT or membership or any money obtained through a commercial transaction." In reality, unions and corporations can exert subtle pressure on executives and members to make contributions. Moreover, an FEC ruling in 1975 allowed sponsoring groups to pay for the PAC's organizational costs, so corporations can use PROFITS to pay for the expenses involved in raising money for the PAC.

Under FEC laws, PACs are limited in what they can collect and what they give in federal elections. Most states also have limits that apply to PACs operating at the state level. At the national level, PACs can collect no more than $5,000 from any individual in a single calendar year. However, multiple members of families or different executives in a corporation are all separate individuals. PACs can contribute up to $5,000 per candidate per election; thus, $10,000 for a primary and general election, with an additional $5,000 if there is a run-off. One way to bypass this limit is to create multiple PACs, and another way is to conduct "independent campaigns" either for or against a candidate. To be independent, the PAC may not coordinate its activities with the candidate. The 2002 campaign finance reform law banning soft money also attempts to place limits on independent-issue ads, but the full impact will not be known until after court challenges of the reforms.

The number of PACs has grown dramatically. In 1972, before the reforms, only 113 PACs were registered with the FEC. By 2000 the number hovered around 4,000. This does not count PACs active only at the state level, of which there are thousands more. One estimate is that about 12,000 exist below the federal level.

Most PACs are "affiliated" PACs—that is, affiliated with some organized interest group. For example, the AB-PAC (Anheuser-Bush PAC), affiliated with the well-known brewery, raised and contributed about $400,000 to federal candidates in the 2000 election cycle.

About 25 percent of PACs are "nonaffiliated"—that is, they have no parent or sponsoring organization but collect money from individuals and contribute it to political candidates. What the individuals have in common is some concern or goal that they support through giving money. One of the most important nonaffiliated PACs is EMILY's List, which stands for Early Money Is Like Yeast. EMILY raises money for feminist candidates across the nation using a technique called "bundling," which allows it to evade contribution limits. Donors give $100 to the PAC directly and then give separate checks made out to candidates that the list supports. EMILY uses the PAC contribution to cover internal costs and then bundles the checks made out to candidates together and delivers them. Thus, technically the contributions come from individuals and not the PAC, so the $5,000 per candidate per election limit that normally applies to PACs does not apply to EMILY. Only the $1,000 individual-contribution limits apply (raised to $2,000 following the 2002 elections). This technique makes EMILY, which bundles contributions from about 50,000 members, the number one PAC in the nation, contributing over $10 million in election cycle since 1995–96.

"Leadership" PACs are formed by political candidates for several purposes; for example, they may be for the purpose of collecting money to help explore a possible candidacy before the official announcement takes place. Virtually all presidential candidates do this in the years preceding the presidential primaries. Candidates may collect money to contribute to the campaigns of other candidates. Typically members of Congress will make contributions to fellow members or challengers who share their party label to help like-minded people get elected. This practice also furthers incumbents' own aspirations within Congress as they seek some leadership position that requires the support of fellow members.

The well-publicized campaign finance reforms passed in 2002 and aimed at ending soft money could have an impact on PACs. If the ban stands up in a court challenge, much money that went to candidates through the soft-money route will either be lost to the political process or find other ways to reach candidates. One possible route is through PACs that use all existing ways to give money to candidates or independently spend it on their behalf.

While reformers aim many complaints at PACs, to the extent that they allow the public to track the collection and contribution of money to candidates and causes, they are a vast improvement over the pre-1974 status quo. In those days a few wealthy people, dubbed "fat cats," gave large amounts of unreported money to unnamed politicians for unreported purposes. While it is true that the public can never be sure what PAC contributions are buying, at least some limits apply, and the public can find out who is giving how much to whom. Until the public demands complete public financing of campaigns at all levels, PACs are likely to be a fact of life.

Further reading

Alexander, Herbert E. *Financing Politics: Money, Elections, and Political Reform*, 3d ed. Washington, D.C.: Congressional Quarterly, 1984; Nownes, Anthony. *Pressure and Power: Organized Interests in American Politics*. Boston: Houghton Mifflin, 2001; Sabato, Larry J., and Bruce Larson. *The Party's Just Begun: Shaping Political Parties for America's Future*, 2d ed. New York: Longman, 2002; Schlozman, Kay Lehman, and John T. Tierney. *Organized Interests and American Democracy*. New York: Harper and Row, 1986.

—Robert Botsch

pollution rights

Pollution rights are a market-based system for dealing with environmental problems. At first, the idea of pollution rights may seem like an oxymoron—i.e., who gave anyone the "right" to pollute? The logic behind pollution rights is based on economics. First, most environmental systems can accept certain amount of pollution without seriously harming the environment (often called carrying capacity). If the marginal (extra) cost of reducing or eliminating pollution is greater than the cost to the environment, it does not make economic sense to continue to reduce pollution. Second, if the current level of pollution is unacceptably high, encouraging those who can most easily reduce pollution to do so will cost less than making all polluters reduce their discharges into the environment.

Requiring all polluters to reduce their discharges—called regulation or the command-and-control approach—has been the traditional method of addressing pollution problems. Because of such regulations, companies have installed pollution-control equipment, made operational changes in production, and replaced existing machinery with more efficient technologies. In some firms and industries, the costs of pollution reduction are modest. Some firms actually saved money by installing more energy-efficient equipment in response to environmental regulation, but in other firms and industries the cost of pollution reduction can be significant.

Economists have long debated the issue of pollution rights. With Title IV of the 1990 CLEAN AIR ACT (CAA), the United States created the first pollution-rights market for sulfur dioxide (SO_2). The system established a market for transferable emission allowances among electric utilities. Utilities facing significant marginal pollution-abatement COSTS could purchase the right to emit SO_2 from firms with lower costs of pollution abatement. The firms with lower cost of abatement profit by the difference in the price of the pollution right they sell and their cost of pollution reduction. The most controversial part of the system is the allocation of pollution rights—i.e., since society owns common property resources like air and water, why should producers be given the rights to polluting these resources? Nevertheless, the system went into effect in 1995.

According to the ENVIRONMENTAL PROTECTION AGENCY (EPA), in the first year SO_2 emissions decreased by 3 million tons. Further reductions dropped emissions by 6 million tons below the base year (1980) level, and in 2002 emissions were running more than 30 percent below allowable levels. Costs associated with emissions reductions were 75 percent below the initial industry estimates.

The SO_2 pollution-rights program has been hailed as a major success by some and a questionable success by others. The utility industry aggressively opposed the pollution rights program and, like "Chicken Little" and the falling sky, claimed it would force them to significantly raise electricity prices. One of the reasons the costs of pollution reduction were so much lower than projected was because early estimates exaggerated the true cost. Critics also point to some studies indicating that SO_2 reductions have not decreased acid rain (high-acidity rain that changes the pH of water, thereby harming the ecosystem) proportional to the decrease in emissions. Critics also question whether the pollution-rights program is resulting in environmental injustice, with poor neighborhoods continuing to experience environmental problems while wealthier neighborhoods are experiencing pollution abatement. A *Journal of Political Economy* article on the SO_2 pollution-rights market concludes the claims for the program

> . . . are misleading, especially the suggestion that formal trading has lowered the cost of SO_2 abatement several-fold. In contrast, we reach the following conclusions.

1. Marginal abatement costs for SO_2 are much lower today than those estimated in 1990 . . .
2. This decline in marginal abatement cost, if one assumes that it was not caused by Title IV, has lowered the cost of achieving the SO_2 emission cap under both the least-cost solution and enlightened command and control . . .
3. Comparing the least-cost solution to achieving actual emission reductions with actual abatement cost indicates that actual compliance costs exceed the least-cost solution by $280 million in 1995 and $339 million in 1996. This suggests that the allowance market did not achieve the least-cost solution, even though marginal abatement costs under the solution were approximately equal to allowance prices. . . .

The 1990 CAAA represents a dramatic departure from the pollution regulations which utilities were previously subject, and taking full advantage of their flexibility may require time.

With the perceived success of the SO_2 pollution-rights market, in 1999 the EPA instituted a pollution-rights market for nitrous oxide (NO_2), which reacts with volatile organic compounds to form ground-level ozone, contributing to global warming. The EPA program requires 392 facilities in 13 states to reduce annual NO_2 emissions by a total of 510,000 tons. The 392 producers will participate in a pollution cap and trade program, with each "allowance" equal to 1 ton of emissions. The EPA also created an Online Allowance Transfer System to facilitate trade in SO_2 and NO_2 markets. One criticism of the program is it puts the EPA in a situation where it is acting like the SECURITIES AND EXCHANGE COMMISSION (SEC), a role that is not typically the domain of an environmental management agency.

In theory, individuals and environmental groups can buy pollution rights, decreasing the supply in the market and increasing the market price, which will encourage firms to reduce pollution rather than purchase higher-priced pollution rights. For a few hundred dollars, one junior high school environmental science class purchased a sulfur emissions right.

A third pollution-rights market has been proposed as part of the 1997 KYOTO PROTOCOL, the global agreement to reduce carbon dioxide (CO_2) emissions. Increased levels of carbon dioxide are considered a major cause of global warming. While the current Bush administration withdrew U.S. participation in the Kyoto Protocol, the participants are developing a pollution-rights market based on the SO_2 program in the United States. One problem with carbon dioxide is that the savings through fuel switching are not as great as in sulfur dioxide. According to the ORGANIZATION FOR ECONOMIC COOPERATION AND DEVELOPMENT (OECD), another concern is that with the United States not participating in the protocol, demand for carbon-emissions rights will decrease significantly, possibly reducing the market price from $100 to $10 per ton.

In 2002 President George W. Bush announced his atmospheric-emissions effort, labeled the Clear Skies Initiative. The initiative sets fixed limits on power-plant emissions of SO_2, NO_2, and mercury, but ties carbon-emissions cuts to the country's GROSS DOMESTIC PRODUCT (GDP). Nitrous oxide emissions are to be cut from 5 million tons to 2.1 million tons by 2008 and 1.7 million tons by 2018. Sulfur dioxide emissions will be cut from 11 million tons to 4.5 million tons by 2010 and 3 million tons by 2018, and mercury cut by 69 percent during the same time period. (Mercury is found in coal and released in the air through burning.) The programs are all voluntary.

Unlike the Kyoto Protocol, the Clear Skies Initiative cuts U.S. carbon dioxide emissions based on greenhouse-gas intensity, meaning the amount of carbon dioxide emitted per economic output. The Bush program would decrease U.S. greenhouse gas intensity by 18 percent in the next 10 years, from an estimated 183 tons of CO_2 per million dollars of GDP to 151 tons of carbon per million dollars of GDP. (U.S. GDP has been decreasing in greenhouse intensity as the economy has become more service-oriented and less manufacturing-oriented.) The administration hopes to use a pollution-rights approach to meet these objectives. Critics point out that if the administration's ECONOMIC GROWTH projections are correct, U.S. CO_2 emissions will increase by 14 percent, and voluntary compliance will probably not have the same impact as mandatory measures espoused in the EUROPEAN UNION and elsewhere. *The Economist* criticizes the Clear Skies Initiative for not putting either a tax or mandatory limits on carbon emissions. Many environmental economists have advocated a carbon tax as the simplest way to achieve a reduction in carbon emissions. The United States is the world's largest consumer of hydrocarbons and emitter of carbon dioxide. Most of the rest of the industrialized world uses carbon taxes to reduce CONSUMPTION and therefore emissions.

See also EXTERNALITIES; SUSTAINABLE GROWTH AND DEVELOPMENT.

Further reading

Carlson, Curtis, Dallas Burtraw, Maureen Cropper, and Karen L. Palmer. "Sulfur Dioxide by Electric Utilities: What are the Gains from Trade?" *Journal of Political Economy*, December 2000; "Nuts and bolts of pollution trading," *PECD Observer*, September 2001; "Tax or Trade: Economics Focus," *The Economist*, 16 February 2002; "U.S. launches pollution initiative and carbon plans," *Power Economics*, March 2002; Zingale, Nick. "Market-Based Pollution-Reduction Incentives: Are They a Bull Market?" *Industrial Heating* (March 2002).

Ponzi scheme

A Ponzi scheme is a fraudulent financial-INVESTMENT proposition in which initial investors are promised extraordinarily high rates of return, usually to be realized after a short period of time. These very high rates of return attract a few initial investors who are paid with the funds of subsequent investors. Word quickly spreads that these investments do, indeed, pay off, and hoards of new "pigeons" flock to the scheming investment promoter. The scheme usually collapses either when new investment funds slow, making it impossible for the scheme operator to continue, or when the promoter disappears with large amounts of investors' money.

The scheme is named after Charles Ponzi, who, in 1919, created the Securities and Exchange Company (SEC), promising investors a 40-percent PROFIT on their investment in 90 days. At the time, prevailing INTEREST RATES were around 5 percent, making the Ponzi proposition very attractive to investors. Ponzi's proposition was based on International Postal Reply Coupons, which were redeemable at fixed rates of exchange negotiated by the participating governments. However, EXCHANGE RATES for currency, fluctuate. Ponzi convinced investors he would take their funds, invest in International Postal Reply Coupons in countries where the currency had depreciated significantly, and then redeem the coupons in strong-currency countries, making a significant profit.

In early 1920, Ponzi's prospectus was circulated around Boston, and a few investors put their money into the proposition. Within two months the inflow picked up and the SEC raised its rate to 100 percent on 90-day notes. So much money flowed into the company, reportedly waste-baskets had to be used to store the funds. Ponzi opened an additional office, used the funds to buy interests in other companies, and would occasionally appear in his chauffeur-driven limousine. Finally, in July 1920, the *Boston Post* ran an article stating the postal-coupon scheme was impossible: there were not enough coupons sold to justify what Ponzi claimed.

Some investors panicked and demanded their money back, which the SEC provided. Ponzi convinced most investors that the postal-coupon story was a way to shield his real investment strategy, but he had a secret method to invest their funds for the huge returns he promised. While most investors were satisfied, the local district attorney was not impressed and ordered the SEC to stop taking new funds until the company's books were audited. When the

books were finally tallied, the SEC had a loss of $3 million. Ponzi, charged with mail FRAUD, conspiracy, and grand larceny, was convicted and spent three and a half years in jail. He then moved to Florida, was arrested for real-estate fraud, skipped bail, and was recaptured and sent back to Massachusetts's jail for seven more years. He was then deported and later died in a charity ward in Rio de Janeiro.

Ponzi schemes, also called pyramid schemes, continue to plague economies. In 1997 over 500,000 Albanians bought into a scheme set up by a charismatic woman, Maksude Kaderni, promising huge returns. When the scheme collapsed, the country was bankrupted, and Albanians who had mortgaged their homes and farms to invest in the promise of high returns were left heavily in debt. A similar scheme, known as MMM, also bilked unsophisticated Russians out of their savings.

Further reading

Train, John. *Famous Financial Fiasco*. New York: Clarkson N. Potter, 1985.

positioning

Positioning is a company's use of its MARKETING STRATEGY to create and maintain a particular image in the minds of its consumers. After identifying a target market, marketers attempt to influence how consumers view their PRODUCT or brand and how their organization is perceived relative to the COMPETITION. Marketers recognize that individuals formulate mental positions for products, and often these images are based on a single attribute or limited experience. Many marketers conduct research to understand how consumers develop positions and what position their products have among consumers.

To develop a positioning strategy, marketers typically engage in a three-step process. First, they select a positioning concept, attempting to determine what is important to consumers. In the late 1990s, a British condom manufacturer conducted a series of FOCUS GROUPS in order to position their product. They found consumers were interested in both protection and freedom, and since their competitors emphasized protection, the company emphasized freedom. Second, marketers design the dimension or feature that effectively conveys the position to the target market. A position can be communicated by appearance, slogan, brand name, the place where a product is sold, and many other ways. Third, marketers coordinate the marketing mix components to convey a consistent position.

Over time, marketers may need to adjust or change their positioning strategy as consumer needs and market competition changes. Repositioning is an attempt to change the image of a product in consumers' minds. One of the classic cases of repositioning was Philip Morris's shift of Marlboro cigarettes. Marlboros were initially targeted to women, but with the advent of the Marlboro Man, the company completely changed their product's image without changing the product itself.

When developing a positioning strategy, marketers can engage in a variety of alternatives. One option is to position a product directly against the competition. For example, Southwest Airlines has successfully positioned itself as the low-cost alternative to the major airlines in short-haul airline travel. Another option is to position a product relative to a product class or attribute. In the 1990s many companies attempted to position their products as environmentally friendly. (One egg company distinguishes its product as coming from "happy hens," allowed to exist in pens rather than cages.) A third option is to distinguish products or brands based on price and quality. Many hotel chains segment themselves from the competition based on price and quality images.

Crucial to success in positioning is creating a differential advantage—i.e., any feature perceived as desirable and different from that of the competition. Some dry-cleaning stores promote their use of environmentally friendly cleaning agents. Universities have found that success on the sports fields generates a positive image of the institution as a whole.

See also BRANDS, BRAND NAMES; MARKET RESEARCH; MARKET SEGMENTATION; TARGET MARKETS.

Further reading
Etzel, Michael, Bruce Walker, and William Staunton. *Marketing,* 12th ed. Boston: McGraw-Hill, 2001.

predatory lending

Predatory lending is the use of high fees, charges, and other unscrupulous lending practices to strip homeowners' EQUITY. Federal government regulators define predatory lending as one or more of the following:

- unaffordable LOANS based on a borrower's ASSETS rather than his or her ability to repay the loan
- inducing borrowers to repeatedly refinance their MORTGAGE so that the lender can charge high fees or points
- engaging in FRAUD or deception to hide some of the costs of a loan

Studies have found predatory lending especially hurts minorities and the elderly. A study of North Carolina residents who borrowed from finance companies estimated that predatory lending costs U.S. borrowers over $9 billion annually. Predatory lending differs from subprime lending in that subprime lending focuses on individuals who do not qualify for loans from traditional financial institutions. Predatory lending targets people with assets, often forcing these people into bankruptcy or foreclosure through excessive lending charges. Citibank offers the following "tell-tale signs" of predatory lenders.

- steering—deliberately putting borrowers with good credit into loans with high INTEREST RATES and away from affordable options
- unnecessary INSURANCE—jacking up the cost of credit by needlessly selling credit-life, credit-disability, and involuntary-UNEMPLOYMENT insurance to borrowers at staggering rates
- prepayment penalties—charging fee if a customer wants to pay off the loan early
- flipping—repeated refinancing of loans by rolling the balance of an existing loan into a new loan, with added fees charged each time
- hidden balloon payments—setting up loans so at the end of the loan period the borrower still owes most of the principal amount borrowed

Predatory lending has replaced denial of access to credit as the major ethical and legal concern in consumer lending. Until the 1980s, many states had usury laws limiting interest rates that lenders could charge borrowers. During that period, market rates for some types of loans exceeded maximum rates allowed by law. States responded by replacing usury laws with truth-in-lending statutes requiring full disclosure of fees and rates but placing no limits on the rate lenders could charge.

New state laws and policies implemented by the FEDERAL NATIONAL MORTGAGE ASSOCIATION (Fannie Mae) are attempting to curb predatory lending practices. In 2000 Fannie Mae, the largest purchaser of home mortgage loans from lenders, created limits on certain types of loans, refusing to buy loans where the fees and "points" (up-front payments paid in order to get a loan) exceeded 5 percent of the loan value. It also barred mortgages with prepaid single-premium credit-life insurance policies, a questionable product often sold to less-sophisticated homeowners that generates significant commissions to issuers. Fannie Mae also established guidelines on prepayment penalties, as many predatory lenders include significant prepayment penalties to keep duped borrowers from refinancing their loans.

Further reading
Barta, Patrick. "Fannie Mae in Tiff over Abusive Loans," *Wall Street Journal,* 24 April 2002; End Predatory Lending. Org website. Available on-line. URL: www.endpredatorylending.com/predatorylending.htm; Godon, Marcy. "Predatory-lending cost put at $9.1 billion," *The San Diego Union Tribune,* 26 July 2001, p. A2.

preferred provider organization   See HEALTH MAINTENANCE ORGANIZATION.

preferred stock   See COMMON STOCK, PREFERRED STOCK, TREASURY STOCK.

present value See DISCOUNTING, PRESENT VALUE.

price ceilings, price controls

Price ceilings are government-mandated maximum prices for goods and SERVICES. In the United States, local governments and the federal government have passed laws stating that the prices for certain goods and services could not go above a set amount. Unlike PRICE FLOORS, which are intended to keep prices high to protect producers, price ceilings are designed to keep prices low to help consumers. There are two general uses of price ceilings in the United States: local rent-control laws, and federal price ceilings on goods and services during times of market pressure.

Rent-control laws, which set the maximum price a landlord may charge for rent, were often enacted in cities during the 1960s and 1970s. During that period there was a huge influx of people to urban areas around the country. Landlords who were faced with a limited SUPPLY of apartments and significant DEMAND often raised their rents. Consumer groups claimed this was price gouging and portrayed landlords as unfair monopolists taking advantage of powerless consumers. The goal of rent control was to protect tenants from constantly rising prices. Rent controls or any price ceiling have no impact if the market price is less than the maximum price allowed. If, however, the market price is greater than the price ceiling, quantity demanded will exceed quantity supplied, and a shortage will exist. In response, people looking for apartments will often pay thousands of dollars in "key money" to people vacating their rent-controlled apartments for the privilege of taking over those apartments.

One effect of rent control is that owners of rent-controlled buildings will often minimize or eliminate maintenance, arguing that they cannot afford it. Eventually this leads to a decrease in the supply of apartments, further exacerbating the shortage in the market. Developers, unwilling to build new apartments in rent-controlled areas, will build in areas outside the city limits. Over 125 U.S. cities have rent controls.

The other use of price controls is to restrict the rise in prices of consumers goods and services when crises occur. During World War II, the federal government bought many RESOURCES and products for the war effort, making it a huge source of increased demand. It was therefore necessary to place price controls on many goods, since without controls market prices would go up, increasing the cost to the government and causing INFLATION. Shortages created by the price ceilings created opportunities for black markets, where consumers willing to pay the market price were able to find the products they desired.

In 1971 President Richard Nixon imposed price and wage controls an attempt to control inflation. These laws, in effect for three years, were blamed for the shortages of gasoline during the 1970s oil EMBARGOes. In 1989 the mayor of Charleston, South Carolina, Joe Riley Jr., imposed price controls immediately after Hurricane Hugo devastated his city. Retailers were banned from charging prices higher than what they had charged the day before the hurricane hit. Critics contended the price controls reduced the incentive for suppliers to ship needed food and repair goods to the city, while others supported the measure to protect citizens in markets where it was difficult for them to access information needed to make rational choices during a time of crisis.

Many Eastern European countries and EMERGING MARKETS have also instituted price ceilings at times, usually for necessity items such as gasoline or food. To pay for controlled prices, governments are frequently forced to resort to monetary finance, accelerating the creation of MONEY in the economy. This usually results in inflation, which further exacerbates the problem of price ceilings.

See also WAGE AND PRICE CONTROLS.

Further reading

Huizinga, Harry. "The Political Economy of Price Ceilings for Necessities," *The Journal of Development Economics* 47, no. 2 (August 1995); Miller, Roger Leroy. *Economics Today.* Boston: Addison Wesley, 2001.

price discrimination

Price discrimination occurs when firms sell the same PRODUCTS to different customers at different prices. Some forms of legal price discrimination are widely practiced in U.S. markets and based on economic logic. However, price discrimination is illegal when it is used to reduce or eliminate COMPETITION.

The economic basis for price discrimination is differences in elasticities of demand among consumer groups. ELASTICITY OF DEMAND concerns consumers' sensitivity or responsiveness to price changes. Movie-theater pricing provides an example of price discrimination based on elasticity of demand. In most situations, such as when one can vote or drink alcohol, a person becomes an adult at age 18 or 21. At movie theaters, however, adulthood is achieved at 12 or 15, the age at which one must pay the adult price (usually 50 percent or more than the youth price). Since teenagers are sociable but still too young to drive, they provide a major market segment for movie theater operators. Recognizing that teenagers have few options and therefore are likely to go to the movies even if prices are raised, theaters will charge teenagers adult prices. Similarly, many theaters charge a lower price to senior citizens, who have more alternative entertainment options, do not need outings to the movies as an excuse to get out of their homes, and are therefore more sensitive to movie-theater prices.

Charging teenagers higher prices and seniors lower prices is practicing price discrimination based on differences in their elasticity of demand. This type of price discrimination works if the firm can prevent ARBITRAGE, buying products at lower prices lower in one market and selling at higher prices in another market. In 2000, drug companies began selling and giving away anti-AIDS vaccines in developing countries while charging significantly higher prices in the United States. Although this practice is partly based on humanitarian needs, it is also based on the difference in elasticity of demand in developing versus industrialized countries. One of the drug companies' fears is that medications sold or given away in EMERGING MARKETS will be resold in markets where they are charging higher prices.

Price discrimination when used to drive smaller competitors out of the marketplace was made illegal under the CLAYTON ANTITRUST ACT (1914). During the AMERICAN INDUSTRIAL REVOLUTION, large companies would frequently reduce their prices in targeted markets, eliminating competitors and becoming monopolists. Section 2 of the Clayton Act was designed to address this primary (first-line) price discrimination. In the 1930s Congress passed the ROBINSON-PATMAN ACT (1936) in response to complaints that chain stores used their size to gain lower prices and other special arrangements from manufacturers that were not available to small retailers. The act outlawed price discrimination based on favoring particular buyers; secondary price discrimination; and tertiary discrimination, injury to competitors of favored buyers (i.e., a WHOLESALER receiving discriminatorily low prices from a manufacturer and then passing the saving on to its retailers, enabling them to undersell their competitors).

Since its enactment, the Robinson-Patman Act has been criticized and challenged. Critics state the act reduces rather than increases competition by limiting pricing options. Government enforcement of the act has varied over the years. In a widely watched case during the 1990s, Wal-Mart was accused of price discrimination by small-town merchants but was found not guilty.

Further reading
Mallor, Jane P., A. James Barnes, Thomas Bowers, Michael J. Phillips, and Arlen W. Langvardt. *Business Law and the Regulatory Environment,* 11th ed. Boston: McGraw-Hill, 2001.

price fixing

Price fixing is an agreement between or among firms in an industry to set prices jointly in order to increase PROFITS. Horizontal price fixing is an agreement among directly competing firms, while vertical price fixing involves attempts by manufacturers to control the resale price of their PRODUCTS. Price fixing, which is illegal under Section 1 of the SHERMAN ANTITRUST ACT (1890), undermines the social benefit of COMPETITION. In competitive markets, firms compete on the basis of product quality, service, and price, resulting in lower prices. Price fixing results in higher prices than would occur if competition existed.

In one of the most famous price-fixing cases, during the 1950s executives from General Electric, Westinghouse,

Allis-Chalmers and other leading electrical manufacturing firms met secretly to conspire to rig bids for major government CONTRACTS. They developed what was later known as the "phase of the moon" bidding system, taking turns being the low bidder for the government contract, but at a price that was extremely profitable to the winning firm. Brought to trial in 1961, seven executives were found guilty; given fines (which were paid by their companies); served short jail sentences, during which time they were paid their salaries; and, upon release, were given their old positions.

In addition to covert agreements on fixed prices, market share, quota, and output limitations are sometimes used to support price fixing. While CARTELS are open agreements to restrict output in order to raise prices, firms sometimes agree to divide up markets—i.e., "I will not sell in your territory if you will not sell in mine"—or restrict SUPPLY to create an artificial shortage (something U.S. oil companies were accused of doing during the 1970s oil crises) as strategies to increase market prices.

Price fixing and other collusive activities occur most frequently in oligopolies, markets where there are only a few competitors. In markets where there are many competitors, it is usually difficult or impossible to gain agreement. When there are only a few firms in a market, executives often know each other on a first-name basis, engaged in continual MARKET INTELLIGENCE to keep track of what their competitors are doing, and can readily benefit from agreements not to compete on a price basis. About 1900, U.S. Steel president Judge Gary hosted dinners at which steel prices would be agreed on.

After price fixing became illegal, firms in oligopolistic markets developed new ways to reduce price competition. Price leadership is a system in which one firm announces a price change and the few other firms in the industry quickly follow by matching the change. Done openly in a press conference, price leadership is not a covert action, and many oligopolistic U.S. industries practice it.

See also OLIGOPOLY.

Further reading
Slavin, Steven. *Economics,* 5th ed. Boston: McGraw-Hill, 2001.

price floors, price supports

Price floors are government-mandated minimum prices for goods and SERVICES. The U.S. federal government has passed laws stating that the price for certain goods and services cannot go below a set amount. Unlike PRICE CEILINGS, which are intended to keep prices low to protect consumers, price floors are designed to keep prices high to help producers. In the United States there are two kinds of price floors: MINIMUM WAGE laws and price supports for agriculture.

A minimum-wage law sets the lowest hourly rate that firms may legally pay workers. Minimum-wage laws were first enacted in 1938 during the GREAT DEPRESSION with the goal of ensuring that low-income workers have a decent STANDARD OF LIVING. In 1938 the minimum wage was set at 25 cents per hour, which was approximately 40 percent of the average manufacturing wage at that time.

The impact of minimum-wage laws depends on the prevailing wage in the marketplace. In 2001 the minimum wage was $5.25, but in many markets even the lowest-paid workers received more than the minimum amount mandated by law. In these markets, minimum-wage laws have no impact on the number of people employed. In markets where employers could hire workers for less than the minimum wage, the minimum-wage law causes employers to reduce the number of workers they hire because the price is higher and increases the number of workers willing to work because the wage is higher. Those workers who find jobs at the minimum wage earn a higher level of INCOME, but other workers who would have been willing and able to find jobs at the lower market wage cannot find work. Critics of minimum-wage laws argue the laws do not help people maintain a decent standard of living, because most people working at minimum wages are not the primary breadwinner in poor families but rather teenagers or part-time workers adding to a family's income.

Price supports for farm PRODUCTs were also initiated during the Great Depression (1933). Minimum prices were established for many basic agricultural products, including cotton, wheat, soybeans, sorghum, tobacco, and dairy products. The goal of price supports for agricultural products was PARITY, keeping the prices of farm products, adjusted for INFLATION at historical levels. This would aid the FAMILY FARM and maintain RESOURCES in agriculture. Like minimum-wage laws, if the market price for products covered by the price-support system was greater than the price floor, the laws had no effect on the market. If, however, the market price was lower than the support price, farmers could sell their output to the government at the support price. The government would sell excess SUPPLY in world markets at the lower price, absorbing the loss, or would sometimes give excess output to school-meal programs or poor foreign countries through the Food for Peace Program. In 1996 the federal government eliminated price supports for most agricultural products, but within a few years agricultural interests were again lobbying for the supports.

See also WAGE AND PRICE CONTROLS.

Further reading
Miller, Roger Leroy. *Economics Today*. Boston: Addison Wesley, 2001.

price indexes
Price indexes are composite INDICATORS of the level of prices in the market being studied. Price indexes are used primarily to measure changes in the level of prices, or INFLATION. The BUREAU OF LABOR STATISTICS (BLS) maintains numerous price indexes for the U.S. economy. The three

most widely quoted BLS price indexes are the CONSUMER PRICE INDEX (CPI), PRODUCER PRICE INDEX (PPI), and Gross Domestic Product Implicit Price Deflator (GDP deflator).

The CPI is a statistical measure of the average prices paid by consumers for a typical "market basket" of goods and SERVICES. Measuring the rate of change in consumer prices is important to policy makers. Price changes are a critical concern in MONETARY POLICY, essential in evaluating economic conditions and indexing spending and taxes. The CPI is an important but controversial measure of price changes. The controversy centers on whether the CPI is truly representative of inflation; most U.S. economists agree it overstates the rate of inflation experienced by American consumers.

On a monthly basis, the CPI samples prices around the country on typical goods and services. The sampling procedure determines an average price for each good and service, which is then multiplied by the assumed amount households typically purchase. This process "weights" the goods and services by their relative importance in consumers' budgets. The sum of the prices times quantities are then divided by the cost of the same goods and services in a base year to create a price index.

Price index = [(cost of market basket today) / (cost of market basket in base year)] × 100

The PPI, a monthly measure of prices received by producers, measures prices at the wholesale level. In 1978 the Wholesale Price Index (WPI) was renamed the Producer Price Index, which is actually a series of price indexes measuring the average changes in selling prices received by domestic producers. The BLS maintains over 500 industry price indexes, over 10,000 PRODUCT-line indexes, and 3,200 commodity price indexes. New PPIs are introduced as new products are created. Unlike the CPI, which measures prices paid by consumers, the PPI measures price changes from the seller's perspective.

The PPI is the oldest continuous statistical series maintained by the federal government. Its data are used by businesses and government as

- an economic indicator; PPIs signal price changes prior to changes at the retail level
- a deflator of other economic series; PPIs are used to adjust other economic time series for price changes (adjusting for inflation)
- a basis for CONTRACT escalation; PPI data are used to index and adjust purchase and sales contracts

The GDP deflator measures changes in the average price of all final goods and services in the economy. As such, it is the broadest measure of changes in the price level. The GDP deflator is implicit, or inferred, from measures of GROSS DOMESTIC PRODUCT (GDP). Current nominal GDP is compared to GDP adjusted to a base year (in 2001, the 1996 GDP was used as the base year) to obtain a ratio. For example, in 1999 nominal GDP was $9,248 billion, while 1999 GDP adjusted to the base year was $8,861 billion. Dividing the first number by the second yields a ratio of 1.043, which, when multiplied by 100 (as is customarily done), results in a GDP deflator value of 104.3 This says inflation, as measured by the GDP deflator, was 4.3 percent between 1996 and 1999.

Further reading
U.S. Bureau of Labor Statistics website. Available on-line. URL: www.bls.gov.

pricing strategies
Pricing, an essential part of any business strategy, creates the revenue to support existing and future opportunities. While it is often assumed that the goal of pricing is to generate the most revenue, there are a number of pricing objectives businesses pursue, each leading to a different pricing strategy. These objectives include PROFIT MAXIMIZATION, market share or sales growth, survival, targeted return, return on-investment, and price matching.

Profit maximization considers marginal revenue and marginal cost at various levels of output. Price is determined by market DEMAND at the level of output where the extra (marginal) revenue from the last unit of output produced and sold equals the extra (marginal) cost to produce that unit of output.

Market-share or sales-growth objectives lead managers to increase or decrease price to obtain a specified level of sales. Penetration pricing, setting a low initial price to stimulate sales and gain access to the market, is often associated with market-share or sales-growth pricing strategies.

Sometimes a firm will desperately need cash in order to stay in business. In these situations, previous pricing strategies are replaced with a survival strategy. Prices are cut and discounts offered to generate enough revenue to stay in business.

Targeted-return objectives lead to markup and return on INVESTMENT pricing strategies. In markup pricing, a popular strategy used in wholesaling and retailing, a standard amount or percentage is added to the cost of the product in order to determine price. In many retail stores, keystoning (doubling the cost of the PRODUCT), is used. Percentage markups can be confusing. From a retailer's perspective, if the cost of an item is $1 and it is sold for $2, this is a 50-percent markup. Logically, if the change in price ($2–$1 = $1) is compared to the cost ($1), it would appear to be a 100-percent markup. But in the retail industry, the change price ($1) is compared to the sales price ($2), which is a 50-percent markup.

Return on investment (ROI) pricing compares the expected INCOME to the total ASSETS associated with the product or project. Prices are then determined based on a target return on investment.

Price matching (or competitive pricing) is, as the term suggests, an objective to keep prices consistent with competitors' prices. A price-matching strategy leads to nonprice competition, whereby firms compete for customers based on service, quality, SALES PROMOTION, product differences, and availability—basically anything but price. Price matching is prevalent in markets where there are only a few competing firms (see OLIGOPOLY) and reduces the potential for price wars, severe reductions in prices matched by the other firms in the market. To reduce consumer concerns about getting the lowest price effectively, some retail firms use price-matching guarantees.

Pricing strategies also involve psychological pricing and PRODUCT LIFE CYCLE pricing. Psychological pricing considers how consumers' perceptions and beliefs affect their price evaluations. Premium (or prestige pricing) uses high prices to convey an image of quality to buyers. Odd-even pricing, the use of, for instance, $9.99 rather than $10, leads consumers to think of the product in the lower (less than $10) category rather than in the $10–$20 range.

Product life cycle pricing strategies recognize that products and product categories generally go through a cycle, including introduction, growth, maturity and decline. During the introductory stage, often there is only one firm in the market, and higher prices are used to recoup initial expenditures. As with a price-skimming strategy, such high prices appeal only to those consumers most willing and able to buy the product. During the growth stage, prices are lowered as competing products enter the market; and in the maturity stage, prices are lowered again as the market becomes saturated. During the final decline stage, prices are lowered to sell off final inventory.

As products go through LIFE CYCLES, the number of competitors fluctuates, changing the nature of demand in the market. All pricing strategies must consider demand, the willingness and ability of consumers to purchase products. The law of demand states that as producers raise prices, the quantity demanded decreases, and as they lower prices, the quantity demanded increases, assuming nothing other than price is changed in the market. Price ELASTICITY OF DEMAND is the degree of percentage response of consumers to a price change.

There are also a number of ethical issues associated with pricing strategy. First, the FEDERAL TRADE COMMISSION provides price-comparison guidelines to avoid deceptive price ADVERTISING. Retailers thus must be able to document their claims about comparison prices. A second pricing issue is "bait-and-switch" schemes, in which firms advertise low-priced products but do not have reasonable quantities of the product available for purchase; they do, however, have similar, higher-priced products available. Bait-and-switch practices are illegal. Third, predatory pricing, the use of low prices to weaken and eliminate competitors, is a hard-to-prove but controversial pricing strategy.

Further reading

Bearden, William, Thomas Ingram, and Raymond la Forge. *Marketing, Principles and Perspectives,* 2d ed. Boston: Irwin McGraw-Hill, 1998; Lamb, Charles, Joseph Hair, and Carl McDaniel. *Marketing,* 5th ed. Cincinnati: South Western 2000.

primary markets, secondary markets

Primary markets are the markets where new issues of stocks and BONDS are sold. CORPORATIONS selling such newly created issues receive the proceeds from primary-market transactions. Thus, these are the markets within which new CAPITAL is raised. In primary markets, INVESTMENT BANKING firms (specialists in designing, marketing, and selling new issues) are the FINANCIAL INTERMEDIARIES between the issuers of new securities and their buyers.

Secondary markets are exchanges where outstanding (previously issued) stocks and bonds are traded among investors. Corporations whose securities are being traded are not involved in these secondary-market transactions and consequently receive no funds from them. Nonetheless, secondary markets are vital to corporations, since it is in these markets that a firm's MARKET VALUE is determined, and the exchanges also provide an important source of liquidity for stock and bond investors. Brokers and dealers are secondary-market intermediaries.

See also INITIAL PUBLIC OFFERING; STOCK MARKET, BOND MARKET.

privacy

Privacy, generally defined as the right to be left alone, is an important issue in American business. Privacy issues in the United States have existed since the creation of the country, but they have changed over time. In the 18th century, Americans held government in distrust, based on their experiences with a monarchy, and resisted government knowledge of individual activities. Postal secrecy was a concern first expressed by Benjamin Franklin. As technology changed, privacy concerns arose regarding telegraph and telephone communications and, more recently, surveillance activities. Numbers, such as those issued by SOCIAL SECURITY, data banks, and the U.S. CENSUS BUREAU, have also evoked privacy concerns. The Civil War general William Sherman supposedly used census data to locate and destroy industrial production in the South.

With today's electronic data systems and INTERNET technology, privacy is a major concern for both consumers and businesses. Generally Americans are more ambivalent about privacy issues than Europeans, although in 2000 the EUROPEAN UNION passed strong information-protection (safe harbor) laws.

Privacy issues include employer/employee relationships, customer/firm relationships, and individual and firm relationships with government. The Fourth Amendment to the U.S. Constitution protects people against arbitrary and unreasonable government violations of their privacy rights. The key word in the Fourth Amendment is *unreasonable.* Various rulings have defined and refined what is considered reasonable and unreasonable practices related to privacy. Most business records were found not to be protected by privacy laws, and often material found in garbage and Dumpsters have not been subject to privacy protection.

During President Richard Nixon's administration, abuses of privacy protections, including INTERNAL REVENUE SERVICE audits of political "enemies," led to passage of the Privacy Act of 1974. This act allows individuals to inspect federal agency files that contain information about them and to request that erroneous or incomplete records be corrected. Access to credit reports, an important factor in business decisions, is also protected under the Privacy Act. Businesses must seek approval from customers to access credit data, and employees have gained greater rights of access to personnel files held by employers, allowing job seekers to see what former employers have written about them. Medical records have become an important area of individual and individual/firm concern. A major issue is that employers can use medical-payments information to determine which employees are ill and what illnesses they have.

The biggest change in privacy concerns in American business surrounds Internet data collection and use. "Cookies," electronic tracers allowing companies to track CONSUMER BEHAVIOR on the Internet, provide valuable information about individual consumers and are placed without the knowledge of most Internet users. Business interests are lobbying for a system of opt-out Internet data collection, where consumers can choose not to have information about them collected and disseminated. Consumer groups are pressing for an opt-in system where data can only be collected with the prior approval of Internet users.

privatization

The term *privatization* is used in two distinct but related ways. First, privatization is what occurs when an industry previously owned by the government is returned to the private sector. In the past a country may have "nationalized" an industry by either starting it or taking ownership of it. In either case the government owns the industry within the country. Through privatization, the government sells the various companies in the industry and thus relinquishes its ownership of the industry itself. In many cases this produces a great deal of cash for the country and is seen as a move toward CAPITALISM. Great Britain experienced massive privatization under Prime Minister Margaret Thatcher's administration.

Within the United States, the word *privatization* is used to refer to the practice of governments to hire private companies to carry out SERVICES normally done by the government. For example, many city and state governments outsource services for garbage collection, school buses, drivers' license issuance, and penal corrections.

Proponents of privatization say that it produces cost savings resulting from ECONOMIES OF SCALE, higher labor productivity, fewer legal requirements, and lack of COMPETITION in government. Opponents assert that there is not as much competition among suppliers as privatization's supporters suggest and that privatization entails many hidden COSTS, such as those connected to monitoring the services being provided, and this actually make the alternative more expensive. Opponents also argue on the philosophical grounds that nongovernmental providers should not handle some services, no matter what the savings. For example, they question whether private companies should handle such matters as imprisonment, noting that the removal of someone's liberty should only be carried out by governments, not by private businesses. Related to this is the concern that certain kinds of privatization may erode citizens' legal rights when it is only a case of the lowest bidder is providing the service.

Further reading

Bennett, Robert. *Decentralization, Intergovernmental Relations and Markets: Toward a Post-Welfare Agenda?* Oxford, U.K.: Clarendon Press, 1990; Moe, Ronald. "Exploring the Limits of Privatization." *Public Administration Review* 47 (Nov/Dec 1987): 453–460; Savas, E. S. *Privatization: The Key to Better Government.* Chatham, N.J.: Chatham House, 1987; Starr, Paul. *The Limits of Privatization.* Washington, D.C.: Economic Policy Institute, 1987.

—Mack Tennyson

problem solving

The ability to solve complicated problems quickly is of vital importance in today's economy. From childhood, people are taught to solve problems by trial and error, but this method is not practicable for managers who are confronted daily by economic, technical, political, and other problems. In business, many key problem-solving concepts seem obvious but are often overlooked, causing delays and frustration in finding solutions and accomplishing goals. However, managers can use a variety of strategies to solve messy problems quickly and easily.

- *First define the problem*—that is, what went wrong, and what impact the problem will have on the firm. This should be written down so that everyone who reads it will have a thorough understanding of what the problems is and why it is important. It is important at this stage to simply describe the problem and not offer solutions as yet.
- *Spend time only on problems that are truly important.* Managers should ask themselves, "What will happen if I don't solve this problem?" If the answer is "not much," then attention should be turned to more important matters.

- *Test assumptions about everything and check all the facts.* Managers should be sure that they and their teams understand the problem the same way and that their data confirm the problem is important. Assumptions about proposed solutions should be tested to improve the chances that the problem will be solved.
- *Measure.* The key question managers need to answer is, "How will I know when the problem is solved?" Managers should define specific measurements that will tell them objectively whether a problem has been solved.
- *Measure the right things.* A common measurement trap is to measure something because it is "interesting." If knowing a measurement will not change anything (e.g., help one to make a decision, verify an assumption, or prove the problem is solved), then time should not be wasted in measuring it.
- *Use project-management skills.* Solving a big problem is a project and should be treated like one. This means identifying tasks, making and adjusting assignments, and keeping track of what is due when. It is important to obtain appropriate management support for the project.
- *Look for solution owners rather than problem owners.* Everyone participating in the situation owns the problem, like it or not—and nobody likes it. Managers can avoid the finger-pointing trap by looking for solution owners—i.e., the people who can do something to help solve the problem. This helps ensure a desirable outcome, since helping with a solution is much more fun than being blamed for a problem.
- *Take action on purpose, not by default. Do it on purpose—that is, with conviction.* Taking no action is a weak way to decide not to solve the problem—and is likely to leave someone making awkward explanations when the problem resurfaces.
- *Communicate—don't leave key stakeholders guessing.* Being human, people are often bad about keeping others informed about the progress they are making, especially if there is little or no progress. Support and understanding is more probable if open and honest communication is maintained regarding what is happening.
- *Avoid "bug mentality."* Fixing specific defects only fixes symptoms; like taking aspirin for a headache, it may provide relief but does nothing to prevent the next headache. Relieving symptoms is fine as a temporary measure but does little to prevent problems from recurring.
- *Identify and fix the right root causes.* Complicated problems have multiple root causes, probably more than can be fixed in a reasonable amount of time. Neither time nor money should be wasted on causes that are either insignificant in impact or are only peripheral causes of the problem.
- *Choose solutions that are effective and implement them completely.* Identifying the right root causes is necessary, but unless a solution is implemented, there will still be

a problem. Solutions should be double-checked to ensure the causes of the problem will be eliminated. When this is done, the solution plan can be executed.

- *Reward prevention.* Although it is generally understood that it costs more to deal with crises than to prevent them, many companies do not recognize and reward those who push past the symptoms to the root causes, thus preventing future occurrences. Managers should focus on prevention by rewarding those who successfully prevent problems from occurring.

- *Have the courage to say "no" when appropriate.* If someone believes the problem can't be solved in the time frame allowed or with the RESOURCES available, the best option is to say so right away. Accepting an impossible assignment is setting oneself up for failure. However, it is important to choose strategies for refusing to take on the project—i.e., gather evidence, explain what it will take to accomplish the desired results, provide documentation, etc.

- *Meet all commitments.* Problem solvers must do what they promise to do and not promise to do what they cannot deliver. Meeting commitments strengthens relationships and builds trust, both of which are needed to solve messy problems. If the situation changes and a commitment has to be changed, everyone involved needs to be informed immediately so they can make appropriate changes to their own plans.

- *Solve the problem completely, and avoid being sidetracked by other things that do not address the immediate issue.* The concept here is "everything necessary, nothing extraneous."

- *Make sure everybody who can contribute to the problem-solving effort is appropriately involved.* The team should only include people who can work actively on solving the problem; people who need to know what is going on can be informed more efficiently in other ways. The concept here is "everyone necessary, no one extraneous."

- *Plan for things to go wrong.* As the old saying goes, if something can go wrong, it will go wrong. Managers should determine what could get in the way of the problem-solving effort and develop appropriate contingency plans.

- *Define specifically what successful completion of each task entails.* Completion criteria should specify when tasks are due and what standard must be met to avoid misunderstandings and delays. Someone who has worked hard to complete a task does not want to then learn that he misunderstood and his manager wanted a sledgehammer rather than an ordinary hammer.

- *Acknowledge and thank everyone who helps.* Solving an important problem deserves recognition, and MANAGEMENT and other key stakeholders should be told what the problem-solving team has achieved.

See also GOAL SETTING.

Further reading
Sawyer, Jeanne. *When Stuff Happens: A Practical Guide to Solving Problems Permanently.* Available on-line. URL: www.sawyerpartnership.com.

—Jeanne Sawyer

process theories

Process theories deal with how EMPLOYEE MOTIVATION arises and initiated, redirected, and halted by employees' behavior. There are four types of process theories: expectancy, equity, reinforcement, and GOAL SETTING. All tend to focus on an individual's behavior in specific settings.

EXPECTANCY THEORY, formulated by psychologist Victor Vroom, assumes that people are motivated to exert effort based on their expectations of success. The theory is based on the belief that employee effort will lead to performance, and performance will lead to rewards, which are either positive or negative. An employee's motivation will increase when he or she highly values a particular outcome and feels a reasonably good chance of achieving the desired goal. It is not enough to offer the person something to satisfy his or her important needs if the person is not reasonably sure they have the ability to obtain the reward. The more positive the reward, the more likely the employee will be highly motivated. The more negative the reward, the less likely the employee will be motivated. Expectancy theory assumes that motivational strength is determined by a person's perceived probabilities of success. Employees tend to work harder when they believe they have a good chance of getting rewards that are personally meaningful.

The strengths of the expectancy theory are that it accounts for multiple goals and preferences, real-world differences, and a variety of situations. However, the theory is weak in that it is too complex for most people and in making decisions and that one cannot get a full commitment to a marginally more important goal. Expectancy theory can be used to link performance to pay systems, to facilitate performance, to recognize competing goals, and to align organizational goals.

Equity theory, developed by human resource theorist J. Stacy Adams, focuses on workers' perceptions of fairness regarding their work outcomes and inputs. Individuals compare their job inputs and outcomes with those of others and then respond to eliminate any inequities. Rewards must be perceived as being equitable and fair if they are to motivate people. Employees strive for equity between themselves and other workers, and this is achieved when the ratio of an employee's outcomes over inputs is equal to other employees' outcomes over inputs. Individuals are concerned with their rewards but also with how they compare with what others receive. People are strongly motivated to maintain a balance between what they perceive as their inputs, or contributions, and their rewards. If someone perceives an inequity, that person becomes motivated to reduce or eliminate it. For example, if an employee learns that a coworker earns more money for doing the same job, that employee may request a pay raise. If he does not receive the pay raise, his performance may diminish as he tries to reduce what he sees as an inequity.

The strengths of the equity theory are that it accounts for internal assessment, comparison procedures, and quality changes. The theory's weaknesses include a fixation on underpayment and a lack of clarity about what people "key-in on." Reinforcement theory, based on the work of the psychologist B. F. Skinner, states that employees will repeat behaviors leading to a positive outcome and not repeat those behaviors that lead to negative outcomes. Managers should positively reinforce employee behaviors that lead to positive outcomes and negatively reinforce employee behaviors leading to negative outcomes. Employees will then recognize the connection between a behavior and its consequences. Employers can change employees' behavior by providing the proper reward. For example, an employee will learn to engage in specific behaviors, such as responding to customer requests, in order to receive certain consequences, such as a bonus.

The strengths of the reinforcement theory are that it is straightforward, is outcome-oriented, and works well with overt behaviors. The theory's weaknesses are that it may be fallible when the employee fixates on outcome, that it can be very time-consuming to monitor, and that it may not be consistent with organizational situations. Nevertheless, reinforcement theory is useful in changing behaviors and can be revised easily if necessary.

Goal-setting theory, as researched by leadership and motivation professor Edwin Locke and organizational behavior professor Gary Latham, is the process of improving an individual's or a group's job performance with formally stated objectives, deadlines, or quality standards. The goals that are set for the individual or group should be specific, challenging, and difficult but not impossible for most employees to attain. Goals motivate by directing attention, encouraging effort and persistence, and fostering goal-attainment strategy and action plans. Specific, difficult goals lead to higher motivation and performance. Employees should accept goals and want to attain them if managers set the goals for them.

Good goals should be consistent with organizational goals and are easily monitored. Goal setting is a simple, concrete process and can encourage participation among employees; however, it can also be time-consuming and subordinates may differ with bosses on goals and objectives.

See also MOTIVATION THEORY.

Further reading
St. Louis University website. Available on-line. URL: www.slu.edu/departments/management/650. Downloaded May 28, 2003; Winston Brill & Associates website. Available on-line. URL: www.winstonbrill.com/ bril001/html/article_index/articles/201-250/article240_body.html.

—Judy Mims

Producer Price Index
The Producer Price Index (PPI) is a monthly measure of wholesale prices received by producers. Created in 1902 as the Wholesale Price Index, the PPI was renamed the Producer Price Index in 1978 and is the oldest continuous statistical series maintained by the federal government.

The PPI is actually a series of PRICE INDEXES measuring the average changes in selling prices received by domestic producers. The BUREAU OF LABOR STATISTICS maintains over 500 industry-price indexes, over 10,000 product-line indexes, and 3,200 commodity-price indexes. New PPIs are introduced as new industry PRODUCTs are created. Unlike the CONSUMER PRICE INDEX (CPI), which measures INFLATION experienced by consumers, PPIs measure price change from the seller's perspective.

The most widely quoted PPI is the Finished Goods Price Index, which includes price changes for producers' durable equipment. Unlike the CPI, which is calculated for specific areas of the country, the Finished Goods Index is calculated only on a national basis.

Because the PPI measures changes in prices of domestic goods, it does not include changes in prices of IMPORTS. Price data collected for PPIs consist of the revenue received by producers and thus sales and excise taxes are not included in PPIs.

Producer Price Index data are used by businesses and government as

- economic INDICATORS, signalling price changes prior to changes at the retail level
- a deflator of other economic series used to adjust other economic time series for price changes (adjusting for inflation)
- a basis for CONTRACT escalation, with data used to index and adjust purchase and sales contracts

Further reading
U.S. Bureau of Labor Statistics website. Available on-line. URL: http://stats/bls.gov.

product
A product is a combination of physical, service, and symbolic attributes designed to create utility and benefit for buyers. Most people think of a product as the "thing" they purchase, but as the definition above implies, a product is much more than the physical item or direct service purchased. Good marketers recognize that people do not purchase products; they purchase benefits, utility, wants, and satisfaction. When developing new products or selecting products to offer to their TARGET MARKETS, marketers think in terms of what their customers want or need.

In addition to the physical item, a product includes BRANDS, PACKAGING, design, color, WARRANTY, and SERVICES. Brands enhance a product's image and recognition; many new products are purchased based on consumer satisfaction with other brand-name products purchased from the same company. Packaging has many functions, including protection, facilitating shipping, SALES PROMOTION, and meeting environmental concerns or requirements. Product design can appeal to either functional needs or aesthetic desires. Color is often an important consideration in consumers' purchasing decision and should be considered in product development. Henry Ford once said that customers could have any color car they wanted as long as it was black. While Ford focused on production efficiency and keeping COSTS and pricing affordable, Alfred Sloan of General Motors realized that consumers preferred to choose the color of their car. Similarly, for decades a major contributing factor to the success of Sears was their warranty and service offerings. Customers knew they could trust Sears to honor and even extend their warranties and to service the machines and appliances they bought.

Marketers divide consumer products into four categories: convenience, shopping, specialty, and unsought products. For each category of products, marketers develop different marketing strategies. Convenience goods are things people purchased frequently or impulsively, with minimal comparison of alternatives. Impulse items (snack foods, drinks, candy), everyday items (milk, bread, gasoline), and emergency items (batteries, home medical supplies, minor home-repair items) are all convenience goods. The major marketing consideration for convenience goods is availability. Since consumers do not compare choices or do price comparisons for convenience goods, the key to success for marketers of convenience goods is widespread distribution and point-of-purchase promotion of their products.

Shopping goods are products that consumers purchase after comparing alternatives. Typical shopping goods include electronic equipment, automobiles, and appliances. These products are purchased less frequently than convenience goods; more time is spent comparing price, quality, and features; and location is fairly important to consumers' consideration of alternatives. Marketers of shopping goods emphasize ADVERTISING to create consumer awareness of their offerings and PERSONAL SELLING to demonstrate their products' features and promote the differences between their products and those of competitors. The marketer's reputation and store atmosphere are also important considerations to consumers.

Specialty products are goods consumers seek out and choose for their uniqueness or status value. Specialty goods include luxury cars, designer apparel, and custom home furnishings. Since consumers seek out marketers of specialty items, distribution and location are less important. Store image and atmosphere ave very important, and customer service and personal selling are critical to success in selling specialty products. Marketers of specialty products like Waterford crystal, Rolls-Royce cars, and Rolex watches will intentionally limit the number of retail outlets for their products and scrutinize retailers who market their merchandise in order to maintain their status image.

Unsought products are goods and services people need but do not want. There is an old saying, "There are only two sure things in life, death and taxes." Funeral services and tax preparation are two examples of unsought goods, along with the oxymoronically named life INSURANCE. Because unsought goods are things people need but do not want to purchase, marketers of these products have to design their promotional messages craftily and use considerable personal-selling efforts. Advertising messages for both funeral planning and life insurance appeal to peoples' sense of responsibility and to their desire to benefit their loved ones.

See also MARKETING STRATEGY.

Further reading
Boone, Louis E., and David L. Kurtz. *Contemporary Marketing,* 10th ed. Fort Worth, Tex.: Dryden Press, 2001; Etzel, Michael J., Bruce J. Walker, and William J. Staunton. *Marketing,* 12th ed. Boston: McGraw-Hill, 2001.

production

Production—the relationship between inputs and outputs—is most often associated with images of ASSEMBLY LINES and manufacturing, but production concepts apply to SERVICES, RETAILING businesses, households, and government. In production, inputs—RESOURCES such as labor, materials, energy, and equipment (often referred to as factors of production or land, labor, CAPITAL, and ENTREPRENEURSHIP in economics textbooks)—are combined to produce outputs. For example, to produce this entry in the encyclopedia required labor (the author), materials (printing materials), and capital (the computer and printing system). Logically, more inputs results in more outputs most of the time.

Whether or not more inputs result in more outputs depends on whether all inputs are variable (changing with the level of output) or fixed (not changing within a range of output). Often a businessperson is confronted with a situation in which some resources are variable and some are fixed. A typical example is found in the operations of a typical fast-food restaurant. When planning a day's output, a manager is aware of fixed inputs, including the size of the building and equipment inside; and variable inputs, including labor, energy, and ingredients. As more variable inputs are added to the fixed-production process, total output initially increases. If this restaurant had only one worker, he or she would have to take orders, prepare and assemble meals, take payment, and clean up after customers. Running around the building doing all these tasks would involve a lot of wasted motion and time, and total output (meals) would be small. With the addition of a second, third, and fourth worker, however, total output would increase rapidly. Through specialization, total production would likely be greater than what each worker could have produced individually. Adding a fifth, sixth, or seventh worker would probably result in an increase in total meal production, but it would not be not as rapid, and the fast-food restaurant would experience diminishing marginal returns.

The law of diminishing marginal returns states that as equal successive amounts of a variable resource are combined with a fixed amount of another resource, marginal increases in output will eventually decline and can even become negative. Using the fast-food restaurant example, at some point added workers doing specialized parts of the meal-production process are not fully utilized. If a worker is assigned to the french-fry machine and customers aren't ordering many french fries, that worker's contribution to total product will be minimal. In addition, more workers trying to produce meals in a confined space would result in disrupted production as they constantly bumped into each other. In this situation, added units of a variable resource would create declining total production (negative marginal returns).

Production analysts carefully evaluate COSTS, including total cost, average cost, and marginal cost. Fixed costs occur in any production process where some resource is fixed. As output increases, the cost of the fixed resource is spread over a larger quantity of production, and average fixed cost declines as production increases. Declining fixed costs per unit of output and increased productivity through specialization lead to ECONOMIES OF SCALE (declining average costs). When larger quantities of output result in higher average costs, the firm faces diseconomies of scale. One of the critical decisions managers must make is the size of the operation to establish. Whether a fast-food restaurant, assembly line, or other venue, the size of the operation and fixed inputs associated with its range of production determine the range of economies and diseconomies of scale within which the firm can operate.

See also MARGINAL ANALYSIS.

production-possibilities curve

A production-possibilities curve (PPC), also referred to as a production-possibilities frontier, is a graph used to convey basic economic concepts, including efficiency and inefficiency, tradeoffs, and ECONOMIC GROWTH. The actual PPC is a line on a graph displaying the maximum possible output of any combination of goods using existing RESOURCES and technology. PPCs are typically used for illustrative rather than analytical purposes.

The most frequently generated PPC compares an economy's output of defense versus nondefense goods, often referred to as the "guns and butter" tradeoff. The PPC shows the possible combinations of military and civilian goods an economy can produce. Logically, during periods of war a government will command resources (through drafting soldiers and making military production CONTRACTs with industry), in essence shifting PRODUCTION in the economy from butter to guns. During periods of peace, output will shift from guns to butter.

The PPC also shows tradeoffs. For instance, if a society wants more military goods, then it will have to forego non-defense goods. Resources allocated to production of certain goods are not available to produce other goods. As Rutgers University economist Dr. A. Robert Koch says, "There is always an OPPORTUNITY COST."

A combination of production on the PPC is an efficient level of output—that is, all resources are being utilized, including full EMPLOYMENT of labor resources. If an economy is not fully utilizing all its resources, it will be producing at a point inside the PPC, illustrating inefficiency. Inefficiency is typically caused by misallocation of resources, restrictions on resource use, and waste. Cultural practices, such as discrimination, also cause inefficiency. Not allowing people to do what they do best reduces the potential output of an economic system.

A PPC portrays economic growth through combinations of output outside or beyond the current PPC that are not possible with the current resources and technology. Increases in the quantities of resources, improvements in the quality and use of resources, and changes in technology can all shift the PPC outward.

Production-possibilities curves can also be used to illustrate individuals' or firms' choices and output combinations. For example, say a student has two exams tomorrow, one in economics and the other in English. She has eight hours (her resource) that she can allocate to studying for either exam or some combination. The more time she allocates to studying for one exam, the higher the likely grade will be on that exam (her production outcome). But the more time she allocates to studying for the one exam, the lower the likely grade will be on the other exam (the tradeoff). The student's likely production-possibility curve includes combination of A in economics and F in English if she allocates all of her resources to studying economics, and the opposite if she allocates all of her time to studying English. She could also allocate half of her scarce resources to studying for each exam and possibly achieve a C on both exams. Her ideal outcome, an A on both exams, is beyond her current production-possibilities curve. To achieve an A on both exams requires 16 hours, but she only has 8 hours left to study, and if she does not study efficiently (i.e., studies with distractions like music or friends), she will likely not produce at her maximum possible production.

Further reading

Boyes, William, and Michael Melvin. *Microeconomics,* 5th ed. Boston: Houghton Mifflin, 2002; Ruffin, Roy J., and Paul R. Gregory. *Principles of Economics.* Boston: Addison Wesley, 2000.

product liability

Product LIABILITY is the concept that consumers can be compensated for injuries or losses caused by defective or unsafe products. A manufacturer is legally liable if a PRODUCT can be shown to be unreasonably dangerous to the user or consumer, or if it is defective. Product defects can be design defects, manufacturing defects, or marketing defects. A design defect is a problem that makes the product inherently dangerous by nature of a flaw in its design. Manufacturing defects are problems that occur when the product is made in a way that causes it to be unsafe or defective. Marketing defects are failures to provide proper use or installation instructions with the product or to warn the consumer of the dangers of improper use of the product.

Product liability was initially limited to the manufacturer, although sellers, WHOLESALERS, distributors, and others in the chain of supply, from manufacturers to consumers, may be held liable for personal injury or damage to PERSONAL PROPERTY in some situations. Generally the losses that can be claimed are limited to those caused by physical injury or property damage. Under modern U.S. product-liability law, a nonuser or bystander who is injured or suffers a loss due to a defective product may seek compensation. The concept "product" has also been broadened from its original meaning of tangible personal property (automobiles, mechanical equipment, or other consumer goods) and now includes intangibles such as water (as water-supply contamination) or real estate. Product-liability litigation has involved such diverse products as asbestos insulation, cigarettes, dietary supplements, breast implants, MTBE (reformulated gasoline products), latex products, handguns, and automobile tires.

There are three legal theories that may apply in products-liability law: NEGLIGENCE, WARRANTY, and strict tort liability. Under the negligence theory, a manufacturer has a duty to make its product safe for users and is liable for damage or injuries caused by a product that is negligently or carelessly manufactured. Negligence is failure to make a safe product or to take steps to test a product to ensure that it is properly constructed for its intended use. One example of a negligence case is *MacPherson v. Buick Motor Company* (1916). MacPherson, the owner of a Buick automobile, sued Buick Motor Company of Detroit for injuries sustained in an automobile accident that resulted from a defective wheel made of inferior-quality wood. The New York Court of Appeals found that the defect could have been discovered by a manufacturer's inspection and the manufacturer had a duty to ensure the product was safe to be marketed to consumers. Therefore Buick was found liable for MacPherson's injuries and the damage to his automobile.

The warranty theory implies that there are some expectations associated with a product, and the manufacturer or seller can be held liable if the product fails to meet those expectations. Warranties can be implied or express.

Implied warranties are the assumption of a certain quality of a product based on the fact that it is being offered for sale—i.e., it is implied to be suitable for the purpose for which it is being sold. Express warranties are specific representations made by the manufacturer or seller about the quality of the product or its fitness for an intended purpose. An example of an express warranty is found in the state of Washington case *Baxter v. Ford Motor Company et al.* (1932). The windshield of the plaintiff's car was shattered by a pebble, which resulted in his losing an eye. He sued Ford Motor Company and the car dealer who sold him the car on the grounds that the company had advertised that the windshields on the cars were shatterproof. The Washington state court held that Ford's marketing statements were an express warranty, and thus the company was liable for failure of its product to perform as expected.

Strict tort liability arises if the product is defective and unreasonably dangerous. Under strict liability, the manufacturer, seller, or distributor of a product can be held liable if the product is defective and is unreasonably dangerous to the consumer. A consumer can recover DAMAGES by proving the manufacturer made the product and that it was defective; the plaintiff does not need to prove that the manufacturer knew of the defect or could have prevented it. An example is the California case *Greenman v. Yuba Power Products Inc.* (1962). The plaintiff sued the manufacturer of a lathe for injuries caused when wood he was working on came loose from the machine and struck him. The basis of his claim against the manufacturer was that information provided with the lathe led him to believe the wood would be securely held when the machine was in use. Since that was not the case, the machine was therefore defective and an unreasonably dangerous product. The court ruled in favor of the plaintiff.

As indicated in the cases cited above, product-liability law evolved gradually through COMMON LAW. Also known as case law, common law is comprised of the decisions made by state court judges, while statutory law made by the legislative branch of the government at either the state or federal level. One of the most important cases in the development products-liability law was New York's *MacPherson v. Buick*, which opened the door for consumers to sue manufacturers for faulty products. Laws up until that time were based on the concept of CONTRACT privity, which prevented a consumer from suing the manufacturer of a product on the grounds that he had no direct contractual relationship with the manufacturer. This was true of MacPherson, who purchased his automobile from a car dealer and therefore had no direct dealings with Buick Motor Company. However, Judge Benjamin Cardozo held that Buick was liable to its cars' purchasers if it was shown that the cars were negligently made or not properly inspected after manufacture. The effect of the *MacPherson* decision was that products liability was no longer limited to a contractual relationship, and it became a part of tort law. Consumers could sue based on a tort, a private wrong, rather than a breach of contract.

Consumers' rights were expanded under later product-liability cases. In *Baxter v. Ford,* the court provided a means for protecting consumers from false ADVERTISING by manufacturers regarding the quality of products being sold. As a result of *Greenman v. Yuba,* consumers could sue for damages or injuries caused by a defective or inherently dangerous product without having to prove the defect or danger was intentional or known by the manufacturer. The importance of CONSUMER PROTECTION and manufacturer responsibilities was further delineated in the California case *Grimshaw v. Ford Motor Company, et al.* (1981). Ford had manufactured a 1972 Pinto hatchback in which the gas tank was located behind the car's rear axle. It thus lacked additional "crush space" between the gas tank and the rear bumper or structural reinforcements for the gas tank that aid in withstanding impact during an accident. In the events leading to *Grimshaw,* a Pinto was struck from behind and burst into flames, resulting in the death of the driver and her young passenger. Ford was held liable on the grounds that the car was defective and unreasonably dangerous. However, this landmark case was especially notable because it involved punitive damages against the manufacturer. Because Pintos had failed standard safety tests performed prior to going on the market, Ford knew it was selling an unsafe product, and the court awarded the plaintiff punitive damages, an additional sum Ford had to pay as punishment for knowingly selling a dangerous product.

The combined effect of these key cases was the establishment a body of law that provides a method for consumers to be compensated for injuries or loss caused by defective products and at the same time gives businesses an incentive to design, produce, and sell products that are reasonably safe for the public. Although this has resulted in higher design and production costs that are not faced by companies in other countries lacking product-liability laws, product quality and consumer safety have been improved in the United States.

All American states have some form of product-liability law, and many have product-liability statutes. In addition to the common law of each state, product-liability law is also found in Article 2 of the UNIFORM COMMERCIAL CODE (UCC), which covers warranties and consumer rights and has been adopted in all states except Louisiana. While there is no federal product-liability law, and laws can vary considerably from one state to another, the U.S. Department of Commerce has established a Model Uniform Products Liability Act that states can use voluntarily.

Attempts to make product-liability laws more uniform from state to state have been occurring in two areas. One key issue under current consideration is the extent to which consumers can recover for losses or injuries. Many businesses are concerned by the increase in product-liability litigation and the ease with which consumers can sue

manufacturers and others. The effect of numerous lawsuits and dubious or fraudulent claims by some consumers has placed a financial burden on businesses and overloaded the courts. As a result, proposals are being considered by some states and the U.S. Congress to place limits on the amount of compensation that can be claimed by the injured parties in product-liability cases. In the wake of recent lawsuits for products such as dietary supplements and recalled car tires, the imposition of criminal penalties against manufacturers who knowingly allow defective products to be sold or to remain on the market is a second matter being considered by Congress. Both of these proposals are attempts to balance the protection of consumer rights with businesses' ability to develop new products and remain commercially competitive.

—Laurie MacWhinnie

product life cycle

Product life cycle is the series of stages products go through in the marketplace. In marketing, products are known to go through four stages: introduction, growth, maturity, and decline. While the time it takes for PRODUCTS to go through their LIFE CYCLES can vary from days to decades, products have a life and logical marketing goals and marketing strategies differ, depending on the stage in the life of a product.

During the introduction stage, the goal is to stimulate DEMAND for a new product or service. To do this requires creating consumer awareness and interest as well as trials of the new product. Marketers of personal health-care products know it is difficult to get most people to consider alternative products. Placement of samples in hotels, clubs, and spas are typical promotional strategies used to introduce consumers to such new alternatives. Marketers of electronic equipment and technological consumer products know that during the introduction stage they need to reach opinion leaders, people who seek out the latest technology and whose opinions influence others. To gain the attention of these opinion leaders, marketers will promote their new products in special-interest magazines and consumer shows to introduce their new products to people who influence others. Marketers also know that opinion leaders vary. For example, somebody who is not knowledgeable about cars or computers will consult somebody else who *is* knowledgeable before making a major purchase decision.

Gaining the support of DISTRIBUTION CHANNEL members is often critical to success in the introduction stage. There are tens of thousands of new food products introduced each year but not enough room for all of them on supermarket shelves. Most retail stores do not have unused space, and thus for almost every new product, something is removed. To help introduce products, marketers will often provide special display racks and banners and will pay part of a retailer's ADVERTISING cost. With all these expenses, typically during the introduction stage, a firm focuses on stimulating sales, not maximizing PROFITS.

During the growth stage, sales begin to expand rapidly, new customers make their first purchases, and early buyers repurchase the product. During this stage, marketers expand their advertising, changing their messages from "Look, we have a new product" to "This is a great product, and here are the benefits." Also at this stage, competitors, seeing sales taking off, enter the market, which increases price competition and COMPETITION for access through distribution channels. Improvements in the original product are often necessary to match competitors and respond to consumer concerns. Generally profits are maximized during the growth stage of a product life cycle.

During the maturity stage, sales peak and profits begin to decline. There are usually many competitors in the market, and most consumers who want the product have already made an initial purchase. Marketers tend to advertise heavily, emphasizing differences in their products and offering additional benefits such as warranties and customer services. Because there are many producers and market demand is peaking, price competition becomes more aggressive during the maturity stage.

During the decline stage, both sales and profits decrease or disappear. Declining sales often foster price cuts, which then decrease profits. Some competitors leave the market, while other firms consider strategies to extend the lives of their products, for instance introducing new and improved versions. Evaluation is made of new uses or new markets that were previously considered not profitable, and EXIT STRATEGIES are developed to minimize losses and damage to relationships with loyal customers. Sometimes small numbers of loyal customers result in a niche market for one of a few firms remaining during the product's decline stage.

See also MARKETING STRATEGY; PRICING STRATEGIES; SALES PROMOTION.

product-market growth matrix

The product-market growth matrix, first proposed by Igor Ansoff, is a tool managers use to consider growth options and strategies. Ansoff, called the master of corporate strategy, was a professor of strategic management at U.S. International University in San Diego, California. Most businesses have growth as a goal—i.e., expanded sales and increased PROFITS. In seeking these goals, managers consider both its markets and its products.

The product-market growth matrix, as displayed below, suggests four options: market penetration, market development, product development, and diversification.

Market penetration involves expanding the sales of existing PRODUCTS in existing markets. A manager considering a market-penetration strategy will increase ADVERTISING, PERSONAL SELLING, and SALES PROMOTION of their products. Building stronger relationships with DISTRIBUTION CHANNEL members can also foster market penetration. Markets with overcapacity among producers and saturated consumer DEMAND offer few opportunities for market penetration.

Market development involves attempting to sell a firm's existing products in new markets. Decisions to expand into new areas of the country and international markets are examples of market development. A wholesale company that decides to offer its products and SERVICES directly to retail consumers and a retail business

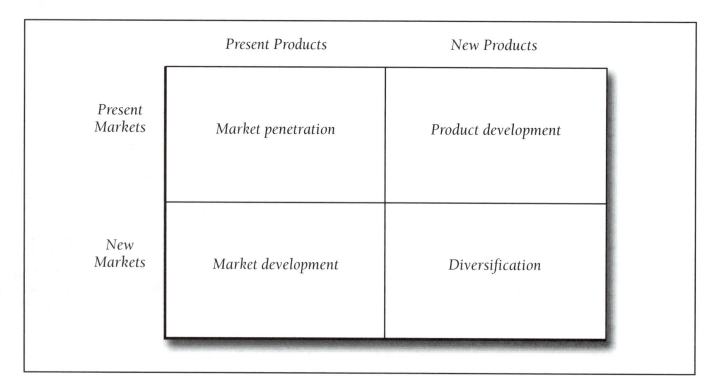

	Present Products	*New Products*
Present Markets	*Market penetration*	*Product development*
New Markets	*Market development*	*Diversification*

considering competing for government contracts are examples of market development.

Product development involves creating new products for existing markets. Many companies grow by identifying or anticipating current customers' additional needs. For retailers, requests from customers for products a company does not currently offer can lead to product development. Customers using a manufacturer's product in an unanticipated way can also lead to ideas for product development. Often a company's sales force is an excellent source of suggestions for opportunities to grow due to knowledge of their customers' wants and needs. One limitation of product development is cannibalization—situations where expanded sales of new products come with decreased sales of existing products. However, a company that does not create new products leaves itself vulnerable to competitors who do offer new and improve products. The rapid level of innovation in consumer technology products in the last 10 years is an example of constant product-development strategies.

Diversification involves creating new products for new markets. This is a more difficult and risky growth strategy, because it involves two unknowns: new products and new markets. Like financial diversification, though, successful diversification into new products and new markets reduces a firm's overall business RISK. Major CORPORATIONS in the United States often diversify by acquiring another company in a market they wish to pursue.

Further reading
Etzel, Michael J., Bruce J. Walker, and William J. Staunton. *Marketing*, 12th ed. Boston: McGraw-Hill, 2001.

product placement

Product placement is the inclusion of a company's PRODUCT within the context of a non-ADVERTISING situation. Typical product placements include insertion of BRANDS and brand-name products within a television show or movie. In product placement, a marketer's product is either shown or even discussed as part of the show or movie.

Product placement is an increasingly popular promotional effort in the United States. Marketers know consumers are frequently zapping or ignoring traditional 30-second television advertising messages and thus need new, innovative ways to capture consumers' attention. Consequently, they are now paying TV networks and movie producers to include their products as part of the script or background. One of the earliest product placements occurred in the 1993 movie *The Firm*, when Tom Cruise casually ordered a Red Stripe beer at the firm's party. During *The Firm*'s filming, Red Stripe lavishly provided cases of their beer to the crew and actors. U.S. distributors saw a quick rise in Red Stripe sales after the film was released.

With the thousands of advertising messages broadcast, published, and transmitted daily, it has become increasingly difficult for marketers to communicate with their customers. Product placement ensures viewers will see a company's products and provides the implicit endorsement of the actor or actress associated with the placement. Companies often pay considerable sums for product placement.

Further reading
Vranica, Suzanne, and Joe Flint. "Omnicom Seeks More for Clients on UPN," *Wall Street Journal,* 24 August 2001. p. B8.

product proliferation

Product proliferation is the expansion of the number of PRODUCT offerings in a product category. The cereal shelves in typical American grocery stores are an example of product proliferation. There may be 200 different boxes of cereal on the shelves, but most of the choices offer only slight variations from each other.

Product proliferation is a common MARKET STRATEGY in industries characterized as oligopolies, markets where there are only a few competitors. Because there are only a few firms, the actions of one firm visibly affects the well-being of other firms in the industry. If, for example, one firm in an industry lowers its prices, it will probably see an increase in sales, and their competitors will see sales decrease. To avoid losing customers, the other firms in the market will match the first firm's price decrease. Likewise, if one firm in an OLIGOPOLY raises its prices, its sales will likely decrease, and the other firms' sales will increase correspondingly. The other firms, happy to see increases in their sales, will probably not match the price increase. (This is known in economics as kinked-demand curve behavior.)

Firms in markets where there are only a few competitors recognize their actions are mutually interdependent. One option in these markets is to not compete on a price basis. Firms in oligopolies often develop price-matching policies and then compete based on other strategies including product features and offerings. The cereal industry is a classic example of nonprice competition resulting in product proliferation. In the United States, the cereal industry is a multibillion-dollar market dominated by four firms. If one firm can develop a slightly different product that increases their sales by 1 percent, it can mean millions of dollars.

Marketers have learned that product proliferation affects consumers. Overwhelmed by slightly different features and options, consumers often think they are doing a research project when deciding which product to buy. To overcome consumer confusion and frustration, "attribute-based" promotion and PERSONAL SELLING can guide customers through product features, overcoming the problem of product proliferation.

See also MUTUAL INTERDEPENDENCE; PRICING STRATEGIES.

Further reading
Lissy, Dana. "Helping Customers Cope with Product Proliferation," *Harvard Business Review* 77, no. 3 (May 1999): 21.

profit

Profit is the increase in a company's net ASSETS—its assets minus its liabilities—over a period of time. The typical way to calculate profit is to subtract net assets from the beginning of the accounting period from end-of-period net assets. If a company had assets of $10,000 and liabilities of $6,000 at the beginning of the year and assets of $15,000 and liabilities of $8,000 at the end of the year, then net assets at the beginning of the year would be $4,000 and at the end of the year would be $7,000. The firm's profit for the year would be $3,000, assuming there had not been any transactions with the owners. If, however, the owners had taken out $2,000 during the year, then the overall profit would have been $5,000, since the year-end net assets would have been $9,000.

Economists are theoretically careful to include both explicit and implicit COSTS in determining profit. Implicit costs would include the value of alternative uses of owner's labor and CAPITAL in making profits. There is further differentiation between a normal profit and excess profits. A normal profit is what a business needs to earn to adequately reward the entrepreneur for his or her efforts in organizing the elements of PRODUCTION. Excess profits—the profits above the normal profit—are what attract other entrepreneurs into the industry.

Accountants tend to concentrate on calculating a company's profits in a way that looks only at explicit costs, without considering implicit costs. To distinguish their calculation from the theoretical, accountants use the term *net income* to refer to profits and report their profit calculation on the INCOME STATEMENT, one of a company's basic FINANCIAL STATEMENTS. (Businesspeople sometimes casually call the income statement the "P and L," short for "profit and loss statement.") Profit is calculated by subtracting the company's expenses from its revenue. Revenue is the firm's increases in net assets resulting from its operations and good fortune and not from cash injections supplied by the owners. Expenses are decreases in the company's net assets relating to operations and not any withdrawal of net assets the owners may make.

—Mack Tennyson

profit maximization

The assumed goal of a private enterprise is to maximize PROFITS. Simply measured, profits are the difference between total revenue and total cost at any level of output. However, determining the profit-maximizing level of output is not that easy and requires a manager to first estimate COSTS.

Costs are categorized as either fixed costs (those that do not change within a range of output) or variable costs (those that do change with the level of output). Costs can also include both accounting costs and economic costs. Accounting costs include all the payments a business owner makes for RESOURCES. Literally, accounting costs are costs for which the business has a payment receipt. In addition to accounting costs, many firms—particularly small, family-owned enterprises—often have OPPORTUNITY COSTS, which are the value of owner resources used in the PRODUCTION of goods and SERVICES. Opportunity costs are estimated as the highest valued alternative forgone by the resource owner and can include the value of owner labor, natural resources, or CAPITAL resources. Accounting costs plus opportunity costs equals economic costs.

To compute profits, a manager must also estimate the price at which he or she can sell the output. Estimating price can be a difficult task. Depending on whether the firm is a small or large part of a large market (see MARKET STRUCTURE), the firm's actions can affect the market price, and its impact on price will depend on the ELASTICITY OF DEMAND for its PRODUCT. The firm may also use a variety of PRICING STRATEGIES, including selling the same product at different prices in different markets. It is important to recognize that the firm is "estimating" price. Often in the time between when a manager decides to produce a product and when it is ready for sale in the market, prices change.

Assuming a manager can estimate both costs and price, profit maximization is achieved at the level of output in which the marginal (extra) revenue from producing and selling one more unit of output equals or just exceeds the marginal (extra) cost of producing that unit of output. This is known as the first condition of the SUPPLY rule: A firm will always maximize profits or minimize losses at the level of output where marginal revenue equals marginal cost.

To determine whether the firm is making a profit at the supply rule–dictated level of output, a manager compares average cost (cost per unit) with price. If price is greater than or equal to average cost, the firm is at least breaking even. If price is less than average cost but greater than average variable cost per unit, the firm is "covering its variable costs" (usually labor and materials) but not covering all costs. If price were less than average variable cost, the firm would be better off (lose less money) by terminating production. That output level where price is less than average variable cost is known as the shutdown point.

The first part of the profit maximization process is to consider the output in which marginal revenue equals marginal costs. To decide whether or not to produce at that level, a manager compares price to average cost and average variable cost. If price is less than average variable cost, shut down; if price equals or exceeds average cost, produce that level of output.

If price is between average cost and average variable cost, managers will need to consider their options and review their credit. Most businesspeople are optimists and believe in their product. To stay in business when it is not breaking even, a firm will need financial capital to pay for the shortfall between total revenue and total costs. A major cause of small-firm BUSINESS FAILURE is the lack of capital to cover initial losses until it can get established. To improve their profit situation, managers will look to see if they can reduce costs or increase revenues, leading to reconsideration of the rules for profit maximization.

Further reading

Boyes, William, and Michael Melvin. *Microeconomics,* 5th ed. Boston: Houghton Mifflin, 2002.

profit sharing, gain sharing

Profit sharing is an agreement between a company and its employees that entitles employees to receive a portion of the company's earned PROFITS. The first profit-sharing plan was introduced in a Pennsylvania glass works in 1794. Approximately one in eight workers in industrialized countries around the world participate in some form of profit sharing.

Some profit-sharing plans pay cash distributions, but most plans provide variable annual distributions contingent on the company's success. Many plans deposit employees' distributions into tax-deferred accounts, which may be invested in stocks, BONDS, or other securities. Often profit-sharing plans allow employees to borrow against their accounts for major purchases such as homes or spending for dependents' education.

Economists suggest profit sharing provides three major benefits. First, it can increase EMPLOYEE MOTIVATION and productivity as workers see their INCOME tied to the success of the company. Second, profit sharing increases the flexibility of wages. One of the arguments in KEYNESIAN ECONOMICS is that wages and prices tend to be "sticky," not adjusting quickly to changes in SUPPLY and DEMAND. By paying workers in part based on profits, a company's COSTS adjust more rapidly to changing market conditions. Third, economists suggest profit sharing can increase EMPLOYMENT because the marginal cost of hiring another worker is the MINIMUM WAGE guaranteed, not the wage plus shared profits. Studies show profit sharing tends to increase productivity, and in the United States this increases wage flexibility. There is only limited evidence that it influences employment.

Gain sharing is similar to profit sharing, except that it is based on cost savings to the company—that is, employee contributions to reducing the cost of PRODUCTION. Most gain-sharing plans are instituted in companies where groups of workers have a "shared economic fate," or combined efforts that influence productivity and costs. Gain-sharing programs typically pay monthly cash bonuses.

Stock-option plans provide similar incentives for executives and managers in CORPORATIONS. Logically, as a company's profits increase, the share price of its stock will also increase. In the United States during the 1990s, STOCK OPTIONS became an increasingly popular incentive program.

Further reading

Graham-Moore, Brian. "Compensation Strategies at Work." *Texas Business Review,* (June 1996): 1–2. "Sharing the Spoils," *The Economist* 341, no. 7994 (30 November 1996): 80.

program evaluation and review technique (PERT)

PERT stands for program evaluation and review technique, and a PERT chart is a PROJECT MANAGEMENT tool used to schedule, organize, and coordinate tasks within a project. The methodology was developed by the U.S. Navy in the 1950s to manage the Polaris submarine missile program. Employing what is referred to as a time-event network, PERT is similar to the CRITICAL PATH METHOD technique, which developed in the private sector at about the same time that PERT was developed.

The advantages of using a PERT diagram include the following.

- PERT charts force managers to contemplate personnel assignment for a project in detail, which can be complex but helpful if detailed networks exist.
- To demonstrate best- and worst-case project scenarios, most PERT charts identify three time estimates: most optimistic, most pessimistic, and most realistic.
- PERT charts are useful in large, complex studies where overlooking details may create irresolvable problems.
- PERT charts are frequently used for detailed evaluation planning.
- The critical path of a PERT chart highlights important interim deadlines that must be met if the overall project is to be completed on time.

In a complex production process, such as automobile manufacturing, PERT charts incorporate a variety of terms and symbols, including event nodes, job activity, immediate predecessors, immediate successors, initial and terminal nodes, duration, earliest start time, earliest finish time, and latest finish time.

- Event node is the beginning and the finish of a job, and each is the connecting point to another job. Each event node has a unique number for ease of reference.
- Job activity is the task that requires a length of time for completion. The event-node numbers that mark its beginning and end refers to each job activity. For example, Job 1, 2 is the task between event numbers 1 and 2.
- The immediate predecessor is a job that must be completed before another job can begin. For example Job 1, 2 is an immediate predecessor for both Jobs 2, 3 and Job 2, 4.
- The immediate successor is a job that cannot be started until another job is finished. For example, Job 3, 5 and Job 4, 6 are immediate successors to Job 1, 2.
- Initial and terminal nodes refer to which nodes start a job and which nodes end a job. For example, node 1 is the initial node for Job 1, 2 and node 2 is the terminal node in Job 1, 2.
- Duration is the length of time required for the completion of any job.
- The earliest start time (ES) is, given the cumulative duration of all of the predecessor activities, is the earli-

est any job can start. For example, Job 2, 3 cannot start until Job 1, 2 is completed and Job 1, 2 will take three days. Therefore the ES for Job 2, 3 is three days.

- The earliest finish time (EF) is the shortest amount of time needed to complete the overall project given the duration of each job and the order of immediate predecessor jobs.
- The latest finish time (LF) is, given the job(s) that any job must feed into, the latest that the job in question can finish without delaying the start of the job where two or more paths merge. Finishing any later would result in delays in the overall project schedule.
- The latest start time (LS) is, given the job(s) that any job must feed into, the latest that the job in question can begin without delaying the start of the job where two or more paths converge. Missing this start time would result in delaying the immediate successor's start.

The major advantage of PERT is that it forces managers to plan their activities.

Further reading
Hodgetts, Richard M. *Management Theory, Process, and Practice,* 5th ed. San Diego, Calif: Harcourt Brace Jovanovich, 1990.

program trading

Program trading is the purchase or sale of large numbers of stock shares based on price differences between the value of the stocks and the FUTURES indexes associated with those shares. The NEW YORK STOCK EXCHANGE (NYSE) defines program trading as any trade of $1 million or more in which more than 15 different stocks are bought or sold at once. In reality, program trading is conducted by computers "programmed" to automatically place orders whenever differences between stock-market indexes and their futures indexes create a PROFIT opportunity. Program trading is an electronic version of ARBITRAGE, the simultaneous buying and selling of ASSETS based on small differences in prices in different markets.

Program trading began in the early 1980s with the creation of computerized trading technology. One of the criticisms of program trading is that it is something available only to large, market-trading companies. Initially the practice was used mostly by large brokerage firms and by HEDGE FUNDS. Recently MUTUAL FUNDS have expanded their use of program trading, representing the interests of their SHAREHOLDERS, who are often small investors.

Another criticism of program trading is that it increases market volatility, adding large volumes of trades to the market as the market is rising or falling. As a *Wall Street Journal* article reports, "In practice, program trades often are much larger, with individual transactions routinely topping $100 million and some reaching $2 billion or $3 billion, often on behalf of WALL STREET's biggest brokerage firms and INVESTMENT banks." In one week in June 2002,

program trades accounted for over 50 percent of trades on the New York Stock Exchange. (In 2002 program trading usually accounted for about 30 percent of all trades.)

After the STOCK MARKET crash in 1987, the NYSE established trading curbs to reduce the impact of program trading. Under current rules, if the Dow Jones Industrial Average rises or falls 180 points, the NYSE requires all program trading to go against the trend in the market. This prevents huge buy and sell orders from exacerbating the market trend.

See also DOW JONES AVERAGES.

Further reading
McKay, Peter A., and Karen Talley, "Rise in Program Trades Fuels Stock Volatility," *Wall Street Journal,* 24 July 2002, p. C1.

project management

Project management is the application of knowledge, skills, tools, and techniques that are necessary to meet the requirements of a particular "project." A project is a unique and temporary endeavor, undertaken to achieve a particular goal, to which MANAGEMENT can be applied regardless of the project's size, budget, or time line. In order to be considered a project, the endeavor must be unique; have a well-defined start, middle, and end date or time; have objectives; and result in an end PRODUCT. The goal of project management is to assure that the project will produce a product/work with the highest quality for the least cost and in the most efficient manner.

People have been planning and managing projects since the beginning of time. Whenever a civilization took root, there were buildings to erect, roads to pave, and laws to write. Since these people did not have the advanced tools, techniques, and methodologies that exist today, they began to create project time-line materials and resources as they started to weigh the risks involved with beginning a new endeavor. Over time, people realized that the techniques for cost control, time-line development and RISK MANAGEMENT were applicable to a wide range of projects, such as erecting bridges and deciding how to govern their newly created communities. These early ideas were the precursors to project management.

The phrase *project management* emerged in the late 1950s when size, scope, duration, and RESOURCES required for new projects began to attract more attention. The development of project management is often traced to the U.S. Navy and the development of the Polaris missile system. This was such a complex and multifaceted project that it required a new type of management. The U.S. Navy developed a process to find the critical path through a series of planned tasks that interconnect during the life of a project. Project management came about as a result of this newly created technique, called PROGRAM EVALUATION AND REVIEW TECHNIQUE, or PERT.

Today project management is used globally by CORPORATIONS, governments, and smaller organizations alike as a means of meeting their customers' needs by both standardizing and reducing the basic tasks necessary to complete projects in the most effective and efficient manner. Intense global COMPETITION demands that new business developments be completed on time and within a specified budget. Project management is practiced by many groups, such as business owners, consultants, suppliers, and is found across all industries. Opportunities in project management include being a project manager, team leader, or part of the support team in a project. Project management not only focuses on planning but also incorporates human attributes such as LEADERSHIP skills and the ability to motivate others.

There are four processes that make up project management: organizing, monitoring, planning and controlling. The delivered product or work helps the STAKEHOLDERS to reach their objectives. The first process in project management is to organize a suitable environment; the project can only succeed in an environment that suits the needs activities involved. This includes items like organization, having the needed resources, and anticipating and solving problems as soon as possible. The second process is to keep the working conditions vibrant by monitoring how the project is being run. These conditions will evolve and be prone to outside influence, causing additional problems or pressures. The project manager has to adapt the project environment when necessary to make it possible to work efficiently. The third process is to plan the activities necessary to create the product, a plan that defines what will take place in order to build the information system. The final process is to control the plan's execution. As the project develops, its outcome will become clearer and more detailed, and new facts or problems may appear. The project's execution plan will have to be detailed and possibly changed or adapted to assure efficient work.

Integration is one of the most basic elements of project management. It brings together the skills that are necessary to achieve project success and ensures that the necessary activities are accomplished properly. It is important to understand that project management is not just implementation management but also the discipline of defining and delivering successful projects. The object of project management is the project itself and how to manage it successfully.

There are many things that can go wrong with the project-management philosophy—poor communication, for example. Many times a project may fail because the project team does not know exactly what to get done or what has already been done. Other barriers include disagreements, failure to comply with standards and regulations, inclement weather, union strikes, personality conflicts, poor management, and poorly defined goals.

Project-management professionals are people who best understand the project process and practices; who can form and shape project strategy; who can best judge how to obtain resources, arrange work flows, and optimize cash flows and financial returns; and who can motivate teams, monitor, and replan. If all of these actions are performed from the beginning of the project's conception to its completion, then it will benefit immensely.

Because modern businesses want projects completed in an effective and efficient manner, project management has become a highly desirable and sought-after skill, especially now that global competition demands that new business development be completed on time and within budget. Consequently, it has became both a way to control business projects and a specialized career path.

See also CRITICAL PATH METHOD.

Further reading
"Evolution of an Idea," Project Management Institute, Inc. Available on-line. URL: http://www.pmi.org/info/; Downloaded May 28, 2003, Lientz, Bennet P. *Project Management for the 21st Century*. San Diego, Calif.: Academic Press, 1998; Pinto, Jeffrey K., ed. The *Project Management Institute: Project Management Handbook*. San Francisco: Jossey-Bass Publishers, 1998.

—Beth Braccia

promissory note
A promissory note is an unconditional promise to pay. Debentures (a bonds backed only by the reputation of the issuing company), MORTGAGES, BONDS, and notes (promises to pay debt) are examples of promissory notes. The borrower is the maker of the note, and the lender is the payee. For the maker, the promissory note is a note payable; for the payee, it is a note receivable. The maker will incur interest expense over the life of the note, while interest INCOME will accrue to the payee. The note has a due date or maturity date, at which time the principal and interest must be repaid. Regardless of what may have happened during the life of the note or what events may occur on the maturity date, the note must be repaid on its due date, unconditionally. Notes that are not repaid at their maturities are defaulted notes, and they can damage the borrower's reputation and ability to borrow in the future.

Because promissory notes have maturity dates, holders of these notes must wait until the notes mature before they can collect on them. If the notes are negotiable, however, they can be sold to an investor before their maturity dates, providing cash to the payee before the notes mature. This common occurrence is known as DISCOUNTING.

promotion See MARKETING COMMUNICATIONS; SALES PROMOTION.

property taxes
Property taxes can be either taxes on ownership of property of taxes on WEALTH, depending on the base used. Measurable characteristics of property that could be used as a

base include weight, size, or value. Most property taxes collected in the United States are *ad valorem* taxes (assessed in relation to the value of the property). Ad valorem taxes on real property, fixtures, and PERSONAL PROPERTY provide a significant source of revenue for local governments (municipalities) and are sometimes collected by state governments. The existence and level of property taxes often influence consumers' and business managers' decisions where to locate. Often homes and businesses are located beyond city limits in order to reduce property taxes.

Most local governments impose a property tax, but the taxing systems differ from county to county and from state to state. Each jurisdiction (state, county or city) has its own rates, assessment dates, exceptions to the tax, and methods for determining the value of the property subject to the tax. Property taxes are usually computed by the government, which then sends a bill to the property owner.

Because ad valorem taxes are based on value, the process requires the application of judgment to a variety of acceptable valuation theories to derive a mutually agreeable valuation level for both the taxpayer and the taxing jurisdiction. A significant portion of the revenue for local governments is collected via property taxes, which are considered to be among the least regressive of taxes collected in the United States.

—Linda Bradley

proprietary information

Proprietary information is information regarding a company's strategy, customers, or PRODUCTs that, if divulged to competitors, would harm the company. Businesses go to great lengths to protect their competitive advantage. PATENTs are often used to protect inventions and technology, noncompete clauses in EMPLOYMENT contracts are used to protect INTELLECTUAL PROPERTY, and security measures are used to limit MARKET INTELLIGENCE and corporate espionage.

Proprietary information can also include the minutes of corporate meetings and even simple items like with whom a corporate executive is meeting. With the rise of technology-based enterprises in the United States and the rapid turnover of workers in the industry, concerns over the loss of TRADE SECRETS and other proprietary information have expanded. Customer lists, technical data, and top-secret research-project information are critical to a company's long-term success but also easy to carry in electronic files.

Chemical formulae are often trade secrets; customer lists that could be recreated by looking in the phone book are not generally recognized as trade secrets. Reasonable steps must be undertaken by businesses possessing and claiming protection for proprietary information. Unlike patents, COPYRIGHTs, and TRADEMARKs, which can be registered with governments in order to protect a company's rights, disclosure of proprietary information would elimi-

nate its value. However, proprietary information can, if protected, last forever, something that is not true of patents and copyrights. The world's best-kept trade secret, for example, is probably the Coca-Cola formula.

Many cases concerning proprietary information wind up in the courtroom, and judges often question what is truly proprietary. In 2002 Wal-Mart won an appeal of a case brought by a company claiming Wal-Mart had used its proposal to handle credit transactions when negotiating a CONTRACT with another company. The court ruled that the proposal was a common wholesale practice and not proprietary information. However, courts have also tended to reject noncompete clauses in contracts when they are too restrictive and limit an individual's ability to earn a living.

See also ECONOMIC ESPIONAGE ACT.

Further reading

Gallun, Alby. "Ex-employees Targeted: Keeping secrets; more firms suing to protect proprietary information." *Crain's Chicago Business,* 28 January 2002; Dan Zehr. "Arkansas Supreme Court Reverses Trade Secrets Ruling, Benefits Wal-Mart," *Arkansas Democrat-Gazette,* 25 February 2002.

proprietorship

A proprietorship is an unincorporated business owned by one person. In the United States, approximately three-fourths of all businesses are proprietorships. The major advantage of a proprietorship is control—the owner makes all decisions and does not have to answer to partners or a BOARD OF DIRECTORS. A proprietor, having total control over the business, receives all the PROFITs (and losses) and is liable for all the actions of the business. Unlimited LIABILITY is a major concern for proprietors. They can be sued for all of the proprietorship's ASSETs as well as for their own personal assets. For example, if a worker for a small home-repair contractor (operating as a proprietorship) starts a fire, the contractor could lose his or her business and personal assets. For this reason proprietors often purchase liability INSURANCE.

A proprietorship is usually easy to establish. In most situations, all that is needed is a business license and, if it is a retail business, a sales-tax license. In addition to the problem of liability, another concern for proprietors is bearing all the responsibilities of their business. In many cases of first-time ENTREPRENEURSHIP, owners are quickly overwhelmed by the many duties that are part of running a business. While their focus is to provide a good or service, proprietors must manage personnel, taxes, ACCOUNTS RECEIVABLE, ACCOUNTS PAYABLE, regulatory compliance, legal issues, and a myriad of other concerns. In addition, without a business history and without partners or stock to sell to investors, it is often difficult for proprietors to raise CAPITAL.

In the United States, proprietorships report their business INCOME or loss on Schedule C of their personal income-tax return. Because proprietorships are not incorporated (that is, they are not legal entities), their income is taxed as the proprietor's personal income. Proprietors pay both the employer and employee parts of SOCIAL SECURITY taxes but are eligible for KEOGH PLAN retirement funds.

prospectus

A prospectus is a document that either describes an offer to sell securities to potential investors or describes the history, goals, and financial performance of a mutual fund. When a company conducts an INITIAL PUBLIC OFFERING (IPO), it must provide a detailed statement of the proposed use of funds, and facts about the company soliciting funds, as per SECURITIES AND EXCHANGE COMMISSION (SEC) guidelines. Sometimes referred to as a "red herring" among financial analysts, an IPO prospectus also includes information about the backgrounds of company officers, RISKS associated with the INVESTMENT, and any legal matters of concern to potential investors. During the peak of the DOT-COMS IPO era (1999–2000), many entrepreneurs with little experience and a BUSINESS PLAN that included not much more than an idea successfully "floated" IPOs, raising hundreds of millions of dollars. Careful scrutiny of their prospectuses would have shown the high degree of risk associated with these investments.

A mutual-fund prospectus is similar to an IPO prospectus, listing the fund's holdings, its investment objectives, and strategies the fund manager uses or may use to achieve its objectives. Until 1998, mutual-fund prospectuses were highly complex, legal documents designed mostly to protect the fund management from lawsuits. One study found that almost 50 percent of investors did not read the prospectuses of funds they invested in. In 1998 the SEC began requiring mutual-fund managers to create "user-friendly" prospectuses, replacing legal jargon with English and providing a standardized summary including the fund's investment objectives, strategies, risk, performance, and fees.

Investment advisors recommend investors scrutinize mutual-fund prospectuses, focusing on

- whether the fund's investment objectives are consistent with their own investment objectives
- the free schedule
- the experience of the current fund managers
- the fund's performance history
- the risk statement

Many investors tend to focus on the mutual fund's current holdings and recent performance in deciding whether to invest in it. Studies have shown that past performance is often hard to replicate, and investors who "chase earnings" are frequently disappointed. Also, many fund managers engage in what is known as "window dressing"—selling poor-performing stocks or stocks that have received negative publicity and purchasing current "hot" stocks just before the end of a quarter, in order to suggest to investors that they correctly purchased the winning stocks.

See also MUTUAL FUNDS.

Further reading
Simon, Ruth. "Invest Smarter by Ferreting Out the Secrets in Fund Prospectuses," *Money* (October 1997): p. 41.

proxy

COMMON STOCK carries voting rights, one vote per common share. SHARE HOLDERS can exercise these voting rights by attending the annual meeting of stockholders. However, most stockholders do not attend annual meetings and do not exercise their voting rights. They can, however, transfer their voting rights by means of a proxy, a document that formally gives another individual or group the power to vote shares of common stock.

When there is dissatisfaction with MANAGEMENT or displeasure over lower-than-expected earnings, an individual or group of individuals will solicit proxies in an attempt to amass enough votes to overthrow and replace the management. This is known as a proxy fight.

public administration

Public administration, the MANAGEMENT of public programs, is about getting things done or about making and carrying out public policies. Scholars who study public administration draw on research gleaned from a number of disciplines, including political science, sociology, psychology, economics, and business. Researchers from each of these disciplines bring their own perspectives on the structure of organizations, what motivates people to work and to be more productive, how people communicate in organizations, HUMAN RESOURCES management, LEADERSHIP, and decision making. Public administration also includes the BUDGETING process, taxation, program evaluation, EMPLOYEE/LABOR relations, ethics, policy making, public-private sector relations, and federalism (the relationship of the national, state, and local governments). Comparative public administration focuses on the similarities and differences between the structures of government in different countries.

Public administration has gradually developed as a profession with a body of scholarly knowledge, a professional organization (the American Society for Public Administration), and a code of ethics. Through much of the 20th century, there were few public managers with formal training in public administration. Most administrators worked their way up in an organization, with city managers often beginning their careers in a department like public works. Although some colleges offer undergraduate courses in public administration today (usually through the political science program), most people who desire a career in public service seek specialized training in graduate school.

Many colleges and universities offer master's degrees in public administration, public policy, or public management for recent undergraduates or for those already working in government. People who are interested in an academic career generally seek a doctoral degree in public administration, political science, or a related area.

The beginning of public administration as a discipline or field of study separate from its "mother" discipline of political science is usually dated to 1887. In that year a college professor named Woodrow Wilson wrote an essay entitled "The Study of Administration." Wilson, who later became the 28th president of the United States, believed that politics did not belong in administration and said that the role of administrators was to carry out policies made by elected politicians. He believed that public administration was very much like private business, and he decried the influence of partisan politics on government administration. Wilson's views were in tune with those of the reformers in the late 1800s and early 1900s who were disgusted by corruption in government and by a spoils system that rewarded political loyalty. They sparked a nationwide government-reform movement. Hiring based on merit (more objective qualifications like a test score) began at the federal level with passage of the Pendleton Act in 1883 and gradually filtered down to the state and local levels. Beginning in 1907, some communities adopted a form of government in which elected officials hire a professional manager or administrator to implement programs.

The scholars of the early 1900s built on Wilson's work as public administration began to emerge as a separate field. In the 1920s and 1930s, their primary focus was how to make government more efficient and how to help the executive gain more control over the organization. Luther Gulick developed a set of managerial principles that described the role of the executive. Along with his colleague Lyndall Urwick, he argued that these "principles," like planning and organizing, could be applied to all organizations.

In the 1940s scholars began to study public administration scientifically. Herbert Simon, a leader in this field, criticized the "principles" approach as contradictory and of little practical value. He believed that the study of how decisions are made in organizations was a central part of an administrative science. However, despite the widespread use of empirical research methods (research based on observation and use of the scientific method), some other late 20th-century scholars have argued that it is difficult to quantify administration. George J. Gordon, for example, points out that many decisions are made in secret and that decision making is often an informal process.

After World War II, with a larger government that was playing a more active role in people's lives, scholars and administrators began to realize that it was impossible for politicians to make all the day-to-day decisions necessary to carry out government programs. Today most students of the discipline know that administrators must have the discretion to interpret laws and to make policy decisions. Politics has always played a role in public administration, even from the earliest days of the republic, when those who governed came from the upper strata of society. Democratic accountability requires government to be responsive to the varied and conflicting demands of many different constituencies and to seek a balance between their needs and desires.

Scholars have also realized that organizations are not static but rather dynamic. Systems theorists study the interaction of organizations with their environment, both internal and external. For example, a manager's decision can have an impact throughout the organization; or, in response to outside criticism, an organization may decide to hold public hearings before implementing a new policy. Scholars have developed a number of new subdiciplines based on the concepts of systems theory, such as cybernetics, information theory, GAME THEORY, organizational change, and organizational development.

In a sense, the country has come full circle since Woodrow Wilson's day. Public confidence in government has been low since the 1960s, and the words *politics* and BUREAUCRACY have negative connotations for much of the public. In an era where there is much overlap and much blurring of the lines between the public and private sectors, some people think the private sector can do a better job of handling many traditional government services, from schools to prisons to trash collection. They favor increased contracting out of PRIVATIZATION of certain government SERVICES to the private sector.

Many people believe that it is possible to resolve the problems inherent in government by applying a business model, arguing that there are many similarities between organizations in the public and private sector, such as their bureaucratic structure. Such critics note that managers in both the public and private sectors must address many of the same problems in administering organizations, such as hiring and firing employees. Reform efforts seek to apply to the government principles that have worked in the private sector. One such reform was the National Performance Review of the Clinton-Gore administration in the 1990s, with its emphasis on customer service and increasing efficiency.

Others, however, point out there are substantial differences between the public and private sectors. The mission of government is to provide service to its various constituencies, while the private sector's goal is to make MONEY. As a result, it is often difficult to determine whether a government program is effective, since its goals may not be so clear-cut. For example, a business's success is generally measured by whether it makes a PROFIT, but how can people determine if a school is successful? Should the criteria be how many of its students graduate, how many have good writing and math skills, or how many find a job after finishing their education?

Because government in the broadest sense belongs to the people, it must operate in a fishbowl, where most decisions are made openly and are subject to public and media scrutiny. A private company can cut an unprofitable route or limit its hours of service to save money. When a public agency attempts to do the same, members of the public who object may place pressure on the elected officials who have the final say. Another critical difference is that all government operations are subject to law and legal scrutiny to a far greater extent than are private businesses. This includes questions of hiring and firing, the extent to which public employees and employers have immunity, and the use of public monies. Court decisions frequently play a role in determining what public managers can and cannot do, as courts interpret and reinterpret various laws.

The field of public administration will have to address these and many other issues in a changing world. New technology will change the way that services are delivered, at least in some respects, and perhaps make government more accessible to a wider range of citizens. There will be disagreements concerning the extent to which government should regulate the private sector and to what extent it should protect citizens from the various harms inherent in modern life. Continuing issues include how to better set goals, measure the accomplishments and failures of government programs, and pay for the services that the public wants. Perhaps most important is the related issue of how to change the political climate from one that denigrates to one that respects and values public service.

Further reading

Berkley, George, and John Rouse. *The Craft of Public Administration,* 7th ed. Madison, Wisc.: Brown and Benchmark Publishers, 1997; Gordon, George J., and Michael E. Milakovich. *Public Administration in America.* 6th ed. New York: St. Martin's Press, 1998; Johnson, William C. *Public Administration: Policy, Politics, and Practice.* Guilford, Conn.: Dushkin Publishing Group, 1992; Rosenbloom, David H. *Public Administration: Understanding Management, Politics, and Law in the Public Sector.* 4th ed. New York: McGraw-Hill, 1998; Shafritz, Jay M., and E. W. Russell. *Introducing Public Administration.* 2d ed. New York: Addison Wesley Longman, 2000; Stillman, Richard J., II. *Public Administration: Concepts and Cases,* 7th ed. Boston: Houghton Mifflin, 2000.

—Carol Sears Botsch

public relations

The term *public relations* (PR) refers to an organization's attempts to improve its image and its relationship with customers, employees, stockholders, community members, news media, and government. Public relations are not limited to businesses; many nonprofit groups also use public relations to communicate with their audiences. For example, by sponsoring presidential debates every four years, the League of Women Voters gains significant national media exposure. Most large organizations have public-relations staff or departments.

Public-relations efforts can be either proactive—designed to increase the organization's visibility and credibility—or reactive—responding to criticism, crises, or rumors. Typical proactive PR activities include membership in civic groups, speaker bureaus, and sponsorship or support of community projects. Communications with employees, financial STAKEHOLDERS, and government regulatory groups are usually proactive PR efforts, but they are also sometimes reactions to crises and conflicts.

Public relations are a critical element in a firm's MARKETING STRATEGY during crises. Any lack of quick, direct, and forthright responses to a crisis or rumor can permanently damage a firm's reputation in the marketplace. In 2000, Firestone failed to respond directly to the accusation of defective tires and instead attempted initially to blame the automobile manufacturer, seriously diminishing their credibility with U.S. consumers.

The basic PR tool is a press release. Andrew Kantor, senior editor of *Internet World,* provides the following eight tips for people writing press releases, from an editor's point of view.

- Know who you're writing to and what I want.
- Think whether it's something I cover.
- Know my lead time.
- Don't annoy me with follow-ups.
- Keep your database up-to-date.
- Remember that I'm an editor on a deadline.
- Get my name right.
- Don't be familiar.

In author "Ban the Press Release!" Michael Daly writes that PR people should instead use the

- captioned photo
- media alert
- pitch letter
- press conference
- phone call
- editorial briefing
- one-on-one meeting

In summary, Daly states that PR personnel should dare to be different whenever they can.

In recent years, many organizations in the United States have increased their PR efforts. ADVERTISING is perceived to be less creditable, while publicity through PR activities continues to be viewed favorably. Another important trend in public relations is monitoring INTERNET communications. Prnewswire and other media-service companies now provide "e-watch"—Internet monitoring of Web publications, sites, portals, message boards, and newsgroups, providing companies an "early warning system to act quickly on false, inaccurate, or misleading information." Some companies utilize the speed of Internet communications to create favorable publicity, a process called viral marketing, in which firms circulate cartoons, stories, and jokes using company products. Internet users frequently forward these messages to their friends.

Further reading
Daly, Michael. "Ban the Press Release!" *Business Marketing* (October 1987): 86–88; Andrew Kantor. Andrew Kantor website "Tips for PR People." Available on-line. URL: www.kantor.com/prtips

public service announcements
Public service announcements (PSAs) are noncommercial announcements created to provide information to the public. A PSA contains information designed to inform and benefit the intended audience, rather than the organization or CORPORATION that created it. Most PSAs are produced for or by nonprofit organizations, though sometimes businesses use them to promote their community activities or events. PSAs, like news stories about businesses, have greater credibility than most ADVERTISING activities and are part of a company's marketing strategies.

PSAs often used by organizations to publicize community events, provide health and safety information, assist in fund-raising for nonprofit groups, and inform and influence public opinion. Typically PSAs are short (usually 10–60 second spots) on television and radio provided at no charge to nonprofit and advocacy groups. Television and radio stations are expected to donate airtime to meet the FEDERAL COMMUNICATIONS COMMISSION's public service requirements. In recent years the huge government settlement with tobacco manufacturers has resulted in powerful PSA messages delivered during prime-time shows; one anti-tobacco message broadcast during the Super Bowl; annually the most expensive television-advertising event in the U.S. market.

Radio PSAs are provided either as audiotapes or as live COPY, scripted announcements to be read on-air. Short PSAs of 10, 15, 30, or 60 seconds in length are preferred by radio stations so they will fit in with advertising time allotments. PSAs should be delivered well in advance, be clearly labeled and easy to read, and use the active voice and everyday language.

Television PSAs need a visual component to the story. Language formatting is similar to radio PSAs, and the audio portion is coordinated with the video segment. Many local TV stations will assist nonprofit organizations in creating PSAs.

Further reading
U.S. Small Business Administration website. Available on-line. URL: www.onlinewbc.gov/docs/market/mk_ PSA_PR.html

public utilities
Public utilities are firms or industries regulated by government agencies (usually public-utility commissions). Public utilities are generally private companies given exclusive rights to provide a service in a particular area. In effect, a public utility is a government-created and regulated MONOPOLY.

There is a long history of government-created monopolies. The Commons House of Assembly, in prerevolutionary South Carolina, granted monopolies to local ferry operators between coastal islands. The House named the recipient of the monopoly and dictated the fare that could be charged. Between Beaufort, South Carolina, and Lady's Island, the ferry operator was allowed to charge 7½ shillings for a man and his horse. As historian Larry Rowland and coauthors report, the ferry operator had a complaint: "What he desired was relief from the many disputes and inconveniences that arise from want of a law to fix . . . rates and other regulations." Similarly, in 1843 Oregon passed laws regulating granaries in the public interest.

There are many public utilities, ranging from telephone and electric services to pay-phone providers, local water companies, local cable companies, and even cotton gins. Public utilities are created based on the concept of natural monopolies, industries and markets where ECONOMIES OF SCALE exist over a wide range of output and cost per unit declines as PRODUCTION is increased. Industries where there are significant start-up or fixed COSTS and low additional or marginal costs when output is increased are likely to experience economies of scale. For example, in a local telephone service, the cost of creating a wire and connection system is significant, but the extra cost of providing local service to another customer is minimal. By spreading the fixed costs of creating the communication system over a larger number of consumers, the average cost of service declines. One large telephone-service provider can provide local service at a lower cost than many small companies could. It would be a waste of RESOURCES and inefficient to have multiple firms providing local telephone service. This was the case in the early 20th century, when business owners often subscribed to five or more telephone services, each a separate phone system, in order to communicate with customers and other businesses. In such a situation, it is natural to create a monopoly.

A monopoly is a market with only one producer and no close substitutes. Without regulation, monopolists will operate at a level that maximizes PROFITs. This usually results in higher prices and lower levels of output than if the market was competitive. In situations where natural monopolies exist for basic consumer goods, government frequently creates public utilities. Because such SERVICES are the only source of what most consumers consider necessity goods, government regulation is necessary, since otherwise monopolists could charge very high prices and consumers would have no recourse.

Every state has a public-utility commission (PUC, also called a public-service commission) regulating electricity, natural gas, railroads, water, and telephone services. These commissions usually assert their mission is to "provide, safe, reliable service at reasonable rates." "Reasonable rates" can be interpreted in many ways. Utilities are allowed a "fair" return, usually calculated as a percentage return to their INVESTMENTS (ROI). For example, if an electric utility company invests $100 million, and the utility commission allows them an 8-percent return, the company would earn an $8 million PROFIT annually over the life of the investment. With this type of regulation, the more the utility invests, the greater their absolute level of profit (though the percentage return would remain constant). Fair-return pricing encourages utility spending rather than cost controls.

Most utility commissions set utility prices equal to the average cost (including profit) of providing the product or service. With this method, total revenue will just cover the utility's total cost. PUCs also allow pricing such that the average price equals the average cost. Using this method, the utility charges different prices for different quantities or levels of service, but overall, total revenue will equal total cost.

With changing technologies, public-utility commissions have often deregulated and even reregulated certain industries. For example, AT&T was created in the early 1900s as a federally mandated monopoly for long-distance telephone service. The company argued to Congress that only with a monopoly could they safely invest in national telephone service using one technology. (At the time there were hundreds of small, local telephone companies, often using different, incompatible technology.) In 1984 Congress ended AT&T's monopoly, allowing Sprint and MCI to compete in long-distance service using new technology (satellites and microwave systems) that bypassed AT&T's long-line system.

The regional telephone systems, known as the Baby Bells, continue to operate as regulated monopolies. Before 1984, AT&T's profits from long-distance service subsidized local service. After the end of regulation, long-distance prices fell while local-service prices rose. The 1996 Telecommunications Reform Act was supposed to increase COMPETITION by allowing Baby Bells to offer long-distance service and let the long-distance companies enter local-service markets. While consumers often benefit when monopoly markets are made more competitive, monopolists, including public utilities, usually resist opening their markets to new competitors. To date, local telephone-service utilities have resisted DEREGULATION, limiting the impact of the reform measures.

The most widely reported attempt at utility deregulation was the 1990s attempt to deregulate electricity prices in California. The California public-utility commission, after years of study and contentious debate, allowed electricity producers to compete and charge market prices.

Prices to consumers were still regulated, and charges for distribution through the electrical grid were also regulated. The major utility companies in California began buying power from independent producers for delivery to their customers. In the late 1990s, a combination of increased DEMAND, shutdowns at power plants, and structural problems with the distribution grid lead to a power shortage and huge increases in the PRODUCTION price. There were also charges that major electrical power brokers manipulated the producer market. With retail prices regulated but the cost of power skyrocketing, mandatory rolling blackouts were instituted, and California electrical utilities lost billions of dollars.

Members of state public-utility commission boards are usually appointed by the governor subject to the approval of the state senate. Frequently consumer groups have questioned the objectivity of PUCs, complaining that the commissions often have too-cozy relationships with the utilities they have jurisdiction over. Most state consumer-advocate offices scrutinize the proceedings of PUCs to ensure the interests of the general public are represented in their decisions.

See also PROFIT MAXIMIZATION.

Further reading
Abel, Amy. *Electricity Restructuring Background: The Public Utility Regulatory Policies Act of 1978 and Energy Policy Act of 1992.* Congressional Research Service Report 98-419. Washington, D.C.: Congressional Research Service, 4 May 1998; Rowland, Larry, et al. *History of Beaufort, South Carolina.* Vol. 1, 1514–1861, edited by Alexander Moore and George C. Rogers Jr. Columbia, University of South Carolina Press, 1996.

purchasing (supply-chain management)
Purchasing refers to the responsibility to procure supplies, materials, PRODUCTS, and SERVICES for use in business. Purchasing agents or buyers are part of the operational strategy in any organization. Retail businesses need the right combination of goods and services available at the right time to meet customer needs. Manufacturers need the right combination of materials, components, and services available at the right time in order to produce goods in an efficient, cost-effective manner.

The major goals of purchasing are to make sure needed goods and materials are available, to secure delivery in a timely manner, and to minimize costs. Typical functions of purchasing departments in a business include

- identifying sources of SUPPLY
- coordinating resource requirements for the different parts of the organization
- developing requests for proposals
- selecting sources of supply
- meeting with and negotiating details of supplier CONTRACTS

- overseeing supply contracts
- managing supplier delivery and payment processes

Purchasing agents are frequently part of business buying centers. The BUYING-CENTER CONCEPT is the idea that in businesses and organizations, many people with different roles and priorities participate in purchasing decisions. Unlike consumer buying, where the consumer—alone or with assistance or influence from acknowledged opinion leaders—makes his or her own purchase decisions, in business buying a group often determines which products or services are purchased.

The typical business buying center will include a variety of roles.

- initiators—people who start the purchase process by defining a need
- decision makers—people who make the final decision
- gatekeepers—people who control the flow of information and access to individuals in an organization
- influencers—people who have input into the purchase decision
- purchasing agent—the person who actually places the purchase order
- controller—the person who oversees the budget for the purchase
- users—people who use the product or service.

In a buying center, purchasing agents often address the questions of "what to buy, where to buy it, and what will it cost?" Purchasing departments usually control vendor analysis, the monitoring and reviewing of the performance of suppliers with respect to timeliness and quality. Purchasing managers would probably be involved in MAKE-OR-BUY DECISIONS.

Since the 1950s, the role of purchasing in most businesses has become more important. Traditionally purchasing was seen as a clerical function, symbolized by clerks surrounded by paper in a windowless office far in the back of company headquarters. With the evolution of systems management, just-in-time delivery systems, TOTAL-QUALITY MANAGEMENT and other MANAGEMENT strategies, purchasing became recognized as a cost-control center and a "player" in management decision making.

The importance of purchasing can be illustrated by what happens when purchasing decisions are isolated within a business organization. A story in the *Wall Street Journal* described how Ford Motor Company took a write-off of $1 billion associated with purchases of palladium, a precious metal used in catalytic converters (pollution-control devices in exhaust systems). Ford found it had too much palladium and that they had paid too much for it, and now palladium prices were falling "drastically and seem unlikely to return to their highs."

In 2000 Ford managers approved purchasing-department plans to begin stockpiling the metal and make arrangements for long-term CONTRACTs with producers from other countries. Ford's treasury department regularly used HEDGING to offset interest-rate and currency RISK, but their treasury department did not work with the purchasing department, and purchasing managers were not involved in hedging strategies. In addition, the purchasing department apparently did not keep in contact with Ford's research department, which was aggressively working on finding new ways to reduce the need for palladium while still meeting pollution standards. By 2001, Ford's research staff had results showing the company could reduce its use of the metal by half, significantly reducing DEMAND.

Palladium prices kept rising, eventually spiking at over $1,000 per ounce in 2000—but then the prices fell. High prices had induced other producers, particularly South African companies, to expand output. Combined with reduced demand, world palladium prices dropped by over 50 percent, and Ford found itself with a huge stockpile of metal bought at high prices, now worth considerably less. According to the *Wall Street Journal,* "Ford has instituted new procedures to ensure that treasury-department staffers with experience in hedging are involved in any major commodities purchase in the future."

Today purchasing includes e-procurement, using Internet-based automated acquisition and management systems to reduce COSTS. The Institute for supply management, formerly the National Association of Purchasing Managers "claims that the use of e-procurement can slash the average cost associated with generating a purchasing order from $150 to $30. . . . In addition, the technology may speed up the buying process, eliminate maverick buying, help negotiate bulk discounts, and improve employee productivity." *Supply-chain management* is now a more widely used term than *purchasing*. Supply-chain management combines purchasing functions with LOGISTICS management.

A major resource used by purchasing managers in the United States is *Thomas' Register of American Manufacturers*. This huge, green series of reference books, available in larger libraries or electronically, lists 170,000 manufacturers and 72,000 products and is used by purchasing managers to identify sources of materials and supplies. In addition, purchasing managers can submit orders and request quotations at the Thomas Register website.

See also DISTRIBUTION CHANNEL; JUST-IN-TIME PRODUCTION.

Further reading

Hayes, Heather B. "Reaping the Benefits of E-Procurement: Not just a quick fix, e-procurement requires a thoughtful and thorough approach to produce the most rewards." *BioPharm,* February 2002; Hodgetts, Richard M. *Management Theory, Process, and Practice.* Harcourt Brace Jovanovich, 1990; Institute for Supply Management website. Available on-line. URL: www.ism.ws; Thomas Register website. Available on-line. URL: www.thomas-register.com; Gregory L. White, "How Ford's Big Batch of Rare Metal Led to $1 Billion Write-off," *Wall Street Journal,* 6 February 2002, p. A1.

push and pull strategies

Push and pull strategies are ADVERTISING and other promotional efforts that assist in getting PRODUCTS through DISTRIBUTION CHANNELS. Push strategies are designed to support and reward participants in the distribution channel, usually WHOLESALERS and retailers. Pull strategies are direct communications with final users of a product or service.

Push strategies are used to motivate wholesalers and retailers to take the extra time and effort needed to promote a manufacturer's product. They typically involve PERSONAL SELLING, cooperative advertising allowances, trade discounts, and other rewards and remuneration. For example, a heating-system manufacturer offered an expense-paid trip to Las Vegas to any dealer who sold 20 or more systems in a year. Manufacturers of brand-name products reimburse retailers for part of their expense when the retailer includes pictures and logos of the manufacturer's products in their advertising.

Pull strategies are efforts to stimulate end-user DEMAND, so that consumers will ask the firms they do business with to carry the products they want. Television advertisements stating, "Ask your doctor about . . ." is one example of a pull-marketing strategy. Manufacturers use DIRECT MAIL advertisements and coupons to help draw consumers into retailer's stores.

Marketers know gaining access to distribution channels is critical to success. There are thousands of new products created each year, and only a small percentage will make it to retailers' shelves. Most companies thus use combinations of push and pull strategies.

pyramid of corporate responsibility

The pyramid of corporate responsibility model suggests CORPORATE SOCIAL RESPONSIBILITY is composed of four components: economic, legal, ethical, and philanthropic. The model uses economic responsibility as its foundation, arguing a company must be profitable in order to survive and contribute to the other levels in the pyramid.

While pursuing PROFITS is the foundation, the next level of the pyramid is legal responsibility; playing by the rules of the competitive-market "game." The third level is ethical responsibilities includes doing what is right, just and fair, avoiding harm to people and the environment. At the top of the pyramid are philanthropic corporate responsibilities, contributing to and improving the quality of life in a community.

Critics of the pyramid of corporate responsibility suggest that the "business of business is business," and efforts that distract from the pursuit of profits are a disservice to STAKEHOLDERS, whether owners or workers. Supporters of corporate social responsibility point out the right to establish a CORPORATION is a charter granted by society, one that, in theory, can be revoked. Advocates of SUSTAINABLE GROWTH AND DEVELOPMENT challenge the tendency to focus on short-term profits versus the long-term social and economic impact of business decisions.

Further reading

Boone, Louis E., and David L. Kurtz. *Contemporary Marketing,* 10th ed. Fort Worth: Dryden Press, 2001; Lamb, Charles W., Joseph F. Hair Jr., and Carl McDaniel. *Marketing,* 6th ed. Cincinnati: Southwestern, 2002.

quality control

Quality control is a system for ensuring the maintenance of proper standards in manufactured goods using periodic random inspection of the PRODUCTS. It is also used for optimizing PRODUCTION.

Quality control incorporates the concepts of quality circles, in which groups of 10–20 workers are given responsibility for the quality of the products they produce. Quality circles are thought to have originated in Japan in the 1960s, but the U.S. Army also adopted the practice soon after 1945. It gradually evolved into various techniques involving both workers and statistical measures used by managers to maximize productivity and quality.

Under quality-control guidelines, companies attempt to minimize scrap materials, wastes, and defective products. While many quality-control ideas were developed in the United States, Japanese manufacturers, under the tutelage of Dr. W. Edward Deming, greatly expanded its use in the 1950s. The Japanese term *kaizen* is the concept of continuous improvement through incremental change. Using quality circles and *kaizen,* Japanese manufacturers were global leaders in quality control by the 1980s. So many American managers visited Japan during that decade that the term *kaizen* became part of American business jargon.

In the United States, the AMERICAN SOCIETY FOR QUALITY (ASQ) is the leading organization promoting and training people in the concepts of quality control. Many International Organization for Standardization (ISO) guidelines for environmental-management practices incorporate the ideas of quality control.

From a marketing and MANAGEMENT perspective, quality control reduces COSTS and improves customer RELATIONS/SATISFACTION. Marketers know word of mouth is almost always the most important form of promotion for a product, and dissatisfied customers will often discuss their experiences with other potential consumers. Quality control attempts to address problems before the product is placed in the hands of consumers.

See also DEMING'S 14 POINTS; ISO STANDARDS.

Further reading

Ishikawa, Kaouru. *Introduction to Quality Control.* New York: 3A Corporation, 1993; Juran, J. M. *Juran on Quality by Design.* New York: The Free Press, 1992; Rust, Ronald T., and Anthony J. Zahorik. *Return on Quality.* Chicago: Probus Publishing, 1994.

—Jim Nix

questionnaires

Questionnaires are used to collect data in MARKET RESEARCH. Whether used in MAIL SURVEYS and INTERNET SURVEYS or TELEPHONE SURVEYS and PERSONAL-INTERVIEW SURVEYS, questionnaire design is critical to successfully obtaining the information needed to achieve the research objectives.

While there will be some variation depending on how the questionnaire is being administered, most questionnaire introductions

- state who is conducting the research
- introduce the surveyor
- indicate to respondents that the questionnaire is for a research study, not a sales effort
- describe the general topic of the research
- state approximately how long the interview will take
- assure individual respondents that their answers will be kept confidential
- state any honorarium or other incentive for participating

Generally market researchers try to use close-ended questions rather than open-ended questions. Close-ended questions include dichotomous choice, yes or no type questions, and multiple-choice questions are easy for respondents to answer and easy to tabulate. Sometimes researchers use FOCUS GROUPS to help identify the likely responses to questions in advance of conducting a survey. Likert scale questions, ranging from "strongly agree" to "strongly disagree" or "poor" to "excellent," are used to elicit more information about people's feelings and opinions. The scale used and the number of choices in the scale can influence responses. Researchers have to decide in advance whether to include "neutral" or "no opinion" choices. For example, the first scale below forces respondents to agree or disagree, while the second allows respondents to not express an opinion.

- strongly agree / agree / disagree / strongly disagree
- strongly agree / agree / neither agree or disagree / disagree / strongly disagree

While researchers try to avoid using open-ended questions, the "other" choice in a multiple-choice question and the "Is there anything else you can tell us" question sometimes can be the most important source of information. Researchers are often so involved in their work that they cannot anticipate what consumers are thinking. Open-ended questions can be a valuable source of new ideas.

Question design is a critical part of successful business research. Five types of errors are common in question design

- *Double-barreled questions:* How would you rate our burgers and fries?

     Excellent   good   fair   poor

What if the respondent thought the burgers were excellent but the fries were poor? Most people would probably just circle "good," and the researcher would never know there was a problem with the fries.

- *Ambiguous wording:* Do you eat at Fast Freddy's regularly?
     Yes   No

What is "regularly"? For some people it might be once a week, for others once a day.

- *Unanswerable question:* When did you eat your first hamburger?

Most consumers cannot remember when. Questions asking people to recall events or experiences even just a week or two earlier are difficult to answer accurately.

- *Missing alternatives:* Where do you live?
     dormitory   apartment   own your own home

What if the person rents a home?

- *Leading question:* Why do you like Freddy's fries?
     hot   spicy   crisp   salty

What if the respondent does not like Freddy's fries?

Market researchers pretest questionnaires to avoid problems with question design. In addition, researchers create mock data results. Reviewing a set of hypothetical data allows researchers to evaluate whether the question will generate the information needed and whether the question is needed at all. Most first-draft questionnaires can usually be reduced in length by pretesting and doing mock data analysis. Market-research companies charge a design fee and a fee per question. Critical analysis during the questionnaire design stage can reduce the cost of a study.

Further reading
Pride, William M., and O. C. Ferrell. *Marketing Concepts and Strategies,* 12th ed. Boston: Houghton Mifflin, 2003.

queuing theory
The queuing theory addresses problems involved in waiting. Typical examples of queuing in business include the lines of people waiting for service at banks and supermarkets and the queues caused by PRODUCTION shutdowns, public transport delays, and slow computer response times. In each of these situations, COSTS and benefits must be weighed. Shorter queues increase customer satisfaction but also are more costly to businesses. Reduced response time on a computer can be compared to the increased cost of hardware or INTERNET service connection. The cost associated with a shutdown of a production line can be compared to the cost of maintaining a supply of parts and machines to restart production quickly.

The most typical queuing theory situation is a system where customers arrive and form a line waiting for a service. Analysis of the arrival process includes

- how the customers arrive (singly or in groups)
- how the arrivals are distributed over time (randomly or in segments)
- whether there is a finite population of customers or potentially infinite number

Arrival patterns can include completely regular arrivals (the same constant time interval between successive arrivals), batch arrivals, and time-dependent arrivals.

Next, queuing theory analyzes the service mechanism available including

- how long the service will take
- whether the servers are in series (each server has a separate queue) or in parallel (one queue for all servers)
- whether preemption is used (whether customer emergencies move people ahead in a queue)

Queuing theory also includes analysis of queue behavior or discipline. Are people served on a first-come-first-served basis? Do customers decide to not join a queue if it is too long, or leave a queue after waiting?

Using formulas or simulating, queuing theory can be used to measure the performance of a system, addressing questions such as

- How long does a customer expect to wait?
- How long will he or she have to wait before a service is completed?

- What is the probability of a customer having to wait longer than a given time interval before he or she is served?
- What is the average length of a queue?

Further reading

J. E. Beasley. "OR-Notes: Queuing theory." Available on-line. URL: http://mscmga.ms.ic.ac.uk/jeb/or/queue.html. Downloaded May 28, 2003.

R

Racketeer Influenced and Corrupt Organization Act (RICO)

The Racketeer Influenced and Corrupt Organization Act, passed as part of the Organized Crime Control Act of 1970 and better known as RICO, was intended to control the activities and influence of mobsters and drug traffickers in legitimate businesses. Under RICO, it is a federal crime to use INCOME derived from a "pattern of racketeering activity" to acquire or maintain an interest in a business, or to conduct or participate in the affairs of a business through a pattern of racketeering activity, or to conspire to do any of the preceding acts.

Critical to understanding RICO and its implications for American business are two terms, *racketeering activity* and *pattern*. Racketeering activity includes the commission of any of more than 30 federal or state criminal offenses, including arson, gambling, extortion, BRIBERY, and mail and wire FRAUD. Many of these crimes are commonly associated with criminal business activity, though others are less so. Under RICO, a pattern is defined as the commission of at least two related acts of racketeering within a 10-year period.

RICO violators are subject to substantial fines and prison sentences of up to 20 years. In addition, they can lose any interest gained in enterprises through racketeering activity as well as property derived from MONEY generated through racketeering. Another important aspect of RICO is that it allows prosecutors to freeze a defendant's ASSETS pretrial. This reduces a racketeer's ability to hide or dispose of assets before conviction.

While intended for use against organized-crime activities, RICO has been used to prosecute other criminal activity and poses a potential problem for American businesspeople. Since a "pattern" is defined as two or more action during a 10-year period, and common business practices such as DIRECT MAIL and TELEMARKETING are included as potential racketeering activities, on occasion nonorganized-crime businesses have been charged with RICO violations. Because a firm's assets can be seized in advance of conviction, many individuals have plea bargained with prosecutors rather than risk having their businesses seized and disrupted under RICO.

Critics of the law argue prosecutors have extended RICO well beyond its original intent. RICO also allows private individuals harmed by violations to recover treble DAMAGES (three times the amount of their actual loss). Opponents contend this encourages lawsuits that would normally have been brought forth under civil suits. RICO defenders counter that the law provides an effective deterrent to unscrupulous businesses. Deceptive pricing, false ADVERTISING, and selling products of poorer quality than advertised, if committed through the mail or over the telephone, have been prosecuted under RICO.

Further reading

Mallor, Jane P., A. James Barnes, Thomas Bowers, Michael J. Philips, and Arlen W. Langvardt. *Business Law and the Regulatory Environment,* 11th ed. Boston: McGraw-Hill, 2001.

random-walk theory

The premise of the random-walk theory is that the STOCK MARKET's past movement cannot predict its future movement. The direction that a stock price will take cannot be determined by its past price history. In other words, the rise and fall of the stock market is completely random, so it is impossible to outperform the market on a consistent basis by predicting how it will perform. The theory also contends that although stocks move up and down in a completely random manner, they will maintain an upward trend over time.

The French mathematician Louis Bachelier (1870–1946) presented the random-walk theory in his dissertation "Theorie de la Spéculation" in 1890. In this work he talked about the random walk of financial market prices, among other topics. The term *random walk* derived from his analogy that trying to forecast market prices was like trying to predict the meandering steps of a drunkard. Unfortunately for Bachelier, his professors and colleagues did not support his ideas; he received a poor grade on his dissertation, was subsequently blackballed, and eventually dropped out of sight. He ended his days at an undistinguished teaching post in Besancon, and very little more is known of his life or his work. In 1953 statistician Maurice Kendall reexamined the random-walk theory, and in 1973 it gained great popularity with the publication of Burton Malkiel's book *A Random Walk Down Wall Street,* which has gone through many subsequent editions.

Today the basic idea of the random-walk theory is that the stock market is so efficient (information being dispersed so rapidly in the modern technology age) that it is impossible for anyone to take advantage of the information quickly enough to successfully buy and sell stocks without fear of losses. Trying to forecast the ups and downs of a stock is futile, because stocks have no regular pattern. In order to outperform or to at least try to outperform the market, one must be prepared to assume additional RISK. Malkiel, in fact, believes that a buy-and-hold strategy is statistically the best ways to go, as history has shown.

The random-walk theory has never been particularly popular on WALL STREET, because it promotes the belief that one cannot predict the rise and fall of the stock market and which stocks to choose, making it difficult for the financiers on Wall Street to capitalize on their INVESTMENT knowledge with the investing public. Wall Street's specialty is MONEY management and strategy, which is the opposite of the random-walk theory's posture. Today investment information is widely available to the general public, who now can do their own investing online without hiring professional investors to help them. If the public takes to heart the random-walk theory and its belief that it is difficult if not impossible to accurately predict a stock's path, they will likely have no need or desire for investing professionals at all.

There are three different versions of the random-walk theory, which is considered a major component of the EFFICIENT MARKET THEORY. The first is the "weak" version, a rather bare-bones theory that future stock or market prices cannot be predicted from past stock or market prices only. The "semi-strong" version promotes the idea that even by using all publicly available information (e.g., ANNUAL REPORTS, analyst reports) one still cannot predict future stock prices. This theory says that this published information has already been factored into a stock price, which leaves no surprise element. The third version is the "strong," which states that even insider knowledge of a stock will not help predict that stock's future price. Given today's efficient high-speed technology, the "strong" version holds that the stock market already knows everything there is to know, so the investor can never hold an advantage.

Not all experts believe that these three versions are entirely accurate. Many do believe in the market's effi-

ciency but also think there are some inefficiencies that may perhaps help the investor get an occasional advantage. For example, because market analysts do not always follow smaller firms, this information is sometimes not factored into their open-market prices. This means that the market is not really 100-percent accurate and opens the door to some investment opportunities. The strong-market theory is also diminished somewhat by the work of questionable individuals who gain insider information and throw the market somewhat off course.

There is another theory that views the markets as efficient but predictable. Andrew Lo, a professor of finance at the Sloan School of Management at the Massachusetts Institute of Technology, has published a book, *A Non-Random Walk Down Wall Street,* (2001) that goes against many of Burton Malkiel's theories. Lo believes that it is possible to outperform the markets to some degree if one is willing to commit the time to financial research and the money to current technology.

As it happens, most in the academic world do support the random-walk theory, but as the investment world for professionals and nonprofessionals becomes more technological and as more information becomes freely available, it is difficult to say how the theory will hold up in the coming years. With increasingly advanced financial tools, perhaps it is possible that investment predictions will become more accurate, but on the other hand, the market will have the same (if not even more advanced) tools, which would keep the market that one step ahead necessary to keep the random-walk theory vital.

Further reading
Lo, Andrew, and A. C. MacKinlay. *A Non-Random Walk Down Wall Street.* Princeton, N.J.: Princeton University Press, 2001; Malkiel, Burton G. *A Random Walk Down Wall Street,* 8th ed. New York: Norton, 2003.

—Patty Bergin

"rank and yank"   See FORCED-RANKING SYSTEMS.

real estate investment trusts
Real estate investment trusts (REITs) are companies that own and, in most cases, operate INCOME-producing real estate. Typically owners of apartments, shopping centers, offices, and warehouses, REITs take funds from investors and purchase real-estate ASSETS. REITs were created in 1960 to allow individual investors to participate in real-estate INVESTMENT. As of 2001, there were 300 REITs in the United States with approximately $300 billion in assets.

There are three general categories of REITs: EQUITY, MORTGAGE, and hybrid. Equity REITs own and operate income-producing real estate. They engage in leasing, or development of property and tenant management. Unlike other real-estate developers, REITs develop and acquire properties, which are then part of their investment portfolio rather than being resold to other investors. From 1960 to 1986, REITs were not allowed to directly manage properties; they could only invest in real estate. The Tax Reform Act of 1986 expanded the power of REITs to include owning and operating real estate. Mortgage REITs purchase mortgage-backed securities and lend MONEY directly to real-estate owners and operators. Most mortgage REITs extend credit on existing properties and do not engage in real-estate development. Hybrid REITs own properties and also make LOANS to real-estate owners. Some REITs own or lend in all areas of real estate, but most REITs specialize in one or two categories of real-estate investment, such as shopping malls, health-care facilities, apartments, etc. Some REITs invest throughout the United States, while others specialize in one region or city.

The major advantage of a REIT as a business organization is tax treatment. Unlike CORPORATIONS, REITs are allowed to deduct DIVIDENDs from their corporate tax bill. They are also required to distribute at least 90 percent of their taxable income to SHAREHOLDERS. REITs are thus effectively exempted from corporate taxation. The major disadvantage of REITs is the fact that they are required to distribute almost all of their income to shareholders. Many corporations retain all or most of their taxable income to reinvest in business activities. REITs have to find new investment CAPITAL in order to expand. Unlike PARTNERSHIPS, REITs are not allowed to pass through losses to shareholders, who would then deduct those losses on their personal income-tax return.

To qualify as a REIT for the INTERNAL REVENUE SERVICE, a REIT must

- be an entity that is taxable as a corporation
- be managed by a BOARD OF DIRECTORS or trustees
- have shares that are fully transferable
- have a minimum of 100 shareholders
- have no more than 50 percent of shares held by five or fewer individuals
- invest at least 75 percent of total assets in real-estate assets
- derive at least 75 percent of gross income from rents or interest on mortgages on real property.
- have no more than 20 percent of its assets of stocks in taxable REIT subsidiaries
- pay dividends of at least 90 percent of its taxable income in the form of shareholder dividends

REITs are considered relatively conservative, income-producing STOCK MARKET investments. REIT stockholders have suffered during periods of real-estate overexpansion but benefited during periods of peak demand for space. Stock-market analysts differ in evaluating the investment performance of REITs. Traditionally they estimated REITs' funds from operations (FFO) rather than net income. FFO was used because under GENERALLY ACCEPTED ACCOUNTING PRINCIPLES (GAAP), a real-estate company must depreciate the value of its properties, even though most real-estate properties appreciate in value. FFO standards, created by the National Association of Real Estate Investment Trusts in 1991, allowed REITs to add back real-estate DEPRECIATION and ignore gains from sales of properties when calculating FFO. Since 1991, some REITs have also excluded losses from investments (particularly, losses from technology and foreign-currency investments) and included funds for sales of depreciated property. In short, FFO has come to have many meanings among REIT managers and market analysts. In 2001, three WALL STREET firms agreed to review and forecast REITs' performances based on GAAP standards rather than the industry FFO figures.

Further reading
National Association of Real Estate Investment Trusts website. Available on-line. URL: www.nareit.org; Smith, Ray A. "REIT Wrangle: A Debate over Earnings Puts Major Wall Street Analysts at Odds," *Wall Street Journal,* 29 August 2001, p. C1.

real income
Real income is the INCOME purchasing power of an individual, group, or nation adjusted for changes in prices. If an individual's income rises faster than INFLATION, his or her real income has increased. Often the opposite occurs, and people's incomes rise at less than the rate of inflation. Frequently in the United States, workers and UNIONS representing workers begin wage negotiations by asking for a wage increase equal to the inflation rate of the previous year. Pensions and SOCIAL SECURITY payments include COLAs (COST-OF-LIVING ADJUSTMENTS) designed to allow recipients to maintain their level of real income. Many U.S. AGRICULTURAL SUPPORT PROGRAMS were initiated with the goal of increasing farm incomes equal to the increase in nonfarm incomes, thereby encouraging workers to remain in agriculture.

While support programs and COLAs can increase people's real incomes, it often results in "bracket creep," the movement into higher marginal tax brackets. The U.S. personal income-tax system is a progressive tax system; as nominal income increases, tax rates increase. Increased income to offset inflation may push individuals' taxable incomes into higher brackets, reducing their real and disposable incomes. Similarly, tax cuts without an increase in inflation increases people's real incomes.

recession
There are several ways to define a recession. The most commonly quoted definition is two consecutive quarters of declining real GROSS DOMESTIC PRODUCT (GDP). The "cocktail party" definition is "when your neighbor is unemployed but you still have your job." The NATIONAL

BUREAU OF ECONOMIC RESEARCH (NBER) Business Cycle Dating Committee is the ultimate arbiter of when recessions and expansions take place. The NBER defines a recession as "a recurring period of decline in total output, INCOME, EMPLOYMENT, and trade, usually lasting from six months to a year, and marked by widespread contractions in many sectors of the economy." This definition depends on how much of a decline, how long it lasts, and how many sectors in the economy are declining. The Business Cycle Dating Committee thus looks at the three Ds: depth, duration, and dispersion of an economic downturn.

Recessions comprise the contraction phase in BUSINESS CYCLES, the normal ups and downs of business activity in an economy. Unlike a depression, which is a severe, prolonged period of economic contraction, a recession usually lasts for less than a year. A "growth recession" is a period of slow growth (but not decline) in total output, income, employment, and trade, usually lasting a year or more.

Defining when a recession begins and ends is a difficult but important task. The NBER is a nonpartisan, nonprofit economic-research organization whose mission is to provide unbiased economic research among public policymakers, business professionals, and the academic community. Much to the dissatisfaction of Nobel Prizewinning economist Milton Friedman, the NBER defined the downturns in 1980–81 as two separate recessions. Some Reagan administration members wanted the period defined as one recession so it could be attributed to the Carter administration. The defeat of President George H. W. Bush in 1992 is largely attributed to the economic decline preceding the election. The NBER found the recession actually ended in March 1991, well before the election, but voters perceived a recession was still taking place in November.

Government leaders naturally want to intercede to counteract or minimize the impact of a recession. FISCAL POLICY and MONETARY POLICY can be used to stimulate economic activity. AUTOMATIC STABILIZERS (UNEMPLOYMENT and WELFARE benefits) help reduce the impact of falling incomes during a recession. In the period from World War II to the end of the century, there were seven recessions.

Further reading

Kulish, Nicholas. "What's a Recession? Two Negative Quarters? Not Really," *Wall Street Journal*, 10 January 2001, p. A2; National Bureau of Economic Research website. Available on-line. URL: www.nber.org.

reciprocity

Reciprocity includes the special allowances, preferences, and favors businesses extend to important customers and suppliers who are also customers. Often businesses will direct purchases toward companies that also buy products from them. Special credit arrangements, accelerated delivery, or customized service is offered to firms with which a company has developed reciprocity. Many reciprocal agreements are informal arrangements among area businesspeople to "take care" of each other. The U.S. Justice Department and FEDERAL TRADE COMMISSION scrutinize formal reciprocal business agreements, often viewing them as an attempt to reduce COMPETITION.

Reciprocity also refers to mutual recognition agreements among business professions. Historically many business professions were licensed by state agencies, requiring individuals wishing to work in more than one state to pass the certification requirements of each state in which they wanted to work. This limited competition within the state and required nonstate-licensed professionals to work with licensed professionals in the state. INSURANCE, law, contracting, and cosmetology are just a few business professions controlled by state licensing. Some states have signed reciprocity agreements, accepting the license from another state as a basis of certification.

On the international level, the WORLD TRADE ORGANIZATION adopted its Guidelines for Mutual Recognition Agreements, providing a common approach to negotiating reciprocity arrangements for business professionals operating in international trade. The NORTH AMERICAN FREE TRADE AGREEMENT (NAFTA) also expanded reciprocity agreements for business professionals working in North America. Thanks to U.S. LEADERSHIP in international SERVICES trade, reciprocal agreements allowing professionals to practice their trade in other countries has expanded opportunities for U.S. professionals abroad.

Further reading

Boone, Louis E., and David L. Kurtz. *Contemporary Marketing*, 10th ed. Fort Worth: Dryden Press, 2001.

recruiting   See EMPLOYEE RECRUITING.

reductions in force

Reductions in force (RIFs) are business decisions to reduce the number of employees, usually in order to reduce COSTS. Also called LAYOFFS, downsizing, and even rightsizing, RIFs became a common business decision in the 1990s. Most companies and organizations have RIF policies, which are usually based on SENIORITY (i.e., last in, first out). Part of the problem is that this does not always allow a company to keep its most productive workers, and depending on EMPLOYMENT contracts, may not save the company money immediately.

In addition to stipulations in employment CONTRACTS, RIFs are often subject to COLLECTIVE BARGAINING agreements. One difficulty is defining seniority, which can be interpreted based on how long a worker has been with the company or has been part of a particular organization or division within the company. Most RIF policies give terminated workers first option for reemployment should the company later hire workers for the same or similar jobs.

Companies considering reductions in force have a variety of alternatives to achieve the goal of reducing costs. In addition to layoffs, reductions in force can be accomplished through attrition, early retirement incentives, job sharing, part-time employment, voluntary time-off programs, and across-the-board salary reductions. After September 11, 2001, many companies, particularly in the tourism and travel industries, instituted many of these programs in order to reduce costs in a time of reduced DEMAND.

Two federal programs affect reductions in force determinations. the WORKER ADJUSTMENT AND RETRAINING NOTIFICATION ACT (WARN) and TRADE-ADJUSTMENT ASSISTANCE (TAA) program. WARN requires employers covered by the act to provide 60-day advance notice of large-scale employment loss, generally resulting from plant closings and mass layoffs. WARN became law in 1989 and generally applies to companies and nonprofit groups with 100 or more employees. Hourly, salaried, and managerial workers are all entitled to notification under WARN, including when the sale of a business will result in mass layoffs of plant closings.

WARN defines employment loss as

- employment termination, other than a discharge for cause, voluntary departure, or retirement
- a layoff exceeding 6 months
- a reduction in an employee's hours of work of more than 50 percent in each month of any 6-month period.

Trade-adjustment assistance refers to government-sponsored training programs and supplemental cash unemployment compensation provided to workers who lose their jobs due to increased foreign competition. TAA grew out of programs intended to aid Americans who were dislocated when the European Community (now the EUROPEAN UNION) was established. The first assistance program was authorized in the Trade Expansion Act of 1962; however, no assistance was actually provided until 1969.

Under TAA, workers may petition the U.S. secretary of labor for assistance. The secretary must certify that workers have been or are threatened with job losses, that the firm's sales or PRODUCTION or both have decreased absolutely, and that increased IMPORTS of articles like or directly competitive with those made by the workers or the firm for which the workers provide essential goods or SERVICES "contributed importantly" to job separation or decline.

The most visible trade-adjustment assistance program is the NAFTA-TAA. Between 1994 and 1997, almost 100,000 American workers were certified for trade-adjustment assistance. This number was often used to show the adverse impact of the NORTH AMERICAN FREE TRADE AGREEMENT (NAFTA), but TAA certification does not necessarily mean workers have been displaced, only that there is the potential for workers to lose their jobs due to imports. In NAFTA's first three years, slightly more than 12,000 workers received NAFTA-TAA. Many workers who have lost their jobs are encouraged by state officials to apply for TAA, thereby reducing the state costs for UNEMPLOYMENT compensation.

Further reading

Fisher, Cynthia D., Lyle F. Schoenfeldt, and James B. Shaw. *Human Resource Management,* 5th ed. Boston: Houghton Mifflin, 2003; Folsom, Ralph H., and W. Davis Folsom. *NAFTA Law and Business.* The Hague: Kluwer International, 1999; U.S. Department of Labor WARN fact sheet. Available on-line. URL: www.doleta.gov/programs/factsht/warn.htm.

relationship marketing

Relationship marketing is an ongoing interaction between buyers and sellers in which sellers actively work to improve their understanding of buyers' needs, and buyers become increasingly loyal to the sellers because their needs are being so well satisfied. Relationship marketing is based on the understanding that, in most market situations, it is infinitely easier and less expensive to maintain and cultivate relationships with existing customers than to find and build relationships with new customers.

Marketers adopting relationship marketing strategies take a long-term perspective, emphasize retaining customers, emphasize customer service, engage customers frequently, are committed to their customers, attempt to build cooperation and trust, and commit everyone in the organization to providing quality products and services. Relationship marketing contrasts with transaction marketing, in which buyer-seller exchanges are characterized by limited communications and little or no ongoing relationship between the two parties. For example, when traveling, consumers often purchase products or services from street vendors whom they will likely never see or purchase from again. The relationship exists only as long as it takes to make the transaction.

In some countries, even travelers' exchanges can evolve into relationships. Often merchants will begin the selling process by serving copious amounts of tea and then have a customer return for fitting a dress or ring spending hours in the exchange process. These merchants have been practicing relationship marketing for centuries, though the practice is relatively new in the United States.

Relationship marketing is based on promises that go beyond the obvious assurances customers expect. Any company that earns CUSTOMER LOYALTY probably does so by exceeding expectations, providing exceptional service or quality, or taking the time to get to know its customers. Relationship marketing involves bonding, empathy, reciprocity, and trust. Bonding means developing mutual interests or needs that tie customers and marketers together. Empathy is the ability to see situations from the perspective of the other person. Reciprocity is the give-and-take between buyers and sellers to address unforeseen circumstances and problems. Trust is the confidence buyers and sellers have in each other.

There are three levels of trust in relationship marketing: financial, social, and structural. Financial relationships are based on incentives for the customer to continue to do business with the firm. Airline frequent-flyer programs are an example of a financial relationship. Social relationships are based on interactions at a social level. Newsletters and events engaging customers on a social level build relationships. Many universities recognize their alumni are their best sales representatives and cultivate those relationships through alumni organizations. Structural relationships are close partnerships between buyers and sellers. Previously in the United States, most business buyers had only a transactions-based relationship with their vendors. In the 1990s, businesses found trusted partners could be a valuable source of ideas and cost savings. Vendors now often have representatives working directly with their customers, reordering materials as needed without negotiations. Just-in-time delivery systems are an example of structural relationships between buyers and sellers.

Relationship marketers often use the saying, "The only way I want to lose a customer is if they DOMA (Die Or Move Away)!" They also recognize the lifetime value of a customer, the revenues and intangible benefits, including customer referrals and feedback over the life of the relationship less the cost to acquire, market to, and service the customer. Even so, sometimes marketers will terminate a relationship, as will customers. A highly demanding, small-volume customer may not be valuable enough to build and sustain a relationship.

Further reading

Boone, Louis E., and David L. Kurtz. *Contemporary Marketing.* 10th ed. Fort Worth: Dryden Press, 2001.

rent-control laws   See PRICE CEILINGS, PRICE CONTROLS.

repurchase agreements, reverse repurchase agreements

Repurchase agreements are lending agreements between borrowers and lenders. The borrower gets MONEY by entering into an agreement in which he or she sells securities that he/she owns and simultaneously agrees to repurchase them at a specific time and price. Since the repurchase is for a specific time and price, the RISK of ownership in fact continues to rest on the borrower. In other words, if the security's price should fall, it hurts the borrower and not the lender, since the borrower has to buy it back at the end of the loan at the agreed price. The contrary is also true. If the security goes up in value during the time of the loan, the benefits of the increase falls on the borrower, since he or she is going to buy it back at the specific price. Since this ownership risk continues to rest on the borrower, the transaction is properly thought of as a borrowing/lending arrangement instead of a security sale. The lender can feel better about the loan, since the collateral is actually owned by the lender.

The difference between repurchase agreements and reverse repurchase agreements is only a matter of perspective. The case described above is from the borrower's perspective. The borrower sells the stock and agrees to repurchase it, so it is called a repurchase agreement. A reverse repurchase agreement is when someone has some money he or she would like to lend and buy stock with a simultaneous agreement to sell the stock back to the original owner/borrower for an agreed price and on an agreed date. The correct term to use depends on who initiated the arrangement. If the borrower initiated the agreement, it is a repurchase agreement. If the lender initiated the agreement, it is a reverse repurchase agreement.

These repurchase agreements (often called "repos" or "RPs") are usually for very short periods of time—maybe just overnight or for a couple of days. A long-term RP may last a few months. As explained above, the borrower still maintains the risk of ownership, but during the time of the RP agreement, the borrower has lost control over the security. Thus, if the price should be falling, the borrower is losing money and is not able to do anything about it, such as sell the stock until it is redeemed from the lender. For this reason RPs make sense for only a short period of time.

In many cases the RP CONTRACT is organized using government and other low-risk securities. This reduces the lender's risk of the loan's collateral falling below the amount loaned. Often the lenders require the underlying security collateral to be greater than the loan. This excess of collateral over the amount loaned is humorously named "a haircut." A haircut protects the lender if security price falls during the time of the agreement.

The repo contracts usually involve large amounts of money, which are often arranged in blocks of $10 million and are usually overnight contracts. The agreement normally specifies a certain interest rate paid by the borrower when the stocks are repurchased. Any appreciation in the stock or security payments such as DIVIDENDs paid during the loan reverts to the borrower.

Since the amounts involved are fairly large, usually institutional investors (instead of individuals) are involved in repurchase agreements. These INVESTMENTs are subject to some restrictions regarding to the risk investors can assume. For example, a city government may restrict its treasurer to only low-risk investments such as treasury BONDS issued by the U.S. government. However, buying these bonds as an outright purchase may involve a relatively long-term commitment of the city's funds. The treasurer can lend money in the repurchase agreements and only involve the city's money for a short period of time. The treasurer can specifically design the repos' maturities to fit his overall cash-flow needs.

Interestingly, the FEDERAL RESERVE SYSTEM (the Fed) uses repurchase agreements as one of its OPEN-MARKET OPERATIONS. If it desires to exert upward pressure on INTEREST RATES, the Fed enters into repurchase agreements as the borrower. If it wants to exert downward pressure on interest rates, it enters into repurchase agreements as the lender. The duration of the agreement may be for just a night but is often for a couple of weeks. Any effect on the interest rate that is accomplished when the Fed enters into one of these agreements is reversed when the agreement matures. It is not unusual for the Fed to enter into as much as $6 billion of these agreements a day.

—Mack Tennyson

request for proposal, invitation to bid

A request for proposal (RFP) solicits offers from suppliers of goods or SERVICES needed by an organization. Similar terms are invitation to bid and request for quotation. Each term is associated with a different degree of request specificity and different procedures and expectations on the part of all parties involved.

In the RFP process, the buyer typically transmits a precise statement of its requirements to several potential suppliers who are qualified to provide the goods or services required. The buyer does not develop precise specifications (e.g., military specifications) but does expect suppliers to present their own design and/or specifications, either standard or customized PRODUCTS, to fulfill the requirements. Often the successful supplier is required to provide substantial performance guarantees.

The RFP process is often used in the procurement of major CAPITAL EXPENDITURE, large information-technology systems, commercial building development, etc. In some cases, financing of the purchase is a required component of the proposal. The buyer is free to accept the proposal it deems best. Often negotiations between the buyer and one or more potential suppliers take place before a decision is made. To balance this apparently superior position for the buyer, the bidder can withdraw a proposal at any time before an award is made. The RFP is more commonly used by businesses than by government bodies, which have more rigid guidelines to follow.

In an invitation to bid, more precise specifications and/or detailed plans are given to the bidders, who are expected to comply with them exactly. Typically less effort is put into prequalifying bidders, and there are larger numbers of bidders. Usually the buyer is obligated to accept the lowest price bid, provided it meets the specifications and all other given terms and conditions. Often in the construction industry, bidders are obligated to provide bonding to insure that they be able to fulfill their obligations. The most rigid procedures involve "sealed bids," which are opened in a public setting, with pricing and other details of bids revealed to all interested parties. This process is often used in governmental PURCHASING and less frequently in private-sector settings.

The request for quotation process has implications similar to bidding, but the term is generally used when dealing with services and goods outside the construction industry. The potential supplier is commonly called the "bidder" regardless of whether asked for bids, proposals, quotations, offers, etc., in order to avoid awkward wording situations. Sample documents and typical terms and conditions to be used in the RFP (or similar) processes are available from many trade or business organizations. Commercially available print resources include Baker's *Purchasing Factomatic: A Portfolio of Successful Forms, Reports, Records and Procedures*, published 1976 and still in print. At the INSTITUTE FOR SUPPLY MANAGEMENT website, one can obtain resource guides and other materials (with prices reduced for members).

Further reading

Baker, R. Jerry. *Purchasing Factomatic: A Portfolio of Successful Forms, Reports, Records and Procedures.* Upper Saddle River, N.J.: Prentice Hall 1977; Cavinato, Joseph. *Purchasing Handbook,* 6th ed. New York: McGraw-Hill, 2001; Institute for Supply Management website. Available on-line. URL: www.ism.ws.

—David G. Spoolstra

research and development

Research is an investigation or experiment aimed at the discovery and interpretation of facts, revision of accepted theories or laws in the light of new facts, or practical application of such new or revised theories or laws. Development is the act of putting new information, research, or ideas into practice.

Research and development (R&D) is critical to growth at both the company and national economy levels. One business saying goes, "If you are not growing, you are dying." One way a firm can grow is through finding or creating new PRODUCTs. When many firms in a country engage in R&D, the overall economy is likely to grow. One measure of R&D used by development economists is the number of PATENTS issued within a country each year. In some industries, STOCK MARKET analysts use the amount or percentage of sales that a company spends on R&D as an indicator of likely future growth.

There are two basic types of research: basic and applied. Basic research is directed toward a generalized goal. Applied research directs the results of basic research towards the needs of a specific firm or industry, with the goal of developing new or modified products or processes. In addition to carrying out basic and applied research, an R&D staff may also be asked to evaluate the efficiency and cost of PRODUCTION using different technologies.

In the United States, the federal government funds a considerable portion of basic research. The National Institutes of Health (NIH), U.S. Department of Agriculture (USDA), and National Science Foundation (NSF) and other agencies oversee the allocation of funds for research. Competition for funds is intense, and federal allocation decisions significantly influence the direction of basic research. Federal funds are also often used to finance specific industry research. For example, the federal government supports R&D efforts for the creation of alternative vehicles, subsidizing efforts by the major automobile manufacturers.

See also ECONOMIC GROWTH.

Further reading
Gaither, Norman, and Greg Frazier. *Operational Management*, 9th ed. Cincinnati, Ohio: South-Western Publishing, 2002.

reserve requirements
Reserve requirements, imposed by the FEDERAL RESERVE SYSTEM, mandate that commercial banks and other depository institutions keep a certain percentage of their deposits in accounts with the Federal Reserve Bank (the central bank in the United States, known as the Fed) or as cash in their vaults. Reserve requirements ensure liquidity in the BANKING SYSTEM and allow the Fed to exercise greater control over the MONEY SUPPLY.

Along with changes in the DISCOUNT RATE and OPEN-MARKET OPERATIONS, changes in the reserve requirements comprise one of the major tools used in MONETARY POLICY, whose goals are ECONOMIC GROWTH and price stability, with primary emphasis on price stability. By changing the percentage of deposits banks must keep in their vault or on deposit, the Fed can influence the ability of banks to make LOANS and in the process create MONEY in the economy. An increase in the reserve requirement will reduce the money supply, while a decrease will allow expansion of the money supply.

The Federal Reserve was first given authority to change reserve requirements in the 1930s. During the GREAT DEPRESSION, many U.S. banks, alarmed by "runs" (large numbers of customers demanding their deposits back), increased their holdings of excess reserves. Fearing banks would lend out these excess reserves and create an uncontrollable expansion of the money supply, the Fed raised reserve requirements three times in 1936 and 1937. This resulted in a slowdown in the growth of the money supply, increasing INTEREST RATES and contributing to the RECESSION of 1937–38. Since then, the Fed has made much more limited use of changing reserve requirements as a policy tool.

As of 1999 all depository institutions were subject to the following reserve requirements.

- 3 percent on the bank's first $44.3 million of checkable deposits
- 10 percent on checkable deposits greater than $44.3 million

Checkable deposits include noninterest-bearing checking accounts, NOW accounts, super-NOW accounts, and automatic transfer savings accounts. The Fed has authority to change the 10-percent requirement in a range of 8–14 percent, and in extraordinary conditions it could be raised as high as 18 percent.

Further reading
Mishkin, Frederic S. *The Economics of Money, Banking, and Financial Markets*, 6th ed. Boston: Addison Wesley, 2001.

residual value (salvage value)
Associated with the accounting for long-term ASSETS, residual value, alternatively called salvage value, is the estimated disposal value of an asset at the end of its useful life. Residual value is the proceeds a firm expects to receive if a long-term asset is sold after it has been fully depreciated.

Because the residual value is expected to be recouped when the asset is sold, the BOOK VALUE (or carrying value) of a long-term asset cannot be less than the asset's residual value. In other words, assets cannot be depreciated to the extent where the accumulated DEPRECIATION results in a book value lower than salvage value. Thus, a long-term asset is fully depreciated when its book value is equal to its salvage value. In terms of the asset's depreciation schedule, this occurs at the end of the asset's useful life.

Resolution Trust Corporation
The Resolution Trust Corporation (RTC) was created in 1989 as part of the Financial Institutions Reform, Recovery, and Enforcement Act to manage, sell, and liquidate bankrupt SAVINGS AND LOAN ASSOCIATIONS (S&Ls). The RTC seized the ASSETS of 750 S&Ls, one-fourth of all the savings and loan organizations in the country. In doing so, it resolved the savings and loan crisis that had begun in the early 1980s.

Historically, most S&Ls were mutual associations aggregating funds from members—often people from one community, ethnic group or working in one industry—and then lending the funds to members. They primarily made fixed-interest-rate LOANS to individuals purchasing homes. Changes in banking laws during the GREAT DEPRESSION allowed S&Ls to pay a slightly higher interest rate to depositors than commercial banks were allowed to pay. For decades they followed what was known as the "3-6-3 rule": pay depositors 3 percent, lend to borrowers at 6 percent, and play golf at 3 P.M. However, in the early 1980s, with high rates of INFLATION (then exceeding 10 percent) and government-restricted rates on deposits, at the time around 5 percent, S&L depositors were losing purchasing power of their savings and so began looking for alternative places to deposit their savings. In addition, the value of S&L assets—specifically home MORTGAGES—was declining in value. During periods of inflation, INTEREST RATES rise, decreasing the value of fixed-INCOME securities, mortgages, and BONDS.

Initial government attempts to address the S&L crisis included DEREGULATION of the industry (Depository Institutions Deregulation and Monetary Control Act, 1980) and granting greater authority to S&Ls to invest in alternatives to home mortgages (Depository Institutions Act, 1982). To many observers, these legislative initiatives appeared to be using Band-Aids to try to stop a hemorrhage, and many S&L industry members took an attitude of "when this crisis gets big enough, the government will step in and resolve it."

The RTC, using funds from government-backed bonds, increased INSURANCE premiums to S&Ls, and assessments to the FEDERAL HOME LOAN BANK SYSTEM reorganized insolvent S&Ls. Most insolvent thrifts were sold to solvent banks and thrift institutions, and the RTC transferred deposits and assets to the purchasing institution at a discount. Critics noted that most failed S&Ls were sold to already large lending institutions, hastening the consolidation of the banking industry at terms attractive to existing institutions. Primarily using taxpayer funds, the RTC sold off the insolvent institutions and went out of business at the end of 1995. The estimated cost of the S&L bailout to U.S. taxpayers differs, depending on how COSTS are estimated. Conservative estimates state the cost at $150 billion, while others estimate it at over $500 billion.

Further reading
Ely, David P., and Nikhil P. Variaya. "Opportunity costs incurred by the RTC in cleaning up S&L insolvencies," *Quarterly Review of Economics and Finance* 36, no. 3 (Fall 1996); Mishkin, Frederic. *The Economics of Money, Banking, and Financial Markets,* 6th ed. Boston: Addison Wesley, 2001.

Resource Conservation and Recovery Act
The Resource Conservation and Recovery Act (RCRA, 1970) regulates the identification, transportation, treatment, storage, and disposal of solid and hazardous wastes. The act directs the ENVIRONMENTAL PROTECTION AGENCY (EPA) to regulate hazardous waste "from cradle to grave." Specifically, the act regulates such matters as

- hazardous waste generators and transporters
- land-disposal restrictions
- federal procurement of PRODUCTS containing recycled materials
- municipal solid-waste landfill criteria
- solid and hazardous waste recycling
- treatment, storage, and disposal facilities
- waste minimization and hazardous waste combustion

As amended in 1984, RCRA also covers the siting, constructing, and monitoring of underground petroleum storage tanks.

The RCRA's goals are to

- protect human health and the environment from the hazards posed by waste disposal
- conserve energy and natural resources through waste recycling and recovery
- reduce or eliminate the amount of waste generated
- ensure that wastes are managed in a manner that is protective of human health and the environment

While the SUPERFUND addresses previously mismanaged hazardous wastes, the RCRA attempts to regulate waste management to prevent threats to human health and the environment. The RCRA involves a variety of government agencies, including the EPA's Office of Solid Waste and Emergency Response (OSWER) and EPA regional offices, states, and communities.

Prior to the RCRA's passage, there were many predictions of landfills brimming at capacity and the threat of not having access to waste disposal in the near future. Landfills were often a major environmental problem unto themselves, contaminating ground and surface waters. Since its passage, the RCRA has had significant impact on business practices, primarily in the areas of waste minimization and recycling. With the 1984 amendments, many companies were forced to remove and replace old, leaking petroleum storage tanks. Medical businesses also had to change their waste-disposal practices in response to the new regulations. One of the most controversial management issues associated with RCRA is control of hazardous-waste combustion, or burning of hazardous materials. Many communities and environmental groups have challenged safety and management practices at hazardous waste incineriary sites.

Further reading
Environmental Protection Agency website. Available on-line. URL: www.epa.gov.

resources
Resources, also referred to as factors of PRODUCTION, are the inputs used in production of goods and SERVICES. Economists typically categorize resources into three groups: human, natural, and CAPITAL. HUMAN RESOURCES include physical and mental labor and ENTREPRENEURSHIP, the actions people take in organizing and creating risk-taking enterprises. Natural resources include minerals, land, water, and forests. Capital resources include buildings, machinery, and human capital, the investments in training and education that increase labor productivity. Economists also differentiate between renewable resources and nonrenewable resources (those that cannot be replenished). Control of land, mineral, and human resources has been a major factor in most of the world's wars and revolutions over the last 500 years.

The abundance or scarcity of resources combined with the DEMAND for particular resources determines their market prices. In the CIRCULAR FLOW MODEL of capitalist economic systems, households control most resources (the source of supply). Businesses purchase resources (the source of demand) in order to produce goods and services for the marketplace. Those businesses that provide what consumers want and need are able to purchase additional resources and grow, while those businesses that do not use resources efficiently will decline or disappear. The 18th-century Scottish philosopher, Adam Smith, described the process of resource (and PRODUCT) allocation in a market system "as if guided by an invisible hand," producing a result not intended by businesses or consumers. This is known as ECONOMIC EFFICIENCY.

Control and allocation of collective resources presents a difficult issue. In a socialist economic system, most resources are owned and allocated by the governing group. Even in capitalist economic systems, numerous resources are collectively controlled and allocated. In many countries, mineral resources such as oil and natural gas are collectively owned. Decisions regarding extraction and use of these nonrenewable resources are a source of debate and are influenced by current prices and the OPPORTUNITY COSTS of not selling them.

Decisions regarding collectively owned renewable resources face the problem of sustainable development, limiting the resource's utilization and harvesting so that it will be available and productive in future time periods. Resource managers have devised many different methods to conserve renewable resources. For example, fisheries managers limit the harvesting season, the type of equipment used, and the number of licenses available in order to prevent resource depletion. For decades Long Island Sound oyster harvesters working public beds were restricted to using two-foot-wide dredges operated under sail power. Economists refer to this as institutionalized inefficiency.

Resource allocation is also illustrated in PRODUCTION-POSSIBILITIES CURVES. Only when resources are achieving their most productive uses will an economic system be operating along its production-possibilities curve. Changes in technology frequently influence the productivity and demand for resources. Often technological advances reduce or eliminate the demand for resources. A classic example is the whaling industry. Whalers searched dangerous and distant places for whales to make whale oil until the development of oil-refining technology made them obsolete. One of the challenges for workers, particularly college students, is the fact that by the time they finish college, "hot" job markets are often saturated with new workers (resources), limiting opportunities for new entrants.

See also CAPITALISM; SUSTAINABLE GROWTH AND DEVELOPMENT; SOCIALISM.

restraints of trade

Restraints of trade of various types are unlawful according to COMMON LAW and under state and federal ANTITRUST LAWS. In common law, covenants not to compete given by employees to employers and sellers of businesses to buyers are the most commonly contested restraints of trade. The law on covenants not to compete varies substantially from state to state, although courts generally are more willing to enforce sellers' promises not to compete than those of employees whose livelihoods may be at stake upon termination of EMPLOYMENT.

Restraints of trade are prohibited under most state antitrust laws and the federal SHERMAN ANTITRUST ACT. Courts have interpreted these prohibitions over many years to cover PRICE FIXING and market-division agreements among competitors, resale price maintenance and market division rules in distribution CONTRACTS, "tying arrangements" (the coerced purchase of unwanted goods or SERVICES), group BOYCOTTS (collective refusals to deal), exclusive dealing contracts, and other trade-restrictive business agreements and practices.

Broadly speaking, only "unreasonable" restraints of trade are illegal. Many of the types of restraints of trade noted above have been deemed unreasonable.

Further reading
Gelhorn, Ernest, and William E. Kovacic. *Antitrust Law and Economics in a Nutshell,* 4th ed. Eagan, Minn.: West Group, 1994.

restrictive covenants

Restrictive covenants limit the ability of a seller or employee to compete in the future with the firm with which they are doing business or currently employed. Restrictive covenants are most frequently found in CONTRACTS for the sale of businesses and professional practices and in EMPLOYMENT contracts. Managers and employees with business KNOW-HOW are often required to sign contracts with restrictive covenants as a condition of employment. Limitations stipulated in contracts often concern time, geographic area, and subject matter. COMMON LAW, RESTRAINTS OF TRADE doctrine, and statutes employing a rule of reason analysis traditionally govern restrictive covenants. Restrictive covenants are generally enforceable if they are reasonable as to time, geographic range, and subject matter. However, covenants not to compete are considered by courts relative to the individual market circumstances, and as such they make each situation unique.

For example, the Connecticut Supreme Court found that restrictive covenants must be reasonable within the context in which they appear. In the sale of a barbershop, a covenant restricting the seller from establishing another barbershop for five years in the same city was considered reasonable. The Connecticut Supreme Court also determined that covenants not to compete found in employment contracts must meet certain requirements to be binding and valid. First, the covenant must be limited with regard to time and place. Second, it must be reasonable in the sense that it should afford only fair protection to the interests of the party seeking the covenant and not be so restrictive that it might interfere with the public's interests. The court found that a covenant precluding an employee from pursuing an occupation was unenforceable. The court did find a contract restricting an employee from management of a specific type of business anywhere in the state for five years was reasonable and enforceable. But covenants in employment contracts covering areas in which the employer does not do business or is unlikely to do business are likely to be held unreasonable.

Further reading
Folsom, Ralph H., and Michael Gordon. *International Business Transactions,* 5th ed. Eagan, Minn.: West Group, 2002.

retailing

Retailing is the selling of goods and SERVICES to final consumers. Retailing in the United States is big business; approximately one-fifth of all U.S. GROSS DOMESTIC PRODUCT is transacted through retailers. Wal-Mart, the country's largest retail company, sells nearly $140 billion annually and now operates in dozens of countries around the world.

Within marketing DISTRIBUTION CHANNELS, retailers serve the functions of providing small quantities for frequent and assorted consumer purchases, customer service, and an environment conducive to shopping. One retailing slogan is, "Have the right product in the right place at the right time for the right price."

One distinguishing feature about retailing is environment, including the layout, color, sound, lighting, displays, and other features created to stimulate consumer interest and PURCHASING. Simple measures like the amount of lighting in a store and its sounds and smells can affect CONSUMER BEHAVIOR. For PRODUCTS consumers want to inspect closely, bright lighting is important; for other products, lower levels of lighting can enhance the store's atmosphere. Some bookstores have learned to place a coffee shop near the front of the store so consumers can immediately smell coffee aromas as they walk in. Fish departments are often placed in the rear of a store for just the opposite effect.

Customer service is another important consideration in retailing strategy. Credit, delivery, check cashing, gift wrapping, rest rooms, repair services, warranties, return privileges, sales assistance, play areas for children, and waiting areas for spouses are just some of the customer-service issues that retailers have to address.

It is often said that the three most important factors in retailing success is location, location, and location. Retailers generally develop locations accessible to TARGET MARKETS with sufficient numbers of potential customers and adjacent to stores with either complementary or competing products. Major retail companies have departments whose sole function is to evaluate future locations using DEMOGRAPHICS, highway traffic counts, and local zoning laws.

In addition to location considerations, retailers vary their retailing strategy depending on the type of business they are developing. Retail strategy includes number of outlets, merchandise number and assortment of items, PRICING STRATEGIES, environment, and MARKETING COMMUNICATIONS (ADVERTISING, SALES PROMOTION, and PERSONAL SELLING). For example, convenience-store strategy includes numerous outlets, easy access, less variety, higher prices, and minimal advertising and promotion. By contrast, warehouse stores have few outlets, large selection, low prices, and advertising that emphasizes expanding membership. Department stores also have few outlets, extensive assortment, and depth in product offerings; they also put less emphasis on price competitiveness but more on the store's environment and heavy use of advertising, sales staff, and displays.

Retailers face a variety of ethical and legal issues, including shoplifting, consumer FRAUD, supplier practices, and use of customer information. Shoplifting, or "shrink" as retail managers often call it, is a major cost. Retailers use many different methods to reduce shoplifting losses, including electronic tags, guards, observation booths, and monitors. One of the major sources of shoplifting losses is employee theft.

Consumer fraud—whether changing price tags, taking a product off the shelf and then "returning" it for a refund, or purchasing products with the intention of returning them for a refund when finished—reduce retailer PROFITs. In recent years retailers have increasingly needed to address criticism for using unethical suppliers. Reports of "sweatshops" employing children and of environmentally irresponsible manufacturers have forced retailers to monitor their suppliers more closely. Lastly, the nature of their work means that retailers have access to considerable information about their customers. How they use that information is of increasing concern to consumers.

retained earnings   See DIVIDENDS, RETAINED EARNINGS.

retirement plan

A retirement provides retirement INCOME to an employee or results in a deferral of income by employees during their EMPLOYMENT or beyond. It is a cash benefit created by government, the employer, or the employee to cover the period after the employee retires. In the United States, retirement plans include SOCIAL SECURITY (Old Age and Survivors Income), KEOGH PLANS, INDIVIDUAL RETIREMENT ACCOUNTS (IRAs), 401(K) PLANS and 403(b) and 457 plans. In most cases the employer governs the options available to employees. In some plans, employers determine whether the company pays all or part of the contributions; in other plans, employees determine contributions.

The most popular and mandatory plan is Social Security, which was designed as a safety net for retired and disabled workers. President Franklin D. Roosevelt introduced the Social Security Act in 1935 as part of his New Deal legislation. In the United States today, over 90 percent retirees age 65 and older receive Social Security. In 2002 Social Security was funded through a payroll tax of 15.3 percent of wage income up to approximately $80,000, divided equally between employers and employees. Self-employed individuals pay both parts of the tax. By 2006 workers will have to be 66 years of age to receive full benefits, a figure that will rise gradually for future generations.

IRAs are employee-controlled advisor-managed retirement plans. Created in 1974 under the EMPLOYEE RETIREMENT INCOME SECURITY ACT (ERISA), IRAs encourage employees to save and supplement Social Security benefits. Congress frequently changes IRA laws, but as of 2003 traditional IRAs allow workers and their spouses (subject to income limits) to contribute $3,000 each to their IRA accounts. These contributions are tax-deferred, meaning the amount is reduced from a worker's current taxable income and taxes are paid when the individual withdraws the funds from his or her IRA account. Retirees can begin withdrawing at age 59½ and must begin withdrawing by age 70½. The penalty for early withdrawal of IRA funds is steep—10 percent of the amount withdrawn. Both the contributions to and the income generated from IRA INVESTMENTs are tax-deferred, providing greater returns than if the individual invested after-tax income.

In the 1990s, Congress created so-called Roth IRAs (named after Senator William V. Roth Jr. of Delaware). Roth IRAs allow anyone to contribute up to $2,000 per year to an investment account, without income restrictions. The contribution is not tax deductible, but the income earned is tax-deferred until the funds are withdrawn.

Self-employed individuals can create their own IRAs or Keogh retirement plans. Keogh plans, which are also sometimes called "qualified plans" or "H.R. 10 plans," were named after U.S. Representative Eugene James Keogh and were first introduced in the 1960s. These plans offer significant benefits over traditional IRA plans for self-employed individuals and their employees. Like traditional IRAs, Keogh plans allow for contribution to a retirement account, and the worker's contribution is pretax, which reduces his or her taxable income. This MONEY can be invested, and the interest from investments is tax-free until the money is withdrawn from the plan. There is an additional tax advantage to employers who receive a "dollar for dollar" tax write-off for any money contributed to an employee's plan. The chief advantage of a Keogh plan over a traditional retirement account is the fact that it is possible to contribute more money annually. The amount of contribution possible depends on the Keogh plan chosen, but it is generally a maximum of $40,000 per year in 2002 (although this changes often due to legislation and INFLATION).

Most CORPORATIONs in the United States offer retirement plans to their employees. A major distinction is whether the plan is a defined-benefit or defined-contribution. A defined-benefit plan is set up to give individuals a desired income upon retirement. Employees and their employers contribute to a retirement account, which is controlled by an employer-designated trustee. The employee has no input into how the funds are invested. At retirement, the employee receives a pension, usually based on a percentage of the employee's income and years of service with the organization. The employee is usually given an option to take a lower monthly benefit and extend the payment over his/her life and the life of his/her spouse. With defined-benefit plans, employees who leave a company can leave their funds in the employer's retirement plan, "roll over" their pensions into an IRA, or buy into the retirement plan offered by their new employer.

In most U.S. corporations, defined-benefit plans have been replaced by defined-contribution plans. This transfers the RISK and responsibility for retirement income from the employer to the employee. It also allows employees to control their retirement funds as they move from one employer to another, in effect creating a portable retirement plan. Many times employers impose vesting requirements on their contributions to employees' retirement plans. In 2002 employer restrictions prevented Enron employees from liquidating their holdings of Enron stock in their retirement plans, resulting in both the loss of their jobs and pension funds. Enron imposed a "blackout" period on employee access to their retirement funds just as the company's financial problems were being exposed. The blackout had been announced in advance as the company was changing the plan administrator.

Defined-contribution plans are known as the 400 plans (401(k), 403(b), and 457). Like defined-benefit plans and IRAs, contributions to 400 plans are tax-deferred. With defined-contribution plans, there are several ways that the money can be contributed. One option is the PROFIT SHARING plan, which allows employers to disburse a percentage of the firm's profits to employees. Another option is a money-purchase plan in which the employer is required to contribute a set percentage of the employee's compensation regardless of whether the company makes a profit or not. It is also possible to combine the profit-sharing and money-purchase options so that a portion is at the discretion of the employer and a portion is set. Many employers have set matching-contribution plans whereby the employer will match up to a set percentage of the employee's income contributed to the plan.

See also SIMPLIFIED EMPLOYEE PENSION.

Further reading
Cross, W. *Retirement Handbook.* New York: Henry Holt, 1993.

—Lourdes Owens

revenue expenditure   See CAPITAL EXPENDITURE, REVENUE EXPENDITURE.

RICO   See RACKETEER INFLUENCED CORRUPT ORGANIZATION ACT.

right-to-know laws

Right-to-know laws are state laws that expand upon federal laws requiring employers to inform employees about hazardous substances that they may encounter in the workplace. Federal laws overseen by the OCCUPATIONAL SAFETY AND HEALTH ADMINISTRATION (OSHA) provide the primary rules regarding workplace safety. Approximately 30 states have passed additional right-to-know laws. Cynthia Lyle Fisher, Schoenfeldt, and James Shaw cite typical features in state right-to-know laws, including the following.

1. Employers have an obligation to post on bulletin boards in the work area and the employees have a right to request information about toxic substances in the work area. And these notices commonly require the employer to state that no reprisals will be taken against employees who exercise their right to request information.

2. Employers have an obligation in some states to inform prospective and current employees of reproductive hazards, including whether radioactive materials are used in the workplace.

3. Employers have an obligation in some states to label containers of toxic substances.

4. In some states, employers must conduct training programs for employees, which inform employees of the properties of the toxic substances in the workplace, train employees concerning the safe handling of the substances, and instruct employees on emergency treatment for overexposure to the substances.

Further reading
Fisher, Cynthia D., Lyle F. Schoenfeldt, and James B. Shaw. *Human Resource Management,* 5th ed. Boston: Houghton Mifflin, 2003.

right-to-work laws

Right-to-work laws are state laws mandating that workers cannot be required to join or pay dues to a UNION as a condition of EMPLOYMENT. The 1947 TAFT-HARTLEY ACT allowed states to pass right-to-work laws, and right-to-work laws exist in 22 states. Most southern states have passed right-to-work laws, but most northeastern and all Pacific Coast states have not passed similar legislation. In right-to-work states, workers can resign from union membership but still be covered by the COLLECTIVE BARGAINING agreement negotiated with the union. Some right-to-work states also prohibit state agencies from negotiating with unions.

In 2001 Oklahoma was the first state to pass right-to-work legislation in over 15 years. Proposed as a single-issue election, the legislation passed with a 54-percent approval. Business leaders in the state promoted the legislation, while union groups opposed it. Oklahoma had last attempted to pass a right-to-work law in 1964. According to its wording, the new law

- bans contacts that require joining or quitting a labor organization to get or keep a job
- bans CONTRACTS that require remaining in a labor organization to get or keep a job
- bans contracts that require the payment of dues or other payments to labor organizations to get or keep a job
- requires employee approval to deduct payments to labor organizations from wages

In 2002 an appeals court in California, which is not a right-to-work state, ruled that 20,000 faculty members in the California State University must pay at least their "fair share" of union dues that go to cover the cost of collective bargaining and contract administration. In a right-to-work state, it is likely that these workers would not have union representation nor have to pay for the cost of collective bargaining.

See also WAGNER ACT.

Further reading
Cleeland, Nancy. "Court Upholds Dues by College Employees," *Los Angeles Times,* 21 March 2002; "Oklahoma Passes Right to Work Law," *PR Newswire,* 26 September 2001.

risk management

After a huge marketing campaign, a computer company sends out a defective game. The same people who stood hours in line to be the first to own it cram the stores demanding their money back. The company loses millions of dollars.

A professional bungee jumper using a brand new bungee cord makes a flawless jump from 500 feet in a televised extreme sporting event. The cord breaks and she falls, injuring her ribs and breaking her nose. She sues the bungee cord manufacturer.

A fire whirls through a textile mill. During the event, five employees are injured and require hospital care. Afterward, the company can't deliver the 500 bolts of cloth it promised in writing to another business. The injured employees and the other business sue, the employees because they had complained for years about the sparks coming from one of the weaving machines, the other company because the loss of the cloth will put them out of business.

A hospital patient is given 100 times the amount of medication he should have received. It turns out that the pharmacy staff could not accurately read the handwriting on the original prescription. The patient dies.

The above scenarios are business RISKS. In order to understand what risk management is, it is important to understand what risk is. Used in the business sense, the word *risk* means something that in some way poses a threat to the stability and well-being of an organization.

There are as many types of risks as there are types of businesses. However, some broad categories apply to many businesses. Some common examples of risk include

- when a business loses money unexpectedly
- when the business incurs damages to its physical or electronic PRODUCTS
- when employees are injured on the job
- when a business's client or clients are injured or suffer a loss as a result of using the firm's products or SERVICES

Risk management is the specialty of trying to minimize risks to businesses. Risk managers—people who specialize in the field of risk management—do four basic things. First, they try to identify the risks that are common to their type of business before risky events happen. Second, they work on strategies to prevent risks they know about, and if they can't prevent them, they try to lessen the impact of risk on the business.

These first two aspects of risk management, which are very positive for businesses, are known by many different names, such as performance improvement, continuous quality improvement (CQI), total quality improvement (TQI), or TOTAL-QUALITY MANAGEMENT (TQM). Basically all of these names mean that businesses encourage their employees to look for ways to improve how the business operates. Employee suggestions for improvement are welcomed, and there is often a special committee formed to discuss risks and explore suggestions. This committee then writes plans and policies regarding how the company will deal with risks.

The third aspect of a risk manager's job comes into play when something actually happens that causes a serious problem. In some cases this is called an untoward event or a sentinel event. To deal with it, risk managers try to figure out exactly what happened and will ask a lot of questions. Who was involved? What happened? When did it happen? Where did it happen? Why did it happen? How did it happen? They try to get to the bottom of the problem without blaming those involved. By asking questions, particularly WHY, over and over again and stressing that their purpose isn't to get anyone in trouble, risk managers get beyond employees' fears of being fired because of what happened, and they find out the truth. The process is a lot like peeling an onion. Risk managers peel back the layers of the problem to expose its root cause, or what made the problem happen in the first place. Once they gather all of the information, they can study it and then find ways to fix the problem so that it doesn't happen again. This is called root-cause analysis.

Finally, risk managers help clean up messy situations in the sense that they handle claims, which are the legal obligations a business has to pay to correct a problem when it occurs—that is, its LIABILITY. Liability and risk management go hand in hand, and risk-management people must understand the way the law works.

Risk management is a critically important aspect of business practice. Without diligent people on the lookout for the bumps in the road of business life, businesses would be in serious trouble. No one wants their business to lose money, which leads to worker LAYOFFS and other drastic measures. No business wants to injure anyone or even to be forced to close as the result of a lawsuit. By taking a proactive approach and tackling risks before they happen as well as looking at serious problems honestly, businesses can avoid very serious consequences.

Further reading
Alliance Online. Nonprofit Management Association. Available on-line. URL: www.allianceonline.org; Brown, Bernard L., Jr. *Risk Management for Hospitals.* Germantown, Md.: Aspen Systems Corp., 1979; Goldberg, Steven H., Steven C. Davis, Andrew M. Pegalis. *Y2K Risk Management: Contingency Planning, Business Continuity, and Avoiding Litigation.* New York: Wiley, 1999; Rejda, George E. *Principles of Risk Management and Insurance,* 6th ed. Reading, Mass.: Addison Wesley, 1998; U.S. Small Business Administration, Management Assistance Division, Support Services Section. For sale by the Supt. of Docs., U.S. G.P.O., 1981.

—Donna Beales
Special thanks to Carla Destramp, R.N., J.D., Director of Quality and Risk Management, Lowell General Hospital, Lowell, Mass.

risk, uncertainty

Risk exists when a probability of occurrence can be assigned to each of a set of possible outcomes. Thus, risk is measurable. Uncertainty exists when it is impossible to determine the probability of occurrence for each of a set of possible outcomes or when the entire set of possible outcomes is not known. As a result, uncertainty is not measurable. Because risk is quantifiable, it is easier to deal with risk than with uncertainty.

In most fields of study, it is assumed that individuals are rational and base their actions on rational decision making. In economics a rational person is one who maximizes his or her utility. In accounting and finance, a rational person is one who is risk-averse. Risk aversion occurs when individuals will not assume risk unless compensated for it.

Assume a situation where there are two options. The first option is a coin toss; an individual will receive $100,000 for heads and $0 for tails. Since there is a 50-percent probability that heads will turn up and a 50-percent probability that tails will turn up, the expected value of the toss is [(.5)(100,000) + (.5)(0)] = $50,000. The second option offers a sure $50,000. If the individual chooses the first option, he would be risk-seeking; if he chooses the second option, he is risk-averse. If a group of people were asked which option they would choose, the overwhelming majority of them would choose the second option, the sure $50,000. Few people would choose the first option, the chance of receiving either $100,000 or nothing. Both options have the same $50,000 expected value, but the first option is a risky $50,000, while the second option is a certain $50,000. Because the first option has the same expected value but is riskier, few people would choose it over the second option. This is evidence of risk aversion among the population.

BONDS with higher levels of DEFAULT risk offer higher coupon-interest rates than bonds with less risk of default. Junk bonds carry very high coupon rates to induce investors to purchase such bonds and to bear considerable risk of default. Based on the CAPITAL asset pricing model, investors require higher returns from stocks with high BETA COEFFICIENTS than they do from stocks with lower betas. Drivers with bad driving records pay higher INSURANCE premiums to cover the riskiness of their driving than do safe drivers, and smokers pay higher health insurance premiums than do nonsmokers. In general, debentures have higher interest COSTS than do MORTGAGES. These are just a few of the many examples of risk aversion in business, economics, and finance.

See also COUNTRY-RISK ANALYSIS; EXCHANGE-RATE RISK.

Robinson-Patman Act

The Robinson-Patman Act of 1935, as amended, is found in Section 2 of the CLAYTON ANTITRUST ACT. Adopted in the middle of the GREAT DEPRESSION, Robinson-Patman was intended to protect small retailers from the growing number of price-cutting chain stores. In that basic purpose it clearly failed, yet the act remains on the books and is still used by small businesses to challenge chain-store practices.

The Robinson-Patman Act prohibits seller PRICE DISCRIMINATION in goods (not SERVICES) that may tend to create a MONOPOLY or substantially lessen COMPETITION. It is also unlawful to knowingly induce or receive an illegal discriminatory price (buyer LIABILITY). However, volume discounts and discounts granted to meet a competitor's price are lawful. Price discrimination is lawful if the differences are justifiable by differences in the cost of manufacturing, sale, or delivery of goods. These "defenses" for price discrimination are often invoked in legal battles over how cost differences were measured.

The Robinson-Patman Act additionally prohibits discriminatory payments by sellers for services or facilities furnished by customers or discriminatory furnishing of services or facilities to purchasers. Discriminatory ADVERTISING allowances, for example, could violate these provisions.

Victims of Robinson-Patman Act offenses often sue in federal court for "treble damages," an automatic trebling of their actual DAMAGES. The remedy of treble damages found in the Clayton Act is a powerful incentive to file such suits.

Further reading

Gellhorn, Ernest, and Kovacic, William E. *Antitrust Law and Economics in a Nutshell*, 4th ed. Eagan, Minn.: West Group, 1994.

rule of 72

Compounding is the process of finding an unknown future value from a known present value—that is, moving forward in time from a known amount in the present to an unknown amount at some point in the future. Obviously, in dollar terms, future values are larger amounts than are present values because of the time value of money (INTEREST RATES are always positive, never negative).

An ever-popular compounding question is, "How long will it take for my money to double?" or "How long will it take for the account to double?" The rule of 72 estimates with a surprising degree of precision how long it will take for a sum to double at some given rate of interest, compounded annually. The number 72 is the numerator, and the denominator is the rate of interest applicable to the situation in question. For example, at 10-percent interest compounded annually, it will take approximately 72/10 = 7.2 years for a sum to double. At 7-percent interest compounded annually, it will take approximately 72/7 = 10 years to double.

The rule of 115, also a compounding technique, will approximate how long it takes for a sum to triple at some given rate of interest, compounded annually. The number 115 is the numerator, and the denominator is the rate of interest applicable to the situation in question. For example, at 10-percent interest compounded annually, it takes approximately 115/10 = 11.5 years for a sum to triple.

While these two rules are fast and easy to use, more accurate results are obtained by using an interest table of future-value interest factors. However, the published interest factor tables carrying the interest factors to only four places to the right of the decimal. The interest factors are therefore rounded off to four decimal places. The most accurate results are obtained by using a financial calculator.

See also COMPOUNDING, FUTURE VALUE.

rules of origin

Rules of origin define the country of origin for exports and IMPORTS. Rules of origin are important in determining what, if any, TARIFF applies to the importation of a PRODUCT. Many products contain components and materials produced around the world and then assembled in another country. For instance, in the case of a personal computer, the keyboard may be assembled in Mexico using parts from the United States, Taiwan, and Indonesia; the "mouse" may be made in China; the monitor may be produced in the United States but assembled in Mexico; and the hard drive may be produced in Canada. Determining the country of origin can be difficult. Rules of origin define whether a product is considered domestically produced or imported. Many trade agreements are designed to give preferential treatment to imports from trading partners and preclude benefits to products originating in other countries.

Rules of origin have been called "the key to unlocking NAFTA," the NORTH AMERICAN FREE TRADE AGREEMENT among the United States, Canada, and Mexico. Under NAFTA, products made in any of the three countries with nonoriginating materials may be freely traded when each material undergoes a change in tariff classification based on the HARMONIZED TARIFF SYSTEM (HTS). If a product undergoes a two-digit product-classification change under the HTS system, it may be freely traded. Also under NAFTA, a product can be classified as North American if the regional value content of the product meets certain standards. Many new cars sold in the United States have stickers on their windows displaying regional value content.

Some rules of origin in NAFTA are quite specific, including those for televisions and textiles. To be considered as originating in North America, television sets must contain picture screens made in the region. In general, textiles must meet a "yarn forward" requirement, which mandates use of North American–spun yarns to make fabrics that are cut and sewn into clothing, all in North America.

See also EXPORTING; UNITED STATES–CANADA FREE TRADE AGREEMENT.

Further reading

Folsom, Ralph H., and W. Davis Folsom. *Understanding NAFTA and its International Business Implications*. New York: Matthew Bender/Irwin, 1996.

S

safety and health

Safety and health rules assure that employees work in an environment that is free from recognized hazards. Although safety and health activities are usually MANAGEMENT-led, everyone in an organization shares responsibility for safety. Safety committees are often established within each department. These employee groups conduct safety inspections and search out unsafe conditions that could result in accidents or poor health. Safety committees also implement safety programs and assist in accident investigations.

There are four primary sources of safety and health concerns in the workplace: physical, chemical, and biological conditions; and stress. Physical conditions include exposure to temperature changes involving heat or cold, loud noises, adequacy of ventilation, and sanitary conditions. Chemical conditions include exposure to dust, fumes, gases, and carcinogens (cancer-causing substances such as asbestos). Many of these conditions are associated with working in an industrial plant; however, smoking or otherwise using tobacco and leaving an office file-cabinet drawer open so that others may hit it are also two examples of unsafe physical conditions. Biological conditions include exposure to mold, fungi, and bacteria. An increasing health concern is stress in the employee's personal and work life. In many states, stress caused by psychological factors as well as physical and chemical conditions in the workplace has been the basis of successful disability claims.

Many companies go beyond efforts to minimize physical and environmental hazards and implement programs designed to increase the health and well-being of their employees. These programs encompass physical fitness, smoking cessation, weight reduction, and stress management. EMPLOYEE ASSISTANCE PROGRAMS are popular voluntary programs some companies offer their employers and close family members to help cope with emotional difficulties, alcohol and drug abuse, and family and marital problems; legal counseling may also be provided. Efforts like these and other programs help the company send the message that the business cares for its employees and gives it a reputation as a preferred place to work.

The Occupational Safety and Health Act, a federal law, has many industry-specific safety regulations. But even when there are no specific guidelines, the act contains the General Duty Clause, which requires employers to conform to the intent of the law requiring safe and healthful working conditions.

See also OCCUPATIONAL SAFETY AND HEALTH ADMINISTRATION.

—John B. Abbott

sales force compensation

Sales force compensation is the basis for paying salespeople for their efforts. Compensation is a critical component in SALES MANAGEMENT. An effective sales-compensation plan

- bases rewards on results and efforts
- provides equal rewards for equal results
- provides rewards that are competitive in the marketplace
- is easy to understand and implement

Most salespeople want to be rewarded for their effectiveness. Typically sales-compensation plans are one of three types: straight salary, straight commission, or a combination plan. Straight-salary compensation plans usually include performance quotas used to determine annual raises. Straight-salary plans are used when sales efforts are made as part of a team and when customer service (rather than selling) is the major function.

Straight-commission plans pay no salary, only a fixed amount or percentage for each sale. Most salespeople on commission plans are paid a "draw"—a set amount per pay period against their sales commission. The draw is, in effect, a loan by the employer. Salespeople keep close track of their commissions and know when they have "made their draw" in a week or month. Repeatedly not making draw will lead to dismissal. Salespeople who excel are often paid bonuses above their standard commission or are awarded prizes, often electronic equipment and vacation trips.

Most U.S. companies pay salespeople based on combination plans, which include salary plus bonus or salary plus commission. Typically retail-store employees are paid a base wage plus a small commission. For example, Julia Roberts in the film *Pretty Woman* returned to the store where she was treated poorly to show the sales clerk the commission she lost. Salary-plus-bonus plans are often difficult to administer. Bonuses are usually based on exceeding a target sales level, determined by a percentage above the previous year's sales. During the booming U.S. economy in the 1990s, many salespeople easily met their target amounts, often well before the end of the year. Selling more would increase the base amount they had to achieve the following year. Since the next year's bonus would be based on exceeding the previous year's sales, once they had met their target level, salespeople then had an incentive not to sell more.

Salespeople tend to be competitive, and therefore sales-compensation plans should reward equal results equally. Unequal reward plans create dissention within an organization. Sales managers often create special incentives for their staff known as "pearl-diving contests."

Sales-compensation plans also have to be competitive. Sales is a skill that is often easily transferable from one firm or industry to another. Salespeople talk with each other and have a good idea how well they are being compensated relative to other opportunities.

Sales-compensation plans need to be easily understood and implemented. When personnel know the basis of compensation, they adjust their efforts to meet the goals. Salespeople often complain about complex and time-wasting paperwork. They know if they are filling out reports, they are not selling.

Further reading
Dwyer, F. Robert, and John F. Tanner Jr. *Business Marketing*, 2d ed. Boston: McGraw-Hill, 2001.

sales forecasting

Sales forecasting is used by businesses to estimate future sales or INCOME. Sales-forecasting techniques, which can range from quite sophisticated to very simple, are grouped as quantitative or qualitative methods. The major qualitative methods used are jury of executive opinion, DELPHI TECHNIQUE, sales force composite, and survey of buyer intentions. The major quantitative techniques include market tests, trend analysis, and exponential smoothing.

The jury of executive opinion technique involves, as the label suggests, gathering the opinions of executives within the organization. A simple, in-house survey asking executives what they think sales will be in the next quarter or year can yield a forecast. The technique is quick and inexpensive but assumes executives are knowledgeable about market conditions.

The Delphi technique is similar to the jury of executive opinion, except that opinions from people outside the organization may be solicited, and a series of QUESTIONNAIRES are used. In the Delphi technique (named after the Oracle of Delphi to whom ancient Greeks would travel and seek advice), results of each round of SURVEYS are aggregated and returned to the participants until a consensus forecast is reached. The Delphi technique is more time-consuming and expensive to administer than a simple jury of executive opinion but is based on the considered opinions of those participating.

The sales-force-composite technique asks the sales team to forecast sales in their particular market. These forecasts are aggregated to yield an overall market forecast. The argument for sales-force-composite forecasting is that the sales team is closest to the customer and therefore most in touch with changing conditions in the marketplace. The weakness in the technique is that the sales team, particularly if the SALES FORCE COMPENSATION plan is based on exceeding a quota, will have an incentive to underestimate DEMAND. Then, when sales exceed the forecast, the salespeople will look good and receive bonuses.

The survey of buyer intentions simply asks customers what they expect to purchase in the next time period. Similarly, a survey of purchasing managers' intentions is a widely quoted indicator of expected changes in manufacturing output. The weakness of any buyer intentions' survey is the difference between what people say they will do and what they actually do. For example, how often do people, both friends and in business, say, "I will call you" or "I will be in touch" but fail to follow through? Surveys of buyer intentions work well in situations where buyers and vendors have developed strong relationships, trusting and depending on each other.

Market tests are often used to forecast demand for new PRODUCTS. Most of the major franchise companies in the United States test new products in sample markets before rolling out the product for national distribution. Market tests give researchers quantitative data and, if representative of the overall market, can yield a predicted market demand. The disadvantages of markets tests are the time they take to implement, their COSTS, and the fact that they alert competitors to a company's new product plans.

Trend analysis, or naïve forecasting, estimates future sales through analysis of historical trends. If sales have been growing by 4 percent annually in recent years, then they are likely to increase 4 percent in the next year. Trend analysis is quick, inexpensive, and usually accurate when market conditions are stable. Trend analysis assumes the future will be similar to the past and assumes there will be no changes in the marketing environment.

Exponential smoothing is similar to trend analysis, but greater consideration is given to recent data over data from the more distant past. In exponential smoothing, the last five years' sales data might be used to forecast the next year's sales, but instead of taking a simple average of the last five years, each year's sales is weighted or multiplied by a factor greater or lesser than one. The benefits and weaknesses of exponential smoothing are the same as trend analysis, but exponential smoothing implicitly incorporates the impact of recent changes in market conditions.

Further reading
Boone, Louis E., and David L. Kurtz. *Contemporary Marketing*, 10th ed. Fort Worth, Tex.: Dryden Press, 2001.

sales management
Sales management, a critical component in the success of any business, includes recruitment and selection, training, organization, supervision, motivation, compensation, evaluation, and control of salespeople to ensure their effectiveness and to accomplish the firm's objectives.

Recruitment and selection of successful salespeople is the major concern for a sales manager. Generally college students say they do not want to pursue a career in sales, but upon graduation they often find that many of the best opportunities are in that field. Sales careers provide opportunities for success based on one's own efforts and can offer higher earnings, independence, and job security. As one former student stated, "By going into sales supported by a large, national organization, I got to start my own business without having to invest a lot of CAPITAL."

Students look at sales positions as being riskier than traditional salaried MANAGEMENT positions, but sales is a business skill, and people with demonstrated sales success can transfer that skill to many different opportunities. From a sales manager's perspective, one question is whether to recruit trained salespeople or people who are new to sales. Many small firms find it less expensive to hire trained salespeople, even though they will demand higher compensation. Small companies often cannot afford to develop and maintain training programs. Hiring trained salespeople reduces the cost of training staff and usually results in faster adaptation of new staff into the organization.

Training can take place on the job or through individual instruction, in-house classes, and external seminars. Some companies use videotapes, interactive computer programs, role-playing and shadowing of other salespeople in their training programs. To people considering a career in sales, the time and effort a company is willing to invest in their new salespeople is an important measure of how much a company values its sales team. For example, McDonalds is famous for sending managers to their hamburger university. U.S. Gypsum sends trainees to a two-week program in its Chicago headquarters, while other companies put new sales staff in a back room to watch videos and then shadow (follow) other salespeople for a day or two.

Organization of sales personnel presents another difficult sales-management question. Do managers organize geographically, by PRODUCT categories, by type of customers, or by some combination of these three methods? Geographic organization reduces sales representatives' travel time but forces them to understand all of the company's products and the needs of different types of customers. Many industrial-products companies have found organization by categories of the company's products to be more effective than geographic organization. For example, General Electric sells everything from turbines to medical-imaging equipment. It would be nearly impossible to find and train salespeople who could effectively sell GE's many highly technical products. Recognizing that in many markets a few customers account for a large portion of the company's sales, many companies divide their sales force geographically but separate out national sales accounts.

Supervision is a "touchy" issue in sales management. As stated earlier, one of the motivations for people to choose sales careers is independence. Salespeople often complain that too much of their time to spent complying with requirements imposed by managers. Sales managers must choose how closely to monitor and what support is needed for their staff.

Motivation and compensation are related but different sales-management responsibilities. Salespeople are motivated by rewards, but monetary incentives are only part of motivation and compensation. Motivation can include emotional support, information sharing, and financial encouragement. Sales managers often use incentive programs, including prizes, trips and awards, to motivate their staffs. A sales manager once inspired his telephone-sales team by simply saying if they sold so many more thousands of dollars' worth of product that day, he would cover all the office duties the next day, the Friday before Christmas. It worked!

Some managers have adopted the EXPECTANCY THEORY of motivation, whereby salespeople know what is expected in terms of sales and other organizational goals. Sales representatives are assigned to tasks based on their needs and capabilities, making goals achievable, providing immediate feedback, and offering rewards that reinforce the values of each salesperson.

SALES FORCE COMPENSATION is based on salary, commission, or a combination of both. Commissions can be "straight commissions," a percentage of the value of the sale, or be based on a sales quota. Many industrial-sales firms set an annual sales quota, often a percentage above the average sales for the previous two years, and then award a bonus to those who achieve their sales quotas. Some U.S. companies have instituted pay-for-profits compensation plans, recognizing that sales goals and company PROFITS are not the same. 3M Corporation's sales goals include requirements for sales representatives to increase sales of the company's new products. Effective sales-quota systems are difficult to develop. They need to be achievable but also substantial enough to keep salespeople motivated throughout the year. If a salesperson achieves their sales quota by September, and next year's sales objective will be based on their current year's sales, they actually have an incentive not to increase their sales for the rest of the year.

Sales managers must also evaluate their personnel. Sales volume can usually be easily measured, but managers also evaluate new-account development, CUSTOMER RELATIONS/SATISFACTION, and long-term sales efforts. Most sales organizations have well-defined evaluation criteria to guide employee assessment.

See also MOTIVATION THEORY.

Further reading

Boone, Louis E., and David L. Kurtz. *Contemporary Marketing*, 10th ed. Fort Worth, Tex.: Dryden Press, 2001.

sales promotion

A sales promotion is a marketing effort other than ADVERTISING, PUBLIC RELATIONS, and PERSONAL SELLING designed to stimulate consumer sales. In the United States, expenditures on sales-promotion activities grew significantly in the 1990s, attributable to the increased power of retailers in marketing channels; slow growth in population, creating COMPETITION for existing customers; changes in computer scanner technology, allowing marketers to quickly measure the impact of sales-promotion efforts; and the fact that Americans simply like and respond to sales promotions.

Sales promotions may be directed toward the final customers or toward retailers and WHOLESALERS. Direct-consumer sales promotions include price deals, coupons, rebates, cross-promotions, contests, sweepstakes, games, samples, and advertising specialty PRODUCTS. Retailer and wholesaler promotions, called trade promotions, include trade allowances, dealer loaders (gifts), trade contests, point-of purchase displays, TRADE SHOWS, and training programs. Marketers use a variety of sales promotions, depending on their goal and target audience.

Generally the goals of consumer sales promotions are to stimulate trial and impulse purchases, encourage repurchase, increase sales of complimentary products, and increase consumer inventory and CONSUMPTION. Price deals, temporary decreases in the price of a product, and coupons offering free or reduced prices are often used to stimulate consumers into trying products. In some categories, such as personal-care products, American consumers are very loyal to their current BRANDS. Marketers often use samples to stimulate impulse purchases and trial of alternative products. Rebates are also used to attract price-conscious consumers.

Cross-promotions, also called "tie-ins," are the collaboration of two or more firms in a sales-promotion effort. Fast-food restaurants offering children's toys, hotels, providing discounts at area golf courses, and INTERNET sites linked to other firm's sites are all examples of cross-promotion. Cross-promotion can be a very effective marketing method, reinforcing the image of each firm and allowing low-cost access to consumers.

Sweepstakes, contests, and games create consumer interest and involvement. American consumers like opportunities to win. In addition to creating interest and awareness of a firm's products, these sales promotions can result in low-cost lists of consumers for future DIRECT MARKETING efforts.

Advertising specialty products, either given away or purchased by consumers, comprises a growing area of sales promotion. Calendars, pens, magnets, and clothing with a company's logo and address are all used for reminder advertising. Many companies have been surprised to find how many consumers are willing to pay for such products. Word of mouth is almost always the best form of advertising, and specialty products stimulate word-of-mouth promotion.

The goals of trade promotion differ slightly from consumer sales promotion. In trade promotion, marketers are attempting to build or maintain good relationships with important members of their DISTRIBUTION CHANNELS. Especially for manufacturers who do not sell directly to final consumers, trade relationships are critical to success, and trade promotions contribute to that success. Specific trade-promotion goals include gaining or maintaining distribution, influencing resellers, increasing reseller inventory, and defending against competitors.

Trade allowances, or short-term special discounts, are often payment for cooperative advertising, shelf space, or volume purchases and stimulate reseller buying. Dealer loaders, gifts such as a free trip or free displays, enhance reseller relationships and provide added visibility in reseller's stores. Point-of-purchase displays also give manufacturers added floor space in retail stores and stimulate impulse purchases. Trade contests, in which resellers win prizes and trips based on selling one firm's products, give resellers incentives to promote one company's products over other products they also sell. For example, a heating and air conditioning installation company sells three brands of equipment but highly recommends only one company's brand. When asked why the one firm's equipment is so superior to the others, one of the installation crew responds, "Oh, the boss gets a free trip to Las Vegas if he sells ten of these systems."

Trade shows, usually sponsored by an industry or professional association, are a major area of trade promotion. U.S. businesses spend billions of dollars annually to display and promote their products at trade shows. Trade shows are particularly important for firms that cannot afford a sales force and for entrepreneurs with new products to promote. Trade shows are also sometimes used to train people in the distribution channel. Whether at trade shows or at other locations, company-sponsored training programs are often needed to provide resellers with the information needed to sell products to final consumers.

Sales promotion can stimulate demand, increase consumer purchases, and gain reseller cooperation, but most sales promotions are easily copied by competitors, and while sales volume may increase, copycats could hurt company PROFITS. One questionable sales-promotion practice is purchasing a retailer's inventory of a competing firm's products as part of a deal to gain shelf space in the retailer's store. Sales promotions are also sometimes deceptive. The FEDERAL TRADE COMMISSION has sometimes intervened, particularly in sweepstakes promotions.

Further reading
Bearden, William O., Thomas Ingram, and Raymond LaForge. *Marketing Principles & Perspectives,* 4th ed. Boston: Irwin/McGraw-Hill, 2004.

Sallie Mae See STUDENT LOAN MARKETING ASSOCIATION.

sanctions
Government officials use a wide variety of tools to influence the policies of other governments: diplomatic persuasion, public appeals, economic and noneconomic sanctions, and military action. These tools are sometimes applied unilaterally, with the enforcing government acting alone, and sometimes applied multilaterally with several countries. The government inflicting the sanctions is referred to as the "sender," and the government receiving the sanctions is referred to as the "target."

Noneconomic sanctions are aimed at denying the foreign government legitimacy or prestige. They include such things as canceling summit meetings, denying VISAS, withdrawing ambassadors, and blocking the government's bid to join international organizations.

Economic sanctions are imposed by the sender to disrupt the target's international commerce. The sender may limit such things as IMPORTS from the target and EXPORTING to the target, restrict INVESTMENT in the target country, prohibit travel to the country, or prohibit private financial transactions between the citizens of the two countries. Two notable economic sanctions are the United States' (sender) decades-old economic sanctions against Cuba (target) and the North's (sender) blockade of Southern (target) ports during the American Civil War. Prior to the recent war in Iraq, U.S. sanctions against that nation were initially supported by most industrialized countries but subsequently opposed or ignored as a reaction against U.S. policy. Economic sanctions usually result in active black-market trade with the target countries.

—Mack Tennyson

saving
In economics, saving is not spending one's INCOME (i.e., postponed CONSUMPTION). Saving is distinguished from savings in that it is a flow of income over time, while savings is the accumulated amount of funds not spent (i.e., the result of past saving). Economists have identified many factors influencing saving, including income, INTEREST RATES, and precautionary motives. Generally higher interest rates, greater incomes, and lowered consumer confidence induce greater saving, which also increases in anticipation of major consumer expenditures.

Moral, religious, and cultural values also influence saving. Most families begin saving as soon as children are born. Ben Franklin's advice of "a penny saved is a penny earned" influenced early American values, and many cultures traditionally had dowry systems requiring the payment of precious metals or animals as part of a wedding arrangement. Social commentators frequently labeled the 1980s as the "me first" decade with heavy emphasis on consumption as a goal. Similarly, nearly a century earlier, social critic Thorstein Veblen, describing the "Robber Baron" era of the AMERICAN INDUSTRIAL REVOLUTION, introduced terms like leisure class and conspicuous consumption.

Saving is critical to the growth of any economic system; as one saying puts it, "There can be no INVESTMENT without saving." In the CIRCULAR FLOW MODEL of economic systems, household income (income after taxes) that is not spent on consumption typically is deposited with FINANCIAL INTERMEDIARIES—commercial banks and other financial institutions. Financial intermediaries aggregate savings from households and provide LOANS to businesses, which in turn use the borrowed funds to make investments. This is what economists call voluntary savings. Savings that are hoarded and not used in any way do not contribute to investment and ECONOMIC GROWTH. During the GREAT DEPRESSION, over 10,000 banks failed, and depositors lost their savings. In response many Americans returned to the practice of keeping unspent income under their mattresses or buried in jars. The FEDERAL DEPOSIT INSURANCE CORPORATION was created in part to overcome consumer fears of depositing their savings in financial intermediaries.

In many poor economies, households consume nearly 100 percent of their income. In this so-called circle of poverty, low incomes yield low savings, which yield low investment, which yields low incomes. ECONOMIC DEVELOPMENT experts often focus on the role of saving for economic growth in EMERGING MARKETS.

Many economic systems include forced saving, whereby portions of household income are removed by government through taxation. SOCIAL SECURITY is a forced-savings program. In 2000, the U.S. savings rate was zero as Americans were consuming 100 percent or more of their income. Much of the investment CAPITAL in the U.S. economy was coming from saving by international households. The U.S. government attempts to induce greater domestic saving through programs like INDIVIDUAL RETIREMENT ACCOUNTS and KEOGH PLANS. Low rates of saving increase interest rates, reducing investment. In Singapore, at one time the government required workers to deposit 20 percent of their income in a national retirement fund.

Retained earnings by businesses are also a source of savings. Businesses either utilize PROFITS to make new investments or distribute profits in the form of DIVIDENDS and bonuses. The latter become income for recipients, who then choose whether to consume or save.

Further reading

Koch, A. Robert. *Economic Principles: Growth and Environment.* Westport, Conn.: AVI Publishing, 1986.

savings and loan associations (thrifts)

Savings and loan associations (S&Ls), also known as thrifts, are depository institutions serving as major FINANCIAL INTERMEDIARIES. Among all depository institutions, they are second in size of ASSETS only to commercial banks. S&Ls use funds acquired through savings deposits (often called shares), TIME DEPOSITS, and checkable deposits to make home MORTGAGES. They are organized as CORPORATIONS and are either state or federally chartered.

Previous to 1980, S&L activities were restricted to offering only savings and time deposits and making only mortgage LOANS. (Checking accounts and consumer loans were offered only by commercial banks.) Because mortgages are typically long-term loans, often with 30-year maturities, and these mortgages had fixed INTEREST RATES (adjustable-rate mortgages weren't popular until the late 1970s), S&L earnings from mortgage activity suffered greatly in the late 1980s. As the author Frederic S. Mishkin wrote, "When interest rates rose, S&Ls frequently found that the INCOME from their mortgages was well below the cost of acquiring funds. Many of them suffered large losses, and many went out of business."

In the 1980s, high interest rates and the simultaneous decline of the real-estate market created an S&L crisis. In 1989 Congress created the RESOLUTION TRUST CORPORATION (RTC), an agency established to manage insolvent thrifts placed in conservatorship or receivership. The RTC seized the ASSETS of about 750 insolvent S&Ls, comprising over 25 percent of the industry, and sold over 95 percent of them. The subsequent recovery rate was over 85 percent. The RTC sold more than $450 billion of real estate this way, and then went out of business on December 31, 1995.

Beginning in 1980, in an effort to put S&Ls on a more equal footing with commercial banks, Congress passed a series of that expanded S&L activities, allowing them to offer checking accounts and consumer loans, for example. Today the distinction between S&Ls and commercial banks is a blurry one, and both types of depository institutions now offer essentially the same intermediary services.

Further reading

Mishkin, Frederic S. *The Economics of Money, Banking, and Financial Markets,* 6th ed. Boston: Addison Wesley, 2001.

S corporation

Congress enacted the S corporation (originally called subchapter S corporation) rules in 1958 to minimize the role of tax considerations in the type of business form choice, to allow single-level (pass-through) taxation at the shareholder level, and to allow owners to offset losses against other INCOME at the shareholder level. Prior to the 1958 tax-law change, businesses had to choose between being taxed as a CORPORATION (with the benefit of limited LIABILITY but the disadvantage of double taxation; DIVIDENDS paid to owners are not tax-deductible) or as a PARTNERSHIP (with the benefit of single-level, or pass-through, taxation but the disadvantage of unlimited liability). The S corporation rules benefit the small businesses. S corporations are organized as corporations and thus are treated as corporations for legal and business purposes. However, for federal income-tax purposes, they are treated much like partnerships. To become an S corporation, an eligible corporation makes an S election through a filing with the INTERNAL REVENUE SERVICE, which must be signed by all SHAREHOLDERS.

The S corporation requirements are somewhat restrictive. The shareholders-related requirements are that the corporation may not have more than 75 shareholders, the shareholders must be individuals/estates/certain TRUSTS/certain tax-exempt organizations, and none of the individual shareholders can be nonresident aliens. The corporation-related requirements are that the corporation must be a domestic corporation, the corporation must not be an "ineligible" corporation (financial institutions, INSURANCE companies), and the corporation must have only one class of stock. The S election terminates if the corporation fails one or more of the five requirements. Events that can terminate the election include exceeding the 75-shareholder limit, selling an ineligible shareholder one or more share of stock, inadvertently creating a second class of stock (for example distributions not proportionate to ownership percentages), selecting an improper tax year (based on the tax year of the shareholders) or failing the passive INVESTMENT income test for three consecutive years (if a former corporation with earnings and PROFITS).

The advantages of S-corporation treatment include the income being exempt from corporate-level taxation (pass-through taxation). Corporate losses can be used at the shareholder level against other income; CAPITAL GAINS, tax-exempt income, deductions, losses, and tax credits are separately stated and retain their character when passed through to the shareholder; splitting income among family members is possible (after reasonable compensation is paid to shareholders who provide SERVICES or CAPITAL); and earnings that flow through to individual shareholders as anything other than wages are not subject to the self-employment tax. Disadvantages of S-corporation treatment include taxation of excessive net passive investment income (if a former C corporation) and built-in gains tax (if a former C corporation). Special allocations and disproportionate distributions are not permitted (as they are in partnerships), and a dividends-received deduction/separate tax-rate schedule is not permitted (as they are in C corporations). In addition, an S corporation is not exempt from the at-risk rules, passive-activity limitations (when investors are not actively involved in management of the business) or the hobby-loss provisions (limitations on deductability of losses associated with a hobby as opposed to business) as are C corporations.

Many new small businesses that would have formerly chosen to operate as an S corporation are now electing to operate as a LIMITED LIABILITY COMPANY (LLC) or LIMITED LIABILITY PARTNERSHIP (LLP). As a reaction to this, the Small Business Job Protection Act of 1996 liberalized a number of the S-corporation rules relating to forming, operating, and restructuring S corporations. This was perceived to be an effort by Congress to reinvigorate the S corporation as a viable alternative to the LLC/LLP entity choice.

Many small businesses currently operate as an S corporation and will continue to do so into the future. Because there is a significant tax cost involved in corporate liquidation, businesses that might prefer the LLC/LLP form of business will continue their S status. Some small businesses prefer the S-corporation form because the owners perceive it as a possible mechanism of managing the owners' self-employment tax expense.

Further reading

Pope, Thomas R., Kenneth E. Anderson, and John L. Kramer. *Prentice Hall's Federal Taxation 2003.* Upper Saddle River, N.J.: Pearson Education, 2003; Willis, Eugene, William A. Hoffman, David M. Maloney, and William A. Rabbe. *West Federal Taxation, Comprehensive Volume, 2002.* Eagan, Minn.: West Publishing Company, 2001.

—Linda Bradley

secondary markets   See PRIMARY MARKETS, SECONDARY MARKETS.

Section 301, Special 301, Super 301

Section 301, Special 301, and Super 301 refer to trade remedies available to the United States under the Trade Act of 1974 and subsequent revisions of that act. Initially Section 301 of the act applied when U.S. rights or benefits under international trade agreements were at risk or when foreign nations engaged in unjustifiable, unreasonable, or discriminatory conduct. Section 301 focused primarily on the activities of foreign governments, not foreign businesses. It has been used primarily to open up foreign markets to U.S. exports and INVESTMENTs and to protect INTELLECTUAL PROPERTY rights.

Most Section 301 disputes have been resolved through negotiations leading to changes in foreign country practices. If the U.S. president or the U.S. trade representative (USTR) is not satisfied with the negotiated results in connection with a Section 301 complaint, the United States may undertake unilateral retaliatory trade actions. Created as a result of U.S. frustration with multilateral trade resolution methods and procedures, Section 301 was a U.S. legislative decision, not sanctioned by the General Agreement on Tariffs and Trade (GATT) or the WORLD TRADE ORGANIZATION (WTO), and is thought to be inconsistent with multilateral trade relations.

Section 301 was amended in 1988 (through the Omnibus Trade and Competitiveness Act), creating Super 301 and Special 301 procedures. The 1988 act introduced the concept of mandatory rather than discretionary retaliation against Section 301 offenses. Offenses requiring retaliation include unjustifiable trade practices and the breach of international trade agreements to which the United States is a party.

Membership in the WTO since 1995 has committed the United States to multilateral dispute settlement of issues covered by WTO agreements. Section 301 petitions that are within the scope of WTO agreements are routinely sent to the WTO Dispute Settlement Body. The United States has been involved in more WTO disputes (as a complaining and responding party) than any other member country. When a petition concerns issues not covered by a WTO agreement or a country that is not a WTO member, Section 301 remedies are often pursued.

Super 301 procedures refer to a requirement that the USTR identify "trade liberalization priorities." These priorities focused on major TRADE BARRIERS and other trade-distorting practices of foreign countries, which, if eliminated, would likely have the most potential to increase U.S. EXPORTING. The revised act of 1988 also required the USTR to investigate harmful practices under Section 301. This resulted in a practice of creating "watch lists," by which the USTR would identify countries whose practices were of most concern without initiating a Section 301 investigation. Shortly after the law was passed, many countries and practices were placed on the Super 301 watch list, including

- Japanese procurement restraints on purchases of U.S. super computers and space satellites, and Japanese technical barriers to trade in wood products
- Brazilian import bans and LICENSING controls
- Indian barriers to FOREIGN INVESTMENT and foreign INSURANCE

Intergovernmental negotiations resolved the Japanese and Brazilian disputes, opening these markets to U.S. exporters, but India refused to discuss super 301 listing.

Sometimes Super 301 procedures and designations were used as "bargaining chip" in advance to GATT/WTO negotiations, and sometimes they used as an alternative to efforts for calls for stricter measures against other trading nations. In September 1995, President Bill Clinton extended Super 301 for two years. No countries were prioritized that year, but China and Japan were identified for special scrutiny. Korea negotiated a last-minute arrangement to avoid citation under Super 301. In 1996 Brazil, Argentina, Australia, and Indonesia were all subject to Super 301 investigations, but Super 301 watch lists were suspended in 1997.

Unlike Super 301 procedures, which were allowed to expire, the Special 301 procedures established in the 1988 Omnibus Trade and Competitiveness Act are permanent parts of U.S. trade legislation. Under these procedures, the USTR is required to identify foreign countries that deny adequate and effective protection of intellectual-property rights or deny fair and equitable access for U.S. citizens who rely on intellectual-property protection. Countries identified under Special 301 as "priority countries" are subject to a mandatory Section 301 investigation within six months unless there is a determination that this would be detrimental to U.S. economic interests or the dispute is settled through negotiation.

In identifying priority foreign countries for intellectual-property rights violations, the USTR is directed to focus on only those countries that have the most "onerous or egregious" practices—that is, whose practices have the greatest adverse impact on U.S. products. Like the Super 301 legislation, Special 301 rules have resulted in "priority watch lists" and "secondary watch lists." This has created pressure for offending nations to enter into intellectual-property rights negotiations with the United States. During the early 1990s, many countries were placed on Special 301 lists, but now most intellectual-property disputes go to the WTO as alleged breaches of the Trade-Related Intellectual Property Agreement.

Further reading
Folsom, Ralph H., and Michael Gordon. *International Business Transactions,* 5th ed. Eagan, Minn.: West Group, 2002.

Securities and Exchange Commission

The Securities and Exchange Commission (SEC) is a federal agency created to oversee the U.S. securities market. The SEC has legislative, executive, and judicial authority over securities matters. It creates and amends securities laws, proposes new rules to address changing market conditions, and enforces existing rules and laws.

Under the Securities Act of 1934, the SEC was created as a response to the STOCK MARKET crash in 1929, which is often called the starting point of the GREAT DEPRESSION. While the U.S. economy was already in a severe RECESSION before the crash, the collapse of the securities markets con-

tributed heavily to economic decline. Investors and banks, often with borrowed funds, purchased numerous securities based on speculative rumors and questionable prospectuses. When these securities became worthless, both individuals and financial institutions went bankrupt.

The Securities Act of 1934 required registration of securities offerings with the SEC unless an exemption applied. The act broadly defined securities as

> Any note, stock, bond, debenture, evidence of indebtedness, certificate of interest of participation in any PROFIT-sharing agreement, . . . preorganization certificate or subscription, . . . INVESTMENT contract, voting TRUST certificate, . . . fractional undivided interest in oil, gas, or mineral rights, . . . or, in general, any interest or instrument commonly known as a "security."

The act emphasized disclosure rather than approval. Thus, with proper disclosure, one may sell securities in nearly any activity. The federal goal was not to approve or disapprove but to inform investors and allow the public to make its own choice.

Disclosure is accomplished through a registration statement that includes a PROSPECTUS and other information. The prospectus must be given to purchasers of securities. Certain securities and transactions are exempt from registration requirements, including private placements (sale of investment securities directly to institutional investors such as INSURANCE companies) and the sale of securities by people other than issuers, underwriters, and dealers. This allows the resale of securities in secondary markets by investors without violation of SEC disclosure rules.

The SEC has five members appointed by the U.S. president, with no more than three members from one political party. Joseph P. Kennedy, father of President John Kennedy, was the first chairman of the SEC. Commissioners are appointed for five-year terms, with one member rotating off the commission each year. The Securities Act excluded from disclosure requirements notes and drafts that mature in less than nine months from the date of issuance, but it increased antiFRAUD provisions addressing INSIDER TRADING, prohibiting "manipulative or deceptive" practices in connection with the sale or purchase of securities. The act imposed LIABILITY on those persons who make inadequate and erroneous disclosures of information. The SEC can impose civil penalties (fines) up to $500,000 and issue cease-and-desist orders. These orders, which must be enforced by federal district courts, direct defendants to stop violating securities laws.

The 1934 act also mandated continual filing of information about companies and the securities they issued. Companies are required to file annually a Form 10-K financial statement report. Since 1934 the SEC's role has continued to change. The commission oversees disclosure requirements for participants in stock exchanges, broker-dealers, investment advisors, MUTUAL FUNDS, and public utility holding companies. The SEC requires public companies to disclose meaningful financial and other information to the public. In 2000 a controversial SEC ruling required FAIR DISCLOSURE, prohibiting advance communication to stock-market analysts.

Further reading
Mallor, Jane P., A. James Barnes, Thomas Bowers, Michael J. Phillips, and Arlen W. Langvardt. *Business Law and the Regulatory Environment,* 11th ed. Boston: McGraw-Hill, 2001; Securities and Exchange website. Available on-line. URL: www.sec.gov.

Securities Industry Association

The Securities Industry Association (SIA) is the WALL STREET trade association representing the interests of the STOCK MARKET industry in the U.S. political and regulatory environment. The SIA was established in 1972 through the merger of the Investment Banker's Association and the Association of Stock Exchange Firms. Included in its 700 members are investment banks, broker-dealers, and mutual fund companies.

Following is the SIA's mission statement.

Recognizing their fundamental role in the continued growth and development of the CAPITAL MARKETS, as well as their responsibility to issuers and investors, SIA member firms hold these values: adherence to ethical and professional standards; commitment to the best interests of clients; and exercise of unquestioned integrity in business and personal dealings in the industry and within the firms.

Some issues on which the SIA has taken advocacy positions include federal securities transaction fees, regulation of capital markets, Regulation FD (full disclosure), and the creation of "best practices" guidelines for stock-market analysts. In 2001 the SIA responded to criticisms that analysts are pressured to recommend stocks of companies their company is soliciting INVESTMENT BANKING services business from (typically BOND issues and stock offerings) by creating a series of guidelines. Some of the SIA's best practices include the following.

- "CORPORATE GOVERNANCE. Research should not report to investment banking; it should also not report to any other business unit in a way that compromises its integrity.
- Recommendations should be transparent and consistent. . . . A formal rating system should have clear definitions that are published in every report or otherwise readily available. MANAGEMENT should encourage analysts to indicate both when a security should be bought and when it should be sold . . . and . . . should support use of the full ratings spectrum.
- Assessment of compensation. While compensation will inevitably vary with market conditions and a firm's

overall profitability, a research analyst's pay should not be directly linked to specific investment banking transactions, sales and trading revenues, or ASSET management fees . . .
- Personal interests should be disclosed. Analysts should disclose whether they or members of their households hold direct ownership positions in securities they cover . . ."

Part of the basis for criticism of the role of security analysts is how few sell recommendations they offer. Even with a significant stock-market decline, that began spring 2000, in 2001 only 1 percent of analysts' ratings were sell recommendations.

Further reading
Opdyke, Jeff D. "Guidelines Aim to Polish Analysts' Image," *Wall Street Journal,* 13 June 2001, p. C1; Securities Industry Association website. Available on-line. URL: www.sia.com.

securitization

Securitization is the process of pooling and repackaging homogeneous FINANCIAL INSTRUMENTS in the form of marketable securities. In each pool of LOANS, the financial instruments are similar with regard to maturity and type of loan (MORTGAGE, automobile, consumer, etc.). The pools of loans are transferred to a TRUST, which then, with the assistance of an underwriter, sells securities (usually called certificates and backed by the pool of loans) to ultimate investors. Often the financial institution instituting the securitization will enhance the credit rating of the securities by insuring the payments against DEFAULT.

In the United States, securitization began in the early 1970s with the sale of bundles of mortgage loans by the GOVERNMENT NATIONAL MORTGAGE ASSOCIATION (Ginnie Mae). These were followed in the 1980s by similar mortgage securitizations by the FEDERAL NATIONAL MORTGAGE ASSOCIATION (Fannie Mae), and FEDERAL HOME LOAN MORTGAGE CORPORATION (Freddie Mac). Because these securities were backed by a government agency (Ginnie Mae) or by GOVERNMENT-SPONSORED ENTERPRISES (Fannie Mae and Freddie Mac), they received high credit ratings.

Private CAPITAL MARKET participants quickly jumped into the securitization market and began offering collateralized mortgage obligations (CMOs), mortgage-backed securities (MBSs), and asset-backed securities (ABSs). By insuring the repayment of principal, the government-sponsored obligations retain the credit or default risk, while private-label securitizations transfer the credit risk to investors. By 1998 securitized loans amounted to over $2 trillion.

Securitization has been applied to automobiles, CREDIT CARDS, leases, and other classes of loans. Securitized obligations are fixed-INCOME and DERIVATIVE SECURITIES. They are fixed income in that they pay a set amount to holders but are also derivatives in that the payments are derived from the underlying pool of ASSETS. For lenders, the benefits of securitization are that it releases CAPITAL that can be loaned out to others and, since the lender usually services the loan, generates fees. Lenders PROFIT from loan origination, servicing, and UNDERWRITING fees. For investors, securitized assets are much more liquid than loans and can be adapted to meet the investor's maturity needs.

Most loans are repaid before they mature. While Americans frequently take out 15- and 30-year mortgage loans, the average homeowner stays about seven years in a home. This usually results in repayment of the loan well before maturity. Some investors want earlier return of their money, while others are willing to invest for a longer period of time. INSURANCE companies, using actuarial tables, can accurately predict when they will have to pay off life-insurance obligations and will invest the insurance premiums received to match the predicted payout schedule. To accommodate the needs of investors like insurance companies, many issuers of mortgage-backed and asset-backed securities divide the securities into classes called tranches. Each tranche will have a different priority of payment of interest and principal from the pool of loans. For example, if a pool of automobile loans contained $4 million in loans, the underwriter might divide the pool into four tranches of $1 million each (A,B,C,D), with each tranche to be paid after the other. Almost all automobile loans are for a maximum of five years, but many loans will be paid off in two or three years as consumers trade in their cars. Overall the pool of loans may average 10 percent, but investors in tranche A, to be paid the first $1 million, would accept a lower interest rate because they would be paid back in the first year or two. Investors in tranche D, the last $1 million in payments, would want a higher rate, because they will not be paid back until much later. The underwriter will adjust the rate offered for each tranche to attract investors but also, preferably, at a rate low enough to provide a profit for its securitization effort.

One of the problems associated with mortgage- and asset-back securities is called negative convexity, or price compression. When INTEREST RATES decline, borrowers are more likely to refinance their loans, paying off old loans. Holders of mortgage- and asset-backed securities will receive more repayment of principal, reducing the yield to investors and giving the investor principal to reinvest in a lower-interest-rate market. When interest rates rise, prepayments fall, but since asset-backed securities are priced based on the average life, a longer average life caused by slower repayment will reduce the security's value.

Further reading

Gangwani, Sunil. "Securitization 101." Deloitte & Touche. Available on-line. URL: www.stern.nyu.edu/~igiddy/ABS/securitization101.pdf; Kidwell, David S., Richard L. Peterson, and David W. Blackwell. *Financial Institutions, Markets, and Money,* 7th ed. Forth Worth, Tex.: Dryden Press, 1997.

seniority

Seniority is a system of job allocation and EMPLOYMENT protection based on how long an employee has worked for a company. The length of continuous employment until resignation, transfer, discharge, or LAYOFF often defines seniority. Seniority systems are most prevalent in UNION and government work environments. There are many detailed, legal aspects of seniority, dividing it into categories of employment, series, and class. Employment seniority concerns the original date of hire into a company. All transfers, promotions, and discharges are usually based on employment seniority. Series and class seniority results in exceptions to the employment-date seniority. Laws regarding seniority vary by state laws and corporate rules.

Series seniority is the number of continuous months (of qualifying service) as a regular employee in a series. A class is usually a specific work section within a series. For example, an electrical worker would be part of the electrical series, but may work in the high-power section, which would be a specific class. His seniority would be based on his class, the high-power section, rather than as part of the series, electrical workers. When a person transfers to another section (class), they become the most junior person in that class.

Series and class seniority affects job activities and, more importantly, layoffs. A worker with significant time as an electrician but is relatively new in the high-power section could be laid off before someone who has less time as an electrician but more time in the high-power class. Similar seniority rules are applied to REDUCTIONS IN FORCE (RIFs) of public-sector employees.

Just as there are different ways to classify seniority, there are different ways to lose it. Employees may lose seniority through quitting, resigning, discharge, release, retirement, transfer, or not returning to work when recalled from a layoff. When a recall occurs, the most senior person in the class is the first rehired.

One problem with seniority systems is they discourage workers from changing classes, especially during periods of economic decline. This can contribute to boredom and job dissatisfaction, lowering morale and productivity. Another problem is that seniority can prevent an employer from hiring or promoting the most qualified person because someone else with greater seniority has to be given the position ahead of a junior person. In addition, there is the question of what to do with the seniority system when companies merge. Do employees from one company have seniority over the employees from the company with which it is being merged, or is seniority based on length of service to either company?

Economists are usually critical of seniority systems in that they discourage efficient allocation of RESOURCES. Workers in seniority systems counter that the systems encourage worker loyalty and prevent employer discrimination against older workers.

Further reading

C. Dustman. "Seniority System, and Wages, Experience and Seniority." Available on-line. URL: http://english.townpage. isp.ntt.jp/jtd/biss/jpn/prot6.htm; Seniority: Article 11. University of California-Berkeley Office of Human Resources website. Available on-line. URL: http://hrweb.berkeley.edu/labor/contracts/ prnt11.htm.

—Lourdes Owens

services

Services are intangible activities that are the main object of a transaction between a buyer and seller. They are probably best described by what they are not: PRODUCTS. Services are the fastest-growing component of the U.S. economy. Approximately two-thirds of U.S. GROSS DOMESTIC PRODUCT is comprised of expenditures for services. Spending on services tends to be higher in developed countries than developing economies (EMERGING MARKETS).

Marketers understand that customers make purchase decisions to satisfy needs or wants. Many purchase decisions include both products and services; for example, a restaurant meal is both a product, the meal, and the service provided. In a famous article, marketing professor Theodore Levitt described marketing myopia, the failure of businesses to recognize their full scope. Product orientation rather than customer-benefits orientation endangers an enterprise's growth. Product orientation can lead to failure to recognize the service component of a firm's offerings.

Services have many unique characteristics requiring different marketing strategies. First, services are intangible; customers usually cannot use their senses to evaluate a service prior to purchase. For example, how can a consumer evaluate a haircut before she has hired the stylist? Because most services are intangible, marketers attempt to demonstrate tangible benefits associated with a service.

Services also are often inseparable from the service provider. This is an important consideration in service-promotion strategy. Most attorneys, accountants, doctors, and other professional-service providers depend heavily on building relationships. Service professionals participate in community organizations, offer pro bono services to nonprofit organizations, frequently offer to be quoted as an expert in local media, and carefully manage their public image. Inseparability of services from the provider results in direct DISTRIBUTION CHANNELS, usually with no market intermediaries.

Services also tend to be heterogeneous, meaning they are difficult to standardize. For example, how can one compare realtor services? Heterogeneity can be turned into a strategy to personalize and customize services, which results in price variability. Variation in service quality also presents a challenge to marketers to meet and exceed customer-service expectations.

Most services are also perishable. Service businesses generally do not hold inventories; hotel occupancy, for example, is determined daily, and if a room is not rented for the evening, that service opportunity is lost. This leads to last-minute PRICING STRATEGIES, on-line discounting, and alternative SALES PROMOTION efforts.

Lastly, services often involve considerable buyer involvement. Accountants need information from clients; hairdressers need preferences from customers; airlines need preferences, schedules, and special-needs information from customers. Because most services are contingent on buyer involvement, service marketers have greater opportunity to develop relationships, anticipate customer needs, and customize marketing mixes.

Many service industries are plagued with productivity problems. The inherent nature of services minimizes opportunities for productivity gains. INTERNET technology is providing some efficiency benefits through automation of routine procedures and providing consumers with vast amounts of information. In the process, some service providers, such as travel agents, are facing increasing pressure to demonstrate their service benefits. With an aging population and continued affluence, most service markets will continue to grow in the United States.

See also MARKETING STRATEGY.

sexual harassment

Sexual harassment is a form of EMPLOYMENT discrimination. It involves unwelcome sexual advances, requests for sexual favors, and verbal or physical behavior of a sexual nature at a workplace. Victims may include individuals who are not being harassed directly but are affected by the sexual conduct. The harasser may be the victim's supervisor or boss, a supervisor of another department, a coworker, or a nonemployee. In addition, the harasser and the victim may be of the same gender.

Sexual harassment is considered a form of gender discrimination and is prohibited by federal law under Title VII of the CIVIL RIGHTS ACT of 1964. The U.S. EQUAL EMPLOYMENT OPPORTUNITY COMMISSION (EEOC), an independent federal agency, is empowered to enforce Title VII of the Civil Rights Act of 1964. Thus the EEOC is empowered to enforce laws against sexual harassment, which is also prohibited under state laws.

Sexual harassment can occur in two types of situations. The first, known as quid pro quo harassment, is sexual harassment that occurs when an individual's employment status implicitly or explicitly depends on their submission to or rejection of sexual advances or other actions of a sexual nature. This includes situations in which decisions to hire, fire, promote, or demote an individual are dependent on whether that individual acquiesces to the harasser's sexual requests. The second, known as hostile environment harassment, is sexual harassment that occurs when the unwelcome sexual advances or sexual actions create a hostile or intimidating work atmosphere or interfere with the victim's work performance, even when the victim is not fired or loses any pay for failing to comply with the unwelcome advances or actions. This may include constructive discharge, which refers to the practice of making working conditions uncomfortable in an effort to cause employees to resign.

An individual who believes he or she is a victim of sexual harassment can file a charge of discrimination with the EEOC or the appropriate state agency if state or local law also covers the charge. Charges of sexual harassment must be filed with the EEOC before private lawsuits concerning sexual harassment may be pursued. Charges must be filed with the EEOC within 180 days from the date of the alleged violations. This deadline may be extended to 300 days from the date of the alleged violations if state or local laws also cover the charge. If the EEOC finds that the charges are valid, the EEOC may prosecute them on the victim's behalf. If the EEOC decides not to prosecute the charges, then it may issue the victim a "right to sue" notice that allows the victim to file a private lawsuit in an appropriate court. The lawsuit must be filed within strict time limits, generally within 90 days of receiving a "right to use" notice from the EEOC.

If a court finds that sexual harassment occurred, the DAMAGES awarded to the victim may include back pay, hiring, promotion, reinstatement, or other remedies that would put the victim in the position he or she would have been if the sexual harassment had not occurred. A court may also order the employer to pay the victim's attorney's fees, expert-witness fees, and court costs. The victim may also receive punitive damages if the employer acted with malice or reckless indifference (as defined legally). In addition, a court may order the employer to take corrective or preventive measures to ensure that sexual harassment does not recur in the future.

In 1995 the EEOC prosecuted Del Laboratories, Inc. (Del), a cosmetics and pharmaceutical manufacturer, in a sexual-harassment lawsuit. Del settled the lawsuit for approximately $1.2 million dollars to be paid to the 15 victims who filed the charges against the company. As part of the settlement, the court ordered Del to provide all its employees with training for the prevention of sexual harassment and to revise its sexual-harassment policy.

In 1998 Mitsubishi Motor Manufacturing of America (Mitsubishi) settled a sexual-harassment lawsuit (prosecuted by the EEOC) for $34 million to be paid to 350 victims. The settlement agreement required Mitsubishi to revise its sexual-harassment policy; revise its corporate policy to encourage employees to file complaints about sexual-harassment policy violations; impose substantial discipline (including termination of EMPLOYMENT) on managers and supervisors who engage in sexual harassment; and provide mandatory sexual-harassment training for managers, supervisors, and employees. The court also appointed monitors to assess whether Mitsubishi was complying with the requirements of the settlement agreement. In 2000 the court-appointed monitors reported that Mitsubishi was in compliance and that sexual harassment was under control at the Mitsubishi plant.

Given the high COSTS arising out of claims of sexual harassment including litigation costs, the costs of implementing court-ordered corrective or preventative measures, possible loss of employee productivity due to a hostile work environment, and the loss of reputation if an organization is found guilty of sexual harassment, it is prudent for organizations to take steps to prevent sexual harassment. Organizations should develop an effective sexual-harassment policy and effective complaint procedures so that charges of sexual harassment are dealt with speedily and discipline is imposed on harassers. Organizations should also continually train all employees to be sensitive to issues of sexual harassment and continually remind employees of the organization's policy and the consequences of violating it.

Further reading
Equal Employment Opportunity Commission website, www.eeoc.gov; Levy, Anne C. *Workplace Sexual Harassment,* 2d ed. Upper Saddle River, N.J.: Pearson Education, March 2001.

—Gayatri Gupta

shareholder rights plans   See POISON-PILL STRATEGIES.

shareholders (stockholders)
Shareholders are individuals, MUTUAL FUNDS, and other groups who collectively own a CORPORATION. The concept of shareholders and joint-stock corporations evolved in Europe during the 17th and 18th centuries. In the United States, WALL STREET in New York City became the center of stock trading during the early 1800s.

Shareholders, also called stockholders, typically are entitled to a share of the corporation's ASSETS in proportion to the number of shares they hold compared to the number of shares issued by the company. (For decades, American Telephone and Telegraph (AT&T) was the mostly widely held corporation in America.) In addition to owning part of the assets of a company, shareholders hold voting rights equal to the number of shares they own, are entitled to DIVIDENDS when declared by the BOARD OF DIRECTORS, and have first rights to purchase additional shares when the corporation authorizes additional stock offerings.

There are two types of shareholders, holders of COMMON STOCK and holders of preferred stock (called ordinary and preference shares respectively in Britain). The rights described above apply to shareholders of common stock. Shareholders of preferred stock typically do not have voting rights, are paid a fixed dividend, and have claims against the assets ahead of common-stock shareholders. Preferred stock is similar to a corporate bond, with a fixed payment rate but, unlike BONDS, preferred shares typically do not have a set maturity date. Preferred stock can be either cumulative or noncumulative. Cumulative shares must be paid any passed dividends before dividends can be paid to common-stock shareholders. Most preferred stock in the United States is cumulative stock. For example, in the 1980s, when Chrysler Corporation (now Chrysler-Daimler) returned to profitability after a government bailout (similar to the airline industry bailout after September 11, 2001), investors holding preferred shares received all back payments owed before the company resumed dividends to common-stock shareholders.

The board of directors determines dividends and announces the amount of the dividend, the date the dividend will be paid to shareholders, and the ex-dividend date. Ex-dividend dates are typically about two weeks before the dividend payment date, allowing the corporation time to issue the dividend to the shareholder of record on that date. STOCK MARKET reporting services indicate with an "x" shares that have gone ex-dividend that day. Dividend payments are taxable as personal INCOME under U.S. tax laws. Critics argue this amounts to double taxation, because corporations pay corporate taxes on PROFITS earned before distribution of dividends.

While shareholders own a corporation, managers direct the day-to-day affairs of the company, and the board of directors represents shareholders in guiding overall corporate strategy. Shareholders' LIABILITY is limited to their INVESTMENT in the company. Shareholder ownership interest in a corporation is usually freely transferable to other investors. After an INITIAL PUBLIC OFFERING, inside investors are usually restricted from selling their shares for a specified period of time. During the DOT-COMS frenzy of the late 1990s and early 2000, many dot-com employees with STOCK OPTIONS and preauthorized shares saw the value of their assets drop from millions to nothing before the holding period expired and they were allowed to sell their shares.

Unlike shareholders in a corporation, owners of shares of a PARTNERSHIP typically cannot freely transfer their ownership to others. Unless specified in the partnership agreement, transfer of partnership shares entitle the recipient to the financial benefits attached to those shares but do not make the recipient a partner in the enterprise.

Sherman Antitrust Act

The Sherman Antitrust Act of 1890 was designed to prevent the concentration of economic power in the hands of a few firms and individuals. Along with the Interstate Commerce Act of 1887, the Sherman Act (named after its sponsor, Senator John Sherman of Ohio) was one of the first major efforts by the U.S. government to constrain the power of leaders in the AMERICAN INDUSTRIAL REVOLUTION.

Beginning in the mid-19th century, large manufacturing companies and combinations of companies gained greater control of the American economy. Referred to as the "robber barons," industrialists including Andrew Carnegie, John D.

Rockefeller, William Henry Vanderbilt, and others engaged in a variety of activities to maximize their gains, usually by restraining COMPETITION. Dominant firms often conspired to monopolize markets and eliminate competitors, actions that were not new to legal experts. In 1414 Englishman John Dyer was accused of agreeing not to compete within his town for half a year. In 1711 the English case of *Mitchel v. Reynolds* established the rule that not all agreements restraining trade were illegal, only the unreasonable ones. This became known as the rule of reason, by which general restraints designed to limit competition were illegal.

The Sherman Act contains only two important sections.

SECTION 1. TRUSTS, ETC., IN RESTRAINT OF TRADE ILLEGAL; PENALTY

Every CONTRACT, combination in the form of TRUST or otherwise, or conspiracy, in restraint of trade or commerce among the several States, or with foreign nations, is declared to be illegal. Every person who shall make any contract or engage in any combination or conspiracy hereby declared to be illegal shall be deemed guilty of a felony, and, on conviction thereof, shall be punished by fine nor exceeding one million dollars if a CORPORATION, or, if any other person, one hundred thousand dollars or by imprisonment not exceeding three years, or by both said punishments, in the discretion of the court.

SECTION 2. MONOPOLIZING TRADE A FELONY; PENALTY

Every person who shall monopolize, or attempt to monopolize, or combine or conspire with any other person or persons, to monopolize any part of the trade or commerce among the several States, or with foreign nations, shall be deemed guilty of a felony, and, on conviction thereof, shall be punished by fine not exceeding one million dollars if a corporation, or, if any other person, one hundred thousand dollars or by imprisonment not exceeding three years, or by both said punishments, in the discretion of the court.

The Sherman Act allows both criminal and civil cases to be brought against parties. The federal government can pursue criminal prosecutions, and a private party can sue civilly for DAMAGES. To encourage civil suits, the act allows private parties to collect treble (three times) damages if they prevail in a lawsuit.

ANTITRUST LAWS are tied to economic theory. Economists argue competition encourages ECONOMIC EFFICIENCY. Producers provide what consumers most want and do so using RESOURCES in their most productive capacity. Those firms that do the best job of providing for consumers' needs in least-cost manner prosper and do not decline or disappear from the market. The natural outcome is that some firms will expand and eventually dominate markets where they are the most efficient producers. Often as companies become very large, they lose their competitive edge, either by losing touch with consumer needs or by expanding beyond their areas or levels of productive efficiency. This leads to opportunities for new firms to enter markets, revitalizing those markets through competition. The Austrian school of economic thought calls this process "creative destruction."

If, however, the large firm can build effective BARRIERS TO ENTRY, it can continue to dominate a market. The Sherman Act was designed to address this problem. Not all economists or antitrust lawyers agree on when to enforce the act. The "traditional" school, associated with Harvard University, condemns any concentration of economic power. They tend to scrutinize any proposed merger for potential adverse effects on the dynamic benefits of having many independent firms in a market. The Chicago school (University of Chicago) of thought focuses on economic efficiency, claiming that large firms are not necessarily anticompetitive. According to the Chicago school, if large firms can allocate resources more efficiently, they should not be subject to antitrust challenges.

The Antitrust Division of the U.S. Justice Department has primary responsibility for enforcement of the Sherman Act. Enforcement has varied depending on the political party in control of the executive branch of the federal government and its economic philosophy. Generally, the Chicago school, advocating a more lenient approach to antitrust enforcement, dominated antitrust policy during the 1980s, while Harvard's traditional approach was more prevalent in the 1970s and 1990s.

While the Sherman Act applies to most interstate commerce, a number of activities and specific groups are exempt from the act. As authors Bruce Fisher and Michael Phillips suggest, "the reasons these areas are exempt run the gamut from pure political power to policy reasons." Exempt areas include

- most labor UNION activities. Logically the goal of unions is to increase their benefits to workers through bargaining power with employers. Initially the Sherman Act was used against the Danbury Hatters (*Loewe v. Lawlor,* 1908) who attempted to use BOYCOTTS to pressure the company.

- intrastate activities having no effect on interstate commerce. The federal government has no authority to regulate intrastate commerce, but most activities by firms of any size, impact interstate commerce and therefore makes them subject to federal antitrust laws.

- farmer and fisherman organizations. Under the Capper-Volstead Act and Fisheries Cooperative Marketing Act (1934), fishermen and farmers can organize (see COOPERATIVE) to increase their market power, either through selling collectively or buying collectively.

- export associations. U.S. companies can create associations to increase their market power in international trade. The federal government allows this otherwise anticompetitive activity in response to foreign governments' support and subsidies of domestic companies.

- baseball. In an historic oddity, the actions of professional baseball clubs are exempt from antitrust regulation. This allows baseball club owners to meet and determine where clubs will be located and approve transfers of clubs from one city to another.

- certain regulated industries. Some industries, like INSURANCE, which are regulated by other federal agencies, are exempt from antitrust regulation.

- small businesses. Under the Small Business Act of 1953, small businesses are allowed to engage in certain actions that would otherwise be considered antitrust violations.

Certain actions are considered "per se"—that is, obviously harmful violations of the Sherman Act. These include horizontal division of markets, horizontal PRICE FIXING, vertical price fixing, group boycotts, and certain TYING CONTRACTS. Horizontal division of markets occurs when firms divide up markets geographically. For example, sales representatives of competing firms often wind up staying in the same hotels. If two sales reps agreed, "You take Tennessee and I take Kentucky," they are engaging in horizontal division of markets. If the two sales reps agreed to charge the same price to customers and compete on a nonprice basis, they are engaging in horizontal price fixing.

Vertical price fixing occurs when participants in the marketing chain (manufacturers, WHOLESALERS, retailers) agree to set prices, called resale price maintenance. If a manufacturer refuses to sell to a wholesaler unless it agrees to charge set prices, the manufacturer is potentially impairing competition. The enforcement of resale price maintenance, as part of the Sherman Act, has varied over time; until 1937 it was a per se violation. The 1937 Miller-Tydings Act excluded resale price maintenance from the Sherman Act, but in 1976 Congress repealed the Miller-Tydings Act.

Group boycotts, usually involving groups of sellers refusing to sell to certain wholesalers, are also illegal under the Sherman Act. A seller can refuse to sell to a particular buyer or group of buyers without violating the act. If a group of sellers organize to boycott certain types of buyers, often discount companies, they are in violation of the Sherman Act.

Some tying agreements, whereby the seller requires the buyer to purchase certain items as a condition for purchasing other items, are illegal under the Sherman Act. An agreement involving patented PRODUCTS or unique items are more likely to be per se violations of the act.

See also CLAYTON ANTITRUST ACT; INTERSTATE COMMERCE COMMISSION; MONOPOLY.

Further reading

Fisher, Bruce D., and Michael J. Phillips. *The Legal, Ethical and Regulatory Environment of Business,* 8th ed. Cincinnati, Ohio: Thomson/South-Western, 2003.

short selling

Short selling is an INVESTMENT technique that makes MONEY when the price of stock is falling. The investor sells stock that he or she does not own for delivery on a future date. At first glance this seems impossible. However on the delivery date, the investor must buy the stock from the open market, upon which he or she can fulfill the commitment to deliver the stock in the original sale agreement. If, during the time between the original sale date and the delivery date, the stock price has fallen, the investor buys the stock to be delivered at a lower price and so makes a PROFIT on the falling price. The reverse is also true; if, during the delayed delivery time, the price rises, the investor must buy the stock at a higher price and therefore loses money. As a result, during a time when stocks are falling in value, it is possible to make money on the STOCK MARKET.

Stock brokerage firms facilitate short selling, often lending shares owned by the brokerage house. Most brokerage firms will allow short selling only on an "up tick"—that is, when the price of the stock advances. This prevents investors from "jumping on the bandwagon," selling short a stock whose price is plummeting.

—Mack Tennyson

shut-down point

The shut-down point is the point at which a firm would be better off closing its operations and producing zero output. Shutting down is not the same as going out of business; it is temporarily suspending production. If a firm shuts down, it will still incur fixed COSTS, often labor, rent, and other payments the firm has committed to paying. In some situations, if the firm's total revenue were very low, it would lose more MONEY by continuing to produce than by shutting down. For the owners of many seasonal businesses, there is likely to be so few sales at certain times of the year that they are better off temporarily closing down. For years ski areas logically closed down for the summer, and beach resorts closed in the winter. Some ski areas have found there is summer demand from mountain-bike riders and people just wanting a scenic view and thus have reopened in the summertime. While ski-area operators are probably not making a PROFIT from their summer business, total revenue is greater than total variable costs, contributing to paying some of the fixed costs. The ski area is losing less money in the summertime by being open than by closing.

In economic analysis, the shut-down point is the point at which total revenue just equals total variable costs, or price just equals average variable cost. If price just equals average variable cost, the firm is losing money, its fixed costs, but is "covering" its variable costs. At the shut-down point, the firm is losing the same amount of money regardless of whether it is operating or closed.

In the real world, most owners are optimistic about their business, which is why they started their firm. Many small-business owners, especially new entrepreneurs, will ignore the shut-down point rule. They expect to quickly increase sales or be able to raise their price to overcome their losses. These owners can stay in business as long as they have CAPITAL or financing from creditors.

See also SUPPLY RULE.

simplified employee pension (SEP-IRA)

The simplified employee pension (SEP) is a defined-contributions pension plan. The SEP is also known as a SEP-IRA because companies contribute to INDIVIDUAL RETIREMENT ACCOUNTS (IRA) for their employees. A defined-contributions plan allows companies or their employees to determine how much will be invested in a pension. These differ from defined-benefits plans, which regulate how retirement INCOME is disbursed. SEPs appeal to small businesses that often do not have the time or CAPITAL to manage a defined-benefits plan.

Defined-contribution plans such as SEPs derive from the EMPLOYEE RETIREMENT INCOME SECURITY ACT of 1974 (ERISA). In creating SEPs, Congress was responding to the fact that nearly all companies of 5,000 or more employees provided some type of pension or RETIREMENT PLAN, while few companies of under 100 employees did not. Congress legislated that any business with 25 employees or fewer could set up an SEP, including CORPORATIONS, PARTNERSHIPS, and sole PROPRIETORSHIPS. SEPs are regulated by the Internal Revenue Code, Title 26, section 408(k).

SEPs are attractive to small-business owners and the self-employed because they are relatively easy to set up, inexpensive to manage, and tax deductible. Employees benefit because contributions are made by their company and can be far greater than those allowed by ordinary IRAs: up to 15 percent of an employee's annual salary or $30,000, whichever is less. In addition, employees may contribute $2,000 annually to an SEP as they would to any other IRA, although they are not required to invest anything.

Setting up a SEP is simple. The employer must fill out IRS Form 5035-SEP—the Simplified Employee Pension–Individual Retirement Accounts Contribution Agreement—and distribute it to all eligible employees. Eligible employees are those who have worked for the company for three of the previous five years, earned more than $450 (annually adjusted for INFLATION), and are 21 years of age or older. They may not be part of a COLLECTIVE BARGAINING agreement or nonresident immigrants. The employer must then determine what percentage of salary will be contributed to the SEP. The amount can vary from 0 to 15 percent, but the percentage must be the same for all eligible employees. Self-employed company owners may contribute up to 13.04 percent of their salary. There is a $170,000 salary maximum after which the 15 percent contribution is no longer allowed. In lean years, employers are not required to contribute anything, removing one impediment to setting up a retirement plan in the first place.

Salary deductions are not allowed as contributions to a SEP. Prior to 1997, companies could deduct employee wages and invest them in a Salary-Reduction Simplified Employee Pension (SARSEP), but that is no longer the case. Employees who were invested in a SARSEP before 1997 are still able to contribute through payroll deduction, but no new SARSEPs can be created.

Once employees have been notified of the company's intention to begin a SEP, either the company or the employees will set up an IRA at a financial institution. Financial institutions comprise banks, SAVINGS AND LOAN ASSOCIATIONS, INSURANCE companies, and CREDIT UNIONS, among others. Stocks, MUTUAL FUNDS, money market funds, and savings accounts are all acceptable INVESTMENT vehicles. Employees are fully vested from the moment the SEP is created, meaning they are entitled to the full amount the company has contributed to their account. Other types of pensions may require the employee to wait as long as five to seven years before they are so entitled.

An SEP is a tax-deferred retirement savings account; employees will not be taxed on the investment as long as the funds remain in the account. Just as with a regular IRA, an employee may withdraw funds once they are 59½ years of age, at which time he or she will be taxed. Withdrawal prior to retirement will be taxed at a rate of 10 percent, unless it is placed or rolled over into another IRA within a year. If the employee becomes disabled, the distribution tax will be waived. All employees are required to begin withdrawing by the time they turn 70½. Employees may name a beneficiary to receive their distribution should they die prematurely.

Business owners benefit from enrolling their employees in an SEP for a number of reasons. An SEP is considered a tax-deductible business expense. Set-up requires minimal effort, and there are no ANNUAL REPORTS to file with the INTERNAL REVENUE SERVICE, keeping administrative costs low. Employers can also tailor an SEP by annually reviewing the percent of salary that they contribute and adjusting that figure according to their company's present fiscal situation. Also, once contributions are made, investment decisions become the responsibility of the employee, thus reducing the company's LIABILITY for poor investment returns. The employer does not need to convince employees to participate as in some other plan, because the company is required to contribute for all eligible employees, whether they agree or not. Even if an employee terminates his or her EMPLOYMENT or dies before the year's end, he or she will still be vested.

There are drawbacks to SEPs. Business owners must consider carefully whether it makes financial sense to set up an SEP, because although the cost of administering the plan is small, the company is the sole contributor. Additionally, employees are fully vested in an SEP from the outset and can roll the money over at any time into another IRA. This reduces the leverage employers might have to retain employees as they would with a pension that vests employees gradually. Employees may change jobs, taking their pension with them. Employers must also be careful to compensate all employees at the same rate and are forbidden from requiring that employees take a cut in pay to enroll. Part-time employees who meet the criteria must be included, and in the case of bankruptcy, the vested party may not be able to protect his or her investment from creditors.

There are a number of alternatives to the SEP. For instance, 401(K) PLANS are extremely popular and allow employees to contribute up to 15 percent of their income along with company matching, but they are expensive and cumbersome to administer. Employees in companies of 100 or fewer workers can contribute up to $6,000 annually to a savings incentive match plan (simple), but the company is required to contribute a percentage as well. The KEOGH PLAN permits deferring 25 percent of salary (up to $30,000) from taxes each year. Keogh contributions are higher than SEPs, but they are more difficult and costly to administer.

Business owners must carefully assess their present position and select the plan that provides the greatest benefit for both the company and its employees. In general, a 401(k) plan may be more attractive to a larger company undaunted by the administrative costs. A simple plan may appeal to self-employed individuals with low income and no employees or with high income and a few employees. An SEP would more likely attract a self-employed, high-income individual with few or no employees.

Further reading

Blakely, Stephen. "Pension Power." Nation's Business, July 1997, p. 12; Fraser, Jill Andresky. "The ABCs of Retirement Plans," Inc 19, no. 5 (April 1997): 103; Grudzien, Larry L. "SEPs Worth Consideration by Smaller Employers," Pension Management 32, no. 4 (April 1996): 52; Maynard, Philip. "You Can Pick the Right Retirement Plan for a Small Business." Financial Services Advisor 144, no. 4 (July/August 2001): 36; Thomas Madden Sources; 101st Congress; 2nd Session in the Senate of the United States as Reported in the Senate. S. 685 - 1989 S. 685; 101 S. 685; United States Code, Title 26, Section 408(k).

—Tom Madden

sinking fund

A sinking fund is a series of regular payments to provide for the orderly retirement (payoff) of a bond issue. Sinking-fund provisions may call for the annual retirement of a portion of a bond issue or may call for annual deposits into a fund, often managed by a trustee, which will accrue to the amount sufficient to retire the BONDS at their maturity. Designed as protection for bondholders, sinking funds are a drain on a firm's cash and can be disastrous for firms with cash-flow problems. Failure to meet sinking-fund provisions causes the bonds to be in DEFAULT, which, in turn can lead to insolvency and bankruptcy (see BUSINESS FAILURE).

Small Business Administration

The Small Business Administration (SBA), created in 1953, provides LOANS, loan guarantees, and business counseling and advice to owners and would-be owners of small businesses. In 2000, the SBA portfolio included over 200,000 loans worth more than $45 billion. The SBA is part of the U.S. Department of Commerce.

The SBA expanded upon the roles of two previous government agencies, the Reconstruction Finance Corporation (RFC), and the Smaller War Plants Corporation (SWPC). The RTC, created in 1932, made loans to all businesses, small and large, hurt by the GREAT DEPRESSION. The SWPC, created in 1942, provided direct loans to small enterprises, supported lending by large financial institutions to small businesses, and advocated small-business efforts to gain part of federal procurement needs during World War II.

Since its creation in 1953, the SBA's role has been expanded numerous times. In 1958 it established the Small Business Investment Company (SBIC) to license, regulate and provide funding for VENTURE CAPITAL investment firms. In 1964 it created the Equal Opportunity Loan Program (EOL) to provide loans for low-income individuals unable to attract CAPITAL for the creation of new businesses.

SBA programs support small businesses and low-income entrepreneurs through financing, counseling, and technical assistance. Critics suggest many SBA programs discriminate against noneligible small businesses and unfairly subsidize businesses in the programs. The SBA manages a wide array of programs, including

- *Basic 7(a) Loan Guarantee.* SBA's primary short- and long-term loan program for start-up and existing businesses cannot obtain financing through normal private-lending channels. Loan guarantees are used through participating, commercial lenders; maximum amount, $750,000
- *CAPLines.* Short-term and cyclical working capital loan guarantees; maximum, $750,000
- *Defense Loan & Technical Assistance (DELTA).* Assistance for small businesses hurt by cuts in defense spending, using loan guarantees
- *Community Adjustment and Investment (CAIP).* Assistance to businesses affected by changes due to NAFTA (North American Free Trade Agreement)
- *Export Working Capital (EWCP).* Loan guarantees to finance export transactions
- *International Trade Loan (ITL).* Long-term loan guarantees for companies engaged in or preparing to engage in international trade
- *Energy & Conservation Loan.* Loan guarantees for eligible small businesses engaged in energy-conservation markets
- *Pollution Control Loan.* Loan guarantees for businesses planning or installing pollution-control facilities

- *Second Market.* Facilitates buying and selling of SBA-guaranteed loans
- *SBAExpress.* Allows participating lenders to use their own documentation to approve, service, and liquidate loans up to $150,000
- *CommunityExpress.* Loan guarantees up to $250,000 for job creation in designated rural and inner-city areas
- *Microloan (7m) Loan Program.* Provides loans up to $25,000 to small businesses through approved nonprofit groups
- *Small Business Investment Company (SBIC).* Provides EQUITY capital, long-term loans, and other financing through licensed SBICs, privately owned, for PROFIT venture capital firms, about 350 in the United States
- *Surety Bond Guarantee.* Guarantees bid, performance, and payment BONDS for up to $1.25 million for eligible small businesses, which cannot obtain surety bonds through commercial channels
- *Prime contracting.* Establishes small business set-aside programs in federal projects
- *Small Business Development Center (SBDC).* Provides MANAGEMENT and technical assistance for small business owners through SBDCs
- *Service Corps of Retired Executives (SCORE).* Offers counseling and training for small-business owners through volunteer services of retired executives
- *Disaster Assistance.* Loans, at reduced rates, for homeowners and businesses affected by disasters
- *Export Assistance Centers.* Coordinates RESOURCES of various federal programs supporting EXPORTING activity
- *Empowerment Zones/Enterprise Communities.* Provides centralized access to community small-business programs
- *Welfare to Work.* Coordinates small businesses and former WELFARE recipients in job-search efforts.

Further reading
Small Business Administration website. Available on-line. URL: www.sba.gov.

Smoot-Hawley Tariff Act

The Smoot-Hawley Tariff Act, officially the Tariff Act of 1930, significantly raised TARIFFS on IMPORTS into the United States. Intended to protect U.S. agricultural PRODUCTS, by the time the act was signed by President Herbert Hoover, it raised tariffs an average of 60 percent on a wide array of goods.

The act is named after Senator Reed Smoot from Utah and Congressman Willis Hawley from Oregon. Senator Smoot was chair of the Senate Finance Committee and Representative Hawley chaired the House Ways and Means Committee. At the time, U.S. agriculture was in a serious economic slump. Drought had reduced output in much of the country. Over-INVESTMENT strapped farmers' limited INCOME, and prices lower than the cost of PRODUCTION eliminated hope of recovery. As the Tariff Act proceeded through Congress, a process known as "log-rolling" took over. Individual items beyond the initial goal of increasing agricultural tariffs were added to the bill as each subcommittee considered the legislation. Senate floor proceedings during debate of the bill were described as chaotic. Though the bill barely passed the Senate (44-42) and more than 1,000 economists signed a petition warning of its harmful effects, President Hoover signed it into law.

Although the U.S. economy was already in a RECESSION before Smoot-Hawley was signed, most economists agree the act added significantly to the severity of the GREAT DEPRESSION. As predicted at the time, other countries quickly passed similar legislation, and world trade declined dramatically. Between 1930 and 1931, U.S. exports declined 33 percent, and imports fell 29 percent. Increased uncertainty associated with protectionist trade legislation reduced investment, adding to the economy's problems.

In 1934 Congress passed the Reciprocal Trade Agreement Act, allowing the president to lower tariffs in return for reductions in foreign tariffs on U.S. goods. This began the process of redeveloping trade relations. Followed by the General Agreement on Tariff and Trade (GATT, 1947), the various GATT "Rounds" of trade negotiations, and the creation of the WORLD TRADE ORGANIZATION (WTO) in 1997, the United States has significantly expanded its international trade.

Further reading
Feldman, David H. "Investment during the great depression: uncertainty and the role of the Smoot-Hawley tariff," *Southern Economic Journal* 64, no. 4 (April 1998).

social audit
A social audit is an analysis of a company's environmental and social impact. Social audits evaluate a company's relationships with its employees. SHAREHOLDERS, and the local communities affected by its activities. Many CORPORATIONS have developed BUSINESS ETHICS standards. Social audits, usually conducted by an outside agency, review a company's performance against its standards and make recommendations for improvement.

A social audit will usually include analysis of a company's

- health and safety practices
- environmental practices
- community development
- working conditions
- labor practices
- human-rights protection
- training and promotion

Social audits are increasingly important to a company's image; positive results are sometimes used as part of mar-keting strategies. In recent years multinational companies have faced increased scrutiny and pressure to improve CORPORATE SOCIAL RESPONSIBILITY. Reports of working conditions in textile factories around the world have influenced major U.S. retailers to review and take increased responsibility for practices in companies they purchase from.

Social audits can be time-consuming and expensive. Some companies attempt to demonstrate their social responsibility through philanthropic and community services and socially responsible INVESTMENT efforts.

Further reading
Helms, Marilyn M. *Encyclopedia of Management,* 4th ed. Detroit: Gale Group, 2000.

social facilitation
Social facilitation occurs when one's behavior or performance is affected in some manner by the presence of other people. Either the simple presence of a coactor, someone performing the same task but who is not in COMPETITION, or the presence of an audience may influence how a person does a job. Typically the presence of others enhances the performance of simple or well-learned tasks, while the performance of complex or unpracticed tasks tends to deteriorate.

Social facilitation may be the product of increased levels of energy (arousal), evaluation apprehension, or the distracting effect of having an audience. Psychologist Robert Zajonc proposed that the presence of other people increases physiological arousal, or excess physical energy. This arousal then facilitates the performance of whatever response is dominant for the actor. Thus, performance of easy or well-learned (dominant) tasks should get better with an audience, but performance of difficult or poorly learned tasks should suffer.

However, psychologist Nickolas Cottrell argued that evaluation apprehension, or nervousness about having one's performance judged by others, also could account for social facilitation. This explanation suggests that people are aware that others' evaluations of them often dictate future rewards or punishments. Thus, actors may experience increased nervousness in social situations because they are concerned with what type of impression they may convey to their audience. Evaluation apprehension subsequently increases arousal, which, as Zajonc proposed, then facilitates performance of the actor's dominant response.

Psychologist Robert S. Baron suggested that the presence of others might be distracting for the actor. When an actor's attention is divided between the task at hand and the audience, a mental conflict arises regarding the focus of attention. This mental conflict might increase arousal, which then tends to facilitate the dominant response. Performance of very simple and well-learned tasks probably is less affected by the distraction of an audience than by performance of complex or unpracticed tasks.

All three explanations of social facilitation predict that the tendency for an audience to facilitate or hinder performance depends on how challenging the task is and on the actor's level of expertise. However, in some instances, expertise may completely override task difficulty. For example, experts at difficult tasks, such as golfing, typically have practiced so often that successfully executing the task has become their dominant response. Therefore, throngs of spectators at a professional golf tournament tend to enhance the professional's game but likely would hinder the novice.

Overall, the effects of social facilitation are very well documented, lending additional credence to the saying that "practice makes perfect."

See also HAWTHORNE EXPERIMENTS; INDUSTRIAL-ORGANIZATIONAL PSYCHOLOGY; SOCIAL LOAFING.

Further reading

Baron, Robert A., and Donn Byrne. *Social Psychology,* 9th ed. Boston: Allyn and Bacon, 2000; Baron, R. S., D. Moore, and G. Sanders. "Distraction as a source of drive in social facilitation research." *Journal of Personality and Social Psychology* 36 (1978): 816–24; Cottrell, N., K. Wack, G. Sekerak, and R. Little. "Social facilitation of dominant responses by the presence of an audience and the mere presence of others." *Journal of Personality and Social Psychology* 9 (1968): 245–50; Forsyth, Donelson R. *Group Dynamics,* 3d ed. Belmont, Calif.: Wadsworth Publishing, 1999; Zajonc, R. B., and S. M. Sales. "Social facilitation of dominant and subordinate responses." *Journal of Experimental Social Psychology* 2 (1966): 160–68.

—Elizabeth L. Cralley

socialism

Socialism is a political and economic theory advocating the reduction of poverty and improvement in social well-being through the collective control and allocation of RESOURCES. Every nation has some degree of socialism. Even the free-market political and economic systems include government control of resources to provide national defense, INFRASTRUCTURE development, and usually education. In the United States, most people equate socialism with communism. Socialism, as espoused and as put into practice, has many variations; two major divisions are social democracy and Marxist socialism.

Social democracy, as practiced in some Scandinavian countries, involves greater collective control and allocation of resources. Social democracies tend to offer free national health INSURANCE, free public education through the university level, free or subsidized housing, and access to WELFARE with few restrictions or requirements. In social democracies, any citizen, not just adults with children, can seek and receive public support. One of the major political parties in most European countries will be social democrats or a similarly named organization. While the Democratic Party in the United States is usually associated with

advocating greater government involvement in the economy and more social programs, in the last 30 years Republican administrations have expanded government spending and deficit spending more than Democratic administrations. (The party controlling the House of Representatives and the U.S. Senate also significantly affects government-spending policies.)

President Franklin Roosevelt (1932–45) significantly increased social spending in the United States. Roosevelt established SOCIAL SECURITY as well as a variety of public-spending programs, and he supported the rights of workers to organize in UNIONS and pursue COLLECTIVE BARGAINING with employers. The 1920s are referred to by some as the era of the "robber barons." Names like Rockefeller, Carnegie, and Vanderbilt exemplified the huge division between the rich and poor in America. Some historians credit Franklin Roosevelt with saving CAPITALISM by providing support for the very poor and limits on wealthy industrialists. Few Americans today are old enough to remember that, in 1932, military personnel with machine-gun bunkers were brought in to insure that Roosevelt's inauguration would be peaceful and not be overwhelmed by protests from the "masses."

Marxist socialism, based on the ideas of Karl Marx and others, advocated workers' control of resources and PRODUCTION. (Many Americans mistakenly think socialism and communism were created in Russia. In fact the term *socialism* was first used in France in the 1830s.) Marx was German-born but spent much of his lifetime in England. Observing the horrible working conditions and barely subsistence wages in industrial revolution factories, Marx predicted and supported a worker's revolution to take control of the means of production. Marx divided the population into two groups, the "bourgeois" and the "proletariat." The bourgeois were the elite, owners of CAPITAL, while the proletariat, were the laborers. Marx predicted the proletariat would rise up, seizing control of the factories. With worker control of the factories, Marx envisioned a classless society, where everyone was equal.

As developed in the 20th century, authoritarian socialism and communism grew and then declined. The Soviet Union and Warsaw Pact countries were the "evil empire" in the cold-war conflict with the United States from the 1940s until 1989. Some economists argue the United States "spent" the Soviet Union into self-destruction. With the cold war, both sides continually escalated military weaponry. The Soviet Union, with its collective control of resources, could not produce military weapons (or other goods) as efficiently as the United States, forcing the Soviet leadership to use a greater share of their limited resources to keep up the "weapons race." This constantly reduced the resources and therefore the goods and SERVICES available for Soviet citizens, eventually leading to the unrest that toppled the government.

One of the major criticisms of socialism is that it does not provide incentives to be efficient or innovative. Capitalism, with private control of resources and PROFIT incentives, provides greater incentives to be productive. Most socialist economies (as of 2002, Cuba, North Korea, and to a lesser degree China) are not leaders in economic output and growth, but critics of capitalism argue that it operates on a system of fear—i.e., if one is not productive, continually replacing technology, updating skills, and responding to threats from competitors, one will be replaced and go hungry. Many people feel that socialism, with collective control and allocation of resources for the collective benefit of the group, works well for family economic decision making.

See also COMPETITION.

social loafing

Social loafing occurs when a person contributes less effort to a group task than he or she would when working on the same task alone. For example, research has shown that two people pulling on one rope together often exert less total strain on the rope than a combination of their individual efforts. The "team" atmosphere actually may tempt individuals to decrease their efforts rather than work harder. Social loafing can be especially problematic for organizations that rely heavily on group efforts in the workplace.

People tend to loaf during group work when individual accountability for their efforts is low or when they think other group members might already be loafing. When individual accountability is low, supervisors and other group members have a difficult time judging how hard any particular group member may be working, perhaps because efforts are all pooled together. When the chances of getting caught loafing are low, people can engage in social loafing without tremendous risk of negative consequences.

People also tend to loaf when they suspect other group members are slacking. Hesitant to become the "sucker" who works harder than other group members, people may decrease their own efforts to a level perceived as comparable to the other social loafers in the group. In either case, individuals are considered "free riders" if they contribute less than the other group members yet share equally in the group's rewards for the work.

On occasion, group members engage in social compensation, which involves taking on extra work in order to offset the negative effects of social loafing. People who are highly committed to a project tend to compensate for others because they wish to see a successful result. In addition, sometimes others will compensate for a group member who appears to lack the skills or ability to contribute equally to the group project.

Rather than rely solely on social compensation, organizations can take straightforward steps to decrease social loafing. First, when individual contributions can be identified and evaluated by a supervisor or other group members, even if a formal evaluation never takes place, social loafing tends to decrease. It appears that evaluation apprehension, or nervousness over the possibility that one's efforts could be judged, helps motivate group members to contribute equally. Second, when tasks are made important both to the individual and to the group, social loafing decreases. People tend to work harder when they have a personal stake in achieving a successful outcome. Finally, social loafing decreases for members of tightly knit groups. Not surprisingly, people generally are willing to work harder for groups that they like.

Organizations tend to assign group work because they assume that a group will be more productive than will a host of individuals working alone. Typically they expect that the positive effects of social facilitation in group settings will lead to better results. Taking steps to decrease social loafing is critical to ensuring that group efforts truly are worth more than the sum of individual contributions.

See also INDUSTRIAL-ORGANIZATIONAL PSYCHOLOGY; SOCIAL FACILITATION.

Further reading

Baron, Robert A., and Donn Byrne. *Social Psychology,* 9th ed. Boston: Allyn and Bacon, 2000; Forsyth, Donelson R. *Group Dynamics,* 3d ed. Belmont, Calif.: Wadsworth Publishing, 1999.

—Elizabeth L. Cralley

socially responsible investing

Socially responsible investing is making INVESTMENT decisions with consideration of social and ethical issues as part of the determination process. Investor decisions typically have goals of INCOME, CAPITAL GAINS, and/or preservation of CAPITAL. Socially responsible investing adds to the decision-making process consideration of issues and concerns such as the environment, military spending, nuclear waste, and tobacco.

Many groups have implemented the concept of socially responsible investing. Churches and universities have long applied what is known as the "sin screen"—no investments in companies that are engaged in tobacco, liquor, or gambling. Opposition to the Vietnam War in the 1960s and early 1970s increased interest among investors concerned with weapons PRODUCTION. Television coverage of the use of defoliants designed to kill vegetation and napalm, a chemical dropped from planes during the war to ignite fires, often burning people, stirred the consciousness of many Americans, including investors. In the 1970s, opposition to companies doing business in apartheid-practicing South Africa expanded efforts toward socially responsible investing. MULTINATIONAL CORPORATIONS (MNCs) came under scrutiny for their investments in South Africa, pressuring many companies to withdraw from the country. Multilateral coordination lead to the creation of the Sullivan Rule, guiding international investment in South Africa. Rev. Leon Sullivan, an American Southern Baptist minister, while on the board of General Motors in 1976, authorized the Sullivan Principles in 1977 as a means for US corporations to bring change while doing business in South Africa. He called for a code of ethics, and his work set the standard for nondiscriminatory employment practices in South Africa under apartheid.

The California Public Employees' Retirement System (CALPERS), the largest state pension fund in the country, uses "basic democratic principles" as part of its international investment guidelines. These guidelines cover such issues as labor standards, political stability, and corporate disclosure. In 2002, CALPERS withdrew investments from Indonesia, Malaysia, the Philippines, and Thailand citing financial and political factors. The fund already does not invest in China, Russia, Pakistan, Venezuela, and 10 other countries.

By the mid-1990s, socially responsible investing expanded from a few firms to over 100 MUTUAL FUNDS allocating approximately $1 trillion. Proponents of traditional investment decision making deride those who practice socially responsible investing as a liberal fringe group. Critics of CAPITALISM contend that socially responsible investing is "participation in capitalism made to feel good."

Two methods or standards for socially responsible investing are offered by goodmoney.com and moneyandvalues.com. Ethicalinvesting.com suggests there are three basic values shared by most people.

- Avoid causing, illness disease and death.
- Avoid destroying or damaging the environment.
- Avoid treating honest people with disrespect.

Using these criteria, it is argued that no ethical person would invest in companies doing business with a drug CARTEL or tobacco companies because these firms contribute to illness and death. Similarly, companies that produce chemicals harmful to the environment and companies that take advantage of consumers by deceiving people with dangerous or poor-quality PRODUCTs should be shunned. Ethicalinvesting.com suggests *Multinational Monitor* and *Mother Jones Magazine* as sources of information to help socially responsible investors evaluate companies.

Moneyandvalues.com offers a unique service to socially responsible investors. At this website, viewers check which issues they want to "screen" for and then input the names of mutual funds to evaluate. Viewers can screen for tobacco, same-sex lifestyle, pornography, nuclear power, gambling, environment, defense contracting, alcohol, affirmative action, and abortion. The site then reports investments made by specified mutual funds in companies engaged in each category of activity. In the cases of environment and affirmative action, the site reports on companies that have poor records or lack policies regarding these issues.

To describe the status of socially responsible investing in the United States, Dr. Ritchie Lowry, professor of sociology at Boston College, quotes the German philosopher Arthur Schopenhauer: "There are three steps in the revelation of any truth: in the first, it is ridiculed; in the second, resisted; in the third, it is considered self-evident." Dr. Lowry contends socially responsible investing is now between the second and third steps.

Further reading
"Calpers Pulls Out of 4 Countries, Dealing Blow to Southeast Asia," Wall Street Journal, 22 February 2002, p. C12; "Ethical Investing: Techniques and Philosophy of Ethical Investing." Available on-line. URL: www.ethicalinvesting.com; Lowry, Dr. Ritchie. "Capitalism with a Conscience." Available on-line. URL: www.goodmoney.com; "Select Your Values." Available on-line. URL:www.moneyandvalues.com.

Social Security
Social security is the general term used in the United States to refer to three major government-administered programs:

- Old Age and Survivors Income (OASI)
- SUPPLEMENTAL SECURITY INCOME (SSI)
- Medicaid

The Social Security Act of 1935 was legislated in response to the GREAT DEPRESSION, during which millions of Americans lost their jobs and had few resources on which to fall back. In arguing for the act, President Franklin Roosevelt stated, "Security was attained in the earlier days through the interdependence of members of families upon each other and of the families within a small community upon each other. The complexities of great communities and of organized industry make less real these simple means of security."

Initially Social Security only included retirement benefits. Social Security taxes were first collected in 1937, and the first recipient, Ernest Ackerman, received a lump-sum payment of 17 cents that year. Social Security was intended to be a modest INCOME insurance program for retiring workers. In 1939 survivor benefits were added, and in 1940 the Social Security Administration (SSA) began paying monthly benefits. In 1956 disability benefits were added to the program, and in 1965 Medicaid, health benefits for poorer Americans were added to Social Security.

The OASI program is funded through matching employer and employee contributions. In 2003 each contributed 6.2 percent of wages and salary income up to a maximum of $87,000 annual income. Income greater than $87,000 is not taxed for OASI. It is still taxed for Medicare (1.45 percent of income), and the maximum income taxed increases annually. Self-employed people pay both the employer and employee amounts, though they can deduct part of the payment from their federal income taxes.

In 1999, the OASI program alone took in over $450 billion in taxes and paid out $340 billion to recipients. For many Americans, Social Security is a "social compact"—a promise to successive generations that they will be supported in their old age. To others Social Security is an intergenerational income-transfer program or a WELFARE program for the elderly. Many Social Security recipients, when asked whether they are getting welfare, will probably respond, "I paid into the system, and now I am getting back what I deserve." Most recipients of OASI get back what they paid into the program in less than four years. Of course there are Americans who pay into the system but die before receiving any benefits, but then there are people like Ida Mae Fuller, the first American to receive regular monthly benefits. Her first check was for $22.45, and by the time she died just after her 100th birthday, she had received over $20,000 in benefits. Her total payment into the Social Security Trust Fund had been $22.00.

Even today the Social Security Administration accounts are referred to as a TRUST fund, but as Americans learned in the 2000 presidential debates, the trust fund is an accounting illusion. Many Americans think their Social Security payments are gaining value in a trust account, like an insurance ANNUITY, but the difference between what the SSA takes in and pays out, about $124 billion in 1999, is deposited in the account of the U.S. Treasury Department. This adds to the federal government's annual budget surplus (in previous years it reduced the government's budget deficit) but is in fact "borrowed" by the federal government to fund current spending. This action changes Social Security from a prefunded system to a pay-as-you-go operation. As long as there are more funds coming into the system than payments made to recipients, the system will remain solvent, but with the pending retirement of "baby boomers," the Social Security system will need to change.

In the 1960s, the emergence of the baby-boom generation as workers contributing to the system resulted in a huge flow of payments into the system. Given the natural political propensity to spend tax revenue and the fact that older Americans are much more likely to vote than younger Americans, Congress readily agreed to link the level of OASI benefits to changes in INFLATION. Benefits began to grow annually, taxes were raised to match the increase, and Social Security changed from a modest retirement INSURANCE program to a major government allocation.

To overcome the future problem of increasing numbers of recipients and smaller numbers of contributors to Social Security, Americans face four possibilities.

- Raise taxes.
- Reduce eligibility to the program.
- Reduce benefits to recipients.
- Change the funding basis for Social Security.

In the year 2000, Social Security was funded through a payroll tax of 15.3 percent of wage INCOME up to about $80,000, levied against both employer and employee.

Eliminating or raising the maximum amount of wages taxed, a move opposed by upper-income Americans, could generate added revenue. Reducing eligibility for the Social Security system has already been planned. In 2000, workers had to be 65 years old to receive full benefits. By 2006 workers will have to be 66 years old, with the age for full benefits gradually rising for future generations. Reducing benefits could be accomplished by reducing benefits for nonworking spouses, using "means testing" to deny benefits to upper-income Americans, or by changing the cost-of-living allowance.

In theory Social Security investing in better-returning securities could attain solvency. U.S. government securities are low-risk and low-return INVESTMENTS. Some argue that investing in the U.S. STOCK MARKET would yield higher returns. This assumes the stock market will continue to provide better returns and that a method can be developed to invest trust funds without political intervention. Investing Social Security funds in stocks would make the trust fund a major investor in the stock market and provide temptation for politicians to direct investment toward strategies that are politically based rather than financially based.

Each part of the Social Security system is a complex and important consideration in American business. OASI is many workers' primary retirement income. Depending on how OASI and medicare change, workers will push for changes in benefits from their employers. The system will likely change dramatically in future years, but how it will change is a hotly debated topic.

Further reading
Miller, Roger Leroy. *Economics Today.* Boston: Addison Wesley, 2001. Social Security Administration website. Available on-line. URL: www.ssa.gov.

Society for Competitive Intelligence Professionals

The Society for Competitive Intelligence Professionals (SCIP) is an international nonprofit organization with a mission to "enhance the skills of knowledge professional in order to help their companies achieve and maintain a competitive advantage." Established in 1986, there are now over 70 SCIP chapters around the world and members from over 50 nations.

The SCIP's basic functions are to provide educational and networking opportunities for competitive-intelligence professionals. Competitive intelligence (CI), also referred to as MARKET INTELLIGENCE and business intelligence, is the gathering, analyzing, and disseminating of external information that impact companies' business strategies. Competitive intelligence is not spying; rather it is the legal collection and analysis of information about competitors' capabilities, vulnerabilities, and plans. Competitive intelligence is conducted using information databases and other "open sources" of information.

Information gathered in competitive intelligence is analyzed using a variety of tools, including competitor profiles, financial analysis, SWOT (strengths, weaknesses, opportunities, and threats) analysis, scenario development, win/loss ratios, war games, conjoint analysis, and simulation/modeling. According to a 1998 survey of SCIP members, competitor profiles was the most frequently used CI tool, while SWOT analysis was rated the most effective tool.

Competitive intelligence complements company efforts in KNOWLEDGE MANAGEMENT (KM). KM is a business activity through which organizations generate value utilizing their explicit and tacit intellectual ASSETS. This is accomplished through the dissemination and utilization of knowledge. The practice of KM involves combining explicit assets (information technologies) with tacit assets (competencies and experiences possessed by employees).

Competitive intelligence is often perceived as a less-than-ethical business activity. The goals of the SCIP Code of Ethics for CI Professionals are

- to continually strive to increase the recognition and respect of the profession
- to comply with all applicable laws, domestic and international
- to fully respect all requests for confidential of information
- to avoid conflicts of interest in fulfilling one's duties
- to provide honest and realistic recommendations and conclusions in the execution of one's duties
- to promote this code of ethics within one's company, with third-party contractors and within the entire profession
- to faithfully adhere to and abide by one's company policies, objectives, and guidelines

Further reading

Society for Competitive Intelligence Professionals website. Available on-line. URL: www.scip.org.

spillover effects   See EXTERNALITIES.

stakeholders

Stakeholders are the various individuals and groups affected by and influencing business decisions. Traditionally in American business, companies perceive three groups as having an interest in the affairs of an enterprise: employees, investors, and customers. The interests of employees are represented by UNIONS or by choice to stay or leave, investors by the BOARD OF DIRECTORS, and customers by their purchasing power.

In the 1990s, as businesses engaged in a broader realm of interests, *stakeholders* became a popular term suggesting that companies also needed to include the interests and concerns of communities and society as a whole in their decision making. CORPORATE SOCIAL RESPONSIBILITY inferred companies were responsible to stakeholders for greater environmental management, recycling and reuse, community involvement, and citizenship. Interest groups often purchased a symbolic one share of stock in companies, allowing them to speak at SHAREHOLDERS meetings and propose amendments to corporate policies.

Standard & Poor's

Standard & Poor's (S&P), a subsidiary of McGraw-Hill Inc., is a leading U.S. financial services company. Standard & Poor's is best known for its S&P 500 Index and its S&P bond-rating system. In 1860 Henry Poor published *The History of Railroads and Canals in the United States,* supplying financial information for investors, primarily Europeans, wanting to increase participation in the country's INFRASTRUCTURE's growth. Poor's publications emphasized "the investor's right to know." The Standard Statistics Bureau was formed in 1906 and in 1916 began assigning ratings to corporate and sovereign debt. In 1941 Poor's publishing operations merged with Standard Statistics to create Standard & Poor's Corporation.

The S&P 500 Index is a broad-based measure of changes in U.S. STOCK MARKET conditions based on the average performance of 500 widely held COMMON STOCKS. The index includes large industrial, financial, transportation and utility stocks. The composition of the index, determined by Standard & Poor's, varies over time. Announcement that a company is being added to the S&P 500 usually boosts the price of the company's stock. This is a result of the influence of the S&P 500 on investing. In 2000, over $1 trillion worth of investors' funds were indexed to the S&P 500, meaning mutual-fund managers were committed to purchasing a portfolio of stocks that matched the index. Adding a stock to the index increases DEMAND for that company's stock. Likewise, removal of a stock from the index results in the sale of that stock by index-fund managers. In addition to the S&P 500 Index, Standard & Poor's also publishes 90 other market and industry indexes.

Like MOODY'S RATINGS, Standard & Poor's also maintains a rating system for BONDS, COMMERCIAL PAPER, and other financial securities. The S&P bond-rating system ranks bonds from AAA to D, with AAA having the lowest DEFAULT risk and D, the highest default risk. Any bond rated BBB or above is considered investment grade, with relatively low RISK of default. Any bond rated below BBB is considered speculative grade and is referred to as a "junk bond" in U.S. financial markets.

The distinction between investment-grade and speculative-grade bonds is important, because many INVESTMENT groups (MUTUAL FUNDS, commercial banks, INSURANCE companies, and pension funds) direct their investment managers to only purchase investment-grade bonds. S&P bond ratings are based on the firm's expected cash flow, other contractual obligations, the firm's past profitability, and variability of the firm's earnings. Bonds receiving higher ratings will be purchased at lower interest-rate yields by investors, saving companies considerable sums in financing COSTS. Lower-rated securities must offer investors a higher interest-rate yield because of the potential for default. Corporate and municipal bonds typically pay higher interest yields than the U.S. Treasury bond of the same maturity, and the lower the bond rating, the greater the spread between its yield and that of comparable Treasury bonds. For example, in February 2001 high quality 10+ year corporate bonds were paying on average 7.05 percent, while comparable U.S. Treasury bonds yielded 5.59 percent, a spread of 1.46 percent. Medium-quality corporate bonds yielded 7.84 percent on average, 2.25 percent more than comparable U.S. TREASURY SECURITIES.

Further reading
Standard & Poor's website. Available on-line. URL: www.standard andpoors.com.

standardization   See ISO STANDARDS.

standard of living
The term *standard of living* refers to a measure of consumer welfare. Economists measure a country's standard of living by the level of real per capita INCOME. If a country's real output (output after adjustment for INFLATION) increases at a rate faster than the population growth rate, its standard of living increases. Individuals whose incomes do not increase with the level of inflation find their standard of living decreases.

Two problems with standard-of-living measures are the distribution of income and the assumption that an increasing standard of living is synonymous with an improved quality of life. During the AMERICAN INDUSTRIAL REVOLUTION (late 1800s to early 1900s), REAL INCOME rose dramatically, but the distribution of income became more unequal. Similarly, in the 1980s per capita income rose but the LORENZ CURVE became more skewed as the upper 20 percent of Americans received a larger percentage of income (approximately 45 percent), while the lowest 20 percent of Americans received less (approximately 4.5 percent).

Followers of BUDDHIST ECONOMICS and other social advocates question whether increased material output and CONSUMPTION lead to a better standard of living. For example, the purchase of security devices for one's home is an increase in consumption, but the necessity of having security devices is surely not an improvement in one's standard of living.

Maintaining or attaining a certain minimum standard of living is often one of society's goals. MINIMUM WAGE laws and UNEMPLOYMENT benefits are the basic social "safety nets" used to give Americans a minimum standard of living. Many social critics have called for a "living wage," one that allows workers to maintain an acceptable rather than minimal standard of living. In 2001 Santa Monica, California, adopted a living-wage law requiring area employers to pay a minimum of $12.25 per hour, almost twice the state's minimum wage of $6.25 per hour. Santa Monica is an affluent, expensive city in the Los Angeles area. To be able to live there, workers would have to earn considerably more than the state minimum wage. Many other cities and counties have adopted living-wage laws, but most only apply to a small percentage of local workers.

Standard-of-living measures vary from country to country. Per capita real income has to be compared with the prices of goods and SERVICES in order to measure the PURCHASING power of a given level of income.

Further reading
Ruffin, Roy J., and Paul R. Gregory. *Principles of Economics,* 7th ed. Boston: Addison Wesley, 2000.

Standard Rate and Data Service
Standard Rate and Data Service (SRDS) is a widely used ADVERTISING-rate information source in the United States. Established in 1921, SRDS, maintains information about advertising rates, circulation, and personnel contacts for more than 80,000 magazines, newspapers, television, radio, and electronic advertising alternatives.

SRDS continually updates what are known as "rate cards," the published prices for advertising in various U.S. media. Traditionally major U.S. companies paid MADISON AVENUE advertising agencies to create and manage their advertising efforts. Agencies would place advertisements in appropriate media, billing customers based on the rate card and receiving a standard commission (usually 15 percent) from the magazine, newspaper, or other media channel.

During the 1980s, COMPETITION in the industry removed fixed-price and fixed-commission standards. SRDS-published advertising rates became the starting point for negotiating price, and 15 percent commissions also became negotiable. In addition, some major companies began developing in-house advertising departments, bypassing ad agencies to create and directly place their own advertising messages. Nevertheless, SRDS remains a major source of information for marketers in the United States.

Further reading
Standard Rate and Data Service website. Available on-line. URL: www.srds.com.

stock market, bond market
A stock is a financial instrument with an infinite life because it has no maturity date. As long as the issuing

CORPORATION exists, a stock will have value. The existence of stock markets provides liquidity for these infinitely long-term securities. Additionally, because stock markets are instrumental in establishing MARKET VALUES for stocks, they are integral in determining market values for corporations.

A bond is also a long-term debt instrument, but unlike stocks, BONDS have finite lives as determined by their maturity dates. Common bond maturities are from 5 to 30 years. The existence of bond markets provides liquidity for bondholders who decide not to hold bonds until their maturities.

The DEMAND for stocks and bonds and the ability of corporations to sell them would be greatly diminished were it not for the existence of the stock and bond markets. These are exchanges where buyers and sellers of securities are brought together. In advanced nations, stock and bond markets are highly organized, creating great efficiencies in the spread of information and minimizing exchange transactions COSTS. In fact, the existence of highly organized securities markets fosters continued ECONOMIC GROWTH by efficiently channeling funds to their best uses. (Lackluster economic growth in lesser-developed countries is often attributed to their lack of well-organized financial markets.)

The U.S. stock market is comprised of organized exchanges and the over-the-counter (OTC) market. The organized exchanges are the NEW YORK STOCK EXCHANGE (NYSE) and the AMERICAN STOCK EXCHANGE (AMEX). Corporations whose stocks are traded on one of these exchanges are said to be "listed." It is prestigious for a corporation to meet the stringent requirements for listing. Unlisted stocks are those traded in the OTC market. While NYSE dominates the stock exchanges in dollar volume traded, the OTC market is the largest stock exchange in terms of the number of different corporations whose stocks are traded there. The backbone of the OTC market is NASDAQ, the NATIONAL ASSOCIATION OF SECURITY DEALERS AUTOMATED QUOTATIONS. Geographically dispersed securities dealers connected by computers are the intermediaries for the OTC stock traders. The enormous size of the OTC market is illustrated by the fact that NASDAQ surpasses NYSE in annual share volume.

Stock and bond exchanges are also classified as being PRIMARY MARKETS or secondary markets. In primary markets, new issues of stocks and bonds are sold to the public. INITIAL PUBLIC OFFERINGS are primary-market transactions, and INVESTMENT BANKING firms are the FINANCIAL INTERMEDIARIES. The secondary markets are the exchanges where outstanding stocks and bonds are traded.

Bond markets provide liquidity for bondholders. There is an inverse relationship between bond prices and *interest rates* in the economy; prices for outstanding bond are as volatile as interest rates. When interest rates rise above the coupon rate on a bond, this will force the bond to sell at a discount, below par (face) value. When interest rates fall below a bond's coupon rate, this will cause the bond to sell

at a premium, above par value. Stable interest rates lead to stable prices for outstanding bonds.

See also NASDAQ, NEW YORK STOCK EXCHANGE, RANDOM-WALK THEORY; STOCK RATING SYSTEMS.

stock options

Stock OPTIONS are the right to purchase shares of a company's stock at a given price for a set period of time. Individuals can purchase stock options for most major companies through stock exchanges. These stock options give the purchaser the right to sell or purchase 100 shares of stock at any time until the expiration date. "Put" options give the purchaser the right to sell the shares, while "call" options give the purchaser the right to buy the shares at the specified price.

In addition to options bought and sold through stock exchanges, many U.S. CORPORATIONS offer senior managers and executives stock options as part of their COMPENSATION AND BENEFITS. Executives are only offered call options, the right to purchase shares at a specified price. An executive might be given the option to purchase 100,000 shares of XYZ stock at the current market price of $20 for the next three years. If the price of XYZ stock raises to $30, the executive can simultaneously purchase the 100,000 shares for $200,000 and sell the shares for $300,000, earning a $100,000 PROFIT.

The logic of the practice of offering stock options to executives is that corporate leaders will then have a vested interest in seeing the price of a company's stock rise. Rising stock prices create CAPITAL GAINS for the company's owners, the SHAREHOLDERS. If the stock price rises, usually as a result of increased earnings, the executives can execute the stock options and profit. This is referred to as "aligning the interests" of MANAGEMENT and shareholders. Critics note that shareholders are at RISK because they have invested their CAPITAL, and if the price of the stock declines, they lose all part of their INVESTMENT. However, managers with stock options do not really suffer any risk if the company's stock price declines; although their options may become worthless, they have not invested any capital and so lose nothing. In addition, if the company's stock price declines, the BOARD OF DIRECTORS will often rewrite executive stock options at lower prices so that executives profit if or when the price of the stock rises.

In recent years, partly in response to the Enron bankruptcy, the practice of corporate stock options has received increased scrutiny from both shareholders and financial markets. Corporation managers have been accused of manipulating their companies' earnings in order to induce short-term price increases at the expense of the companies' long-term growth and profitability.

FEDERAL RESERVE SYSTEM chairman Alan Greenspan and others have also criticized FINANCIAL ACCOUNTING practices related to stock options. As of 2002, companies do not have to include the cost of stock options as an employee expense and, therefore, a deduction against earnings. Critics argue this overstates earnings and transfers INCOME from shareholders to corporate managers. In 2002, STANDARD & POOR'S, the largest financial information source in the United States, announced it would begin including the expense of stock options when calculating companies' earnings. A *New York Times* article reported that stock-options expense at Microsoft Corporation was $3.3 billion in 2001, representing almost one-third of the company's net income.

While financial-accounting rules do not require companies to include the cost of stock options, the profit earned by executives when they execute options is an allowable expense against federal corporate-profit taxes. Differences in financial-accounting and tax-accounting rules allow this anomaly.

Further reading
Morgenson, Gretchen. "As Pressure Grows, Option Costs Come Out of Hiding," *New York Times,* 19 May 2002.

stock-rating systems
Stock-rating systems are rankings generated by analysts at stock-brokerage firms. Stock ratings are an important and controversial part of STOCK MARKET trading. Traditionally the major, full-service brokerage firms provide INVESTMENT advice to clients as part of the services offered. Stock ratings, usually ranking from "strong buy" to "strong sell" summarize the brokerage house's recommendation regarding a stock. Announcement by one of the major firms of a change in rating will often influence sales or purchases of the stock.

Stock-rating systems came under scrutiny after investigations by the SECURITIES AND EXCHANGE COMMISSION (SEC) and state attorneys general showed that in 2001, when the stock market in general was falling, less than 2 percent of the stocks rated by the major brokerage houses were rated as sell; in the previous year, only 1 percent of stocks were rated as sell. Brokerage firms are hesitant to issue sell recommendations, often because the INVESTMENT BANKING part of the firm is attempting to recruit business from the same companies, managing new-stock sales, issuing debt securities, and providing financial consulting services. The investment banking part of a brokerage firm can be quite profitable, and a sell recommendation by the company's research analyst can cause executives to take their business elsewhere. Analysts at most brokerage firms understood that an unwritten rule was not to issue sell recommendations on companies that were important investment banking clients. This, of course, compromised the analysts' objectivity and the information they provided to retail-stock customers.

In 2002, WALL STREET leader Merrill Lynch paid a $100 million fine and agreed to separate research analysts' pay from the investment banking side of the business. In September that same year, U.S. brokerage firms were required by the SEC to issue research ratings in terms of buy, hold,

or sell. The firms' overall research-rating system must be based on the three rankings, but individual stocks can still be rated using other terms. For example, Lehman Brothers announced a new rating-system structure that includes three tiers (trimmed down from the previous five tiers) and rate stocks relative to the analyst's sector, not the overall market. The three rankings are "overweight," "equal weight," "underweight."

> *Overweight:* The stock is expected to outperform the unweighted expected total return of the industry sector over a 12-month investment horizon.
> *Equal weight:* The stock is expected to perform in line with the unweighted expected total return of the industry sector over a 12-month investment horizon.
> *Underweight:* The stock is expected to underperform the unweighted expected total return of the industry sector over a 12-month investment horizon.

Analyst teams also rate the attractiveness of their respective sectors on a positive, neutral, negative basis.

> *Positive:* Fundamentals are improving.
> *Neutral:* Fundamentals are steady, neither improving nor deteriorating.
> *Negative:* Fundamentals are deteriorating.

Lehman Brothers and most brokerage firms also provide price targets, expected prices within a specified period of time, on all stocks under coverage.

Goldman Sachs changed its system to rate stocks as "outperform," "in line," or "underperform." Previously the company had used a five-tier rating system of recommended list, trading buy, market outperformer, market performer, and market underperformer. Credit Suisse First Boston (CSFB) changed their system to "outperform," "neutral," and "underperform." Charles Schwab began rating stocks from A to F, based on a computer analysis of whether the company will outperform or underperform the overall market.

In none of these rating systems do the companies use the "s" word: sell. Analysts and knowledgeable investors have long known that a "hold" rating or "market perform" rating were, in effect, a sell rating. After the new rules went into effect, the percentage of what were effectively "sell" ratings rose to 7 percent.

Behind each stock-rating system is each firm's analysis system. Most brokerage firms use a wide variety of data, including momentum, financial strength, earnings, sales volume, cash flow, price/earnings ratios, and DIVIDENDS. One company (Quadrix) uses 100 variables in seven categories to generate its stock ratings.

Further reading
Craig, Suzanne. "Securities Firms Find New Ways to Issue 'Sells'," *Wall Street Journal,* 13 September 2002, p. C1; Lehman Brothers website. Available on-line. URL: www.lehman.com.

strategic alliances

Strategic alliances are agreements between companies to work together. Alliances can be created in many forms, through referral networks, CONTRACTS, limited PARTNERSHIPS, general partnerships, or corporate JOINT VENTURES. The basis for strategic alliances is the complementary strengths of the companies agreeing to work together. Alliances are designed to take advantage of the capabilities each company brings to the effort and to reduce RISK by reducing the unknowns and diversifying. The benefit of strategic alliances depends on the flexibility and commitment of each partner to the alliance, although this is also a potential weakness. As one author states, "Strategic alliances are, in essence, marriages of unrelated parties."

Business analysts stress four factors important to the success of strategic alliances: proper strategy, aligned structure, clear governance rules, and effective monitoring. Proper strategy addresses the question of why is the company entering a strategic alliance. Like consumers, business managers are affected by trends, and throughout the 1990s, strategic alliances were a very popular trend. Numerous U.S. businesses, particularly in banking and telecommunications, entered strategic alliances as their way of responding to the NORTH AMERICAN FREE TRADE AGREEMENT (NAFTA). The prevailing logic was "we know our industry and our Mexican partner knows how to do business in Mexico." But like all consumer fads, strategic alliances were not necessarily the right thing for all businesses. Many alliances soured due to unclear communication, governance rules, and definition of objectives. Proper strategy incorporates proposed alliances into overall corporate strategic plans.

The term *aligned structure* in strategic alliances refers to the relationship between the alliance's structure and its objectives. Joint ventures are usually significantly structural relationships. Strategic alliances should be consistent with the goals of each participant, neither overstating nor understating the nature of the agreed relationship. Writer John Graham satirically but poignantly suggests, "Never do business with anyone who talks freely about 'partnering' because it will cost you. It's worth noting that there are also strategic partners. This term is reserved for those who do not capitulate so easily or egomaniacal CEOs who want to believe they're actually important. . . . Strategic alliances is pure puff and simply a gimmick to make someone feel important enough so that they are lured into a costly proposition."

Clear governance rules in strategic alliances attempt to allow for flexibility as the nature of the business venture evolves, creating a process for resolving business disputes among partners. Regardless of the type of strategic alliance reached, the agreement should clearly address four issues: partner contributions and distributions, control, allocation of RISKS and rewards, and termination strategies. When strategic alliances are made between firms of similar size and RESOURCES, partner contributions and distributions are usually easily defined. Often, especially in international business, alliances are made between unequals, and defining CAPITAL contributions, control of INTELLECTUAL PROPERTY, RESEARCH AND DEVELOPMENT efforts and control, market-access efforts, and distributions are more difficult. Control should also be addressed in the alliance governance documents, including issues such as

- admission of new partners or the sale of additional securities by the alliance
- appointment of board members, managers, and officers
- compensation of the alliance's MANAGEMENT
- terms of transactions with partners and/or their affiliates
- circumstances under which the terms of the alliance may be modified
- allocation of risks and rewards among partners
- when and how the alliance terminates

Like a prenuptial agreement, a strategic alliance should anticipate a time when the relationship might end and set up a process for termination. For example, two small-business partners, recognizing the potential for disagreement, included in their partnership agreement a requirement that if they reached an impasse, they would agree to meet on three occasions to resolve the conflict. If after three meetings they could not resolve the conflict, they would sell the partnership ASSETS and distribute returns based on the agreement.

Monitoring is the fourth aspect of a strategic alliance. Alliance members should establish in advance clear understandings regarding

- annual budgets
- BUSINESS PLANS with detailed marketing, financial, and operating plans
- capital requirements and timing of capital needs
- methods used to establish overhead costs
- period summaries of financial and marketing results

While many strategic alliances are entered into like a Las Vegas wedding, clearly stated understandings and expectations among alliance members improve the success rate in business relationships.

Further reading

Graham, John R. "A Glossary of Business BS: How to Make Sense out of What You Hear." *Supervision*, January 1994; Pietras, Thomas, and Christian Stormer. "Making Strategic Alliances Work," *Business & Economic Review* 47, no. 4 (July–September 2001).

strategic planning

Business strategic planning is a dynamic, controlled, and continuous process of review that focuses corporate thinking on consistency of purpose and long-term economic gain. It requires answers for questions like why the business exists, who its clients are, what unique PRODUCTS differentiate it from competitors, where it wants to go, what marketing and financial strategies it needs, and how the identified strategies can be implemented to move the business forward.

Strategic planning has a history that dates back to the fourth century B.C., when Sun Tzu, a military strategist, wrote the classic book *The Art of War*, a treatise still widely read by Asian business leaders and even Western military strategists and one that contains important strategic logic applicable for both eastern and Western businesses. Early American business strategic planning centered on solving the immediate problems of SUPPLY and DEMAND, daily events, opportunities, and threats. World War II, with its logistic complexity, global orientation, and need for sophisticated technology and coordinated decision making, changed the focus of companies like Ford Motor Company to a more strategic one, though many other companies kept their primary orientation on supplying postwar consumer demand. By the 1960s the general consensus was that strategic planning was a separate and deliberate business function that could be managed to improve margins and generate revenues. Since that time, various permutations of the basic concept of strategic planning have occurred.

It is theorized that strategic planning is guided by a dominant logic that exists within an organization. The three logical frameworks that govern strategic planning are capability logic, guerrilla logic, and complexity logic. Capability logic assumes the premise that businesses look for strategies that will create a sustainable competitive advantage by protecting and nurturing ASSETS, building on excellence, and creating a future that needs exactly what the business has to offer.

Guerrilla logic is based on the assumption that competitive success is achieved when a business is able to generate new ideas that create new demands and new arenas of action faster than their competitors. Competitive advantage is fleeting under this framework of logic, and organizational energy is seen to be best used in transforming weaknesses rather than building on strengths. Long-term success is achieved by implementing short-term tactics that take advantage of emerging opportunities and keep the COMPETITION off balance.

Complexity logic links success to the ability to understand, maintain, and encourage the individual functions of cooperation and competition as well as the creative and destructive forces that shape business systems. According to complexity logic, the success of any business is directly related to the health of the community in which it operates. Therefore the goal of a strategic plan with a complexity-logic basis would be to set in motion events that are profitable for the business and consequently favorable for the community.

The first step most successful businesses take in strategic planning is to focus on the future that they want to create. In this way they are able to focus on the potential of doing things differently to provide better SERVICES, make better PRODUCTS, etc. Second, they make innovation a priority, a norm, a part of the routine; they look for the needs of clients and prospective clients, focusing not so closely on how to improve current services but more on what services clients really need. Third, they look for ways to make themselves different from and more valuable than their competitors. They set radical goals and involve participation from all levels of the business hierarchy among people who care most about the organization and its future. Often a bottom-up method is employed to generate recommendations from rank-and-file employees that are then taken to higher levels of MANAGEMENT and executive staff for further development and coordination. Finally, they develop a strategy that evolves through experimentation, thought, adjustment and implementation.

Further reading

Doerle, C. "Strategic Planning Is for Everybody," *Institutional Distribution* 27, no. 15 (Dec. 1991): 16–18; Lengnick-Hall, C. A., and J. A. Wolff. "Achieving consistency of purpose," *Strategy and Leadership* 26, no. 2 (March–April 1998): 32–37; McKenna, Patrick A. "Why Strategic Planning Does Not Work—And What You Should Be Doing About It," Available on-line. Patrick McKenna's website. www.patrickmckenna.com/pdfs/ strategyinnovation2.pdf. Downloaded 28 May 2003; Oliver, R. W. "The Future of Strategy: Historic Prologue," *Journal of Business Strategy* 23, no. 4 (2002): 6–10; Rarick, Charles A. "Ancient Chinese Advice for Modern Business Strategists," *SAM Advanced Management Journal* 61, no. 1 (1996): 38–44; Ray, Douglas E. "Strategic Planning for Non-Profit Organizations," *Fund Raising Management* 28, no. 6, (Aug. 1997): 22–24.

—Jill Briggs

strengths, weaknesses, opportunities, and threats (SWOT) analysis

Strengths, weaknesses, opportunities, and threats (SWOT) analysis is a marketing/management tool used to evaluate a company's competitive position. SWOT analysis begins with assessing a firm's strengths. Strengths include what the firm does well, what competitive advantages the firm has over rivals, and what resources the firm has to utilize. Strengths are relative to competitors' strengths and relative to the firm's target markets. Analysis of strengths, if done objectively, provides ideas for future growth of the firm.

Weaknesses are what the firm does not do well and areas that could be improved. Weaknesses create limitations on the growth of a firm. Weaknesses can include lack of human or financial capital, market access, sales capability, product quality, or other problems. Weaknesses should be assessed from the customer's perspective. What is it that the firm is not doing well?

Opportunities are favorable situations that could create benefits to the firm if pursued. Often managers wait for opportunities to arise, but creative and assertive managers seek out and capitalize on opportunities ahead of competitors. Changes in government policies, changes in technology, competitors' action or inaction, and market conditions can create opportunities.

Threats are obstacles or conditions that may prevent a firm from achieving its objectives. Threats can include competitors' actions, changing technology, financial constraints, and government policy. Analysis of threats helps a firm anticipate problems rather than react to them.

SWOT analysis is often incorporated as part of environmental scanning, assessment of the political, legal, economic, cultural, and competitive environment in which a firm operates.

Further reading
Pride, William M., and O. Ferrell. *Marketing Concepts and Strategies*, 12th ed. Boston: Houghton Mifflin, 2003.

Student Loan Marketing Association (Sallie Mae; USA Education, Inc.)

The Student Loan Marketing Association (SLMA), better known as Sallie Mae, was established in 1972 as a federally chartered, stockholder-owned CORPORATION providing funding for education. Because most beginning college students have little INCOME or credit history, it is difficult for them to borrow for their education.

Sallie Mae's primary activity is funding educational LOANS through loan guarantees. Sallie Mae guarantees loans made under the Federal Family Education Loan Program (FFELP). Federal student-loan programs include Stafford loans, Perkins loans, and Parent Loan for Undergraduate Students. Through a variety of subsidiaries, Sallie Mae is the leading student lending, servicing, and loan-guaranteeing organization in the country. As of 2002, Sallie Mae owned or managed over 5 million loans.

As a government-sponsored enterprise (GSE), Sallie Mae created a secondary market for student loans. GSEs have implied federal-government guarantees, reducing the risk associated with borrowing, which reduces the cost of funds to the lender. Like other GSEs, Sallie Mae packages and services government-guaranteed loans, selling these loans to investors. This releases funds back into the lending market for additional student loans.

During the 1980s and 1990s, Sallie Mae was criticized for poor management and high rates of DEFAULT on government-sponsored loan programs. Reforms in the 1990s, particularly termination of loan programs at institutions with significant default rates, have decreased the problem of non-payback of loans. The GSE part of Sallie Mae must be dissolved by 2008.

In 1997 Sallie Mae was reorganized with SLM Holding Company, and in 2000 it was renamed USA Education,

Inc. In addition to the SLMA, Sallie Mae controls SLM Financing Corporation and Sallie Mae Solutions. Through these subsidiaries, Sallie Mae offers consumer-credit loans, including continuing education, K–12 loans for parents whose children attend private school, and business and technical OUTSOURCING services for colleges throughout the United States.

See also GOVERNMENT-SPONSORED ENTERPRISES.

Further reading
Sallie Mae website. Available on-line. URL: www.salliemae.com.

sufficient cause See JUST CAUSE.

Superfund

As quoted on the Environmental Protection Agency's website The Superfund, created by the Comprehensive Environmental Response, Compensation, and Liability Act (CERCLA) in 1980, is a TRUST fund used to clean up "abandoned, accidentally spilled, or illegally dumped hazardous waste that poses a current or future threat to human health or the environment." Managed by the ENVIRONMENTAL PROTECTION AGENCYS' (EPA) Office of Emergency and Remedial Response (OERR), Superfund monies are used to identify hazardous waste sites, test for pollutant levels, formulate plans to address the problems, and clean up sites. (Environmentalists often take issue with the term *clean* with respect to hazardous wastes. Many hazardous wastes cannot be cleaned like cleaning a home. At best they can be contained and stored in a less-threatening manner and location.)

The EPA uses a Hazard Ranking System (HRS) to assess the "relative threat associated with actual or potential releases of hazardous substances at sites." The HRS ranking is based on actual or potential groundwater, surface waterway, air, and soil migration pathways and their risk to human health and the environment. The HRS is the primary method of determining whether a site is to be included on the Superfund's National Priorities List (NPL).

The NPL is a published list of hazardous waste sites that are being cleaned up under the Superfund program. As of August 2001, there were 1,235 sites on the NPL. There were also 43,806 potential hazardous waste sites listed on the Comprehensive Environmental Response, Compensation, and Liability System.

The Superfund is funded through a tax on chemical and petroleum products. Superfund managers work with scientists, contractors, local authorities, and potentially responsible parties (PRPs) in identifying and addressing hazardous waste sites. Environmental laws often create LIABILITY for any business associated with a hazardous waste site. Purchases of properties and lenders receiving ownership of property through DEFAULTS on LOANS have become liable for environmental problems caused by past owners. Communities have sometimes been stymied in redevelopment efforts due to environmental liability, labeled "brownfields." In 1996 the government introduced legislation to clean up environmental contamination on industrial sites in order to stimulate ECONOMIC DEVELOPMENT.

Further reading
Superfund website. Available on-line. URL: www.epa.gov/super fund/about.html.

Supplemental Security Income

Supplemental Security Income (SSI) is a federally financed and administered program created in 1974. SSI is managed by the Social Security Administration but funded through general tax revenues. Designed to assist needy Americans, SSI provides monthly cash payments to Americans with limited INCOME and resources who are age 65 and older, blind, or disabled. Unlike the Old Age and Survivors Income (OASI) part of SOCIAL SECURITY, SSI is not based on prior work or contributions into the Social Security system.

Supplemental Security Income is available to U.S. citizens and "certain qualified aliens." In 2002, 7.2 million Americans received SSI benefits. SSI rules regarding income and resources are quite severe, limiting eligibility to the program to only the most needy people. Critics contend SSI discourages people from returning to work after being disabled. SSI, under the Ticket to Work and Work Incentives Improvement Act (1999), allows SSI recipients to return to work without immediately losing benefits.

In the year 2000, SSI restrictions included a resources limit of $2,000 for individuals and $3,000 for couples. Resources include cash, land, life INSURANCE, and PERSONAL PROPERTY but excluded an individual's home and a car. The maximum SSI payment was $512 for individuals and $769 for couples in the year 2000. SSI recipients' benefits are reduced for any earned income greater than $65 per month. Some states provide supplements to SSI payments. In most states, SSI recipients also receive Medicaid, a joint federal-state health payment program. Federal spending on SSI has grown from $8 billion in 1974 to $35 billion in 2000.

Further reading
Social Security Administration website. Available on-line. URL: www.ssa.gov.

supply

Supply, or the law of supply, is the relationship between price and the quantity supplied of a good or service in a market. The law of supply states there is a positive relationship between price and quantity supplied; that is, the higher the price the greater the quantity supplied, and the lower the price the lower the quantity supplied, ceteris paribus (all other things being equal, or nothing else has changed).

When discussing supply in a market, it is important to clearly define what market is being considered. If one says "the television market," does this refer to the local, national, or global market? And which level is meant—retail, wholesale, or manufacturing? When discussing market supply, it is important to clarify the level and location under consideration and to define the time frame and other assumptions associated with analysis of supply in a market. It is often difficult for producers to adjust output in a short period of time. Supply relationships are usually studied with the ceteris paribus assumption.

A supply curve, or graph portrays the relationship between price and quantity supplied in a market in a period of time, ceteris paribus. Producers respond to price changes by increasing or decreasing the quantity they are willing and able to provide to the market. Price is the independent variable, and quantity supplied is the dependent variable. A change in price causes a change in quantity supplied in the same direction as the price change.

Other factors cause a change in supply, which is a shift of the whole price/quantity relationship in a market. An increase in supply means that at every price, producers are willing and able to provide more of a good or service. Likewise, a decrease in supply means producers are willing to provide less of a good at each price.

While only a price change can cause a change in quantity supplied, economists have identified six factors that can cause a change in supply.

- price of factors (RESOURCES)
- price of related PRODUCTS
- expectations (producer)
- taxes and subsidies
- technology
- number of producers

Changes in the price of factors alter the cost of producing goods and SERVICES. If the cost of labor increases, either through increased COMPETITION for workers or changes in MINIMUM WAGE laws, firms will adjust their output. Increases in resource COSTS cause firms to decrease their supply in a market.

Changes in the price of related goods motivate producers to increase or decrease their supply of what they produce. For example, if a television manufacturer can produce both small- and large-screen TVs, and the price of large-screen televisions increases, the firm will shift production away from small TV production into production of large-screen televisions. For centuries this has been the dilemma for farmers: Do they produce more corn and fewer soybeans, more cotton and less wheat? Farmers often make their choices based on last season's prices, but by the time their products are available for market, prices have usually changed. If too many farmers shift PRODUC-

TION to crops with high prices the previous season, the market price will probably drop significantly.

Producer expectations can affect their current supply decisions. If producers anticipate higher resource costs in the future, they may increase current production. If firms anticipate that new technology will make their current products less marketable, they may cut production to avoid having inventory they cannot sell or even increase current production to sell as much as possible before their current products become less competitive in the market.

Changes in taxes and subsidies have the same effect on producer supply decisions as changes in resources. Taxes increase the cost of production, causing firms to decrease their supply. Similarly, subsidies decrease firms' costs of production and result in an increase in supply. Many international trade disputes are centered on government subsidies for domestic industries, reducing their firms' costs of production and making it difficult or impossible for foreign firms to compete.

Changes in technology generally increase productivity. This allows firms to increase output, an outward shift of their supply curves. A major factor in the growth of the U.S. economy in the 1990s was the implementation of new cost-saving technology allowing firms in many industries to increase output.

As the number of firms in a market increases or decreases, the market-supply curve shifts accordingly. Few firms want increased COMPETITION, but more firms in a market increases the supply available at every price.

supply-chain management   See PURCHASING.

supply rule
The supply rule is a two-part set of theoretical guidelines for businesses in determining whether to produce and how much to produce. According to the supply rule, in the long run (when all RESOURCES are variable and subject to change), a firm should only produce quantity where marginal revenue (MR) is equal to or greater than marginal cost (MC). The choice of whether or not to produce is then determined by the second part of the supply rule: Produce the quantity where MR ≥ MC if total revenue is greater than or equal to total cost (which is the same as price is greater than or equal to average total cost). In other words, a firm should produce if it is at least breaking even and produce nothing, in the long run, if it is not at least breaking even.

In the short run—a time frame in which some resources are fixed (usually building and equipment)—the supply rule states that the firm should produce quantity where MR ≥ MC if total revenue is greater than or equal to total variable costs (TR ≥ TVC). If total revenue does not at least equal total variable costs (labor, materials, energy, etc.), the firm should produce nothing. In other words, if it is not at least covering the variable costs of production, it should not produce. Economists call this the SHUT-DOWN POINT.

The basis of the supply rule is that no other level of output other than that quantity where MR ≥ MC makes sense to produce. Marginal revenue is the extra revenue derived from producing and selling another unit of a good. Marginal cost is the extra cost of producing that unit of output. If the extra revenue exceeds the extra cost, keep producing. Either PROFITS will increase or losses will decrease. If the extra cost of another unit of output exceeds the extra revenue, the supply rule says do not produce. Profits will decrease or losses increase.

While the supply rule makes sense in theory, it is difficult to use in practice. First, costs are difficult to allocate, especially in firms with multiple PRODUCTS. Second, it is even more difficult to estimate revenues—that is, to make projections about what consumers are willing and able to pay for the firm's products—and in the time it takes to produce additional output, markets may change. The supply rule nevertheless provides logical guidelines for business decision making.

supply-side economics
Supply-side economics centers on the idea that lower marginal tax rates increase peoples' incentives to work. First articulated by economist Arthur Laffer in 1974, supply-side economics increases labor productivity by allowing workers to keep more of their added INCOME. This, in turn, increases taxable output and income, resulting in greater revenue for government.

According to Laffer and his supporters, including politician Jack Kemp, economist Lawrence Lindsey, and former president Ronald Reagan, high marginal tax rates discourage workers. At the beginning of the Reagan administration (1980), the highest marginal tax rate on personal income was 70 percent, which meant that someone earning an extra $1,000 in this tax bracket would be allowed to keep only $300 of that extra income. Because the United States' income-tax system is progressive, only higher-income taxpayers paid at the 70 percent marginal tax rate. Supply-side economists argued that these were the most productive members of the economy, and high marginal tax rates discouraged their productive activities. Reducing marginal taxes rates would result in flurry of new economic effort, expanding the economy and increasing tax revenues. By the end of the Reagan administration (1988), the rate had decreased to 28 percent.

Opponents of supply-side economics note that decreasing the highest marginal tax rates benefits only the wealthiest Americans, reducing their taxes while lower- and middle-income workers receive no decrease in their taxes. Supply-side advocates respond that the increased economic activity provides new jobs and greater income to everyone, noting the increasing number of women who entered the workforce in the 1980s. Opponents of supply-side economics label this TRICKLE-DOWN ECONOMICS, in which the benefits might eventually flow to the rest of society after the wealthy got their tax cut.

Supply-side arguments also influenced tax and economic policies in other industrialized countries. Sweden, long known for its high tax rates, cut the top rate from 80 percent to 56 percent. France, Britain, and Japan all cut their rates, concerned that high tax rates cause a national outflow of CAPITAL and high-income workers.

During the 1990s, supply-side economics was largely discredited and held partly responsible for the massive increase in the national debt, which more than doubled during the Reagan years. Supply-side economists predicted doom when the Clinton administration raised the top marginal tax rate to 39.6 percent, but the economy continued to grow. With the election of George W. Bush on a platform of cutting taxes, supply-side economics again became a source of debate among economists and politicians.

Further reading
Henderson, David R. "Rehabilitation the supply-side," *Fortune* 128, no. 6 (28 September 1998): 64–66.

sustainable growth and development (sustainability)

Sustainable growth and development, sometimes referred to as sustainability, was defined by the Brundtland Commission (World Commission on Environment and Development, 1987) as ECONOMIC GROWTH that "meets the needs of the present without compromising the ability of future generations to meet their own needs." Paul Hawken, owner of the Williams-Sonoma catalog company, described sustainability as an economic golden rule: "Leave the world better than you found it, take no more than you need, try not to harm life or other environment, make amends if you do." Others have defined sustainability as eco-efficiency and the foresighted utilization, preservation, and/or renewal of forests, waters, lands, and minerals for the greatest good for the greatest numbers for the longest time.

Sustainable growth and development is a relatively new topic among economic-development specialists. For decades GROSS DOMESTIC PRODUCT (GDP) and growth in GDP were widely accepted as the measure of economic and social well-being. Only in the 1970s did economists, led by the efforts of Herman Daly, challenge the assumption that increases in output (GDP) equal improvements in the quality of life of citizens. Daly and John Cobb Jr. developed an alternative, the Index of Sustainable Economic Welfare (ISEW). Their index adjusts GDP to account for environmental and social factors, including the distribution of INCOME, value of household labor, environmental damage, and social and environmental spending. Daly and Cobb found that in the United Kingdom, GDP and ISEW were positively related for the period from 1950 to 1970, but since that time GDP has continued to grow while the ISEW has stagnated and declined. Their analysis suggests a growing disparity between GDP and sustainable growth and development.

More recently, collaboration among the Global Leaders for Tomorrow, the Yale Center for Law and Environmental Policy, and the Columbia University Center for International Earth Science Information Network resulted in a Pilot Environmental Sustainability Index (PESI). The PESI is a massive study that uses 64 variables to quantify 21 factors measuring sustainability. Preliminary analysis found that decisions to pursue economic growth and environmental sustainability appear to be separate choices, or even that high levels of economic growth encourage sustainability. Often political leaders in industrialized and developing countries rationalize environmental degradation, saying that once they have economic growth, then they will be able to afford environmental controls. (President George Bush once said, "I am an environmentalist, but we just cannot afford it now.") The PESI study suggests a cause-and-effect relationship that, if proven in further analysis, would be a significant addition to the study of sustainable growth and development.

ECONOMIC DEVELOPMENT analysis requires full accounting of negative and positive environmental impacts of development activities. Internalizing these EXTERNALITIES is critical to evaluating the total impact of economic changes. Similarly, economic development analysis often weighs the utility or well-being of present consumers and CONSUMPTION versus the opportunities of future generations. Economists use DISCOUNTING—adjusting the value of future streams of COSTS, income, or benefits to the present time period—and benefit-cost analysis to analyze the economic impact of economic development efforts.

In his Declaration of Sustainability, Paul Hawken lists 12 strategies for sustainability.

- Take back the charter . . . eliminate businesses that violate the public trust.
- Adjust price to reflect cost . . . internalize externalities.
- Throw out and replace the entire tax system . . . the current system encourages waste and discourages conservation.
- Allow resource companies to be utilities . . . encourage resource companies to conserve rather than expand.
- Change linear systems to cyclical ones . . . incorporate recycling and reuse into PRODUCTION systems.
- Transform the making of things . . . design would include plans for decomposition or return and discourage creation of unrecyclables.
- Vote, don't buy . . . know who are responsible CORPORATIONS and who are not responsible.
- Restore the "guardian" . . . restore the role of government as guardian of the interests of society.
- Shift from electronic literacy to biologic literacy . . . improve Americans' understanding of ecosystems.

- Take inventory . . . of our planet and the species that are threatened.
- Take care of human health . . . address the present dangers faced by people worldwide.
- Respect the human spirit . . . have businesses support hope and initiate change toward sustainability.

Further reading

Daly, Herman. *Beyond Growth: the Economics of Sustainable Development.* 1992; Hawken, Paul. "A Declaration of Sustainability." *Utne Reader,* September/ October 1993; Yale Center for Environmental Law and Policy. "Pilot Environmental Sustainability Index." 2000.

sweatshop

As defined by sweatshopwatch.org, a sweatshop is a "workplace where workers are subject to extreme exploitation, including the absence of a living wage or benefits, poor working conditions, and arbitrary discipline." The difficulty in defining sweatshop is the word *extreme*. What some labor activists call extreme, some employers consider necessary but dirty jobs that need to be done. LAISSEZ-FAIRE advocates suggest sweatshops are a voluntary choice. Workers accept the working conditions and pay because they have no better alternative. When they have better options, they will move on.

The term *sweatshop* originated in the 19th century. Middlemen would contract to provide PRODUCTS to companies and then hire workers on a piecemeal rate to produce the products. The difference between the price paid to the middleman and the price paid to workers was the middleman's PROFIT, "sweated" from the labor of workers.

Most Americans' images of sweatshops are associated with 19th-century industrialization and abuse of child labor. The Triangle Factory fire in 1911 was a galvanizing force in the U.S. history of sweatshops. More than 500 women were working on the ninth floor of a building in downtown New York when the fire broke out. Since doors were locked to keep workers from leaving early, many women jumped to their death.

Throughout the early 1900s, what most people would agree are sweatshop conditions existed in both the textile and agricultural industries. Textile workers were often immigrants, thankful to not be in the country they had fled and willing to take any job opportunity. Huge numbers of immigrants arrived annually in most U.S. port cities, creating a steady stream of workers. The number of sweatshops diminished—or diminished from public view—after labor legislation in the 1930s increased the rights of workers to unionize and created a MINIMUM WAGE.

With increasing prosperity in the United States after World War II, many textile jobs moved overseas. In the 1990s college students, aware of extreme working conditions in overseas factories where workers produced logo products for their college bookstores, began organizing efforts to address international sweatshops. In one of the worst cases, young women from the Philippines were brought to Saipan, a Pacific island, and kept in slave-like conditions. Most governments in EMERGING MARKETS overlook sweatshops, accepting them as the price of creating jobs. When major U.S. apparel makers like Nike, Kathie Lee Gifford, and Liz Claiborne were associated with international sweatshops, pressure from U.S. consumers forced change.

Today sweatshops still exist in the United States, most often in the garment industry. In 2002, 19 workers at a Los Angeles sewing factory began to protest against their employer, complaining that they were not paid for overtime nor were they paid minimum wage for their work. The workers organized a BOYCOTT of one of the retail stores selling the factory's clothing; the retailer countered with a defamation lawsuit.

Agricultural workers continue to organize against poor working conditions and underpayment of wages. In both the garment and agricultural industries, often workers are illegal aliens in the United States and therefore are not willing to pressure for change.

Further reading

Sweatshop Watch website. Available on-line. URL: www.sweatshopwatch.org; "The Story of the Fire: Sweatshops and Strikes." Available on-line. URL: www.ilr.cornell.edu/trianglefire.narrative.html.

—Jonathan R. Sullivan

synergy

According to *Webster's New World Dictionary,* synergy is the positive result that occurs when "the simultaneous action of separate agencies have greater total effect than the sum of their individual effects." Management professor Stephen Robbins relates positive and negative synergy to business in the following way:

> Synergy is a term used in biology that refers to an action of two or more substances that results in an affect that is different from the individual's summation of the substances. We can use the concept to better understand group processes. SOCIAL LOAFING, for instance, represents negative synergy. The whole is less than the sum of its parts. On the other hand, research teams are often used in research laboratories because they can draw on the diverse skills of various individuals to produce more meaningful research as a group than could be generated by all of the researchers working independently. That is, they produce positive synergy. Their process gains exceed their process losses.

According to prominent MANAGEMENT theorists, including Robert Blake and Jane Mouton in their classic management-development theory, synergy is a critical element of the managerial grid. In managerial-grid theory, managers (leaders) have as much concern for developing their people as they do for attaining their goals or objectives. The grid provides a visual framework for considering leadership approaches with axes of concern for production and concern for people. Simply put, if synergy is fully utilized, one plus one should be more than two. Managerial-grid training became quite popular in the 1970s and 1980s as a mechanism for developing managers; extensive public and custom programs were developed. A critical component of the training process is basic PROBLEM SOLVING or decision making through the use of *critique,* or constructive criticism. Managerial-grid workshops focus on how to use this in a positive fashion to obtain optimum operational solutions while maximizing teamwork.

In addition, work by Janis discusses the phenomenon of groupthink and the loss of synergy if the leader or manager allows this process to take place. Groupthink is social conformity and pressure to conform. Groupthink reduces individual initiative, creative problem solving, and the benefits of synergy through teamwork.

Further reading

Blake, Robert R., and Jane S. Mouton. *The Managerial Grid.* Houston: Gulf, 1964; Janis, Irving L. *Groupthink.* 2d ed. Boston: Houghton Mifflin, 1982; Robbins, Stephen P. *Organizational Behavior,* 10th ed. Upper Saddle River, N.J.: Prentice Hall, 2003.

—Howard Rudd

T

t-account

The accounts in a firm's ledger are physically represented by t-accounts, so named because of their "T" formation. The "T" creates two sides for each account, a debit (left) side and a credit (right) side. Amounts are entered into the t-accounts by posting, a phase in the accounting cycle when journal entries are transferred to the ledger accounts. Alone, debit and credit mean nothing more than left and right, respectively. When associated with ASSETS and expense accounts, a debit increases these accounts; credits decrease them. When associated with liabilities, equities, and revenues, a credit increases these accounts; debits decrease them.

See also DEBIT, CREDIT.

Taft-Hartley Act (Labor-Management Relations Act)

The Taft-Hartley Act (Labor-Management Relations Act, 1947) attempted to reduce the power of organized labor in the United States through changes in the WAGNER ACT (National Labor Relations Act, 1935). After World War II, pent-up consumer DEMAND created ECONOMIC GROWTH, and workers who had been constrained from strikes or other labor actions during the war asserted their demands. Political sentiment shifted from pro-labor during the Roosevelt years to a more conservative, pro-business environment. Taft-Hartley was passed over President Harry Truman's veto and included the following provisions.

- declared certain acts by labor as unfair UNION practices
- prohibited closed-shop agreements
- granted states the right to enact right-to-work laws
- restricted the use of secondary pressure by unions
- created the FEDERAL MEDIATION AND CONCILIATION SERVICE
- expanded membership on the NATIONAL LABOR RELATIONS BOARD
- granted the president power to intervene in "national emergency" disputes
- created the right for unions to sue and be sued

- recognized free-speech rights of union members
- recognized the right of individuals to refrain from union activity
- restricted the power of unions to control pension and other funds

Taft-Hartley declared certain union activities as unfair, including refusal to bargain with employers, coercing employees to join unions, and causing an employer to discriminate against a worker who is not a union member. Unions requiring membership as a condition of EMPLOYMENT (closed shops), and conducting strikes or BOYCOTTS against third parties with which the union has no real dispute in order to gain leverage against an employer (secondary pressure) were in violation of Taft-Hartley. FEATHERBEDDING—using a union CONTRACT to force an employer to pay for work not actually performed—was also declared an unfair labor practice.

Taft-Hartley is most known for its "cooling-off" period for strikes. The president can invoke a 60-day injunction period for strikes that would endanger national safety or health. Presidents have often used this provision to intervene in disputes by police and sanitation unions and during periods of national emergencies.

Further reading

Mallor, Jane P., A. James Barnes, Thomas Bowers, Michael J. Philips, and Arlen W. Langvardt. *Business Law and the Regulatory Environment.* 11th ed. Boston: McGraw-Hill, 2001.

takings clause

The phrase *takings clause* refers to the U.S. Constitution's Fifth Amendment, which provides that no "private property [shall] be taken for public use without just compensation." Individuals and businesses before the U.S. Supreme Court have extensively disputed the meaning and scope of the takings clause. Traditional takings disputes, such as government acquisition of private land by EMINENT DOMAIN to build roads, focus on questions of just compensation. Broadly speaking, the duty of governments is to pay fair MARKET VALUE for their takings, although determining fair market value is often elusive.

In recent decades, the concept of a "taking" that triggers the duty of just compensation has been expanded somewhat to include so-called "regulatory takings." The basic idea is that by issuing regulations, for example concerning land use or environmental protection, governments may take private property by reducing the scope of the full range of options that normally comes with ownership that (unlike the road example above) remains in private hands. Gradually the U.S. Supreme Court has recognized the concept of regulatory takings of private property.

Further reading
Siegan, Bernard H. *Property and Freedom: The Constitution, the Courts, and Land Use Regulation.* Somerset, N.J.: Transaction Publishers, 1997.

target markets

Target markets are groups of buyers toward whom a business or organization directs its marketing efforts. Target markets can include groups of consumers, businesses, government, or users of SERVICES or PRODUCTS from nonprofit organizations.

Target markets and target marketing can be compared to the idea of hitting the bull's-eye. The term *bull's-eye* comes from the ancient sport of archery, where the black center of the target is surrounded by a white circle and resembles the eye of a bull. Similar to aiming at the bull's-eye in a target's center, good marketing aims at a specific grouping of customers. The idea of choosing the right target market—hitting the bull's-eye—comes from the reality that no firm has the ability to sell all products to all customers.

When choosing target markets, managers consider the size of target group, the PROFIT potential, accessibility to that group of consumers, and the potential interest of those consumers. In the United States, the number of potential customers and their PURCHASING power is usually available using U.S. CENSUS BUREAU data. Access to potential target markets (i.e., availability of DISTRIBUTION CHANNELS to get products or services to customers) and ADVERTISING and SALES PROMOTION methods to make potential customers aware of a firm's offerings can be assessed through informal MARKET RESEARCH. Assessing consumers' interest in a firm's offerings is often done through FOCUS GROUPS, market tests, and SURVEYS,

For any organization, the benefit of defining target markets is marketing efficiency. The more marketers know about their customers or potential customers, the better opportunity they have to meet the needs of those consumers. Good marketers anticipate their customers' needs, often even before the customers recognize them.

Many companies think in terms of their products rather than the benefits they are providing to consumers. One of the failures of many marketing executives is to not think in terms of their consumers, termed *marketing myopia* by Harvard business professor Theodore Levitt.

Marketers in nonprofit organizations often have additional problems. Typically they have at least two distinct target markets, donors and recipients. User groups are different from donors to nonprofit groups, whether they are financial contributors or people giving their time. Donors typically have different motives, interests, INCOME, and other demographic characteristics from users. This requires nonprofit marketers to develop different marketing strategies for each audience. Often target user groups for nonprofit organizations are hard to identify and difficult to communicate with.

Whether for nonprofit organizations or businesses, once viable target markets have been identified, marketers then decide what type of MARKETING STRATEGY to use. Generally there are three choices: undifferentiated, concentrated, or multisegment. An undifferentiated strategy involves using one marketing mix for all target markets. Undifferentiated strategies minimize marketing costs by using the same message, promotions, signs, products, etc., for all target groups. On the other hand, an undifferentiated approach may not be appropriate for some target audiences. Many U.S. companies have failed in their initial INTERNATIONAL MARKETING efforts by not adjusting their marketing mix for target markets abroad.

A concentrated strategy involves focusing a firm's efforts on one target market and developing products, pricing, promotion, and distribution strategies for this group of consumers. Small firms without sufficient resources to compete in many markets often use a concentrated strategy.

A multisegment strategy involves identifying a few target markets, a basic marketing mix, and adapting product offerings, pricing, promotional efforts, and distribution strategies for each group. Business-to-business marketers often use multisegment strategies employing different distribution and promotional methods for large versus small and domestic versus foreign customers.

See also MARKET SEGMENTATION.

Further reading
Boone, Louis E., and David L. Kurtz. *Contemporary Marketing,* 11th ed. Cincinnati, Ohio: South-Western, 2003.

tariff

A tariff is a tax or duty imposed on goods imported into a nation. Tariffs increase the price of imported PRODUCTS. The U.S. Constitution authorizes Congress to levy uniform tariffs on IMPORTS. There are several types of U.S. tariffs, the most common being an ad valorem ("according to the value") rate. Ad valorem rates are assessed in proportion to the value of the good, for example 10 percent of the value.

Tariffs may also be assessed at specific or compound rates. Specific rates are based on weight measures (i.e., pounds, ounces), while a compound rate is a mixture of an ad valorem and a specific-rate tariff. Tariff-rate quotas impose a limit on imports at a specific rate up to a certain amount. Imports in excess of that amount are subject to a higher rate of tariff. Thus tariff-rate quotas discourage imports in excess of the specified quota at the lower tariff level.

In the 18th century, tariffs were initially used to generate revenue for the federal government. In many developing countries, where government oversight of INCOME and sales activities is minimal, tariffs continue to be used for revenue generation, but by 1816 the United States had begun using tariffs for openly protectionist goals. Raising the price of imported goods protected American producers from foreign COMPETITION.

Throughout the 19th century, the United States legislated heavy tariffs, justified as being needed to protect "infant" industries, and to force the South to engage in more trade with the North rather than with Europe. Exceptions to the tariff laws were granted through most-favored-nation RECIPROCITY treaties. The first of these treaties involved Canada (Elgin-Marcy, 1854) and Hawaii (1875). Pressure from U.S. manufacturers (mostly northern) and the perception that Britain had been sympathetic to the Confederacy led to abrogation of the 1854 treaty with Canada in 1866.

In the late 19th century, additional "countervailing duties" were created to combat export subsidies of European countries, particularly Germany. After 1916, additional tariffs could also be imposed if foreign countries were found to be DUMPING, selling goods at unfairly low prices in the United States. Most early American dumping legislation was a response to the practices of foreign CARTELS. On many occasions, the U.S. Supreme Court debated the constitutionality of protective tariffs, finally ruling they were constitutional in 1928. This decision, along with the STOCK MARKET crash in 1929, led to enactment of the infamous SMOOT-HAWLEY TARIFF ACT of 1930. Smoot-Hawley raised tariffs on over 12,000 products to an average of approximately 60 percent of their import values. President Herbert Hoover, ignoring a petition signed by more than 1,000 economists warning of the act's harmful effects, signed the legislation. A trade war resulted as foreign countries quickly enacted retaliatory legislation. Many economists believe the Smoot-Hawley Tariff Act contributed significantly to the GREAT DEPRESSION. This would be the last time the U.S. passed tariff legislation without international negotiations.

Since 1930, Congress has achieved changes in the levels of tariffs for goods entering the United States through international trade agreements negotiated by the president. The Reciprocal Trade Agreements Act of 1934 gives the president the authority to negotiate bilateral agreements, reducing Smoot-Hawley tariffs with selected countries. The Trade Agreements Extension Act of 1945, anticipating the creation of the General Agreement on Tariffs and Trade (GATT), authorized the president to conduct multilateral trade negotiations.

GATT became effective in 1948 and was implemented in the United States by executive order. Even though the U.S. Congress never ratified GATT, which was replaced by the WORLD TRADE ORGANIZATION in 1997, it resulted in significant reductions in U.S. tariffs. Under GATT, duties known as most-favored-nation (MFN) tariffs or "Column 1 tariffs" have been successively reduced through "rounds" of trade negotiations. Since 1948, multilateral tariff agreements have been the predominant basis for tariff negotiations.

The term *most-favored-nation* is misleading, suggesting special tariff arrangements. It is more appropriate and, since 1998, officially correct to consider MFN tariffs as the normal level of U.S. tariffs, to which there are exceptions resulting in higher or lower tariffs. After the Tokyo Round of GATT negotiations in 1978, the average MFN tariff applied to manufactured imports into the United States was approximately 5.6 percent. The Uruguay Round in 1994 reduced MFN tariffs to an average of 3.5 percent.

See also MOST-FAVORED NATION CLAUSE; NONTARIFF BARRIERS.

Further reading

Boyes, William, and Michael Melvin. *Microeconomics*, 5th ed. Boston: Houghton Mifflin, 2002; U.S. Customs Service website. Available on-line. URL: www.customs.ustreas.gov.

taxes   See BUSINESS TAXES; LOCAL OPTION SALES TAX; PAYROLL TAXES; PROPERTY TAXES; TRANSFER TAXES.

tax incremental funding (tax incremental financing)

Tax incremental funding (TIF) is the use of tax revenues to address specific funding priorities. Most often TIF, also called tax incremental financing, involves the commitment of increased property-tax revenue from increased values of properties that are rehabilitated. Development funds are used to redevelop a "blighted" area, raising the value of the properties and adjoining properties. The increased PROPERTY TAXES are used to pay for the cost of redevelopment. Once a TIF district is created, the government agency can borrow against the anticipated tax revenue and use the funds for redevelopment.

TIF districts are a method to fund and then recapture the cost of development, but they can adversely affect other parts of the municipality or county. The funds from increased property values that pay for redevelopment also decrease the general revenue to the city or county. The city or county then must either increase their tax rates or decrease government SERVICES. In most areas of the United States, property taxes are a significant portion of the funding for public schools. Decreased tax revenues to the city or county have the greatest impact on school funding.

From a property owner's perspective, TIF districts can be quite beneficial. Rather than pay taxes to pay for all government services, their taxes, specifically the increase in their taxes from increased property values, pay for the cost of increasing the property values in their area. Most TIF districts are created for a specific purpose and a defined time period, typically ranging from 10 to 25 years.

tax shelter

A tax shelter is a method of giving investors certain tax benefits by allowing them to avoid, reduce, or defer payment of taxes. Tax shelters may be legitimate or abusive. The INTERNAL REVENUE SERVICE (IRS) prohibits the use of abusive tax shelters.

The federal government loses tax revenues by allowing taxpayers to avoid, reduce, or defer payment of taxes through the use of tax shelters. However, Congress has determined that the loss of tax revenues is acceptable as a side effect of encouraging investors to participate in transactions that promote society's economic and social well-being. Thus the Internal Revenue Code (IRC) has special tax provisions designed to encourage investors to invest in legitimate tax shelters. Examples of legitimate tax shelters include DEPRECIATION of ASSETS such as land, plants, and equipment used in business operations. Depreciation reduces a firm's taxable INCOME and therefore reduces the amount of taxes a firm must pay. Other examples of legitimate tax shelters include tax-exempt municipal BONDS and INDIVIDUAL RETIREMENT ACCOUNTS (IRAs).

Abusive tax shelters, which are strongly motivated by a desire to reduce or avoid taxes, are not legal and produce little or no societal benefit. Often abusive tax shelters offer tax savings far in excess of the actual INVESTMENT placed at risk, but they also often produce little or no income. In order to reduce the use of abusive tax shelters, the IRS has registration and reporting requirements to help identify violations. Organizers of certain tax shelters must register their shelters with the IRS, which then issues them tax registration numbers. Sellers of the tax shelters must provide buyers with the registration numbers of the tax shelters being purchased, and buyers are required to report the tax shelters' registration numbers in their tax returns. Organizers and sellers of tax shelters must also maintain a list of individuals or organizations that invest in the shelters; this list must be made available to the IRS for inspection. The registration of tax shelters may assist the IRS in identifying investments that qualify as abusive tax shelters and thus penalize users and providers of those shelters.

Further reading

Black, Henry Campbell, et al. *Black's Law Dictionary,* 6th ed. St. Paul: West Publishing Co., 1991; Department of the Treasury, Internal Revenue Service. *Publication 550: Investment Income and Expenses (Including Capital Gains and Losses).* Cat. No. 15093R, 26–28; Downes, John, and Jordan Elliot Goodman. *Finance and Investment Handbook,* 6th ed. New York: Barron's Educational Series, 2003; Internal Revenue Service. "Frequently Asked Questions—How Can I Recognize an Abusive Tax Shelter?" Available on-line. URL: http://www.irs.gov/faqs/display/0,,i1=52&genericId=15793,00.html. Downloaded on February 13, 2002; Internal Revenue Service. *"Topic 454—Tax Shelters."* Available on-line. URL: http://www.irs.gov/file/display/0,,i1=52&genericId=16225,00.html. Downloaded on February 13, 2002; Johnson, Calvin H. "What's A Tax Shelter?" *68 Tax Notes,* 14 August 1995, pp. 879–83; Jack Warren Wade Jr. "Tax Shelters." Available on-line. URL: http://www.unclefed.com/Audit-Proofing/step4-3.html. Downloaded on February 13, 2002.

—Gayatri Gupta

technical analysis

Technical analysis is a STOCK MARKET prediction method based on the analysis of changes in a stock's price and volume of trading. Technical stock analysts (known as technicians or "elves" on Louis Rukeyser's *Wall Street Week* television show) construct a variety of charts plotting stock-price changes. Based on these charts, technicians predict future price movement.

Technicians differ from other stock-market analysts in that they do not use changes in the fundamentals of a stock in making their predictions. Most investors and INVESTMENT analysts study a company's fundamentals: its PROFITS, sales, market share, PRODUCTS, RESEARCH AND DEVELOPMENT, and MANAGEMENT. If a company's fundamentals are perceived as positive, it is likely the company will grow and increase its profits, and thus its stock price will increase. In technical analysis, however, a technician may chart a stock's 50-day moving average and purchase shares whenever the stock's price moves higher than the average, regardless of any change in fundamental conditions affecting the company.

Richard Schalbacker, author of *Technical Analysis and Stock Market Profits,* is considered the father of modern technical analysis. Schalbacker and other technicians use a language of their own. In addition to moving averages (50-, 100-, or 200-day average of the stock's closing price), technicians discuss *support and resistance levels, momentum investing stochastic, Bollinger bands, Dow theory, head-and-shoulders,* and *plunging neckline,* among other special terms. *Support and resistance levels* are lows (support) and highs (resistance) in a stock's price. Technicians watch closely as a stock's price approaches a new low. If the price goes below the lowest price traded in the last year, this is a negative signal, and technical analysts will often sell the stock. If the stock trades above its recent high, it has broken a resistance level. This is considered a positive sign and is an indication to buy the stock.

Momentum investing is a variation of technical analysis in which investors buy and sell stocks based on whether the stock's price is increasing or decreasing in relation to the volume of shares being traded. Momentum investing was a popular strategy among day traders in the late 1990s.

Stochastic is a calculation comparing the current price of a stock with its trading range in the recent past. Stochastic is used to predict reversals in a stock's price.

Bollinger bands are lines plotted at standard deviation levels (variations from the average) above and below a stock's moving average. Movement of a stock's price out of the bands signals a "break-out" of the stock and either a buy or sell recommendation.

Dow theory refers to the ideas of Charles Dow (of the DOW JONES AVERAGES), who held that the overall stock market would not change course unless the Dow Jones Transportation and Industrial Indexes were moving in the same direction.

Head-and-shoulder and *plunging neckline* are descriptions of the pattern of movement of stock prices, usually using the Dow Jones Industrial Average. A head-and-shoulder pattern would indicate the market has peaked and is on the decline. If the average were to fall below the recent lowest point, this would be a plunging neckline and, if accompanied by a high volume of trading, would forecast a significant decline.

There are many other technical-analysis descriptions of stock-market movements. A number of websites provide examples of technical-analysis interpretation. For many years, technical analysis was compared to the psychological interpretation of inkblots. Traditional, fundamental stock-market analysts rarely admit to using technical analysis but quietly check technical signals when making their recommendations and investment decisions.

Further reading
Smith, Gary B. "We're Off to See The Wizard . . . Three technical analysis site illuminate stock picking's dark side," *Money* 28 (1 July 1999).

Teamsters Union   See INTERNATIONAL BROTHERHOOD OF TEAMSTERS.

technology transfer
Technology transfer occurs when the developer or owner of certain technology shares that technology with organizations or individuals who wish to have access to it. The technology may be in the form of a PRODUCT, a PRODUCTION process, a design, information, KNOW-HOW, or some combination of these.

Technology transfers may occur between parties in different nations. Often companies or individuals in developed nations are the owners of technology, and they may have nationally and internationally recognized proprietary rights in what they own or have developed. Parties in EMERGING MARKETS may be interested in acquiring that technology, and owners may choose from a variety of options to bring about the technology transfer.

One way for technology owners to share their technology is through a license or franchise agreement, whereby the owner receives fees from licensees or royalties from franchisees as compensation for the use of the technology. Owners who wish to establish a more substantial presence in another nation or market may engage in direct FOREIGN INVESTMENT in that nation by forming JOINT VENTURES with local companies or individuals or forming subsidiaries in foreign nations. The owner would share the technology with the joint venture or with its foreign subsidiary and could be compensated in a variety of ways, including PROFITS from sales.

Nations may have laws that protect the proprietary interest of owners of various types of technology, such as PATENT, COPYRIGHT, and TRADEMARK laws. Some protection, such as that for patents, may only protect the owner in the nation in which they have been granted the patent. Thus, an inventor of U.S.-patented technology may need to apply for a patent in every nation in which he or she seeks protection against the unauthorized use of his technology. However, some nations refuse to grant patents for certain technology. For example, some less-developed nations do not grant patents for pharmaceuticals, which has led to the production of generic pharmaceuticals based on technology developed elsewhere, but without any compensation to the technology's developer or owner. U.S. businesses that are considering technology transfer to parties outside in other countries should consider the laws of the nation to which they are transferring technology and obtain protection from the unauthorized use of their technology in those nations whenever possible.

U.S. businesses should also consider various international agreements and treaties to assess whether their technology may be internationally protected from unauthorized use. However, some of the principles of international agreements or treaties may not override domestic laws. Some important international agreement and treaties are the General Agreement on Tariffs and Trade (GATT, 1947), the agreement on Trade-Related Intellectual Property Rights (TRIPS, 1994), the Paris Convention, the Patent Cooperation Treaty, and the 1957 Arrangement of Nice Concerning the International Classification of Goods and Services.

See also FRANCHISING; LICENSING.

Further reading
Folsom, Ralph H., Michael Wallace Gordon, and John A. Spanogle. *International Business Transactions in a Nutshell,* 6th ed. Eagan, Minn.: West Publishing Co., 2000.

—Gayatri Gupta

telemarketing
Telemarketing is DIRECT MARKETING conducted entirely by telephone; the term includes both inbound and outbound telemarketing. Inbound telemarketing usually involves a

toll-free number that customers can call to obtain information or make purchases. Outbound telemarketing involves a sales force using the telephone to contact customers and potential customers. The advantages of telemarketing are that it offers the quickest and most direct way to reach consumers, provides immediate feedback to the seller, and allows sellers the opportunity to overcome consumer objections. It is also often the least costly method of direct marketing.

Telemarketing programs are managed either in-house or by a service bureau. In-house operations allow for greater control over personnel, scripts, budgets, and incentive policies. They are often appropriate for companies with technical PRODUCTS requiring considerable explanation to consumers and for companies with rapidly changing products. Service bureaus are often cheaper than in-house operations for small companies and companies that do not have 24-hour operations. Service bureaus reduce the time and CAPITAL cost to get started, in addition to providing experienced telephone sales staff and knowledge from past telemarketing operations.

Telemarketing is almost as old as the telephone; stockbrokers began "cold calling" in the 1930s. In the 1940s and 1950s, many magazine publishers found telemarketing was an effective way to sell to new subscribers and keep customers whose subscriptions were ending. With the introduction of 800 numbers in the 1960s, inbound telemarketing grew rapidly. Today predictive-dialer systems automatically dial numbers from the company's database and instantly connect calls when consumers respond. Computer database systems have combined with on-line scripts and ordering and information systems to make telemarketing a high-technology industry. In the United States, over 900 companies employing almost 5 million people work in telemarketing.

Telemarketing is an alternative to the DIRECT MAIL business, in which a 2 percent response rate is considered a good standard. In outbound telemarketing, 6 to 8 percent response rates are normally achieved. Like direct mail, the success of outbound telemarketing is tied to the quality of the database being used. Even if the telemarketer has a good database, his or her efforts are not often positively received; virtually every household has been interrupted during dinnertime by a telemarketer. In 1996 the FEDERAL TRADE COMMISSION created telemarketing sales rules, including the following.

- Identify the caller.
- Restrict calls to daytime and early evening (none after 9 P.M.).
- Maintain do-not-call lists.
- Disclose the total cost of all goods, SERVICES, and refund policies.
- Release the phone line within five seconds once the other party has hung up the phone.
- Never send unsolicited advertisements by fax.

- Disclose the odds of winning prizes and any restrictions on receiving prizes or merchandise. Also specify that the customer does not have to make a purchase to win a prize.

In recent years, many states created "do-not-call lists" that citizens can subscribe to. Telemarketers operating in the state are required to purge these consumers from their databases. The Direct Marketing Association also maintains a Telephone Preference Service and a do-not-call list, and in 2003 over 50 million Americans signed on to a national do-not-call list.

Further reading
American Telemarketing Association website. Available on-line. URL: www.ataconnect.org; Boone, Louis E., and David L. Kurtz. *Contemporary Marketing,* 10th ed. Fort Worth: Dryden Press, 2001; Direct Marketing Association website. Available on-line. URL: www.the-dma.org.

telephone surveys
Telephone SURVEYS are one method market researchers use to collect information. Telephone surveys can be formal or informal and are used to interview both businesses and consumers. They are distinguished from TELEMARKETING by the fact that the surveyor is not attempting to sell anything but is only gathering information. Some MARKET RESEARCH companies use telephone surveys to fill in missing information about consumers in their database. Information about the number of dependents, their ages, and other DEMOGRAPHICS is useful in target-marketing consumer groups.

The advantages of telephone surveys are they allow for quick collection of data, centralized control over data collection, and are less expensive than PERSONAL-INTERVIEW SURVEYS. Telephone-survey work is often contracted out to specialized companies with the equipment and expertise to conduct surveys. The survey questionnaire is loaded into computer software programs that allow interviewers to enter respondents' answers directly into a database. Results can be tabulated and analyzed quickly with predetermined statistical measures generated from the database. More than 500 telemarketing and telephone-survey firms operate in the United States.

The disadvantages of telephone surveys are the limited amount of information that can be collected, consumer resistance to being questioned, unlisted numbers, and caller ID and message machines that can block calls. Telephone surveys frequently collect information from a disproportionate percentage of elderly consumers. If the target population of the survey is the general public, therefore, telephone surveys often are not representative.

While five minutes is typically the longest time for a telephone survey, with a well-organized survey, an interesting topic, a motivated interviewer, and sponsorship from a credible organization, surveys can be used to collect large amounts of information. A computer company once surveyed businesses to ask only the names of the people involved in making computer PURCHASING decisions. The company was acting on the BUYING CENTER CONCEPT—the fact that a number of people with a variety of interests would likely be involved in computer purchasing decisions.

While telephone surveys do not allow the use of visual materials or observation of respondents, they do provide a degree of anonymity for respondents and allow for some probing and follow-up questioning.

See also QUESTIONNAIRES.

Further reading
Pride, William O., and O. C. Ferrell. *Marketing Concepts and Strategies*, 12th ed. Boston: Houghton Mifflin, 2003.

tender offer
A tender offer is an offer from a firm or INVESTMENT group to buy shares of stock. In a tender offer, stockholders are usually offered a price above the stock's current market price. This premium is used to induce SHAREHOLDERS to sell. A tender offer is a means for an outside group to take control of a company and can come in the form of a friendly or hostile takeover. In the case of a friendly takeover, MANAGEMENT and the BOARD OF DIRECTORS will recommend shareholders "tender" (sell) their shares to the group making the offer. In the case of a hostile-takeover attempt, companies often adopt a variety of strategies to prevent or eliminate the incentive for the takeover. These strategies include a variety of colorful terms such as "poison pills" (issuing new debt or preferred shares to make the company less attractive financially), a "bear hug" (where the terms are so attractive that a company's board of directors is afraid not to accept the offer), and "cram-down" deals (where an unattractive tender offer is made, but the company being acquired has no other alternatives).

The SECURITIES AND EXCHANGE COMMISSION (SEC) requires any corporate "suitor" who accumulates 5 percent or more of the shares of a target company to disclose its holdings to the SEC, the target company, and the stock exchange where the shares are traded.

See also POISON-PILL STRATEGIES.

Tennessee Valley Authority
The Tennessee Valley Authority (TVA) is a federal CORPORATION providing public power services in seven southeastern states. The TVA, created by the U.S. Congress in 1933, was part of President Franklin Roosevelt's "New Deal" legislation designed to stimulate the U.S. economy out of the GREAT DEPRESSION. Roosevelt asked Congress to create "a corporation clothed with the power of government but possessed of the flexibility and initiative of a private enterprise."

The TVA's initial goal was to provide flood control, navigation, and electric power to the Tennessee Valley region; their slogan was "TVA, Electricity for All." Over the years, the TVA has become a major utility provider and was the country's largest public power company in 1997. The TVA operates 49 dams as well as coal-fired and nuclear power plants. While the TVA no longer receives any federal funding, it was created with public funds and pays tax-equivalent payments in lieu of state and local taxes.

The TVA is, as President Roosevelt had intended, both a public and a private enterprise. As such it has the advantages of lower-cost financing for current projects and no debt from construction of initial power plants. It also does not pay taxes on PROFITs, which allows it to produce relatively low-cost electricity. This was and continues to be used as a source of COMPARATIVE ADVANTAGE in the Tennessee Valley area. Critics complain the TVA is such a dominant economic force in the region, its influence cannot be questioned. Competitors complain TVA has unfair economic advantages due to its status as a federal corporation. However, at the time it was created, TVA brought jobs and ECONOMIC DEVELOPMENT to one of the poorest regions of the country.

Further reading
Tennessee Valley Authority website. Available on-line. URL: www.tva.gov.

theory of constraints
Webster's defines the word *theory* as "the analysis of a set of hypothetical facts and their relationship to each other." *Constraints* are restrictions placed on those facts, inhibiting the desired outcomes. The theory of constraints (TOC) is a philosophy of "how to think" associated with Dr. Eliyahu M. Goldratt, author of *The Goal* (1992). According to Goldratt, if people know "how to think," they can greatly influence the outcome of any situation where constraints exist. *The Goal* is a novel in which the main character, Alex Roga, uses Goldratt's ideas to save the local factory and his marriage. The author includes himself in the novel as the character Jonah. Managers who have gone through the extensive theory of constraint training often refer to themselves as "Jonahs."

The theory of constraints includes three distinct but interrelated concepts: performance measurement, LOGISTICS, and logical thinking. Performance measurement emphasizes throughput rather than cost control. Throughput is the rate at which the organization generates sales revenue. In traditional accounting procedure, PRODUCTION is considered output. In TOC thinking, output, which is not sold, is not relevant. What counts is MONEY generated through sales. Anything that restricts the company from the goal of attaining sales is a constraint, which can include production capacity, RESOURCES, distribution, market DEMAND, and MANAGEMENT.

Goldratt emphasizes the role of corporate policies and procedures as constraints to performance. Requirements act as barriers, limiting managers' decision-making ability. TOC focuses on overcoming constraints, first by identifying the constraint and then by establishing goals and objectives that will remove the barriers.

The second concept in TOC is logistics. In TOC language, logistics include drum-buffer-rope scheduling and VAT analysis. Professors Mokshagundam Srikanth and Michale Umble define *drum* as the detailed master production schedule that sets the pace for the entire system and *buffer* as the additional planned lead time allowed, beyond the required setup and run times. The buffers protect the system against uncertainty. *Rope* is defined as the set of instructions needed to release materials into the system, flowing to the buffers in a way that supports the planned overall throughput. In other words, it is the coordination of inputs, governed constraints, that maximizes throughput.

VAT analysis is a conceptualization of the organization with respect to the interaction of parts of the process. Goldratt suggests there are three logical structures. A "V" structure starts with one or a few raw materials which, when used in a variety of production processes, ultimately leads to a variety of products. The few materials are the bases of a "V," and the many products are the tops of the V. An "A" structure is the opposite of a V structure. In an A structure, many materials go through a series of processes, resulting in one or a few final products. A "T" structure involves a few processing or assembly operations working in parallel, which coordinate at later stages, resulting in a variety of final products using the output of the early processing systems. The shape of the production process defines where constraints on throughput occur.

The third TOC concept is logical thinking. Goldratt coined a number of terms to describe tools to address logical thinking, including *effect-cause-effect diagramming, current reality tree, the evaporating cloud,* and other colorful descriptors for analyzing logical thinking.

During the 1980s and 1990s, theory-of-constraint analysis, along with JUST-IN-TIME PRODUCTION (JIT) and TOTAL-QUALITY MANAGEMENT (TQM) was three of the most widely applied production management techniques. Executives embraced each as a revolutionary new way of thinking about management and developed almost cult-like followings among managers. Each contributed to improving efficiency, quality, and productivity in the United States and other industrial countries.

Further reading
Goldratt, Eliyahu M. *The Goal,* 2d ed. Croton-on-Hudson, N.Y.: North River Press, 1992; Srikanth, Mokshagundam L., and Michale M. Umble. *Synchronous Management: Profit-based Manufacturing for the 21st Century.* Guilford, Conn.: Spectrum Publishing, 1997; Sytsma, Sid. "Theory of Constraints: Making Process

Decisions under Conditions of Limited Resources." Available online. URL: http://www.sytsm.com/cism700/toc.html.

—Kimberly Jeffers

Theory X and Theory Y

Post-World War II manager assumptions about subordinate workplace ethics and their affect on HUMAN RESOURCES management significantly changed in 1960 with management theorist Douglas McGregor's Theory X and Theory Y propositions. Improving management techniques by understanding what motivates workers supports McGregor's theories. Furthermore, his propositions were strongly influenced by Abraham MASLOW'S HIERARCHY OF NEEDS, a model demonstrating the motivational need for self-actuation leading to self-fulfillment. Maslow argued that worker dissatisfaction was not the fault of the worker but due to poor job design, inappropriate managerial techniques, and lack of self-fulfillment. McGregor's Theory X and Theory Y are based on a set of assumptions that managers have about people's attitude toward work and the value they place on it. These assumptions establish managerial practices and workplace environment guidelines and serve as the basis for personnel development and managerial policies, while directly affect business productivity.

McGregor did not oppose authoritative managerial techniques or instructions (appropriate or necessary), but if these tools were ineffective, then alternate employee-oriented methodologies were needed. His theories indicated that managerial beliefs toward employee work ethics directly influence the development of human-resource MANAGEMENT policies and procedures. Organizational policies determined the motivational technique managers used to improve employee productivity. Theory X represents the traditional (authoritarian) management style using close supervision, direction, and control in directing employee behavior. Theory X managers make four assumptions about workers.

1. Workers dislike work.
2. Workers must be closely supervised.
3. Workers avoid responsibility.
4. Workers value job security and have very little ambition.

According to Theory X managers, the main motivator for workers is MONEY. With these assumptions, management felt they must force people to work through coercion and threats of punishment.

Theory X organizations/managers use "soft" and "hard" approaches in controlling workers, such as rewards, incentives, close supervision, rules and regulations, and coercion. Soft approaches use rewards and incentives—i.e., more money for more work—whereas hard approaches use coercive and abusive language and other authoritarian methods in directing worker behavior. The saying "a day's work for a day's pay" supports the soft approach, and both methods have a wage-work relationship as a motivational factor. However, McGregor argued that extrinsic (external) motivational factors such as money are not necessarily as effective as the intrinsic (internal) motivational factor of self-actuation/self-fulfillment (realizing one's own potential). He realized the need for a more humanistic management style—Theory Y.

In Theory Y, the organizational relationship between managers and workers is based on participatory management. Theory Y enumerates four basic behavioral assumptions of employee work values.

1. If the work is satisfying, employees find work as natural as play.
2. When employees agree with organizational objectives, they use initiative, self-direction, and self-control.
3. Employees value creativity and being involved in the decision-making process.
4. If the work conditions allow, employees not only accept responsibility, they will seek it.

McGregor demonstrated that open-minded, progressive managers accept and use Theory Y principles for motivating employees and improving human-resource management techniques. Generally managers use Theory X with less motivational and managerial success than managers who use Theory Y.

In conclusion, Theory X and Theory Y are two fundamental principles used in managing people at work. Based on employee work-ethic assumptions, the theories offer opposing behavioral factors in human-resource management and underpin an organization's work environment, productivity, and ultimately its success. The traditional approach, Theory X, is often considered less desirable and less effective than Theory Y, because of its authoritative management style resulting from negative and inaccurate assumptions about employee work ethics. Money and job security are the main employee motivational factors assumed by Theory X managers. A more progressive, humanistic, and acceptable approach, Theory Y, presumes a more positive and participatory role toward EMPLOYEE MOTIVATION and development in an organization. Self-fulfillment—ingenuity, creativity, and decision making—is the main motivational factor for employees holding Theory Y assumptions.

See also MOTIVATION THEORY.

Further reading

"Douglas McGregor—Theory X and Theory Y," Business Open Learning Archive. Available on-line. URL: http://sol.brunel.ac.uk/~jarvis/bola/motivation/mcgregor.html. Downloaded on July 24, 2002; Huitt, W. G. "Maslow's Hierarchy of Needs." Available on-line. URL: http://chiron.valdosta.edu/whuitt/col/regsys/maslow.html. Downloaded on July 29, 2002; "Theory X and Theory Y," NetMBA. Available on-line. URL: http://www.netmba.com/mgmt/ob/motivation/mcgregor/. Downloaded on July 24, 2002; Owens, R. G. "Theory X and Theory Y." In Organizational Behavior in Education, 8th ed. Old Tappan, N.J.: Allyn & Bacon, 2003.

—Frank Ubhaus Jr. and Jerry Merwin

think tanks

Think tanks are nonprofit organizations, usually institutes, created to study and advocate positions on social, political, and business issues. An INTERNET search would lead to a listing of almost 200 think-tank institutes. Think tanks have considerable influence on American public policy, including policies affecting business. Think-tank forums are frequently quoted in the media, and their scholars often testify at congressional hearings. Think tanks often provide temporary homes for politicians and high-level administrators of the political party not in control of the White House. While the terms conservative and liberal are politically charged, think tanks frequently embrace the terms, in part to attract support and contributors for their causes.

One conservative-leaning think tank is the American Enterprise Institute (AEI). The AEI states as its mission "preserving and strengthening the foundations of freedom—government, private enterprise, vital cultural and political institutions, and strong foreign policy and national defense—scholarly research, open debate, and publications." Vice President Dick Cheney, former UN representative Jeane Kirkpatrick, and Judge Robert Bork are all associated with the AEI.

Another conservative/libertarian think tank, the Cato Institute, advocates ideas such as abolishing CAPITAL GAINS taxes, "real" term limits for politicians, and devolution of power from the federal government to the states. The Cato Institute describes itself as providing "24 years of promoting public policy based on individual liberty, limited government, free markets and peace."

For many years Harvard's Kennedy School of Government provided an orientation program for newly elected members of Congress. In the 1990s the Kennedy School, associated with Democratic Party ideas, was displaced by the conservative Heritage Foundation think tank. The Heritage Foundation, created in 1973, states that its mission is "to formulate and promote conservative public policies based on principles of free enterprise, limited government, individual freedom, traditional American values and a strong national defense."

Former House Speaker Newt Gingrich is a member of the American Enterprise Institute and Stanford University's Hoover Institute. The Hoover Institute, started in 1919 by Herbert Hoover (later president of the United States) to study the causes and consequences of World War I, is another widely quoted conservative think tank. It is most associated with the ideas of Nobel Prize–winning economist Milton Friedman, whose Free to Choose video series was widely viewed during the 1970s.

The Brookings Institution, created in 1916 as the Institute for Government Research, is one of the most widely quoted think tanks associated with Democratic Party ideas. Presidential advisor Vernon Jordan is a member of the executive board of the Brookings Institute. There are also many think tanks that focus on specific areas of public policy. One of the most widely quoted is the Rand Institute, created in 1948 to "promote scientific, educational, and charitable purposes for the public welfare and security of the U.S."

Further reading
American Enterprise Institute website. Available on-line. URL: www.aei.org; Brookings Institution website. Available on-line. URL: www.brook.edu; Heritage Institute website. Available on-line. URL: www.heritage.org; Hoover Institute website. Available on-line. URL: www.hoover.org; Rand Institute website. Available on-line. URL: www.rand.org.

360-degree feedback

In the 360-degree feedback evaluation system, assessments of employee performance are gathered from a variety of sources and used in PERFORMANCE APPRAISALS. A typical system may include 10 or more peers, managers, customers, underlings and others who are asked to write up an evaluation.

The 360-degree feedback system was a 1990s response to criticism of MANAGEMENT evaluation systems. With the implementation of FORCED-RANKING SYSTEMS, managers recognized the need for documentation to support their evaluations, especially when negative appraisals led to termination of workers. According to Management Professors Dr. John E. Jones and William L. Beasley, 360-degree feedback solves the problem of IDKWIS—"I don't know where I stand." IDKWIS = NEAMO + NETMA + INA where

NEAMO = nobody ever asks my opinion
NETMA = nobody ever tells me anything
INA = I never ask

Jones and Beasley describe 360-degree feedback as a nine-step process.

1. Determine the need for and purpose of the assessment.
2. Establish a competency model.
3. Write data sources and select and develop assessment items.
4. Develop an assessment questionnaire.
5. Administer the questionnaire.
6. Process the data and develop a feedback-report.
7. Deliver the feedback-report.
8. Brief the executive on group trends.
9. Evaluate the intervention.

Systems utilizing 360-degree feedback are popular, and there are numerous model systems and questionnaires available on the INTERNET. Jones and Beasley state 10 benefits of the typical system.

1. defines corporate competencies
2. increases the focus in customer service
3. supports team initiatives
4. creates a high-involvement workforce
5. decreases hierarchies and promotes streamlining
6. detects barriers to success
7. assesses developmental needs
8. identifies performance thresholds
9. is easy to implement

Critics contend 360-degree feedback systems are not easy to implement and, if based on subjective criteria, can be biased.

Further reading
Bruman, John. "Performance Reviews: Perilous Curves Ahead." Available on-line. URL: http://deming/eng.clemson.edu/pub/den/archive/2001.05/msg00114.html; Jones, John E., and William L. Beasley. "360-degree Feedback—Strategies, Tactics and Techniques for Developing Leaders." Available on-line. URL: http://homeroom.idnstate.edu/ite695/Assignments/360/sld003.htm.

thrifts   See SAVINGS AND LOAN ASSOCIATIONS.

time deposits (certificates of deposit, CDs)

Time deposits (also called certificates of deposits, or CDs) are nontransaction deposits at banks. Checks cannot be written on these accounts, and they carry substantial penalties for withdrawal before maturity, which can range from a few months to 5 years. In return for sacrificing liquidity, savers earn higher rates of return on time deposits than on savings accounts. Time deposits are a major source of funds for banks.

Time deposits of less than $100,000 are generally nonnegotiable. They are not liquid, unless one is willing to pay the rather costly penalty for early withdrawal. Time deposits of $100,000 or more are negotiable and can be traded in secondary markets before their maturity, making them liquid.

time management

Time management, simply stated, is controlling the use of one's most valuable resource: time. Proper time management allows for the elimination of wasted time, the refusal of excessive workloads, and the allocation of time appropriate to a task's importance. It leads to greater efficiency and effectiveness, and it reduces the effort needed to accomplish goals.

The absence of time management is characterized by last-minute rushes to meet deadlines, days that seem to somehow slip by unproductively, and unexpected crises. Lack of time management increases stress and interferes with performance. Poor time management is sometimes associated with being overconfident. Perhaps the reason time management is not widely practiced is because it is seldom included as a measured part of PERFORMANCE APPRAISALS and standards, although it has been shown to lead to improved performance.

Time management has many facets. The simple concepts of planning activities and keeping an organized journal can help anyone with a hectic schedule. Since time management is a process, it must be planned, monitored, and reviewed. With a little self-discipline, anyone can manage their time better by planning each day and each week effectively.

A good way to start gaining control of time is to track how time is used for one week, after which the activities and time spent in each activity can be reviewed. One can then determine which activities were necessary (a good use of time) and those that were not. Time is often wasted in changing direction between activities. Organizing similar tasks together can reduce start-up time, and a journal can be used to identify where time savings can be made.

One positive aspect of time management is that a balance can be chosen objectively and self-imposed. Personal time can be set aside when it is convenient and needed and still allow work productivity. Vacations, meetings, social outings, and appointments can all be coordinated through regular time management.

Once people have implemented time management into their lives, that control can be used to augment their careers. Good time management promotes efficient work practices, focuses on chosen activities, and helps people meet long-term goals and objectives. It does not solve problems but will help reveal them and provide guides to reviewing and implementing solutions. Time management requires little effort and allows people to take control of their time in the ways they see necessary and most effective.

Further reading
Blair, Gerald M. "Personal Time Management for Busy Managers." Available on-line. URL: www.ee.ed.ac.uk/~gerard/Management/art2.html.

—Melissa Luma

tobacco settlement

On November 23, 1998, attorneys general of 46 states, who had sued five of the largest tobacco companies in the United States (Philip Morris Inc., Brown & Williamson Tobacco Corp., R. J. Reynolds, Lorillard Tobacco Company, and Liggett & Myers) to recover COSTS associated with treating smoking-related illnesses, entered into an agreement to collectively settle their claims in exchange for monetary and other relief. Four states (Florida, Minnesota, Texas, and Mississippi) settled their tobacco cases separately.

Pursuant to the written settlement by the parties, referred to as the Master Settlement Agreement (MSA), the "participating manufacturers" agreed to pay substantial sums to the 46 "settling states" and to fund a national foundation devoted to the interests of public health, as well as to make substantial changes in their ADVERTISING and marketing practices and CORPORATE CULTURE, with the intention of reducing underage smoking.

According to the MSA, the participating manufacturers agreed to pay the settling states in excess of $200 billion over a 25-year period, to fund a foundation to support programs that reduce youth tobacco-product usage, and to fund educational programs to prevent diseases associated with the use of tobacco products in the United States. Pursuant to the MSA, the tobacco companies also agreed to not target the youth market in their advertising, marketing, or promotion of tobacco products; to discontinue the use of cartoons in their advertising, promotion, PACKAGING, or labeling of tobacco products; to eliminate outdoor and transit advertising of tobacco products except in adult-only establishments; and to discontinue payments to persons and organizations in exchange for promoting tobacco products in film and live entertainment.

The participating manufacturers also agreed to limit their brand-name sponsorship by not sponsoring concerts or events in which a significant number of the intended audience or participants are youths and by banning the distribution of free samples and gifts based on proof of purchase to underage persons. The MSA further prohibits participating tobacco manufacturers from opposing states' legislation intended to reduce youth access to tobacco products and the incidence of youth CONSUMPTION of tobacco; from participating in trade associations whose actions are contrary to the MSA's provisions; and from making any material misrepresentation of fact regarding the health consequences of using tobacco products, including additives, filters, paper, and other materials.

The MSA cases, unlike previous lawsuits against the tobacco manufacturers, succeeded to settlement because of a unique theory of recovery proposed by Dr. Ray Gangarosa, research fellow at the Center for Ethics, Emory University, to the lawyers who initiated the first state suit against the tobacco companies on behalf of the state of Mississippi. Although Mississippi settled its case separately for over $3 billion, its suit began the process that led to 46 state actions and the resulting MSA. Previous lawsuits by individual plaintiffs failed because the juries in those cases applied the theory of assumption of the risk—that is, the smokers knew the risks and voluntarily began to smoke and continued to do so—and/or because the plaintiffs could not prove that smoking had in fact caused their cancer. Dr. Gangarosa's theory was that states or public hospitals could bring their own suits to recover their costs of treating disease and illness caused by cigarette smoking, and a direct action by the state would not be subject to the assumption-of-risk and cause-in-fact defenses that defeated the individual plaintiffs' cases.

Although adolescent cigarette use reportedly declined after the Master Settlement Agreement, the *New England Journal of Medicine* reported in August 2001 that studies showed tobacco companies were continuing to promote cigarettes to youths and that the amounts spent by the tobacco companies in advertising certain BRANDS popular to young people had actually increased since the MSA's signing. In fact, several states have sued the tobacco companies for violating the MSA's provisions.

The *New England Journal of Medicine* also reported in October 2002 that the settling states were not spending adequate amounts of their tobacco settlement funds on programs to control tobacco usage by youth, but were in fact using portions of the monies to balance their budgets in bad economic times. Such disappointment with the MSA's implementation has prompted many to call for jurisdiction to be given to the FOOD AND DRUG ADMINISTRATION to regulate tobacco products. In fact, legislation (H.R. 1097) supported by all major health organizations is currently pending in Congress to do just that.

Further reading
National Assoc. of Attorneys General website. Available on-line. URL: http://www.naag.org/issues/issue-tobacco.php; Thomas Legislative Information on the Internet Library of Congress. Available on-line. URL: http://thomas.loc.gov/cgi-bin/query; University of Dayton website. Available on-line. URL: http://academic.udayton.edu/health/syllabi/tobacco/summary.htm.

—Terrye Conroy

total-quality management
Total-quality management (TQM) is a MANAGEMENT philosophy and strategy designed to involve all members of an organization in the process and responsibility for producing quality PRODUCTs and SERVICES. TQM is based on the ideas of W. Edward Deming, Philip B. Crosby, and Joseph M. Juran, quality-control experts in the United States and Japan. TQM was first associated with the Toyota PRODUCTION system. Companies using a TQM system typically incorporate

- JUST-IN-TIME PRODUCTION (JIT) systems
- business process reengineering, analyzing and redesigning the work environment
- traditional quality systems such as ISO 9000

As a corporate philosophy, TQM includes eight principles.

- Define quality in terms of customers and their requirements.
- Pursue quality at the source.
- Stress objectives rather than subjective measurement and analysis.

- Emphasize prevention rather than detection of defects.
- Focus on process rather than output.
- Strive for zero defects.
- Establish continuous improvement as a way of life.
- Make quality everyone's responsibility.

The nine TQM principles lead to sets of activities that will vary, depending on the nature of the organization. Management professor Robert J. Trent developed a set of activities for applying TQM to supply-chain management (PURCHASING), including the following.

- Identify internal supply-chain customers and establish communication linkages.
- Conduct regular performance reviews.
- Create performance measures that quantify expectations and requirements.
- Involve suppliers early in product and process development.
- Develop a consistent source-selection procedure.
- Upwardly migrate supplier-performance targets.
- Use longer-term CONTRACTs selectively.

Traditionally issues of product inspection and quality are associated with manufacturing processes, but in a TQM system quality is perceived to be the concern of all members of the organization. TQM consultant Rod Collard describes the implications of TQM programs as

- reductions in staff numbers, particularly those previously responsible for directing others
- changes to a flatter management style, including team-working and cross-functional teams
- less control of tasks by individuals, since everyone is responsible for quality

While TQM remains a popular and widely used management practice (a 1997 United Kingdom survey indicated over two-thirds of the country's 500 largest companies had implemented TQM), it is subject to a variety of criticisms. Dr. Edward Lestrade, one of the leading critics of TQM practices in the United Kingdom, describes the goal of TQM as being "designed to be motivational, in that it increase the responsibilities of the employees in the organization and widens the scope of their duties. However, the reality is that the natural outcome of the organizational TQM system is to drive the employee to work harder and longer hours thereby increasing the potential for incidences of stress-related illness." In Japan the term *karoshi* (death from overwork) is associated with the stress and demands made in organizations practicing TQM. Lestrade concludes, "I recommend therefore that organizations using TQM, should, for legal, ethical as well as commercial reason, investigate other methods of management as a matter of some urgency."

Other critics of TQM are less dramatic than Dr. Lestrade. Many organizations have found TQM too deliberative and quantitatively oriented to utilize in fast-changing markets. Author John Addey identified a variety of myths associated with quality systems, one of which is the idea that staff follow QUALITY CONTROL procedures during their daily work. Addey suggests that workers actually tend to do what they think will work, ignoring often-boring and inaccurate or inappropriate quality-control guidelines. Another myth is that quality audits are a good way to find problems, and managers welcome auditors as a means of identifying opportunities to improve. As Addey points out, though, quality audits review only the past, not current situations. Since they are based on samples and are usually carried out by external staff, they may be resisted by workers in the affected unit. Addey notes, "In quality management systems effectiveness is rarely assessed; most audits only check compliance." He provides many other myths about quality management as well, including the statement, "If everything is controlled, all will be well." Addey suggests instead that sometimes the best control is no control at all.

While it is still espoused in many organizations, TQM probably peaked as a management system in the United States in the mid-1990s.

See also DEMING'S 14 POINTS.

Further reading
Addey, John. "Quality Myths and Legends," *Total Quality Management,* July 2000; Lestrade, Dr. Edward. "Total Quality Management in Trouble," *Monday Business Briefing,* 22 March 2002; Trent, Robert J. "Applying TQM to SCM," *Supply Chain Management Review,* May 2001.

trade-adjustment assistance

In the United States, trade-adjustment assistance (TAA) refers to government-sponsored training programs and supplemental cash UNEMPLOYMENT compensation provided to workers who lose their jobs due to increased foreign COMPETITION. Some TAA programs require participation in job-training and job-search programs.

Trade-adjustment assistance grew out of programs intended to aid Americans who were dislocated when the European Community (now the EUROPEAN UNION) was established. The first assistance program was authorized in the Trade Expansion Act of 1962, although no assistance was actually provided until 1969. Congress has often been reluctant to fund TAA programs, but during the early 1980s, payments to workers dramatically increased, and the Reagan administration responded with efforts to repeal the program. Tighter eligibility standards and reduced budget allocations diminished the program's scope. It was not until the Omnibus Trade and Competitiveness Act of 1988 that significant funding was committed to TAA.

Under TAA, workers may petition the U.S. secretary of labor for assistance. The secretary must certify that work-

ers have been or are threatened with job losses, that sales or PRODUCTION or both of the firm in question have decreased absolutely, and that increased IMPORTS of articles like or directly competitive with those made by the workers or the firm for which the workers provide essential goods or SERVICES "contributed importantly" to job separation or decline.

The most visible trade adjustment assistance program is the NAFTA-TAA. Between 1994 and 1997, almost 100,000 American workers were certified for trade-adjustment assistance. This number was often used to show the adverse impact of the NORTH AMERICAN FREE TRADE AGREEMENT (NAFTA), but TAA certification does not necessarily mean workers have been displaced, only that there is the potential for workers to lose their jobs due to imports. In the first three years of NAFTA, slightly more than 12,000 workers received NAFTA-TAA. Many workers who have lost their jobs are encouraged by state officials to apply for TAA, thereby reducing the state COSTS for unemployment compensation.

Further reading
Folsom, Ralph H., and W. Davis Folsom. *NAFTA Law and Business.* The Hague: Kluwer International, 1999.

trade balance (balance of trade)

Trade balance (or balance of trade) is the difference between merchandises exports and IMPORTS in a country's BALANCE OF PAYMENTS. While a country's balance of payments must, by definition, be balanced, its trade balance can be either positive or negative. Trade balance is the merchandise account in a country's current account—that is, the sum of merchandise imports, SERVICES, INVESTMENT, and unilateral transfers into and out of a country. For decades after World War II, the United States had a favorable (positive) trade balance, but beginning in the 1970s U.S. merchandise imports exceeded exports, creating a negative trade balance.

According to MERCANTILISM, a favorable trade balance was desirable, since it meant a country would accumulate greater quantities of gold. In *Political Discourses* (1752), Scottish philosopher David Hume challenged the mercantilist view, arguing that increases in gold would increase a country's MONEY SUPPLY, thereby increasing prices and wages, which would eliminate the trade surplus.

Trade balances can be influenced by a country's international trade policies. For example, for many years Mexico pursued import-substitution-industrialization, actively subsidizing domestic companies to produce PRODUCTs that were previously imported. More recently, with the NORTH AMERICAN FREE TRADE AGREEMENT (NAFTA), Mexico is pursuing export development, importing equipment and technology to produce goods for export to the United States and elsewhere.

See also EXPORTING.

Further reading

Appleyard, Dennis R., and Alfred J. Field Jr. *International Economics.* Boston: Irwin, 1994.

trade barriers (barriers to trade)

Trade barriers may be loosely defined as laws, regulations, policies, or practices on the part of a government to either protect domestic PRODUCTs from foreign COMPETITION or artificially stimulate EXPORTING of a particular domestic product. The most straightforward way that this can be done is to institute a duty on the IMPORTS of an item. However, most countries have entered into agreements that limit such activity, and such a direct action can result in a trade war in which other countries place their own duty on imports from the original offending country. To be less obvious and to avoid direct retaliation, countries have invented a vast array of what is referred to as technical trade barriers (or barriers to trade). Countries hope that using technical trade barriers will protect their domestic goods without appearing to directly violate trade agreements and, therefore, precipitate a trade war. Following is a list of some of the technical trade barriers that some countries use.

- *Standards, testing labeling and certification.* This includes refusing to accept a manufacturers' test or other outside product testing such as the testing done by Underwriters Laboratories. By instituting unjust or unnecessary safety standards, countries hope to limit the imports of foreign goods and to advance domestically manufactured goods.
- *Government procurement.* This is when a government limits its own purchases to domestically manufactured goods.
- *Export subsidies.* These can be direct or hidden in the form of preferential financing or agricultural subsidies.
- *Lack of* INTELLECTUAL PROPERTY *protection.* This takes such forms as inadequate PATENT, COPYRIGHT, and TRADEMARK protection.
- *Services barriers.* These impose limits on the range of SERVICES that can be offered by foreign companies. They are most often seen in the financial and banking industries.
- *Investment barriers.* This is usually seen in limits on foreign ownership of domestic business or limits on transferring earnings and CAPITAL to foreign owners.
- *Trade restrictions affecting electronic commerce.* This relatively new trade barrier may impose limits on such things as access to the INTERNET or certain Internet sites.
- *Toleration of anticompetitive practices.* This is seen in the toleration of such practices as BRIBERY, monopolies, CARTELs, etc.

Unfortunately in many cases it is difficult to distinguish between trade barriers and legitimate public-policy actions not motivated by trade protectionism. For example, countries should be able to limit certain types of imports based on safety, environmental, or child labor issues. These issues may not be considered relevant to the exporting country, and thus legitimate concerns get lost in discussions relative to trade barriers.

Many countries use environmental and safety concerns as trade barriers. These concerns are especially notable in such organizations as the WORLD TRADE ORGANIZATION. The WTO is a massive trade alliance whose purpose is to advance FREE TRADE among its members. However, often the advancement of free trade and the removal of trade barriers, which are admirable economic objectives, puts the WTO at odds with other admirable goals such as environmental protection and those fighting child labor, who in turn are often rebuffed by countries hiding behind WTO antitrade barrier rules to excuse their inappropriate behavior.

—Mack Tennyson

trade credit   See ACCOUNTS PAYABLE, TRADE CREDIT.

trademark

A trademark is a distinctive word, name, symbol, or device which enables consumers to identify PRODUCTs or SERVICES. Trademarks support business efforts to create brand recognition, preference, and EQUITY, providing marketers a strategic advantage over generic products. Service marks that distinguish services; certification marks that certify origin, method of PRODUCTION, quality, or some other aspect of a product; and collective marks that are trademarks for organizations are all protected under federal legislation.

In the United States, trademarks are protected by state and federal registrations and by COMMON LAW. The principal U.S. trademark law is the Lanham Act (1946). The major consideration in federal trademark registration is whether the mark distinguishes the seller's product from competitors' offerings. Distinctiveness is categorized as

- arbitrary or fanciful marks that are unique but do not describe a product's qualities. *Coke* is an example of a unique trademark. The Coca-Cola Company has protected the distinctiveness of its product to avoid losing its trademark status. Cola was a trademark but is now a generic name.
- suggestive marks conveying a product's nature. *Dietene* is a trademark for a dietary supplement, suggesting but not fully describing the product.
- descriptive marks that directly describe the product or service. *Rubbermaid* is an example of a descriptive trademark.

Federal registration of trademarks protects the user for 10 years. Unlike U.S. PATENTS and COPYRIGHTS, trademarks may be renewed every 10 years. Businesses can lose trademark rights by abandonment or if a mark acquires a generic meaning, referring to a class of products or services rather than a particular product or service. Aspirin, linoleum, nylon, and kerosene are all examples of once-protected trademarks that are now generic names.

The Federal Trademark Dilution Act (1995) increased trademark holders' right to sue for infringement on their rights. The act allows a trademark holder "to seek legal relief when another party's commercial use of a substantially similar version of the famous mark causes 'dilution of [the mark's] distinctive quality'." Infringement can also be claimed when similar versions of a trademark are likely to cause confusion concerning source, endorsement, or affiliation of a product or service.

Further reading
Mallor, Jane P., A. James Barnes, Thomas Bowers, Michael J. Phillips, and Arlen W. Langvardt. *Business Law and the Regulatory Environment,* 11th ed. Boston: McGraw-Hill, 2001.

trade promotion authority   See FAST TRACK.

trade secrets
Trade secrets involve commercially valuable business information not generally known or readily accessible to persons normally dealing with that information. Chemical formulae are often trade secrets; customer lists that could be recreated by looking in the phone book are not generally recognized as trade secrets. Reasonable steps must be undertaken by businesses possessing and claiming protection for trade secrets. Unlike PATENTS, COPYRIGHTS, and TRADEMARKS, trade secrets are not remittable with governments; indeed, disclosure of the secrets would eliminate their value. However, trade secrets can, if protected, last forever, something that is not true of patents and copyrights. The world's best-kept trade secret, for example, may well be the Coca-Cola formula.

Protecting trade secrets is difficult, even in the legal jurisdictions where they are recognized. Angry employees or retirees are common sources of disclosure of trade secrets. Though they breach promises made in their CONTRACTS of EMPLOYMENT, suing to recover DAMAGES will never recover the secret's full value. If competitors were involved in the unauthorized disclosure, broader remedies may be available, but a trade secret that has been for example, posted, on the INTERNET is lost forever. Thus, trade secrets are a high-stakes environment.

The NORTH AMERICAN FREE TRADE AGREEMENT (NAFTA) was the first international agreement to require protection of trade secrets in each country by making it illegal to disclose them by "dishonest commercial practices." To obtain protection, the owner of the trade secret must be willing to document its existence to the satisfaction of a court or administrative authorities. Similar duties to protect trade secrets are provided in the WORLD TRADE ORGANIZATION's agreement on Trade-Related Intellectual Property Rights (TRIPs).

See also ECONOMIC ESPIONAGE ACT; PROPRIETARY INFORMATION.

Further reading
Miller, Arthur R., and Michael A. Davis. *Intellectual Property in a Nutshell,* 3d ed. Eagan, Minn.: West Group, 2000.

trade shows
Trade shows are industry- or association-organized displays of companies' PRODUCTS. In the United States, businesses spend billions of dollars on trade shows annually. Trade shows provide businesses with the opportunity to demonstrate and write orders for their products, provide information to DISTRIBUTION CHANNEL members, generate sales leads, build relationships, and compare products to competitors' offerings. There are trade shows for almost every imaginable industry segment.

In North America there are more than 4,000 industry trade shows each year. Trade shows rank second to ADVERTISING in U.S. businesses' MARKETING COMMUNICATIONS budgets. Shows are expensive; often the display fee alone can be $5,000–$10,000, so companies determine which shows to display in based on potential or past sales and the number of vendors and visitors. Most shows are open only to industry members, while some, like automobile, boat, and home shows, are open to both the general public and industry members. Comdex, the leading computer-industry trade show, is held annually in Las Vegas. Many technology companies use Comdex to display their latest products, and competitors have found it to be a valuable source of MARKET INTELLIGENCE, often gaining new ideas for their companies from competitors' presentations.

The PGA golf show in Orlando each winter is another example of an industry trade show; more than 5,000 golf products firms participate each year. Convention centers in major cities are often hosts to trade shows. The World Trade Center in Miami, Atlanta Merchandise Mart, and Las Vegas Convention Center host a variety of trade shows annually. In addition to national trade shows, there are also many smaller regional shows.

Trade shows can be found in various ways. Since many are hosted by industry associations, the *Encyclopedia of Associations,* available is almost any library, is an excellent resource, and www.tscentral.com is a searchable website listing many shows.

Further reading
Boone, Louis E., and David L. Kurtz. *Contemporary Marketing,* 11th ed. Fort Worth, Tex.: Dryden Press, 2003; *Encyclopedia of Associations,* 37th ed. Detroit: Gale Press, 2001.

training and development

Training and development, components of HUMAN RESOURCES, assure that an organization has employees with the appropriate knowledge, skills, and abilities to perform the necessary job duties. Training has the connotation of learning specific job skills necessary to performing the current job. Development, however, has the longer-term goal of educating employees to perform future jobs that have higher knowledge, skills, and abilities requirements.

Training needs are identified by examining operational results for performance decrements—instances where the level of performance is less than desired. Performance decrements can be found on either an individual, group/departmental, or organizational basis. Examples of organizational needs are the desire to change the MANAGE-MENT style from autocratic to participative or to implement a culture of EMPOWERMENT throughout the organization. A group/department need could be a matter of increasing the department's educational level in order to be sure that INVESTMENTS in new, highly technical equipment will be justified. An individual need could be a matter of improving a specific employee's level of production.

Before the low-producing employee is sent to a training program, two "quick fixes" should be evaluated. Does the employee know that his/her production level is unsatisfactory? Perhaps the supervisor has not conveyed this to the employee. This quick training fix reinforces the need for honest PERFORMANCE APPRAISALS to let each employee know how he or she is doing, as evaluated by the company. Another question is: Does the employee already know how to do perform the task correctly? If someone has already learned the correct job techniques but does not use them, it may be because the techniques are strange and feel awkward. Reinforcement by the supervisor and others combined with repetition by the employee is the second quick fix.

After the needs analysis is conducted and the decision is made to put the employee in a training program, objectives must be determined. The training program must be developed and its content designed for the specific need. Sometimes training programs already exist and can be purchased from outside vendors. These off-the-shelf programs usually teach concepts that are generic to a particular industry or teach widely accepted techniques, such as TIME MANAGE-MENT or supervisory skills. Companies will probably decide to design and develop their own custom training program if PROPRIETARY INFORMATION or specialized techniques are involved. To enhance the program's efficacy, potential instructors may have to learn effective teaching techniques. They must also know their audience and understand the training needs of adults compared to children.

The key to a training program's success is to actively involve the participants. Lecturing is a frequently used technique that dispenses information to large numbers of people in a very cost-effective setting; however, it is the least-effective training method when measured by retention rate. Retention of learned information increases with reading assignments, demonstrations, class discussions, and practice by doing. The most effective training technique, however, is to put the information to immediate use after learning it.

The effectiveness of a training program can be measured by a variety of techniques. Having the participants complete an evaluation form after the program has ended is the easiest method, but it also provides the least-valuable information. Responses are often based on initial reactions to the speaker, physical surroundings, and other superficial considerations.

Questionnaires do not measure what the training participant has learned; it is tests that measure student learning. A well-designed test procedure would assess the participants' knowledge before and after training. In test design, this group is known as the experimental group. The experimental group's results should be compared to a control group that is tested at the same time but does not participate in the training program.

The crucial question in evaluating the effectiveness of a training program is: Did the training graduates change their behavior? Another evaluation technique, therefore, is to observe over an extended length of time whether the participants' behaviors have changed. If behavior change does not occur or if the behavior change is of short duration and the participants revert to their original behavior, then the training was not worthwhile.

Finally, if the student has learned, and behavior has changed, there should be improvements in the performance measures used by the company. PROFITs, operational efficiencies, customer-service levels, and employee-satisfaction indices should be examine for improvement.

—John B. Abbott

transaction costs

Transaction costs are the COSTS associated with exchanges between buyers and sellers. They typically include the cost of travel, negotiation, defining and transferring property rights, and the cost of acquiring information. Consumers and businesses use markets to reduce transaction costs. Markets allow buyers and sellers to find each other, learn current prices, negotiate, and exchange goods and SERVICES. Well-organized markets reduce transaction costs more than less-organized markets.

When transaction costs are significant, consumers will either not participate in the market or find alternatives to markets to fulfill needs. For example, one of the reasons for increased participation of Americans in STOCK MARKETS is the advent of on-line trading. Previously investors had to call stockbrokers and pay significant fees to trade stocks. Similarly, one of the reasons for the growth in home-repair stores like Home Depot and Lowes is the cost of trying to find a repair person. In addition to paying for a plumbing or electrical repair, many homeowners have to wait for the repair person to show up, get the needed part, and make the repair. These transaction costs encourage people to fix things themselves.

The emergence of on-line auctions illustrates how reductions in transaction costs are creating market exchanges that were previously too expensive. On-line auctions dramatically reduce the search costs and overcome geographical separation of buyers and sellers. Previously buyers and sellers would have to travel to auction sites or advertise in specialty newspapers to find each other. One of the major factors contributing to the growth of the U.S. economy in the 1990s was the use of electronic information technology to reduce transaction costs in both consumer and resource markets. On a macroeconomic level, a unified currency, like the euro, reduces the cost of exchanges among members of the monetary union in that it eliminates the cost of converting currencies and makes pricing simpler.

transfer payments

Transfer payments are expenditures by government for which no goods or SERVICES are received in return. In the United States, transfer payments consist mostly of SOCIAL SECURITY, Medicare, Medicaid, UNEMPLOYMENT benefits, and other WELFARE programs. Transfer payments are primarily administered by the federal government, while state and local governments are responsible for some INCOME REDIS-TRIBUTION and in-kind transfers. Repatriation payments from one country to another are also considered transfer payments, because they involve no exchange of goods or services.

Depending on which programs are included, transfer payments account for over 40 percent of U.S. government expenditures. The largest program, Social Security, is an intergenerational transfer program, with payments by current workers being redistributed by government to current retirees. As long as the inflow of funds continues to grow, the transfer program can continue indefinitely. If, however, the inflow of funds begins to drop, the program is in trouble.

In addition to intergenerational transfer, transfer payments redistribute income from the employed to the unemployed (unemployment benefits and welfare), from taxpayers to specific industries (AGRICULTURAL SUPPORT PRO-GRAMS), and from individuals to CORPORATIONS (CORPORATE WELFARE). Transfer payments alter the DEMAND for goods and services in favor of the desires of INCOME recipients. Transfer payments, particularly unemployment benefits and government subsidies, act as AUTOMATIC STABILIZERS during downturns in the economy.

Further reading

Ruffin, Roy J., and Paul R. Gregory. *Principles of Economics,* 7th ed. Boston: Addison Wesley, 2001.

transfer taxes

Transfer taxes are those taxes imposed when property is transferred from one party to another. The estate tax and the gift tax are WEALTH-transfer taxes that combine to create the unified transfer-tax system. Gift taxes apply if a person transfers property while alive; estate taxes apply when a property is transferred after death. Gift and estate taxes are calculated on a property's fair MARKET VALUE on the date of the gift or on the date of death (or six months later if eligible to so elect). These taxes can also be considered an "excise tax" on the privilege of transferring property to another. The vast majority of all property transfers are exempt from these property transfer taxes due to the annual gift-tax exclusion ($11,000/person/year) and various deductions and credits. Transfer taxes can affect small business owners when transferring ownership to their children. Critics of estate and gift taxes often portray these measures as forcing the break-up of the family farm or business.

The current system of estate and gift-transfer taxes will be in place until December 31, 2009. The Economic Growth and Tax Relief Reconciliation Act of 2001 repealed the estate tax, effective for deaths occurring after December 31, 2009. Gift taxes were not repealed, however, and are slated to continue into the future unabated. The tax rate for taxable gifts after December 31, 2009, will be the highest individual income-tax rate.

There is a certain amount of uncertainty about planning for estate taxes, because the Economic Growth and Tax Relief Reconciliation Act of 2001 also contains a "sunset clause" that results in all of the act's provisions being repealed as of December 31, 2010. As a result, the estate, gift, and generation-skipping transfer provisions in effect in 2001 will become law once again on January 1, 2011, if Congress takes no intervening action.

For the period up to December 31, 2009, the gift tax and the estate tax are calculated on a cumulative basis. The transfer-tax rates range from 18 to 55 percent, depending on the value of the decedent's estate and the sum of the prior taxable gifts. Generally estate tax is owed to the federal government if the decedent's taxable estate exceeds a specified exemption equivalent amount at the date of death. The exemption equivalent amount is $1 million for 2002 and 2003, $1.5 million for 2004 and 2005, $2.0 million for 2006–08, and $3.5 million for 2009. The gift-tax exclusion is constant at $1 million for all years from 2002 into the future. These generous exclusion amounts result in only a fraction of all estates or gifts being subjected to tax at transfer.

Until 2010, the same tax rates that apply to the estate tax apply to the gift tax. These are considered companion taxes because gifts made during a person's lifetime reduce the value of the estate and thus the amount of the estate tax that will be owed after the person dies. Using the same tax rates for both recognizes that gifts and estates serve the same purpose: the transfer of wealth. By applying the same rate structure, the government is leveling the playing field between lifetime and post-death transfers. Whether a person chooses to transfer wealth during his/her lifetime or after death, the tax on that transfer will be the same. If an individual uses the $1 million exclusion for lifetime gifts, the amount of the estate that can pass estate-tax-free will be reduced by that amount. In essence, with each taxable gift, all prior taxable gifts are added back to the tax calculation, and the tax is then reduced by the tax calculated on the prior taxable gifts. The effect of this calculation is that successive gifts (and the eventual estate) are forced into higher marginal transfer-tax rates.

The recipient of gifted property takes a tax basis in the property equal to the donor's carryover basis plus a portion of the gift tax paid. If the full market value (FMV) of the gift is less than the donor's basis, the recipient will take the lower amount (FMV) as basis. The recipient of property that passes at death generally takes a basis in the property equal to the fair market value on the date of the decedent's death (for decedents dying before December 31, 2009).

There exists a gift-tax exclusion of $11,000 per donee per year for gifts of a present interest (one whose recipient is allowed to enjoy the gift currently). If a donor is married, the donor's spouse could agree to "split" the gift, resulting in a total possible transfer of $22,000 (2 × $11,000) tax-free per year. A donor may claim exclusions for transfers to an unlimited number of donees.

Another federal transfer tax, the generation-skipping transfer tax, originated in the realization that when property is bequeathed (transferred at death) from grandparents directly to grandchildren, a transfer is skipped and less total tax is collected. The generation-skipping tax's purpose is to ensure that some form of transfer taxation is imposed one time per generation. The generation-skipping tax is imposed at the highest estate-tax rate. The tax applies to direct-skip gifts and bequests and to taxable terminations of and taxable distributions from generation-skipping transfers. However, every grantor is entitled to a $1,060,000 exemption from the generation-skipping transfer tax (2002–03), $1.5 million (2004–05), $2 million (2006–08), and $3.5 million (2009). The generation-skipping tax is also repealed as of December 31, 2009.

After the estate tax is repealed in 2010, there will be a limited amount of basis "step up" available. Recall that for deaths occurring before December 31, 2009, all the ASSETS passing through the estate receive a stepped-up (or stepped-down) basis to fair market value. After December 31, 2009, there will be a total amount of $1.3 million that an estate can increase the basis of assets transferred (basis increase can not increase basis higher than the fair market value of the assets). An estate can increase the basis of assets transferred to a surviving spouse by an additional $3 million. The total step-up in basis for a surviving spouse can be $4.3 million of increase, given an estate with sufficient FMV of assets.

Transfers to an individual's spouse, either by gift or estate, are exempt from taxation. This "unlimited marital deduction" allows all spousal transfers to be free from tax.

In addition, a marital deduction can be taken for property where the recipient spouse is not entitled to designate which parties eventually receive the assets. This "qualified terminable interest property" (QTIP) gives the surviving spouse all the INCOME from the property, payable at least annually. In addition, no person has the power to appoint any portion of the property to anyone other than the surviving spouse unless the power cannot be exercised during the spouse's lifetime.

—Linda Bradley

treasury stock   See COMMON STOCK, PREFERRED STOCK, TREASURY STOCK.

trial balance   See ADJUSTING ENTRY, TRIAL BALANCE, ADJUSTED TRIAL BALANCE.

trickle-down economics

The theory of trickle-down economics posits that ECONOMIC GROWTH benefits all members of society, including the poor. One analogy is the idea that "a rising tide raises all ships," suggesting that when the economy expands, everyone benefits. Logically, if economic growth benefits everyone in society, then efforts by government to stimulate economic growth are good for society.

Most associated with the Reagan administration and SUPPLY-SIDE ECONOMICS, trickle-down economics justifies tax cuts for wealthy citizens and incentives for business INVESTMENT. Since the wealthy are more likely to save and thereby provide funds for investment, and incentives for business (which critics call CORPORATE WELFARE) stimulate business expansion, trickle-down economic logic suggests benefits eventually will flow to everyone in the economy.

Critics of trickle-down economics sometimes use a horse-and-sparrow metaphor: If a horse is fed well, some of the nutrients will pass through it and be available on the ground to benefit sparrows. But if the goal is to benefit sparrows, then why not do it directly? Most critics of trickle-down theory advocate DIRECT INVESTMENT in poorer groups through education, training, and small-business development.

In the United States, supporters of trickle-down economics point to the tax cuts of 1981 and 1986, which were followed by upswings in the economy, as evidence to support their ideas. Opponents note that while the economy grew, business and household SAVING did not. Instead, investment during that period was due largely to the flow of foreign CAPITAL into the U.S. economy.

trust

A trust is a legal arrangement in which an individual (the grantor) transfers legal ownership of ASSETS to one party (the trustee) and the legal right to enjoy and benefit from those assets to a second party (the beneficiary). This arrangement is generally designed for the protection of the beneficiary, who is often a minor child or family member incapable of competently managing the assets themselves. However, a trust is sometimes used to split benefits between two classes of beneficiaries, the INCOME beneficiaries (persons who receive the current income arising from the trust assets) and the remaindermen (persons who receive the trust assets upon a future termination of the trust). In other situations the income beneficiary and the remainderman could be the same individual. Trusts are often used to control the transfer of family businesses from one generation to the next.

The terms of the trust, the duties of the trustee and the rights of the various beneficiaries are specified in a legal document (the trust instrument). The assets placed into the trust are the trust corpus or trust principal. The role of the trustee is that of a fiduciary who is required to act in the best interest of the trust beneficiaries rather than for his/her own interest. A competent friend, knowledgeable family member, or the professional trust department of a bank usually fills the position of trustee. Professional trustees receive an annual fee to compensate them for services rendered.

The purpose of a trust is to protect and conserve its assets for the sole benefit of the trust beneficiaries. Traditionally, unless a trust specified a different standard, a trustee was required to manage trust assets under a "prudent-man" rule whereby cautious INVESTMENTS are required. Most recently, states have adopted laws providing a "prudent-investor" rule, permitting trustees to play the STOCK MARKET prudently, unless the trust itself imposes a more restrictive standard. The trustee is often concerned about a lawsuit for DAMAGES under a "breach of fiduciary duty" claim whereby the beneficiaries assert that the trustee mismanaged the fund investments.

The taxation of a trust is a hybrid concept. A trust files a form 1041 with K-1 schedules that report income (if any) to be taxed to the beneficiaries. To the extent that the trust distributes the current year's income, the income is taxed to the beneficiaries who received the income, resulting in the income being taxed at the beneficiary's marginal tax rate. To the extent the trust does not distribute current income, the trust pays the tax on the income, and the income is taxed at the trust's marginal tax rate. The marginal income-tax rates for trusts rise to the maximum level at approximately $9,000 of annual income, compared to the maximum rate for single or married individuals, approximately $290,000 of annual income. Trusts that do not currently distribute income thus pay a high tax burden compared to trusts that do currently distribute income to beneficiaries, if the receiving beneficiaries are not themselves at the maximum marginal rate level.

Currently trusts are used in various situations. Many wills are written in such a way that trusts are established upon an individual's death. For example, a husband might place assets at his death in trust for the lifetime benefits of his wife (the income beneficiary), and at her death the trust would terminate and the assets distributed to his children (the remaindermen). During the surviving spouse's life, as she receives the income, she reports it to be taxed on her individual return.

Another example of a common trust created under a will would be an individual stipulating that assets be placed into a trust for the benefit of a minor child at the decedent's death. The decedent might name a family member as the trustee. The trust could exist until the minor child reaches a specified age (for example, 30), at which time the trust would terminate and the child would receive the assets outright.

Many individuals use trusts set up during the individual's lifetime to obtain estate-planning and investment-management benefits. For example, an individual could place a valuable building into a trust that ran for the joint lives of the individual and his/her spouse (current income being paid to individual and spouse), with the trust terminating at the death of the survivor and the assets then transferring to a charity. Thus, the individual and spouse are the income beneficiaries and the charity is the remainderman. The individual receives a double benefit in this case: The asset will be managed by the charity, with the income stream being paid to the individual (or spouse) for life; and the individual can take a current tax deduction for the future gift to the charity. The income stream could be set up as an ANNUITY interest (a set annual amount to be paid each year), or it could be set up as a unitrust interest (a set percentage of the assets to be paid each year). If the income stream is an annuity interest, the trust is known as a CRAT (Charitable Remainder Annuity Trust). If the income stream is a unitrust interest, the trust is known as a CRUT (Charitable Remainder Unitrust). The charity deduction would be the fair MARKET VALUE of the building minus the present value of the retained income stream.

Another variation on charitable trusts set up during an individual's lifetime is the Charitable Lead Trust (CLT). In these trusts, the income beneficiary is the charity and the remainderman is usually a family member of the person setting up the trust (for example, a grandchild). In this case, the charitable contribution deduction would be the present value of the income stream to the charity. The trust might last until the remaindermen reached a certain age (for example 30 years old).

There are also noncharitable retained-interest trusts that could be set up during an individual's lifetime to obtain estate-planning benefits. A valuable asset (for example, an apartment complex) could be set up in a trust that ran for a specified period of time (e.g., 15 years). The individual would retain an income interest for the specified years, either an annuity interest or a unitrust interest. At the end of the period of time (15 years in this case), the trust would terminate and ownership would transfer to the beneficiaries specified in the trust document. The individual would owe gift tax on the gift to the beneficiaries, valued at the fair market value of the assets minus the present value of the retained-income interest. If the individual lived longer than the trust term (15 years in this case), the trust assets would not be included in the taxable estate of the individual establishing the trust. If the individual died during the trust term, the fair market value of the assets would be included in his/her taxable estate.

A final retained-interest trust that is a popular estate-planning strategy is a Qualified Personal Residence Trust. In this trust, the individual places a personal residence in the trust, which will terminate after a set period of time, upon which the assets will transfer to the beneficiaries specified in the trust document. The current gift tax to be paid on the future transfer to the beneficiaries is calculated as the present value of the fair market value of the residence, with the discount period being the term of the trust. If the individual outlives the term of the trust, it is not included in his/her taxable estate. If the individual dies during the trust term, the fair market value of the residence would be included in his/her taxable estate.

Trusts are often used to protect assets and preserve them for the future benefit of other individuals (usually family members). They are also used in estate and financial-planning strategies and in charitable giving endeavors. A common distinction is made between the income beneficiaries (who receive the income during the life of the trust) and the remainder beneficiaries (who receive the assets at trust termination). To the extent that income is currently distributed, the receiving beneficiaries pay tax on the income. To the extent that income is not currently distributed, tax is paid on the income by the trust. Trusts' marginal rates reach the highest level at a relatively low level of income. If the trustee has discretion over whether to distribute the income or retain it at the trust level, the trust is categorized as a complex trust. If the trustee is required to distribute the income currently, has no charitable organizations as beneficiaries, and does not distribute trust corpus during the year, the trust is categorized as a simple trust. If the trustee can determine, within guidelines established by the trust, the timing of income or corpus distributions and who will receive them (among a specified class of beneficiaries), the trust is known as a sprinkling trust.

Further reading
Pratt, James W., and William N., Kulsrud. *Federal Taxation.* Charlotte, N.C.: ARC Publishing Company, Inc. 2001; Willis, Eugene, William Hoffman, David M. Maloney, and William A. Rabbe. *West Federal Taxation, Comprehensive Volume,* 2004. Eagan, Minn.: West Publishing Company, 2001.

—Linda Bradley

Truth in Lending Act

The Truth in Lending Act (TILA) requires lenders to provide uniform disclosure of credit terms. Initially passed by Congress in 1968, the TILA, amended several times, was designed to increase consumer knowledge and understanding of credit offerings. With uniform disclosure requirements, consumers could compare credit offerings and make better decisions.

Anyone who imposes finance charges or, by agreement, requires payment in more than four installments is subject to the TILA. In most circumstances borrowers have a three-day rescission right to any credit agreement they have signed.

The TILA makes different disclosure requirements depending on the type of credit being offered. For open-ended credit, one that involves repeated transactions between the same parties, the TILA requires an initial statement and periodic statements, including disclosure of when a finance charge is imposed, the amount of additional charges and method of computing them, the creditor's security interest in the debtor's property, and the debtor's billing rights. For closed-end credit such as a car loan or consumer loan from a finance company, the TILA requires disclosure of the total finance charge, the annual percentage rate (APR), the amount financed, the total number of payments, their due dates and amounts, the total dollar value of all payments, late charges imposed for past-due payments, and any security interest taken by the creditor. Applications and solicitations for CREDIT CARDS have similar requirements but also force lenders to disclose the grace period for paying without incurring finance charges and the method used for computing the balance on which the finance charge is based.

The TILA also established other important lending/borrowing rules, including regulations with regard to consumer credit ADVERTISING, home equity LOANS, and credit-card holder liability. The act prevents "bait and switch" advertisements and promoting terms not usually made available and requires disclosure of the APR in advertisements. In response to deceptive advertising offering "free money" loans against home EQUITY, the TILA requires detailed disclosures on home equity loans. The act also limits credit-card holders' LIABILITY to $50 for unauthorized used of the card.

Enforcement of the TILA was given to the FEDERAL TRADE COMMISSION for most circumstances. Civil actions, including CLASS-ACTION LAWSUITS are also possible under the act.

Further reading
Mallor, Jane P., A. James Barnes, Thomas Bowers, Michael J. Philips, and Arlen W. Langvardt. *Business Law and the Regulatory Environment,* 11th ed. Boston: McGraw-Hill, 2001.

two-factor theory of motivation

Management theorist Fredrick Herzberg's two-factor theory of motivation suggests that there are two components to

EMPLOYEE MOTIVATION in the workplace. In 1959 Herzberg suggested that the sets of circumstances that make people unsatisfied at work (hygiene factors) are a different set from the sets of circumstances that make people satisfied (motivating factors). This was the result of interviews he conducted with 200 engineers and accountants in Pittsburgh, Pennsylvania, who were asked what made them feel bad about their jobs (dissatisfier) and what made them feel good about their jobs (satisfier). Hertzberg concluded that man has a dual set of needs, "his need as an animal to avoid pain and his need as a human to grow psychologically"; thus, the two-factor theory of motivation.

The first factor is the dissatisfier (or hygiene) factor. Hygiene is something that preserves and promotes the physical, mental, and emotional health of an individual and community; the lack of it creates a dissatisfying situation. The existence of hygiene creates an EQUILIBRIUM in which satisfaction is maintained and pain is avoided. In the work environment, hygiene includes company policies, supervision, salary, interpersonal relations, and working conditions, a list that Herzberg compiled from responses given to the question "What makes you feel bad about your job?" The items on this list need to be present to avoid pain. More of any of them does not promote happiness, and a lack of one or more of them will promote unhappiness. For example, a lowered salary, or one perceived as lower than one's coworkers, would certainly create dissatisfaction. As professor Gerald Blair writes, "Once a fair level of pay is established, money ceases to be a significant motivator for long term performance."

The second factor, motivators, includes achievement, recognition, nature of work, responsibility and advancement, all of which created satisfaction for the 200 engineers and accountants. Motivators intrinsically promote satisfaction, and according to Herzberg, managers encourage these factors in order to "increase profitability through greater creativity and commitment in employees." Without motivators, employees will perform their jobs as required, but with them, employees will exceed the minimum requirements. Add to salary the incentive of recognition and/or advancement, and employees will probably perform to the best of their ability and derive a high level of personal satisfaction.

The difference between hygiene and motivators is indicated in the following table.

Hygiene Factors	Motivating Factors
Company Policies	Achievement
Administration	Recognition
Supervision	Growth
Working Conditions	Advancement
Interpersonal Relations	Interest in Job
Salary	Responsibility
Status	Challenges
Security	

External	Internal
Animal	Human
Maintain	Promote
Basic	Added Value

Without	With	Without	With
Dissatisfied	Not dissatisfied	Not satisfied	Satisfied
Demotivated	Limited motivation	Not Motivated	Motivated

Herzberg reported, "In the motivator factors, the underlying dynamic is psychological growth. It is the human source for happiness." He acknowledged that not all jobs can be stimulating but thought that employees should be chosen for their particular position. Some people are hygiene seekers and some are motivation seekers. Often managers ignore this reality and rely on less-sophisticated means for motivating hygiene seekers. According to Herzberg, they attempt to apply the "kick in the a**" approach, or KITA, which leads to "short-range results, but rarely generates any actual motivation. . . . KITA yields movement—the avoidance of pain—not motivation. . . . KITA techniques fail to instill self-generating motivation in workers. Job content factors, such as achievement and responsibility, are motivators, while job environment factors are hygiene or KITA factors. Motivators are the key to satisfaction."

The two-factor theory of motivation is often associated with Abraham MASLOW'S HIERARCHY OF NEEDS theory. Maslow asserted that there are physiological needs (food and shelter), security needs (safety), social needs (acceptance), esteem needs, and the need for self-actualization. Once one set of needs is satisfied, these kind of needs cease to motivate. Both theories acknowledge different types of motivation and the need to surpass a minimum standard in order to motivate people. Managers, both in the United States and internationally, continue to try to find ways to improve morale within the work environment. Motivation theories abound, and Herzberg's theory is not novel. However, it is considered one of the important contributions in the field.

See also MOTIVATION THEORY.

Further reading
Blair, Gerald M. "The Human Factor," University of Edinburgh website. Available on-line. URL: http://www.see.ed.ac.uk/~gerald/Management/art6.html; Herzberg, Frederick. *On Management.* New York: Harper & Row, 1975; ———. *Work and the Nature of Man.* New York: World Publishing, 1966.

—Kate Anderson Young

tying contracts
Tying contracts are agreements in which a producer requires a buyer (usually a retailer) to purchase one or more other PRODUCTS as a condition of PURCHASING the product the buyer wants to acquire. Tying contracts potentially limit

COMPETITION and can be challenged under the SHERMAN ANTITRUST ACT and the CLAYTON ANTITRUST ACT. Under the Clayton Act, only tying contracts that "substantially lessen competition or tend to create a monopoly" are illegal.

Sometimes manufacturers have required retailers to carry a full line of a company's products as a condition for selling any of their products. For example, a building-materials manufacturer refuses to sell contractors wall-board (the tying product), unless they also agree to buy its joint compound, steel studs, and nails (the tied products). The potential anticompetitive effect of the tying agreement reduces competition in the sale of the tied products. During a 1980s shortage of wallboard, sellers raised prices and still had contractors begging for product. Contractors, whose building projects were stopped due to a lack of wallboard, offered a variety of incentives to sellers to get the needed materials. If, however, the manufacturer required the purchase of other products as a condition for the purchase of wallboard, the manufacturer could be accused of requiring a tying contract.

To be illegal per se under the Sherman Act, (1) a tying contract must involve two separate and distinct items rather than integrated components of a larger product, (2) the tying product cannot be purchased unless the tied product is also purchased, (3) the seller must have sufficient power to restrain competition in the tied product, and (4) a "not insubstantial" amount of commerce in the tied product must be affected by the agreement. In a widely discussed case in 2000, a federal court held that Microsoft unlawfully tied its INTERNET Explorer Web browser to its Windows operating system. However, in a case involving McDonalds, a FRANCHISING agreement requiring the franchisee to lease a store from the franchiser as a condition for the acquiring the franchise was considered an integral part of a BUSINESS PLAN and not a tying contract.

Further reading
Mallor, Jane P., A. James Barnes, Thomas Bowers, Michael J. Philips, and Arlen W. Langvardt. *Business Law and the Regulatory Environment,* 11th ed. Boston: McGraw-Hill, 2001.

U

uncertainty See RISK, UNCERTAINTY.

underground economy (informal economy, parallel economy)

The underground economy, also called informal or parallel economy, is economic activity that is not recorded in NATIONAL INCOME ACCOUNTING. Generally underground economic activity includes BARTER, illegal business activity (black markets), and unreported payments for goods and SERVICES.

The most frequently cited unreported activity is EMPLOYMENT of household help. Many candidates for executive positions in the U.S. government have been rejected when it became known that they hired people to work as nannies or household help without paying taxes for their services. Barter, by its nature, does not include cash exchanges. In some U.S. communities there are small, local barter exchanges. Because records are kept of these exchanges, participants usually report the value of these exchanges as INCOME, but in many markets barter goes unreported. With the 1990s, collapse of the Russian currency, even more exchanges in that country have been made using barter. One economist estimated 90 percent of business activity in Russia is not reported to tax authorities.

Illegal economic activities such as drugs, gambling, and prostitution are also part of a country's underground economy. One of the arguments for making some illegal activities legal is to then be able to generate tax revenue. During the period known as Prohibition in the United States, alcohol was easily available but not subject to taxation because such sales were illegal and thus not reported.

High tax rates and overregulation of economic activity are the major forces stimulating underground economies. In the 1990s, Italy's underground economy was estimated at over 25 percent of GROSS DOMESTIC PRODUCT (GDP). At the time, employer's COSTS for workers, taxes, and government-mandated benefits were 200 percent of wages. This encourages employers and workers to agree to work "off the books." U.S. estimates of underground economic activity range from approximately 5 percent to over 16 percent of GDP. Given the size of the U.S. economy, this represents a significant amount of unreported and untaxed income. In many countries, home-based subcontract work such as sewing operations, even though they are linked to formal business activity, are not included in official statistics, also reducing reported income. One way the U.S. Treasury Department estimates the value of illegal drugs coming into the country is by measuring the relative deposits of cash versus checks in known drug-importation cities such as Miami and Los Angeles. Officials found a significantly higher amount of cash transactions in these cities compared to rest of the country and used this disparity to estimate the value of drug business coming into the country.

Estimating underground economic activity is difficult. In a groundbreaking study, economist Hernando DeSoto conducted in-depth surveys of people in the barrios around Lima, Peru, documenting the organization and cooperation of participants in what he called the parallel economy. Because they were not legally allowed to be living where they were, residents in the barrios created their own system to supply basic goods and services, in full view of the country's capital but unreported to authorities.

While the popular image of underground economic activity is associated with illegal businesses and EMERGING MARKETS, economists recognize significant amounts of unreported income occur in the United States among high-income citizens and among self-employed people. Higher marginal tax rates encourage underreporting of income, and self-employment creates greater opportunities to control the amount of income reported and deductions taken from gross income. Antigovernment political attitudes are also reported as encouraging misrepresentation of income to tax authorities.

Further reading
DeSoto, Hernando. *The Other Path: Invisible Revolution in the Third World.* Boulder, Colo.: Basic Books, 2002; Kacapyr, Elia,

Peter Francese, and Diane Crispell. "Are You Middle Class?" *American Demographics* 18, no. 10 (October 1996): 30–36; Miller, Roger LeRoy. *Economics Today*. Boston: Addison Wesley, 2001.

undertime

Undertime is time taken off during the workday to compensate for workload and stress. Tom DeMarco coined the term *undertime* in his book *Slack*. Workers typically engage in two types of undertime: time away from the office and time spent in the office doing personal affairs. Managers know workers engage in undertime but generally do not talk about it. Some managers recognize that undertime diversions and relaxation can lead to greater creativity and efficiency as workers rejuvenate themselves during a workday.

In many work environments, time spent in the office is automatically equated to productivity. "Face time"—visibility in the office—often helps lower and MIDDLE MANAGERS get promoted. Recognizing that face time is important, workers will sit at their desk, looking busy while really engaging in undertime. They may be surfing the INTERNET, playing Internet games, making purchases for their personal use, or looking for a new job. Conspicuous undertime activities in the office are generally not acceptable. One exception is in technology companies, where workers will often engage in electronic games as a means of taking a break from their efforts.

Undertime also involves getting out of the office. In some situations, extended lunch hours are accepted and ignored. In others, working out in a health center during the workday is acceptable. Workers often look to office leaders or supervisors to determine what is acceptable undertime activities. *Wall Street Journal* reporter Sue Shellenbarger reports there are gender differences in what is considered acceptable undertime activities: "It's OK for women at some offices to attend their kids' events, for instance—but not for men . . . [I]t was OK for men to make dates or even set trysts with lovers over the lunch hour. But women were expected to avoid making dates or even talking to spouses or lovers from the office."

Undertime differs from SOCIAL LOAFING in that social loafing occurs when a person contributes less effort to a group task than he or she would when working on the same task alone. Social loafing involves a "team" atmosphere that may tempt individuals to decrease their efforts rather than work harder. It can be especially problematic for organizations that rely heavily on group efforts in the workplace. Undertiming is an individual rather than a team workplace activity.

See also FAMILY-FRIENDLY BUSINESS PRACTICES.

Further reading

Shellenbarger, Sue. "Why You Can Hit the Gym—But Not Get a Manicure—On Company Time," *Wall Street Journal,* 18 April 2002.

Underwriters Laboratory

Underwriters Laboratory (UL) is an independent, nonprofit PRODUCT safety, testing and certification organization. UL, in existence over 100 years, evaluates 100,000 products annually and conducts over 500,000 compliance audits each year. UL has developed 750 standards and certifies products in 89 countries around the world. UL certification, like ISO STANDARDS certification, is an internationally recognized symbol of safety and QUALITY CONTROL. PURCHASING agents for major CORPORATIONS often require UL certification. Manufacturers subscribe to UL certification newsletter, which alert companies to pending and approved safety standards.

UL certifies thousands of products ranging from AC and DC power circuit breakers to X-ray equipment. Recent UL certification criteria include standards for low-voltage fuses and tests for flammability for parts and devices and appliances. UL often works with industry groups to design safety standards. For instance, UL has worked for years with appliance manufacturers to reduce clothes-dryer fires. In addition to working with industry groups, UL publishes Consumer Safety Guides and an Appliance Safety Quiz.

The American National Standards Institute (ANSI) approves many UL standards. ANSI is the United States' representative to the International Organization for Standardization (ISO).

Further reading

Underwriters Laboratory website. Available on-line. URL: www.ul.com.

underwriting

Underwriting, financial intermediation provided by INVESTMENT BANKING firms in PRIMARY MARKETS, is the purchase and subsequent resale to the public of new issues of securities. Investment banking firms assist in the design and creation of new securities issues for CORPORATIONS wishing to raise additional CAPITAL. Once a new issue is created, an investment banking firm purchases from the corporation the entire new issue at a discount below the anticipated MARKET VALUE of the issue. ADVERTISING by way of a PROSPECTUS, an investment banking firm promotes and sells these new issues to the public.

When the new issue is large, if there is a significant amount of money required to purchase the new issue or if there is considerable RISK associated with the new issue, a consortium of investment banking firms, called an underwriting syndicate, will be formed to manage the new issue. The investment banking firm that organized the underwriting syndicate is known as the lead underwriter.

unemployment

Unemployment is measured as the percentage of the LABOR FORCE not currently working. *Labor force* is defined as people working plus people actively seeking work. "Actively seeking work" usually means people are currently registered with their state EMPLOYMENT service.

The U.S. CENSUS BUREAU estimates unemployment (expressed as a percentage of the labor force not working) by sampling U.S. households regarding their employment status. By defining the labor force as those people working and actively seeking work, unemployment statistics do not include discouraged workers (people no longer actively looking for work), and the statistics do not distinguish between people working full-time and those working part-time. Of course, unemployment statistics may include people collecting unemployment benefits but working "off the books." In the United States, unemployment benefits last only for 26 weeks, considerably shorter than in most European countries, which minimizes the problem of people collecting benefits while in fact working.

Unemployment rates in the United States vary by age, gender, and race. The highest unemployment rates are among young female minorities, while the lowest unemployment rates are among older white males.

Economists distinguish among four types of unemployment: seasonal, structural, frictional, and cyclical. *Seasonal unemployment* is, as the term suggests, unemployment associated with seasonal conditions. Agricultural and construction workers become seasonally unemployed, while retail employment jumps during the holiday season. Unemployment rates are adjusted for seasonal variations.

Structural unemployment refers to people who are out of work because there is no longer demand for their skills. With today's rapid increases in the use of technology, people who worked at repetitive tasks or efforts that involve counting are often being replaced by technology. For example, where one used to reach an operator when calling for directory assistance, nowadays most calls are answered by a computer-based voice recognition system. Telephone directory assistance people are thus becoming structurally unemployed. Similarly, 100 years ago there were thousands of coopers, highly skilled craftsmen who made wooden containers. With the invention of cardboard, aluminum, and plastic PACKAGING, today the only coopers still employed are demonstrators in antique museums.

Structural unemployment is a serious economic problem. People who lose their jobs because there is no longer a need for their skills either become retrained and return to the workforce, retire, or join the WELFARE rolls when their unemployment benefits end. Training programs and government incentives to business to hire and train structurally unemployed people provide long-term benefits to both the individuals and society.

Frictional unemployment refers to people who choose to leave their jobs in search of other opportunities. Sometimes referred to as turnover unemployment, frictional unemployment is a normal and healthy part of an economy. Generally people are paid based on their productivity. When workers seek employment where they can more

fully utilize their skills, they are more productive. An economic system that does not provide opportunities for people to improve their opportunities discourages productivity and collectively impairs ECONOMIC GROWTH.

Cyclical unemployment is associated with BUSINESS CYCLES. Though the U.S. economy consistently grew throughout the 1990s, historically economies go through periods of expansion and contraction. Unemployment associated with contractions in the economy is cyclical unemployment.

Full employment is defined as the absence of cyclical unemployment; this means there is still frictional, seasonal, and structural unemployment. Defining full employment has significant implications. The goal of macroeconomic policy is an economy operating at its potential level of output, which entails full utilization of its RESOURCES, including labor. During periods of economic expansion, an unemployment rate that is too low will lead to pressure to increase wages, causing INFLATION. Throughout the 1990s, economists in the United States debated whether 4 percent unemployment would lead to inflation.

Uniform Commercial Code

The Uniform Commercial Code (UCC) is a set of statutes that govern various types of commercial transactions, and its principles are meant to be followed uniformly by the various American states. However, the UCC is not completely uniform, because a state may choose not to adopt it or may choose to adopt a modified version in order to accommodate that state's commercial objectives. Fifty states, the District of Columbia, Guam, and the Virgin Islands follow the UCC; Louisiana has adopted only some parts of the code.

In 1942 the American Law Institute and the National Conference of Commissioners on Uniform State Laws began a project to create a set of laws governing commercial transactions that would be followed collectively by all American states. The purpose of the project was to provide organizations with greater certainty as to the laws of commercial transactions across states, so that organizations would be more comfortable with conducting interstate business. In 1952 this project led to the creation of the official text of the UCC. The official text has been revised and amended several times over the years; however, the states are not required to continually adopt revised versions of the UCC. Despite the possibility of differences in the adoption of UCC provisions among states, the code has created greater uniformity in the COMMERCIAL LAWS of the various American states than there was prior to the UCC.

As the UCC laws for each state may differ, businesses need to consult its rules, any official comments to the rules (generally printed after each rule), and any corresponding case law for each of the states in which they conduct business before engaging in commercial transactions covered by the UCC.

The UCC consists of nine articles.

- Article 1 contains general provisions such as purposes of the UCC; and general definitions, including the definition of good faith.
- Article 2 governs the sale of goods; provides various definitions, including the definitions of goods, merchant, CONTRACT, agreement and termination; and regulates the form and formation of contracts for sales of goods. Article 2 also governs matters related to leases of goods.
- Article 3 governs NEGOTIABLE INSTRUMENTS such as notes, checks, and certificates of deposit (TIME DEPOSITS).
- Article 4 governs bank deposits and collections and attempts to provide uniformity for the collection processes of banks, and specifically deals with ELECTRONIC FUNDS TRANSFERS.
- Article 5 governs matters related to letters of credit issued by banks.
- Article 6 governs matters related to bulk sales of a seller's inventory whereby the seller will not continue to operate the same or a similar business after the sale of the inventory.
- Article 7 deals with matters related to warehouse receipts, bills of lading, and other documents of title for wholesale transactions.
- Article 8 regulates the transfer and registration various types of INVESTMENT securities.
- Article 9 governs secured transactions, such as liens on PERSONAL PROPERTY and the use of personal property as collateral.

The UCC does not govern the sale of or secure interests in real estate, EMPLOYMENT agreements, or contracts that require the use of significant labor.

See also BILL OF LADING; LEASING; LETTER OF CREDIT; WARRANTY.

Further reading

Uniform Commercial Code, 2001. Available on-line. Cornell University Legal Information Institute. URL: http://www.law.cornell.edu.ucc.table.html. Fullerton, James D. "Sale of Goods Under the Uniform Commercial Code." Available on-line. URL: http://www.fullertonlaw.com/chapt12.htm. Downloaded on March 20, 2002; Klein, Joseph. "Uniform Commercial Code." Available on-line. URL: http://www.libsci.sc.edu/bob/class/clis748/UCC.htm. Downloaded on March 22, 2002; Stone, Bradford. *Uniform Commercial Code in a Nutshell,* 4th ed. Eagan, Minn.: West Publishing Co., 1995.

—Gayatri Gupta

union

A union is an organization of workers established to protect members' rights when dealing with employers. A popular and often true statement about unions is "bad MANAGEMENT creates unions." Today about 15 percent of the U.S. LABOR FORCE is unionized. Membership in unions varies significantly among regions of the country and industries; it is lowest in the southern and Rocky Mountain areas of the country. Unions in the United States have a long history, and there are many different types.

The first U.S. unions were the craft guilds of the 1790s. Printers, shoemakers, and other skilled craftsmen organized to increase wages, reduce working hours, and establish systems where only union labor was used (called a closed shop) by securing control of entry into the crafts. In 1794 printers in New York became the first union to strike, and in the 1820s unions attempted to reduce workdays from 12 to 10 hours. The New York printers strike lasted 10 years but was unsuccessful. During the 19th century, unions were often subjected to prosecution under criminal conspiracy laws. In spite of government prosecution, as industrialization replaced agricultural labor, more unions were formed. Union membership tended to grow during periods of economic expansion and tight LABOR MARKETS and to decline during RECESSIONS.

In the late 19th century, mass PRODUCTION and larger factories aided the expansion of unions, some of which sought political power. During that period, Samuel Gompers, considered the "father" of the American labor movement, organized the American Federation of Labor (AFL), an association of craft unions providing services to local unions and lobbying on behalf of all members in national politics. As a child in London, Gompers was apprenticed to a cigar maker. When his family sailed to New York, he joined the Cigar Makers Union, and by age 24 he was president of the local union. In 1886, when the AFL was created, Gompers led union efforts for an 8-hour day and expansion of union efforts to include women.

Eugene Debs was also an important leader in the union movement, founding the American Railway Union in 1893 and leading the Pullman strike in 1894. Debs was imprisoned for violating an INJUNCTION against the strike. While in jail, he studied SOCIALISM, and after his release he joined and later led the Socialist Party. Debs ran for president five times, including the 1920 election, when he was imprisoned for speaking against participation in World War I.

In the early 1900s there were many violent confrontations between organized labor and management, one of the worst being the 1914 strike by coal miners in Ludlow, Colorado. John D. Rockefeller, America's first billionaire, owned the Colorado Fuel and Iron Company. During the strike, workers and their families were forced out of company housing. Living in tents near the mine, strikers were harassed by company "deputies" who one night poured oil on the strikers' tents, setting them on fire. Thirteen women and children died.

Union membership declined during the early years of the GREAT DEPRESSION and then grew in the period from the mid-1930s to the mid-1950s, reaching a peak of slightly more than 30 percent of the labor force. A shift of workers from agrarian regions to urban areas during the period and the 1935 passage of the National Labor Relations Act (NLRA) contributed to union growth. The NLRA, also known as the WAGNER ACT, was a major turning point in government intervention into labor/management relations. The NLRA expanded the process by which unions were recognized as representing groups of workers and also required COLLECTIVE BARGAINING between employers and unions to negotiate wages and benefits. Between 1935 and 1945, union membership grew from 3 million to 14 million.

Union membership began to decline in the 1950s as employers moved jobs to employer-friendly areas of the country and as the United States moved from a predominantly manufacturing base to a service-based economy. Service industries have typically been less unionized than manufacturing industries. Part of this is attributable to the history of unions. The largest U.S. unions are industrial unions, which represent many different types of workers and industries. Industrial unions long ago organized many sectors of manufacturing, foremost the mining, construction, and transportation industries. Service industries are newer and also more fragmented, with fewer large employers.

The only unions continuing to grow in the United States are public and professional unions. Part of the growth in public unions was due to an executive order signed by President John F. Kennedy in 1962, granting federal Civil Service employees the right to organize. The American Federation of Teachers (AFT) is one of the oldest public/professional unions in the United States. The AFT, along with the National Education Association (NEA), represents many public schoolteachers in the country. Similarly, the American Association of University Professors (AAUP) represents college teachers in areas of the country where collective bargaining is allowed. In many states, predominantly in the Southeast and Southwest, state RIGHT-TO-WORK LAWS limit public-sector employees' ability to unionize.

The economic impact of unions varies, depending on who is speaking. Unions have apprentice programs for members, providing skilled workers to employers and thus increasing output and productivity. Unions also attempt to negotiate higher salaries for their members and focus on safe working conditions. Upton Sinclair's book *The Jungle* is an early 20th-century tale describing abusive management and horrendous working conditions in the meatpacking industry. While Sinclair's book is extremely critical of management abuse of labor, unions have also been criticized for excessive demands and unreasonable expectations. The term FEATHERBEDDING refers to union demands to maintain jobs even though changes in technology have made some jobs unnecessary. For example, many trains were required to have a fireman on board as part of a union contract, long after coal-fired engines had been replaced. Union work rules often frustrate business manager's efforts to "get the job done." Although union membership in the United States is declining, unions still represent a significant political and economic force.

See also AMERICAN FEDERATION OF LABOR–CONGRESS OF INTERNATIONAL ORGANIZATIONS.

Further reading
Boyes, William, and Michael Melvin. *Microeconomics,* 5th ed. Boston: Houghton Mifflin, 2002; Ziegber, Robert H. *American Workers, American Unions,* 2d ed. Baltimore: Johns Hopkins University Press, 1994.

United Farm Workers

The United Farm Workers (UFW) is a small but politically and socially active UNION representing agricultural workers in the western United States. The UFW attempts to increase farmworkers' salaries, benefits, housing, and working conditions. Farmworkers—many of them illegal workers in the United States and legal immigrants who do not speak English and are not familiar with American labor laws—have historically been subject to the demands of agricultural employers. During World War II, the bracero program, an agreement between the United States and Mexico, began allowing farmworkers to come into the country temporarily as guest workers. After the war, many of them stayed in the United States.

In the 1940s–60s, several attempts were made to organize farmworkers. Ernesto Galarza led the National Farm Labor Union, representing U.S. workers, but was undermined by the use of bracero workers willing to work without union representation. In 1959 the powerful AFL-CIO (AMERICAN FEDERATION OF LABOR–CONGRESS OF INTERNATIONAL ORGANIZATIONS) supported the creation of the Agricultural Workers Organizing Committee (AWOC), an outgrowth of the Agricultural Workers Association founded by Dolores Huerta. Cesar Chavez, a young Chicano born in Yuma, Arizona, created the National Farm Workers Association (NFWA) in 1962. The NFWA supported efforts to gain better wages for grape pickers in California. In 1965 the NFWA joined with the AWOC in a strike against grape farms in Delano, California, uniting Chicano and Filipino workers in an effort to get a $1.25 per hour wage. Chavez called for a consumer BOYCOTT of grapes without a union label, creating the first major national publicity for farmworkers. Supported by people involved in the civil rights movement of the 1960s, American consumers significantly reduced their purchases of table grapes. In 1966 Chavez led a march of workers through the agricultural valleys in California, gaining additional national attention and support and concession from one major grower to the union demands.

The UFW was created in 1966 by the merger of the NFWA and the AWOC. By 1970 the UFW had 50,000 dues-paying members. The union established a health clinic, CREDIT UNION, COOPERATIVE, and hiring hall. At its peak in 1973, the UFW had more than 80,000 members, but membership declined to, at one point, only 5,000 workers. Farm-grower resistance to unions has continued, and changes in labor laws reduced the union's role. The death of Cesar Chavez in 1993 left a void in the political and social connections that supported the union. In 2001 the UFW signed a CONTRACT with the country's largest strawberry grower, giving 750 workers a 7 percent pay raise over three years and free medical and dental care, in addition to establishing a grievance and ARBITRATION procedure for firings.

Further reading
DeArmond, Michelle. "UFW Signs Contract to Represent Strawberry Pickers," *SF Gate News,* 8 March 2001; United Farm Workers website. Available on-line. URL: www.ufw.org.

United States–Canada Auto Pact　See AUTO PACT.

United States–Canada Free Trade Agreement

The United States–Canada Free Trade Agreement (CFTA, 1989) reduced and eliminated TARIFFS on PRODUCTs traded between the two countries, initiated a trade agreement on SERVICES, increased investor access in each country, and created new mechanisms for trade-dispute resolution. While few Americans paid much attention to CFTA, it was the blueprint for the much more widely debated NORTH AMERICAN FREE TRADE AGREEMENT (NAFTA).

During the early 1980s, the Reagan administration, pursuing a FREE TRADE agenda, created the Caribbean Basin Initiative increasing access to the U.S. market for noncommunist countries in the Caribbean and Central America, completed a trade agreement with Israel, and pushed for liberalization in the Uruguay Round of the General Agreement on Tariffs and Trade (GATT; see WORLD TRADE ORGANIZATION). The GATT negotiations were stalled, and at a meeting in Canada known as the Shamrock Summit, U.S. president Ronald Reagan and Canadian prime minister Brian Mulroney agreed to pursue a bilateral trade agreement.

Historically Canadian leaders have entered into negotiations with the United States very cautiously. Few Americans know that one of the first acts during the American Revolution was sending a delegation led by Benjamin Franklin to Canada, inviting Canadians to join in the rebellion against Britain. Later, during an economic slowdown (1849), some Canadian leaders called for Canada's annexation to the United States. While geographically the larger country, Canada has one-tenth the U.S. population and has often resented the United States' economic, political, and cultural dominance in North America. Canada had also found in the past that it was easier to negotiate with the United States as part of a multilateral trade agreement than to "go it along." In spite of these reservations, Canada has needed continued access to the huge U.S. mar-

ket, and the United States buys over three-fourths of Canadian exports.

The United States and Canada are each other's largest trading partner, and before CFTA, 75 percent of products already traded duty-free. Most existing tariffs were at a rate of 5 percent of the value of the product. CFTA immediately eliminated some tariffs and phased out others over 5- and 10-year schedules with a goal of "virtual free trade" between the two countries. A few nontariff barriers were allowed to remain, based on national security interests.

The U.S. agenda in pursuing CFTA was multifaceted. The United States was shaken by the oil EMBARGOes during the 1970s, and Canadian nationalism in the early 1980s added to U.S. anxiety over access to Canada's gas, oil, and other mineral RESOURCES. The United States was also frustrated by the lack of progress of GATT negotiations, particularly on issues concerning trade in services, INVESTMENT, and INTELLECTUAL PROPERTY.

CFTA gave the United States access to Canadian minerals, created new rules for trade in services, and reduced government control of DIRECT INVESTMENT by U.S. nationals. One of CFTA's important features was the RULES OF ORIGIN. Free-trade agreements have a critical problem in that since the parties have not established a common set of tariffs for trade with the rest of the world, producers in other countries can ship their goods into the free-trade partner with the lowest applicable tariff and then export the goods to another free-trade partner. U.S. negotiators recognized the potential for this problem and in CFTA created rules for defining which products could be shipped from one country to the other without tariff. CFTA rules thus allow all goods "wholly obtained or produced," "substantially transformed," and meeting U.S./Canadian "content" rules. "Wholly obtained or produced" included minerals, fish, and agricultural goods. "Substantially transformed" has often been a subject of trade disputes and lawsuits; under CFTA it became defined as a good that has changed category in the HARMONIZED TARIFF SYSTEM. This meant that if any product imported from a third country, such as apples, was substantially transformed (used to make an apple pie), it could be shipped without duty between the two countries. In CFTA the two countries agreed products containing at least 50 percent U.S. and Canadian materials could trade freely.

CFTA also created new rules regarding trade in services. At the time, GATT negotiations on services trade were stalled, and U.S. negotiators recognized that new rules on free trade in services could affect those negotiations. Since the United States is highly competitive in services markets, it pushed hard for as much trade liberalization as the Canadians would tolerate. CFTA expanded trade in services, but only in "covered" services. Many services important to international trade, including legal, telecommunications, and customs brokers, were excluded from the agreement.

One of CFTA's innovations was the creation of new trade-dispute mechanisms. The agreement created the

Canada–United States Trade Commission (TC), ordinarily comprised of just the international trade representatives of the two countries (or their designees), and ad hoc committees and working groups. The TC provides each side of a trade dispute with a forum to discuss issues and resolve disputes. If a dispute cannot be resolved, it is sent to binding ARBITRATION before a qualified panel. In addition, CFTA created binational panels to hear complaints about DUMPING and countervailing duties. These panels have been used often, mostly by Canadian companies to pursue claims against U.S. companies.

Further reading

Folsom, Ralph H., and W. Davis Folsom. *Understanding NAFTA and its International Business Implications*. New York: Matthew Bender/Irwin, 1996.

U.S. Agency for International Development

The U.S. Agency for International Development (USAID) is an independent federal agency that works to support ECONOMIC GROWTH and agricultural development, global health, and disaster assistance in developing areas of the world. Created in 1961 by President John F. Kennedy, the USAID was based on the objectives of the MARSHALL PLAN for the reconstruction of Europe after World War II, and the Truman Administration's Point Four Program.

The USAID is headquartered in Washington, D.C., and has field offices around the world. Working with a variety of organizations, both private and governmental, the USAID provides financial assistance and technical advice for development efforts. The USAID is one of the more controversial U.S. government programs. Though the United States allocates less than 1 percent of its budget for foreign aid, USAID programs have long been criticized for waste, FRAUD, and abuse. Numerous reports document unfinished projects, disappearance of funds, and inappropriate development schemes recommended by U.S. "experts" traveling around the world in a style consistent with that of politicians' "fact-finding" junkets.

To help remedy the problems with the USAID, one proposal recommended giving more aid to private agencies rather than the governments in developing countries. Another suggestion has been to eliminate the agency entirely. U.S. businesses have sometimes complained the USAID subsidizes projects that cause the loss of American jobs. Support for export-processing zones, in particular, are criticized on this basis. On the other hand, the majority or USAID funding is tied to the purchase of goods and SERVICES from U.S. companies, creating lucrative EXPORTING opportunities.

Further reading

Stryk, Thomas. "Milkshakes in the African Desert," *Washington Monthly* 26 (May 1994): 14; U.S. Agency for International Development website. Available on-line. URL: www.usaid.gov.

U.S. Census Bureau

The U.S. Census Bureau generates and provides general statistical information about the U.S. population. The Census Bureau and census data are important sources of information for marketers and PUBLIC ADMINISTRATION. The need for a national census arose during the Constitutional Convention in 1789, when delegates agreed to use population as the basis for representation in the U.S. House of Representatives. Since then, a census of the United States has been conducted every 10 years and is used as the basis for redistricting political representation both on national and state levels. As the U.S. economy has grown, the quantity of data collected has expanded over time.

During the 1990s, a significant debate arose regarding whether to continue to collect information from all Americans or to use statistical sampling. Demographers recognize that census-taking typically undercounts homeless people, rural populations, and illegal residents in the country. Advocates for sampling argue it is less expensive and more accurate. Opponents point to the constitutional requirement for a census, and they won in a legal decision. The courts ruled a census rather than a sample will continue to be taken.

For businesspeople, the U.S. Census and the Topographically Integrated Geographic Encoding and Referencing (TIGER) system are valuable sources of secondary data. Census data are quite detailed, including information about peoples' INCOME, gender, household size, age, and ethnicity. Data are available free from the Census Bureau by city block or census tract. Many MARKET RESEARCH companies repackage census data for commercial customers.

Census Bureau data are frequently used as a basis for MARKET SEGMENTATION and identifying TARGET MARKETS. Knowing which areas of a city or town have higher or lower income, more or fewer elderly consumers, and which ethic groups live in a community helps marketers determine where to locate new stores, prices to charge, and what PRODUCTS to provide. U.S. Census Bureau information is available on-line and in almost any library.

See also DEMOGRAPHICS.

Further reading

U.S. Census Bureau website. Available on-line. URL: www.census.gov.

U.S. Commercial Service

The U.S. Commercial Service, an agency within the Department of Commerce, promotes exports of goods and SERVICES from the United States, particularly by small and medium-sized business. The service also acts to protect U.S. business interests abroad. Founded in 1980, the Commercial Service has over 100 offices in the United States and 160 international offices in 82 countries.

The Commercial Service evolved out of the Bureau of Foreign Commerce, established as part of the Department of State in 1897. Over the years, the function of trade promotion has been housed in the departments of state, labor, and commerce. Before the creation of the Commercial Service, foreign attachés working for the Department of State operated out of U.S. embassies around the world.

With a goal of promoting U.S. exports, the Commercial Service provides information about overseas markets, facilitates contacts with foreign buyers, and provides trade promotion support. Small companies rarely have the RESOURCES to investigate and pursue international business deals. The Commercial Service maintains a list of trade opportunities, conducts international partner searches, and publishes an INTERNATIONAL MARKETING magazine promoting U.S. PRODUCTS and services. For a fee the service will provide a customized market analysis. The Commercial Service also assists U.S. businesses with trade delegations, catalog and video shows, and TRADE SHOWS.

Further reading
U.S. Commercial Service website. Available on-line. URL: www.usatrade.gov.

U.S. Customs Clearance

All goods coming into the United States must "clear customs." Many disputes in the customs area arise over the classification of imported goods—basically, what is it? While this may seem a simple question, sometimes it is not; the TARIFF-duty rate depends on classification, and a substantial amount of tariff may depend on the outcome. Customs classifications are often overlapping, and where overlaps exist, logically the importer wants to choose the category with the least duty.

Other customs-clearance disputes concern the place of origin: Where did it come from? Many imported PRODUCTS contain components or materials from many countries, complicating the question of the place of origin. The country of origin may determine whether the goods enter subject to tariff or duty-free.

Lastly, customs disputes over the value of the imported goods can occur: What is its value? Customs duties are calculated as percentages of these values, which are principally derived from the transaction or invoice price. But often imported goods are intra-company transfers, from one division of a company to another. The companies use transfer pricing rather than invoicing, resulting in potentially different prices on which to base duties.

The formalities for imported goods entering the United States are usually handled by a customs broker. Customs brokers are licensed and regulated under federal law as administered by the U.S. CUSTOMS SERVICE. The customs broker, or agent, files an "entry" form with the U.S. Customs Service, supplying documentation which the customs officer uses do determine whether to release the goods or not. At the same time, or within 10 days the agent must submit an "entry summary," which is used by the

official to determine duties, collect statistics, and determine conformity of the merchandise with U.S. health and safety requirements. Estimated customs duties are deposited at the time of filing customs documentation.

The U.S. Customs clearance procedure was streamlined in 1978 to allow immediate release of imported goods after only entry documentation has been filed, without posting of bond to cover customs duties. Using a national, electronic automation program implemented in 1993, the Customs Service sends importers consolidated statements for all goods imported during a billing period.

See also RULES OF ORIGIN.

Further reading
U.S. Customs and Clearance Border Protection website. Available on-line. URL: www.cbp.gov.

U.S. Customs Service

The United States Customs Service oversees all import and export activity to ensure that international trade activity complies with U.S. laws and regulations. Most Americans' images of the Customs Service are the signs and questionnaires filled out when returning to the country from abroad, but the Customs Service has many other roles and responsibilities, which have changed over time.

The Customs Service collects revenues, guards against smuggling, and is responsible for

- assessing and collecting customs duties, excise taxes, fees, and penalties due on imported PRODUCTS
- searching for and seizing contraband, particularly illegal drugs and banned products or materials
- processing persons, baggage, mail, and cargo coming into and out of the country
- detecting and apprehending people engaged in fraudulent practices
- enforcing U.S. laws intended to prevent illegal trade practices including those involving INTELLECTUAL PROPERTY, rights violations, and anti-DUMPING laws
- enforcing restrictions on EXPORTING of critical technology, money laundering, and weapons
- collecting international trade data
- enforcing other agency statutes related to motor vehicle safety, emission controls, water pollution standards, pesticide controls, and endangered wildlife

The Customs Service has a long history, having been established by the fifth act of Congress in 1789. For over 100 years, customs-duty revenues funded virtually all of federal government activity. Today many EMERGING MARKETS depend on customs duties to fund government spending. Often, control of IMPORTS is one of the few parts of an economy that can be closely monitored and then taxed. In the United States, customs revenue represents only a small percentage of total tax revenue, having been replaced with taxes on INCOME (primarily personal-income and SOCIAL SECURITY taxes). The United States is a leading force in reducing TARIFFS among countries around the world, pursuing a goal of increased world trade through reduced TRADE BARRIERS.

Further reading
U.S. Customs Service website. Available on-line. URL: www.uscs.gov.

U.S. Trade Representative
The U.S. Trade Representative (USTR) is the chief trade negotiator in America as well as the chief advisor on trade policy to the president of the United States. According to its website the office of USTR is, responsible for "developing and implementing trade policies which promote world growth and create new opportunities for American businesses, workers and agricultural products." The term *USTR* refers to not only the head of the office but to the office itself.

Congress created the Office of Special Trade Representative, in the Trade Expansion Act of 1962, and in 1963 President John F. Kennedy implemented the act under Executive Order 11075. The office's main responsibility was negotiating trade agreements under the Tariff Act of 1930 and the Trade Expansion Act. Passage of the Trade Act of 1974 shifted the agency to the cabinet level under the president, and with that came more powers and responsibilities. In 1980 President Jimmy Carter's Executive Order 12188 renamed it the Office of the United States Trade Representative and made it responsible for all trade policy and the chief trade negotiator in all international matters.

The head of the office holds the title of ambassador. On February 7, 2001, Robert B. Zoelick was sworn in as the newest USTR ambassador. The USTR's major role involves developing U.S. international trade and INVESTMENT policy. It is also the leader for negotiations concerning trade with other countries and directly advises the president on national and international trade matters. The USTR is involved with other government agencies and is also vice chairman of the OVERSEAS PRIVATE INVESTMENT CORPORATION as well as a nonvoting member of the WORLD TRADE ORGANIZATION (WTO). The office provides leadership in matters of expansion of market access for American goods and services and in industrial and services trade policy.

The USTR is not an isolated agency; it works to foster communication between different groups. The private-sector advisory committee (which includes business and labor groups) consults with the office on trade agreements and U.S. trade policy, playing an integral role in China's accession into the WTO. The USTR also works directly with Congress; five members from each house are appointed as advisors on trade policy.

Further reading
U.S. Trade Representative website. Available on-line. URL: www.ustr.gov.

—Tara Lynn McDonald

U.S. Treasury securities
There are three major types of U.S. Treasury securities: bills, notes, and BONDS. In financial markets they are referred to as T-bills, T-notes, and T-bonds. The U.S. Treasury sells these securities on a continuing basis to finance the public (national) debt. When the government runs a budget deficit (spending more than what is taken in during a FISCAL YEAR), the U.S. Treasury sells additional securities to finance the deficit. As current Treasury securities mature, the department "rolls over" debt by selling replacement securities.

Of the three types of Treasury securities, T-bills are the most important. T-bills are short-term debt with maturities of three months, six months, and one year. They are issued in denominations of $10,000, $15,000, $50,000, $100,000, $500,000, and $1 million, are generally sold to securities dealers in lots of $5 million; and are priced on a discount basis. This means T-bills pay no coupon-interest rate. Instead they are sold at a price less than the face value, with the investor receiving the difference between the price and the face value received at maturity as interest. Treasury bills are priced using a "bank discount rate," calculated by multiplying the percentage price discount (the difference between the current price and the face value expressed as a percentage) by 360 (days) and then dividing by the number of days to maturity. For example, if a $10,000 T-bill is priced at $9,700, with 90 days until its maturity, the DISCOUNT RATE would be $r_d = (10,000 - 9,700 \div 10,000) \times (360 \div 90) \times 100$ percent = 12 percent.

On a regular basis, the U.S. Treasury announces its sale of 13-week and 26-week T-bills. Bids are received through the FEDERAL RESERVE SYSTEM and can be either competitive or noncompetitive. A competitive bid means the investor (lender) states the quantity of T-bills he or she want to purchase and what price he/she is bidding. The higher the price bid, the lower the interest-rate return. Likewise, the higher the bid price, the more money the government receives. In noncompetitive bids, the investor states what quantity of securities he/she wants to purchase and agrees to pay the weighted average of the competitive bids accepted. The Treasury Department then decides which competitive bids to accept, resulting in the price for noncompetitive bids; this process is called a Dutch auction. Most competitive bids are made by "primary dealers," market intermediaries who buy and sell Treasury securities in multimillion-dollar volumes. Noncompetitive bids typically are made by individuals and small commercial banks. In the 1970s, the Treasury Department stopped issuing physical securities, replacing them with a book-entry system, recorded in the Federal Reserve's computer records. Trading these securities is then a matter of electronic transfer of the security from one account to another.

T-notes and T-bonds are longer-term securities issued with coupon rates of interest. T-notes and T-bonds, like corporate bonds, are issued in $1,000 denominations. T-notes have maturities of 1–10 years, and T-bonds have maturities over 10 years. In recent years, T-notes and T-bonds have become less important, as the Treasury Department has financed most public debt using T-bills. With the decline in the public debt, in 2001 the Treasury Department announced it would eliminate the benchmark 30-year Treasury bond. Like T-bills, longer-term Treasury securities are sold through auctions but with less frequency than T-bills.

In addition to the three major types of Treasury securities, there are also savings bonds and inflation-indexed T-notes and T-bonds. Savings bonds have maturities up to 30 years, can be purchased directly by individuals, and can be redeemed any time after 6 months. In the late 1990s, the Treasury Department created inflation-indexed notes and bonds. The interest rate for these securities changes with INFLATION, as measured by the CONSUMER PRICE INDEX. Inflation-indexed securities protect investors against unexpected changes in inflation. Major securities dealers also create U.S. Treasury "strips"—securities (electronic book entries) whereby investors choose between buying the interest payments (a 10-year T-note consists of 20 payments every six months) or repayment of the principal at maturity. The second part of strips is known as a zero-coupon Treasury. Investors purchase strips coupon payments for a steady stream of income. They purchase zero-coupon Treasuries to lock in an interest rate of return for a longer period of time.

The Federal Reserve is a major purchaser of Treasury securities, first as an ASSET and second for use in OPEN-MARKET OPERATIONS. The Fed uses the purchase and sale of Treasury securities to member banks as a means of increasing or decreasing banks' reserves, funds available to make LOANS. This limits or expands the MONEY SUPPLY.

As of January 2002, U.S. Treasury securities held by the public (much of the national debt is held by other government agencies) consisted of

- T-bills: $792 billion
- T-notes: $1,411 billion
- T-bonds: $602 billion
- Indexed T-notes and bonds: $145 billion

Further reading

Kidwell, David S., Richard L. Peterson, and David W. Blackwell. *Financial Institutions, Markets, and Money*, 7th ed. Fort Worth, Tex.: Dryden Press, 2000; U.S. Treasury website. Available online. URL: www.ustreas.gov.

V

venture capital

In its rawest form, venture capital is the money invested in young, rapidly growing businesses—in essence, the important startup CAPITAL needed by new businesses. It is invested in high-risk situations with a compensating high expectation of return. To produce such compensations, usually a notable portion of the startup ownership is apportioned to these investors, the venture capitalists.

Venture capitalists typically purchase only EQUITY securities in new and rapidly growing businesses but usually bring more than just financial RESOURCES to a company. Normally they also become active participants in the new enterprise by utilizing their expertise and business relationships on the company's behalf. For example, a venture-capital firm may invest only in restaurant startups, so they not only invest financial resources but can bring in skills and processes useful to the startup. Venture capitalists like to characterize themselves as entrepreneurs first and investors second.

Most commonly, venture capital is raised from a venture-capital firm, the use of which allows the investor to offset the risk of a single INVESTMENT with a portfolio of projects. Venture-capital firms usually consist of a small group of fairly wealthy individuals who have been successful in previous startup situations, very often as the startup entrepreneurs. These individuals serve as the general partner and manage the MONEY invested in the fund by other limited partners. The limited partners realize that the fund is a high-RISK, high-return investment, but they want to benefit from the investment insights of the general partner.

Venture-capital investment firms most often focus on a certain industry and on investments at particular stages in a company's emergence. Venture capital jargon breaks the emergence of a new company into three stages of financing. "Seed capital" is needed at the earliest "start-up" stage. This is money to help a company that is just starting out and does not yet have PRODUCTS or customers. The next stage is "early stage financing," which is designed to fund the early growth after the company starts delivering a product. The final venture capital state is "expansion stage financing" to fund the expansion of the company into new markets or product lines. Each stage is less risky and so demands a lower expected return on investment.

Though venture capitalists claim to have a long-term orientation, they most often include provisions for an EXIT STRATEGIES in their plans that will allow them to boost their returns within three to five years. The most exciting exit is for the company to have an INITIAL PUBLIC OFFERING (IPO), listing its stock on a stock exchange. This raises the money to buy out the stock owned by the venture capitalist, in many cases producing very good returns for the existing capitalist. However, the most likely exit is for the company to be bought by another company, and very often the original company founder buys the stock owned by the venture-capital firm.

—Mack Tennyson

vertical integration

There are several different business models for companies to create sound business practices. Vertical integration is the model that allows a company to control aspects of its business by owning other companies. In contrast to horizontal integration, vertical integration involves buying companies that are either up or down from the existing company in the SUPPLY chain. For instance, a clothing store buys a manufacturing plant to make sure it has a stable supply of clothing. The clothing store not only gains a stable supply source but can also create its own fashions unique to its store.

There are two kinds of vertical integration: forward and backward. Both types can be used either simultaneously or separately, depending on the company's goals and/or problems.

Forward integration involves buying the aspects of the business that deal with the public, such as marketing or ADVERTISING. A good example of forward integration occurred when GFI Premium Foods, a meat-processing company, bought its own freight line and storage company so it could make sure its meat reached its customers on time.

Backward integration involves buying the aspects of the business that entail supplying the PRODUCT, such as manufacturing. American Tower Corporation began by selling communications towers, but through backward integration they now own a company that creates the towers and a paint company that finishes them as well as the construction company that assembles them.

A good example of total vertical integration is seen in Abbott Labs, a company that started out selling medicines. Today Abbott owns the manufacturing plants that create the medicines, the marketing companies that sell it, and the machines that administer the medicines in hospitals.

Further reading

Affuso, Luisa. "An Empirical Study on Contractual Heterogeneity within the Firm: The 'Vertical Integration-Franchise Contracts' Mix." *Applied Economics* 34, no. 8 (20 May 2002): 931; Kumpe, Ted, and Piet T. Bolwijn. "Manufacturing: The New Case for Vertical Integration," *Technology Management* 37, no. 1 (January–February 1994): 38–45; Malburg, Chris. "Vertical Integration." *Industry Week* 249, no. 20 (11 December 2000): 17; Mpoyi, Richard. "Vertical Integration: Strategic Characteristics and Competitive Implications." *Global Competitiveness* 9, no. 1 (2001): 108.

—Michelle Mitchell

viral marketing

Viral marketing occurs when a marketing message influences people to pass on the message to other potential customers. Similar to a biological virus, viral marketing has the potential to never end. The idea motivating viral marketing is to succeed by means of numerical power. With viral marketing consumers to pass the message on to others. A message forwarded from a friend or colleague has much more credibility than most advertising messages. In this way, a marketing message can initially be targeted to a few consumers but over time be seen and considered by millions.

According to Dr. Ralph F. Wilson, viral marketing has six elements:

1. Gives away products or services
2. Provides for effortless transfer to others
3. Scales easily from small to very large
4. Exploits common motivations and behaviors
5. Utilizes existing communication networks
6. Takes advantage of others' resources

Viral marketing has grown rapidly with the advent of the World Wide Web. Examples of this include AOL offering free Internet, MSN promoting free e-mail through Hotmail.com, and various promotional offers making their way to our private e-mail inbox. A Dallas, Texas, automobile dealership bought a local e-mail list and sent a message offering a chance to win a new car. They received more entries than the number of people they initially sent the message to when recipients forwarded the message to their friends.

Nonprofit groups and political organizations utilize viral marketing to promote their causes. In one viral marketing effort, Planned Parenthood sent a message to their e-mail distribution list warning about a change in government policy and providing a link to the White House for members to voice their concerns. The message was passed to thousands of people beyond the initial distribution list, increasing the number of people writing to voice their concern and increasing Planned Parenthood's membership. Similarly, an e-mail message comparing the relative IQs of President George W. Bush and former president Clinton was shared by millions over the Internet before it was proven to be a hoax.

Businesspeople recognize the power and potential of viral marketing to benefit and harm their enterprises. Many large companies monitor Internet chat rooms, posting responses and even issuing press releases when negative information or misinformation is being distributed.

Further reading

Wilson, Ralph F. "The Six Simple Principles of Viral Marketing." Wilson Internet website. Available on-line. URL: www.wilsonweb.com. Downloaded on June 4, 2003.

—Frank Check

visas

A visa is an endorsement in a passport allowing an individual to enter a country for purposes of travel or work. Business visas allow foreigners to enter and work in the United States. Often mistakenly referred to as GREEN CARDS because of their color, business visas are temporary nonimmigrant visas, while true green cards are for immigrants entering the country permanently based on having relatives in United States or due to EMPLOYMENT preferences. Visas and green cards are a confusing and ever-changing part of U.S. political and social policy. From an economic perspective, visas allow people with special skills and investments to enter and contribute to the U.S. LABOR FORCE, adding to the productive potential of the economic system. From a business perspective, work visas allow U.S.-based companies to utilize their personnel in the best capacity by bringing in specialty workers, transferring managers, and directing contact with trade partners.

Work and investor visas include specialty-occupation (H-1B), intra-company transfer (L-1), treaty-trader (E-1), and investor visas (E-2). Specialty-occupation visas require documentation that the worker has special theoretical and practical knowledge and has completed required courses of higher education. The United States issues 115,000 specialty-occupation visas annually, all with a six-year maximum duration. Employers must attest to the specialty skills of immigrants for whom they are seeking work visas. In effect, H-1B workers are "tied" to their employer, much like indentured servants brought into the United States centuries ago. However, the American Competitiveness in the 21st Century Act (2000) increased the speed with which H-1B workers can transfer from one U.S. employer to another without losing their visas.

Intra-company visas are available for executive, managerial, or special-knowledge workers being transferred into the United States. The company must have employed the foreign worker for at least three years. These visas have a maximum length of seven years for executives and managers and five years for employees with specialized knowledge.

Treaty-trader visas are available to individuals from countries with which the United States has a trade treaty (most of the world) and represent a firm doing "substantial trade" with the United States. These E-1 visas are available to executives or supervisory personnel. E-2 (investor) visas are available to individuals willing to put a substantial amount of CAPITAL at RISK in the United States. The INVESTMENT must earn more than what is required to support the investor and his or her family. These visas are renewable indefinitely. For example, if a citizen of Mexico starts or purchases a restaurant in the United States that creates more INCOME than is required to support him and his family, he is eligible for an investor visa. The law requires the investment be made before applying for the visa and that the capital comes from sources outside the United States.

The NORTH AMERICAN FREE TRADE AGREEMENT (NAFTA) created a special class of visas (TN) that are available to certain Canadian and Mexican professionals wishing to work temporarily in the United States. Article 16 of the NAFTA agreement defines and implements the immigration provisions of the agreement. Because the agreement was virtually identical to the UNITED STATES–CANADA FREE TRADE AGREEMENT, it had little impact on Canadian-U.S. business labor movement, but it significantly impacted U.S./Mexican business labor mobility. TN visas are available for North Americans with skills ranging from accounting to vocational counseling. Unlike many other work visas, the TN visa is relatively easily accessible and issued on an annual basis.

Further reading
Folsom, Ralph H., and W. Davis Folsom. *NAFTA Law and Business.* The Hague, Netherlands: Kluwer Law International, 1998;

U.S. Immigration and Naturalization Service website. Available on-line. URL: www.ins.usdoj.gov.

vision statement
A brief, concise statement by an organization of what it needs to become is called a vision statement. The vision statement should motivate and inspire the organization's employees and be shared with the businesses' owners, customers, and suppliers. The vision statement, therefore, gives direction to the organization's long-term goals and objectives. Three to five years into the future is the typical time frame for this forward-looking introspection.

The vision statement for the business administration department at the University of South Carolina at Beaufort (USCB) is:

> The USCB School of Business Administration leads the way in providing business education in the South Carolina Lowcountry thereby helping students to succeed in their professional activities, and achieve personal satisfaction while building the area's economic and societal levels thereby enhancing quality of life for all.

This long-term statement reflects the faculty's desire not only to provide quality education but also have a meaningful impact on the entire geographical area and the personal happiness of its residents.

Writing the vision statement is only one step, perhaps the easiest step, in an organization's growth and development. Making the vision become reality is the real task. An effective vision statement must be a living document and be supported by the values and actions of the organization or group that developed it. The next step is to develop ways of progressing from what the organization is now to what the organization wants to be. Identifying what the organization believes and the values it cherishes that are fundamental to its actions is the next step. These guiding ethical values become the road map that the organization uses to progress from its present status to its desired future.

Some of the guiding values for the USCB business administration department are:

- Emphasize the development of fundamental ideals, values, and guiding principles for professional and personal life.
- Base each course on sound business theory and principles, with a practical emphasis.
- Curriculum has a strong quantitative component based on statistical applications in business research to help prospective business professionals make effective business decisions.
- Assist business administration students find meaningful employment by emphasizing career development and linking students with prospective employers.

These and the other guiding values influence all facets of the department's activities, including daily contact and discussions with students, course development and presentation, and interaction within the community.

Identifying the organization's current position also requires an honest introspection. The mission statement summarizes where the organization currently is in terms of products and services offered to customers in the market-place. It is a statement of why the organization exists today. The mission statement is static because it looks at the organization as of a particular point in time. The vision statement is dynamic because identifies what the organization wants to be in the future. The mission statement does, however, provide a baseline against which progress in attaining the organization's vision can be measured.

—John B. Abbott

W

wage and price controls (incomes policies)

Wage and price controls are government-imposed limits on increases in wages and prices. Also called incomes policies, wage and price controls are typically imposed during wartime to limit INFLATION. During wars, government spending usually expands rapidly to provide the materials and weapons needed for defense. At the same time, governments conscript or enlist large numbers of young adults, reducing the supply of labor available in the private sector.

During World War II, the federal government enforced wage and price controls through the National War Labor Board and the Office of Price Administration. Citizens were encouraged to voluntarily reduce their CONSUMPTION of needed war materials. Families reduced the number of vehicles driven, and women sacrificed new PRODUCTS (at the time), including nylon hosiery, but rationing was also needed in order to have sufficient supplies for the military. In a market system, price acts as the basis of rationing. If DEMAND exceeds SUPPLY, prices rise, and only those consumers willing and able to pay the new, higher price will purchase the product. During World War II, rationing coupons were used to limit consumer demand. Coupons were needed to purchase gasoline and other necessities. This gave rise to a "black market," where, for a higher price, consumers could purchase additional quantities of the price-controlled product.

When the price of a specific product is controlled, it is called a price ceiling. When the prices of many or most goods are controlled, it is called price controls. In 1989 the government of Nepal, after a trade blockade by India (Nepal is landlocked and has no domestic source of hydrocarbons), imposed price controls on gasoline and kerosene. The government restricted prices to what they were before the blockade. The responses were amazing. On the demand side, consumers switched to wood for cooking and heat, driving up the price of firewood in a country already facing a serious deforestation problem and horrible air pollution in the Katmandu valley. The price of rickshaw rides rose as wealthy citizens put away their automobiles. Buses, with no changes in prices, became incredibly crowded and dangerously overweighted as they crept through the Himalayan Mountains. On the supply side, entrepreneurs hoarded fuels in their 17th-century wooden homes, selling gasoline at the equivalent of $8.00 per gallon. Hard-working traders smuggled gas and kerosene across the border from India, literally carrying the now-precious resource on their backs.

Wage controls are less frequently used than price controls. During World War II, government-imposed wage controls led to many changes, some of them good. First, with fewer male workers available, employers were forced to end discriminatory practices toward women. Second, because they were not allowed to pay higher wages, employers began offering their workers extra COMPENSATION AND BENEFITS, including health-care benefits.

The most recent American use of wage and price controls was during the Nixon administration. In 1971 President Richard Nixon imposed a 90-day wage and price freeze in the hope of breaking inflationary expectations. The controls continued beyond the 90-day period but had mixed results, and while they slowed inflation, it returned after they were removed.

During the 1960s, the Kennedy administration established wage and price "guideposts"—government-recommended increases in wages and prices. Though they were not backed by any penalty for violations, the guideposts helped stabilize prices during the period. Government can also influence wages and prices through their purchases. The U.S. government spends approximately $2 trillion annually. Government-negotiated prices for pharmaceuticals, defense materials, and other public goods as well as government salaries for military and civilian workers influence market prices and wages.

See also PRICE CEILINGS, PRICE CONTROLS; PRICE FLOORS, PRICE SUPPORTS.

Further reading

Ruffin, Roy J., and Paul R. Gregory. *Principles of Economics,* 7th ed. Boston: Addison Wesley, 2001.

Wagner Act (National Labor Relations Act)

The Wagner Act (officially the National Labor Relations Act, 1935) is considered by most labor specialists as the most important 20th-century labor statute. The act, named after New York Senator Robert F. Wagner gave American workers the right to organize, allowed COLLECTIVE BARGAINING, prohibited certain unfair labor practices, and created the NATIONAL LABOR RELATIONS BOARD (NRLB).

Before the Wagner Act, UNION-organizing efforts were often judged as being illegal criminal conspiracies, resulting in the use of police to disperse workers and the imprisonment of union organizers. Collective bargaining meant workers could be represented in negotiations with MANAGEMENT concerning wage, hours, and working conditions. In prohibiting certain unfair labor practices, the act enjoined owners and managers from

1. interfering with employees' rights to form, join, and assist labor unions
2. dominating or interfering with the formation or administration of a labor union
3. discriminating against employees in hiring, tenure, or any term of EMPLOYMENT due to their union membership
4. discriminating against employees because they have filed charges or given testimony under the NLRA
5. refusing to bargain collectively with any duly designated employee representative

By creating the NLRB, the Wagner Act established a forum for union-management DISPUTE SETTLEMENT outside of the FEDERAL COURTS (which up to that time had been decidedly promanagement). Future labor laws, particularly the TAFT-HARTLEY ACT (1947) and the LANDRUM-GRIFFIN ACT (1959), have amended the Wagner Act, both expanding and contracting the provisions of the law.

Further reading

Mallor, Jane P., A. James Barnes, Thomas Bowers, Michael J. Philips, and Arlen W. Langvardt. *Business Law and the Regulatory Environment,* 11th ed. Boston: McGraw-Hill, 2001.

Wall Street

Wall Street is both a street in the lower part of Manhattan in New York City and a generic reference to the financial district located there. The NEW YORK STOCK EXCHANGE is located on the corner of Wall and Broad Streets, while the AMERICAN STOCK EXCHANGE is located nearby on Trinity Street. Historically, Wall Street was a wall created by early Dutch settlers to keep wild animals from eating their crops.

In most business situations, "Wall Street" refers to buyers and sellers in STOCK MARKETS. News stories often start with the phrase, "Wall Street reacted positively (or negatively) today in response to . . ." Traditionally the New York Stock Exchange has dominated trading in stocks, but more recently the NATIONAL ASSOCIATION OF SECURITY DEALERS AUTOMATED QUOTATIONS (NASDAQ) system has challenged Wall Street control. Wall Street is also the location of many law firms specializing in securities and MERGERS AND ACQUISITIONS law.

For 30 years, *Wall Street Week with Louis Rukeyser* aired on public television networks around the country. The commentator, Louis Rukeyser, educated many Americans about the stock market, always defining INVESTMENT jargon used by guests on the program. In 2002 program executives decided to remove Rukeyser, who was quickly hired by a television network to continue *Wall Street Week* on cable television.

warranty

A warranty is an expressed or implied promise that PRODUCTS sold will perform as represented by the seller's words, actions or writings. Many consumer goods come with a written "limited warranty" of performance for a certain period of time ("three months parts and labor"), indicating the seller will repair or replace the goods without charge within that period. Products sold with limited warranties must clearly be labeled as such. Some goods come with "lifetime warranties," essentially unlimited in time. The UNIFORM COMMERCIAL CODE creates two well-known "implied warranties" that are legally binding unless the seller expressly disclaims them in writing. The first is the implied warranty of the fitness or suitability of the good for a buyer's special purposes, which are known to the seller. The second implied-at-law warranty is that the good is "merchantable"—i.e., fit for the ordinary purposes for which it is used. Other warranties may concern rental residences, including the implied warranty of "habitability," that the property is fit to live in and will remain so during the life of the lease.

To consumers, a warranty is a confirmation of the quality or performance of a product or service. Warranties help overcome consumer resistance in the buying process. In the United States, marketers often promote warranties as a selling feature. In 1975 Congress passed the Magnuson-Moss Warranty-Federal Trade Commission Improvement Act to help consumers better understand warranties and get warranties acted on by manufacturers and dealers. Under the act, a manufacturer must meet certain warranty standards, including repair "within a reasonable time and without charge" and replacement of merchandise or full refund if the product does not work "after a reasonable number of attempts" at repair.

Further reading

Lamb, Charles W. Jr., Joseph F. Hair Jr., and Carl McDaniel, *Marketing*, 6th ed. Cincinnati: Southwestern-Thomson Learning, 2002; Marsh, Genett. *Consumers Protection Law in a Nutshell*, 3rd ed. Eagan, Minn.: West Group, 1999.

wealth

Wealth is usually defined as an abundance of RESOURCES. A country's wealth is its natural, CAPITAL, and HUMAN RESOURCES. Individuals and households typically define wealth as their net worth, the value of their ASSETS (dwellings, land, stocks, BONDS, cash, and collectibles) minus the amount owed on those assets. Many people think of wealth as having lots of MONEY, which can result from the accumulation of wealth and can be used to create wealth. Wealth is distinguished from INCOME in that individuals and countries have a fixed level of wealth at any point in time, while income is a flow of payments over time. Bill Gates is probably the wealthiest person in the world; one website (www.webho.com/WealthClock) continually updates its estimate of Gates's wealth ($70 billion in 2002).

Wealth has been the subject of inquiry and concern for hundreds if not thousands of years. The Hindu deity Lakshmi is the goddess of wealth. In the 16th and 17th centuries, MERCANTILISM dominated economic thinking. Under mercantilism, a country's wealth came from the accumulation of gold and silver. Physiocrats, who opposed mercantilism, believed that agriculture was the primary source of economic wealth and advocated a LAISSEZ-FAIRE (let be) doctrine, supporting the private control and allocation of resources rather than government domination.

Adam Smith (1723–91), considered the "father of modern economics," wrote *The Wealth of Nations* (1776), in which he argued that the market system best promoted society's interests. Smith believed that in a perfect world, a "self regulating market system would automatically satisfy the needs of society," which was to "produce the greatest good for society as a whole." At the time, governments readily granted monopolies to favored interest groups and used protective subsidies to assist local manufacturers to compete against foreign rivals. Smith stated that individuals, pursuing rational self-interest, would create wealth through efficient PRODUCTION and COMPETITION, and consumers would allocate their scarce resources to maximize well-being.

In recent years, with the huge increase in U.S. ECONOMIC GROWTH and wealth, one organization, Responsible Wealth, has questioned the distribution of wealth. The group states its goal is to put "a spotlight on the dangers of excessive inequality of income and wealth in the United States." To address these dangers, Responsible Wealth advocates fair taxes, a living wage, greater corporate responsibility, and broadened asset ownership for all Americans. The group's tax-fairness proposals include pre-

serving the estate tax and pledging to give the proceeds from the 1997 CAPITAL GAINS tax cut to support groups that organize for tax fairness. Their living-wage proposal suggests that an increase of the federal MINIMUM WAGE by at least 60 percent would be needed to bring workers up to the federal poverty level. In 2001 Santa Monica, California, instituted a citywide living-wage regulation, significantly raising the wages of all city employees.

Responsible Wealth and other groups challenge what is known as TRICKLE-DOWN ECONOMICS. This theory suggests that as a nation's wealth grows, everyone will benefit. Trickle-down economics is associated with the policies of the Reagan administration (1980–88), during which significant tax benefits were provided to businesses and affluent Americans. Part of the argument for this was that these groups would save and invest increasing output, income, and wealth in society. Critics of the trickle-down theory asked that they "not be the last drip."

In recent years one of the interesting debates regarding wealth is the so-called "wealth effect." The wealth effect is the degree to which changes in wealth influence CONSUMPTION spending. FEDERAL RESERVE SYSTEM chairman Alan Greenspan and others debated to what extent increases in paper wealth—the value of peoples' INVESTMENT and retirement portfolios—affected their present consumption spending. Most analysts agree that part of the economic boom in the late 1990s was attributable to the wealth effect.

See also CAPITALISM.

Further reading

"Major Schools of Economic Theory," Federal Reserve Bank of California. Available on-line. URL: www.frbs.org. Responsible Wealth website. Available on-line. URL: www.responsiblewealth.org.

welfare

Welfare, also referred to as public charity, is educational, medical, and financial assistance to people identified as needy. In the United States, welfare includes a variety of programs benefiting senior citizens, low-INCOME families, and people with disabilities.

In western society, welfare began with the Greeks and Romans, who provided assistance to people who qualified as citizens. In early times, most welfare was associated with church activities rather than government programs. The Elizabeth poor law (1601) was the first major European government welfare program. The poor law attempted to provide assistance through local parishes. With the Industrial Revolution, business leaders claimed welfare programs impeded on market forces, discouraging productive efforts. Renowned social reformer Robert Owen challenged industrial practices, arguing welfare was essential in a capitalist system but should be administered jointly by private and public programs.

In the United States, poor houses and religious charities were the major welfare activities from the 1700s until the 1930s. The Social Security Act (1935) was the first federally funded assistance program. SOCIAL SECURITY was a response to the GREAT DEPRESSION, during which millions of Americans lost their jobs and had few resources to fall back on. In arguing for the act, President Franklin Roosevelt stated, "Security was attained in the earlier days through the interdependence of members of families upon each other and of the families within a small community upon each other. The complexities of great communities and of organized industry make less real these simple means of security."

Initially Social Security included only retirement benefits. Social Security taxes were first collected in 1937, and the first recipient, Ernest Ackerman, received a lump-sum payment of 17 cents that year. Social Security was intended to be a modest income INSURANCE program for retiring workers. In 1939 survivor benefits were added, and in 1940 the Social Security Administration (SSA) began paying monthly benefits. In 1956 disability benefits and in 1965 Medicaid health benefits for poorer Americans were added to the Social Security program.

Most Americans do not consider Social Security—specifically Old Age, Survivors, and Disability Insurance (OASDI)—as a welfare program. Some consider it is a "social compact," a promise to successive generations that they will be supported in their old age. To others Social Security is an intergenerational income-transfer program or a welfare program for the elderly. Social Security recipients will deny that they are getting welfare, saying, "I paid into the system, and now I am getting back what I deserve."

Assuming OASDI is a welfare program, the second largest cash-assistance program in the United States is SUPPLEMENTAL SECURITY INCOME (SSI). SSI is a federally financed and administered program created in 1974. It is managed by the Social Security Administration but funded through general tax revenues. Designed to assist needy Americans, SSI provides monthly cash payments to Americans with limited income and resources who are 65 and older, blind, or disabled. Unlike the Old Age and Survivors Income (OASI), SSI is not based on prior work or contributions into the Social Security system.

Supplemental Security Income is available to U.S. citizens and "certain qualified aliens." In 2002, 7.2 million Americans received SSI benefits. SSI rules regarding income and resources are quite severe, limiting eligibility to the program to only the most needy people. Federal spending on SSI has grown from $8 billion in 1974 to $35 billion in 2000.

AID FOR FAMILIES WITH DEPENDENT CHILDREN (AFDC) is the third largest cash-assistance program in the United States and the one most associated with the term *welfare*. Title IV of the Social Security Act, originally titled "Aid to Dependent Children," was enacted to provide financial assistance for disadvantaged dependent children and did not provide assistance for parents or guardians involved in the raising of the children. In 1950 the federal government expanded the provision to provide funds to aid in the care of the adults responsible for the children.

Critics of the AFDC argue that the program created a set of incentives that were harmful to the nation's "social fabric." The welfare system was allegedly dehumanizing; encouraged dependency; supported female-headed families, divorce, and unmarried childbearing; and encouraged low levels of work effort among recipients. Supporters argue that AFDC has helped to reduce poverty, provided work and skill training, and succeeded in keeping intact poor female-headed families with young children.

On August 22, 1996, President Bill Clinton signed into law the Personal Responsibility and Work Opportunity Reconciliation Act (PRWORA) of 1996 (Public Law 104-193), replacing the AFDC program. PRWORA gave states a lump sum to fund their own welfare programs, with the stipulation that recipients work or receive training as a condition of welfare assistance. The law also limited benefits to two years at a time and lifetime benefits to five years. Welfare rolls subsequently dropped as recipients reached term limits. Supporters of the reforms claimed success, while critics argued removing poor people from the welfare rolls did not reduce poverty. (Economists also noted that during the period 1998–99, the economy grew rapidly, creating many new job opportunities.)

In most states SSI and AFDC recipients also receive Medicaid, a joint federal-state health-payment program. Medicaid is the largest in-kind welfare program. Food stamps are the second largest in-kind welfare program, providing low-income households with coupons redeemable for specific categories of food items at grocery stores. Other in-kind welfare programs include public housing, Head Start educational assistance, college LOANS and grants, vocational rehabilitation training programs, and TRADE-ADJUSTMENT ASSISTANCE.

Government also provides aid to CORPORATIONS. CORPORATE WELFARE includes a wide variety of technical assistance, export promotion, low- or no-interest loans, free personnel training, tax holidays, and other measures subsidizing the COSTS of businesses.

Further reading
"The History of Social Welfare." Available on-line. URL: www.uic.edu/classes/socw/socw550?HISWEL/; Social Security Administration website. Available on-line. URL: www.ssa.gov.
—Carrie Wilson

Wheeler-Lea Act

The Wheeler-Lea Act of 1938 amended the Federal Trade Commission Act of 1914 to give the FEDERAL TRADE COMMISSION (FTC) jurisdiction over false or misleading ADVERTISING in addition to special powers to regulate advertising on food, drugs, cosmetics, and therapeutic devices. The

1914 act, which had established the FTC, declared "unfair methods of COMPETITION" to be unlawful. The FTC broadly interpreted the act to include jurisdiction in certain cases of deceptive and false advertising of the character of goods that was likely to mislead the public. In 1922 the U.S. Supreme Court upheld the FTC's jurisdiction in this area with its approval of an FTC order to cease and desist from deceptive advertising.

During the 1930s, however, several cases began to roll back the boundaries of the FTC's jurisdiction, the most damaging of these cases being *FTC v. Raladam Co.* (1931). In *FTC v. Raladam Co.*, the Supreme Court unanimously ruled that one of the facts necessary to support the FTC's jurisdiction to issue an order to cease and desist a false advertisement was proof that the advertisement affected competitors. If there was no proof that the advertisement affected any competitors, then the FTC was without jurisdiction, even if the advertisement admittedly deceived the public. *FTC v. Raladam Co.* effectively limited the scope of the FTC to injury to the competition and not injury to the public. The consumer could not claim any protection under the Federal Trade Commission Act.

In 1938, after years of intense lobbying, Congress legislatively overruled *FTC v. Raladam Co.* case by passing the Wheeler-Lea Act. The Wheeler-Lea Act amended Section Five of the Federal Trade Commission Act to read, "Unfair methods of competition in or affecting commerce and unfair or deceptive acts or practices in or affecting commerce, are hereby declared unlawful." The FTC was empowered to issue cease-and-desist orders against firms that make false and misleading advertising claims. Proof of injury to the competitors was no longer a requirement. The Wheeler-Lea Act further strengthened the FTC's power in dealing with false and deceptive advertising of food, drugs, cosmetics and other therapeutic devices by providing definitive and significant penalties for violation of orders to cease and desist from illegal practices.

—Lisa Vincent Gagnon

wheel of retailing

The wheel of RETAILING is the theory or observation that new competitors come into established retail markets offering lower prices, greater selection of a limited line of PRODUCTS, or unique products challenging a portion of the market of established firms. The new competitors can do this (and still earn a PROFIT) by minimizing costs through limiting SERVICES, smaller stores, or control of inventories. In effect, the new firm is attempting to establish a niche market, attracting a portion of the established firm's customers.

Logically the new competitor is going to attempt to attract the segment of customers that is potentially the most profitable. The "wheel" analogy is used to suggest that this is an ongoing, circular process. The new firm

becomes established by offering lower prices or added selection of a limited line of products. Once it has developed a customer base (assuming it is successful), the new firm will begin to offer additional products and services to its customers. This will require additional COSTS but should (it hopes) result in increased profits. Eventually the new firm becomes an established retailer, upon which new competitors will probably attempt to compete by taking away profitable segments.

One way of visualizing the wheel of retailing is the children's story of the little fish eats the bigger fish, which eats the bigger fish, which becomes the biggest fish and then is nibbled on by the little fish. An example is today's specialty clothing stores. In the early 20th century, Sears, J. C. Penney, Nordstrom, and others were individual stores that, over time, expanded to become national retailers. New competitors often choose to locate in the same shopping malls as these established companies, attracting a portion of the traditional stores' consumers. The most successful of these specialty retailers become national chain stores, which will attract new COMPETITION.

Even in retail markets like fast-food restaurants, the wheel of retailing can be observed. In the 1960s, as Americans worked longer hours and two-income families became the norm, fast-food restaurants challenged local diners and at-home meals. By the 1990s fast-food companies had become established leaders. Then, led by Starbucks, new retailers challenged one part of the fast-food market—coffee—and, by turning a commodity into a gourmet food, created a niche market.

In 2002 a *Wall Street Journal* article reported another example of the wheel of retailing, gourmet sandwiches. New, small restaurant chains are challenging the fast-food industry by offering custom-made sandwiches using "artisanal" bread. In addition, the sandwiches and stores are given upscale-sounding names to help justify the higher prices. Unlike traditional fast-food restaurants, which target children and younger adults, gourmet sandwich stores are attempting to attract "baby boomers," adults 45–64 years old.

Further reading

Leung, Shirley. "Fast-Food Chains Vie to Carve Out Empire in Pricey Sandwiches," *Wall Street Journal*, 5 February 2002, p. A1.

whisper numbers

Whisper numbers are unofficial earnings estimates for companies. Brokerage houses employ STOCK MARKET analysts who closely watch and make predictions about a narrow range of stocks they "cover." Major brokerage houses will probably have analysts who cover just oil stocks, utility companies, retailers, etc. Market analysts regularly predict the quarterly earnings-per-share for the companies they follow. The industry analysts' official estimates are then compared to yield a consensus estimate.

During the DOT-COMS' boom in 1999–2000, earnings estimates were a constant and rapidly changing concern for technology companies. Official analysts' estimates often did not change as fast as market conditions. Thus unofficial market estimates, made either by industry analysts and distributed privately among clients and brokerage house personnel or by individual investors and distributed over INTERNET stock-market discussion groups, flourished.

Day traders, individual stock-market investors who buy and sell stock in a matter of minutes or hours, often used whisper numbers as compared to official estimates in determining which stocks to invest in. At the time of the dot-com boom, whisper numbers were often a better estimate of companies' earnings than official estimates, and stock prices advanced or declined based on whether the company's earnings exceeded or fell short of whisper numbers rather than consensus estimates.

As the dot-com market crashed and earnings disappointments replaced those exceeding estimates, and with introduction of the FAIR DISCLOSURE regulation (Reg FD) by the SECURITIES AND EXCHANGE COMMISSION (SEC) in 2000, the number of whisper numbers reported declined. Reg FD bars companies from selectively disclosing information. Previously, stock-market analysts often received advanced notice of news or privileged information from the companies they cover. For companies, relationships with analysts would generally lead to more positive recommendations, which in turn helped raise their company's stock price. For analysts, advance notice allowed them to inform important customers about impending news.

Since the introduction of Reg FD and with the decline of the dot-com industry, whisper numbers all but disappeared. One website, EarningsWhisper.com, tracks earnings projections from on-line message boards. The number of whisper estimates reported has dramatically declined, and in 2001 the website reported whisper numbers for technology stocks tended to be within a penny per share of consensus estimates.

Further reading

Edmundston, Peter. "Shhh! Focus on 'Whisper Numbers' Fades as Pundits Sidestep the Informal Targets," *Wall Street Journal,* 26 July 2001, p. C1.

whistle-blower (whistleblower)

According to Janet P. Near and Marcia Miceli of Indiana University, a whistle-blower is an "employee or member of an organization (former or current) who discloses the illegal, immoral, or illegitimate practices of their employers to persons or organizations that may be able to effect action." Near and Miceli cite three instances when whistle-blowing occurs in organizations: A person or persons must commit a wrongdoing; somebody else must observe, define, and report it; and another person or persons must

be a victim of the wrongdoing. They conclude, "From a legal standpoint, a whistle-blower should believe the wrongdoing has implications for public policy, or some portion of society is endangered by the organization's actions."

A whistle-blower can report wrongdoings to parties either inside or outside the organization. There is no law that mandates whistle-blowers must report wrongdoing within an organization; they come forward themselves for many reasons. According to Near and Miceli, "From a legal perspective, effectiveness of whistle-blowing can be defined in terms of win/loss ratio in lawsuits entered into by whistle-blowers. However, many define whistle-blower success as the extent to which the questionable or harmful practice is terminated as a result of the whistle-blower's complaint."

Whistle-blowers risk potential discrimination or retaliation by the organization they report for wrongdoing. Examples of discrimination include firing, demotion, job transfer, LAYOFF, and losing an opportunity for overtime or promotion. If a whistle-blower suffers such consequences, he or she must be able to prove the employer had acted in a discriminatory or a retaliatory manner. There are four elements of a whistle-blower reprisal violation: The employee must make a protected disclosure, the official responsible for the action must have knowledge of the disclosure, the employee must be subjected to personnel action, and there must be a connection proved sufficient to establish that the protected disclosure was a contributing factor in the personnel action. Federal legislation has been enacted to protect whistle-blowers from such discrimination or reprisal, although currently there is no comprehensive federal whistle-blower protection law.

The whistle-blower protection law, the False Claims Act (1986), allows a private individual or whistle-blower with knowledge of past or present FRAUD to sue on behalf of the government and receive a monetary reward. The first whistle-blower act was first enacted during the American Civil War was known as the Lincoln Law. It was strengthened in 1986 to make it easier for private citizens to sue. The government has the right to intervene and join the action. If the government does not join the action, the plaintiff can proceed alone.

Other federal legislation with whistle-blower protection statutes include laws with employee protection provisions, such as the Sarbanes-Oxley Act 2002, and the Whistle-blower Protection Act of 1989. Under the Sarbanes-Oxley Act, companies are required to set up confidential whistle-blower hotlines so corporate employees can report misdeeds. The Whistle-blower Protection Act of 1989 provides protection for federal employees, whose complaints are handled through the government Office of Special Counsel. There are also many states with statutes or provisions for whistle-blower protection. Employees who face retaliation for whistle-blowing can be reinstated and receive back pay and compensatory DAMAGES.

Supporters of whistle-blower protection argue that whistle-blower's actions can save lives and billions of dollars, and the individuals who report the fraud should be afforded protection. Strong laws allow employees to be comfortable about voicing concerns and to work for change. When the employee is comfortable working within the system, MANAGEMENT is able to address potentially harmful situations and rectify them before a crisis occurs.

Critics of whistle-blower protection maintain that the inconsistent application of the laws discourage employees from pursuing administrative remedies and instead pursue punitive damage suits. There is also argument that narrow legal interpretations and inconsistent application of the law actually discourages insiders from reporting corporate wrongdoings. Finally, critics point out that the Department of Justice only takes 20 percent of the complaints filed under the False Claims Act, which further discourages whistle-blowers to come forward.

Some of the more notable whistle-blowers include Sharon Watkins in the Enron case, Colleen Rowley in the FBI case, Mary Schiavo in the FAA case, Winston McCully in the Hanford Nuclear Reservation case, and Karen Silkwood in the Kerr-McGee plutonium case.

Further reading

Devine, Tom. "A Whistle-blower's Checklist." Available on-line. URL: www.whistle-blower.org/www/ checklist.htm. Downloaded on November 7, 2002; Keenan, John P., and Charles A. Krueger. "Whistle-blowing and the Professional," *Management Accounting* 74, no. 2 (August 1992): 21; Koch, Kathleen Day, and Paul S. Ellis. "Protecting Whistle-blowers (Office of Special Counsel)," *The Public Manager: The New Bureaucrat* 23, no. 1 (Spring 1994): 51; "Legal Resources for Whistle-blowers." Available on-line. URL: www.whistle-blower.org/getall.php?scid=100&cid=32. Downloaded on June 2, 2003; Near, Janet P., and Marcia Miceli. "Whistle-blowing: Myth and Reality," *Journal of Management* 22, no. 3 (Fall 1996): 507; ———. "Effective Whistle-blowing," *Academy of Management Review* 20, no. 3 (July 1995): 679; "Q&A: False Claims Act." Available on-line. URL: www.quitamonline. com/whatis.html. Downloaded on November 9, 2002; Weber, Joseph. "A Whistle-blower's New Ally: The Web." *Business Week*, 21 October 2002, p. 16; "Whistle-blower Disclosures." Available on-line. URL: www.osc.gov/wbdisc.htm. Downloaded on November 9, 2002.

—Abbey Gehman

white-collar

White-collar refers to employees who typically wear white, collared shirts: professionals, administrators, and office workers. White-collar contrasts with BLUE-COLLAR, the traditional color of clothing worn by ASSEMBLY LINE or other laborers. White-collar is often used to describe specific groups or conditions, including white-collar salaries, crime, UNIONS, and RECESSIONS.

A March 6, 1997, Knight Ridder/Tribune Business News headline read "General Motors Struggles to Balance Blue-, White-Collar Salaries." The article described differences in employee compensation for office versus factory workers. Another article entitled "Crack Down on Corporate Crime" described white-collar crime as the theft of PROPRIETARY INFORMATION, EMBEZZLEMENT, vendor kickbacks, and misappropriation of company funds.

Jill Fraser titled her book *"White-Collar" Sweatshop: The Deterioration of Work and its Reward in Corporate America*, describing office working conditions and motivation of white-collar workers through the fear of LAYOFFS. Another writer, suggesting unions are needed for professional groups as well as industrial workers, posed the question, "Is it Time for White-collar Unions?" During the mid-1990s, as part of corporate downsizing, many MIDDLE MANAGERS lost their jobs, creating what was called a white-collar recession.

wholesaler

A wholesaler is a market intermediary who purchases PRODUCTS from manufacturers and then distributes them to retailers. Wholesalers act as an alternative to manufacturer or retailer-owned DISTRIBUTION CHANNELS. Wholesalers have existed as long as trade has existed. While today many firms are using the INTERNET to increase their direct communications and transactions with customers, wholesalers continue to be an important part of the U.S. economy. In 1997 wholesalers' sales in the United States equaled $4.2 trillion.

Wholesalers exist because they provide two primary benefits: ECONOMIES OF SCALE in distribution and transactions economies. For many small manufacturers, the cost of establishing and maintaining a distribution system would be prohibitive. Just the cost of selling to retailers for a small firm could make the venture unprofitable. Wholesalers contact many retailers to sell a variety of products, also creating assortments to meet retailers' needs; maintaining inventories; handling order taking and fulfillment, transportation, and information to both manufacturers and retailers; and sometimes providing financing.

In addition to economies of scale, wholesalers provide transactions economies, efficiency in communication and selling between manufacturers and retailers. For example, in a market with six manufacturers and six retailers, if each manufacturer attempts to directly interact with each retailer, there will be a total of 36 (6 × 6) marketing interactions. If, instead, the manufacturers sell to a wholesaler who then markets to each retailer, there will be 12 transactions.

In many international markets, wholesalers have considerable market power, determining which products gain access to retail markets. U.S. companies that expand abroad often develop cooperative relationships with existing wholesale networks in their target countries.

work council

A work council is a representative body of employees selected to provide direct input into the company's operational activities. Typically seen only in European nations, the work council provides MANAGEMENT with ideas of what the employees would like to see at their particular company.

The councils are open to all employees, unionist or nonunionists. Council members, who are elected by a ballot of all employees to represent the company's employee pool with regard to business functions, address topics such as the financial state of the business, the forecasted plans, EMPLOYMENT trends, new working methods and any organizational changes that may take place. Councils can act as a negotiating team for wages and conditions but are not required to do so. In most cases, UNIONS still maintain the right to conduct any salary negotiations.

U.S. MULTINATIONAL CORPORATIONS that operate in Europe currently consult with the elected work councils to provide for easier flow of information between management and employees. Studies have shown that only 30 percent of employees think that they are adequately consulted about workplace issues, and 70 percent do not think that their thoughts are considered. On the other hand, 70 percent of managers believe that they sufficiently consider employees' thoughts and concerns.

Union memberships in the United States has been declining over the last two decades from one in every two workers to one in five. Academics have identified the development of a representational gap between management and employees as one result of the decrease in union membership. With decreased union involvement, firms are starting to see that employee representation is needed to increase employee moral and are implementing work councils. Employees who think that their opinions are taken into consideration have a higher level of JOB SATISFACTION than those who do not think their opinions are considered.

The best-known work council is the European Works Council (EWC), which was originally established to inform employees about future business decisions and engagements. The EWC's goal is to ensure that any decision made that affects employees will be properly communicated to all workers.

European companies with over 1,000 employees typically elect 150 members to participate in the work councils. The involvement of employees in decision making gives them a sense of interest in the company's direction and profitability and often assists in achieving organizational goals.

Further reading
ACTU pushes for non-union "work councils." The Age. Available on-line. URL: www.theage.com.au/news/2001/03/08/FFX259PUOkc.html; Downloaded on February 24, 2002; The European Works Council website. Available on-line. URL: www.lawinternational. com/articles/euroworks.html. Downloaded on February 27, 2002; "Works Councils." Available on-line. URL: www.diazresearch.com/work_councils.htm. Downloaded on February 25, 2002; "Work Councils—A better way of talking to the boss?" Available on-line. URL: http://flinders.edu.au/news/articles/?story=fj15v12s03. Downloaded on February 24, 2002.

—Carrie Wilson

Worker Adjustment and Retraining Notification Act

The Worker Adjustment and Retraining Notification Act (WARN) requires employers covered by the act to provide 60-day advance notice of large-scale EMPLOYMENT loss, generally resulting from plant closings and mass LAYOFFs. WARN became law in 1989 and generally applies to companies and nonprofit groups with 100 or more employees. Hourly, salaried, and managerial workers are all entitled to notification under WARN. Also, if the sale of a business results in mass layoffs or plant closings, the parties to the sale must give WARN notice. The act defines employment loss as

- employment termination, other than a discharge for cause, voluntary departure, or retirement
- a layoff exceeding 6 months
- a reduction in an employee's hours of work of more than 50 percent in each month of any 6-month period

The act provides a variety of exceptions, including when a company is faltering or suffering unforeseeable business circumstances, in addition to natural disasters. Failure to give notice of impending job loss can lead to penalties, including back pay and benefits for the period of violation of the act. Many states have WARN-like disclosure laws alerting workers to the possibility of layoffs.

Further reading
U.S. Department of Labor WARN Fact Sheet. Available on-line. URL: www.doleta.gov/programs/factsht/warn.htm.

workers' compensation

Workers' compensation is a no-fault system developed by the government in response to serious societal problems that occurred with the significant rise in the number of workers injured in industrial settings. The idea of compensating workers for work-related injuries and that government should ensure such compensation spread to America from Europe during the first decade of the 20th century. The courts at that time generally held that mandatory, government-administered workers' compensation programs denied employers property rights without DUE PROCESS of law. To ease objections, most states made laws that allowed employers to choose whether or not to participate in the program. In 1911 Wisconsin became the first state to enact a workers' compensation law that would stand in court. In 1917 the U.S. Supreme Court ruled that states could legally require employers to provide compensation to injured workers. As a result, many states revised their laws to include mandatory workers' compensation.

Although each state has its own workers' compensation laws, there are three major components to general compensation law.

- medical expenses: the cost for hospitals, doctors, medical treatment, etc.
- disability pay: temporary coverage while workers recover from injuries, or permanent coverage in the event workers do not fully recover; the amount varies but can be as high as one-half to two-thirds of normal pay
- vocational rehabilitation: physical therapy to assist in recovery and/or retraining for a new occupation

Since workers' compensation imposes strict liability without inquiry into fault, an employer could be penalized when its conduct is found to be an egregious violation of federal or state safety standards.

Further reading
Texas Workers' Compensation Commission website. Available on-line. URL: www.twcc.state.tx.us.

workforce   See LABOR FORCE.

Works Progress Administration (Work Projects Administration)

The Works Progress Administration (WPA) was a federal program created during the GREAT DEPRESSION, a time of severe UNEMPLOYMENT, that was intended to stimulate the economy and boost morale by paying unemployed laborers and artisans to do useful projects. Approved by Congress on April 8, 1935, as part of the Emergency Relief Appropriation Act, the WPA, renamed the Work Projects Administration in 1939, was one of the key components of President Franklin D. Roosevelt's New Deal program. The importance Roosevelt attached to the program is illustrated by the fact that he appointed one of his closest lieutenants, Harry Hopkins, to lead the WPA until 1938.

Over its seven years of existence, the WPA's building program included the construction of 116,000 buildings, 78,000 bridges, and 651,000 miles of road as well as the improvement of 800 airports. Altogether more than 8.5 million people worked for the WPA, with 3.5 million employed at its peak. The WPA's National Youth Administration gave work to nearly 1 million students. Federal funding totaled $11 billion.

In addition to its sizable building program, the WPA's Federal Theater, Arts, Music and Writers' Projects supported cultural initiatives around the country. Rising authors such as Zora Neale Hurston, Richard Wright, and

eventual Nobel laureate Saul Bellow wrote state guidebooks and recorded the life stories of more than 10,000 men and women from a variety of regions, occupations, and ethnic groups.

Although the WPA was very popular among the workers and communities it benefited, it was frequently attacked by President Roosevelt's enemies, particularly those in Congress who charged that it led to waste and political manipulation. The WPA was finally disbanded in 1943 as wartime PRODUCTION demands greatly reduced unemployment.

Further reading
Adams, Grace Kinckle. *Workers on Relief.* New York: Arno Press, 1971; Burns, James MacGregor. *Roosevelt: The Lion and the Fox 1882–1940.* New York: Harcourt, Brace, 1956; Hopkins, Harry Lloyd. *Spending to Save: The Complete Story of Relief.* New York: W. W. Norton, 1936.

—Megan Fennessy

World Bank (International Bank for Reconstruction and Development)

The World Bank is a joint effort of 180 member countries to provide development assistance to more than 100 developing "client" countries. In the countries where it operates, the World Bank uses a combination of strategic poverty-reduction measures and LOANS to promote health, education, social development, environment protection, institutional development, and governmental self-reliance. The bank operates in five overarching programs.

- The International Development Association provides interest-free loans to the poorest of countries in the greatest economic and development stress.
- The International Bank for Reconstruction and Development provides loans and development assistance to middle-income countries and credit-worthy poorer countries.
- The International Finance Corporation promotes private-sector INVESTMENT within the client country. It tries to serve as an impartial broker to reassure both foreign investors and local partners. It advises businesses entering new countries, and it guides governments trying to create a more hospitable business environment.
- The Multilateral Investment Guarantee Agency promotes direct FOREIGN INVESTMENT in a country by providing what it calls "political risk INSURANCE" or guarantees to investors and lenders.
- The International Centre for Settlement of Investment Disputes (ICSID) provides a forum for settling investment disputes between foreign investors and the host countries.

A BOARD OF DIRECTORS representing the 180 member countries governs the World Bank. Its president is, by tradition, a national from the United States, which is the bank's largest contributor.

The World Bank has been criticized for being too bureaucratic and slow about acting in the cases of regional emergencies. It has also been accused (to a lesser degree than the INTERNATIONAL MONETARY FUND) of meddling in a country's internal affairs and of allowing countries to become too heavily indebted. In recent years, the World Bank has slightly reduced its emphasis on big project loans, providing greater assistance for small-scale local ECONOMIC DEVELOPMENT efforts. The idea for a World Bank was proposed at the 1944 BRETTON WOODS meeting.

—Mack Tennyson

World Intellectual Property Organization

The World Intellectual Property Organization (WIPO) is an agency of the United Nations charged to promote INTELLECTUAL PROPERTY rights worldwide. Intellectual property rights are "works of the mind," including inventions, designs, books, music, and films; TRADEMARKS, COPYRIGHTS, and PATENTs are all considered intellectual property. Protection of intellectual property is critical to stimulating research, development, and ENTREPRENEURSHIP. In a political/economic system where others could usurp peoples' (or businesses) new ideas with no compensation to the inventor, creativity and product improvement would be discouraged.

WIPO administers over 20 intellectual-property treaties among the 177 signatory member states. The treaties can be grouped into three categories: intellectual-property protection, global protection systems, and classification. The first group of treaties defines internationally agreed basic standards of intellectual-property protection. The second group ensures that one international filing registration will have effect in any of the relevant signatory states, thereby simplifying and reducing the cost of registering intellectual property globally. The third group of treaties creates classification systems that organize information about intellectual property into indexed, manageable structures for easy retrieval.

The WIPO evolved out of 19th-century industrialization. The need for international protection of intellectual property became evident when international exhibitors refused to attend the International Exhibition of Inventions in Vienna, Austria, in 1873, because inventors feared their ideas would be stolen. This led to the 1883 Paris Convention for Protection of Industrial Property, the first major international treaty to help protect inventions, trademarks, and industrial designs in other countries. Originally there were 14 member states to the Paris Convention.

In 1886 the Berne Convention for the Protection of Literary and Artistic Works expanded international protection to copyrighted material. Like the Paris Convention, the Berne Convention set up an International Bureau to administer the agreement. Seven years later (1893), the two groups merged to create the United International Bureau for the Protection of Intellectual Property (best known by its French acronym BIRPI). In 1970, following the Convention Establishing the World Intellectual Property Organization, BIRPI became WIPO, and in 1974 it became an agency of the United Nations.

One of the most visible and dynamic roles of the WIPO is overseeing protection of information technology and the INTERNET. The WIPO administers the Arbitration and Mediation Center, created to resolve intellectual property rights disputes. The Center maintains a list of specialized mediators and arbitrators from more than 70 countries, who conduct dispute resolution according to rules determined by the WIPO.

The Center has become a leader in resolving disputes over abusive registration and use of Internet domain names, commonly known as "cybersquatting." To challenge an abusive registration of a domain name, a complainant must prove

- the domain name is identical or confusingly similar to a trademark or service mark in which the complainant has rights
- the person who registered the domain name has no rights or legitimate interests in it
- the domain name was registered or is being used in bad faith to extract payment from the trademark owner or prevent the trademark owner from using the domain name for his or her benefit

In 2000 the Center handled 1,850 cases. The process is conducted on-line, resulting in enforceable decisions within two months.

Further reading

World Intellectual Property Organization website. Available online. URL: www.wipo.org.

World Trade Organization

The World Trade Organization (WTO) is the major global organization involved in negotiating, establishing, and resolving international trade rules and disputes. In 1995 the WTO replaced the General Agreement on Tariffs and Trade (GATT), which was created at the end of World War II to reduce TRADE BARRIERS through multilateral negotiations. The WTO, a powerful and controversial organization, includes more than 140 member countries; China was accepted as a member in 2001.

The WTO and its predecessor, the GATT, were conceived at a conference held at the Mount Washington Hotel in BRETTON WOODS, New Hampshire, in 1944. At Bretton Woods, representatives of allied countries proposed the creation of three important international institutions, the WORLD BANK (International Bank for Reconstruction and

Development), the INTERNATIONAL MONETARY FUND (IMF), and the International Trade Organization (ITO). The ITO was chartered to oversee the GATT, which originally focused on reducing TARIFFs on manufactured goods. One of the reasons for the Bretton Woods conference was the impact of 1930s trade wars on international trade relations. Beginning with the SMOOT-HAWLEY TARIFF ACT in 1930, the United States and its trading partners dramatically increased tariffs (60 percent), devastating international trade and global economic activity. Many economists consider Smoot-Hawley a significant cause of the length and depth of the GREAT DEPRESSION. The proposed ITO and GATT were designed to reduce the likelihood of future trade wars.

The United Nations was given responsibility to manage the ITO and would have had a broad regulatory mandate over trade, EMPLOYMENT rules, and international business practices. However, after initially supporting the ITO, the United States, under pressure from business interests, failed to ratify legislation supporting the organization's creation. That left the GATT, with its focus on reduction in tariffs, without the larger international trade forum, the ITO.

The GATT, administered from Geneva, Switzerland, initially included 23 countries, with Canada and the United States acting as major participants. Central to the GATT (and now the WTO) is the principle of most-favored-nation status. Membership in GATT entitled countries to pay the lowest tariffs applied to another country's goods. Many countries, particularly as a result of past colonial relationships, allowed PRODUCTs from some countries to enter their country at a lower tariff than the same products coming from another country. This created an advantage for products from countries receiving favored treatment. Membership in GATT gave each country the right to similar treatment. In addition, GATT membership gave countries the right to use the GATT dispute resolution procedures and to participate in future trade-liberalization negotiations.

After its inception, the GATT went through a number of "rounds" of trade negotiations, including those held at Geneva (1947); Annecy, France (1948); Torquay, England (1950); Geneva (1956); Geneva (1960–61); "Kennedy" Geneva (1964–67); "Tokyo" Geneva (1973–79); and Uruguay (1986–93). As can be observed from this, the rounds of GATT negotiations became longer over time. First, membership expanded and, acting on a basis of mutual consensus, the process became more complex. Second, the early rounds involved mostly reductions in tariff barriers, while later rounds expanded trade-liberalization efforts into new territory, including NONTARIFF BARRIERS, barriers to trade in services, and special provisions for EMERGING MARKETS. Given the United States' growing international trade power since World War II, most countries preferred GATT as a multilateral forum for negotiations rather than bilateral negotiations.

However, frustrated by the protracted nature of the Uruguay Round, Canadian interest in direct negotiations with the United States increased, resulting in the UNITED STATES-CANADA FREE TRADE AGREEMENT (1989), which became the basis for the NORTH AMERICAN FREE TRADE AGREEMENT (NAFTA).

In 1995, after eight years of negotiation, the GATT was replaced by the WTO. Today over 90 percent of international trade is governed by WTO rules. In addition to efforts to reduce tariffs, the WTO is committed to eliminating nontariff barriers. Critics argue the WTO represents a significant shift of power from citizens and national governments to a "global authority run by unselected bureaucrats." The WTO strengthened the trade-dispute resolution process established in the GATT, making WTO panel decisions binding, with authorization to impose trade sanctions if a country does not comply with the decisions.

Under the WTO, member countries have the right to challenge other countries' federal, state, or local laws as impediments to international trade. In the United States, if the WTO panel finds a law to be WTO-illegal, the federal government may overturn local or state laws or face international trade sanctions. U.S. businesses have used WTO authority to challenge Mexican laws, and Mexican labor groups have used this to challenge U.S. business practices. Critics suggest this undermines democratic practices and will lead to changes in laws and regulations to the least-trade-restrictive level, reducing the right and ability of a nation to control labor and environmental standards. In December 1999 the WTO attempted to hold meetings in Seattle, Washington, to begin the process of a new round of negotiations, including a multilateral INVESTMENT agreement liberalizing rules regarding the flow of CAPITAL among countries. President Bill Clinton and his administration had visions of this being part of his presidential legacy. Administration and WTO leaders were shocked by the level of protests by environmental, labor, and social activist groups and ended the meetings abruptly.

WTO supporters and opponents have developed "Top 10" lists for the benefits of the WTO and reasons to oppose it. The Global Exchanges' "Top 10 Reasons to Oppose the World Trade Organization" include

1. The WTO only serves the interests of MULTINATIONAL CORPORATIONS.
2. The WTO is a stacked court.
3. The WTO tramples over labor and human rights.
4. The WTO is destroying the environment.
5. The WTO is killing people.
6. The U.S. adoption of the WTO is undemocratic.
7. The WTO undermines local development and penalizes poor countries.
8. The WTO is increasing inequality.
9. The WTO undermines national sovereignty.
10. The tide is turning against FREE TRADE and the WTO.

The WTO lists "10 benefits of the WTO trading system."

1. The system helps keep the peace.
2. The system allows disputes to be handled constructively.
3. A system based on rules rather than power makes life easier for all.
4. Freer trade cuts the cost of living.
5. It gives consumers more choice, and a broader range of qualities to choose from.
6. Trade raises INCOMES.
7. Trade stimulates ECONOMIC GROWTH, and that can be good news for EMPLOYMENT.
8. The basic principles make the system economically more efficient, and they cut COSTS.
9. The system shields governments from narrow interests.
10. The system encourages good government.

Further reading
Anderson, Sarah, and John Cavanagh. "World Trade Organization." *Foreign Policy in Focus* 2, no. 14 (January 1997). Available on-line. URL: www.foreignpolicy-infocus.org; Folsom, Ralph H., and W. Davis Folsom. *Understanding NAFTA and Its International Business Implications.* New York: Matthew Bender/Irwin, 1996; "Top Ten Reasons to Oppose the World Trade Organization." Global Economy. Available on-line. URL: www.globalexchange. org; World Trade Organization website. Available on-line. URL: www.wto.org.

World Wide Web

The World Wide Web (WWW) is a system that connects computer networks around the world. Software engineer Tim Berners-Lee is credited with the creation of the Web through the application of hypertext to networked computers. Hypertext includes hypertext markup language (HTML), which is used for creating documents with hypertext links; and hypertext transfer protocol (HTTP) for specifying how networks respond when a user clicks on the link. In addition, a system of universal resource locators (URLs) provides each item on the Web with a unique "address." Hypertext was first proposed by engineer Vannevar Bush in 1945 and had been used by researchers to interlink material among different files on individual computers.

During the 1980s, while working at CERN (a European particle-physics laboratory in Geneva, Switzerland), Berners-Lee developed a system to allow nuclear physicists at CERN using a closed computer network to access documents created by different individuals and groups within the laboratory. In 1991 Berners-Lee expanded the hypertext system he had created at CERN and made it available on the INTERNET. As he stated in an interview, "What was really new with the Web was the idea that you could code all the information needed to find any document on the network into a short string of characters." These strings, originally called universal document identifiers, are now known as URLs. Berners-Lee did not set out to create the Web. Instead, as he states, "It was something I needed in my work. CERN is composed of a variety of bright and creative people from institutes in many countries. When they work together on a project, the result can be a tangle of complexity. . . . I found a tremendous need to be able to find out what was going on, particularly the interdependencies—what work was related to what."

It did not take long for the Web to move from a resource for document sharing among physicists to a global system of information access. In 1995 Netscape co-founder Mark Andreessen received the Stewart Alsop Industry Achievement Award for his "choice of HTML as the Web standard." Andreessen introduced the Netscape Navigator in 1994, significantly improving access to the Web. For several "generations," Netscape Navigator dominated World Wide Web access before being surpassed by Microsoft's Internet Explorer, the subject of a major antitrust lawsuit.

In addition to serving as a system of access to documents, the World Wide Web facilitated the creation of cyber-businesses, businesses with no "brick and mortar" locations, existing only in the electronic files on computers around the world. Even though the dot-com industry first flourished and then imploded, the Web will continue to evolve and expand as a home for E-BUSINESS, E-COMMERCE, and INTERNET MARKETING.

See also CYBERSPACE.

Further reading
Alsop, Stewart. "Marc Andreessen: Vice President of Technology, Netscape Communications Corp." *Infoworld,* 29 January 1996; Brody, Herb. "The Web Maestro: An Interview with Tim Berners-Lee." *Technology Review,* July 1996.

wrongful discharge

Wrongful discharge occurs when an employee is terminated for a reason other than JUST CAUSE. The concept of wrongful discharge is one of the results of the development of the concept of EMPLOYMENT-AT-WILL. Most employee/employer relationships are "at will," meaning that either party can terminate the relationship at any time and for any reason. Over the years, however, certain protections have been put in place for employees. An employer can be sued for wrongful discharge if he or she is seen to have violated any of these protections.

There are several federal laws that try to prevent wrongful discharge. The WAGNER ACT protects the activities of UNION members. The FAIR LABOR STANDARDS ACT (FLSA) demands that covered employees are paid a MINIMUM WAGE and overtime wages for any hours over 40 worked in any one week. An employer who fires a worker who tries to exercise his or her FLSA rights can be sued for wrongful discharge. Title VII of the CIVIL RIGHTS ACT of

1964 protects workers who may otherwise be discriminated against on the basis of race, color, religion, gender, or national origin. The Age Discrimination Employment Act protects against age discrimination, and the AMERICANS WITH DISABILITIES ACT protect employees with physical or mental disabilities. The EMPLOYEE RETIREMENT INCOME SECURITY ACT of 1974 prohibits the firing of employees in order to deny them retirement benefits. The Occupational Safety and Health Act protects workers who try to assert their rights to a safe workplace. The FAMILY AND MEDICAL LEAVE ACT (FMLA) gives employees up to 12 weeks to care for themselves or family members with serious medical conditions and also provides time off following the birth or adoption of a child. An employer cannot discharge an employee who wishes to take advantage of the FMLA. Finally, the CONSUMER CREDIT PROTECTION ACT prohibits the discharge of employees on the basis of garnishment of wages. States can also enact their own employee-protection laws, and most have done so.

Beyond federal and state laws, there are other exceptions to employment-at-will rules. Both written CONTRACTS and oral agreements have been used to challenge an employee's discharge, as have expectations that can be reasonably made from personnel manuals and policy handbooks. Many companies now try to delineate just causes for termination in contracts or employee handbooks. A wrongful discharge suit may be brought against an employer who fires an employee for reasons that would be considered against public policy. Examples of this type of wrongful discharge would include an employee fired for refusing to violate a law during the performance of his or her duties, or the discharge of an employee who reports violations by the employer to law enforcement agencies or other authorities ("whistle-blowing").

An at-will employee cannot guarantee that he or she will not be a victim of wrongful discharge, and an employer cannot be sure that what he or she considers a just termination will not be challenged. However, both parties can try to protect themselves by documenting expectations of performance before EMPLOYMENT has begun.

See also DOT-COMS; OCCUPATIONAL SAFETY AND HEALTH ADMINISTRATION; WHISTLE-BLOWER.

—Gretchen Wade

Y

yield curve

In finance, the relationship between short-term rates and long-term rates is known as the term structure of INTEREST RATES. A yield curve is a picture of the term structure of interest rates. For securities, on a graph where the horizontal axis represents years to maturity and the vertical axis represents interest rates, a yield curve illustrates the relationship between yields and maturities. Short-term securities (money-market instruments, for example) are represented on the horizontal between zero and one years to maturity, and longer-term securities (capital market instruments) are represented on the horizontal axis beyond the one-year point.

Most yield curves are upward-sloping and are known as normal yield curves. They have positive slopes because, historically, short-term rates have been lower than long-term rates. The longer a security's term to maturity, the higher its yield. Thus, when plotted, the yield curve, consisting of yields of all securities from short-term to long-term ones, must be upward-sloping.

During periods of high INFLATION, which in turn causes higher interest rates, especially for short-term securities, yield curves can have negative slopes. Such yield curves are known as inverted yield curves. Because investors expect the high rates of inflation to subside in the future, they expect long-term rates to be lower than current short-term rates. When plotted, these yield curves will have negative slopes. For example, in early 1980, when inflation had risen to double-digit levels, yield curves plotted at that point in time were inverted yield curves. Since that time, inflation has been better controlled and has subsided to single-digit levels, and yield curves have been normal ones.

Z

zero-sum game

A zero-sum game is a game or situation where the gains by winners are offset by losses to losers. Zero-sum games are sometimes used to describe market situations in which increased sales by one firm come at the expense of other firms. The total sales remain the same, only each firm's share of the total changes. If, in a market, there are only a fixed number of potential buyers, increased sales by one competitor result in lost sales by other competitors. Zero-sum games are one form of GAME THEORY, models used to describe results of market strategies depending on the strategies other participants in the market employ.

Well-known MIT economist Lester Thurow popularized the term *zero-sum game* in his 1981 book *Zero-sum Society: Distribution and Possibilities for Economic Change.* Written during a period of economic stagnation, Thurow suggested MACROECONOMICS comprised a zero-sum game, and as such, well-off members of society must bear the brunt of taxation and other government-sponsored economic actions for the benefit of all members of the society.

Recently the term was used to describe growth of the INTERNET, one writer suggesting that Internet growth represents a shift of RESOURCES rather than an expansion of resources and economic output. Zero-sum game is also used to describe the conflict between work and personal life, with additional time and resources being given to one outcome at the expense of the other. Technology companies created the term *zero-drag* to describe employees who did not have spouses or dependents and therefore had nothing to prevent them from devoting more time to the company.

It is often argued that COMPETITION in consumer goods markets results in a win-win situation in which both buyers and sellers seek out the most return for their limited resources and, in the process, create economic efficiency. Market exchanges could be viewed as a zero-sum game, whereby the benefits to either buyer or seller come at the expense of the other. Financial markets can exemplify the zero-sum game, since for every buyer there is a seller. In early 2001 the *Wall Street Journal* described "dot-com" insiders who sold their shares before the collapse of the technology market. Some insiders sold their shares for more than the current market value of the companies for which they worked.

Further reading

Miller, Roger Leroy. *Economics Today,* 11th ed. Boston: Addison Wesley, 2001.

zero-base budgeting (zero-based budgeting)

Zero-base budgeting (also called zero-based budgeting, or ZBB) is a system of BUDGETING in which all expenditures are justified each year. This is in contrast to the typical budgeting process that evaluates only amounts in excess of the previous year's budget. In ZBB each department must justify all of its funding for the next year. This process starts with an assumed "zero base" and must show how every expenditure helps the organization meet its objectives.

Peter A. Pyhrr at Texas Instruments first introduced ZBB; nonprofit and government organizations quickly adopted it and are its most enthusiastic users. ZBB usually involves the following steps.

1. Define the organization's mission and goals.
2. Identify the organization's decision units. A ZBB decision unit is an operating division of the organization, usually a cost center or budget center. The decision unit develops decision packages.
3. Identify a decision unit's decision packages. These are descriptions of each program that will be operated by the decision unit. A decision package states a specific contribution it makes toward reaching the organization's objectives and usually presents several alternate ways that it could make its contribution towards the

objectives. For each alternative, the decision package will specify objectives, activities, RESOURCES, COSTS, etc.

4. Analyze decision packages. Managers must review each decision package to determine if in fact it contributes to the mission and objectives. They must consider the impact of eliminating the decision package and must review the alternatives to determine which decision package alternative is most cost-effective.

5. Rank decision packages. After the analysis, management must rank the decision packages relative to its cost-effectiveness and how well it contributes to the overall goals and objectives.

6. Prepare a budget. This pulls together the cost of each of the decision packages that have been approved.

7. Monitor and evaluate actual budget performance. This is relatively easy after the work already done to develop the decision packages' objectives.

The process of developing goals, identifying decision units, and developing, analyzing, and ranking decision packages is more beneficial than the actual budget savings that the process produces. The organization can use the process to organize their thinking relative to the organization's overall priorities. Everything and everyone has to justify their continued existence in light of the organization's mission.

Most ZBB critics point out that it sounds good to consider everything starting from a zero base. However, most of the items in an organization's budget are not as flexible as ZBB assumes. Many organization costs are a product of previous ORGANIZATIONAL COMMITMENTS. Interest, LEADERSHIP salaries, utilities, DEPRECIATION, and INSURANCE are more or less fixed and must be immediately added to any budget that assumes the organization's continuation. In many organizations this leaves precious little to be evaluated from a zero base.

zoning

The term *zoning* may be used for "zoning laws," "zoning ordinances," or "zoning regulations." The statuary laws governing zoning may be at the local, state, or federal level. Zoning controls how the land may be used in a particular region or community. A local community may be classified as residential, commercial, industrial, or agricultural. An example of federal government zoning is preserving natural RESOURCES through establishing National Parks. The classification of the land will dictate the ability to operate a business in a particular area.

Historically, as the nation became more populated and space started to become an issue, zoning was used to maintain the space in a community. Unfortunately, it was used at the same time to segregate against various populations by limiting the number of multifamily apartments affordable to lower-income residents. New York City established the first zoning ordinance in 1916.

Two acts by the federal government laid the groundwork for future zoning. The Standard Zoning Enabling Act of 1922 and the Standard State Planning Enabling Act of 1928 gave states and local governments the ability to establish their own zoning laws. In addition, in 1926 the U.S. Supreme Court upheld zoning as a legal way to control land use with the case *Village of Euclid v. Ambler Realty Co.* In this case, zoning had been for single-family only. As a result of these federal government actions, most states enacted zoning laws in the 1930s.

Today zoning has an impact on businesspeople, including local and home-based entrepreneurs. The ability to operate a small business, especially a home-based business may be affected by zoning. A prospective business owner should investigate the local zoning laws prior to establishing a business. If zoning is for residential use, a home-based business may or may not be allowed. In addition, there may be restrictions on client parking, storage, the number of employees who work at the site, and outdoor signage.

In any case where zoning is prohibitive, a prospective businessperson may choose to file for a "variance" with the zoning board to waive the restrictions. Some home-based business owners operate illegally, ignoring zoning laws. Balancing the interests of business owners and residents is often difficult. Neighborhoods want to prevent overcrowding and maintain a safe environment, and one argument against businesses in a community is the potential for increased traffic. In addition, some home-based businesses use materials that are potentially dangerous.

Home-based business owners argue their businesses benefit local neighborhoods. Home-based businesses reduce rush-hour traffic; increase local jobs; and position people in the neighborhood during the day when most houses are unoccupied, adding to neighborhood security.

Zoning is also used to control the types of business activities in a community. Many towns have zoning ordinances controlling adult stores, drug and rehabilitation centers, and religious institutions. Often zoning regulations are challenged under the first amendment of the U.S. Constitution, guaranteeing freedom of speech.

Further reading
American Association of Home-Based Businesses website. Available on-line. URL: www.aahbb.org.

—Diane Zydlewski

BIBLIOGRAPHY

Anderson, Carl R. *Management: Skills, Functions, and Organization Performance.* Boston: Allyn and Bacon, 1988.

Appleyard, Dennis R., and Alfred J. Field Jr. *International Economics.* Homewood, Ill.: Irwin Publishing, 1994.

Archer North's Performance Appraisal website. Available on-line. URL: http:/www.performance-appraisal.com.

Axelrod, Karen, and Bruce Brumberg. *Watch It Made in the USA,* 2d ed. Santa Fe, N. Mex.: John Muir Publishing, 1998.

Baker, R. Jerry. *Purchasing Factomatic: A Portfolio of Successful Forms, Reports, Records, and Procedures.* Upper Saddle River, N.J.: Prentice Hall, 1977.

Bearden, William O., Thomas Ingram, and Raymond LaForge. *Marketing Principles & Perspectives,* 4th ed. Boston: Irwin/ McGraw-Hill, 2004.

Bender, David, pub. *Business Ethics.* Opposing Viewpoints Series. San Diego, Calif.: Greenhaven Press, Inc., 2001.

Berkley, George, and John Rouse. *The Craft of Public Administration.* 7th ed. Madison, Wisc.: Brown and Benchmark Publishers, 1997.

Birnbaum, Michael H., ed. *Psychological Experiments on the Internet.* San Diego, Calif.: Academic Press, 2000.

Black, Henry Campbell, et al. *Black's Law Dictionary,* 6th ed. St. Paul: West Publishing Co., 1991.

Bly, Robert W. "Persuasion Secrets of Marketing Pros." *DM News,* 21 October 2002.

Boone, Louis E., and David L. Kurtz. *Contemporary Marketing,* 10th ed. Fort Worth, Tex.: Dryden Press, 2001.

————. *Contemporary Marketing,* 11th ed. Fort Worth, Tex.: Dryden Press, 2003.

Boyes, William J., and Michael Melvin. *Fundamentals of Economics,* 2d ed. Boston: Houghton Mifflin, 2002.

————. *Microeconomics,* 5th ed. Boston: Houghton Mifflin, 2002.

Burke, Barlow D. *Personal Property in a Nutshell,* 2d ed. Eagan, Minn.: West Group, 2003.

Busby, Michael. *Demystifying EDI.* Plano, Tex.: Wordware Publishing, 2000.

Cammack, Mark E., and Norman Garland. *Advanced Criminal Procedure in a Nutshell.* Eagan, Minn.: West Group, 2001.

Cammarano, James. "Project Management: How to Make It Happen." *IIE Solutions* 29, No. 12. Available from Dialog, Expanded Academic ASAP, article A20331320, 1997.

Carroll, Archie B., and Ann K. Buchholtz. *Business & Society,* 5th ed. Mason, Ohio: Thomson Learning, 2003.

Cavinato, Joseph. *Purchasing Handbook,* 6th ed. New York: McGraw Hill, 2001.

Champy, James A. "From Reengineering to X-Engineering." In *Organization 21C: Someday All Organizations Will Lead This Way.* Edited by Subir Chowdhury. Upper Saddle River, N.J.: Prentice Hall, 2003.

Cooper, Robin, and Robert Kaplan. *Cost and Effect: Using Integrated Cost Systems to Drive Profitability and Performance.* New York: Harvard Business School Publishing, 1997.

Daft, Richard. *Organization Theory and Design,* 6th ed. Eagan, Minn.: West Group, 1997.

Dark, Taylor E. *The Unions and the Democrats: An Enduring Alliance, Updated Edition.* Ithaca, N.Y.: Cornell University Press, 2001.

DeGeorge, Richard T. *Business Ethics.* Upper Saddle River, N.J.: Prentice Hall, 1999.

Department of the Treasury, Internal Revenue Service. *Publication 550: Investment Income and Expenses (Including Capital Gains and Losses).* Cat. No. 15093R, 26–28.

Deresky, Helen. *International Management,* 2d ed. Reading, Mass.: Addison-Wesley, 1997.

Dessler, Gary. *Human Resource Management,* 9th ed. Upper Saddle River, N.J.: Prentice Hall, 2003.

Downs, John, and Jordan Elliot Goodman. *Finance and Investment Handbook.* 6th ed. New York: Barron's Educational Series, 2003.

Dunphy, Dexter. "The Sustainability of Organizations." In *Organization 21C: Someday All Organizations Will Lead This Way.* Edited by Subir Chowdhury. Upper Saddle River, N.J.: Prentice Hall, 2003.

Dwyer, F. Robert, and John F. Tanner Jr. *Business Marketing,* 2d ed. Boston: McGraw-Hill, 2002.

Engdahl, David E. *Constitutional Federalism in a Nutshell.* Eagan, Minn.: West Group, 1987.

Ethics Resource Center website. Available on-line. URL: http://www.ethics.org.

Etzel, Michael J., Bruce J. Walker, and William J. Staunton. *Marketing.* 12th ed. Boston: McGraw-Hill, 2001.

Fabozzi, Frank J. *The Handbook of Fixed Income Securities,* 5th ed. New York: McGraw-Hill, 1997.

Faerber, Esme. *All About Bonds and Bond Mutual Funds,* 2d ed. New York: McGraw-Hill, 2000.

Federal Home Loan Bank website. Available on-line. URL: http://www.fhlb.gov.

Fisher, Bruce D., and Michael J. Phillips. *The Legal, Ethical, and Regulatory Environment of Business,* 8th ed. Cincinnati: Thomson/South-Western, 2003.

Fisher, Cynthia D., Lyle F. Schoenfeldt, and James B. Shaw. *Human Resource Management,* 5th ed. Boston: Houghton Mifflin, 2003.

Folsom, Ralph H., Michael Gordon, and John Spanogle. *International Business Transactions in a Nutshell,* 6th ed. Eagan, Minn.: West Group, 2000.

Folsom, Ralph H., and W. Davis Folsom. *NAFTA Law and Business.* The Hague, Netherlands: Kluwer Law International, 1998.

———. *Understanding NAFTA and Its International Business Implications.* New York: Matthew Bender/Irwin, 1996.

Friedenthal, Jack H., and Arthur R. Miller. *Civil Procedure: Sum & Substance.* 4th ed. Encino, CA: Herbert Legal Series, 1988.

Gaither, Norman, and Greg Frazier. *Operational Management,* 9th ed. Cincinnati, Ohio: South-Western, 2002.

Galbraith, John Kenneth. *The Affluent Society.* Boston: Houghton Mifflin, 1958.

Gale Group, *Encyclopedia of Associations,* 37th ed. Detroit: Gale Press, 2001.

Gordon, George J., and Michael E. Milakovich. *Public Administration in America,* 6th ed. New York: St. Martin's Press, 1998.

Gitman, Lawrence J., and Michael D. Joehnk. *Personal Financial Planning,* 9th ed. Cincinnati: South-Western, 2001.

Goffee, Rob, and Gareth Jones. *The Character of a Corporation: How Your Company's Culture Can Make or Break Your Business.* New York: Harper Business, 1998.

Gunn, Ronald A. "Five Not So-easy Pieces of Matrix Management." Available on-line. URL: http://www.stategic-futures.com/articles/matrix/5pc-1.htm.

Hellriegel, Don, Susan E. Jackson, and John W. Slocum Jr. *Management,* 8th ed. Cincinnati: Southwestern, 1999.

———. *Management: A Competency-Based Approach,* 9th ed. Cincinnati: Southwestern, 2002.

Helms, Marilyn M. *Encyclopedia of Management,* 4th ed. Detroit: Gale Group, 2000.

Hodgetts, Richard M. *Management Theory, Process, and Practice,* 5th ed. San Diego: Harcourt Brace Jovanovich, 1990.

———, and Fred Luthans. *International Management: Culture, Strategy, and Behavior,* 4th ed. New York: Irwin McGraw-Hill, 2000.

Hofstede, Geert. *Culture's Consequences: International Differences in Work-related Values.* Newbury Park, Calif.: Sage Publishing, 1980.

Institute for Supply Management website. Available on-line. URL: http://www.ism.ws.

Internal Revenue Service. "Frequently Asked Questions—How Can I Recognize an Abusive Tax Shelter?" Available on-line. URL:http://www.irs.gov/faqs/display/0,,il=52&genericID=157 93,00.html. Downloaded on February 13, 2002.

———. "Topic 454—Tax Shelters." Available on-line. URL: http://www.irs.gov/file/display/0,,il=52&genericID=16225,00. html. Downloaded on February 13, 2002.

"Investing Basics: Bonds." Available on-line. URL: http://www. motleyfool.com

Jilovec, Nahid. *The A to Z of EDI & Its Role in E-Commerce,* 2d ed. Loveland, Colo.: 29th Street Press/NEWS/400 Books, 1998.

Johnson, Calvin H. "What's a Tax Shelter?" *Tax Notes* 68 (14 August 1995): 879–888.

Johnson, William C. *Public Administration: Policy, Politics, and Practice.* Guilford, Conn.: Dushkin Publishing Group, 1992.

Kane, Mary K. *Civil Procedure in a Nutshell,* 4th ed. Eagan, Minn.: West Group, 1996.

Kidwell, David S., Richard L. Peterson, and David W. Blackwell. *Financial Institutions, Markets and Money,* 7th ed. Fort Worth, Tex.: Dryden Press, 2000.

Klonoff, Robert H. *Class Actions and other Multi-Party Litigation in a Nutshell.* Eagan, Minn.: West Group, 1999.

Koch, A. Robert. *Economic Principles: Growth and Environment.* Westport, Conn.: AVI Publishing, 1986.

Lamb, Charles W., Jr., Joseph F. Hair Jr., and Carl McDaniel. *Marketing.* 6th ed. Cincinnati: South-Western, 2002.

Lo, Andrew, and A. C. Mackinlay. *A Non-Random Walk Down Wall Street.* Princeton, N.J.: Princeton University Press, 2001.

Management Learning. Available on-line. URL: http: //www. management learning.com/topi/mngtmtrx.html.

Mangum, Garth L. *Union Resilience in Troubled Times: The Story of the Operating Engineers, AFL-CIO, 1960–1993.* Armonk, N.Y.: M. E. Sharp, 1994.

Malkiel, Burton G. *A Random Walk Down Wall Street,* 8th ed. New York: Norton, 2003.

Mallor, Jane P., A. James Barnes, Thomas Bowers, Michael J. Philips, and Arlen W. Langvardt. *Business Law and the Regulatory Environment.* 11th ed. Boston: McGraw-Hill, 2001.

Marsh, Gene H. *Consumer Protection Law in a Nutshell,* 3d ed. Eagan, Minn.: West Group, 1999.

Mauer, John G., et al., eds. *Encyclopedia of Business.* New York: Gale Research Group, 1995.

McFarland, Dalton E. *Management and Society.* Upper Saddle River, N.J.: Prentice Hall, 1982.

Miller, Roger LeRoy. *Economics Today,* 11th ed. Boston: Addison Wesley, 2001.

Mishkin, Frederic S. *The Economics of Money, Banking, and Financial Markets.* 6th ed. Boston: Addison Wesley, 2001.

Moorman, Jerry, and James W. Halloran. *Contemporary Entrepreneurship.* Cincinnati, Ohio: South-Western, 1995.

Mortgage Bankers Association website. Available on-line. URL: http://www.mbaa.org.

Mort, Jo-Ann, ed. *Not Your Father's Union Movement: Inside the AFL-CIO.* New York: Verso, 1998.

Myers, David G. *Exploring Psychology,* 5th ed. New York: Worth Publishers, 2002.

Nolan-Haley, Jacqueline M. *Alternative Dispute Resolution in a Nutshell,* 2d ed. Eagan, Minn.: West Group, 2001.

O'Connell, John T. *Remedies in a Nutshell,* 2d ed. Eagan, Minn.: West Group, 1984.

Oskamp, Stuart, and P. Wesley Schultz. *Applied Social Psychology,* 2d ed. Upper Saddle River, N.J.: Prentice-Hall, 1998.

O'Sullivan, Arthur, and Steven M. Sheffrin. *Economics: Principles and Tools.* Upper Saddle River, N.J.: Prentice Hall, 2001.

"Other Types of Bonds: Callable Bonds." Available on-line. URL: http://www.cnet.com.

Perreault, William D., Jr., and E. Jerome McCarthy. *Basic Marketing.* Boston: McGraw-Hill, 1999.

Peter, Dr. Laurence J., and Raymond Hull. *The Peter Principle— Why Things Always Go Wrong.* New York: William Morrow, 1971.

Pride, William O., and O. C. Ferrell. *Marketing Concepts and Strategies,* 12th ed. Boston: Houghton Mifflin, 2003.

Render, Barry, and Ralph M. Stair Jr. *Quantitative Analysis for Management.* Boston: Allyn and Bacon, 1988.

Robbins, Stephen P. *Organizational Behavior.* Upper Saddle River, N.J.: Prentice Hall, 2003.

Rosenbloom, David H. *Public Administration: Understanding Management, Politics, and Law in the Public Sector,* 4th ed. New York: McGraw-Hill, 1998.

Ruffin, Roy J., and Paul R. Gregory. *Principles of Economics,* 7th ed. Boston: Addison Wesley, 2000.

Schemerhorn, John R., Jr., James G. Hunt, and Richard N. Osborn. *Basic Organizational Behavior,* 2d ed. New York: John Wiley & Sons, 1998.

Schultz, Duane, and Sydney Ellen Schultz. *Psychology and Work Today: An Introduction to Industrial and Organizational Psychology,* 8th ed. New York: Macmillan Publishing, 2001.

Schumacher, E. F. *Small Is Beautiful: Economics as If People Mattered.* New York: HarperCollins, 1973; Schumacher Society website. Available on-line. URL: http://www.schumachersociety.org.

Shafritz, Jay M., and E. W. Russell. *Introducing Public Administration,* 2d ed. New York: Addison Wesley Longman, 2000.

Sheldon, Jonathan, and Carolyn L. Carter. *Unfair and Deceptive Acts and Practices,* 5th ed. Boston: National Consumer Law Center, 2001.

Sherriton, Jacalyn, and James L. Stern. *Corporate Culture/Team Culture: Removing the Hidden Barriers to Team Success.* Atlanta: American Management Association, 1997.

Slavin, Stephen L. *Economics,* 6th ed. Boston: Irwin-McGraw Hill, 2001.

Stevenson, William J. *Production Operations Management,* 6th ed. Boston: McGraw-Hill, 1999.

Stillman, Richard J., II. *Public Administration: Concepts and Cases,* 7th ed. Boston: Houghton Mifflin, 2000.

"A Stock Buyer's Guide to Investing: Fourth Quarter 2001." Available on-line. URL: http://www.solomonsmithbarney.com.

Stockton, John M., and Frederick H. Miller. *Sales and Leases of Goods in a Nutshell,* 3d ed. Eagan, Minn.: West Group, 1992.

Stoner, James F., and R. Edward Freeman. *Management,* 5th ed. Upper Saddle River, N.J.: Prentice Hall, 1992.

Sullivan, Jeremiah J. *Exploring International Business Environments,* 1st ed. New York: Pearson Custom Publishing, 1999.

Tillman, Ray M., and Michael S. Cummings. *The Transformation of U.S. Unions: Voices, Visions, and Strategies from the Grassroots.* Boulder, Colo.: Lynne Rienner Publishers, Inc., 1999.

Train, John. *Famous Financial Fiascos.* New York: Clarkson N. Potter, 1985.

Tribe, Laurence H. *American Constitutional Law,* 2d ed. Minelo, N.Y.: The Foundation Press, 2001.

Wade, Jack Warren, Jr. "Tax Shelters." Available on-line. URL: http://www.unclefed.com/Audit-Proofing/step4-3.html. Downloaded on February 13, 2002.

Werhane, Patricia H., and Edward R. Freeman, eds. *The Blackwell Encyclopedic Dictionary of Business Ethics.* Cambridge, Mass.: Blackwell Business, 1997.

Woelfel, Charles J. *Encyclopedia of Banking and Finance,* 10th ed. Chicago: Probus Publishing Company, 1994.

Wright, Sharon Saltzgiver, *Getting Started in Bonds.* New York: John Wiley & Sons, 2003.

Zant, Peter. *Microchip Fabrication.* New York: McGraw-Hill, 2000.

INDEX

Boldface page numbers denote extensive treatment of a topic. *Italic* page numbers refer to illustrations.

A

AAUP (American Association of University Professors) 469
ABA. *See* American Bankers Association; American Bar Association
Abbott Labs 476
ABC (activity-based costing) 4
Abercrombie, Neil 268
AB-PAC (Anheuser-Busch Political Action Committee) 359
ABSs. *See* asset-backed securities
ACAs (Agricultural Credit Associations) 184
accounting. *See* financial accounting; managerial accounting; national income accounting
Accounting Oversight Board (AOB) 1–2
accounts payable, trade credit 2, 57
accounts receivable 2–3, 24, 36, 57, 178
accrual basis, cash basis 3, 5
ACH (automatic clearing house) 151
achievement motivation 3–4, 157
acid rain 360–361
acid-test (quick) ratio 198
Ackerman, Ernest 429, 482
acquisitions. *See* mergers and acquisitions
ACSI. *See* American Customer Satisfaction Index
action call 60–61
activity-based costing (ABC) 4
ADA. *See* Americans with Disabilities Act
Adams, Stacy J. 370
adaptability screening 4
Addey, John 455
adjustable rate mortgages (ARMs) 317
adjusted gross income (AGI) 235
adjusting entry, trial balance, adjusted trial balance 4–5
administrative law 5
adoption process 5–6
ADRs. *See* American depositary receipts
ad valorem taxes 382, 444–445
Advanced Research Projects Agency (ARPA) 255
advertising 6–7
    Better Business Bureau 30
    brand names 38

break-even analysis 39
copy 93
deceptive trade practices 116
demographics 120
distribution channels 130
infomercials 243
Internet 256
marketing, communications 293
product placement 377
push and pull strategies 389
sales promotions 412
Standard Rate and Data Service 432
Wheeler-Lea Act 482–483
advertising agencies 7, 285
AE. *See* aggregate expenditures
AEI (American Enterprise Institute) 451
AFDC. *See* Aid for Families with Dependent Children
affinity programs 147
affirmative action. *See* equal employment opportunity and affirmative action
affluent society 7
AFL. *See* American Federation of Labor
AFL-CIO. *See* American Federation of Labor and Congress of Industrial Organizations
Africa 346
African Americans 242
AFT (American Federation of Teachers) 469
Age Discrimination in Employment Act of 1967 260, 491
agency theory 7–8
agents, manufacturers' 290
aggregate expenditures (AE) 262, 270, 284, 324, 325
aggregate income 235
AGI (adjusted gross income) 235
aging of accounts. *See* bad debts, aging of accounts
agribusiness 9, 74, 182
Agricultural Adjustment Act of 1938 348
Agricultural Credit Associations (ACAs) 184
Agricultural Marketing Act of 1929 184

agricultural support programs 8–9, 74–75, 395
Agricultural Workers Association 469
A. H. Robins 46
agriculture 14, 61–62, 75–76, 144, 181–182, 184, 348, 366, 441
AICPA. *See* American Institute of Certified Public Accountants
AIDA. *See* attention, interest, desire, action concept
Aid to Families with Dependent Children (AFDC) 9–10, 215, 482
Aiken (South Carolina) 119
AIO. *See* attitude, interests, opinions statements
airline industry 64–65, 167, 185–186, 257, 338
air pollution control 68–69
Alaskan oil spill 224
Albania 362
Algeria 344
AlliedSignal 359
Allis-Chalmers 365
AMA. *See* American Medical Association
Amazon.com 29, 48, 257, 258, 271, 302
American Airlines 65, 147
American Association of University Professors (AAUP) 469
American Bankers Association (ABA) 10–11
American Bar Association (ABA) 11, 309
American Competitiveness in the 21st Century Act (2000) 477
American Customer Satisfaction Index (ACSI) 11, 111
American depositary receipts (ADRs) 12, 217, 218
American dream 12
American Enterprise Institute (AEI) 451
American Federation of Labor (AFL) 12–13, 15, 358, 468
American Federation of Labor and Congress of Industrial Organizations (AFL-CIO) 12–13, 469
American Federation of Teachers (AFT) 469
American Industrial Revolution 13–15, 160, 421

American Institute of Certified Public Accountants (AICPA) 15, 59–60, 195, 215
American Legacy Foundation 316
American Medical Association (AMA) 15, 359
American National Standards Institute (ANSI) 149, 264, 265, 466
American Revolution 312
American Society for Public Administration 383
American Society for Quality (ASQ) 15–16, 390
American Stock Exchange (AMEX) 16, 433, 480
Americans with Disabilities Act (ADA) 16–17, 260, 491
American Telephone & Telegraph (AT&T) 99, 232, 292, 314, 359, 387, 420
American Tobacco Company 14
American Tower Corporation 476
AMEX. *See* American Stock Exchange
AMOCO 359
amortization 17. *See also* depreciation, depletion, amortization
amortized loan 17
Amway Corporation 319
Andean Common Market (ANCOM) 212
Andreesen, Mark 490
Anheuser-Busch Political Action Committee (AB-PAC) 359
annual percentage rate (APR) 248
annual reports 17–18, 22, 128, 249
annuity 17, 18, 81, 128
ANSI. *See* American National Standards Institute
Ansoff, Igor 376
antitrust law 18, 28, 177, 192, 267, 292, 300, 305, 325, 402. *See also* Clayton Antitrust Act; Sherman Antitrust Act
AOB. *See* Accounting Oversight Board
AOL 476
APEC (Asia-Pacific Economic Cooperation) 217
Apple 115
applied research 399

appraisals 50. *See also* performance appraisal
appreciation 172
apprenticeship 336
APR (annual percentage rate) 248
ARAMCO (Arab American Oil Company) 140
arbitrage 12, **18–19**, 340, 348, 380
arbitration 19, 30, 129, 190
Arbitron 296
ARCO 359
Arctic wilderness 122, 344
ARMs (adjustable rate mortgages) 317
arousal theory 318
ARPA (Advanced Research Projects Agency) 255
Arthur Andersen 1, 131
The Art of War (Sun Tzu) 436
ASEAN (Association of Southeast Asian Nations) 212
Asian financial crisis 104
Asia-Pacific Economic Cooperation (APEC) 217
aspirin 457
ASQ. *See* American Society for Quality
assembly line 2, **19–20**, 266
assembly plants 20
assessment center 20
asset-backed securities (ABSs) 417, 418
assets **20–21**
    amortization 17
    balance sheet 25
    capital expenditure 54
    capital gain, capital loss 54
    corporate divestiture 95–96
    equity 168
    five Cs of credit 201
    guaranteed investment contracts 226–227
    profit 378
    residual value 400
    shareholders 420–421
    trust 460–461
    wealth 481
asset-turnover ratio 198
Association of Caribbean States 211
Association of Southeast Asian Nations (ASEAN) 212
Atlanta Merchandise Mart 457
ATMs (automated teller machines) 105
AT&T. *See* American Telephone & Telegraph
Attaturk, Mustafa 285
attention, interest, desire, action concept (AIDA) 21, 93
"at the money" 340
attitude, interests, opinions statements (AIO) **21–22**, 298
attrition 133, 258
auctions 256, 257
auditing 22, 83, 250, 426
austerity programs 255
Australian Human Rights & Equal Opportunity Commission 216–217
automated teller machines (ATMs) 105
automatic clearing house (ACH) 151
automatic stabilizers (built-in stabilizers) 22, 200, 325, 396, 459
automobile industry 22–23, 51, 94, 149, 175, 257, 331, 338
Auto Pact **22–23**
average total cost 102
Avon 319
Axner, Marya 109

B
Baby Bells 359, 387
baby-boom generation 120, 430
Bachelier, Louis 393, 394
background checks 158
backward-bending supply curve 275
backward integration 476
bad debts, aging of accounts 2–3, **24**
Baker, James 38, 168
Baker, Jerry R. 399
balance of payments **24–25**, 40, 455
balance of trade. *See* trade balance
balance sheet 5, **25**, 42, 54, 198, 346
Baldrige, Malcolm 25
Baldrige Award **25–26**
balloon payments 363
ballot stuffing 285
BankAmericard 105
banking system **26–27**. *See also* Federal Reserve System; financial intermediaries; savings and loan associations
    American Bankers Association 10–11
    American depositary receipts 12
    American Industrial Revolution 13–14
    Bank of International Settlements 27
    Comptroller of the Currency 81–82
    discount rate 128–129
    electronic funds transfer 150–151
    Electronic Fund Transfer Act 150
    Federal Deposit Insurance Corporation 188
    Great Depression 223
    investment banking 263–264
    letter of credit 278
    monetary policy 311
    New York Clearing House Association 329
    reserve requirements 400
    Resolution Trust Corporation 400–401
Bank of America 105, 112
Bank of International Settlements (BIS) 27, 356
Bank of Mexico 356
Bank of New York 217–218
Bank of North America 26, 312
Bank of the United States 26, 312
bankruptcy. *See* business failure; consumer bankruptcy
Bankruptcy Act 46
Baron, Robert S. 426
barriers to entry 28, 92, 175, 253, 299, 314, 338
barriers to trade. *See* trade barriers
barter **28–29**, 102–103, 311–312, 465
baseball 422
basic goods/materials 75–76
basis of accounting. *See* accrual basis, cash basis
Baxter v. Ford Motor Company 374, 375
BBB. *See* Better Business Bureau
BEA. *See* Bureau of Economic Analysis
bearer (negotiable instruments) 327
bear hug 449
Beasley, William L. 452
BECC. *See* Border Environmental Cooperation Commission
"beige book" 284, 339
Bellow, Saul 487

Bell South 359
benchmarking **29**
beneficiary, trust 461
benefit-cost analysis 291
benefits. *See* compensation and benefits; employee benefits
Ben & Jerry's 98, 169
Bergstresser, Charles 132
Berners-Lee, Tim 490
best practices 29, 417
beta coefficient, capital asset pricing model **29–30**, 226, 407
Better Business Bureau (BBB) **30–31**, 85
Bevin, Ernest 300
Bezos, Jeff 48
Bidault, Georges 300
Biggs, John 1
Big Three auto makers 94
bilateral monopoly 103
billboards, Internet 257
bill of lading **31**
BIS. *See* Bank of International Settlements
Blair, Gerald 463
Blake, Robert 441–442
blind trust **31–32**
BLM. *See* Bureau of Land Management
block grants 44
blocking statutes 177
BLS. *See* Bureau of Labor Statistics
"blue book" reports 214
blue-chip stocks 32
blue-collar 32
BlueCross/BlueShield Associations 359
blue laws **32–33**
Bly, Robert W. 93
BMW 94, 99, 347
board of directors 17, **33–35**, 83, 248–249, 357, 358
Board of Governors (Federal Reserve) 192
Body Shop 98
Boeing 98–99, 359
Boesky, Ivan 245
Bollinger bands 447
bonding (relationship management) 397–398
bonds **35–36**. *See also* stock market, bond market
    American Industrial Revolution 14
    annuity 18
    Brady bonds 38
    callable bond 53
    default 117
    duration 136
    investment 262–263
    investment clubs 264
    leveraged buyouts 279
    mergers and acquisitions 305
    Moody's ratings 315
    parity 348
    promissory notes 381
    risk 407
    sinking fund 424
    Standard & Poor's 431–432
    T-bonds 473–474
book value (carrying value) **36–37**, 400
Border Environmental Cooperation Commission (BECC) 37, 332, 334
Bork, Robert 451
Boston Consulting Group 298
Boston Tea Party 37, 49, 304
"Boulwareism" 72
bourgeois 427

boycotts 37, 85, 276, 422, 443, 469, 470
bracero program 469
Brady, Nicholas 38
Brady bonds **38**
brand insistence 38
brand preference 38
brands, brand names **38–39**, 102, 257, 280, 362–363, 371–372, 377, 412
Brazil 415, 416
break-even analysis 39, 290, 439
break-even point 100
break-up, corporate 96
Bretton Woods 27, **39–40**, 173, 488–489
bribery **40–41**, 203–204
bricks and clicks 139
Brookings Institution 452
brownfields 438
Brown v. Board of Education 66
Brown & Williamson Tobacco Corp. 453
browsers, Internet 255
Brundtland Commission Report 224, 440
Bryan, William Jennings 312
Buchwald, Art 344
Buddhist economics 41, 432
Budget and Accounting Act 214
budget deficit 473
budgeting, capital budgeting **41–42**, 57, 87–88, 325, 353, 493–494. *See also* federal budget
Buick Motor Company 374
built-in stabilizers. *See* automatic stabilizers
bulk mailing 127, 208–209
bundling 359–360
Bureau of Apprenticeship and Training 336
Bureau of Economic Analysis (BEA) **42–43**
Bureau of Indian Affairs 122
Bureau of Labor Statistics (BLS) **43**, 88, 275, 366, 371
Bureau of Land Management (BLM) **43**, 122
Bureau of Reclamation 122
Burma (Myanmar) 37
Burnett, Leo 285
burn rate 132
Bush, George H. W. 44, 176, 182, 219, 332–334, 337, 396
Bush, George W.
    agricultural support programs 9
    consumption tax 91
    corporate welfare 98
    cyberspace 112
    Department of the Interior, U.S. 122
    Export-Import Bank of the United States 175
    government debt 219
    individual retirement account 240
    Kyoto Protocol 272, 273
    macroeconomics 284
    national income accounting 324
    pollution rights 361
    supply-side economics 440
    sustainable growth 440
    viral marketing 476
Bush, Vannevar 490
business and the U.S. Constitution **43–44**, 73, 76, 104, 134, 154, 187, 443, 444
business cycles **44–45**, 139, 239, 272, 323, 396, 467

business ethics **45–46**. *See also* fraud
  churning 63
  Coalition for Environmentally
    Responsible Economies
    70–71
  conflict of interest 83
  corporate social responsibility
    97–98
  deceptive trade practices
    116–117
  earnings management 137–138
  fair disclosure 180
  Institute for Supply
    Management 245–246
  market intelligence 295
  moral suasion 316
  Office of Government Ethics
    337
  organization behavior 342
  pyramid of corporate
    responsibility 389
  social audit 426
  socially responsible investing
    428–429
  sweatshop 441
  whistle-blower 484–485
business failure (bankruptcy) 46, 378
business forecasting 46–47,
  118–119, 324–325, 410–411
business goals 96
business intelligence 47, 295–296.
  See also market intelligence
business language 47
business logistics (physical
  distribution) **47–48**
business methods 247, 350
business plan 47, **48**
Business Roundtable **48–49**
business taxes **49–50**
  American Bankers Association
    10
  automatic stabilizers 22
  capital gain, capital loss 54
  consumption tax 91–92
  corporate welfare 98–99, 99
  empowerment/enterprise zones
    160–161
  externalities 176
  federal courts 187
  fiscal policy 200
  401(k) plan 207
  independent contractors 238
  individual retirement account
    240
  Internal Revenue Service 249
  limited liability company 281
  limited liability partnership 281
  local option sales tax 282
  macroeconomics 284
  marginal analysis 291
  national income accounting 325
  partnership 348, 349
  payroll taxes 350–351
  property taxes 381–382
  real estate investment trusts 395
  real income 395
  S corporation 414–415
  simplified employee pension
    424
  supply 439
  supply-side economics
    439–440
  tax shelter 446
  transfer taxes 459–460
  trickle-down economics 460
  trust 461
business-to-business commerce 298
business travel 97
business valuation 50

Buy American Act and campaigns
  50–51
buy-and-hold strategy 394
buy class 51
buyer intentions 410
buy-grid model **51**
buying-center concept **52**, 388
buy phase 51
bylaws **52**, 237

C

CAB. *See* Civil Aeronautics Board
"cabotage" law 267
CACM (Central American Common
  Market) 211
CAD/CAE/CAM (computer-aided
  design, engineering, and
  manufacturing) 82
CAFE. *See* corporate average fuel
  efficiency
cafeteria plans **53**, 155
California 125, 387, 405, 429
California Public Employees'
  Retirement System (CALPERS)
  429
callable bond 36, **53**
call option contracts 340
Calvert Group 98
Calvin Klein 280
campaign finance 191, 360
Campaign Finance Institute 358
Campbell Soup Company 7
Canada 22–23, 110, 320, 332–333,
  348, 445, 470, 477
Canada–United States Trade
  Commission 471
cannibalization 377
Canon 222
capability logic 436
capacity/capacity utilization 201,
  262, 324–325
capital 2, 13, 21, 24, **54**, 143, 197,
  201, 346, 475
capital account 24
capital asset pricing model (CAPM)
  30
capital budgeting. *See* budgeting,
  capital budgeting
capital consumption allowance 225
capital expenditure, revenue
  expenditure **54**, 124
capital gain, capital loss 54, 353
capitalism **54–55**, 161–162, 168,
  276, 309, 427, 428
capital markets, money markets **55**,
  354
capital resources 401
CAPM (capital asset pricing model)
  30
Capper-Volstead Act and Fisheries
  Cooperative Marketing Act of
  1934 422
carbon tax 361
Cardoza, Benjamin 374
career development 20
Cargill, Inc. 182
Caribbean 247, 343
Caribbean Basin Initiative 470
Caribbean Community (CARICOM)
  211
Carnegie, Andrew 421
Carnegie Mellon University 303
carrying capacity 176, 286
carrying value. *See* book value
Carson, Rachel 90, 162
cartel **55–56**, 72, 322, 344
Carter, Jimmy 31, 58, 65, 396
case law. *See* common law

cash account 57
cash basis. *See* accrual basis, cash
  basis
cash budget 57
cash cow 299
cash-flow analysis 2, **56–57**,
  201–202
cash-flow statement. *See* flow of
  funds
cash management 57
cash transactions 465
Castro, Fidel 58, 59
catalog marketing 127
"catch up" provision 206–207
categorical grants 44
Cato Institute 451
Catton, William 286
cause, just. *See* just cause
CBOE (Chicago Board of Options
  Exchange) 340
CBOT. *See* Chicago Board of Trade
CCC. *See* Civilian Conservation
  Corps; Commodity Credit
  Corporation
CCCS. *See* consumer credit
  counseling service
CCPA. *See* Consumer Credit
  Protection Act
CDs (certificates of deposit) 452
CEAO (West African Economic
  Community) 211
cease and desist orders 244
Celanese 218
Celestial Seasonings Tea 178, 347
cellular manufacturing 269
Center for Science in the Public
  Interest (CSPI) **57–58**
Central America 343
Central American Common Market
  (CACM) 211
centrally planned economy **58–59**
Central Pacific Railroad 14
CEO. *See* chief executive officer
CERCLA (Comprehensive
  Environmental Response,
  Compensation, and Liability Act)
  437
cereal industry 322, 338, 377
CERES. *See* Coalition for
  Environmentally Responsible
  Economies
CERN 490
certificates of deposit (CDs) **452**
certification 275, 456
Certified Financial Planner (CFP)
  197
Certified Public Accountant (CPA)
  15, **59–60**
CFCs. *See* chlorofluorocarbons
CFO. *See* chief financial officer
CFP (Certified Financial Planner)
  197
CFTA. *See* United States-Canada Free
  Trade Agreement
CFTC. *See* Commodity Futures
  Trading Commission
chain-of-command principle **60**
Chamber of Commerce **60–61**, 186
champions 52
Champy, James A. 281
channel power 130
channels, distribution. *See*
  distribution channels
Chapter 7 bankruptcy 46, 85
Chapter 11 bankruptcy 46
Chapter 13 bankruptcy 85
character 201
Charitable Remainder Annuity Trust
  (CRAT) 461

Charitable Remainder UniTrust
  (CRUT) 461
charity 461, 462
Charles Schwab Company 197, 434
Chase, Salmon P. 81
Chavez, Cesar (César Chávez) 37,
  469, 470
checks 329
Cheney, Dick 451
Chevron 359
Chicago Board of Options Exchange
  (CBOE) 340
Chicago Board of Trade (CBOT) **61**,
  212
Chicago Mercantile Exchange (CME)
  61–62
chief executive officer (CEO) 48, **62**
chief financial officer (CFO) **62–63**
child labor 180
China 222, 253, 318, 416
CHIPS. *See* Clearing House Interbank
  Payments System
chlorofluorocarbons (CFCs) 69, 272,
  315
Chrysler Corporation 120, 297, 305,
  421
churning **63**
Cifra 267
Cigar Makers Union 468
CIGNA 359
CII. *See* Council of Institutional
  Investors
CIM (computer-integrated
  manufacturing) 82
CIO (Committee for Industrial
  Organization) 13
circular flow model **63–64**, 118, 168,
  172, 225, 284, 324, 402, 413
circular letter of credit 278
CISG (Convention on the
  International Sale of Goods) 92
Citibank 217, 363
citizenship behaviors 341
Civil Aeronautics Board (CAB)
  64–65, 125, 185
Civilian Conservation Corps (CCC)
  65, 200, 310
civil procedure 65, 66–67
civil rights 16–17
Civil Rights Acts 65–66, 164, 165,
  216, 260, 490–491
Civil Service 469
Civil War 13, 14, 26–27, 312, 368,
  413
class-action lawsuits 66–67
classical economics 67, 284
class seniority 418
Clayton Antitrust Act 18, **67–68**,
  193, 223, 365, 407, 464
Clean Air Acts **68–69**, 163, 360,
  361
Clean Water Act **69–70**
Clearing House Interbank Payments
  System (CHIPS) 151, 329
Clear Skies Initiative 361
climate change/global warming
  272–273, 315, 361
Climate Change Treaty. *See* Kyoto
  Protocol
Clinton, Bill
  Aid for Families with
    Dependent Children 10
  blind trust 31
  consumption tax 91
  Family and Medical Leave Act
    180
  fast track 185
  Federal Aviation Administration
    186

North American Free Trade Agreement 333, 334
Organization of American States 343
peso crisis 356
public administration 384
Section 301, Special 301, Super 301 416
supply-side economics 440
viral marketing 476
welfare 482
World Trade Organization 489
Clinton, Hillary 31, 212
closed-end funds 321
closed-shop 468
closed systems, input-output 244
closely held corporation 70
CME. *See* Chicago Mercantile Exchange
CMOs (collateralized mortgage obligations) 417
Coalition for Environmentally Responsible Economies (CERES) 70–71
CoBank 184
Cobb, John 226, 440
Coca-Cola Company 103, 173–174, 217, 247, 271, 297, 354, 382, 456, 457
cognitive dissonance 87
coincidence of needs 28
coincident indicators 239
COLA. *See* cost-of-living adjustment
Colclasure, Sheila 111
cold calling 448
Colgate 222
Collard, Rod 454
collateral 201
collateralized mortgage obligations (CMOs) 417
collective bargaining 71–72, 169, 233, 274, 325–326, 405, 469, 480
collective marks 456
collusion 56, 72–73, 322, 338
colonialism 344
Colorado Fuel and Iron Company 468
Columbia University 440
combination plans (compensation) 410
Comdex Trade show 355, 457
Commerce Business Daily 73
Commerce Clause 43, 73
commercial law 73, 467–468
commercial letter of credit 278
commercial paper 73–74
Committee for Industrial Organization (CIO) 13
commodities 61–62, 212
Commodity Credit Corporation (CCC) 74–75, 181
Commodity Futures Trading Commission (CFTC) 61, 62, 75, 212, 330
commodity markets 75–76, 212, 329–330, 351–352
Common Cause 358
common law (case law) 76–77, 160, 187, 374–375
Commons, British 386
common stock, preferred stock, treasury stock 77–78. *See also* bonds; shareholders; stock market, bond market
　beta coefficient 29–30
　blue-chip stocks 32
　closely held corporation 70
　employee stock-ownership plan 158–159

global shares 217
growth stocks 226
initial public offering 244
parity 348
proxy 383
Standard & Poor's 431
communication. *See* cross-cultural communication; marketing communications
Communications Act of 1934 186
Community Work and Training (CWT) 10
comparable worth (comparable pay, pay equity) 78, 156, 166–167, 169
comparative advantage 78–79, 164, 174, 449
comparative advertising 6
compensating balance 282
compensation and benefits 79–80.
　See also employee benefits
　agency theory 8
　comparable worth 78
　cost-of-living adjustment 101
　employee stock-ownership plan 158–159
　Equal Pay Act 166–167
　equity income theory 169
　Fair Labor Standards Act 180
　human resources 233
　independent contractors 238
　minimum wage 308
　sales force compensation 409–410
　sales management 411
　simplified employee pension 423–424
　stock options 433–434
　wage and price controls 479
　workers' compensation 486–487
competition 80. *See also* antitrust law; barriers to entry; free trade
　American Industrial Revolution 14–15
　cartel 55
　Clayton Antitrust Act 67–68
　conglomerate 84
　contestable market theory 92
　deceptive trade practices 116
　economies of scale 145
　environmental scanning 164
　Federal Trade Commission 193
　Herfindahl Index 231–232
　import restraints 234
　laissez-faire 276
　market intelligence 295
　market structure 299
　monopolistic competition 313–314
　mutual interdependence 322
　oligopoly 338
　perfect competition 351–352
　public utilities 387
　trade barriers 456
competitive advantage 80, 157
competitive intelligence. *See* market intelligence
complaints, customer 30
complexity logic 436
compounding, future value 80–81, 407
Comprehensive Environmental Response, Compensation, and Liability Act (CERCLA) 437
Comptroller of the Currency 81–82, 192
computer-aided design, engineering, and manufacturing (CAD/CAE/CAM) 82

computer-integrated manufacturing (CIM) 82
computerized trading 323
computers 52, 97, 350
concentrated strategy 444
condemnation 154
Conduit IRA 241
Confederate flag 37–38
Conference Board 82–83
confirmed letter of credit 278
conflict of interest 31, 32, 83, 246, 337
Confucian dynamism 232
conglomerates 84, 130, 182
Congress, U.S. 89, 98, 186, 214, 337, 358, 471
congressional campaigns 358
Connecticut 32, 402–403
consent decree 84
conservation 43, 161
Conservation Reserve Program (CRP) 9
conservatism 36
consideration 278
consignment 84–85
Constitution, U.S. *See* business and the U.S. Constitution
Constitutional courts 187
construction projects 162
consumer advocacy (consumerism) 85, 89–90
consumer bankruptcy (insolvency) 85–86, 88
consumer behavior 86–87. *See also* boycotts; customer loyalty
　adoption process 5–6
　American Customer Satisfaction Index 11
　Buy American Act and campaigns 50–51
　Consumer Price Index 89
　demographics 120
　family life cycle 183–184
　globalization 217
　gross domestic product 225
　Index of Consumer Expectations 238–239
　observation 335
　parallel markets 348
consumer buying process 86, 87
Consumer Confidence Index 82–83, 324
consumer credit 85–86, 91, 104–106, 201, 278
consumer credit counseling service (CCCS) 87–88, 353
Consumer Credit Protection Act (CCPA) 88, 90, 248, 491
consumer education 30–31
consumer expectations 239
Consumer Federation of America 85
consumer fraud 403
consumer goods 11
consumer innovators 200
consumerism. *See* consumer advocacy
consumer orientation 294
Consumer Price Index (CPI) 43, 88–89, 101, 170, 243, 366
Consumer Product Safety Act 90
Consumer Product Safety Commission (CPSC) 85, 89–90
consumer protection 90, 150, 192–194
Consumer Sentiment Index 324
Consumers Union (CU) 85, 90
consumption 7, 41, 90–91, 143, 324, 413, 432
consumption tax 91–92
contestable market theory 92
Continental Grain Company 182

contingency model 342
continuous flow manufacturing 269
continuous quality improvement (CQI) 390, 406
contra asset accounts 124
contract 92. *See also* futures, futures contracts; options, option contracts
　agency theory 7
　arbitration 19
　bill of lading 31
　business valuation 50
　Commercial Business Daily 73
　derivative securities 125–126
　employment-at-will 160
　escalator clause 170
　financial instrument 196
　franchising 207
　fraud 207
　guaranteed investment contract 226–227
　insurance 246
　labor-employee relations 274
　market value 300
　negotiable instruments 327
　New York Mercantile Exchange 329–330
　outsourcing 345
　restrictive covenants 402
　tying contracts 463–464
contractionary fiscal policy 200
contractors. *See* independent contractors
contributed capital 346
contribution margin 289–291
controls 174–175, 261–262, 479–480
convenience goods 372
convenience samples 297
Convention on the International Sale of Goods (CISG) 92
convertible bonds 348
cookies 368
cooperatives 56, 93, 106–107, 181
copay 229
copy 93–94
copyright, fair use 94, 247, 488
core competency 309
corporate average fuel efficiency (CAFE) 94–95
corporate culture 95, 216, 269
corporate divestiture 95–96
corporate espionage 295
Corporate Fraud Task Force 45
corporate governance 96–97
corporate responsibility, pyramid of 389
corporate scandals 45
corporate security 97
corporate social responsibility (CSR) 97–98, 389, 426, 431
corporate welfare 98–99, 175, 460, 482
corporation 99–100. *See also* multinational corporation
　board of directors 33–35
　business taxes 49
　bylaws 52
　closely held corporation 70
　corporate culture 95
　dividends, retained earnings 131
　document-retention policy 131
　employee stock-ownership plan 158–159
　fair disclosure 180
　fiscal year 200
　holding companies 232–233
　interlocking directorate 248–249
　limited liability company 281

corporation (continued)
  limited liability partnership 281
  Model Business Corporation
    Act 309
  partnership 349
  political action committee
    358–359
  project management 380–381
  S corporation 414–415
  shareholders 420–421
  stock market 433
  stock options 433–434
corruption 40–41, 100
cost accounting. See managerial
  accounting
cost-benefit analysis 100
cost drivers 4
cost-efficiencies 100
cost of goods sold 3, 100–101, 237
cost-of-living adjustment (COLA)
  89, 101, 243, 395
cost-push inflation (supply-shock
  inflation, sellers' inflation) 101,
  242
costs 101–102, 170, 176, 291,
  339–340, 345, 373, 378, 439,
  458–459
Cottrell, Nickolas 426
Council of Institutional Investors
  (CII) 33, 35
Council on Environmental Quality
  162
counseling, outplacement 345
counterfeit goods 102
counterfeit money 26
countertrade 102–103
countervailing power 103
Country Life Commission 184
country-risk analysis 103–104
coupon-interest rate 35–36
Court of International Trade 104
courts. See federal courts
covenants 402–403
Covey Leadership Center 287
CPA. See Certified Public Accountant
CPI. See Consumer Price Index
CPM. See critical path method
CPSC. See Consumer Product Safety
  Commission
CQI. See continuous quality
  improvement
craft system 19
craft unions 242, 468
Cram, Tony 148
"cram-down" deals 449
crash time 107
CRAT (Charitable Remainder
  Annuity Trust) 461
crawling-peg exchange-rate system
  173
credit. See consumer credit; debit,
  credit
credit cards 104–105, 150, 353
credit guarantees 175
credit policy 24
credit-reporting services (credit
  bureaus) 105–106, 135–136, 201
credit risk 226
credit scoring 105, 106
Credit Suisse First Boston (CSFB) 434
credit union 93, 106–107
credit worthiness 197
Crest toothpaste 39
critical path method (CPM) 107–108
Crosby, Philip B. 454
cross-cultural communication
  108–109
cross-price elasticity of demand 109
cross-promotion 412

crowding-out effect 200
Crown Zellerbach 357
Cruise, Tom 377
CRUT (Charitable Remainder
  UniTrust) 461
CSFB (Credit Suisse First Boston)
  434
CSPI. See Center for Science in the
  Public Interest
CSR. See corporate social
  responsibility
CSX Corporation 216
Cuba 58, 59, 152, 413
Cuban Democracy Act 152
cultural industries 109–110
culture/cultural differences 86, 95,
  108–109, 164, 232, 252, 254, 295
cumulative dividend preference 77
cumulative shares 421
currency/currency risk 14, 19,
  81–82, 172–173, 204, 205, 356
current account 24
current assets 20
current dividend preference 77
current liabilities 280
current ratio 197, 198
customer-comment cards 111
customer complaints 30
customer loyalty (customer retention)
  39, 98, 110, 257, 302, 397–398
customer-relationship management
  (CRM) 110–111, 111–112, 138,
  147–148, 294
customer relations/satisfaction 11,
  111–112, 213–214, 269, 293–294,
  390
Customfan 302
customization 258, 295, 302
customs union 112
Customs Union of Central Africa 211
CWT (Community Work and
  Training) 10
cyber-business 490
cyber hustlers 257–258
cyberspace 112–113
cyber squatters 258, 488
cycle time 113
cyclical unemployment 467

D

Daimler-Benz AG 305
DaimlerChrysler 217, 218, 305, 319,
  421
Daly, Herman 226, 440
Daly, Michael 385
damaged goods 347
damages 114, 374, 393, 407, 420,
  457, 461, 484, 485
Danbury Hatters 422
Dartmouth's Tuck School of Business
  302, 303
Darwin, Charles 286
database management 112, 114–115
data interchange (electronic)
  149–150
data mining 294
data storage 97
Davis-Bacon Act 115
days sales outstanding (DSO) ratio 2,
  198
day traders 484
D&B. See Dun & Bradstreet
death tax 459–460
DeBeers 56, 314
debentures 381
debit, credit 115, 215, 443
debit cards 150
Debs, Eugene 468

debt(s) 24, 117–118, 181
debt collection 88, 178–179
Debt Collection Improvement Act
  (DCIA) 151
debt instruments 35–36, 73–74
debt-management service 88
debtor nations 254–255
debt overhang 38
debt ratio 198, 279
debt restructuring 38
deceptive trade practices 116–117
decision making 160, 285–286, 343
decision-support systems 294
decision tree 117
declaration date 131
deductions, income 235
default 35, 117–118, 178, 201, 315,
  356, 407
defective products 327, 374
defense contractors 359
deficiency needs 301
defined-benefit plans 270, 351, 404
defined-contribution plans 270, 351
deflation 118, 222–223
Delano (California) 469, 470
Delaware 358
Dell, Michael 302
Del Laboratories, Inc. 420
Dell Computer Company 261–262,
  302
Delphi technique 118–119, 410
Delta & Pine Land Company 339–340
demand 119–120
  consumption 91
  cross-price elasticity of demand
    109
  elasticity of demand 148–149
  income elasticity of demand
    235–236
  indicators 239
  inflation 242
  macroeconomics 307
  marginal analysis 291
  national income accounting 324
  product life cycle 375
  product proliferation 377
  push and pull strategies 389
demand curve 39, 221, 321–322
demand-deposit multiplier 339
demand-pull inflation 242–243
DeMarco, Tom 466
Deming, W. Edwards 390, 454
Deming Award 26
Deming's 14 points 120, 288
demographics 21–22, 87, 120–121,
  124, 164, 258, 297, 354, 471. See
  also market segmentation; target
  markets
Denison, Edward 143
Department of Agriculture, U.S.
  (USDA) 74, 181, 203, 348, 400
Department of Commerce, U.S.
  (DOC) 42, 121, 176, 225, 262,
  324, 375, 425, 471
Department of Defense, U.S. 50, 215,
  255, 304
Department of Housing and Urban
  Development, U.S. (HUD) 220
Department of Justice, U.S. 232, 256,
  314, 336, 340, 396, 422
Department of Labor, U.S. (DOL) 43,
  121–122, 158, 166, 181, 216, 335,
  336
Department of State, U.S. 471–472
Department of the Interior, U.S.
  (DOI) 43, 122, 161
Department of the Treasury, U.S.
  123–124, 214, 219, 356, 430, 465,
  473–474

Department of Transportation, U.S.
  (DOT) 122–123, 185
dependency ratios 124
depletion. See depreciation,
  depletion, amortization
Depository Institutions Deregulation
  and Monetary Control Act of 1980
  189, 401
Depository Institutions (Garn-St.
  Germain) Act of 1982 189, 401
depreciation, depletion, amortization
  119–120, 124, 172, 395, 400, 446
depression. See Great Depression
deregulation 64–65, 106, 124–125,
  387, 401
derivative securities 75, 125–126
DeSoto, Hernando 465
Dessler, Gary 268
Deutsche Bank 218
developing countries 38, 140, 273,
  320. See also emerging markets
development. See economic
  development; new-product
  development; training and
  development
Dietene 456
Dilbert (cartoon character) 357
Di Meglio, Francesca 218
diminishing marginal returns 373
Diners Club 105
DINKS 184
dioxin 163
diplomatic risk 205
direct e-mail 127
direct investment 103–104, 126,
  205, 262
Directive for Packaging and
  Packaging Waste (1996) 347
direct mail 37, 126–127, 393
direct marketing 127–128, 293,
  447–448
Direct Marketing Association 448
direct sales 130
disability 16–17, 336, 487
disclosure 180, 416, 462
disclosure duties 128, 133, 137
discontinued products 173–174
discounted cash flow 42, 56
discounting, present value 56, 128,
  381
discount-interest loans 282
discount rate 50, 128–129, 311
discount-store industry 302
discrimination 65–66, 166–167, 260,
  336, 364–365, 419–420, 484
disintermediation 126
Disney corporation 37
dispute settlement 19, 129
distribution channels (marketing
  channels) 28, 47, 129–130, 231,
  254, 375, 389, 412–413
distributions, forced 203
diversification 130, 377
divestiture. See corporate divestiture
dividends, retained earnings 77, 131,
  226, 346, 395, 420, 421
DOC. See Department of Commerce,
  U.S.
document-retention policy 131–132,
  244
DOI. See Department of the Interior,
  U.S.
DOL. See Department of Labor, U.S.
dollar (U.S.) 172
domain names 112, 132, 258, 488
domestic goods 235
domestic suppliers 50
Donohue, Tom 61
do-not-call lists 448

Dorgan, Bryan 182
Dorny, Brett 131
DOT. *See* Department of
    Transportation, U.S.
dot-coms 132
    churning 63
    conglomerate 84
    first-mover advantage 199
    growth stocks 226
    initial public offerings 244
    Internet 256
    Internet marketing 257
    New York Stock Exchange 330
    opportunity cost 339
    prospectus 383
    shareholders 421
    whisper numbers 484
    zero-sum game 493
Double-click Corporation 335
double-entry accounting. *See*
    financial accounting
double taxation 100
Dow, Charles 132, 447
Dow Jones averages 32, **132–133**,
    380, 447
downsizing **133**, 396–397
downstream 319
Dow theory 447
draft 327
draws 409–410
Drexel Burnham Lambert 305
drive-reduction theory 318
Drucker, Peter 153, 320
drug companies. *See* pharmaceuticals
drug testing 158
drug trafficking 393, 465
DSO. *See* days sales outstanding ratio
due diligence **133**
due process 67, **134–135**
Duke, James B. 14
dumping 104, 135, 445
Dun & Bradstreet (D&B) 8,
    135–136
Duncan, David 131
DuPraw, Marcell 109
durable consumer expenditures 262
duration 136
Dyer, John 421

E

E-1 visas 477
E-2 visas 477
EAC (East African Community) 211
EAEC (European Atomic Energy
    Community) 171
EAP. *See* employee assistance
    program
early withdrawals (IRAs) 240
earnings (retained) **131**
earnings before interest and taxes
    (EBIT) 279
earnings management **137–138**
earnings per share (EPS) 237, 279
Earth Day 163
East African Community (EAC) 211
Eastern Europe 103
eBay 257
EBIT (earnings before interest and
    taxes) 279
EBT. *See* electronic benefits transfer
e-business 138, 256–258
e-commerce 91, **138–139**, 150,
    256–258
economic conditions **139–140**, 201,
    243–244, 339
economic development 70, 102,
    140–141, 211, 247, 321–322, 343,
    413, 440, 487–488

economic efficiency 55, 99, **141**,
    144–145, 402
Economic Espionage Act **141–142**
economic freedom **142–143**, 144
economic growth **143**
    agricultural support programs 8
    Buddhist economics 41
    Business Roundtable 48
    capital 54
    economic freedom 142, 143
    economic policy 144
    Export-Import Bank of the
        United States 175
    monetary policy 310–311
    national income accounting 324
    production-possibilities curve
        373
    reserve requirements 400
    trickle-down economics 460
    USAID 471
    wealth 481
Economic Growth and Tax Relief
    Reconciliation Act (EGTRRA)
    240, 459
economic investment 262
economic policy **143–144**, 167, 192
economic rent **144**
Economic Research Services 181
economic responsibility 389
economic sanctions 413
economics/economic theory
    affluent society 7
    agency theory 7–8
    Buddhist economics 41
    business cycles. *See* business
        cycles
    centrally planned economy
        58–59
    circular flow model. *See* circular
        flow model
    classical economics 67
    comparative advantage 78–79
    countervailing power 103
    cross-price elasticity of demand
        109
    deflation 118
    demand 119–120
    efficient market theory 145
    equation of exchange 167
    equilibrium 167–168
    equity income theory 169
    income elasticity of demand
        235–236
    inflation. *See* inflation
    Keynesian economics 270–271
    Kondratev waves 272
    Lorenz curve 282–283
    macroeconomics. *See*
        macroeconomics
    Malthusian trap 286
    marginal analysis 291–292
    market failure 292
    mercantilism. *See* mercantilism
    microeconomics 306–307
    mixed economy 309
    modern portfolio theory 310
    monetary policy. *See* monetary
        policy
    opportunity cost 339–340
    production-possibilities curve
        373
    random-walk theory 393–394
    socialism 427–428
    supply 438–439
    supply rule 439
    supply-side economics 439–440
    trickle-down economics 460
    underground economy
        465–466

wealth 481
    zero-sum game 493
economic stimulus 65, 144
economies of scale, economies of
    scope 28, **144–145**, 314, 373,
    386, 485
Ecuador 38, 344
EDI. *See* electronic data
    interchange
EDIFACT standard 149
Edison, Thomas A. 14
education 176, 437
Education IRA (EIRA) 241
EEC (European Economic
    Community) 171
EEOC. *See* Equal Employment
    Opportunity Commission
efficiency. *See* economic efficiency
efficient market theory (efficient
    market hypothesis) 145, 394
EFT. *See* electronic funds transfer
EFTA (Electronic Fund Transfer
    Act) **150**
e-government 145, **145–147**
EGTRRA. *See* Economic Growth
    and Tax Relief Reconciliation
    Act
80-20 principle **147–148**, 298
EIRA (Education IRA) 241
EIS (environmental impact
    statement) **162**
Eisenhower, Dwight D. 249
elasticity of demand 49, 109,
    148–149, 239, 307, 364, 365
elderly-dependency ratio 124
election campaigns 61, 358–360
electricity 387
electronic benefits transfer (EBT)
    150–151
electronic data interchange (EDI)
    149–150
Electronic Federal Tax Payment
    System 351
electronic funds transfer (EFT)
    150–151
Electronic Fund Transfer Act (EFTA)
    150
Elgin-Marcy 445
Elizabeth poor law (1601) 481
Elmuti, Dean 29
El Salvador 37
e-mail 127, 207–209, 255–259, 476
embargoes **151–152**, 234
embezzlement **152**, 207
Emergency Relief Appropriation Act
    487
emerging markets **153–154**, 231,
    345–346, 356, 447
EMILY's list 359–360
eminent domain **154–155**, 444
emissions 69, 176, 272, 273
e-money 151
Emory University 453
empathy 398
employee assistance program (EAP)
    155, 409
employee benefits 53, **155–156**,
    230. *See also* compensation and
    benefits
employee handbook 274, 491
employee motivation 3–4, **156–157**,
    266, 352, 370–371, 379, 426–428,
    450–451, 452, 463
employee recruiting **157–158**,
    159–160, 259–261
employee relations 233, 274
Employee Retirement Income
    Security Act (ERISA) 158, 351,
    404, 423, 491

employee(s). *See also* compensation
    and benefits
    blue-collar 32
    comparable worth 78
    Consumer Credit Protection
        Agency 88
    equity income theory 169
    Hawthorne experiments 229
    job satisfaction 266–267
    just cause 268
    Maslow's hierarchy of needs
        301
    minimum wage 308
    motivation theory 318–319
    National Mediation Board 326
    Occupational Safety and Health
        Administration 335
    organizational commitment 341
    training and development 458
    undertime 466
    white-collar 485
    work council 486
employee stock-ownership plan
    (ESOP) 130, **158–159**
Employer and Employee Association
    Trust Account 241
Employer Information Survey 166
employment **159–160**, 274–275
    adaptability screening 4
    classical economics 67
    compensation and benefits
        79–80
    dependency ratios 124
    downsizing 133
    due process 134
    equal employment opportunity
        and affirmative action
        164–165
    Equal Employment
        Opportunity Commission
        165–166
    expectancy theory 174
    Fair Labor Standards Act 180
    Family and Medical Leave Act
        180–181
    family-friendly business
        practices 182–183
    forced-ranking systems 203
    fraud 207
    layoff 276–277
    nepotism 327–328
    outplacement 344–345
    payroll taxes 350
    profit sharing 379
    restrictive covenants 402
    right-to-work laws 405
    seniority 418
    sexual harassment 419–420
    sweatshop 441
    underground economy 465
    visas 476–477
    wrongful discharge 490–491
employment-at-will 160, 268, 490,
    491
employment taxes 350–351
empowerment 160
empowerment zones, enterprise
    zones **160–161**
Endangered Species Act **161**
energy futures 329–330
energy policies 250–251
England 78, 304, 344
English common law 76–77, 187
English language 108–109
Enron
    Accounting Oversight Board 1
    agency theory 8
    conflict of interest 83
    document-retention policy 131

Enron (continued)
    equity income theory 169
    forced-ranking systems 203
    401(k) plan 207
    fraud 207
    personal finance 353
    retirement plan 404
    stock options 433
    whistle-blower 485
enterprise-resource planning (ERP)
    138
enterprises, government-sponsored
    220–221
enterprise zones. See empowerment
    zones, enterprise zones
entrepreneurship 132, 161–162, 382
environment
    Coalition for Environmentally
        Responsible Economies
        70–71
    externalities 176
    family farm 182
    green marketing 224
    organizational theory 342
    packaging 347
    pollution rights 360
    Resource Conservation and
        Recovery Act 401
    social audit 426
    Superfund 437–438
    sustainable growth 440
    takings clause 444
environmental impact statement
    (EIS) 162
environmental infrastructure projects
    37
environmentally sensitive products
    224
Environmental Protection Agency
    (EPA) 68, 69–70, 162–163, 176,
    224, 315, 332, 338, 360, 361, 401,
    437
environmental scanning 164, 295,
    436–437
EOL (Equal Opportunity Loan)
    Program 425
EPA. See Environmental Protection
    Agency
e-procurement 388
EPS. See earnings per share
Equal Credit Opportunity Act 90
equal employment opportunity and
    affirmative action 164–165, 336
Equal Employment Opportunity
    Commission (EEOC) 66,
    165–166, 216, 275, 336, 419, 420
Equal Opportunity Loan Program
    (EOL) 425
Equal Pay Act 78, 166–167, 169
equation of exchange 167
equilibrium 67, 167–168, 271
equity 21, 25, 54, 99, 168, 346, 363,
    475
equity account 131
equity income theory 169
equity REITs 394–395
equity security 77
equity theory 370–371
ergonomics 169–170
ERISA. See Employee Retirement
    Income Security Act
ERP (enterprise-resource planning)
    138
escalator clause 170
ESOP. See employee stock-ownership
    plan
espionage, corporate 295
Essex Investment Company 31
estate-planning 461–462

estate tax 459–460
esteem needs 301
ethical hackers 97
ethics. See business ethics
Ethics in Government Act of 1978 337
EU. See European Union
euro 172
Europe 125
European Atomic Energy Community
    (EAEC) 171
European Commission 171
European Economic Community
    (EEC) 171
European Recovery Program. See
    Marshall Plan
European Union (EU) 170–172
    exchange rate 173
    extraterritorial jurisdiction 177
    free-trade areas 211
    globalization 217
    harmonization 228
    international marketing 253
    nontariff barriers 331
    packaging 347
    parallel markets 347–348
    privacy 368
    reductions in force 397
European Works Council (EWC) 486
evaluation. See performance appraisal
evaluation apprehension 426, 428
EWC (European Works Council) 486
exchange 167, 204. See also barter;
    foreign exchange; market exchange
exchange-rate risk 173
exchange rates 24, 27, 40, 124,
    172–173, 175, 204, 362
Exchange Stabilization Fund 356
excise tax 49, 91–92
exclusion orders 350
exclusive rights 349–350
ex-dividend dates 421
Executive MBA programs 303
executive order 5
Executive Order 11246 164–165, 336
Ex-Im Bank. See Export-Import Bank
    of the United States
exit strategies 173–174
expansionary fiscal policy 200
expectancy theory 91, 174, 370
expenditures. See capital expenditure,
    revenue expenditure
expense 3, 54
expense account 100–101
experience and learning curves 174
experimental designs 296
exponential smoothing 411
Export Administration Act 174
export controls 174–175
Export-Import Bank of the United
    States (Ex-Im Bank) 175, 176
exporting 175–176. See also
    imports/exports
express warranties 374
externalities (spillover effects) 176,
    292, 440
extraterritorial jurisdiction 177
ExxonMobil 104, 319
Exxon Valdez 163, 224
eye contact 108

F
FAA. See Federal Aviation
    Administration
face time 466
factoring 178, 178
factory tours 178
Facts On File 294–295
failure, fear of 3

Fair Credit Billing Act of 1975 90,
    248
Fair Credit Reporting Act 90,
    105–106
Fair Debt Collections Practices Act
    (FDCPA) 88, 178–180
fair disclosure (SEC Regulation FD)
    32, 180, 484
Fair Isaac and Company (FICO) 106
Fair Labor Standards Act (FLSA)
    180, 308, 490
fair market value 50, 154
The Fair Packaging and Labeling Act
    of 1990 347
fair use. See copyright, fair use
False Claims Act of 1986 484
Family and Medical Leave Act
    (FMLA) 180–181, 182, 491
family brand 39
family farm 181–182, 366
family-friendly business practices
    182–183
family life cycle 183–184
Fannie Mae. See Federal National
    Mortgage Association
Farm Credit Administration (FCA)
    184
Farm Credit Council (FCC) 184
Farm Credit System (FCS) 184, 220,
    221
Farm Security and Reinvestment Act
    of 2002 9
FASB. See Financial Accounting
    Standards Board
fast track (trade promotion authority)
    185, 332, 333, 343
FBI. See Federal Bureau of
    Investigation
FCA (Farm Credit Administration)
    184
FCC. See Farm Credit Council;
    Federal Communications
    Commission
FCPA. See Foreign Corrupt Practices
    Act
FCS. See Farm Credit System
FCUA (Federal Credit Union Act)
    106
FDA. See Food and Drug
    Administration
FDCPA. See Fair Debt Collections
    Practices Act
FDI. See foreign direct investment
FDIC. See Federal Deposit Insurance
    Corporation
featherbedding 185, 469
FEC. See Federal Election Campaign
    Act of 1974
Federal Agriculture Improvement and
    Reform Act (FAIR) 9, 181–182
Federal Aviation Act of 1958 185
Federal Aviation Administration
    (FAA) 185–186, 485
federal budget 89, 186, 219, 225,
    337
Federal Bureau of Investigation (FBI)
    256, 485
Federal Communications
    Commission (FCC) 186–187, 386
federal courts 65, 187
Federal Credit Union Act (FCUA)
    106
Federal Deposit Insurance
    Corporation (FDIC) 27, 188, 189,
    226, 338, 413
Federal Election Campaign
    Commission 358
Federal Election Campaign (FEC)
    Act of 1974 358

Federal Emergency Management
    Agency (FEMA) 215
Federal Family Education Loan
    Program (FFELP) 437
Federal Farm Loan Act of 1916 184
Federal Financial Institutions
    Examinations Council (FFIEC)
    188–189
federal funds market 189, 248
Federal Glass Ceiling Commission
    216
Federal Highway Administration
    (FHWA) 123
Federal Home Loan Bank System
    (FHLBS) 189–190, 220, 221
Federal Home Loan Mortgage
    Corporation (Freddie Mac)
    (FHLMC) 190, 191, 220, 221,
    417
Federal Housing Administration
    (FHA) 220
Federal Housing Enterprises
    Financial Safety Act 190
federalism 43, 44
Federal Land Bank Associations
    (FLBAs) 184
Federal Land Credits Associations
    (FLCAs) 184
Federal Mediation and Conciliation
    Service (FMCS) 190
Federal National Mortgage
    Association (Fannie Mae) 190,
    191–192, 220, 221, 363, 417
Federal Open Market Committee
    (FOMC) 192, 339
Federal Reserve Bank of New York
    356
Federal Reserve System 192
    American Industrial Revolution
        14
    banking system 26, 27
    discount rate 128–129
    electronic funds transfer 151
    Federal Deposit Insurance
        Corporation 188
    federal funds market 189
    five Cs of credit 201
    flow of funds 201–202
    government debt 219
    macroeconomics 284
    monetary policy 311
    money 312
    money supply 313
    moral suasion 316
    open-market operations 339
    repurchase agreements 399
    reserve requirements 400
    stock options 433
    U.S. Treasury securities 473,
        474
Federal Savings and Loan Insurance
    Corporation (FSLIC) 189
Federal Theater, Arts, Music and
    Writers' Projects 487
Federal Trade Commission (FTC)
    192–194
    advertising 6
    consumer protection 90
    deceptive trade practices 116
    Fair Debt Collections Practices
        Act 180
    franchising 207
    fraud 207
    pricing strategies 367
    primary activities of 192
    reciprocity 396
    review of mergers by 192
    telemarketing 448
    Wheeler-Lea Act 482–483

Federal Trade Commission Act of 1914 482, 483
feedback 352–353
FEMA (Federal Emergency Management Agency) 215
FFELP (Federal Family Education Loan Program) 437
FFIEC. *See* Federal Financial Institutions Examinations Council
FFO (funds from operations) 395
FHA. *See* Federal Housing Administration
FHLBS. *See* Federal Home Loan Bank System
FHLMC. *See* Federal Home Loan Mortgage Corporation
FHWA (Federal Highway Administration) 123
FIBO-B (Fundamental Interpersonal Relations Orientation-Behavior) 20
FICA (Federal Insurance Contributions Act) 350, 351
FICO (Fair Isaac and Company) 106
fiduciary duties 194–195, 249
Fielding Tariffs 320
FIFO 199
Fifth Amendment 134, 154, 443
financial accounting (double-entry accounting) 195. *See also* managerial accounting; national income accounting; *specific headings*
 accounts payable, trade credit 2
 accounts receivable 2–3
 accrual basis, cash basis 3
 activity-based costing 4
 adjusting entry, trial balance, adjusted trial balance 4–5
 American Institute of Certified Public Accountants 15
 amortization 17
 amortized loan 17
 book value 36–37
 business valuation 50
 capital expenditure, revenue expenditure 54
 capital gain, capital loss 54
 Certified Public Accountant 59–60
 cost of goods sold 100–101
 factoring 178
 FIFO/LIFO 199
 Financial Accounting Standards Board 195
 residual value 400
 stock options 433–434
 t-account 443
Financial Accounting Standards Board (FASB) 195, 215
financial engineering 340
Financial Institutions Reform, Recovery, and Enforcement Act (FIRREA) 189–190, 400
financial instrument 195–196, 327
 American depositary receipts 12
 annuity 18
 bond. *See* bond
 Brady bonds 38
 callable bond 53
 CDs 452
 commercial paper 73–74
 derivative securities 125–126
 promissory note 381
 securitization 417–418
 Treasury securities 473–474
financial intermediaries 54, 64, 126, 196, 263, 321

financial investment 262
financial leverage 279
financial planning 196–197
Financial Planning Association (FPA) 196–197, 354
financial ratios 124, 197–198, 215–216
Financial Stability Institute (FSI) 27
financial statements 17–18, 25, 48, 197, 198–199, 378. *See also* income statement
Finished Goods Price Index 371
Firestone 385
FIRREA. *See* Financial Institutions Reform, Recovery, and Enforcement Act
first impressions 260
first in, first out (FIFO); last in, first out (LIFO) 199
first-mover advantage (first-to-market) 199–200
fiscal policy 22, 144, 200, 243, 337
fiscal year 200
Fish and Wildlife Service (FWS) 161
Fisher, Bruce 63, 72, 309, 422
Fisher, Cynthia 155, 160, 405
five Cs of credit 201
fixed costs 101–102
flat-file systems 114, 115
FLBAs (Federal Land Bank Associations) 184
FLCAs (Federal Land Credits Associations) 184
flip-in poison-pill strategy 357
flip-over strategy 357
flipping 244, 363
floating exchange-rate systems 173
floor specialist 330
flowchart 201
flow of funds 201–202
FLSA. *See* Fair Labor Standards Act
FMCS (Federal Mediation and Conciliation Service) 190
FMLA. *See* Family and Medical Leave Act
FM Watch 190, 191
FOB. *See* free on board
focus groups 7, 202, 354, 362
FOIA. *See* Freedom of Information Act
Folgers coffee 37
follow-up (sales) 355–356
FOMC. *See* Federal Open Market Committee
Food and Drug Administration (FDA) 202–203, 454
Food and Drugs Act of 1906 202
Food for Peace Program 366
food safety 58
food stamps 482
forced-ranking systems (forced distributions, "rank and yank") 203, 452
Ford, Henry 19–20, 293, 372
Ford Motor Company 203, 307, 319, 352, 375, 388, 436
forecasting. *See* business forecasting; sales forecasting
foreign aid 141, 142, 471
Foreign Assistance Act 300
foreign competition 104
Foreign Corrupt Practices Act (FCPA) 40, 203–204
foreign direct investment (FDI) 126, 141, 253
foreign exchange 172, 204, 329
foreign investment 12, 126, 204–205, 447
foreign-sales corporations (FSCs) 98

Foreign Sovereign Immunities Act (FSIA) 205–206
foreign trade. *See* trade
Foreign Trade Zone Act of 1934 206
foreign-trade zones 206
Form 10-K 416
forward integration 476
fossil fuels 272, 273
Fosters Lager 217
four-firm concentration ratio 232, 292
401(k) plan 197, 206–207, 270, 404
four Ps of marketing 253–254
Fourteenth Amendment 134
FPA. *See* Financial Planning Association
fractional reserve banking 26
franchising 128, 207, 253, 447, 464
Franklin, Benjamin 93, 246, 312, 368, 413, 470
Franklin National Bank (New York) 105
Fraser, Jill 485
Fraser Institute 142
fraud 208–209
 bribery 40–41
 business ethics 45
 churning 63
 collusion 72–73
 counterfeit goods 102
 deceptive trade practices 116–117
 earnings management 137
 Economic Espionage Act 141–142
 embezzlement 152
 insider trading 244–245
 Internet Fraud Complaint Center 256
 Ponzi scheme 362
 predatory lending 363
 price fixing 365
 Racketeer Influenced and Corrupt Organization Act 393
 whistle-blower 484
Freddie Mac. *See* Federal Home Loan Mortgage Corporation
freedom, economic. *See* economic freedom
Freedom House 142
Freedom of Information Act (FOIA) 209–210
Freedom to Farm Act 181–182
free enterprise system 55, 276
free on board (FOB) 210, 228
free trade 78, 109–110, 210–211, 332–334, 343, 456, 470
free-trade areas 211–212
free-trade zones (FTZs) 206
frequent flyers 298
frictional unemployment 467
Friedman, Milton 167, 276, 310, 323, 396, 451
friendly takeovers 306
FSCs (foreign-sales corporations) 98
FSI (Financial Stability Institute) 27
FSIA. *See* Foreign Sovereign Immunities Act
FSLIC (Federal Savings and Loan Insurance Corporation) 189
FTC. *See* Federal Trade Commission
FTC v. Raladam Co. 483
FTZs (free-trade zones) 206
fuel efficiency 94
full employment 467
Fuller, Ida Mae 430
Fundamental Interpersonal Relations Orientation-Behavior (FIRO-B) 20

funds-flow statement 201
funds from operations (FFO) 395
Furfine, Craig 316
FUTA (Federal Unemployment Tax Act) 350
futures, futures contracts 61–62, 75–76, **212**, 231, 329–330, 380
future value 80–81, 407
FWS (Fish and Wildlife Service) 161

G

G10 27
GAAP. *See* generally accepted accounting principles
Gabon 344
Gadsden Purchase 333
gain sharing. *See* profit sharing, gain sharing
Galarza, Ernesto 469
Galbraith, John Kenneth 7, 103
game theory 213, 322, 493
Gangarosa, Ray 453
GAO. *See* General Accounting Office
gap analysis 213–214
Gardiner, Brian 272
Garfield, Sidney 230
garnishments 88
Gary, Judge 365
Gastil, Raymond 142
Gates, Bill 245, 355, 481
GATT. *See* General Agreement on Tariffs and Trade
GCC. *See* Gulf Cooperation Council
GDP. *See* gross domestic product
GE. *See* General Electric
General Accounting Office (GAO) 214, 337
General Agreement on Tariffs and Trade (GATT)
 dumping 135
 exporting 175
 family farm 182
 globalization 217
 monopoly 314
 most-favored-nation clause 318
 multinational corporation 320
 North American Free Trade Agreement 333
 patents 350
 Section 301, Special 301, Super 301 415
 Smoot-Hawley Tariff Act 426
 tariff 445
 United States–Canada Free Trade Agreement 470
 World Trade Organization 488
General Electric (GE) 177, 203, 293–294, 332, 359, 365, 411
generally accepted accounting principles (GAAP) 2–3, 17, 18, 195, 198, 214–215, 289
General Mills 322, 338
General Motors (GM) 71, 85, 319, 372
general partnerships 349
General Services Administration (GSA) 215
generation-skipping tax 460
Generation X 120
geographic information system (GIS) 146
geographic segmentation 297, 306
George III (king of England) 76
Germany 103, 106, 243, 300, 445
Gibbons, Robert 8
Gibbs, Lois 163, 224
GIC. *See* guaranteed investment contract

gift tax 459–460
Gingrich, Newt 451
Gini ratio **215–216**
Ginnie Mae. *See* Government
    National Mortgage Association
GIS (geographic information system)
    146
glass ceiling **216–217**
Glass-Steagall Act of 1933 188, 263
globalization **217**. *See also* World
    Trade Organization
        arbitrage 19
        assembly plants 20
        Bank of International
            Settlements 27
        business ethics 45
        comparative advantage 78–79
        Conference Board 82–83
        country-risk analysis 103–104
        cross-cultural communication
            108–109
        cultural industries 109–110
        emerging markets 153
        European Union 170–172
        extraterritorial jurisdiction 177
        Foreign Sovereign Immunities
            Act 205
        harmonization 228–229
        International Monetary Fund
            254
        Internet marketing 257
        ISO standards 264–265
        maquiladoras 290–291
        marketing strategy 295
        mergers and acquisitions 305
        middle managers 307
        Montreal Protocol 315
        multinational corporation
            319–321
        outsourcing 345
        trade-adjustment assistance 455
Global Leaders for Tomorrow 440
global shares **217–218**
global warming. *See* climate change
Gloria Vanderbilt 280
GM. *See* General Motors
goal setting **218**, 341, 342, 371, 436,
    493, 494
going concern. *See* goodwill, going
    concern
"going naked" 340
gold 223, 312
"golden rule" 440
Goldman Sachs 263, 434
Goldrau, Eliyahu M. 449–450
Goldschmid, Harvey J. 1
Goldsmith, James 357
Gompers, Samuel 12, 468
"gone long" 212
"gone short" 212
goodwill, going concern 102,
    218–219
Gordon, George J. 384
Gore, Al 224
government, U.S. *See also* e-
    government
        affirmative action 164–165
        capitalism 55
        circular flow model 64
        Commercial Business Daily 73
        deregulation 125
        economic policy 143–144
        eminent domain 154
        federal budget 186
        fiscal year 200
        national income accounting
            325
        public administration 383–384
government debt **219–220**

Government National Mortgage
    Association (Ginnie Mae) 190,
    191, **220**, 417
government-sponsored enterprises
    (GSEs) 184, **220–221**, 417, 437
Graham, John 435
Gramlich, Edward 129
The Grange 93
graphs **221–222**
Graves, Lucas 199
gray markets **222**, 280, 348
Grayson, C. Jackson, Jr. 29
Great Depression **222–223**. *See also*
    New Deal
        AFL-CIO 13
        agricultural support programs 8
        automatic stabilizers 22
        banking system 26
        business and the U.S.
            Constitution 44
        business cycles 44
        classical economics 67
        Commodity Credit Corporation
            74
        Davis-Bacon Act 115
        deflation 118
        Department of Labor, U.S. 121
        family farm 181
        Fannie Mae 191
        Federal Deposit Insurance
            Corporation 188
        fiscal policy 200
        foreign-trade zones 206
        government debt 219
        government-sponsored
            enterprises 220–221
        investment banking 263
        Keynesian economics 271
        laissez-faire 276
        macroeconomics 284
        Marshall Plan 301
        monetary policy 310
        National Industrial Recovery
            Act 325
        price floors 365, 366
        reserve requirements 400
        Robinson-Patman Act 407
        saving 413
        Smoot-Hawley Tariff Act 426
        Social Security 429
        tariff 445
        TVA 449
        welfare 482
        Works Progress Administration
            487
        World Trade Organization 489
Great Society 43
greenbacks 14
green cards **223–224**, 476
Green Gauge Report 224
greenhouse gases 272, 273, 361
Greenman v. Yuba Power Products Inc.
    374, 375
green marketing **224–225**
Greenspan, Alan 91, 284, 311, 316,
    433
Grimshaw v. Ford Motor Company
    375
gross domestic product (GDP)
    225–226
        Bureau of Economic Analysis
            42–43
        business cycles 44
        classical economics 67
        economic conditions 139
        economic growth 143
        emerging markets 153
        government debt 219
        imports/exports 235

Index of Consumer
    Expectations 238
        indicators 239
        inflation 243
        international marketing 252
        macroeconomics 284
        monetary policy 310
        national income accounting
            325
        price indexes 366–367
        recession 395
        sustainable growth 440
        underground economy 465
gross income 235
gross margin. *See* income statement,
    gross margin
group boycotts 422
group IRA 241
groups 202, 342
growth. *See* economic growth;
    product-market growth matrix;
    sustainable growth and
    development
growth stage 376
growth stocks **226**
GSA (General Services
    Administration) **215**
GSEs. *See* government-sponsored
    enterprises
GTE 359
Guadalupe Hidalgo, Treaty of 333
guanxi 253
guaranteed investment contract
    (guaranteed income contract)
    (GIC) **226–227**, 354
guerrilla logic 436
Guess 280
Gulf Cooperation Council (GCC)
    211–212
Gulf War 267, 344
Gulick, Luther 384
Gunn, Ronald 304
"guns and butter" tradeoff 373

H

habitability 480
hackers 146
Halley, Edmond 246
halo effect 203
Hamilton, Alexander 312
Hammer and Company 288
handshake 108
Hanford Nuclear Reservation 485
Hanke, Steve H. 143
harassment, sexual 419–420
harmonization 228
Harmonized Tariff System (HTS)
    228–229, 408
Hart, Stuart 225
Harvard University 344, 451
Hawaii 268, 445
Hawken, Paul 440–441
Hawley, Willis 425
Hawthorne experiments **229**, 242,
    266
Haywood, Big Bill 242
hazardous occupations 180
hazardous substances 224, 401, 405
Hazard Ranking System (HRS) 437
health care 15, 180, 229–230,
    246–247
health maintenance organization
    (HMO) **229–230**
Heartland By-Products 104
Heckscher-Ohlim theorem 79
hedge fund **230–231**
hedging 75, 76, 172, 212, **231**
Hepburn Act of 1906 259

Herfindahl Index (Herfindahl-
    Hirschman Index) 292
Heritage Foundation 142, 451
Herzberg, Frederick 301, 462, 463
hierarchy of needs. *See* Maslow's
    hierarchy of needs
Hill, Joe 242
Hinjosa, Raul 37
H. J. Heinz Company 8
HMO. *See* health maintenance
    organization
Hoffa, Jimmy 250
Hoffman, Paul G. 300–301
Hofstede's dimensions **232**
holding company **232–233**
home-based business 494
Home Depot 458–459
Homeland Security Act of 2002 123
Home Mortgage Disclosure Act of
    1975 189
homeowners insurance 247
Home Shopping Network 127
Honeywell 177, 332
Hong Kong 142
Hooker Chemical Company 163
Hoover, Herbert 44, 67, 115,
    425–426, 445
Hoover Institute 451
Hopkins, Harry 487
Horne, Stephen 111
hospitality taxes 282
Host, Kevin 155
hostile environment harassment
    419–420
hostile takeovers 279, 306, 357–358,
    449
Hotmail.com 476
House of Representatives, U.S. 214,
    358, 471
housing loans 190–192
H.R. 10 plans 270, 404
HRS (Hazard Ranking System) 437
HTS. *See* Harmonized Tariff System
HTTP. *See* hypertext transfer protocol
HTTP (hypertext transfer protocol)
    490
HUD (Department of Housing and
    Urban Development) 220
Hull, Raymond 357
human resources **233**
        assessment center 20
        chain-of-command principle 60
        downsizing 133
        employee recruiting 157–158
        employment 159
        equity income theory 169
        international management 252
        nepotism 328
        outplacement 344–345
        resources 401
        training and development 458
human rights 251
Hume, David 455
Hurricane Hugo 364
Hurston, Zora Neale 487
hyperinflation 243
hypertext 490
hypertext markup language (HTML)
    150, 490
hypertext transfer protocol (HTTP)
    490

I

I-banking. *See* investment banking
IBT. *See* International Brotherhood of
    Teamsters
ICC. *See* Interstate Commerce
    Commission

ICSID (International Centre for Settlement of Investment Disputes) 487
IDB (Inter-American Development Bank) 247
IEA. *See* International Energy Agency
IEC (International Electrotechnical Commission) 264
IFCC (Internet Fraud Complaint Center) 256
ILO (International Labor Organization) 251
IMA (Institute of Management Accountants) 246
IMF. *See* International Monetary Fund
immigration 13, 223, 476–477
Immigration Reform and Control Act (IRCA) 336
implied warranties 480
import restraints 151–152, 234
imports/exports 235
    Auto Pact 22–23
    consignment 85
    dumping 135
    economic development 140
    embargo 151–152
    exchange rate 173
    Export-Import Bank of the United States 175
    free trade 211
    national income accounting 325
    nontariff barriers 331
    rules of origin 407–408
    Smoot-Hawley Tariff Act 425–426
    tariff 444–445
    trade balance 455
    trade barriers 456
    U.S. Commercial Service 471–472
    U.S. Customs Clearance 472
    U.S. Customs Service 472–473
    U.S. Trade Representative 473
import-substitution-industrialization (ISI) 140
in-bond production operations. *See* maquiladoras
incentives, external 3
incentive theory 318
income 235. *See also* national income accounting
    capital gain, capital loss 54
    equity income theory 169
    five Cs of credit 201
    gini ratio 215
    income elasticity of demand 235–236
    income statement, gross margin 236–237
    indicators 239
    inflation 242
    Lorenz curve 282–283
    minimum wage 308
    personal finance 353
    profit sharing 379
    proprietorship 382–383
    real income 395
    retirement plan 403
    sales forecasting 410
    saving 413
    standard of living 432
    trust 461
income disparity 7
income elasticity of demand 235–236
income funds 321
income redistribution 236, 459

income statement, gross margin 42, 54, 100–101, 198, 235, 236–237, 289, 378
income taxes 49, 249, 350, 351
incorporation 52, 99, 237, 309
independent contractors 237–238, 336
India 415, 479
indicators 44–45, 139, 239–240, 245, 366
indirect compensation 79
individual retirement account (IRA) 240–241, 270, 403, 414, 423–424, 446
Indonesia 104, 344
industrial-organizational psychology (I/O) 4, 229, 241–242
Industrial Revolution 19, 55, 327. *See also* American Industrial Revolution
Industrial Workers of the World (IWW) 242
inefficiency 373, 402
inequality gap 282
inflation 242–243
    automatic stabilizers 22
    compounding 80–81
    Consumer Price Index 88–89
    cost-of-living adjustment 101
    cost-push inflation 101
    equation of exchange 167
    escalator clause 170
    Great Depression 222
    Index of Consumer Expectations 239
    Keynesian economics 271
    money 311
    peso crisis 356
    price ceilings 364
    price indexes 366
    real income 395
    standard of living 432
    wage and price controls 479
    yield curve 492
inflation-indexed securities 474
infomercials 127, 243
informal economy 465–466
informal investigations 296
information risk 205
information systems 294
infrastructure 37, 99, 243–244, 300, 332
initial public offering (IPO) 63, 99, 132, 244, 383, 421, 475
Initiating structure 278
injunctions 151–152, 244
input-output (I/O) 244
Insiders Trading Sanctions Act 244
insider trading 244–245, 416
Insider Trading and Securities Fraud Enforcement Act 245
insolvency. *See* business failure; consumer bankruptcy
Institute for Governmental Research 452
Institute for Supply Management (ISM) 245–246, 388
Institute of Certified Financial Planners 196
Institute of Management Accountants (IMA) 246
institutional investors 358
institutionalized inefficiency 402
institutional memory 307
insurance 155–156, 188, 220, 226–227, 246–247, 345–346, 350, 351, 354, 407, 422
integrated marketing communications. *See* marketing communications

Intel 203, 226
intellectual property 247. *See also* patents
    benchmarking 29
    copyright 94
    corporate security 97
    counterfeit goods 102
    franchising 207
    international management 252
    licensing 280
    proprietary information 382
    Section 301, Special 301, Super 301 416
    trade barriers 456
    trademark 456–457
    trade secrets 457
    World Intellectual Property Organization 488
intelligence. *See* business intelligence; market intelligence
Inter-American Development Bank (IDB) 247
interdependence, mutual. *See* mutual interdependence
interest rates 247–248
    callable bond 53
    capital markets, money markets 55
    credit cards 105
    credit union 106
    deflation 118
    derivative securities 125
    duration 136
    fiscal policy 200
    five Cs of credit 201
    government debt 219
    Great Depression 223
    guaranteed investment contracts 226
    hedge fund 231
    Index of Consumer Expectations 238–239
    macroeconomics 284
    Moody's ratings 316
    open-market operations 339
    personal finance 353
    predatory lending 363
    repurchase agreements 399
    reserve requirements 400
    savings and loan associations 414
    stock market, bond market 433
    yield curve 492
interlocking directorate 68, 72, 248–249
intermediate products 225
Intermediate Technology Development Group 41
internal rate of return (IRR) 42, 56–57
Internal Revenue Service (IRS) 249–250
    Department of the Treasury 123
    financial accounting 195
    401(k) plan 207
    generally accepted accounting principles 215
    income 235
    ombudsmen 338
    partnership 349
    payroll taxes 351
    privacy 368
    real estate investment trusts 395
    tax shelter 446
Internal Revenue Service Restructuring and Reform Act of 1998 249

International Association for Financial Planning 196
International Bank for Reconstruction and Development. *See* World Bank
International Brotherhood of Teamsters (Teamsters Union) (IBT) 250, 358
International Centre for Settlement of Investment Disputes (ICSID) 487
International Development Association 487
International Electrotechnical Commission (IEC) 264
International Energy Agency (IEA) 250–251
International Federation of the National Standardizing Associations (ISA) 264
International Finance Corporation 487
International Labor Organization (ILO) 251
international management 251–252
international marketing 252–254, 471–472
International Monetary Fund (IMF) 40, 254–255, 356, 489
International Organization for Standardization (ISO) 228, 390. *See also* ISO standards
International Postal Reply Coupons 362
International Standard Industrial Classification System (ISIC) 334
International Trade Commission (ITC) 135, 228, 255
International Trade Organization (ITO) 489
Internet 255–256
    arbitrage 19
    assessment center 20
    barriers to entry 28
    barter 28, 29
    Better Business Bureau 31
    cash management 57
    consumption tax 91
    customer loyalty 110
    cyberspace 112
    distribution channels 130
    dot-coms 132
    e-business 138
    e-commerce 138–139
    e-government 145–147
    electronic data interchange 149–150
    fraud 209
    gray markets 222
    infrastructure 243
    privacy 368
    public relations 385–386
    viral marketing 476
    World Intellectual Property Organization 488
Internet Fraud Complaint Center (IFCC) 256
Internet marketing 139, 256–258
Internet surveys 258–259, 297
internships 259
interstate commerce 73
Interstate Commerce Act of 1887 421
Interstate Commerce Commission (ICC) 125, 259
interstate highway system 243
interstate transportation 259
interviewing 157–158, 241, 259–261
"in the money" 340
intrafirm trade 175

inventory control 199, **261–262**, 269
investment **262–263**
   bonds 35–36
   break-even analysis 39
   compounding 80–81
   direct investment 126
   economic growth 143
   foreign investment 204–205
   guaranteed investment contract
     226–227
   Institute for Supply
     Management 246
   international marketing 253
   national income accounting
     324
   Overseas Private Investment
     Corporation 345–346
   personal finance 353
   Ponzi scheme 362
   real estate investment trusts
     394–395
   repurchase agreements 398–399
   socially responsible investing
     428–429
   stock-rating systems 434
   trust 461
   venture capital 475
   World Bank 487–488
investment banking (I-banking) 83,
  262, **263–264**, 434, 466
investment clubs 262, **264**
Investment Company Act of 1940
  230
investment-grade bonds 35, 431–432
investor visas 477
invisible hand 141, 276, 402
invitation to bid 399
invoices 2, 207
I/O. *See* industrial-organizational
  psychology; input-output
IPO. *See* initial public offering
IRA. *See* individual retirement
  account
Iran 344
Iraq 344, 413
IRCA (Immigration Reform and
  Control Act) 336
IRR. *See* internal rate of return
IRS. *See* Internal Revenue Service
ISA (International Federation of the
  National Standardizing
  Associations) 264
ISIC (International Standard
  Industrial Classification System)
  334
ISI (import-substitution-
  industrialization) 140
ISM. *See* Institute for Supply
  Management
ISO. *See* International Organization
  for Standardization
ISO 9000 265
ISO 14000 265
ISO Information Network (ISONET)
  265
ISO standards 16, **264–265**, 331
Italy 147, 465
ITC. *See* International Trade
  Commission
ITO (International Trade
  Organization) 489
IWW (Industrial Workers of the
  World) **242**

J

Jackson, Andrew 26
Jackson, Jess 37
Jacobson, Michael 57

Japan
  conglomerate 84
  corporate average fuel
    efficiency 94
  deflation 118
  demand 119–120
  exporting 175
  gray markets 222
  interlocking directorate 248
  international marketing 253
  inventory control 261
  just-in-time production 269
  nontariff barriers 331
  quality control 390
  Section 301, Special 301, Super
    301 415, 416
J. C. Penney 483
Jefferson, Thomas 312
Jevons, Stanley 291
JIT. *See* just-in-time production
job satisfaction **266–267**, 341, 463,
  486
job training 10
Johns-Manville Corporation 46
Johnson, Lyndon B. 66, 164, 336
Johnson & Johnson 347
joint venture 253, **267**, 320, 435, 447
Jones, Edward 132
Jones, John E. 452
Jones Act (Merchant Marine Act)
  267–268
Jordan, Vernon 452
journal entries 4
J.P. Morgan 217
judicial interpretation 43
junk bonds 117, 279, 305, 315,
  431–432
Juran, Joseph M. 454
juries 187
jurisdiction, extraterritorial **177**
just cause (sufficient cause) 160,
  268, 490
just-in-time production (JIT) 20,
  149, 261, **268–269**
J. Walter Thompson 285

K

Kabin, Bonnie 203
Kaderni, Maksude 362
Kahn, Alfred 65
Kaiser, Henry J. 230
kaizen 390
Kameda, Naoki 108
kanban 261
Kantor, Andrew 385
karoshi 454
Kathie Lee Gifford 441
Katona, George 238
Kellogg 322, 338
Kelly, J. E. 107
Kemp, Evan 216
Kemp, Jack 440
Ken Blanchard Companies 287
Kendall, Maurice 394
Kennedy, John F. 66, 416, 469, 471,
  473
Kennedy, Joseph P. 416
Kennedy administration 480
Kennedy School of Government
  (Harvard) 451
Keogh plan **270**, 403, 404, 414
Kerr-McGee 485
key money 364
Keynes, John Maynard 40, 200, 223,
  270, 291, 310
Keynesian economics 67, **270–271**,
  276, 284, 310
keystoning 367

Kirkpatrick, Jeane 451
KKR. *See* Kohlberg Kravis, Roberts
KM. *See* knowledge management
Kmart 302, 306
Knight-Ridder/Tribune Business
  News 485
Knights of Labor 12, 15
know-how 271, 350, 402
knowledge management (KM) 138,
  271–272, 431
Koch, A. Robert 339, 373
Kohlberg Kravis, Roberts (KKR) 279,
  305
Kondratev waves **272**
Korten, David 58
Kroc, Ray 207
Kuwait 344
Kuznets, Simon 284, 324
Kyoto Protocol (Kyoto Accord,
  Climate Change Treaty) **272–273**,
  361

L

labor-employee relations **274**. *See
also* collective bargaining; union(s)
labor force (workforce) **274–275**
  American Industrial Revolution
    15
  blue-collar workers 32
  Buddhist economics 41
  Bureau of Labor Statistics 43
  Department of Labor, U.S.
    121–122
  economic growth 143
  Fair Labor Standards Act 180
  family-friendly business
    practices 183
  Federal Mediation and
    Conciliation Service 190
  human resources 233
  National Labor Relations Board
    325–326
  National Mediation Board 326
  North American Agreement on
    Labor Cooperation 331–332
  reductions in force 396–397
  unemployment 466–467
  union 468–469
  visas 476–477
  work council 486
Labor Law Study Committee 48
Labor-Management Relations Act. *See*
  Taft-Hartley Act
Labor Management Reporting and
  Disclosure Act 276
labor markets **275**
Laffer, Arthur 440
lagging indicators 239
laissez-faire 141, **276**, 309, 441
"Lake Wobegon" evaluations 203
Lakshimi 481
Landrum-Griffin Act (Labor
  Management Reporting and
  Disclosure Act) 276, **276**
land use 43, 122, 444, 494
last in, first out (LIFO) **199**
Las Vegas Convention Center 457
Latham, Gary 371
Latin America 211, 247
law and legislation. *See also* litigation;
  specific headings
  administrative law 5
  American Bar Association 11
  blue laws 32–33
  commercial law 73
  common law 76–77
  copyright 94
  federal courts 187

Internal Revenue Service
  249–250
  right-to-know laws 405
  right-to-work laws 405
  Uniform Commercial Code
    467–468
law of comparative advantage 235
law of diminishing marginal returns
  373
law of supply 438
layoff 133, **276–277**, 344, 396–397,
  418
LBO (leveraged buyout) 279
LDCs (less-developed countries) 153
leadership 62–63, 157, 241, 266,
  277–278, 287, 307, 343
"leadership" political action
  committees 360
Leading Indicator Composite Index
  239
leading indicators 239
League of Woman Voters 385
leakage (market intelligence) 296
lean production 269
learning curves. *See* experience and
  learning curves
leasing **278**
leave time, employee 156, 181
legislation. *See* law and legislation
legislative courts 187
lending. *See* loans
less-developed countries (LDCs) 153
Lestrade, Edward 454, 455
letter of credit 278
leverage 212, **278–279**
leveraged buyout (LBO) **279**
Levine, Dennis 245
Levi Strauss 98
Levitt, Theodore 419, 444
Levittown 12
liabilities **279–280**
  balance sheet 25
  book value 36
  business failure 46
  corporation 99
  incorporation 237
  independent contractors 238
  insurance 246, 247
  limited liability company 281
  limited liability partnership
    281–282
  owner's equity 346
  partnership 349
  product liability 374–375
  proprietorship 382
  risk management 406
  Superfund 437–438
Libya 344
licensing 175, 187, 207, 253, **280**,
  314, 396, 447
life cycle 183–184, **280–281**, 367,
  375–376
life insurance 246–247, 354
LIFO 199
Liggett & Myers 453
Likert scale questions 391
Limbaugh, Rush 37
limited liability 279
limited liability company (LLC) 99,
  281, 349
limited liability partnership (LLP)
  281–282, 349
limited partnership 349
Lincoln, Abraham 249
Lincoln Law 484
Lindsey, Lawrence 440
Lipton, Martin 357
liquidation 85
liquidity crisis 356

list brokers 127
litigation
    civil procedure 65
    class-action lawsuits 66–67
    consent decree 84
    contract 92
    Court of International Trade
      104
    damages 114
    dispute settlement 129
    document-retention policy 131
    due process 134–135
    eminent domain 154–155
    extraterritorial jurisdiction 177
    Foreign Sovereign Immunities
      Act 205–206
    injunctions 244
    liability. *See* liabilities
    negligence 327
    product liability 374–375
    tobacco settlement 453–454
living wage 432, 481
Liz Claiborne 441
LLC. *See* limited liability company
Lloyds 246
LLP. *See* limited liability partnership
Lo, Andrew 394
load funds 321
loan certificates 329
Loan Prospector 190
loans **282**
    amortized loan 17
    annuity 18
    credit bureaus 105
    credit scoring 106
    credit union 106–107
    default 117–118
    Export-Import Bank of the
      United States 175
    Federal Financial Institutions
      Examinations Council 189
    financial intermediaries 196
    five Cs of credit 201
    401(k) plan 207
    Freddie Mac 190
    Ginnie Mae 220
    interest rates 248
    International Monetary Fund
      254
    mortgage 316–317
    predatory lending 363
    repurchase agreements 398
    Sallie Mae 437
    savings and loan associations
      414
    securitization 417
    Small Business Administration
      425
    Truth in Lending Act 462
    World Bank 487–488
lobbying 10–11, 28, 48–49, 57–58,
    60–61, 164, 186, 191
local government websites 146
local option sales tax (LOST) **282**
local taxes 381–382
lockboxes 57
Locke, Edwin 371
Lockheed Martin 359
lock-up periods 230–231
Loewe v. Lawlor 422
logic 436, 450
logistics. *See* business logistics
Long Island Sound 402
long-term assets 20–21
long-term capital gains 54
Long Term Capital Management
    (LTCM) 191, 231, 316, 340
long-term debt instruments 55
long-term interest rates 248, 492

long-term liabilities 280
Lorenz, Max Otto 282
Lorenz curve 215, **282–283**, 432
Lorillard Tobacco Company 453
Los Angeles 465
LOST (local option sales tax) **282**
Lott, Trent 268
The Louvre 335
Love Canal 163, 224
Lowes 458–459
Lowry, Ritchie 429
LTCM. *See* Long Term Capital
    Management
Lucky Supermarkets 37
lump sum discounting 128
luxury items 148–149
Lyman, George D. 329

M

M1 (monetary aggregate) 313
M2 (monetary aggregate) 313
M3 (monetary aggregate) 313
MacPherson v. Buick Motor Company
    374–375
macroeconomics 67, 101, 139, 200,
    284–285, 493
Madison Avenue 285, 432
Magnuson-Moss Warranty-Federal
    Trade Commission Improvement
    Act 90, 480
mail (corporate security) 97
mail surveys 258, **285**, 297
make-or-buy decisions **285–286**
Malkiel, Burton 394
Mallor, Jane 52, 83, 160, 327
Mallor et. al 238
Malthus, Thomas 286
Malthusian trap **286**
managed care 229–230
management **287**
    business failure 46
    corporate culture 95
    customer-relationships
      management 110–111
    database management 114–115
    decision tree 117
    earnings management 137–138
    empowerment 160
    experience/learning curves 174
    gap analysis 213–214
    goal setting 218
    human resources 233
    industrial-organizational
      psychology 241
    Institute for Supply
      Management 245
    international management
      251–252
    ISO standards 264–265
    knowledge management
      271–272
    masters of business
      administration 302–303
    matrix management 303–304
    middle managers 307
    nepotism 327–328
    performance appraisal 352
    poison-pill strategies 357
    problem solving 369–370
    project management 380–381
    public administration 383–384
    quality control 390
    risk management 405–406
    sales management 411–412
    supply-chain management
      387–388
    synergy 441–442

360-degree feedback 452
    time management 452–453
    total-quality management
      454–455
management gurus **287–289**
management theory 7–8, 51, 60,
    213–214, 301, 357, 449–451,
    462–463
managerial accounting (cost
    accounting) 4, 39, **289–290**, 439
managerial grid theory 441–442
manufacturers' representatives
    (manufacturers' agents) **290**
manufacturing 14–15, 15–16, 19–20,
    20, 32, 39, 82, 113, 129–130, 327.
    See also quality control
maquiladoras (twin plants, in-bond
    production operations) 20, 37,
    290–291, 320–321, 334
March Group 48
marginal analysis **291–292**
marginal costs 102, 378, 439
marginal product 275, 291
marginal revenue (MR) 275, 378, 439
marginal tax rate 439
marginal utility 291
marine insurance 246
Maritime Administration 123
market capitalization 226
market-clearing price 167
market concentration 72–73,
    231–232, **292**
market exchange 61–62, 329–330
market failure 125, 176, **292**
market-growth matrix. *See* market-
    share, market-growth matrix
marketing
    adoption process 5–6
    AIDA concept 21
    brands. *See* brands, brand names
    buying-center concept 52
    customer-relationship
      management 110–111
    customer relations/satisfaction
      111
    demographics 120
    direct mail 126–127
    direct marketing 127–128
    e-business 138
    exit strategies 173–174
    gap analysis 213–214
    green marketing 224–225
    international marketing
      252–254
    Internet marketing 256–258
    multilevel 319
    network marketing 319
    product placement 377
    relationship marketing 397–398
    target markets 444
    telemarketing 447–448
    viral marketing 476
marketing channels. *See* distribution
    channels
marketing communications
    (integrated marketing
    communications) 6, 126, 127,
    243, **293**, 355, 457–458
marketing concept **293–294**
marketing-information systems **294**
marketing strategy **294–295**
    buy-grid model 51
    consumer behavior 86
    80-20 principle 148
    environmental scanning 164
    exporting 175
    factory tours 178
    family life cycle 183–184
    first-mover advantage 199

    game theory 213
    international marketing
      253–254
    market segmentation 297
    North American Industry
      Classification System 334
    packaging 347
    positioning 362
    product-market growth matrix
      376–377
    product proliferation 377
    public relations 385
    relationship management
      397–398
    relationship marketing 397–398
    target markets 444
market intelligence (competitive
    intelligence, business intelligence)
    80, 164, 272, **295–296**, 382,
    430–431, 457
market interdependence 299
market-manipulation schemes 256
market penetration 376
market research **296–297**
    AIO statements 21–22
    brand names 38
    customer relations/satisfaction
      111
    80-20 principle 148
    focus groups 202
    international marketing
      252–253
    mail surveys 285
    observation 335
    personal-interview surveys 354
    questionnaires 390–391
    sales forecasting 410
    telephone surveys 448–449
    U.S. Census Bureau 471
markets 75–76, 153–154, 189, 222,
    275, 347–348, 368, 438, 444
market segmentation 222, **297–298**,
    364, 471
market-share, market-growth matrix
    298, **298–299**, 367
market structure **299–300**, 307,
    313–314, 338. *See also* monopoly
market theory 92, 145, 394
market value 50, 167, 168, **300**, 368,
    433, 444
Markowitz, Harry 310
Marks and Spencer 217
markup pricing 367
Marlboro 362–363
Marshall, Alfred 167, 291
Marshall, George C. 300
Marshall, John 205
Marshallian cross 167
Marshall Plan (European Recovery
    Program) **300–301**, 319, 343, 471
Marx, Karl 55, 427
marxist socialism 427
Mary Kay 319
M&As. *See* mergers and acquisitions
masculinity-femininity 232
Maslow, Abraham 301, 318, 342, 450
Maslow's hierarchy of needs 86, **301**,
    318, 450
Massachusetts Institute of Technology
    (MIT) 394
mass customization 302
mass merchandising 302
Masstricht Treaty 171
MasterCard 105
master of business administration
    (MBA) **302–303**
Master Settlement Agreement (MSA)
    453, 454
matching contributions 207

matching principle 3, 17
material corporate developments 244
material information 245
materials-requirements planning (MRP) 261
materials-resource planning (MRPII) 261
matrix management *303*, **303–304**
MBA. *See* master of business administration
MBCA (Model Business Corporation Act) 83
MBTI (Myers Briggs Type Indicator) 20
McCain, John 268
McCarron-Ferguson Act of 1945 246
McClelland, David 301
McCully, Winston 485
McDonald's 207, 217, 281, 411, 464
McGraw-Hill, Inc. 431
McGregor, Douglas 450
MCI 232, 387
MCI WorldCom 292
Meat Inspection Act 202
mediation 190, 326
Medicaid 10, 236, 429, 430, 482
medical expenses 487
medical records 368
Medicare 49, 236, 350
mercantilism 211, 276, **304**, 455, 481
Mercedes-Benz 94, 99
merchandise account 24
"merchantable" 480
Merchant Marine Act **267–268**
MERCOSUR 112, 211–212
mergers and acquisitions (M&As) 68, 96, 192, **304–306**
Merrill Lynch 83, 263, 434
Merton, Robert 340
MES (minimum efficient scale) 145
metropolitan statistical area (MSA) **306**
Mexico
    Border Environment Cooperation Commission 37
    Brady bonds 38
    economic development 141
    gray markets 222
    international marketing 253
    joint venture 267
    maquiladoras 290
    multinational corporation 320–321
    North American Agreement on Labor Cooperation 332
    North American Development Bank 332
    North American Free Trade Agreement 332–334
    Organization of Petroleum Exporting Countries 344
    parallel markets 348
    peso crisis 356
    strategic alliances 435
    trade balance 455
    United Farm Workers 469
    visas 477
    World Trade Organization 489
MFN clause. *See* most-favored-nation clause
Miami 343, 465
microeconomics **306–307**
Microloan (7m) Loan Program 425
Microsoft
    corporate divestiture 96
    corporation 100
    database management 115
    growth stocks 226
    infomercials 243

insider trading 245
monopoly 314
NASDAQ 323
personal selling 355
stock options 434
tying contracts 464
World Wide Web 490
middle managers 277, **307–308**
military-industrial complex, U.S. 339
Milken, Michael 305
minimum efficient scale (MES) 145
minimum wage 180, **308**, 365–366
Mishkin, Frederic S. 414
mission statement 45, 48, **308–309**, 478
Mississippi 453
Mitchell, Wesley 323
Mitchel v. Reynolds 421
MIT (Massachusetts Institute of Technology) 394
Mitsubishi Motor Manufacturing of America 420
mixed economy 63–64, **309**
MLM (multilevel marketing) **319**
MNC. *See* multinational corporation
Mobil Oil 359
Model Business Corporation Act (MBCA) 83, **309**
Model Uniform Product Liability Act 375
modernization theory 153
modern portfolio theory (MPT) **310**
Molotov, Vyacheslav 300
momentum investing 446
monetarists 167
monetary aggregate 313
monetary policy 27, 44, 64, 129, 144, 200, 243, 284, **310–311**, 324, 400
money 4, 26, **311–312**, 481
money markets. *See* capital markets, money markets
money-purchase plan 270, 404
money supply 26, 128, 167, 192, 310–311, **312–313**, 339, 455
Mongolia 168
monopolistic competition 299, **313–314**, 352
monopoly 28, 103, 145, 231, 232, 299–300, 307, 313–314, **314–315**, 350, 386, 387. *See also* antitrust law
Monsanto 339–340
Montgomery Ward 127, 250
Montreal Protocol 69, **315**
Moody's ratings 35, 136, 279, **315–316**
Moorman, Jerry 162
moral suasion **316**
Morgenstern, Oskar 213
Morgenthau, Henry M. 40
mortgage **316–317**
    amortization 17
    amortized loan 17
    credit scoring 106
    Fannie Mae 191
    Federal Home Loan Bank System 189
    Freddie Mac 190
    Ginnie Mae 220
    personal finance 353
    predatory lending 363
    promissory notes 381
    real estate investment trusts 395
    Resolution Trust Corporation 400–401
    savings and loan associations 414
mortgage-backed securities 417, 418

most-favored-nation clause (MFN) 206, **317–318**, 445
motivation theory 3–4, 301, **318–319**, 342, 411, 462–463. *See also* employee motivation
Motor Carrier Act 259
Mouton, Jane 441–442
Mowatt, Jeff 110
MPT (modern portfolio theory) **310**
MR. *See* marginal revenue
MRPII (materials-resource planning) 261
MRP (materials-requirements planning) 261
MSA. *See* Master Settlement Agreement; metropolitan statistical area
MSN 476
muckraking 85
Mulroney, Brian 470
Multilateral Investment Guarantee Agency 487
multilevel marketing (network marketing) (MLM) **319**
multinational corporation (MNC) **319–321**
    country-risk analysis 104
    cross-cultural communication 108–109
    direct investment 126
    economic development 140
    emerging markets 153
    exchange-rate risk 172
    Export-Import Bank of the United States 175
    exporting 175
    international management 251–252
    maquiladoras 290–291
    Marshall Plan 301
    socially responsible investing 428
    work council 486
multiple use management 43
multisegment strategy 444
municipal bonds 37
Murray, Henry A. 301
Muskie, Edmund 68
mutual funds 16, 153, **321**, 353–354
mutual interdependence 63–64, **321–322**, 338, 377
Mutual Security Agency 301
Myanmar (Burma) 37
Myers Briggs Type Indicator (MBTI) 20

N

NAACP (National Association for the Advancement of Colored People) 37
NAALC. *See* North American Agreement on Labor Cooperation
NABPAC (National Association of Business Political Action Committees) 359
NADBank. *See* North American Development Bank
Nader, Ralph 85, 90
NAFTA. *See* North American Free Trade Agreement
NAIC (National Association of Investment Clubs) 264
NAICS. *See* North American Industry Classification System
naïve forecasting 410
NASDAQ. *See* National Association of Securities Dealers Automated Quotation System

NASD (National Association of Securities Dealers) 323
Nash, John 213, 322
National Association for the Advancement of Colored People (NAACP) 37
National Association of Business Political Action Committees (NABPAC) 359
National Association of Foreign Trade Zones 206
National Association of Independent Insurers 359
National Association of Investment Clubs (NAIC) 264
National Association of Life Underwriters 359
National Association of Purchasing Managers
National Association of Real Estate Investment Trusts 395
National Association of Realtors 359
National Association of Securities Dealers Automated Quotation System (NASDAQ) 16, 168, **323**, 330, 433, 480
National Association of Securities Dealers (NASD) 323
National Bank Act 27, 81, 82
National Bureau of Economic Research (NBER) **323–324**, 396
National Collegiate Athletic Association (NCAA) 37–38, 56
National Cooperative Research Act (NCRA) 267
National Credit Union Share Insurance Fund (NCUSIF) 106–107
National Education Association (NEA) 469
National Environmental Policy Act (NEPA) 162
National Farm Labor Union 469
National Foundation for Credit Counseling (NFCC) 87–88
National Futures Association 75
National Highway Traffic Safety Administration (NHTSA) 123
National Housing Act of 1934 191, 220
national income accounting 91, 284, 323, **324–325**, 465
National Industrial Recovery Act (NIRA) **325**
National Institute of Standards and Technology (NIST) 25
National Institutes of Health (NIH) 400
National Labor Relations Act. *See* Wagner Act
National Labor Relations Board (NLRB) 71–72, **325–326**, 480
National Mediation Board (NMB) **326**
National Mortgage Association of Washington 191, 220
National Organization of Women (NOW) 37
National Performance Review 384
National Priorities List (NPL) 437
National Pure Food and Drug Congresses 203
National Science Foundation (NSF) 400
national security 146, 147, 267
National Transportation Safety Board 185
National War Labor Board 479

National White Collar Crime Center 256
natural resources 401
Nautica 280
Navigation Acts 304
NBER. *See* National Bureau of Economic Research
NCAA. *See* National Collegiate Athletic Association
NCRA (National Cooperative Research Act) 267
NCUSIF. *See* National Credit Union Share Insurance Fund
NEA (National Education Association) 469
Near, Janet P. 484
necessity goods 148–149
negligence 250, 279, 327, 374
negotiable instruments 73, 196, **327**
Neighbor to Neighbor 37
Nepal 479
NEPA (National Environmental Policy Act) 162
nepotism **327–328**
Netherlands 344
net income 378
net present value (NPV) 42
Netscape 490
Net Solutions 112, 258
netting 57
network diagram (critical path method) 107
networking 49
net working capital 197–198
network marketing **319**
net worth 25, 201
New Africa Infrastructure Fund 346
New Deal
   AFL-CIO 13
   business and the U.S. Constitution 43
   Civilian Conservation Corps 65
   Commodity Credit Corporation 74
   family farm 181
   fiscal policy 200
   General Accounting Office 214
   Keynesian economics 271
   national income accounting 324
   National Industrial Recovery Act 325
   retirement plan 404
   Works Progress Administration 487
New Jersey 338
Newmont Mining 104
new-product development **328–329**
New York City 158
New York Clearing House Association 329
New York Convention 129
New York Federal Reserve Bank 340
New York Mercantile Exchange (NYMEX) **329–330**
New York Stock Exchange (NYSE) 16, 168, 323, 330, 380, 433, 480
NFCC. *See* National Foundation for Credit Counseling
NFSNet 255
NHTSA (National Highway Traffic Safety Administration) 123
Nielsen 296
Nigeria 344
Nigerian money-order scam 256
NIH (National Institutes of Health) 400
Nike 441
NIRA (National Industrial Recovery Act) **325**

NIST (National Institute of Standards and Technology) 25
Nixon, Richard M. 44, 163, 364, 368, 479
NLRB. *See* National Labor Relations Board
NLRB v. Bildisco 72
NLRB v. Burns International Security Services 72
NMB (National Mediation Board) **326**
no-load funds 321
noncompete clause 382
noneconomic sanctions 413
non-interest-bearing note 17, 36–37
nonprice competition 80, 322, 367
nonprivileged foreign merchandise 206
nonprofit organizations 93, 106–107, 295, 386, 444
nontariff barriers 210, 234, **331**
nontaxable benefits 53
Nordstrom 483
normal completion time 107
"normal" goods 236
normal yield curve 492
Norris-LaGuardia Act **331**
North American Agreement on Labor Cooperation (NAALC) 290, **331–332**, 334
North American Development Bank (NADBank) 37, **332**
North American Free Trade Agreement (NAFTA) **332–334**
   Auto Pact 22
   Border Environment Cooperation Commission 37
   corporate welfare 98
   Court of International Trade 104
   cultural industries 110
   economic development 141
   European Union 170
   fast track 185
   free trade 210, 211
   free-trade areas 211
   globalization 217
   harmonization 228
   import restraints 234
   imports/exports 235
   international marketing 253
   maquiladoras 290
   multinational corporation 320, 321
   nontariff barriers 331
   North American Industry Classification System 334
   Organization of American States 343
   reciprocity 396
   reductions in force 397
   rules of origin 407–408
   strategic alliances 435
   trade-adjustment assistance 455
   trade balance 455
   trade secrets 457
   visas 477
   World Trade Organization 489
North American Industry Classification System (NAICS) 120, **334**
North Dakota 155
North Korea 58
Northrop Grumman 359
Northwestern University 303
Norway 344
NOW (National Organization of Women) 37

NPL (National Priorities List) 437
NPV (net present value) 42
NSF (National Science Foundation) 400
NuSkin 319
Nutrilite Products, Inc. 319
The Nutrition Labeling Act of 1990 347
Nutrition Labeling and Education Act 57
nylon 457
NYMEX. *See* New York Mercantile Exchange
NYSE. *See* New York Stock Exchange

O

OAS. *See* Organization of American States
OASDI. *See* Old Age, Survivors and Disability Insurance
OAU (Organization of African Unity) 211
OB. *See* organization behavior
object-oriented database-management systems (ODBM) 115
observation 229, 296, **335**
obstruction of justice 131
Occidental Petroleum (OXY USA) 359
OCC (Option Clearing Corporation) 340
Occupational Safety and Health Act of 1970 233, 335, 405, 409, 491
Occupational Safety and Health Administration (OSHA) 169–170, **335–336**
ODBM (object-oriented database-management systems) 115
odd-even pricing 367
OECD. *See* Organization for Economic Cooperation and Development
OEM parts. *See* original equipment parts
OFCCP. *See* Office of Federal Contract Compliance Programs
Office of Energy Efficiency and Renewable Energy 273
Office of Federal Contract Compliance Programs (OFCCP) **336–337**
Office of Federal Housing Enterprise Oversight (OFHEO) 191
Office of Government Ethics (OGE) 31, 40, **337**
Office of Management and Budget (OMB) 186, **337**
Office of Personnel Management Employment Service 345
OFHEO (Office of Federal Housing Enterprise Oversight) 191
OGE. *See* Office of Government Ethics
Ogilvy & Mather 285
oil and oil industry 101, 250–251, 344, 356, 359
Oklahoma 405
Old Age, Survivors and Disability Insurance (OASDI) 49, 350, 429, 430, 482
oligopoly 231, 292, 299, 320, 321, **338**, 344, 365, 367, 377
OMB. *See* Office of Management and Budget
ombudsmen 5, **338**
Omnibus Trade and Competitiveness Act of 1988 277, 415, 416, 455
Omnicom 285

O'Neil, Tip 358
on-line auctions 459
on-line retailing 127–128
on-line surveys 285
OPEC. *See* Organization of Petroleum Exporting Countries
open-market operations 192, 311, **339**, 399
Open Secrets 358
open systems 244, 342
operating leverage 279
OPIC. *See* Overseas Private Investment Corporation
opportunity cost 78, **339–340**
opt-in e-mail 257
Option Clearing Corporation (OCC) 340
options, option contracts 61–62, 75–76, 329–330, **340–341**, 433–434
Oracle 115
Orbitz.com 257
Oregon 78
organic acts 5
organizational charts. *See* chain-of-command principle
organizational commitment **341**
organizational life cycles 281
organizational structure 303–304
organizational theory **341–342**
organization behavior (OB) **342–343**
Organization for Economic Cooperation and Development (OECD) 41, 96–97, 343, 361
Organization for European Economic Co-operation 343
Organization of African Unity (OAU) 211
Organization of American States (OAS) **343–344**
Organization of Petroleum Exporting Countries (OPEC) 56, 101, 139, 242, 251, **344**
organized crime 393
Organized Crime Control Act of 1970 393
organized labor 12–13
original equipment (OEM) parts 22, 23
Ortiz, Guillermo 356
OSHA. *See* Occupational Safety and Health Administration
OTC market. *See* over-the-counter market
outbound telemarketing 448
"out of money" option contracts 340
outplacement **344–345**
outsourcing 52, 78, 174, 285–286, **345**
overhead 4
Overseas Private Investment Corporation (OPIC) 175, 176, **345–346**, 473
over-the-counter (OTC) market 168, 433
Owen, Robert 481
owner's equity (owners' equity) **346**
OXY USA (Occidental Petroleum) 359
ozone 272, 273, 315, 361

P

Pacific Telesis 359
Pacioli, Fra Luca 115, 195, 214
packaging 116, **347**
palladium 388
parallel economy. *See* underground economy

parallel markets 347–348
Parent Loan for Undergraduate
Students 437
Pareto, Vilfredo 141, 147
Pareto Optimality 141
Paris 335
Paris Convention for Protection of
Industrial Property 488
parity 74, **348**
Parity Program 181
Parker Pen 222
partnership 49, 230, 267, 281–282,
346, **348–349**
par value 77
passive losses 281
patents 228, 247, 314, **349–350**,
399, 447, 488
Patton, George 47
pay. See compensation and benefits
payback period 42, 56, 100
pay equity. See comparable worth
pay-for-performance appraisal
systems 352
pay-per-service model 230
payroll taxes (employment taxes)
350–351
PBGC (Pension Benefit Guaranty
Corporation) **351**
PC. See perfect competition
PCAs (Production Credit
Associations) 184
"pearl-diving contests" 410
pegged exchange-rate system 173
PEMEX (Petroleos Mexicanos) 356
Pendleton Act (1883) 384
Pennsylvania Land Bank 312
Pension Benefit Guaranty
Corporation (PBGC) **351**
pension funds 158, 358
pension plans. See retirement plans
PepsiCo 96, 103
P/E ratio. See price/earnings ratio
perfect competition (PC) 92,
351–352, 352
performance 268, 406, 449
performance appraisal (performance
evaluation) 20, 203, 241, 342,
352–353, 452, 458
performance letter of credit 278
Perkins loans 437
Perot, Ross 234
perpetual inventory system 100
personal finance 85–86, 87–88, 130,
235, **353–354**
personal-interview surveys 296, **354**
personal property 278, **354–355**
Personal Responsibility and Work
Opportunity Reconciliation Act
(PRWORA) 10, 482
personal selling **355–356**, 389
PERT. See program evaluation and
review technique
PESI (Pilot Environmental
Sustainability Index) 440
peso crisis 173, 204, 222, 290, 334,
348, **356–357**. See also
maquiladoras
Peter, Laurence 357
Peter principle **357**
Petroleos Mexicanos (PEMEX) 356
PGA golf show (Orlando) 457
pharmaceuticals 328, 347–348, 365,
447
Phar-mor 152
Philadelphia Contribution 246
Philadelphia Contributorship for the
Insurance of Houses from Loss by
Fire 93

philanthropic corporate responsibility
389
Philip Morris 226, 359, 362–363, 453
Philippines 441
Phillips, Michael J. 63, 72, 309, 422
physical distribution. See business
logistics
Physiocrats 481
Pilot Environmental Sustainability
Index (PESI) 440
pilot fish 52
Pinto (Ford automobile) 375
PITI (principal, interest, taxes and
insurance) 316
Pitt, Harvey 1
planned economy. See centrally
planned economy
Planned Parenthood 476
planning 48, 56–57, 196–197, 287,
381, 452–453. See also strategic
planning
Plessy v. Ferguson 66
plunging neckline technical analysis
447
PMI (Purchasing Managers Indexes)
245
Point Four Program (Truman
administration) 471
points, mortgage 317
poison-pill strategies (shareholder
rights plans) 52, 249, 279, 306,
357–358, 449
Polaris submarine program 379, 380
Policy Management Systems, Inc. 82
political action committee (PAC) 15,
358–360
political environment 252
Political Money-Line 358
political risk 205, 345–346
pollution rights 176, **360–362**
Ponzi, Charles 209, 362
Ponzi scheme 209, 236, **362**
Poor, Henry 431
pop-up promotions 258
portfolio investments 25
positioning **362–363**
Post 322, 338
poverty 9–10, 140, 147, 153
power distance 232
PPC. See production-possibilities
curve
PPI. See Producer Price Index
PPOs (preferred provider
organizations) 229
PR. See public relations
precedent, legal 76
precious metals 304
predatory lending **363**
predatory pricing 135
predictive models 4
preferred provider organizations
(PPOs) 229
preferred stock. See common stock,
preferred stock, treasury stock
prepayment penalties 363
present value discounting. See
discounting, present value
presidential election campaigns 358
Presidential Emergency Board 326
pretests, market research 297
prevailing local wage 115
price ceilings, price controls **364**. See
also wage and price controls
price changes
Consumer Price Index 88–89
cross-price elasticity of demand
109
price controls. See price ceilings, price
controls; wage and price controls

price discrimination 68, 135,
364–365, 407
price/earnings (P/E) ratio 198, 226
price fixing 85, **365**, 422
price floors, price supports 308,
365–366
price indexes 88–89, **366–367**
Priceline.com 257
price matching 367
price/pricing
collusion 72
economic policy 144
elasticity of demand 148
equilibrium 167
escalator clause 170
international marketing 254
oligopoly 338
parity 348
profit maximization 378
public utilities 387
supply 438–439
price supports. See price floors, price
supports
pricing strategies 80, 109, 148–149,
367–368
primary-care physicians 229
primary markets, secondary markets
368, 433
primary production 140
prime rate 248
principal, interest, taxes and
insurance (PITI) 316
principal-agent relationship 7–8
print advertising 7
"prior art" (intellectual property) 247
privacy 111, 127, 146–147, 179, 257,
368
Privacy Act of 1974 368
private brands 39
privatization 124, 252–253,
368–369, 384
privileged foreign merchandise 206
problem solving **369–370**
process technology 285–286
process theories **370–371**
Procter and Gamble 37, 302
Producer Price Index (PPI) 43, 243,
366, **371**
product development 377
product differentiation 313–314
production 19, 20, 54, 58–59, 82,
113, 201, 268–269, 293, **372–373**
Production Credit Associations
(PCAs) 184
production-possibilities curve (PPC)
141, **373**, 402
productivity 155, 229, 379, 450–451
product liability 327, **374–375**
product life cycle 173, 367, **375–376**
product-market growth matrix 376,
376–377
product placement 377
product proliferation 377
product-related segmentation 298
product(s) **371–372**
adoption process 5–6
break-even analysis 39
consumer buying process 87
Consumers Union 90
harmonization 228–229
international marketing
253–254
Internet marketing 257
inventory control 261–262
life cycle 280
mass customization 302
mass merchandising 302
new-product development
328–329

packaging 347
perfect competition 351
price discrimination 364
price fixing 365
product liability 374
product life cycle 375
tariff 444–445
warranty 480
Professional Insurance Agents 359
profit 45, 131, 147–148, 237, 262,
263, 324, 365, **378**
profit margin 198
profit maximization 367, **378–379**
profit sharing, gain sharing 270, **379**,
404
pro forma earnings 137
pro forma statements 42
program evaluation and review
technique (PERT) 107, 108,
379–380, 380
program trading 231, **380**
Prohibition 465
project management 107–108,
379–380, **380–381**
promissory note 73–74, 282, **381**
promotion. See sales promotion
property 134, 142, 154, 247,
354–355
property taxes **381–382**, 445–446
proprietary information 29, 141,
246, **382**
proprietorship 346, **382–383**
prospectus 128, 263, **383**, 416
protectionism 73
protective tariffs 444
proxy 383
prudent-investor rule 461
prudent-man rule 158, 461
PRWORA. See Personal
Responsibility and Work
Opportunity Reconciliation Act
PSAs (public service announcements)
386
psychographic segmentation 297–298
psychological pricing 367
public administration **383–385**
public charity 481
public health 202
public information 245, 296
public land management 43
publicly owned corporation 70
public relations (PR) 51, 97–98, 293,
385–386
public service announcements (PSAs)
386
public utilities 224, 314, 360–361,
386–387, 449
Pullman strike 468
punitive damages 375
purchasing decisions 21, 52, 86–87
Purchasing Managers Indexes (PMI)
245
purchasing power 101, 242, 348
purchasing (supply-chain
management) 51, 215, 245,
387–388, 463–464
Purdue University 303
push pull strategies **389**
put option contracts 340
Pyhrr, Peter A. 493
pyramid of corporate responsibility
389
pyramid schemes 362

Q

Qatar 344
Quadrix 434
Quaker 322, 338

Qualified Personal Residence Trust 462
qualified plans 270, 404
qualifying customers 355
quality control 15–16, 120, 214, 265, 288, **390**, 454–455, 466
quality management 25–26
quantity theory of money 310
quasi rent 144
Quesnay, François 276
questionnaires 118, 285, **390–391**
queuing theory **391–392**
quick ratio 198
quid pro quo harassment 419
quotas 206, 210, 211, 234, 331, 344, 445
QVC 127

R

racetracks 120
Racketeer Influenced and Corrupt Organization Act (RICO) 40, **393**
racketeering activity 393
rack jobbers 130
railroads 14, 125, 154, 243, 259
Ralph Lauren 280
Rand Corporation 118
Rand Institute 452
random samples 297
random-walk theory 145, **393–394**
"rank and yank." See forced-ranking systems
rate cards 432
ratios. See financial ratios
RCRA (Resource Conservation and Recovery Act) **401**
R&D. See research and development
RDBM (relational database-management systems) 115
Reagan, Ronald 219, 276, 396, 440, 455, 460, 470, 481
real estate 119, 340, 414
real estate investment trusts (REITs) **394–395**
real income **395**
rebuys 51
receivables. See accounts receivable
recession 44, 219, 324, 344, **395–396**
Reciprocal Trade Agreement Act 426, 445
reciprocity **396**, 445
Reconstruction Finance Corporation (RFC) 191, 220, 425
recruiting. See employee recruiting
recycling 347
redevelopment 445–446
red herring prospectus 383
redistribution, income 236
Red Stripe (beer) 377
red tape 335
reductions in force (RIFs) 277, **396–397**
reengineering 281, 288–289
reference group 86–87
Reflect.com 302
regional trade 112
registered agents 309
registration statement 263
regulated monopolies 387
regulatory takings 154, 444
Rehnborg, Carl 319
Reich, Robert 51
reinforcement theory 371
REITs. See real estate investment trusts
relational database-management systems (RDBM) 115

relationship marketing 173, **397–398**
remaindermen 461
renewable energy sources 224, 273
rent-control laws 364
repeat customers 356
repetitive-stress syndrome 169
repos. See repurchase agreements
repurchase agreements, reverse repurchase agreements **398–399**
request for proposal (RFP), invitation to bid **399**
research and development (R&D) 267, 328, **399–400**
reserve requirements 129, 339, **400**
residual equity 346
residual value (salvage value) **400**
Resolution Trust Corporation (RTC) 190, **400–401**, 414
Resource Conservation and Recovery Act (RCRA) **401**
resources **401–402**
    economic development 140
    economic rent 144
    human resources 233
    Malthusian trap 286
    market failure 292
    Marshall Plan 301
    opportunity cost 339
    Organization of Petroleum Exporting Countries 344
    price ceilings 364
    production 372–373
    production-possibilities curve 373
response rates 285
responsible wealth 481
restraints of trade 234, **402**
restrictive covenants **402–403**
résumés 157, 260
retailing 39, 297, 302, **403**, 483
retained earnings. See dividends, retained earnings
retained-interest trusts 461–462
retaliatory trade actions 415
retirement plans 156, 206–207, 226–227, 240–241, 264, 270, 351, 353, **403–404**, 423–424, 429–430
return on equity (ROE) 198
return on investment (ROI) 262, 310, 367
revenue 148, 439. See also income
revenue expenditure. See capital expenditure, revenue expenditure
revenue principle 3
reverse repurchase agreements 398
revolving letter of credit 278
reward system 266
RFC. See Reconstruction Finance Corporation
RFP (request for proposal, invitation to bid) **399**
Ricardo, David 78, 211
Richard Schalbacker 446
RICO. See Racketeer Influenced and Corrupt Organization Act
"riffed" 277
RIFs. See reductions in force
rightsizing 396–397
right-to-know laws **405**
right-to-work laws **405**
Riley, Joe 364
risk, uncertainty **406–407**
    American depositary receipts 12
    beta coefficient, capital asset pricing model 29–30
    bonds 36
    country-risk analysis 103–104
    derivative securities 125–126

diversification 130
duration 136
exchange-rate risk 172
factoring 178
Federal Financial Institutions Examinations Council 188
financial intermediaries 196
five Cs of credit 201
foreign investment 205
futures, futures contracts 212
hedging 231
insurance 246–247
investment 262
modern portfolio theory 310
Moody's ratings 315
peso crisis 356
prospectus 383
repurchase agreements 398
risk management 405–406
tobacco settlement 453–454
venture capital 475
risk-free rate 248
risk management **405–406**
Ritchey, Tom 218
R. J. Reynolds 453
RJR Nabisco 279, 305, 359
Robbins, Stephen 441
Robinson-Patman Act 365, **407**
Rochdale Equitable Pioneers Society 93
Rockefeller, John D. 14, 56, 421, 468
ROE (return on equity) 198
ROI. See return on investment
Rolex 372
Rollover IRA 241
Rolls-Royce 372
Romania 168
Roosevelt, Franklin. See also New Deal
    AFL-CIO 13
    classical economics 67
    credit union 106
    fiscal policy 200
    General Accounting Office 214
    Keynesian economics 271
    macroeconomics 284
    monetary policy 310
    national income accounting 324
    National Industrial Recovery Act 325
    retirement plan 404
    socialism 427
    Social Security 429
    Taft-Hartley Act 443
    TVA 449
    welfare 482
    Works Progress Administration 487
Roosevelt, Theodore 184
root causes 369, 406
Rostow, Walt 143, 153
Roth, William 240, 404
Roth IRA 240, 404
Rowland, Larry 386
Rowley, Colleen 485
royalties 280
RTC. See Resolution Trust Corporation
Rubbermaid 456
Ruckelshaus, William 163
Rukeyser, Louis 446, 480
rule of 115 407
rule of origin **407–408**, 470
rule of reason 421
rule of 72 353, 407, **407**
Russia 222, 465. See also Soviet Union
Rutgers University 339

S

Saatchi & Saatchi 285
SACU (Southern African Customs Union) 112
safety and health 185, 335, **409**
Saipan 441
sale or return agreements 84
sales 84–85, 147–148, 290
sales discounts 2
sales force compensation **409–410**, 411–412
sales forecasting 46–47, **410–411**
sales management 174, 409, **411–412**
sales promotion 130, 139, 254, 293, 329, **412–413**. See also marketing
sales taxes 91, 282
Salinas, Carlos 333, 356
Sallie Mae. See Student Loan Marketing Association
salvage value **400**
sanctions **413**
S&Ls. See savings and loan associations
S&P. See Standard & Poor's
Santa Monica (California) 432, 481
Sarbanes-Oxley Act of 2002 1, 484
Saudi Arabia 56, 140, 344
saving 140, 353, **413–414**
savings and loan associations (thrifts) (S&Ls) 136, 188, 189, 400, **414**
savings bonds 36, 474
Savings Incentive Match Plan for Employees IRA (SIMPLE-IRA) 241
Say's law 67
SBA (Small Business Administration) 425
SBC Communications 359
SBIC (Small Business Investment Company) 425
Scherer, F. M. 72
Schiavo, Mary 485
Schoenfeldt, Lyle 155, 160, 405
Scholes, Myron 340
The Schooner Exchange v. McFaddon 205
Schopenhauer, Arthur 429
Schumacher, E. F. 41
Schumpeter, Joseph 143
Schweiger, David M. 305, 306
SCIP. See Society for Competitive Intelligence Professionals
SCORE (Service Corps of Retired Executives) 425
S corporation **414–415**
Sears 8, 483
seasonal businesses 423
seasonal unemployment 467
Seattle (Washington) 217, 489
SEC. See Securities and Exchange Commission
SECA (Self-Employment Contributions Act) 350
secondary boycotting 276
secondary markets. See primary markets, secondary markets
Section 301, Special 301, Super 301 **415–416**
secure server 139
Securities Act of 1933 263
Securities and Exchange Commission (SEC) 362, **416–417**
    Accounting Oversight Board 1
    annual report 17
    blind trust 32
    churning 63
    earnings management 137
    fair disclosure 180

Securities and Exchange Commission
(SEC) *(continued)*
financial accounting 195
financial statements 198
generally accepted accounting
principles 215
insider trading 244–245
pollution rights 361
prospectus 383
stock-rating systems 434
tender offer 449
whisper numbers 484
Securities Exchange Act of 1934 168,
203, 263, 416
Securities Industry Association (SIA)
180, **417**
securitization 190, 191, **417–418**
seed capital 475
self-actualization 301
self-concept 86
self-directed teams 343
self-employment 237–238, 270, 350,
404, 423
Self-Employment Contributions Act
(SECA) 350
sellers' inflation. *See* cost-push
inflation
selling, personal 355–356
selling agents 290
sell-offs 96
Sells, Saul 4
Senate, U.S. 214, 358
seniority 266, 271, 341, 396–397,
418–419
SEP-IRA. *See* simplified employee
pension
September 11, 2001 terrorist attacks
97, 129, 131, 155, 245, 261, 324,
397
service companies 32, 92
Service Corps of Retired Executives
(SCORE) 425
service marks 247, 456
services 333, **419**
7m Loan Program 425
sexual harassment **419–420**
shareholder rights plans. *See* poison-
pill strategies
shareholders (stockholders) **420–421**
agency theory 7–8
board of directors 33–35
business ethics 45
closely held corporation vs. 70
corporate governance 96–97
equity 168
poison-pill strategies 357
proxy 383
real estate investment trusts 395
stock options 433
tender offer 449
Shaw, James 155, 160, 405
Shellenbarger, Sue 466
Sherman, William 368
Sherman Antitrust Act **421–422**
American Industrial Revolution
15, 421
antitrust law 18
cartel 55
Clayton Antitrust Act 67
extraterritorial jurisdiction 177
Great Depression 223
monopolizing trade, section
two of 421
monopoly 315
price fixing 365
restraint of trade, section one of
421
restraints of trade 402
tying contracts 464

Shewhart, Walter 16
shipping 31, 149, 210, 267–268
shoplifting 403
short selling 231, 256, **423**
short-term debt instruments 55,
73–74, 128, 248, 492
shut-down point **423**
SIA. *See* Securities Industry
Association
SII (Strong Interest Inventory) 20
Silkwood, Karen 485
Simon, Herbert 384
simple-interest loans 282
SIMPLE-IRA (Savings Incentive
Match Plan for Employees IRA)
241
simplified employee pension (SEP-
IRA) 241, **423–424**
Sinclair, Upton 85, 203, 469
sinking fund **424**
skin cancer 273
Skinner, B. F. 371
slack time 108
slang 47
SLMA. *See* Student Loan Marketing
Association
SLM Financing Corporation 437
SLM Holding Company 437
Sloan, Alfred 372
small business 84, 423
Small Business Administration (SBA)
425
Small Business Investment Company
(SBIC) 425
Small Business Job Protection Act of
1996 415
Smaller War Plants Corporation 425
Smith, Adam 19, 55, 141, 210–211,
276, 304, 402, 481
smoking 453–454
Smoot, Reed 425
Smoot-Hawley Tariff Act 222,
425–426, 445, 489
Snow, John W. 124, 216
social audit **426**
social class 86
social customs 140
social democracy 427
social facilitation 229, **426–427**, 428
social insurance 350
socialism 58–59, **427–428**
social loafing 241, **428**, 466
socially responsible investing 71,
428–429
social needs 301
Social Security **429–430**
annuity 18
business taxes 49
Consumer Price Index 89
cost-of-living adjustment 101
gross domestic product 225
income redistribution 236
payroll taxes 350
real income 395
retirement plan 403–404
saving 413
SSI 438
transfer payments 459
welfare 482
Social Security Act 9, 10, 404, 429,
482
Social Security Administration (SSA)
429
Society for Competitive Intelligence
Professionals (SCIP) 295,
430–431
soft-money contributions 358, 359
Sonoco 71
Soros, George 231

South Africa 37, 428, 429
South America 343
South Asia 253
South Carolina 32–33, 347, 386
Southern African Customs Union
(SACU) 112
Southern Baptist Convention 37
Southern Methodist University 303
Southwest Airlines 65, 363
Southwest System 15
Soviet Union 59, 103, 152, 300, 427
spam 257
SPDRs (Standard & Poor's Depository
Receipts) 16
specialists 330
specialization 19, 373
specialty products 372
speculative bonds 279, 431–432
speculators 75, 76
spillover effects. *See* externalities
spin-offs 96
split-offs 96
spoils system 384
sports leagues 103
sport utility vehicles (SUVs) 94
spotted owl 161
Spousal IRA 241
Sprint 232, 292, 332, 359, 387
SRDS (Standard Rate and Data
Service) **432**
Srikanth, Mokshagundam 450
SSA (Social Security Administration)
429
SSI. *See* Supplemental Security Income
Stafford, Robert 69
Stafford loans 437
stakeholders 45, **431**
Stalin, Joseph 272
Standard & Poor's (S&P) 35, 279,
431–432, 434
Standard & Poor's Depository
Receipts (SPDRs) 16
standard of living 12, 58, 308, 366,
432
Standard Oil Company 14, 56
Standard Rate and Data Service
(SRDS) **432**
Standard State Planning Enabling Act
of 1928 494
Standard Zoning Enabling Act of
1922 494
Stanford University's Hoover Institute
451
Starbucks 483
stare decisis 76
statements. *See* financial statements
Staten, Michael 111
state taxes 50, 350, 351
State Unemployment Taxes (SUTA)
350
statistical measures. *See also specific
measures*
Bureau of Economic Analysis
42
dependency ratios 124
economic conditions 139–140
economic growth 143
indicators. *See* indicators
metropolitan statistical area 306
national income accounting
324–325
North American Industry
Classification System 334
price indexes 366–367
standard of living 432
underground economy 465
Statute of Frauds 207
statutory law 77
Stephenson, George 14

Stewart Alsop Industry Achievement
Award 490
Stigler, George 308
stock funds 321
stockholders. *See* shareholders
stockless production 269
Stockman-Vines, Linda 218
stock market, bond market **432–433**.
See also bonds; common stock,
preferred stock, treasury stock
American Stock Exchange 16
beta coefficient, capital asset
pricing model 29–30
blue-chip stocks 32
capital markets, money markets
55
churning 63
Dow Jones averages 132–133
economic conditions 139
efficient market theory 145
equity 168
fair disclosure 180
fiscal year 200
foreign exchange 204
Great Depression 222
guaranteed investment
contracts 226
Index of Consumer
Expectations 239
investment clubs 264
NASDAQ 323
New York Stock Exchange 330
personal finance 353
primary markets 368
program trading 380
random-walk theory 393–394
repurchase agreements
398–399
Securities and Exchange
Commission 416–417
short selling 423
Standard & Poor's 431
stock-rating systems 434
technical analysis 446–447
Wall Street 480
whisper numbers 483–484
stock options 99–100, 245, 340, 379,
433–434
stock-rating systems 434
straight-commission plans 409–410
straight-salary compensation 409
strategic alliances **435**
strategic management 267
strategic planning 236, 309,
435–436
strengths, weaknesses, opportunities,
and threats (SWOT) analysis
436–437
stress 409, 454
strict scrutiny 134–135
strict tort liability 374
strike price 340
strikes 15, 250, 331, 443, 468
strips 474
Strong, E. K. 21
Strong Interest Inventory (SII) 20
structural unemployment 467
structured job interviews 260
Student Loan Marketing Association
(Sallie Mae; USA Education, Inc.)
(SLMA) 220, 221, **437**
subleasing 278
sub-S classification 49
subsidies 8–9, 98–99, 110, 135, 439
success, fear of 3
sufficient cause. *See* just cause
sugar lobby 104
Suharto 104
sulfur dioxide 360, 361

Sullivan, Leon 428, 429
Sullivan Rule 428, 429
Summit of the Americas 343
sunset provisions 5
Sun Tzu 436
Super Bowl 38
supercomputers 175
Superfund 163, 401, **437–438**
Supplemental Security Income (SSI)
  101, 351, 429, 430, **438**, 482
suppliers 285–286
supply 275, 312–313, 344, 378,
  438–439, 475–476
supply and demand 67
supply-chain management. *See*
  purchasing
supply curve 101
supply rule **439**
supply-shock inflation. *See* cost-push
  inflation
supply-side economics **439–440**, 460
Supreme Court, U.S. 72, 129, 134,
  325, 445, 494
Survey of Consumers (University of
  Michigan) 238–239
surveys 258–259, 285, 296–297,
  354, 410, 448–449
survival strategy 367
sustainable growth and development
  (sustainability) 70–71, 225–226,
  265, 272, 273, 402, **440–441**
SUTA (State Unemployment Taxes)
  350
SUVs (sport utility vehicles) 94
sweatshop **441**
Sweden 338, 440
Sweeny, John J. 12, 13
sweep account 57
swing producers 344
SWOT analysis. *See* strengths,
  weaknesses, opportunities, and
  threats (SWOT) analysis
syndicated market research 296
synergy 84, **441–442**
systems 342

T

TAA. *See* trade-adjustment assistance
Tab 174
t-account **443**
Taft, William Howard 60
Taft-Hartley Act (Labor-Management
  Relations Act) 13, 72, 190, 244,
  326, 405, **443**
takings clause **443–444**
TANF (Temporary Assistance to
  Needy Families Act) 9
Target 302
target markets 6, 111, 126, 294–295,
  328, 362, **444**, 471
tariff **444–445**
  Auto Pact 22
  business taxes 49
  customs union 112
  foreign-trade zones 206
  free trade 210
  free-trade areas 211
  globalization 217
  Harmonized Tariff System
    228–229
  import restraints 234
  International Trade
    Commission 255
  maquiladoras 290
  most-favored-nation clause
    317–318
  multinational corporation 319
  rules of origin 407–408

Smoot-Hawley Tariff Act
  425–426
  United States-Canada Free
    Trade Agreement 470
  U.S. Customs Clearance 472
Tariff Act of 1930 425–426, 473
taxable income 235
taxes. *See* business taxes
tax incremental funding (tax
  incremental financing) (TIF)
  445–446
Tax Reform Act of 1986 395
tax shelter **446**
Taylor, Frederick W. 174, 352
T-bills 473–474
T-bonds 473–474
team leaders 307
Teamsters. *See* International
  Brotherhood of Teamsters
technical analysis **446–447**
technology 41, 439
technology transfer **447**
Telecommunications Reform Act of
  1996 187, 387
telemarketing 393, **447–448**
Telemarketing and Consumer Fraud
  and Abuse Prevention 90
telephone service 314, 386, 387
telephone surveys 296–297, **448–449**
Telephone Workers Union of Mexico
  332
Temporary Assistance to Needy
  Families Act (TANF) 9
tender offer **449**
Tennessee Valley Authority (TVA)
  449
termination-at-will 268
test marketing 328–329
Texaco 37, 166
Texas Instruments 173, 493
textiles 20, 441
Textron 359
Thatcher, Margaret 368
theft 152
theory of constraints (TOC) 288,
  449–450
Theory X and Theory Y **450–451**
think tanks **451–452**
3M Corporation 411–412
Three Mile Island 163, 224
360-degree feedback **452**
thrifts. *See* savings and loan
  associations
Thurow, Lester 493
Ticket to Work and Work Incentives
  Improvement Act of 1999 438
Tide detergent 39
tie-ins 412
TIF. *See* tax incremental funding
Tijuana (Mexico) 290–291
TILA. *See* Truth in Lending Act
timber 98, 161
time deposits (certificates of deposit,
  CDs) 452
time management **452–453**
Times Beach (Missouri) 163
time value of money 42, 56, 128
Timm, Paul R. 110
Title IV. *See* Aid to Families with
  Dependent Children
Title VII of the Civil Rights Act of
  1964 419
TI (Transparency International) 41
T-notes 473–474
tobacco manufacturers 359, 386
tobacco settlement 49, 77, 316,
  453–454
Tobacco Tax and Trade Bureau (TTB)
  123–124

TOC. *See* theory of constraints
Tom Peters Company 289
total quality improvement (TQI) 406
total-quality management (TQM)
  406, **454–455**
toxic waste 163, 224
Toyota 90, 261, 269, 297
TQI (total quality improvement) 406
TQM. *See* total-quality management
trade. *See also* free trade; globalization;
  imports/exports; tariff
    barter 28–29
    countertrade 102–103
    Court of International Trade
      104
    deceptive trade practices
      116–117
    demand 119–120
    Foreign Corrupt Practices Act
      203–204
    foreign exchange 204
    ISO standards 264–265
    Marshall Plan 301
    Organization of American
      States 343–344
    restraints of trade 402
    sanctions 413
    Section 301, Special 301, Super
      301 415
    U.S. Commercial Service
      471–472
Trade Act of 1974 415, 473
trade-adjustment assistance (TAA)
  277, 397, **455**
Trade Agreements Extension Act of
  1945 445
trade balance (balance of trade)
  24–25, 173, 235, **455–456**
trade barriers (barriers to trade) 112,
  126, 170, 175, 211, 217, 331, **456**,
  488
trade credit. *See* accounts payable,
  trade credit
Trade Expansion Act of 1962 277,
  397, 455, 473
trademark 207, 247, **456–457**, 488
trade promotion authority. *See* fast
  track
Trade-Related Intellectual Property
  Agreement 416, 447, 457
trade secrets 247, 271, 382, 457
trade shows 412–413, 457
training and development 233, 241,
  254, 411, **458**
tranches 418
transaction costs **458–459**
transfer payments 236, **459**
transfer taxes **459–460**
Transparency International (TI) 41
travel agents 257
traveler's letter of credit 278
Treasury securities 36, 339
treasury stock. *See* common stock,
  preferred stock, treasury stock
trend analysis 410
Trent, Robert J. 454
trial balance. *See* adjusting entry, trial
  balance, adjusted trial balance
Triangle Factory fire 441
trickle-down economics 440, 460,
  481
trucking industry 250, 259
Truman, Harry S. 300, 443
trust 14–15, 18, 31–32, 398,
  460–462
Truth in Lending Act (TILA) 105,
  193, **462**
TTB. *See* Tobacco Tax and Trade
  Bureau

Tupperware 319
TVA (Tennessee Valley Authority)
  449
TWA Flight 800 185–186
twin plants. *See* maquiladoras
two-factor theory of motivation 301,
  462–463
tying contracts 68, 422, **463–464**
Tylenol 347

U

UBS Financial Services 218
UCC. *See* Uniform Commercial Code
UDEAC (Union Douaniere et
  Economique de L'Afrique
  Centrale) 211
UDSA. *See* Department of
  Agriculture, U.S.
UFW. *See* United Farm Workers
UL (Underwriters Laboratory) **466**
Umble, Michale 450
uncertainty. *See* risk, uncertainty
uncertainty avoidance 232
underground economy (informal
  economy, parallel economy) 348,
  465–466
undertime **466**
Underwriters Laboratory (UL) **466**
underwriting 263, **466**
unemployment **466–467**
  Bureau of Labor Statistics 43
  fiscal policy 200
  income redistribution 236
  Index of Consumer
    Expectations 239
  indicators 239
  labor force 275
  National Industrial Recovery
    Act 325
  recession 396
  trade-adjustment assistance 455
  transfer payments 459
  Works Progress Administration
    487
unemployment tax 350
unfair labor practices 326
Uniform Commercial Code (UCC)
  73, 84, 92, 118, 327, 375, **467–468**
Union Douaniere et Economique de
  L'Afrique Centrale (UDEAC) 211
Union Pacific Railroad 14, 15
union(s) **468–469**. *See also* collective
  bargaining
  AFL-CIO 12–13
  countervailing power 103
  employment-at-will 160
  featherbedding 185
  Industrial Workers of the World
    242
  International Brotherhood of
    Teamsters 250
  International Labor
    Organization 251
  labor-employee relations 274
  Landrum-Griffin Act 276
  layoff 277
  National Labor Relations Board
    326
  National Mediation Board 326
  Norris-LaGuardia Act 331
  North American Agreement on
    Labor Cooperation 332
  political action committee
    358–359
  right-to-work laws 405
  seniority 418
  Sherman Antitrust Act 422
  Taft-Hartley Act 185, 443

union(s) (continued)
    United Farm Workers 469
    Wagner Act 480
    white-collar 485
    wrongful discharge 490
United Arab Emirates 344
United Farm Workers (UFW) 37, 85, 469–470
United Fruit Company 319
United Nations 251, 272
United Parcel Service (UPS) 214, 250
United States–Canada Auto Pact. See Auto Pact
United States–Canada Free Trade Agreement (CFTA) 22, 23, 110, 185, 320, 332, 470–471
unity of command 60
University of Chicago 303, 310
University of Michigan 303
University of South Carolina at Beaufort 477
University of Texas at Austin 303
unpaid leave 156
UPS. See United Parcel Service
USA Education, Inc. 437
USAID (U.S. Agency for International Development) 471
U.S. Agency for International Development (USAID) 471
U.S. Army 390
U.S. Census Bureau 215, 306, 334, 368, 467, 471
U.S. Commercial Service 471–472
U.S. Court of Appeals (Ninth Circuit) 258
U.S. Customs Clearance 472
U.S. Customs Service 472–473
U.S. Gypsum 411
U.S. International University (San Diego, California) 376
U.S. Mint 123
U.S. Model Business Principles 45
U.S. Navy 379, 380
U.S. Patent Office 350
U.S. Tariff Commission 255
U.S. Trade Representative (USTR) 415, 473
U.S. Treasury securities 25, 189, 473–474
US Steel 307, 365
USTR. See U.S. Trade Representative
US West 359
utilities. See public utilities

V
VA (Veterans Administration) 220
valuation, business 50
value-added network (VAN) 149–150
value-added tax (VAT) 92
values 110, 341
VAN. See value-added network
Van den Berg, Joroen P. 261
Vanderbilt, William Henry 421
variable costs 101–102
VAT (value-added tax) 92
Veblen, Thorstein 413
Vecchio, Robert P. 301
vendors 398
Venezuela 344
venture capital 48, 475

Versailles, Treaty of 27, 251
vertical integration 130, 475–476
vesting 207, 404, 424
veterans 336
Veterans Administration (VA) 220
Vietnam Era Veterans Readjustment Assistance Act 336
Vietnam War 428
Village of Euclid v. Ambler Realty Co. 494
viral marketing 386, 476
virtual corporation 345
Visa (credit card) 105
visas 223, 476–477
vision statement 309, 477–478
vocational rehabilitation 487
volatility 29–30
Volcker, Paul 311
Von Neumann, John 213
voting rights (stock) 383
Vroom, Victor 174, 342–343, 370

W
W-4 form 351
Wabash Railroad 15
wage and price controls (incomes policies) 144, 479–480
wages 156, 169, 308
Wagner, Robert F. 480
Wagner Act (National Labor Relations Act) 13, 71–72, 325, 443, 469, 480, 490
Wahid, Abdurrahman 104
Walker, M. R. 107
Wall Street 330, 394, 417, 434, 480
Wal-Mart
    benchmarking 29
    Buy American Act 51
    growth stocks 226
    international marketing 254
    inventory control 261
    joint venture 267
    know-how 271
    marketing-information systems 294
    market segmentation 297
    mass merchandising 302
    metropolitan statistical area 306
    multinational corporation 319
    price discrimination 365
    proprietary information 382
    restrictive covenants 403
Walters, Stephen J. K. 143
Walton, Sam 51
wampum 312
WARN. See Worker Adjustment and Retraining Notification Act
Warnaco 280
War Production Board 16
Warren (Michigan) 32
warranty 374, 480–481
Warsaw Pact 427
Washington, D.C. 343
Washington Public Power Supply System (WPPSS) 117–118
watchdog groups 358
Waterford crystal 372
Watergate scandals 359
water pollution 69–70
Watkins, Sharon 485

Watt, James 122
waybills 31
wealth 91, 147, 201, 304, 481
wealth effect 91, 201–202
Web-based banking 11
websites 138–139, 258
Webster, William 1
Welch, Jack 203
welfare 481–482
    Aid for Families with Dependent Children 9–10
    automatic stabilizers 22
    corporate welfare 98–99
    fiscal policy 200
    gini ratio 215
    gross domestic product 225
    income redistribution 236
    recession 396
    Social Security 430
    transfer payments 459
    trickle-down economics 460
West African Economic Community (CEAO) 211
Western Electric Company 229
Western Federation of Miners 242
Western Union 104–105
Westinghouse 365
Wheeler-Lea Act 482–483
wheel of retailing 483
Whiskey Rebellion 49
whisper numbers 483–484
Whistle-blower Protection Act of 1989 484
whistle-blower (whistleblower) 268, 484–485, 491
White, Harry Dexter 40
white-collar 152, 485
wholesaler 130, 485
Wiley, Harvey 203
Williams-Sonoma 440
wills 461
Wilson, Ralph F. 476
Wilson, Woodrow 384
Wilson Tariff Act of 1894 249
window dressing 383
Windows (operating system) 464
WIN (Work Incentive) 10
WIPO. See World Intellectual Property Organization
Wolfensohn, J. 96
women 78, 166. See also comparable worth
work council 486
work environment 95, 169–170
Worker Adjustment and Retraining Notification Act (WARN) 277, 397, 486
workers' compensation 238, 247, 350, 486–487
work ethic 451
workforce. See labor force
Work Incentive (WIN) 10
working capital 197
working-capital loans 175
workplace policies 95
Work Progress Administration (WPA) 200, 310, 487
work visas 476–477
World Bank (International Bank for Reconstruction and Development) 40, 487–488, 488–489

WorldCom 1
World Commission on Environment and Development 440
World Intellectual Property Organization (WIPO) 112, 258, 488
World Trade Organization (WTO) 488–490
    agricultural support programs 8, 9
    Buy American Act 50
    corporate welfare 98
    counterfeit goods 102
    European Union 170
    exporting 175
    family farm 182
    free trade 210, 211
    free-trade areas 211
    globalization 217
    ISO standards 265
    licensing 280
    most-favored-nation clause 318
    multinational corporation 320
    reciprocity 396
    Smoot-Hawley Tariff Act 426
    tariff 445
    trade barriers 456
    trade secrets 457
    U.S. Trade Representative 473
World War I 121
World War II 13, 16, 40, 47, 155, 175, 219, 300, 333, 479
World Wide Web (WWW) 112, 127–128, 255–258, 476, 490
WPA. See Work Progress Administration
WPPSS. See Washington Public Power Supply System
Wright, Lindsay 142
Wright, Richard 487
writing covered calls 340
wrongful discharge 345, 490–491
WTO. See World Trade Organization
WWW. See World Wide Web

X
X-engineering principles 281

Y
Yale University 310, 440
Yamani, Sheik Zaki 344
yen 172
yield curve 492
Young, James Harvey 202, 203
Young Plan 27
Young & Rubicam 285
youth-dependency ratio 124

Z
Zajonc, Robert 426
zero-based budgeting (ZBB) 493–494
zero-coupon bonds 36
zero-coupon Treasuries 474
zero-drag employees 493
zero-sum game 322, 493
Zoelick, Robert 473
zoning 494